COGNITIVE NEUROSCIENCE

THE BIOLOGY OF THE MIND

THIRD EDITION

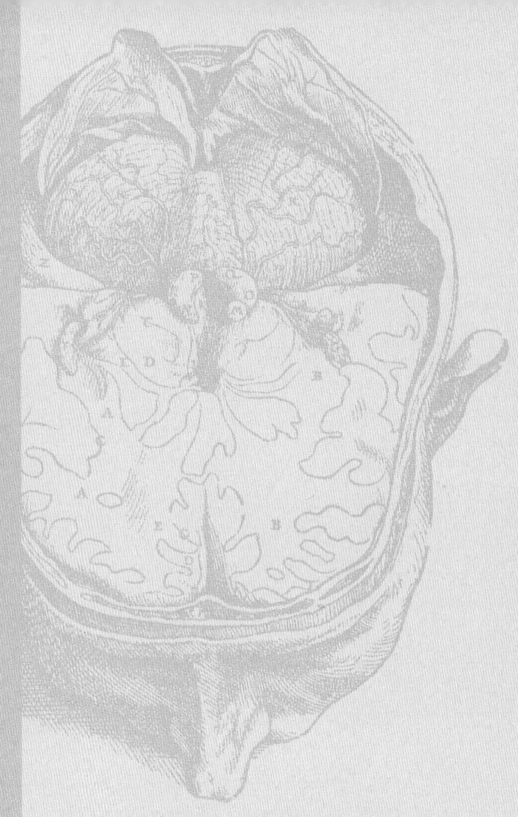

Michael S. Gazzaniga
UNIVERSITY OF CALIFORNIA,
SANTA BARBARA

Richard B. Ivry
UNIVERSITY OF CALIFORNIA,
BERKELEY

George R. Mangun
UNIVERSITY OF CALIFORNIA,
DAVIS

With
Megan S. Steven
DARTMOUTH COLLEGE

COGNITIVE NEUROSCIENCE

THE BIOLOGY OF THE MIND

THIRD EDITION

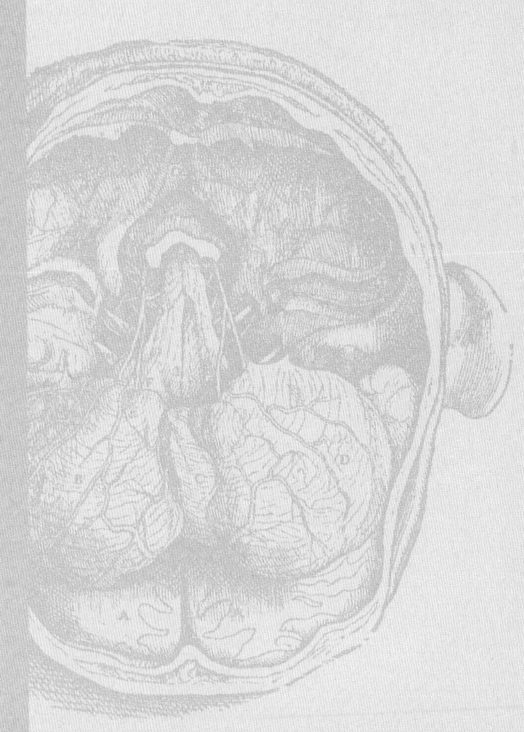

W • W • NORTON & COMPANY
NEW YORK • LONDON

PRINTED IN THE UNITED STATES OF AMERICA

Editor: Jon W. Durbin.
Senior project editor: Kim J. Yi.
Senior production manager: Ben Reynolds.
Copy editor: Stephanie Hiebert.
Editorial assistants: Alexis Hilts and Jason Spears.
Book design: Jack Meserole and Rubina Yeh.
Illustrations: Frank Forney and ElectraGraphics, Inc.

The text of this book is composed in Minion with the display set in Myriad.
Composition: TSI Graphics.
Manufacturing: R. R. Donnelley—Willard Division.

Library of Congress Cataloging-in-Publication Data

Gazzaniga, Michael S.
Cognitive neuroscience : the biology of the mind / Michael S. Gazzaniga, Richard B. Ivry, George R. Mangun ; with Megan S. Steven. —3rd ed.
p. ; cm.
Includes bibliographical references and index.
ISBN 978-0-393-92795-5 (hardcover)
1. Cognitive neuroscience. I. Ivry, Richard B. II. Mangun, G. R. (George Ronald), 1956– III. Title.
[DNLM: 1. Brain—physiology. 2. Cognition—physiology. 3. Cognitive Science. 4. Neuropsychology. WL 300 G291c2009]
QP360.5.G39 2009
612.8'233—dc22

2008016822

W. W. Norton & Company, Inc., 500 Fifth Avenue, New York, NY 10110
www.wwnorton.com

W. W. Norton & Company Ltd., Castle House, 75/76 Wells Street, London W1T 3QT

1 2 3 4 5 6 7 8 9 0

FOR LILLY, EMMY, AND GARTH
M.S.G.

FOR HENRY AND SAM
R.B.I.

FOR NICHOLAS AND ALEXANDER
G.R.M.

BRIEF OVERVIEW

PART I: BACKGROUND AND METHODS

PART II: CORE PROCESSES

PART III: CONTROL PROCESSES

CONTENTS

9 Emotion 364

10 Language 388

11 Hemispheric Specialization 445

PART III: CONTROL PROCESSES

BOXES

MILESTONES IN COGNITIVE NEUROSCIENCE

HOW THE BRAIN WORKS

THE COGNITIVE NEUROSCIENTIST'S TOOLKIT

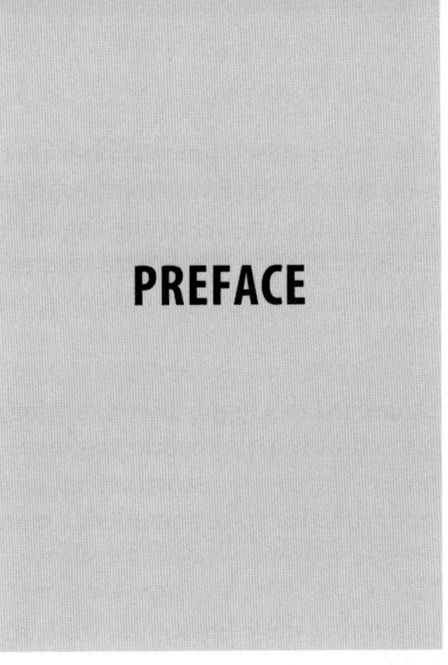

PREFACE

Welcome to the third edition! When new enterprises like cognitive neuroscience emerge, it is not always clear if they will survive. The youthful enthusiasm of a new field is not unlike a young doe standing up for the first time after birth. Can she make it? Will this new life develop and grow? Will true meaning emerge from the new life?

Ten years later, cognitive neuroscience has blossomed in spectacular fashion. We can measure this progress in many ways. Leading universities have undertaken major initiatives to develop dedicated cognitive neuroscience programs, providing researchers with the tools of the trade and opportunities that promote interdisciplinary research. New journals are introduced each year, dedicated to new specialties within the cognitive neurosciences, with the number of papers in the field increasing at an exponential rate. The annual meeting of the Cognitive Neuroscience Society has burst its seams, with attendance increasing dramatically—growing from an initial tally of 400 at the first meeting to over 1,800 at the fifteenth annual meeting in 2008.

As the field of cognitive neuroscience has grown and evolved, so has our survey text. We began a decade and a half ago with a basic question: What constitutes the first principles that make cognitive neuroscience distinct from physiological psychology, neuroscience, cognitive psychology, or neuropsychology? This question was the fundamental challenge we faced in laying the groundwork for our first edition, and it constituted our defining point. We concluded that it is indeed a critical question—but paradoxically, not a question at all. Cognitive neuroscience certainly overlaps with and synthesizes these traditional approaches. We sought to help identify how future cognitive neuroscientists would address the neural bases of cognition in the years ahead.

We continue to seek a balance between cognitive theory and neuropsychological and neuroscientific evidence, adding examples that use computational techniques to complete the story. We make liberal use of patient case studies to illustrate essential points for understanding the architecture of cognition rather than providing an exhaustive description of brain disorders. In every section, we strive to include the most current information and theoretical views, supported by evidence from the cutting-edge technology that is such an important part of cognitive neuroscience. In contrast to purely cognitive or neuropsychological approaches, this text emphasizes the convergence of evidence that is a crucial aspect of any science, particularly studies of higher mental function.

Getting students to think like cognitive neuroscientists is a second key goal of our text. Cognitive neuroscience examines mind–brain relationships with a wide range of techniques, such as fMRI, MRI, PET, and ERPs. The field requires becoming knowledgeable about the strengths and weaknesses of these methods, and understanding how these techniques can be used in a complementary manner. This book is intended to prepare students of cognitive neuroscience to do just that.

Since the first edition, there have been many major developments, both methodological and theoretical. There has been an explosion of brain imaging studies—almost 1,500 a year for the last decade. New technologies, such as transcranial magnetic stimulation, have been added to the arsenal of the cognitive neuroscientist. New links to genetics, comparative anatomy, and robotics have emerged. Parsing all of these studies and deciding which ones should be included so that we capture the cutting-edge trends in the field, while keeping in mind that this is an undergraduate survey text, has been our final key goal for the text.

So far, the evidence suggests that our efforts have led to a highly useful text for undergraduates taking their first course in cognitive neuroscience. Over 400 colleges and universities worldwide have adopted the first two editions, and the sales between editions have more than doubled. Moreover, instructors tell us that in addition to our interdisciplinary approach, they like that our book has a strong narrative voice and offers a manageable number of chapters to teach in a one-semester survey course.

With this new, third edition, we focused on refining these principles, while making the text even more user-friendly. Chief highlights of the third edition include the following:

- *A reorganized table of contents that follows a clear micro to macro outline.* Students will start with basic foundational topics, and then move to more complex, higher order functions. As before, the chapters are organized by function rather than anatomy, consistent with the organization of the brain, in which distributed networks of neural regions are engaged for even the simplest of tasks. Part I of the new edition focuses on Background and Methods, Part II on Core Processes, and Part III on Control Processes. The most significant change along these lines was the merging of the chapter on development and neural plasticity from the second edition into a new chapter on neuroanatomy and development, enabling us to carry the theme of neuroplasticity through the entire book.
- *Substantial rewriting of all chapters to ensure a uniform voice, style, and presentation throughout, with particular attention paid to making more connections across chapters.* Our primary goal here was to strengthen the book's underlying pedagogy and make it even more useful for students.
- *Fully up-to-date material, including over 400 new research citations, and a brand-new chapter on social cognition.* Reinforcing the text's reputation for capturing the field's most important new trends, Jennifer Beer (University of Texas, Austin), one of the leading researchers in the field of social cognitive neuroscience, has written a highly engaging overview of this exciting new area of research.
- *New Instructor's Neuroscience Media DVD.* This two-disc set contains interviews with leading cognitive neuroscientists about major topics in the field, and footage of interviews with human neuropsychology patients. Instructors will easily be able to incorporate these clips into their PowerPoint presentations.

This book has been an interactive effort among us, our colleagues, our students, and our reviewers! The product has benefited immeasurably from these interactions, but we will not rest here. We stand ready to modify and improve any and all of our work. In our earlier editions, we asked readers to contact us with suggestions and questions, and we do so again. We live in an age where interaction is swift and easy. We are to be found as follows: gazzaniga@psych.ucsb.edu; mangun@ucdavis.edu; ivry@socrates.berkeley.edu. Good reading and learning!

ACKNOWLEDGMENTS

As usual, we are indebted to a number of people. Of special note are three colleagues who brought their expertise and abilities to the text. Megan Steven (Dartmouth College) lent her considerable writing skills to make the book as student-friendly as possible. Jeff Hutsler (University of Nevada, Reno) ably revised the chapter on evolutionary perspectives that now serves as a capstone chapter for the text. Jennifer Beer (University of Texas, Austin) brought her exceptional abilities and insights to bear on our new social cognition chapter. We thank again Tamara Y. Swaab, Liz Phelps, and Leah Krubitzer for their work on the language, emotion, and evolution chapters, respectively, in earlier editions of the book. Tim Justus, Chadd Funk, Adam Riggal, Karl Doron, Kristin McAdams, and Todd Heatherton, our longtime friend and colleague, are all to be thanked for sharing their advice and wisdom and for helping along the way. As in the previous two editions, we make a special effort to bring cognitive neuroscience alive with color. Frank Forney is again the book's artist and is to be congratulated for his continued fine work. We also thank our many colleagues who provided original artwork or scientific figures.

In addition, we are indebted to many scientists and personal friends. Writing a textbook is a major commitment of time, intellect, and affect! Those who helped significantly are noted below. Some reviewed our words and critiqued our thoughts. Others allowed us to interview them. To all we owe our deep gratitude and thanks.

Eyal Aharoni, University of California, Santa Barbara; David G. Amaral, University of California, Davis; Franklin R. Amthor, University of Alabama, Birmingham; Michael Anderson, St. Andrews University; Adam Aron, University of California, San Diego; Ignacio Badiola, Florida International University; David Badre, Brown University; Juliana Baldo, VA Medical Center, Martinez, California; Gary Banker, Oregon Health Sciences University; Horace Barlow, Cambridge University; Kathleen Baynes, University of California, Davis; N. P. Bechtereva, Russian Academy of Science; Mark Beeman, Northwestern University; Marlene Behrmann, Carnegie Mellon University; Robert S. Blumenfeld, University of California, Davis; Elizabeth Brannon, Duke University; Rainer Breitling, San Diego State University; Silvia Bunge, University of California, Berkeley; Valerie Clark, University of California, Davis; Clay Clayworth, VA Medical Center, Martinez, California; Asher Cohen, Hebrew University; Jonathan Cohen, Princeton University; J. M. Coquery, Université des Sciences et Technologies de Lille; Michael Corballis, University Auckland; Paul Corballis, Georgia Tech University; Anders Dale, Massachusetts General Hospital; Antonio Damasio, University of Iowa; Hanna Damasio, University of Iowa; Daniel C. Dennett, Tufts University; Mark D'Esposito, University of California, Berkeley; Nina Dronkers, University of California, Davis; Martha Farah, University of Pennsylvania; Harlen Fichtenholtz, Duke University; Peter T. Fox, University of Texas; Karl Friston, Institute of Neurology, London; Rusty Gage, Salk Institute; Jack Gallant, University of California, Berkeley; Priyanka Ghosh; Mitchell Glickstein, University College London and Dartmouth College; Gail Goodman, University of California, Davis; Elizabeth Gould, Princeton University; Jay E. Gould, University of West Florida; Scott Grafton, University of California, Santa Barbara; Charlie Gross, Princeton University; Nouchine Hadjikhani, Massachusetts General Hospital; Peter Hagoort, Max Planck Institute for Psycholinguistics;

Todd Handy, University of British Columbia; Eliot Hazeltine, University of Iowa; Hans-Jochen Heinze, University of Madgeberg; Steven A. Hillyard, University of California, San Diego; Hermann Hinrichs, University of Madgeberg; Jens-Max Hopf, University of Magdeburg; Joseph Hopfinger, University of California, Davis; Richard Howard, National University of Singapore; Drew Hudson, University of California, Berkeley; Akira Ishiguchi, Ochanomizu University; Lucy Jacobs, University of California, Berkeley; Amishi Jha, University of California, Davis; Cindy Jordan, Michigan State University; Tim Justus, VA Medical Center, Martinez, California; Nancy Kanwisher, Massachusetts Institute of Technology; Larry Katz, Duke University; Steven Keele, University of Oregon; Leon Kenemans, University of Utrecht; Steve Kennerley, University of California, Berkeley; Alan Kingstone, University of British Columbia; Robert T. Knight, University of California, Berkeley; Stephen M. Kosslyn, Harvard University; Neal Kroll, University of California, Davis; Leah Krubitzer, University of California, Davis; Marta Kutas, University of California, San Diego; Joseph E. Le Doux, New York University; Matt Lieberman, University of California, Los Angeles; Steven J. Luck, University of California, Davis; Jennifer Mangels, Graduate Center at the City University of New York; Chad Marsolek, University of Minnesota; Nancy Martin, University of California, Davis; James L. McClelland, Stanford University; George A. Miller, Princeton University; Teresa Mitchell, Duke University; Amy Needham, Duke University; Kevin Ochsner, Columbia University; Ken A. Paller, Northwestern University; Jasmeet K. Pannu, University of Arizona; Steven E. Petersen, Washington University School of Medicine; Steven Pinker, Harvard University; Lara Polse, University of California, San Diego; Michael I. Posner, University of Oregon; David Presti, University of California, Berkeley; Robert Rafal, University of Bangor; Marcus Raichle, Washington University School of Medicine; Charan Ranganath, University of California, Davis; Mikko E. Sams, University of Tampere; Donatella Scabini, University of California, Berkeley; Daniel Schacter, Harvard University; Ariel Schoenfeld, University of Magdeburg; Michael Scholz, University of Magdeberg; Art Shimamura, University of California, Berkeley; Michael Silverman, Oregon Health Sciences University; Allen W. Song, Duke University; Larry Squire, University of California, San Diego; Michael Starks, 3DTV Corporation; Thomas M. Talavage, Massachusetts General Hospital; Keiji Tanaka, Riken Institute; Michael Tarr, Brown University; Ed Taylor; Sharon L. Thompson-Schill, University of Pennsylvania; Roger Tootell, Massachusetts General Hospital; Anne M. Treisman, Princeton University; Carrie Trutt, Duke University; Endel Tulving, Rotman Research Institute, Baycrest Center; John Vollrath; C. Mark Wessinger, University of Nevada, Reno; Kevin Wilson, Gettysburg College; Ginger Withers, Oregon Health Sciences University; Marty G. Woldorff, Duke University; Andrew Yonelinas, University of California, Davis.

1

A Brief History of Cognitive Neuroscience

On December 14, 1650, Anne Green walked to the gallows in the courtyard of the city of Oxford, England. She was to be executed for murdering her newborn child (a crime she did not commit). As she faced certain death, it must have been the furthest thought from her mind that she was about to play a role in the founding of clinical neurology and neuroanatomy. She proclaimed her innocence to all who were watching, and after a psalm was read she was hanged. She hung there for a full half hour before she was taken down, pronounced dead, and placed in a coffin provided by Drs. Thomas Willis and William Petty. Willis and Petty were physicians in Oxford, and by order of Charles I, then king of England, they had permission to dissect, for medical research, the bodies of any criminals killed within 21 miles of Oxford.

An autopsy, however, was not what would take place on that fateful day. When Willis and Petty brought Anne's body back to their office, they heard a grumbling sound from her throat. They poured spirits in her mouth and rubbed a feather on her neck to make her cough. They rubbed her hands and feet for several minutes, bled 5 ounces of her blood, and swabbed her neck wounds with turpentine. They cared for her through the night, and the next morning she was able to drink fluids (in fact, she asked for a beer!). Five days later she was out of bed and able to eat normally (Molnar, 2004; Zimmer, 2004).

Although the authorities wanted to hang Anne again, Willis and Petty fought in her defense. She had been accused of killing her baby, but the doctors argued that her baby had been stillborn and its death was not her fault. They also argued that her miraculous escape from death by execution was a divine providence proving her innocence. Their arguments prevailed. Anne was set free and later went on to marry and have three more children.

This miraculous experience was well publicized in England (Figure 1.1) and helped bring fame to Willis and Petty. Thomas Willis (Figure 1.2) would go on to become the Sedleian professor of natural philosophy at Oxford University, an inquisitive neurologist (indeed, he coined the term *neurology*), and the first anatomist to link abnormal human behaviors to changes in brain structure. Although Willis might have been successful without such publicity, he owed much to Anne Green and the fame brought to him by the events of her resurrection. With it came money he desperately needed and the prestige to publish his work and disseminate his ideas.

Willis became one of the best-known doctors of his time. He treated the richest people in England and charged them heavily so that he could, in turn, treat the poorest in England for free. He treated patients throughout their lives and then autopsied them after their deaths, allowing him to understand how changes in their brains might have caused the behaviors and diseases that he had monitored during their lives.

Figure 1.1 An artistic rendition of the miraculous resurrection of Anne Green in 1650.

Willis was among the first to link specific brain damage to specific behavioral deficits, and to theorize how the brain transfers information in what would later be called *neuronal conduction*. He appreciated that the human brain differs from the brains of other animals in the amount of cortex, and that this difference might be responsible for human intelligence (or even, he pondered, the additional cortex might be the seat of the human soul).

Willis would discover symptoms of the neuromuscular disease myasthenia gravis, the brain abnormalities of people with congenital mental retardation, and the fact that unilateral degeneration of the cerebral peduncle (a part of the brainstem) could lead to unilateral paralysis. Together with his colleague and friend Christopher Wren (known to most now as the architect who designed St. Paul's Cathedral in London, England), he would draw the most accurate representations of the human brain of the time and for at least 200 years following (Figure 1.3). He would also coin names for a myriad of brain regions (Table 1.1) (Molnar, 2004; Zimmer, 2004). In short, Willis would set in motion the ideas and knowledge base that took hundreds of years to ruminate and develop into what we know today as the field of *cognitive neuroscience*.

In this chapter we discuss the scientists and physicians who have made important contributions to the field of neuroscience. You will discover how the field began and how it has developed into what it is today: a discipline geared toward understanding how the brain works, how its structure and function affect behavior, and ultimately how the brain enables the mind.

Figure 1.2 Thomas Willis (1621–1675), a founder of clinical neuroscience.

Figure 1.3 The human brain (ventral view) drawn by Christopher Wren for Thomas Willis, published in Willis's *The Anatomy of the Brain and Nerves.*

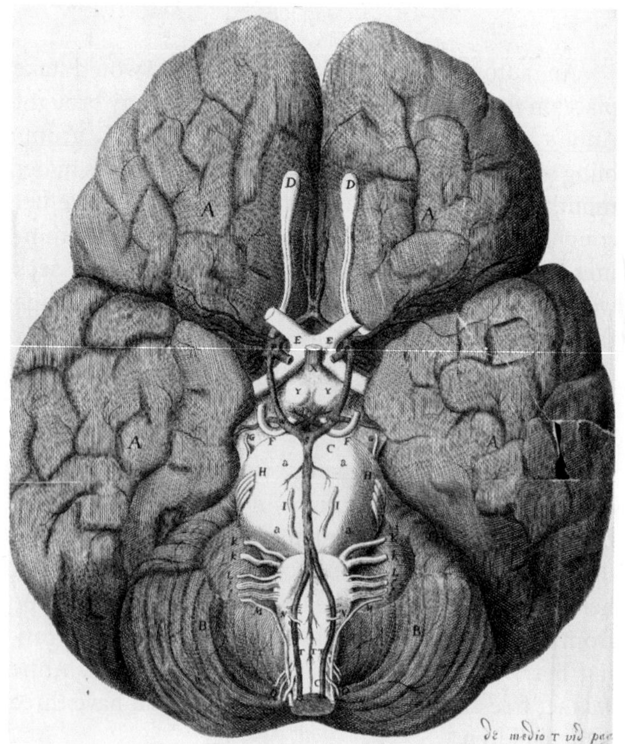

A HISTORICAL PERSPECTIVE

The scientific field of **cognitive neuroscience** received its name in the late 1970s in the back seat of a New York City taxi. One of us (M.S.G.) was riding with the great cognitive psychologist George A. Miller on the way to a dinner meeting at the Algonquin Hotel. The dinner was being held for scientists from Rockefeller and Cornell universities, who were joining forces to study how the brain enables the mind—a subject in need of a name. Out of that taxi ride came the term *cognitive neuroscience,* from *cognition,* or the process of knowing (i.e., what arises from awareness, perception, and reasoning), and *neuroscience* (the study of the nervous system). This seemed the perfect term to describe the question of understanding how the functions of the physical brain can yield the thoughts and ideas of an intangible mind. And so the term took hold in the scientific community.

Table 1.1 A Selection of Terms Coined by Thomas Willis

Term	Definition
Anterior commissure	Axonal fibers connecting the middle and inferior temporal gyri of the left and right hemispheres.
Cerebellar peduncles	Axonal fibers connecting the cerebellum and brainstem.
Claustrum	A thin sheath of gray matter located between two brain areas: the external capsule and the putamen.
Corpus striatum	A part of the basal ganglia consisting of the caudate nucleus and the lenticular nucleus.
Inferior olives	The part of the brainstem that modulates cerebellar processing.
Internal capsule	White matter pathways conveying information from the thalamus to the cortex.
Medullary pyramids	A part of the medulla that consists of corticospinal fibers.
Neurology	The study of the nervous system and its disorders.
Optic thalamus	The portion of the thalamus relating to visual processing.
Spinal accessory nerve	The 11th cranial nerve, which innervates the head and shoulders.
Stria terminalis	The white matter pathway that sends information from the amygdala to the basal forebrain.
Striatum	Gray matter structure of the basal ganglia.
Vagus nerve	The 10th cranial nerve, which, among other functions, has visceral motor control of the heart.

To grasp the miraculous properties of brain function, bear in mind that Mother Nature, not a team of rational engineers, built it. Although the Earth formed approximately 5 billion years ago and life first appeared about 3.5 billion years ago, human brains in their present form have been around only about 100,000 years. The primate brain appeared during the Oligocene epoch, between 34 million and 23 million years ago, evolving to produce the progressively larger brains of the apes in the Miocene epoch between roughly 23 million and 5 million years ago. The juggernaut of evolution continued, yielding the brains of great apes and chimpanzees, and finally fashioning the present human brain, capable of all sorts of wondrous feats.

During most of history, humans were too busy to think about thought. Although there can be little doubt that human brains could engage in such activities, life was given over to more practical work, such as surviving in tough environments, developing ways to live better by inventing agriculture or domesticating animals, and so forth. However, as soon as civilization developed to the point at which day-to-day survival did not occupy every hour of every day, our ancestors began to spend time constructing complex theories about the motives of fellow humans. Examples of attempts to understand the world and our place in it include *Oedipus Rex* (the ancient Greek play that deals with the nature of the child–parent conflict) and Mesopotamian and Egyptian theories on the nature of religion and the universe. The brain mechanisms that enabled the generation of theories about the nature of human nature thrived inside the heads of ancient humans. Yet they had one big limitation: They did not have the methodology to systematically explore the mind through experimentation.

In a diary entry of 1846, the brilliant philosopher Søren Kierkegaard wrote:

> That a man should simply and profoundly say that he cannot understand how consciousness comes into existence—is perfectly natural. But that a man should glue his eye to a microscope and stare and stare and stare—and still not be able to see how it happens—is ridiculous, and it is particularly ridiculous when it is supposed to be serious. . . . If the natural sciences had been developed in Socrates' day as they are now, all the sophists would have been scientists. One would have hung a microscope outside his shop in order to attract custom, and then would have had a sign painted saying: "Learn and see through a giant microscope how a man thinks (and on reading the advertisement Socrates would have said: 'That is how men who do not think behave')."

The Nobel laureate Max Delbrück (1986) began his fascinating account of the evolution of the cosmos in his book *Mind from Matter?* with the foregoing quote of Kierkegaard. Delbrück is part of the modern tradition that started in the 19th century: Observe, manipulate, measure, and start to determine how the brain gets its job done. Armchair thinking is a wonderful thing and has produced fascinating science such as theoretical physics and mathematics. But to understand how a biological system works, a laboratory is needed and experiments have to be performed. Ideas derived from introspection can be eloquent and fascinating, but are they true? Philosophy can add perspective, but is it right? Only scientific method can move a topic along on sure footing. And just think about the rich phenomena to study.

THE BRAIN STORY

You are given a problem to solve. A hunk of biological tissue is known to think, remember, attend, solve problems, want sex, play games, write novels, exhibit prejudice, and do a zillion other things. You are supposed to figure out how it works. Before starting, you might ask a few questions. Does the blob work as a unit with each part contributing to a whole? Or is the blob full of individual processing parts, each carrying out specific functions, with the result being something that looks like it is acting as a whole unit? After all, the blob that is the city of New York looks like an integrated whole from a distance, but it is actually composed of millions of individual processors—that is, people. Perhaps people, in turn, are made of smaller, more specialized units.

This central issue—whether the mind is enabled by the whole brain working in concert or by specialized parts of the brain working at least partly independently—is what fuels much of modern research. As we will see, the dominant view has changed over the years, and it continues to change today. Thomas Willis foreshadowed cognitive neuroscience with the notion that isolated brain damage could affect behavior. In the 19th century, people who studied **phrenology**, called *phrenologists*, declared that the brain was organized around some 35 or more specific functions (Figure 1.4). These functions, which ranged from cognitive basics such as language and color perception to more ephemeral capacities such as hope and self-esteem, were thought to be supported by specific brain regions.

The phrenology movement was led by Franz Joseph Gall and J. G. Spurzheim, who believed that if a person used one of the faculties with greater frequency than the others, the part of the brain representing that function would grow (Gall & Spurzheim, 1810–1819). According to the phrenologists, this increase in local brain size would cause a bump in the overlying skull. Logically, then, Gall and his colleagues believed that a careful analysis of the skull could go a long way in describing the personality of the person inside the skull. Gall called this technique *anatomical personology* (Figure 1.5).

Gall, an Austrian physician and neuroanatomist, was not a scientist, in the sense that he did not test his ideas; but he did contribute to the field by carrying on Willis's scientifically tested notion: Different brain functions are localized to discrete brain regions.

At the time of Gall, however, not everyone believed in this "localizationist" view, including physiologist Marie-Jean-Pierre Flourens (Figure 1.6). A large group of people rejected the idea that specific processes such as language and memory were localized within circumscribed brain regions, and Flourens became their champion. He studied animals, especially birds, and discovered that lesions in particular areas of the brain did not cause certain deficits in behavior. No matter where he made a lesion in the brain, the bird recovered. Flourens developed the notion that the whole brain participated in behavior, a view later known as the **aggregate field theory**. In 1824, Flourens wrote, "All sensations, all perceptions, and all volitions occupy the same seat in these (cerebral) organs. The faculty of sensation, percept and volition is then essentially one faculty."

Figure 1.4 **(a)** Franz Joseph Gall (1758–1828), one of the founders of phrenology. **(b)** The right hemisphere of the brain, according to Gall and Spurzheim in 1810.

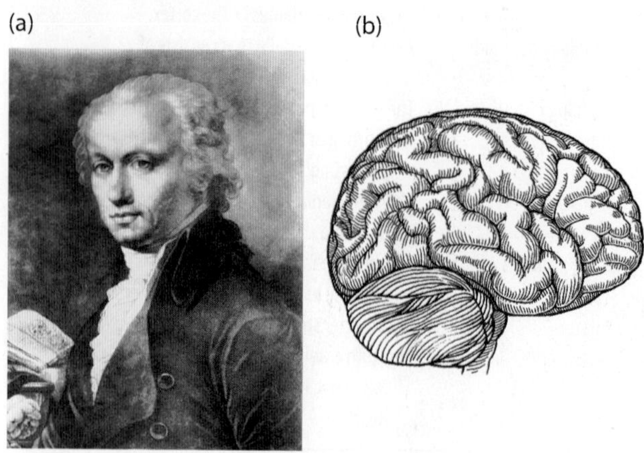

(a) (b) (c)

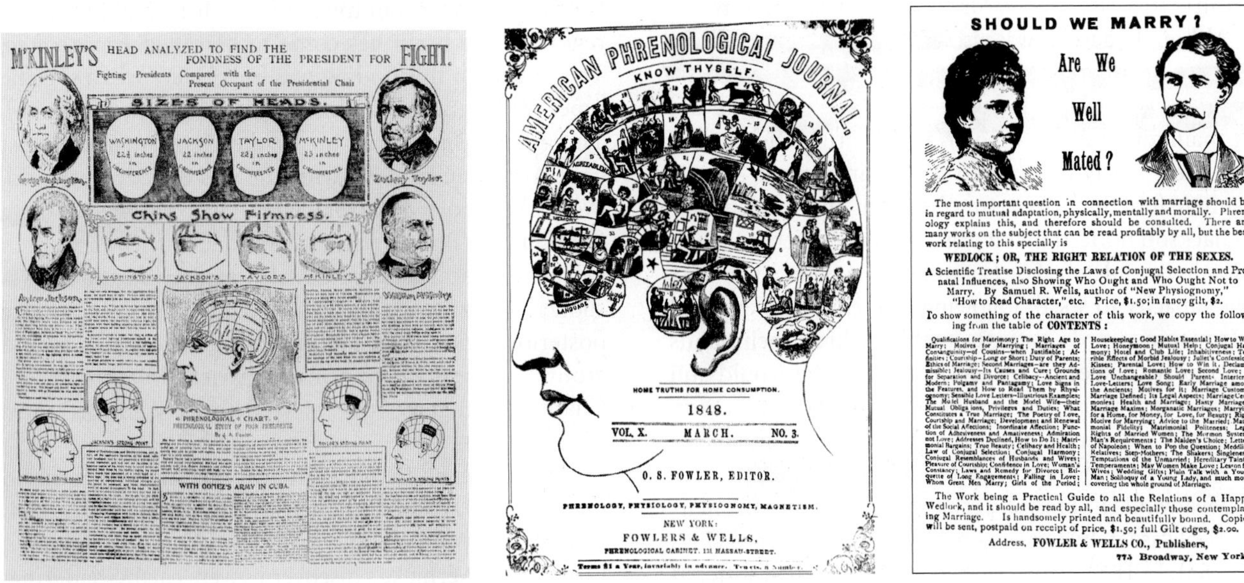

Figure 1.5 **(a)** An analysis of Presidents Washington, Jackson, Taylor, and McKinley by Jessie A. Fowler, from the *Phrenological Journal*, June 1898. **(b)** The phrenological map of personal characteristics on the skull, from the *American Phrenological Journal*, March 1848. **(c)** Fowler & Wells Co. publication on marriage compatibility in connection with phrenology, 1888.

However, work in Europe helped swing the notion back to the localizationist view. In England, for example, the neurologist John Hughlings Jackson (Figure 1.7) began to publish his observations on the behavior of persons with brain damage. One of the key features of Jackson's writings was the incorporation of suggestions for experiments to test his observations. He noticed, for example, that during the start of their seizures, some epileptic patients moved in such characteristic ways that the seizure appeared to be stimulating a set map of the body in the brain; that is, the clonic and tonic jerks in muscles, produced by the abnormal epileptic firings of neurons in the brain, progressed in an orderly way from one body part to another. This phenomenon led Jackson to propose a *topographic* organization in the cerebral cortex: In this view, a map of the body was represented

Figure 1.6 **(a)** Marie-Jean-Pierre Flourens (1794–1867), who supported the idea later termed the *aggregate field theory*. **(b)** The posture of a pigeon deprived of its cerebral hemispheres, as described by Flourens.

(a) (b)

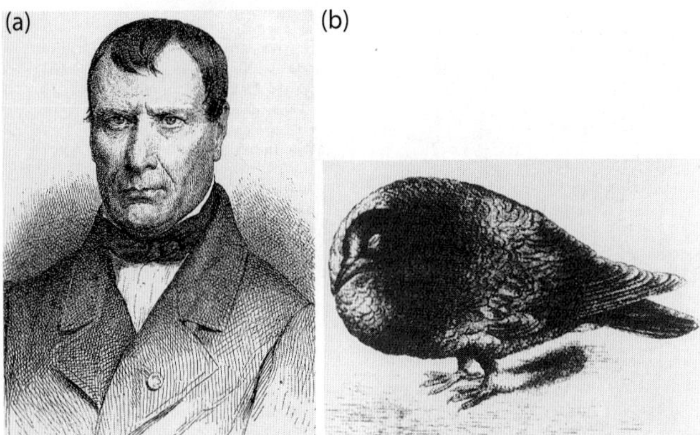

Figure 1.7 John Hughlings Jackson (1835–1911), an English neurologist who was one of the first to recognize the localizationist view.

in a particular cortical area. Jackson was one of the first to realize this essential feature of brain organization.

Although Jackson was also the first to observe that lesions on the right side of the brain affect visuospatial processes more than do lesions on the left side, he did not maintain that specific parts of the right side of the brain were solely committed to this important human cognitive function. Being an observant clinical neurologist, Jackson noticed that it was rare for a patient to lose a function completely. For example, most people who lost their capacity to speak following a cerebral stroke could still say some words. Patients unable to direct their hands voluntarily to specific places on their bodies could still easily scratch those places if they itched. When Jackson made these observations, he concluded that many regions of the brain contributed to a given behavior.

Meanwhile in France, perhaps the most famous neurological case in history was reported by Paul Broca (Figure 1.8a). In 1861, Broca treated a man who had suffered a stroke; the patient could understand language but could not speak. Consistent with Jackson's observations, though, the patient could utter something: the word *tan*. Such patients could also usually speak automatically, so although they might say, "Tan, tan, tan, …" in response to the question "Who are you?," they might easily count to 10 or sing well-known songs like "Happy Birthday."

The exact part of the brain that was damaged in Broca's patient was in the left inferior frontal lobe. This region of the brain has come to be called *Broca's area*. The impact of this finding was huge. Here was a specific aspect of language that was impaired by a specific lesion. This theme was picked up by the German neurologist Carl Wernicke. In 1876, when he was only 26 years old, Wernicke reported a stroke victim who could talk quite freely, unlike Broca's patient, but made little sense when he spoke. Wernicke's patient also could not understand spoken or written language. He had a lesion in a more posterior region of the left hemisphere, an area in and around where the temporal and parietal lobes meet (see Chapter 3) that is now referred to as *Wernicke's area* (Figure 1.8b).

Today these differences in how the brain responds to focal disease are well known (H. Damasio et al., 2004; R. J. Wise, 2003). A little over 100 years ago, however, Broca's and Wernicke's discoveries were earth-shattering. Willis's first observations that isolated brain damage could affect behavior had largely been forgotten. Thus, with the discoveries of Broca and Wernicke, attention was again paid to this startling point: Focal brain damage causes specific behavioral deficits. In those days investigators were limited in their ability to identify a patient's lesion. Physicians could observe the site of injury—for

Figure 1.8 **(a)** Paul Broca (1824–1880). **(b)** The connections between the speech centers, from Wernicke's 1876 article on aphasia. A = Wernicke's sensory speech center; B = Broca's area for speech; Pc = Wernicke's area concerned with language comprehension and meaning.

(a)

(b)

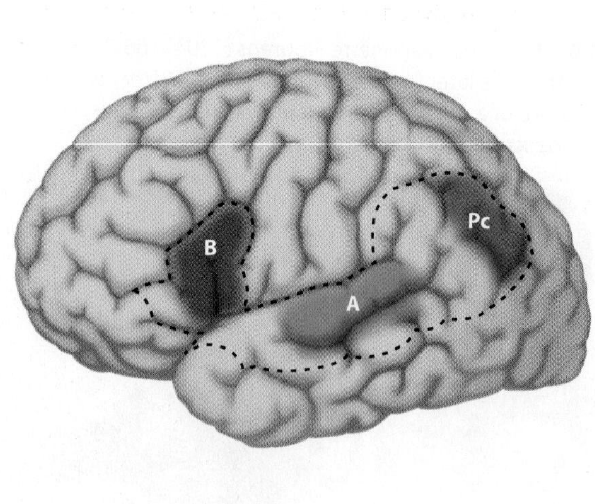

example, a penetrating head wound from a bullet—but they had to wait for the patient to die in order to determine the site of the brain lesion. The latter might take months or years, and usually was not possible: The physician would lose track of the patient after he or she recovered, and when the patient eventually died the physician was generally not informed and thus could not examine the brain to correlate brain damage with the person's behavioral deficit(s).

Today the site of brain injury can be determined in a few minutes with imaging methods that scan the living brain and produce a picture (Osborn et al., 2004; see Chapter 4). We will discuss these techniques as we progress through this book. (As an interesting historical footnote, the brain of Broca's famous patient has been preserved and is still housed in a laboratory in Paris. Recent scanning of the brain revealed the patient's lesion to be much larger than what Broca had originally described; Castaigne et al., 1980; Naeser et al., 1989.)

As is so often the case, the study of humans leads to questions for those who work on animal models. Shortly after Broca's discovery, the German physiologists Gustav Fritsch and Eduard Hitzig electrically stimulated discrete parts of a dog brain and observed that this stimulation produced characteristic movements in the dog (Figure 1.9). This discovery led neuroanatomists to a closer analysis of the cerebral cortex and its cellular organization; they wanted support for their ideas about the importance of local regions. Because these regions performed different functions, it followed that they ought to look different at the cellular level.

Following this logic, German neuroanatomists began to analyze the brain by using microscopic methods to view the cell types in different brain regions. Perhaps the most famous of the group was Korbinian Brodmann, who analyzed the cellular organization of the cortex and characterized 52 distinct regions (Figure 1.10). Brodmann used tissue stains, such as the one developed by Franz Nissl, which permitted him to visualize the different cell types in different brain regions. How cells differ between brain regions is called **cytoarchitectonics**, or *cellular architecture.*

Soon many now-famous anatomists, including Oskar Vogt, Vladimir Betz, Theodor Meynert, Constantin von Economo, Gerhardt von Bonin, and Percival Bailey, contributed to this work, and several subdivided the cortex even further than Brodmann had. To a large extent, these investigators discovered that various cytoarchitectonically described brain areas do indeed represent functionally distinct brain regions. For example, Brodmann first distinguished area 17 from area 18—a distinction that has proved correct in subsequent functional studies. The characterization of the primary

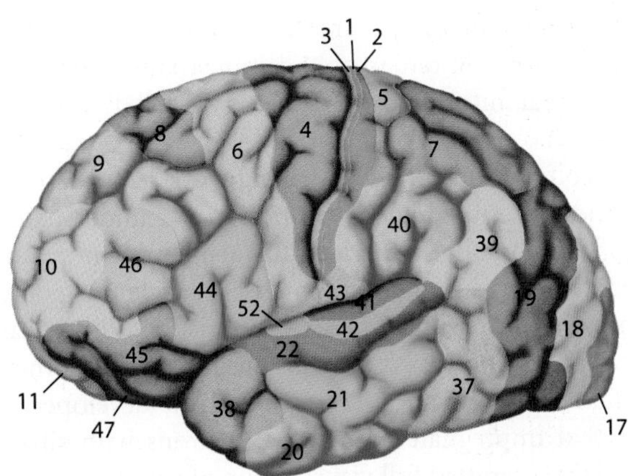

Figure 1.10 Sampling of the 52 distinct areas described by Brodmann on the basis of cell structure and arrangement.

Figure 1.9 **(a)** Gustav Theodor Fritsch (1838–1927), physiologist and anatomist. **(b)** Eduard Hitzig (1838–1907), professor of psychiatry. **(c)** The original illustration of the dog's cortex by Fritsch and Hitzig.

(a)

(b)

(c)

visual area of the cortex, area 17, as distinct from surrounding area 18, remarkably demonstrates the power of the cytoarchitectonic approach, as we will discover in Chapter 3.

Despite all this groundbreaking work in cytoarchitectonics, the truly huge revolution in our understanding of the nervous system was happening down south, in Italy and Spain. There, an intense struggle was going on between two brilliant neuroanatomists. Oddly, it was the work of one that led to the insights of the other. Camillo Golgi (Figure 1.11), an Italian, developed a stain that impregnated individual neurons with silver. This stain permitted full visualization of single neurons. Using Golgi's method, Santiago Ramón y Cajal (Figure 1.12), a Spaniard, went on to find that, contrary to the view of Golgi and others, neurons were discrete entities. Golgi had believed that the whole brain was a **syncytium**, a continuous mass of tissue that shares a common cytoplasm. Ramón y Cajal extended Golgi's findings and was the first to identify not only the unitary nature of neurons, but also their transmission of electrical information in only one direction, from the dendrites down to the axonal tip (Figure 1.13).

Shepherd (1992) recounted the fascinating story of Camillo Golgi and contrasted it with Ramón y Cajal's. Born near Milan, Golgi, the son of a physician, received his medical degree at the age of 22 from the University of Pavia in Italy, yet he was outside the mainstream of research in Germany's great universities—a fact that haunted him throughout his career. Still, Pavia produced many spectacular scientists, including physicist Alessandro Volta, Christopher Columbus, and a host of great biologists. Among this august group, Golgi was a well-trained physician and scientist.

Although his career started off with great promise, Golgi was forced, out of financial necessity, to take a job outside of Pavia, in the town of Abbiategrasso, where he became the resident physician at the Hospital of the Chronically Ill. Under such circumstances, it was highly unlikely that Golgi would continue his scientific life. But he persevered, and, working by the candlelight in his kitchen, he developed the most famous cell stain in the history of the world: the silver method for staining neurons—*la reazione nera*, "the black reaction."

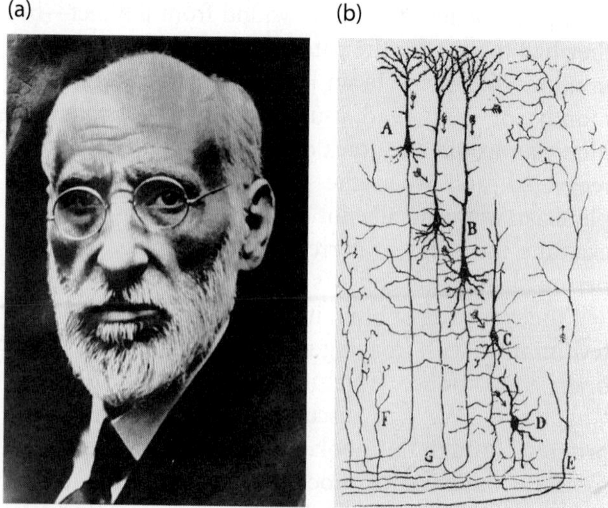

Figure 1.12 **(a)** Santiago Ramón y Cajal (1852–1934), cowinner of the Nobel Prize in 1906. **(b)** Ramón y Cajal's drawing of the afferent inflow to the mammalian cortex.

Figure 1.11 **(a)** Camillo Golgi (1843–1926), cowinner of the Nobel Prize in 1906. **(b)** Golgi's drawings of different types of ganglion cells in dog and cat.

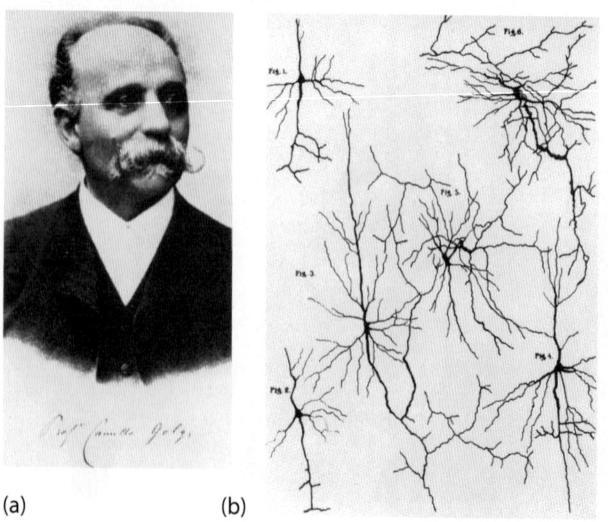

Figure 1.13 A bipolar retinal cell, illustrating the dendrites and axon of the neuron.

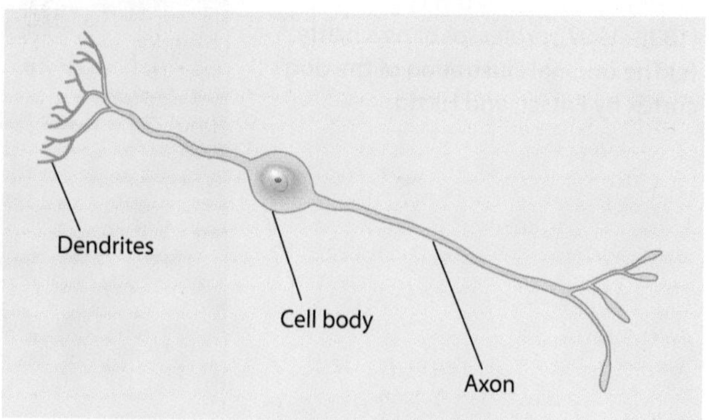

MILESTONES IN COGNITIVE NEUROSCIENCE

Interlude

In textbook writing, authors use broad strokes to communicate milestones that have become important to our thinking over a long period of time. It would be folly, however, not to alert the reader to the complex and intriguing cultural, intellectual, and personal setting. The problems that besieged the world's first scientists remain today, in full glory. Issues of authorship, ego, funding, and credit are all integral to the fabric of intellectual life. Much as teenagers never imagine that their parents once had the same interests and desires as they do, novitiates in science believe they are tackling new issues for the first time in human history. Gordon Shepherd (1991), in his riveting account *Foundations of the Neuron Doctrine,* detailed the variety of forces at work on the figures we now feature in our brief history.

Shepherd noted how the explosion of research on the nervous system started in the 18th century as part of the intense activity swirling around the birth of modern science. As examples, Robert Fulton invented the steam engine in 1807, and Hans Christian Ørsted discovered electromagnetism. Of more interest to our concerns, Leopoldo Nobili, an Italian physicist, invented a precursor to the galvanometer—a device that laid the foundation for studying electrical currents in living tissue. Many years before, in 1674, Anton van Leeuwenhoek in Holland had used a primitive microscope to view animal tissue (Figure 1). One of his first observations was of a cross section of a cow's nerve in which he noted "very minute vessels." This observation was consistent with René Descartes's idea that nerves contained fluid or "spirits," and these spirits were responsible for the flow of sensory and motor information in the body (Figure 2). To go further, however, this revolutionary work would have to overcome the problems with early microscopes, not the least of which was the quality of glass used in the lens. Chromatic aberrations made them useless at higher magnification. It was not until lens makers solved this problem that microscopic anatomy again took center stage in the history of biology.

Figure 1 **(a)** Antoni van Leeuwenhoek (1632–1723). **(b)** One of the original microscopes used by Leeuwenhoek, composed of two brass plates holding the lens.

Figure 2 René Descartes (1596–1650). Portrait by Frans Hals.

The Golgi stain became famous, as did Golgi himself. His intense interest in disease led him to several discoveries in pathobiology, and eventually he was recruited back to Pavia to be a professor. Still, his writings were not widely known outside of Italy, so he translated them, publishing them in the *Italian Archives of Biology*—which, oddly, was in French. Golgi's reputation grew, and in 1906 he was awarded the Nobel Prize in Physiology or Medicine jointly with Ramón y Cajal.

Meanwhile, Ramón y Cajal was the rambunctious son of another physician. Not until his ambitious father started tutoring him at home did he develop an interest in biology. From a complex childhood, Ramón y Cajal emerged as what some call the *father of modern neuroscience.* He is credited as the first to articulate fully the neuron doctrine.

The irony in the story, as we already mentioned, is that Ramón y Cajal made many of his discoveries as a result of the Golgi stain. He first saw the stain in the Madrid home of a colleague, Luis Simarro, who had learned the technique while attending a meeting in Paris. Ramón y Cajal said that it was there, in Simarro's home laboratory—not unlike the laboratory where Golgi invented the stain—that he saw for the first time "the famous sections of the brain impregnated by the silver method of the Savant of Pavia" (Sherrington, 1935).

Ramón y Cajal's response to seeing the stain remains fascinating (translated by Sherrington, 1935):

> Against a clear background stood black threadlets, some slender and smooth, some thick and thorny, in a pattern punctuated by small dense spots, stellate or fusiform. All was sharp as a sketch with Chinese ink on transparent Japanese paper. And to think that that was the same tissue which stained with carmine or logwood left the eye in a tangled thicket where sight may stare and grope for ever fruitlessly, baffled in its effort to unravel confusion and lost forever in a twilit doubt. Here, on the contrary, all was clear and plain as a diagram. A look was enough. Dumbfounded, I could not take my eye from the microscope. (p. 430)

Many truly gifted scientists were involved in the early history of the **neuron doctrine** (Shepherd, 1991). For example, Jan Evangelista Purkinje (Figure 1.14), a Czech trained in German-controlled Prague who had to travel to Poland to get a university position, not only described the first nerve cell in the nervous system but also invented the stroboscope, described common visual phenomena, and made a host of other major discoveries.

Even Sigmund Freud (Figure 1.15) got into the neuron act. As a young man, Freud studied microscopic anatomy with the great German anatomist Ernst Brücke. Freud even wrote an essay about his subsequent and independent work with crayfishes. Indeed, some of Freud's biographers suggest that he, too, had come up with the idea of the neuron as a separate and distinct physiological unit.

Hermann von Helmholtz (Figure 1.16), perhaps one of the most famous scientists of all time, also contributed to the early study of the nervous system. Helmholtz was the first to suggest that invertebrates would be good models for studying vertebrate brain mechanisms. This was the same Helmholtz who went on to make major contributions to physics, medicine, and psychology.

British physiologist Sir Charles Sherrington vigorously pursued the neuron's behavior as a unit and, indeed, coined the term *synapse* to describe the junction between two neurons.

With Golgi, Ramón y Cajal, and these other bright minds, the neuron doctrine was born—a discovery

(a)

(b)

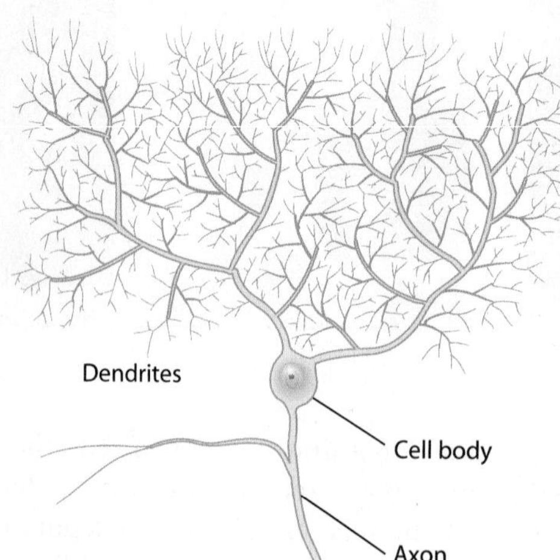

Figure 1.14 **(a)** Jan Evangelista Purkinje (1787–1869), who described the first nerve cell in the nervous system. **(b)** A Purkinje cell of the cerebellum.

(a)

(b)

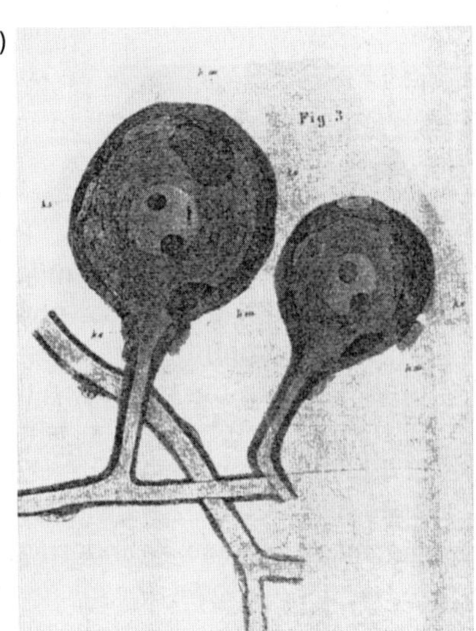

Figure 1.15 **(a)** Sigmund Freud (1856–1939). **(b)** From his work with crayfishes, Freud published this illustration as an example of how two nerve fibers connect—a concept that Ramón y Cajal disproved.

whose importance was highlighted by the 1906 Nobel Prize shared by Golgi and Ramón y Cajal, and later by the 1932 Nobel Prize awarded to Sherrington.

As the 20th century progressed, the localizationist views became mediated by those who saw that, even though particular neuronal locations might serve independent functions, the network of these locations and the interaction between them are what yield the integrated, holistic behavior that humans exhibit.

French biologist Claude Bernard (1865) wrote,

> If it is possible to dissect all the parts of the body, to isolate them in order to study thm in their structure, form and connections it is not the same in life, where all parts cooperate at the same time in a common aim. An organ does not live on its own, one could often say it did not exist anatomically, as the boundary established is sometimes purely arbitrary. What lives, what exists, is the whole, and if one studies all the parts of any mechanisms separately, one does not know the way they work.

Thus scientists have come to believe that the knowledge of the parts (the neurons and brain structures) must be understood in conjunction with the whole (i.e., what the parts make when they come together: the mind). Next we explore the history of the mind.

Figure 1.16 **(a)** Hermann Ludwig von Helmholtz (1821–1894). **(b)** Helmholtz's apparatus for measuring the velocity of nerve conduction.

(a)

(b)

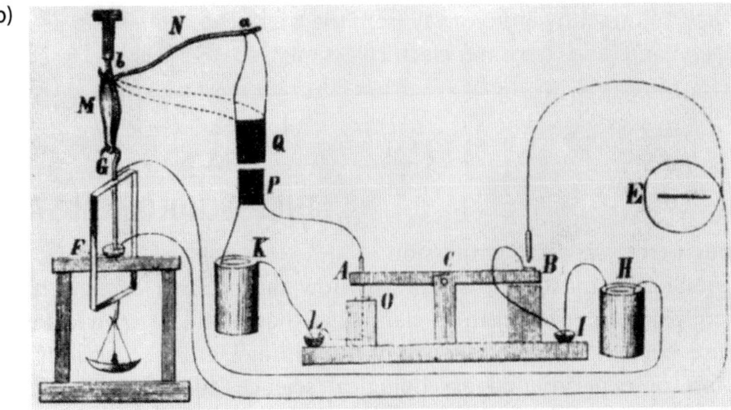

MILESTONES IN COGNITIVE NEUROSCIENCE

Female Pioneers in Neuroscience

As in most other scientific fields, until relatively recently few women have been recognized for their contributions to neuroscience. Although it is easy to draw the conclusion that the reason is a lack of participation by women, all too frequently the reason is that women have been involved but have not been fully credited for their work. Consider the case of the microelectrode. An important tool in electrophysiological studies today, the microelectrode is used to deliver discrete electrical or chemical stimulation to a cell and to record the electrical activity from within individual nerve and muscle cells. Ralph Gerard is the scientist credited with discovery of the microelectrode, among many other distinguished accomplishments. However, two notable women made significant contributions to the microelectrode's discovery, though they were not formally recognized.

In 1902, Ida Hyde (see part [a] of the figure) was the first woman to be elected to the American Physiological Society; she remained the only woman in the society until 1914. She was the first woman to be awarded a doctorate in physiology from a German university (the University of Heidelberg) and to do research at Harvard Medical School. She invented the first microelectrode for intracellular work with lower organisms (see part [b] of the figure) by combining instruments used by F. H. Pratt in 1917 and by M. A. Barber in 1912. Hyde constructed a salt solution–filled electrode of very small diameter (3 μm or so) and connected it to a small column of mercury whose level could be altered by the introduction of varying amounts of positive or negative electrical current. This mercury, in turn, could force the salt solution toward or away from the tip of the capillary and also transmit electrical stimuli to the cell through the salt solution. In 1921, using this method, Hyde provided the first evidence that the recently discovered principle of all-or-nothing contraction was not true for all contractile cells. The microelectrode was subsequently lost during World War II and had to be reinvented.

The first report that a microelectrode had been used to record resting potentials from the membranes of a frog muscle was published in 1942 by Judith Graham Pool (1917–1975; under Graham), G. R. Carlson, and Ralph Gerard. Their electrodes (2–3 μm in diameter) were also bent capillary tubes drawn out to a tip and filled with an isotonic salt solution of potassium chloride that allowed the recording of resting potentials and action potentials evoked with the electrode. Although Gerard was fully credited with the microelectrode discovery because he decreased the diameter to 0.25 μm, it appears that, at the least, Pool was instrumental in its development; and according to her, she actually invented it without any credit for her achievement.

In addition to being unrecognized for their work, women have been overshadowed by similar work done by their male contemporaries, as exemplified by studies of the recording of single nerve cells. Though most neuroscience textbooks discuss the work of Alan Hodgkin and Andrew Huxley on the giant axon of the squid, another scientist who is less recognized, Angelique Arvanitaki (1901–1983), made significant contributions to the study of the single neuron.

By the 1940s, neurobiologists had learned to penetrate electrically active cells with microelectrodes and wanted to study the properties of nerves from within a single cell. Although vertebrate nerves are minute and housed in a brain and nervous system, the large nerve

THE PSYCHOLOGICAL STORY

Although the medical profession was pioneering most early studies of how the brain worked, psychologists began to claim that they could measure behavior and indeed study the mind. Until the start of experimental psychological science, the mind had been the province of philosophers, who wondered about the nature of knowledge and how we come to know things. The philosophers had two main positions: **rationalism** and **empiricism**. Rationalism grew out of the Enlightenment period. It replaced religion, and among intellectuals and scientists it became the only way to think about the world. Through this thinking, rationalists would determine true beliefs. They would reject beliefs that,

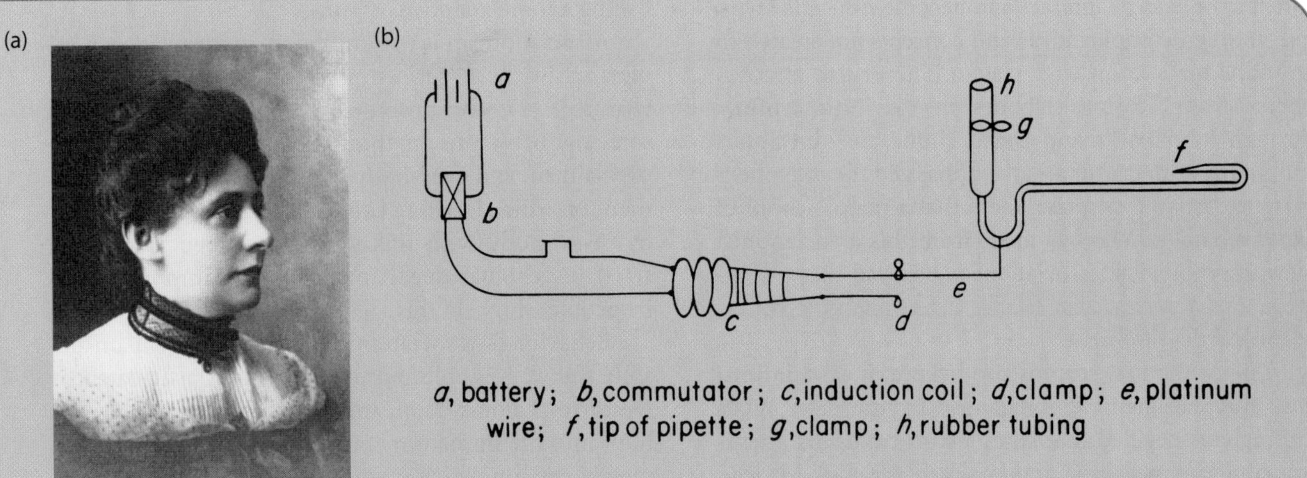

(a) Ida Hyde (1857–1945), the first woman elected to the American Physiological Society, 1902. **(b)** Ida Hyde's microelectrode.

cells of certain invertebrates are not. Arvanitaki (1939) developed the ganglion preparation of large identifiable nerves in the snails *Aplysia* (sea hare) and *Helix* (land snail). She also discovered that, in low-calcium solutions, isolated nerve fibers of the cuttlefish *Sepia* (a relative of the octopus) produced regular electrical oscillations that periodically became larger and larger, until from time to time the nerve fired a series of action potentials. Arvanitaki was the first to demonstrate that spontaneous, rhythmically recurring activity could be an inherent property of a single nerve without the requirement of an entire neuronal circuit to generate it. In addition, she found that, when two or more nerves run close together, the activity in one nerve can entrain the activity in its neighbor. Hodgkin and Huxley won the 1963 Nobel Prize in Physiology or Medicine for analyzing the ionic basis of the action potential in the squid axon and are recognized in most neuroscience textbooks, overshadowing Arvanitaki's significant contributions to this area of study.

Since Brenda Milner's memory work in the 1960s, many women in numerous areas of neuroscience have been recognized as leading scientists in their field: Patricia Goldman-Rakic (neurophysiology and neuroanatomy of the frontal cortex), past president of the Society for Neuroscience; Margaret Livingstone (visual neurophysiology); Leslie Ungerleider (cortical functional neuroimaging); Carol Colby (vision and the parietal cortex); Mary Hatten (developmental cellular neurophysiology); Carla Shatz (visual neurophysiology), past president of the Society for Neuroscience; Christine Nussellin-Volhard (molecular neurophysiology); and perhaps the best recognized, Rita Levi-Montalcini, the neurobiologist who shared the 1986 Nobel Prize in Physiology or Medicine for the discovery of nerve growth factor, and Linda B. Buck, who with Richard Axel earned the 2004 Nobel Prize in Physiology or Medicine for her work on the organization of the olfactory system. Although the field of neuroscience still contains more male members than females, this inequality is quickly disappearing, as the number of female graduate students pursuing degrees in neuroscience indicates.

although perhaps comforting, were unsupportable and even superstitious.

Although rationalism frequently is equated with logical thinking, it is different. Rationalism takes into account such issues as the meaning of life, whereas logic does not. Logic simply relies on inductive reasoning, statistics, probabilities, and the like. It does not concern itself with such personal mental states as happiness, self-interest, and public good. Each person weighs these issues differently, and as a consequence a rational decision is more problematic than a simple logical decision.

Empiricism, on the other hand, is the idea that all knowledge comes from sensory experience. Direct sensory experience produces simple ideas and concepts. When simple ideas interact and become *associated* with one another, complex ideas and concepts are created in an individual's knowledge system. The British philosophers—from Thomas Hobbes in the 17th century, through John Locke and David Hume, to John Stuart Mill in the 19th century—all emphasized the role of experience. It is no surprise, then, that a major school of experimental psychology arose from this associationist view. Psychological associationists believed that the aggregate of a person's experience determined the course of mental development.

One of the first scientists to believe in **associationism** was Hermann Ebbinghaus. In the late 1800s Ebbinghaus decided that complex processes like memory could be measured and analyzed. He took his lead from the great psychophysicists Gustav Fechner and Ernst Heinrich Weber, who were hard at work relating the physical properties of things like light and sound to the psychological experiences that they produce in the observer. These measurements were rigorous and reproducible. Ebbinghaus was one of the first to understand that one could also measure mental processes that are more internal, such as memory (see Chapter 8).

Even more influential was the classic 1911 monograph *Animal Intelligence: An Experimental Study of the Associative Processes in Animals* by Edward Thorndike (Figure 1.17). In this volume Thorndike articulated his law of effect, which was the first general statement about the nature of associations. Thorndike simply observed that a response that was followed by a reward would be stamped into the organism as a habitual response. If no reward followed a response, the response would disappear. Thus, rewards provided a mechanism for establishing a more adaptive response.

Figure 1.17 Edward L. Thorndike (1874–1949).

Associationism is committed to an idea widely popularized by the American psychologist John B. Watson (Figure 1.18), who promoted the notion that he could turn any baby into anything. Learning was the key, he proclaimed, and everybody had the same neural equipment on which learning could build. American psychology was giddy with this idea. Consumed with it, all strong psychology departments in the country were run by people who held this view.

Behaviorist–associationist psychology went on despite the well-established position—first articulated by Descartes, Leibniz, Kant, and others—that complexity is built into the human organism. Sensory information is merely data on which preexisting mental structures act. This idea, which dominates psychology today, was blithely asserted in that golden age.

The behaviorist view was challenged when Gestalt psychologists, working with perceptual phenomena, reported that percepts were best understood in relation to the emergent properties of a stimulus. Apparent motion, for instance, was an emergent property of real-world stimuli. It existed only as a function of built-in properties of the brain; it was not learned. The Gestalt psychologists developed hundreds of demonstrations making similar points.

The true end of the dominance of **behaviorism** and stimulus–response psychology did not come until the late 1950s. Almost overnight, psychologists began to think in terms of cognition, not just behavior. George Miller (Figure 1.19), who had been a confirmed behaviorist, had a change of heart in the 1950s. In 1951, Miller wrote an influential book entitled *Language and Communication* and noted in the preface, "The bias is behavioristic." Eleven years later he wrote another book, called *Psychology, the Science of Mental Life*—a title that signals a complete rejection of the idea that psychology should study just behavior.

Upon reflection, Miller determined the exact date of his rejection of behaviorism and cognitive awakening to be September 11, 1956, during the second Symposium on Information Theory, held at the Massachusetts Institute of Technology (MIT). That year had been a rich one for several disciplines. In computer science, Allen Newell and Herbert Simon successfully introduced Information Processing Language I, a powerful program that simulated the proof of logic theorems. The computer guru John von Neumann wrote the Silliman lectures on neural organization. A famous meeting on artificial intelligence was held at Dartmouth College, with Marvin Minsky, Claude

(a)

(b)

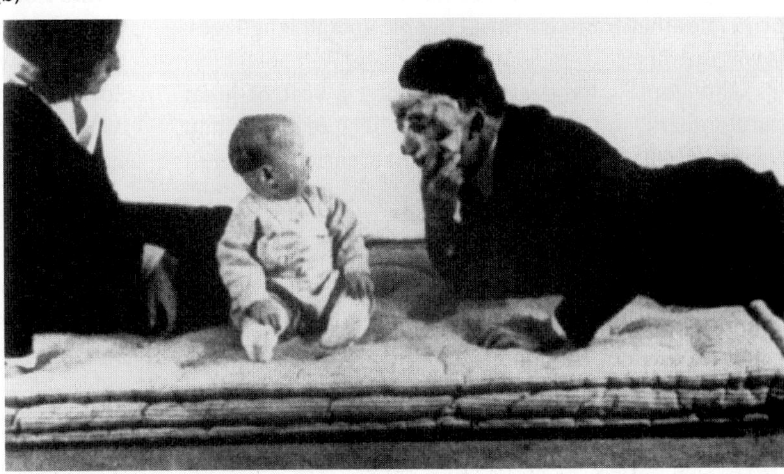

Figure 1.18 **(a)** John B. Watson (1878–1958). **(b)** Watson and "Little Albert" during one of Watson's fear-conditioning experiments.

Shannon (known as the father of information theory), and many others in attendance.

Big things were also happening in psychology. As a result of World War II, new techniques were being applied. James Tanner and John Swets used signal detection and computer technology to study perception. (These techniques had been developed, in large part, to help the U.S. Department of Defense detect submarines.) In 1956 Miller wrote his classic paper "The Magical Number Seven, Plus-or-Minus Two," in which he showed that there is a limit on the amount of information that can be apprehended in a brief period of time. In addition, the developmental psychologist Jerome Bruner was working on the problem of thinking. Although Bruner saw limited utility to associationist ideas in childhood learning, he believed in higher level processes involved in thinking that were built on representations and mental maps.

Perhaps the most important development, however, was from Noam Chomsky's work (Figure 1.20; for a review see Chomsky, 2006). A preliminary version of his ideas on syntactic theories was published in September 1956 in an article titled "Three Models for the Description of Language." Chomsky's effort transformed the study of language virtually overnight. The deep message was that learning theory—that is, associationism, then heavily championed by B. F. Skinner—could in no way explain how language was learned. The complexity of

Figure 1.19 George A. Miller.

Figure 1.20 Noam Chomsky

language was built into the brain, and it ran on rules and principles that transcended all people and all languages. It was universal.

Thus, on September 11, 1956, after a year of great development and theory shifting, Miller realized that, although behaviorism had important theories to offer, it could not explain all learning. He set out to understand how the brain works as an integrated whole—to understand the workings of the brain *and* the mind. Many followed his new mission, and a few years later a new field was born: cognitive neuroscience.

SUMMARY

Thomas Willis first introduced us, in the mid 1600s, to the idea that damage to the brain could influence behavior and that the cerebral cortex might indeed be the seat of what makes us human. Phrenologists expanded on this idea and developed a localizationist view of the brain. Patients like those of Broca and Wernicke later supported the importance of specific brain locations on human behavior (like language). Ramón y Cajal, Sherrington, and Brodmann, among others, provided support that the microarchitecture of distinct brain regions could support a localizationist view of the brain, but that these areas are interconnected. Soon scientists began to realize that the integration of the brain's neural networks might be what enables the mind.

At the same time that neuroscientists were researching the brain, psychologists were studying the mind. Out of the philosophical theory of empiricism came the idea of associationism, that any response followed by a reward would be maintained and that these associations were the basis of how the mind learned. Associationism was the prevailing theory for many years, until Chomsky and Miller realized that it couldn't explain all learning or all actions of the mind.

Neuroscientists and psychologists both reached the conclusion that there is more to the brain than just the sum of its parts, that the brain must enable the mind—but how? The term *cognitive neuroscience* was coined in the late 1970s because fields of neuroscience and psychology were once again coming together. Neuroscience was in need of the theories of the psychology of the mind, and psychology was ready for a greater understanding of the working of the brain. The resulting marriage was cognitive neuroscience.

KEY TERMS

aggregate field theory
associationism
behaviorism
cognitive neuroscience
cytoarchitectonics
empiricism
neuron doctrine
phrenology
rationalism
syncytium

TAKE-HOME MESSAGES

General

- Thomas Willis was among the first to link specific brain damage with specific behavioral deficits in humans.
- The field of cognitive neuroscience joins the methods of psychology, philosophy, and neuroscience to help us understand how the brain enables the mind.

History of Cognitive Neuroscience: The Brain Story

- Phrenologists believed that specific locations in the brain were specialized to enable specific faculties; if such faculties were used with greater frequency, the brain region would grow and cause a bump in the overlying skull. By "reading" the bumps in a person's skull, they believed they could learn about that person's skills and personality.
- John Hughlings Jackson was the first to bring scientific experimentation to the localizationist view.
- Paul Broca was the first to observe that a patient could lose the ability to generate speech following localized brain damage to the left hemisphere. Carl Wernicke later discovered that a person could lose the ability to comprehend speech (while retaining the ability to generate speech) when a distinct area on the left side of the brain was damaged.

- Korbinian Brodmann divided the brain into 52 distinct regions on the basis of cytoarchitectonics. His characterization of the anatomical divisions of the brain are still used today.
- Camillo Golgi developed a stain that allowed scientists to view individual neurons. Using Golgi's stain, Ramón y Cajal determined that neurons are distinct units and helped develop the neuron doctrine.

History of Cognitive Neuroscience: The Psychological Story

- Associationists believe that the aggregate of a person's experiences determines the course of mental development. Associationism is closely tied to behaviorism, the idea that the environment and learning are the most important factors in mental development.
- George A. Miller showed that there was a limit on the amount of information that could be apprehended in a brief amount of time. The limit was seven plus or minus two.
- Noam Chomsky studied language and realized that the principles of associationism and behaviorism were not sufficient for explaining language acquisition.

THOUGHT QUESTIONS

1. Can we study how the mind works without studying the brain?
2. Will modern brain-imaging experiments become the new phrenology?
3. What do cognitive psychologists mean by the term *representation*? What do neuroscientists mean by the term?
4. How do you think the brain might be studied in the future?

SUGGESTED READING

KASS-SIMON, G., and FARNES, P. (1990). *Women of science: Righting the record.* Bloomington: Indiana University Press.

LINDZEY, G. (Ed.). (1936). *History of psychology in autobiography* (Vol. 3). Worcester, MA: Clark University Press.

MILLER, G. (2003). The cognitive revolution: A historical perspective. *Trends in Cognitive Sciences, 7,* 141–144.

RAICHLE, M. E. (1998). Behind the scenes of functional brain imaging: A historical and physiological perspective. *Proceedings of the National Academy of Sciences, USA,* 95, 765–772.

SHEPHERD, G. M. (1991). *Foundations of the neuron doctrine.* New York: Oxford University Press.

ZIMMER, C. (2004). *Soul made flesh: The discovery of the brain—and how it changed the world.* New York: Free Press.

2

Cellular Mechanisms and Cognition

G.W. was a 21-year-old student when her life hit a bump in the road. During her senior year at college she began to have difficulties managing the details of her life. Although she attended classes regularly, her grades suffered, she performed poorly on exams, and she even failed courses. Her parents worried that she might have become involved with illicit drugs or be suffering from depression, but neither one was the reason for her problems. Her behavior during holiday visits home caused her parents further unease.

G.W. talked of plans they had never heard before. She spoke of traveling the world or of attending law school or medical school—each not an uncommon idea for a college student—but the organization of her plans had some clear flaws, of which she seemed to be unaware or unconcerned. When her parents asked her why she was having trouble in school, she insisted that her instructors did not appreciate or understand her ideas, and she hinted that they were out to get her. Her family believed she was suffering the stress of too many demands in college, so they offered support and encouragement, and G.W. returned to school. Several months later she came home again, unable to continue with college; she was on a leave of absence at the suggestion of her college adviser.

During the next few months, matters took a dramatic turn for the worse. G.W. began to express, sometimes aggressively, the idea that she was being persecuted by friends and family, and later she described voices that warned her of dangers all around. She complained of difficulty with a tooth and seemed convinced that her dentist had done something terrible to her during a past visit—something that might explain her current emotional problems. A new dentist found no evidence of anything wrong with her teeth. Her family doctor referred her to a specialist.

On the advice of that physician, G.W. was hospitalized in a private psychiatric hospital for observation and treatment. After a month of treatment she seemed much better and returned home, and the next semester she returned to school. She was given medication that her physician wanted her to continue taking for the foreseeable future. G.W. did not finish college, however, and over the next few years she was in and out of the hospital several times. She lived at home, where her parents tried their best to help her. Although their support seemed to make a difference, she had sudden downturns characterized by bouts of paranoia, disordered thinking, and emotional outbursts. G.W. wrote long stories in letters to her grandmother. These notes became progressively disordered in both style and content, showing strange associations between topics and sometimes referring to conspiracies against her and naming prominent individuals with whom she claimed some sort of connection. It seemed to her grandmother that G.W. could no longer distinguish between the real and the imaginary.

G.W. suffered from a psychiatric disease, once called *dementia praecox*, but now named *schizophrenia*, a term coined by Swiss psychiatrist Eugen Bleuler (1857–1939) in his 1911 book on the subject. What is schizophrenia? Simply put, it is a disorder of cognition, sometimes called a *thought disorder*. Schizophrenia affects nearly 1% of the population worldwide. It has a genetic component: A person who has a family member with the disorder is more likely to develop schizophrenia; the odds of developing the disorder are nearly 50% for the identical twin of a person with schizophrenia. These findings are clear evidence that schizophrenia has a biological component (Riley & Kendler, 2006).

What, however, is the neurobiological basis of the disorder? At present this question remains unanswered, but one of the major clues is the finding that certain drugs acting on major chemical transmitter systems in the brain can positively influence the symptoms of the disease. It is for this reason that we begin Chapter 2 with a story about a psychiatric disorder. The delicate balance in communication between neurons in the brain yields cognition, and when this balance is disrupted by damage or disease, perception, movement, and thought itself may be at risk. In the rest of this chapter we examine how neural cells communicate, returning later to the story of schizophrenia and chemical transmission.

In Chapter 1 we painted the historical canvas of modern cognitive neuroscience to describe how psychology and biology have coalesced to create this new subdiscipline. In so doing, we introduced the theories, thoughts, and personalities of the history of psychology and neuroscience. Although thinking about the mind and brain can be traced to ancient civilizations, most of what we now consider to be the basic biology of the nervous system began from humble beginnings in the last half of the 19th century. Only in the last 100 years have the neurosciences laid the foundation for understanding how the human brain's cells and circuits enable behavior.

Neuroscientists now understand key aspects of neuronal signaling, synaptic transmission, and neuronal coding of information for storage and processing. Researchers have worked intensively to relate elementary molecular and cellular processes to the activity of both individual neurons and neuronal circuits. Although the precise manner by which biological events give rise to behavior is only just beginning to be understood, a vast amount of knowledge has accumulated about events at the neuronal level. Some findings are sufficiently well understood to form a set of elementary principles of brain science. In this chapter we briefly review these first principles of neuroscience, which provide a necessary foundation for the chapters that follow. Here we focus on the cellular anatomy and physiology of neurons; in Chapter 3 we will turn to the gross anatomy and development of the nervous system. To develop an understanding of the biology of information processing, we ask the following questions: How do neurons communicate? What are the chemical signals that mediate that communication? How do drugs modify these interactions, sometimes for the good and sometimes to the detriment of the individual?

CELLS OF THE NERVOUS SYSTEM

Scientists often adopt a reductionist strategy in the hope of understanding the whole by first identifying the parts. For example, in physics and chemistry the fundamental building blocks of matter were pursued with a vengeance over the past 400 years—a chase that led to the identification of the basic elements from which all molecules are made and the principles of subatomic structure. This fascination with the essential building blocks of the world around us was also shared by the early biologists, who in the 17th and 18th centuries attempted to visualize the constituents of biological tissues by using a magnifying lens. Out of this effort, a fundamental principle, the cell theory, was derived. The cell theory posited that the body was composed of elementary units, or cells. As we noted in Chapter 1, however, the idea that individual cells formed elementary functional units of the nervous system was controversial even as late as the start of the 20th century. In the end, Ramón y Cajal's concept that the nervous system is composed of individual neurons prevailed.

Ramón y Cajal observed that, although neurons are close to each other, they are separated by small gaps. From these observations he defined two main principles of neurons:

1. *Connectional specificity* incorporates the ideas that cells are separate because the cytoplasms of neurons are not in contact and that the connections between neurons are not random: Circuits pass information through specific pathways.
2. *Dynamic polarization* is the appreciation that some parts of neurons are specialized for taking information in, while others are specialized for sending it out to other neurons or muscles.

These two principles, and the overarching theory of the *neuron doctrine*, provide the focus for the first part of this chapter, which reviews the cellular structure and function of the nervous system.

The nervous system has two main classes of cells: neurons and glial cells. Neurons not only share similarities with all other cells but also have unique morphological and physiological properties for special functions. Glial cells are a class of nonneural cells located in the nervous system that serve various purposes, including, but not limited to, providing both structural support and insulation to neurons to make neural transmission more efficient.

The Structure of Neurons

Neurons, the basic signaling units, are distinguished by their form, function, location, and interconnectivity within the nervous system (Figure 2.1). As Ramón y Cajal and others of his time deduced, neurons take in information, make a "decision" about it following some relatively simple rules, and then, by changes in their activity levels, pass it along to other neurons. These functions have close relations to the morphological, or structural, specializations of neurons.

The neuron consists of a cell body, the **soma**, Greek for "body" (Figure 2.2). As with most cells, the cell body contains metabolic machinery that maintains the neuron. The components of the machinery include a nucleus, endoplasmic reticulum, ribosomes, mitochondria, Golgi apparatus, and other intracellular organelles common to most cells. These structures are surrounded by the neuronal membrane, which is composed of a lipid bilayer, and are suspended in cytoplasm, the intracellular fluid that is present inside all cells of the body.

In addition to the cell body, neurons have specialized processes, the **dendrites** and **axon**, which extend away from the cell body. The role of these two types of structures reflects the principle of dynamic polarization. Dendrites are (usually) large treelike processes that receive inputs from other neurons at locations called **synapses**. As a result of being located *after* the synapse with respect to information flow, the dendrites of a neuron are said to be **postsynaptic**. The axon, situated *before* the synapse with respect to information flow, is said to be **presynaptic**. More generally, then, we can refer to neurons as either presynaptic or postsynaptic with respect to any particular synapse. Most neurons are both presynaptic and postsynaptic: They are presynaptic

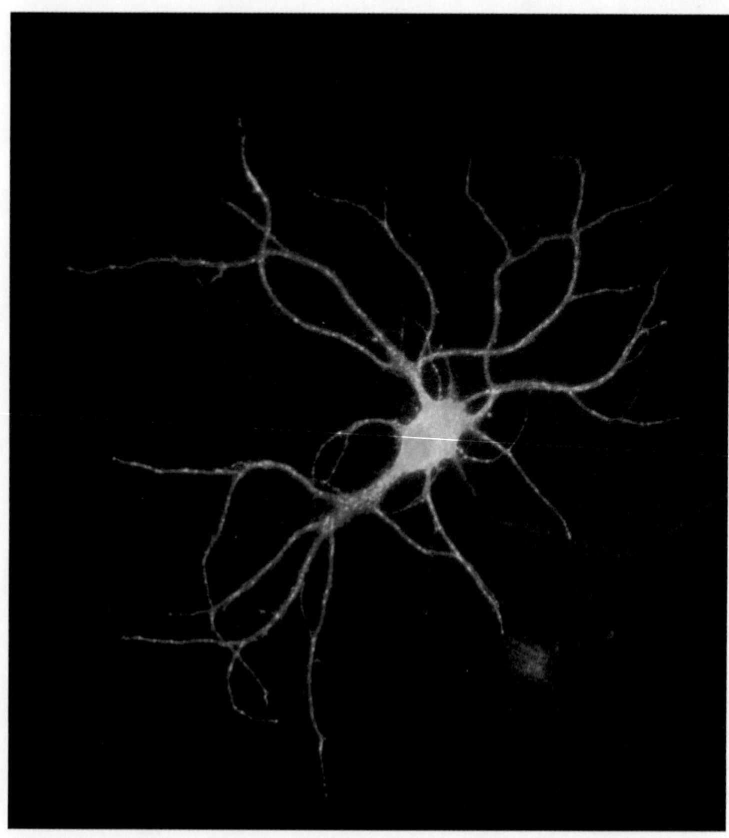

Figure 2.1 Mammalian neuron showing the cell body (soma) in the center surrounded by dendrites. The axon is visible as a hair-thin line emerging from the lower right quadrant of the soma and trailing off to the right of the image. This image shows a neuron expressing transferrin (TfR) receptor, a dendritic protein, tagged with green fluorescent protein (GFP) (green); TfR was produced in the cell body and transported to the dendrites. The red stain is anti-TfR, which distinguishes another source of TfR. Staining for MAP2, a dendrite-specific cytoskeletal protein, is blue. Though similar to the idealized neuron in Figure 2.2, this neuron has a relatively large dendritic field compared to its soma.

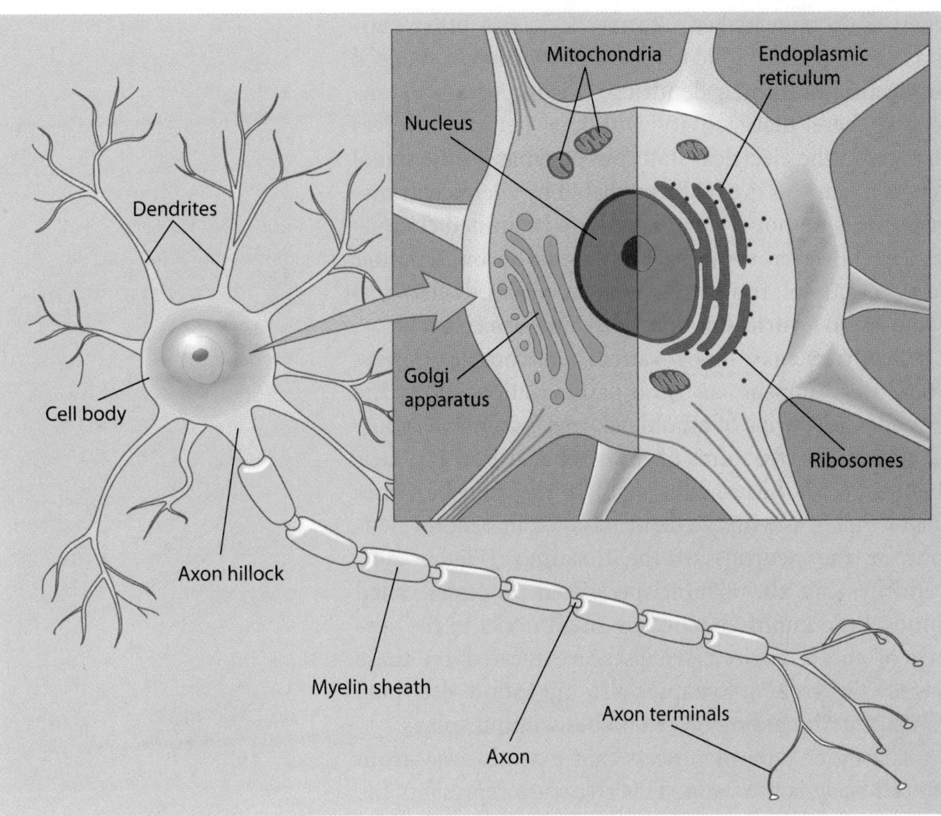

Figure 2.2 Idealized mammalian neuron. The cell body contains the cellular machinery for the production of proteins and other cellular macromolecules. Like other cells, the neuron contains a nucleus, endoplasmic reticulum, ribosomes, mitochondria, Golgi apparatus, and other intracellular organelles (inset). These structures are suspended in the intracellular fluid—cytoplasm—and are contained by a cell membrane composed of a lipid bilayer. Extending from the cell body are various processes that are extensions of the cell membrane and contain cytoplasm that is continuous with that in the cell body. These processes are the dendrites and axon.

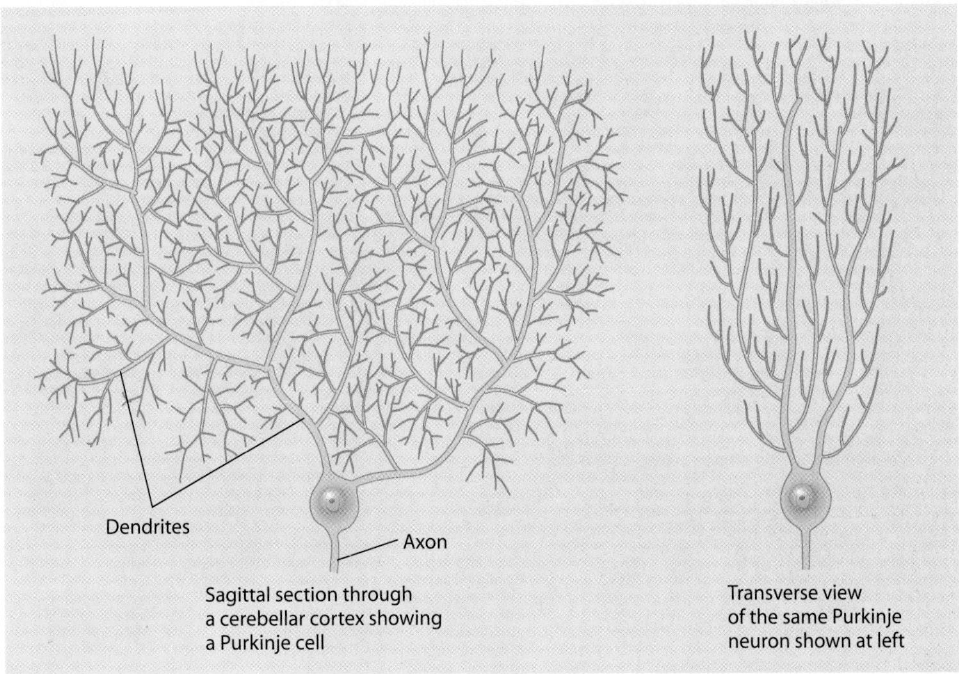

Figure 2.3 Soma and dendritic tree of a Purkinje cell from the cerebellum. The Purkinje cells are arrayed in rows in the cerebellum. Each one has a large dendritic tree that is wider in one direction than the other.

when their axon makes a connection onto other neurons, and postsynaptic when other neurons make a connection onto their dendrites. It is important to emphasize here that activity within a neuron involves changes in the electrical state, but at synapses the signal between neurons is usually mediated by chemical transmission, as Ramón y Cajal surmised. In limited circumstances, however, some neurons signal to one another using electrical transmission at specialized electrical synapses, so it turns out that Golgi was also correct.

Dendrites take many varied and complex forms. They may appear as large arborizations like the branches and twigs of an old oak tree, as with the complex dendritic structures of the cerebellar Purkinje cells (Figure 2.3, on the previous page), or they may be somewhat simpler, as with the dendrites of spinal motor neurons or the neurons of the thalamus (Figure 2.4). Dendrites can also exhibit specialized processes called **spines**, little knobs attached by small necks to the surface of the dendrites; synapses are located on these spines (Figure 2.5). Synapses also are found elsewhere on neurons, including on cell bodies without spines.

The other type of process that extends away from the cell body is the axon. This structure represents the output side of the neuron: Electrical signals travel to the axon terminals, where synapses are located. As noted, these axons, and axon terminals of the neuron, are

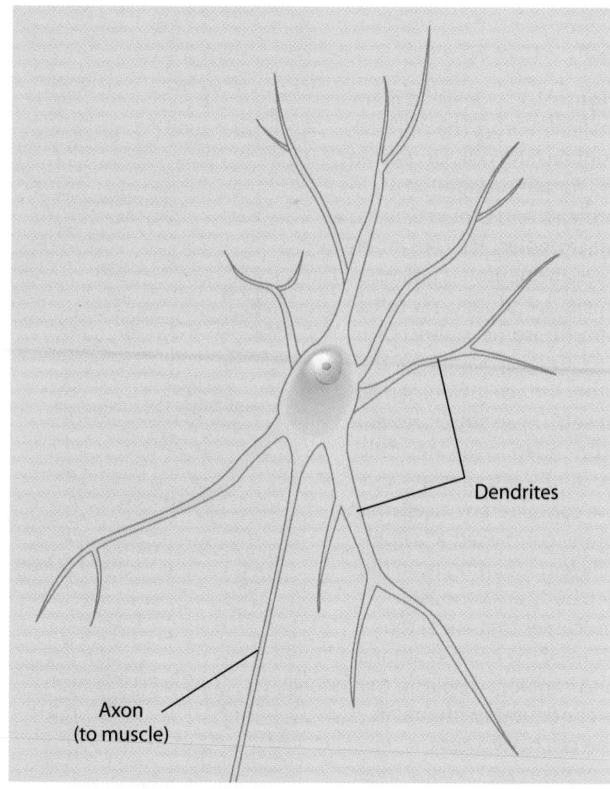

Figure 2.4 Ventral-horn motor neuron. Multipolar neurons located in the spinal cord send their axons out the ventral root to make synapses on muscle fibers.

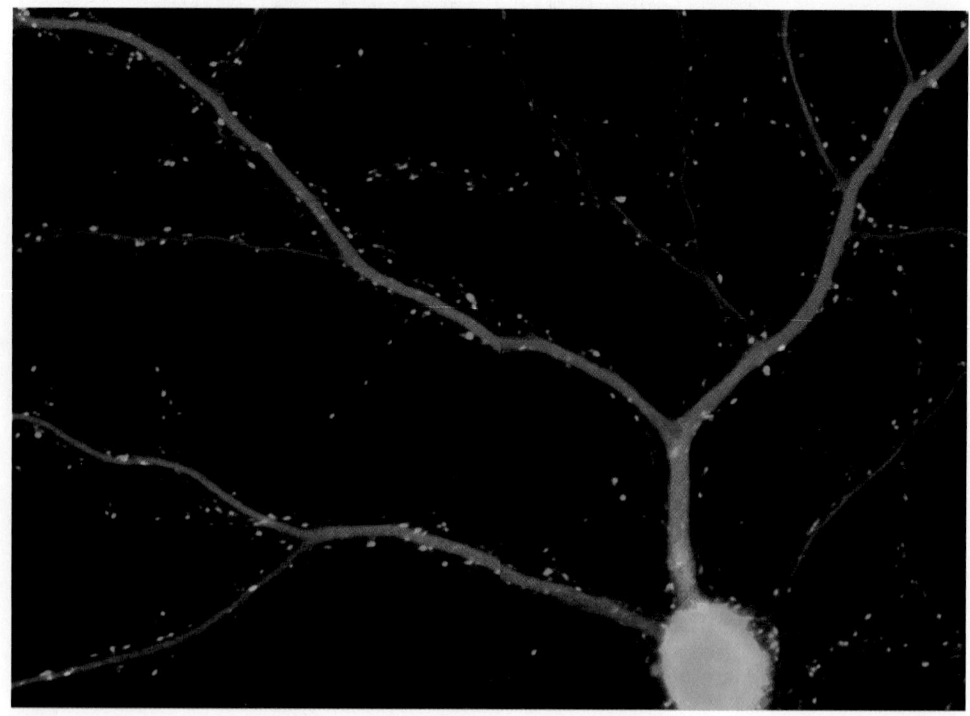

Figure 2.5 Cultured rat hippocampal neuron double labeled using immunofluorescent methods. Shown are presynaptic terminals (small green dots) making contact with spines located on the dendrites (red).

presynaptic with respect to the synapses they form. The axon terminals have specialized intracellular structures that enable communication via the release of **neurotransmitters**, the chemical substances that transmit the signal between neurons at chemical synapses. The dendrites and the axon of a neuron are extensions of the cell body; their internal volume is filled with the same cytoplasm that fills the cell body. Hence, the cell body, dendrites, and axon are parts of one neuron. The continuity of the intracellular space between these neuronal components is necessary for the electrical signaling that neurons perform, as we will see.

The idealized neuron depicted in Figure 2.2 is modeled after a spinal motor neuron, but neurons have many forms. Indeed, the variation in the morphology of neurons is impressive; descriptions of the multitudes in the human nervous system would take a lot of space—more than we have here. Early anatomists described this morphological variation in great detail and grouped neurons into three or four broad categories according to their shapes. These distinctions have largely to do with how the cell's dendrites and axon are oriented with respect to each other and to the soma. Figure 2.6 presents four general morphological classes of neurons: unipolar, bipolar, pseudounipolar, and multipolar. Neurons with similar morphologies tend to be localized in specific regions of the nervous system and have a similar functional role, but the morphology of neurons in all areas of the nervous system varies widely.

Figure 2.6 Various forms that mammalian neurons may take. Some have few processes extending from their cell bodies; others have many. The short axons shown on these neurons are not representative of all neurons. For example, motor neurons in the spinal cord have axons a meter or more in length, depending on the muscle innervated or the animal or human in question.

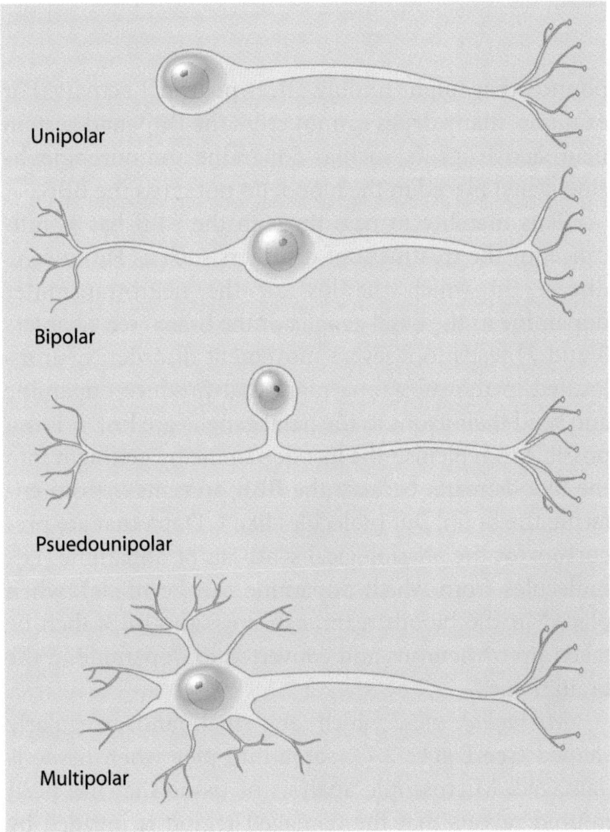

In general, the *unipolar* neuron has only one process extending away from the cell body; it can branch to form dendrites and axon terminals—a pattern common in invertebrate nervous systems. *Bipolar* neurons participate in sensory processes; for example, bipolar neurons convey information in the auditory, visual, and olfactory systems. These neurons have two processes, one axon and one dendrite, and thus in some sense might be considered the prototypical neuron: Information comes in one end via the dendrite and leaves through the other end down the axon, as, for instance, in the bipolar cells of the retina in the eye (see Figure 1.13). These neurons process information within the retina and do not send projections outside it.

Pseudounipolar neurons are so named because they have the appearance of unipolar neurons but were originally bipolar sensory neurons whose dendrites and axon have fused. An example is found in the dorsal-root ganglia of the spinal cord. These neurons are somatosensory cells that convey information from receptors in joints, muscles, and skin to the central nervous system.

Finally, *multipolar* neurons exist in several areas of the nervous system and participate in motor and sensory processing. They have one axon but can have a few or many dendrites emerging from their cell bodies. The myriad of multipolar cells include spinal motor neurons, cortical sensory neurons such as stellate cells and pyramidal neurons, and some neurons of the autonomic nervous system. Figures 2.1 and 2.5 show stained multipolar neurons. For the most part, when we think about neurons in the brain, we are thinking about this class of neurons.

The Role of Glial Cells

The other type of cell in the nervous system is the **glial cell** (also called *neuroglial cell*). Glial cells are more numerous than neurons, by perhaps a factor of 10, and they may account for more than half of the brain's volume. Neuroglial cells probably do not conduct signals

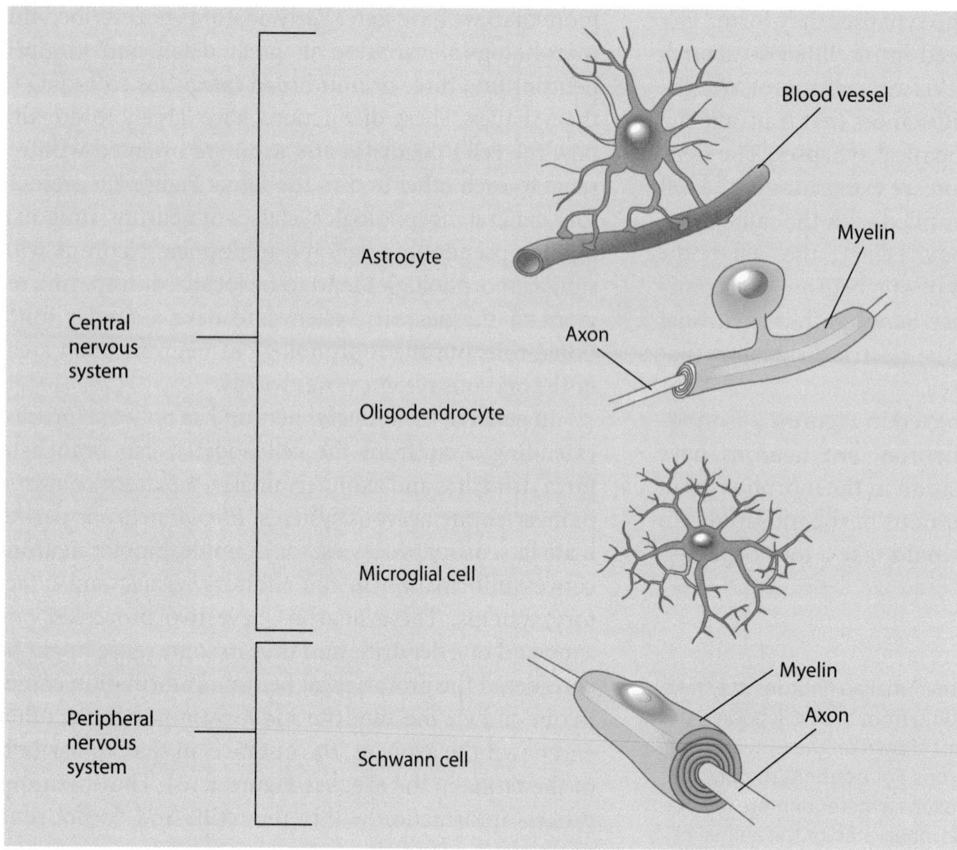

Figure 2.7 Various types of glial cells in the mammalian central and peripheral nervous systems. An astrocyte is shown with end feet attached to a blood vessel. Oligodendrocytes and Schwann cells produce myelin around the axons of neurons—oligodendrocytes in the central nervous system, and Schwann cells in the peripheral nervous system. A microglial cell is also shown.

themselves, but without them, the functionality of neurons would be severely diminished. The term *neuroglia* means, literally, "nerve glue," because anatomists in the 19th century believed that the main role of neuroglial cells in the nervous system was structural support.

Glial cells are in the central nervous system (brain and spinal cord) and the peripheral nervous system (sensory and motor inputs and outputs to the brain and spinal cord). The types of glial cells in each system are different, though. The central nervous system has three main types of glial cells: astrocytes, oligodendrocytes, and microglial cells (Figure 2.7).

Astrocytes are large glial cells having round or radially symmetrical forms; they surround neurons and come in close contact with the brain's vasculature. Astrocytes make contact with blood vessels at specializations called *end feet,* which permit the astrocyte to transport ions across the vascular wall and to create a barrier between the tissues of the central nervous system and the blood. This astrocytic barrier between neuronal tissue and blood is called the **blood–brain barrier** (**BBB**). It plays a vital role in protecting the central nervous system from blood-borne agents or chemical compounds that might unduly affect neuronal activity. For example, many drugs cannot cross the BBB, and certain neuroactive agents, such as dopamine and norepinephrine, when placed in the blood, do not cross the BBB.

This inability to pass through the BBB has significance for the treatment of disorders such as Parkinson's disease, in which the loss of the neurotransmitter dopamine in the basal ganglia of the brain (see Chapters 3 and 7) leads to a severe movement disorder; neurons located in the substantia nigra that produce dopamine and send their axons to the basal ganglia are lost. It is not possible to replenish the lost dopamine by getting it into the bloodstream, because the BBB prevents it from entering the brain. But molecules like L-Dopa that are precursors for the physiological synthesis of dopamine (i.e., molecules from which dopamine can be made), when placed in the bloodstream, can cross the BBB, then be taken up by neurons and converted to dopamine in the brain tissue.

Microglial cells, which are small and irregularly shaped (see Figure 2.7), come into play when tissue is damaged. Microscopic analysis of tissue that has been injured reveals that the damaged region is invaded by these glial cells. They also serve a phagocytic role, literally devouring and removing damaged cells. Microglial cells can proliferate even in adults (as do other glial cells), whereas neurons in the central nervous system are typically prevented from proliferating (but see Chapter 3 for exciting new information on the birth of neurons in the adult brain).

The most obvious role of glial cells in the nervous system is to form myelin. **Myelin** is a fatty substance that surrounds the axons of many neurons. In the central nervous system, *oligodendrocytes* form myelin; in the peripheral nervous system, *Schwann cells* carry out this task (see Figure 2.7). Both glial cell types create myelin by wrapping their cell membranes around the axon in a concentric manner during development and maturation, and the cytoplasm in that portion of the glial cell is squeezed out. This squeezing out of the cytoplasm leaves primarily the lipid bilayer of the glial cell membrane, which is responsible for the characteristic appearance of myelin as a fatty-looking material (under normal physiological conditions it looks white and shiny because fat is made up of lipids, which appear white). But there are differences in how oligodendrocytes and Schwann cells produce myelin, as Table 2.1 outlines.

One oligodendrocyte of the central nervous system can form myelin sheaths around several axons. Figure 2.8 shows the wrappings of oligodendrocytes around the axons of several adjacent neurons in a white matter tract. The analogous situation is shown for a Schwann cell in the peripheral nervous system. However, the Schwann cell produces myelin only for a single axon in a peripheral nerve. The goal of each is similar: to provide electrical insulation around the axon that changes the way intracellular electrical currents flow in axons. In myelinated axons (many axons are unmyelinated), the myelin is interrupted at locations called *nodes*. First described in the late 19th century by the French histologist and anatomist Louis-Antoine Ranvier, these nodes are commonly referred to as the **nodes of Ranvier**. At the nodes, important membrane specializations permit the generation of electrical signals, called **action potentials**, that are conducted down the axon. Thus, both the portions of the axon where glial cells form myelin and the regions where myelin is absent, at the nodes, are significant for the way neurons are able to signal electrically. However, each of these segments has a different role in signaling.

Figure 2.8 Oligodendrocytes and Schwann cells produce myelin around axons. The oligodendrocytes in the central nervous system wrap around more than one axon to form myelin for many axons, but the Schwann cells in the peripheral nervous system wrap around a segment of only one axon. Whether in the central or the peripheral nervous system, many glial cells are necessary to produce myelin for the length of an axon because each wraps only a short segment of the axon.

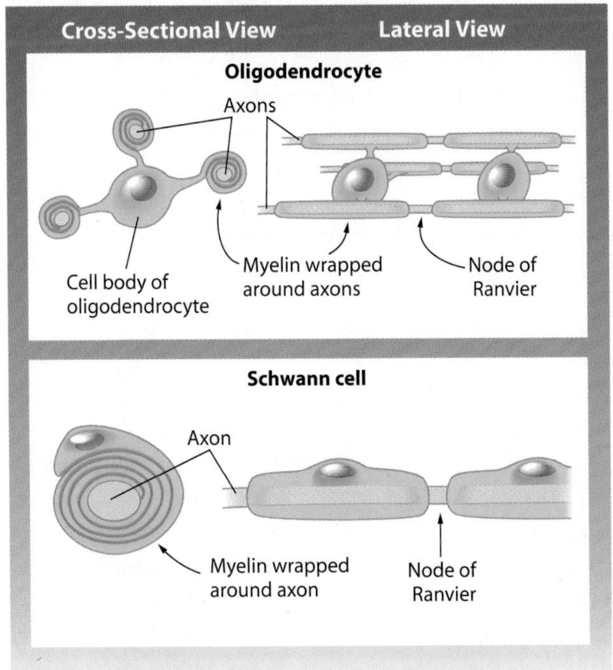

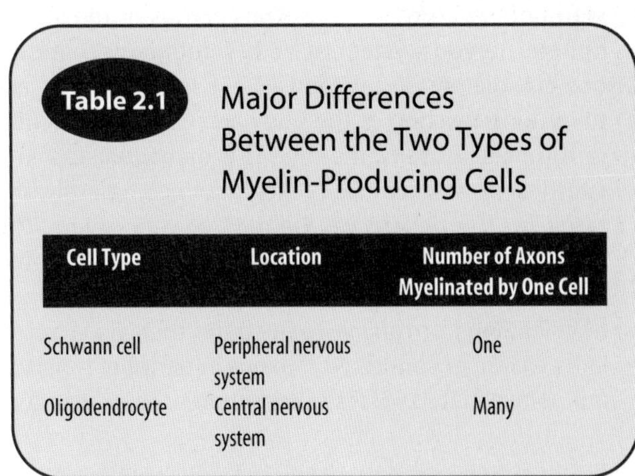

Table 2.1 Major Differences Between the Two Types of Myelin-Producing Cells

Cell Type	Location	Number of Axons Myelinated by One Cell
Schwann cell	Peripheral nervous system	One
Oligodendrocyte	Central nervous system	Many

HOW THE BRAIN WORKS

Myelin and Disease

J.C. was 32 years old when she stumbled while walking down her level, clean driveway. Embarrassed at her clumsiness, she laughed and told her friend that she should have the driveway repaired. Two weeks later she fell while walking across her living room. Six months after these seemingly trivial instances of clumsiness, some minor but annoying visual problems developed but disappeared over the next 6 months. During the next year J.C. experienced some strange numbness in her hands and weakness in her left leg, which prompted her to seek medical treatment. Following a series of tests, J.C. was diagnosed with a neuromuscular disease called *multiple sclerosis* (*MS*). What is this disease, why did it lead to the varied symptoms, and why was J.C. sometimes clumsy?

Moment to moment, on a millisecond scale, the human nervous system processes sensory information and executes motor responses. Some of these are under voluntary control; perhaps the vast majority are reflexive or automatic in one fashion or another. With respect to standing, for example, not only do we decide voluntarily whether to stand or sit, but we also use reflexive systems to maintain balance and posture. To accomplish all this in real time takes speed and accuracy of timing. Thus, in many ways the nervous system is a high-speed machine. The timing of this machine is compromised in some disease states when the integrity of the neurons and their component parts is destroyed.

MS is one disease among many that manifests itself, in part, as a loss of coordination among information transactions within specified neural systems. Specifically, MS is manifest as damage of the myelin sheaths surrounding axons in the central nervous system or peripheral nervous system, or both. Through mechanisms not completely understood (likely some form of autoimmune reaction of the body against the molecules in the myelin itself), the myelin is damaged, and in a spotty fashion it may be broken down completely. The result for the patient can be mild or very severe. The symptoms of MS depend on which axons are affected by demyelination. If the affected axons are in the optic tract leading from an eye to the brain, then visual problems will be encountered. If axons in peripheral nerves are demyelinated, losses of sensation or muscular control and strength may result. If the demyelination occurs in white matter tracts interconnecting regions of cerebral cortex involved in higher function, the damage may affect cognition or personality.

Why does damage to myelin lead to these problems? Damage to myelin can lead to slowing or complete disruption of neural signaling and, hence, a loss of function in the portion of the neural circuitry affected. In addition, however, inflammation that occurs as a result of the demyelination can lead to damage of the axons themselves and ultimately to their destruction. So the symptoms of MS may have two causes: demyelination and neuronal damage. The role of myelin in axonal conduction is discussed in the text. After reading about neuronal signaling, try to deduce how intermittent damage in myelin leads to the symptoms of MS.

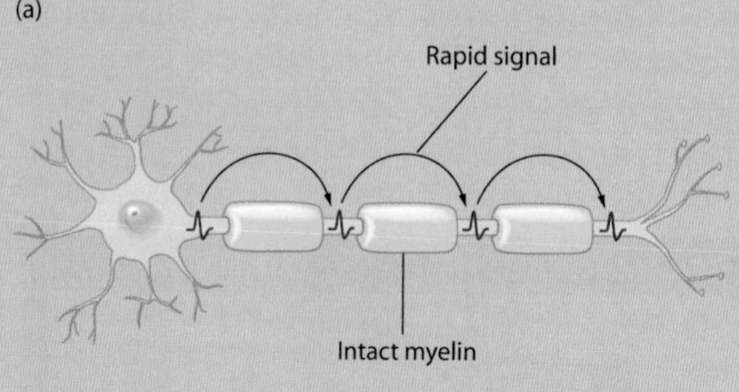

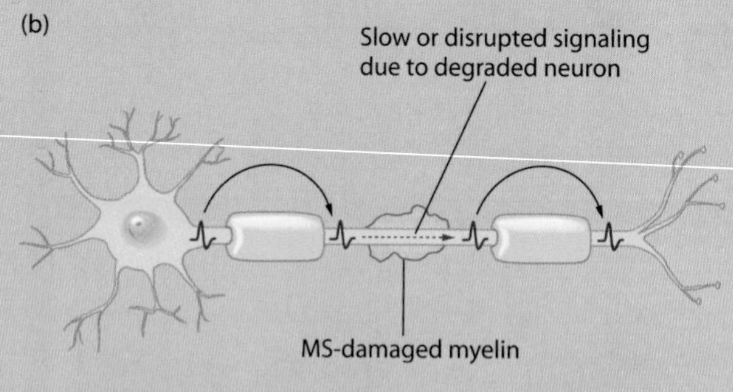

(a) Healthy neuron. **(b)** Neuron of a person with multiple sclerosis.

NEURONAL SIGNALING

In reviewing the morphology of neurons, we noted that their function is to analyze and transmit information—the basic goal of nervous systems. Now we turn to how this transfer of information between neurons, which we refer to globally as *neuronal signaling*, is accomplished.

Neuronal signaling has several requirements. As with most things in the physical world, energy is a primary requirement. How do neurons provide energy for neuronal signaling? How is this energy used to create a signal within a neuron? How is this intraneuronal signal transmitted to other neurons? In this section we will answer these questions and learn how the electrical activity of neurons can be recorded as a way to investigate their physical properties. We begin with an overview, followed by the details of each step.

Overview of Neuronal Communication

Neurons are the integral units of the nervous system, and each neuron communicates with other cells at synapses, usually on dendrites or the cell body, or both. For outgoing information the synapses are at axon terminals. The goal of neuronal processing is to take in information, evaluate it, and pass a signal to other neurons, thereby forming local and long-distance circuits and networks of neurons.

The process of signaling has several stages. Neurons first receive a signal that is in either a chemical form (a neurotransmitter, or a chemical in the environment for sensations such as smell) or a physical form (such as touch in somatosensory receptors in the skin, or light in photoreceptors in the eye, or electrical signals at electrical synapses). These signals initiate changes in the membrane of the postsynaptic neuron, changes that make electrical currents flow in and around the neuron. The electrical currents act as signals within the neuron, potentially affecting the neuronal membrane at sites remote from the input synapse. The current flow is mediated by ionic currents carried by electrically charged atoms (ions), such as sodium, potassium, and chloride, that are dissolved in the fluid inside and outside of neurons. These ionic currents are related to but also different from the electrical currents that flow in metal wires, which are mediated by electrons rather than ions in solution.

Long-distance signals, action potentials, can be generated in a region of the neuron that integrates the currents from many synaptic inputs, or from the

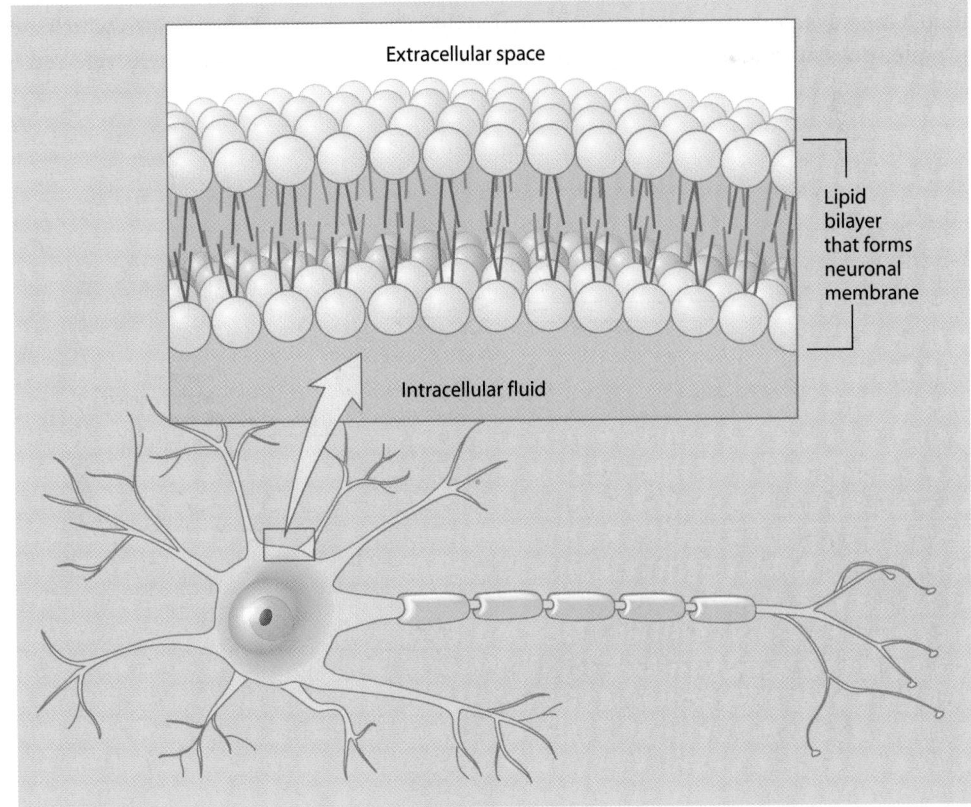

Figure 2.9 Idealized neuron and the lipid bilayer (inset) that separates the intracellular from the extracellular space. The lipid bilayer makes up the cell membrane. The lipids (fatty material) are not water soluble and thus form a barrier to materials dissolved in watery solution such as sodium and potassium ions, proteins, and other molecules.

stimulation of a sensory receptor; this region of the neuron is referred to as the **spike-triggering zone**, where *spike* refers to an action potential. What results in most cases is a signal that travels down the axon to its terminals, where it eventually causes the release of neurotransmitters at synapses.

Remember that this review highlights aspects of neuronal signaling that might be considered typical, but numerous variations on this pattern are present in the nervous system. For example, many neurons communicate without ever generating an action potential. Such neurons are located in the retina, and elsewhere where electrical synapses can be found.

Properties of the Neuronal Membrane and the Membrane Potential

The *neuronal membrane* is a bilayer of lipid molecules that separates intracellular space from extracellular space. Because the membrane is composed of lipids (fatty molecules), it does not dissolve in the watery environments inside and outside the neuron (Figure 2.9, on the previous page). This is how the membrane remains intact and controls the flow of water-soluble substances across its breadth. That is, the membrane does not allow some things to cross it; it is a barrier to ions, proteins, and other molecules dissolved in the intracellular and extracellular fluid. One way to think of it is that anything that dissolves in water does not dissolve well in the membrane's lipids, so it cannot readily cross into or out of the cell. This principle is a familiar one: Oil and water do not mix.

THE BASIS OF THE RESTING MEMBRANE POTENTIAL

The neuronal membrane, though, is not merely a lipid bilayer. It has numerous transmembrane proteins that form a variety of specialized structures in the membrane, including ion channels and active transporters or pumps. Other transmembrane proteins of interest include the class known as *receptor molecules.* We will discuss all of these channels in more detail later. For now, however, it is important to define a few special properties of ion channels and pumps in order to understand how the neuronal membrane creates the **resting membrane potential**, the difference in voltage across the neuronal membrane (Figure 2.10).

Ion channels are formed by transmembrane proteins that create pores, actual passageways across the membrane through which ions (charged atoms in solution) of sodium, potassium, and chloride (Na^+, K^+, and Cl^-, respectively) might pass (Figure 2.11). Thousands of ion channels exist in the neuronal membrane. Some ion channels are passive (nongated) and are always in the same state (open to certain ions). Other channels are gated; that is, they can be opened or closed by electrical, chemical, or physical stimuli. We will discuss gated channels later, when we consider active membrane processes.

The extent to which a channel permits ions to cross the membrane is referred to as **permeability**. Although

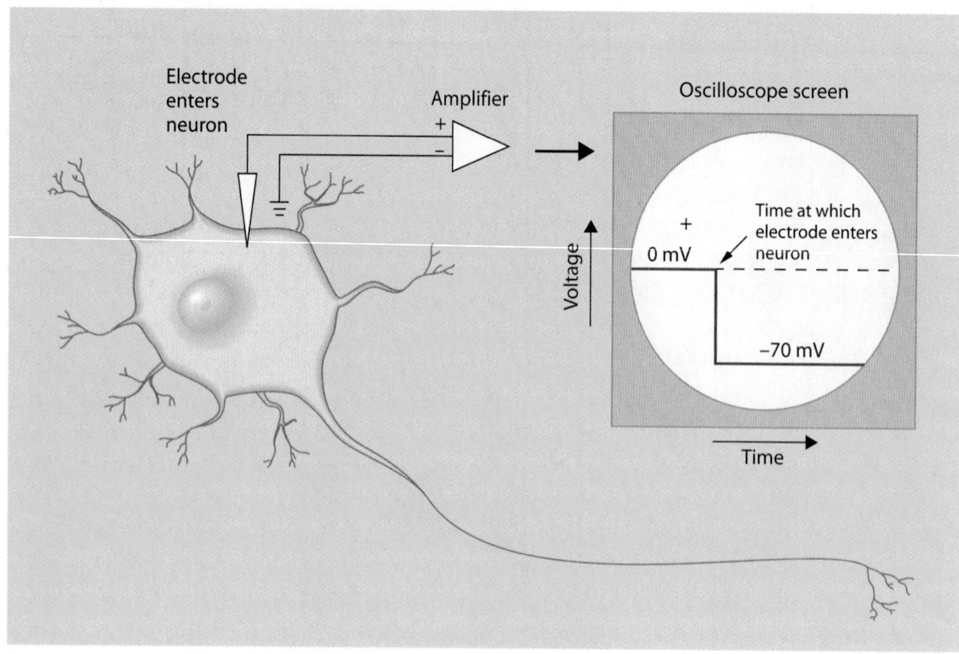

Figure 2.10 Intracellular recordings are used to measure the resting membrane potential. One method is to use a small glass pipette electrode with a fine tip, to penetrate the neuronal cell membrane without damaging it too severely. Then, recordings of the differences between the voltages measured by the electrodes inside and outside the neuron (transmembrane differences) can be obtained. When the electrode enters the neuron, the difference in voltage between the two electrodes reflects the membrane potential, as shown in the idealized oscilloscope record on the right.

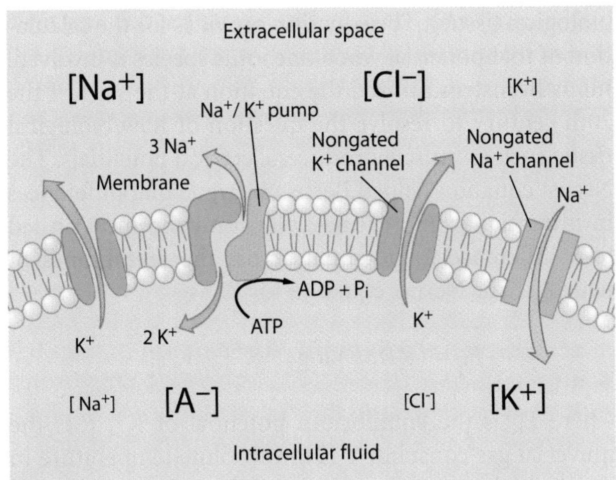

Figure 2.11 Ion channels in a segment of neuronal membrane. The ionic species to which each ion channel and pump are related are shown. The brackets around the letters representing the ions are symbols for concentration, and the print size of the letters in brackets corresponds to the relative concentration inside and outside the neuron. For example, there is a higher concentration of sodium (Na^+) outside than inside the cell. Properties of the membrane combined with the active pumping of ions across the neuronal membrane lead to ionic concentration gradients for sodium (Na^+), potassium (K^+), chloride (Cl^-), and large charged proteins (A^-) across the membrane.

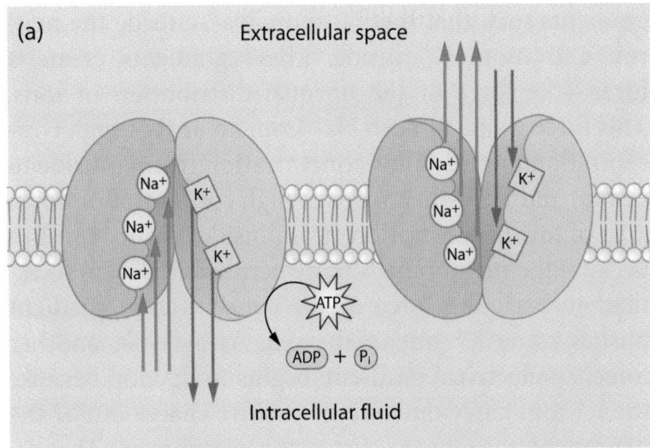

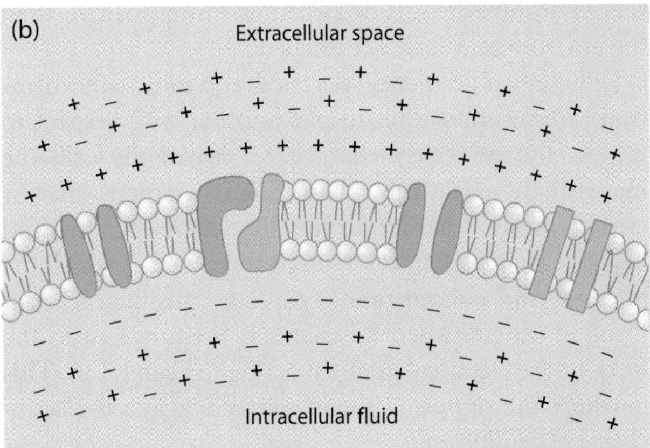

Figure 2.12 **(a)** The sodium–potassium pump preserves the cell's resting potential by maintaining a larger concentration of K^+ inside the cell and Na^+ outside the cell. The pump uses ATP as energy. **(b)** The membrane's selective permeability to some ions and the concentration gradients formed by active pumping lead to a difference in electrical potential across the membrane called the *resting membrane potential*. The membrane potential, represented here by the greater number of positive charges outside the neuron along the membrane than inside, is the basis for the transmembrane voltage difference shown in Figure 2.10.

the membrane itself is relatively impermeable to ions crossing it, some ion channels (nongated in this case) allow ions to move from inside to outside or vice versa. The membrane is more permeable to some ions (K^+) than to others (Na^+, Cl^-), and therefore is said to be *selectively permeable*. The reason why the neuronal membrane is more permeable to K^+ than to Na^+ is that it has many more nongated K^+-selective channels than nongated Na^+ channels (or other nongated channels).

Active transporters, such as the Na^+–K^+ ATPase pump (Figure 2.12a), can move ions across the membrane. Energy-storing molecules called *adenosine triphosphate* (*ATP*) provide a form of fuel that the neuron uses to operate these small transmembrane pumps. The pumps are actually enzymes (proteins) located in the neuronal membrane; they can break a chemical bond in the ATP molecule and release energy that moves Na^+ out of the cell and K^+ into the cell. Every molecule of ATP can provide enough energy to move two K^+ ions inside for every three Na^+ ions extruded (see Figure 2.11). Over time, pumping changes the internal-to-external neuronal concentrations of Na^+ and K^+ and creates ionic concentration gradients across the membrane (Figure 2.12b). The relative impermeability of the neuronal membrane tends to keep these ions from traveling back across the membrane, even though the natural tendency is for diffusion to push ions down their concentration gradients (from areas of high concentration to areas of low concentration) to eliminate the differential in concentration. Hence, in the *resting state*, a higher concentration of Na^+ exists outside the neuron and a higher concentration of K^+ exists inside.

The property of selective membrane permeability and the establishment of transmembrane ionic concentration gradients act together to create differences in charge across the membrane. Here's how this works: As we just discussed, the pumps establish concentration gradients such that there is more Na^+ outside the neuron and more K^+ inside. These gradients create a force—the force of the unequal distribution of ions. This force wants to push Na^+ from an area of high concentration to one of low concentration (from outside to inside) and K^+ from an area of high concentration to an area of low concentration (from inside to outside). But because the membrane is more permeable (leaky) to K^+ than to Na^+, the force of the concentration gradient pushes some K^+ out of the cell. As a result, another force, an **electrical gradient**, begins to develop because the K^+ ions carry one unit of positive charge out of the neuron as they move across the membrane. That is, the environment outside becomes more positive than the environment inside the neuron.

These two gradients (electrical and ionic concentration) are in opposition to one another with respect to K^+. As the positively charged K^+ leaves the cell, the increasingly negatively charged environment that is created makes it harder for the K^+ to leave (positive and negative charges attract). A point is reached at which the force of the concentration gradient pushing K^+ out through the nongated K^+ channels is equivalent to the force of the electrical gradient acting to keep K^+ in. This is where the opposing forces are said to reach *electrochemical equilibrium.*

The small difference in charge across the membrane at equilibrium is the basis of the resting membrane potential. The transmembrane potential can be measured with electrodes as shown in Figure 2.10. At equilibrium, the difference can range from –40 to –90 millivolts (mV); that is, the electrical potential inside the neuron is more negative with respect to the potential outside the neuron. In essence, the neuron now is equivalent to a battery; that is, it has a form of potential energy that enables neurons to generate electrical signals by varying the membrane potential via active membrane processes, as we'll learn later in this section.

MODELING THE MEMBRANE POTENTIAL

The difference in the concentrations of ions across the selectively permeable membrane of the neuron leads to the resting membrane potential. The values for the resting membrane potential that are typically observed can be quantified, and the 19th-century German chemist Walter Nernst provided the means. His equation, the *Nernst equation*, is derived from principles of physical chemistry and thermodynamics, and it describes how unequal distributions of ions in solution will develop a difference in potential across a permeable membrane (either an artificial membrane or a membrane made of biological tissue). The equation provides for the calculation of that potential when one ionic species is involved. Julius Bernstein utilized the equation at the start of the 20th century to resolve the question of how biological tissue such as muscle produces electrical potentials. The Nernst equation helped Bernstein argue that differences in intracellular and extracellular ion concentration led to a difference in potential across the membranes of neurons. The Nernst equation for K^+ is

$$E_K = (RT/zF)\ \log_e([K^+]_o/[K^+]_i)$$

where E_K is the equilibrium potential of K^+, R is the universal gas constant, T is the absolute temperature in degrees Kelvin, z is the valence of the ion (which for K^+ is 1), F is Faraday's constant, $[K^+]_o$ is the concentration of K^+ outside, and $[K^+]_i$ is the concentration of K^+ inside the cell; $\log_e$ is the natural logarithm. By inserting values of 400 mM for the concentration of K^+ inside and 20 mM for the concentration outside the neuron (from studies in the squid axon), one can simplify the Nernst equation for K^+ at 25 °C to

$$E_K = 59.8\ \log_{10}(20/400) = -75\ \text{mV}$$

which is the **equilibrium potential** for K^+. In essence, this is the membrane voltage at which there is no net flow of ions in or out.

Bernstein performed measurements in muscle tissue that were in fair agreement with the results of his calculations using the Nernst equation. In neurons, then, the resting membrane potential is roughly equal to the equilibrium potential of K^+. The actual value is different because of the contribution of other ions. K^+ is not the only ion to which the membrane is permeable; one must also account for Na^+ and Cl^-. In the 1940s, David Goldman derived an equation that permits this calculation by taking into consideration the permeability of all relevant ionic species; we refer to this equation as the *Goldman equation.*

The findings from simulations with the Nernst and Goldman equations were tested in the classic studies of Alan Hodgkin and Andrew Huxley and their students and colleagues in the 1930s, 1940s, and 1950s. They conducted an ingenious series of studies that included artificial manipulation of extracellular and intracellular ion concentrations to observe the effects on the membrane potential. They also injected current while recording the membrane potential, to see how it changed and to identify the associated transmembrane currents. They found that, indeed, the equations did a good job of characterizing the changes in membrane potential that they

HOW THE BRAIN WORKS

History of the Action Potential

As recently as about 70 years ago, we did not know much about the mechanisms underlying the generation of action potentials. That is, humans had built devices like airplanes and radios, both of which are sophisticated pieces of machinery for war and peace, but no living human had recorded an action potential from inside a neuron, although many wanted to. Two key figures in the story of the action potential are Alan Hodgkin and Andrew Huxley, who from 1938 to 1952 published a series of foundational articles on the action potential. In a classic 1939 report in the journal *Nature*, they published the first recording of an action potential, shown in part (a) of the figure, from the giant axon of the squid. (Note that we're talking here about the giant axon of the squid—an animal about 20 cm long—not the axon of a giant squid; Hodgkin and Huxley may have been pioneers of the nervous system, but they left giant squids to the likes of Jacques-Yves Cousteau, preferring to challenge the natural world in the laboratory.)

The details of Hodgkin and Huxley's work led to the "ionic hypothesis" and ultimately to the Hodgkin–Huxley theory of the action potential. The bottom line of their model was that ionic currents, the Na^+ and K^+ currents, acted independently to create the action potential, and that these currents became active in a specified time period as the result of rapid changes in the conductances of the neuronal membrane. Hodgkin and Huxley made use of an ingenious technique, invented by Kenneth Cole, called the *voltage clamp*. This technique, in which an electrical circuit is connected to the intracellular recording system, permits the voltage of the membrane to be maintained at a constant value ("clamped") even during changes in ionic concentration in the extracellular fluid and after injections of electrical current that cause currents to flow across the membrane through ion channels. Using these techniques, Hodgkin and Huxley and their colleagues demonstrated that separate Na^+ and K^+ currents contribute to the different phases of the action potential, via changes in conductances for Na^+ (g_{Na}) and K^+ (g_K), as part (b) of the figure illustrates.

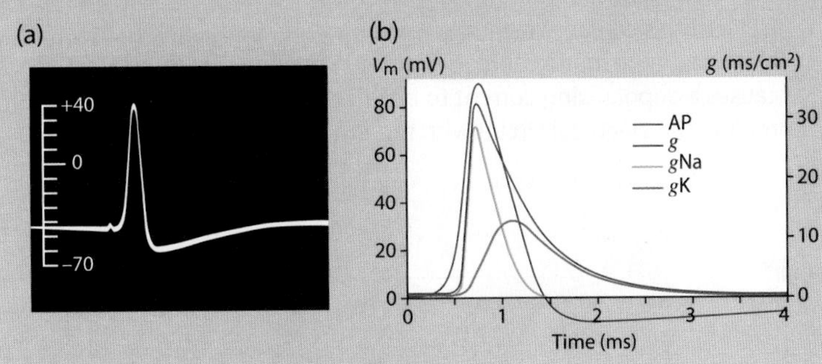

(a) First recorded axon potential, reported in 1939 by Hodgkin and Huxley. **(b)** This plot shows transmembrane voltage (V_m, membrane potential) and membrane conductance (g) as a function of time during an action potential (AP).

recorded. Their use of novel methods for recording is discussed in "How the Brain Works: History of the Action Potential."

Electrical Conduction in Neurons

Neurons have two properties important for cellular signaling. First, they are *volume conductors*, and hence currents can flow through them and across their membrane. Second, they generate a variety of electrical currents, called **receptor potentials**, **synaptic potentials**, and **action potentials**. Before delving into passive electrical properties, let's look at how to measure the flow of current across membranes and within neurons.

RECORDING THE MEMBRANE POTENTIAL

In the 1940s and early 1950s, techniques were developed to record the neuronal membrane potential with high accuracy. Although the basic principles and tools for these measurements are not complex, new techniques were required because of the small size of neurons (50–100 μm in diameter) and axons (1–3 μm in diameter). To record the transmembrane difference in potential, one must have a very small recording electrode (fine wire or micropipette electrode) inside a neuron and one outside; the difference in potential between these two electrodes is the value of the membrane potential (see Figure 2.10).

To create a micropipette electrode, we heat and stretch a small glass tube to a fine point (1 μm). When the microelectrode is filled with a conductive solution, it acts as both the recording tip and a kind of harpoon for puncturing the neurons under a microscope. The signal representing the difference between the voltage recorded from the electrode inside the cell and that recorded from the electrode outside the cell can be amplified and displayed on an oscilloscope for viewing. Typically, the outside of the neuron is arbitrarily defined to be at zero voltage; thus, the inside of a resting neuron is observed to have a negative voltage.

This technique has been adapted so that current can be injected into the neuron. A current source instead of an amplifier is attached across the two electrodes. When one electrode is placed inside a neuron and the other is outside the neuron, current can be injected and the changes in the neuron's membrane potential recorded (Figure 2.13). The action of the stimulating electrode can approximate the role of synaptic potentials in a neuron, or of receptor potentials at a sensory receptor. Thus, neuroscientists are able to observe how a postsynaptic neuron is affected by tiny changes in current. Variations of this technique are now sophisticated enough to enable us to investigate the properties of individual ion channels.

PASSIVE ELECTRICAL PROPERTIES OF NEURONS

We now know the gross morphology of neurons, and we know (a) that they have a potential difference across their membranes that arises from the properties of the neuronal membrane and the distributions of ions across the membrane, and (b) that this electrical power source can be used by the neuron for signaling and can also be measured by investigators. The next question we turn to is this: How does the membrane potential permit neurons to communicate with one another? The first things to understand are the passive physical properties of neurons, and how these properties influence current flowing in their intracellular space; this information is important to know because the flow of ionic current is involved in all aspects of neuronal signaling.

Neurons are essentially sacks of electrically conductive fluid (cytoplasm) bounded by an electrical insulator (the cell membrane), making them excellent volume conductors; that is, they are conductive volumes (as is

Figure 2.13 Intracellular recording and injection of current. Electrodes can be attached to current-generating equipment and used to pass current into the neuron. The effect that this current has on the membrane potential can then be measured. Here, making the tip of the electrode inside the neuron more positive causes a depolarizing current to be injected. As a result, the membrane becomes depolarized as the current flows out across it to complete the electrical circuit with the other electrode outside the cell.

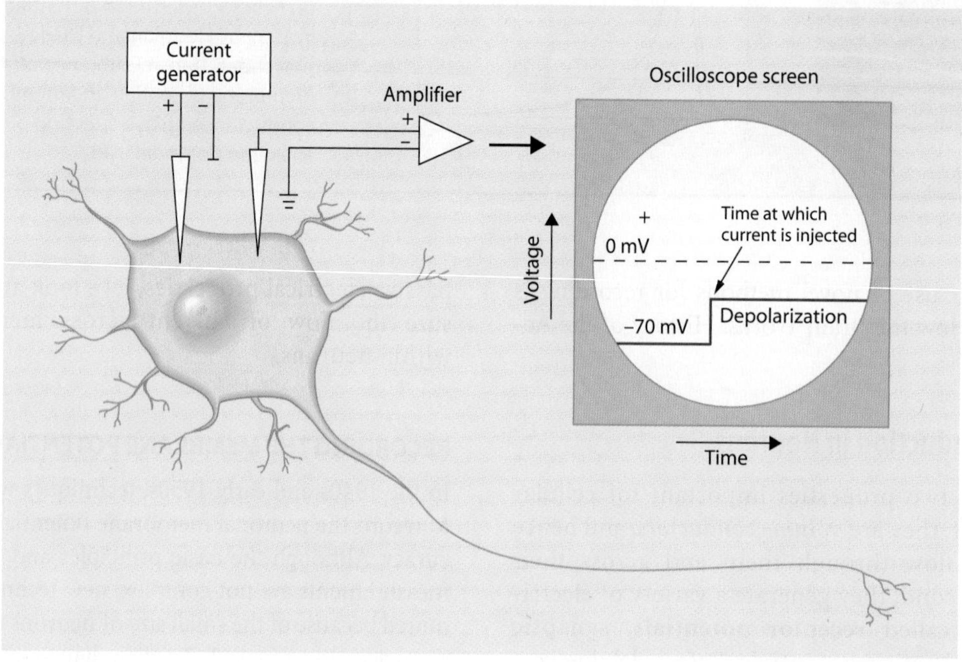

your entire body, which is why sticking your finger into a light socket while standing in a puddle of water is an especially bad idea!). All this sits in a salty sea of extracellular fluid that has a conductivity similar to that of the cytoplasm. Thus, neurons and their environment can be broken down into conductors (cytoplasm and extracellular fluid) and insulators (membranes). Membranes have high but variable resistance, as well as the ability to store charge briefly (capacitance). We can model these components, plus the membrane potential and ion channels, by using equivalent electrical circuits (see "The Cognitive Neuroscientist's Toolkit: Building Neurons Out of Batteries and Baling Wire," on p. 34).

We can also grasp the behavior of neurons in simple, qualitative terms. The first goal is to learn how electrical currents flow passively through neurons, owing to sensory stimulation or synaptic activity. In so doing, we make a distinction between active membrane processes such as those that generate action potentials, synaptic potentials, or receptor potentials, all of which involve the opening of ion channels, and the passive currents that result. How well these passive currents flow through the neuron is what constrains how far a neuron can conduct a signal, as well as whether and how the neuron will use action potentials to aid in communication. We will return to the action potential later, when we discuss active membrane processes.

Overview of Signaling: Active Versus Passive Currents

Let's begin with an overview of some of the steps in neuronal signaling—in this case, between neurons. Figure 2.14 shows the steps from synaptic input to the generation of action potentials in the axon. When a synapse is activated (Step 1 in Figure 2.14), active electrical currents are generated across the cell membrane near the synapse, and these currents generate synaptic potentials (Step 2).

Figure 2.14 Overview of signaling between neurons. Synaptic inputs (1) affect the postsynaptic membrane, leading to postsynaptic currents at synapses (2). These currents are active, but they are conducted by electrotonic (passive) conduction through the intracellular space (3). They depolarize the membrane, and, if large enough, the depolarization can trigger action potentials to be generated in the axon (4). Each action potential represents an active process that occurs when voltage-gated Na^+ channels open in the membrane. The inward current generated during this phase of the action potential is then conducted down the axon following principles of electrotonic conduction (5). The result is depolarization of adjacent regions of the membrane, which can then generate another action potential, and the process continues down the axon (6).

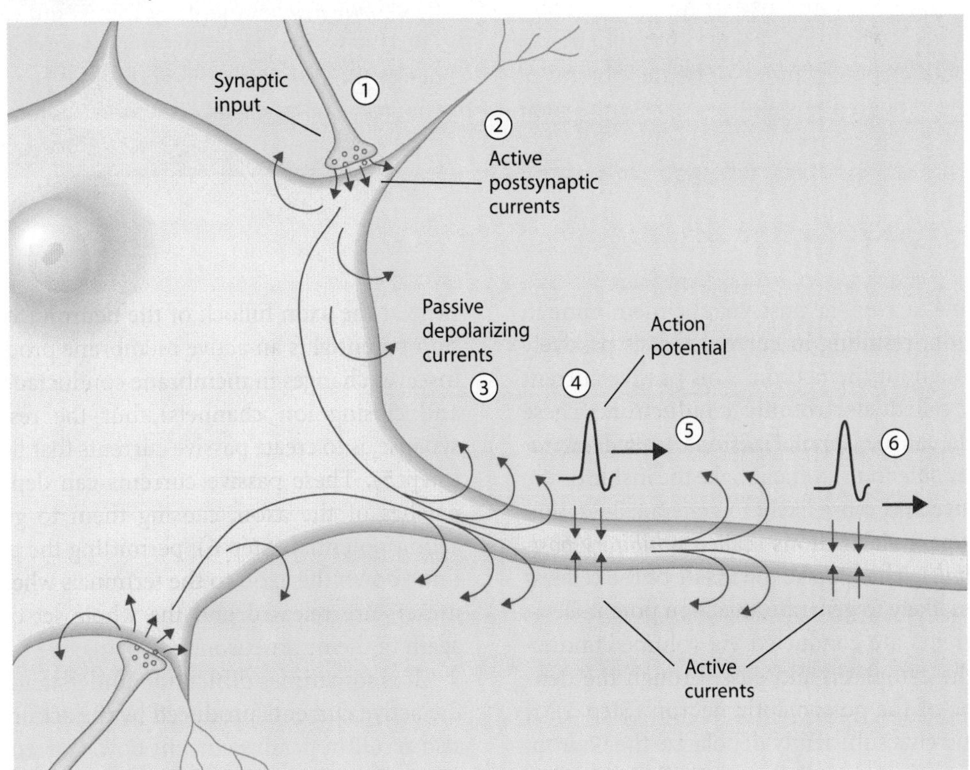

THE COGNITIVE NEUROSCIENTIST'S TOOLKIT

Building Neurons Out of Batteries and Baling Wire

The components of the neuron have physical properties that determine how it conducts currents. These properties include the resistivities of the neuronal membrane, cytoplasm, and extracellular fluid, and the amplitude of the current generated by the power of the membrane potential. To model these components of the neuron in an effort to understand the electrical behavior of dendrites, neurons, and axons, physiologists have developed the concept of the *equivalent circuit*. The equivalent circuit uses terminology and principles from electronics to approximate the neuron, and thus to provide quantitative values for modeling the state of the neuron, given a specific set of conditions. For example, as the figure shows, we can assign specific resistances and capacitances (the ability to store charge) to the membrane, the intracellular fluid, and the extracellular fluid. Thus, diagrammatically the neuronal membrane becomes a set of resistors and capacitors in parallel, and the intracellular and extracellular fluids are represented as resistors in series.

The membrane of the neuron contains variable resistors because ion channels can open and close, thereby changing the resistance of the membrane to current flow (i.e., when ions move through the ion channels, conductance increases). The membrane potential can be modeled as a battery across the membrane because the membrane potential represents a steady power source that can direct current through the equivalent circuit.

Modeling the neuron as an electrical circuit permits quantitative predictions as to how the neuron should behave in the laboratory setting and under normal physiological conditions. By modeling the neuron in this fashion, physiologists have been able to attain theoretical explanations for the behavior of neurons from which they actually recorded data using microelectrodes. For example, the giant axon in the squid has a diameter of about 0.5 mm, whereas the diameter of a muscle fiber in a frog may be as small as 0.1 mm. In these two cells, the resistance of the cytoplasmic fluid itself is approximately equivalent, but in the larger of the two cells, the resistance inside is lower because of the greater volume, and we can model this situation by decreasing the value of the resistors in series that represent the internal resistance of the intracellular space. Using such a model, we can calculate the differential effect that a given change in current at one location would have on the membrane potential at any given distance away. Experimentally, this *length constant* (see the text) is known to be different, and changes in the values of the resistors in an equivalent circuit model of the neuron can effectively describe this effect.

This current flows across the postsynaptic membrane in a localized region, resulting in current that is passively conducted throughout the neuron. This passive current conduction is called **electrotonic conduction**. These passive currents can be **depolarizations** (called *excitatory postsynaptic potentials*), which make the inside of the cell more positive and more likely to generate an action potential, or **hyperpolarizations** (called *inhibitory postsynaptic potentials*), which make the inside of the cell less positive and less likely to generate an action potential.

Passive currents are conducted via volume conduction through the cytoplasm and pass through the dendrites and soma of the postsynaptic neuron (Step 3). If these passive currents sufficiently depolarize the neuron, they can trigger action potentials in the spike-triggering zone at the axon hillock of the neuron (Step 4). The action potential is an active membrane process (because it involves changes in membrane conductances by opening and closing ion channels), but the result, as at the synapse, is to create passive currents that flow in the axon (Step 5). These passive currents can depolarize nearby patches of the axon, causing them to generate a new action potential (Step 6), permitting the process to continue down the axon to the terminals where neurotransmitters are released and the whole set of steps occurs again in the next neuron.

It is sometimes difficult to understand precisely how the active currents produced by the action potential can also result in passive current flow. Currents that flow in neurons are said to be active when they are in the neigh-

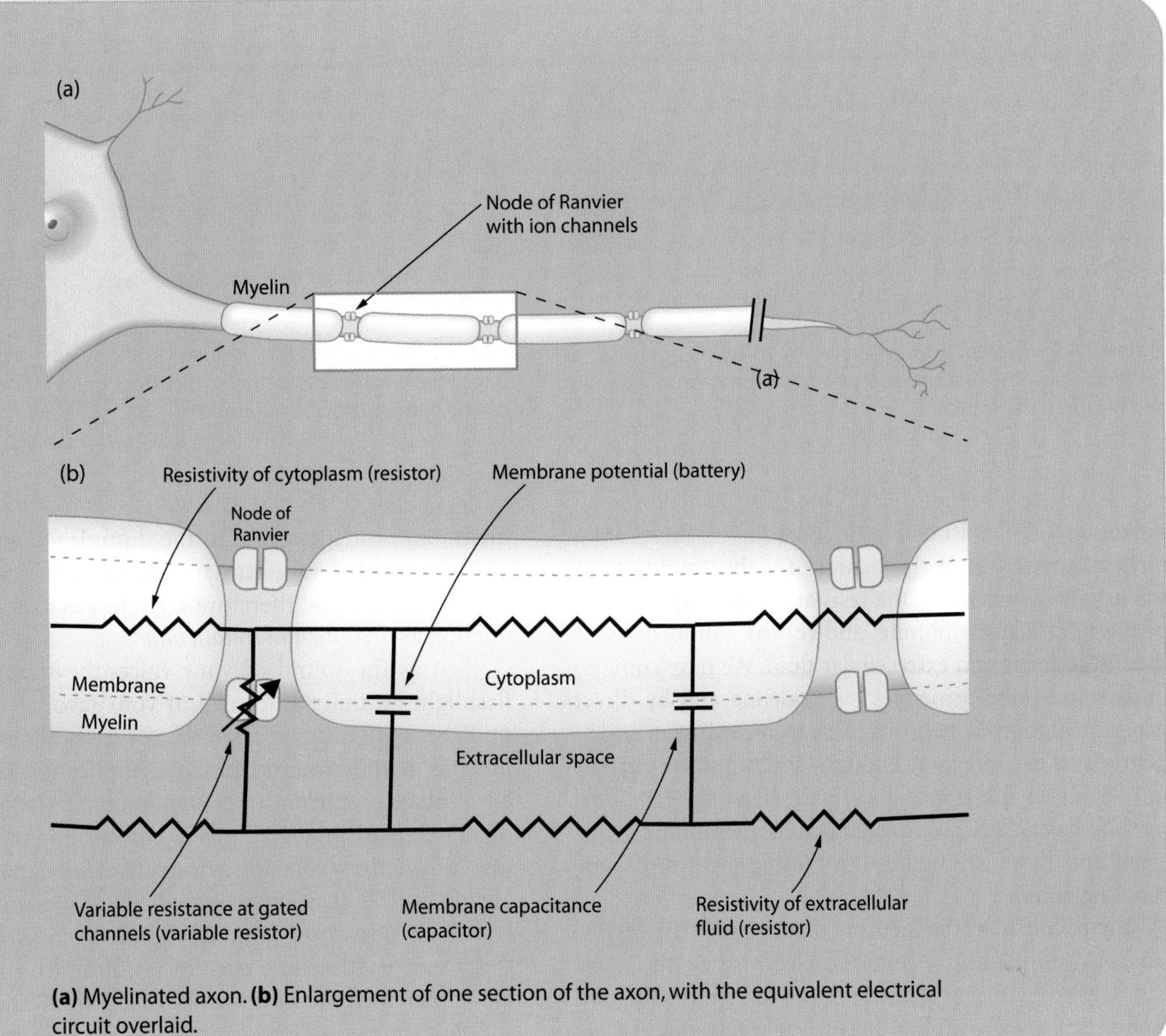

(a) Myelinated axon. **(b)** Enlargement of one section of the axon, with the equivalent electrical circuit overlaid.

borhood of active membrane processes that involve the opening of ion channels to let ionic currents flow (described later). The same currents then also flow through the cell passively by electrotonic conduction; we refer to these currents as *passive* because, as they flow through the cell and across nearby portions of the membrane, they are mediated not by openings of ion channels but by the physical properties of the membrane and the nature of electrical circuits. Current must always flow to complete an electrical circuit; thus, the movement of ions to the inside of a neuron is accompanied by the return of currents to the outside of the neuron, forming a complete circuit (Figure 2.15).

As described earlier, electrical current in neurons is ionic; that is, it is carried by charged atoms (ions) in solution. With neurons, the charge carriers are primarily Na^+, K^+, and Cl^- ions, but there are also large charged proteins in solution. Because transmembrane currents are carried by the smaller ions, we usually speak of sodium currents, potassium currents, and chloride currents across the membrane and of ionic currents more generally inside or outside the neuron. These currents typically occur when ionic species such as Na^+ or K^+ cross the neuronal membrane through ion channels that open in response to chemical, electrical, or physical stimuli.

Electrotonic (Decremental) Conduction A key question for understanding signaling is this: How far down a dendrite, axon, or cell body will passive ionic currents flow when not replenished by active processes (i.e., action

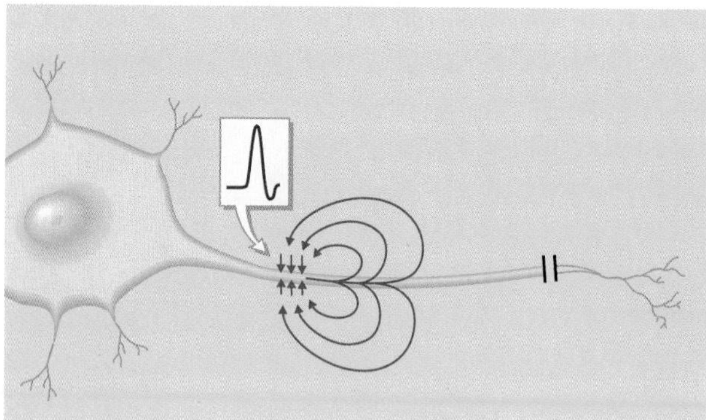

Figure 2.15 Current flow generated by an action potential. Currents cross the membrane, travel down the neuron, exit, and return to the source.

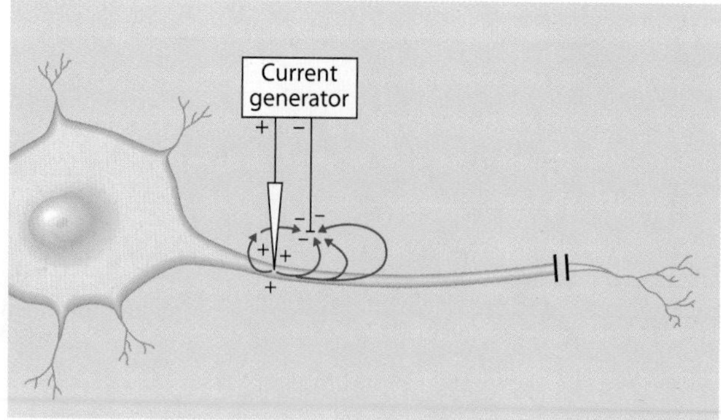

Figure 2.16 Current flow induced artificially. By use of an intracellular electrode attached to a current generator, currents can be made to flow in neurons.

potentials)? The distance is a function of three main physical properties of the neuron: (a) the amplitude of the original current, (b) the resistance (and capacitance) of the neuronal membrane, and (c) the conductivity of the intracellular and extracellular fluid. We have come to understand these principles by modeling and by direct experimentation in neurons; we can record from inside neurons (if they are large enough) and can inject current into them to investigate the result (Figure 2.16). This method has greatly illuminated passive membrane properties and how they figure into the big picture of neuronal signaling.

First, consider the neuron diagrammed in Figure 2.17a. A stimulating electrode placed inside the axon can be used to inject current into the cell, mimicking the action of synaptic inputs. Recording electrodes are inserted into the axon at varying distances from the point at which a stimulating electrode is located. When the stimulating electrode injects positive current into the axon at that location (i.e., the electrode tip is made positive by a current generator), the current flows down the axon and emerges through the axonal membrane, creating return currents that flow toward the other electrode located in the extracellular fluid, and thereby completing the circuit. In the example shown here, the depolarization induced by the current injection is below the threshold for generating action potentials (see the next section). Near the electrode inside the axon, the current is strongest, and the passive electronic currents that flow down the axon decrease with distance away from the source. If we measure the voltage across the membrane, we see a large voltage change near the stimulating electrode and progressively smaller voltage changes as we move farther away from it. If we assume that the membrane's resistivity does not change, then the change in membrane voltage is due to the diminished amplitude of the current at more distant loci (i.e., decrements in the signal), and we therefore refer to electrotonic conduction as *decremental conduction.*

Just as the sound of your voice, the strength of a flashlight beam, or the smell of your favorite pizza diminishes with distance from the source, so does current flowing in and around the axon. Application of Ohm's law (voltage = current × resistance, or $V = IR$) can help us understand this relationship. As current moves farther down the axon, the cumulative resistance (R) is greater, so the drop in voltage (V) is greater in the circuit. We can rearrange the equation as $I = V/R$, showing that the strength of the current (I) diminishes as resistance increases. Note, however, that Ohm's law in this simple expression does not capture the details of neuronal properties, although it is nonetheless useful in developing an intuitive sense of the relevant factors in electrotonic conduction (see "The Cognitive Neuroscientist's Toolkit: Building Neurons Out of Batteries and Baling Wire," on p. 34).

Now remember, the goal of electrical conduction in neurons is to conduct signal changes that, when strong enough, will cause axon terminals to release neurotransmitter, resulting in synaptic transmission between neurons. The question of the most interest now is whether passive electrotonic conduction is sufficient to allow this communication. The answer is that it depends on the circumstances. Because the current's strength diminishes with distance from the source, such a signal is not appropriate for *long-distance* communication, but it can work well for short distances.

As noted earlier, the distance from the source that electrotonic currents can still be effective for communication depends in part on the size of the original current. The

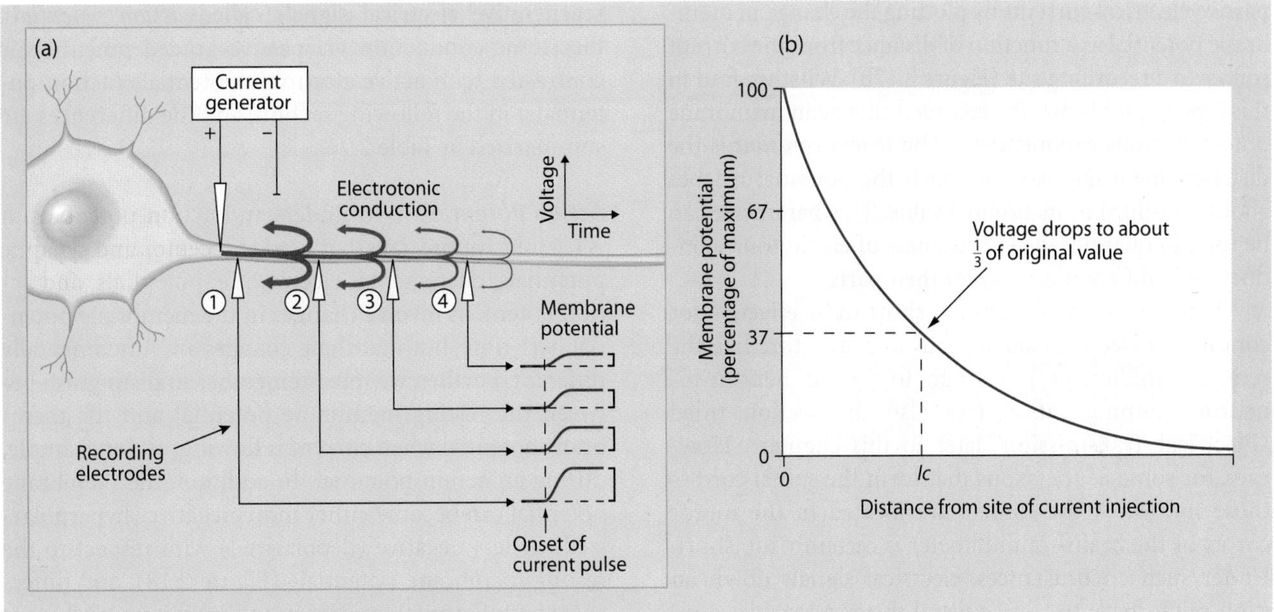

Figure 2.17 **(a)** Neuron with an electrode injecting current at one end of the axon and recording electrodes positioned at varying distances down the axon away from the soma. The amplitude of the membrane depolarization that is induced by the injection of current with an amplitude below threshold drops systematically with increasing distance from the site of injection. **(b)** The decline in membrane depolarization induced by passive currents flowing down the axon follows an exponential function as distance increases, and a value known as the *length constant* (*lc*) can be defined as the distance from the origin at which the change in membrane potential reaches 37% of its original value

greater the current, the farther it will conduct. In the laboratory, we can manipulate the extent of conduction by increasing the size of the current injected in the neuron. Under normal physiological conditions, however, the amplitude of the current is determined by physiological factors such as the intensity of a physical stimulus at a receptor, or the strength and number of synaptic inputs onto the neuron. Because these events may be associated with currents of different sizes, the changes in membrane potential that they induce are said to be *graded.*

We can also ask about the influence of the membrane's resistivity on the conduction of electrotonic potentials. Put simply, as the membrane resistivity increases, more current will be shunted down the axon and less will leak out. Consider the analogy of a garden hose. If the tubing of the hose is intact (i.e., has high resistance to water crossing it), then water put in one end is forced down the hose. Yet if the hose is full of holes (i.e., has low resistance to water), the water forced in one end does not move as far down the hose, because some of it leaks out. If the hose is leaky enough, the water may move only a short distance before the water pressure falls to the level where water no longer flows to the end of the hose. Similarly, the resistivity of the neuronal membrane influences the distance down an axon that a current can travel (this will be relevant later, when we discuss myelination and conduction).

Finally, the inverse of resistivity—the conductivity of the intracellular space—also affects how far through a neuron a current will flow. Usually the intracellular and extracellular fluids have high conductivities because, as salt solutions, they are generally good conductors of electrical current (although they are vastly inferior to metal wire). Even so, the resistivity of dendrites, cell bodies, and axons changes as a function of their size. Returning to the garden hose analogy, we find that, if the hose has a large diameter, water flows easily, but in a thin hose, water pressure, and thus resistivity, rises because of the restricted flow. In a similar way, if the axon is large, the current flow is greater. Thus, high-amplitude receptor or synaptic currents, high membrane resistance, and low-resistance intracellular pathways enhance the electrotonic conduction of currents by permitting them to affect the neuronal membrane at loci more distant from their site of generation.

Under the best of conditions, however, how far can electrotonic conduction provide an effective means of electrical communication? Not far—generally only about a millimeter. We can describe the decremental nature of passive electrical currents by plotting the change in membrane potential as a function of distance from the current source to a recording site (Figure 2.17b). What we find in this type of plot is that the recorded change in membrane potential drops exponentially. The *length constant* is the distance down the axon at which the potential reaches about one-third of its original value. This parameter can be used to quantify the effectiveness of electrotonic conduction in different neurons or their parts.

A millimeter may seem too short to be effective for conducting electrical signals, but in a structure like the retina, a millimeter is enough to permit neuron-to-neuron communication (see also the section titled "Electrical Transmission" later in this chapter). However, for some of the axons that form the spinal cord—those for which the somata are located in the motor cortex of the brain—a millimeter is certainly too short. Under such circumstances, electrical signals down an axon might have to cover several meters; consider a giraffe, an elephant, or a whale! Another mechanism, an active regenerative mechanism, has evolved to conduct electrical signals long distances in the central and peripheral nervous systems.

ACTIVE ELECTRICAL PROPERTIES OF NEURONS

In the preceding section we described how the physical properties of neurons affect the way electrical currents passively flow through them, as a result of synaptic inputs or sensory stimulation at receptors. We showed that electrotonic conduction is good for short-distance communication but fails for long-distance communication. Long-distance communication requires active or regenerative electrical signals called *action potentials.* Electronic conduction via passive graded potentials is contrasted with active electronic potentials (action potentials) in the following section, and the differences are summarized in Table 2.2.

Action Potentials To understand action potentials, it is useful to appreciate that graded receptor and synaptic potentials, decremental electrotonic potentials, and action potentials involve changes in the membrane potential over time, but that these changes are fundamentally different. Further, we must remember to distinguish between the resting membrane potential and the membrane potential when current is flowing, as, for example, during an action potential. In addition, the membrane potential can become either more negative (hyperpolarized) or less negative (depolarized) with respect to the resting membrane potentials (Figure 2.18), and different types of inputs (excitatory and inhibitory) influence these changes. And finally, active processes such as action potentials are initiated by passive electrotonic currents that alter the local membrane potential, thereby triggering action potentials in specific regions of the neuronal membrane. Hence, the two types of electrical conduction in neurons—passive electrotonic and active regenerative—are intimately related (see Figure 2.14).

Stimulating neurons with excitatory currents (depolarization) can generate action potentials in axons. We can observe these action potentials without intracellular recording by simply placing recording electrodes on the outsides of axons or bundles of axons (i.e., nerves) (Figure 2.19). To find out about the mechanisms that generate action potentials, however, researchers use

Table 2.2 Major Differences Between Graded and Action Potentials

Feature	Graded Potentials	Action Potentials
Amplitude	Varies with stimulus	All or none; always same amplitude
Summation	Can be summed (compare to an analog code)	Cannot be summed (compare to a digital code)
Threshold	No	Yes
Refractory period	No	Yes, both relative and absolute
Conduction	Decremental	Nondecremental
Duration	Varies	Constant for given type of cell under constant conditions
Polarization	Can be depolarization or hyperpolarization	Can be only depolarization
Initiation	Initiated by signal transduction and neurotransmission	Initiated by a graded potential
Channels	Not voltage-gated (mostly ligand-gated)	Voltage-gated

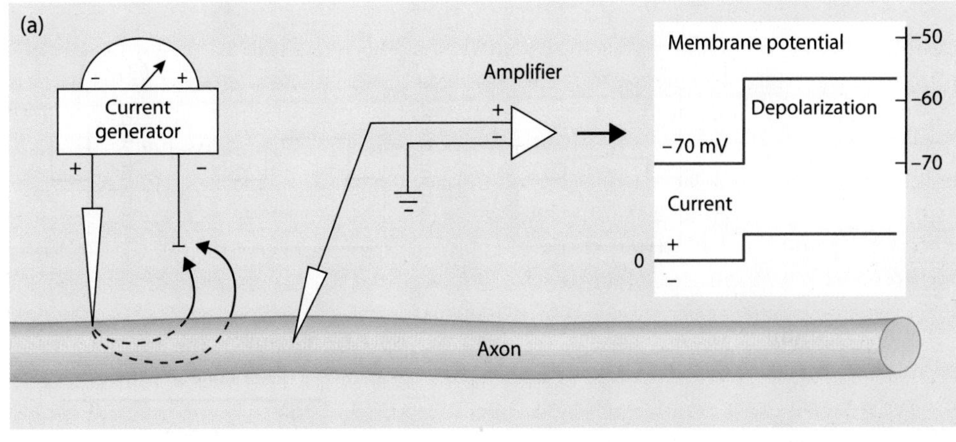

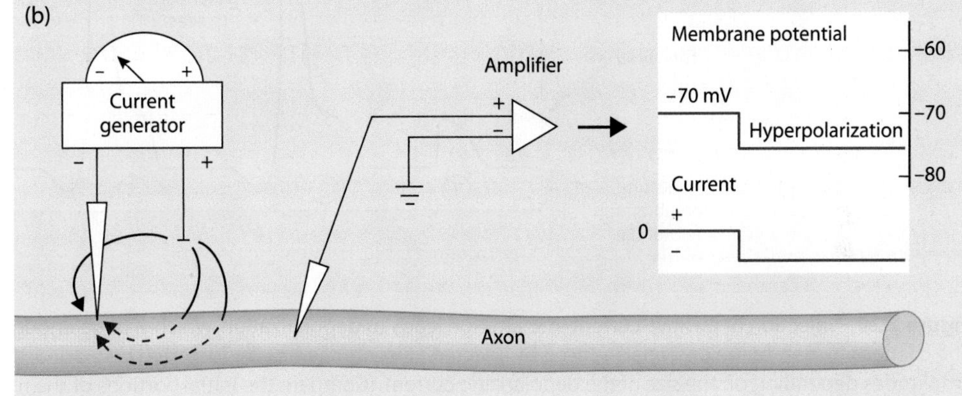

Figure 2.18 Axon with stimulating and recording electrodes placed inside. **(a)** Injection of current by making the electrode tip more positive depolarizes the membrane. **(b)** Current flow in the opposite direction can hyperpolarize the neuronal membrane.

Figure 2.19 Extracellular stimulating and recording electrodes and recorded compound action potentials. A large electrode placed extracellularly can also depolarize the membrane and generate action potentials. Here a peripheral nerve composed of many individual axons is being stimulated, and the compound action potential (the summation of the action potentials from all the axons) is recorded with an extracellular electrode. The electrodes pictured are hook electrodes, pieces of wire curled into hooks against which the nerve lies.

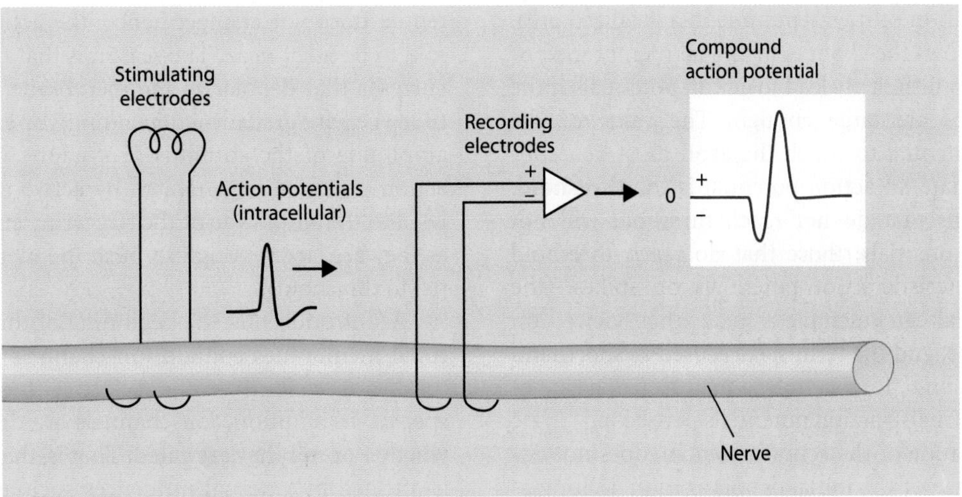

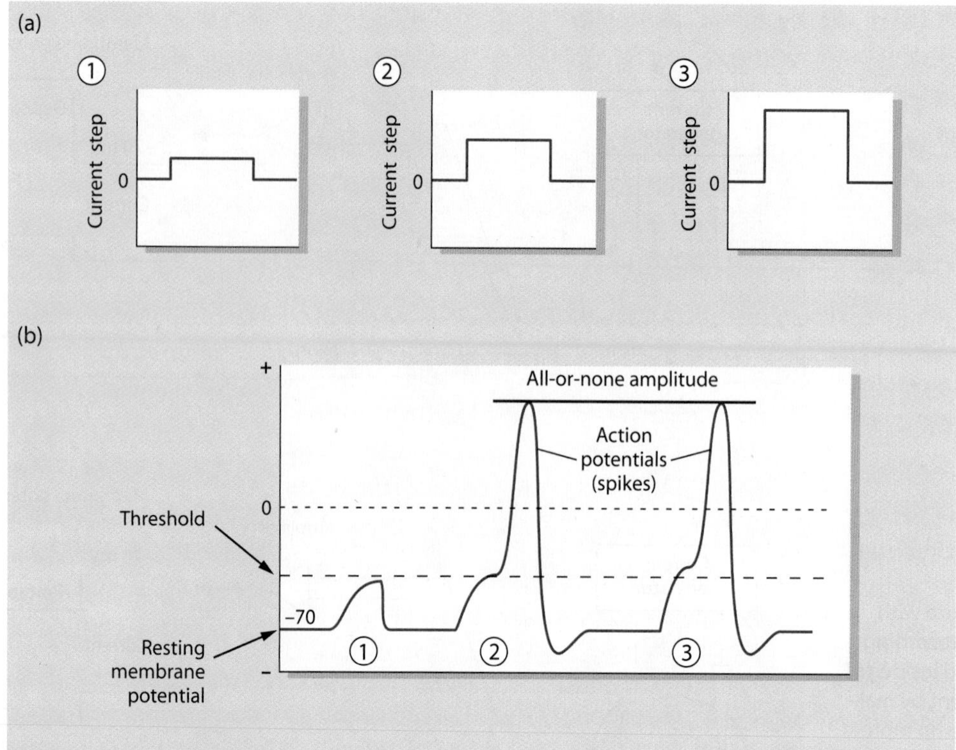

Figure 2.20 Injection of positive current into an axon leads to depolarization, which, if large enough, triggers an action potential. The changes in membrane potential induced by injected currents can be considered to be graded; that is, they can take on varying amplitudes depending on the size of the depolarizing current. (Compare the initial portions of the membrane depolarizations in Steps 1 through 3 in **(b)** as a function of the size of the injected current indicated in 1 through 3 in **(a)**.) However, when the depolarization reaches threshold, the action potential that is generated reaches an amplitude that is not related to the size of the original depolarizing current. That is, the action potential is said to be all or none (compare 2 and 3 in (b)).

intracellular recording and stimulation. In axons, if stimulation is continued with successively higher and higher amplitudes of current, an action potential can be elicited. The action potential is a rapid depolarization and repolarization of the membrane in a localized area. Figure 2.20 shows the changes in axonal membrane potential that can ultimately lead to action potentials if the depolarizations are large enough. The value of the membrane potential to which the axon must be depolarized to initiate an action potential is the **threshold.** Depolarizations that do not reach threshold will not elicit action potentials; those that do reach threshold lead to characteristic action potentials, or "spikes" (the action potential can resemble a spike when viewed on an oscilloscope, and the term *spike* is used as shorthand for *action potential*; for example, a neuron firing rate of 10 spikes/s means 10 action potentials per second).

The amplitude of the action potential, does not depend on the size of the initial depolarization, as long as that depolarization is great enough to reach threshold for triggering the action potential. Thus, even if the depolarizing current is raised higher than the level needed to reach threshold, the value of the generated action potential does not change; hence, the action potential is said to be *all or none.* The reason is that the electrotonic currents that depolarize the membrane vary in amplitude (i.e., are graded)—depending, for example, on the amplitude of the stimulus or synaptic input—but the action potential is generated by active processes unrelated to the amplitude of the triggering currents (as long as they are large enough to push the membrane potential to threshold).

As introduced at the beginning of this section, neuronal membranes contain ion channels that are structurally specialized to be selective to specific ionic species. In addition, ion channels are distinguished by whether or not they are gated. That is, their conductivity is affected by external influences such as voltage (e.g., from passive currents), chemicals (e.g., neurotransmitters), or physical stimulation (e.g., stretch or pressure such as at sensory receptors). The gated channels have different physical states; essentially they can be open or closed, like small gates in the membrane. If the channels are open, ions can move through them by being driven by electrical and ionic concentration gradients. Voltage-gated ion channels are of prime importance in generating action potentials.

Voltage-gated ion channels open and close according to the membrane potential. They are closed at the resting membrane potential but open as the membrane becomes depolarized. When a passive current flows across the neuronal membrane following a synaptic or receptor potential, the membrane depolarizes and affects voltage-gated Na^+ channels. At this point, some of the channels begin to admit Na^+ into the neuron, which further depolarizes the neuron. In turn, additional voltage-gated Na^+ channels open, and thus the neuron becomes more depolarized, continuing the cycle by causing even more Na^+ channels to open. This process, the *Hodgkin–Huxley cycle*, is depicted in Figure 2.21.

Figure 2.21 Hodgkin–Huxley cycle. Depolarization of the axonal membrane leads to the opening of voltage-gated Na^+ channels. The inward Na^+ current then adds to the depolarization, thereby causing even more Na^+ channels to open. When the membrane potential reaches threshold, the Na^+ channel currents dominate the membrane potential, leading to the action potential's positive-going initial phase (see Figure 2.22).

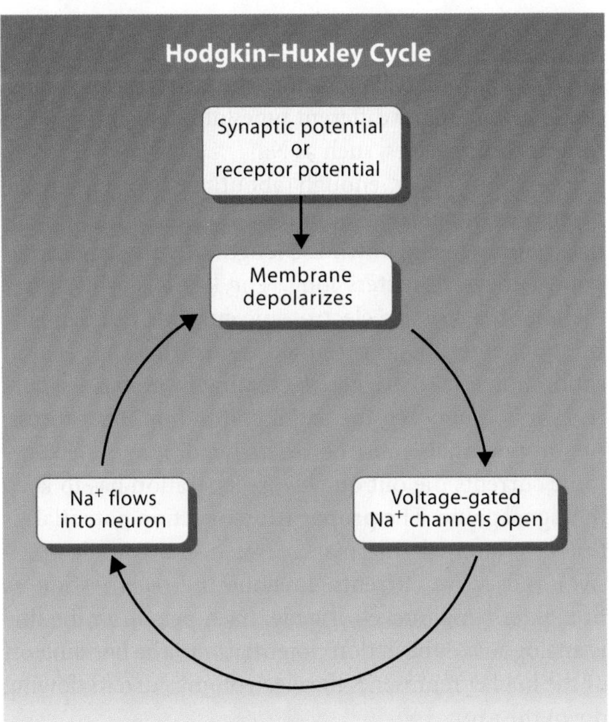

This rapid, self-reinforcing cycle generates the large depolarization that is the first portion of the action potential (Figure 2.22). Then, with a short delay, membrane depolarization leads to an opening of voltage-gated K^+ channels, which allow K^+ to flow out of the neuron and begin to repolarize it—and to reestablish the value of the resting membrane potential. The opening of the K^+ channels outlasts the closing of the Na^+ channels. The efflux of K^+ without the influx of Na^+ leads to the second repolarizing phase of the action potential, which brings the membrane potential back to the level of the resting membrane potential. The K^+ efflux drives the membrane potential below the level of the original membrane potential, toward the equilibrium potential of K^+, which is more negative than the resting potential. As a result, the action potential undershoots the resting membrane potential (see Figure 2.22). During this transient period following an action potential, the membrane is actually hyperpolarized; that is, it is even more negative inside compared to outside than it is at rest. This transient hyperpolarization lasts only a couple of milliseconds, as the membrane gradually returns to the resting membrane potential.

The result of membrane hyperpolarization following the depolarization and repolarization of the action potential leaves the neuron in a temporary state in which it is less able to generate an action potential. This temporary state, known as the **refractory period**, occurs when the membrane is hyperpolarized because the membrane potential is even farther from the threshold required for triggering an action potential. However, one other factor also influences the neuron's ability to generate another immediate action potential. Immediately following the repolarizing phase of the action potential, the voltage-gated Na^+ channels are inactivated and unable to be opened, regardless of how much the membrane is depolarized. This inactivation of Na^+ channels produces the *absolute refractory period*, which is followed by the *relative refractory period*, during which the neuron can generate action potentials, but only with larger-than-normal depolarizing currents.

A consequence of the refractory period is that the neuron's speed for generating action potentials is limited. In contrast to computers, which have essentially limitless transmission speeds between bits of information, neurons are relatively slow. Time is required for current changes to lead to action potentials, and refractory periods limit the rate at which the neuron can generate successive action potentials. This limitation of the neuron is reflected in how it can be used for temporal coding. For

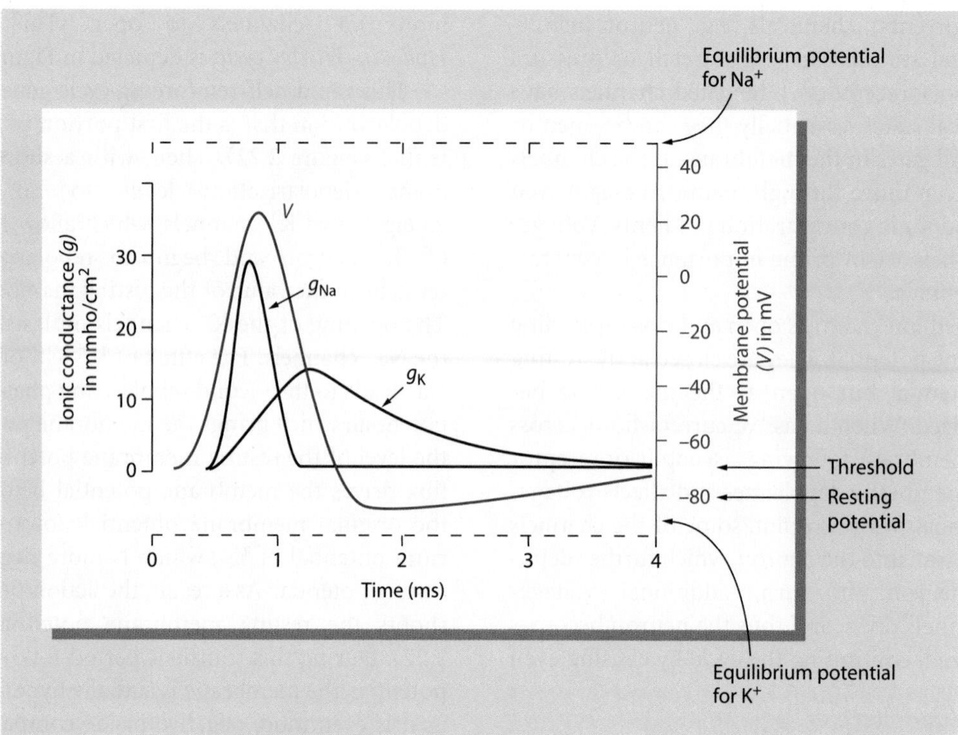

Figure 2.22 Relative time course of changes in membrane voltage during an action potential, and the underlying causative changes in membrane conductance to Na^+ (g_{Na}) and K^+ (g_K). The initial depolarizing phase of the action potential is mediated by Na^+ current, and the later repolarizing, descending phase of the action potential is mediated by an increase in K^+ conductance that occurs when the K^+ channels open. The Na^+ channels have closed during the last part of the action potential, when repolarization by the K^+ current is taking place. The action potential undershoots the resting membrane potential at the point where the membrane becomes more negative than the resting membrane potential.

example, consider the coding of sound frequency in the auditory system. Some sounds have frequencies in the tens of thousands of cycles per second (hertz, abbreviated Hz); that is, the periodic changes in sound pressure can occur very rapidly. Our auditory system is sensitive to this information; we can, for example, hear the high-pitched sounds of a songbird or fire siren. However, the fastest sensory neurons of the auditory system can fire at rates only up to about 1000 Hz. Thus the firing rate, at least from a single neuron, would not be sufficient to code the sound frequency if it had to fire in tandem with the cyclic nature of the sound. Rate-based firing alone is not a sufficient mechanism for neural coding (see the section on auditory perception in Chapter 5).

Note that not all Na^+ channels show a rapid deactivation. Some Na^+ channels in mammalian axons do not inactivate, and therefore they lead to action potentials that last longer, although most show rapid inactivation. The classic picture we described here was derived from studies in the squid axon by Hodgkin and Huxley, but more recent molecular genetic approaches have revealed that there are many different types of ion channels, even for one ionic species, such as Na^+.

We now know enough about passive and active properties of neurons to understand how action potentials can propagate down the length of very long axons, even if they are meters long. The key is simply to remember that passive electrotonic currents can depolarize the membrane to threshold. When this happens, an action potential is triggered, creating more passive currents to travel down the axon, continuing this process. Action potentials must be regenerated because electrotonic currents die out quickly; regeneration has to keep the signal going. The **propagation** of action potentials is thus a continual interplay between electrotonic (passive) and active currents. Imagine the regeneration as firefighters in a bucket brigade: Each person in the line is analogous to the action potential, and the handing off of the bucket represents the electrotonic current flowing down the axon.

The analogy would be better if the firefighters threw the water out of their buckets as far as they could to the next person, but analogies and firefighters have their limitations. Consider for a moment what would happen if the firefighters in the bucket brigade were too far apart: They would not be able to get the water to the next firefighter in the chain, so the water would not be passed along. Something analogous would also occur in axons if the next segment of axon with voltage-dependent Na^+ and K^+ channels were too distant. As a result, the electronic currents might be decremented until too weak to trigger an action potential in the distant voltage-dependent Na^+ and K^+ channels. When the axon is myelinated and conducts via saltatory conduction, the neuron faces this situation and overcomes it by the benefits of myelination, as described in the next section.

SALTATORY CONDUCTION AND THE ROLE OF MYELIN

A key aspect of neuronal communication is the speed of signaling between neurons, or between neurons and muscles. For example, as noted earlier, in animals as large as a giraffe or whale, the motor neurons located in the brain's motor cortex project axons down to the spinal cord and therefore may have to send signals over many meters. In addition, the alpha motor neurons that originate in the spinal cord receive the signal from the brain and then send axons to innervate muscles. These muscles, such as in the hand or foot, might also be a considerable distance away. If these signals did not occur rapidly, the coordination of motor activity would be compromised. It is not enough that the signals can travel that distance; they must also do it quickly.

The physical properties of neurons affect how currents flow through them, and the resistances of the intracellular fluid and neuronal membrane are of prime importance. If the resistance of the membrane increases, or the resistance of the axon decreases, then currents flow down the axon more effectively, following the path of least resistance, and therefore flow down the axon farther.

One way to lower the axon's internal resistance is to expand its diameter; larger-diameter axons conduct axon potentials faster. In the squid, one of the favorite species for studying action potentials, large axons allow for rapid neural conduction, allowing the animal to quickly contract its muscles and avoid predators. The question is this: How big would an axon's diameter have to be to achieve the speed required to communicate signals from a giraffe's brain to the motor neurons of the hind limbs? The answer is that it would have to be too big, given the constraint that a large number of neurons is needed to drive the muscles and these must be packed into the spinal cord. For large animals to evolve, this dilemma had to be solved in another way.

Myelination holds the key. Myelin wrapped around the axons of peripheral and central neurons increases membrane resistance. Myelin is formed by the concentric multiple wrappings of glial cell membrane around the axon (Figure 2.23); the cytoplasm in this portion of

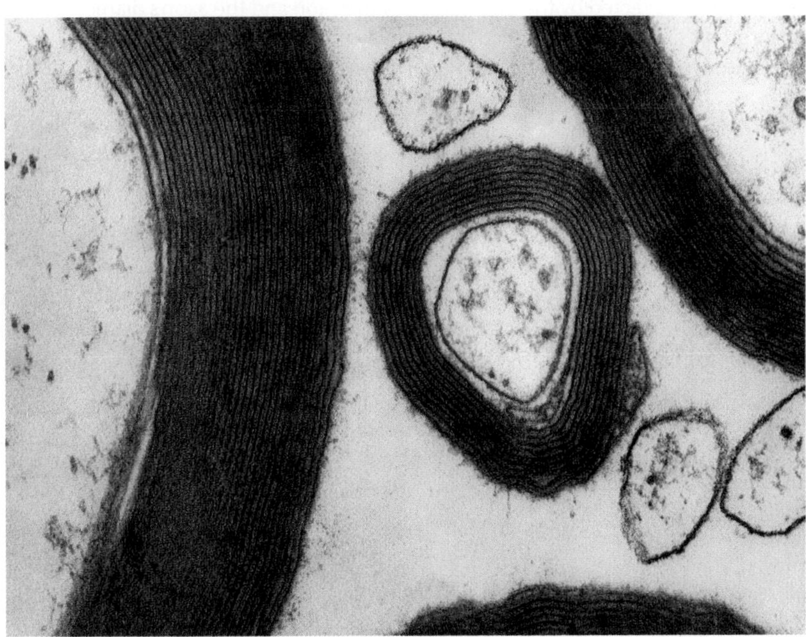

Figure 2.23 Cross section through a peripheral nerve showing concentric wrappings of myelin around the axon.

the glial cell is essentially squeezed out, leaving layer upon layer of cell membrane, the myelin. These layers of lipid membrane have high electrical resistance. The increased electrical insulation produced by the myelin causes currents to be shunted a greater distance down the axon. The result is that action potentials do not have to be generated as often, and they can be spread out along the axon at wider intervals. Indeed, action potentials in myelinated axons need occur only at the nodes of Ranvier, where myelination is interrupted.

At the nodes, voltage-gated Na^+ channels can trigger action potentials that regenerate fast electrotonic currents that flow to the next node, where another action potential is generated. So the action potential appears to jump along the axons from node to node—hence the name **saltatory conduction**, from the Latin *saltare*, which means "to jump" (Figure 2.24). By such conduction, mammalian nerves can transmit signals at roughly 120 m/s—or, in more concrete terms, the length of a football field in one second. Now that's quite fast!

Transmembrane Proteins: Ion Channels and Pumps

In the preceding sections we discussed how the resting membrane potential arises and how changes in membrane permeability permit electrical signaling. We introduced the concept of transmembrane proteins and defined two main types: the active transporters and the ion channels—the former using energy to pump ions across the membrane to create ionic concentration gradients, and the latter contributing to the membrane permeability of ions. These molecules come in a variety of forms. For example, some ion channels are gated and others are not. Here we describe the structure and properties of ion channels in more detail.

ION CHANNELS

Ion channels are proteins, which are polypeptides (chains of many peptides). Peptides, in turn, are formed from the molecular building blocks called *amino acids*. Any two amino acids can form a peptide, but many can come together to form small and large proteins. For example, human myoglobin contains 153 amino acid residues (individual amino acid molecules). There are 21 amino acids, including familiar ones like leucine, lysine, methionine, phenylalanine, threonine, and tryptophan that you can find on the labels of products in any health food store, and others such as glutamate that are important in their own right as neurotransmitters, as we will discover later.

Figure 2.24 Saltatory conduction in a myelinated nerve. Action potentials in a myelinated nerve occur only at the nodes of Ranvier, where there are gaps in the myelin. The current generated at the nodes flows in the internode region under the constraints determined by the principles of electrotonic conduction. The distance between the nodes is determined by the length constant of the axon, which is affected by the myelination of the axon and the axon's diameter. Hence, the nodes are optimally spaced such that electrotonic currents from the action potential at the last node are still strong enough to depolarize the membrane to threshold at the present node, thus handing the signal down the axon and regenerating it at the nodes of Ranvier.

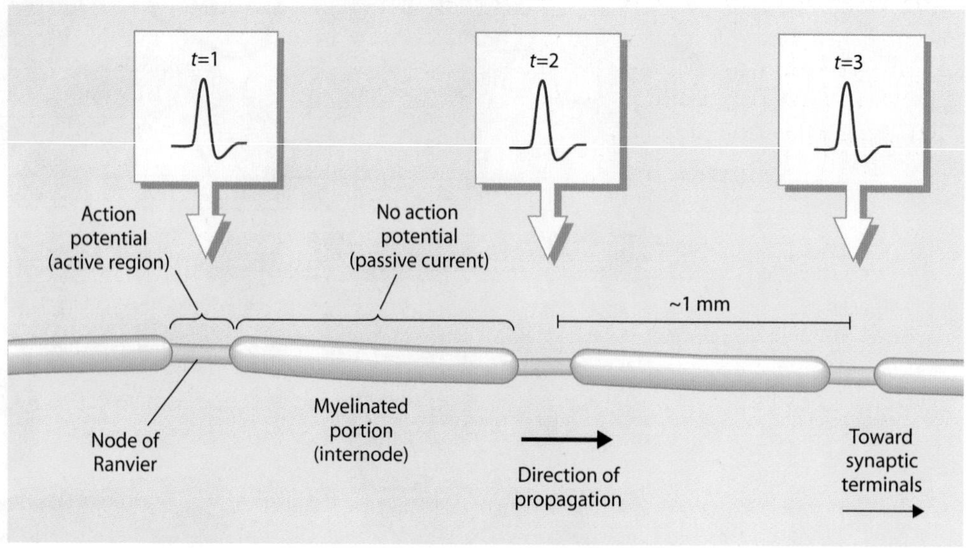

Proteins are not only long strings of amino acids. They also have a three-dimensional structure that is important for their function. We can define several levels of structure in proteins. The *primary structure* is simply the order of the amino acids. The *secondary structure* refers to how the long chains of amino acids coil to form characteristic patterns such as the alpha-helix (a helical coiling). The *tertiary structure* of proteins reflects the fact that the long strands of coiled amino acids can fold on themselves to form complex three-dimensional structures. Finally, many large proteins are composed of subunits, each itself a tertiary protein, that come together to create the final structure: the *quaternary structure* (Figure 2.25).

The molecular structure of ion channels has been investigated by the use of methods such as X-ray crystallography in simple model systems. From these types of studies we know that ion channels are composed of subunits, giving them an important quaternary three-dimensional structure. An example is the formation of a pore through their centers that serves as the conduit for ions to traverse the membrane. The crystallographic approach with bacteria has led to our understanding of how K^+, Na^+, and Cl^- channels operate at the molecular level. Roderick MacKinnon, Declan Doyle, and their colleagues at Rockefeller University (Doyle et al., 1998) identified the three-dimensional structure of an ion channel as composed of four subunits (Figure 2.26). Their crystallographic analysis led them to propose that the ion channel has the shape of an inverted *V* or a teepee, created by the three-dimensional relationships of the four subunits of the protein (Figure 2.27).

Figure 2.25 General structure of proteins. **(a)** The amino acid sequence is the *primary* structure. **(b)** The strings of amino acids can coil into helical shapes, forming the *secondary* structure. **(c)** Folding of the helix—the *tertiary* structure—can give rise to globular proteins (many are enzymes, for example). **(d)** The *quaternary* structure is a complex three-dimensional structure (such as an ion channel) composed of globular proteins.

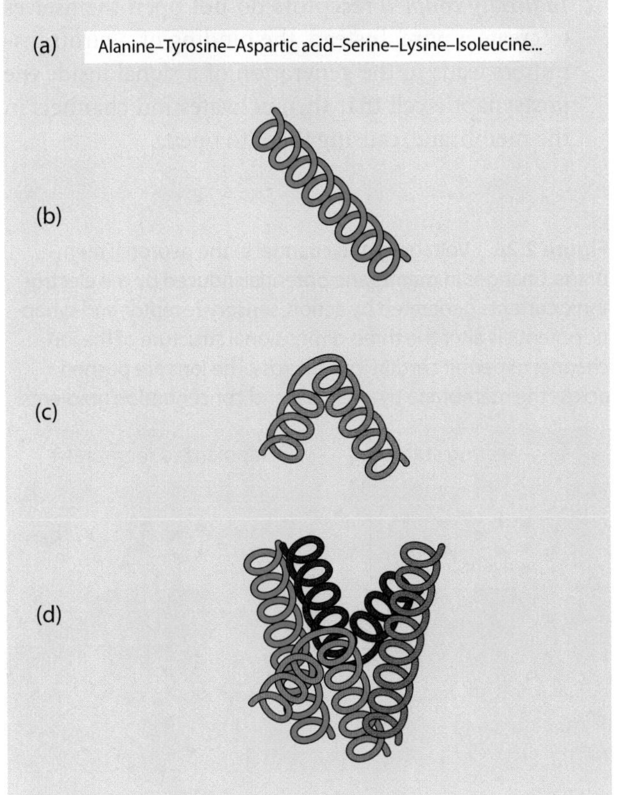

At the wider end of the ion channel is a region serving as a filter that imparts permeability only to the ion for which it is selective (in this case K^+); this region is about 12 angstroms (Å) wide. The selectivity filter opens into a central space filled with water that is continuous with the cytoplasm. The chemical environment created by the portions of the subunits lining the pore and the dimensions of the pore help K^+ to cross the membrane, down the K^+ concentration gradient. Other ions, such as Na^+, are not able to use K^+ channels to cross the membrane, because the chemical environment inside the pore is not effective in enabling Na^+ to pass through. However, other ion channels that are specialized to be selective for Na^+, Cl^-, or Ca^{2+} probably act by similar principles as the K^+ ion channel.

Gated and Nongated Ion Channels Ion channels are either passive (*nongated*) or active (*gated* by electrical, chemical, or physical stimuli). The Na^+ and K^+ channels involved in the generation of the action potential are voltage-gated channels. Electrotonically conducted currents that pass out across the membrane can depolarize the neuron, causing the channels to open like gates. The opening permits ions to be driven through the pores by the concentration and electrical gradients across the membrane. The channels are selective; that is, they allow the passage of only some ions.

Voltage-gated channels exist for Na^+, K^+, Cl^+, and Ca^{2+}. Voltage-gated Cl^- channels are involved in homeostatic processes, including stabilization of the membrane potential. Voltage-gated Ca^{2+} channels are, among other things, relevant for the release of neurotransmitters from presynaptic terminals. You might wonder how the voltage triggers the channels to open and close. Changes in the transmembrane potential influence the molecular structure of the proteins in the

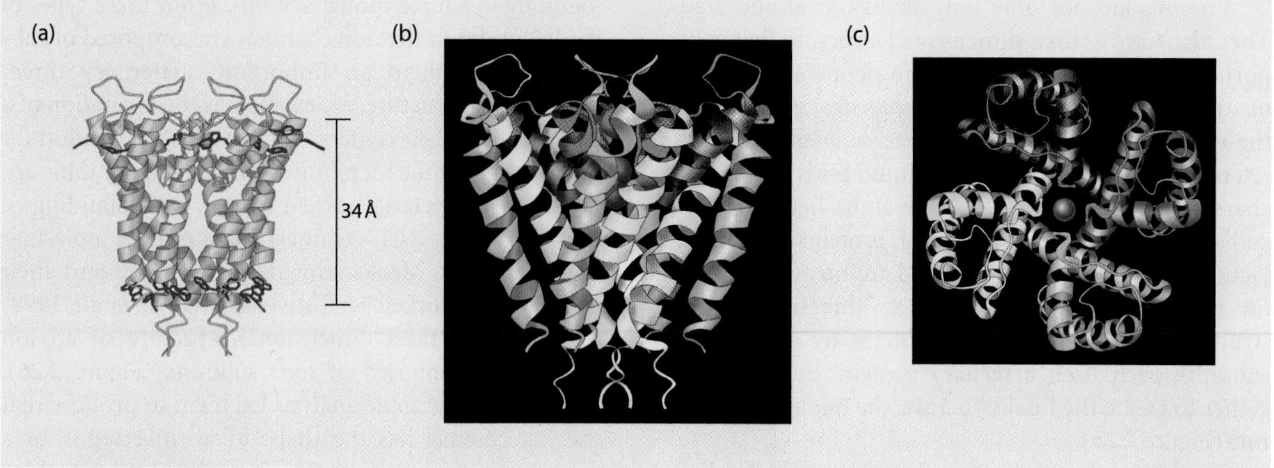

Figure 2.26 Helical structure of the transmembrane K^+ ion channel. **(a)** Cross-sectional diagram of the four subunits spanning the membrane from the extracellular (top) to the intracellular space, a length of about 34 Å. **(b)** Individual subunits in cross-sectional view as in (a), shown in different colors. **(c)** "Top" view of the ion channel, showing the central pore. K^+ ions are represented by the purple spheres in **(b)** and **(c)**.

channels, changing the three-dimensional configuration of the pore region (Figure 2.28).

Chemically gated ion channels located chiefly on the postsynaptic membrane serve as neurotransmitter receptors; examples are found on the dendrites of cortical neurons, or on muscle cells at the neuromuscular junction where motor neurons innervate muscle fibers. The chemicals, also called *ligands*, are typically neurotransmitters such as glycine, dopamine, and acetylcholine. Thus, **receptors** are specialized ion channels that mediate signals at synapses; we will describe the process of synaptic transmission in the next section.

There are two general classes (and many subclasses) of postsynaptic receptors (Figure 2.29):

1. *Directly coupled* receptors chemically interact with, or bind, neurotransmitters on their extracellular surfaces. This binding leads to structural changes in the receptor that permit the passage of ions.
2. *Indirectly coupled* receptors do not open themselves to create a pore. Instead, the binding of neurotransmitters leads to the generation of a signal inside the postsynaptic cell that then activates ion channels in the membrane, causing them to open.

Figure 2.27 K^+ channel in the membrane. In cross-sectional view, the channel is shown embedded in the membrane (the lipid bilayer is to the left and right of the channel). The extracellular space is at the top. K^+ ions (green) are shown traversing the membrane via the pore.

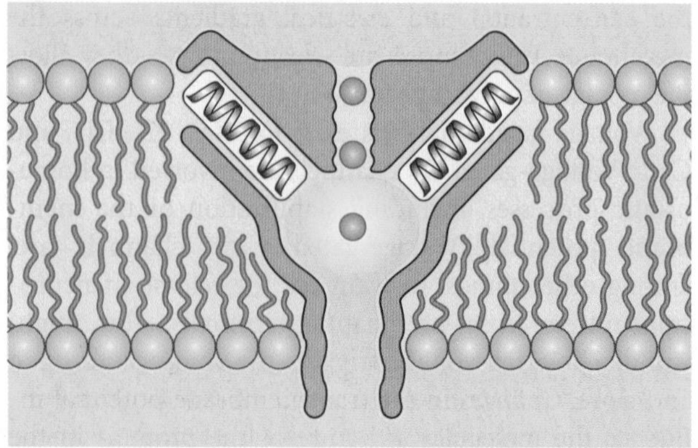

Figure 2.28 Voltage-gated channel in the neuronal membrane. Changes in membrane potential induced by the electrotonic currents generated by action, sensory receptor, and synaptic potentials alter the three-dimensional structure of the ion channel to permit certain ions to cross. The ions are pushed across the membrane by electrical and concentration gradients.

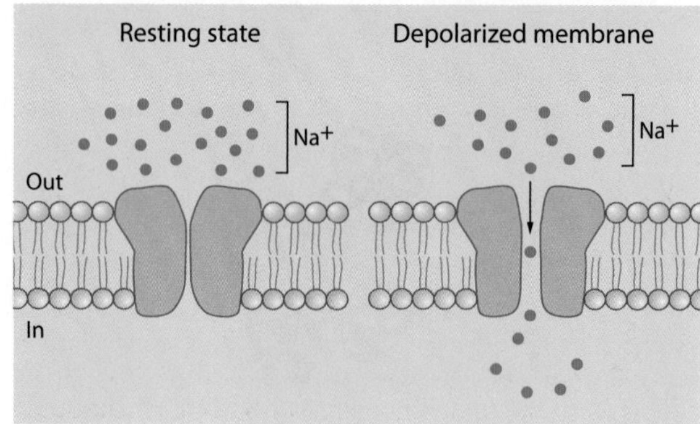

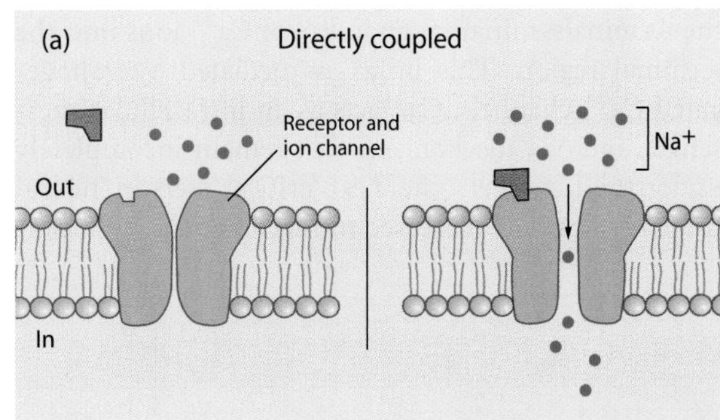

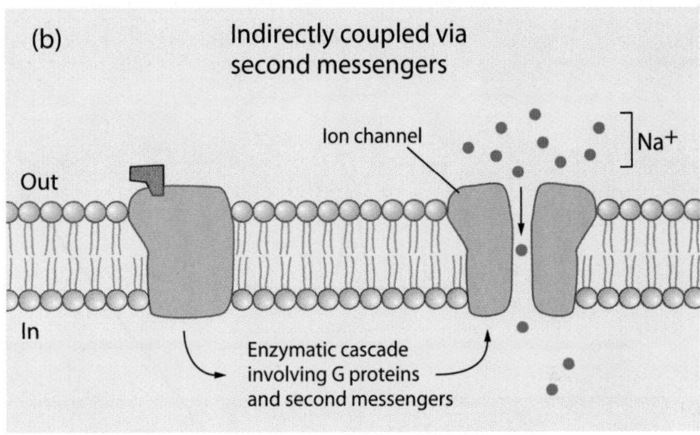

Figure 2.29 Mechanisms of neurotransmitter receptor molecules. **(a)** After binding with a neurotransmitter, a directly coupled receptor undergoes a conformational (structural) change that opens the pore to permit ions to cross the membrane, leading to (in this case) depolarization of the postsynaptic neuron. **(b)** An indirectly coupled receptor binds the neurotransmitter but is not itself an ion channel and hence forms no pore. Instead, the binding of the neurotransmitter leads to a series of intracellular biochemical events, beginning with the action of G proteins and the subsequent generation of second messengers, ultimately leading to a signal that affects ion channels in the postsynaptic membrane, which then open and (in this case) depolarize the postsynaptic neuron.

The latter mechanism involves so-called G proteins (intracellular proteins that bind guanosine triphosphate, or GTP) and **second messengers** such as Ca^{2+}, cyclic nucleotides including cyclic guanosine monophosphate (cGMP) and cyclic adenosine monophosphate (cAMP), nitric oxide, and other substances.

One advantage of second-messenger systems is that they can permit signal amplification by triggering enzymatic cascades. These cascades exponentially increase the final signal via several intermediate biochemical steps, thereby allowing a relatively small neurotransmitter signal to lead to a large postsynaptic response. The second-messenger systems not only act to modulate ion channel conductances but also are essential for intracellular signaling that leads, for example, to changes in gene expression in response to neurotransmitters and hormones. There are a variety of receptor subtypes, and they play specific roles in neuronal communication, disease, and cognitive processes. An example is the role of the NMDA receptor in learning and memory, which we will discuss in Chapter 8.

SYNAPTIC TRANSMISSION

The ultimate act in neuronal signaling is for a neuron to communicate with other neurons or muscles. In order for neurons to do this, they must transmit signals—an action called *synaptic transmission.* Synaptic transmission (as its name implies) occurs at synapses. There are two major kinds of synapses—chemical and electrical—each using very different mechanisms from the other. The essentials of synaptic transmission have been understood for decades, but the details continue to be unraveled with some recent exciting discoveries illuminating mechanisms that only a few years ago had been mysteries.

Chemical Transmission

Chemical transmission involves a series of fairly well understood steps. First, in most cases, an action potential must arrive at the axon terminals where the synapses are located. The invasion of the axon terminals by the action potential leads to depolarization of the terminals, initiating an influx of Ca^{2+} ions into the terminal region. This influx is mediated by voltage-gated Ca^{2+} channels. Ca^{2+}acts as an intracellular messenger and, via mechanisms that remain incompletely understood, triggers the next critical step in neural transmission. The increased intracellular Ca^{2+} concentration causes small **vesicles** containing neurotransmitter to fuse with the membrane at the synapse and release this transmitter into the *synaptic cleft*, the space between the presynaptic and postsynaptic neuronal membranes. The transmitter diffuses across the cleft and, on reaching the postsynaptic membrane, binds

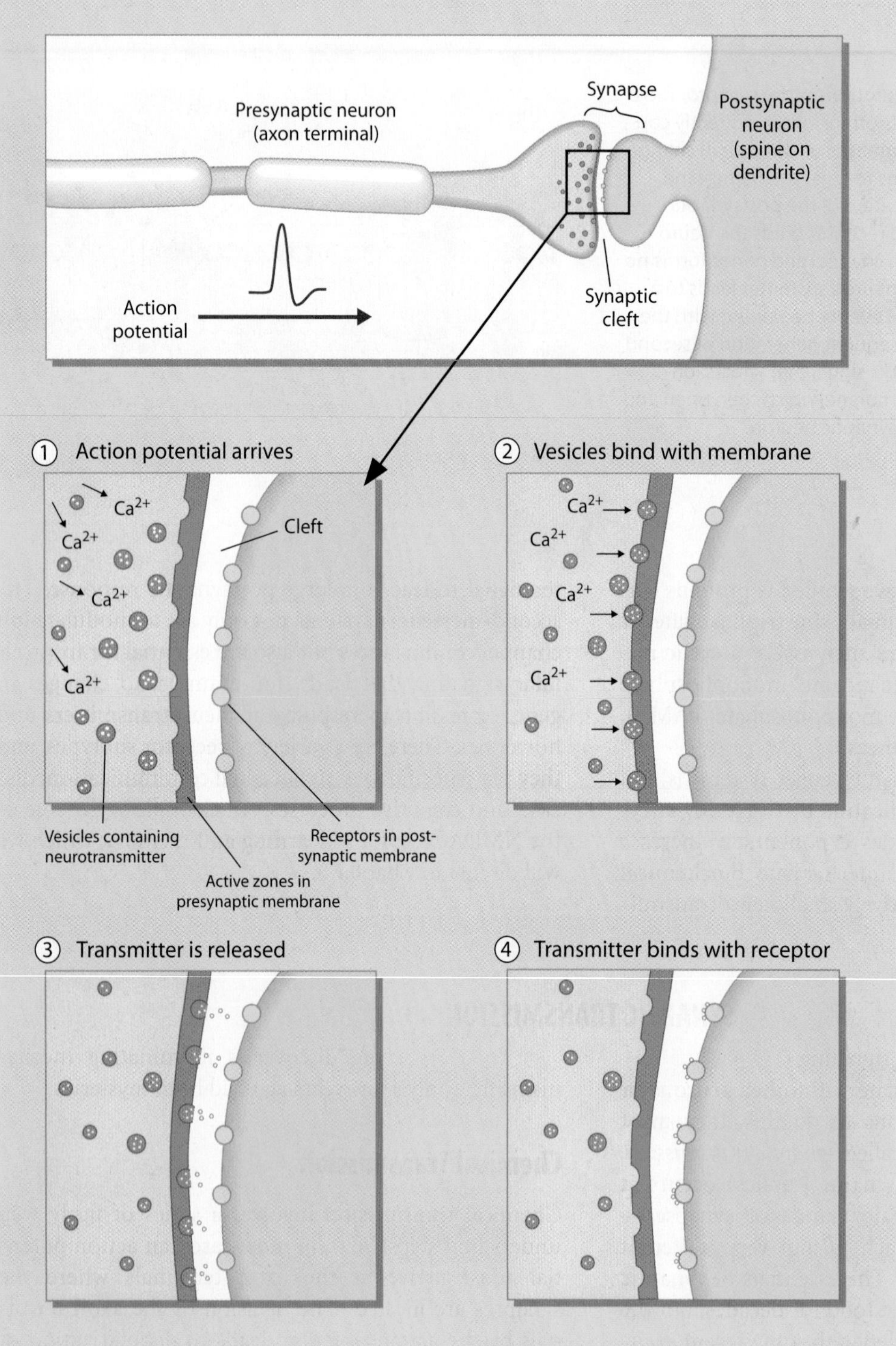

Figure 2.30 Neurotransmitter release at the synapse. The synapse consists of various specializations where the presynaptic and postsynaptic membranes are in close apposition. When the action potential invades the axon terminals, it causes voltage-gated Ca^{2+} channels to open (1), which triggers vesicles to bind to the presynaptic membrane (2). Neurotransmitter is released into the synaptic cleft by exocytosis and diffuses across the cleft (3). Binding of the neurotransmitter to receptor molecules in the postsynaptic membrane completes the process of transmission (4).

with protein molecules (receptor molecules) embedded in the postsynaptic membrane, initiating changes in the postsynaptic membrane via the mechanisms reviewed in the previous section (Figure 2.30).

The chemical interaction of the neurotransmitter and the postsynaptic receptor initiates events that lead to either depolarization (excitation) or hyperpolarization (inhibition) of the postsynaptic cell (Figure 2.31). If the postsynaptic cell is a neuron, then an *excitatory postsynaptic potential* (*EPSP*) might lead to the generation of action potentials, depending on a variety of factors. In most neurons, action potentials are initiated at the interface between the cell body and the axon (axon hillock), where synaptic currents are summed electrically. That is, the influences of many synaptic potentials sum together. This principle of summation is key, especially since the axon hillock region of the postsynaptic neuron may be quite distant from the many spines on its dendrites that received the signals in the first place. The summation of EPSPs may be sufficient to reach threshold. In neurons, postsynaptic summation can lead to the generation of action potentials and subsequent release of transmitter at the axon terminals. If the postsynaptic cell is a muscle cell, the EPSP leads to action potentials in the muscle and to muscular contraction.

If the neurotransmitter has an inhibitory action on the postsynaptic neuron, the membrane potential will usually become hyperpolarized, causing an *inhibitory postsynaptic potential* (*IPSP*). Hyperpolarization would make the postsynaptic neuron less likely to generate an action potential, because the membrane potential would become more negative and hence be farther away from threshold. This hyperpolarization can result from opening of Cl^- channels on the postsynaptic membrane. The concentration of Cl^- is much higher outside the neuron than inside. Therefore, if the Cl^- channels are open, Cl^- will be forced into the neuron by the concentration gradient, making the inside of the cell even more negative. Or, even if no hyperpolarization of the neuron occurs, the opening of Cl^-channels will minimize the effects of any simultaneous excitatory inputs that would open Na^+ channels. The effects are minimized because the open Cl^- channels and the open Na^+ channels have opposite influences on the membrane potential; hence, via summation, their effects tend to cancel each other. Thousands of inputs to a single neuron may try to influence its behavior, and summation helps determine the outcome.

Interestingly, inhibitory synaptic inputs might even lead to slight *depolarization* of the postsynaptic neuron and still act to inhibit the neuron from being depolarized

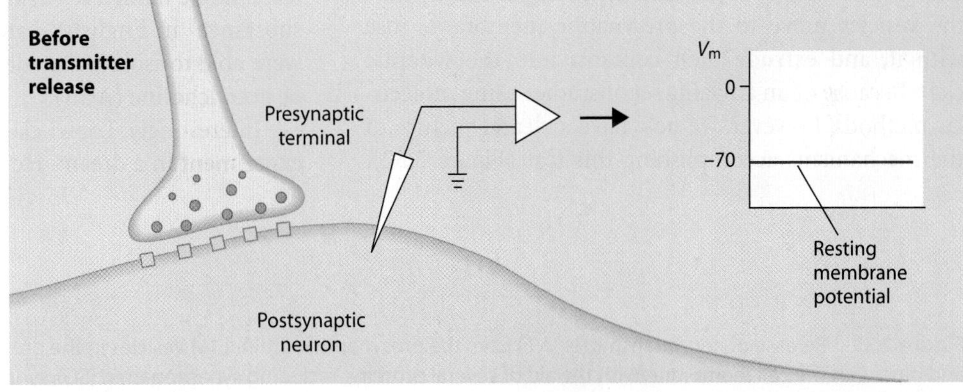

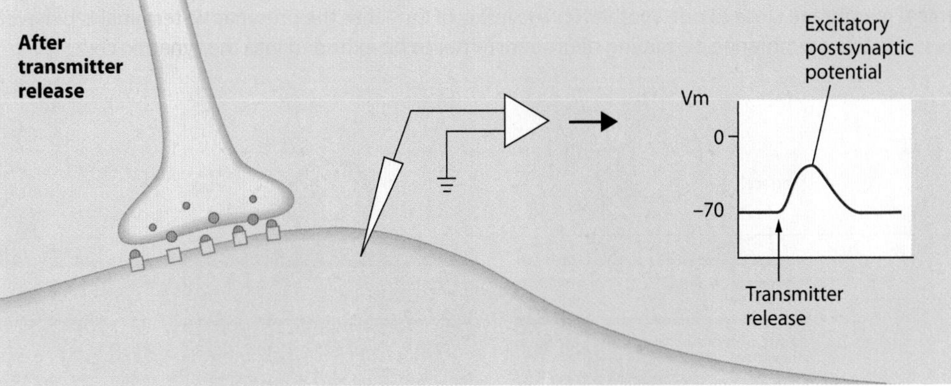

Figure 2.31 Neurotransmitter leading to postsynaptic potential. The binding of neurotransmitter to the postsynaptic membrane receptors changes the membrane potential (V_m). These postsynaptic potentials can be either excitatory (depolarizing the membrane), as shown here, or inhibitory (hyperpolarizing the membrane).

to threshold by other (excitatory) inputs. How can this be? The answer is relatively straightforward. The equilibrium potential for Cl^- is about –60 mV; recall that the equilibrium potential, which is described by the Nernst equation, is the membrane potential that yields no net flux of ions, in this case Cl^-, across the membrane. If the *resting membrane potential* is –70 mV, then opening Cl^- channels would tend to move the membrane potential toward –60 mV, the equilibrium potential for Cl^-. However, further depolarization past –60 mV would be resisted because the action of the Cl^- ions entering the neuron would cause the potential to remain near –60 mV. Hence, if the *threshold* to generate an action potential were about –40 mV, the result of depolarizing to –60 mV by such a mechanism would still be to inhibit the neuron. So inhibitory inputs do not always hyperpolarize the postsynaptic neurons, but they do act to maintain the membrane potential in the direction of hyperpolarization with respect to threshold.

TRANSMITTER RELEASE

One of the mysteries of neuronal transmission has been how neurotransmitter is released. Not until the 1980s did researchers confirm that the release of neurotransmitter from presynaptic terminals is usually the result of exocytosis of the vesicles in the terminals. Even as recently as the mid 1990s, it remained unclear exactly how the vesicles move to the presynaptic membrane, fuse with it, and extrude their contents into the synaptic cleft. Because of an amazing set of studies using molecular methods, however, we now have a clearer picture of the mechanisms accomplishing this feat (Figure 2.32). The story has to do with a group of specialized intracellular proteins, some of which are attached to vesicles and some of which are attached to the neuronal membrane in the terminals where the synapses are located. These proteins act as structural elements that can bring the vesicle up to the membrane and "dock" it there, like a ship next to a pier. Then, via biochemical processes triggered by the influx of Ca^{2+}, the vesicle fuses with the neuronal membrane, permitting neurotransmitter to be extruded into the synaptic cleft.

Neurotransmitters

An important element in the story of neuronal transmission is the neurotransmitter itself. In the early 20th century in Germany, Otto Loewi designed a clever experiment to demonstrate that chemical transmission is possible. He prepared the hearts from two frogs, keeping them as intact as possible, including their innervation by the vagus nerve. He then electrically stimulated the vagus nerve of one frog, causing the heartbeat to slow, and collected the fluid perfusing (running through) that heart. He then transferred this perfusate from the stimulated heart to the second, unstimulated heart and observed a fascinating sight: The second heart, although not stimulated by Loewi, also slowed its rate of pumping. He surmised that a chemical agent mediated this effect, and he named it *Vagusstoff* ("vagus stuff" or "vagus substance" in English). Later, Loewi and his colleagues were able to isolate the substance, which turned out to be acetylcholine (ACh).

Interestingly, Loewi claimed he had the idea for the experiment in a dream. He woke up, wrote it down, and

Figure 2.32 Release of neurotransmitter (NT) from the presynaptic terminal. **(a)** Vesicles in the presynaptic terminal move toward and bind with the cell membrane, with the aid of several proteins, including synaptogamin (SG), synaptobrevin (SB), syntaxin (ST), and SNAP-25 (S25). **(b)** These proteins act a bit like ropes on a ship and dock, and are used to bring the vesicle and presynaptic terminal membrane close to one another. **(c)** The influx of Ca^{2+} into the presynaptic terminal is believed to induce synaptogamin to fuse the two membranes, permitting neurotransmitter to be extruded into the synaptic cleft.

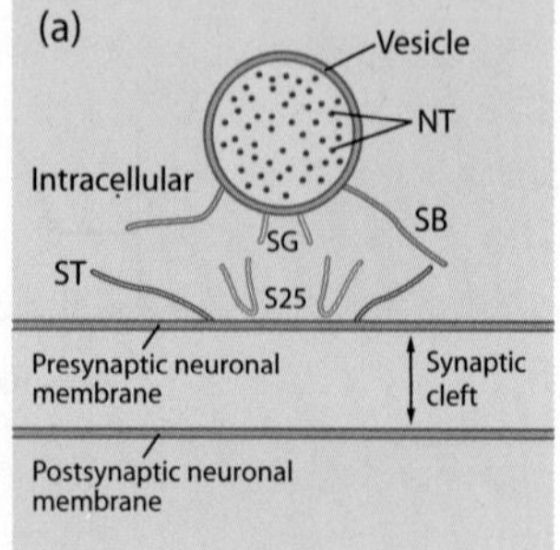

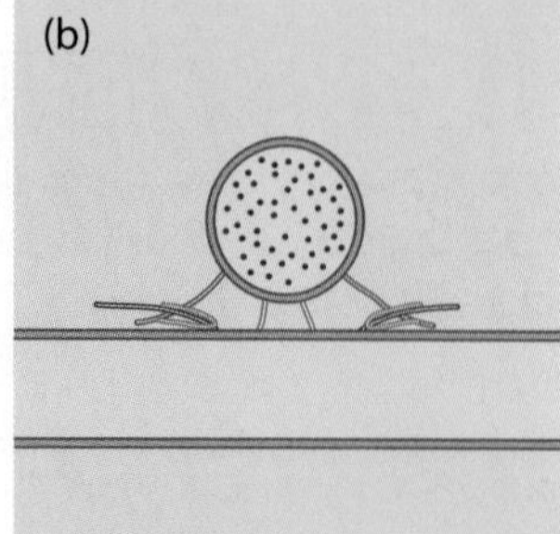

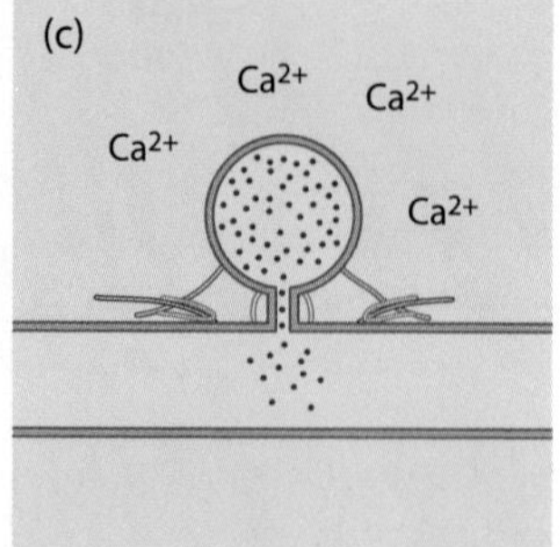

went back to sleep. But upon waking in the morning, he could not decipher the writing in his note. Later (luckily) he had the dream again, and this time he remembered the idea long enough to carry out the history-making experiment. A few years later, British physiologist Henry Dale demonstrated that ACh is also the neurotransmitter for skeletal muscles, not merely cardiac muscles or other parts of the autonomic nervous system. The age of neurotransmitters was firmly established in neuroscience.

Today more than 100 neurotransmitters are recognized. But precisely what are they? Because they vary significantly in their molecular structures, the best general definition is that they are molecules, varying in size and chemical composition, that share some common properties: All are synthesized by the presynaptic neuron; transported to the axon terminals, stored in vesicles that extrude the transmitter into the synaptic cleft; and, after binding with the postsynaptic cell, removed or degraded by enzymatic action.

Several criteria have been established to classify a substance as a neurotransmitter. These guidelines are important because thousands of substances are present in the brain and nervous system, and determining which of these are involved in neural transmission is not easy. Candidates (putative neurotransmitters) must meet the following four criteria:

1. They should be synthesized by and localized within the presynaptic neuron, and stored in the presynaptic terminal prior to release.
2. They must be released by the presynaptic neuron when action potentials invade and depolarize the terminal (mediated by Ca^{2+}).
3. The postsynaptic neuron must contain receptors specific for them.
4. When artificially applied to the postsynaptic cell, they should elicit the same response that stimulating the presynaptic neuron would.

CLASSES OF NEUROTRANSMITTERS

There are several ways to categorize neurotransmitters. They can be classified biochemically as particular substances, like ACh. Some transmitters are *amino acids*, such as aspartate, gamma-aminobutyric acid (GABA), glutamate, and glycine. Others are *biogenic amines*, including dopamine, norepinephrine, and epinephrine (these three are known as *catecholamines*); serotonin (5-hydroxytryptamine); and histamine. Another class consists of the *neuropeptides*, of which there are more than 100.

Recall that peptides are strings of amino acids. Neuropeptides typically vary in length from 3 to more than 30 amino acid residues (the numbers are changing constantly as new ones are identified). In any case, neuropeptides are large molecules relative to the nonpeptide neurotransmitters. The peptides can be subdivided further into five major groups:

1. *Tachykinins* (brain/gut peptides), such as substance P, which affects vasoconstriction and is a spinal neurotransmitter involved in pain
2. *Neurohypophyseal hormones*: oxytocin and vasopressin, the former involved in mammary functions and the latter as an antidiuretic hormone
3. *Hypothalamic releasing hormones*, including corticotropin-releasing hormone and somatostatin
4. *Opioid peptides* (so named for their similarity to opiate drugs, permitting them to bind to opiate receptors) such as the endorphins and enkephalins
5. Other peptides (those that do not fit neatly into another category)

In general, each neuron typically produces one or more neurotransmitters, and these may be released together or separately, depending on the conditions of stimulation. For example, the rate of stimulation can induce the same neuron to release one or another neurotransmitter. In most cases, the effect that a neurotransmitter has on the postsynaptic neuron is determined by that postsynaptic neuron rather than by the transmitter itself. That is, the same transmitter released from the same presynaptic neuron onto two different postsynaptic cells might cause one to increase firing and the other to decrease. Nevertheless, neurotransmitters can be classified by the typical effect that they induce in the postsynaptic neuron.

Excitatory neurotransmitters include ACh, the catecholamines, glutamate, histamine, serotonin, and some of the neuropeptides. Inhibitory neurotransmitters include GABA, glycine, and some of the peptides. In addition to acting directly to excite or inhibit a postsynaptic neuron, some neurotransmitters act only in concert with other factors and are sometimes referred to as *conditional neurotransmitters*; that is, their action is conditioned on the presence of another transmitter in the synaptic cleft or activity in the neuronal circuit. These types of mechanisms permit the nervous system to achieve complex modulations of information processing via modulation of the effectiveness of neurotransmission.

SYNTHESIS OF NEUROTRANSMITTERS

Large-molecule transmitters (peptides) are synthesized in the cell body; small-molecule transmitters are synthesized in the synaptic terminals. The enzymes (biological catalysts) necessary for the synthesis (biochemical production of specific molecules) of small-molecule transmitters are produced in the cell body. They are then transported down the axon via slow axonal transport, at a rate of about 1 mm/day, to the terminals where the small-molecule transmitters are synthesized. In contrast, after synthesis in the cell body, peptides are placed in vesicles and transported down the axon via fast axonal transport, at a rate up to 400 mm/day. Intra-axonal microtubules transport the vesicles using energy from ATP.

Synthesis of the catecholamines is one of the most interesting chemical pathways, and it has important implications in the treatment of Parkinson's disease, a disease in which dopamine-containing neurons in the midbrain nucleus, the substantia nigra, lead to a loss of dopamine in the basal ganglia. The synthesis of dopamine, norepinephrine, and epinephrine begins with the amino acid tyrosine; the metabolic pathway for dopamine and norepinephrine is shown in Figure 2.33.

Figure 2.33 Biochemical synthesis of dopamine and norepinephrine from the amino acid tyrosine. The synthetic enzymes are tyrosine hydroxylase (TH), dopa decarboxylase (DD), and dopamine beta-hydroxylase (DBH). Norepinephrine can be converted to epinephrine in neurons containing phenylethanolamine *N*-methyltransferase (not shown).

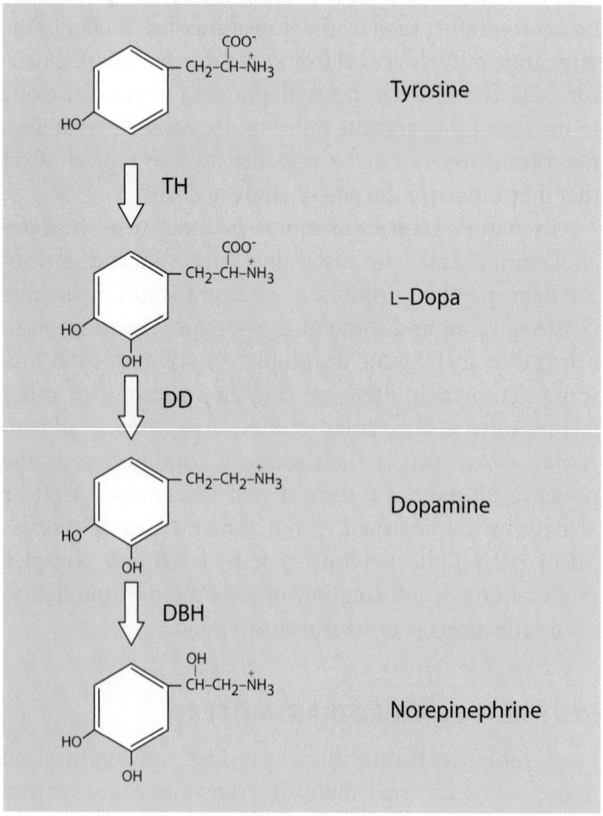

INACTIVATION OF NEUROTRANSMITTERS AFTER RELEASE

Following the release of neurotransmitter into the synaptic cleft and its binding with the postsynaptic membrane receptors, the remaining transmitter must be removed. This removal can be accomplished (a) by active reuptake of the substance back into the presynaptic terminal, (b) by enzymatic breakdown of the transmitter in the synaptic cleft, or (c) merely by diffusion of the neurotransmitter away from the region of the synapse or site of action (e.g., in the case of hormones that act on target cells distant from the synaptic terminals).

Neurotransmitters that are removed from the synaptic cleft by reuptake mechanisms include the biogenic amines (dopamine, norepinephrine, epinephrine, histamine, and serotonin). The reuptake mechanism is mediated by active transporters, which are transmembrane proteins that pump the neurotransmitter back across the presynaptic membrane.

An example of a neurotransmitter that is eliminated from the synaptic cleft by enzymatic action is ACh. The enzyme acetylcholinesterase (AChE), which is located in the synaptic cleft, breaks down ACh after it has acted on the postsynaptic membrane. In fact, special AChE stains (chemicals that bind to AChE) can be used to label AChE on muscle cells, thus revealing where motor neurons innervate the muscle.

To monitor the level of neurotransmitter in the synaptic cleft, presynaptic neurons have autoreceptors. These autoreceptors are located on the presynaptic terminal and bind with the released neurotransmitter, allowing the presynaptic neuron to regulate the synthesis and release of the transmitter.

ANATOMICAL PATHWAYS OF THE BIOGENIC AMINES

Neurotransmitters are both localized and widely distributed in the brain. Glutamate is located almost everywhere in the brain. In contrast, the biogenic amines are more specifically localized. Indeed, the biogenic amines form major neurotransmitter systems from the nuclei (groups of cells) containing the cell bodies in the midbrain (or in the hypothalamus in the case of histamine). Their axons project to widespread regions of the cortex and can play key modulatory roles. An example is the norepinephrine system (also called the *noradrenergic system*). The widespread projections of the norepinephrine neurotransmitter system to the cortex are involved in arousal and attentive behavior. Figure 2.34 shows the major projection pathways of the biogenic amines.

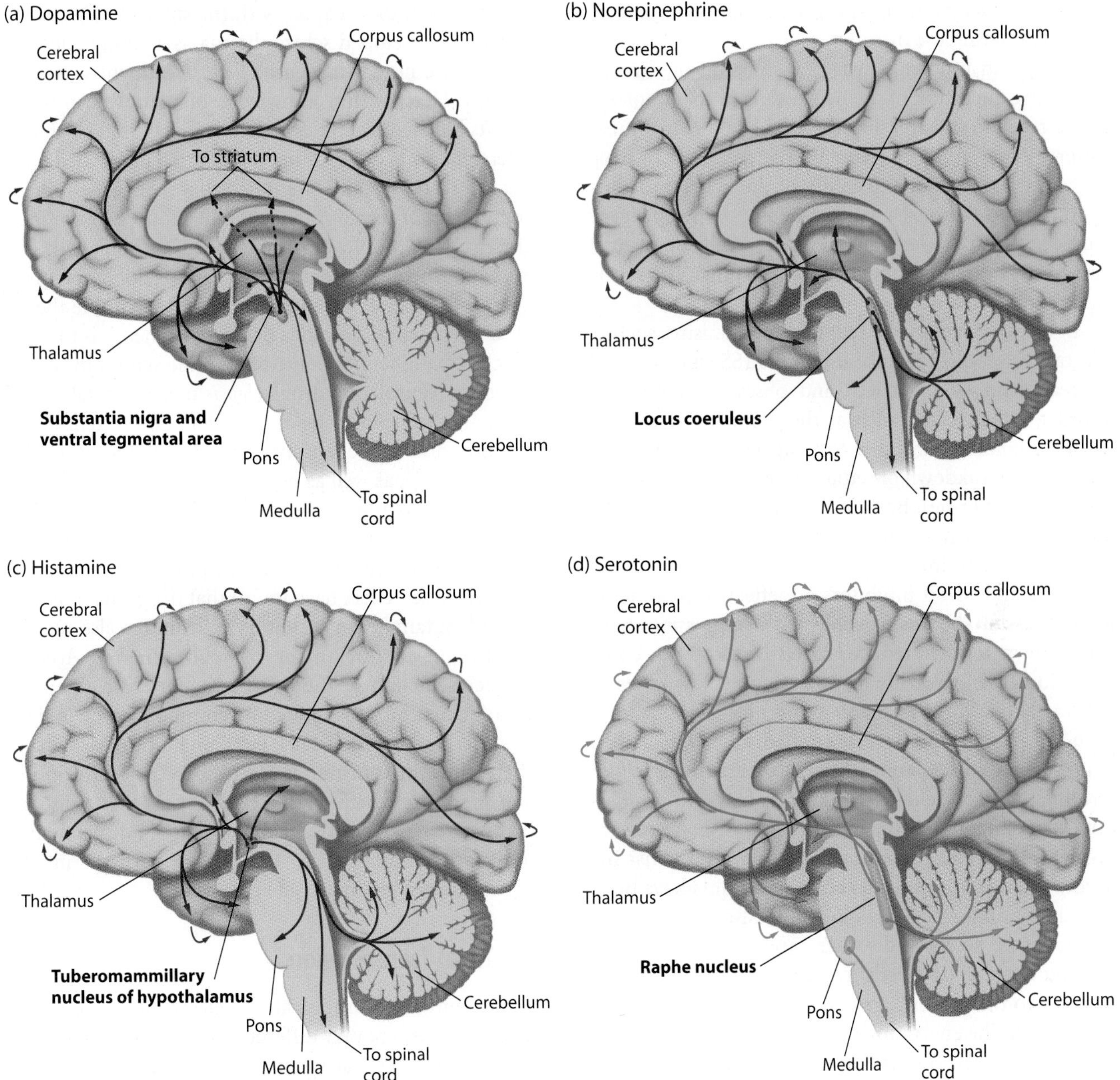

Figure 2.34 Major projection pathways of the biogenic amine neurotransmitter systems in the human brain. Shown are the projections of the dopamine **(a)**, norepinephrine **(b)**, histamine **(c)**, and serotonin **(d)** systems. The views are midsagittal cuts through the human brain, showing the medial surface of the right hemisphere; the frontal pole is at left (see Chapter 3 for anatomical information).

Drugs, Neurotransmission, and Disease

Many classes of drugs act to modify neurotransmission and are useful in treating psychiatric and neurological disorders. Other drugs can actually induce depression, psychosis, and other symptoms of psychiatric disorders. For example, abuse of amphetamines, which increases the release of dopamine and norepinephrine, leads to amphetamine psychosis. The individual may exhibit symptoms similar to those found in schizophrenia. These observations have led to important insights into the biochemical basis of mental disorders. Indeed, some psychiatric disorders are thought to reflect an improper functioning of specific brain neurotransmitter systems. If that idea is correct, then drug therapies targeting neurotransmitter action might be useful in treating the disorder.

Drugs can influence neurotransmission by directly mimicking the action of the neurotransmitter at postsynaptic receptors, increasing the release of neurotransmitter or preventing its reuptake. Alternatively, a drug might act by reducing the ability of the neurotransmitter to bind to the postsynaptic receptors. The effects of drugs can also be less direct, acting like conditional transmitters to fine-tune neural signaling via subtle modulatory influences.

Drugs that manipulate reuptake mechanisms, such as selective serotonin reuptake inhibitors (SSRIs), are used to treat depression, anxiety, and obsessive-compulsive disorder. Other drugs, such as the monoamine oxidase (MAO) inhibitors, are used to treat depression by preventing the breakdown of serotonin (as well as dopamine and norepinephrine). Both of these types of drugs allow the targeted transmitter to remain in the synaptic cleft for longer periods of time.

SSRIs and MAO inhibitors are effective treatments for depression because people with depression have been shown to have reduced levels of serotonin compared to healthy individuals. For example, low levels of the metabolic precursor of serotonin, 5-HIAA, are found in people who have attempted suicide related to major depression (Mann, 2003). Do these low levels of serotonin reflect genetic variation across the population, suggesting that some individuals have a propensity for depression and related mental health problems? Indeed, various serotonin-related gene variants have been linked not only to depression, but also to attention deficit hyperactivity disorder and panic disorder (Huang et al., 2004). Reduced serotonin may also be a reaction to the person's mental state and current interactions with the environment.

Environmental factors clearly influence the development of such antisocial behavior. For example, maltreatment or abuse during childhood increases the risk of criminality by 50%. Note, however, that not every child who is maltreated or abused develops violent or criminal tendencies later in life. Might genes contribute to these differential developmental outcomes? Caspi and colleagues found that the level of expression of the *MAOA* gene modulated the effect of maltreatment on the development of violence later in life. Subjects who were maltreated but had high levels of *MAOA* expression were less likely to become violent in young adulthood than were subjects who were maltreated and had low levels of *MAOA* expression. Here we see an elegant example of the interplay of genes and environment on the behavioral outcome of altered brain chemistry.

We began this chapter with the story of G.W., a patient who developed schizophrenia as a young adult. In passing, we noted that part of her treatment was drug therapy. Here, with a knowledge of neurotransmission and its biochemical bases in hand, you should be able to infer what sorts of drugs her psychiatrist prescribed. Let's put the story together. We noted that psychosis, a major component of schizophrenia, can be induced by amphetamine abuse. Moreover, amphetamines stimulate the release of some neurotransmitters, such as dopamine. This and other related evidence led to the "dopamine theory of schizophrenia." The idea behind this theory is that too much dopamine may contribute to the symptoms of the disorder. Neuroleptic drugs (*lepsis* means "to take hold of"), also referred to as *antipsychotic drugs*, relieve the paranoia and hallucinations associated with psychosis in schizophrenia, as well as psychosis induced by amphetamines. Some common neuroleptic drugs are antagonists of dopamine. *Antagonists* bind to receptors and prevent the normal action of neurotransmitters. More recently, however, researchers have found that drugs that are agonists of glutamate, an excitatory transmitter, also may be effective in the treatment of schizophrenia. *Agonists* mimic the action of the neurotransmitter on the postsynaptic neuron. It is now quite common for physicians to prescribe "drug cocktails," combinations of drugs that affect different transmitter systems, to treat schizophrenia. So we can conclude that patient G.W. has a disease, schizophrenia, that causes a disruption of normal neurotransmitter function in the brain, perhaps in the dopamine or glutamate systems, or both.

Electrical Transmission

Some neurons communicate via electrical synapses. But these synapses are very different from chemical synapses because, in electrical synapses, no synaptic cleft separates the neurons. Instead, the neuronal membranes are touching, and the cytoplasms of the two neurons are essentially continuous. This continuity is maintained via specialized transmembrane channels called *gap junctions* that create pores connecting the cytoplasms of the two neurons (Figure 2.35). As a result, the two neurons are *isopotential* (i.e., have the same potential), meaning that electrical changes in one are reflected in the other, virtually instantaneously. Following the principles of electrotonic conduction, however, the passive currents that flow between the neurons when one of them is depolarized (or hyperpolarized) decrease and are therefore smaller in the postsynaptic neuron than in the presynaptic neuron. Under most circumstances the communication is bidirectional, but so-called rectifying synapses limit current flow in one direction, as is typical in chemical synapses.

Electrical synapses are useful when information must be conducted rapidly, such as in the escape reflex of some invertebrates. Groups of neurons with these synapses can activate muscles fast to get the animal out of harm's way quickly. For example, the well-known tail flip reflex of crayfishes involves powerful rectifying electrical synapses. Electrical synapses are also useful when groups of neurons should operate synchronously, as with some hypothalamic neurosecretory neurons. The disadvantages of electrical synapses are that they cannot transmit inhibitory information, they are much less plastic than chemical synapses, and they cannot amplify a signal (whereas an action potential that triggers a chemical synapse could cause a large release of neurotransmitter, thus amplifying the signal).

Are electrical synapses merely an odd type of synapse found in invertebrates on the run, and in hormonal systems that are just plain running? No; there is well-accepted evidence for a role of these synapses in the mammalian retina and some subcortical nuclei. Barry Connors and his colleagues Jay Gibson and Michael Beierlein at Brown University provided a powerful demonstration of electrically coupled neurons in the somatosensory cortex of the rat (Gibson et al., 1999). They investigated inhibitory interneurons (in cortical layers IV and VI), neurons that make local circuit connections within the cerebral cortex, by recording from them in slice preparations using microelectrodes. The slice preparation is literally a slice of brain taken from an animal killed moments before. The slice is then placed in a dish with physiologically friendly solutions. With the use of a microscope and micromanipulators to position electrodes, electrical activity is recorded from the neurons within the slice where the local circuitry remains intact. When Connors and his colleagues (Figure 2.36)

Figure 2.35 Electrical synapse between two neurons. Gap junctions are the transmembrane proteins in the presynaptic and postsynaptic neurons that are aligned to create a pore.

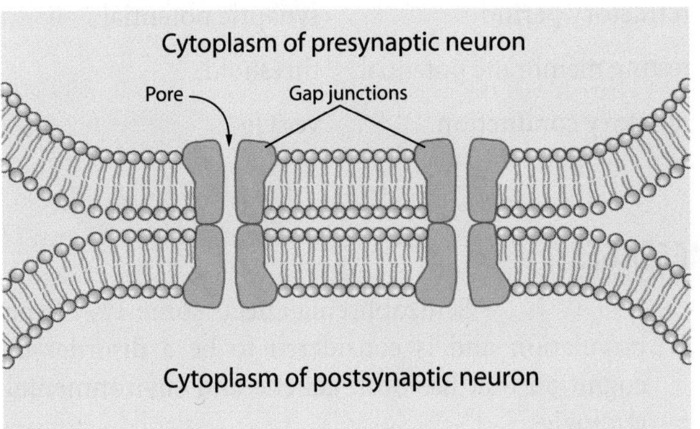

Figure 2.36 Activity of two cortical interneurons in the rat somatosensory cortex connected by electrical synapses. **(a)** Electrodes were placed in two coupled neurons, and a current whose amplitude varied at about 40 Hz was injected into Cell 1 while Cell 2 was maintained below spontaneous spike threshold with constant current. Cell 2 showed a tendency to spike at the peaks of the depolarizing phases in Cell 1. **(b)** Depolarizing current was injected into two different neurons simultaneously, and the neurons were found to spike in synchrony. **(c)** To test the synchrony of the firing of the two neurons, the cross-correlogram method was used. The activity of Cell 2 was cross-correlated with the firing of Cell 1. If they were firing in synchrony, the cross-correlogram should show a strong peak at about 0 ms, and this was indeed observed. The peak is at 2 ms, demonstrating a very close coupling between the electrical activity in the two neurons. These neurons did not have chemical synaptic interactions.

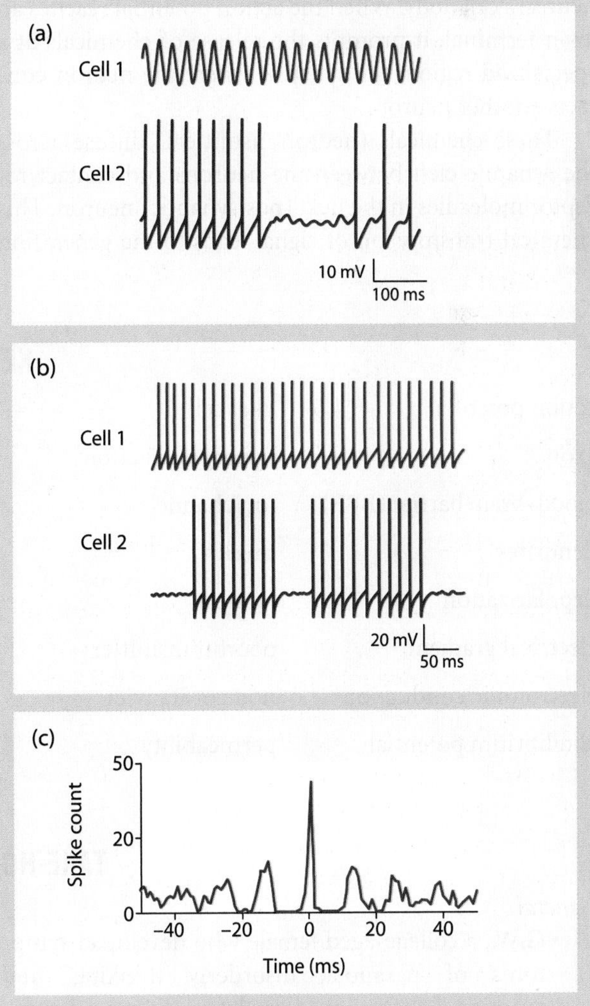

recorded from neurons that were electrically but not chemically coupled, they were able to show high synchrony of electrical activity between two neurons when one or both were stimulated, and the delay between the activity in the two neurons was too short to be due to traditional chemical synapses. Thus, in the mammalian brain, neuronal communication involves both chemical and electrical transmission.

SUMMARY

Cells are the elementary units of the body. In the nervous system, nerve cells (neurons) provide the mechanism for information processing. At rest, the neuronal membrane has properties that allow some materials (primarily ions) dissolved in intracellular and extracellular fluids to pass through better than others. In addition, active transport processes pump ions across the membrane to separate different species of ions, thereby setting the stage for differences in electrical potential inside and outside the neuron. These electrical differences are a form of energy that can be used to generate electrical currents, which, via action potentials, can travel great distances down axons away from the neuron's cell body. When the action potential reaches an axon terminal, it prompts the release of chemicals at a specialized region, the synapse, where the neuron contacts another neuron.

These chemicals (neurotransmitters) diffuse across the synaptic cleft between the neurons and contact receptor molecules in the next (postsynaptic) neuron. This chemical transmission of signal leads to the generation of currents in the postsynaptic neuron and the continuation of the signal through the system of neurons that make up a neuronal circuit. Ion channels are the specialized mediators of neuronal membrane potential. They are large transmembrane proteins that create pores through the membrane. Transmembrane proteins also form receptors on postsynaptic neurons. These are the receptors that bind with neurotransmitters, leading to changes in the membrane potential.

Neurotransmitters come in a large variety of forms. Small-molecule transmitters include amino acids, biogenic amines, and substances like ACh; large-molecule transmitters are the neuropeptides. All neurotransmitters share the following characteristics: They are synthesized and then transported to the terminal (or synthesized in the terminal), stored in vesicles, released, and removed. Neurological and psychiatric diseases can involve disturbances in neurotransmission, and major therapies rely on drugs that modulate neurotransmitter function with the hope of reestablishing the delicate balance of function that characterizes normal neuronal communication.

KEY TERMS

action potential
axon
blood–brain barrier (BBB)
dendrites
depolarization
electrical gradient
electrotonic conduction
equilibrium potential
glial cell
hyperpolarization
ion channel
myelin
neuron
neurotransmitter
node of Ranvier
permeability
postsynaptic
presynaptic
propagation
receptor
receptor potential
refractory period
resting membrane potential
saltatory conduction
second messenger
soma
spike-triggering zone
spine
synapse
synaptic potential
threshold
vesicle

TAKE-HOME MESSAGES

General

- G.W., a college-aged female who developed symptoms of paranoia, disorderly thinking, and emotional behavior was later diagnosed with schizophrenia.
- Schizophrenia affects some 1% of the population and is considered to be a disorder of cognition that has both genetic and environmental etiologies.

Cells of the Nervous System

- Neurons and glial cells make up the nervous system.
- Neurons are the cells that transmit information throughout the nervous system. Most neurons consist of a cell soma (body), axon, and dendrites.
- Neurons come in many shapes and sizes, but they can be classified into four morphological types: unipolar, bipolar, pseudounipolar, and multipolar.
- Synapses occur at various locations along the neuron, primarily at the dendrites, and often on the dendritic spines, where information is received.
- The presynaptic cell is located before the synapse with respect to information flow; the postsynaptic cell is located after the synapse with respect to information flow. Nearly all neurons are both pre- and postsynaptic, since they both receive and transmit information.
- Glial cells aid in the speed of information transfer by forming myelin around the axons of the neurons; they also carry out other roles in the nervous system, such as providing structural support and forming the blood–brain barrier.
- An astrocyte is a type of glial cell that forms the blood–brain barrier.
- An oligodendrocyte is a type of glial cell that forms myelin in the central nervous system.
- A Schwann cell is a type of glial cell that forms myelin in the peripheral nervous system.
- Nodes of Ranvier are the spaces between sheaths of myelin where voltage-gated Na^+ and K^+ channels are located and action potentials occur.

Membrane Potentials and Passive Currents

- The resting membrane potential is the difference in the voltage across the neuronal membrane during rest (i.e., not during any phase of the action potential).
- The permeability of a membrane for a specific ion depends on the extent to which the ion channel permits ions to cross the membrane.
- ATP is the main source of energy for the neuron and is used to operate the Na^+–K^+ pump.
- The electrical gradient results from the asymmetrical distribution of ions across the membrane. The electrical difference across the membrane is the basis of the resting potential.
- The Nernst equation is used to find the equilibrium potential for an ion. The Goldman equation takes into account the permeability of several ions in determining the membrane potential.
- Passive current conduction is called electrotonic conduction or decremental conduction. A depolarizing current makes the inside of the cell more positive and therefore more likely to generate an action potential; a hyperpolarizing current makes the inside of the cell less positive and therefore less likely to generate an action potential.

Action Potentials

- The spike-triggering zone is the part of the neuron where the action potential is generated.
- Action potentials are an all-or-none phenomenon: The amplitude of the action potential does not depend on the size of the triggering depolarization, as long as that depolarization reaches threshold for initiating the action potential.
- Voltage-gated channels are of prime importance in generating an action potential because they open and close according to the membrane potential.
- The large depolarization that is characteristic of the initial phase of the action potential is driven by the self-reinforcing cycle of the voltage-gated Na^+ channels. During this phase of the action potential, the membrane depolarizes and nears the equilibrium potential for Na^+.
- K^+ channels open more slowly than Na^+ channels, but K^+ efflux out of the cell is much greater than Na^+ influx into the cell. After the Na^+ channels have closed, some K^+ channels will remain open, bringing the membrane potential closer to the K^+ equilibrium potential, which is below the resting potential of the membrane.
- The inactivation of the Na^+ channels leads to the absolute refractory period, during which no action potentials can be generated.
- During the relative refractory period, which follows the absolute refractory period, the membrane is hyperpolarized because of the slow closure of K^+ channels. During this time it is more difficult, but not impossible, for an action potential to be generated.
- Myelin allows for the rapid transmission of an action potential down an axon via saltatory conduction.

Ion Channels

- Ion channels are formed by transmembrane proteins that create passageways through which ions can flow.
- The proteins that make up ion channels have several levels of structure: primary (order of the amino acids), secondary (how the amino acid chains coil, as in an alpha-helix), tertiary (folding of coiled amino acids upon themselves to create complex three-dimensional structures), quaternary (combining of tertiary structures to create a final structure).

- Ion channels can be either passive (always open) or gated (open only in the presence of electrical, chemical, or physical stimuli).
- Chemically gated ion channels serve as neurotransmitter receptors. Neurotransmitters are also referred to as ligands.
- Postsynaptic receptors can be either directly coupled or indirectly coupled, the latter requiring second-messenger systems.

Synaptic Transmission and Neurotransmitters

- Chemical transmission results in the release of neurotransmitters from the presynaptic neuron and the binding of those neurotransmitters on the postsynaptic neuron, which in turn causes excitatory or inhibitory postsynaptic potentials (EPSPs or IPSPs), depending on the neurotransmitter that was released.
- Neurotransmitters are released by exocytosis of vesicles in the synaptic terminals.
- The criteria for classifying a substance as a neurotransmitter are as follows:

1. A neurotransmitter should be synthesized by and localized within the presynaptic neuron.
2. A neurotransmitter must be released by the presynaptic neuron when action potentials invade and depolarize the terminal (mediated by Ca^{2+}).
3. The postsynaptic neuron must contain receptors that are specific for the substance.
4. When artificially applied to the postsynaptic cell, a neurotransmitter should elicit the same response that stimulating the presynaptic neuron would elicit.

- Classes of neurotransmitters include amino acids, biogenic amines, and neuropeptides.
- Neurotransmitters must be removed from the receptor after binding. This removal can be accomplished by (a) active reuptake back into the presynaptic terminal, (b) enzymatic breakdown of the transmitter in the synaptic cleft, or (c) diffusion of the neurotransmitter away from the region of the synapse.
- Agonists are chemical agents that can influence neurotransmission by mimicking the action of the neurotransmitter at the postsynaptic receptor, increasing the release of neurotransmitter, or preventing reuptake of the neurotransmitter. Antagonists, in contrast, are chemicals that reduce the ability of the neurotransmitter to influence the postsynaptic neuron.

THOUGHT QUESTIONS

1. If action potentials are all or none, how does the nervous system code differences in sensory stimulus amplitudes?
2. What property (or properties) of ion channels makes them selective to only one ion, such as K^+, and not another, such as Na^+? Is it the size of the channel, other factors, or a combination?
3. Given that synaptic currents produce electrotonic potentials that are decremental, how do inputs located distantly on a neuron's dendrites have any influence on the firing of the cell?
4. What would be the consequence for the activity of a postsynaptic neuron if reuptake or degradation systems for neurotransmitters were damaged?
5. How do drugs modify brain chemistry to alleviate disorders such as schizophrenia?

SUGGESTED READING

BLOOM, F., NELSON, C. A., & LAZERSON, A. (2001). *Brain, mind and behavior* (3rd ed.). New York: Worth.

DOYLE, D., CABRAL, J., PFUETZNER, R., KUO, A., GULBIS, J., COHEN, S., ET AL. (1998). The structure of the potassium channel: Molecular basis of K^+ conduction and selectivity. *Science, 280*, 69–77.

HAEUSSER, M. (2000). The Hodgkin-Huxley theory of the action potential. *Nature Reviews. Neuroscience, 3*, 1165.

KATZ, B. (1966). *Nerve, muscle and synapse.* New York: McGraw-Hill.

3

Neuroanatomy and Development

The relationship between brain anatomy and cognition has been the source of fascination and puzzlement for hundreds of years. For example, many studies have attempted to relate aspects of brain organization to intelligence in humans. Consider the story of one of the greatest brains in human history, that of Albert Einstein. Einstein was clearly a person of exceptional ability. During his life he mentally tiptoed among atoms and stars and brought his incredible insights about the physics of the universe to humankind in the form of concrete mathematical descriptions. In a letter to his colleague Jacques Hadamard, Einstein said of his own scientific thinking that "words do not seem to play any role," yet there is an "associative play" involving "more or less clear images" of a "visual and muscular type" (Hadamard, 1945, p. ix).

Numerous efforts have been made to identify unique anatomical features of Einstein's brain that might explain his genius. When Einstein died in 1955 at the age of 76, his brain was extracted and saved. It was weighed, perfused with a solution of the chemical preservative formalin, measured, and photographed. The brain was then sectioned and embedded in a material that permitted it to be thinly sliced to make histological slides for microscopic analysis. These specimens and materials documenting their original three-dimensional relationships in the whole brain were stored for future scientific study. Sandra Witelson and her colleagues at McMaster University in Canada performed one such study (Witelson et al., 1999). They investigated the dimensions and gyral morphology of Einstein's brain, comparing the original measurements to their own new measurements of the brain and to measurements calculated from the original calibrated photographs taken shortly after his death.

The characteristics of Einstein's brain were compared to those of brains from a few dozen normal persons that had been donated for scientific research. These researchers found two prominent features of Einstein's brain that were very different from the normal control group of brains. The first observation was that the **Sylvian fissure**, the division that separates the temporal lobe from the frontal and parietal lobes, in Einstein's brain had an unusual anatomical organization (see the description of gross anatomy later in the chapter to appreciate the anatomical features described here). Unlike the control brains, Einstein's brain showed a strange confluence of the Sylvian fissure with the central sulcus on the brain's lateral surface; most brains have a Sylvian fissure that projects posteriorly to end in an area surrounded by the supramarginal gyrus. The second unusual feature resulted from this anatomy: Einstein's inferior parietal lobe was actually larger, and indeed thicker (15%) in lateral to medial extent.

Witelson and her colleagues hypothesized that the increased size of Einstein's inferior parietal cortex might have been related to his intellectual capacity, although they pointed out that it is difficult to make any conclusions about causal relationships from their data. Nonetheless, it is remarkable that they found gross anatomical features that were so strikingly different in Einstein's brain in comparison to the brains of the rest of us, who for the most part are merely trying to understand what Einstein said, never mind attempting to generate new insights ourselves. From such investigations, hypotheses can be generated and then tested in brains removed at autopsy or, in the modern age of neuroimaging, in brains in the living human. Perhaps the next Einstein, like the last one, who permitted electroencephalograms to be recorded from electrodes on his head, will lie inside a scanner so that young cognitive neuroscientists can measure his or her living, thinking brain and its function.

From form is derived function. This is a central tenet in biology. Throughout the history of neuroscience, researchers have probed the organization of the nervous system, hoping that, by doing so, they would unlock its secrets. In Chapter 1 we saw how the great neuroanatomists Santiago Ramón y Cajal of Spain and Camillo Golgi of Italy used information from cellular neuroanatomy to argue for different theories of information processing in the nervous system. This work continues to the present, with a march toward new and higher-resolution techniques for probing the biological foundations of the mind.

In the next chapter we will learn about some of these new techniques for revealing the functional anatomy of the brain—techniques that are based on understanding the relationships between form and function. In later chapters we will see many examples of the anatomical correlates of different aspects of cognition. It will become clear that gross anatomy must be interpreted in light of the functional interactions of structures, circuits, and systems in the nervous system because similar structures may perform very different computations, and the same structure may participate in different functions at different times. Understanding how the form of the nervous system supports the myriad functions of the mind is one of the major challenges of cognitive neuroscience.

In this chapter we review the gross anatomy and microanatomy of the brain and nervous system. We describe the major anatomical structures of the brain and make note of the vasculature and ventricular systems. We discuss how the brain develops prenatally and how it changes even in adulthood. Some discussion of the functional organization of the mental functions that the brain supports begins here; subsequent chapters will describe in more detail the many functions of the human brain in perception and cognition. Hence, the aim of this chapter is to provide a reference for the material to be covered later, and to introduce the neuroanatomical and neurodevelopmental terms that will be important throughout the book. Refer back to the content of this chapter and Chapter 2 as needed to interpret the complexities of the form and function of the nervous system that are introduced later.

NEUROANATOMY

Neuroanatomy is the study of the nervous system's structure. It is concerned with identifying the parts of the nervous system and describing how the parts are connected. As with all of anatomy, descriptions can be made at many levels. For the neuroanatomist, investigations occur at one of two levels: *gross neuroanatomy*, which focuses on general structures and connections visible to the naked eye, and *fine neuroanatomy* (also referred to as *microscopic anatomy*), in which the main task is to describe the organization of neurons and their connections and subcellular structure. In Chapter 2, to provide the background necessary to consider the physiology of the nervous system in signaling, we introduced cellular neuroanatomy. (Refer back to the first part of Chapter 2 for an overview of cells of the nervous system.) Here we begin with a short description of the methods that help reveal the gross, microscopic, and functional neuroanatomy of the nervous system, the latter being the anatomical organization of cells, circuits, and systems that support a particular function, such as object perception.

Methods in Neuroanatomy

Different approaches are used to investigate the nervous system at different levels of description, and indeed, these methods are highly specialized such that they represent different subdisciplines of neuroanatomy. Their development follows roughly the historical story laid out in Chapter 1, for the field of neuroanatomy developed in step with the development of new techniques.

GROSS DISSECTION

For identification of gross anatomy, the first challenge is to figure out how to view the brain. Until recently, when neuroimaging made it possible to view the living brain within the heads of animals and humans in vivo (see Chapter 4), the only available approach was the tried-and-true method of removing the brain from the head and putting it on the table, or more accurately, in a container filled with a preservative such as formalin. A neuroanatomist undertaking this procedure immediately is made aware of the specialized defenses that protect the brain. Not only is the brain enclosed within the skull's protective bony structure, but also it is surrounded by the **dura mater**, which consists of dense layers of collagenous fibers (*dura* is Latin for "hard" or "tough," and *mater* is Latin for "mother").

After the dura mater is removed, superficial examination reveals many prominent structures (Figure 3.1). The **gyri** (singular *gyrus*; the protruding rounded surfaces) and primary **sulci** (singular *sulcus*; the numerous smaller invaginations seen as creases) and *fissures* (the less numerous, larger invaginations) of the cerebrum; the gradual narrowing of the brainstem; and the elaborate folding of the cerebellar cortex can be identified without the aid of a microscope. Further dissections expose internal structures and reveal organizational principles. For example, slicing through the brain reveals the dichotomy of **gray matter** and **white matter**: The gray matter forms a continuous cortical sheath enshrouding a seemingly homogeneous mass of white matter. Gray matter is so named because it appears darker and even a bit grayish in preserved brains, although it is more typically pinkish to reddish in the living brain, owing to its vascularization. The gray matter contains cell bodies of neurons and glial cells. The white matter is so termed because it looks lighter than the gray matter in preserved tissues; it actually appears quite milky white in the living brain. This coloring is due to the fatty myelin surrounding the axons (see Chapter 2).

Neuroanatomical dissection of the brain can provide a relatively detailed description of the organization of the major systems, structures, and connections of the brain. For example, gross dissection will reveal the inputs to and outputs from peripheral sensory structures or motor effectors (muscles), via nerve bundles. It is also possible to follow the trajectory of axons grouped in large fiber **tracts** (bundles of axons) as they course through the brain and connect with different regions. Such dissection will show the geniculostriate projections from the thalamus to the visual cortex that we touch upon later in this chapter and will learn about in detail in Chapter 5. In another good example, dissection will reveal the arcuate fasciculus, a prominent fiber tract interconnecting Broca's and Wernicke's areas in support of language functions (see Chapter 10). These interconnections observable at the gross level are revealed in greater detail with tract-tracing methods using chemical substances in animals and degeneration and neuroimaging methods in animals and humans. Some of these methods are reviewed in the next section.

MICROANATOMY AND HISTOLOGY: CELL STAINING AND TRACT TRACING

If we simply looked at the brain in gross dissections, we would not know that structures such as the white matter

Figure 3.1 **(a)** Midsagittal section through the human cerebral cortex. This medial view of the right hemisphere of a postmortem brain reveals prominent features of the gross anatomy, including cortical, subcortical, cerebellar, and brainstem regions. The frontal pole is on the left. On the surface of the cortex (top portions mostly), the crowns of the various cortical gyri can be seen; the folded regions of the cortex (the sulci) appear as lines or creases. **(b)** A horizontal (also called *axial*) section through the human brain at approximately the level diagrammed in the drawing at right (dark line). The left and right cerebral hemispheres (frontal pole now at the top), the underlying subcortical structures, and portions of the cerebellum (bottom) can be seen in the horizontal section. The gray matter (darker regions) and white matter (lighter regions) are clearly visible.

(a)

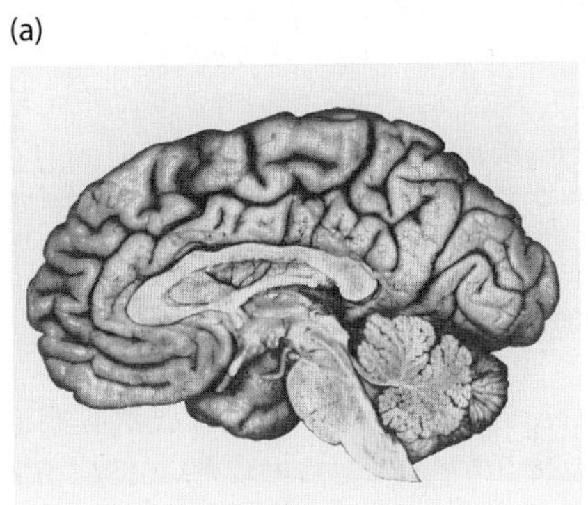

(b)

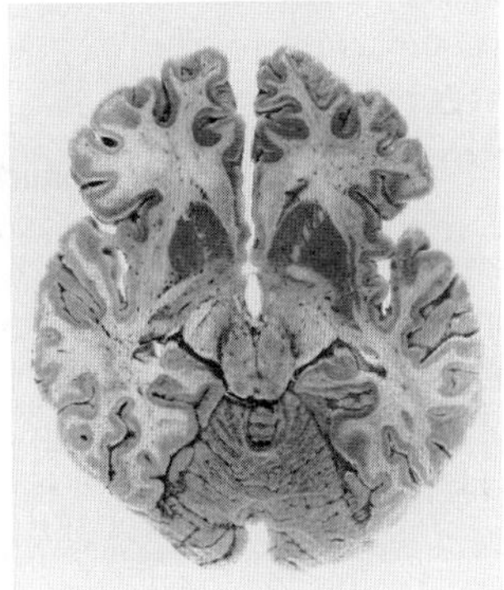

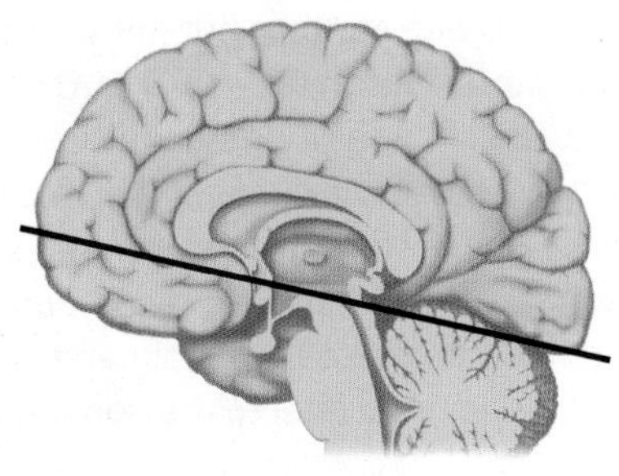

THE COGNITIVE NEUROSCIENTIST'S TOOLKIT

Navigating in the Brain

Because the brain is a complex three-dimensional object with numerous structures and pathways that are difficult to imagine in two-dimensional pictures, it is important to utilize conventions for describing the relations of regions. In general, the terms we use were derived from those used by anatomists to describe similar relations in the body as a whole; therefore, the brain's orientation with respect to the body determines the coordinate frame of reference that is used to describe anatomical relationships in the brain. But some confusing aspects of the terminology arise from differences in how the head and body are arranged in animals that walk on four legs versus humans, who are upright. Consider a dog's body surfaces. The front end is the *rostral* end, meaning "nose." The opposite end is the *caudal* end, the "tail." The back is the *dorsal* surface and the bottom surface is the *ventral* surface **(a, top)**. We can refer to the dog's nervous system by using the same coordinates **(a, bottom)**. The part of the brain toward the front is the rostral end, toward the frontal lobes; the posterior end is the caudal end, toward the occipital lobe; and the top and bottom are, respectively, the dorsal and ventral surfaces of the brain. This seems to be a reasonable set of conventions, or is it? Consider the human **(b)**.

Humans are atypical and thus create confusing problems with respect to anatomical nomenclature. The reason is simple: Humans stand upright and therefore tilt their heads down in order to be parallel with the ground. Thus, the dorsal surface of the body and brain are now at right angles to each other. But the conventions still apply, though there may be some confusion unless we remember that humans have tilted their heads. *Rostral* still means "toward the frontal pole," and *caudal* still means "toward the occipital pole," as long as we are referring to the brain; however, when we discuss the spinal cord, the coordinate systems shift with respect to one another but not with respect to the local body axis. Thus, in the spinal cord *rostral* means "toward the brain," just as it does in the dog.

In humans, perhaps in part because of the differences in posture between humans and quadrupedal animals, we also use terms like *superior* and *inferior* to refer to the top of the brain and bottom, and *anterior* and *posterior* to refer to the front and back, respectively.

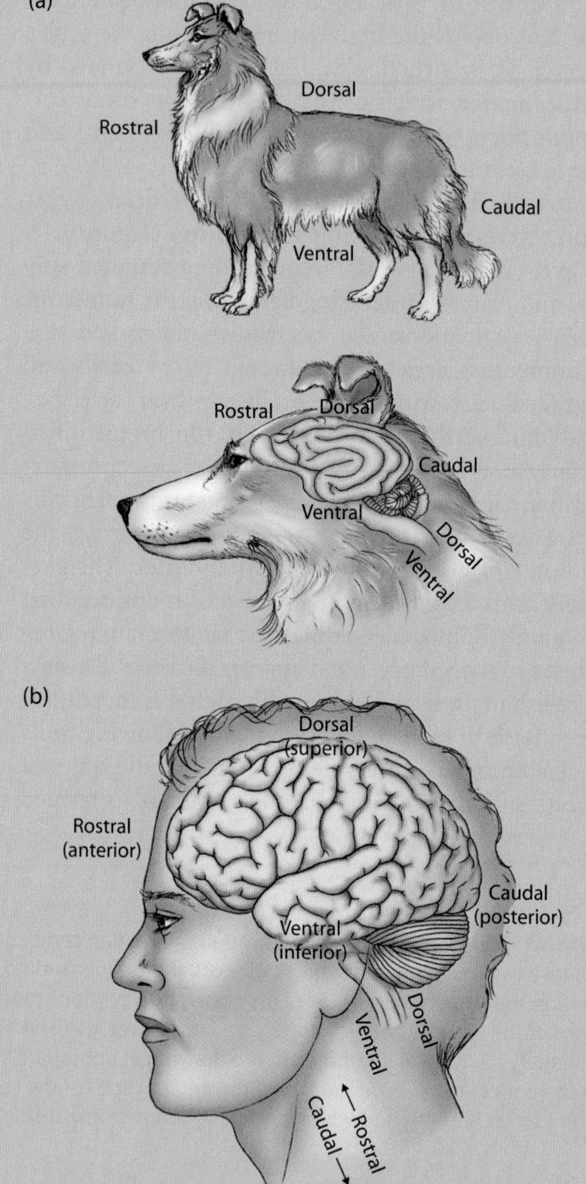

Anatomical terms for describing various views of anatomy and sections through brain and body. The relationship between a bipedal human and quadruped animal leads to some important considerations in describing the surfaces of the brain and spinal cord.

are neural elements rather than supportive tissues. To make this inference, neuroanatomists must probe for finer detail with high-power microscopes. For example, microscopic examination reveals that the white matter is actually composed of millions of individual fibers, each surrounded by myelin. This level of analysis is the domain of the histologist. *Histology* is the study of tissue structure through microscopic techniques like those introduced in Chapter 1 in the work of the early neuroanatomists Ramón y Cajal, Golgi, and Purkinje.

A primary concern for neuroanatomists is to identify the patterns of connectivity in the nervous system in order to lay out the neural "highways" that allow information to get from one place to another. This problem is made complex by the fact that neurons are not wired together in a simple, serial circuit. A single cortical neuron is likely to be innervated by (i.e., receive inputs from) large numbers of neurons, and the axons from these input neurons can originate in widely distributed regions. That is, there is tremendous convergence in the nervous system, as well as divergence, in which a single neuron can receive inputs from many neurons and/or project to multiple target neurons in different regions.

Most axons are short projections from neighboring cortical cells. Others can be quite long, originating in more distant cortical regions and reaching their target only after descending below the cortical sheath into the white matter, traveling through long fiber tracts, and then entering another region of cortex, subcortical **nucleus**, or spinal layer to synapse on another neuron. Neighboring and distant connections between two cortical regions are referred to as *corticocortical connections*, following the convention that the first part of the term identifies the source and the second part identifies the target. Inputs that originate in subcortical structures such as the thalamus would be referred to as *thalamocortical connections*; the reverse are *corticothalamic*, or more generally, *corticofugal*, *projections* (projections from more central structures like cortex, outward toward the periphery).

Much of the progress in neuroanatomy has been prompted by the development and refinement of new *stains*, chemicals of various sorts that are selectively absorbed by specific neural elements (see Chapter 1). Staining methods were discovered by trial and error or by intention, such as when the interaction of a chemical with tissues yielded an interesting pattern of staining that then became useful. Cell staining allows different levels of analysis. For example, we can stain pieces of neural tissue to reveal the laminar organization of the retina (Figure 3.2a), or we can zoom in on individual cells that have either taken up or been injected with

(a)

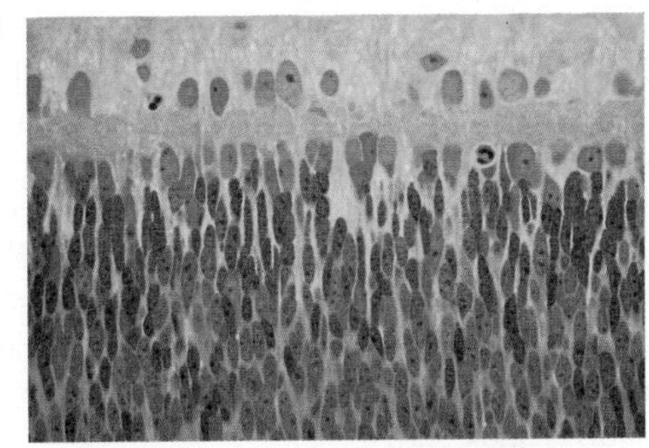

(b)

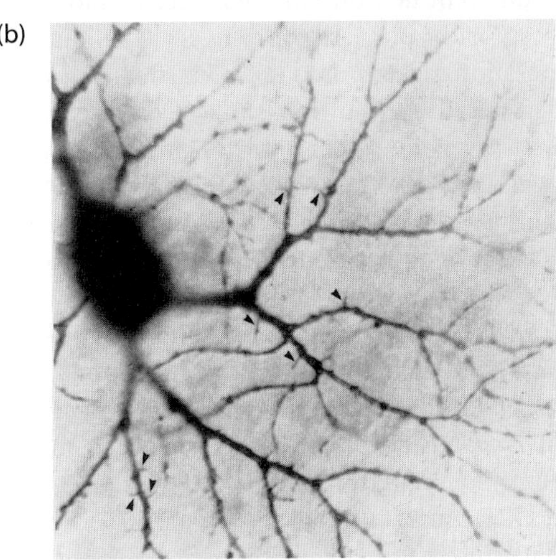

(c)

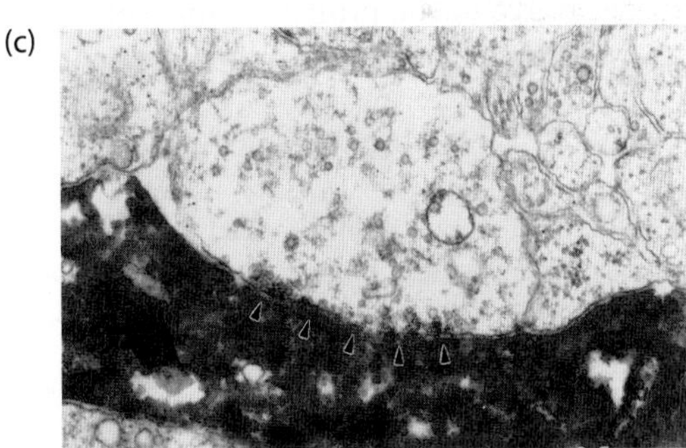

Figure 3.2 Neuroanatomical analysis at different scales. **(a)** Cells from the retina of a young ferret, stained and magnified by a light microscope. This section of the retina spans approximately 1.5 mm. **(b)** A ganglion cell from the cat retina that has been injected with stain to highlight its dendritic arborization. The magnification by light microscopy here is much greater than in (a). The arrowheads highlight places where short dendritic extensions, or spines, are visible. Processes along one dendritic branch can be visualized with the electron microscope. **(c)** The dark region of this electron micrograph is one of the stained dendrites of the cell shown in (b). The light regions are axons forming synapses along the dendrite. At this magnification, it is possible to see the synaptic vesicles (arrowheads) in the axon terminals. These vesicles contain neurotransmitter as described in Chapter 2.

intracellular stains that show the neural architecture (Figure 3.2b). We can examine such stained cells with a light microscope. At a higher level of resolution, we can examine subcellular organelles such as synaptic vesicles inside an axon terminal with an electron microscope, which, as the name suggests, uses a beam of electrons rather than light to "illuminate" neural tissues (Figure 3.2c). Another approach is to use fluorescent stains and ultraviolet light to visualize the structures that take up the stains (Figure 3.3).

Tract-tracing methods permit the connections between different neurons and brain regions to be identified. An old, but still effective, technique is the degeneration method used to trace axonal pathways that are degenerating following damage or disease. At the simplest level, one can look for missing myelinated axons in damaged brains. At a more advanced level, the Marchi stain can be applied. The Marchi stain selectively stains the myelin in degenerating axons—a process that can result when the cell bodies die or the axons are cut off from the cell body. A more modern but now common method makes use of the enzyme *horseradish peroxidase* (*HRP*). HRP is a *retrograde* tracer (Figure 3.4) in that it is taken up by the axons when it is injected at axon terminals and transported back to their cell bodies. Thus, HRP provides a tool to visualize where the input to a particular neural region originates (Figure 3.5).

Researchers who want to know which subcortical structures project to the primary visual cortex can use HRP as a retrograde transport tool, injecting it into the input layers of the visual cortex. HRP is absorbed

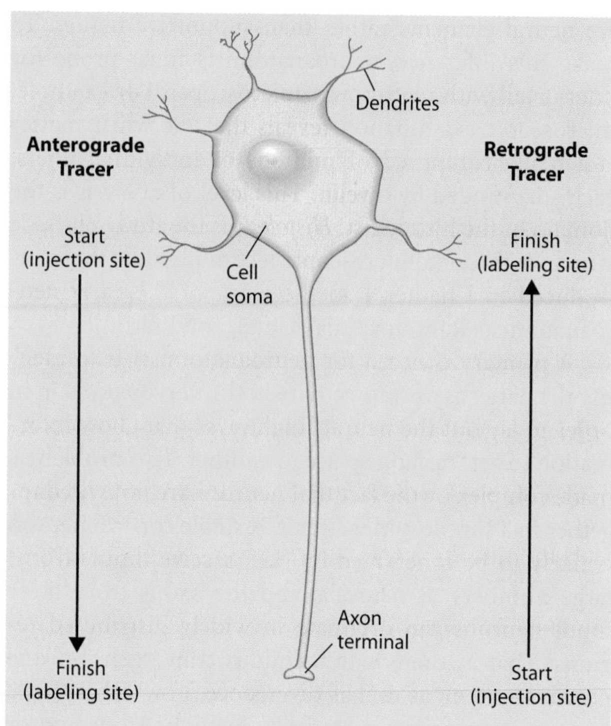

Figure 3.4 Directionality of anterograde and retrograde tracers. Anterograde tracers **(left)** are injected near and taken up by the cell soma. They then travel along the axon and label it with a tracer. Retrograde tracers **(right)** are injected near the axon terminal and are taken up there. They travel up the axon, where they terminate and label the cell soma.

Figure 3.3 Fluorescent staining method. **(a)** The soma and dendritic arbor of a retinal neuron in the prenatal cat, 8 days before birth. **(b)** The soma and dendritic arbor of a neuron from this same structure in the adult cat. Many dendritic branches are eliminated during development, and staining permits this developmental change to be visualized and quantified. Fluorescent stains come in a variety of types and may include adding a fluorescent molecule to an antibody or other molecule that binds with material in a neuron, or injecting a fluorescent material into a neuron and allowing it to diffuse throughout the cell.

(a)

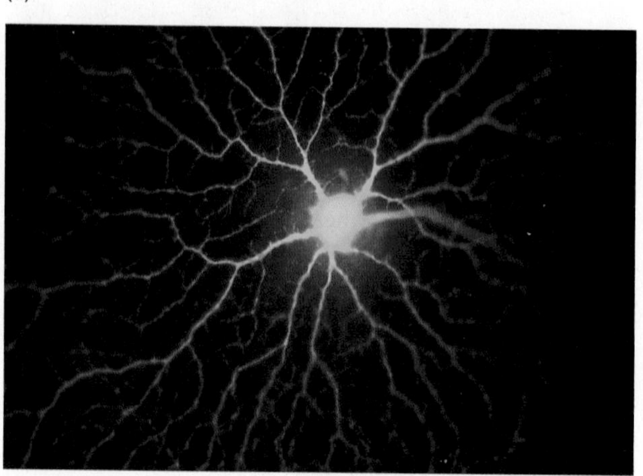

(b)

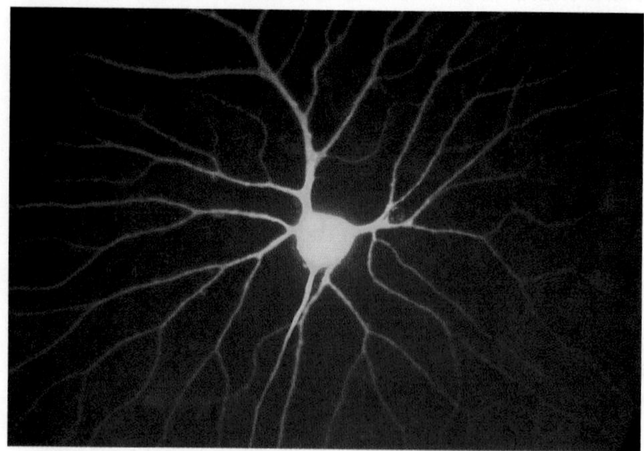

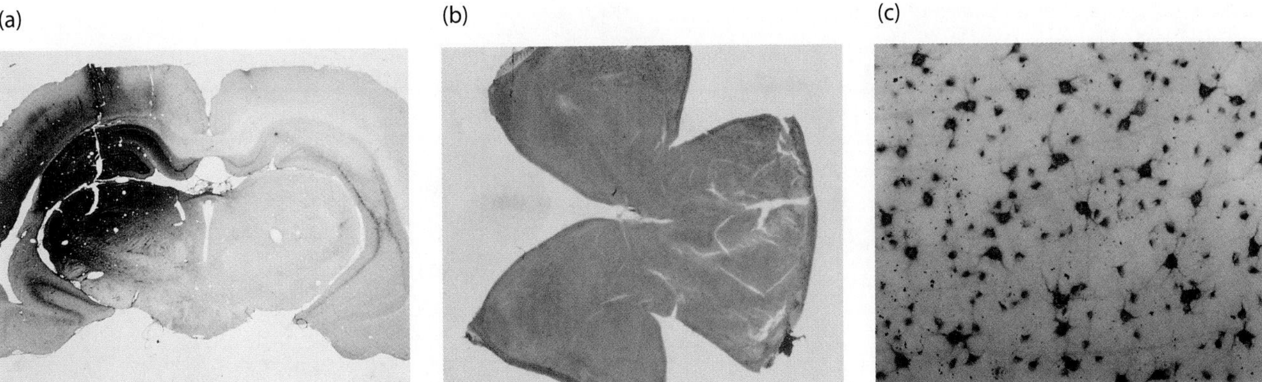

Figure 3.5 Staining techniques reveal connections between distant neural structures. Horseradish peroxidase (HRP) is a commonly used tracer. When used as a retrograde label, HRP is taken up by axon terminals and is transported back to the cell bodies. The animal is then killed, and histological methods are used to identify the location of the stain. **(a)** Injection site in the lateral geniculate nucleus of the thalamus of a rat. **(b)** A flattened retina, shown under very low-level magnification. **(c)** Individual neurons (the black spots are cell bodies of neurons filled with stain) under high magnification. If you look closely, you can see the shapes of many of these neurons and their dendrites.

through the same axonal channels that allow neural transduction via the inflow and outflow of sodium, potassium, and calcium ions. Once inside, the HRP diffuses up the axon to the cell body. The animal is then sacrificed and its brain removed. The HRP-injected tissue can then be treated with chemicals that turn the HRP a variety of colors from black to blue or brown. Examining thin slices of brain tissue cut with a sharp mechanical knife called a *microtome*, researchers can identify regions containing cell bodies labeled by HRP.

HRP is just one of many retrograde tracers. Other chemicals serve as *anterograde* tracers (see Figure 3.4), in that they are absorbed at the dendrites or soma and then diffuse along the axons. One popular approach is to use radioactively labeled materials as tracers—for example, radiolabeled amino acids. Autoradiography then can be used to visualize the pattern of staining. In this technique, tissue is sliced, labeled, and placed on a photographic material to let the radioactivity expose the photographic emulsion, producing a picture of the distribution of label in the tissue. In combination, retrograde and anterograde tracers allow researchers to identify the inputs to a specific region and determine where the axons from a particular region terminate. In this manner, the neuroanatomist can construct projection maps of the patterns of connectivity for small and large circuits of the nervous system.

Neuroanatomists have used histological techniques to classify neurons into groups based on their morphology (form). Upon close examination, it is clear that, despite the commonalities across neurons (most have cell bodies, axons, and dendrites), they are very heterogeneous, varying in size and shape. For some neurons, such as the giant pyramidal cells in the cerebral cortex, the dendritic arbor is relatively small. In contrast, the Purkinje cells of the cerebellar cortex have vast dendritic arbors, allowing for more than 200,000 synaptic input contacts (Figure 3.6; see also Chapter 2).

This level of detail was available early on to neuroanatomists. Recall that the silver impregnation stain introduced by Golgi allows an entire cell to be visualized, providing observers with the kinds of details seen in the drawings in Figure 3.6. However, this mysterious procedure stains only about 1% of the cells exposed to the stain. Such selectivity is advantageous in that it becomes possible to visualize individual cells without visual interference from their anatomical neighbors. With the Golgi technique and a host of other methods—such as those using the Nissl stain, which stains rough endoplasmic reticulum (an intracellular organelle, also referred to as *Nissl substance*), revealing the distribution of cell bodies (somata), or the Weigert stain, which selectively stains myelin, revealing the axons of neurons—a researcher can (painstakingly) catalog the cellular architecture and layering patterns of different brain regions. Indeed, as noted in Chapter 1 and described in more detail later in this chapter, Korbinian Brodmann used this technique to devise his **cytoarchitectonic map** of the brain. He methodically applied stains to samples from the entire surface of the cortex and obtained a picture of regional variations in cellular architecture. Brodmann partitioned cortical areas according to these differences in cell morphology, density, and layering (Figure 3.7) and introduced a numbering scheme that continues to be widely employed in the neurosciences today.

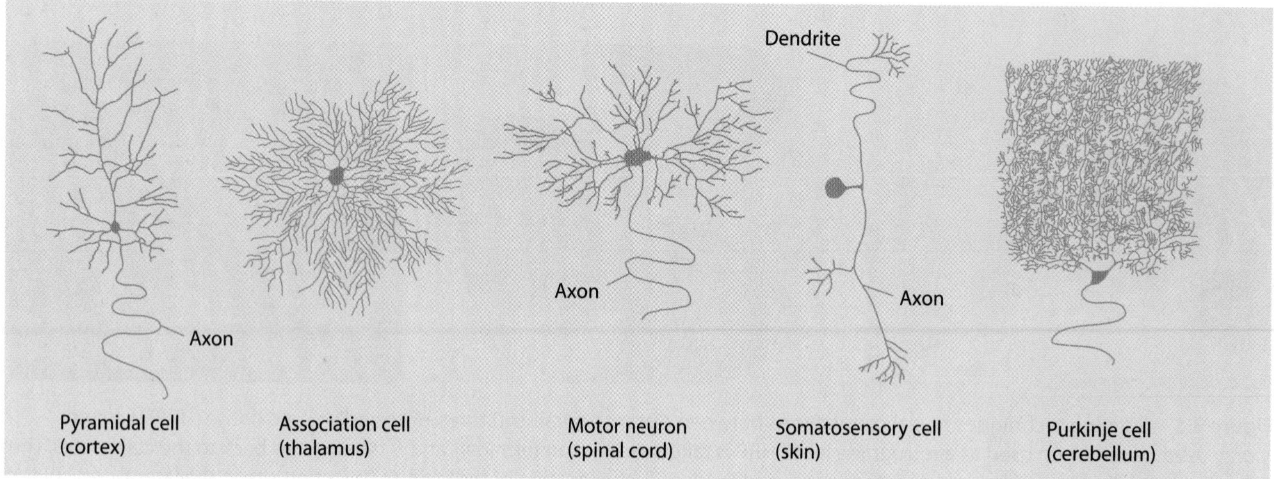

Figure 3.6 Five different neurons in the central and peripheral nervous systems. These neurons vary greatly in size (they are not drawn to scale); for example, the axon of an association cell in the thalamus may extend less than 1 mm, whereas the axon of the pyramidal cell may traverse the length of the spinal cord

The methods that we have described here and others related to these general neuroanatomical approaches have been used to investigate and describe how the nervous system is organized. Now let's turn to an overview of the organization of the human brain and nervous system.

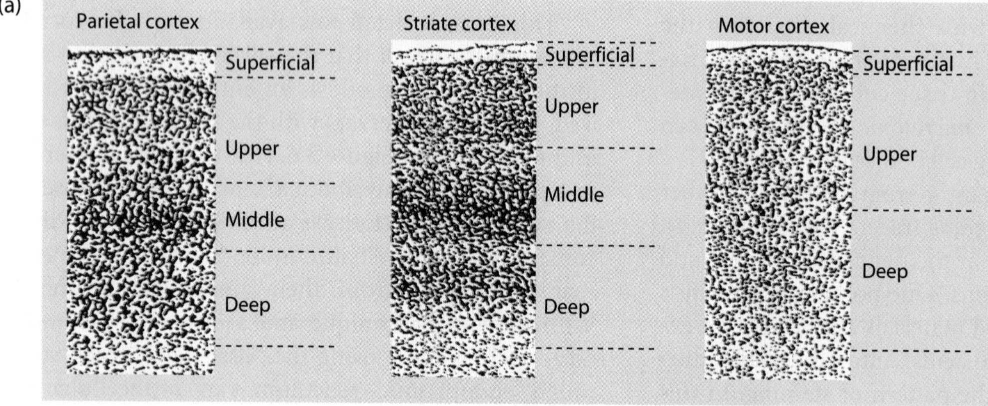

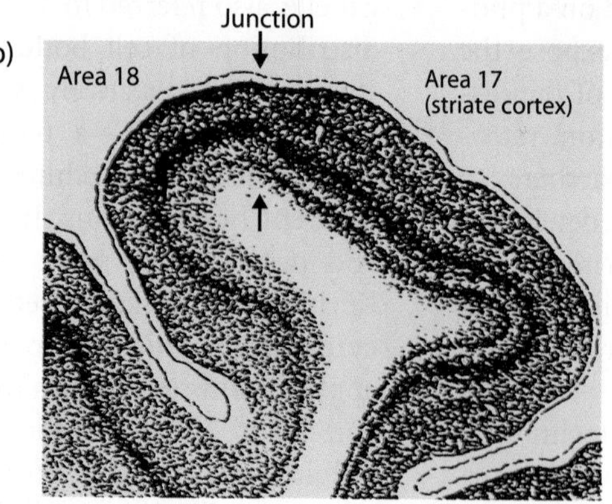

Figure 3.7 The gray matter of the cerebral cortex is composed of unmyelinated cell bodies that give a layered appearance as a function of the different cell types and their groupings in cross-sectional views (cortical surface at top). **(a)** As shown in these examples from the macaque monkey, across different cortical areas the density and layering of the cell types vary. Brodmann used these variations in density and layering, as well as neuronal morphology to define the boundaries between different cortical areas. **(b)** This example shows a cross section through the visual cortex. The arrows identify the border between two cytoarchitectonically defined Brodmann's areas. Note the change in the pattern of layering.

GROSS AND FUNCTIONAL ANATOMY OF THE NERVOUS SYSTEM

Signaling in the nervous system occurs along well-defined pathways, and via specific anatomical relays to circumscribed areas of the brain, spinal cord, and peripheral musculature. A review of the nervous system's anatomical organization clarifies this organization. We begin with a global view; in later chapters we'll focus on specific anatomical and physiological systems relevant to specific sensory, cognitive, and motor processes.

The nervous system has two major subdivisions: the **central nervous system** (**CNS**) consisting of the brain and spinal cord, and the **peripheral nervous system** (**PNS**), consisting of everything outside the CNS. The CNS can be thought of as the command-and-control portion of the nervous system. The PNS represents a courier network that delivers sensory information to the CNS and carries the motor commands of the CNS to the muscles, to control the voluntary muscles of the body (somatic motor system) and the involuntary activity of the smooth muscles, heart, and glands (autonomic motor system). In most of the remainder of this chapter, we focus on describing the CNS, to lay the groundwork for the studies of cognition that follow.

Cerebral Cortex

The **cerebral cortex** has two symmetrical hemispheres that consist of large sheets of (mostly) layered neurons. It sits over the top of core structures, including parts of the limbic system and basal ganglia, and surrounds the structures of the diencephalon, all of which will be considered later. Together, the cerebral cortex, basal ganglia, and diencephalon form the forebrain. The term *cortex* means "bark," as in tree bark, and in higher mammals and humans it contains many infoldings, or convolutions (Figure 3.8). As noted earlier, the infoldings of the cortical sheet are further defined as sulci (the folded regions) and gyri (the crowns of the folded tissue that one observes when viewing the surface). Many mammalian species, such as the rat or even New World monkeys like the owl monkey, have smoother, less folded cortices with few sulci and gyri.

The folds of the human cortex serve a functional purpose: to pack more cortical surface into the skull. If the human cortex were smoothed out to resemble that of the rat, for example, humans would need to have very large heads. Folding of the cortex provides about a one-third savings in space. The total surface area of the human cerebral cortex is about 2,200 to 2,400 cm^2, but because of the folding, about two thirds of this area is confined within the depths of the sulci. Another advantage of having a highly folded cortex is that neurons are brought into closer three-dimensional relationships to one another, saving axonal distance and hence neuronal conduction time between different areas. This savings occurs because the axons that make long-distance corticocortical connections run under the cortex through the white matter and do not follow the foldings of the cortical surface in their paths to distant cortical areas. In addition, by folding, the cortex brings some nearby regions closer together; for example, the opposing layers of cortex in each gyrus are in closer linear proximity than they would be if the gyri were flattened.

Although the cortex is composed of several cell layers in most regions, its thickness averages only 3 mm and ranges from 1.5 to 4.5 mm in different cortical regions. The cortex itself contains the cell bodies of neurons, their dendrites, and some of their axons. In addition, the cortex includes axons and axon terminals of neurons projecting to the cortex from other brain regions, such as the subcortical thalamus. The cortex also contains blood vessels. Because the cerebral cortex has such a high density of cell bodies, it appears grayish in relation to underlying regions that are composed primarily of axons of neurons and appear slightly paler or even white. As described earlier, for this reason anatomists used the terms *gray matter* and *white matter* when referring to areas of cell bodies and axon tracts, respectively. The latter tracts represent the billions of axons that connect the neurons of the cerebral cortex to other locations in the brain (Figure 3.9).

ANATOMICAL SUBDIVISIONS

The cerebral hemispheres have four main divisions, or *lobes*—and a fifth, if you consider that the limbic system is sometimes referred to as the *limbic lobe*, as described later. These regions have different functional properties and can usually be distinguished from one another by prominent anatomical landmarks such as pronounced sulci. The names of the brain areas were derived from names originally given to the overlying skull bones; for example, the temporal lobe lies underneath the temporal bone. The temporal bone derived its name from the Latin *temporalis* (meaning "of time") probably because of the graying of hair overlying the temporal bone—a sign of passing time if there ever was one.

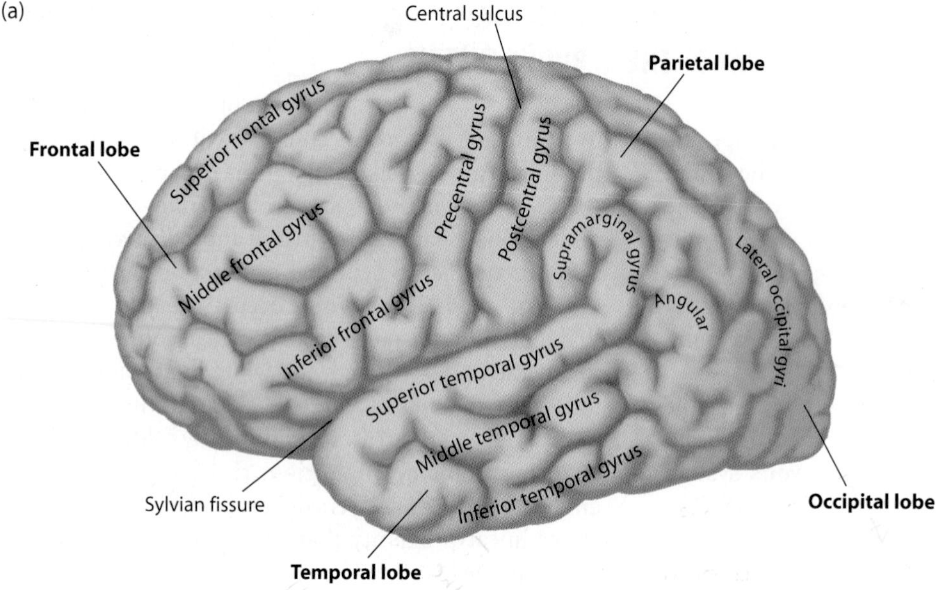

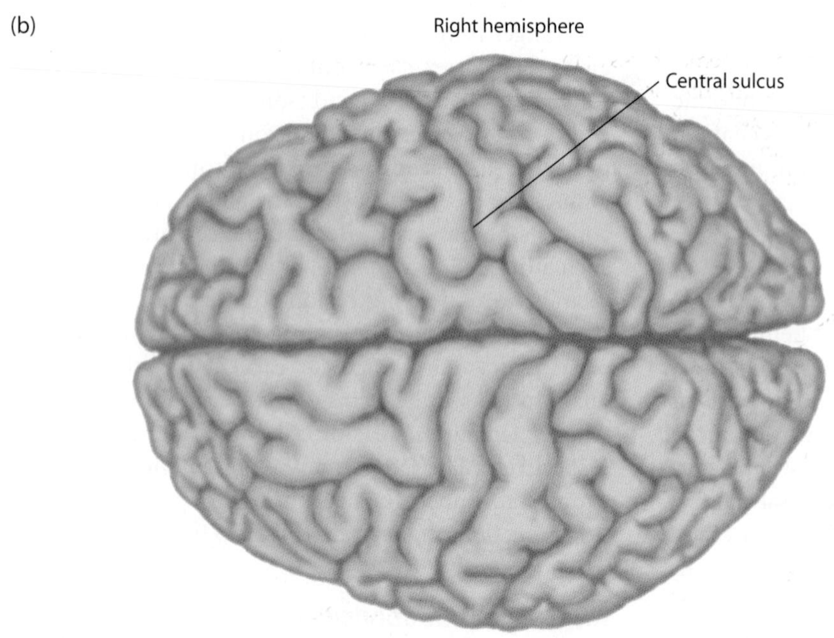

Figure 3.8 Lateral view of the left hemisphere **(a)** and dorsal view of the cerebral cortex **(b)** in humans. The major features of the cortex include the four cortical lobes and various key gyri. Gyri are separated by sulci and result from the folding of the cerebral cortex that occurs during development of the nervous system, to achieve an economy of size.

The four lobes are the frontal, parietal, temporal, and occipital lobes (Figure 3.10). The central sulcus divides the **frontal lobe** from the **parietal lobe**, and the Sylvian (lateral) fissure separates the **temporal lobe** from the frontal and parietal lobes. The **occipital lobe** is demarcated from the parietal and temporal lobes by the parieto-occipital sulcus on the brain's dorsal surface and the preoccipital notch located on the ventrolateral surface. The left and right cerebral hemispheres are separated by the interhemispheric fissure (also called the *longitudinal fissure*) that runs from the rostral to the caudal end of the forebrain.

Connections between the cerebral hemispheres are accomplished by axons from cortical neurons that travel through the **corpus callosum**, which represents the largest white matter **commissure** in the nervous system. *Commissure* is a special term for the white matter tracts that cross from the left to the right side, or vice versa, of

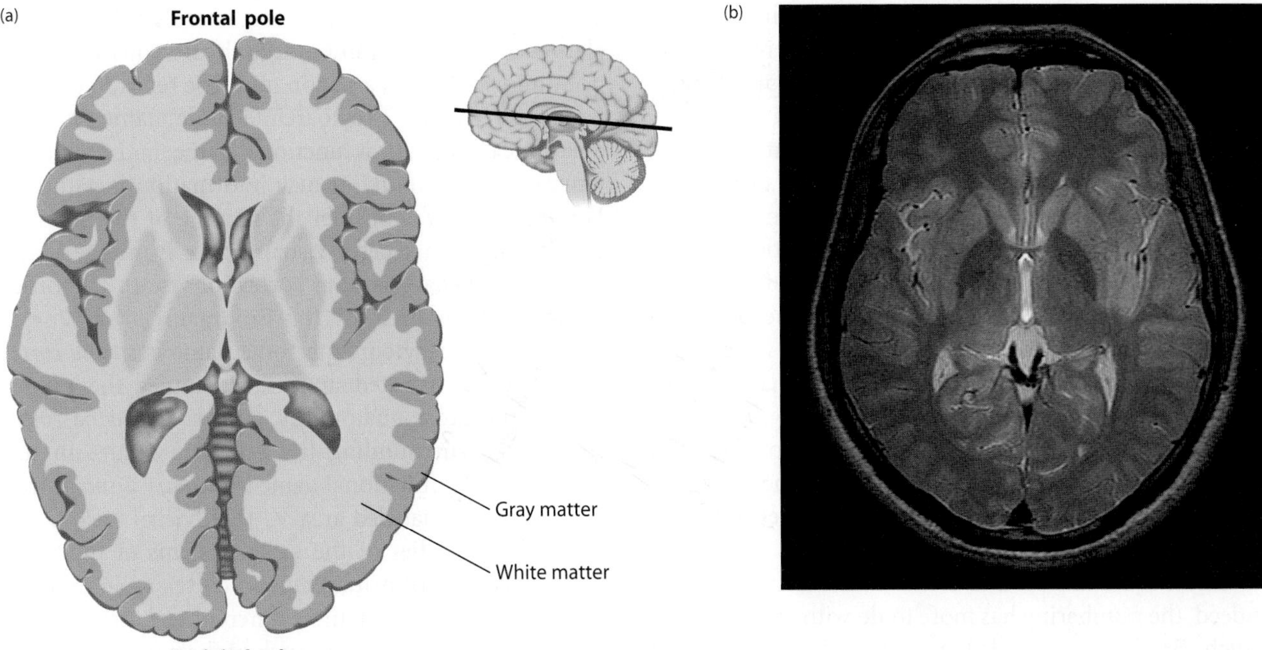

Figure 3.9 **(a)** Horizontal section through the cerebral hemispheres at the level indicated at upper right. White matter is composed of myelinated axons, and gray matter is composed primarily of neurons. This diagram shows that the gray matter on the surface of the cerebral hemispheres forms a continuous sheet that is heavily folded. **(b)** High-resolution structural MRI in a similar plane of section in a living human. This T2 image was obtained on a 4-tesla scanner (a high-magnetic-field scanner) using a 512 × 512 matrix for acquisition. Note that on T2 images the white matter appears darker than the gray matter. The skull and scalp can be seen here but are not shown in (a).

the CNS. The term *corpus callosum* means "hard body," so named because of its tough consistency. Indeed, very early anatomists incorrectly believed that the corpus callosum served a structural function in supporting the cerebral hemispheres because it prevented them from collapsing onto structures below. As we will discuss later in the book, the corpus callosum carries out valuable integrative functions for the two hemispheres.

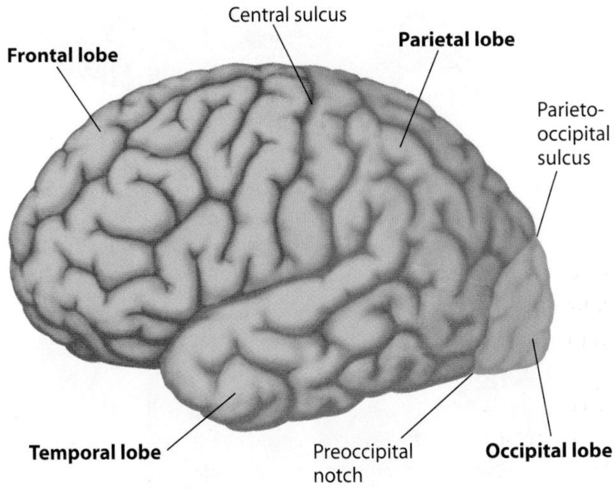

Figure 3.10 Four lobes of the cerebral cortex, in lateral view of the left hemisphere. See text for details.

CYTOARCHITECTONICS

The cerebral cortex can be divided more finely than the four or five main lobes, in various ways. For example, it can be divided according to functional subdivisions of the cortex. But there are other, more purely anatomical criteria for subdividing the cortex. One is by the microanatomy of cell types and their organization. This method of subdividing is generally referred to as *cytoarchitectonics*—*cyto-* means "cell" and *architectonics* means "architecture"—and has to do with how cells in a region appear morphologically and are arranged with respect to each other. Cytoarchitectonic investigations entail the performance of detailed histological analysis of the tissue from different regions of the cerebral cortex. The goal is to define the extent of regions in which the cellular architecture looks similar and therefore might indicate a homogeneous area of the cortex that represents, perhaps, a functional area. This work began in earnest with Korbinian Brodmann at the beginning of the 20th century.

Brodmann (1909/1960) identified approximately 52 regions of the cerebral cortex. These areas were categorized according to differences in cellular morphology and organization, and numbered (Figure 3.11). Other anatomists further subdivided the cortex into almost 200 cytoarchitectonically defined areas, but many classified transition zones as separate areas when perhaps they should not be considered so. A combination of cytoarchitectonic and functional descriptions of the cortex is probably most effective in dividing the cerebral cortex into meaningful units; this type of work will likely continue into the foreseeable future because we are only beginning to learn the functional organization of the cerebral cortex. In the sections that follow, we use Brodmann's numbering system to describe the cerebral cortex, as well as anatomical names (e.g., superior temporal gyrus).

The Brodmann system often seems unsystematic. Indeed, the numbering has more to do with the order in which Brodmann sampled a region than with any meaningful relation between areas. Nonetheless, in some regions the numbering system has a rough correspondence with the relations between areas that carry out similar functions, such as vision—Brodmann areas 17, 18, and 19. It is worth noting here that the nomenclature of the cortex (and indeed the nervous system) is not uniform. Hence, a region might be referred to by its Brodmann name, a cytoarchitectonic name, a gross anatomical name, or a functional name; and functional names change rapidly as new information is gathered. For example, let's consider the naming of the first area in the cortex to receive visual inputs from the thalamus—the primary sensory cortex for vision. The Brodmann name is area 17 (or Brodmann area 17; i.e., BA17), another cytoarchitectonic name is *striate cortex* (owing to its striated appearance under the microscope), the gross anatomical name is *calcarine cortex* (the cortex surrounding the calcarine fissure in humans), and the functional name is *primary visual cortex*, which has been labeled area *V1* (for "visual area 1") on the basis of studies of the visual systems of monkeys. The choice here of primary visual cortex as an example is fortuitous because all these different terms refer to the same cortical area. But for much of the cortex this is not the case; that is, different nomenclatures often do not refer to precisely the same area with a one-to-one mapping. *BA18* of the visual system, for example, is not synonymous with *V2* (for "visual area 2").

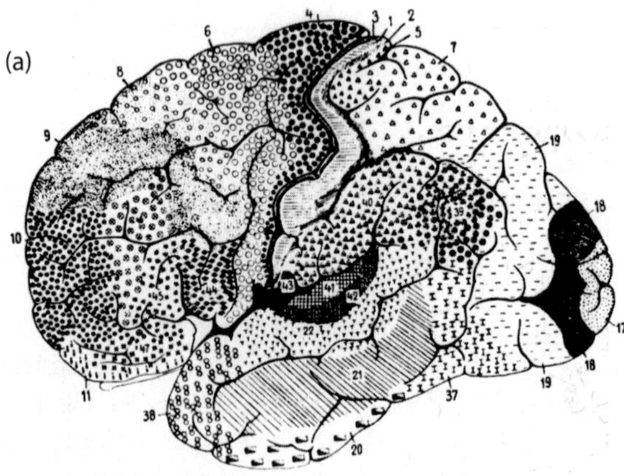

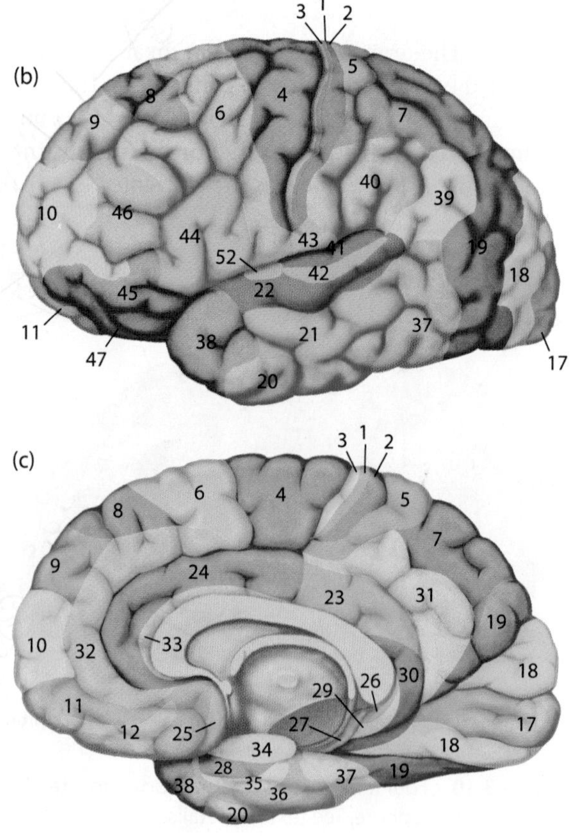

Figure 3.11 **(a)** Brodmann's original cytoarchitectonic map from his work around the start of the 20th century. Different regions of cortex have been demarcated by histological examination of the cellular microanatomy. Brodmann divided the cortex into about 52 areas. **(b)** Lateral view of the left hemisphere showing Brodmann's areas. Over the years, the map has been modified, and the standard version no longer includes some areas. **(c)** Medial view of the right hemisphere showing Brodmann's areas. Most of Brodmann's areas are symmetrical in the two hemispheres.

It is also possible to subdivide the cerebral cortex according to the general patterns of layering (Figure 3.12). Ninety percent of cortex is composed of **neocortex**, which typically contains six main cortical layers with a high degree of specialization of neuronal organization (see Figure 3.12c). Layer IV is typically the input layer, receiving information from the thalamus, as well as information from other, more distant cortical areas. Layer VI, on the other hand, is typically considered an output layer that sends information from the cortex back to the thalamus, facilitating feedback. Each layer is anatomically and functionally distinct, though it is important to note that information is shared between the layers via axonal projections.

Neocortex includes areas like primary sensory and motor cortex and association cortex (areas not obviously primary sensory or motor). *Mesocortex* is a term for the so-called paralimbic region, which includes the cingulate gyrus, parahippocampal gyrus, insular cortex, and the orbitofrontal cortex, all of which will be defined later. Mesocortex is interposed between neocortex and allocortex and has six layers. *Allocortex* typically has only one to four layers of neurons and includes the hippocampal complex (sometimes referred to as *archicortex*) and primary olfactory cortex (sometimes referred to as *paleocortex*). The take-home message here is that the cerebral cortex can be subdivided into major regions that differ according to the degree of complexity of the neuronal layering.

FUNCTIONAL DIVISIONS

The lobes of the cerebral cortex have a variety of functional roles in neural processing. Major identifiable systems can be localized within each lobe, but systems of the brain also cross different lobes. That is, these brain systems do not map one to one onto the lobe in which they primarily reside, but in part the gross anatomical

Figure 3.12 Cerebral cortex, color-coded to show the regional differences in cortical layering that specify different types of cortex. **(a)** The lateral surface of the left hemisphere. **(b)** The medial surface of the right hemisphere. Neocortex is shown in red, mesocortex in blue, and allocortex in green. **(c)** Idealized cross section of neocortex showing a variety of cell types and the patterns of three different types of staining techniques. On the left, the Golgi preparation is apparent: Only a few neurons are stained, but each is completely visualized. In the middle, we see primarily cell bodies from the Nissl stain. On the right, we see the fiber tracks in a Weigert stain, which selectively stains myelin.

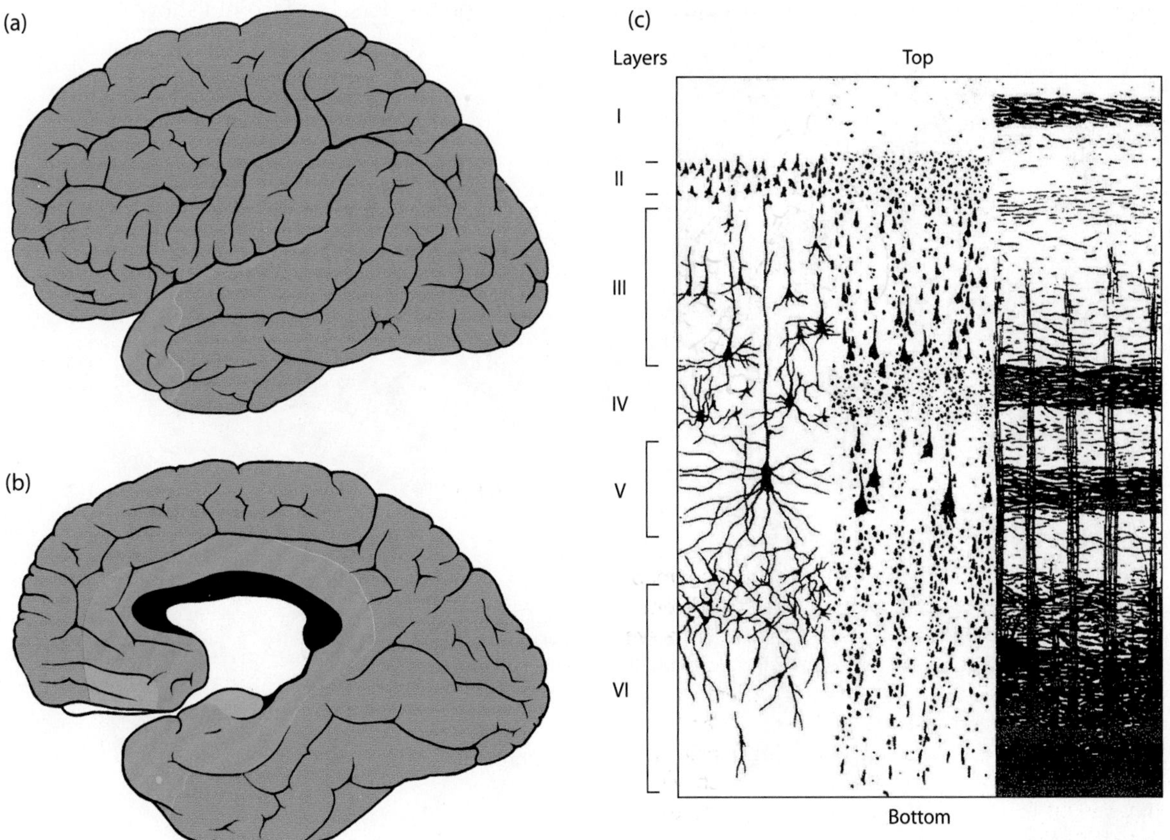

HOW THE BRAIN WORKS

The Chambers of the Mind

We have understood for many decades that neurons in the brain are functional units, and that how they are interconnected yields specific circuits for the support of particular behaviors. Centuries ago, early anatomists, believing that the head contained the seat of behavior, examined the brain to see where the conscious self (soul, if you wish) was located. They found a likely candidate: Some chambers in the brain seemed to be empty (except for some fluid) and thus were possible containers for higher functions. These chambers are called *ventricles* (see the figure). What is the function of these chambers within the brain?

The brain weighs a considerable amount but has little or no structural support; there is no skeletal system for the brain. To overcome this potential difficulty, the brain is immersed in a fluid called *cerebrospinal fluid* (*CSF*). This fluid allows the brain to float to help offset the pressure that would be present if the brain were merely sitting on the base of the skull. CSF also reduces shock to the brain and spinal cord during rapid accelerations or decelerations, such as when we fall or are struck on the head.

The ventricles inside the brain are continuous with the CSF surrounding the brain. The largest of these chambers are the lateral ventricles, which are connected to the third ventricle in the brain's midline. The cerebral aqueduct joins the third to the fourth ventricle in the brainstem below the cerebellum. The CSF is produced in the lateral ventricles and in the third ventricle by the choroid plexus, an outpouching of blood vessels from the ventricular wall. Hence, CSF is similar to blood, being formed by the transport of what resembles an ultrafiltrate of blood plasma; essentially, CSF is a clear fluid containing proteins, glucose, and ions, especially potassium, sodium, and chloride. It slowly circulates from the lateral and third ventricles through the cerebral aqueduct to the fourth ventricle and on to the subarachnoid space surrounding the brain, to be reabsorbed by the arachnoid villi in the sagittal sinus (the large venous system located between the two hemispheres on the dorsal surface; not shown).

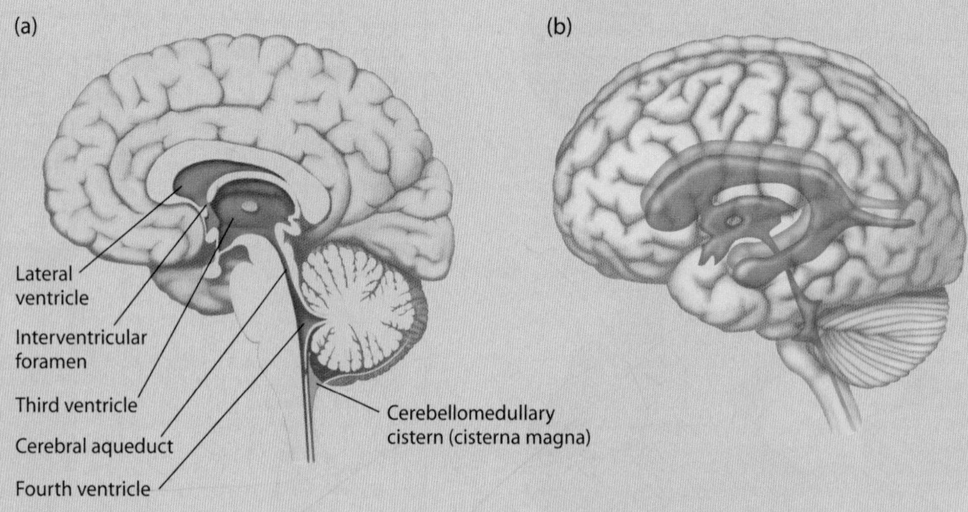

Ventricles of the human brain. **(a)** Midsagittal view. **(b)** Three-dimensional view.

subdivisions of the cerebral cortex can be related to different sensorimotor functions. In their principal organization, cognitive brain systems are often composed of networks whose component parts are located in different lobes of the cortex. Finally, most functions in the brain—whether sensory, motor, or cognitive—rely on both cortical and subcortical components. Because one of the goals of this book is to review what we know about the functional localization of higher cognitive and perceptual processes, what follows in this section is a beginner's guide to the functional anatomy of the cortex.

Motor Areas of the Frontal Lobe The frontal lobe plays a major role in the planning and execution of movements. It has two main subdivisions: the motor cortex and the prefrontal cortex. The motor cortex begins in the depths of the central sulcus and extends in the anterior direction. The primary motor cortex (M1) corresponds to BA4. It includes the anterior bank of the central sulcus and much of the precentral gyrus (the prefix *pre-* in neuroanatomy means "in front of"). Anterior to this area are two more main motor areas of cortex (within BA6): the premotor cortex on the lateral surface of the hemisphere, and the supplementary motor cortex that lies dorsal to the premotor area and extends around to the hemisphere's medial surface. These motor cortical areas contain motor neurons whose axons extend to the spinal cord and brainstem and synapse on motor neurons in the spinal cord. The output layer of motor cortex contains some of the most amazing neurons in the nervous system: the large pyramidal neurons known as *Betz's cells*, named after Vladimir Aleksandrovich Betz, who described them. Betz's cells are the largest neurons in the cerebral cortex, reaching 60 to 80 mm in diameter at the cell body, with some sending axons several feet long down the spinal cord.

The more anterior regions of the frontal lobe, the **prefrontal cortex**, take part in the more complex aspects of planning and executing behavior—tasks that require the integration of information over time. The prefrontal cortex has three or more main areas that are commonly referred to in descriptions of the gross anatomy of the frontal lobe (although different definitions can be used): the dorsolateral prefrontal cortex, the orbitofrontal cortex (Figure 3.13), and the anterior cingulate and medial frontal regions (not visible in Figure 3.13, but refer to Figure 3.18).

Somatosensory Areas of the Parietal Lobe The somatosensory cortex is in the posterior bank of the central sulcus and encompasses the postcentral gyrus and adjacent areas (Brodmann areas 1, 2, and 3). These cortical regions receive inputs from the somatosensory relays of the thalamus and represent information about touch, pain, temperature sense, and limb proprioception (limb position). The primary somatosensory cortex (or S1) is immediately caudal to the central sulcus, and a secondary somatosensory cortex (S2), receiving information via projections primarily from S1,

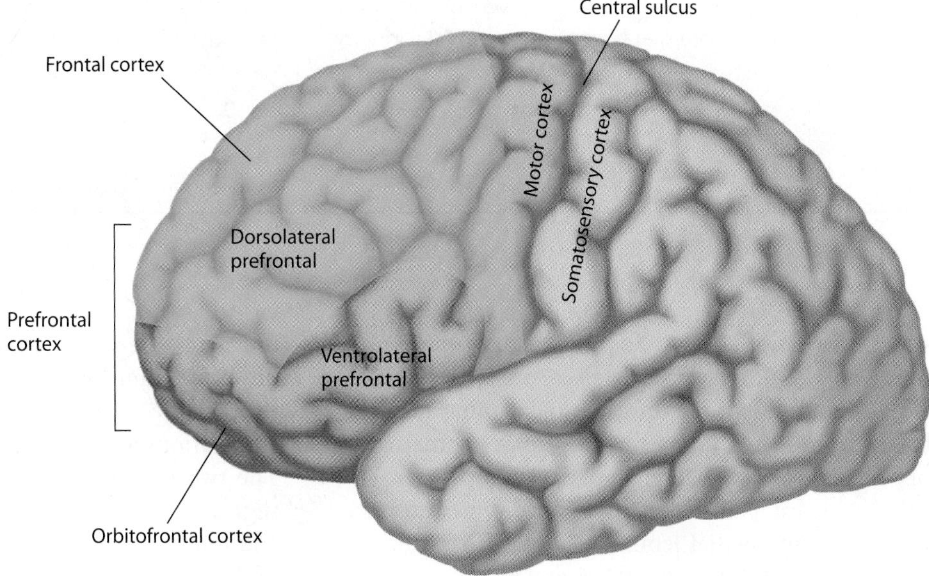

Figure 3.13 Divisions of the frontal cortex. The frontal lobe contains both motor and higher order association areas. For example, the prefrontal cortex is involved in executive functions, memory, and other processes.

HOW THE BRAIN WORKS

Cortical Topography

Early insights into human cortical organization were made possible by studies that involved direct stimulation of the cortex of awake humans undergoing brain surgery. Wilder Penfield and Herbert Jasper (1954) at the Montreal Neurological Institute carried out such pioneering work in the 1940s. Taking advantage of the fact that the cortex is exposed during surgery, these surgeons removed damaged brain tissue and systematically explored the effects of small levels of electrical current applied to the cortical surface. Panel **(a)** of the figure shows the exposed cortex of an epileptic patient and panel **(b)**, a gridwork of electrodes laid over the surface for stimulation and recording; stimulation during surgery can be done with a single electrode rather than a grid. Because there are no pain receptors in the central nervous system, patients experience no discomfort from stimulation. Thus, stimulation can be applied even when they are awake and fully conscious, enabling researchers to gather the patients' subjective experiences—a relative impossibility in animal studies.

In their studies, Penfield and his associates found a topographic correspondence between cortical regions and body surface with respect to somatosensory and motor processes. This correspondence is represented in panel **(c)** by overlaying drawings of body parts on drawings of coronal sections of the motor and somatosensory cortex. These coronal sections are from the regions indicated by the color codes in the lateral view of the whole brain at the top of panel **(c)** (only the left hemisphere is shown here, representing the right body surface). The resulting map of the body surface on the cortex is sometimes called a *homunculus*, referring to the fact that there is an organized representation of the body across a given cortical area. Note that there is an indirect relation between the actual size of body parts and the cortical representation of the body's parts. For example, areas within the motor homunculus that activate muscles in the fingers, mouth, and tongue are much larger than would be expected if the representation were proportional. The large drawings of the fingers and mouth indicate that large areas of cortex are involved in the fine coordination required when we manipulate objects or speak.

Is the representation of the homunculus in the figure correct? Recent evidence from brain-imaging studies using a technique described in Chapter 4—functional magnetic resonance imaging (fMRI)—suggests that it may not be. Ravi Menon and his colleagues (Servos et al., 1999) in Canada stimulated the foreheads and chins of healthy volunteers while their brains were being scanned. In contrast to the results of the electrical-stimulation studies, they found that stimulating the forehead produced activity in a region that was below (inferior to) the region for activity related to chin stimulation—the reverse of the drawing in the figure based on the work of Penfield and his colleagues. If the latter pattern from neuroimaging turns out to be accurate, it will constitute a dramatic example of scientific revisionism.

is located ventrally to S1. Somatosensory inputs projecting to the posterior parietal cortex arise from S1 and S2. Somatosensory information coming into the thalamus and then going to the primary somatosensory cortex traverses two main pathways: the anterolateral system for pain and temperature sense, and the dorsal column–medial lemniscal system for information about touch, proprioception, and movement (Figure 3.14). Receptor cells in the periphery transduce physical stimuli into neuronal impulses conducted to the spinal cord and toward the brain, making synaptic connections at relay sites along the ascending pathway. The two systems for somatosensory information take slightly different paths in the spinal cord, brainstem, and midbrain on their route to the thalamus, and then to the cortex.

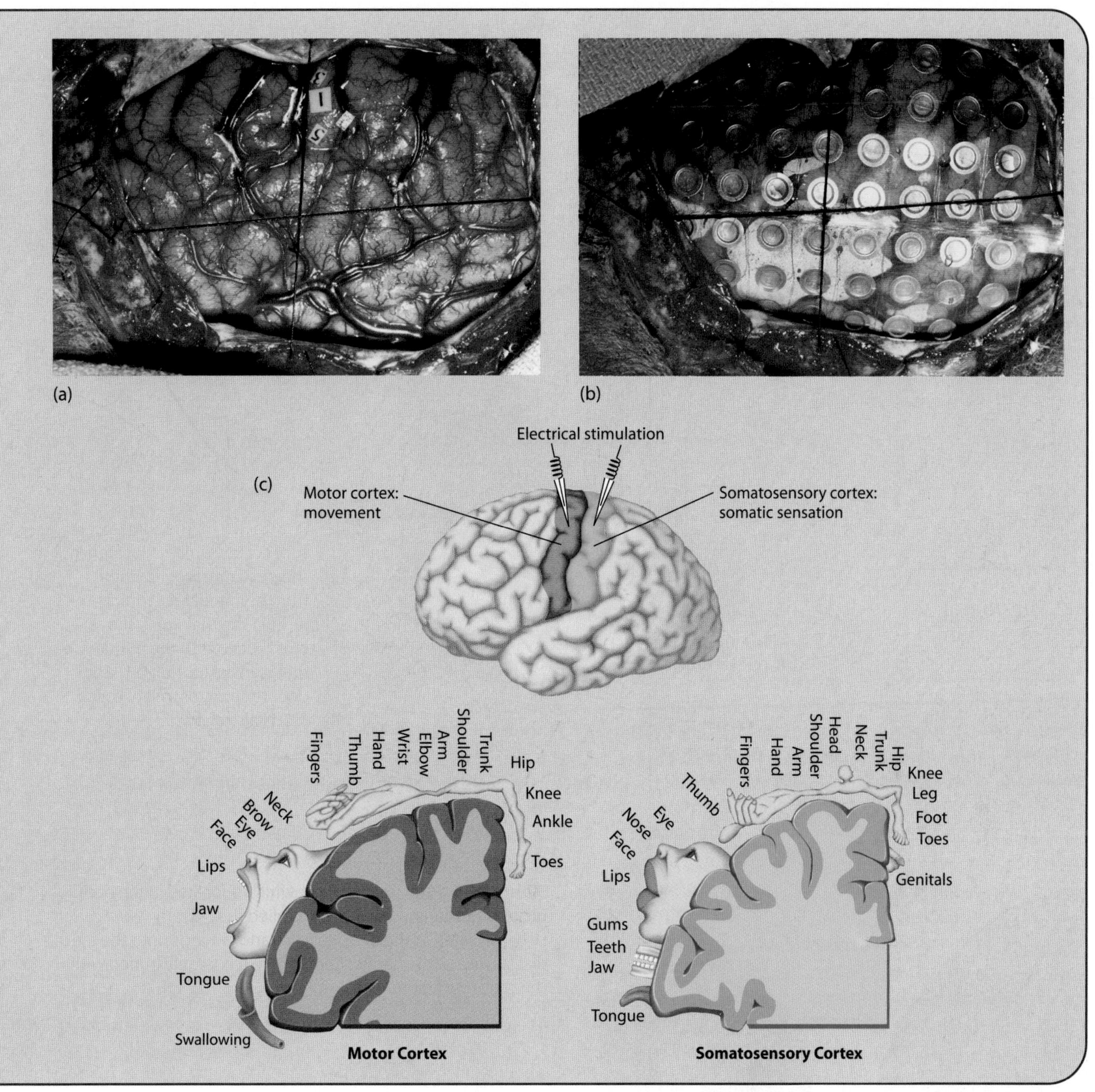

Visual Processing Areas in the Occipital Lobe The primary visual cortex (also known as *striate cortex* because its surface anatomical organization makes it appear striped to the naked eye, *V1* for visual area 1, or *BA17*) receives visual inputs relayed from the lateral geniculate nucleus of the thalamus (Figure 3.15). In humans, the primary visual cortex is on the medial surface of the cerebral hemispheres, extending only slightly onto the posterior hemispheric pole. Thus, most of the primary visual cortex is effectively hidden from view, between the two hemispheres. The cortex in this area has six layers; it begins the cortical coding of visual features like color, luminance, spatial frequency, orientation, and motion—features that we will take up in detail in Chapters 5 and 6.

Visual information from the outside world is processed by multiple layers of cells in the retina and

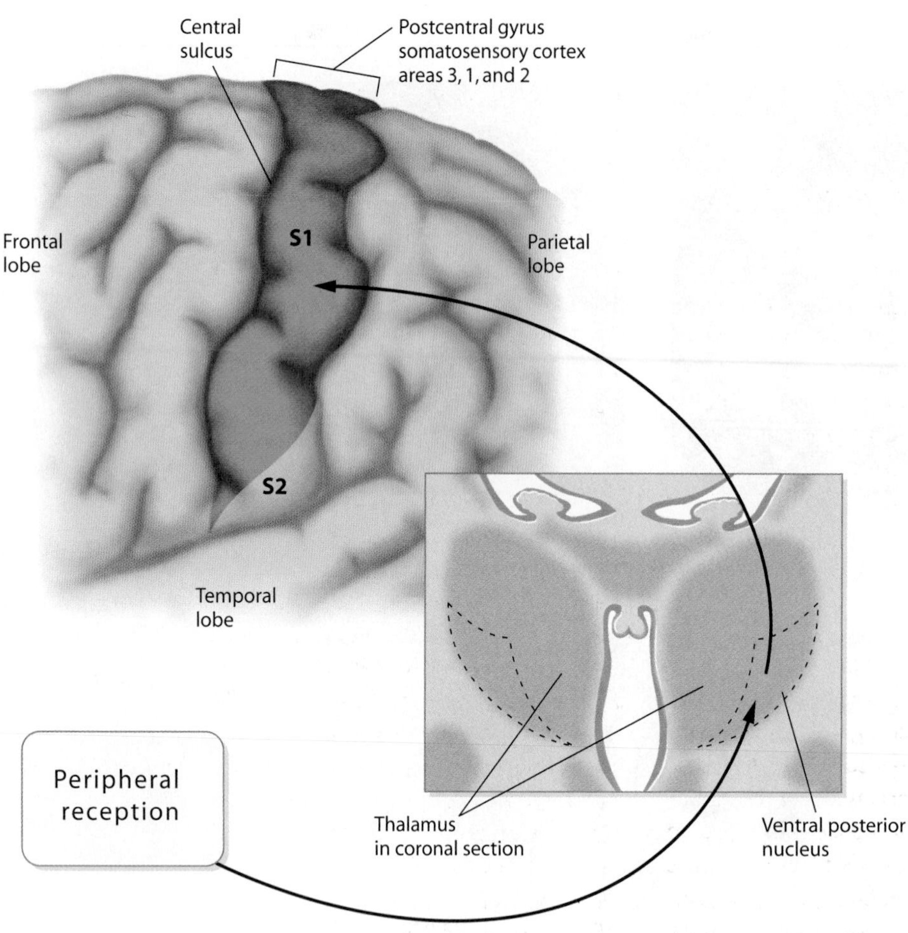

Figure 3.14 The somatosensory cortex, which is located in the postcentral gyrus. Inputs from peripheral receptors project via the thalamus (shown in cross section) to the primary somatosensory cortex (S1). Secondary somatosensory cortex (S2) is also shown.

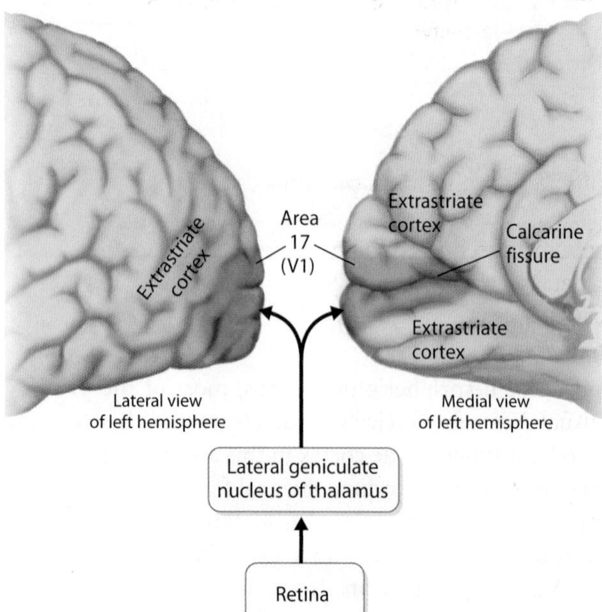

Figure 3.15 The visual cortex, which is located in the occipital lobe. Brodmann area 17, also called the *primary visual cortex* (V1), is located at the occipital pole and extends onto the medial surface of the hemisphere, where it is largely buried within the calcarine fissure.

transmitted via the optic nerve to the lateral geniculate nucleus of the thalamus, and from there to V1—a pathway often referred to as the *retinogeniculostriate*, or *primary visual, pathway.* Note that visual projections from the retina also reach other subcortical brain regions by way of secondary projection systems. The superior colliculus of the midbrain is the main target of the secondary pathway and participates in visuomotor functions such as eye movements. In Chapter 12 we will review the role of the cortical and subcortical projection pathways in visual attention.

Surrounding the striate cortex is a large visual cortical region called the *extrastriate* ("outside the striate") visual cortex (sometimes referred to as the *prestriate* cortex in monkeys, to signify that it is anatomically anterior to the striate cortex). The extrastriate cortex includes BA18 and BA19.

Auditory Processing Areas in the Temporal Lobe The auditory cortex lies in the superior part of the temporal lobe and is buried within the Sylvian fissure (Figure 3.16). The projection from the cochlea (the auditory sensory organ in the inner ear) proceeds through the subcortical relays to the medial geniculate of the thalamus, and then to the supratemporal cortex in a region known as *Heschl's gyri.* This region represents A1, the primary auditory cortex, and A2, the auditory association area surrounding it and posterior to the primary auditory cortex (BA41 and BA42). BA22, which surrounds the auditory cortex, aids in the perception of auditory inputs; when this area is stimulated, sensations of sound are produced in humans. One can represent the sensory inputs to the auditory cortex using a tonotopic map; the orderly representation of sound frequency within the auditory cortex can be determined with several tonotopic maps.

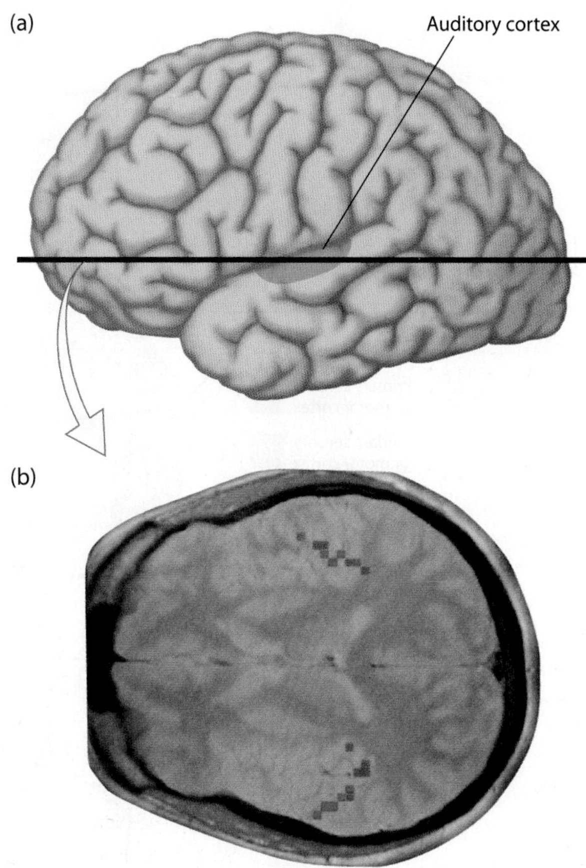

Figure 3.16 **(a)** Primary auditory cortex, which is located in the superior temporal lobe. The primary auditory cortex and surrounding association auditory areas contain representations of auditory stimuli and show a tonotopic organization. **(b)** This MRI shows areas of the superior temporal region in horizontal section that have been stimulated by tones of different frequencies and show increased blood flow as a result of neuronal activity.

Association Cortex The portion of neocortex that is not sensory or motor has traditionally been termed the **association cortex.** These regions receive inputs from many cortical areas, contain cells that may be activated by more than one sensory modality, and have specific functional roles that are not exclusively sensory or motor. For example, take the visual association cortex. Though the primary visual cortex is necessary for normal vision, neither it nor the extrastriate cortex is the sole locus of visual perception. Regions of visual association cortex in the parietal and temporal lobes are important for correct perception of the visual world (see Chapters 5 and 6). Moreover, visual association cortex can be activated during mental imagery when we call up a visual memory even in the absence of visual stimulation. As another example, the association areas of the parietal–temporal–occipital junction of the left hemisphere have a prominent role in language processing, whereas this region in the right hemisphere is implicated in attentional orienting (see Chapter 12). Thus, higher mental processes are the domain of the association cortical areas, in interaction with sensory and motor areas of cortex (Figure 3.17).

Limbic System, Basal Ganglia, Hippocampus, and Diencephalon

In the preceding sections we focused on the neocortex. Here we will consider the mesocortical and allocortical

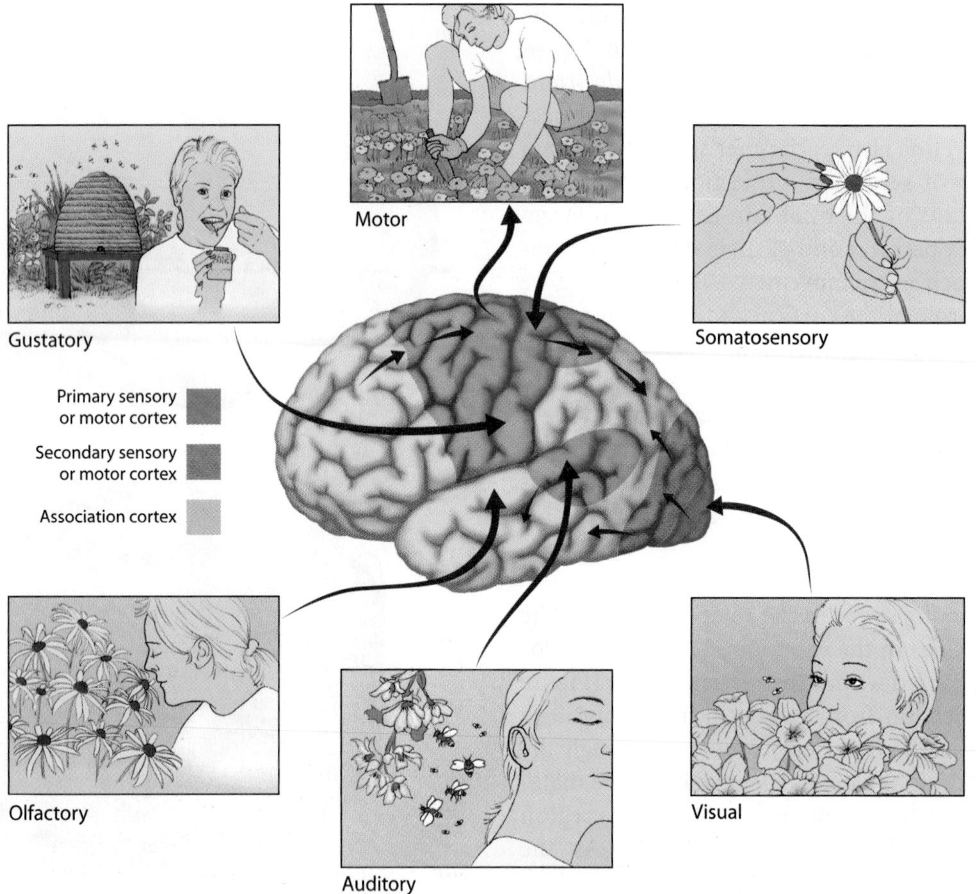

Figure 3.17 Primary sensory and motor cortex and surrounding association cortex. The blue regions show the primary cortical receiving areas of the ascending sensory pathways and the primary output region to the spinal cord. The secondary sensory and motor areas are colored red. The remainder is considered association cortex.

regions of the cerebrum. Then we will look at the subcortical structures of the basal ganglia and the diencephalon.

LIMBIC LOBE

Let's look at the portions of the forebrain that are collectively known as the limbic lobe or **limbic system** (Figure 3.18). These include several structures that form a border (in Latin, *limbus*) around the brainstem, named the *grand lobe limbique* by Paul Broca (see Chapter 1). A band of cortex known as the cingulate gyrus extends above the corpus callosum in the anterior–posterior direction. Together, the cingulate gyrus, hypothalamus, anterior thalamic nuclei, and hippocampus constitute the "classical" limbic lobe (Figure 3.19). In the 1930s James Papez (pronounced "payps") first suggested the idea that these structures were organized into a system for emotional behavior, which led to use of the term *Papez circuit.*

Since that initial formulation, much has been learned about the structures participating in the limbic system, and today the **amygdala**, a group of neurons anterior to the hippocampus, is usually considered a key component, along with the orbitofrontal cortex and parts of the basal ganglia (described in the next section, but not shown in Figure 3.19); in some descriptions, the medial dorsal nucleus of the thalamus is also included. The organization and role of the limbic system are described in more detail in Chapter 9. The limbic system participates in emotional processing, learning, and memory. With each passing year we discover new functions of this system.

BASAL GANGLIA

The **basal ganglia** are a collection of subcortical neuronal groups in the forebrain located beneath the anterior portion of the lateral ventricles (see "How the Brain Works: The Chambers of the Mind," on p. 72). The basal ganglia have a significant role in the control of movement. The three main subdivisions are the globus pallidus, caudate nucleus, and putamen (Figure

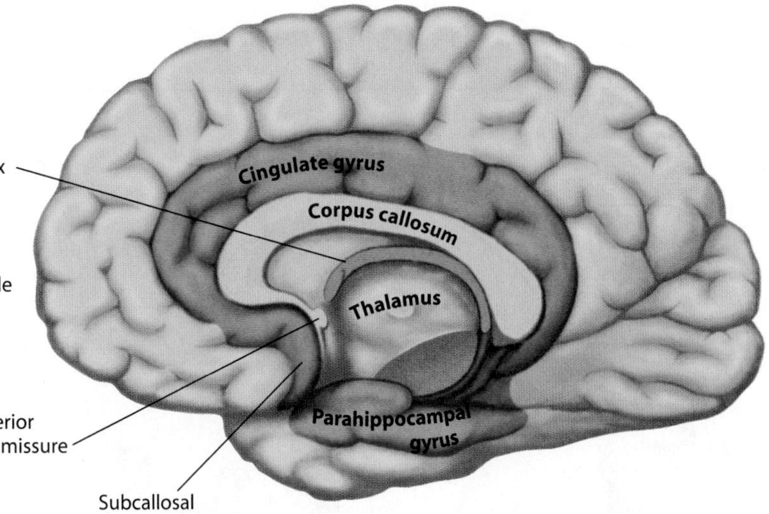

Figure 3.18 The limbic lobe as seen from a medial view of the right hemisphere. The structures that the limbic system comprises are in purple. These include the cingulate gyrus, the parahippocampal gyrus, and the subcallosal gyrus, as well as the dentate gyrus and hippocampal formation, which are not visible in this view.

3.20). The caudate and putamen are referred to together as the *neostriatum.*

Some anatomists have considered the amygdala and associated nuclei (amygdaloid complex) to be part of the basal ganglia, but this is not the convention agreed on by most neuroscientists today. The subthalamic nucleus and the substantia nigra are considered part of the basal ganglia because of their strong interconnectivity with the principal cell groups forming the basal ganglia. Yet these nuclei are quite distant from the rest of the basal ganglia. The substantia nigra is located in the midbrain—actually at the juncture of the midbrain and diencephalon—and the neostriatum and globus pallidus are in the forebrain. This gross anatomical distinction between the substantia nigra and the nuclear groups of the basal ganglia may not be

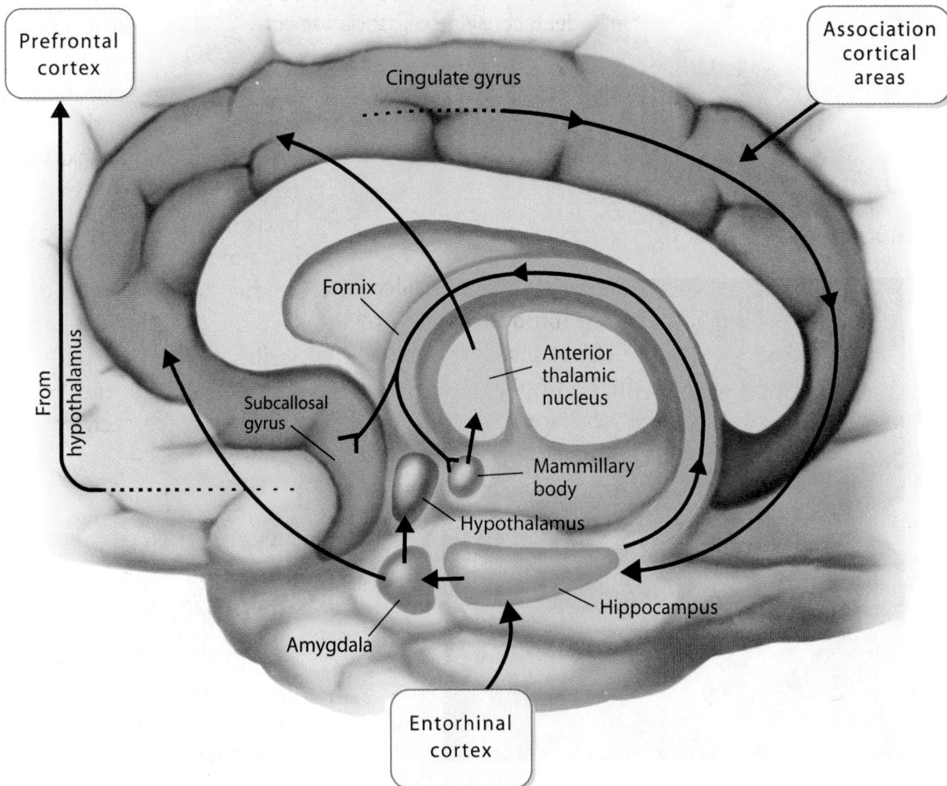

Figure 3.19 Major connections of the limbic system, shown diagrammatically in a medial view of the right hemisphere. The figure zooms in on the region in purple in Figure 3.18. The basal ganglia are not represented in this figure, nor is the medial dorsal nucleus of the thalamus. More detail is shown here than needs to be committed to memory, but this figure provides a reference that will come in handy in later chapters.

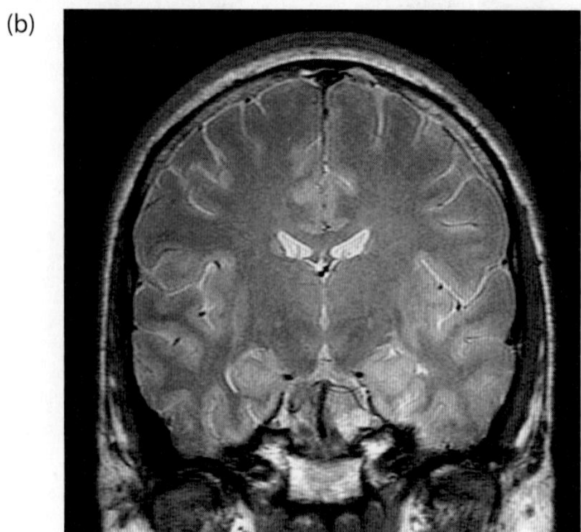

Figure 3.20 **(a)** Cross sections through the brain at two anterior–posterior levels (as indicated), showing the basal ganglia. **(b)** Corresponding high-resolution, structural MRI (4-tesla scanner) taken at approximately the same level as the more posterior drawing in (a). This image also shows the brainstem, as well as the skull and scalp, which are not shown in (a).

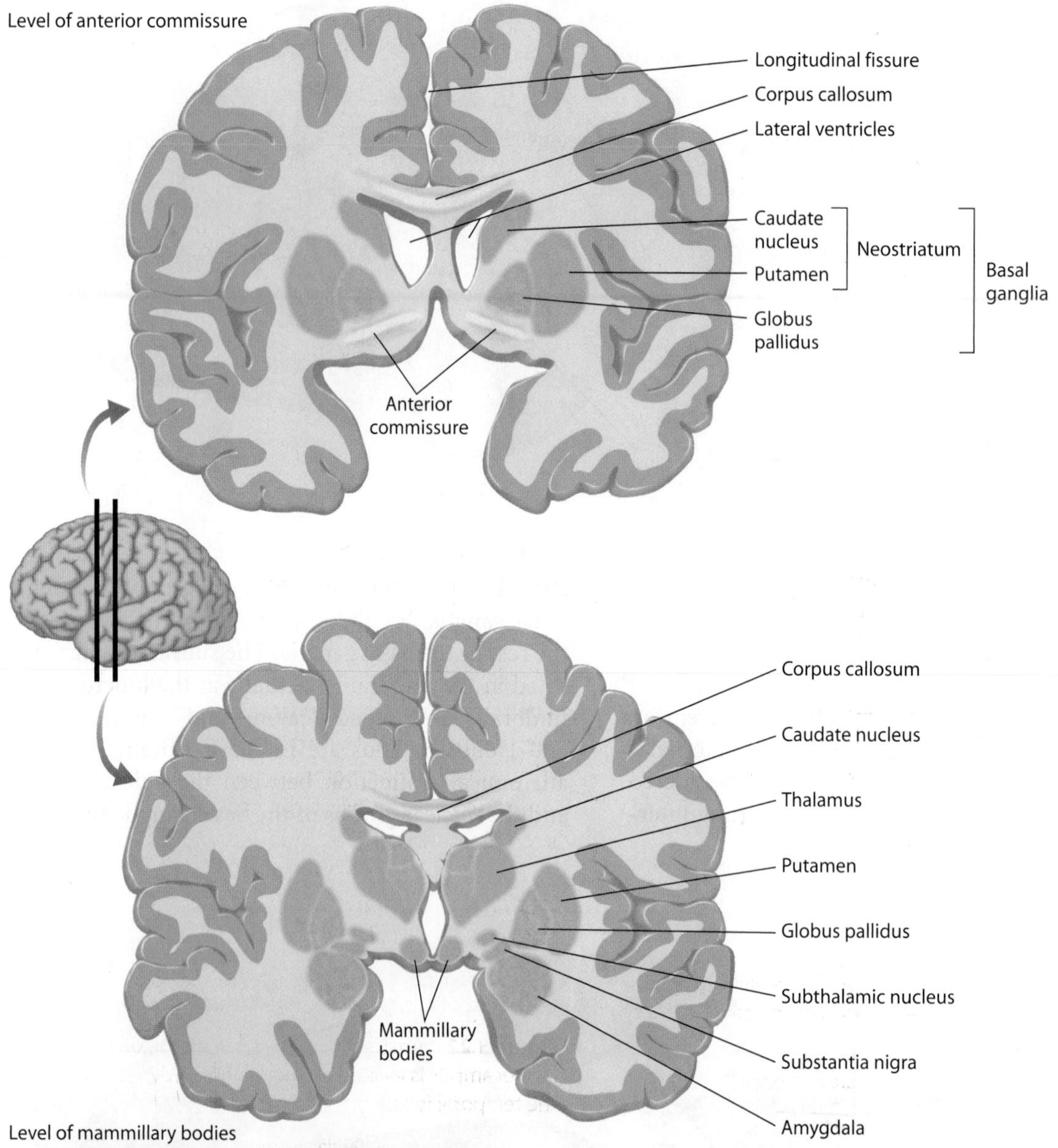

as important as the microanatomical (cellular) and functional relationships, however. We will return to this idea with respect to the basal ganglia in detail in Chapter 7.

The basal ganglia, subthalamic nucleus, and substantia nigra participate in circuits with the cortex and thalamus to mediate aspects of motor control (both somatic motor and oculomotor systems), as well as some cognitive functions.

The primary circuits projecting to the basal ganglia include a corticostriatal projection that contains direct projections from all major cortical regions onto neurons in the caudate and putamen, which are the input structures of the basal ganglia. In addition, motor areas of cortex can project to the basal ganglia via the cell groups in the thalamus and the subthalamic nucleus. The major outputs of the basal ganglia project from the globus pallidus to thalamic nuclei and then to cortex—primarily motor and premotor cortex, as well as prefrontal cortex (Figure 3.21). Thus, the basal ganglia are not in a projection pathway from motor cortical areas to the spinal cord, to control muscular activity directly, but instead are part of a cortical–subcortical motor loop that is thought to monitor aspects of how motor activity, as well as nonmotoric functions are progressing.

Figure 3.21 Major inputs and outputs of the basal ganglia. The basal ganglia form a cortical–subcortical motor loop that monitors motor behavior.

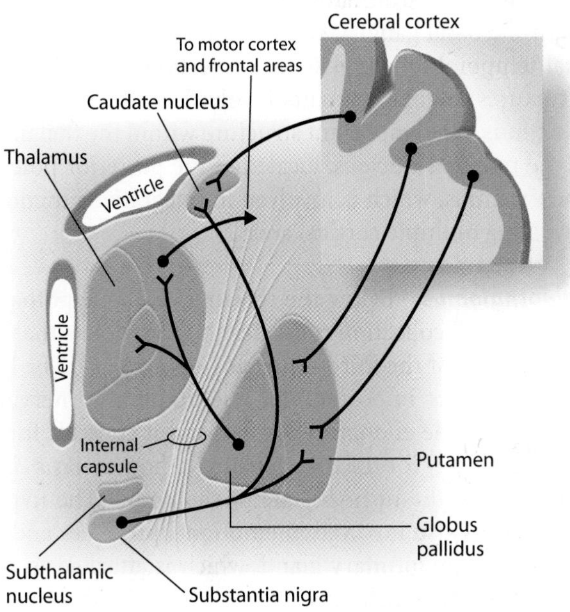

HIPPOCAMPAL FORMATION AND MEDIAL TEMPORAL LOBE

The region of the forebrain along the ventral medial surface of the temporal lobe contains the **hippocampus** and the associated areas of the dentate gyrus, parahippocampal gyrus, and entorhinal cortex—the latter being the anterior portion of the parahippocampal gyrus (BA28) (Figure 3.22). The hippocampus and dentate gyrus are composed of three- or four-layer cortex (archicortex), whereas entorhinal cortex and the parahippocampal gyrus in humans are composed of six-layer cortex (although it is mesocortex, not neocortex).

The hippocampus has been subdivided into zones referred to as the *CA fields* (*cornu ammonis* is Latin for "horn of Ammon"), which are divided into CA1, CA2, CA3, and CA4 based on differences in cellular morphology, connectivity, and development (Figure 3.23). As we will see in Chapter 8, the hippocampus plays a central role in memory or, to be more precise, learning.

DIENCEPHALON

The remaining portions of the forebrain to consider are the **thalamus** and **hypothalamus**, which together constitute the diencephalon. These subcortical nuclei are composed of groups of specialized cells with interconnections to widespread brain areas.

Thalamus Although its name is Greek for "inner chamber," the thalamus is not actually hollow. It lies at

Figure 3.22 Anatomy of the hippocampal formation. The hippocampus is located on the inferior and medial aspect of the temporal lobe.

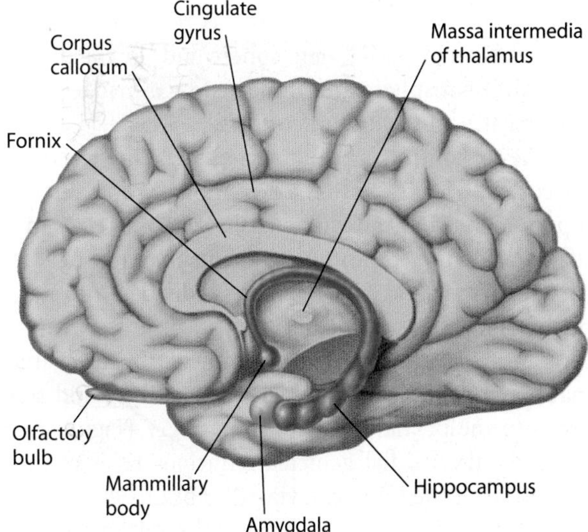

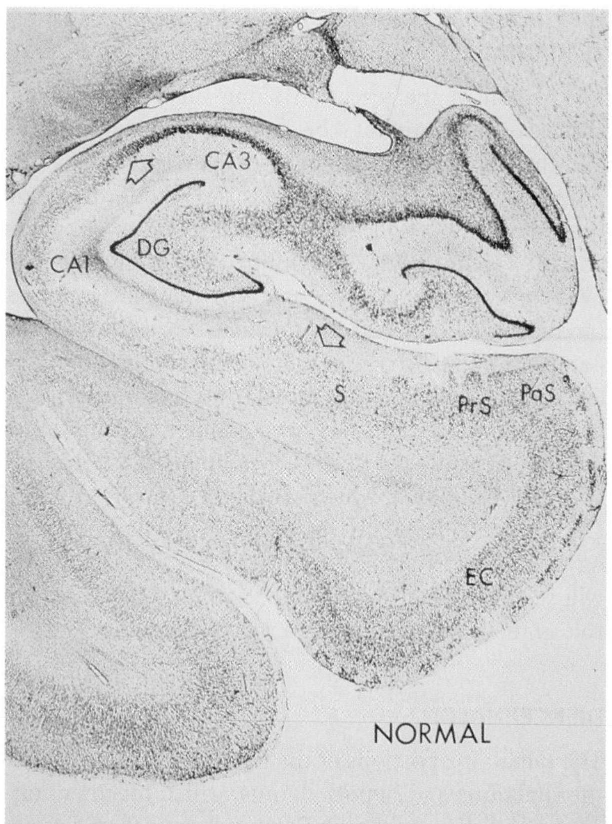

Figure 3.23 Histological slide of a cross section through the hippocampus. The dentate gyrus (DG), entorhinal cortex (EC), and subiculum (S) can be seen, as well as cells of CA fields. The presubiculum (PrS) and parasubiculum (PaS) are also labeled.

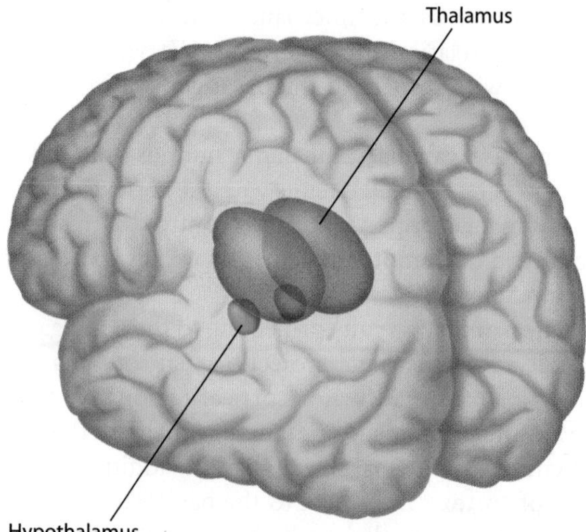

Figure 3.24 Gross anatomy of the thalamus. This diagram shows the thalamus of the left and right hemispheres in a see-through brain. The thalamus is egg shaped. It serves as the gateway to the cortex for the sensory systems and contains reciprocal loops with all cortical regions, organized according to subdivisions of the thalamus. The thalamus also is innervated by brainstem projection systems.

the most rostral end of the brainstem (Figure 3.24), in the dorsal part of the diencephalon in each hemisphere, and is bordered medially by the third ventricle, dorsally by the fornix and corpus callosum, and laterally by the internal capsule—the projection fibers from the motor cortex to the brainstem and spinal cord. In some people, the thalamus in the left hemisphere and the thalamus in the right hemisphere are connected by a bridge of gray matter called the *massa intermedia.*

The thalamus has been referred to as the "gateway to the cortex" because, with the exception of some olfactory inputs, all sensory modalities make synaptic relays in the thalamus before continuing to the primary cortical sensory receiving areas. The thalamus is divided into several nuclei that act as specific relays for incoming sensory information. The lateral geniculate nucleus receives information from the ganglion cells of the retina and sends axons to the primary visual cortex, BA17 (Figure 3.25). Similarly, the medial geniculate nucleus receives information from the inner ear, via other brainstem nuclei in the ascending auditory pathway, and sends axons to the primary auditory cortex (A1). Somatosensory information projects via the ventral posterior (medial and lateral) nuclei of the thalamus and then to primary somatosensory cortex in BA1, BA2, and BA3. Sensory relay nuclei of the thalamus not only project axons to the cortex but also receive heavy descending projections back from the same cortical area that they contact.

Not only is the thalamus involved in relaying primary sensory information, but also it receives inputs from the basal ganglia, cerebellum, neocortex, and medial temporal lobe and sends projections back to these structures to create circuits involved in many different functions. One important structure within the thalamus is the pulvinar nucleus, located at the posterior pole of the thalamus, which is involved in integrative functions involving multiple cortical areas.

Hypothalamus Below the thalamus is the hypothalamus, a small collection of nuclei and fiber tracts that lie on the floor of the third ventricle (Figure 3.26). The hypothalamus is important for the autonomic nervous system and the endocrine system, and it controls functions necessary for the maintenance of homeostasis (i.e., maintaining the normal state of the body). The hypothalamus is also involved in emotional processes and in control of the pituitary gland, which is attached to the base of the hypothalamus.

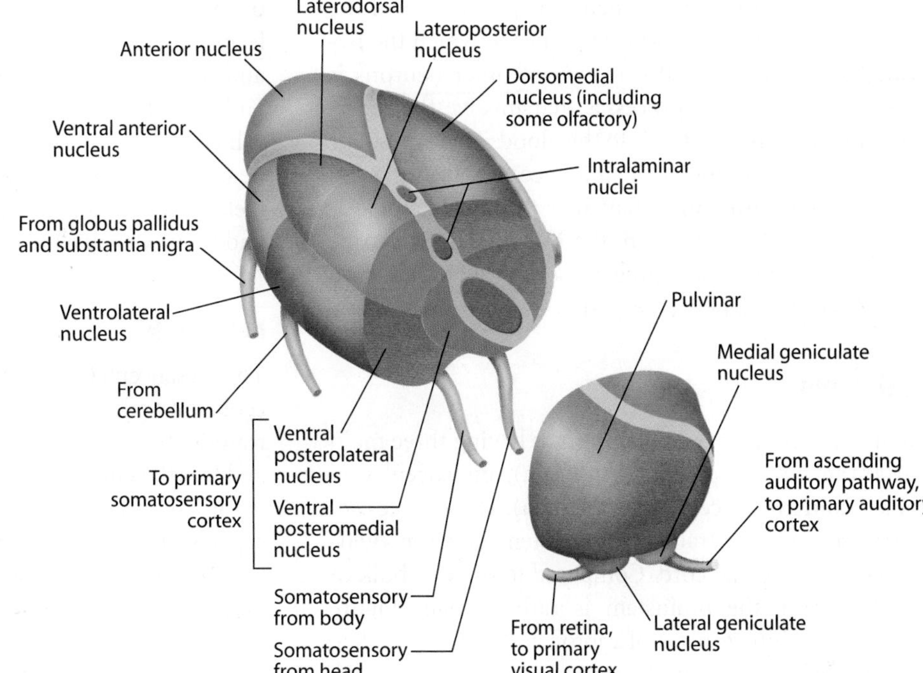

Figure 3.25 The left thalamus, showing inputs and outputs and major subdivisions. The various subdivisions of the thalamus serve different sensory systems and participate in various cortical–subcortical circuits. The posterior portion of the thalamus **(lower right)** is cut away in cross section and separated from the rest of the thalamus to reveal the internal organization of the thalamic nuclei **(upper left)**.

Figure 3.26 Midsagittal view of the hypothalamus. Various nuclear groups are shown diagrammatically. The hypothalamus is the floor of the third ventricle, and, as the name suggests, it sits below the thalamus. Anterior is to the left in this drawing.

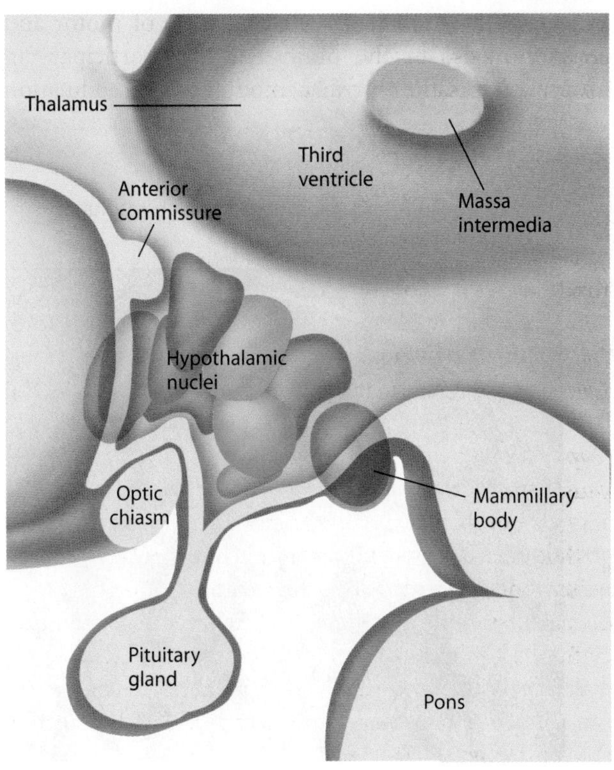

The hormones produced by the hypothalamus control much of the endocrine system. For example, hypothalamic neurons in the region that surrounds the third ventricle send axonal projections to an area at the border of the hypothalamus and pituitary gland—the median eminence—where releasing factors (e.g., peptides) are released into the system that provides circulation to the anterior pituitary gland. In the anterior pituitary, these hypothalamic peptides trigger (or inhibit) the release of a variety of hormones into the bloodstream; growth hormone, thyroid-stimulating hormone, adrenocorticotropic hormone, and the gonadotropic hormones are examples of those released by the cells of the anterior pituitary under hypothalamic control. Hypothalamic neurons in the anteromedial region, including the supraoptic nucleus and paraventricular nuclei, send axonal projections into the posterior pituitary, where they stimulate the posterior pituitary to release the hormones vasopressin and oxytocin into the blood to regulate water retention in the kidneys, and milk production and uterine contractility, respectively. The hypothalamus receives inputs not only from the limbic cortex but also from other brain areas, including the mesencephalic reticular formation, amygdala, and the retina, to control circadian rhythms (light–dark cycles). Projections from the hypothalamus include a major projection to the prefrontal cortex, amygdala, and spinal cord. One of the most prominent projections is the one to the pituitary.

In addition to the direct neuronal projections of the hypothalamus, one important manner in which the hypothalamus influences the activity of other neurons is via neuromodulatory processes that involve the secretion of peptide hormones into the blood. These circulating peptide hormones can influence a wide range of behaviors by acting on distant sites through the bloodstream. In a similar fashion, the hypothalamus can be affected by hormones circulating in the blood, and thereby produce a neural response.

Brainstem

We usually think of the **brainstem** as having three main parts: the mesencephalon (midbrain), metencephalon (pons), and myelencephalon (medulla). These three sections form the central nervous system between diencephalon and spinal cord. Compared to the vast bulk of the forebrain, the brainstem is rather small (Figure 3.27). It contains groups of motor and sensory nuclei, nuclei of widespread modulatory neurotransmitter systems, and white matter tracts of ascending sensory information and descending motor signals.

The organization becomes more complex as it proceeds from the spinal cord through the medulla, pons, and midbrain to the diencephalon and cerebral cortex. This neuronal complexity reflects the increasingly complex behaviors that these regions enable. However, this does not mean that the brainstem is unimportant or simplistic in its processing, nor does it signify that the brainstem's functions are ancillary. Indeed, damage to the brainstem is highly life threatening, in part because of the brainstem's size—being small means that a small lesion encompasses a large percentage of the tissue—and also because brainstem nuclei control respiration and even states of consciousness such as sleep and wakefulness. Therefore, damage to the brainstem can often be fatal, whereas damage to the cerebral cortex may have (relatively) minor consequences, depending on where and how extensive the cortical damage is.

MIDBRAIN

The mesencephalon, or **midbrain**, lies caudal to the diencephalon and is bounded posteriorly by the pons. It surrounds the cerebral aqueduct, which connects the third and fourth ventricles and consists of the *tectum* (meaning "roof," representing the dorsal portion of the mesencephalon), *tegmentum* (the main portion of the midbrain), and ventral regions occupied by large fiber tracts (*crus cerebri*) from the forebrain to the spinal cord (corticospinal tract), cerebellum, and brainstem (corticobulbar tract). The midbrain contains neurons that participate in visuomotor functions (e.g., superior colliculus, oculomotor nucleus, trochlear nucleus), visual reflexes (e.g., pretectal region), and auditory relays (inferior colliculus); and the mesencephalic tegmental nuclei involved in motor coordination (red nucleus) (Figure 3.28).

Much of the midbrain is occupied by the mesencephalic reticular formation, a rostral continuation of the pontine and medullary reticular formation. The reticular formation is best seen as a set of motor and sensory nuclei in the brainstem that participate in arousal, respiration, cardiac modulations, modulation

Figure 3.27 **(a)** Midsagittal section through the head, showing the brainstem, cerebellum, and spinal cord. **(b)** High-resolution structural MRI obtained with a 4-tesla scanner, showing the same plane of section as in (a).

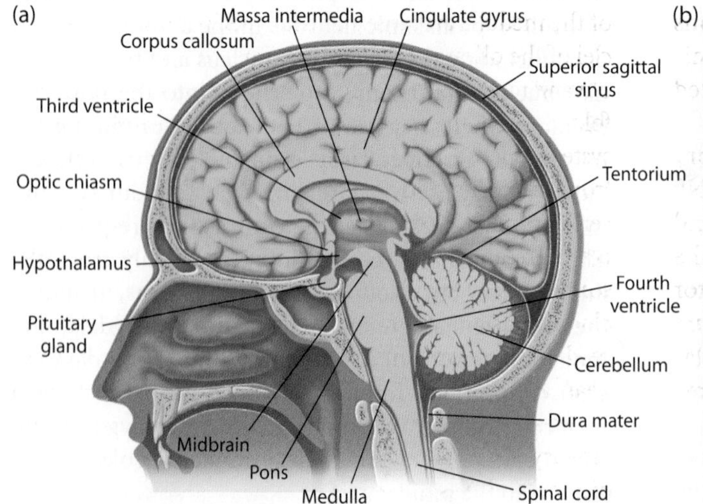

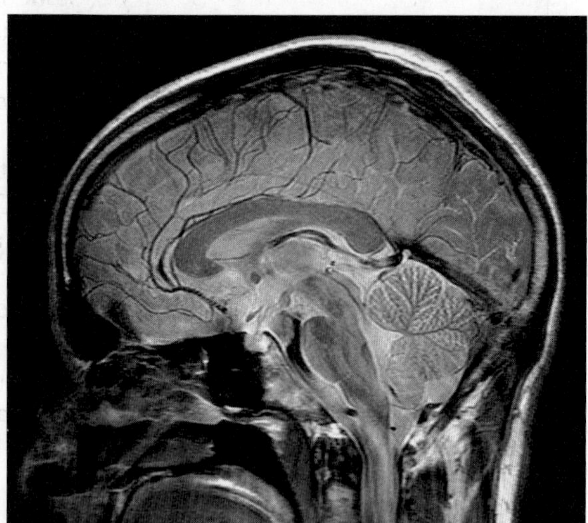

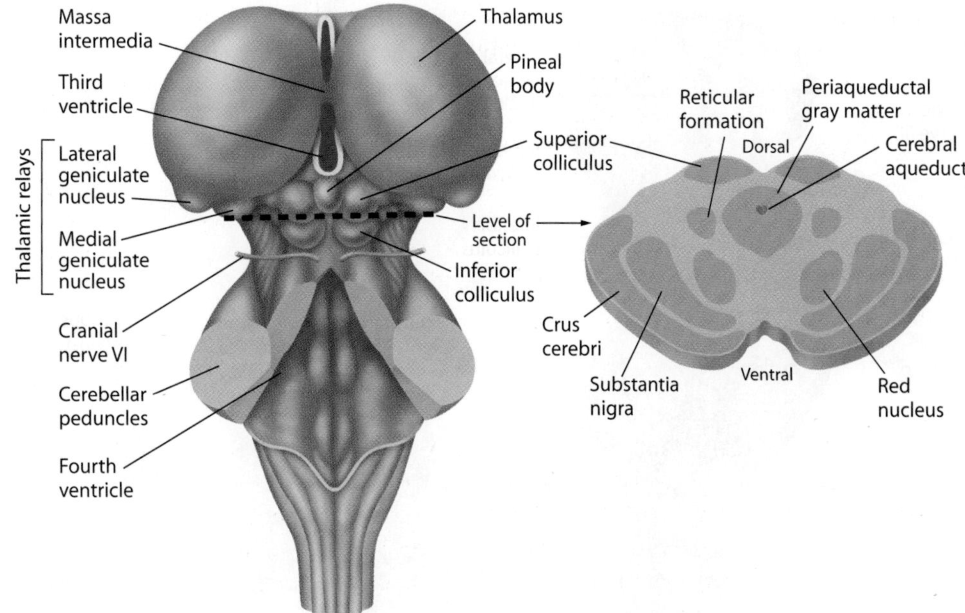

Figure 3.28 Anatomy of the midbrain. The dorsal surface of the brainstem is shown with the cerebral cortex and cerebellum removed. Cross section is through the midbrain at the level of the superior colliculus, the subcortical visuomotor nuclei.

of reflex muscular activity at the segmental level (i.e., in the limbs), and pain regulation.

PONS AND MEDULLA

The last areas of the brainstem to consider are the metencephalon (pons) and myelencephalon (medulla). Together they form the hindbrain. The **pons** includes the pontine tegmental regions on the floor of the fourth ventricle, and the pons itself, a vast system of fiber tracts interspersed with pontine nuclei. The fibers are continuations of the cortical projections to the spinal cord, brainstem, and cerebellar regions; initially they are compact fiber tracts on the ventral surface of the midbrain. At the pons, they explode into smaller tracts that continue to their final destinations as they course around the pontine nuclei, some terminating on neurons in this region (the pons is labeled in Figure 3.27a).

The many nuclei at the pontine level have auditory and vestibular (balance) functions; primary CNS synapses of axons coming from the auditory and vestibular periphery are located in cell groups of the pontine tegmentum. In addition, sensory and motor nuclei from the face and mouth are located here, as are visuomotor nuclei controlling some of the extraocular muscles. This level of the brainstem also contains a large portion of the reticular formation.

Finally, the brain's most caudal portion is the **medulla**, which is continuous with the spinal cord. The medulla has two prominent bilateral nuclear groups on the ventral surface (the gracile and cuneate nuclei) that are the primary relay nuclei for ascending somatosensory information entering the spinal cord. These projection systems continue through the brainstem to synapse in the thalamus en route to the somatosensory cortex. On the ventral surface of the medulla the continuations of the corticospinal motor projections are grouped once again as tight bundles of nerve fibers into the *pyramids*, bilateral bumps on the ventral medulla.

At the level of the medulla these motor axons to the spinal cord cross (forming the pyramidal decussation) in order to project to the contralateral side of the spinal cord; that is, for example, the right-hemisphere motor systems control the left side of the body. At the rostral end of the medulla are large and characteristically formed nuclei of the olivary complex (inferior and medial accessory olivary nuclei). They appear in cross section as highly folded nuclei that are part of the corticocerebellar motor system (Figure 3.29). The olivary nuclei receive inputs from the cortex and red nucleus and project them to the cerebellum. Sensory nuclei that carry out vestibular processing (caudal portions of the vestibular nuclei) and some sensory inputs from the face, mouth, throat (including taste), and abdomen are in the medulla. The medulla also contains motor nuclei that innervate the heart and muscles of the neck, tongue, and throat.

In sum, the brainstem's neurons carry out numerous sensory and motor processes, especially visuomotor, auditory, and vestibular functions, and sensation and

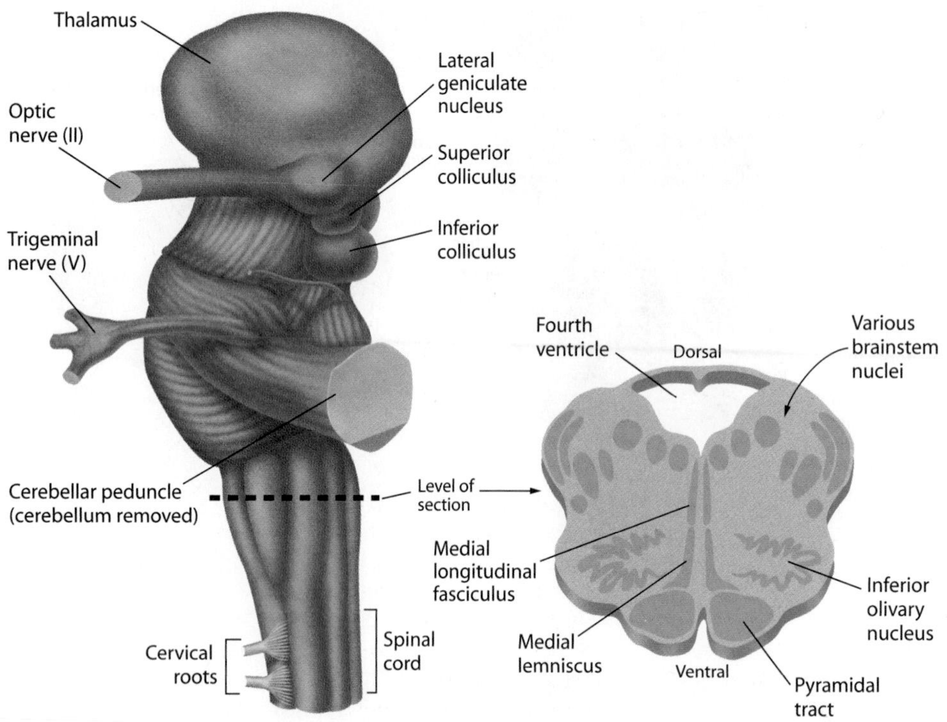

Figure 3.29 Lateral view of the brainstem showing the midbrain, medulla, and spinal cord. Section is through the medulla at the level of the inferior olivary nucleus.

motor control of the face, mouth, throat, respiratory system, and heart. The brainstem houses fibers that pass from the cortex to the spinal cord and cerebellum, and sensory fibers from spinal levels to the thalamus and then the cortex. Many neurochemical systems have nuclei in the brainstem that project widely to the cerebral cortex, limbic system, thalamus, and hypothalamus.

Cerebellum

The **cerebellum** (literally "small cerebrum" or "little brain") is actually a very large neuronal structure overlying the brainstem at the level of the pons (see Figure 3.27). It forms the roof of the fourth ventricle and sits on the cerebellar *peduncles* (meaning "feet"), which are massive input and output fiber tracts of the cerebellum (Figure 3.29, left). The cerebellum has several gross subdivisions, including the cerebellar cortex, the four pairs of deep nuclei, and the internal white matter (Figure 3.30). In this way the cerebellum resembles the forebrain's cerebral hemispheres. The cerebellum is packed with cells; current estimates suggest that the cerebellum contains as many neurons as the rest of the central nervous system combined—about 11 billion!

Although some inputs to the cerebellum terminate in the deep nuclei, the majority of the fibers project to the cerebellar cortex. These inputs come from the parts of the brain that participate in motor and sensory processing; hence, they convey information about motor outputs and about sensory inputs describing body position. Inputs from vestibular projections involved in balance, as well as auditory and visual inputs, also project to the cerebellum from the brainstem. The output from the cerebellum originates in the deep nuclei. Ascending

Figure 3.30 Gross anatomy of the cerebellum. Anterior in the brain is at the top, and the spinal cord is toward the bottom (not shown). This dorsal view of the cerebellum shows the underlying deep nuclei in a see-through projection.

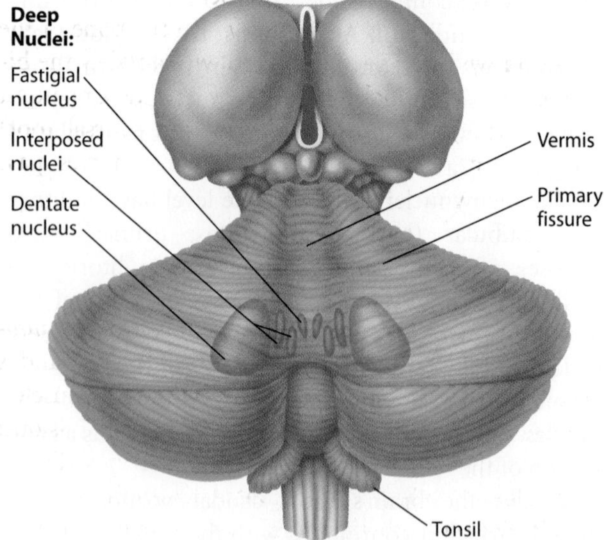

outputs ascend to the thalamus and then to the motor and premotor cortex. Other outputs project to nuclei of the brainstem and are in a position to influence descending projections to the spinal cord. The cerebellum is key to maintaining posture, walking, and performing coordinated movements. By itself, the cerebellum does not control movements directly; instead it integrates information about the body and motor commands and modifies motor outflow to effect smooth, coordinated movements. The cerebellum's role in motor control is given more attention in Chapter 7.

Spinal Cord

The last neural portion of the CNS to review is the spinal cord, which runs from the medulla to its termination in the *cauda equina* (meaning "horse's tail") at the base of the spine. The spinal cord primarily conducts the final motor signals to muscles; it also takes in sensory information from the body's peripheral sensory receptors and relays it to the brain. In addition, at each level of the spinal cord, reflex pathways exist, as, for example, that for the knee jerk reflex. The gross anatomy of the spinal cord is simple: It consists of white matter tracts carrying sensory and motor information (plus intraspinal projection fibers), and neuronal cell bodies organized in a more central gray matter (Figure 3.31). These include motor neurons, interneurons, and sensory neurons. The gray matter, when viewed in cross section, resembles a butterfly, with two separate sections, or horns, called *dorsal* and *ventral* horns. The ventral horn contains the large motor neurons that project to muscles; the dorsal horn contains sensory neurons and interneurons. The latter project to motor neurons on the same and opposite sides of the spinal cord to aid in the coordination of limb movements.

The spinal cord is protected within the bone of the spine, but with the spine removed, we can view the bilateral pairs of spinal nerves that carry motor output (ventral root) and sensory information (dorsal root) into and out of the spinal cord. These nerves pass through small gaps in the spine.

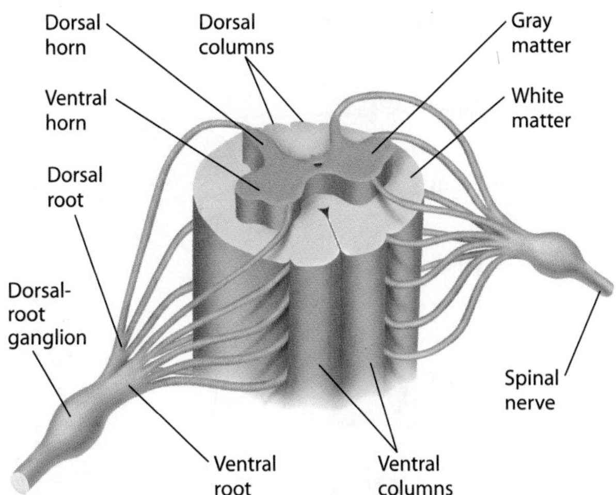

Figure 3.31 Gross anatomy of the spinal cord. This cross-sectional and three-dimensional representation of the spinal cord shows the central butterfly-shaped gray matter, which contains neurons, and the surrounding white matter tracts, which convey information down the spinal cord from the brain to neurons in the cord and up the spinal cord from peripheral receptors to the brain. The dorsal and ventral nerve roots are shown exiting and entering the cord; they fuse to form peripheral nerves. The cell bodies of peripheral sensory inputs reside in the dorsal-root ganglion and project their axons into the central nervous system via the dorsal root. The ventral horn of the spinal cord houses motor neurons that project their axons out the ventral roots to innervate peripheral muscles.

Autonomic Nervous System

The **autonomic nervous system** (also called the *autonomic*, or *visceral, motor system*) is part of the PNS and is involved in controlling the action of smooth muscles, the heart, and various glands. It has two subdivisions: the *sympathetic* and *parasympathetic* branches (Figure 3.32). These two systems innervate smooth muscles and glands. The sympathetic system uses the neurotransmitter norepinephrine, and the parasympathetic system uses acetylcholine as the transmitter. The two systems frequently operate in an antagonistic manner. For example, activation of the sympathetic system increases heart rate, diverts blood from the digestive tract to the somatic musculature, and prepares the body for action (fight or flight) by stimulating the adrenal glands to release adrenaline. In contrast, activation of the parasympathetic system slows heart rate, stimulates digestion, and in general helps the body with normal functions germane to maintaining the body.

There is a great deal of specialization in the autonomic system that is beyond the scope of this chapter, but understanding that the autonomic system is involved in a variety of reflex and involuntary behaviors is useful for interpreting information presented later in the book. In Chapter 9 we will discuss arousal of the autonomic nervous system and the way in which changes in a number of psychophysiological measures tap into emotion-related changes in the autonomic nervous system. One example is the change in skin conductance that is related to sweat gland activity; sweat glands are under the control of the autonomic nervous system.

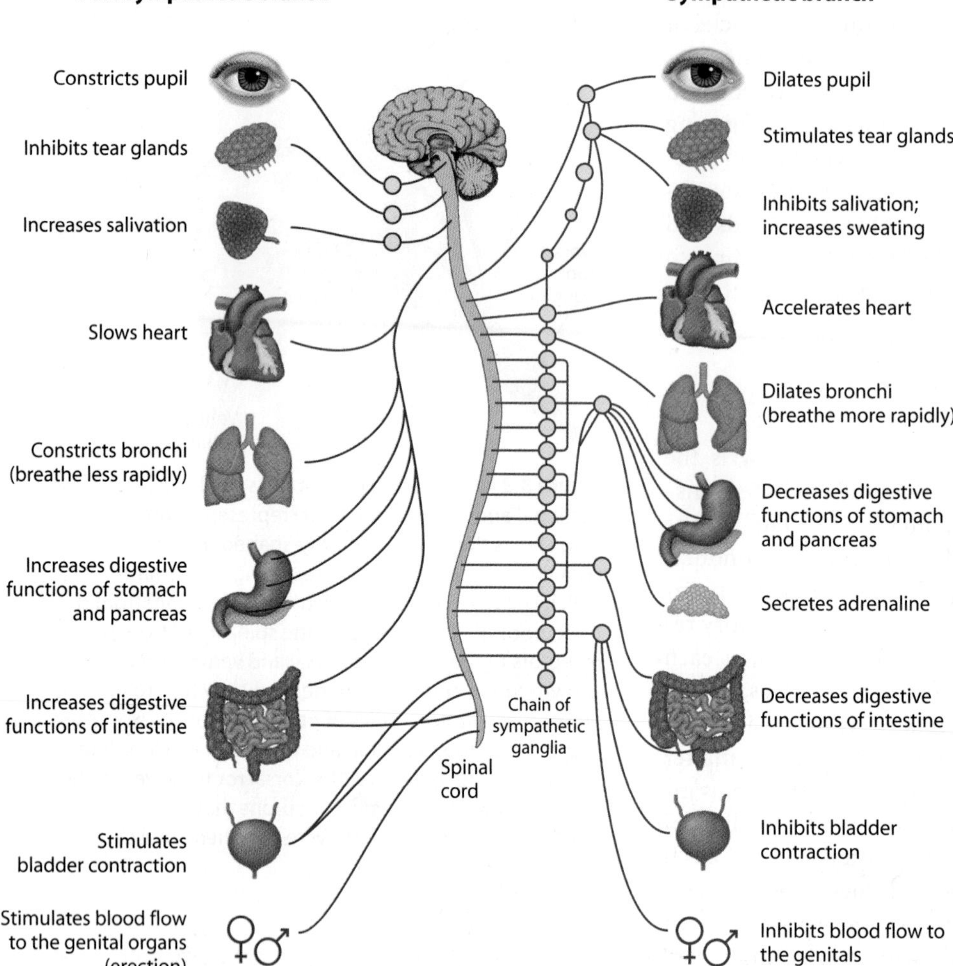

Figure 3.32 Organization of the autonomic nervous system, showing sympathetic and parasympathetic branches.

DEVELOPMENT OF THE NERVOUS SYSTEM

Thus far we have been discussing the neuroanatomy of the developed adult brain. In humans and many other species, the fetal brain is well developed and shows cortical layers, neuronal connectivity, and myelination; in short, it is already extremely complex. To find out how this complex brain develops prenatally and to uncover the rules governing development, let's examine the development of the nervous system with special reference to the neocortex.

Animal models, such as the rhesus monkey, have permitted a close look at how neurons in the cortex achieve their final connectivity with each other and other brain systems. The monkey has a large cortex and well-developed perceptual and motor skills. Although the human brain is larger in volume and has a larger proportion of association cortex than most other mammals have (Figure 3.33 on p. 90), other animals have provided data important for determining the mechanisms of cortical development, which we would not be able to discover by observing only humans. In recent decades, a wealth of information has been derived about the cellular, biochemical, and hormonal influences on the genesis of the cerebral cortex. New and sophisticated methods permit us to do more than merely observe the changes in the developing brain. They provide us with the chance to manipulate the course of development in ways that inform us about the underlying processes. For example, anatomists have developed tracers that target developing cells and can apply genetic manipulations to observe resultant changes in neurodevelopment.

Overview of Gross Development

From a single fertilized egg, an organism of billions of cells with specialized functions will arise. This complexity

HOW THE BRAIN WORKS

Blood Supply and the Brain

Approximately 20% of the blood flowing from the heart is pumped to the brain. A constant flow of blood is necessary because the brain has no way of storing glucose or extracting energy without oxygen. Disruption in the flow of oxygenated blood to the brain lasting only a few minutes can produce unconsciousness and, finally, death. Two sets of arteries bring blood to the brain: the vertebral artery, which supplies blood to the caudal portion of the brain, and the internal carotid artery, which supplies blood to the rostral portions. Although the major arteries sometimes join together and then separate again, there is actually little mixing of blood from the rostral and caudal arterial supplies or from the right and left sides of the rostral portion of the brain. As a safety measure, in the event of a blockage or ischemic attack, blood should be rerouted to reduce the probability of loss of blood supply, but in practice this backup system is relatively poor.

The blood flow in the brain is tightly coupled with metabolic demand of the local neurons. Hence, increases in neuronal activity lead to a coupled increase in regional cerebral blood flow. The increased blood flow is not primarily for increasing the delivery of oxygen and glucose to the active tissue, but rather to hasten the removal of the resultant metabolic by-products of the increased neuronal activity. The precise mechanisms, however, remain hotly debated. These local changes in blood flow permit regional cerebral blood flow to be used as a measure of local changes in neuronal activity. This is the principle on which some types of functional neuroimaging are based. Particular examples are positron emission tomography using techniques such as the ^{15}O-water method, and functional magnetic resonance imaging, which is sensitive to changes in the concentration of oxygenated versus deoxygenated blood in the region of active tissue.

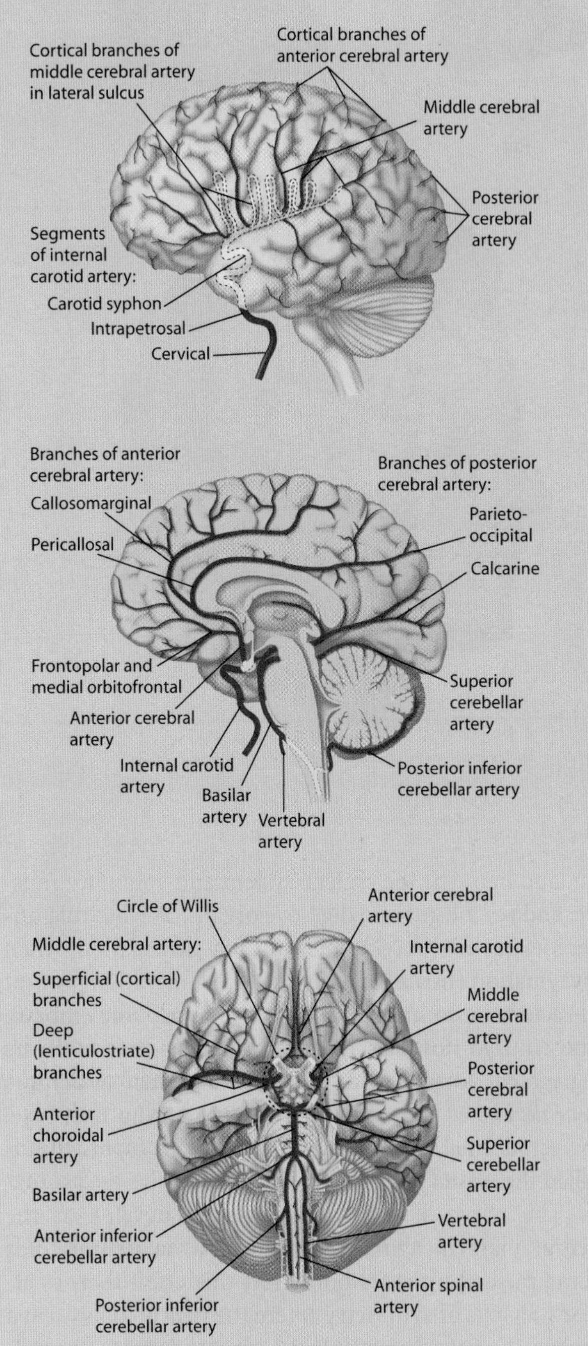

clearly peaks in the nervous system. Figure 3.34 on p. 91 depicts a few stages of human development between fertilization and birth. Following fertilization, events lead to the multicellular *blastula* that has already begun to specialize. The blastula contains three main types of cell lines: the **ectoderm**, the *mesoderm*, and the *endoderm*. In a broad sense, these cell lines form, respectively, (a) the nervous system and the outer skin, lens of the eye, inner

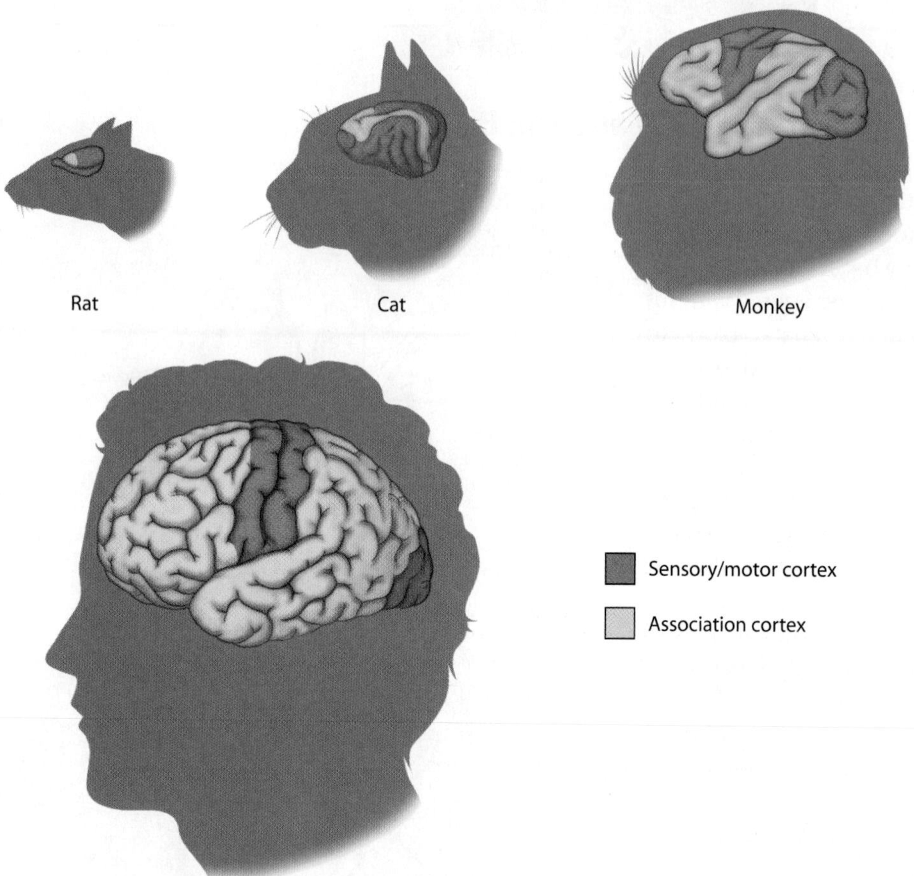

Figure 3.33 As mammalian evolutionary development progresses from rat to cat to monkey to human, the brain (especially the neocortex) increases in size, association cortex is expanded, and fissures are more prevalent, allowing for greater cortical surface.

ear, and hair; (b) the skeletal system and voluntary muscle; and (c) the gut and digestive organs. The blastula undergoes further development during gastrulation, when invagination (tissue infolding) and cell migration prompt the ectoderm to surround the entire developing embryo. The embryo now has mesoderm and endoderm layers segregated dorsally and ventrally, and then undergoes *neurulation*, as shown in Figure 3.35. During this stage, the ectodermal cells on the dorsal surface form what is called the *neural plate*.

The nervous system continues to develop as the neural plate invaginates, or infolds, via neural folds being pushed up at its border. At this point there is already an axis of symmetry where the neural folds form a groove, the *neural groove*. As this groove deepens, the cells of the neural fold region eventually meet and fuse, forming the *neural tube* that runs anteriorly and posteriorly along the embryo. The adjacent nonneural ectoderm then reunites to seal the neural tube within an ectodermal covering that surrounds the embryo. At both ends of the neural tube are openings (the anterior and the posterior neuropores) that eventually close. When the anterior neuropore is sealed, this cavity forms the primitive brain, consisting of three spaces, or ventricles (Figure 3.36a, top, on p. 92). From this stage on, the brain's gross features are formed by growth and flexion (bending) of the neural tube's anterior portions (Figure 3.36a, bottom). The result is a cerebral cortex that envelops the subcortical and brainstem structures. The final three-dimensional relations of the brain's structures are the product of continued cortical enlargement and folding. One interesting feature of the flexions during fetal development is that, at these early stages, there is a striking similarity between fetuses of humans and those of other mammals (Figure 3.36b).

Genesis of the Cerebral Cortex

Let's consider the mechanisms underlying the brain's growth and connectional specificity: **neuronal proliferation, neuronal migration, neuronal determination and differentiation, synaptogenesis,** and **synapse elimination.** Decades of careful studies in animals and

(a)

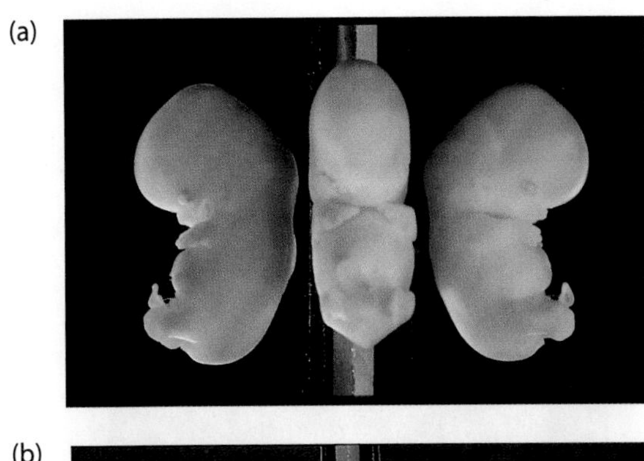

(b)

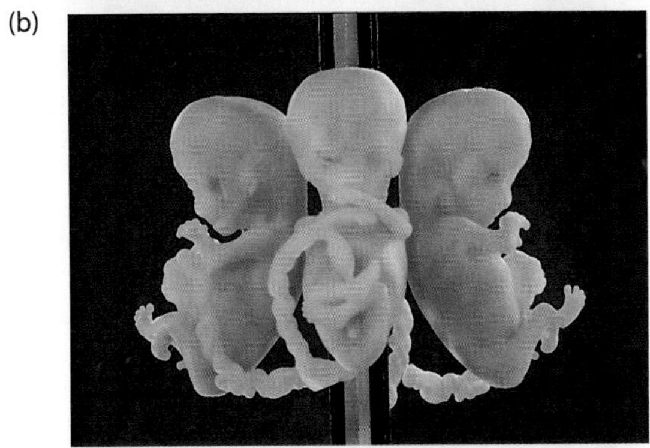

(c)

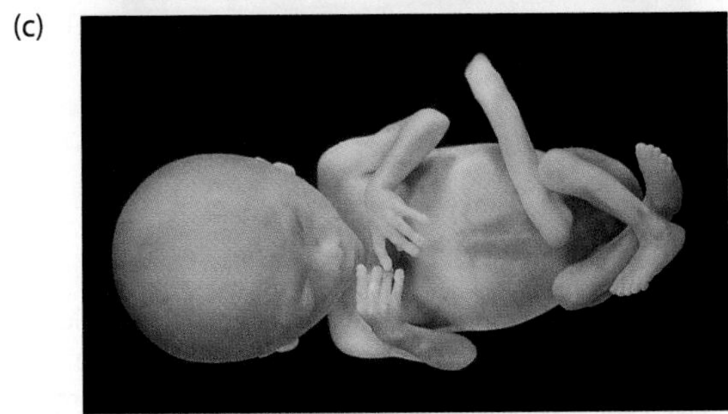

Figure 3.34 Developing human fetus at 7 weeks **(a)**, 9 weeks **(b)**, and 7 months **(c)**.

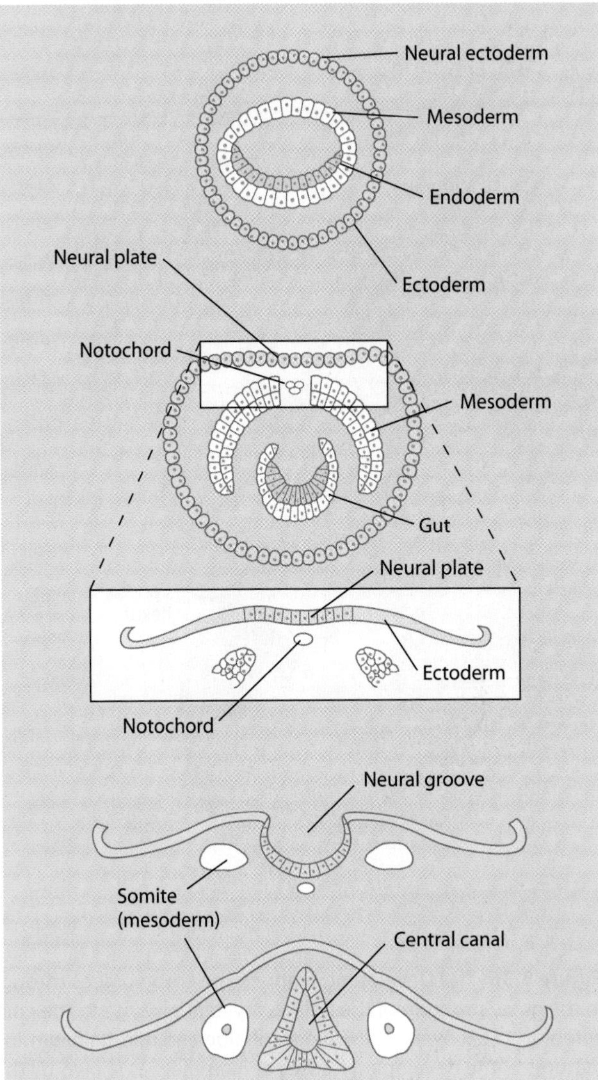

Figure 3.35 Development of the vertebrate nervous system. Cross sections through the blastula and embryo at various developmental stages during the first 21 days of life. Early in embryogenesis, the multicellular blastula **(top)** contains cells destined to form various body tissues. Migration and specialization of different cell lines leads to formation of the primitive nervous system around the neural groove and neural tube on the dorsal surface of the embryo. The brain is located at the anterior end of the embryo and is not shown in these more posterior sections, which are taken at the level of the spinal cord.

humans have provided a relatively detailed understanding of the sequence of these cellular events as they take place on the path to building a mammalian brain.

NEURONAL PROLIFERATION

The first question about the brain's development is this: When in the course of prenatal and postnatal development are neurons in the brain "born"? Examination of the brains of newborn monkeys or humans reveals that virtually the entire adult pattern of gross and cellular anatomical features is present at birth. Although axonal myelination continues for some period postnatally (e.g., until adulthood in the human frontal lobe), the newborn has a well-developed cortex that includes the cortical layers and areas characterized in adults. BA17 (the primary visual cortex) can be distinguished from the motor cortex by cytoarchitectonic analysis of its neuronal makeup. Indeed, in primates there is little generation of neurons after birth; almost all neurons are generated prenatally (but see the section titled "Birth of New Neurons Throughout Life" later in this chapter). So

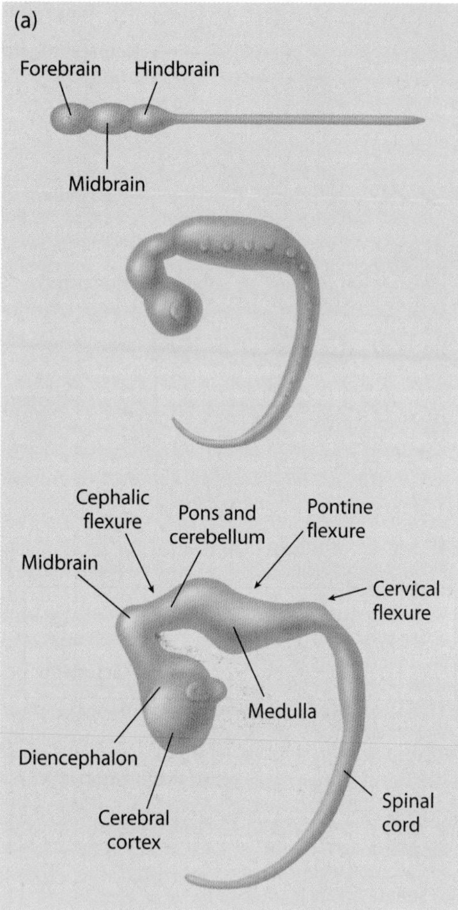

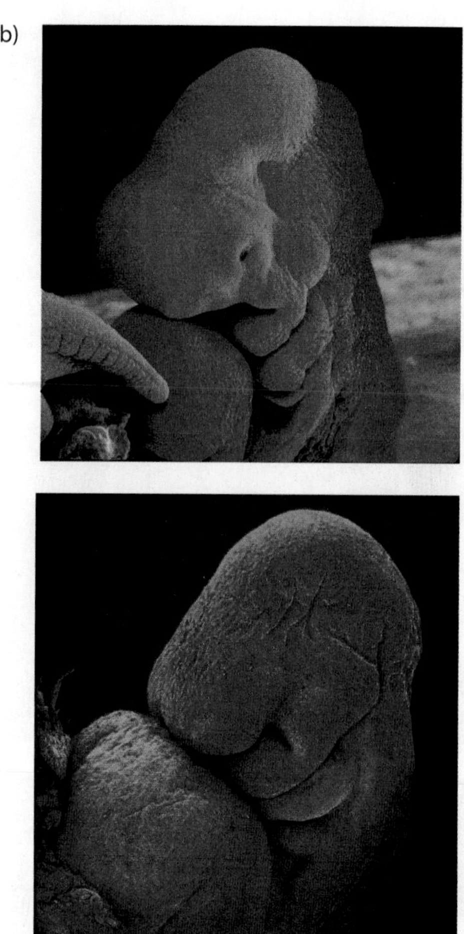

Figure 3.36 (a) Developing embryo. The embryo goes through a series of folds, or flexures, during development. These alterations in the gross structure of the nervous system give rise to the compact organization of the adult brain and brainstem in which the cerebral cortex overlays the diencephalon and midbrain within the human skull. **(b)** There is significant similarity between the gross features of the developing fetuses of mammals, as shown by this comparison of human **(top)** and pig **(bottom)** fetuses.

the question can be refined like this: When during development can specific types of neurons be identified?

The timeline of neuronal development in nonhuman primates has been tracked by clever cell-labeling methods. The classic anatomical methods are unable to provide this information; by merely staining sections of cortex and observing the neurons present during embryogenesis, we cannot accurately determine which neurons arose first. However, some methods can track cells that are undergoing replication. In *3H-thymidine labeling*, radioactively labeled thymidine is injected into an embryo early in development. The thymidine is taken up by neurons and is used to label DNA in cells undergoing cell division. Because the thymidine is labeled with a radioactive tag, the DNA of only the cells undergoing division at the time of injection will contain the radioactive label; hence, the label's distribution in the brain tissue can permit us to identify the final fate of the neurons born at the time of injection (Figure 3.37). An *autoradiographic* method is used to determine the distribution of these cells. Sections of brain tissue are placed against photosensitive film, and the radiation exposes the film, creating an image that can be developed and viewed as a picture. The resultant picture shows the distribution within the brain section that contains the ^{3}H-thymidine label, and therefore the cells that were born at injection time.

These cell-labeling studies using embryonic tissue make possible a clear view of **corticogenesis**. The genesis of the cerebral cortex in primates begins during the first quarter of gestation and continues for several months. For instance, the production of the neurons of

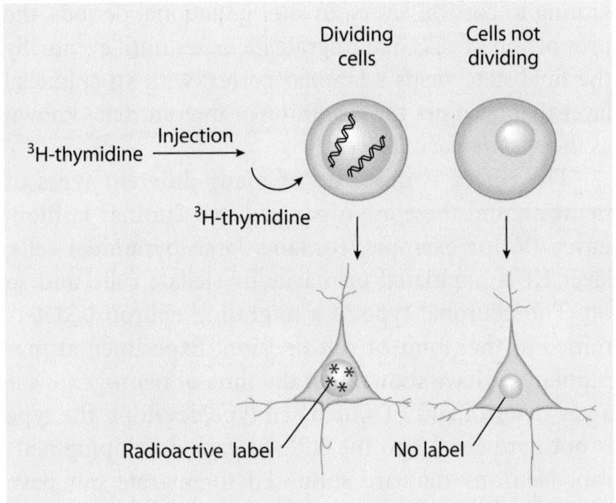

Figure 3.37 ^{3}H-thymidine method used to determine the fate of neurons that arise at a particular time in prenatal development. ^{3}H-thymidine is incorporated into dividing cells and remains within the cell body. The radioactive label can be viewed in the mature neurons and, because the investigator knows when the injection was made, can be used to trace when the neurons arose during development.

BA17 (striate cortex) is not finished until long after the neurons in the other brain areas have been born. Nevertheless, in primates the middle third of the gestational period accounts for the production of all cortical neurons present at birth. The same timeline does not apply to other mammalian species. In mice and rats, for example, all cortical neurons arise during 1 week of the last third of gestation, and in other species neuronal genesis may continue until after birth.

NEURONAL MIGRATION

The neurons that form the cortex arise from a layer of cells located adjacent to the ventricles of the developing brain. This layer, known as the *ventricular zone*, has cells that divide to form cortical neurons. Figure 3.38 shows a cross section through the cortex and the precursor cell layers at various times during gestation. **Precursor cells** are undifferentiated cells from which neurons or glial cells are produced; those for neurons and glial cells coexist in the ventricular zone. After these cells undergo mitosis, they migrate outward from the ventricular zone by moving along a peculiar cell known as the **radial glial cell** and described by Ramón y Cajal at the end of the 19th century (see Chapter 1). These cells stretch from the ventricular zone to the surface of the developing cortex. The work of radial glial cells does not end with development. These cells are transformed into astrocytes in the adult brain, helping to form part of the blood–brain barrier.

The migrating neuron remains in contact with the framework provided by the radial glial cell via interactions of cell surface molecules that keep the two cells intimately associated. The movement of the migrating cells is believed to result from contractions of skeletal-

Figure 3.38 Histogenesis of the cerebral cortex. Cross-sectional views of developing cerebral cortex at early **(left)** and late **(right)** times during histogenesis. The mammalian cortex develops from the inside out as cells in the ventricular zone (VZ) divide, and some of the cells migrate to the appropriate layer in the cortex. Radial glial cells form a superhighway along which the migrating cells travel en route to the cortex. CO = cortex; CP = cortical plate; EL = ependymal layer; IZ = intermediate zone; ML = molecular layer; MZ = marginal zone; SP = subplate; SZ = subventricular zone; WM = white matter.

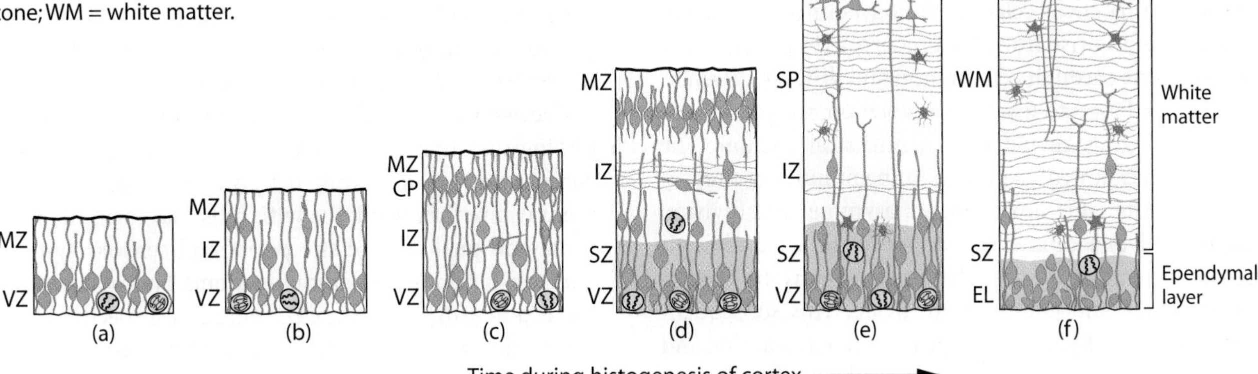

like intracellular molecules initiated by signals conducted across the membrane via ion channels.

Once the first migrating neurons approach the surface of the developing cortex—a point known as the *cortical plate*—they stop short of the surface. Neurons that migrate later pass beyond the termination point of the initial neurons and end up in more superficial positions—positions nearer the outer cortical surface. Thus, it is said that the cortex is built from the inside out because the first neurons to migrate lie in the deepest cortical layers, whereas the last to migrate move farthest out toward the cortical surface. This timeline of cortical cell genesis has been demonstrated with the thymidine-labeling method, as in Figure 3.39.

Early in corticogenesis, injection of radioactive thymidine leads to labeling of neurons in the deepest cortical layers, V and VI, and the underlying white matter, whereas at later stages of corticogenesis, injections of radioactive thymidine label neurons in more superficial cortical layers: II and I. As noted earlier, the timeline of cortical neurogenesis differs across cortical cytoarchitectonic areas, but the inside-out pattern is the same for all cortical areas. Because the timeline of cortical neurogenesis determines the ultimate pattern of cortical lamination, anything that affects the genesis of cortical neurons will lead to an ill-constructed cortex. A good example of how neuronal migration can be disrupted in humans is *fetal alcohol syndrome.* In cases of chronic maternal alcohol abuse, neuronal migration is severely disrupted and results in a disordered cortex, and a consequent plethora of cognitive, emotional, and physical disabilities.

NEURONAL DETERMINATION AND DIFFERENTIATION

So far we have regarded the cells in the ventricular zone as a single population. But how does this population of virtually identical precursor cells give rise to the variety of neurons in the adult cortex? Moreover, where do the glial cells come from? The answers to these questions are known: All cortical cells, including neuronal subtypes and glial cells, arise from the precursor cells of the ventricular zone through cell division and differentiation.

For the first 5 to 6 weeks of gestation, the cells in the ventricular zone divide in a symmetrical fashion. The result is an exponential growth in the number of precursor cells. After this time, though, asymmetrical division begins and one of the two cells present after division becomes a migratory cell. The other remains in the ventricular zone and continues to divide. This subsequent division is also asymmetrical, yielding one remaining and one migratory cell. This process contributes the cells migrating to cortical layers. In later gestational periods, the proportion of cells that migrate increases until eventually the final state yields a laminar cortex, with an epithelial layer that becomes the cell lining of the ventricles known as the *ependymal cell layer.*

The cortex is made up of many different types of neurons, and these are organized in a laminar fashion. Layer IV, for example, contains large pyramidal cells, layer III is populated primarily by stellate cells, and so on. The neuronal type of a migrating neuron is determined at the point of cell division. Experimental manipulations have shown that the time of neurogenesis is a key determinant of which cell type develops; the type is not hardwired into the code of each developing neuron. Neurons that are supposed to migrate but have been prevented from doing so by experimental intervention, such as exposure to high-energy X-rays, eventually form cell types and patterns of connectivity that would be expected from neurons that are created at the same gestational stage. Even though these neurons might remain in the ventricular zone, they display interconnections with other neurons that would be normal had they migrated to the cortical layers.

Similar evidence comes from transplanting cells from one animal to another. If embryonic cells from the ventricular region are removed at a certain stage of gestation and transplanted to the cortex of newborn host animals, such as ferrets, these transplanted neurons migrate to the proper cortical layer expected for their gestational age, regardless of the time during gestation at which the host tissue receives the graft (Figure 3.40). Again, we see here evidence that it is the time of genesis of the cell, not the time of migration, that is key. Even if the host cortex is past the stage when neurons migrate to layers V and VI—for example, when the neurons in the host are migrating past these layers to form layers II and III—a transplanted neuron whose gestational age dictated that it should migrate to layers V and VI will indeed move to these layers. What's more, these transplanted neurons take on the morphological form (i.e., stellate cell, pyramidal cell, etc.) and the connectional pattern predicted by their age; that is, they are predetermined to be a certain neuronal type. The alternative would have been to have the properties (morphology, connectivity, biochemistry, etc.) of each cortical neuron determined by the neuronal environment where they reside, as with cells that form the neuronal and glial cells of the peripheral sensory systems and the autonomic nervous system. For mammalian cortical neurons, neuronal properties are specified long before the migrating neuron reaches its destination in the cortex.

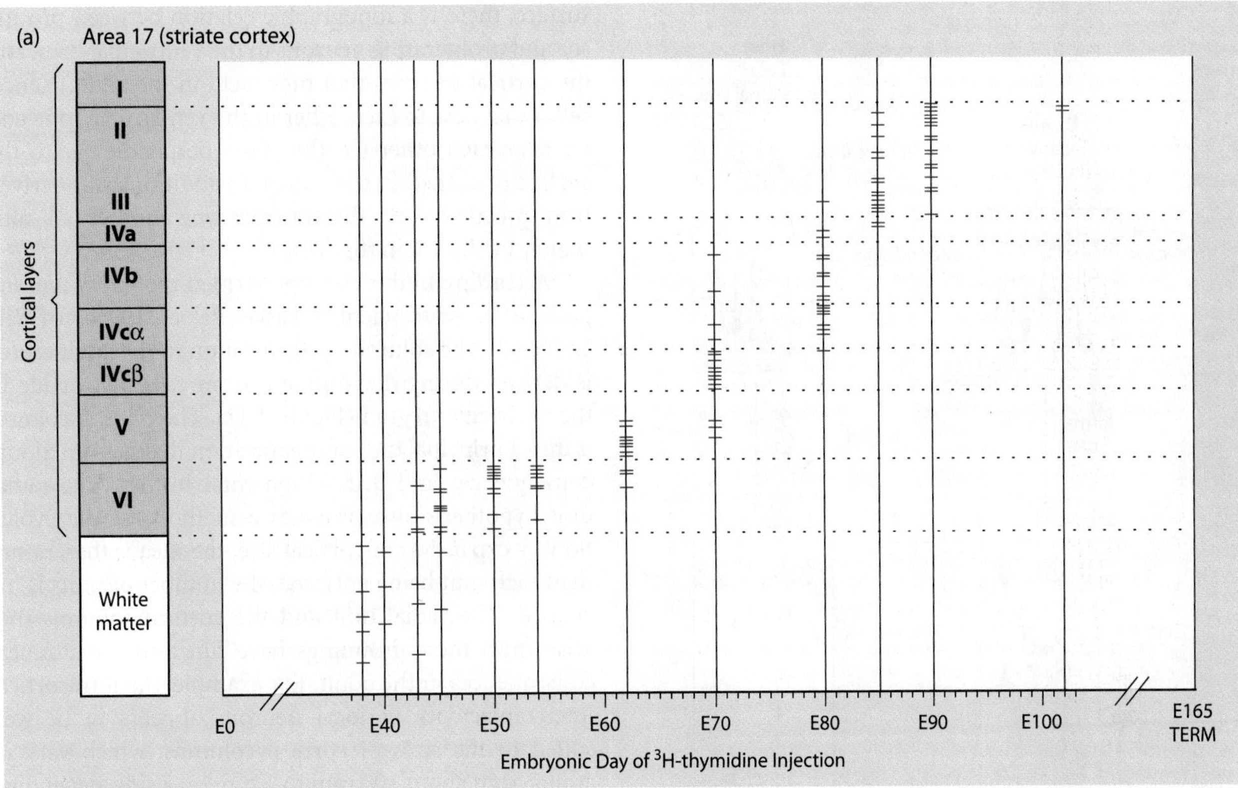

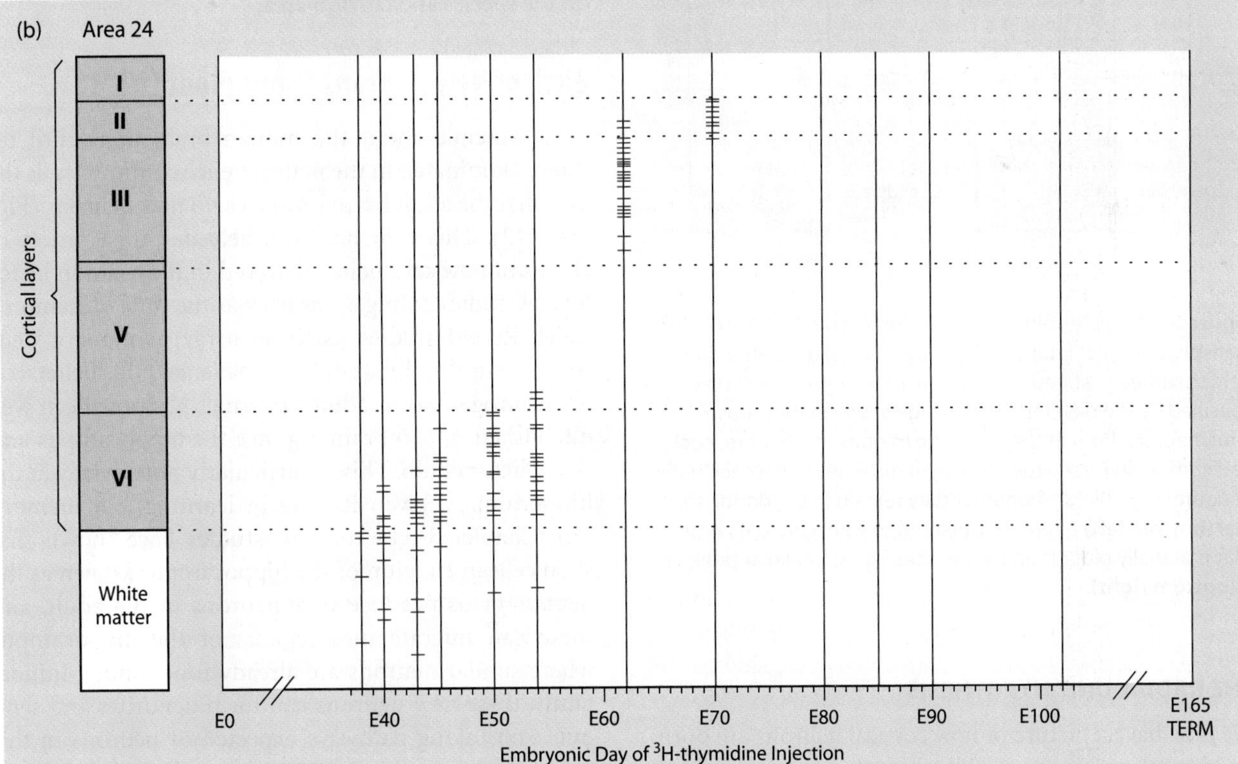

Figure 3.39 Birth ages of cortical neurons. Radiolabeled thymidine was used to label cells at different embryonic days in two cortical areas: **(a)** BA17 and **(b)** BA24. The cortical layers present at birth are shown on the axis at the left, with the cortical surface at the top of each plot. Cells with birth dates later in gestation are found in more superficial cortical layers, but the time course of this development differs for different cortical regions.

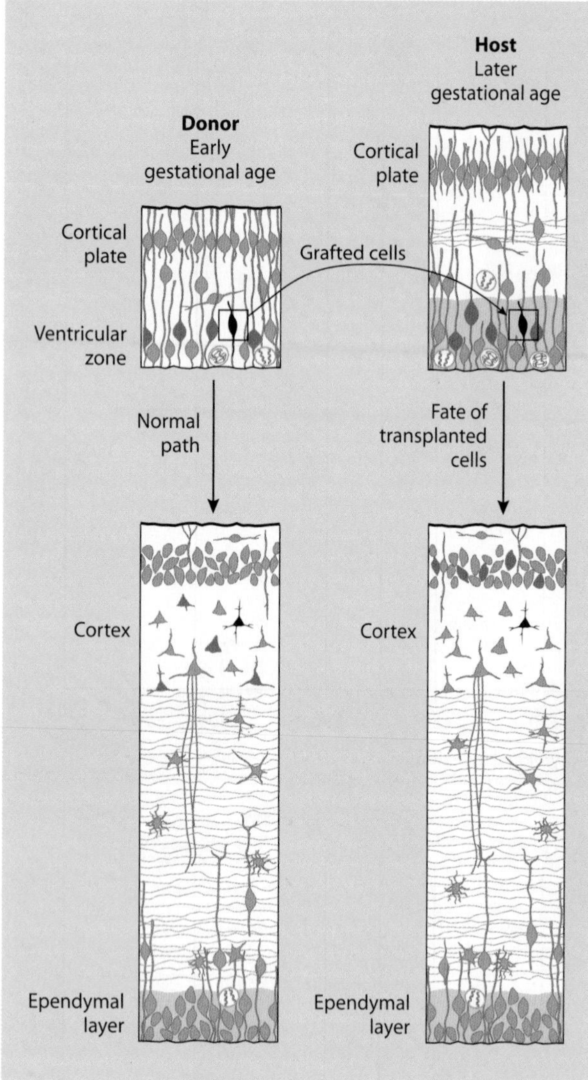

Figure 3.40 Determination of neuronal types in cortex. Transplantation of fetal cells from one animal to another has demonstrated that neurons migrate to the region of cortex specified by the developmental stage at which they arose. Thus, neurons born at the same age migrate to their prespecified cortical layer (see the black pyramidal neuron in each half of figure) regardless of whether they remain in the donor animal **(bottom left)** or are transplanted to a host animal's brain that is actually older than the neurons being transplanted into it **(bottom right)**.

THE RADIAL UNIT HYPOTHESIS

We now have a picture of how cortical neurons are born and how they migrate radially from the ventricular zone toward the surface of the developing cortex. The neurons migrate along the radial glial cells that form a pathway for them. Because the radial glial highway is organized in a straight line from the ventricular zone to the cortical surface, there is a topographic relation between precursor and proliferating neurons in the ventricular area, and the cortical neurons that they yield in the adult. Hence, cells born next to each other in the ventricular zone end up near each other (in the plane perpendicular to the surface of cortex) in the cortex. In addition, cells derived from precursor cells distant from one another will ultimately be distant in the cortex.

According to this concept, termed the *radial unit hypothesis* by neuroscientist Pasko Rakic (1995a) of Yale University, the columnar organization in the adult cortex is derived during development from cells that divide in the ventricular region (Figure 3.41). The cortical column is thus a principal unit of organization that has functional consequences and a developmental history. The radial unit hypothesis also provides a method for the evolutionary expansion of cortical size; the idea is that, rather than each unit being enlarged, the number of units is increased. The radial unit and the cortical columns that arise from these groupings have functional-anatomical consequences in the adult. For example, the intracortical interconnectivity of local neurons appears to be well suited to the sizes of cortical columns, which vary in adults from about 100 mm to 1 mm on a side, depending on the species and cortical area.

Birth of New Neurons Throughout Life

One principle about the human brain that, until recently, dominated in the neuroscience community, is the idea that the adult brain produces no new neurons (Figure 3.42). This view has been held despite a variety of claims of new cells being observed in the brain in histological studies dating as far back as the time of Ramón y Cajal. Recent studies using an array of modern neuroanatomical techniques have challenged this belief.

Neurogenesis in adult mammals has now been well established in two brain regions: the hippocampus and the olfactory bulb. This is particularly noteworthy in the hippocampus, given its role in learning and memory (see Chapter 8). In rodents, studies have shown that stem cells in a region of the hippocampus known as the *dentate gyrus* produce new neurons in the adult, and these can migrate into regions of the hippocampus where similar neurons are already functioning. Importantly, these new neurons can form dendrites and send out axons along pathways expected of neurons in this region of the hippocampus, and also show signs of normal synaptic activity. These findings are particularly interesting because the number of new neurons correlates positively with learning or enriched experience (more social contact or challenges in the physical environ-

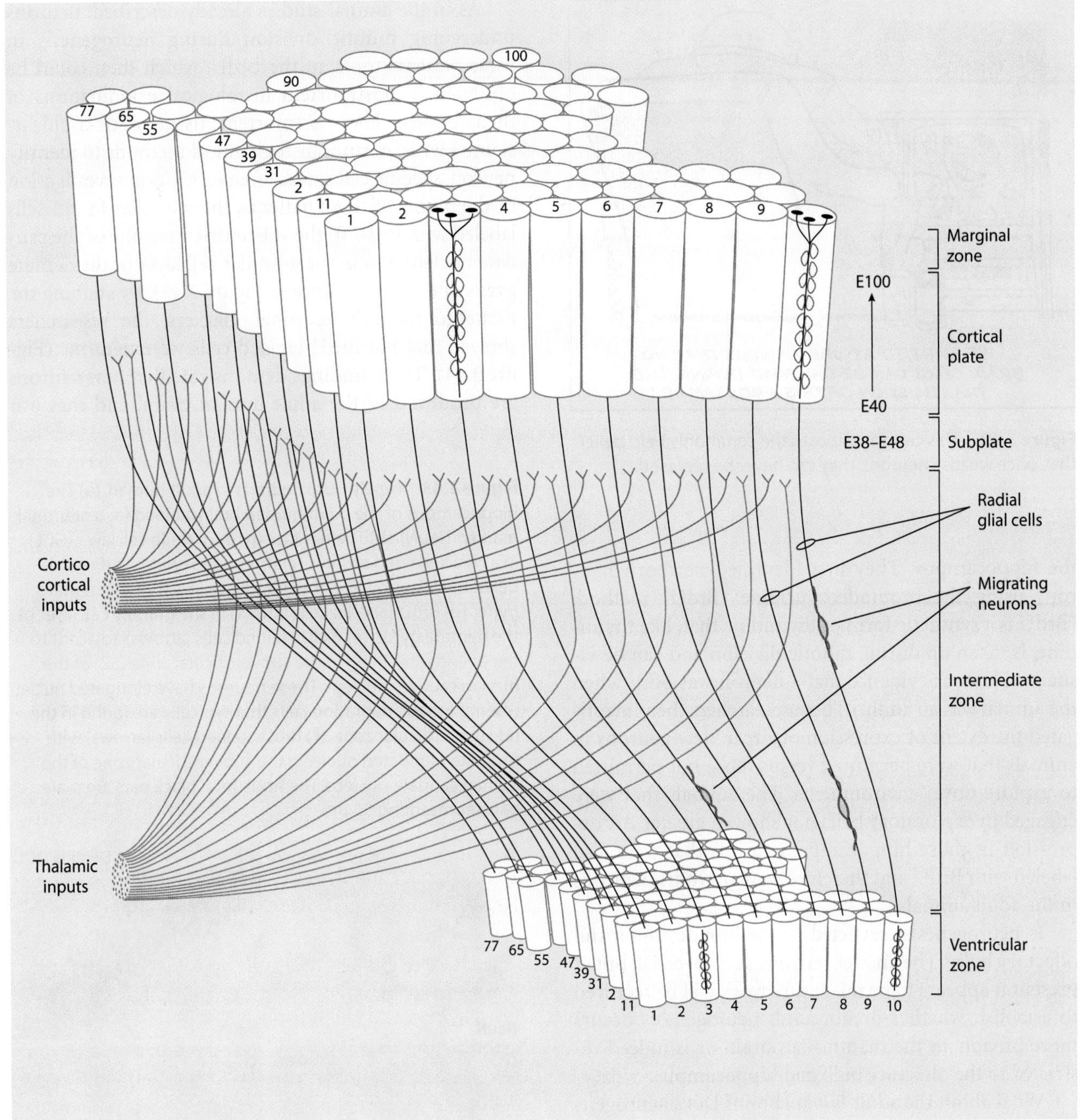

Figure 3.41 Radial unit hypothesis. Radial glial cells in the ventricular zone project their processes in an orderly map through the various cortical layers, thus maintaining the organizational structure specified in the ventricular layer.

ment) and negatively with stress (e.g., living in an overcrowded environment). Moreover, the number of newborn neurons is related to hippocampus-dependent memory (Shors, 2004).

A key remaining question is the extent to which these new neurons become integrated into functional networks of neurons to participate in behavioral and cognitive functions in the same way that those generated during development do. To answer this question, Fred Gage in San Diego, Carol Barnes in Arizona, and their colleagues (Ramirez-Amaya et al., 2006), were able to demonstrate that the immediate early gene *Arc* that is expressed in neurons during exploratory behavior in rodents was also expressed in newborn adult neurons in

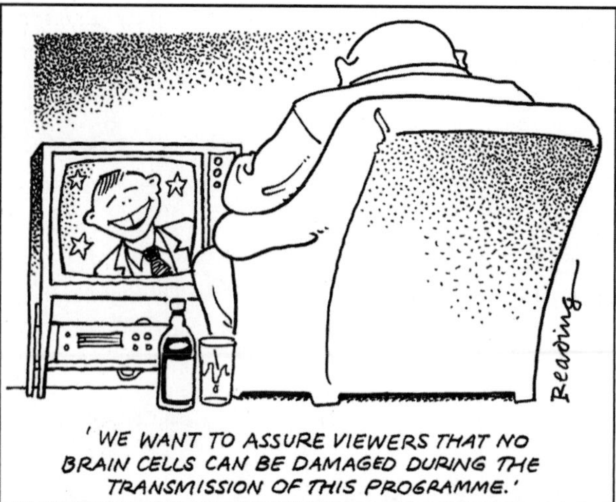

Figure 3.42 This cartoon exposes the commonly held belief that, once we lose neurons, they can never be replaced.

the hippocampus. They first identified newborn neurons using the bromodeoxyuridine (BrdU) method. (BrdU is a synthetic form of thymidine that, like thymidine, is taken up during mitotic division and can be visualized later as evidence that a neuron was born when the animal was an adult.) These researchers then investigated the extent of expression of *Arc* in new neurons in animals that were permitted versus those not permitted to explore novel environments. The animals that were engaged in exploratory behavior showed greater *Arc* expression in those hippocampal neurons that were also labeled with BrdU and therefore were newborn neurons in the adult animals.

Is neurogenesis restricted to the hippocampus and olfactory bulb? The answer remains controversial, but at present it appears to be no. Future work will be required to establish whether or not adult neurogenesis occurs more broadly in the mammalian brain or is indeed restricted to the olfactory bulb and hippocampus.

What about the adult *human* brain? Does neurogenesis also occur in mature humans? In a fascinating line of research, a team of scientists from California and Sweden (Eriksson et al., 1998) used very similar methods to explore this question in a group of terminally ill cancer patients. As part of a diagnostic procedure related to their treatment, the patients were given BrdU, the same synthetic form of thymidine used as a label to identify neurogenesis in animal studies. The purpose was to assess the extent to which the tumors in the cancer patients were proliferating; tumor cells that were dividing would take up BrdU, and this label could be used to quantify the progress of the disease.

As in the animal studies already described, neurons undergoing mitotic division during neurogenesis in these patients took up the BrdU, which then could be observed in postmortem histological examinations of their brains. The postmortem tissue also could be stained with immunohistochemical methods to identify neuron-specific cell surface markers. Upon investigation of the brains of these patients, the scientists found cells labeled with BrdU in the subventricular zone of the caudate nucleus and in the granular cell layer of the dentate gyrus of the hippocampus (Figure 3.43). By staining the tissue to identify neuronal markers, the researchers showed that the BrdU-labeled cells were neurons (Figure 3.44). These findings demonstrate that new neurons are produced in the adult human brain, and that our

Figure 3.43 Newly born neurons in adult human. **(a)** The hippocampus of the adult human brain stained for a neuronal marker (NeuN). **(b)** The dentate gyrus granule cell layer (GCL) in a NeuN-stained section. **(c)** Bromodeoxyuridine (BrdU)-labeled nuclei (arrows) in the granule cell layer of the dentate gyrus. **(d)** BrdU-labeled cells (arrow) in the granule cell layer of the dentate gyrus. **(e)** BrdU-stained cells (arrows) adjacent to the ependymal lining in the subventricular zone (SZ) of the human caudate nucleus. These neurons have elongated nuclei resembling the migrating cells that typically are found in the rat subventricular zone. **(f)** BrdU-stained cells (arrows) with round to elongated nuclei in the subventricular zone of the human caudate nucleus. The horizontal black bars are scale bars representing 50 μm.

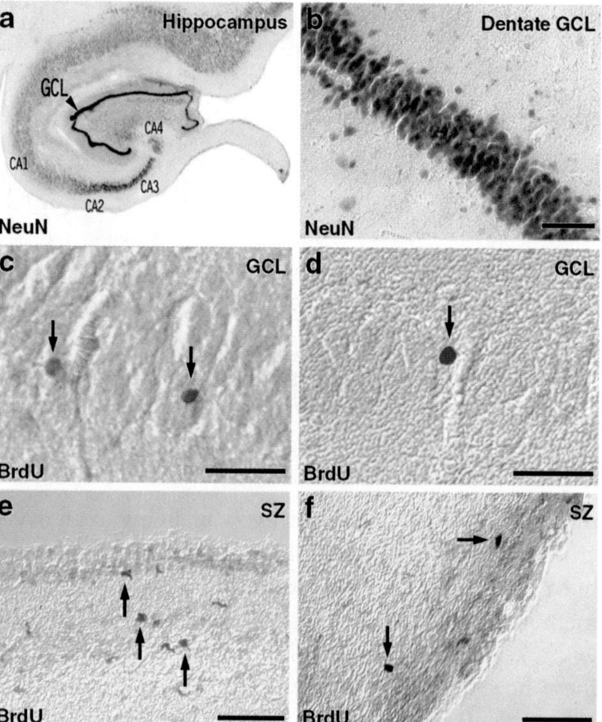

brains renew themselves throughout life to an extent previously thought not possible.

This exciting line of research holds great promise for the future of neuroscience. Research is under way to investigate the functionality of new neurons in the adult brain and to determine whether or not such neuronal growth can be facilitated in order to ameliorate stroke or diseases such as Alzheimer's.

Postnatal Brain Development

A host of behavioral changes take place during the first months and years of life. What accompanying neurobiological changes enable these developments? Even if we assume that neuronal proliferation continues, we know that, at birth, the human has a fairly full complement of neurons, and these are organized intricately to form a human nervous system that is normal, even if not complete in all details. What details are incomplete, and what is known about the time course of the maturation of the brain?

One important aspect of neural development is *synaptogenesis*, the formation of synapses. Synapses in the brain begin to form long before birth, prior to week 27 in humans (counting from conception), but they do not reach peak density until after birth, during the first 15 months of life. Synaptogenesis is more pronounced early in the deeper cortical layers and occurs later in more superficial layers, following the pattern of neurogenesis described earlier. At roughly the same time that synaptogenesis occurs, neurons of the brain are increasing the size of their dendritic arborizations, extending

Figure 3.44 The birth of new neurons in the dentate gyrus of the adult human compared to those in the adult rat. New neurons show simultaneous labeling for different stains. **(a)** A neuron is labeled for NeuN, a neuronal marker. **(b)** The same cell is labeled with BrdU, indicating that it is newly born (full arrow). (Note that the lone arrowheads in (a) through (d) are pointing to neurons that are fluorescing red or green, owing to nonspecific staining; i.e., these are not newly born neurons). **(c)** This same cell is not stained by glial fibrillary acidic protein (GFAP), indicating that it is not an astrocyte. **(d)** The three stained sections are merged. The image shows that a BrdU-labeled cell could specifically coexpress NeuN without expressing GFAP. Confocal microscopy permits examination of the coexpression of NeuN and BrdU in the neuron by focusing the image above **(e, f)** and below **(g, h)** the level of the section shown in panel (d). Note that red blood cells and endothelial cells, present in several small blood vessels, show nonspecific staining, as indicated by the asterisks in (e) through (h). Panels **(i)** through **(l)** show the similarity of the BrdU-labeled neurons in rat dentate gyrus. Note: The scale bar in (a) is 25 μm, and the scale is the same for panels (a) through (h). The scale bar in panel (i) is also 25 μm and is the scale for (i) through (l), but the magnification for (i) through (l) is higher than for (a) through (h).

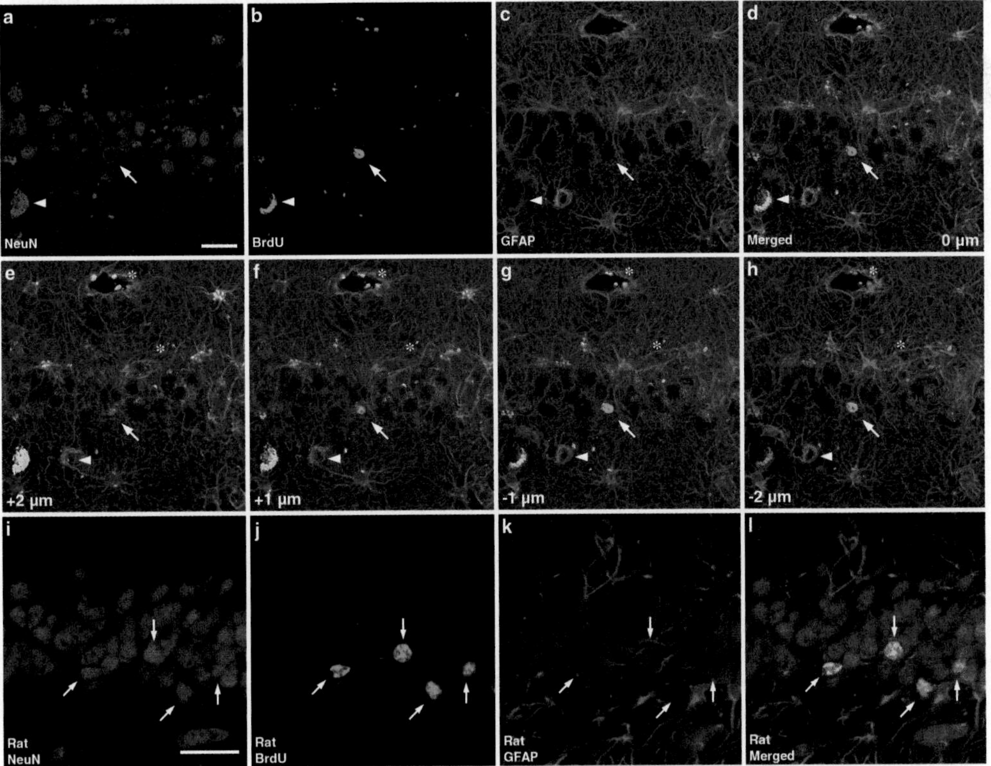

their axons, and undergoing myelination. Synaptogenesis is followed by synapse elimination (sometimes called *pruning*), which continues for more than a decade. Synapse elimination is a means by which the nervous system fine-tunes neural connectivity, presumably eliminating the interconnections between neurons that are redundant or do not remain functional. An example comes from primary visual cortex (BA17), where there is initially more overlap between the projections of the two eyes onto neurons in BA17 than there is when synapse elimination is complete. After synapse elimination, the cortical areas within BA17 (*ocular dominance columns*) are nearly completely segregated with regard to the eye from which the projections are received.

One of the central hypotheses about the process of human synaptogenesis and synapse elimination is that the time course of these events differs in different cortical regions. By contrast, in the brain development of other primates, synaptogenesis and pruning appear to occur at the same rates across different cortical regions. However, differences in methodology must be resolved before these interspecies variations will be wholly accepted. Nonetheless, compelling evidence suggests that different regions of the human brain reach maturity at different times.

Peter Huttenlocher and his colleagues (e.g., Huttenlocher & Dabholkar, 1997) at the University of Chicago investigated the time course of synaptogenesis in auditory cortex and prefrontal cortex (middle frontal gyrus) in postmortem human brains ranging in age from 28 weeks after conception (one premature infant) to 59 years. They stained the tissue from the two cortical areas using the phosphotungstic acid (PTA) method, which stains proteins associated with synapses, and visualized the stained synapses using electron microscopy so that they could count the number of synapses per unit of cortical volume.

They found that synapses in the superior temporal region, in the auditory cortex, reached peak density earlier in postnatal development (around the age of 3 months) than did synapses in the association cortex of the frontal lobe, the density of which peaked around the age of 15 months. Synapse elimination, which occurs later in life, also appeared to end earlier in the auditory cortex than in the prefrontal cortex, although this finding remains less well established. The general pattern is shown in Figure 3.45 as the biphasic plot of the difference between the synaptic density values in the prefrontal cortex and those in the auditory cortex; initially density is greater in the auditory cortex, and later it is greater in the prefrontal cortex. These data suggest that, in humans, synaptogenesis and synapse elimination follow different time courses in sensory (and motor) cortex than in association cortex, like that in the prefrontal cortex.

Measurements of glucose metabolism also can be used in living persons to investigate development of the brain, and a time course similar to that in the foregoing

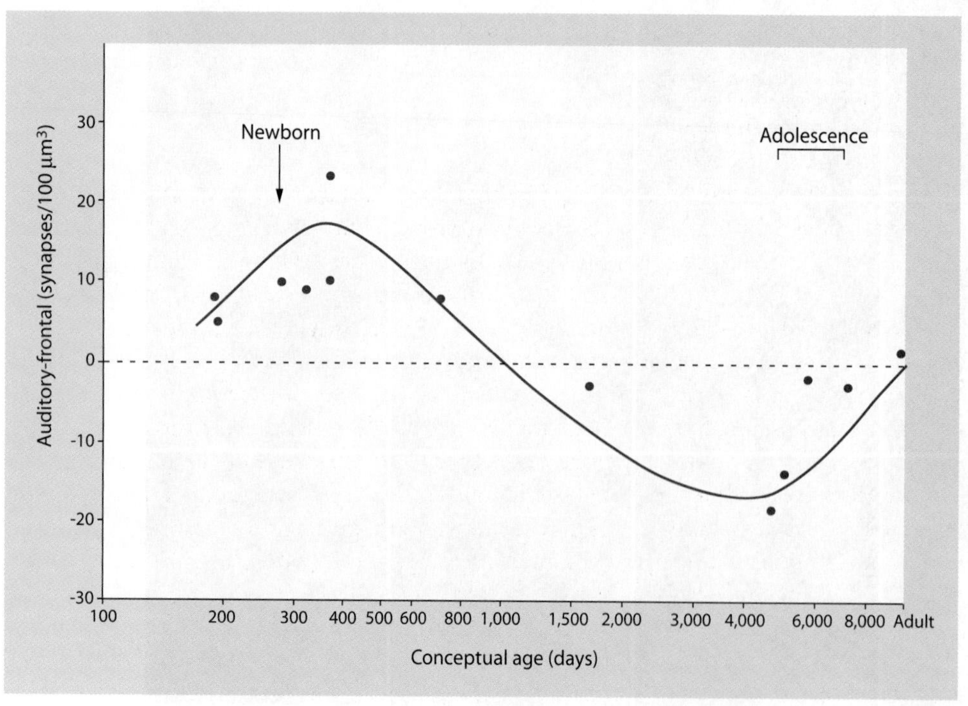

Figure 3.45 Plot of the difference score obtained by subtracting the value for synaptic density in the frontal cortex from that for synaptic density in the auditory cortex, as a function of the conceptual age of humans. Prenatal synaptic density peaks earlier for the auditory cortex, as reflected by the positive difference score, and later for the frontal cortex, as reflected by the negative difference score.

has emerged from studies using positron emission tomography (PET) in infants, children, and adolescents. Harry Chugani (1998) of Wayne State University School of Medicine showed that glucose metabolism measured at rest rapidly increases with age in young infants and decreases during the teenage years. In newborns, glucose metabolism is highest in sensory and motor cortical areas, in the hippocampus, and in subcortical areas including the thalamus, brainstem, and cerebellar vermis. By the age of 2 to 3 months, more glucose starts to be used in parietal and temporal cortex, the primary visual cortex, and the basal ganglia and cerebellar hemispheres. Glucose utilization in the frontal cortex increases between the ages of 6 and 12 months. The overall level of glucose use in the developing brain increases until about the age of 4 years, plateaus through about age 10, and decreases gradually to adult levels between the ages of 16 and 18 years. These data argue for a developmental time course in the human brain that is similar to that described in the results of histological methods, such as measures of synaptic density, and therefore reinforce the idea that different regions of the human brain develop at different rates, with association areas lagging behind sensory and motor structures (see Chapter 15 for an evolutionary perspective on cortical development).

Another trend in postnatal development is the significant increase in brain volume during the first 6 years. The increase appears to be the result of both myelination and the proliferation of glial cells. Jay Giedd and his colleagues at the National Institutes of Health, with Tomas Paus and his colleagues at McGill University in Montreal, Canada, calculated growth curves for gray and white matter volume in the lobes of the developing human brain (Giedd et al., 1999). The research team used magnetic resonance images to quantify white and gray matter volumes in children and young adults (ages between 4 and 20) who were willing to be scanned multiple times over a few different years.

The researchers found that white matter volume increased linearly with age and that the time course was not different for different cortical regions. In contrast, gray matter volume increased nonlinearly, showing a preadolescent increase followed by a postadolescent decrease—a finding in accord with the results from PET studies and postmortem histological measures. In addition, the time courses of the gray matter increases and decreases were not the same across different cortical regions. In general, these data support the idea that postnatal developmental changes in the cerebral cortex may not occur with the same time course across all cortical regions (see also Shaw et al., 2006).

PLASTICITY IN THE NERVOUS SYSTEM

It is obvious from the dramatic cellular events that occur during gestation that the nervous system is tremendously **plastic**, or adaptive, during development. It can change its form, including the type and location of cells and how they are interconnected. This developmental plasticity stands in stark contrast to the relative rigidity of the adult brain. Indeed, until recently it was widely believed that the adult brain was incapable of great change.

However, it is now abundantly clear that plasticity does exist in the adult brain. After all, we learn new things even as adults, and these new skills must be reflected in the anatomy of our brains. Learning involves primarily changes in the synaptic strength between neurons in the brain's circuitry. As we learn, connections that are critical to the learned action or behavior are strengthened, while those that are not used are weakened. The mechanisms underlying such changes are beginning to be understood in great detail at the molecular level (e.g., see the discussion of long-term potentiation in Chapter 8). So there must be some plastic change in the adult brain, given the fantastic behavioral plasticity that adults display.

Cortical Maps and Experience

Since the mid 1980s an amazing revolution in neuroscience has grown out of the work of Michael Merzenich (Merzenich & Jenkins, 1995; Merzenich et al., 1988) at the University of California, San Francisco; and Jon Kaas (1995) at Vanderbilt University. These scientists have investigated how sensory and motor maps (called *homunculi*; see "How the Brain Works: Cortical Topography," on p. 74) in the cortex can be modified with experience. The organization of the body is reflected in the cortical representation of the body—a principle know as **topography**. For example, within somatosensory cortex, neurons that respond to touch of the index finger are adjacent to those that respond to touch of the middle finger, which are also neighbored by neurons that respond to touch of the ring finger. Similarly, the hand area as a whole is adjacent to the lower arm area, which is near the upper arm, and so forth. This mapping of specific parts of the body to areas of the cortex is known as **somatotopy**, resulting in somatotopic maps of the cortical areas. It is interesting to ask why such maps exist, since there is no inherent necessity for the organization. Yet topographic maps are a common feature of the nervous system (see Chapter 5), perhaps reflecting the fact that neighboring body parts are frequently co-recruited, as when we're gripping a ball or stroking a favorite pet.

Merzenich and Kaas discovered that the size and shape of these maps can be altered by experience, even in adult animals. Radical manipulation might involve amputating a digit, cutting the nerves that innervate a limb, or sewing together two fingers of one hand so that they always move in a perfectly synchronized manner. A less radical approach might be to apply a specific stimulus over and over to only one finger. With all of these manipulations, significant changes in the somatotopic maps have been observed. For example, when a finger of a monkey is deafferented—that is, the nerve fibers from that finger to the spinal cord are severed—the relevant part of the cortex no longer responds to the touch of that finger (Figure 3.46). This is perhaps no big surprise; after all, the cortex is no longer receiving input from that finger. But here comes the strange part: The area of the cortex that formerly represented the denervated finger soon becomes active again and responds to stimulation of the finger adjacent to the amputated finger. The surrounding cortical area fills in the silent area and takes over. Similar changes are found with less invasive procedures, such as when a particular finger is given extended sensory stimulation. This functional plasticity suggests that the adult cortex is a dynamic place where changes can still happen. Such phenomena demonstrate a remarkable plasticity.

Are phenomena of cortical functional plasticity limited to monkeys, or do humans also display such cortical plasticity? Professor Vilayanur Ramachandran at the University of California, San Diego, studied the cortical mapping of human amputees and brought the dramatic animal results into the realm of human phenomena. Consider the human cortical somatosensory surface. Starting at one point, the pharynx is represented, then the face, with the sensitive lips having a huge area of representation, and next to the face are the fingers and hand, followed by the arm and leg (Figure 3.47).

Ramachandran reasoned that a cortical rearrangement ought to take place if an arm is amputated, just as had been found for the amputation of a digit in monkeys. Such a rearrangement might be expected to create bizarre patterns of perception. Remember that the face

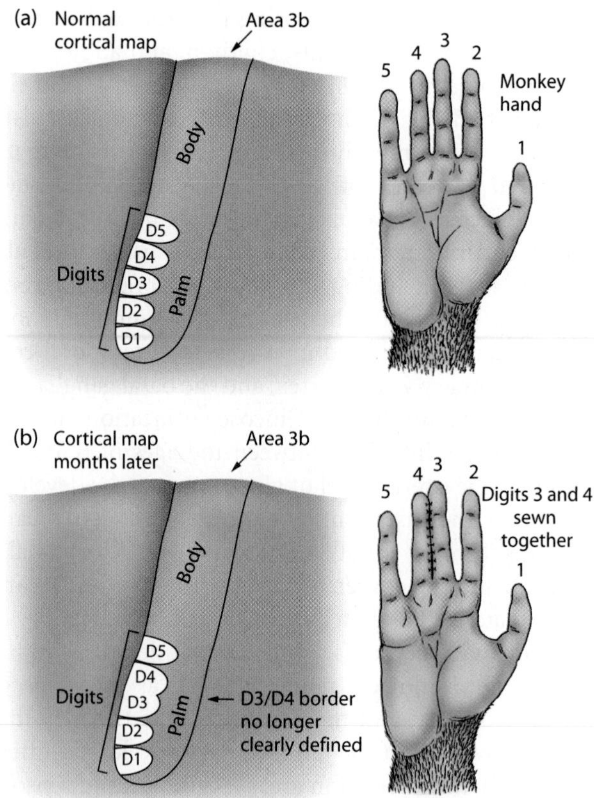

Figure 3.46 Reorganization of sensory maps in the primate cortex. **(a)** In a mapping of the somatosensory hand area in normal monkey cortex, the individual digit representations can be revealed by single-unit recording. **(b)** If the two fingers of one hand are sewn together, months later the cortical maps change such that the sharp border once present between the sewn fingers is now blurred.

area is next to the hand and arm area—an important point for understanding this story. Suppose there were no lower arm or hand to send sensory signals to the brain. According to animal research, the region coding for the arm that had been amputated might become functionally innervated by the surrounding cortex. That is exactly what happened in several spectacular cases.

In one case, Ramachandran studied a young man who had recently had his arm amputated just above the elbow. About 4 weeks after the amputation, the young man was tested. When a cotton swab was brushed lightly against his face, he reported feeling his amputated hand being touched! Feelings of sensation in missing limbs are the well-known phenomenon of *phantom limb sensation*; however, this case is different because the sensation was introduced by stimulating the face. Indeed, with careful examination, a map of his hand could be demonstrated on his face (Figure 3.48)!

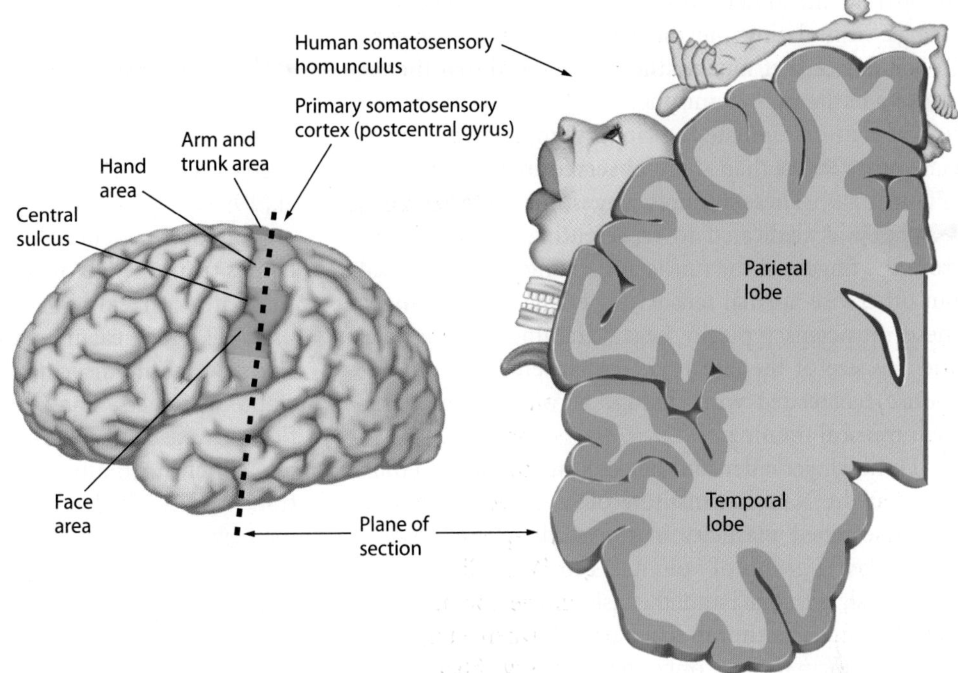

Figure 3.47 Human somatosensory homunculus. The representation of the body surface is mapped in a somatotopic fashion onto the somatosensory cortex of the parietal lobe. At right is a coronal view of the left hemisphere showing the approximate location and relative cortical area (as indicated by distorted sizes of various body parts) dedicated to body parts. The anterior–posterior plane of the coronal section is indicated at left.

Ramachandran's (1993) report of another case is too good not to quote verbatim:

> A neuroscience graduate student wrote to us that soon after her left lower leg was amputated she found that sensation in her phantom foot was enhanced in certain situations—especially during sexual intercourse and defecation. Similarly an engineer in Florida reported a heightening of sensation in his phantom (left) lower limb during orgasm and that his experience . . . actually spread all the way down into the [phantom] foot instead of remaining confined to the genitals: so that the orgasm was much bigger than it used to be. (p. 10417)

Figure 3.48 Hand representation sketched on the face of the amputee studied by Ramachandran.

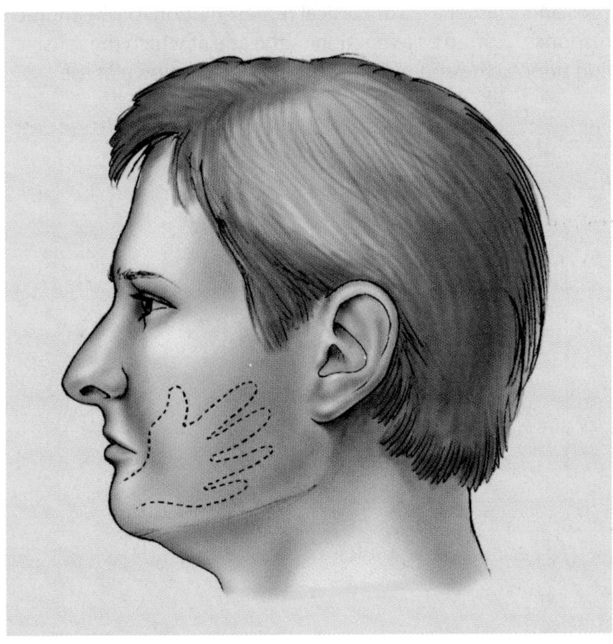

These are dramatic examples of plasticity in humans following significant injury or altered experience. But is there evidence that changes in experience within the normal range—say, due to training—have any ability to influence the organization of the adult human brain?

Plasticity in the Adult Human Brain

We have learned that the brains of adult mammals, including humans, generate new functioning neurons. We have also seen that the organization of the sensory systems can be dramatically altered following injury or damage. Given these facts, we might well expect to see changes in adult human brains as the result of significant training, as, for example, in the acquisition and maintenance of musical skill.

Thomas Elbert and his colleagues at the University of Konstanz used magnetoencephalography (MEG) to investigate the somatosensory representations of the hand area in musicians, specifically violin players (Elbert et al., 1995). Recall that violinists use the right hand to operate the bow and the left hand to finger the strings. Stimulating the fingers with a precisely controlled device that touches the skin showed that the responses in the right hemisphere (which controls the left fingers that manipulate the violin strings) of the musicians were larger than those observed in nonmusicians (Figure 3.49). These findings suggest that a larger cortical area was dedicated to representing the sensations from the fingers of the musicians, owing to their altered but otherwise normal sensory experience. Interestingly, these musicians typically began training early in life, and the size of the effect (the enhancement in the response) correlated with the age at which they began their musical training.

Leslie Ungerleider and her colleagues (Karni et al., 1995) at the National Institute of Mental Health have also researched plasticity in the adult motor system. They asked a group of volunteers to perform a simple motor task with one hand; the task required the subjects to touch finger to thumb in a particular sequence. They had to perform the task only a few minutes each day, but their accuracy and speed of finger–thumb touching improved with this practice. Using functional magnetic resonance imaging (fMRI), which is described in Chapter 4, the scientists measured the size of activity-related changes in blood flow in the motor cortex for the practiced sequences and untrained sequences. Figure 3.50 shows the results: There were greater changes in blood flow in the corresponding motor cortex for trained than for untrained sequences after a few weeks. Indeed, recent evidence indicates that cortical reorganization can occur after just 15 to 30 minutes of practice (Classen et al., 1998).

Further evidence that adult brains show plasticity comes from the lab of Norihiro Sadato at the National Institutes of Health. Sadato and his colleagues (1996) used PET to measure blood flow in the visual cortex during a tactile discrimination task in both blind and sighted subjects. They found that, in the blind, blood flow increased in primary and secondary visual cortex, which normally responds only to visual stimulation, whereas it decreased in sighted subjects during the task.

More recently, Alvaro Pascual-Leone and his colleagues at Harvard Medical School (Kauffman et al., 2002) have studied the cortical plasticity effects of extended blindfolding of *sighted* volunteers. The study included four groups of participants. Two groups were continuously blindfolded for 5 days, during which one group received intensive Braille training and the other did not. Matched control groups were not blindfolded. Regardless of whether the blindfolded subjects were

Figure 3.49 Changes in the cortical representation of the human fingers in musicians who play string instruments. **(a)** Top view of a three-dimensional human brain reconstructed from MRI; anterior is to the left. The arrows over the right hemisphere indicate the calculated locations of neural activity recorded using MEG for the thumb (D1) and fifth finger (D5). The black arrows represent the thumb and fifth finger for musicians; the yellow arrows represent nonmusicians. The arrow size shows the strength of the responses (to stimulation of the thumb and finger). Musicians show larger responses and a larger area of cortical representation for the thumb and fifth finger (distance between arrows). **(b)** The size of the cortical response, plotted as a function of the age at which the musicians begin training. Responses were larger for those who began training prior to the age of 12 years; controls are shown at the lower right of the graph.

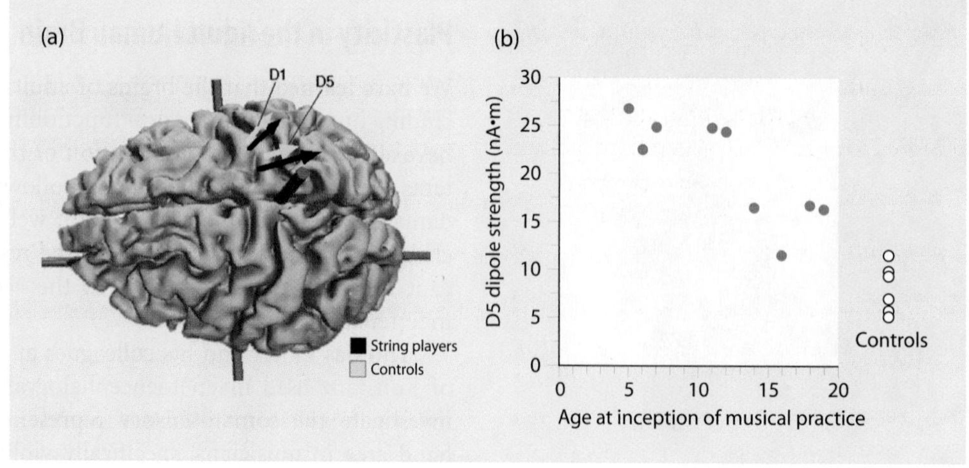

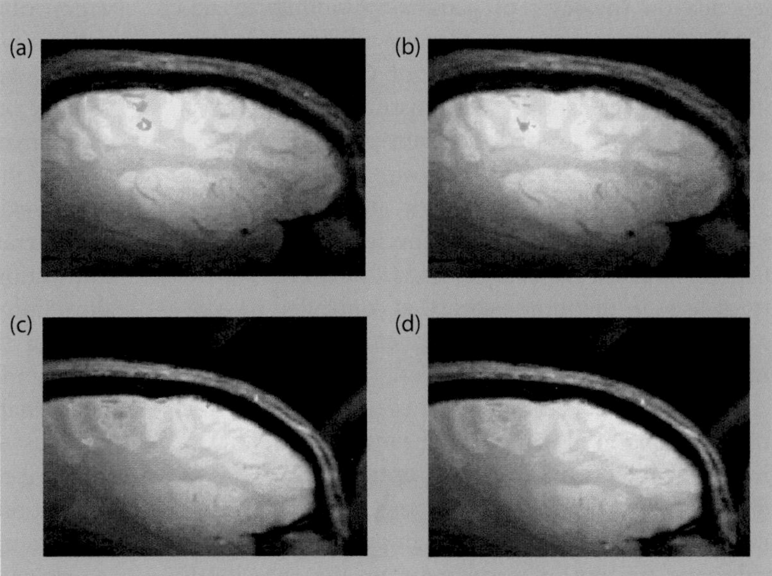

Figure 3.50 Changes in the size of cortical activation of hand movements with training. **(a)** A sagittal section through the right hemisphere of a representative subject shows greater activation (larger area activated—yellow-orange) for motor sequences that were repeated over many sessions in comparison to motor-evoked activity for untrained sequential movements **(b)**. These activations were in M1, the primary motor cortex. The increased activation for trained movements **(c)** in comparison to untrained movements **(d)** lasted up to 8 weeks, even when no training ensued on the task in the interim.

trained, after only 5 days of visual deprivation they could discriminate Braille letters better than nonblindfolded subjects could. This finding implies that, once deprived of normal input, the adult visual system can become engaged in tactile analysis in a very short period of time. Furthermore, fMRI of these subjects revealed activation in the visual cortex during tactile stimulation of the right or left fingertips using a brush (to reduce the likelihood of visual imagery) during the last day of the study (the 5th day). Interestingly, just 20 hours after the blindfold was removed (on day 6) the activation in visual cortex during tactile stimulation disappeared.

Furthermore, transcranial magnetic stimulation (TMS) of the occipital cortex disrupted tactile discrimination abilities during the last day of blindfolding, but not after the blindfold was removed on the 6th day, suggesting a functional role of the visual cortex activation in tactile discrimination during blindfolding. Similarly, auditory stimulation was shown to activate the visual cortex in blindfolded subjects: Left-lateralized activations of the medial occipital lobe and the posterior extension of the superior temporal lobe were found in the blindfolded population during tone and phoneme matching tasks.

These data argue that, in the normal brain, training can induce relatively rapid changes in cortical organization that reflect the plastic ability of the nervous system to acquire and retain new information and skills. The possibility that someday such neural reorganization could serve a clinically beneficial role is enticing. However, before that is possible, neuroscientists must unravel the mechanisms underlying such plasticity.

Mechanisms of Cortical Plasticity

Most of the evidence for the mechanisms of cortical plasticity comes from animal studies (Steven & Blakemore, 2005). The results suggest a cascade of effects, operating across different timescales. In both humans and other animals, changes in cortical mapping can be detected essentially immediately after the change in sensory input or motor activity. But additional components of the plasticity take longer to appear. There appear to be at least three distinct mechanisms: two that account for short-term changes, and a separate mechanism for very long-term effects.

Rapid changes probably reflect both the unveiling of weak connections that already exist in the cortex, through both release from inhibition and changes in the efficacy of synapses. Longer term plasticity may result from the growth of new synapses and/or axons.

Immediate effects (e.g., as a result of amputation) are likely to be due to a sudden reduction in the level of inhibitory synaptic activity in the cortex, which normally suppresses weak inputs onto cortical cells from regions of the receptor surface beyond their classical receptive fields. Ulf Ziemann and his colleagues (2001) at the Johann Wolfgang Goethe-University of Frankfurt report that reorganization in the motor cortex depends on the level of gamma-aminobutyric acid (GABA), the principal inhibitory neurotransmitter. They showed that, as the level of GABA-ergic inhibition was increased by administration of a GABA receptor agonist drug (lorazepam), the capacity for plasticity decreased. The opposite was true when GABA levels were lowered with an ischemic nerve block in the hand (deafferentation leads to a decrease in GABA). These data suggest that short-term plasticity, at least in the motor cortex, is controlled by a release of tonic inhibition on synaptic input (thalamic or intracortical) from remote sources.

Changes in cortical mapping over a period of days following increased or decreased sensory or motor activity probably involve modulation of the effectiveness of initially weak excitatory synapses. After loss of normal sensory input (e.g., through amputation or peripheral nerve section) cortical neurons that previously responded to that input might undergo "denervation hypersensitivity"—up-regulation of the strength of their responses to any remaining weak excitatory input. But remapping as a result of more subtle changes in activity (e.g., through motor or sensory learning) might well depend on regulated changes in synaptic efficacy similar to the forms of long-term potentiation and depression in the hippocampus that are thought to underlie the formation of spatial and episodic memories (see Chapter 8). Finally, some evidence in animals suggests that the growth of intracortical axonal connections and even sprouting of new axons might contribute to these very slow changes.

Less is known about the basis of changes in activity beyond individual cortical areas, such as the tactile activation of visual areas in the blind. It is unlikely that there is wholesale growth of new long-range cortico-cortical association connections, given that Pascual-Leone's work shows that these changes can take place over a matter of days. More plausible is the hypothesis that the plasticity occurs because of changes in the efficacy of existing circuitry, but there is little evidence and no general agreement about which particular form of connections might be involved. A great many pathways allow for feedback from "higher" to "lower" sensory areas in the cortex, and this extensive network may come under the control of inputs from other sensory areas, enabling them to activate regions of cortex normally used for a different sensory system. Alternatively, the long-range influences might be mediated through facilitation of multiple, serial connections, or even of descending and ascending loops via the thalamus.

Helen Neville at the University of Oregon and her colleagues (Neville & Lawson, 1987) have pointed out that some of the areas that show unusual responses after sensory loss (e.g., in the blind and deaf) are normally involved in multimodal sensory processing (including higher visual cortical areas in the temporal lobe and the inferior parietal lobe, among others). Since multimodal areas already have input from several senses, it is not so surprising that loss of input from one sense should lead to the enhancement of response to a remaining sensory input, perhaps through modulation of the strength of synapses from association connections.

This is a hot topic in neuroscience research, and we hope that definitive answers about the mechanisms of each form of cortical plasticity will be revealed in the near future.

SUMMARY

The nervous system is composed of neurons and their supportive counterparts, the glial cells. The neuron is the elementary unit of structure and function within the brain and spinal cord of the central nervous system and the peripheral nervous system, which includes the autonomic nervous system. These elementary units and their interconnections can be viewed directly by use of a variety of gross dissection methods, and analyzed in detail with microanatomical methods. Connections can be traced with special substances that are taken up by neurons and transported down their axons either in an anterograde (from soma to axon terminals) or a retrograde (from terminals to soma) direction.

Neuronal circuits are organized to form highly specific interconnections between groups of neurons in subdivisions of the central nervous system. Different neuronal groups have different functional roles. The functions might be localized within discrete regions that contain a few or many subdivisions, identifiable either anatomically or functionally, but usually by a combination of both approaches. Brain areas are also interconnected to form higher level circuits or systems that are involved in complex behaviors such as motor control, visual perception, or cognitive processes such as memory, language, and attention. Neurodevelopment begins at an early stage in fetal growth and continues through birth and adolescence. New research also suggests that new neurons and new synapses form throughout life, allowing, at least in part, for cortical plasticity.

KEY TERMS

amygdala
association cortex
autonomic nervous system
basal ganglia
brainstem
central nervous system (CNS)
cerebellum
cerebral cortex
commissure
corpus callosum
corticogenesis
cytoarchitectonic map
dura mater
ectoderm
frontal lobe
gray matter
gyri
hippocampus
hypothalamus
limbic system
medulla
midbrain
neocortex
neuronal determination and differentiation
neuronal migration
neuronal proliferation
nucleus
occipital lobe
parietal lobe
peripheral nervous system (PNS)
plastic
pons
precursor cells
prefrontal cortex
radial glial cell
somatotopy
sulci
Sylvian fissure
synapse elimination
synaptogenesis
temporal lobe
thalamus
topography
tract
white matter

TAKE-HOME MESSAGES

General

- Gross neuroanatomy encompasses the large brain structures that can be viewed by the naked eye; fine neuroanatomy, or microscopic neuroanatomy, has to do with the organization of the brain at the cellular or subcellular level.

Neuroanatomy

- The central nervous system consists of the brain and spinal cord. The peripheral nervous system consists of all nerves outside of the central nervous system.
- The lobes of the brain include the frontal, parietal, temporal, occipital (and occasionally limbic) lobes. The frontal lobe is for planning, cognitive control, and execution of movements. The parietal lobe receives sensory input about touch, pain, temperature, and limb position, and is involved in coding space and coordinating actions. The temporal lobe contains auditory, visual, and multimodal processing areas. The occipital lobe processes visual information. The limbic lobe is involved in emotional processing, learning, and memory.
- Gyri are the protruding areas seen on the surface of the cortex; sulci, or fissures, are the enfolded regions of cortex.
- Gray matter is formed by the cell bodies in the brain; white matter is formed by the axons.
- White matter forms tracts that connect various regions of the brain. Tracts are referred to by source and then by target. For example, the corticospinal tract goes from the cortex to the spinal cord.
- Retrograde tracers are injected at the axon terminal and proceed up the axon to label the cell body. Anterograde tracers are injected at the cell body and travel down the axon to label the axon and the axon terminals.
- The corpus callosum is the largest interhemispheric (commissural) white matter tract in the brain.
- Brodmann divided the brain into distinct regions based on the underlying cytoarchitectonics.
- Cerebral cortex can be subdivided into major regions that differ in the degree of complexity of the neuronal layering (e.g., neocortex, allocortex, and paleocortex).
- The basal ganglia are involved in movement processing.
- The hippocampus is involved in learning and memory.
- The thalamus is the relay station for almost all sensory information. Association cortex is neocortex that is neither sensory nor motor in function.
- The hypothalamus is important for the autonomic nervous system and endocrine system. It controls functions necessary for the maintenance of homeostasis. It is also involved in emotional processing and in the control of the pituitary gland.

- The brainstem includes the midbrain, pons, and medulla. Nuclei of the brainstem control respiration, sleep, and wakefulness.
- The cerebellum integrates information about the body and motor commands and modifies motor outflow to effect smooth, coordinated movements.
- The spinal cord conducts the final motor signals to the muscles, and it relays sensory information from the body's peripheral receptors to the brain.
- The autonomic nervous system is involved in controlling the action of smooth muscles, the heart, and various glands. It includes the sympathetic and parasympathetic systems.
- The sympathetic system uses the neurotransmitter norepinephrine. This system increases heart rate, diverts blood from the digestive tract to the somatic musculature, and prepares the body for fight-or-flight responses by stimulating the adrenal glands.
- The parasympathetic system uses acetylcholine as a neurotransmitter. It is responsible for decreasing heart rate and stimulating digestion.

Neurodevelopment

- The nervous system develops from the ectoderm, which forms a neural plate. The neural plate becomes the neural groove and eventually the neural tube.
- Neuronal proliferation is the process of cell division in the developing embryo and fetus. It is responsible for populating the nervous system with neurons.
- Neurons and glial cells are formed from precursor cells. After mitosis these cells migrate along the radial glial cells to the developing cortex.
- The key to the type of cell that will be made (e.g., a stellate or pyramidal cell) appears to be the time at which the cell is born (genesis) rather than the time at which it begins to migrate.
- The radial unit hypothesis states that the columnar organization in the adult cortex is derived during development from cells that divide in the ventricular region.

Neurogenesis and Plasticity

- A belief strongly held by the general public (and, until recently, by most neuroscientists) was that the adult brain produces no new neurons. We now know that that is not the case and that new neurons form throughout life in certain brain regions.
- Synaptogenesis is the birth of new synapses; neurogenesis is the birth of new neurons.
- The adult brain is plastic—that is, able to change or remap its function. The topographic map of the sensory cortex, for instance, will remap to reflect changes in sensory experience (e.g., increased use of the fingers of the left hand as in violin playing, or increased use of part of the body because of the loss of a limb). And the visual cortex is able to remap to process information about touch and audition after sensory deprivation (e.g., the onset of blindness).
- The mechanisms that underlie cortical plasticity are not entirely understood but might include one or both of the following: (a) unveiling of weak connections that already exist in the cortex through the release from inhibition and/or changes in the efficacy of the synapses; (b) growth of new neurons or synapses.

THOUGHT QUESTIONS

1. What is the evolutionary significance of the different types of cortex (e.g., neocortex versus allocortex)?
2. What is the functional advantage of organizing cortex as a sheet of neurons, rather than as groups of nuclei such as those found in subcortical structures?
3. What region of the cerebral cortex has increased in size the most across species during evolution? What does this brain region subserve in humans that is absent or reduced in animals?
4. Why are almost all sensory inputs routed through the thalamus on the way to cortex? Would it not be faster and therefore more efficient to project these inputs directly from sensory receptors to the primary sensory cortex?
5. Although the brainstem is relatively small in comparison with the forebrain, it contains some essential structures. Select one and describe how its anatomical organization supports its role in brain function.
6. Once the human brain is past the critical period in development and is fully developed, damage has less impact on its organization. But how would a person losing a limb in an accident in adulthood feel the missing limb, and why might this feeling be triggered by stimulation of the remaining body parts?
7. Expert violinists may have larger regions of the brain dedicated to somatosensory processing in the hand and finger region of the brain. Are these individuals born with more cortex dedicated to somatomotor processing? What evidence in animals helps resolve the study of this form of plasticity?

SUGGESTED READING

MESULAM, M.-M. (2000). Behavioral neuroanatomy: Large-scale networks, association cortex, frontal syndromes, the limbic system, and hemispheric specialization. In M.-M. Mesulam (Ed.), *Principals of behavioral and cognitive neurology* (pp. 1–34). New York: Oxford University Press.

SHAW, P., GREENSTEIN, D., LERCH, J., CLASEN, L., LENROOT, R., GOGTAY, N., ET AL. (2006). Intellectual ability and cortical development in children and adolescents. *Nature, 440,* 676–679.

SHEPHERD, G. M. (1988). *Neurobiology* (2nd ed.). New York: Oxford University Press.

SHORS, T. J. (2004). Memory traces of trace memories: Neurogenesis, synaptogenesis and awareness. *Trends in Neurosciences, 27,* 250–256.

STEVEN, M. S., & BLAKEMORE, C. (2004). Cortical plasticity in the adult human brain. In M. Gazzaniga (Ed.), *The cognitive neurosciences* (3rd ed., pp. 1243–1255). Cambridge, MA: MIT Press.

4

Methods of Cognitive Neuroscience

The frontiers of scientific discovery are defined as much by the tools available for observation as by conceptual innovation. In the 16th century the Earth was considered the center of the solar system. Simple observation verified it: The sun rose each morning in the east and slowly moved across the sky to set in the west. But the invention of the telescope in 1608 changed astronomers' observational methods. With this new tool, astronomers suddenly found galactic entities that they could track as these objects moved across the night sky. These observations rapidly exposed geocentric theories as painfully wrong. Indeed, within 5 years, Galileo spoke out for a heliocentric universe—a heretical claim that even the powerful Roman Catholic Church could not suppress in the face of new technology.

Theoretical breakthroughs in all scientific domains can be linked to the advent of new methods for observation. The invention of the bubble chamber allowed particle physicists to discover new and unexpected elementary particles such as *mesons*—discoveries that have totally transformed our understanding of the microscopic structure of matter. Gene cloning and sequencing techniques provided the tools for identifying new forms of proteins and for recognizing that these proteins formed previously unknown biological structures, such as the neurotransmitter receptor that binds with tetrahydrocannabinol (THC), the psychoactive ingredient in marijuana. Research in this area is now devoted to searching for endogenous substances that utilize these receptors rather than following the more traditional view that THC produces its effects by binding to receptors linked to known transmitters.

The emergence of cognitive neuroscience has been similarly fueled by new methods, some of which utilize high-technology tools unavailable to scientists of previous generations (Sejnowski & Churchland, 1989). Positron emission tomography (PET), for instance, has enabled scientists to measure, albeit indirectly, activity in the human brain while people perform simple tasks such as reading or memory retrieval. Brain lesions can be localized with amazing precision owing to methods such as magnetic resonance imaging (MRI). High-speed computers allow investigators to construct elaborate models to simulate patterns of connections and processing. Powerful electron microscopes bring previously unseen neural elements into view.

The real power of these tools, however, is still constrained by the types of problems one chooses to investigate. The dominant theory at any point in time defines the research paradigms and shapes the questions to be explored. The telescope helped Galileo plot the position of the planets with respect to the sun. But without an appreciation of the forces of gravity, he would have been at a loss to provide a causal account of planetary revolution. In an analogous manner, the problems investigated with the new tools of neuroscience are shaped by contemporary ideas of how the brain works in perception, thought, and action. Put simply, if well-formulated questions are not asked, even the most powerful tools will not provide a sensible answer.

In the preceding chapters we discussed some of the tools that neuroanatomists use to investigate the cellular and gross structures of the nervous system. In this chapter we turn to methods that form the core of cognitive neuroscience research. We focus on methods for studying brain-behavior relationships that are employed by cognitive psychologists, computer modelers, neurophysiologists, and neurologists. Although each of the areas represented by these professionals has blossomed in its own way, the interdisciplinary nature of cognitive neuroscience has depended on the clever ways in which scientists have integrated paradigms across these areas. The chapter concludes with examples of this integration.

WHAT IS COGNITIVE PSYCHOLOGY?

It would be naive to suppose that people have only recently sought to relate behavior to brain function. What marks cognitive neuroscience as a new field for this endeavor is the advent of the paradigms developed in **cognitive psychology**, the study of mental activity as an information-processing problem. Cognitive psychology rests on the assumption that we do not directly perceive and act in the world. Rather, our perceptions, thoughts, and actions depend on internal transformations or computations. Information is obtained by sense organs, but our ability to comprehend that information, to recognize it as something that we have experienced before, and to choose an appropriate response depends on a complex interplay of processes.

As an introduction to the magic of the mind, see what sense you can make of the following passage:

> ocacdrngi ot a schrehearc ta maccbriegd ineyurvtis, ti edost'n rttaem ni awth rreod eht tlteser ni a rwdo rea, eht ylon pirmtoatn gihtn si atth het rifts nda satl ttelre eb tat het ghitr clepa. eht srte anc eb a otlta sesm dan ouy anc itlls arde ti owtuthi moprbel. ihst si cebusea eth nuamh nidm sedo otn arde yrvee telrte yb stifle, tub eth rdow sa a lohew.

Not much, eh? Now take another shot at it:

> Aoccdrnig to a rscheearch at Cmabrigde Uinervtisy, it deosn't mttaer in waht oredr the ltteers in a wrod are, the olny iprmoatnt tihng is taht the frist and lsat ltteer be at the rghit pclae. The rset can be a total mses and you can sitll raed it wouthit porbelm. Tihs is bcuseae the huamn mnid deos not raed ervey lteter by istlef, but the wrod as a wlohe.

It is surprisingly easy to read the second passage, even though only a few words are correctly spelled. As long as the first and last letters of each word are in the correct position, we can accurately infer the correct spelling, especially when the surrounding context helps generate expectations for each word. Simple demonstrations such as this help us discern the content of mental representations, and thus help us gain insight into how information is manipulated by the mind.

Mental Representations and Transformations

Two key concepts underlie the cognitive approach. The first idea, that information processing depends on internal representations, we usually take for granted. Consider the concept "ball." If we met someone from a planet composed of straight lines, we could try to convey what this concept means in many ways. We could draw a picture of a sphere, we could provide a verbal definition indicating that such a three-dimensional object is circular along any circumference, or we could write a mathematical definition. Each instance is an alternative form of representing the "circular" concept. Whether one form of representation is better than another depends on our visitor. To understand the picture, our visitor would need a visual system and the ability to comprehend the spatial arrangement of a curved drawing. To understand the mathematical definition, our visitor would have to comprehend geometric and algebraic relations. Assuming our visitor had these capabilities, the task would help dictate which representational format was most useful. For example, if we wanted to show that the ball rolls down a hill, a pictorial representation is likely to be much more useful than an algebraic formula.

The second critical notion of cognitive psychology is that mental representations undergo transformations. The need to transform mental representations is most obvious when we consider how sensory signals are connected with stored knowledge in memory. Perceptual representations must be translated into action representations if we wish to achieve a goal. Moreover, information processing is not simply a sequential process from sensation to perception to memory to action. Memory may alter how we perceive something, and the manner in which information is processed is subject to attentional constraints. Cognitive psychology is all about how we manipulate representations.

Consider the categorization experiment, first introduced by Michael Posner (1986) at the University of Oregon, that is illustrated in Figure 4.1. Two letters are presented simultaneously in each trial. The subject's task is to evaluate whether they are both vowels, both consonants, or one vowel and one consonant. The subject presses one button if the letters are from the same category, and the other button if they are from different categories.

One version of this experiment includes five conditions. In the physical-identity condition, the two letters are exactly the same. In the phonetic-identity condition, the two letters have the same identity, but one letter is a capital and the other is lowercase. There are two types of same-category conditions, conditions in which the two letters are different members of the same category. In one, both letters are vowels; in the other, both letters are consonants. Finally, in the different-category condition, the two letters are from different categories and can be either of the same type size or of different sizes. Note that the first four conditions—physical identity, phonetic identity, and the two same-category conditions—require the "same" response: On all three types of trials, the correct response is that the two letters are from the same category. Nonetheless, as Figure 4.1b shows, response latencies differ significantly. Subjects respond fastest to the physical-identity condition, next fastest to the phonetic-identity condition, and slowest to the same-category condition, especially when the two letters are both consonants.

Figure 4.1 Letter-matching task. **(a)** In this version of the task, the subject responds "same" when both letters are either vowels or consonants and "different" when they are from different categories. **(b)** The reaction times vary for different conditions.

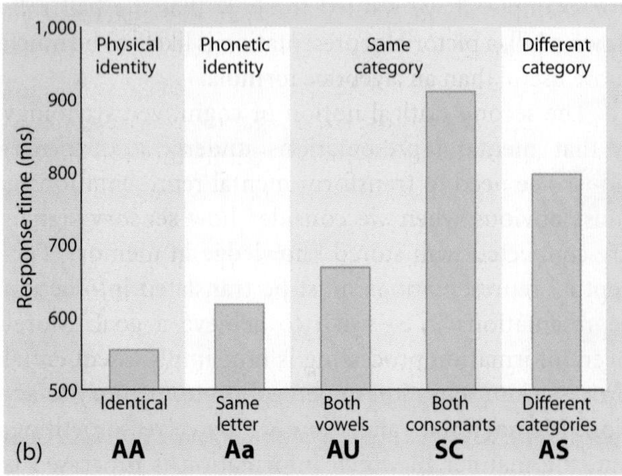

The results of Posner's experiment suggest that we derive multiple representations of stimuli. One representation is based on the physical aspects of the stimulus. In this experiment, it is a visually derived representation of the shape presented on the screen. A second representation corresponds to the letter's identity. This representation reflects the fact that many stimuli can correspond to the same letter. For example, we can recognize that *A*, a, and *a* all represent the same letter. A third level of abstraction represents the category to which a letter belongs. At this level, the letters *A* and *E* activate our internal representation of the category "vowel." Posner maintains that different response latencies reflect the degrees of processing required to do the letter-matching task. By this logic, we infer that physical representations are activated first, phonetic representations next, and category representations last.

This experiment provides a powerful demonstration that, even with simple stimuli, the mind derives multiple representations. Other manipulations with this task have explored how representations are transformed from one form to another. In a follow-up study, Posner and his colleagues used a sequential mode of presentation. Two letters were presented again, but a brief interval (referred to as the *stimulus onset asynchrony*, the time between the two stimuli) separated the presentations for the letters. As Figure 4.2 shows, the difference in response time to the physical-identity and phonetic-identity conditions was reduced as the stimulus onset asynchrony became longer. Hence, the internal representation of the first letter is transformed during the interval. The representation of the physical stimulus gives way to the more abstract representation of the letter's phonetic identity.

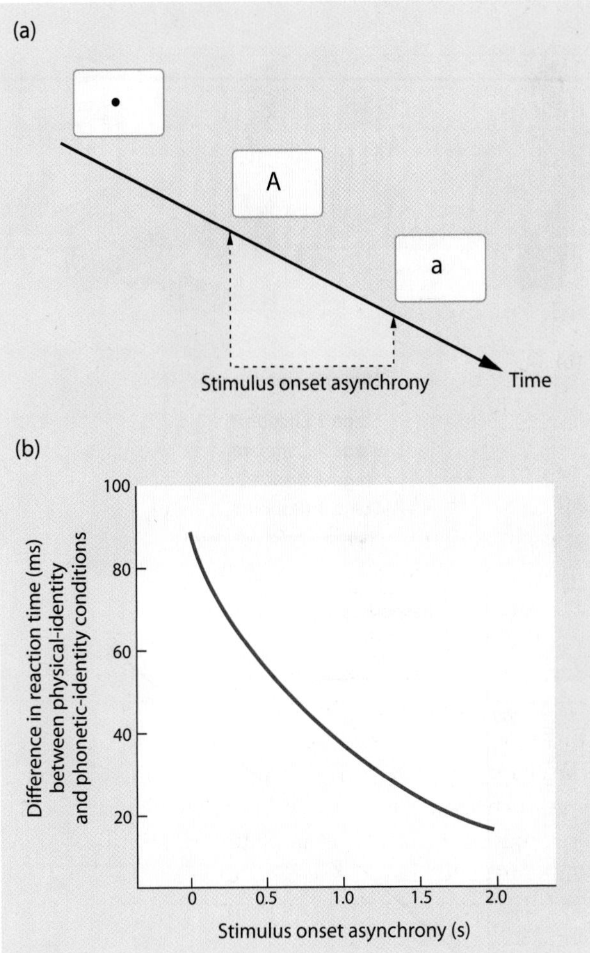

Figure 4.2 **(a)** The same letter-matching task as in Figure 4.1, except that an interval, defined as the stimulus onset asynchrony, separates the presentation of the two letters. **(b)** As this interval is lengthened, the difference in the reaction time to the physical-identity and phonetic-identity conditions becomes smaller, suggesting a transformation of the representation into a more abstract code.

As you may have experienced personally, experiments such as these elicit as many questions as answers. Why do subjects take longer to judge that two letters are consonants than they do to judge that two letters are vowels? Would the same advantage for identical stimuli exist if the letters were spoken? What about if one letter were visual and the other were auditory? Suppose that the task were to judge whether two letters were physically identical. Would manipulating the stimulus onset asynchrony affect reaction times in this version? Cognitive psychologists address these questions and then devise methods for inferring the mind's machinery from observable behaviors.

In the preceding example, the primary dependent variable was reaction time, the speed with which subjects make their judgments. Reaction time experiments utilize the chronometric methodology. *Chronometric* comes from the Greek words *chronos* ("time") and *metron* ("measure"). The chronometric study of the mind is essential for cognitive psychologists because mental events occur rapidly and efficiently. If we consider only whether a person is correct or incorrect on a task, we miss subtle differences in performance. Measuring reaction time permits a finer analysis of internal processes. In addition to measuring processing time as a dependent variable, chronometric manipulations can be applied to independent variables, as with the letter-matching experiment in which the stimulus onset asynchrony was varied.

Characterizing Mental Operations

Suppose you arrive at the grocery store and discover that you forgot to bring your shopping list. As you wander up and down the aisles, you gaze upon the thousands of items lining the shelves, hoping that they will help prompt your memory. Perhaps you cruise through the pet food section, but when you come to the dairy section you hesitate: Was there a carton of eggs in the refrigerator? Was the milk supply low? Were there any cheeses not covered by a 6-month rind of mold?

This memory retrieval task draws on a number of cognitive capabilities. A fundamental goal of cognitive psychology is to identify the different mental operations that are required to perform tasks such as these. Not only are cognitive psychologists interested in describing human performance—the observable behavior of humans and other animals—but also they seek to identify the internal processing that underlies this performance. A basic assumption of cognitive psychology is that tasks are composed of a set of mental operations. Mental operations involve taking a representation as an *input* and performing some sort of process on it, thus producing a new representation, or *output*. As such, mental operations are processes that generate, elaborate on, or manipulate mental representations. Cognitive psychologists design experiments to test hypotheses about mental operations.

Consider an experimental task introduced by Saul Sternberg (1975) when he was working at Bell Laboratories. The task bears some similarity to the problem faced by an absentminded shopper, except that in Sternberg's task, the difficulty is not so much in terms of forgetting items in memory, but rather in comparing sensory information with representations that are active in memory. On each trial, the subject is first presented with a set of letters to memorize (Figure 4.3a). The memory set could consist of one, two, or four letters. Then a single letter is presented, and the subject must decide if this letter was part of the memorized set. The subject presses one button to indicate that the target was part of the memory set ("yes" response) and a second button to indicate that the target was not part of the set ("no" response). Once again the primary dependent variable is reaction time.

Sternberg postulated that, to respond on this task, the subject must engage in four primary mental operations (Figure 4.3b):

1. *Encode.* The subject must identify the visible target.
2. *Compare.* The subject must compare the mental representation of the target with the representations of the items in memory.
3. *Decide.* The subject must decide whether the target matches one of the memorized items.
4. *Respond.* The subject must respond appropriately for the decision made in Step 3.

Note that each of these operations is likely to be composed of additional operations. For example, responding might be subdivided into processes involved in selecting the appropriate finger and processes involved in activating the muscles that make the finger move. Nonetheless, by postulating a set of mental operations, we can devise experiments to explore how putative mental operations are carried out.

A basic question for Sternberg was how to characterize the efficiency of recognition memory. Assuming that all items in the memory set are actively represented, the recognition process might work in one of two different ways: A highly efficient system might compare a representation of the target with all of the items in the memory set simultaneously. On the other hand, the recognition operation might be limited in terms of how much information it can handle at any point in time. For example, it might require the input to be compared successively to each item in memory.

Sternberg realized that the reaction time data could distinguish between these two alternatives. If the comparison process can be simultaneous for all items—what is called a *parallel* process—then reaction time should be independent of the number of items in the memory set. But if the comparison process operates in a sequential, or *serial*, manner, then reaction time should slow down as the memory set becomes larger, because more time is required to compare an item with a large memory list than with a small memory list. Sternberg's results convincingly supported the serial hypothesis. In fact, reaction time increased in a constant, or linear, manner with set size, and the functions for the "yes" and "no" trials were essentially identical (Figure 4.3c).

The parallel, linear functions allowed Sternberg to make two inferences about the mental operations associated with this task. First, the linear increase in reaction time as the set size increased implied that the memory comparison operation took a fixed amount of internal

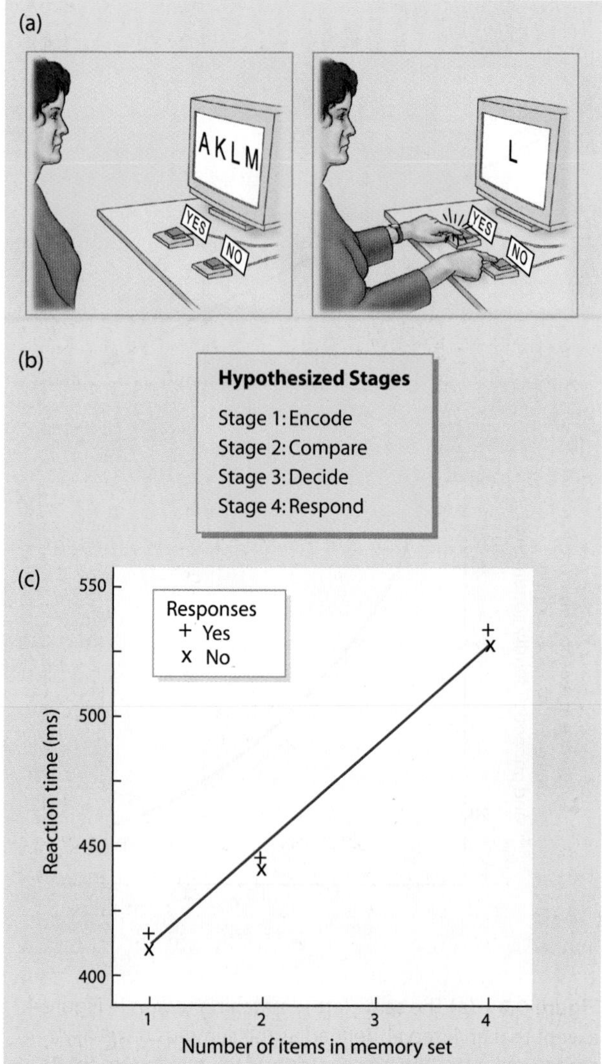

Figure 4.3 Memory comparison task. **(a)** The subject is shown a set of one, two, or four letters and is asked to memorize them. After a delay, a single probe letter appears, and the subject indicates whether that letter was a member of the memory set. **(b)** Performance of this task is hypothesized to require four different mental operations. **(c)** Reaction time increases with set size, indicating that the target letter must be compared with the memory set sequentially rather than in parallel.

processing time. In the initial study, the slope of the function was approximately 40 ms per item, implying that it takes about 40 ms for each successive comparison of the target to the items in the memory set. This does not mean that this value represents a fixed property of memory comparison. It is likely to be affected by factors such as task difficulty (e.g., whether the nontarget items in the memory set are similar or dissimilar to the target item) and experience. Nonetheless, the experiment demonstrates how mental operations can be evaluated both qualitatively and quantitatively from simple behavioral tasks.

Second, the fact that the two functions were parallel implied that subjects compared all of the memory items to the target before responding. If subjects had terminated the comparison as soon as a match was found, then the slope of the "no" function should have been twice as steep as the slope of the "yes" function. This follows because in "no" trials, all of the items have to be checked. With "yes" trials, on average only half the items need to be checked before a match is found. The fact that the functions were parallel implies that comparisons were carried out on all items in what is called an *exhaustive search* (as opposed to a serial, self-terminating search). An exhaustive process seems illogical, though. Why continue to compare the target to the memory set after a match has been detected? One possible answer is that it is easier to store the result of each comparison for later evaluation than to monitor "online" the results of successive comparisons.

Although memory comparison appears to involve a serial process, much of the activity in our mind operates in parallel. A classic demonstration of parallel processing is the word superiority effect (Reicher, 1969). In this experiment, a stimulus is shown briefly and subjects are asked which of two target letters (e.g., *A* or *E*) was presented. The stimuli can be composed of words, nonsense letter strings, or letter strings in which every letter is an *X* except for the target letter (Figure 4.4). Brief presentation times are used so that errors will be observed, with the critical question centering on whether the context affects performance. *Word superiority effect* refers to the fact that subjects are most accurate when the stimuli are words. Somewhat counterintuitively, this finding suggests that we do not need to identify all of the letters of a word before we recognize the word. Rather, when we are reading a list of words, representations corresponding to the individual letters and to the entire word are activated in parallel for each item. Performance is facilitated because both representations can provide information as to whether the target letter is present. A word-level representation is not possible with nonsense words and letter strings, and thus judgments must be based solely on letter-level representation.

Does the stimulus contain an *A* or an *E*?

Condition	Stimulus	Accuracy
Word	**RACK**	90%
Nonsense string	**KARC**	80%
*X*s	**XAXX**	80%

Figure 4.4 Word superiority effect. Subjects are more accurate in identifying the target vowel when it is embedded in a word. This result suggests that letter and word levels of representation are activated in parallel.

Constraints on Information Processing

In the memory search experiment, information processing operates in a certain manner because the memory comparison process is limited. The subjects cannot compare the target item to all of the items in the memory set simultaneously. An important question is whether this limitation reflects properties that are specific to memory or a more general processing constraint. Perhaps the amount of internal processing that people can do at any one time is limited regardless of the task. An alternative explanation is that processing limitations are task specific. Processing constraints are defined only by the particular set of mental operations associated with a particular task. For example, although the comparison of a probe item to the memory set might require a serial operation, encoding might occur in parallel such that it would not matter whether the probe was presented by itself or among a noisy array of competing stimuli.

Exploring the limitations in task performance is a central concern for cognitive psychologists. Consider a simple color-naming task that was devised in the early 1930s by an aspiring doctoral student, J. R. Stroop (1935; for a review, see MacLeod, 1991), and that has become one of the most widely employed tasks in all of cognitive psychology. In this task, a list of words is presented and the subject is asked to name the color of each stimulus as fast as possible. As Figure 4.5 illustrates, it is

Color matches word	Color without word	Color doesn't match word
RED	XXXXX	GREEN
GREEN	XXXXX	BLUE
RED	XXXXX	RED
BLUE	XXXXX	BLUE
BLUE	XXXXX	GREEN
GREEN	XXXXX	RED
BLUE	XXXXX	GREEN
RED	XXXXX	BLUE

Figure 4.5 Stroop task. Time yourself as you work through each column, naming the color of the ink of each stimulus as fast as possible. Assuming that you do not squint to blur the words, it should be easy to read the first and second columns but quite difficult to read the third.

much easier to do this task when the words match the ink colors.

The Stroop effect powerfully demonstrates the multiplicity of mental representations. The stimuli in this task appear to activate at least two separable representations. One representation corresponds to the color of each stimulus; it is what allows the subject to perform the task. The second representation corresponds to the color concept associated with the words. The fact that you are slower to name the colors when the ink color and words are mismatched indicates that this representation is activated even though it is irrelevant to the task. Indeed, the activation of a representation based on the words rather than the colors of the words appears to be automatic. The Stroop effect persists even after thousands of trials of practice, reflecting the fact that skilled readers have years of practice in analyzing letter strings for their symbolic meaning. On the other hand, the interference from the words is markedly reduced if the response requires a key press rather than a vocal response. Thus, the word-based representations are closely linked to the vocal response system and have little effect when the responses are produced manually.

Another method used to examine constraints on information processing involves dual tasks. For these studies, performance on a primary task alone is compared to performance when that task is carried out concurrently with a secondary task. The decrement in primary-task performance during the dual-task situation helps elucidate the limits of cognition. Sophisticated use of dual-task methodology also can identify the exact source of interference. For example, the Stroop effect is not reduced when the color-naming task is performed simultaneously with a secondary task in which the subject must judge the pitch of an auditory tone. However, if the auditory stimuli for the secondary task are a list of words and the subject must monitor this list for a particular target, the Stroop effect is attenuated. It appears that the verbal demands of the secondary task interfere with the automatic activation of the word-based representations in the Stroop task, thus leaving the color-based representations relatively free from interference.

The efficiency of our mental abilities and the way in which mental operations interact can change with experience. The beginning driver has her hands rigidly locked to the steering wheel; within a few months, though, she is unfazed to steer with her left hand while maintaining a conversation with a passenger and using her right hand to scan for a good radio station. Even more impressive is the fact that, with extensive practice, people can become proficient at simultaneously performing two tasks that were originally quite incompatible.

Elizabeth Spelke and her colleagues at Cornell University studied how well college students read for comprehension while taking dictation (Spelke et al., 1976). Prior to any training, their subjects could read about 400 words per minute when faced with difficult reading material such as modern short stories. As we would expect, this rate fell to 280 words per minute when the subjects were required to simultaneously take dictation, and their comprehension of the stories was also impaired. Remarkably, after 85 hours of training spread over a 17-week period, the students' proficiency in reading while taking dictation was essentially as good as when reading alone. The results offer an elixir for all college students. Imagine finishing the reading for an upcoming psychology examination while taking notes during a history lecture!

COMPUTER MODELING

The computer is a powerful metaphor for cognitive neuroscience. Both the brain and the computer chip are impressive processing machines, capable of representing and transforming large amounts of information. Although there are vast differences in how these machines process information, cognitive scientists use computers to simulate cognitive processes. To **simulate** is to imitate, to reproduce behavior in an alternative medium. The simulated cognitive processes are commonly referred to as *artificial intelligence*—artificial in the sense that they are artifacts, human creations—and intelligent in that the computers perform complex functions. Computer programs control robots on factory production lines, assist physicians in making differential diagnoses or in detecting breast cancer, and create models of the universe in the first nanoseconds after the big bang.

Many commercial computer applications are developed without reference to how brains think. More relevant to our present concerns are the efforts of cognitive scientists to create models of cognition (Rumelhart et al., 1986). In these investigations, simulations are designed to mimic behavior and the cognitive processes that support that behavior. The computer is given input and then must perform internal operations to create a behavior. By observing the behavior, the researcher can assess how well it matches behavior produced by a real mind. Of course, to get the computer to succeed, the modeler must specify how information is represented and transformed within the program. To do this, concrete hypotheses regarding the "mental" operations needed for the machine must be generated. As such, computer simulations provide a useful tool for testing theories of cognition. Successes and failures of models give valuable insights to the strengths and weaknesses of a theory.

Models Are Explicit

Computer models of cognition are useful because they can be analyzed in detail. In creating a simulation, the researcher must be completely explicit; the way the computer represents and processes information must be totally specified. This does not mean that a computer's operation is always completely predictable and that the outcome of a simulation is known in advance. Computer simulations can incorporate random events or be on such a large scale that analytic tools do not reveal the solution. But the internal operations, the way information is computed, must be determined. Computer simulations are especially helpful to cognitive neuroscientists in recognizing problems that the brain must solve to produce coherent behavior.

Braitenberg (1984) gave elegant examples of how modeling brings insights to information processing. Imagine observing the two creatures shown in Figure 4.6 as they move about a minimalist world consisting of a single heat source such as a sun. From the outside, the creatures look identical: They both have two sensors and

Figure 4.6 Two very simple vehicles, each equipped with two sensors that excite motors on the rear wheels. The wheel linked to the sensor closest to the sun will turn faster than the other wheel, thus causing the vehicle to turn. Simply changing the wiring scheme from uncrossed to crossed radically alters the behavior of the vehicles. The "coward" will always avoid the source, whereas the "aggressor" will relentlessly pursue it.

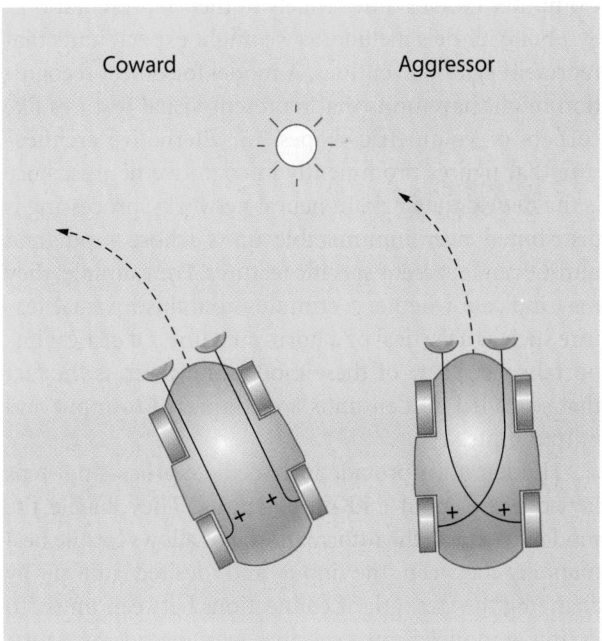

four wheels. Despite this similarity, their behavior is distinct: One creature moves away from the sun, and the other homes in on it. Why the difference? As outsiders with no access to the internal operations of these creatures, we might conjecture that they have had different experiences and so the same input activates different representations. Perhaps one was burned at an early age and fears the sun, and maybe the other likes the warmth.

As their internal wiring reveals, however, the behavioral differences depend on how the creatures are wired. The uncrossed connections make the creature on the left turn away from the sun; the crossed connections force the creature on the right to orient toward it. Thus, the two creatures' behavioral differences arise from a slight variation in how sensory information is mapped onto motor processes.

These creatures are exceedingly simple—and inflexible in their actions. At best, they offer only the crudest model of how an invertebrate might move in response to a phototropic sensor. The point of Braitenberg's example is not to model a behavior; rather, it represents how a single computational change—from crossed to uncrossed wiring—can yield a major behavioral change. When interpreting such a behavioral difference, we might postulate extensive internal operations and representations. When we look inside Braitenberg's models, however, we see that there is no difference in how the two models process information, but only a difference in their patterns of connectivity.

Representations in Computer Models

Computer models differ widely in their representations. Symbolic models include, as we might expect, units that represent symbolic entities. A model for object recognition might have units that represent visual features like corners or volumetric shapes. An alternative architecture that figures prominently in cognitive neuroscience is the **neural network**. In neural networks, processing is distributed over innumerable units whose input and output can represent specific features. For example, they may indicate whether a stimulus contains a visual feature such as a vertical or a horizontal line. Of critical importance in many of these models, however, is the fact that so-called hidden units are connected to input and output units.

Hidden units provide intermediate processing steps between the input and output units. They enable the model to extract the information that allows for the best mapping between the input and desired output by changing the strength of connections between units. To do this, a modeler must specify a *learning rule*, a quantitative description of how processing within the model changes. With most learning rules, changes are large when the model performs poorly and small when the model performs well. Other learning algorithms are even simpler. For example, whenever two neighboring nodes are simultaneously active, the link between them is strengthened; if one is active when the other is silent, then the link between them is weakened.

Models can be very powerful for solving complex problems. Simulations cover the gamut of cognitive processes, including perception, memory, language, and motor control. One of the most appealing aspects of neural networks is that the architecture resembles, at least superficially, the nervous system. In these models, processing is distributed across many units, similar to the way that neural structures depend on the activity of many neurons. The contribution of any unit may be small in relation to the system's total output, but complex behaviors can be generated by the aggregate action of all units. In addition, the computations in these models are simulated to occur in parallel. The activation levels of the units in the network can be updated in a relatively continuous and simultaneous manner.

Computational models can vary widely in the level of explanation they seek to provide. Some models simulate behavior at the systems level, seeking to show how cognitive operations such as motion perception or skilled movements can be generated from a network of interconnected processing units. In other cases, the simulations operate at a cellular or even molecular level. For example, neural network models have been used to investigate how the variation in transmitter uptake is a function of dendrite geometry (Volfovsky et al., 1999). The amount of detail that must be incorporated into the model will be dictated to a large extent by the type of question being investigated. Many of these problems are difficult to evaluate without simulations, either experimentally because the available experimental methods are insufficient or mathematically because the solutions become too complicated given the many interactions of the processing elements.

An appealing aspect of neural network models, especially for people interested in cognitive neuroscience, is that "lesion" techniques demonstrate how a model's performance changes when its parts are altered. Unlike strictly serial computer models that collapse if a circuit is broken, neural network models degrade gracefully: The model may continue to perform appropriately after some units are removed, because each unit plays only a small part in the processing. Artificial lesioning is thus a fascinating way to test a model's validity. At the first level, a model is constructed to see if it adequately simulates normal behavior. Then "lesions" can be made to see if the breakdown in the model's performance resembles the behavioral deficits observed in neurological patients.

Models Lead to Testable Predictions

The contribution of computer modeling usually goes beyond the assessment of whether a model succeeds in mimicking a cognitive process. Models can generate novel predictions that can be tested with real brains. An example of the predictive power of computer modeling comes from the work of Szabolcs Kali of the Hungarian Academy of Sciences and Peter Dayan at the University College London (Kali & Dayan, 2004). Their computer models were designed to ask questions about how people store and retrieve information in memory about specific events—what is called *episodic memory* (see Chapter 8). Observations from the neurosciences suggest that the *formation* of episodic memories depends critically on the hippocampus and adjacent areas of the medial temporal lobe, whereas the *storage* of such memories involves the neocortex. Kali and Dayan used a computer model to explore a specific question: How is access to stored memories maintained in a system where the neocortical connections are ever changing (see the discussion on cortical plasticity in Chapter 3)? Does the maintenance of memories over time require the reactivation of hippocampal–neocortical connections, or can neocortical representations remain stable despite fluctuations and modifications over time?

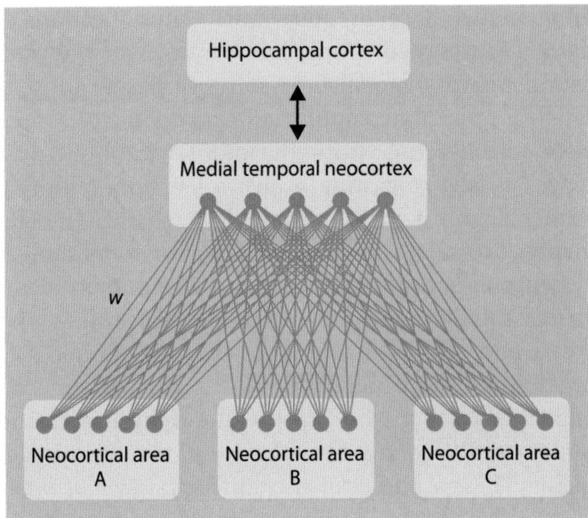

Figure 4.7 Computational model of episodic memory. "Neurons" (•) in neocortical areas A, B, and C are connected in a bidirectional manner to "neurons" in the medial temporal neocortex, which is itself connected bidirectionally to the hippocampus. Areas A, B, and C represent highly processed inputs (e.g., inputs from visual, auditory, or tactile domains). As the model learns, it extracts categories, trends, and correlations from the statistics of the inputs (or patterns of activations) and converts these to weights (*w*) that corresponds to the strengths of the connections. Prior to learning, the weights might be equal or set to random values. With learning, the weights become adjusted to reflect correlations between the processing units.

The model architecture was based on anatomical facts regarding patterns of connectivity between the hippocampus and neocortex (Figure 4.7). The model was then trained on a set of patterns that represented distinct episodic memories. For example, one might correspond to the first time you visited the Pacific Ocean; another, to the lecture in which you first learned about the Stroop effect. Once the model had mastered the memory set by showing that it could correctly recall a full episode when given only partial information, it was tested on a consolidation task. Could old memories remain after the hippocampus was disconnected from the cortex if cortical units continued to follow their initial learning rules? In essence, this was a test of whether lesions to the hippocampus would disrupt long-term episodic memory. The results indicated that episodic memory became quite impaired when the hippocampus and cortex were disconnected. Thus, the model predicts that hippocampal *reactivation* is necessary for maintaining even well-consolidated episodic memories. In the model, this maintenance process requires a mechanism that keeps hippocampal and neocortical representations in register with one another, even as the neocortex undergoes subtle changes associated with daily learning.

This modeling project was initiated because research on people with lesions of the hippocampus had failed to provide a clear answer about the role of this structure in memory consolidation. The model, based on known principles of neuroanatomy and neurophysiology, could be used to test specific hypotheses concerning one type of memory, episodic memory, and to direct future research. Of course, the goal here is not to make a model that has perfect memory consolidation. Rather, it is to ask how human memory works. Thus, human experiments can be conducted to test predictions derived from the model, as well as to generate new empirical observations that must be incorporated into future versions of the computational model.

Limitations of Computer Models

Computer modeling is limited as a method for studying the operation of living nervous systems. For one thing, models always require radical simplifications of the nervous system. Although the units in a typical neural network model bear some similarity to neurons—for example, nonlinear activation rules produce spikelike behavior—the models are limited in scope, usually consisting of just a few hundred or so elements, and it is not always clear whether the elements correspond to single neurons or to ensembles of neurons. Second, some requirements and problems arise in modeling work, particularly in learning, and are at odds with what we know occurs in biological organisms. Many network models require an "all-knowing" teacher who "knows" the right answer and can be used to correct the behavior of the internal elements. These models can also suffer *catastrophic interference*, the loss of old information when new material is presented.

Third, most modeling efforts are restricted to relatively narrow problems, such as demonstrating how the Stroop effect can be simulated by postulating separate word name and word color representations under the control of a common attentional system. As such, they provide useful computational tests of the viability of a particular hypothesis but are typically less useful for generating new predictions. Moreover, as some critics have argued, unlike experimental work that, by its nature, is cumulative, modeling research tends to be conducted in isolation. There may be lots of ways to model a particular phenomenon, but less effort has been devoted to devising critical tests that pit one theory against another.

These limitations are by no means insurmountable, and we should expect the contribution of computer simulations to continue to grow in the cognitive neurosciences. Indeed, the trend in the field is for modeling work to be more constrained by neuroscience, with researchers replacing generic processing units with elements that embody the biophysics of the brain. In a reciprocal manner, computer simulations provide a useful way to develop theory, which may then aid researchers in designing experiments and interpreting results.

EXPERIMENTAL TECHNIQUES USED WITH ANIMALS

The use of animals for experimental procedures has played a critical role in the medical and biological sciences. Although many insights can be gleaned from careful observations of people with neurological disorders, as we will see throughout this book, such methods are, in essence, correlational. We can observe how behavior is disturbed following a neurological insult, but it can be difficult to pinpoint the exact cause of the disorder. For one thing, insults such as stroke or tumor tend to be quite large, with the damage extending across many neural structures. Moreover, damage in one part of the brain may disturb function in other parts of the brain that are spared. There is also increasing evidence that the brain is a plastic device: Neural function is constantly being reshaped by our experiences, and such reorganization can be quite remarkable following neurological damage.

The use of animals in scientific research allows researchers to adopt a more experimental approach. Because neural function depends on electrochemical processes, neurophysiologists have developed techniques that can be used to measure and manipulate neuronal activity. Some of these techniques measure and record cell activity, in either passive or in active conditions. Others manipulate activity by creating lesions through the destruction or temporary inactivation of targeted brain regions. Lesion studies in animals face the same limitations associated with the study of human neurological dysfunction. However, modern techniques allow the researcher to be highly selective in creating these lesions, and the effects of the damage can be monitored carefully following the surgery.

Single-Cell Recording

The most important technological advance in **neurophysiology**—perhaps in all of neuroscience—was the development of methods to record the activity of single neurons in laboratory animals. With this method, the understanding of neural activity advanced a quantum leap. No longer did the neuroscientist have to be content with describing nervous system action in terms of functional regions. **Single-cell recording** enabled researchers to describe response characteristics of individual elements.

In single-cell recording, a thin electrode is inserted into an animal's brain. If the electrode is in the vicinity of a neuronal membrane, electrical changes can be measured (see Chapter 2). Although the surest way to guarantee that the electrode records the activity of a single cell is to record intracellularly, this technique is difficult, and penetrating the membrane frequently damages the cell. Thus, single-cell recording is typically done extracellularly. With this method, the electrode is situated on the outside of the neuron. The problem with this approach is that there is no guarantee that the changes in electrical potential at the electrode tip reflect the activity of a single neuron. It is more likely that the tip will record the activity of a small set of neurons. Computer algorithms are used to differentiate this pooled activity into the contributions from individual neurons.

Neurons are constantly active, even in the absence of stimulation or movement. This baseline activity varies widely from one brain area to another. For example, some cells within the basal ganglia have spontaneous firing rates of over 100 spikes/s, whereas cells in another basal ganglia region have a baseline rate of about 1 spike/s. These spontaneous firing levels fluctuate. The primary goal of single-cell recording experiments is to determine experimental manipulations that produce a consistent change in the response rate of an isolated cell. Does the cell increase its firing rate when the animal moves its arm? Is this change specific to movements in a particular direction? Does the firing rate for that movement depend on the outcome of the action (e.g., the food morsel to be reached)? As interesting, what makes the cell decrease its response rate?

The neurophysiologist is interested in what causes change in the synaptic activity of a neuron. The experimenter seeks to determine the response characteristics of individual neurons by correlating their activity with a given stimulus pattern or behavior. The technique has been used in almost all regions of the brain in a wide range of nonhuman species. For sensory neurons, the experimenter might manipulate the type of stimulus presented to the animal. For motor neurons, recordings can be made as the animal performs a task or moves about the cage. Some of the most recent advances in neurophysiology have come about as researchers probe higher brain centers to examine changes in cellular activity related to goals, emotions, and rewards.

In the typical neurophysiological experiment, recordings are obtained from a series of cells in a targeted area of interest. In this manner, a functional map can describe similarities and differences between neurons in a specified cortical region. One area where the single-cell method has been used extensively is the study of the visual system of primates. In a typical experiment the researcher targets the electrode to a cortical area that contains cells thought to respond to visual stimulation. Once a cell has been identified, the researcher tries to characterize its response properties.

A single cell is not responsive to all visual stimuli. A number of stimulus parameters might correlate with the variation in the cell's firing rate; examples include the shape of the stimulus, its color, and whether or not it is moving (see Chapter 5). An important factor is the location of the stimulus. As Figure 4.8 shows, all visually sensitive cells respond to stimuli in only a limited region of space. This region of space is referred to as that cell's **receptive field**. For example, some neurons respond when the stimulus is located in the lower left portion of

Figure 4.8 Electrophysiological methods are used to identify the response characteristics of cells in the visual cortex. **(a)** While the activity of a single cell is monitored, the monkey is required to maintain fixation, and stimuli are presented at various positions in its field of view. **(b)** The vertical lines to the right of each stimulus correspond to individual action potentials. The cell fires vigorously when the stimulus is presented in the upper right quadrant, thus defining the upper right as the receptive field for this cell.

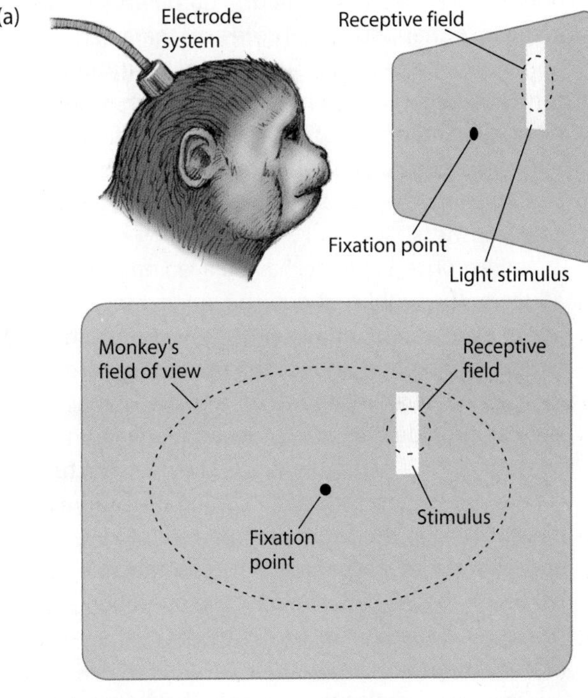

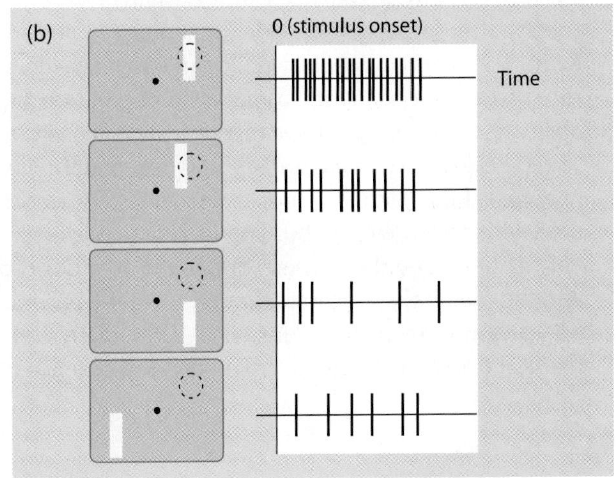

THE COGNITIVE NEUROSCIENTIST'S TOOLKIT

The Ethics and Practice of Animal Research

Students on most university campuses are familiar with the annual protests during World Laboratory Animal Liberation Week by groups opposed to the use of animals for research purposes. These groups hand out inflammatory pamphlets graphically depicting how researchers callously exploit laboratory rats, cats, and especially monkeys in their pursuit of knowledge. Although many of the protests are peaceful and law-abiding, there have been numerous incidents of violence against people and property: Windows have been smashed, equipment destroyed, animals kidnapped, and professors harassed at their homes. The protesters argue that university administrators have become dependent on the money generated by public and private grants supporting "frivolous and unnecessary" research, and thus they are forced to resort to more dramatic measures to raise the public's consciousness.

In response, scientists have played offense, eager to educate the public about the importance of these forms of research. Almost all that we know about the structure and physiology of the nervous system has depended on invasive studies of animals. Human autopsies can provide only the crudest understanding of the anatomy of the nervous system. The fine structure that is revealed by sophisticated staining procedures is not possible unless the stains are injected into live animals and allowed to propagate along metabolically active tissue. All that we know about the operation of single neurons has been made possible only by the use of laboratory animals.

This basic research does not exist in a vacuum, sought after as part of an ephemeral quest for knowledge. Scientists and public policy makers have long recognized that advances in medicine depend on the ability to carry out both basic research and clinically inspired research. Human studies of brain metabolites may reveal that excessive dopamine levels are associated with schizophrenia, but animal research is essential for understanding where dopamine is produced and the metabolic processes that regulate the production and uptake of this transmitter. Only rarely have medical treatments been discovered in the absence of animal models. In most cases, new medical treatments become available only after years of careful experimental work with animals, first involving years of basic research, then followed by the careful development of clinical measures involving animal studies.

The scientific research community has served as a visible target for animal rights groups. One reason has been a few well-publicized cases in which videotapes or photographs were used to demonstrate the extreme experimental manipulations being practiced on laboratory animals. Two of the more well-known cases involved monkeys. In one case the animals were subjected to severe blows to the head as part of a study of head trauma in car accidents. In the other case, the animals were in poor health after undergoing fetal surgery to destroy sensory fibers. The latter case resulted in the only recorded U.S. conviction of a scientist on animal cruelty charges.

Although abuses most certainly exist, research with laboratory animals is closely regulated by both research institutions and federal agencies. All research protocols must be approved by institutional animal care and use committees that include not only scientific peers but also lay members of the community. Three basic principles must be met for any research project to be certified (Rowan & Rollin, 1983). First, the goals of the research must be articulated clearly, showing that the studies are worthwhile and will advance our knowledge of the nervous system. Second, experiments must be conducted so as to minimize pain and distress through the use of anesthetics and analgesics. Any animals that show evidence of suffering must be humanely destroyed. Third, alternative methods that might yield similar knowledge must be considered.

The evidence suggests that these codes are strictly followed. In almost all studies involving surgical procedures, animals are provided with anesthesia. The rare exceptions are those in which the focus is how the brain reacts to pain—an important problem faced by people recovering from surgery. The argument that computer models can serve as realistic substitutes for animal research is specious. Current models can simulate only the simplest of neural functions, and even these models are useful only in terms of how well they converge with the results of studies on living organisms.

Nonetheless, it is important for the public to debate the fundamental question of whether it is ethical for humans to exploit other species for their own benefit. A researcher in 1898 was quoted as saying, "Animals have no more rights than inanimate objects, and it is no worse from an ethical point of view to flay the forearm of an ape or lacerate the leg of a dog than to rip open the sleeve or rend a pair of pantaloons." It is clear that few would take this stance in our modern society. We must understand both the benefits and the costs of animal research in order to form educated opinions on these ethical matters.

The morality of using animals for research purposes has been debated for centuries. People on both sides of the debate have recognized the importance of engaging the public—a point underscored by the fact that members of the U.S. Congress receive more letters on this issue than on any other.

the visible field. For other neurons, the stimulus may have to be in the upper left.

The sizes of the receptive fields of visual cells vary; they are smallest in primary visual cortex and become larger in association visual areas. Thus, a stimulus will cause a cell in primary visual cortex to increase its firing rate only when it is positioned in a very restricted region of the visible world. If the stimulus is moved outside this region of space, the cell will return to its spontaneous level of activity. In contrast, displacing a stimulus over a large distance may produce a similar increase in the firing rate of visually sensitive cells in the temporal lobe.

Neighboring cells have at least partially overlapping receptive fields. As a region of visually responsive cells is traversed, there is an orderly relation between the receptive-field properties of these cells and the external world. External space is represented in a continuous manner across the cortical surface: Neighboring cells have receptive fields of neighboring regions of external space (Figure 4.9). As such, cells form a topographic representation, an orderly mapping between an external dimension such as spatial location and the neural representation of that dimension. In vision, topographic representations are referred to as **retinotopic.**

The retina is composed of a continuous sheet of photoreceptors, neurons that respond to visible light passing through the lens of the eye. Visual cells in subcortical and cortical areas maintain retinotopic information. Thus, if light falls on one spot of the retina, cells with receptive fields spanning this area are activated. If the light moves and falls on a different region of the retina, activity ceases in these cells and begins in other cells whose receptive fields encompass the new region of stimulation. In this manner, visual areas provide a representation of the location of the stimulus. Cell activity within a retinotopic map correlates with (i.e., predicts) the location of the stimulus.

There are other types of topographic maps. In Chapter 3 we reviewed the motor and somatosensory maps along the central sulcus that provide topo-

(a)

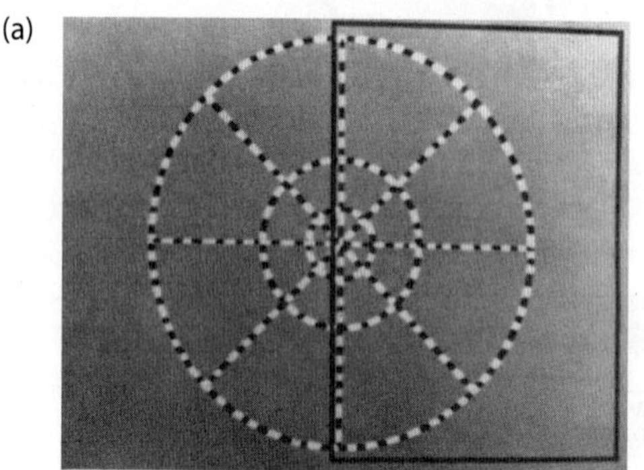

(b)

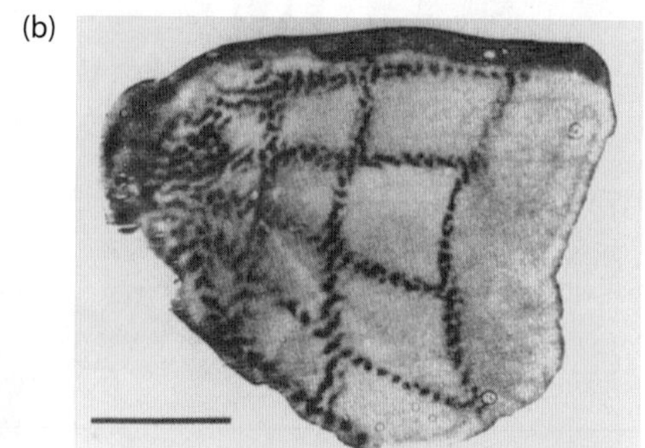

(c)

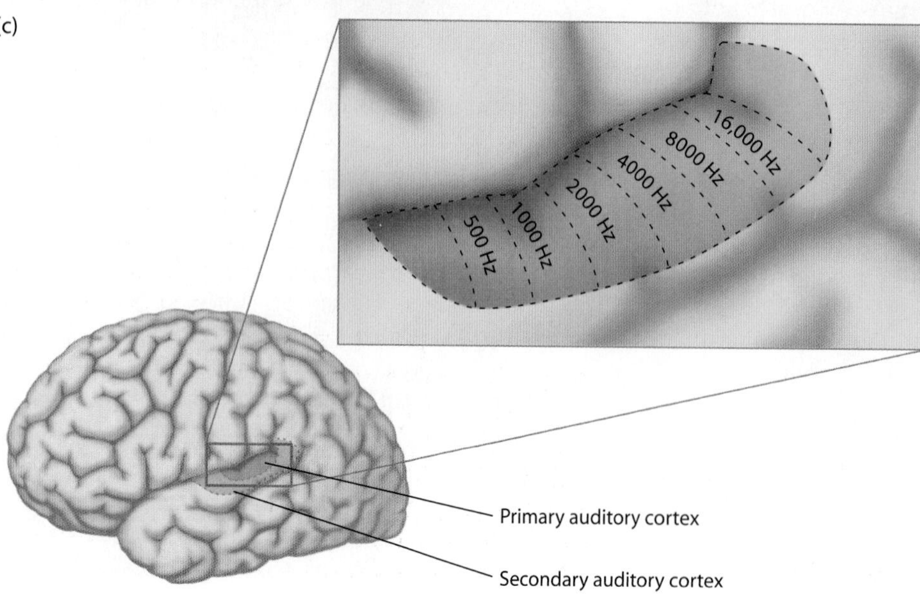

Figure 4.9 Topographic maps of the visual and auditory cortex. In the visual cortex the receptive fields of the cells define a retinotopic map. While viewing the stimulus **(a)**, a monkey was injected with a radioactive agent. **(b)** Metabolically active cells in the visual cortex absorb the agent, revealing how the topography of the retina is preserved across the striate cortex. **(c)** In the auditory cortex, the frequency-tuning properties of the cells define a tonotopic map. Topographic maps are also seen in the somatosensory and motor cortex.

graphic representations of the body surface. In a similar sense, auditory areas in the subcortex and cortex contain tonotopic maps, in which the physical dimension reflected in neural organization is the sound frequency of a stimulus. With a tonotopic map, some cells are maximally activated by a 1000-Hz tone, and others by a 5000-Hz tone. In addition, neighboring cells tend to be tuned to similar frequencies. Thus, sound frequencies are reflected in cells that are activated upon the presentation of a sound. Tonotopic maps are sometimes referred to as *cochleotopic* because the cochlea, the sensory apparatus in the ear, contains hair cells tuned to distinct regions of the auditory spectrum.

When the single-cell method was first introduced, neuroscientists were optimistic that the mysteries of brain function would be solved. All they needed was a catalog of contributions by different cells. Yet it soon became clear that, with neurons, the aggregate behavior of cells might be more than just the sum of its parts. The function of an area might be better understood by identification of the correlations in the firing patterns of groups of neurons rather than by identification of the response properties of each individual neuron. This idea has inspired single-cell physiologists to develop new techniques that allow recordings to be made in many neurons simultaneously—what is called **multiunit recording.**

Bruce McNaughton at the University of Arizona studied how the rat hippocampus represents spatial information by simultaneously recording from 150 cells (M. A. Wilson & McNaughton, 1994)! By looking at the pattern of activity over the group of neurons, the researchers were able to show how the rat coded spatial and episodic information differently. Today it is not uncommon to record from over 400 cells simultaneously (Lebedev & Nicolelis, 2006). As we will see in Chapter 7, multiunit recordings from motor areas of the brain are now being used to allow animals to control artificial limbs, a dramatic medical advance that may change the way rehabilitation programs are designed for paraplegics. For example, multiunit recordings can be obtained while people think about actions they would like to perform, and this information can be analyzed by computers to control robotic or artificial limbs.

Lesions

The brain is a complicated organ composed of many structures, including subcortical nuclei and distinct cortical areas. It seems evident that any task a person performs requires the successful operation of many brain components. A long-standing method of the neurophysiologist has been to study how behavior is altered by selective removal of one or more of these parts. The logic of this approach is straightforward. If a neural structure contributes to a task, then rendering the structure dysfunctional should impair the performance of that task.

Humans obviously cannot be subjected to **brain lesions** as experimental procedures with the goal of understanding brain function (but see the section titled "Functional Neurosurgery" later in this chapter). Typically, human neuropsychology involves research with patients who have suffered naturally occurring lesions. But animal researchers have not been constrained in this way. They share a long tradition of studying brain function by comparing the effects of different brain lesions. In one classic example, Nobel laureate Charles Sherrington employed the lesion method at the start of the 20th century to investigate the importance of feedback in limb movement in the dog (see Chapter 7). By severing the nerve fibers carrying sensory information into the spinal cord, he observed that the animals stopped walking.

Lesioning a neural structure will eliminate that structure's contribution. But the lesion also might force the animal to change its normal behavior and alter the function of intact structures. One cannot be confident that the effect of a lesion eliminates the contribution of only a single structure. The function of neural regions that are connected to the lesioned area might be altered, either because they are deprived of their normal neural input or because their axons fail to make normal synaptic connections. The lesion might also cause the animal to develop a compensatory strategy to minimize the consequences of the lesion. For example, when monkeys are deprived of sensory feedback to one arm, they stop using the limb. However, if the sensory feedback to the other arm is eliminated at a later date, the animals begin to use both limbs (Taub & Berman, 1968). The monkeys prefer to use a limb that has normal sensation, but the second surgery shows that they could indeed use the other limb.

With this methodology we should remember that a lesion may do more than eliminate the function provided by the lesioned structure. Nonetheless, the method has been critical for neurophysiologists. Over the years, lesioning techniques have been refined, allowing for much greater precision. Most lesions were originally made by the *aspiration* of neural tissue. In aspiration experiments, a suction device is used to remove the targeted structures. Another method was to apply electrical charges strong enough to destroy tissue. One problem with this method is the difficulty of being selective. Any tissue within range of the voltage generated by the electrode tip will be destroyed. For example, a researcher might want to observe the effects of a lesion to a certain cortical area, but if the electrolytic lesion extends into underlying white matter, these fibers also will be destroyed. Therefore, a distant structure might be rendered dysfunctional because it is deprived of some input.

Newer methods allow for more control over the extent of lesions. Most notable are neurochemical lesions. Sometimes a drug will selectively destroy cells that use a certain transmitter. For instance, systemic injection of 1-methyl-4-phenyl-1,2,3,6-tetrahydropyridine (MPTP) destroys dopaminergic cells in the substantia nigra, producing an animal version of Parkinson's disease (see Chapter 7). Other neurochemical lesions require application of the drug to the targeted region. Kainic acid is used in many studies because its toxic effects are limited to cell bodies. Application to an area will destroy the neurons whose cell bodies are near the site of the injection, but will spare any axonal fibers passing through this area.

Some researchers choose to make reversible lesions using chemicals that produce a transient disruption in nerve conductivity. As long as the drug is active, the exposed neurons do not function. When the drug wears off, function gradually returns. The appeal of this method is that each animal can serve as its own control. Performance can be compared during the "lesion" and "nonlesion" periods. In a different form of reversible lesion, neural tissue is cooled by the injection of a chemical that induces a low temperature. When the tissue is cooled, metabolic activity is disrupted, thereby creating a temporary lesion. When the coolant is removed, metabolic activities resume and the tissue becomes functional again.

Pharmacological manipulations also can be used to produce transient functional lesions. For example, the acetylcholine antagonist scopolamine produces temporary amnesia such that the recipient fails to remember much of what he or she was doing during the period when the drug was active. Because the low doses required to produce the amnesia have minimal adverse consequences, scopolamine provides a tool for studying the kinds of memory problems that plague patients who have hippocampal damage (Nissen et al., 1987). However, systemic administration of this drug produces widespread changes in brain function, thus limiting its utility as a model of hippocampal dysfunction.

Genetic Manipulations

The start of the 21st century witnessed the climax of one of the great scientific challenges: the mapping of the human genome. Scientists now have a complete record of the genetic sequence on our chromosomes. At present, the utility of this knowledge is limited; we have only begun to understand how these genes code for all aspects of human structure and function. In essence, what we have is a map containing the secrets to many treasures: What causes people to grow old? Why are some people more susceptible to certain cancers than other people? What dictates whether embryonic tissue will become a skin cell or a brain cell? Deciphering this map is an imposing task that will take years of intensive study.

Genetic disorders are manifest in all aspects of life, including brain function. Certain diseases, such as Huntington's disease, are clearly heritable (see the section titled "Degenerative and Infectious Disorders" later in this chapter). Indeed, by analyzing individuals' genetic codes, scientists can now predict whether those individuals will develop this debilitating disorder. This diagnostic ability was made possible by analysis of the genetic code of individuals who developed Huntington's disease and that of relatives who remained disease free. In this particular disease, the differences were restricted to a single chromosomal abnormality. This discovery is also expected to lead to new treatments that will prevent the onset of Huntington's. Scientists hope to devise techniques to alter the aberrant genes, either by modifying them or by figuring out a way to prevent them from being expressed.

In a similar way, scientists have sought to understand other aspects of normal and abnormal brain function through the study of genetics. Behavioral geneticists have long known that many aspects of cognitive function are heritable. For example, controlling mating patterns on the basis of spatial-learning performance allows the development of "maze-bright" and "maze-dull" strains of rats. Rats that are quick to learn to navigate mazes are likely to have offspring with similar abilities, even if the offspring are raised by rats that are slow to navigate the same mazes. Such correlations also are observed across a range of human behaviors, including spatial reasoning, reading speed, and even preferences in watching television (Plomin et al., 1990). This should not be taken to mean that our intelligence or behavior is genetically determined. Maze-bright rats perform quite poorly if raised in an impoverished environment. The truth surely reflects complex interactions between the environment and genetics (see "The Cognitive Neuroscientist's Toolkit: Correlation and Causation," on p. 128).

To understand the genetic component of this equation, neuroscientists are now working with many species, seeking to identify the genetic mechanisms of both brain structure and function. Dramatic advances have been made in studies with the fruit fly and mouse, two species with reproductive propensities that allow many generations to be spawned over a relatively short period of time. As with humans, the genome sequence for these species has been mapped out. More important, the functional role of many genes can be explored. A key methodology is to develop genetically altered animals, using what are referred to as **knockout procedures**. The term *knockout* comes from the fact that specific genes have been manipulated so that they are no longer present or expressed.

Scientists can then study the new species to explore the consequences of these changes. For example, *weaver* mice are a knockout strain in which Purkinje cells, the prominent cell type in the cerebellum, fail to develop. As the name implies, these mice exhibit coordination problems.

At an even more focal level, knockout procedures have been used to create strains that lack single types of postsynaptic receptors in specific brain regions while leaving intact other types of receptors. Susumu Tonegawa at the Massachusetts Institute of Technology (MIT) and his colleagues developed a mouse strain in which they altered cells within a subregion of the hippocampus that typically contain a receptor for *N*-methyl-D-aspartate, or NMDA (M. A. Wilson & Tonegawa, 1997; see Chapter 8). Knockout strains lacking the NMDA receptor in the hippocampus exhibit poor learning on a variety of memory tasks, providing a novel approach for linking memory with its molecular substrate (Figure 4.10). In a sense, this approach constitutes a lesion method, but at a microscopic level.

The New Genomics

Neurogenetic research is not limited to identifying the role of each gene individually; it is widely recognized that complex brain function and behavior arise from interactions between many genes and the environment. Using DNA arrays and knowledge gained from mapping of the human and mouse genomes, scientists can now

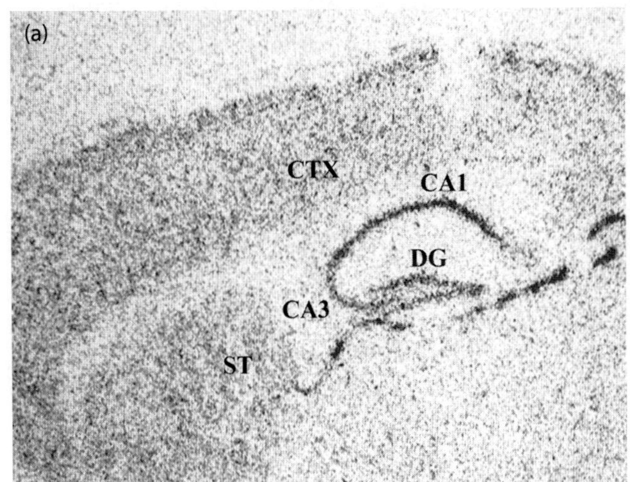

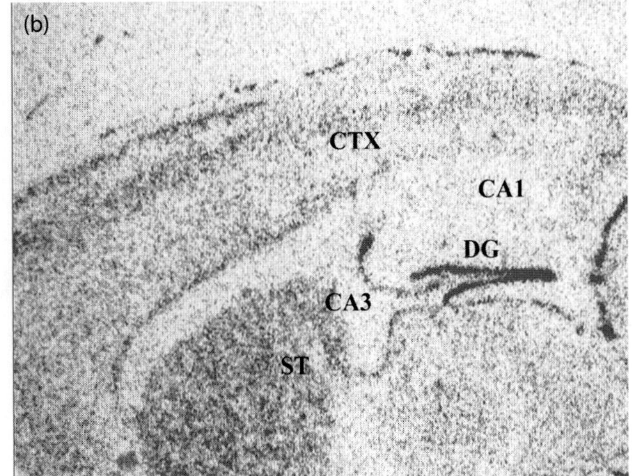

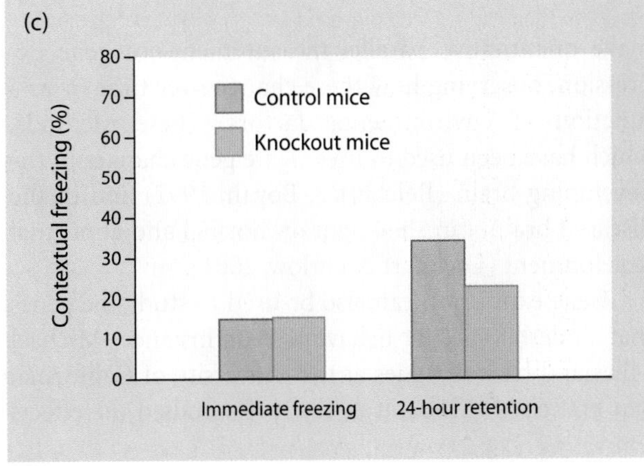

Figure 4.10 Brain slices through the hippocampus, showing the absence of a particular receptor in genetically altered mice. **(a)** Cells containing the gene associated with the receptor are stained in black. **(b)** The gene is absent in the CA1 region of the slice from the knockout mouse. **(c)** Fear conditioning is impaired in knockout mice. After receiving a shock, the mice freeze. When normal mice are placed in the same context 24 hours later, they show strong learning by the large increase in the percentage of freezing responses. This increase is reduced in the knockout mice. CTX = cortex; DG = dentate gyrus; ST = striatum.

THE COGNITIVE NEUROSCIENTIST'S TOOLKIT

Correlation and Causation: Brain Size and Posttraumatic Stress Disorder

The issue of causation is important to consider in any discussion of scientific observation. A recent study examining drinking habits and personal income found that self-reported drinkers earned about 10% more than self-reported abstainers, and that those who drank in bars earned an additional 7% more (Peters & Stringham, 2006). The research team offered the counterintuitive conclusion that the increase in alcohol consumption played a causative role in the higher income levels, at least in men. In their view, social drinking increases social networking and this networking has the benefit of increasing income. Although this causal chain is reasonable, there are certainly alternative ways to account for the relationship of drinking and income. For example, individuals who make a lot of money can afford to go to bars at night and spend their income on drinks! In elementary statistics we all learn to be wary about inferring causation from correlation, but the temptation can be strong.

The tendency to infer causation from correlation can be especially great when we're comparing the contribution of nature and nurture on brain and behavior. Consider the following results that have accumulated concerning the relationship of chronic stress and the hippocampus. From animal studies, we know that exposure to prolonged stress, and the resulting increase in glucocorticoid steroids, can cause atrophy in the hippocampus (Sapolsky et al., 1990). With the advent of neuroimaging, we have also learned that people with chronic posttraumatic stress disorder (PTSD) have smaller hippocampi then individuals who do not suffer from PTSD (Bremner et al., 1997; M. B. Stein et al., 1997). Can we therefore conclude that the stress that we know is associated with PTSD results, over time, in a reduction in the hippocampal volume of people with PTSD? This certainly seems a reasonable way to deduce a causal chain of events between these observations.

However, it is also important to consider alternative explanations. For instance, the causal story may run in the opposite direction: Individuals with smaller hippocampi, perhaps due to genetic variation, may be more vulnerable to the effects of stress, and thus be at higher risk for developing PTSD. How might we contrast these different hypotheses? What study design could distinguish between two hypotheses—one that emphasizes environmental factors (e.g., PTSD, via chronic stress, causes reduction in size of the hippocampus) and one that emphasizes genetic factors (e.g., individuals with small hippocampi are at risk for developing PTSD)?

A favorite approach of behavioral geneticists in exploring questions like these is to study identical twins. Mark Gilbertson and his colleagues (2002) at the New Hampshire Veterans Administration Medical Center studied a cohort of 40 pairs of identical twins. Within each twin pair, one member had experienced

make quantitative parallel measurements of gene expression, observing how these change over time or as a function of environmental factors. These methods, which have been used to investigate gene changes in the developing brain (Reichert & Boyan, 1997) and in the diseased brain, can shed light on normal and abnormal development (Lockhart & Barlow, 2001).

Gene expression can also be used to study the genes that underlie specific behaviors. For instance, Michael Miles and his colleagues at the University of California, San Francisco (Thibault et al., 2000) studied the effects of alcohol on gene expression, asking how specific genes might be related to variations in alcohol tolerance and dependence (Figure 4.11 on p. 130). Similarly, Jorge Medina and his colleagues at the Universidad de Buenos Aires in Argentina (Igaz et al., 2004) used genomic methods to investigate memory consolidation and found that orchestrated, differential hippocampal gene expression is necessary for long-term memory consolidation.

Gene arrays and the new genomics provide great promise for detecting the polygenetic influences on brain function and behavior.

severe trauma during a tour of duty in Vietnam. The other member of the pair had not seen active duty. In this way, each high-stress participant had a very well matched control, at least in terms of genetics: a twin brother.

Although all of the active-duty participants had experienced severe trauma during their time in Vietnam (one of the inclusion criteria for the study), not all of these individuals had developed PTSD. Thus, the experimenters could look at various factors associated with the onset of PTSD in a group of individuals with similar environmental experiences. Consistent with previous studies, anatomical MRIs showed that people with PTSD had smaller hippocampi than unrelated individuals without PTSD had. However, the same was also found for the twin brothers of the individuals with PTSD; that is, these individuals also had smaller hippocampi, even though they did not have PTSD and did not report having experienced unusual trauma in their lifetime. Moreover, the severity of the PTSD was negatively correlated with the size of the hippocampus in both the patient with PTSD [part **(a)** of the figure] and the matched twin control [part **(b)**]. Thus, the researchers concluded that small hippocampal size was a risk factor for developing PTSD and that PTSD alone did not cause the decreased hippocampal size.

This study serves as an example of the need for caution: We must be careful when making causal inferences based on correlational data. This study also provides an excellent example of how scientists are studying interactions between genes and the environment in influencing behavior and brain structure.

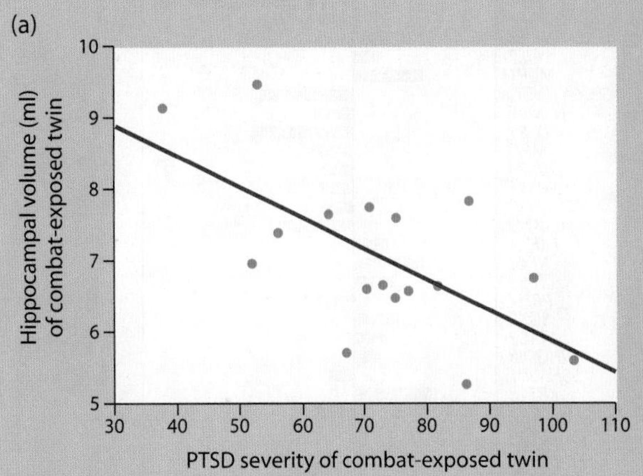

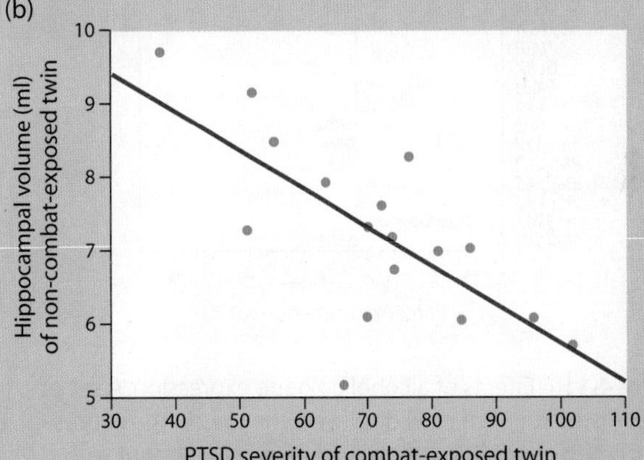

Correlations between hippocampal volume and posttrauma symptoms. Scatter plots illustrate the relationship of symptom severity in combat veterans with PTSD to **(a)** their own hippocampal volumes and **(b)** the hippocampal volumes of their identical twin brothers who were not exposed to combat. Symptom severity represents the total score received on the Clinician-Administered PTSD Scale (CAPS).

NEUROLOGY

Human pathology has long provided key insights into the relationship between brain and behavior. Observers of neurological dysfunction have certainly contributed much to our understanding of cognition—long before the advent of cognitive neuroscience. Discoveries concerning the contralateral wiring of sensory and motor systems were made by physicians in ancient societies attending to warriors with open head injuries. Postmortem studies by early neurologists, such as Broca and Wernicke, were instrumental in linking the left hemisphere with language functions (see Chapter 1). Many other disorders of cognition were described in the first decades of the 20th century, paralleling the emergence of **neurology** as a specialty within medicine.

Even so, there is now an upsurge in testing neurological patients to elucidate issues related to normal and aberrant cognitive function. As with other subfields of cognitive neuroscience, this enthusiasm has been inspired partly by advances in the technologies for diagnosing neurological disorders. As important, studies of patients with brain damage have benefited from the

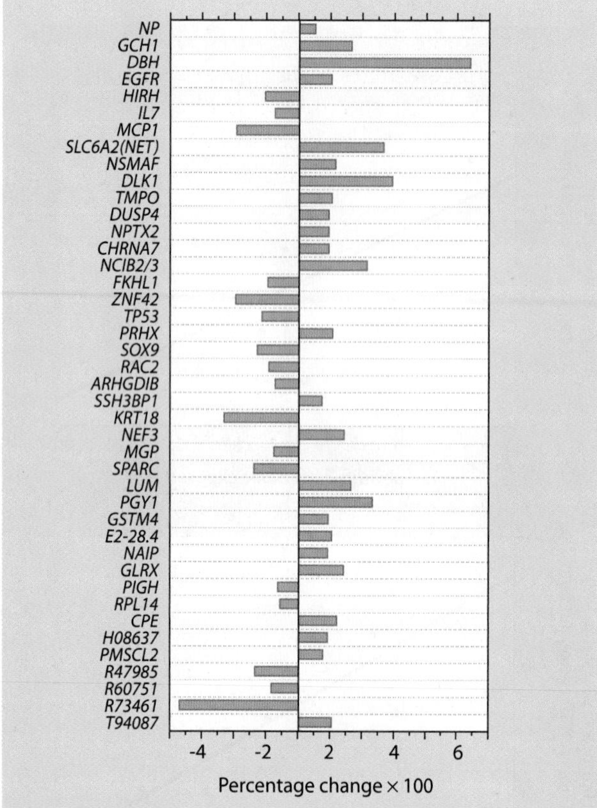

Figure 4.11 Effects of alcohol on gene expression. A set of genes (listed for each row) displayed changes in the expression of messenger RNA following 3 days of treatment with 100-m*M* ethanol. (The colors indicate groups of genes associated with different functions, such as metabolic processes or neural signaling.) For some genes, the change was an increase in RNA expression; for other genes, the change was a decrease in expression.

use of experimental tasks derived from research with healthy people.

Examples of the merging of cognitive psychology and neurology are presented at the end of this chapter; in this section we focus on the causes of neurological disorders and the tools that neurologists use to localize neural pathology. We also take a brief look at treatments for ameliorating neurological disorders.

We can best address basic research questions, such as those attempting to link cognitive processes to neural structures, by selecting patients with a single neurological disturbance whose pathology is well circumscribed. Patients who have suffered trauma or infections frequently have diffuse damage, rendering it difficult to associate the behavioral deficit with a structure. Nonetheless, extensive clinical and basic research studies have focused on patients with degenerative disorders such as Alzheimer's disease, both to understand the disease processes and to characterize abnormal cognitive function.

Structural Imaging of Neurological Damage

Brain damage can result from vascular problems, tumors, degenerative disorders, and trauma. The first charge of neurologists is to make the appropriate diagnosis. They need to follow appropriate procedures, especially if a disorder is life-threatening, and to work toward stabilizing the patient's condition. Although diagnosis frequently can be made on the basis of a clinical examination, almost all hospitals in the Western world are equipped with tools that help neurologists visualize brain structure.

Computed tomography (**CT** or **CAT** scanning), introduced commercially in 1983, has been an extremely important medical tool for structural imaging of neurological damage in living people. This method is an advanced version of the conventional X-ray study; whereas the conventional X-ray study compresses three-dimensional objects into two dimensions, CT allows for the reconstruction of three-dimensional space from the compressed two-dimensional images. Figure 4.12a depicts the method, showing how X-ray beams are passed through the head and a two-dimensional image is generated by sophisticated computer software.

To undergo CT, a patient lies supine in a scanning machine. The machine has two main parts: an X-ray source and a set of radiation detectors. The source and detectors are located on opposite sides of the scanner. These sides can rotate, allowing the radiologist to project X-ray beams from all possible directions. Starting at one position, an X-ray beam passes through the head. Some radiation in the X-ray is absorbed by intervening tissue. The remainder passes through and is picked up by the radiation detectors located on the opposite side of the head. The X-ray source and detectors are then rotated and a new beam is projected. This process is repeated until X-rays have been projected over 180°. At this point, recordings made by the detectors are fed into a computer that reconstructs the images.

The key principle underlying CT is that the density of biological material varies and the absorption of X-ray radiation is correlated with tissue density. High-density material such as bone absorbs a lot of radiation. Low-density material such as air or blood absorbs little radiation. The absorption capacity of neural tissue lies between these extremes. Thus, the software for making CT scans actually provides an image of the differential absorption of intervening tissue. The reconstructed images are usually contrast reversed: High-density regions show up as light colored, and low-density regions are dark.

Figure 4.12b shows a CT scan of a healthy individual. Most of the cortex and white matter appear as homogeneous gray areas. The typical spatial resolution for CT scanners is approximately 0.5 to 1.0 cm in all directions. Each point on the image reflects an average density of that point and the surrounding 1.0 mm of tissue. Thus, it is not possible to discriminate two objects that are closer than approximately 5 mm. Since the cortex is only 4 mm thick, it is very difficult to see the boundary between white and gray matter on a CT scan. The white and gray matter are also of very similar density, further limiting the ability of this technique to distinguish them. But larger structures can be easily identified. The surrounding skull and eye sockets appear white because of the high density of bone. The ventricles are black owing to the cerebrospinal fluid's low density.

MAGNETIC RESONANCE IMAGING

Although CT machines are still widely used, many hospitals have now added a second important imaging tool, the **magnetic resonance imaging** (**MRI**) scanner. In contrast to use of X-rays in CT, the MRI process exploits the magnetic properties of organic tissue. The number of the protons and neutrons in their nuclei makes certain atoms especially sensitized to magnetic forces. One such atom that is pervasive in the brain, and indeed in all organic tissue, is hydrogen. The protons that form the nucleus of the hydrogen atom are in constant motion, spinning about their principal axis. This motion creates a tiny magnetic field. In their normal state, the orientation of these protons is randomly distributed, unaffected by the weak magnetic field created by Earth's gravity (Figure 4.13).

The MRI machine creates a powerful magnetic field, measured in tesla units. Whereas gravitational forces on the Earth create a magnetic field of about 1/1000 tesla, the typical MRI scanner produces a magnetic field that ranges from 0.5 to 1.5 teslas. When a person is placed within the magnetic field of the MRI machine, a significant proportion of the protons become oriented in the direction parallel to the magnetic force. Radio waves are then passed through the magnetized regions, and as the protons absorb the energy in these waves, their orientation is perturbed in a predictable direction. When the

Figure 4.12 Computed tomography provides an important tool for imaging neurological pathology. **(a)** The CT process is based on the same principles as X-rays. An X-ray is projected through the head, and the recorded image provides a measurement of the density of the intervening tissue. By projection of the X-ray from multiple angles and with the use of computer algorithms, a three-dimensional image based on tissue density is obtained. **(b)** In this transverse CT image, the dark regions along the midline are the ventricles, the reservoirs of cerebrospinal fluid.

(a)

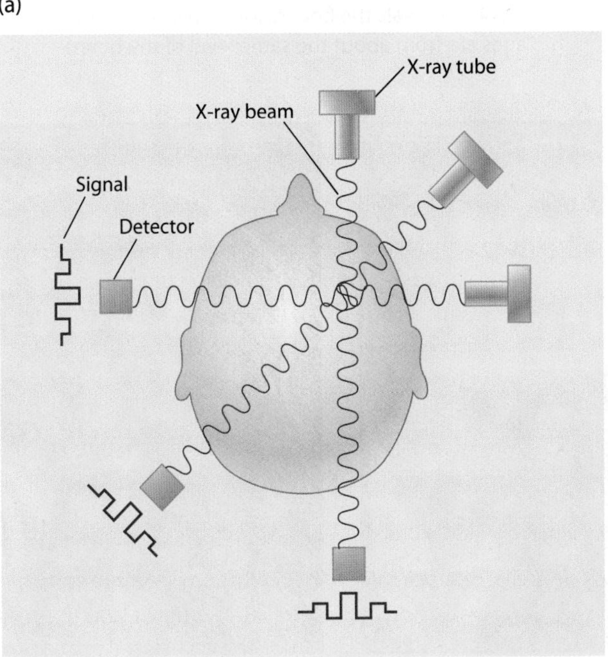

(b)

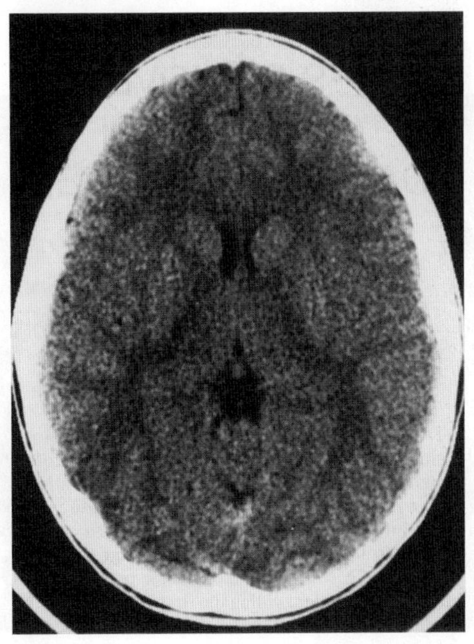

radio waves are turned off, the absorbed energy is dissipated and the protons rebound toward the orientation of the magnetic field. This synchronized rebound produces energy signals that are picked up by detectors surrounding the head. By systematically measuring the signals throughout the three-dimensional volume of the head, the MRI system can then construct an image reflecting the distribution of the protons and other magnetic agents in the tissue.

As Figure 4.13b shows, MRI scans provide a much clearer image of the brain than is possible with CT scans. This improvement reflects the fact that the density of protons is much greater in gray matter compared to white matter. With MRI, it is easy to see the individual sulci and gyri of the cerebral cortex. A sagittal section at the midline reveals the impressive size of the corpus callosum. The MRI scans can resolve structures that are less than 1 mm, allowing elegant views of small, subcortical structures such as the mammillary bodies or superior colliculus.

DIFFUSION TENSOR IMAGING

MRI scanners are now also used to study the microscopic anatomical structure of the axon tracts that form the white matter. This method is called **diffusion tensor imaging** (**DTI**; Figure 4.14). DTI is performed

(a)

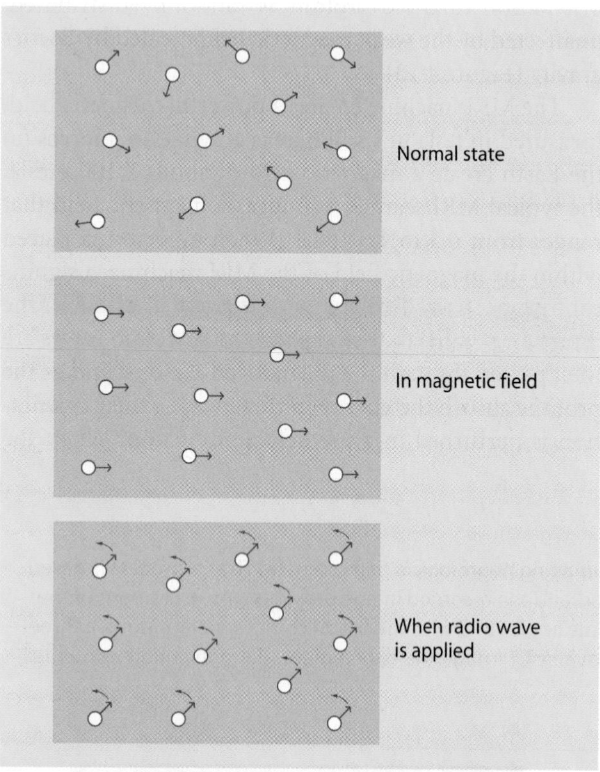

(b)

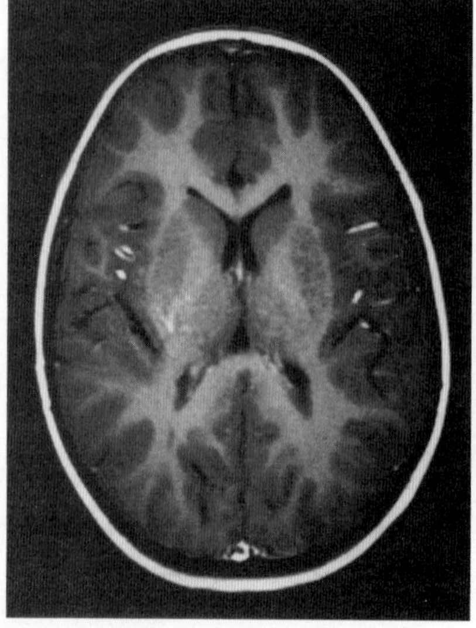

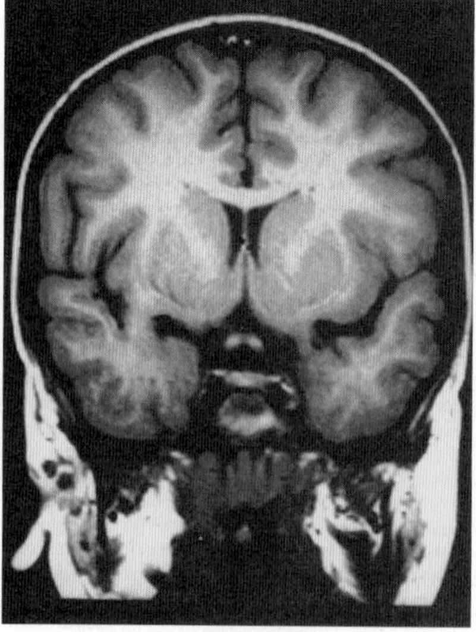

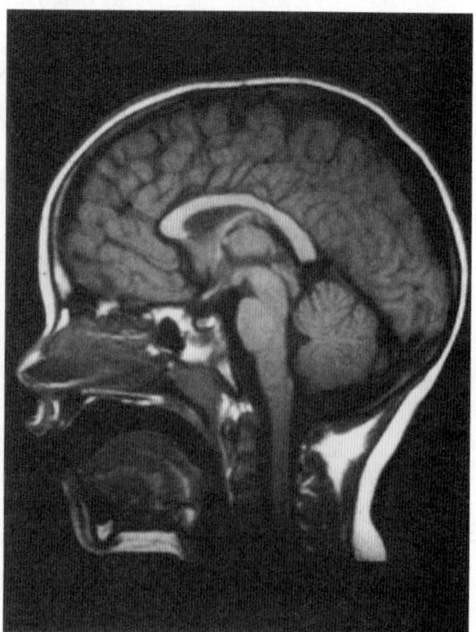

Figure 4.13 Magnetic resonance imaging exploits the fact that many organic elements, such as hydrogen, are magnetic. **(a)** In their normal state, the orientation of these elements is random. When an external magnetic field is applied, the elements become aligned and can be perturbed in a systematic fashion by the introduction of radio waves. The MRI scanner measures the endogenous magnetic fields generated by these elements as they spin. The density of hydrogen atoms is different in white and gray matter, making it easy to visualize these regions. **(b)** Transverse, coronal, and sagittal images. Comparing the transverse slice in this figure with the CT image in Figure 4.12 reveals the finer resolution offered by MRI. Both images are from about the same level of the brain.

with an MRI scanner, but unlike traditional MRI scans, DTI measures the density and, more important, motion of the water contained in the axons. DTI utilizes the known diffusion characteristics of water to determine the boundaries that restrict water movement throughout the brain (Behrens et al., 2003). Free diffusion of water is *isotropic*; that is, it occurs equally in all directions. However, diffusion of water in the brain is *anisotropic*, or restricted, so it does not diffuse equally in all directions. The reason for this anisotropy is that the axon membranes restrict the diffusion of water; the probability of water moving in the direction of the axon is thus greater than the probability of water moving perpendicular to the axon (Le Bihan, 2003). The anisotropy is greatest in axons because myelin creates a lipid boundary, limiting the flow of water to a much greater extent than gray matter or cerebrospinal fluid does. In this way, the orientation of axon bundles within the white matter can be imaged (DaSilva et al., 2003).

MRI principles can be combined with what is known about the diffusion of water to determine the diffusion anisotropy for each region within the MRI scan. These regions are referred to as **voxels**, a term that captures the computer graphics idea of a pixel, but volumetrically. By introducing two large pulses to the magnetic field, we can make MRI signals sensitive to the diffusion of water (Le Bihan, 2003). The first pulse determines the initial position of the protons carried by water. The second pulse, introduced after a short delay, detects how far the protons have moved in space in the specific direction that is being measured. It is standard to acquire DTI images in more than 30 directions.

The functional differences in diffusion anisotropy have been the subject of recent investigations. For instance, fractional anisotropy (a measure of the degree of anisotropy in white matter) in the temporoparietal region of the left hemisphere is significantly correlated with reading scores in adults with and without dyslexia. This correlation might reflect the differences in the strength of communication between visual, auditory, and language-processing areas in the brain (Klingberg et al., 2000).

Causes of Neurological Disorders

Nature has sought to ensure that the brain remains healthy. Structurally, the skull provides a thick, protective encasement. The distribution of arteries is extensive and even redundant for much of the brain. Even so, the brain is subject to numerous disorders, and their rapid treatment is frequently essential to reduce the possibility of chronic, debilitating problems or death.

VASCULAR DISORDERS

As with all other tissue, neurons need a steady supply of oxygen and glucose. These substances are essential for the cells to produce energy and make transmitters for neural communication. The brain uses 20% of all the

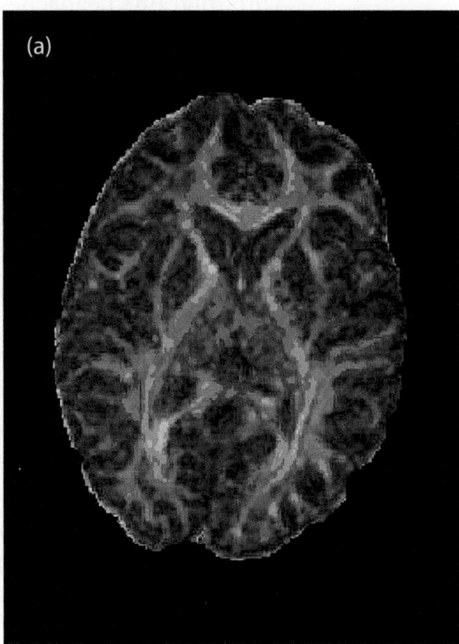

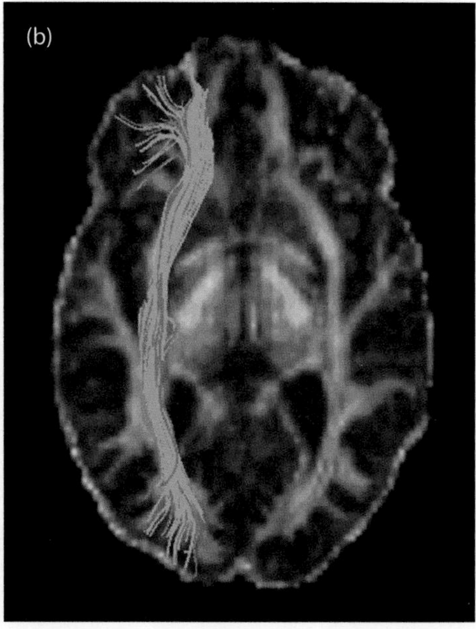

Figure 4.14 Diffusion tensor imaging. **(a)** This axial slice of a human brain reveals the directionality and connectivity of the white matter. The colors correspond to the principal directions of the white matter tracts in each region. **(b)** DTI data an be analyzed to trace white matter connections in the brain. The tracks shown here form the inferior fronto-occipital fasciculus, which, as the name suggests, connects the visual cortex to the frontal lobe.

oxygen we breathe, an extraordinary amount considering that it accounts for only 2% of the total body mass. The continuous supply of oxygen is essential: A loss of oxygen for as little as 10 minutes can result in neural death. **Angiography** is an imaging method used to evaluate the circulatory system in the brain. As Figure 4.15 shows, this method helps us visualize the distribution of blood by highlighting major arteries and veins. A dye is injected into the vertebral or carotid artery, and then an X-ray study is conducted.

Oxygen and glucose are distributed to the brain from four primary arteries: the two internal carotid and two vertebral arteries. Each carotid artery branches into two major arteries—the anterior cerebral artery and the middle cerebral artery—as well as several smaller ones. Together, these arteries act as a network to supply the anterior and middle portions of the cortex with blood. The vertebral arteries join to form the basilar artery. Inferior branches from the basilar artery irrigate the cerebellum and posterior part of the brainstem. More superiorly, this system branches into two posterior cerebral arteries to provide blood to the occipital lobe and the medial temporal lobe. The major cerebral arteries partially overlap in their distribution, in areas referred to as *border zones* or *watershed areas.*

Cerebral vascular accidents, or strokes, occur when blood flow to the brain is suddenly disrupted. The most frequent cause of stroke is occlusion of the normal passage of blood by a foreign substance. Over years, arteriosclerosis, the buildup of fatty tissue, occurs in the heart. This tissue can break free, becoming an embolus that is carried off in the bloodstream. An embolus that enters the cranium may easily pass through the large carotid or vertebral arteries. But as the arteries and capillaries reach the end of their distribution, their size decreases. Eventually, the embolus becomes stuck, or infarcted, blocking the flow of blood and depriving all downstream tissue of oxygen and glucose. Within a short period of time, this tissue will become dysfunctional. If the blood flow is not rapidly restored, the cells will die (Figure 4.16a).

Figure 4.15 The angiogram provides an image of the arteries in the brain.

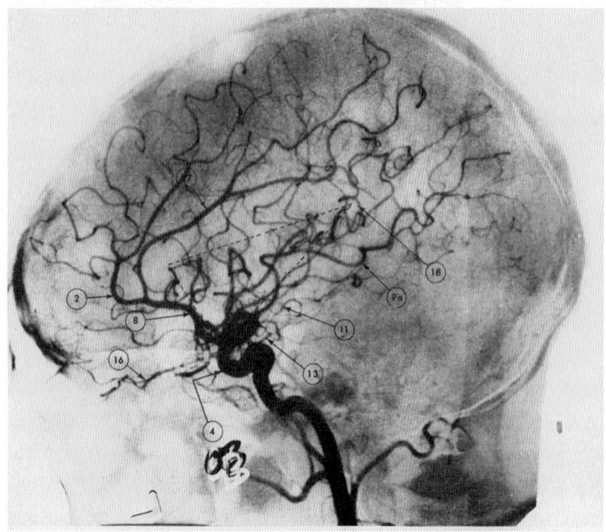

The onset of stroke can be quite varied, depending on the afflicted area. Sometimes the person may lose consciousness and die within minutes. In such cases the infarct is usually in the vicinity of the brainstem. When the infarct is cortical, the presenting symptoms may be striking, such as sudden loss of speech and comprehension. In other cases, the onset may be innocuous. The person may report a mild headache or be unable to use a hand in an appropriate manner. The vascular system is fairly consistent between individuals; thus, stroke of a particular artery typically leads to destruction of tissue in a consistent anatomical location. For example, occlusion of the posterior cerebral artery invariably leads to deficits in visual perception.

There are many other types of cerebral vascular disorders. Ischemia can be caused by partial occlusion of an artery or capillary due to an embolus, or it can arise from a sudden drop in blood pressure that prevents blood from reaching the brain. A sudden rise in blood pressure can lead to cerebral hemorrhage (Figure 4.16b), or bleeding over a wide area of the brain due to the breakage of blood vessels. Spasms in the vessels can result in irregular blood flow and have been associated with migraine headaches.

Other disorders are due to problems in arterial structures. Cerebral arteriosclerosis is a chronic condition in which cerebral blood vessels become narrow because of thickening and hardening of the arteries. The result can be persistent ischemia. More acute situations can arise if a person has an aneurysm (a weak spot or distention in a blood vessel). An aneurysm may suddenly expand or even burst, causing a rapid disruption of the blood circulation. Although some aneurysms appear to develop spontaneously, others can develop in people born with an arteriovenous malformation. An arteriovenous malformation that has remained innocuous for many years may suddenly weaken.

Cerebral vascular accidents require immediate attention. Often a neurological examination and CT can reveal the problem. Arteriovenous malformations or aneurysms, however, may require the more precise MRI or angiography. In these instances, surgery is frequently

(a)

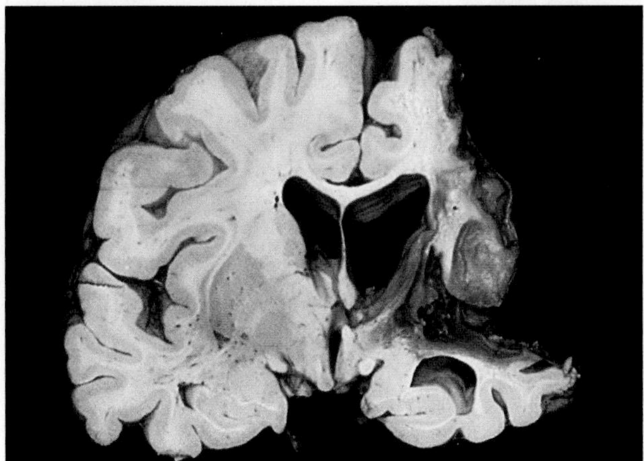

(b)

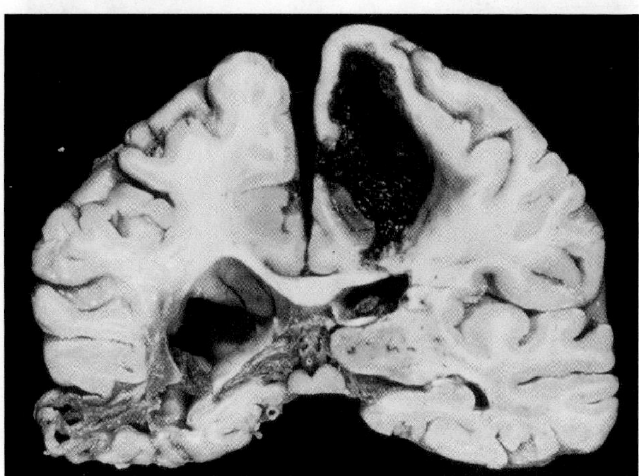

Figure 4.16 Vascular disorders. **(a)** Strokes occur when blood flow to the brain is disrupted. This brain is from a person who had an occlusion of the middle cerebral artery. The person survived the stroke. After death later, postmortem analysis showed that almost all of the tissue supplied by this artery had died and been absorbed. **(b)** This brain is from a person who died following a cerebral hemorrhage. The hemorrhage destroyed the dorsomedial region of the left hemisphere. The effects of a cerebrovascular accident 2 years prior to death can be seen in the temporal region of the right hemisphere.

required to prevent further bleeding. Occlusive strokes, on the other hand, do not generally require surgery. Either the occluded tissue is already completely infarcted, the clot is too small to remove, or the embolus has been absorbed into the surrounding tissue by the time of surgery. Such cases are usually treated by the administration of drugs to dissolve the clot and restore circulation prior to permanent tissue injury.

TUMORS

Brain lesions also can result from tumors. A *tumor*, or *neoplasm*, is a mass of tissue that grows abnormally and has no physiological function. Brain tumors are relatively common, with most originating in glial cells and other supporting white matter tissues. Tumors also can develop from gray matter or neurons, but these are much less common, particularly in adults. Tumors are classified as benign when they do not recur after removal and tend to remain in the area of their germination (although they can become quite large). Malignant, or cancerous, tumors are likely to recur after removal and are often distributed over a number of different areas. With brain tumors, the first concern is not usually whether the tumor is benign or malignant, but rather its location and prognosis. Concern is greatest when the tumor threatens critical neural structures. Neurons can be destroyed by an infiltrating tumor or become dysfunctional as a result of displacement by the tumor.

Three major types of brain tumors are distinguished according to where they originate:

1. *Gliomas* (Figure 4.17a) begin with the abnormal reproduction of glial cells. The rate of growth of different subtypes of gliomas can vary widely: Some escape detection for years; others expand rapidly and are malignant, with a poor prognosis because a lot of tissue is quickly disturbed.
2. *Meningiomas* (Figure 4.17b) originate in the meninges, the protective membrane that surrounds the brain. Although meningiomas do not invade the brain, they can create severe neurological problems by producing abnormal pressure.
3. *Metastatic tumors* (Figure 4.17c) originate in a noncerebral structure such as the lungs, skin, or breasts. The malignant tissue invades the bloodstream or lymphatics and is ultimately carried to the brain. Metastatic tumors are commonly widely distributed, affecting many structures.

DEGENERATIVE AND INFECTIOUS DISORDERS

Many neurological disorders result from progressive disease. Table 4.1 lists some of the more prominent degenerative and infectious disorders. In later chapters we will review some of these disorders in detail, exploring the cognitive problems associated with them and how these problems relate to underlying neuropathologies.

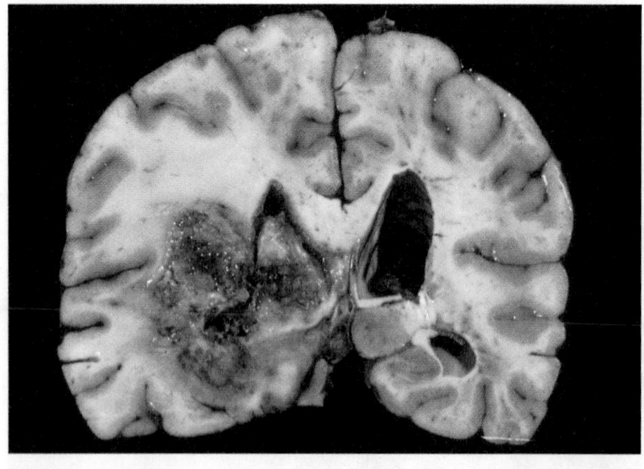

(a)

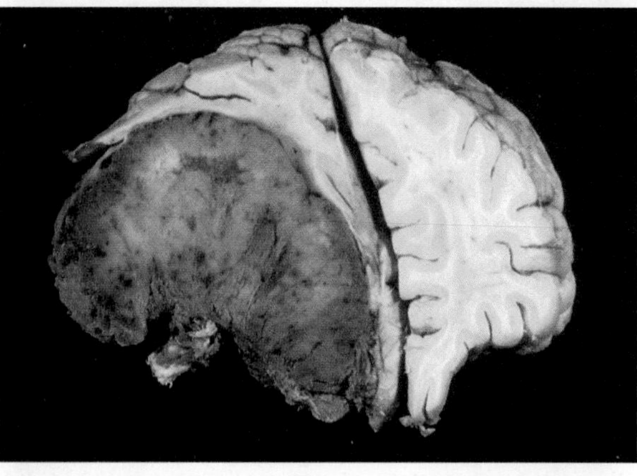

(b)

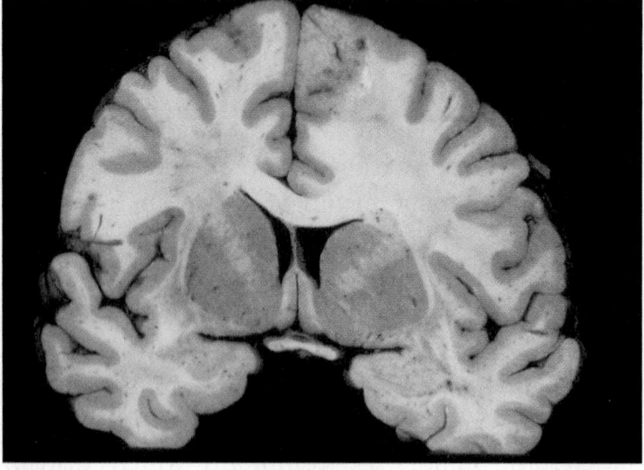

(c)

Figure 4.17 Postmortem views of three types of brain tumors. **(a)** A malignant glioma infiltrated the white matter of the parietal lobe in the right hemisphere in this case. **(b)** Here a large meningioma led to massive compression of the right frontal lobe. This patient had been hospitalized at age 41 for psychotic behavior, quite likely due to the effects of this slow-growing tumor. The tumor was not detected until autopsy. **(c)** A metastatic tumor is seen here in the dorsomedial tip of the left hemisphere. This woman died 5 years after undergoing a mastectomy for breast cancer.

Table 4.1 Prominent Degenerative and Infectious Disorders of the Central Nervous System

Disorder	Type	Most Common Pathology
Alzheimer's disease	Degenerative	Tangles and plaques in limbic and temporoparietal cortex
Parkinson's disease	Degenerative	Loss of dopaminergic neurons
Huntington's disease	Degenerative	Atrophy of interneurons in caudate and putamen nuclei of basal ganglia
Pick's disease	Degenerative	Frontotemporal atrophy
Progressive supranuclear palsy (PSP)	Degenerative	Atrophy of brainstem, including colliculus
Multiple sclerosis	Possibly infectious	Demyelination, especially of fibers near ventricles
AIDS dementia	Viral infection	Diffuse white matter lesions
Herpes simplex	Viral infection	Destruction of neurons in temporal and limbic regions
Korsakoff's syndrome	Nutritional deficiency	Destruction of neurons in diencephalon and temporal lobes

Here we focus on the etiology and clinical diagnosis of degenerative disorders.

Degenerative disorders have been associated with both genetic aberrations and environmental agents. A prime example of a degenerative disorder that is genetic in origin is Huntington's disease. The genetic link in degenerative disorders such as Parkinson's disease and Alzheimer's disease is weaker. Environmental factors are suspected to be important, perhaps in combination with genetic dispositions. The causes of Parkinson's disease are unknown, but it is suspected that the cell death in dopaminergic neurons may be accelerated by unknown toxins accumulating in the environment. Unlike many neurological disorders, there are no descriptions of people with parkinsonian symptoms in the pre–Industrial Age medical literature. The causes of Alzheimer's disease also remain a mystery, despite intense research efforts. The disease in about 5% of patients is clearly linked to a genetic deficiency; in the rest, there is no identifiable genetic component. Many hypotheses regarding the cause of Alzheimer's disease have been proposed. A leading hypothesis is that the production of amyloid, a ubiquitous protein in organic tissue, goes awry and leads to the characteristic plaques found in the brains of patients with the disease.

Progressive neurological disorders can also be caused by viruses. The human immunodeficiency virus (HIV) that causes acquired immunodeficiency syndrome (AIDS)–related dementia has a tendency to lodge in subcortical regions of the brain, producing diffuse lesions of the white matter by destroying axonal fibers. The herpes simplex virus, on the other hand, destroys neurons in cortical and limbic structures if it migrates to the brain. Viral infection is also suspected in multiple sclerosis, although evidence for such a link is indirect, coming from epidemiological studies. For example, the incidence of multiple sclerosis is highest in temperate climates, and a number of isolated tropical islands had not experienced multiple sclerosis until the population came in contact with Western visitors.

Degenerative and infectious disorders are usually characterized by a gradual onset of symptoms. Often the patient may not notice the deterioration of motor or cognitive abilities. Rather, the changes may be more apparent to a spouse or other family members. The neurological examination is especially critical for reliable diagnosis. The first signs of multiple sclerosis may be slight disturbances in sensation or double vision. The insidious onset of the memory problems associated with Alzheimer's disease may be difficult to detect, given our expectations of cognitive changes in normal aging. A patient developing Parkinson's disease may first note difficulty standing up or initiating movement. The experienced clinician will recognize the implications of these signs. CT and MRI may confirm a diagnosis, but usually the scans do not reveal any pathology in the early phases of these disorders. As the diseases progress, evidence of neural atrophy or degeneration becomes obvious (see Figure 4.18).

The pace of deterioration varies enormously, depending on the degenerative disorder. Whereas Huntington's disease invariably results in progressive deterioration and

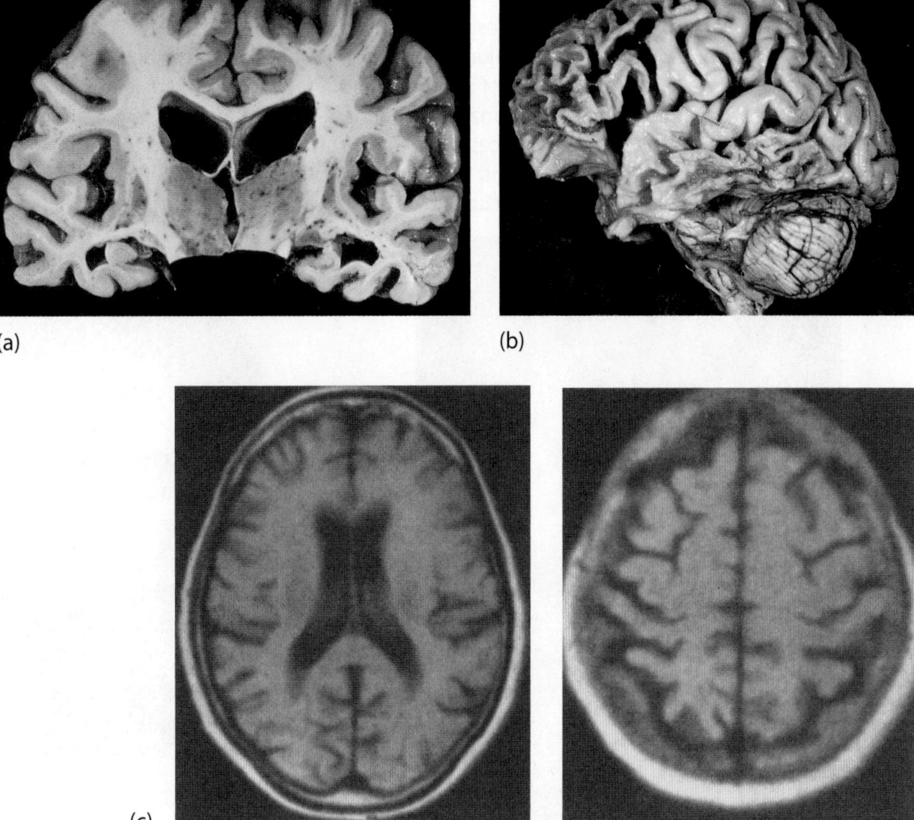

Figure 4.18 Degenerative disorders of the brain. **(a)** This coronal section is from a patient with Alzheimer's disease who died at age 67, 8 years after the first reports of memory problems. Severe cortical atrophy is apparent; at death, her brain weighed only 750 g, less than half the weight of a normal brain. **(b)** In this brain from a patient who died of Pick's disease, the atrophy is limited to frontal and temporal lobe regions. **(c)** These transverse MRI scans from a patient with Alzheimer's disease show that atrophy has led to enlargement of the sulci and ventricles.

death within 5 to 15 years, demyelinating disorders such as multiple sclerosis may go into remission for many years. Part of this variation is due to differences in the underlying mechanisms producing the neural pathology. For example, in multiple sclerosis the disease process affects white matter, whereas Alzheimer's disease involves widespread atrophy of cell bodies. Another important factor affecting a patient's outcome is the use of medication to treat symptoms. Just 40 years ago, patients with Parkinson's disease were generally bedridden within a few years of diagnosis, and the disorder would be listed as the cause of death. With the introduction of drugs categorized as dopamine agonists, the symptoms are greatly minimized for many patients.

TRAUMA

More than any natural cause, such as stroke or tumor, the reason that most patients arrive on a neurology ward is a traumatic event such as a car accident, a gunshot wound, or an ill-advised dive into a shallow swimming hole. The traumatic event can lead to a closed- or an open-head injury. In *closed* head injuries, the skull remains intact, but the brain is damaged by the mechanical forces generated by a blow to the head. The most common cause of closed head injury is a car accident in which a person's head slams against the windshield. The damage may be at the site of the blow, for example, just below the forehead—damage referred to as a *coup*. In addition, reactive forces may bounce the brain against the skull on the opposite side of the head, resulting in a *countercoup*. Occipital deficits are sometimes observed in car accident victims who suffer a countercoup. Certain regions are especially sensitive to the effects of coups and countercoups. The inside surface of the skull is markedly jagged above the eye sockets; and, as Figure 4.19 shows, this rough surface can produce extensive tearing of brain tissue in the orbitofrontal region.

Open head injuries happen when the skull is penetrated by an object like a bullet or shrapnel. With these injuries, tissue may be directly damaged by the penetrating object. The impact of the object can also create reactive forces producing coup and countercoup.

Additional damage can follow a traumatic event as a result of vascular problems and increased risk of infection. Trauma can disrupt blood flow by severing vessels, or it can change intracranial pressure as a result of bleeding. Swelling after trauma might generate further brain damage, and seizures, common after trauma, can originate in scarred tissue.

Figure 4.19 Trauma can cause extensive destruction of neural tissue. Damage can arise from the collision of the brain with the solid internal surface of the skull, especially along the jagged surface over the orbital region. In addition, accelerative forces created by the impact can cause extensive shearing of dendritic arbors. **(a)** In this brain of a 54-year-old man who had sustained a severe head injury 24 years prior to death, tissue damage is evident in the orbitofrontal regions and was associated with intellectual deterioration subsequent to the injury. **(b)** The susceptibility of the orbitofrontal region to trauma was made clear by A. Holbourn of Oxford in 1943, who filled a skull with gelatin and then violently rotated the skull. Although most of the brain retains its smooth appearance, the orbitofrontal region has been chewed up.

(a)

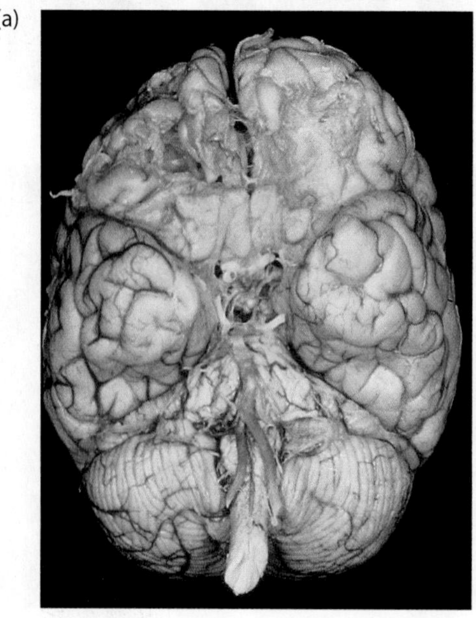

(b)

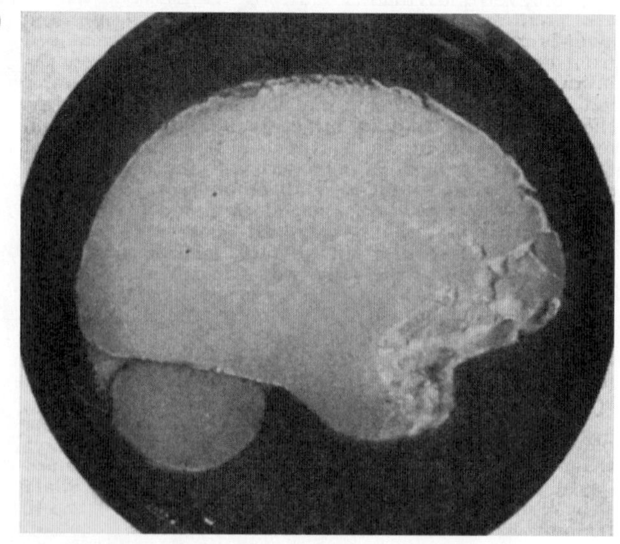

Early work on localizing cognitive function often involved patients with traumatic injuries. The eminent British neurologist Sir Gordon Holmes (1919) provided some of the classic descriptions of cerebellar and occipital lobe function based on his observations of World War I soldiers who had open head injuries. Indeed, prior to the invention of CT, open head injuries offered the best way to localize brain damage while the patient was still alive. Note, however, that trauma patients frequently have multiple neuropsychological problems because the neurological damage is generally extensive and diffuse.

EPILEPSY

Epilepsy is a condition characterized by excessive and abnormally patterned activity in the brain. The cardinal symptom is a seizure, a transient loss of consciousness. The extent of other disturbances varies. Some epileptics shake violently and lose their balance. For others, seizures may be perceptible only to the most attentive friends and family. Seizures are confirmed by electroencephalography (EEG) to record the patient's brain waves (see the section titled "Electrical and Magnetic Signals" later in this chapter). During the seizure, the EEG profile is marked by large-amplitude oscillations (Figure 4.20).

The frequency of seizures is also variable. The most severely affected patients can have hundreds of seizures each day, with each seizure disrupting function for a few minutes. Other epileptics suffer only an occasional seizure, but it may incapacitate the person for a couple of hours. Furthermore, simply having a seizure is not diagnostic of epilepsy. Although 0.5% of the general population has epilepsy, it is estimated that one in 20 people will have a seizure at some point during life. Often the

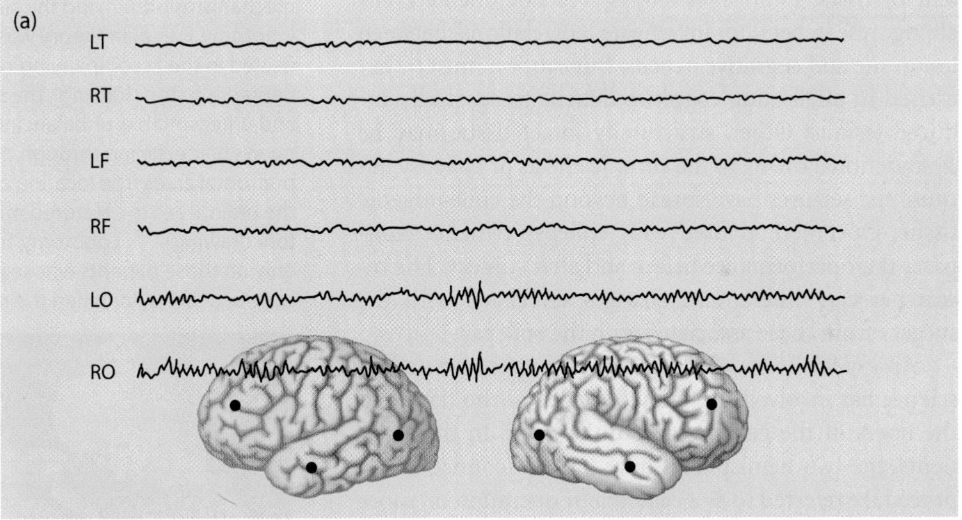

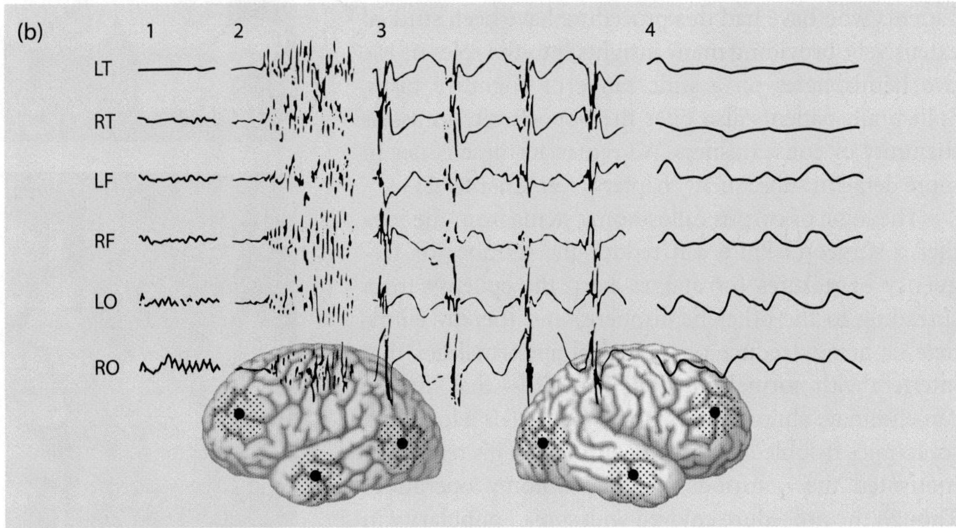

Figure 4.20 Electroencephalographic recordings from six electrodes, positioned over the frontal (F), temporal (T), and occipital (O) cortex on both the left (L) and the right (R) sides. **(a)** Activity during normal cerebral activity. **(b)** Activity during a grand mal seizure.

seizure is triggered by an acute event such as trauma, exposure to toxic chemicals, or high fever. Approximately 50% to 70% of epileptics respond well when treated with antiseizure medication. For the remaining patients, surgery may be an option if the disorder is chronic and severely debilitating.

Neuropsychologists are generally not interested in the cognitive deficits associated with epilepsy as they relate to normal function. Because the seizures disrupt neural activity across large sections of the brain, it is difficult to link behavioral deficits with structural abnormalities.

Functional Neurosurgery

Surgical interventions for treating neurological disorders provide a unique opportunity to investigate the link between brain and behavior. The best example comes from research involving patients who have undergone surgical treatment for the control of intractable epilepsy. The extent of tissue removal is always well documented, enabling researchers to investigate correlations between lesion site and cognitive deficits. But caution must be exercised in attributing cognitive deficits to surgically induced lesions. Other, structurally intact tissue may be dysfunctional owing to the chronic effects of epilepsy because the seizures have spread beyond the epileptogenic tissue. One method used with epilepsy patients compares their performance before and after surgery. The researcher can differentiate changes associated with the surgery from those associated with the epilepsy.

An especially fruitful paradigm for cognitive neuroscience has involved the study of patients who have had the fibers of the corpus callosum severed. In these patients, the two hemispheres have been disconnected—a procedure referred to as a *callosotomy* operation or, more informally, the *split-brain* procedure. The relatively few patients who have had this procedure have been studied extensively, providing many insights into the roles of the two hemispheres on a wide range of cognitive tasks. Split-brain patients also offer the opportunity to assess the unity of consciousness. We return to these issues in more detail in subsequent chapters (e.g., Chapter 11).

The logic of corpus callosotomy stems from the idea that a surgeon's knife can reduce the number or frequency of seizures (or at least keep the epilepsy from spreading to the other hemisphere) and thereby eliminate or greatly reduce physiological abnormalities that interfere with normal function. This idea—that surgery can eliminate abnormal brain function—has a long and sometimes troubled history in neurology. This reasoning motivated the notorious frontal lobotomy operation. Though the procedure enjoyed widespread popularity in the middle of the 20th century as a treatment for depression, schizophrenia, and other psychiatric disorders, its theoretical motivation was weak—perhaps best captured in the *Life* magazine cartoon shown in Figure 4.21. A hyperactive superego, localized in the frontal lobes, was assumed to exert excessive control over posterior brain regions. Slicing the white matter in the frontal cortex (with crude techniques such as inserting an ice pick behind the eye sockets!) was thought to restore balance by reducing the connections between frontal and posterior brain regions.

In the preceding examples, neurosurgery was eliminative in nature, but it has also been used as an attempt to restore normal function. Examples are found in current treatments for Parkinson's disease, a movement disorder

Figure 4.21 *Life* magazine cartoon from 1947, sketching the mechanisms underlying the supposed benefits of the frontal lobotomy. Freudian theory was in its heyday at the time, as reflected in the accompanying caption, which read, "In agitated depression (top drawing), the superego becomes overbearing and unreasonable, unbalancing the whole mind. . . . The surgeon's blade, slicing through the connections between the prefrontal areas (the location of the superego) and the rest of the brain, frees the tortured mind from its tyrannical ruler (bottom drawing). . . . Lobotomy, however, should be performed only on those patients whose intelligence is sufficient to take control of behavior when the moral authority is gone."

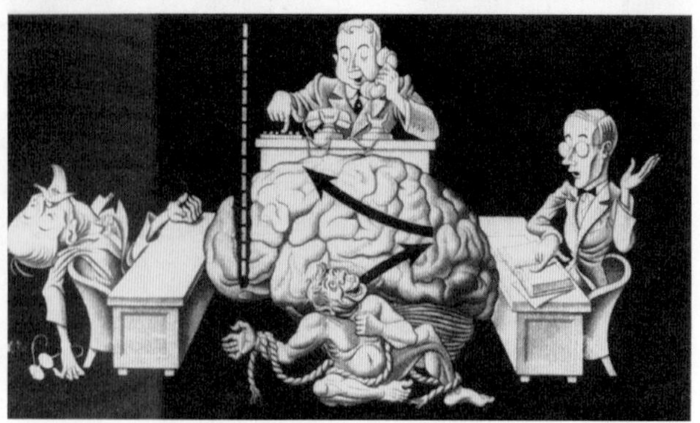

resulting from basal ganglia dysfunction. Although the standard treatment is medication, the efficacy of the drugs can change over time and even produce debilitating side effects. Some patients who develop severe side effects are now treated surgically. One technique that has become widely used is **deep-brain stimulation (DBS)**, in which electrodes are implanted in the basal ganglia. These devices produce continuous electrical signals that trigger neural activity. Dramatic and sustained improvements are observed in many patients who undergo this procedure (Hamani et al., 2006; Krack et al., 1998). DBS is discussed in more detail in Chapter 7.

Another approach for treating severe Parkinson's disease is the use of fetal brain transplants. Neurochemically, Parkinson's disease results from a loss of cells in the substantia nigra, a nucleus that is the source of dopaminergic inputs to the basal ganglia and frontal cortex. To restore function to the basal ganglia, cells from aborted fetuses are placed in structures that receive inputs from the nigra. The fetal tissue is able to develop into dopamine-sensitive neurons (Kordower et al., 1995). In animals, fetal grafts have been placed in the spinal cord to promote reconnectivity of descending motor fibers following spinal resection.

A more dramatic development in clinical research—one that has garnered tremendous attention in public discussion—is the work on stem cells. The idea here is similar to that underlying neural transplants. However, the key difference is that, whereas transplants use tissue that is functionally similar to that of the targeted region, embryonic stem cells are immature cells from the developing embryo that have not yet differentiated and thus have, in theory, limitless potential. That is, these cells have the potential of becoming a cell within any body system: circulatory, digestive, neural, or any other body part. Moreover, within these systems, stem cells can develop into specific cell types. The same stem cells could be used to create visual neurons, motor neurons, or cells in higher association areas.

The goal of stem cell research is to implant stem cells into a region where the adult cells have been damaged or atrophied and to create conditions such that the stem cells will mature, replacing and replenishing the damaged cells to restore function. For instance, someone who has had spinal cord injury could receive stem cell implants or injections in the damaged region. Over time, these neurons would mature into motor neurons, capable of conducting signals between the brain and periphery to allow the person to recover the ability to produce movement. The promise of stem cells is limitless. Researchers already envision a day in the not-too-distant future when stem cells might be used to reverse the effects of atrophic degenerative processes such as Alzheimer's disease.

We are still a long way from this goal, but major advances have occurred in the past decade. Recent studies have found that embryonic neural transplants can survive and even form synapses in an adult host's spinal cord (Fricker-Gates et al., 2002). The most successful growth appears to occur when neurological growth factors are present and the targeted area has not suffered a complete loss of cells. Possibly the remaining tissue helps provide signals for the development of pre- and postsynaptic circuits (Harel & Strittmatter, 2006).

CONVERGING METHODS

So far, we have taken a brief look at the basic methodologies of cognitive psychology, computer modeling, neurosciences, and neurology. Each discipline has unique methodologies for learning about the nature of the mind and the relation between brain and mind. But the real strength of cognitive neuroscience comes from the way in which these diverse methodologies are integrated, which is the subject of this final section.

Cognitive Deficits Following Brain Damage

Perhaps the best-established paradigm of cognitive neuroscience involves the effects of brain injury on behavior. For many centuries lesions have been studied extensively in animals and humans, and, as noted earlier in this chapter, the lesion model has laid an empirical foundation for learning about brain organization. Fundamental concepts, such as the left hemisphere's dominant role in language or the dependence of visual functions on posterior cortical regions, were developed by observation of the effects of brain injury.

Two developments in the past 30 years have led to significant advances in the study of neurological patients. First, with neuroimaging methods such as CT and MRI, we can precisely localize brain injury in vivo. Second, the paradigms of cognitive psychology have provided the tools for making more sophisticated analyses of the behavioral deficits observed after brain injury. Early neuropsychological work focused on localizing complex tasks: language, vision, executive control, motor programming. The essence of the cognitive revolution has been that these complex tasks require the integrative activity of many component operations. Cognitive neuropsychologists have extended this idea to research on brain-injured patients. Indeed, the excitement about neuropsychological research is not restricted to its potential to link mental activities to brain structures. Equally important, many researchers recognize that the study of dysfunctional behavior can help identify the component operations that underlie normal cognitive performance.

The logic of this approach is straightforward. If a behavior depends on processing within a certain brain structure, then damage to this structure should disrupt the behavior. As such, this approach assumes that brain injury is eliminative—that brain injury disturbs or eliminates the processing ability of the affected structure.

Consider the following example. Suppose that damage to brain region A results in impaired performance on task X. One conclusion is that region A contributes to the processing required for task X. For example, if task X is reading, we might conclude that region A is critical for reading. But from cognitive psychology we know that a complex task such as reading has many component operations: fonts must be perceived, letters and letter strings must activate representations of their corresponding meanings, and syntactic operations must link individual words into a coherent stream. By merely testing reading ability, we will not know which component operation or operations are impaired when there are lesions to region A. What the cognitive neuropsychologist wants to do is design tasks that diagnose the function of specific operations. If a reading problem stems from a general perceptual problem, then comparable deficits should be seen on a range of tests of visual perception. If the problem reflects the loss of semantic knowledge, then the deficit should be limited to tasks that require some form of object identification or recognition.

Associating neural structures with specific processing operations calls for appropriate control conditions. The most basic form of control is to compare the performance of a patient or group of patients with that of healthy subjects. Poorer performance by the patients might be taken as evidence that the affected brain regions are involved in the task. Thus, if we had a group of patients with lesions in the frontal cortex who showed impairment on our reading task, we might suppose that this region of the brain was critical for reading. Keep in mind, however, that brain injury can produce widespread changes in cognitive abilities. The frontal lobe patient not only might have trouble in reading but also might demonstrate impairment on just about any task, such as problem solving, memory, or motor planning. Thus, the challenge for the cognitive neuroscientist is to determine whether the observed behavioral problem results from damage to a particular mental operation or is secondary to a more general disturbance. For example, many patients are depressed after a neurological disturbance such as a stroke, and depression is known to affect performance on a wide range of tasks.

SINGLE AND DOUBLE DISSOCIATIONS

Cognitive neuropsychologists typically design experiments that have at least two tasks: an experimental task and a control task. The best experiments are those in which the two tasks are similar in most respects but differ in requiring one hypothetical mental operation. Suppose a researcher is interested in the association between two aspects of memory. One aspect is knowledge about when we learned a particular fact or piece of information. For example, people who were alive in 1963 can recall not only that President Kennedy was killed in Dallas but also where they were when they first heard about the tragedy. A second aspect relates to the familiarity we have with that fact or piece of information. We recognize that our memory of Kennedy's death is not simply the result of that initial experience, but also a product of the countless news documentaries, books, and movies that have rehashed that event.

Our researcher hypothesizes that these two aspects of memory are separable. One way to test this hypothesis is to examine patients with memory disorders. For example, if the hypothesis is that familiarity is associated with the temporal lobe, then the researcher might test patients with temporal lobe lesions on two memory tests: one designed to look at memory of when information was acquired, and the second designed to look at familiarity. Patients with memory problems would be required to perform two tasks. For each task, the stimuli would be identical: a series of abstract drawings in which some items are shown once, others twice, and others three times. To test how well the patients remember when they learned something, the subjects would be presented with a pair of drawings and asked to judge which drawing was presented first—a test of temporal order. To test for familiarity, a frequency judgment task can be used. Here, the subjects would again be presented with a pair of drawings, but now they would have to decide which drawing they had seen more often. If temporal lobe lesions disrupt familiarity but not the ability to remember when something was learned, then the patients should demonstrate selective impairment on the frequency task. To detect the impairment, it would be necessary to include a control group, such as people with no neurological problems.

Assuming the patients were selectively impaired on the frequency task, our researchers would have observed a **single dissociation** (Figure 4.22a). In single dissociations, two groups are tested on two tasks and a between-group difference is apparent in only one task. Two groups are necessary, so that the patients' performance can be compared with that of a control group. Two tasks are necessary to examine whether a deficit is specific to a particular task or reflects a more general impairment. Many conclusions in neuropsychology are based on single dissociations: Compared to control subjects, patients with hippocampal lesions cannot develop long-term memories even though their short-term memory is intact. Patients with Broca's aphasia have intact comprehension but struggle to speak fluently.

Single dissociations have unavoidable problems. In particular, the two tasks are assumed to be equally sensitive to differences between the control and experimental groups. However, often this is not the case. One task may be more sensitive than the other because of differences in task difficulty or sensitivity problems in how the measurements are obtained. For example, the frequency judgment task might be more demanding than the temporal-order task, requiring a greater degree of concentration. If the brain injury produced a generalized problem in concentration, then the patients might have difficulty with this task, but the problem would not be due to a specific problem in memory for familiarity.

As an analogy, consider a comparison between two six-cylinder cars: one with an engine in mint condition, and a second that is running on only five cylinders. It might be difficult to tell the difference between the two cars when driving through the city because the speed must be kept low and frequent stops are necessary. But if the cars were taken out on the highway, it would quickly become apparent that one car drives rougher than the other. However, we would not want to conclude that this car has a selective deficit in highway driving. Rather, our city-driving test was not sufficiently sensitive to detect the persistent problem.

Double dissociations avoid these problems. In double dissociations, group 1 is impaired on task X and group 2 is impaired on task Y (Figure 4.22b). The two groups' performances can be compared to each other, or more commonly, the patient groups are compared with a control group that shows no impairment. With a double dissociation, it is no longer reasonable to argue that a difference in performance results merely from the unequal sensitivity of the two tasks. In our memory example, the claim that temporal lobe patients have a selective problem with familiarity would be greatly strengthened if it were shown that a second group of patients (e.g., frontal lobe patients) showed selective impairment on the temporal-order task. Double dissociations offer the strongest neuropsychological evidence that a patient or patient group has a selective deficit in a certain cognitive operation.

The inferential power of double dissociations has been exploited in many settings beyond the neuropsychology laboratory. Lesion studies in animals are most convincing when the conclusions are based on double dissociations. Cognitive research on healthy subjects has also benefited from the logic of double dissociations. Evidence of separable cognitive operations can be gained by demonstration that one task is affected by one type of manipulation, whereas a second task is selectively affected by a different manipulation. For example, in normal subjects the rate at which the stimuli appear might be found to affect performance on the temporal-order task, whereas the similarity between the stimuli affects familiarity performance. Here, the same subjects

Figure 4.22 Hypothetical series of results conforming to either a single **(a)** or a double **(b)** dissociation. With the single dissociation, the patient group shows impairment on one task and not on the other. With the double dissociation, one patient group shows impairment on one task and a second patient group shows impairment on the other task. Double dissociations provide much stronger evidence for a selective impairment.

(a) Single dissociation

Group	Tasks (% correct)	
	Recency memory	Familiarity memory
Temporal lobe damage	90	70
Controls	90	95

(b) Double dissociation

Group	Tasks (% correct)	
	Recency memory	Familiarity memory
Temporal lobe	90	70
Frontal lobe	60	95
Controls	90	95

serve as their own controls. The double dissociation arises because the two manipulations—rate and similarity—differentially affect performance on the two tasks. Such a result would suggest that the two tasks involve nonoverlapping component operations (Figure 4.23).

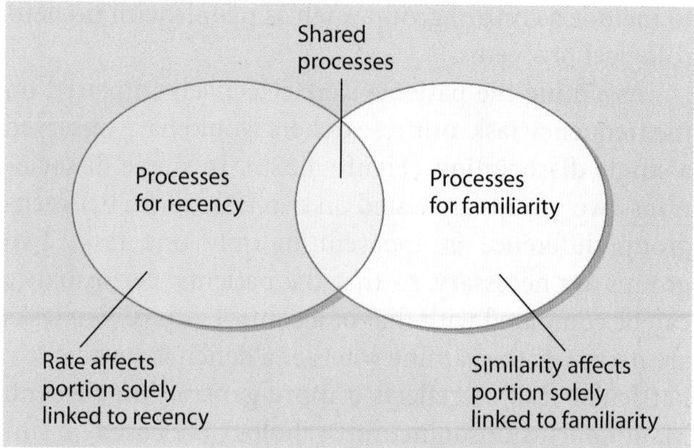

Figure 4.23 We can identify the mental operations required for a particular task by showing that different manipulations selectively influence different aspects of performance. In this example, it is hypothesized that recognition memory depends on both recency and familiarity, and that these two processes can be influenced by separate manipulations.

GROUPS VERSUS INDIVIDUALS

In many neuropsychological studies, groups are defined according to whether patients have a common neurological diagnosis (e.g., Alzheimer's disease) or have pathology in a common neural region (e.g., frontal strokes). Group studies have been criticized as inappropriate for human neuropsychology because of the variability among patients assigned to the same groups. No two strokes or tumors are exactly alike. In a similar sense, neurological and cognitive deficits found in degenerative diseases such as Alzheimer's disease vary from patient to patient. Human neuropsychology will never approximate the type of control that is possible in animal research, where the experimenter can dictate the size and location of the lesion. Even powerful MRI machines provide a relatively crude resolution compared to the histological procedures available to researchers working with animals, and some types of lesions go undetected with either CT or MRI. Given this anatomical variability, the utility of lumping patients into a single group has been questioned, as we should expect a similar lack of correspondence at the behavioral level. Instead, it has been argued that insights into cognitive processes can best be achieved by comprehensive documentation of the performance of individual patients and comparison across case studies (Caramazza, 1992).

In general, proponents of the case study approach want to use patient studies to develop models of cognitive architecture. Double dissociations are especially prominent. Individuals with unique deficits help isolate the component operations of a task. Yet the case study approach is more limited for linking neural structures to cognitive operations. Lesions from strokes or tumors encompass a wide area and affect several disparate structures. It is difficult to know which affected area correlates with a deficit. Group studies offer hope. Though the extent and location of damage may be heterogeneous, reconstruction software can identify regions of overlap, as Figure 4.24 shows. Despite individual differences that might occur because lesions extend into nonidentical regions, the common site of pathology might produce a consistent pattern of deficits on a task being studied.

The debate over group studies versus individual case studies reflects the difference between the root words in cognitive neuroscience and cognitive neuropsychology. The case study method affords powerful insights into the functional components of cognition. For example, case studies have been essential for demonstrating that brain lesions can selectively disrupt restricted semantic classes. One patient studied by Alfonzo Caramazza and his colleagues at Johns Hopkins University showed a peculiar anomia, the inability to name things (Hart et al., 1985). For this patient, the problem was restricted to certain classes of objects. He was unable to generate the names of fruits and vegetables. In contrast, he showed no impairment when asked to name objects such as tools or furniture. If a study had been conducted with a group of patients with anomia, this patient's selective problem might have been attributed to normal between-subject variability. When he was treated as an isolated case, the problem stood out and inspired researchers to look for patients with similar problems, as well as patients with other category-specific anomias. This work has led to sophisticated models of the functional organization of semantic knowledge.

On the other hand, group studies have proved useful for relating cognitive processes to underlying brain structures (Robertson, Knight, et al., 1993). If a brain structure is hypothesized to perform a particular mental operation, then lesions to this structure should be associated with deficits on tasks that depend on the putative operation. This does not mean that all patients will be similarly affected. For some patients, the pathology may not be as extensive or encroach on the critical tissue. Moreover, as with healthy subjects, individuals will differ in how they perform a particular task, or they may have

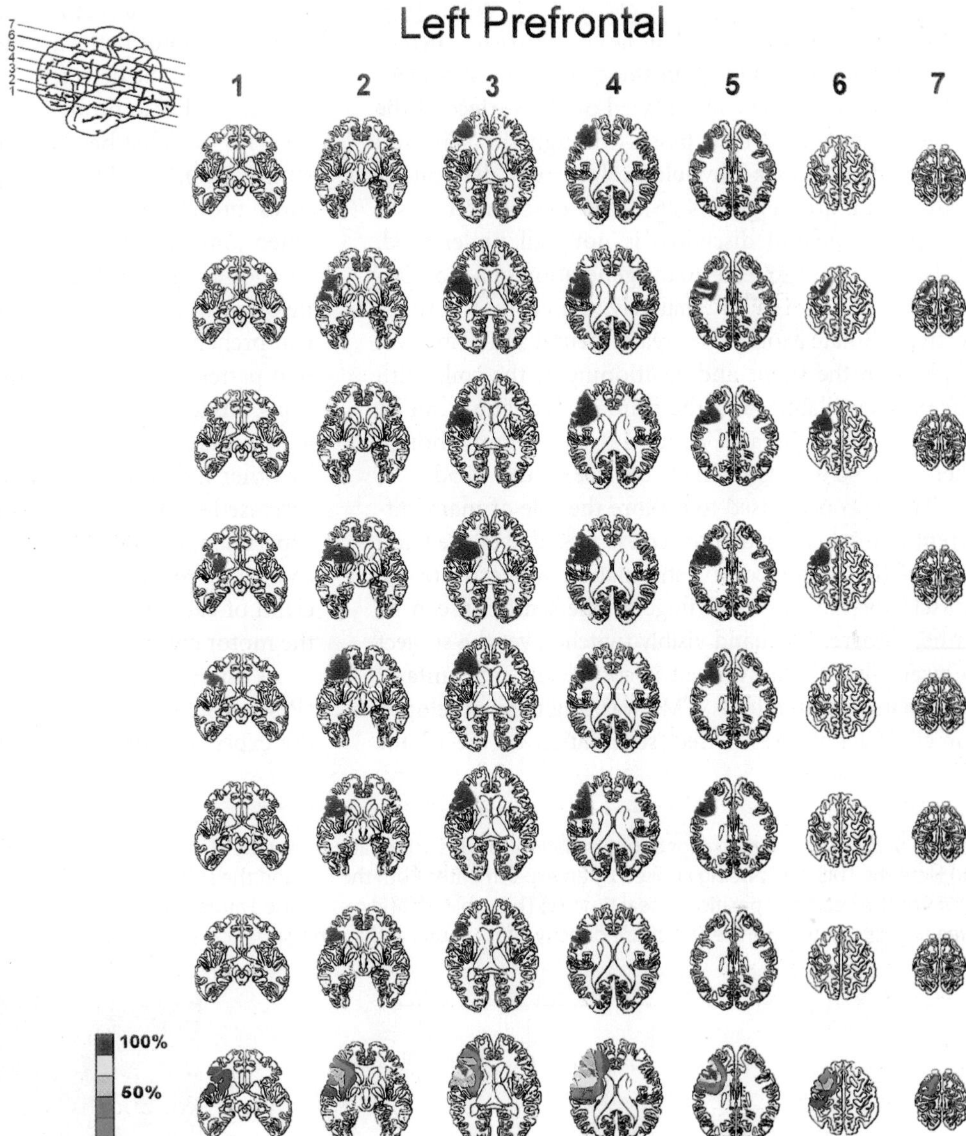

Figure 4.24 Drawing inferences from the study of humans with brain damage is difficult because naturally occurring brain lesions are never identical. Group studies can facilitate the functional analysis of brain structures by identifying regions of lesion overlap. Shown here are sketches of the extent of lesions in seven patients who had strokes in the frontal lobe of the left hemisphere. The individual patients are represented in each row, with the transverse slices going from inferior to superior (as the upper left diagram shows). The bottom row shows the extent of damage for the group in composite form.

developed idiosyncratic strategies. Nonetheless, group studies allow the researcher to look for similarities across patients with related lesions, as well as to make systematic comparisons between the effects of lesions centered in different brain structures.

Virtual Lesions: Transcranial Magnetic Stimulation

Lesion methods have been an important tool for both human and animal studies of the relationship between the brain and behavior. Observations of the performance of neurologically impaired individuals have tended to serve as the starting point for many theories. Nonetheless, it is important to keep in mind that, with human studies, the experimenter is limited by the vagaries of nature (or the types of damage caused by military technology). Lesion studies in animals have the advantage that the experimenter can control the site and size of the damage. Here a specific hypothesis can be tested by comparison of the effects of lesions to one region versus another.

Transcranial magnetic stimulation (**TMS**) offers a methodology to noninvasively produce focal stimulation of the brain in humans. The TMS device consists of a tightly wrapped wire coil that is encased in an insulated sheath and connected to a source of powerful electrical capacitors (Figure 4.25a and b). When triggered, the capacitors send a large electrical current through the coil, resulting in the generation of a magnetic field. When the coil is placed on the surface of the skull, the magnetic field passes through the skin and scalp and induces a physiological current that causes neurons to fire (Figure 4.26). The exact mechanism causing the neural discharge is not well understood. Perhaps the current leads to the generation of action potentials in the soma; alternatively, the current may directly stimulate axons. The area of neural activation will depend on the shape and positioning of the coil. With currently available coils, the primary activation can be restricted to an area of about 1.0 to 1.5 cm^3, though there are also downstream effects (see Figure 4.25d).

TMS has been used to explore the role of many different brain areas. When the coil is placed over the hand area of the motor cortex, stimulation will activate the muscles of the wrist and fingers. The sensation can be rather bizarre: The hand visibly twitches, yet the subject is aware that the movement is completely involuntary! Like many research tools, TMS was originally developed for clinical purposes. Direct stimulation of the motor cortex provides a relatively simple way to assess the integrity of motor pathways because muscle activity in the periphery can be detected about 20 ms after stimulation.

The ability to probe the excitability of the motor cortex with TMS has been exploited in many basic research studies. Consider how we come to understand the gestures produced by another individual—for example, when someone waves at us as a greeting or throws a ball to another friend. Recognition of these gestures surely involves an analysis of the perceptual information. But comprehension may also require relating these perceptual patterns to our own ability to produce similar actions. Indeed, as TMS shows, the motor system is activated during passive observation of actions produced by other individuals. Although we can assume that the increased excitability of the motor cortex is related to our experimental manipulation, we cannot infer that this change is required for action comprehension. Such a claim of causality would require showing that lesions of the motor cortex impair comprehension.

A different use of TMS is to induce "virtual lesions" (Pascual-Leone et al., 1999). By stimulating the brain, the experimenter is disrupting normal activity in a se-

Figure 4.25 Transcranial magnetic stimulation. **(a)** This schematic shows the electrical circuit used to induce the TMS pulse. **(b)** Here the TMS coil is being applied by an experimenter. Both the coil and the subject have affixed to them a tracking device to monitor the head/coil position in real time. **(c)** The subject's MRI can be used along with the tracking system to display the cortical area being targeted. **(d)** The TMS pulse directly alters neural activity in a spherical area of approximately 1 cm^3.

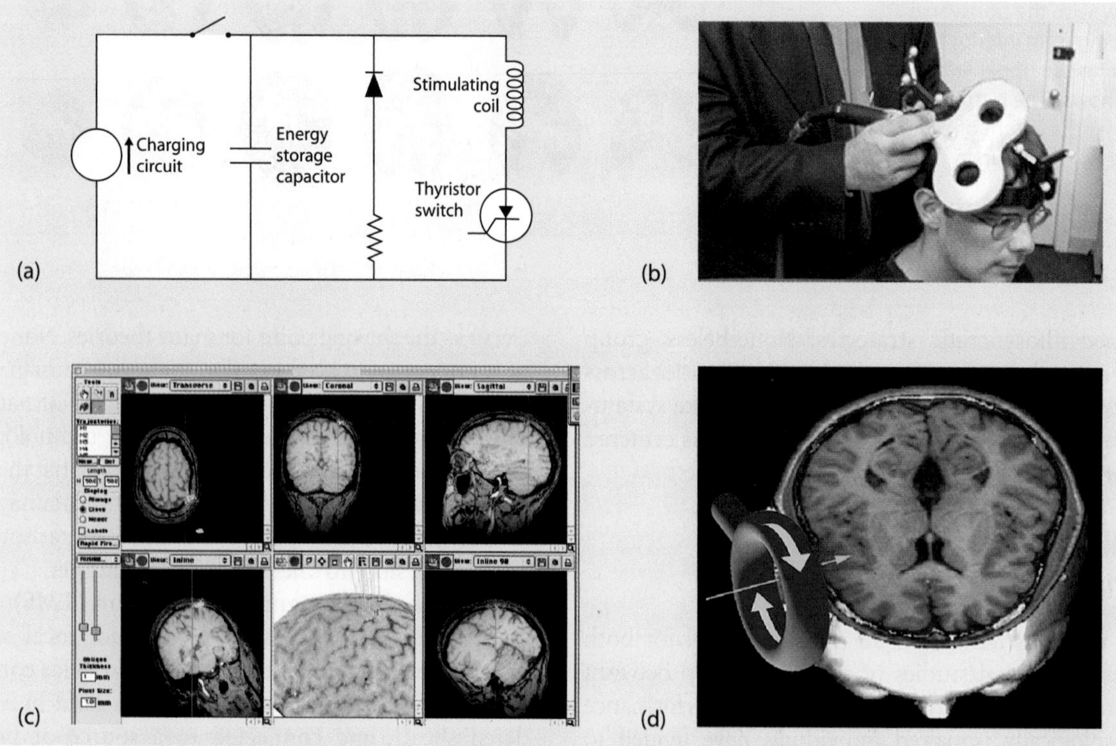

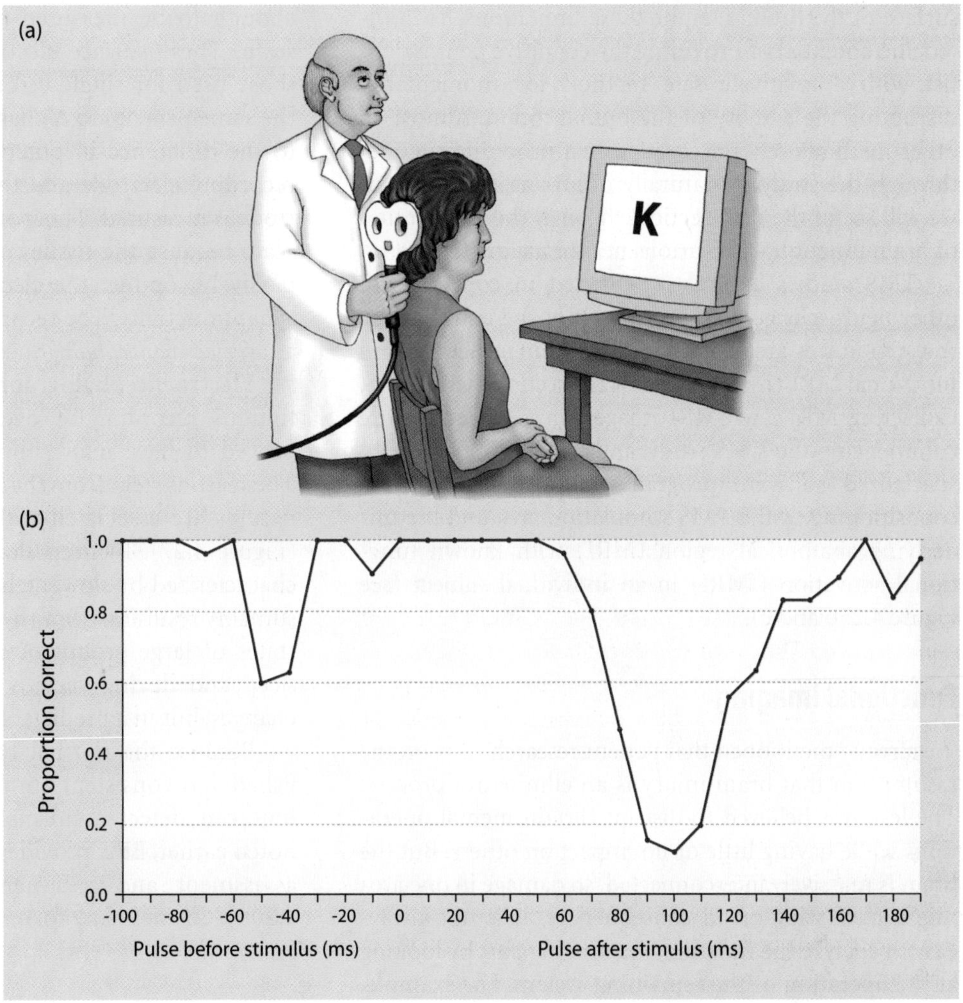

Figure 4.26 Transcranial magnetic stimulation over the occipital lobe. **(a)** The center of the figure-eight coil is placed over the targeted area. When a large electrical field is passed through the coil, a magnetic pulse is generated and passes through the skull. This pulse activates neurons in the underlying cortex. **(b)** The time between the onset of the letter stimulus and the pulse varies. When the pulse follows the stimulus by 70 to 130 ms, the subject fails to identify the stimulus on all trials. Note the failures when the pulse precedes the letter. These occur because the subject briefly blinks on some trials after the pulse.

lected region of the cortex. Similar to the logic in lesion studies, the consequences of the stimulation on behavior are used to shed light on the normal function of the disrupted tissue. What makes this method appealing is that the technique, when properly conducted, is safe and noninvasive, producing only a relatively brief alteration in neural activity. Thus, performance can be compared between stimulated and nonstimulated conditions in the same individual. This, of course, is not possible with brain-injured patients.

The virtual-lesion approach has been successfully employed with stimulation of various brain sites, even when the person is not aware of any effects from the stimulation. For example, stimulation over visual cortex can interfere with a person's ability to identify a letter (Corthout et al., 1999). The synchronized discharge of the underlying visual neurons interferes with their normal operation. The timing between the onset of the TMS pulse and the onset of the stimulus (e.g., presentation of a letter) can be manipulated to plot the time course of processing. In the letter identification task, the person will err only if the stimulation occurs between 70 and 170 ms after presentation of the letter. If the TMS is given before this interval, the neurons have time to recover; if the TMS is given after this interval, the visual neurons have already responded to the stimulus.

TMS has some notable limitations. As the previous example illustrated, the effects of TMS are generally quite brief. The method tends to work best with tasks in which the stimulation is closely linked to either stimulus events or movement. It remains to be seen if more complex tasks can be disrupted by brief volleys of externally induced stimulation. The fact that stimulation activates a restricted area of the cortex is both a plus and a minus. The experimenter can restrict stimulation to a specific area, especially if the coordinates are based on MRI scans. But TMS will be of limited value in exploring the function of cortical areas that are not on the superficial surface of the brain. Despite these limitations, TMS offers the potential of providing the cognitive neuroscientist with a relatively safe method for momentarily disrupting the activity of the human brain. Almost all other methods rely on correlational procedures, either through the study of naturally occurring lesions or, as we will see in the next section, through the observation of brain function with various neuroimaging tools.

TMS studies are best conducted in concert with other neuroscience methods. Much of the cutting-edge research in this area combines data from structural and functional MRI (fMRI; see the next section) with TMS. Collecting MRI and fMRI images on a subject before commencing the TMS study, and feeding the data into specialized software programs, allows for real-time copositioning of the TMS stimulation area and the underlying anatomical region (MRI) with known functional activation (fMRI) in an individual subject (see Figure 4.25b and c).

Functional Imaging

We already mentioned that patient research rests on the assumption that brain injury is an eliminative process: The lesion is believed to disrupt certain mental operations while having little or no impact on others. But the brain is massively interconnected, so damage in one area might have widespread consequences. It is not always easy to analyze the function of a missing part by looking at the operation of the remaining system. For example, allowing the spark plugs to decay or cutting the line distributing the gas to the pistons will cause an automobile to stop running, but this does not mean that spark plugs and distributors do the same thing; rather, their removal has similar functional consequences.

Concerns such as these point to the need for methods that measure activity in the normal brain. Along this front have occurred remarkable technological breakthroughs during the past 25 years. Indeed, new tools and methods of analysis develop at such an astonishing pace that new journals and scientific organizations have been created for rapid dissemination of this information. In the following section we review some of the technologies that allow researchers to observe the electrical and metabolic activity of the healthy human brain in vivo.

ELECTRICAL AND MAGNETIC SIGNALS

Neural activity is an electrochemical process. Although the electrical potential produced by a single neuron is minute, when large populations of neurons are active together, they produce electrical potentials large enough to be measured by electrodes placed on the scalp. These surface electrodes are much larger than those used for single-cell recordings, they but involve the same principles: A change in voltage corresponding to the difference in potential between the signal at a recording electrode and the signal at a reference electrode is measured. This potential can be recorded at the scalp because the tissues of the brain, skull, and scalp passively conduct the electrical currents produced by synaptic activity. The record of the signals is referred to as an *electroencephalogram.*

Electroencephalography, or **EEG**, provides a continuous recording of overall brain activity and has proved to have many important clinical applications. The reasons stem from the fact that predictable EEG signatures are associated with different behavioral states (Figure 4.27). In deep sleep, for example, the EEG is characterized by slow, high-amplitude oscillations, presumably resulting from rhythmic changes in the activity states of large groups of neurons. In other phases of sleep and during various wakeful states, this pattern changes, but in a predictable manner.

Because the normal EEG patterns are well established and consistent among individuals, EEG recordings can detect abnormalities in brain function. As noted earlier, EEG provides valuable information in the assessment and treatment of epilepsy (see Figure 4.20b). Of the many forms of epileptic seizures, gener-

Figure 4.27 EEG profiles obtained during various states of consciousness.

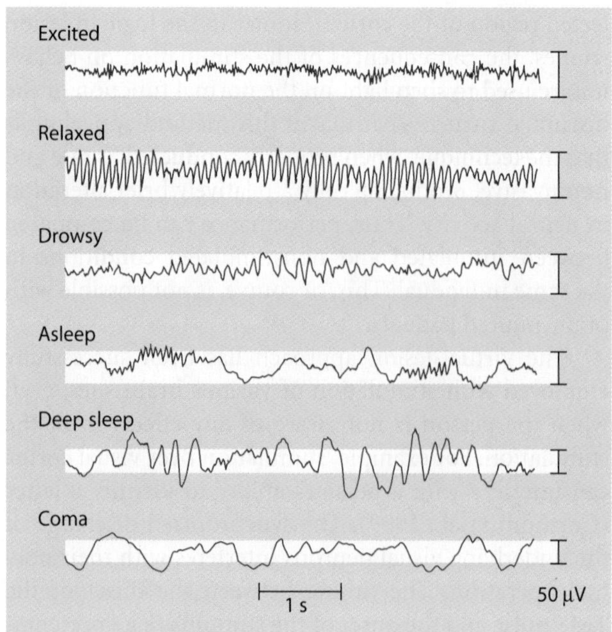

alized seizures have no known locus of origin and appear bilaterally symmetrical in the EEG record. Focal seizures, in contrast, begin in a restricted area and spread throughout the brain. Focal seizures frequently provide the first hint of a neurological abnormality. They can result from congenital abnormalities such as a vascular malformation or can develop as a result of a local infection, enlargement of a tumor, or residual damage from a stroke or traumatic event. Surface EEG can only crudely localize focal seizures, because some electrodes detect the onset earlier and with higher amplitude than other electrodes.

EEG is limited in providing insight to cognitive processes because the recording tends to reflect the brain's global electrical activity. A more powerful approach used by many cognitive neuroscientists focuses on how brain activity is modulated in response to a particular task. The method requires extracting an evoked response from the global EEG signal.

The logic of this approach is straightforward. EEG traces from a series of trials are averaged together by being aligned according to an external event, such as the onset of a stimulus or response. This alignment washes out variations in the brain's electrical activity that are unrelated to the events of interest. The evoked response, or **event-related potential** (**ERP**), is a tiny signal embedded in the ongoing EEG. By averaging the traces, investigators can extract this signal, which reflects neural activity that is specifically related to sensory, motor, or cognitive events—hence the name *event-related potential* (Figure 4.28). A significant feature of evoked responses is that they provide a precise temporal record of underlying neural activity. The evoked response gives a picture of how neural activity changes over time as information is being processed in the human brain.

ERPs have proved to be an important tool for both clinicians and researchers. Sensory evoked responses offer a useful window for identifying the level of disturbance in patients with neurological disorders. For example, the visual evoked potential can be useful in the diagnosis of multiple sclerosis, a disorder that leads to demyelination. When demyelination occurs in the optic nerve, the early peaks of the visual evoked response are delayed in their time of appearance. Similarly, in the auditory system, tumors that compromise hearing by compressing or damaging auditory processing areas can be localized by the use of auditory evoked potentials (AEPs) because characteristic peaks and troughs in the AEP are known to arise from neuronal activity in anatomically defined areas of the ascending auditory system. The earliest of these AEPs indexes activity in the auditory nerve, occurring within just a few milliseconds of the sound. Within the first 20 to 30 ms, a series of responses indexes, in sequence, neural firing in the brainstem, midbrain, thalamus, and cortex (Figure 4.29). These stereotyped responses allow the neurologist to pinpoint the level at which the pathology has occurred. Thus, by looking at the sensory evoked responses in patients with hearing problems, the clinician can determine if the problem is due to poor sensory processing and, if so, at what level the deficit becomes apparent.

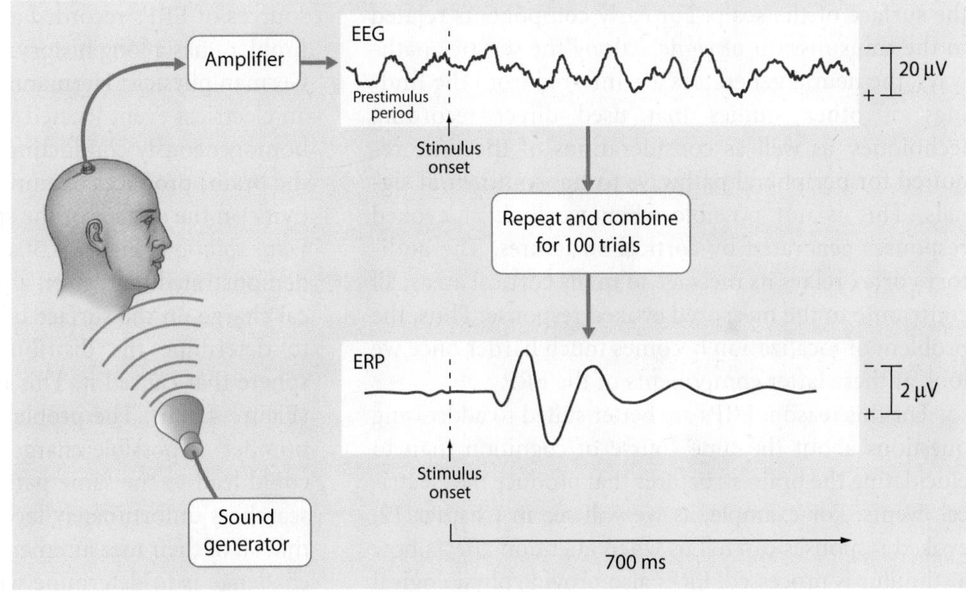

Figure 4.28 The relatively small electrical responses to specific events can be observed only if the EEG traces are averaged over a series of trials. The large background oscillations of the EEG trace make it impossible to detect the evoked response to the sensory stimulus from a single trial. Averaging across tens or hundreds of trials, however, removes the background EEG, leaving the event-related potential (ERP). Note the difference in scale between the EEG and ERP waveforms.

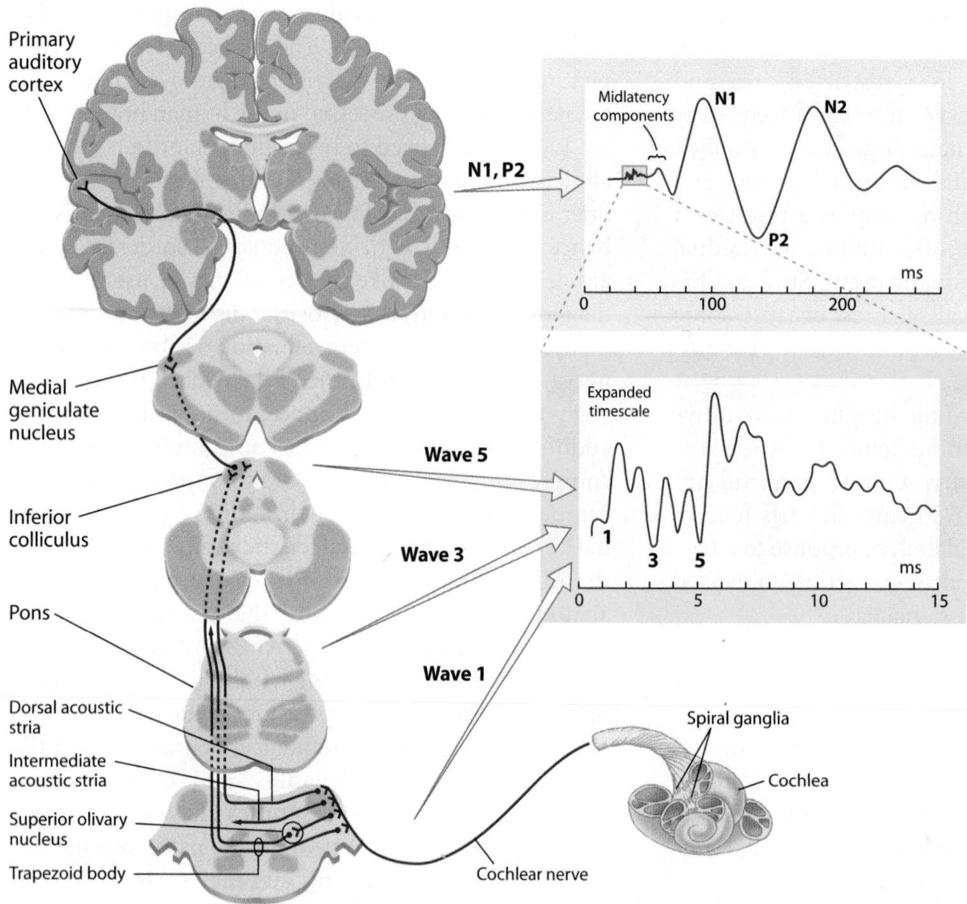

Figure 4.29 The evoked potential shows a series of positive (P) and negative (N) peaks at predictable points in time. In this auditory evoked potential, the early peaks are invariant and have been linked to neural activity in specific brain structures. Later peaks are task dependent, and localization of their source has been a subject of much investigation and debate.

In this example we specified the neural structures associated with the early components of the ERP. Note that these localization claims are based on indirect methods because the electrical recordings are made on the surface of the scalp. For early components related to the transmission of signals along the sensory pathways, the neural generators are inferred from the findings of other studies that used direct recording techniques, as well as considerations of the time required for peripheral pathways to transmit neural signals. This is not possible when we look at evoked responses generated by cortical structures. The auditory cortex relays its message to many cortical areas; all contribute to the measured evoked response. Thus, the problem of localization becomes much harder once we look at these latter components of the ERP.

For this reason, ERPs are better suited to addressing questions about the time course of cognition than to elucidating the brain structures that produce the electrical events. For example, as we will see in Chapter 12, evoked responses can tell us when attention affects how a stimulus is processed. ERPs also provide physiological indices of when a person decides to respond, or when an error is detected.

Nonetheless, researchers have made significant progress in developing analytic tools to localize the sources of ERPs recorded at the scalp. This localization problem has a long history: In the late 19th century, the German physicist Hermann von Helmholtz showed that an electrical event located within a spherical volume of homogeneously conducting material (approximated by the brain) produces one unique pattern of electrical activity on the surface of the sphere. This is called the *forward solution* (Figure 4.30a). However, Helmholtz also demonstrated that, given a particular pattern of electrical charge on the surface of the sphere, it is impossible to determine the distribution of charge within the sphere that caused it. This is called the *inverse problem* (Figure 4.30b). The problem arises because an infinite number of possible charge distributions in the sphere could lead to the same pattern on the surface. ERP researchers unfortunately face the inverse problem, given that all of their measurements are made at the scalp. The challenge is to determine what areas of the brain must

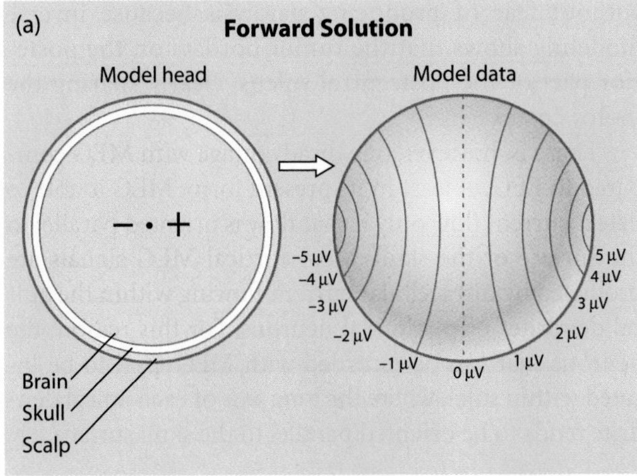

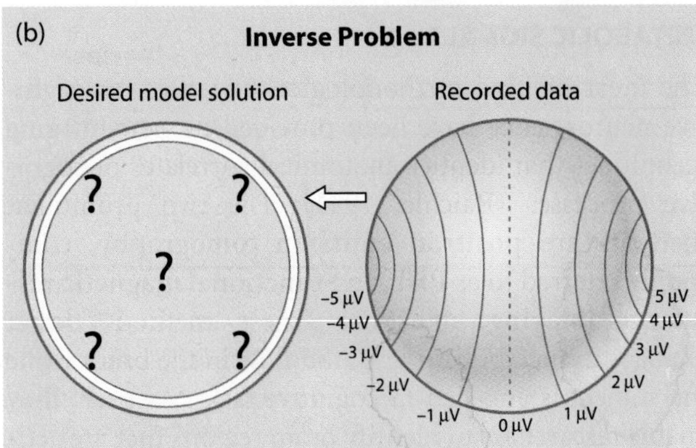

Figure 4.30 **(a)** In the forward solution, a model head is created that is based on known conductivities of various tissues of the brain, skull, and scalp. The pattern results from the location and orientation of a single dipolar charge, used to simulate an active neuronal population. The dipolar charge creates electrical currents that flow to the surface of the sphere, creating a distinct pattern of electrical voltages in the surface. **(b)** The inverse problem arises because a given pattern observed on the surface of the scalp can result from many possible locations of underlying neural generators.

have been active to produce the recorded pattern. In other words, where are the generators of a particular event in the ERP?

To solve this problem, researchers have turned to sophisticated modeling techniques. They have been able to do so by simplifying assumptions about the physics of the brain and head tissues, as well as the electrical nature of the active neurons. Of critical importance is the assumption that neural generators can be modeled as electrical dipoles, conductors with one positive end and one negative end, as shown in Figure 4.31. For example, the excitatory postsynaptic potential generated at the synapse of a cortical pyramidal cell can be viewed as a dipole.

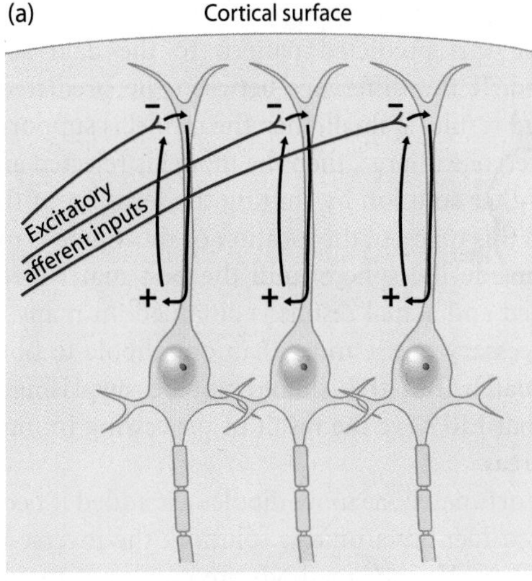

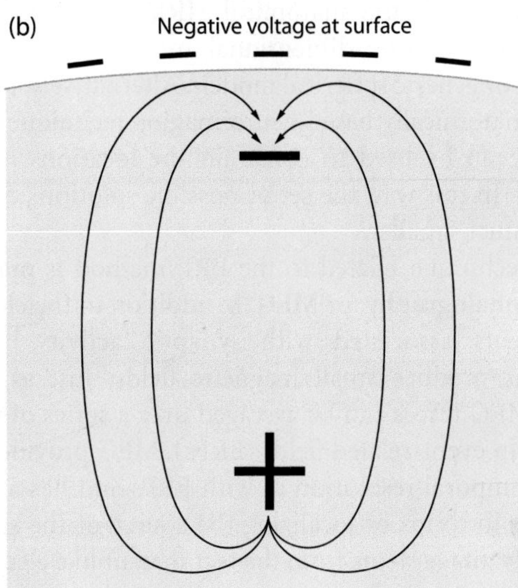

Figure 4.31 Inverse dipole modeling. **(a)** The long axes of these three cortical pyramidal neurons are perpendicular to the cortical surface (top of the figure). Each neuron is receiving an excitatory synaptic input at its apical dendrite. The postsynaptic potential that is created causes current to flow into the neuron near the cell body. This pattern of current flow produces an electrical field with one pole being the negative (–) electrical potential at the apical dendrite, and the other pole being the positive (+) electrical potential near the neuronal cell body. **(b)** The electrical fields of the pyramidal cells sum and can be represented by a single current dipole. In inverse dipole modeling, the source of the neural activity is estimated from the electrical activity that is recorded at the scalp.

Inverse dipole modeling is relatively straightforward. Using a high-speed computer, we create a model of a spherical head and place a dipole somewhere within the sphere. We then calculate the forward solution to determine the distribution of voltages that this dipole would create on the surface of the sphere. Finally, we compare this predicted pattern to the data actually recorded. If the difference between the predicted and obtained results is small, then the model is supported; if the difference is large, then the model is rejected and we test another solution by shifting the location of the dipole. In this manner, the location of the dipole is moved about inside the sphere until the best match between predicted and actual results is obtained. In many cases, it is necessary to use more than one dipole to obtain a good match. But this should not be surprising: It is likely that ERPs are the result of processing in multiple brain areas.

Unfortunately, as more dipoles are added it becomes harder to identify a unique solution; the inverse problem returns. Various methods are employed to address this problem. Using anatomical MRI, investigators can study precise three-dimensional models of the head instead of generic spherical models. Alternatively, results from anatomically based neuroimaging techniques (see below) can be used to constrain the locations of the dipoles. In this way, the set of possible solutions can be made much smaller.

A technique related to the ERP method is **magnetoencephalography**, or **MEG**. In addition to the electrical events associated with synaptic activity, active neurons produce small magnetic fields. Just as with EEG, MEG traces can be averaged over a series of trials to obtain event-related fields (ERFs). MEG provides the same temporal resolution as with ERPs and has an advantage in terms of localizing the source of the signal. This advantage stems from the fact that, unlike electrical signals, magnetic fields are not distorted as they pass through the brain, skull, and scalp. Inverse modeling techniques similar to those used in EEG are necessary, but the solutions are more accurate.

Indeed, the reliability of spatial resolution with MEG has made it a useful tool in neurosurgery (Figure 4.32). Suppose that an MRI scan reveals a large tumor near the central sulcus. Such tumors present a surgical dilemma. If the tumor extends into the precentral sulcus, surgery might be avoided or delayed because the procedure is likely to damage motor cortex and leave the person with partial paralysis. However, if the tumor does not extend into the motor cortex, surgery is usually warranted. MEG provides a noninvasive procedure to identify somatosensory cortex. From the ERFs produced following repeated stimulation of the fingers, arm, and foot, inverse modeling techniques are used to determine if the underlying neural generators are anterior to the lesion. In the case shown in Figure 4.32, the surgeon can proceed to excise the tumor without fear of producing paralysis because inverse modeling shows that the tumor borders on the posterior part of the postcentral sulcus, clearly sparing the motor cortex.

There is, however, one disadvantage with MEG compared to EEG, at least in its present form: MEG is able to detect current flow only if that flow is oriented parallel to the surface of the skull. Most cortical MEG signals are produced by intracellular current flowing within the apical dendrites of pyramidal neurons. For this reason, the neurons that can be recorded with MEG tend to be located within sulci, where the long axis of each apical dendrite tends to be oriented parallel to the skull surface.

METABOLIC SIGNALS

The most exciting methodological advances for cognitive neuroscience have been provided by new imaging techniques that identify anatomical correlates of cognitive processes (Raichle, 1994). The two prominent methods are **positron emission tomography**, commonly referred to as **PET**, and **functional magnetic resonance imaging**, or **fMRI**. These methods detect changes in metabolism or blood flow in the brain while the subject is engaged in cognitive tasks. As such, they enable researchers to identify brain regions that are activated during these tasks, and to test hypotheses about functional anatomy.

Unlike EEG and MEG, PET and fMRI do not directly measure neural events. Rather, they measure metabolic changes correlated with neural activity. Neurons are no different from other cells of the human body. They require energy in the form of oxygen and glucose, both to sustain their cellular integrity and to perform their specialized functions. As with all other parts of the body, oxygen and glucose are distributed to the brain by the circulatory system. The brain is an extremely metabolically demanding organ. As noted previously, the central nervous system uses approximately 20% of all the oxygen we breathe. Yet the amount of blood supplied to the brain varies only a little between the time when the brain is most active and when it is quiet (perhaps because what we regard as active and quiet in relation to behavior does not correlate with active and quiet in the context of neural activity). Thus, the brain must regulate itself. When a brain area is active, more oxygen and glucose are made available by increased blood flow.

PET activation studies measure local variations in cerebral blood flow that are correlated with mental activity (Figure 4.33). To do this, a tracer must be introduced into the bloodstream. For PET, radioactive elements (isotopes) are used as tracers. Owing to their unstable

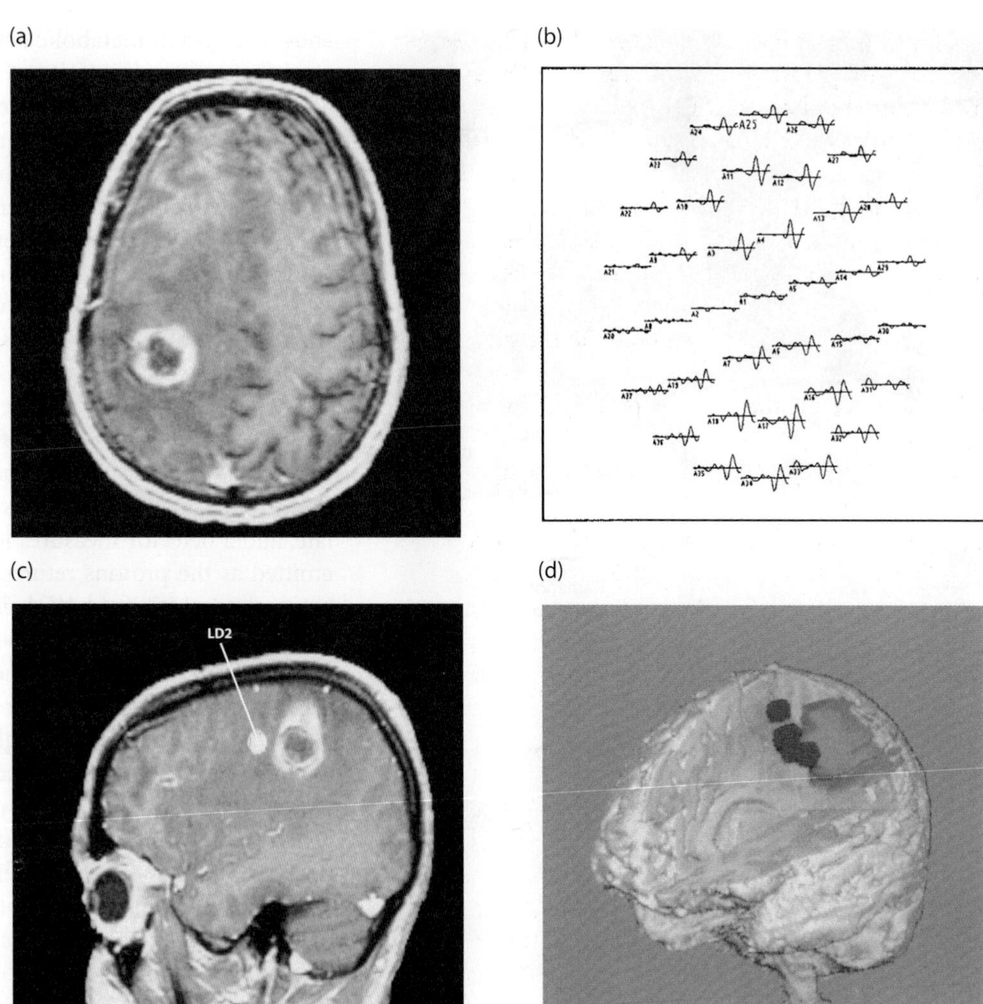

Figure 4.32 Magnetoencephalography as a noninvasive presurgical mapping procedure. **(a)** This MRI shows a large tumor in the vicinity of the central sulcus. **(b)** These event-related fields (ERFs) were produced following repeated tactile stimulation of the index finger. Each trace shows the magnetic signal recorded from an array of detectors placed over the scalp. **(c)** Inverse modeling showed that the dipole (indicated by LD2) producing the surface recordings in (b) was anterior to the lesion. **(d)** This three-dimensional reconstruction shows stimulation of the fingers and toes on the left side of the body in red and the tumor outlined in green.

state, these isotopes rapidly decay by emitting a positron from their atomic nucleus. When a positron collides with an electron, two photons, or gamma rays, are created. Not only do the two photons move at the speed of light, passing unimpeded through all tissue, but also they move in opposite directions. The PET scanner—essentially a gamma ray detector—can determine where the collision took place. Because these tracers are in the blood, a reconstructed image can show the distribution of blood flow: Where there is more blood flow, there will be more radiation.

The most common isotope used in cognitive studies is ^{15}O, an unstable form of oxygen with a half-life of 123 s. This isotope, in the form of water (H_2O), is injected in the bloodstream while a person is engaged in a cognitive task. Although all areas of the body will absorb some radioactive oxygen, the fundamental assumption of PET is that there will be increased blood flow to the brain regions that have heightened neural activity. Thus, PET activation studies do not measure absolute metabolic activity, but rather relative activity. In the typical PET experiment, the injection is administered at least twice: during a control condition and during an experimental condition. The results are usually reported in terms of a change in **regional cerebral blood flow** (**rCBF**) between the two conditions.

Consider, for example, a PET study designed to identify brain areas involved in visual perception: In the experimental condition the subject views a circular checkerboard surrounding a small fixation point (to keep subjects from moving their eyes); in the control condition, only the fixation point is presented. With PET analysis, researchers subtract the radiation counts measured during the control condition from those

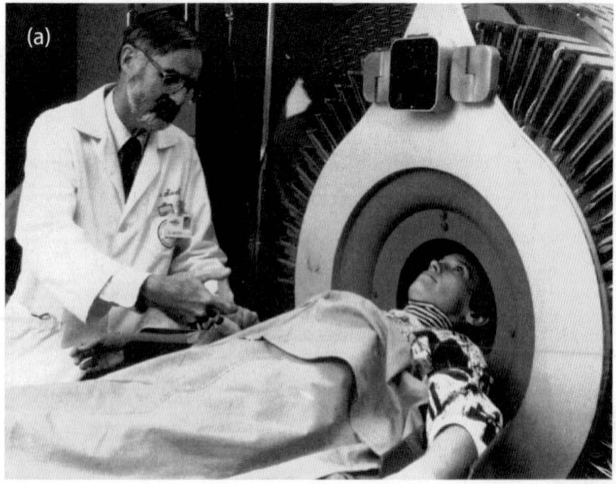

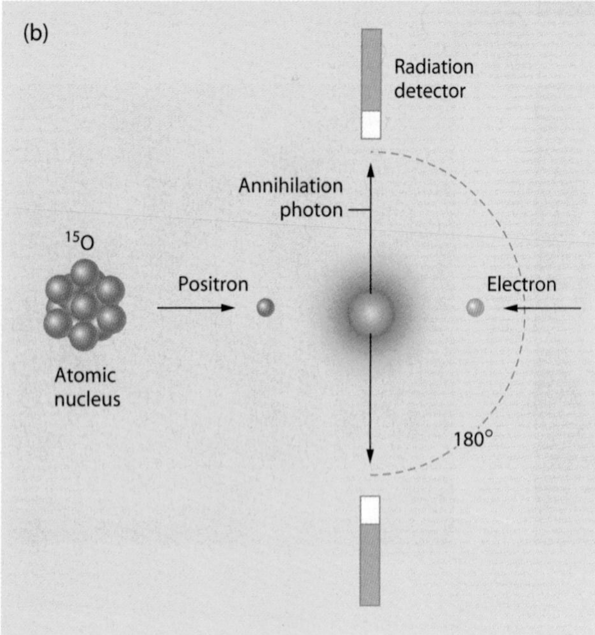

Figure 4.33 Positron emission tomography. **(a)** PET scanning allows metabolic activity to be measured in the human brain. **(b)** In the most common form of PET, water labeled with radioactive oxygen, ^{15}O, is injected into the subject. As positrons break off from this unstable isotope, they collide with electrons. A by-product of this collision is the generation of two gamma rays, or photons, that move in opposite directions. The PET scanner measures these photons and calculates their source. Regions of the brain that are most active will increase their demand for oxygen.

measured during the experimental condition. Areas that were more active when the subject was viewing the checkerboard stimulus will have higher counts, reflecting increased blood flow. This subtractive procedure ignores variations in absolute blood flow between the brain's areas. The difference image identifies areas that show changes in metabolic activity as a function of the experimental manipulation.

PET scanners are capable of resolving metabolic activity to regions, or voxels, that are approximately 5 to 10 mm^3 in volume. Although this size includes thousands of neurons, it is sufficient to identify cortical and subcortical areas and can even show functional variation within a given cortical area. The panels in Figure 4.34 show a shift in activation within the visual cortex as the stimulus moves from being adjacent to the fixation point to more eccentric places.

As with PET, fMRI exploits the fact that local blood flow increases in active parts of the brain. The procedure is essentially identical to the one used in traditional MRI: Radio waves make the protons in hydrogen atoms oscillate, and a detector measures local energy fields that are emitted as the protons return to the orientation of the external magnetic field. With fMRI, however, imaging is focused on the magnetic properties of hemoglobin. Hemoglobin carries oxygen in the bloodstream, and when the oxygen is absorbed the hemoglobin becomes deoxygenated. Deoxygenated hemoglobin is more sensitive, or paramagnetic, than oxygenated hemoglobin. The fMRI detectors measure the ratio of oxygenated to deoxygenated hemoglobin. This ratio is referred to as the **blood oxygenation level–dependent**, or **BOLD**, effect.

Intuitively, one would expect the proportion of deoxygenated tissue to be greater in active tissue, given the intensive metabolic costs associated with neural function. However, fMRI results are generally reported in terms of an increase in the ratio of oxygenated to deoxygenated hemoglobin. This change occurs because, as a brain area becomes active, the amount of blood being directed to that area increases. The neural tissue is unable to absorb all of the excess oxygen. The time course of this regulatory process is what is measured in fMRI studies. Although neural events occur on a scale measured in milliseconds, blood flow is modulated much more slowly, with the initial rise not evident for at least a couple of seconds and peaking 6 to 10 seconds later. This delay suggests that, right after a neural region is engaged, there should be a small drop in the ratio of oxygenated to deoxygenated hemoglobin. In fact, the newest generation of MRI scanners, reaching strengths of 4 teslas and above, are able to detect the initial drop (Figure 4.35). This decrease is small, representing no more than 1% of the total hemoglobin signal. The subsequent increase in the oxygenated blood can produce a signal as large as 5%. Continual measurement of the fMRI signal makes it possible to construct a map of changes in regional blood flow that are coupled with local neuronal activity.

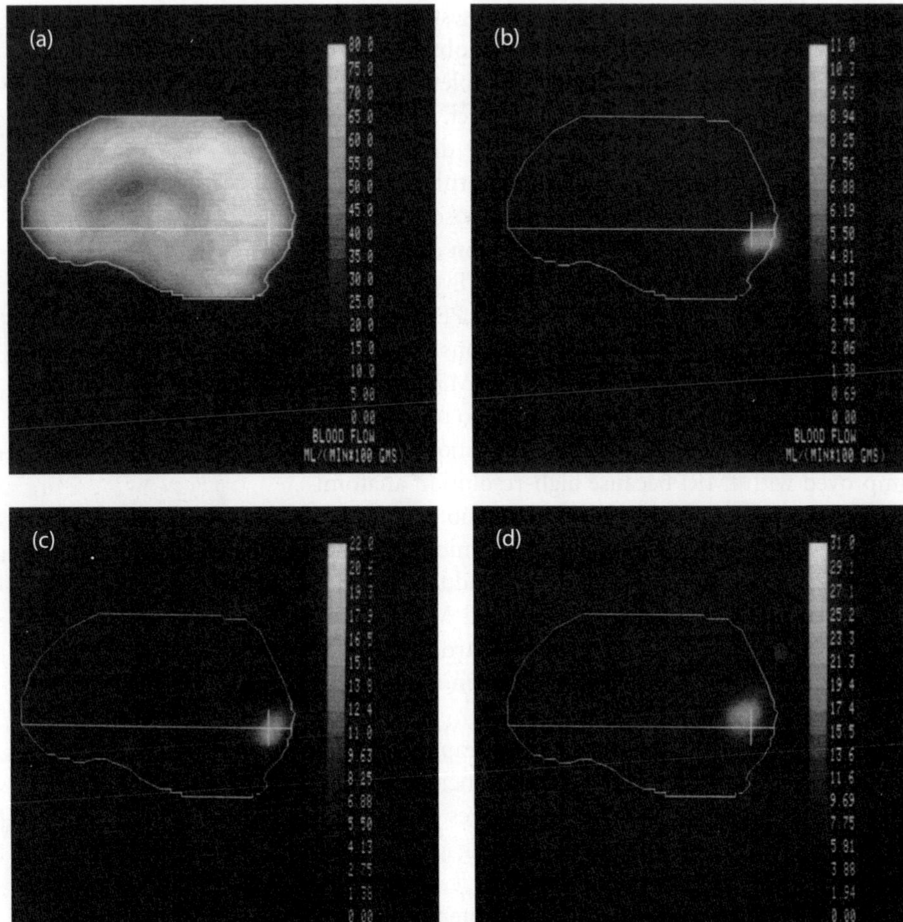

Figure 4.34 Measurements of cerebral blood flow using PET. **(a)** Blood flow when the subject fixated on a central spot. Activity in this baseline condition was subtracted from that in three other conditions in which the central spot was surrounded by a checkerboard in the center of view **(b)**, more toward the periphery **(c)**, or in the far periphery **(d)**. A retinotopic map can be identified, with central vision represented more inferiorly than peripheral vision.

PET scanning provided a breakthrough for cognitive neuroscience, but fMRI has led to revolutionary changes. Only about a decade after the first fMRI papers appeared (in the early 1990s), fMRI imaging studies now fill the pages of neuroscience journals and proceedings of conferences. Functional MRI is popular for various reasons. For one thing, compared to PET, fMRI is a more practical option for most cognitive neuroscientists. MRI scanners are present in almost all hospitals in technologically advanced countries, and with modest hardware modifications most of them can be used for functional imaging. In contrast, PET scanners are available in only a handful of major medical facilities and require a large technical staff to run the scanner and the cyclotron used to produce the radioactive tracers.

In addition, important methodological advantages favor fMRI over PET. Because fMRI does not require the injection of radioactive tracers, the same individual can

Figure 4.35 Functional-MRI signal observed from visual cortex in the cat with a 4.7-tesla scanner. The black bar indicates the duration of a visual stimulus. Initially there is a dip in the blood oxygenation level–dependent (BOLD) signal, reflecting the depletion of oxygen from the activated cells. Over time, the BOLD signal increases, reflecting the increased hemodynamic response to the activated area. Scanners of this strength are now being used with human subjects.

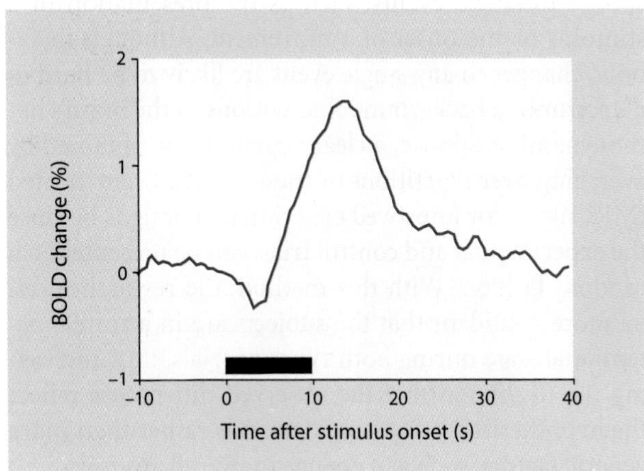

be tested repeatedly, either in a single session or over multiple sessions. With these multiple observations it becomes possible to perform a complete statistical analysis on the data from a single subject. This advantage is important, given the individual differences in brain anatomy. With PET, computer algorithms must be used to average the data and superimpose them on a "standardized" brain because each person can be given only a limited number of injections. Even with the newest generation of high-resolution PET scanners, subjects can receive only 12 to 16 injections.

Spatial resolution is superior with fMRI compared to PET. Current fMRI scanners are able to resolve voxels of about 3 mm^3. Moreover, the localization process is improved with fMRI because high-resolution anatomical images can be obtained when the subject is in the scanner. With PET, not only is anatomical precision compromised by averaging across individuals, but precise localization requires that structural MRIs be obtained from the subjects. Error will be introduced in the alignment of anatomical markers between the PET and MRI scans.

Functional MRI can also be used to improve temporal resolution. It takes time to collect sufficient "counts" of radioactivity in order to create images of adequate quality with PET. The subject must be engaged continually in a given experimental task for at least 40 s, and metabolic activity is averaged over this interval. The signal changes in fMRI also require averaging over successive observations, and many fMRI studies utilize a block design similar to that of PET in which activation is compared between experimental and control scanning phases (Figure 4.36).

However, the BOLD effect in fMRI can be time-locked to specific events to allow a picture of the time course of neural activity. This method is called *event-related fMRI* and follows the same logic as is used in ERP studies. The BOLD signal can be measured in response to single events, such as the presentation of a stimulus or the onset of a movement. Although metabolic changes to any single event are likely to be hard to detect among background fluctuations in the brain's hemodynamic response, a clear signal can be obtained by averaging over repetitions of these events. Event-related fMRI allows for improved experimental designs because the experimental and control trials can be presented in a random fashion. With this method, the researcher can be more confident that the subjects are in a similar attentional state during both types of trials, thus increasing the likelihood that the observed differences reflect the hypothesized processing demands rather than more generic factors, such as a change in overall arousal.

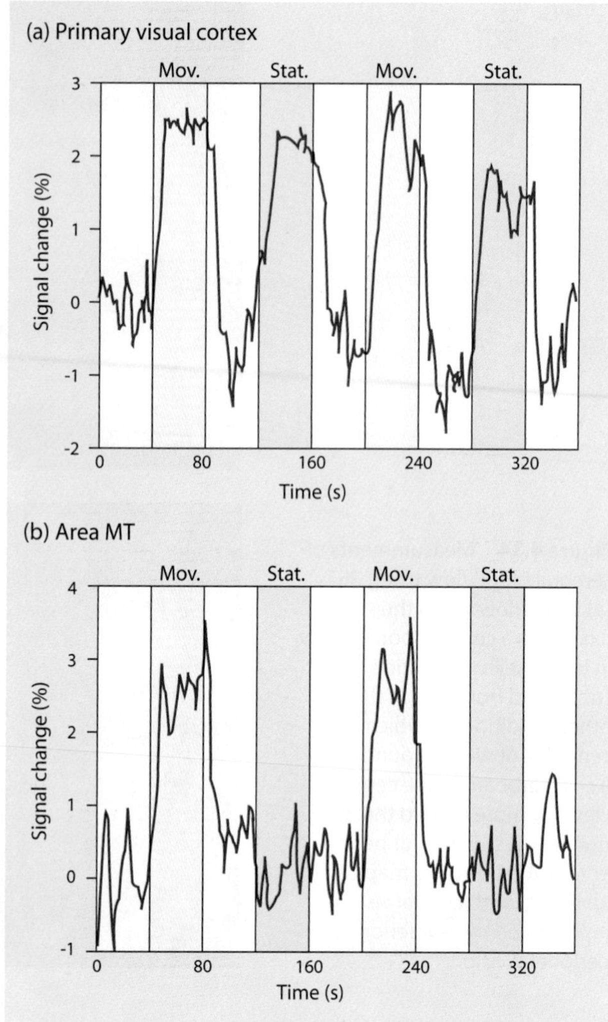

Figure 4.36 Functional MRI measures time-dependent fluctuations in oxygenation with excellent spatial resolution. The subject in this experiment viewed a field of randomly positioned white dots on a black background. The dots would either remain stationary or move along the radial axis. The 40-s intervals of stimulation (shaded background) alternated with 40-s intervals during which the screen was blank (white background). **(a)** Measurements from primary visual cortex (V1) showed consistent increases during the stimulation intervals compared to the blank intervals. **(b)** In area MT, a visual region associated with motion perception (see Chapter 5), the increase was observed only when the dots were moving.

A powerful advantage of event-related fMRI is that the experimenter can choose to combine the data in many different ways after the scanning is completed. As an example, consider memory failure. Most of us have experienced the frustration of being introduced to someone at a party and then being unable to remember the person's name just 2 minutes later. Is this because we failed to listen carefully during the original introduction and thus the information never really entered memory? Or did the information enter our memory stores but, after 2 minutes of distraction, we are unable to access the information? The former would constitute a problem with memory encoding; the latter would reflect a problem with memory retrieval. Distinguishing between these two possibilities has proved very difficult, as witnessed by the thousands of articles on this topic that have appeared in cognitive psychology journals over the past 100 years.

Anthony Wagner and his colleagues at Harvard University used event-related fMRI to take a fresh look at the question of encoding versus retrieval (Wagner et al., 1998). They obtained fMRI scans while the subjects were studying a list of words, with one word appearing every 2 s. About 20 minutes after the scanning session was completed, the subjects were given a recognition memory test. On average, the subjects correctly recognized 88% of the words studied during the scanning session. The researchers then separated the trials on the basis of whether a word had been remembered or forgotten. If the memory failure was due to retrieval difficulties, no differences should be detected in the fMRI response to these two trials, since the scans were obtained only while the subjects were reading the words. However, if the memory failure was due to poor encoding, then one would expect to see a different fMRI pattern following presentation of the words that were later remembered compared to those that were forgotten. The results clearly favored the encoding-failure hypothesis (Figure 4.37). The BOLD signal recorded from two areas, the prefrontal cortex and the hippocampus, was stronger following the presentation of words that were later remembered. As we'll see in Chapter 8, these two areas of the brain play a critical role in memory formation. This type of study would not be possible with a block design method, because the signal is averaged over all of the events within each scanning phase.

The limitations of imaging techniques such as PET and fMRI must be kept in mind. The data sets from an imaging study are massive, and in many studies the contrast of experimental and control conditions produces a large set of activations. This should not be surprising, given what we know about the distributed nature of brain function; for example, asking someone to generate a verb associated with a noun (experimental task) likely requires many more cognitive operations than just saying the noun (control task).

The standard analytic procedure in imaging studies has been to generate maps of all the areas that show greater activity in the experimental condition. However, even if we discover that the metabolic activity in a particular area correlates with an experimental variation, we still need to make inferences about the area's functional contribution. Correlation does not imply causation. For example, an area may be activated during a task but not play a critical role in the task's performance. The area simply might be "listening" to other brain areas that provide the critical computations. New analytic methods are being developed that address these concerns. A starting point is to ask whether the activation changes in one brain area are related to activation changes in another brain area—that is, to look at what is called *functional connectivity* (Sun et al., 2004).

Using event-related designs, it is possible not only to measure changes in activity within brain regions, but also to ask if the changes in one area are correlated with changes in another area. In this manner, fMRI data can be used to describe networks associated with particular cognitive operations and the relationships between nodes within those networks.

Interpretation of the results from imaging studies is frequently guided by other methodologies. For example, single-cell recording studies of primates can be used to identify regions of interest in an fMRI study of humans. Or imaging studies can be used to isolate a component operation that is thought to be linked to a particular brain region because of the performance of patients with injuries to that area.

In turn, imaging studies can be used to generate hypotheses that are tested with alternative methodologies. For example, in one experiment fMRI was used to identify neural areas that become activated when people recognize objects through touch alone (Deibert et al., 1999; Figure 4.38a). Surprisingly, tactile object recognition led to pronounced activation of the visual cortex, even though the subjects' eyes were shut during the entire experiment. One possible reason for the pronounced activation is that the subjects identified the objects through touch and then generated visual images of them. Alternatively, the subjects might have constructed visual images during tactile exploration and then used the images to identify the objects.

A follow-up study with TMS was used to pit these hypotheses against one another (Zangaladze et al., 1999). TMS stimulation over the visual cortex impaired tactile object recognition. The disruption was observed only when the TMS pulses were delivered 180 ms after the hand touched the object; no effects were seen with earlier or later stimulation (Figure 4.38b). Thus, the results indicate that the visual representations generated during tactile exploration were essential for inferring

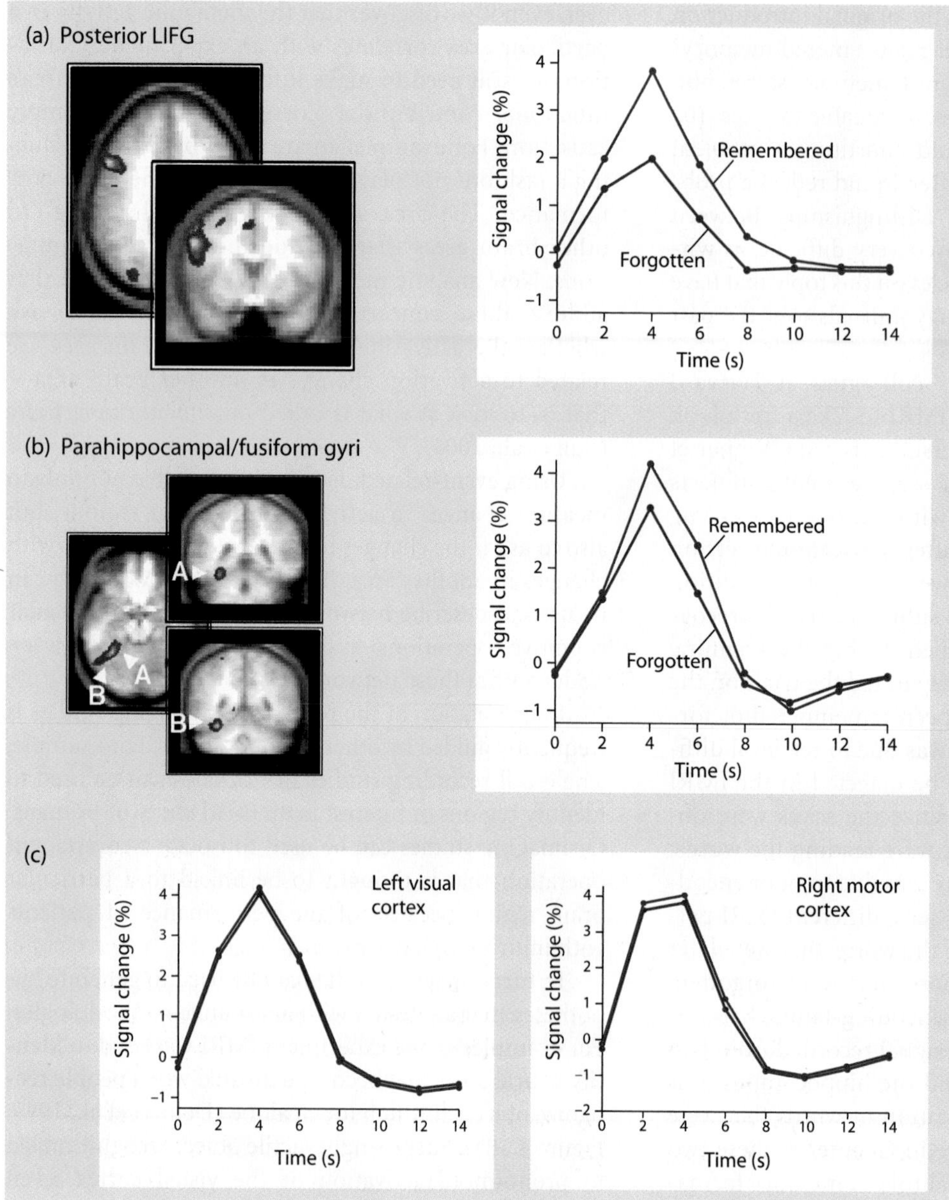

Figure 4.37 Use of event-related fMRI to identify areas associated with failures during memory encoding. Both the left inferior frontal gyrus (LIFG) **(a)** and the parahippocampal region **(b)** in the left hemisphere exhibit greater activity during encoding for words that are subsequently remembered compared to those that are forgotten. (A = parahippocampal region; B = fusiform gyrus.) **(c)** Activity over the left visual cortex and right motor cortex is identical following words that subsequently are either remembered or forgotten. These results demonstrate that the memory effect is specific to the frontal and hippocampal regions.

object shape from touch. These studies demonstrate how the combination of fMRI and TMS allows investigators to test causal accounts of neural function, as well as to make inferences about the time course of processing. Obtaining converging evidence from various methodologies enables us to make the strongest conclusions possible.

Another limitation of PET and fMRI is that both methods have poor temporal resolution in comparison to techniques such as single-cell recording or ERPs. PET is constrained by the decay rate of the radioactive agent. Even the fastest isotopes, such as ^{15}O, require measurements for 40 s to obtain stable radiation counts. Although fMRI can operate much faster, the metabolic changes used to measure the BOLD response occur over many seconds. Thus, PET and fMRI cannot give a temporal picture of the "online" operation of mental operations. Researchers at the best-equipped centers frequently combine the temporal resolution of evoked potentials with the spatial resolution of fMRI for a better picture of the physiology and anatomy of cognition.

One of the most promising methodological developments in cognitive neuroscience is the combination of imaging, behavioral, and genetic techniques into single studies. This approach is widely employed in studies of psychiatric conditions known to have a genetic basis.

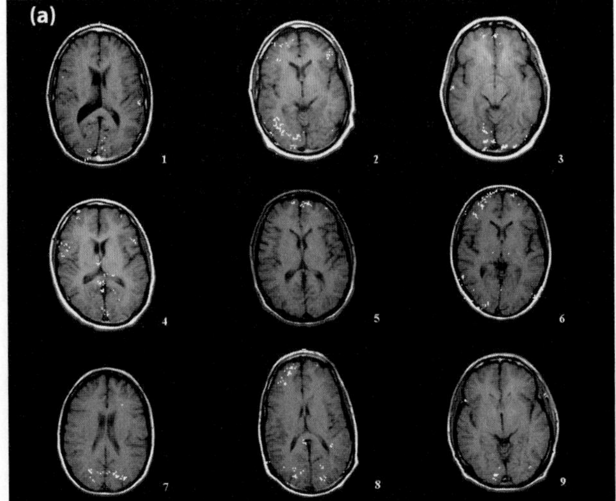

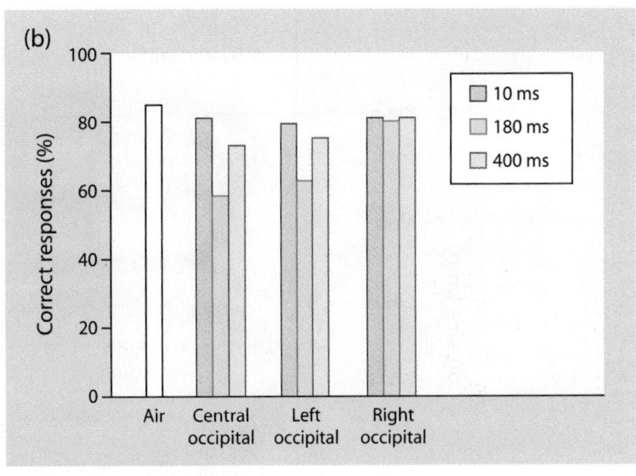

Figure 4.38 Combined use of fMRI and TMS to demonstrate the role of the visual cortex in tactile perception. **(a)** Functional MRI showing areas of activation in nine people during tactile exploration with the eyes closed. All of the subjects show some activation in striate and extrastriate cortex. **(b)** The results graphed here illustrate accuracy in making tactile orientation judgments when a textured object is vibrated against the right index finger. Performance is impaired when the TMS pulse is applied 180 ms after the vibration. This effect is observed only when the pulse is applied over the central occipital cortex or over the contralateral occipital lobe.

Daniel Weinberger and his colleagues at the National Institutes of Health have proposed that the efficacy of antipsychotic medications in treating schizophrenia varies as a function of how a particular gene is expressed, or what is called a *polymorphism* (Bertolino et al., 2004; Weickert et al., 2004). In particular, schizophrenics who express one allelic variant linked to the release of dopamine in prefrontal cortex showed changes in prefrontal activity during working memory tasks following the administration of an antipsychotic drug, as well as improved performance on the tasks. In contrast, schizophrenics with a different allele did not respond to the drugs.

The logic underlying these clinical studies can also be applied to ask how genetic differences within the normal population relate to individual variations in brain function and behavior. A common polymorphism in the human brain is related to the gene that codes for monoamine oxidase A (MAOA). Using a large sample of healthy individuals, Weinberger's group found that the low-expression variant was associated with increased tendency toward violent behavior, as well as hyperactivation of the amygdala when the subject was viewing emotionally arousing stimuli (Meyer-Lindenberg et al., 2006).

SUMMARY

Two goals have guided the overview of cognitive neuroscience methods presented in this chapter: The first was to provide a sense of the methodologies that come together to form an interdisciplinary field such as cognitive neuroscience (Figure 4.39). The practitioners of the neurosciences, cognitive psychology, and neurology differ not only in the tools they use but also in the questions they seek to answer. The neurologist may request a CT scan of an aged boxer to find out if the patient's confusional state is reflected in atrophy of the frontal lobes. The neuroscientist may want a blood sample from the patient to search for metabolic markers indicating a reduction in a transmitter system. The cognitive psychologist may design a reaction time experiment to test whether a component of a decision-making model is selectively impaired. Cognitive neuroscience endeavors to answer these questions by taking advantage of the insights that each approach has to offer and using them together.

The second goal of this chapter was to introduce methods that we will encounter in subsequent chapters. These chapters focus on content domains such as perception, language, and memory, and on how the tools are being applied to understand the brain and behavior. Each chapter

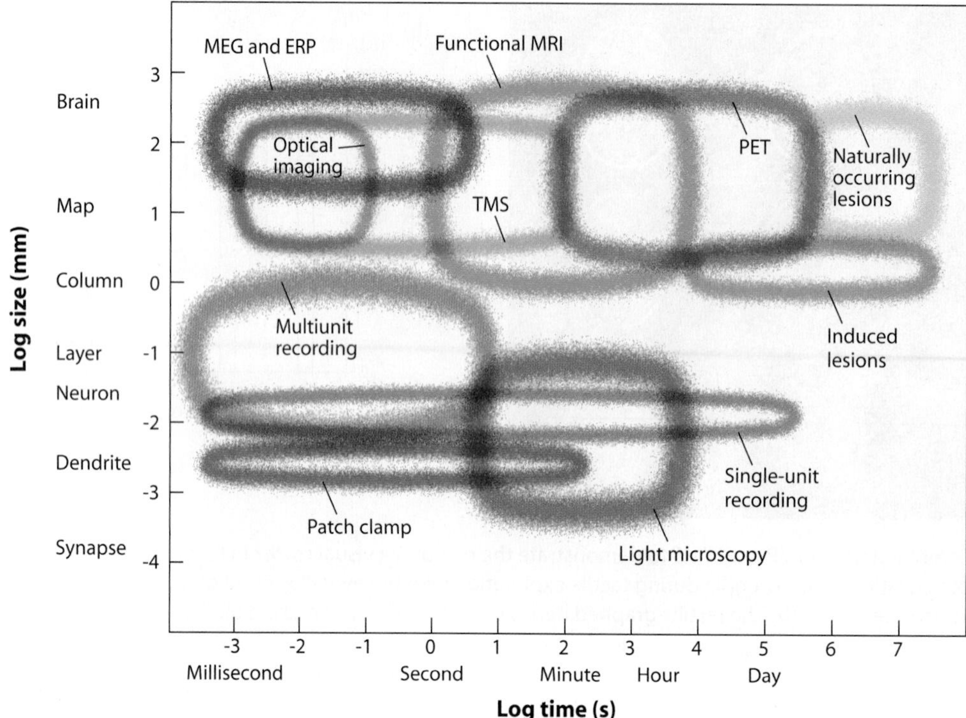

Figure 4.39 Spatial and temporal resolution of the prominent methods used in cognitive neuroscience. Temporal sensitivity, plotted on the *x*-axis, refers to the timescale over which a particular measurement is obtained. It can range from the millisecond activity of single cells to the behavioral changes observed over years in patients who have had strokes. Spatial sensitivity, plotted on the *y*-axis, refers to the localization capability of the methods. For example, real-time changes in the membrane potential of isolated dendritic regions can be detected with the patch clamp method, providing excellent temporal and spatial resolution. In contrast, naturally occurring lesions damage large regions of the cortex and are detectable with MRI.

draws on research that uses the diverse methods of cognitive neuroscience. Often the convergence of results yielded by different methodologies offers the most complete theories. A single method cannot bring about a complete understanding of the complex processes of cognition.

We have reviewed many methods, but the review is incomplete, in part because new methodologies for investigating the relation of the brain and behavior spring to life each year. Neuroscientists are continually refining techniques for measuring and manipulating neural processes at a finer and finer level. Patch clamp techniques isolate restricted regions on the neuron, enabling studies of the membrane changes that underlie the inflow of neurotransmitters. Laser surgery can be used to restrict lesions to just a few neurons in simple organisms, providing a means to study specific neural interactions. The use of genetic techniques such as knockout procedures has exploded in the past decade, promising to reveal the mechanisms involved in normal and pathological brain function.

Technological change is also the driving force in our understanding of the human mind. Our current imaging tools are constantly being refined. Each year we witness the development of more sensitive equipment to measure the electrophysiological signals of the brain or the metabolic correlates of neural activity, and the mathematical tools for analyzing these data are constantly becoming more sophisticated. In addition, entire new classes of imaging techniques are just beginning to gain prominence.

In recent years we have seen the development of *optical imaging* (Gratton & Fabiani, 1998). With this type of imaging a short pulse of near-infrared light is projected at the head. The light diffuses through the tissues and scatters back. Sensors placed on the skull detect the photons of light as they exit the head. Brain areas that are active scatter the light more than areas that are inactive, allowing the measurement of neural activity. Noninvasive optical imaging offers excellent temporal resolution. Its spatial resolution is comparable to that of current high-field MRI systems, although the technique at present is limited to measuring structures near the cortical surface. Furthermore, the method is relatively inexpensive, and the tools are transportable. Whereas an MRI system might cost $5 million and require its own building, optical-imaging systems cost less than $100,000 and can be used at the bedside.

We began this chapter by pointing out that paradigmatic changes in science are often fueled by technological developments. In a symbiotic way, the maturation of a scientific field such as cognitive neuroscience provides a tremendous impetus for the development of new methods. The questions we ask are constrained by the available tools, but new research tools are promoted by the questions that we ask. It would be foolish to imagine that current methodologies will become the status quo for the field, which makes it an exciting time to study brain and behavior.

KEY TERMS

angiography

blood oxygenation level–dependent (BOLD)

brain lesion

cognitive psychology

computed tomography (CT, CAT)

deep-brain stimulation (DBS)

diffusion tensor imaging (DTI)

double dissociation

electroencephalography (EEG)

event-related potential (ERP)

functional magnetic resonance imaging (fMRI)

knockout procedure

magnetic resonance imaging (MRI)

magnetoencephalography (MEG)

multiunit recording

neural network

neurology

neurophysiology

positron emission tomography (PET)

receptive field

regional cerebral blood flow (rCBF)

retinotopic

simulation

single-cell recording

single dissociation

transcranial magnetic stimulation (TMS)

voxel

TAKE-HOME MESSAGES

General

- Our tools for conducting research are only as good as the questions we ask with them.

Cognitive Psychology

- Cognitive psychology focuses on understanding how objects or ideas are represented in the brain and how these representations are manipulated.
- Fundamental goals of cognitive psychology include identifying the mental operations that are required to perform cognitive tasks and exploring the limitations in task performance.
- Computer models are used to simulate neural networks in order to ask questions about cognitive processes and to generate predictions that can be tested in future research.

Neuroscience Techniques and Tools

- Single-cell recording allows neurophysiologists to record from individual neurons in the animal brain in order to understand how increases and decreases in the activity of neurons correlate with stimulation of one of the senses or behavior.
- With multiunit recording, the activity of hundreds of cells can be recorded at the same time.
- Brain lesions, either naturally occurring (in humans) or experimentally derived (in animals), allow experimenters to test hypotheses concerning the functional role of the damaged brain region.
- Gene knockout technology allows scientists to explore the consequences of the lack of expression of a specific gene in order to determine its role in behavior.
- Computed tomography (CT or CAT) uses X-rays to image the structure of the brain.
- Magnetic resonance imaging (MRI) exploits the magnetic properties of the organic tissue of the brain in order to image its structure. The spatial resolution of MRI is superior to CT.
- Diffusion tensor imaging (DTI), performed with magnetic resonance scanners, is used to measure white matter pathways in the brain.
- Angiography is used to evaluate the circulatory system in the brain.

Neurological Disorders and Conditions

- Tumors can cause neurological symptoms either by damaging neural tissue or by producing abnormal pressure on spared cortex and cutting off its blood supply. There are three major types of brain tumors: Gliomas originate in glial cells; meningiomas originate in the meninges; and metastatic tumors originate in a noncerebral structures and are carried to the brain after invading the bloodstream.
- Degenerative disorders include Huntington's disease, Parkinson's disease, Alzheimer's disease, and AIDS-related dementia.
- Neurological trauma can result in damage at the site of the blow (coup) or at the site opposite the blow because of reactive forces (countercoup). Certain brain regions such as the orbitofrontal cortex are especially prone to damage from trauma.
- Epilepsy is characterized by excessive and abnormally patterned activity in the brain.

Treatment of Neurological Disorders

- Intractable epilepsy can be relieved by surgery to remove the focal region causing the epilepsy, or to disconnect the two hemispheres of the brain to limit the spread of the epilepsy via callosotomy.
- In deep-brain stimulation, electrodes are implanted in the brain to relieve conditions like Parkinson's disease.
- In fetal brain transplants, fetal neurological tissue is transplanted into an adult brain in order to replace neurons damaged by diseases like Parkinson's.
- In stem cell implantation, undifferentiated cells are implanted into the brain or spinal cord. The cells can differentiate into neurons, providing a mechanism to replace those that were damaged by trauma or disease—for instance, in spinal cord injury.

Neuroscience Tools

- Research involving patients with neurological disorders is used to examine structure–function relationships. Single and double dissociations can provide evidence that damage to a particular brain region may result in a selective deficit of a certain cognitive operation.
- Transcranial magnetic stimulation (TMS) utilizes magnetic pulses to transiently alter local brain physiology.
- Electroencephalography (EEG) measures the electrical activity of the brain. The EEG signal includes endogenous changes in electrical activity, as well as changes triggered by specific events (e.g., stimuli or movements).
- An event-related potential (ERP) is a change in electrical activity that is time-locked to specific events, such as the presentation of a stimulus or the onset of a response. When the events are repeated many times, the relatively small changes in neural activity triggered by these events can be observed by averaging of the EEG signals. In this manner, the background fluctuations in the EEG signal are removed, revealing the event-related signal with great temporal resolution.
- Magnetoencephalography (MEG) measures the magnetic signals generated by the brain. The electrical activity of neurons also produces small magnetic fields, which can be measured by sensitive magnetic detectors placed along the scalp, similar to the way EEG measures the surface electrical activity. MEG can be used in an event-related manner similar to ERPs, with similar temporal resolution. The spatial resolution can be superior because magnetic signals are minimally distorted by organic tissue such as the brain or skull.
- Positron emission tomography (PET) measures metabolic activity in the brain by monitoring the distribution of a radioactive tracer. The PET scanner measures the photons that are produced during decay of the tracer. A popular tracer is O^{15} because it decays rapidly and the distribution of oxygen increases to neural regions that are active.
- Functional magnetic resonance imaging (fMRI) utilizes MRI to track blood flow changes in the brain, which are thought to be correlated with local changes in neuronal activity.
- Powerful insights can be gained from experiments that combine methods such as genetic, behavioral, and neuroimaging techniques.

THOUGHT QUESTIONS

1. To a large extent, progress in all scientific fields depends on the development of new technologies and methodologies. What technological and methodological developments have advanced the field of cognitive neuroscience the most?
2. Cognitive neuroscience is an interdisciplinary field that incorporates aspects of neuroanatomy, neuro-

physiology, neurology, cognitive psychology, and computer science. What do you consider the core feature of each discipline that allows it to contribute to cognitive neuroscience? What are the limits of each discipline in addressing questions related to the brain and mind?

3. Describe the requirements for establishing single and double dissociations, and explain why double dissociations provide stronger evidence for claims about the brain and behavior. Choose a task that interests you, and generate an example of each type of dissociation you might find if you were to study neurological patients whose ability to perform this task is impaired. Be sure to note what we learn about the brain *and* mind from these examples.
4. A skeptic wrote in the *New York Times* science section in the spring of 2000 that, despite all of the excitement surrounding new imaging techniques like PET and fMRI, these methods were unlikely to lead to profound insights into brain function. The author stressed that these tools were limited in terms of their resolution and were unlikely to provide more insight beyond simply showing which parts of the brain are activated during particular tasks. Describe explicitly the concerns that the writer was expressing, comparing these imaging tools to other methods that might not have similar problems. Discuss whether you share these concerns.
5. In anticipation of the next chapter, consider how you might study a problem such as color perception using the multidisciplinary techniques of cognitive neuroscience. Predict the questions that you might ask about this topic, and outline the types of studies that cognitive psychologists, neurophysiologists, and neurologists might consider.

SUGGESTED READING

CHURCHLAND, P. S. (1986). *Neurophilosophy: Toward a unified science of the mind/brain.* Cambridge, MA: MIT Press.

D'ESPOSITO, M., ZARAHN, E., & AGUIRRE, G. K. (1999). Event-related functional MRI: Implications for cognitive psychology. *Psychological Bulletin, 125,* 155–164.

HILLYARD, S. A. (1993). Electrical and magnetic brain recordings: Contributions to cognitive neuroscience. *Current Opinion in Neurobiology, 3,* 710–717.

HUETTEL, S., SONG, A. W., & MCCARTHY, G. (2004). *Functional magnetic resonance imaging.* Sunderland, MA: Sinauer.

KANDEL, E. R., SCHWARTZ, J. H., & JESSELL, T. M. (1995). *Essentials of neural science and behavior.* Norwalk, CT: Appleton and Lange.

MORI, S. (2007). *Introduction to diffusion tensor imaging.* New York: Elsevier.

POSNER, M. I., & RAICHLE, M. E. (1994). *Images of mind.* New York: Freeman.

RAPP, B. (2001). *The handbook of cognitive neuropsychology: What deficits reveal about the human mind.* Philadelphia: Psychology Press.

5

Sensation and Perception

Patient P.T.'s case was presented in Portland, Oregon, at the Neurology Grand Rounds, a weekly event at which staff neurologists, internists, and residents gather to review the most puzzling and unusual cases being treated on the ward. The cause of P.T.'s existing neurological problems was not a mystery; he had suffered a left-hemisphere stroke 6 years previously. The physician was confident in his diagnosis that P.T. had suffered a second stroke, especially because multiple strokes are not uncommon. P.T. was referred to the hospital, and the current stroke was confirmed by computed tomography (CT) to be in the right hemisphere.

What was unusual about P.T. was the collection of symptoms that he continued to experience 4 months after the second stroke. The dizziness had ended by the second day after the incident, and the left-sided weakness had mostly subsided during the first month. The only remaining sign of these initial symptoms was that P.T. continued to drag his left leg slightly, although he was not aware of it. Yet P.T. experienced some difficulties as he tried to resume the daily routines required on his small family farm, his home of 66 years.

P.T. had particular difficulty recognizing places and objects. While working on a stretch of fence, for example, he might look out over the hills and suddenly realize that he did not know the landscape. It was hard for him to pick out individual dairy cows—a matter of concern lest he attempt to milk a bull! And, most troubling of all, P.T. no longer recognized the people around him, including his wife. The woman whom he had known for so many years and with whom he had spent all his days was completely unrecognizable to him. He had no trouble seeing her and could accurately describe her actions, but in simply looking at her, he failed to identify her as his wife. He knew that her parts—body, legs, arms, and head—formed a person, but P.T. failed to see these parts as belonging to a specific individual. This deficit was not limited to P.T.'s wife; he had the same problem with other members of his family and friends from his small town.

A striking feature of P.T.'s impairment was that his inability to recognize objects and people was limited to the visual modality. Interestingly, when his wife spoke, he immediately recognized her voice. Indeed, he claimed that, on hearing her voice, the visual percept of her would "fall into place." The shape in front of him would suddenly morph into his wife. In a similar fashion, he could recognize specific objects by touching, smelling, or tasting them.

Perception is a remarkable human ability, normally involving the integration of each of the fives senses: vision, audition, touch, smell, and taste. P.T. lost only a relatively small aspect of his visual perception—an issue we return to later in the chapter—and he was able to compensate for this loss by utilizing his other senses. Similarly, a person who is blind is able to compensate to some degree for this deficit, becoming exquisitely sensitive to sound and touch while navigating about the world.

In normal perception, the interplay of all of the senses is critical. Driving a car down a busy highway in an effective and safe manner requires the successful integration of vision, touch, hearing, and perhaps even smell (warning, for example, if the emergency brake has been left on). We cannot enjoy food intensely without smell. Even visual cues enhance our gustatory experience—a perfectly browned hamburger on a tan-colored bun is much more enticing than a hamburger that is artificially colored green.

In this chapter we begin with a description of what is known about the anatomy and function of the individual senses. Then we return to the issue of how information from our different sensory systems is integrated to produce a coherent representation of the world.

AUDITORY PERCEPTION

Knock knock. Beep beep. Ring ring. The sense of hearing, or *audition*, plays an important role in our daily lives and is essential for everything from communication to survival. But how does the brain process sound? What happens as sound waves enter the ear? How does our brain interpret those waves?

Neural Pathways of Audition

An overview of the auditory pathways is presented in Figure 5.1. The complex structures of the inner ear provide the mechanisms for transforming sounds (variations in sound pressure) into neural signals. Sound waves arriving at the ear make the *eardrum* vibrate. These vibrations produce tiny waves in the inner ear's fluid that stimulate tiny *hair cells* located along the surface of the *basilar membrane.* Hair cells are primary auditory receptors. Oscillations of the basilar membrane prompt hair cells to generate action potentials. In this way, a mechanical signal, the fluid oscillations, is converted into a neural signal, the output from hair cells. The basilar membrane and hair cells are located within a

Figure 5.1 Overview of the auditory pathway. The hair cells of the cochlea are the primary receptors. The output from the auditory nerve projects to the cochlear nuclei in the brainstem. Ascending fibers reach the auditory cortex following synapses in the inferior colliculus and medial geniculate nucleus.

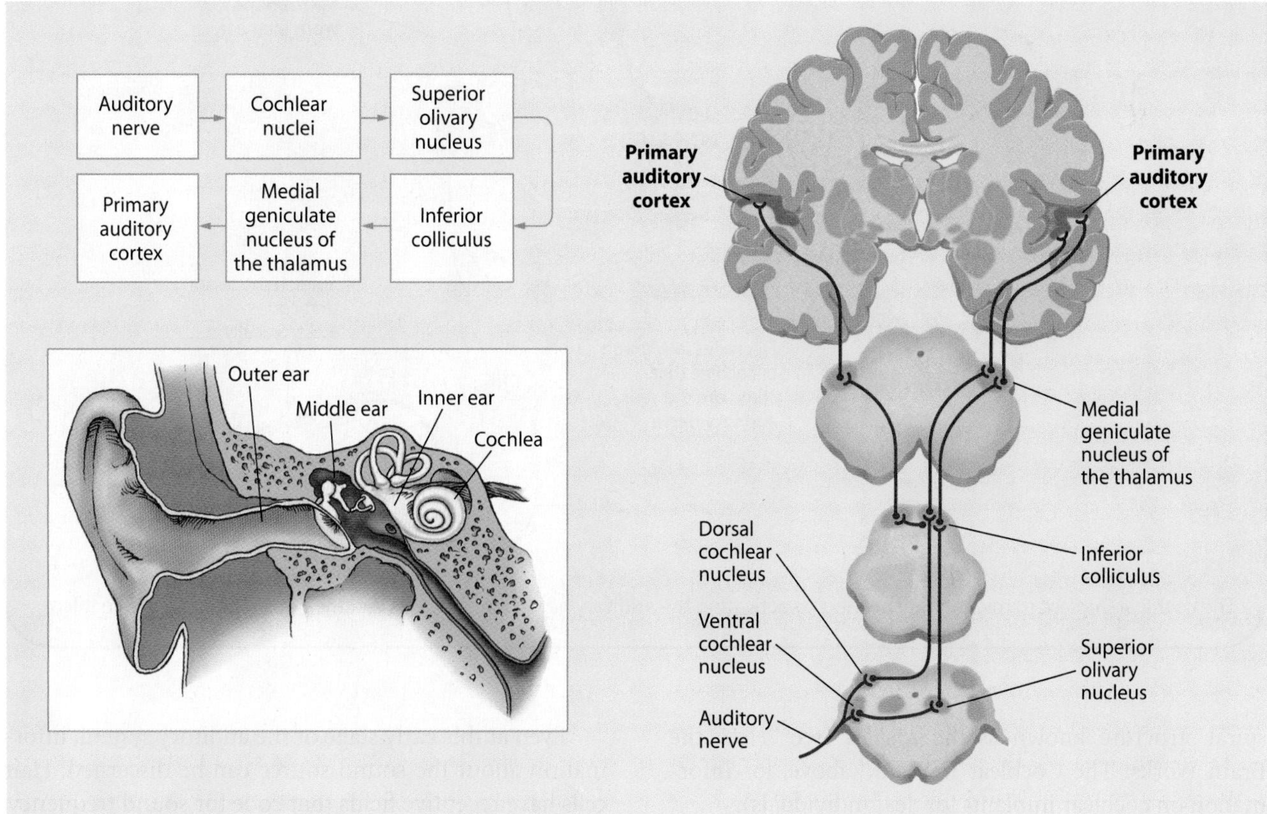

HOW THE BRAIN WORKS

The Cochlear Implant

P.M. became deaf after contracting pneumococcal meningitis when she was 13 months old. She lost the ability to transform sound waves into meaningful neuronal signals that her brain could interpret. At the age of 3 years, she received a cochlear implant. Now 18, P.M. has little difficulty conversing with people and even uses the telephone to talk with her friends.

The cochlear implant is one of the great breakthroughs in biomedical engineering, having partially restored hearing to thousands of individuals. A cochlear implant is not like a traditional hearing aid that amplifies sound. The implant is actually designed to perform the job of the cochlea: to transform sound waves into neuronal impulses that the brain will interpret as sound.

The figure shows the components of the cochlear implant. The sound signal enters the device through a microphone worn over the ear and is then analyzed by a microcomputer called the *speech processor*. The speech processor converts the information into radio waves that are sent to a receiver. The signal is then relayed by a small wire to the cochlea, where the electrodes artificially stimulate the auditory nerve. The brain, of course, doesn't know that the cochlea has been artificially stimulated. It processes the information from the auditory nerve just as it would information relayed from a healthy cochlea.

P.M. has this to say about her cochlear implant: It "changed my life dramatically, in such a beautiful way, that I went from being profoundly deaf to being an auditory learner, a social being, and an independent young woman" (personal communication, April 14, 2005).

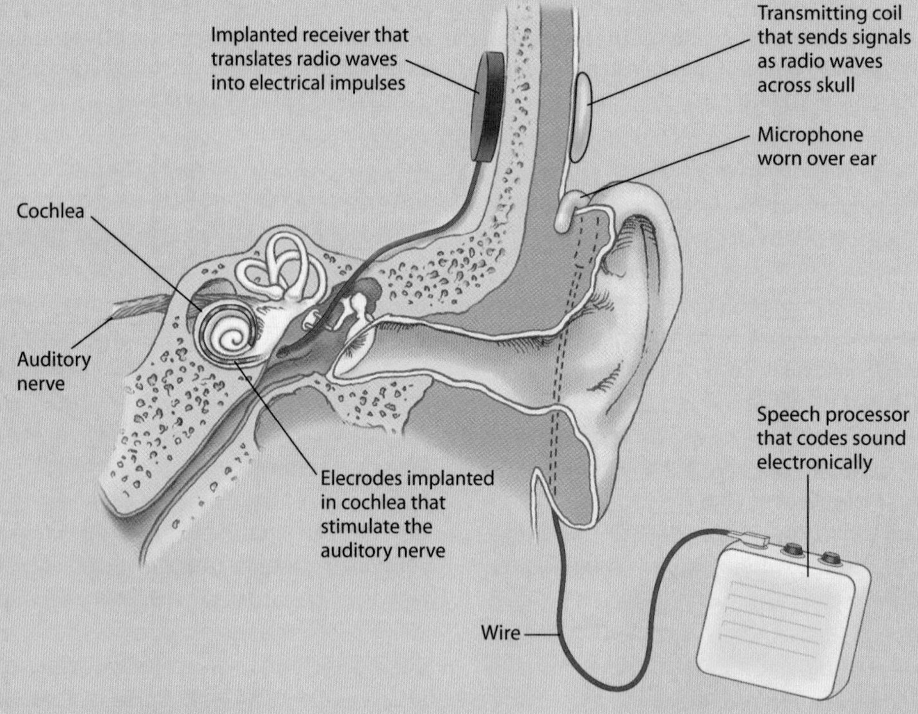

The cochlear implant mimics natural hearing by activating the auditory nerve artificially via electrical stimulation of the cochlea.

spiral structure known as the *cochlea* (see "How the Brain Works: The Cochlear Implant," above, for information on cochlear implants for deaf individuals).

Even at this early stage of the auditory system, information about the sound source can be discerned. Hair cells have receptive fields that code for sound frequency.

Human auditory sensitivity ranges from a low of about 20 Hz to a high of 20,000 Hz, but it is best tuned for 1000 to 4000 Hz, a range that carries much of the information critical for human communication, such as speech or the cries of a hungry infant. Hair cells at the thick end, or base, of the cochlea are activated by high-frequency sounds; cells at the opposite end, or apex, are activated by low-frequency sounds. These receptive fields overlap extensively. Further, natural sounds like music or speech are made up of complex frequencies; thus, sounds activate a broad range of hair cells.

The auditory system contains important subcortical relays. Output from the cochlea is projected to two midbrain structures: the **cochlear nucleus** and the **inferior colliculus**. From there, information is sent to the **medial geniculate nucleus** (**MGN**) in the **thalamus**. As with all other senses, except for olfaction, the thalamus serves as a relay station, taking signals from the periphery and passing the information to the primary sensory cortex. For audition, the thalamic outputs project to the **primary auditory cortex** (**A1**) in the superior part of the temporal lobe.

Neurons throughout the auditory pathway continue to have frequency tuning. As Figure 5.2 shows, the tuning curves for auditory cells can be quite broad. The fact that individual cells do not give precise frequency information but provide coarse coding indicates that our perception must depend on the integrated activity of many neurons. Such integration is probably facilitated by tonotopic maps found in most auditory areas; such maps show an orderly correspondence between the location of the neurons and their specific frequency tuning. For example, cells in one region of an auditory area will respond to low-frequency stimuli; cells in another region will respond to middle or high frequencies. The tonotopic organization can be seen in humans with the resolution provided by fMRI (Figure 5.3). As described in Chapter 4, topographic maps are a defining feature of many cortical areas for the different senses.

Electrophysiological studies of the cat revealed a second general principle of auditory processing. The tuning specificity of auditory receptive fields becomes more refined as the stimulus proceeds through the system. A neuron in the cochlear nucleus that responds maximally to a pure tone of 5000 Hz may also respond to tones ranging from 2000 to 10,000 Hz. A comparable neuron in the auditory cortex is likely to respond over a much narrower range.

Figure 5.2 Frequency-dependent receptive fields for a cell in the auditory nerve of the squirrel monkey. This cell is maximally sensitive to a sound of 1600 Hz, and the firing rate falls off rapidly for either lower- or higher-frequency sounds. The cell is also sensitive to intensity differences, although this sensitivity does not cause a shift in its tuning profile. Other cells in the auditory nerve would be tuned for different frequencies.

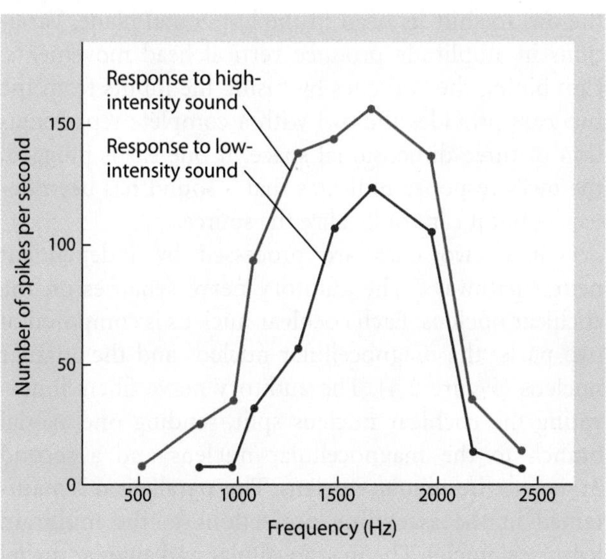

Computational Goals in Audition

Frequency data are essential for deciphering a sound. Sound-producing objects have unique resonant properties that provide a characteristic signature. The same note played on a clarinet and a trumpet will sound differently even though they share the same base frequency. The resonant properties of each instrument will produce great differences in the note's harmonic structure. In a similar way, we produce our range of speech sounds by varying the resonant properties of the vocal tract. Movements of our lips, tongue, and jaw change the frequency content of the acoustic stream produced during speech. Frequency variation is essential for a listener to identify words or music.

Auditory perception does not merely identify the content of an acoustic stimulus. A second important function of audition is to localize sounds in space. Consider the bat, which hunts by echolocation. High-pitched sounds are emitted by the bat and bounce back, as echoes from the environment. From these echoes, the bat's brain creates an auditory image of the environment and the objects within it—preferably a tasty moth. But knowing that a moth ("what") is present will not lead to a successful hunt. The bat also has to determine the moth's precise location ("where"). The cognitive neuroscience of audition has focused primarily on this "where" problem. In solving the "where" problem, the

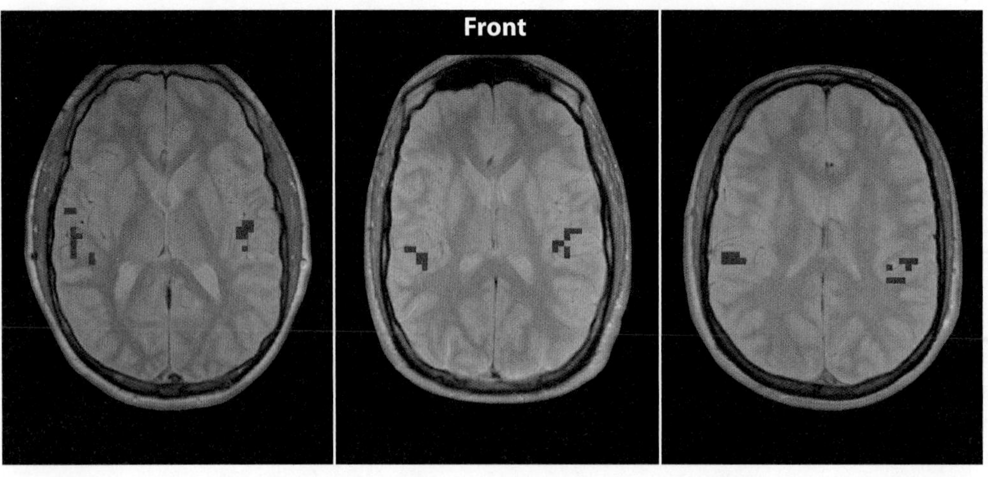

Figure 5.3 Tonotopic representation revealed with fMRI in the human brain. Three horizontal slices are shown with regions responding to low tones shown in blue and regions responding to high tones shown in red. The different clusters indicate the presence of multiple tonotopic maps.

auditory system relies on integrating information from the two ears.

Multiple Cues for Sound Localization

In developing animal models to study auditory perception, we select animals with well-developed hearing. A favorite species for this work has been the barn owl, a nocturnal creature. Barn owls have excellent *scotopia* (night vision), which guides them to their prey. But barn owls also must utilize an exquisitely tuned sense of hearing to locate food because visual information can be unreliable at night. The low levels of illumination provided by the moon fluctuate over the lunar cycle; this and stellar sources can be obscured by dense cloud cover. Sound, such as the patter of a mouse scurrying across a field, offers a more reliable stimulus. Indeed, barn owls have little trouble finding prey in a completely dark laboratory.

Barn owls rely on two cues to localize sounds: the difference in when a sound reaches each of the two ears, the **interaural time**, and the difference in the sound's intensity at the two ears. Both cues result from the fact that the sound reaching two ears is not identical. Unless the sound source is directly parallel to the head's orientation, the sound will reach one ear before the other. Moreover, because the intensity of a sound wave becomes attenuated over time, the magnitude of the signal at the two ears will not be identical. The time and intensity differences are minuscule. For example, if the stimulus is located at a 45° angle to the line of sight, the interaural time difference will be approximately 1/10,000 of a second. The intensity differences resulting from sound attenuation are even smaller—indistinguishable from variations due to noise. However, these small differences are amplified by a unique asymmetry of owl anatomy: The left ear is higher than eye level and points downward, and the right ear is lower than eye level and points upward. Because of this asymmetry, sounds coming from below are louder in the left ear than the right. Humans do not have this asymmetry, but the complex structure of the human outer ear, or *pinna*, may amplify the intensity difference between a sound at the two ears.

Interaural time and intensity differences provide independent cues for sound localization. To show this, stimuli are presented over headphones and the owl is trained to turn its head in the sound's perceived direction. The headphones allow the experimenter to manipulate each cue separately. When amplitude is held constant, asynchronies in presentation times prompt the owl to shift its head in the horizontal plane. Variations in amplitude produce vertical head movements. Combining the two cues by fusing the inputs from the two ears provides the owl with a complete representation of three-dimensional space. If one ear is plugged, the owl's response indicates that a sound has been detected, but it cannot localize the source.

These two cues are processed by independent neural pathways. The auditory nerve synapses on the cochlear nucleus. Each cochlear nucleus is composed of two parts: the magnocellular nucleus and the angular nucleus (Figure 5.4). The auditory nerve fibers innervating the cochlear nucleus split, sending one axonal branch to the magnocellular nucleus and a second branch to the angular nucleus. This parallelism is maintained in the ascending projections to the midbrain lemniscal nuclei. The magnocellular and angular nuclei

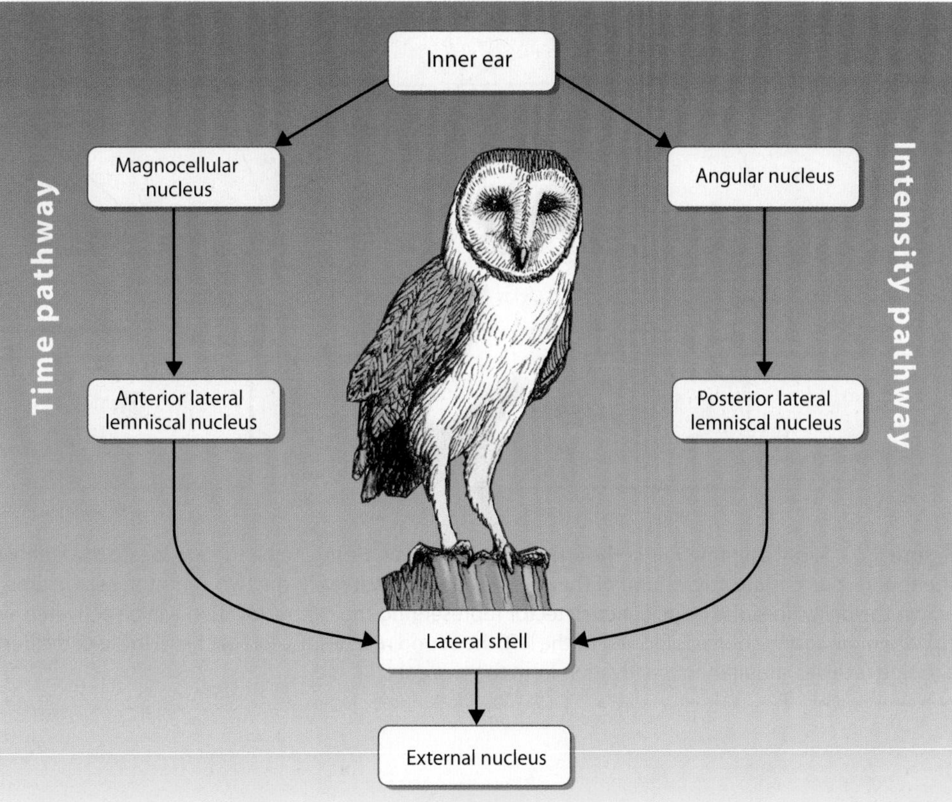

Figure 5.4 Parallel pathways in the auditory system of the barn owl. The cochlear nucleus is composed of two parts: the magnocellular nucleus and the angular nucleus. The magnocellular pathway is specialized to compute interaural time differences—information essential for locating the lateral position of a stimulus. The angular pathway is specialized to compute intensity differences—information essential for locating the distance to a stimulus.

project to the anterior and posterior regions of the lemniscal nucleus, respectively.

Mark Konishi of the California Institute of Technology has provided a well-specified neural model of how the owl brain codes interaural time and intensity differences. For detecting time differences, Konishi assumed that the first site of convergence from the two ears is in the anterior lemniscal neurons. These neurons operate as coincidence detectors. To be activated, an anterior lemniscal neuron must simultaneously receive input from each ear. In computer science terms, these neurons act as AND operators. An input from either ear alone or in succession is not sufficient; the neurons will fire only if an input is received at the same time from both ears. Simultaneous activation from a sound source is restricted to only some of these neurons because the magnocellular axons from each half of the brain converge from opposite directions on the coincidence detectors.

Figure 5.5 explains how this model works. In Figure 5.5a, the sound source is directly in front of the animal. In this situation the coincidence detector in the middle is activated because the stimulus is received at each ear at the same time. In Figure 5.5b, the sound source is to the animal's left, which gives the magnocellular axon from the left ear a slight head start. Simultaneous activation now occurs in a coincidence detector to the left of center. This simple arrangement provides the owl with a complete representation of the sound source's horizontal position. Physiological studies have confirmed that neurons of the anterior lemniscal nucleus act as coincidence detectors.

A different coding scheme represents interaural intensities. The posterior region of the lemniscal nucleus is again the first point of convergence. But the neural code for intensity is based on the input's firing rate. The stronger the input signal, the more strongly the cell fires. Neurons in the posterior region use combined signals from both ears to pinpoint the vertical position of the source.

Localization is incomplete at the level of the lemniscal nucleus; horizontal and vertical positions must be combined. Outputs from each region of the lemniscal nucleus converge on another brainstem nucleus, the external nucleus. Neurons within this nucleus are considered space specific. They are activated only when sound comes from a certain location.

Konishi provided an elegant account of how the barn owl can pinpoint a sound in three-dimensional space. The theory stands as an excellent example of the

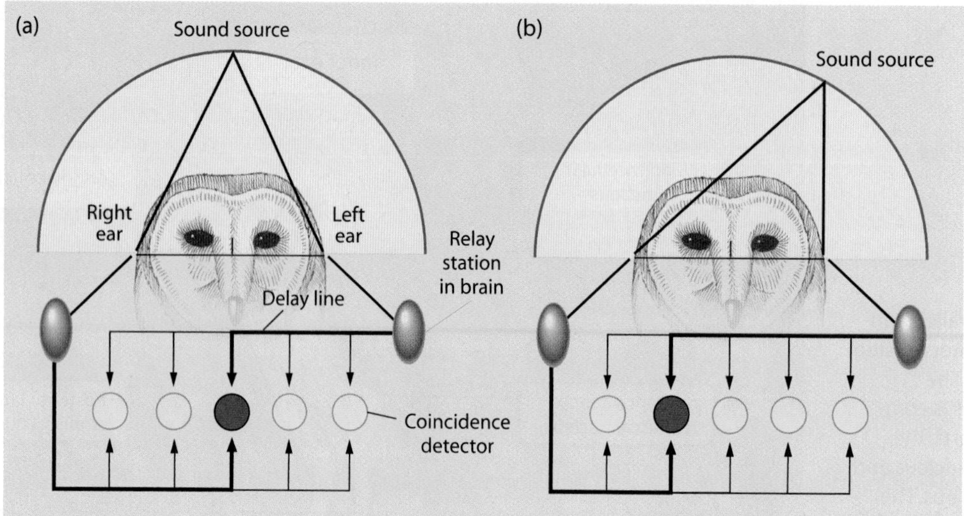

Figure 5.5 Slight asymmetries in the arrival times at the two ears can be used to locate the lateral position of a stimulus. **(a)** When the sound source is directly in front of the owl, the stimulus will reach the two ears at the same time. As activation is transmitted across the delay lines, the coincidence detector representing the central location will be activated simultaneously from both ears. **(b)** When the sound source is located to the left, the sound reaches the left ear first. Now a coincidence detector offset to the opposite side receives simultaneous activation from the two ears.

power of cognitive neuroscience. We know from an owl's behavior that it can localize sounds precisely. As we shall see later in this chapter, the neural representation of space is more straightforward in vision. The sensory detectors in the retina form a topographic map, and this representation is maintained throughout the processing system. In audition, though, the sensors do not code spatial information in a direct way. The location of a sound source must be computed by integration of the signals received from two ears. Anatomy and physiology led Konishi to realize that temporal information and intensity information are processed independently. Computational models of coincidence detectors and neural summation then guided the search for the derivation of location information.

In Konishi's model, the problem of sound localization by the barn owl is solved at the level of the brainstem. To date, this theory has not explained higher stages of processing, such as in the auditory cortex. Perhaps cortical processing is essential for converting location information into action. The owl does not want to simply attack every sound; it must decide if the sound is generated by potential prey. Another way of thinking about this is to reconsider the issues surrounding the computational goals of audition. Konishi's brainstem system provides the owl with a way to solve "where" problems but has not addressed the "what" question. The owl needs a more detailed analysis of the sound frequencies to determine whether a stimulus results from the movement of a mouse or a deer.

OLFACTORY PERCEPTION

Sight, sound, taste, and touch are the senses of which we have the greatest awareness. Yet the more primitive sense of smell is, in many ways, equally essential for our survival. Although the baleen whale probably does not smell the tons of plankton it ingests, the sense of smell *is* essential for terrestrial mammals, helping in the recognition of foods that are nutritious and safe. Observing the interactions of dogs romping about the beach provides a quick reminder of the importance of smell for mammals. Olfaction may have evolved as a mechanism for evaluating whether a potential food is edible, but it now serves other important roles as well—for instance, in social functions. Before discussing the functions of *olfaction*, let's review the neural pathways of the brain that respond to odors.

Neural Pathways of Olfaction

The olfactory pathway to the brain is unique: The receptors are directly exposed to the outside world, and the olfactory nerve arrives at the primary olfactory cortex without going through the thalamus.

Figure 5.6 details the olfactory pathway. First, odor molecules, called **odorants**, enter the nasal cavity. Odorants can enter the nasal cavity in various ways. They flow in during normal breathing or when we sniff. They will also flow into the nose passively, because air pressure in the nasal cavity is typically lower than in the outside environment, creating a pressure gradient. Finally, via *retronasal olfaction*, odorants from the mouth can travel back up into the nasal cavity (e.g., during consumption of food). Odorants then attach to odor receptors embedded in the mucous membrane of the roof of the nasal cavity, called the *olfactory epithelium*. There are over 1,000 types of receptors, and most of these respond to only a limited number of odorants, though a single odorant can bind to more than one type of receptor.

The olfactory receptor is called a *bipolar neuron* because appendages extend from opposite sides of its cell body. When an odorant binds to a bipolar neuron, a signal is sent to the neurons in the *olfactory bulb*, called the **glomeruli**. Tremendous convergence and divergence take place in the olfactory bulb. One bipolar neuron may activate over 8,000 glomeruli, and each glomerulus, in turn, receives input from up to 750 receptors. The axons from the glomeruli then exit the olfactory bulb laterally, forming the olfactory nerve, and travel to the **primary olfactory cortex**. Most fibers in the olfactory tracts connect to the ipsilateral cortex (the cortex on the same side as the tract), though some do cross to the other side of the brain via the anterior commissure. The primary olfactory cortex is located at the ventral junction of the frontal and temporal cortices. Neurons from this area then connect to the *orbitofrontal cortex*, which is considered a secondary olfactory processing center.

The Role of Sniffing in Olfactory Perception

Until recently, very little research had been conducted to explore the cognitive neuroscience of human olfaction. This neglect reflects in part our failure to appreciate the importance of olfaction. In addition, some thorny technical challenges must be overcome to apply tools such as fMRI to study the human olfactory system. First is the problem of delivering odors to the subject in a controlled manner (Figure 5.7a). Nonmagnetic systems must be constructed to allow the odorized air to be directed at the subject's nostrils while the subject is in the fMRI magnet. Second, it is hard to determine when an odor is no longer present. The chemicals that carry the odor can linger in the air for a long time. Third, although some odors overwhelm our senses, most are quite subtle, requiring exploration through the act of sniffing to detect and identify. Whereas it is almost impossible to ignore a sound, we can exert considerable control over the intensity of our olfactory experience.

Figure 5.6 The olfactory receptors lie within the nasal cavity, where they interact directly with odorants. The receptors then send information to the glomeruli in the olfactory bulb, the axons of which form the olfactory nerve that relays information to the primary olfactory cortex. The orbitofrontal cortex has also been shown to be a secondary olfactory processing area.

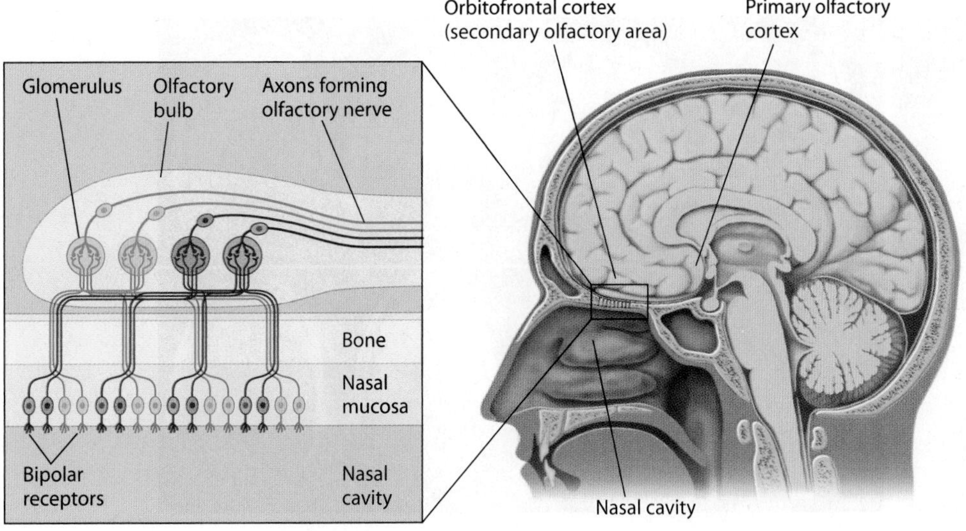

Noam Sobel of the Weizmann Institute in Israel has developed methods to overcome these challenges, conducting neuroimaging studies that have revealed an intimate relationship between smelling and sniffing (Mainland & Sobel, 2006; Sobel et al., 1998). Subjects were scanned while being exposed to either nonodorized, clean air or one of two chemicals: vanillin or decanoic acid. The former smells like vanilla; the latter, like crayons. The odor-absent and odor-present conditions alternated every 40 s. Throughout the scanning session, the instruction, "Sniff and respond, is there an odor?" was presented every 8 s. In this manner, the researchers sought to identify areas in which brain activity was correlated with sniffing and areas in which activity was correlated with smelling (Figure 5.7b).

Surprisingly, smelling failed to produce consistent activation in the primary olfactory cortex. Instead, the presence of the odor produced a consistent increase in the fMRI response in lateral parts of the orbitofrontal cortex, a region typically thought to be a secondary olfactory area. Activity in the primary olfactory cortex was closely linked to the rate of sniffing. Each time the person took a sniff, the fMRI signal increased regardless of whether the odor was present. These results seemed quite puzzling, suggesting that the primary olfactory cortex might be more part of the motor system for olfaction.

Upon further study, however, the lack of activation in the primary olfactory cortex became clear. Neurophysiological studies of the primary olfactory cortex in the rat had shown that these neurons habituate quickly. Perhaps the primary olfactory cortex lacks a smell-related response because the hemodynamic response measured by fMRI exhibits a similar habituation. To test this idea, Sobel's group modeled the fMRI signal by assuming a sharp increase followed by an extended drop after the presentation of an odor—an elegant example

(a)

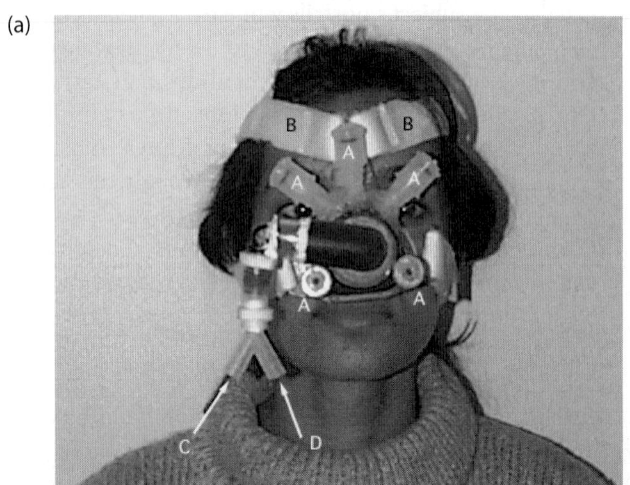

(b)

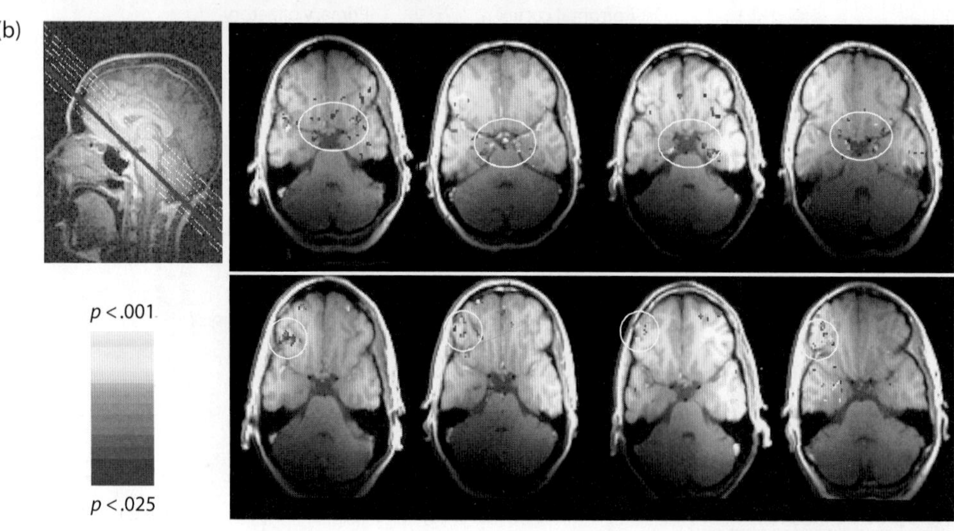

Figure 5.7 Sniffing and smelling. **(a)** This special device was constructed to deliver controlled odors during fMRI scanning. **(b, top)** Regions activated during sniffing. The circled region includes the primary olfactory cortex and a posteromedial region of the orbitofrontal cortex. **(b, bottom)** Regions more active during sniffing when an odor was present compared to when the odor was absent.

of how single-cell results can be used to interpret imaging data. When analyzed in this manner, the hemodynamic response in the primary olfactory cortex was found to be related not only to sniffing, but also to smell. These results suggest that the primary olfactory cortex role might be essential for detecting a change in the external odor, with the secondary olfactory cortex playing a critical role in identifying the smell itself. Each sniff represents an active sample of the olfactory environment, and the primary olfactory cortex plays a critical role in determining if a new smell is present.

One Nose, Two Smells

The importance of sniffing for olfactory perception is underscored by the fact that our ability to smell is continually being modulated by changes in the size of the nasal passages. In fact, the two nostrils appear to switch back and forth—one being larger than the other for a number of hours, and then the reverse. These changes have a profound effect on how smell is processed (Figure 5.8). Why might the nose behave this way?

Maxwell Mozell of the University of Pennsylvania theorizes that the olfactory percept depends not only on how intense the odor is, but also on how efficiently we sample it (Mozell et al., 1991). The presence of two nostrils of slightly different sizes provides the brain with slightly different images of the olfactory environment. Sobel put this theory to test. In each participant, he monitored which nostril was allowing high airflow and which nostril was allowing low airflow, while presenting high-absorption-rate and low-absorption-rate odors to each nostril. As predicted (see Figure 5.8), when sniffed through the high-airflow nostril, the high-absorption-rate odorant was judged to be more intense compared to when the same odorant was presented to the low-airflow nostril. The opposite was true for the low-absorption-rate odorant: here, the odor with a low rate of absorption was judged to be more intense when sniffed through the low-airflow nostril. Some of the participants were monitored when the flow rate of their nostrils reversed. The perception of the odorant presented to the same nostril reversed with the change in airflow.

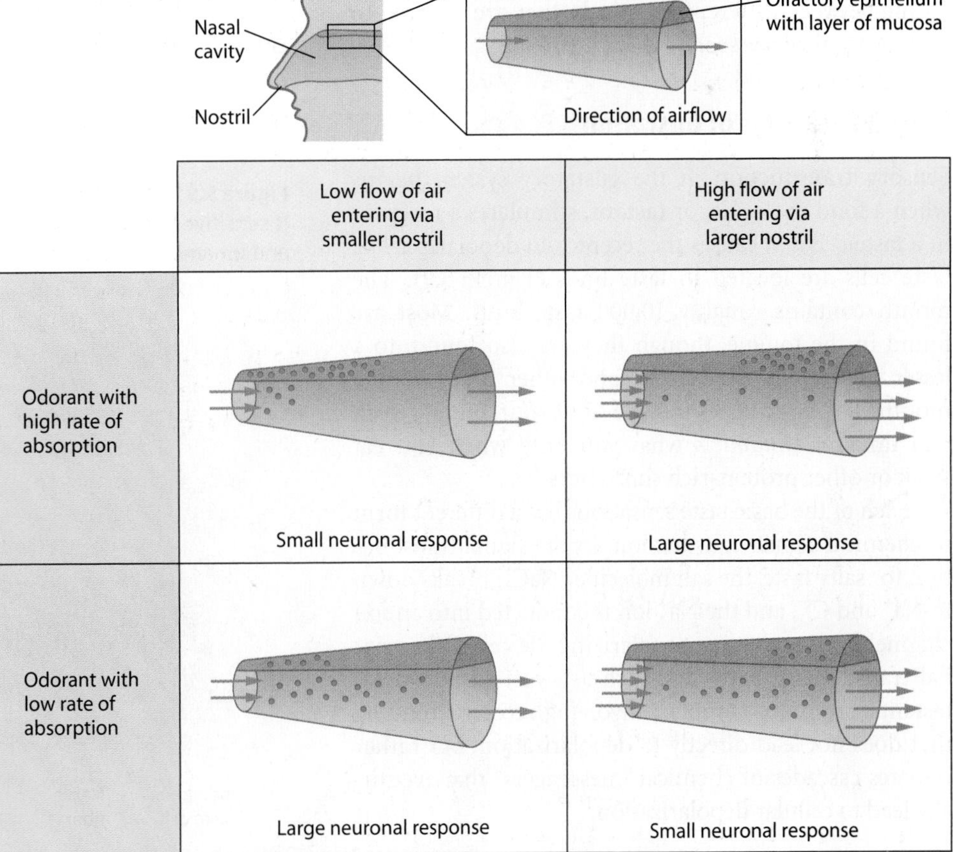

Figure 5.8 Although the same odorants enter each nostril, the response across the epithelium will be different for the two nostrils because of variation in flow rates. One nostril always has a greater input airflow than the other with the nostrils switching between the two rates every few hours. This system of having one low-flow and one high-flow nostril has evolved to give the nose optimal accuracy in perceiving odorants that have both high and low rates of absorption.

As we will see in Chapter 11, asymmetrical representations are the rule in human cognition, perhaps providing a more efficient manner of processing complex information. With the ancient sense of olfaction, this asymmetry appears to be introduced at the peripheral level by modulation of the rate of airflow through the nostrils.

Smell and Memory

Have you ever noticed that a specific smell can bring you back to a memory from long ago? Perhaps a certain perfume or cologne reminds you of an old friend. Or perhaps, like L.W., the smell of an orange reminds you of Christmas. L.W. is now 82 years old, but the smell of an orange immediately triggers a vivid memory of her childhood Christmases on the family farm in Idaho, when her parents would put an orange in the bottom of her stocking.

Why are smells so closely related to memories? Some scientists believe that the reason is the direct connectivity of the olfactory cortex to the limbic cortex, a region that is intimately involved in memory and emotion (see Chapters 8 and 9). Using functional MRI, Rachel Herz of Brown University found that odors activate the limbic system more robustly than a related visual stimulus does when the stimuli are used to trigger meaningful personal memories (Herz et al., 2004). The link between odor and memory is further supported by studies showing that odor recognition is severely compromised in patients with hippocampal lesions (Levy et al., 2004). Perhaps, then, we should invent a new poem: Roses are red, violets are blue, but it's a flower's odor that captures memories so true.

GUSTATORY PERCEPTION

The sense of taste depends greatly on the sense of smell. Indeed, the two senses are often grouped together because they both begin with stimulation by chemicals (odorants or tastants). Because these two senses interpret the environment by discriminating between different chemicals, they are referred to as the **chemical senses.**

Neural Pathways of Gustation

Sensory transduction in the gustatory system begins when a food molecule, or **tastant**, stimulates a receptor in a taste cell *and* causes the receptor to depolarize. The taste cells are located in taste buds (Figure 5.9). The mouth contains roughly 10,000 taste buds. Most are found in the tongue, though they are also found, to a lesser degree, in the cheeks and other areas of the mouth. The basic tastes include salty, sour, bitter, sweet, and umami. *Umami* is what you taste when you eat steak or other protein-rich substances.

Each of the basic taste sensations has a different form of chemical signal transduction. In the signal transduction for salty taste, the salt molecule (NaCl) breaks down to Na^+ and Cl^-, and the Na^+ ion is conducted into an ion channel in the cell, thus depolarizing the cell. Other signal transduction pathways, such as sweet carbohydrate tastants, are more complex, involving receptor binding that does not lead directly to depolarization, but rather initiates cascades of chemical "messengers" that eventually lead to cellular depolarization.

Once a taste cell has been depolarized, it sends a signal to the gustatory nucleus in the dorsal medulla, which in turn synapses on the ventral posterior medial nucleus (VPM) of the thalamus. Finally the VPM synapses with the primary gustatory cortex located in the *insula* and *operculum.* **Primary gustatory cortex** is connected to secondary processing areas of the *orbitofrontal cortex.* Each taste cell is thought to respond

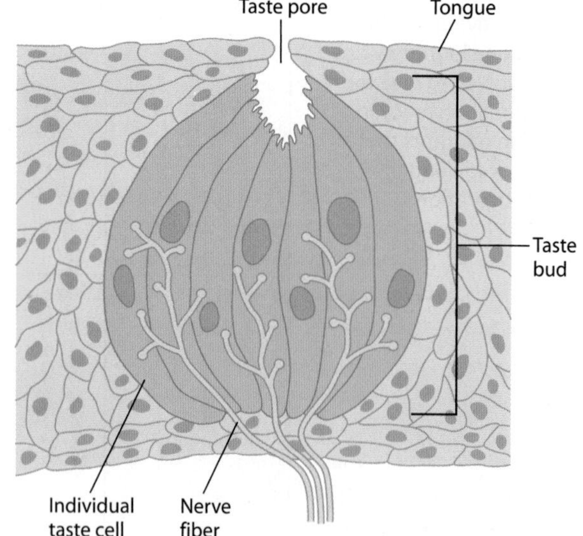

Figure 5.9 Taste cells form pores on the taste bud. Each cell is sensitive to one of five basic tastes: salty, sweet, sour, bitter, and umami.

to only one type of tastant. The complex range of tastes that we experience, however, must result from the integration of information conveyed from the taste cells and processed in areas like the orbitofrontal cortex.

Gustatory Processing

The basic tastes give the brain information about the types of food that have been consumed. The sensation of umami tells the body that protein-rich food is being ingested; sweet tastes indicate carbohydrate intake and salty tastes give us information that is important for the balance between minerals or electrolytes and water. The tastes of bitter and sour likely developed as warning signals. Many toxic plants taste bitter, and a strong bitter taste can induce vomiting. Other evidence suggesting that bitterness is a warning signal is the fact that we can detect bitter substances 1,000 times better than, say, salty substances. Therefore a significantly smaller amount of bitter tastant will yield a taste response, allowing toxic bitter substances to be avoided quickly. Similarly, but to a lesser extent, sour indicates spoiled food (e.g., "sour milk") or unripe fruits.

Humans can readily learn to discriminate similar tastes. For instance, Richard Frackowiak and his colleagues at University College London (Castriota-Scanderberg et al., 2005) studied wine connoisseurs (sommeliers), asking how their brain response compared to that of nonexperts when tasting wines that varied in very subtle ways. In primary gustatory areas, the two groups showed a very similar response. However, the sommeliers exhibited increased activation in the insula cortex and parts of the orbitofrontal cortex in the left hemisphere, as well as greater activity bilaterally in dorsolateral prefrontal cortex, a region thought to be important for high-level cognitive processes such as decision making and response selection (see Chapter 13).

The orbitofrontal cortex also appears to play an important role in processing the pleasantness and reward value of eating food. Dana Small and her colleagues (2001) at Northwestern University scanned the brains of people as they ate chocolate. During testing, the subjects rated the pleasantness of the chocolate and their desire to eat more chocolate. Initially, the chocolate was rated as very pleasant and the subjects expressed a desire to eat more. But as the subjects became satiated, their desire for more chocolate dropped. Moreover, although the chocolate was still perceived as pleasant, the intensity of their pleasure ratings decreased.

Comparing the neural activation in the beginning trials with the trials at the end of the study, the researchers were able to determine which areas of the brain participated in processing the reward value of the chocolate (the pleasantness) and the motivation to eat (the desire to have more chocolate). The posteromedial portion of the orbitofrontal cortex was activated when the chocolate was highly rewarding and the motivation to eat more was strong. In contrast, the posterolateral portion of the orbitofrontal cortex was activated during the satiated state, when the chocolate was unrewarding and the motivation to eat more was low. Thus, the orbitofrontal cortex appears to be a highly specialized taste-processing region containing distinct areas able to process opposite ends of the reward value spectrum associated with eating.

SOMATOSENSORY PERCEPTION

Somatosensory perception is not simply the perception of touch. It includes the interpretation of signals that indicate the position of our limbs (proprioception), as well as our sense of temperature and pain. Perhaps to an even greater degree than with our other sensory systems, the somatosensory system has an intricate array of specialized receptors and vast projections to many regions of the central nervous system.

Neural Pathways of Somatosensation

Somatosensory receptors lie under the skin and at the musculoskeletal junctions (Figure 5.10). Touch and pressure are signaled by receptors in the skin, called **corpuscles**, that include *Merkel's corpuscles* for regular touch, *Meissner's corpuscles* for light touch, and *Pacinian corpuscles* for deep pressure. *Ruffini corpuscles* convey temperature information. Pain is signaled by **nociceptors**, specialized cells, that may either be myelinated or unmyelinated. The myelinated fibers conduct information about pain quickly. Activation of these cells usually produces immediate action. For example, when you touch a hot stove, the myelinated nociceptors can trigger a response that will cause you to quickly lift your hand, possibly even before you are aware of the temperature. The unmyelinated fibers are responsible for the duller, longer-lasting pain that follows the initial burn and reminds you to care for the damaged skin.

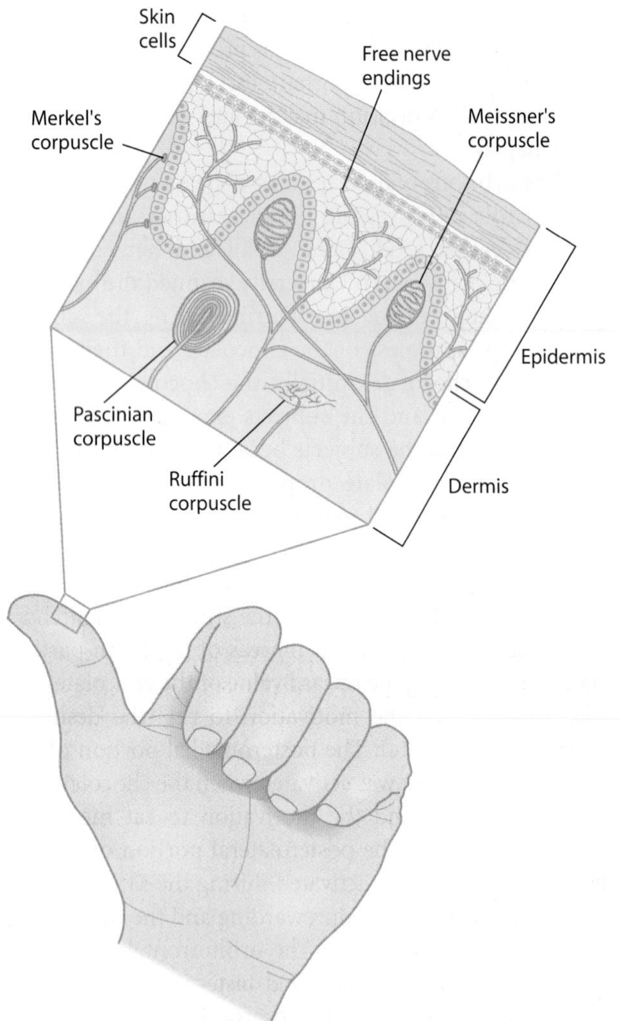

Figure 5.10 Somatosensory receptors underneath the skin. Merkel's corpuscles detect regular touch; Meissner's corpuscles, light touch; Pacinian corpuscles, deep pressure; Ruffini corpuscles, temperature. Nociceptors, or free nerve endings, detect pain.

Specialized nerve cells at the linkage of the muscles and tendons provide proprioceptive cues, allowing the sensory and motor systems to represent information about the state of the muscles and limbs (**proprioception**). Proprioceptive cues, for example, signal when a muscle is stretched and can be used to monitor if that movement is due to an external force such as a shove from another individual or from our own actions (see Chapter 7).

The somatosensory receptors of the body send their signals to the brain via the spinal cord. The ascending, or afferent, signals synapse in the brainstem and then cross over to the thalamus on the opposite side before being projected to the cerebral cortex. As in vision (which will be covered later in the chapter) and audition, the primary peripheral projections to the brain are cross-wired; that is, information from one side of the body is represented primarily in the opposite, or contralateral, hemisphere. In addition to the cortical projections, somatosensory information is projected to many subcortical structures, such as the cerebellum.

Somatosensory Processing

The initial cortical receiving area is called **primary somatosensory cortex**, or **S1** (Figure 5.11), which includes Brodmann areas 1, 2, and 3. S1 contains a somatotopic representation of the body, called the *sensory homunculus.* Recall from Chapter 3 that the relative amount of cortical representation in the sensory homunculus corresponds to the relative importance of somatosensory information for that part of the body. For example, the hands cover a much larger portion of the cortex than the trunk because we use our hands to actively explore surfaces and manipulate objects with great precision (see the figure in "How the Brain Works: Cortical Topography," in Chapter 3, for a picture of the somatosensory homunculus; see also the discussion of plasticity in Chapter 3). When blindfolded, we can

Figure 5.11 Somatosensory cortex lie in the post central gyrus, the most anterior portion of the parietal lobe. S2 is ventral to S1.

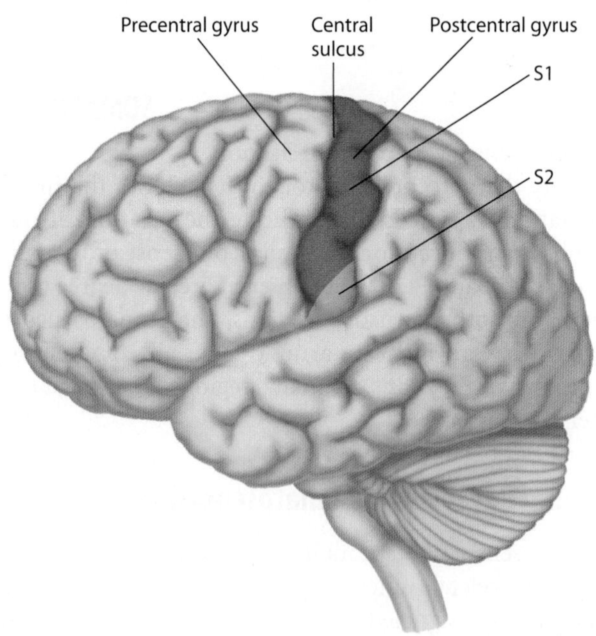

readily identify an object placed in our hand, but we would have great difficulty if the object were rolled across our back.

Somatotopic maps show considerable variation across species. In each species the body parts that are the most important for sensing the outside world through touch are the ones that have the largest cortical representation. The spider monkey uses its tail for exploring objects like food or for grabbing onto tree limbs, so a great deal of the cortex is devoted to the tail. The rat, on the other hand, uses its whiskers to explore the world. A vast portion of the rat somatosensory cortex is devoted to representing information obtained from the whiskers (Figure 5.12).

Secondary somatosensory cortex (**S2**) builds more complex representations. From touch, for example, S2 neurons may code information about object texture and size. Interestingly, because of projections across the corpus callosum, S2 in each hemisphere receives information from both the left and the right sides of the body. Thus, when we manipulate an object with both hands, an integrated representation of the somatosensory information can be built up in S2.

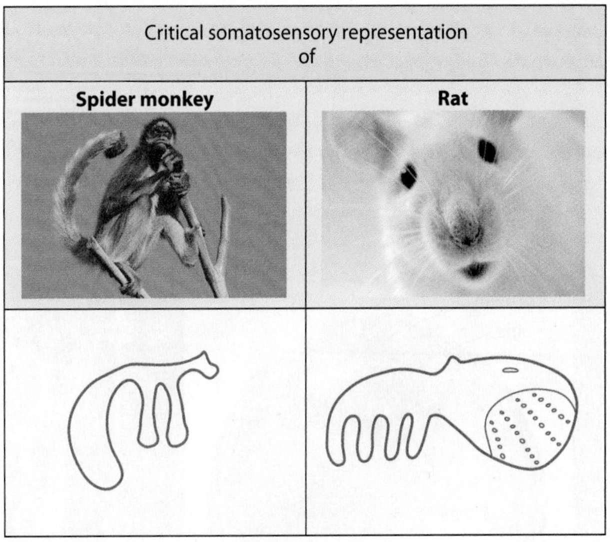

Critical somatosensory representation of	
Spider monkey	**Rat**

Figure 5.12 Variation in the organization of somatosensory cortex reflects behavioral differences across species. The cortical area representing the tail of the spider monkey is large because this animal uses this structure to explore the environment as well as for support. The rat explores the world with its whiskers; clusters of neurons form whisker barrels in the rat somatosensory cortex.

VISION

Now let's turn to a more detailed analysis of the most widely studied sense: vision. Like most other diurnal creatures, humans depend on the sense of vision. Although other senses, such as hearing and touch, are also important, visual information dominates our perceptions and appears even to frame the way we think. Much of our language, even when used to describe abstract concepts with metaphors, makes reference to vision. For example, we say "I see" to indicate that something is understood or "Your hypothesis is murky" to indicate confused thoughts.

Neural Pathways of Vision

One reason why vision is so important is that it enables us to perceive information at a distance, to engage in what is called *remote sensing* or *exteroceptive perception*. We need not be in immediate contact with a stimulus to process it. Contrast this ability with the sense of touch. For touch, we must be in direct contact with the stimulus. The advantages of remote sensing are obvious. An organism surely can avoid a predator better when it can detect the predator at a distance. It is probably too late to flee once a shark's teeth have pierced your skin, no matter how fast your neural response to the pain.

Visual information is contained in the light reflected from objects. To perceive objects, we need sensory detectors that respond to the reflected light. As light passes through the lens of the eye, the image is inverted and focused to project on the back surface of the eye (Figure 5.13), the **retina**. The deepest layer of the retina is composed of millions of **photoreceptors**, each containing light-sensitive molecules, or *photopigments*. When exposed to light, the photopigments become unstable and split apart. Their decomposition alters the flow of the electrical current around the photoreceptors. This light-induced change triggers action potentials in downstream neurons. Thus, photoreceptors provide for translation of the external stimulus of light into an internal neural signal that the brain can interpret.

The two types of photoreceptors are rods and cones. *Rods* are sensitive to low levels of stimulation. They are most useful at night, when light energy is reduced. Rods also respond to bright light, but because replenishing the photopigment in rods takes time, they are of little use during the day. *Cones* require more intense levels of light and use photopigments that can be generated

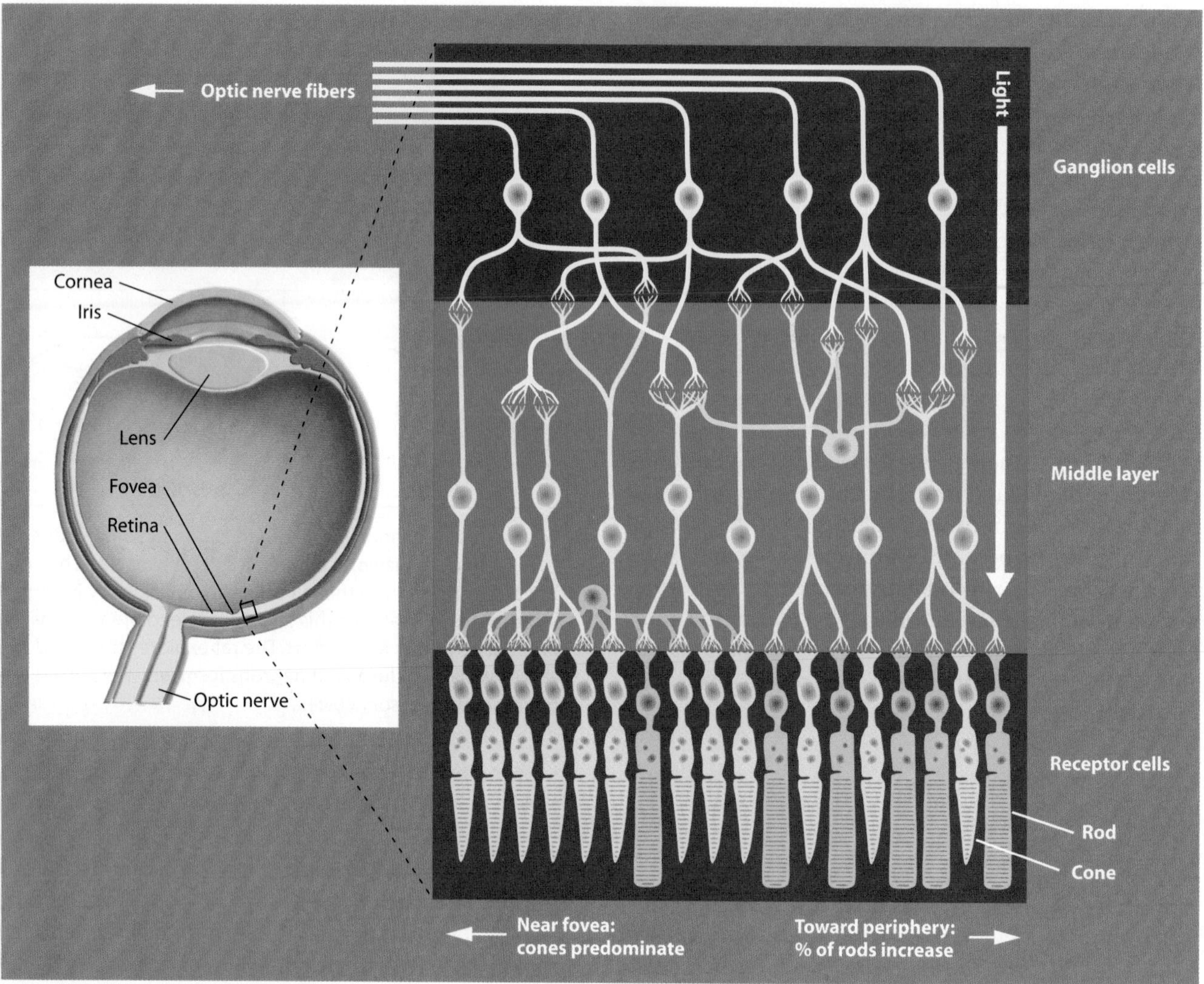

Figure 5.13 Anatomy of the eye **(left)** and retina **(right)**. Light enters through the cornea and activates the receptor cells of the retina located along the rear surface. There are two types of receptor cells: rods and cones. The output of the receptor cells is processed in the middle layer of the retina and then relayed to the central nervous system via the optic nerve, the axons of the ganglion cells.

rapidly. Thus, cones are most active during daytime vision. Cones are essential for color vision, and we commonly speak of them as being one of three types: red, green, or blue. These names are somewhat misleading, though: Cones do not respond to colors per se; rather, as Figure 5.14 shows, they differ in the sensitivity of their photopigments to different wavelengths of visible light.

Rods and cones are not distributed equally across the retina. Cones are densely packed near the center of the retina, in a region called the *fovea*. Few cones are in the more peripheral regions of the retina. In contrast, rods are distributed throughout the retina. You can easily demonstrate the differential distribution of rods and cones by having a friend slowly bring a colored marker into your view from one side of your head. Notice that you see the marker and its shape well before you identify its color because of the sparse distribution of cones in the retina's peripheral regions.

From the Eye to the Central Nervous System

The extensive processing of visual information performed within the retina is characterized by elaborate convergence of information. Indeed, though humans have an estimated 260 million photoreceptors, there are only 2 million ganglion cells, the output neurons from the retina. This compression of information suggests that higher-level visual centers should be efficient processors to recover the details of the visual world. Axons of the ganglion cells form a bundle, the *optic*

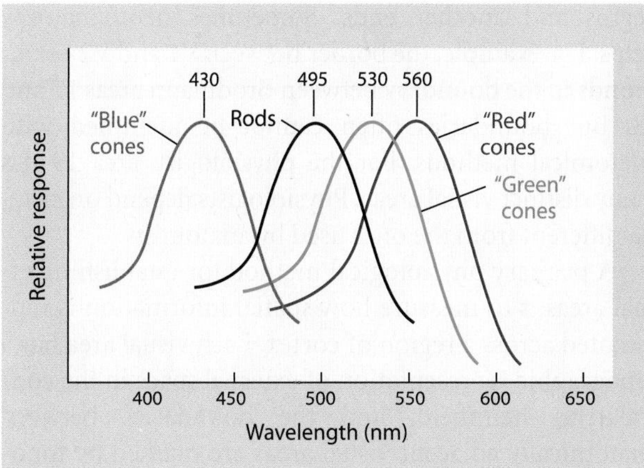

Figure 5.14 Spectral sensitivity functions for rods and the three types of cones. The short-wavelength ("blue") cones are maximally responsive to light with a wavelength of 430 nm. The peak sensitivities of the medium-wavelength ("green") and long-wavelength ("red") cones are shifted to longer wavelengths. White light such as daylight activates all three receptors because it contains all wavelengths.

nerve. By way of this nerve, visual information is transmitted to the central nervous system.

Figure 5.15 diagrams how visual information is conveyed from the eyes to the central nervous system. Before entering the brain, each optic nerve splits into two parts. The temporal (lateral) branch continues to traverse along the same (ipsilateral) side. The nasal (medial) branch crosses over to project to the opposite (contralateral) side; this crossover place is called the *optic chiasm*. Given the eye's optics, the crossover of nasal fibers ensures that visual information from each side of external space will be projected to contralateral brain structures. Because of the retina's curvature, for example, the temporal half of the right retina is stimulated by objects in the left visual field. In the same fashion the nasal hemiretina of the left eye is stimulated by this same region of external space. Because fibers from each nasal hemiretina cross, all information from the left visual field is projected to the right hemisphere, and information from the right visual field is projected to the left hemisphere (see Figure 5.15).

Once inside the brain, each optic nerve divides into pathways that differ with respect to where they terminate

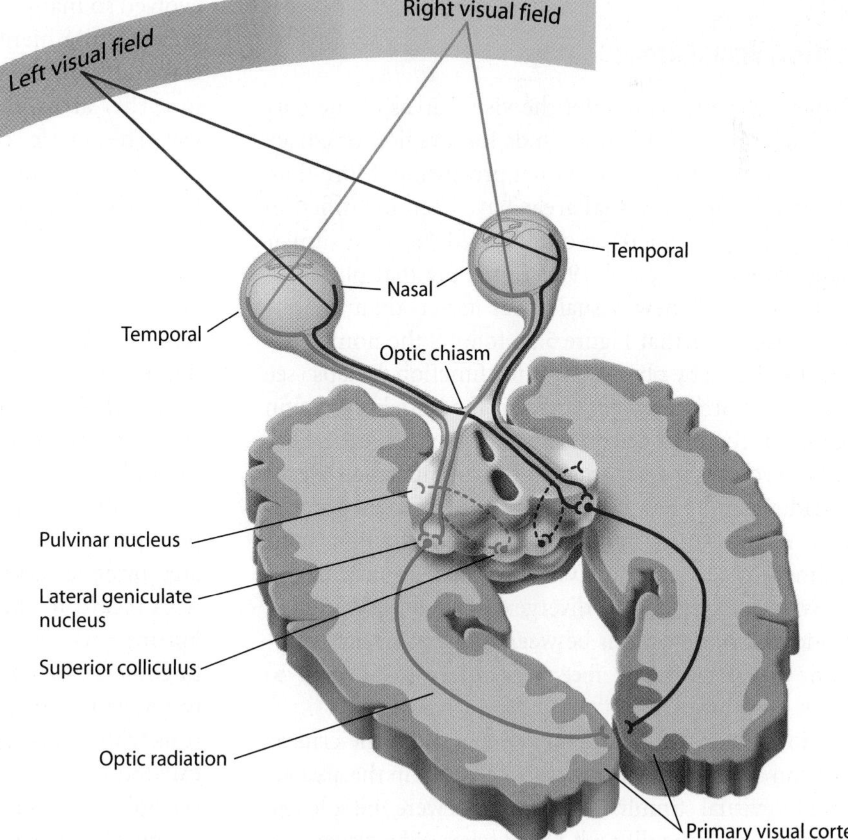

Figure 5.15 The primary projection pathways of the visual system. The optic fibers from the temporal half of the retina project ipsilaterally, and the nasal fibers cross over at the optic chiasm. In this way, the input from each visual field is projected to the primary visual cortex in the contralateral hemisphere after the fibers synapse in the lateral geniculate nucleus (geniculocortical pathway). A small percentage of visual fibers of the optic nerve terminate in the superior colliculus and pulvinar nucleus.

in the subcortex. Figure 5.15 focuses on the retinogeniculate pathway, the projection from the retina to the **lateral geniculate nucleus** (**LGN**) of the thalamus. This pathway contains more than 90% of the axons in the optic nerve and provides input to the cortex via the geniculocortical projections. The remaining 10% of the fibers innervate other subcortical structures, including the pulvinar nucleus of the thalamus and the **superior colliculus** of the midbrain. However, the fact that these other receiving nuclei are innervated by only 10% of the fibers does not mean that these pathways are unimportant. The human optic nerve is so large that 10% of it constitutes more fibers than are found in the entire auditory pathway. The superior colliculus and pulvinar nucleus play a large role in visual attention, and the retinocollicular pathway is sometimes viewed as a more primitive visual system (see the discussion of blindsight later in this chapter).

The final projection to the visual cortex is via the geniculocortical pathway. This bundle of axons exits the LGN and ascends to the cortex, with almost all of the fibers terminating in the **primary visual cortex** (**V1**) of the occipital lobe. Thus, visual information reaching the cortex has been processed by at least four distinct neurons: photoreceptors, bipolar cells, ganglion cells, and LGN cells.

Cortical Visual Areas

Figure 5.16 shows a map of the visual areas of the cortex. Each box in the figure stands for a region of cortex that is a distinct region of visual processing. More than 30 distinct **cortical visual areas** have been identified in the monkey—an increase of about 200% since similar maps were published in 1983. Some say that physiologists "discover" new visual areas faster than rabbits reproduce. Note that Figure 5.16 follows the nomenclature developed by physiologists for functional maps (see Chapter 3). Striate cortex, or V1, is the initial projection region of geniculate axons. Although other areas have names such as *V2*, *V3*, and *V4*, this numbering scheme should not be taken to mean that the synapses proceed sequentially from one area to the next. The lines connecting these **extrastriate visual areas** demonstrate extensive convergence and divergence across visual areas. In addition, connections between many areas are reciprocal; areas frequently receive input from an area to which they project.

How a visual area is defined depends on the criteria used. An obvious criterion is that cells within the area respond to visual stimuli; however, if this were the sole criterion, it would be difficult to tell where one visual area begins and another ends. Sometimes neuroanatomy helps. For example, the border between V1 and V2 corresponds to the boundary between Brodmann areas 17 and 18. But boundaries often cannot be identified with anatomical methods. For the physiologist, area 19 has many distinct visual areas. Physiologists depend on criteria different from the ones used by anatomists.

A primary physiological method for establishing visual areas is to measure how spatial information is represented across a region of cortex. Each visual area has a topographic representation of external space in the contralateral hemifield, and the boundaries between anatomically adjacent visual areas are marked by topographic discontinuities (Figure 5.17). The replication of topography within the cortex does not result from independent inputs to each area. As one area projects to another, topography is preserved. Precise spatial information is preserved by these multiple retinotopic maps, at least in early visual areas, reflecting the fact that the system has to link features that emanate from a common location.

CELLULAR PROPERTIES VARY ACROSS CORTICAL VISUAL AREAS

Why would it be useful for the primate brain to have evolved so many visual areas? One possibility is that the areas form a hierarchy in which each area successively elaborates on the representation derived by processing in earlier areas, representing the stimulus in a specific way. The simple cells of the primary visual cortex calculate edges. Complex cells use the information from many simple cells to represent corners and edge terminations. In turn, higher order visual neurons integrate information from complex cells to represent shapes. Successive elaboration culminates in formatting the representation of the stimulus so that it matches (or doesn't match) information in memory. As Figure 5.16 shows, though, there is not a simple hierarchy; extensive patterns of convergence and divergence result in multiple pathways.

An alternative hypothesis relates to the idea of visual perception as an analytic process. Although each visual area provides a map of external space, the maps differ with regard to the type of information they represent. For instance, neurons in some areas are highly sensitive to color variation. In other areas, they may be sensitive to movement but not to color. By this hypothesis, neurons within an area not only code where an object is located in visual space but also provide information about the object's attributes. Visual perception is a divide-and-conquer strategy. Rather than all attributes of an object

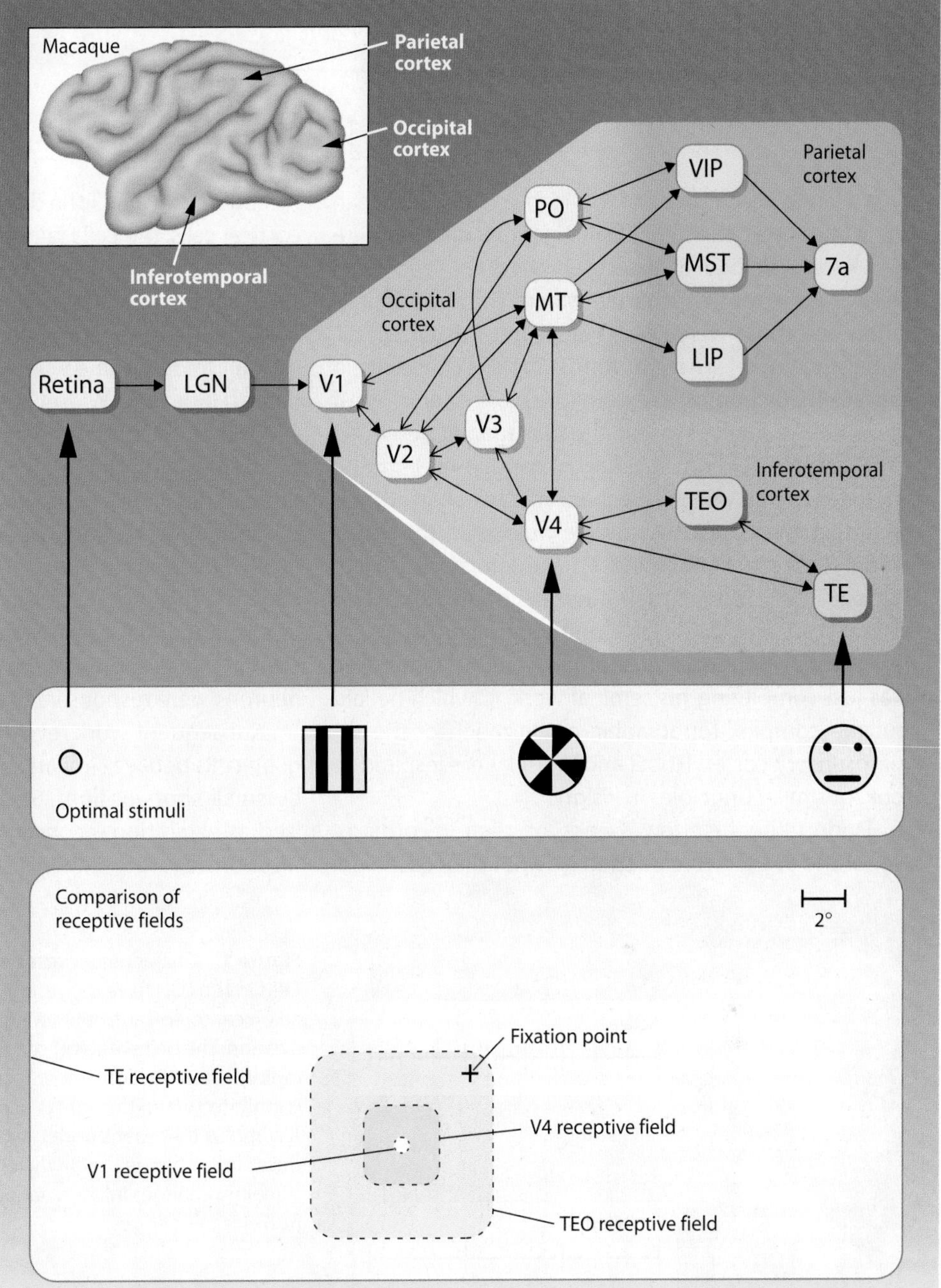

Figure 5.16 Prominent cortical visual areas and the pattern of connectivity in the macaque. Whereas all cortical processing begins in V1, two processing streams extend either dorsally (to the parietal lobe) or ventrally (to the temporal lobe; see Chapter 6). The stimulus required to produce optimal activation of a cell becomes more complex along the ventral stream. In addition, the size of the receptive fields of these cells increases, ranging from the 0.5° span of a V1 cell to the 40° span of a cell in area TE.

being represented by all visual areas, each visual area provides its own limited analysis. Processing is distributed and specialized. As we advance through the visual system, different areas elaborate on the initial information in V1 and begin to integrate this information across dimensions to form recognizable percepts.

Extensive physiological evidence supports the specialization hypothesis. Consider cells in **area MT**, so named because it lies in the *m*iddle *t*emporal lobe region of the macaque monkey, a species used in many physiology studies. Physiologists commonly refer to this region as *visual area 5* (*V5*). Single-cell recordings reveal that neurons in this region do not show specificity in terms of the color of the stimulus. These cells will respond similarly to either a green or a red circle on a white background. Even more striking, these neurons

MILESTONES IN COGNITIVE NEUROSCIENCE

Pioneers in the Visual Cortex

Akin to the voyages of the 15th-century European explorers, the initial investigations into the neurophysiology of the cerebral cortex required a willingness to sail in uncharted waters. The two admirals in this enterprise were David Hubel and Torsten Wiesel. Hubel and Wiesel arrived at Johns Hopkins University in the late 1950s, hoping to extend the pioneering work of Steve Kuffler. Kuffler's research had elegantly described the receptive-field organization of ganglion cells in the cat retina, laying out the mechanisms that allowed cells to detect the edges that define objects in the visual world. Rather than focusing on the lateral geniculate nucleus (LGN), the next relay in the system, Hubel and Wiesel (1977) set their sights on the primary visual cortex. Vernon Mountcastle, another Hopkins researcher, was just completing his seminal work, in which he laid out the complex topographic organization of the somatosensory cortex. Hubel and Wiesel were inspired to look for similar principles in vision.

During the first few weeks of their recordings, Hubel and Wiesel were puzzled by what they observed. Although they had little difficulty identifying individual cortical cells, the cells failed to respond to the kinds of stimuli that had proved so effective in Kuffler's studies: small spots of light positioned within a cell's receptive fields. Indeed, the lack of consistent responses made it difficult to determine where the receptive field was situated. Hubel and Wiesel had a breakthrough, though, when they switched to dark spots, which they created by placing an opaque disk on a glass slide. Although the cell did not respond to the dark spot, Hubel and Wiesel noticed a burst in activity as the edge of the glass moved across part of the retina. After hours of play with this stimulus, the first organizational principle of primary visual cortex neurons became clear: Unlike the circular receptive fields of ganglion cells, cortical neurons were responsive to edges.

Subsequent work revealed that LGN cells and ganglion cells behave similarly: Both are maximally excited by small spots of light. Such cells are best characterized as exhibiting a concentric center–surround organization. Figure 1 shows the receptive field of an LGN

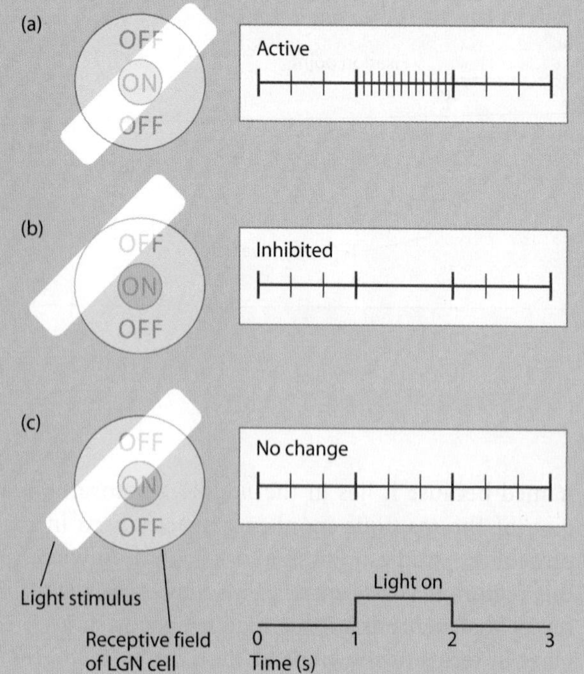

Figure 1 Characteristic response of a lateral geniculate cell. Cells in the LGN have concentric receptive fields with either an on center–off surround or an off center–on surround organization. The on center–off surround cell shown here fires rapidly when the light encompasses the center region **(a)** and is inhibited when the light is positioned over the surround **(b)**. A stimulus that spans both the center and the surround produces little change in activity **(c)**. Thus, LGN cells are ideal for signaling changes in illumination, such as those that arise from stimulus edges.

cell. When a spot of light falls within the excitatory center region, the cell is activated. If the same spot is moved into the surrounding region, the activity is inhibited. A stimulus that encompasses both the center and the surrounding region will fail to activate the cell because the activity from the excitatory and inhibitory regions will cancel. This observation clarifies a fundamental principle of perception: The nervous system is most interested in change. We recognize an elephant not by the homogeneous gray surface of its body, but by the contrast of the gray edge of its shape against the background.

In Figure 2, outputs from three LGN cells with receptive fields centered at slightly different positions are linked to a single cortical neuron. This cortical neuron would continue to have a center–surround organization, but for this cell the optimal stimulus would have to be an edge. In addition, the cell would be selective for edges in a certain orientation. As the same stimulus was rotated within the receptive field, the cell would cease to respond because the edge would now span excitatory and inhibitory regions of the cell. Hubel and Wiesel called these cells *simple cells*, to connote the fact that their simple organization would extract a fundamental feature for shape perception: the border of an object. The same linking principle can yield more complex cells—cells with a receptive-field organization that makes them sensitive to other features, such as corners or edge terminations.

Orientation selectivity has proved to be a hallmark of neurons in the primary visual cortex. Across a 2 mm x 2 mm chunk of cortex, the receptive fields of neurons are centered on a similar region of space (Figure 3). Within the chunk, the cells vary in terms of their preferred orientation, and they alternate between columns that are responsive to inputs from the right and left eyes. A series of such chunks allows for the full representation of external space, providing the visual system with a means of extracting the visible edges in a scene.

Hubel and Wiesel's studies established how a few organizational principles can serve as building blocks of perception derived from simple sensory neurons. The importance of their pioneering studies was acknowledged in 1981, when they shared the Nobel Prize in Physiology or Medicine.

Continued on the following page

Figure 2 Simple cells in the primary visual cortex can be formed by the linking of outputs from concentric LGN cells with adjacent receptive fields. In addition to signaling the presence of an edge, simple cells are selective for orientation. The simple cell illustrated here is either excited or inhibited by an edge that follows its preferred orientation. It shows no change in activity if the edge is at a perpendicular orientation.

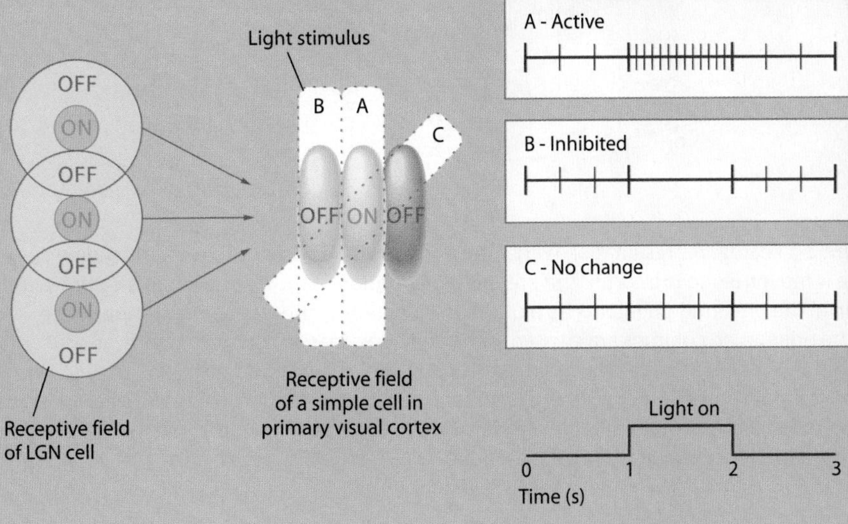

Continued from previous page

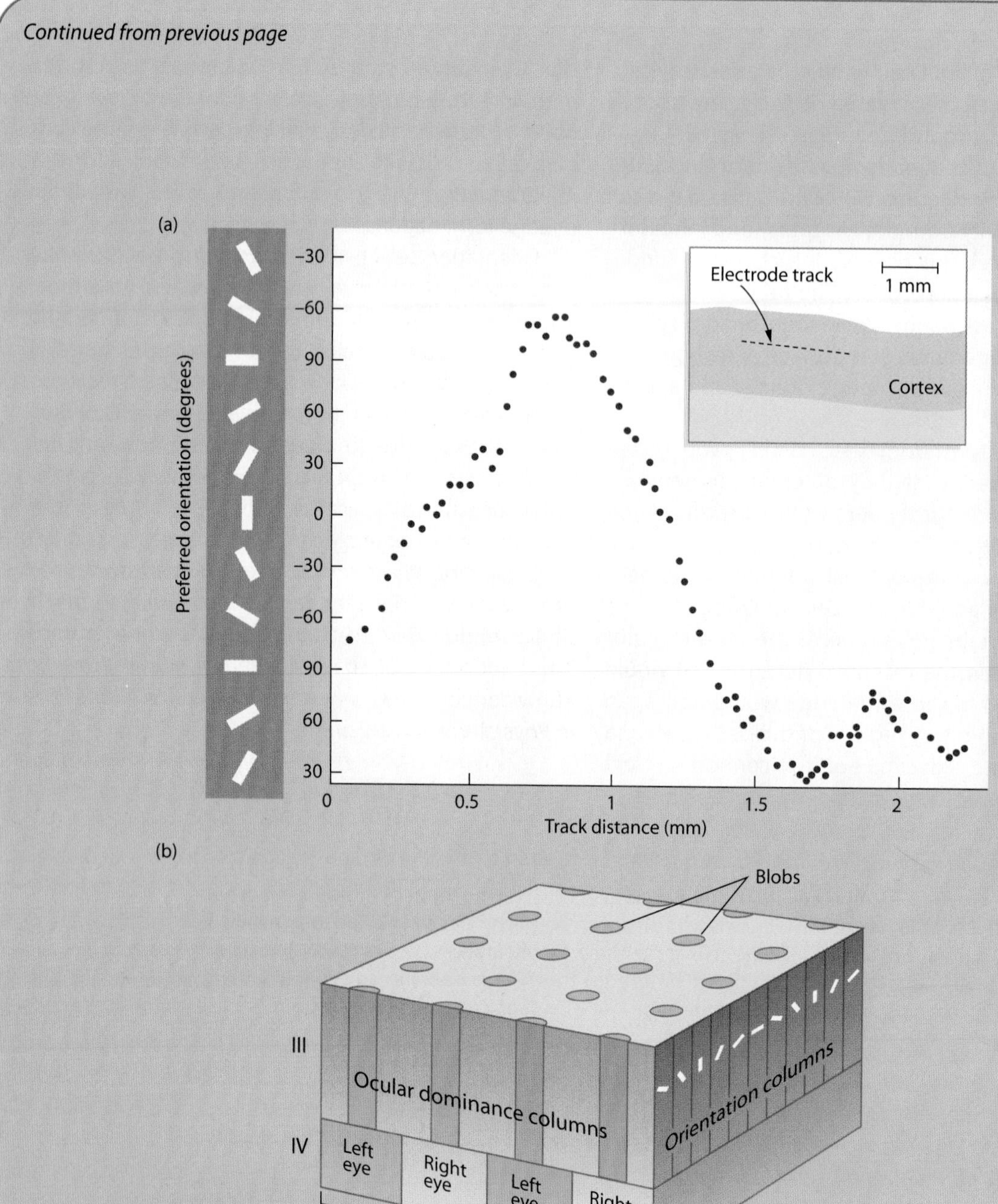

Figure 3 Feature representation within the primary visual cortex. **(a)** As the recording electrode is moved along the cortex, the preferred orientation of the cells varies in a continuous manner. The preferred orientation is plotted as a function of the location of the electrode. **(b)** The orientation columns are crossed with ocular dominance columns to form a cortical module. Within a module, the cells have similar receptive fields (location sensitivity), but they vary in terms of input source (left or right eye), and sensitivity to orientation, color, and size. For example, the so-called blobs contain cells that are sensitive to color and finer details in the visual input. This organization is repeated for each module.

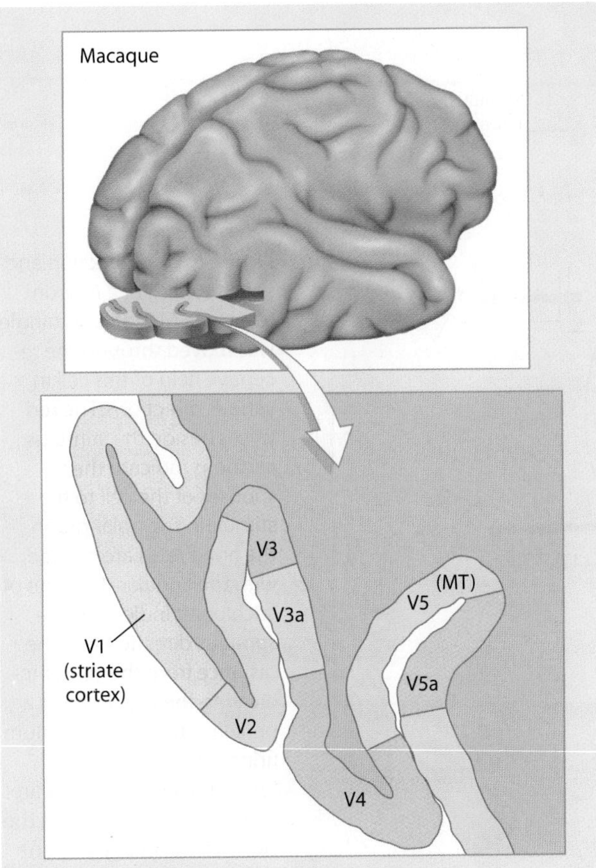

Figure 5.17 Physiological methods are used to identify different visual areas. An area is defined by a discontinuity in the retinotopic representation of the cells. Along the continuous ribbon of cortex shown here, seven different visual areas can be identified. However, processing is not restricted to proceeding from one area to the next in a sequential order. For example, axons from V2 project to V3, V4, and V5/MT.

respond weakly when presented with an alternating pattern of red and green stripes whose colors are of equal brightness.

In contrast, MT neurons are quite sensitive to movement and direction, as Figure 5.18 shows (Maunsell & Van Essen, 1983). The stimulus, a rectangular bar, was passed through the receptive field in varying directions. The cell's response was greatest when the stimulus was moved downward and left. In contrast, this cell was essentially silent when the stimulus was moved upward or to the right. Thus, the cell's activity correlates with two attributes of the stimulus. First, the cell is active only when the stimulus falls within its receptive field. Second, the response is greatest when the stimulus moves in a certain direction. Activity in V5 cells also correlates with the speed of motion. The cell in Figure 5.18 responded maximally when the bar was moved rapidly. At lower speeds, the bar's movement in the same direction failed to raise the response rate above baseline.

HUMAN VISUAL AREAS

Single-cell recording studies have provided physiologists with a powerful tool to map out the visual areas in the monkey brain and characterize the functional properties of the neurons within these areas. This work has provided strong evidence that different visual areas are specialized to represent distinct attributes of the visual scene. Inspired by these results, researchers have employed neuroimaging techniques to ask whether a similar architecture can be discerned in the human brain.

Semir Zeki (1993) of University College London and his colleagues at London's Hammersmith Hospital used position emission tomography (PET) to verify that different visual areas are activated when subjects are processing color or motion information. They used subtractive logic by factoring out the activation in a control condition from the activation in an experimental condition. Consider first the color experiment. For the control condition, subjects passively viewed a collage of achromatic rectangles. Various shades of gray, spanning a wide range of luminances, were chosen. The control stimulus was expected to activate neural regions with cells that are contrast sensitive (e.g., sensitive to differences in luminance).

For the experimental condition, the gray patches were replaced by a variety of colors (Figure 5.19a). Each color patch was matched in luminance to its corresponding gray patch. With this setup, neurons sensitive to luminance information should be equally activated in control and experimental conditions. However, the colored stimulus should produce more activity in neural regions sensitive to chromatic information. These regions should be detected if the metabolic activity recorded when subjects viewed the gray stimulus is subtracted from the activity recorded when subjects viewed the color stimulus.

The same logic was used to design the motion experiment. For this study, the control stimulus consisted of a complex black-and-white collage of squares (Figure 5.19b). The same stimulus was used in the experimental condition, except that the squares were set in motion. They would move in one direction for 5 s and then in the reverse direction for the next 5 s.

The results of the two studies provided clear evidence that the two tasks activated distinct brain regions (Figure 5.20). After subtracting activation during viewing of the achromatic collage, investigators found

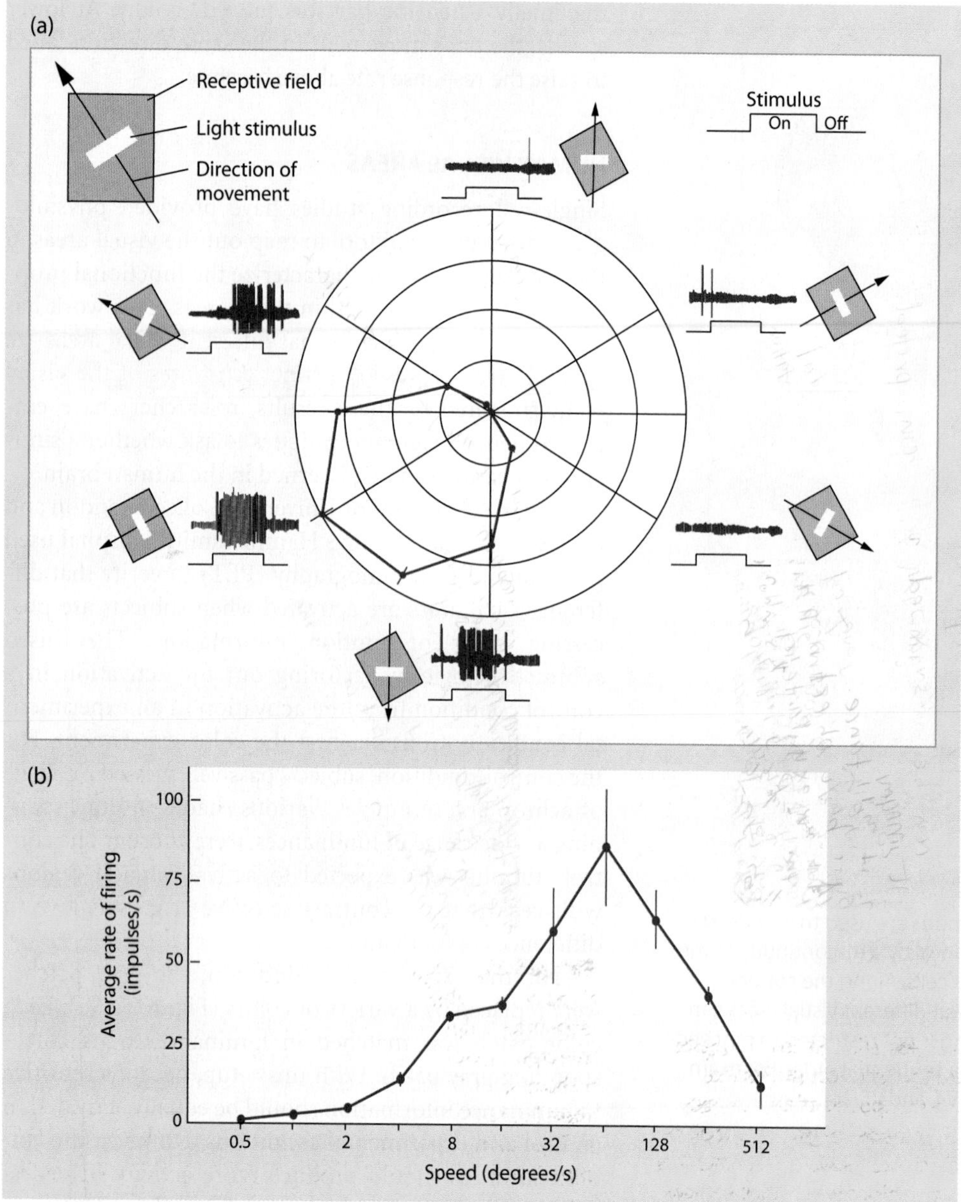

Figure 5.18 Direction and speed tuning of a neuron from area MT. **(a)** A rectangle was moved through the receptive field of this cell in various directions. The red traces beside the stimulus cartoons indicate the responses of the cell to these stimuli. In the polar graph, the firing rates are plotted, with the angular direction of each point indicating the stimulus direction and the distance from the center indicating the firing rate as a percentage of the maximum firing rate. The polygon formed when the points are connected indicates that the cell was maximally responsive to stimuli moved down and to the left; the cell responded minimally when the stimulus moved in the opposite direction. **(b)** The graph shows speed tuning for a cell in MT. In all conditions, the motion was in the optimal direction. This cell responded most vigorously when the stimulus moved at 64°/s.

numerous residual foci of activation when subjects viewed the colored collage. These foci were bilateral and located in the most anterior and inferior regions of the occipital lobe (Figure 5.20a). Although the spatial resolution of PET is coarse, these areas were determined to be in front of the striate (V1) and prestriate (V2) cortex. In contrast, after the appropriate subtraction in the motion experiment, the residual foci were bilateral but near the junction of the temporal, parietal, and occipital cortices (Figure 5.20b). These foci were more superior and much more lateral than the color foci.

Zeki and his colleagues were so taken with this dissociation that they proposed that the nomenclature developed by primate researchers be applied here. They labeled the area activated in the color foci as **area V4** and the area activated in the motion task as *V5*. Note that researchers frequently refer to area V5 as *human area MT*, even though the area is not in the temporal lobe in the human brain. Of course, with PET data we cannot be sure that the foci of activation really consist of just one visual area.

Note that there are also striking between-species differences in terms of the relative position of the color and motion areas (compare Figures 5.17 and 5.20). Such differences probably result from the fact that the surface area of the human brain is substantially larger, and this

Figure 5.19 Stimuli used in a PET experiment to identify regions involved in color and motion perception. **(a)** For the color experiment, the stimuli were composed of an arrangement of rectangles that were either shades of gray (control) or various colors (experimental). **(b)** For the motion experiment, a random pattern of black and white regions was either stationary (control) or moving (experimental).

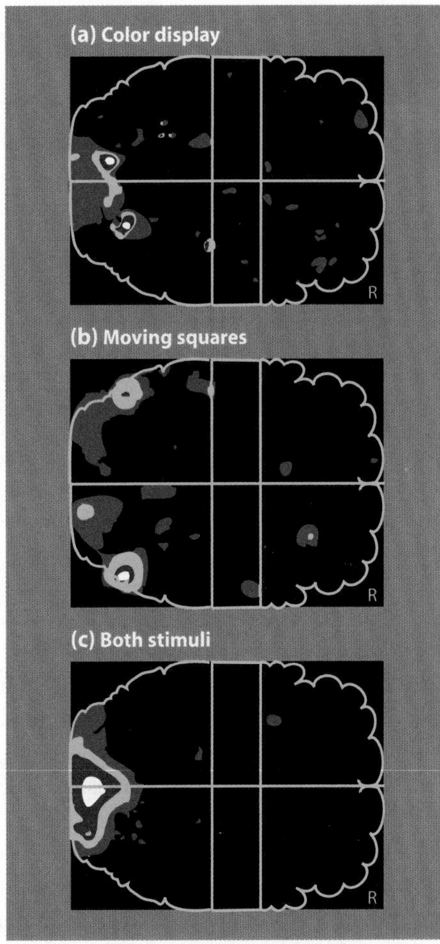

Figure 5.20 Regions of activation when the control conditions were subtracted from the experimental conditions in the experiment illustrated in Figure 5.19. **(a)** In the color condition, the prominent activation was medial, in areas corresponding to human V4. **(b)** In the motion condition, the activation was more lateral, in areas corresponding to human MT. The foci also differed along the dorsoventral axis: The slice showing MT is superior to that showing V4. **(c)** Both stimuli produced significant activation in primary visual cortex, when compared to a control condition in which there was no visual stimulation.

expansion required additional folding of the continuous cortical sheet. Thus, we can ask questions about functional homology (see Chapter 15)—the correspondence in structure and function between species—but we need to be aware that the mapping is unlikely to be straightforward. Indeed, it is quite possible that humans have visual areas that do not correspond to any region in our close primate relatives.

The activation maps in this PET study are rather crude. Many laboratories now employ more sophisticated fMRI techniques to study the organization of human visual cortex. In these studies, a stimulus is systematically moved across the visual field (Figure 5.21). For example, a semicircular checkerboard pattern is slowly rotated about the center of view. In this way, the BOLD response for areas representing the superior quadrant will be activated at a different time than areas representing the inferior quadrant, and in fact, the representation of the entire visual field can be continuously tracked. To compare areas that respond to foveal stimulation and those that respond to peripheral stimulation, a dilating and contracting ring stimulus is used. By combining these different stimuli, the cortical representation of external space is measured.

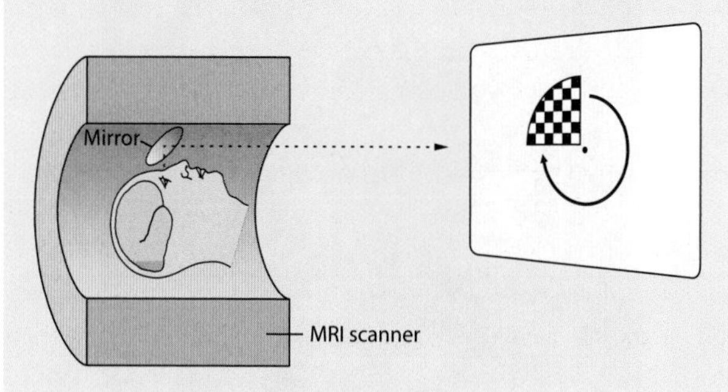

Figure 5.21 Mapping visual fields with functional magnetic resonance imaging (fMRI). The subject views a rotating circular wedge while fMRI scans are obtained. The wedge passes from one visual quadrant to the next, and the blood oxygenation level dependent (BOLD) response in visual cortex is measured continuously to map out how the regions of activation change in a corresponding manner.

(a)

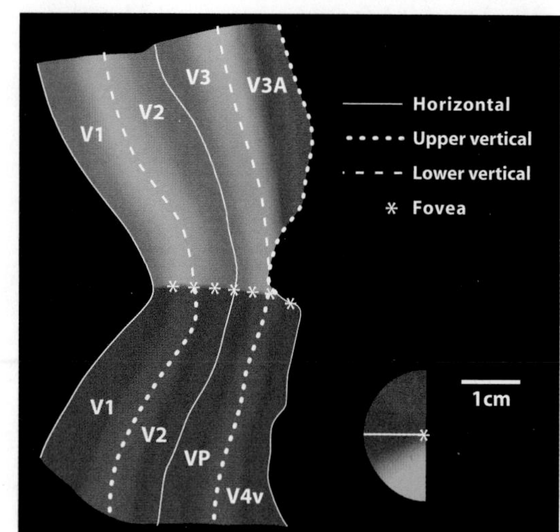

(b)

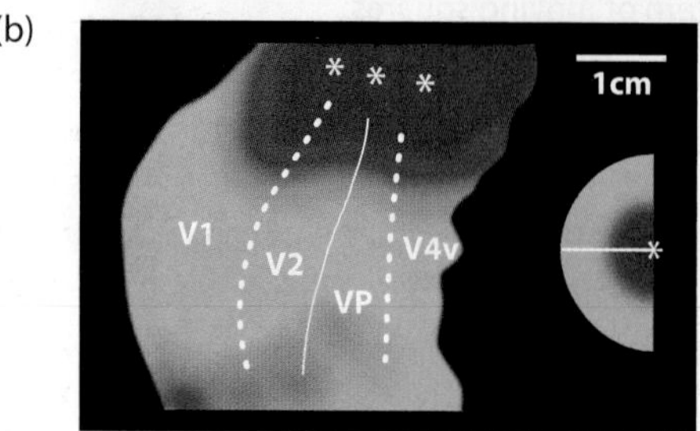

Figure 5.22 Retinotopic mapping in the human. **(a)** The correspondence between the position of the rotating wedge and activation across the visual cortex is coded by color on the flattened map. Boundaries between visual areas are defined by reversals in the retinotopic representation within a quadrant. Note that V3 in the ventral portion is referred to as VP. **(b)** The expanding/contracting stimulus is used to map eccentricity. Only the ventral visual cortex is shown. The foveal regions are marked by the asterisks. Adapted from Hadjikhani et al. (1998).

Because of the convoluted nature of the human visual cortex, the results from such an experiment would be indecipherable if we were to plot the data on the anatomical maps found in a brain atlas. To avoid this problem, a flat map representation is constructed. High-resolution anatomical MRI scans are obtained and computer algorithms transform the folded, cortical surface into a two-dimensional map by tracing the gray matter. The activation signals from the fMRI study are then plotted on the flattened surface, with color coding used to indicate areas that were activated at similar times.

Researchers at the Massachusetts General Hospital used this procedure to reveal the organization of the human visual system in exquisite detail. The flattened map from the visual cortex of the right hemisphere shows the activation map when the checkerboard moves across the left side of space (Figure 5.22). Primary visual cortex (V1) lies along the calcarine sulcus and, as found in all physiological studies, the physical world is inverted. Except for the most anterior aspects of visual cortex, areas above the sulcus are active when the rotating stimulus is in the lower quadrant; the reverse is true when the stimulus is in the upper quadrant.

In addition, the activation patterns show a series of repetitions across the visual cortex. The green and blue repetitions in the superior portion of the visual cortex indicate that the lower quadrant of the visual field is represented multiple times. Similarly, the red and purple alternations in the lower portion indicate the upper quadrant of the visual field is represented multiple times. These repetitions indicate separate topographic maps. Following the conventions adopted in the single-cell studies, the visual areas are numbered in increasing order, with primary visual cortex (V1) most posterior and secondary visual areas (V2, V3/VP, V4) more anterior.

Figure 5.22b shows how eccentricity is represented in the ventral part of the right visual cortex. The cortical representation of the fovea, the regions shown in red, is quite large. Visual acuity is much greater at the fovea due to the disproportionate amount of cortex that encodes information from this part of space.

VISUAL ILLUSIONS

Imaging studies have opened a new window for studying visual illusions that have puzzled philosophers and psychologists alike for many years. Patterns of brain activation during illusory states can be compared with those observed during visual stimulation. In this way, areas of overlap can provide insight into the level of processing at which illusions arise, as well as indicate how information is represented in different visual areas.

Stare at the Enigma pattern shown in Figure 5.23a. After a few seconds, you should begin to see scintillating motion within the blue circles—an illusion created by their opposed orientation to the radial black and white lines. What are the neural correlates of this illusion? We know that moving patterns produce a strong hemodynamic response in V5. Is this same area also activated during illusory motion? Both PET and fMRI have been used to show that viewing displays such as the Enigma pattern do indeed lead to pronounced activity in V5. This activation is selective: Activity in V1 does not increase during illusory motion.

A different illusion is demonstrated in Figure 5.23b. After staring at the bright green circle for about 30 s, shift your gaze to the neighboring gray circle. You should perceive the gray circle as tinged with a reddish purple, the complementary color to green. Scans of subjects while they are perceiving this color illusion reveal a high level of activation in an inferior visual area just anterior to V4 for an extended period of time after a saturated color turns to gray. In a control condition, the color patch alternates between two saturated colors before turning gray, thus negating the illusion. Here, activity quickly returns to baseline when the gray patch is presented. As with the motion illusion, such aftereffects are not seen in V1.

These results show that our percepts are more closely related to activity in higher visual areas than to activity in primary visual cortex. Indeed, illusions can be viewed as an interesting way to link the study of perception and imagery, an issue we return to in Chapter 6. While most of us do not have vivid percepts when we tap into our visual knowledge—for example, think about the color of a banana—imaging studies demonstrate that accessing this knowledge can produce measurable changes of activity in secondary visual areas.

Deficits in Visual Perception

Before the advent of neuroimaging, much of what we learned about visual processing in the human brain came from lesion studies. In 1888, Louis Verrey (cited in Zeki, 1993), described a patient who had lost the ability to perceive colors in her right visual field. Verrey reported that the patient had problems with acuity within restricted portions of this right visual field. But the color deficit was uniform and complete. We can guess that this patient's world looked similar to the drawing in

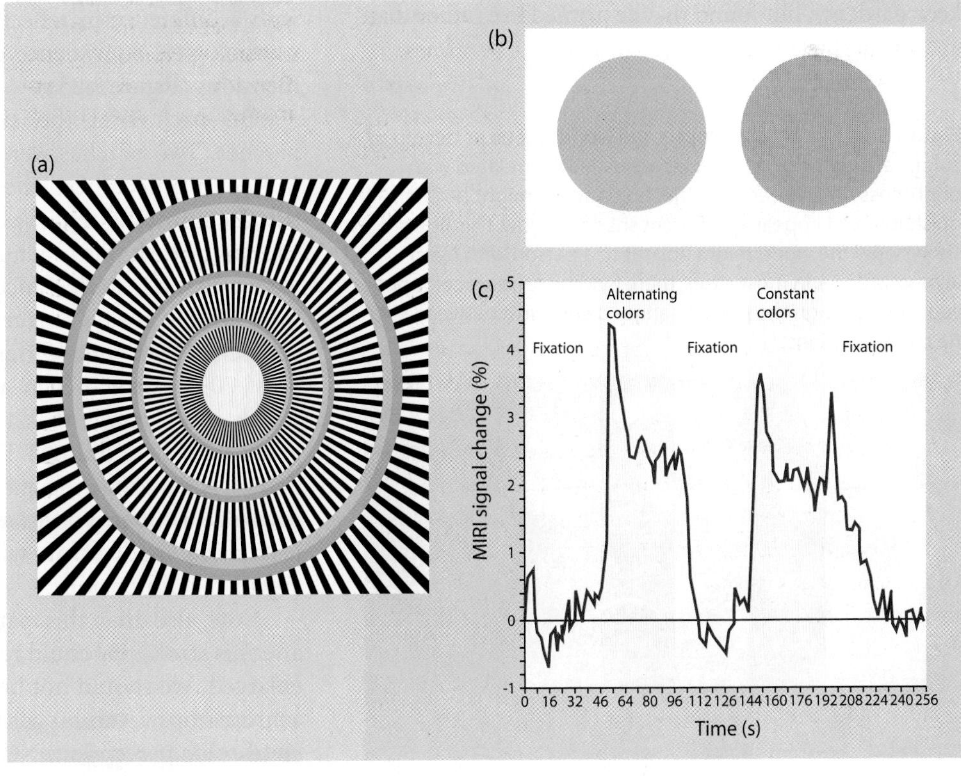

Figure 5.23 The neural basis of visual illusions. **(a)** When viewing the Enigma pattern, we perceive illusory motion. Viewing the pattern is accompanied by activation in area MT. **(b)** Staring at the bright green patch produces color aftereffects. **(c)** Activation in a visual region anterior to V4 is plotted (see text for details).

Figure 5.24: On one side of space, the world was multicolored; on the other, it was a montage of grays.

DEFICITS IN COLOR PERCEPTION: ACHROMATOPSIA

When we speak of someone who is color-blind, we are usually describing a person who has inherited a gene that produces an abnormality in the photoreceptor system. *Dichromats*, people with only two photopigments, can be classified as red–green color-blind if they are missing the photopigment sensitive to either medium or long wavelengths, or blue–yellow color-blind if they are missing the short-wavelength photopigment. *Anomalous trichromats*, in contrast, have all three photopigments, but one has abnormal sensitivity. The incidence of these genetic disorders is high in males: about 8% of the population. The incidence rate is much lower in females: less than 1%.

Much rarer are disorders of color perception that arise from disturbances of the central nervous system. These disorders are called **achromatopsia**, taken from the prefix *a*- ("without") and the stem *chroma* ("hue"). As is evident in Verrey's description, these patients see the world without color. J. C. Meadows (1974) of the National Hospital for Neurology and Neurosurgery in London described one such patient as follows: "Everything looked black or grey. He had difficulty distinguishing British postage stamps of different value, which look alike, but are of different colors. He was a keen gardener, but found that he pruned live rather than dead vines. He had difficulty distinguishing certain foods on his plate where color was the distinguishing mark" (p. 629).

Figure 5.24 In achromatopsia, the world is seen as devoid of color. Because color differences are usually correlated with brightness differences, the objects in a scene might be distinguishable and appear as different shades of gray. This figure shows how the world might appear to a person with hemi-achromatopsia. In most cases, there is some residual color perception, although the person cannot distinguish between subtle color variations.

Patients with achromatopsia often report that colors have become a bland palette of "dirty shades of gray." The shading reflects variations in brightness rather than hue. Other aspects of vision, such as depth and texture perception, also remain intact, enabling someone with achromatopsia to see and recognize objects in the world. Indeed, color is not a necessary cue for shape perception. Its subtlety is underscored when we consider the fact that people often do not notice the change from black and white to color when Dorothy lands in Oz in the movie *The Wizard of Oz*. Nonetheless, when lost forever, this subtlety is sorely missed.

In almost all published cases of achromatopsia, patients exhibit abnormalities in other areas of visual perception as well. What remains clear is that the deficit in color perception is markedly more severe. Consider the performance of an achromatopsia patient on tests of hue discrimination and brightness discrimination conducted by Alan Cowey and his colleagues at Oxford University (Heywood et al., 1987). Although we think of colors as differing in hue, they also vary in other properties, such as saturation (e.g., pink versus deep red) and reflectance, the physical property of reflected light that reaches the eye and determines our psychological impression of the brightness of a visual scene. Although there is no objective way to equate a difference in hue with a difference in reflectance, we can determine the psychological equivalence of differences across the dimensions (Figure 5.25a).

On each trial the subject viewed three color patches. Two patches were identical; the third varied in hue or reflectance. The subject was asked to identify the stimulus that was different. As Figure 5.25b shows, the task was much more difficult when stimuli varied in hue. Reflectance differences, for example, were almost always correctly identified with a 4-step difference. For hue differences, the patient scored only 70% correct even with a 10-step difference, which corresponds to a transition from a yellowish green to a deep orange! Though this hue perception deficit is striking, the patient's performance on reflectance differences was also impaired. Healthy subjects rarely made errors with a one-step difference on any of the dimensions.

Note also that this patient had lost visual acuity after his stroke. He could read, but only if the print was enlarged. We should not be surprised that people with achromatopsia exhibit visual deficits that extend beyond color perception. Neurological disorders such as

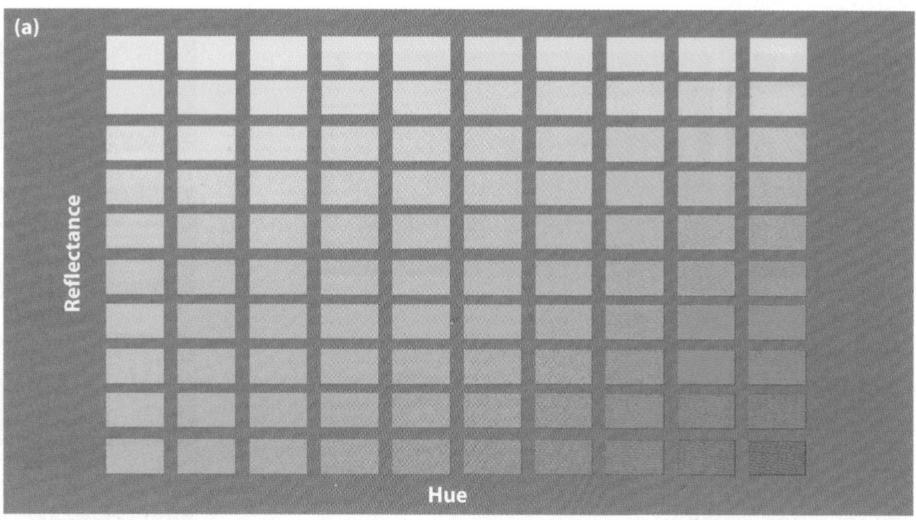

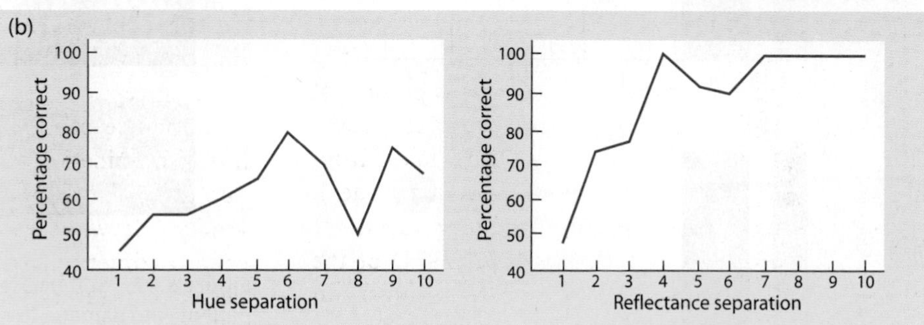

Figure 5.25 Assessing sensitivity to different dimensions of color perception in achromatopsia. **(a)** Psychological scaling techniques can be used with healthy individuals to create stimulus sets in which the similarity of all neighboring pairs is judged as equal. These techniques are used to create norms for the similarity across the different dimensions of a color (hue, saturation, and reflectance, the physical measure that underlies our perception of brightness). **(b)** Three chips were presented, two that were identical and one that differed either in hue or reflectance. A patient with achromatopsia had difficulty identifying chips that differed in hue, even when the stimuli differed by 10 units. His ability to discriminate brightness, although not normal, was much better. Here, he almost always labeled the stimuli as different when they were separated by at least 4 units.

strokes and tumors do not respect the borders of visual areas. Achromatopsia has consistently been associated with lesions that encompass V4 and the region anterior to V4, but the lesions typically extend to neighboring regions of the visual cortex. Color-sensitive neurons are also orientation selective; as such, many achromatic patients have difficulty with form perception.

This hypothesis linking achromatopsia with deficits in form perception was carefully explored in the case study of a patient who suffered a stroke resulting in a small lesion near the temporo-occipital border in the right hemisphere. The damage was centered in area V4 and anterior parts of the visual cortex (Figure 5.26a). To assess the patient's achromatopsia, a hue-matching experiment was performed in which a sample color was presented at the fovea, followed by a test color in one of the four quadrants of space. The patient's task was to judge if the two colors were the same. The difference between the sample and test color was adjusted until the patient was performing correctly on 80% of the trials, and this difference was measured separately for each quadrant. Regardless of the sample hue, the patient was severely impaired on the hue-matching task when the test color was presented in the upper left visual field (Figure 5.26b). The fact that the deficit was found only in the upper *contralesional* visual field is consistent with previous reports of achromatopsia.

The main focus of the study, however, was to examine form perception. Would the patient show similar deficits in form perception in this quadrant? If so, what types of form perception tasks would reveal the impairment? To answer these questions, a variety of tasks were administered. The stimuli are shown in Figure 5.27. On the basic visual discriminations of contrast, orientation, and motion, the patient's performance was similar for all four quadrants and comparable to the performance of control participants. However, he showed impairment on tests of higher order shape perception, and again, this impairment was restricted to the upper left quadrant. For these tasks, shape information requires combining information from neurons that might detect simple properties such as line orientation. For example, the orientation of the line separating the two semicircles is defined only by the combination of the lengths of the individual stripes and their offset.

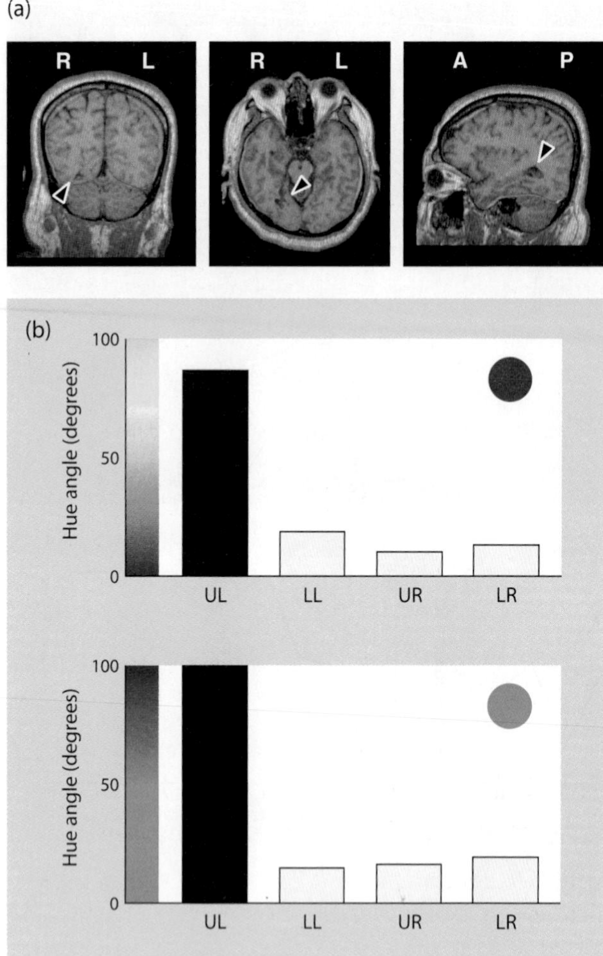

Figure 5.26 Color and shape perception in a patient with a unilateral lesion of V4. **(a)** MRI scans showing a small lesion encompassing V4 in the right hemisphere. **(b)** Color perception thresholds in each visual quadrant. The *y*-axis indicates the color required to detect a difference between a patch shown in each visual quadrant (upper left, UL; lower left, LL; upper right, UR; lower right, LR) and the target color shown at the fovea. The target color was red for the results shown in the top panel and green for the results shown in the bottom panel.

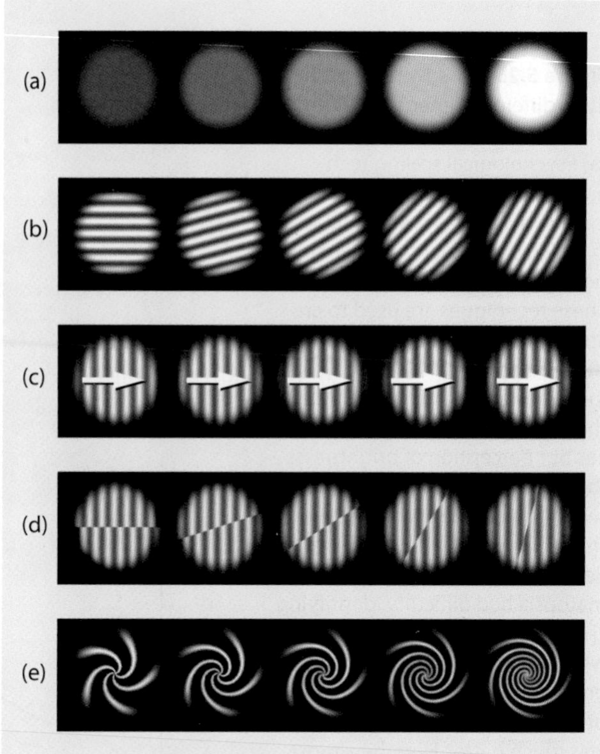

Figure 5.27 Stimuli used to assess form perception in the patient with damage to area V4 illustrated in Figure 5.26. On basic tests of luminance **(a)**, orientation **(b)**, and motion **(c)**, the patient's perceptual threshold was similar in all four quadrants. Thresholds for illusory contours **(d)** and complex shapes **(e)** were elevated in the upper left quadrant.

Characterizing area V4 as a "color" area is too simplistic. This area is part of secondary visual areas devoted to shape perception. Color can provide an important cue about an object's shape. V4 may be invaluable for using color information as one cue to define the boundaries that separate the objects that form our visual environment.

Revisiting Patient P.T. Let's return to patient P.T., who was left with visual agnosia following a stroke to his right hemisphere. In particular, let's turn to a striking demonstration of P.T.'s deficit.

During examination, P.T. was shown two paintings, one by Monet depicting a subdued 19th-century countryman dressed in his Sunday suit, and the other by Picasso of a woman with a terrified expression (Figure 5.28). P.T. was asked to describe what he saw in each painting. When shown the Monet, he looked puzzled. He saw no definable forms, but just an abstract blend of colors and shapes. His problem in interpreting the painting was consonant with the deficits he experienced at home. Yet he readily identified the figure in Picasso's painting and pointed out that it was a woman, or perhaps a young girl. This dissociation is compelling, as most would readily agree that the Monet is more realistic.

Picasso painted the parts of his work as separate units. He used sharp contrasts in brightness and vivid colors to highlight facial regions. Monet opted for a softer approach, in which parts are best seen in a continuous whole, with gradual changes in contrast and color. Can any of these factors account for P.T.'s performance in identifying the figures in Picasso and Monet?

(a)

(b)

Figure 5.28 Two portraits. **(a)** Detail from *Luncheon on the Grass*, painted in the 1860s by the French Impressionist Claude Monet. **(b)** Pablo Picasso's *Weeping Woman*, painted in 1937 during his Cubist period.

The neurologist evaluating P.T. emphasized that the primary problem stemmed from a deficit in color perception. This hypothesis is in accord with one of the primary differences between the Monet and the Picasso. In the Monet painting, the boundaries between the face and the background are blended: Gradual variations in color demarcate the facial regions and separate them from the background landscape. A deficit in color perception provided a parsimonious account of the patient's problems in recognizing faces and landscapes. The rolling green hills of an Oregon farm can blur into a homogeneous mass if one cannot discern fine variations in color. In a similar way, each face has its characteristic coloration.

It seems equally plausible, however, that the problem stemmed from a deficit in contrast or contour perception. These features are salient in the Picasso and absent in the Monet. Indeed, we know from our recent discussion of V4, that color and form perception are often conflated. What is clear is that the patient's stroke affected primarily the cortical projections of the pathways essential for color and form perception. In contrast, the cortical projections of the pathway involved in motion were intact. The patient had no trouble recognizing his wife as she moved from the stove to the kitchen table; indeed, P.T. commented that her idiosyncratic movement enabled him to recognize her.

DEFICITS IN MOTION PERCEPTION: AKINETOPSIA

In 1983, researchers at the Max Planck Institute in Munich reported a striking case of a woman who had incurred a selective loss of motion perception, or **akinetopsia** (Zihl et al., 1983). For this woman, whom we call M.P., perception was akin to viewing the world as a series of snapshots. Rather than seeing things move continuously in space, she saw moving objects appear in one position and then another. When pouring a cup of tea, M.P. would see the liquid frozen in air, like a glacier. She would fail to notice the tea rising in her cup and would be surprised when the cup overflowed (Figure 5.29). The loss of motion perception also made M.P. hesitant about crossing the street. As she noted, "When I'm looking at the car first, it seems far away. But then, when I want to cross the road, suddenly the car is very near" (Zihl et al., 1983, p. 315).

Examination revealed M.P.'s color and form perception to be intact. Her ability to perceive briefly presented objects and letters, for example, was within the normal range. But her ability to judge the direction and speed of moving objects was severely impaired. This deficit was most apparent with stimuli moving at high speeds. At speeds faster than 20°/s, M.P. never reported detecting the motion. She could see that a dot's position had changed and hence could infer motion. But her percept was of two static images; there was no continuity from

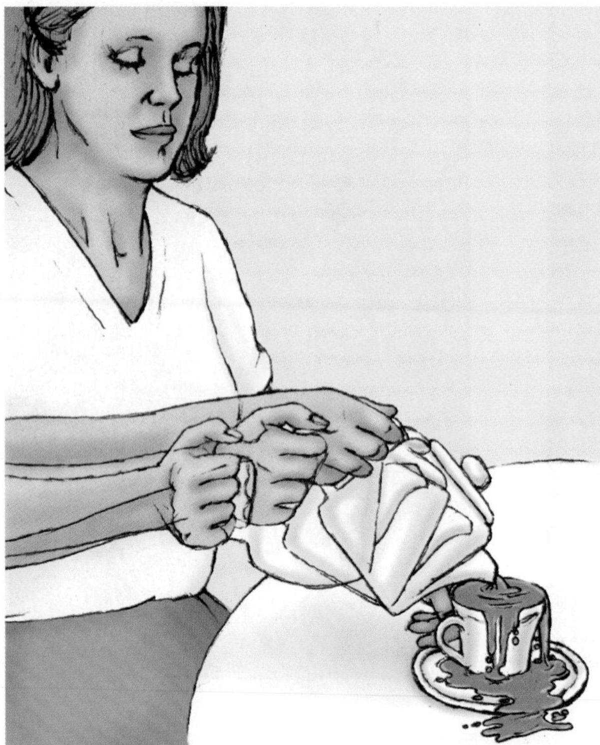

Figure 5.29 For patients with motion blindness (akinetopsia), the world appears as if viewed through a strobe light. Rather than seeing the liquid rise continuously in the teacup, for example, patient M.P. reported seeing the liquid jump from one level to the next.

one image to the other. Even when presented with stimuli moving more slowly, M.P. was hesitant to report a clear impression of motion.

CT scans of M.P. revealed large, bilateral lesions involving the temporoparietal cortices. On each side, the lesions included posterior and lateral portions of the middle temporal gyrus. These lesions roughly corresponded to areas that participate in motion perception. Furthermore, the lesions were lateral and superior to human V4, including the area identified as V5, the human equivalent of area MT.

Although the case of M.P. has been cited widely for many years, the fact that similar patients have not been identified suggests that severe forms of akinetopsia result only from bilateral lesions. With unilateral lesions, the motion perception deficits are much more subtle (Plant et al., 1993). Perhaps people can perceive motion as long as human V5 is intact in at least one hemisphere. Motion, by definition, is a dynamic percept, one that typically unfolds over an extended period of time. With longer viewing times, signals from early visual areas in the impaired hemisphere have an opportunity to reach secondary visual areas in the unimpaired hemisphere. The receptive fields in primate area V5 are huge and have cells that can be activated by stimuli presented in either visual field.

Nonetheless, the application of transcranial magnetic stimulation (TMS; see Chapter 4) over human V5 can produce transient deficits in motion perception. In one such experiment, subjects were asked to judge whether a stimulus moved to the left or right (Beckers & Zeki, 1995). To make the task demanding, the stimulus was visible for only 25 ms. TMS was applied to three locations over the visual cortex, targeted to activate neurons in V5, V1, or, as a control, an extrastriate region lying between these two regions (Figure 5.30). Performance of the motion task was disrupted by stimulation over V5. One advantage of this method is that the timing of the magnetic pulses can be varied to determine the time of maximum disruption in the ability to perform the task. When TMS was applied to V5 just prior to the onset of the stimulus, performance was no better than chance. When the TMS was delayed until 40 ms after stimulus onset, performance was perfect.

These results are puzzling, especially when one considers that only at much longer delays did stimulation over V1 disrupt performance. If V1 provides the gateway to all information processing in the visual cortex, one would expect the optimal time of stimulation over V1 to precede the optimal time of stimulation for V5. Alternatively, it is possible that there are at least two ways for signals to reach V5. The first is a cortical route: the extension of geniculostriate pathways and on to V5. The second route bypasses V1. It may involve direct projections to V5 from the LGN or projections from other subcortical structures that are sensitive to moving stimuli, such as the superior colliculus or pulvinar. Physiological and anatomical studies in primates will likely be needed to address these hypotheses.

PERCEPTION WITHOUT A VISUAL CORTEX

Almost all of the ascending axons from the LGN terminate in the primary visual cortex. We would expect an individual with damaged primary visual cortex to be blind and indeed, this is what is observed. The blindness may not be complete, however. If the lesion is restricted to one half of the visual field, the loss of perception will be restricted to the contralateral side of space; such a deficit is referred to as **hemianopia.** Smaller lesions may produce more discrete regions of blindness, or **scotomas.** Patients with primary visual cortex lesions are unable to report seeing anything presented within a scotoma. As anatomists have shown,

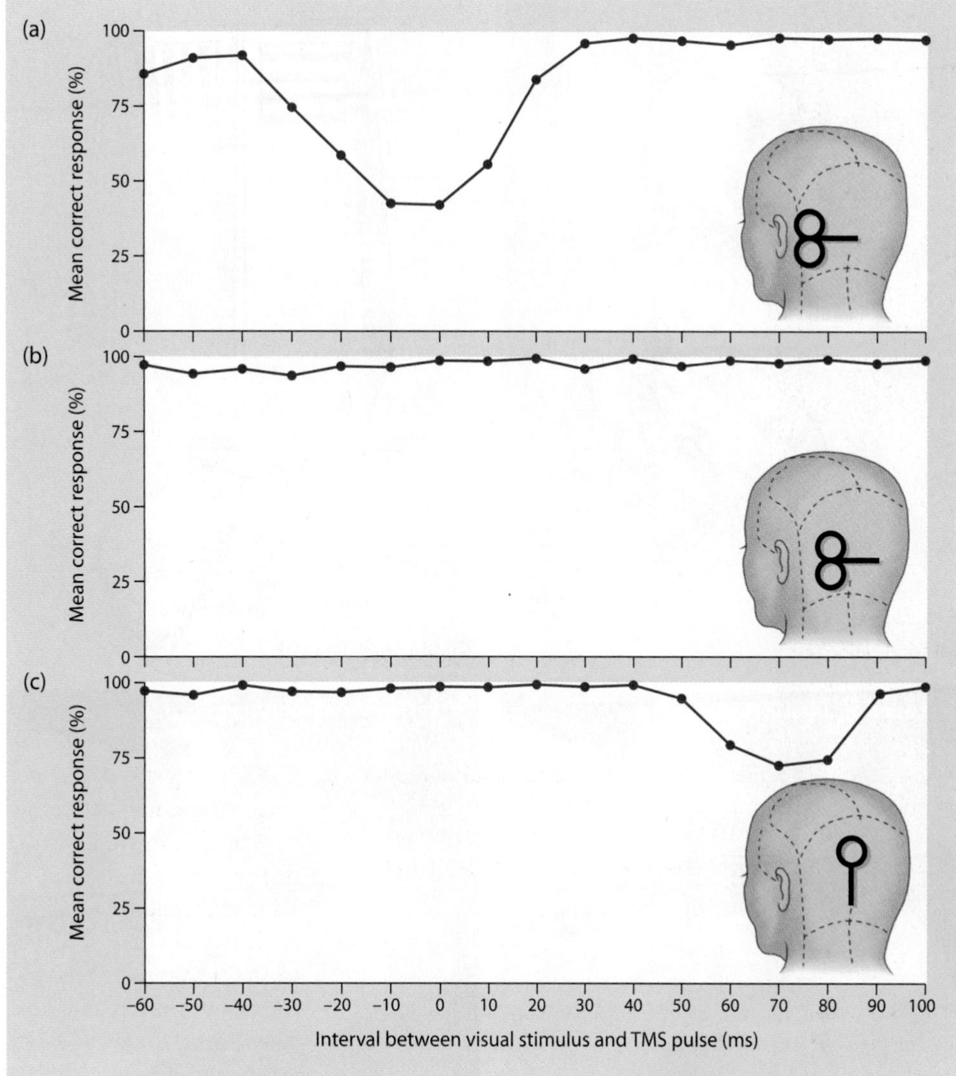

Figure 5.30 Perception of motion during transcranial magnetic stimulation over the visual cortex. Results are rates of accuracy in determining the direction of motion as a function of the time between stimulus onset and the TMS pulses applied over area MT **(a)**, V1 **(c)**, and an extrastriate region between these two **(b)**.

however, there are not only multiple visual pathways within the cortex, but also prominent subcortical visual pathways. These observations have led to some very surprising findings showing that visual capabilities may persist even in the absence of the primary visual cortex.

Cortical and Subcortical Perception in the Hamster Many nongeniculate fibers terminate in the superior colliculus. This structure plays a critical role in producing eye movements. If this midbrain structure becomes atrophied, as with supranuclear palsy, the patient will lose the ability to generate eye movements. It is as if the eyes have become paralyzed. Stimulation studies in primates further demonstrate the role of the superior colliculus in eye movement. When this area is stimulated, the animal's eyes move and the direction of this movement depends on the stimulation site.

Gerald Schneider (1969), working at the Massachusetts Institute of Technology, provided initial evidence of the importance of the colliculus in studies of hamsters. These animals were trained to do the two tasks illustrated in Figure 5.31. In one task, the hamsters were trained to turn their heads in the direction of a sunflower seed held in an experimenter's hand (Figure 5.31a). The task was easy for hamsters because they have a strong propensity to find sunflower seeds and put them in their cheeks.

The second task presented more of a challenge. Here the animals were trained to run down a two-arm maze and enter the door behind which a sunflower seed was hidden (Figure 5.31b). The task required the animals to

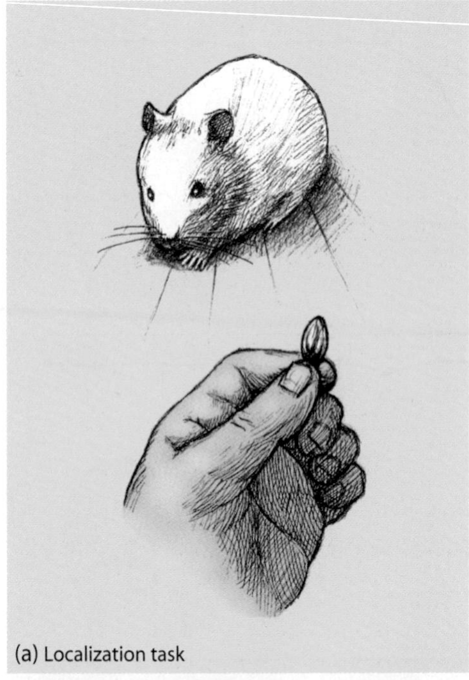

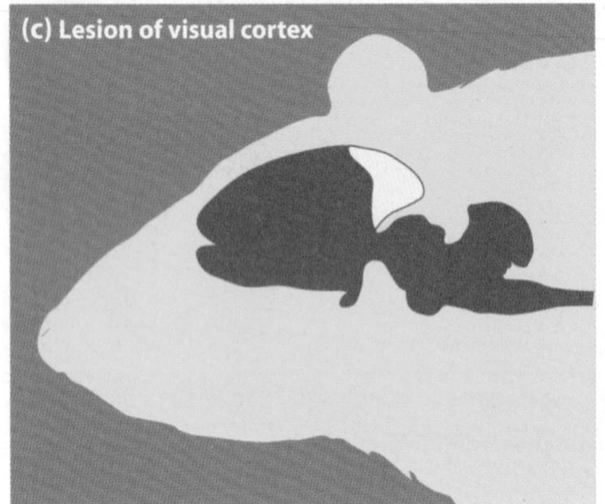

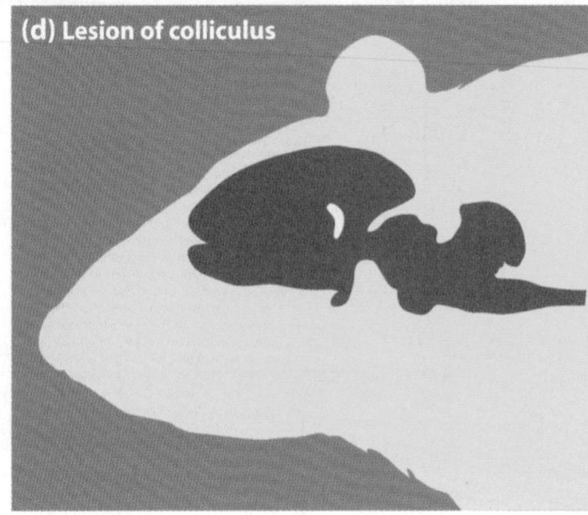

Figure 5.31 Tests to demonstrate the double dissociation between lesions of the superior colliculus and visual cortex. **(a)** In the localization task, hamsters were trained to collect sunflower seeds that were held at various positions in space. **(b)** In the discrimination task, hamsters were trained to run down one of two alleys toward doors that differed in terms of whether the stripes were horizontal or vertical. **(c)** Lesions of the visual cortex selectively impaired performance on the discrimination task. **(d)** In contrast, lesions of the colliculus disrupted performance on the orientation task.

make simple visual discriminations such as to distinguish between black and white doors or between doors with vertical or horizontal stripes. For normal hamsters, the discriminations are not taxing. Within a few trials, they became proficient in selecting the right door in almost all trials.

After training, Schneider divided the hamsters into two experimental groups. One group received bilateral lesions of the visual cortex, including all of areas 17 and 18 (Figure 5.31c). For the second group, the superior colliculus was rendered nonfunctional by the ablation of its input fibers (Figure 5.31d). This strategy was necessary because direct lesions to the colliculus are likely to kill the animals, since the structure borders numerous brainstem nuclei that are essential for life.

The two lesions yielded a double dissociation. Cortical lesions severely impaired the animals' performance on the visual identification tasks. The animals could run down the maze and had sufficient motor capabilities to enter one of the doors, but they could not discriminate black from white or horizontal from vertical stripes. In contrast, the animals with collicular lesions demonstrated no impairment.

The deficits were reversed on the sunflower seed localization task. Animals with cortical lesions were perfect at this task once they had recovered from the surgery. Yet animals with collicular lesions acted as though they were blind. They made no attempt to orient toward the seeds—and not because they were unmotivated or had a motor problem. If the seed brushed against a whisker, the animal rapidly turned toward it and gobbled it up.

These data provide compelling evidence for dissociable functions of the hamsters' superior colliculus and visual cortex. The collicular lesions impaired their ability to orient toward the position of a stimulus, and the cortical lesions disrupted visual acuity. For the hamster, one might think of this double dissociation as reflecting two systems: one devoted to spatial orientation, the other devoted to object identification. As we will see in the next chapter, the ability to distinguish between representing properties of an object and representing the location of the object can also be traced to the cortex itself.

Blindsight: Evidence of Residual Visual Function Following Cortical Blindness Inspired by Schneider's findings that cortically blind hamsters could still locate the sunflower seeds, Lawrence Weiskrantz (1986) at Oxford University tested a hemianopic patient, D.B., to determine whether he could still detect the location of objects presented within his scotoma. Weiskrantz was not satisfied with the usual method of self-report to test for visual function. Rather, he designed a clever behavioral assay for residual function. After presenting a spot of light, the experimenters sounded a tone and D.B. was asked to move his eyes to the location of the stimulus. This task was easy when stimuli were presented in D.B.'s intact right visual field. But when stimuli were presented within the scotoma, the task struck D.B. as utter nonsense. He could not understand how he should know where to move his eyes when he failed to see anything. Nonetheless, the experimenters encouraged D.B. to guess. On control trials, a tone was sounded, requiring D.B. to move his eyes, but it was not preceded by a light. D.B., of course, was not aware of this difference between the control and experimental trials. To him, all of the trials seemed bizarre, in that he was being asked to look at stimuli that he had not been aware of (Figure 5.32).

The results could hardly have been more dramatic. As expected, D.B.'s eye movements on the phantom trials were random. But in the experimental trials, D.B. did much better than chance at localizing the stimuli. When the stimuli were within 20° of the fovea, D.B.'s eye movements were highly correlated with the position of the stimuli.

Weiskrantz named this paradoxical phenomenon **blindsight**. The patient acts and feels as if he is blind yet shows a residual ability to localize stimuli. Although the blindsight phenomenon has been reported in many other patients, the interpretation of the effect remains controversial. It would be premature to conclude that this phenomenon reflects solely processing in subcortical pathways. Information may reach extrastriate visual areas in the cortex, either through direct geniculate projections or via projections from other subcortical structures. Using PET, researchers have shown that extrastriate regions such as human MT can be activated by moving stimuli, even when the ipsilateral striate cortex is completely destroyed (Barbur et al., 1993). Another possibility is that the lesions in the primary visual cortex are incomplete and that blindsight results from residual function in the spared tissue (Fendrich et al., 1992). The representations in the damaged region may be sufficient to guide eye movements, even though they fail to achieve awareness.

DEFICITS IN OTHER ASPECTS OF VISUAL PERCEPTION

The case for specific deficits in other elementary aspects of visual perception is more contentious then for achromatopsia and akinetopsia. A report from the early 20th century (Riddoch, 1917) described a patient to whom the world appeared essentially flat. This depth perception impairment was said to exist despite the patient's ability to perceive variations in color and shading. However, it is not possible to evaluate the selectivity of the deficit, because careful assessments of other visual functions were not performed. In a similar manner, patients who have lost visual acuity after suffering cortical lesions generally have widespread problems in visual perception. Thus, there are no unambiguous reports of selective deficits in form or depth perception.

The visual system is likely to represent form and depth redundantly. Depth perception arises from a multitude of cues. One potent cue, binocular disparity, arises when each eye has a slightly different view of the world. Inputs from the two eyes converge on common cortical neurons. Depth also can be inferred from motion. A moving object will obscure a more distant object or be hidden by a nearer object. In a similar sense, as we move, the change in the retinal image is greater for near objects than for ones far away. All these cues can be used in normal depth perception. This redundancy would be expected to help preserve depth perception even if certain modules were lesioned.

Form perception also stems from multiple sources of information. Indeed, form perception is an essential goal of vision, and all visual processing is devoted to determining what objects are in the visual field and where they are located. Motion perception may be important for a predator anticipating the location of moving prey. Nonetheless, movement also can help to identify prey, to separate it from the background, and

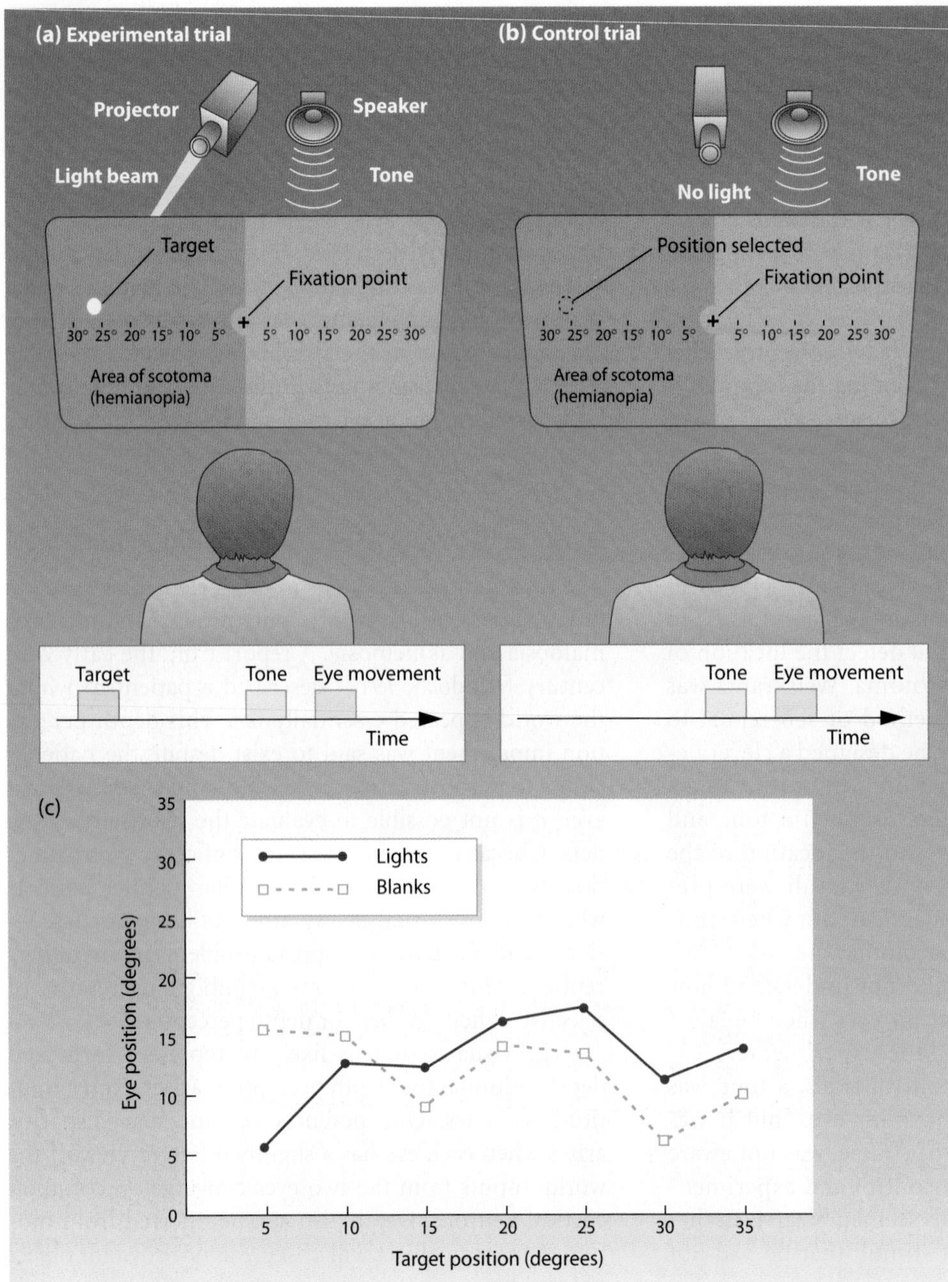

Figure 5.32 Experimental conditions to demonstrate blindsight. **(a)** In the experimental trials, a light beam was projected at one of seven locations within D.B.'s scotoma. Upon hearing a tone, D.B. was required to move his eyes to the target location. **(b)** In the control conditions, a target was selected but not illuminated prior to the tone. To D.B., the two conditions seemed identical, and he had to be encouraged to move his eyes because he reported not seeing anything in either condition. **(c)** Nonetheless, D.B.'s eye movements showed a systematic relationship to the target position in the experimental condition, at least for the targets within 20° of fixation.

to determine if its motion is characteristic of an animal worthy of pursuit. A hungry frog does not want to flick its tongue at every moving object. Rather, the frog can recognize a potential snack by its specific motion—for example, that produced by a fly. Color perception is important only in that it facilitates form perception. Colors do not exist without forms. Color is a potent cue for discriminating an object or part of one from other regions of space. Unlike borders, which can change as a function of illumination conditions—consider the effects of a shadow falling across an object—color remains invariant as long as sufficient light is available for the cones to fire.

Therefore, it is not surprising that we have no clinical reports of patients who are "form-blind." It is reasonable to suppose that the many visual pathways provide multiple inputs to systems devoted to object recognition, one of the primary computational goals of sophisticated perception. In the next chapter we will explore how these higher level aspects of perception operate.

MULTIMODAL PERCEPTION

Each sense provides us with unique information about the world in which we live. Color is a visual experience; pitch is uniquely auditory. However, even though the information that each sense provides is distinct, the resulting representation of the surrounding world is not one of disjointed sensations, but of a unified multisensory experience. Indeed, we are often more accurate or efficient at sensory tasks when information from more than one sense is provided.

How is information from different sensory systems integrated in the brain? What mechanisms allow for sensory summation?

Multimodal Processing in the Brain

The first brain candidates for multisensory interaction are the areas where information from two or more senses converges. Neurophysiological methods are especially useful here: Once the electrode has been placed in the targeted brain region, the animal can be presented with stimuli along different sensory channels. For example, some cells in the superior temporal sulcus (STS) of anesthetized monkeys respond to visual, auditory, and somatosensory stimuli. In one study, recordings were made from over 200 cells in this region. Although 50% of these cells were unimodal (meaning that they responded only to one of the three sensory modalities), over 20% were bimodal or trimodal; the remaining cells did not respond to any of the stimuli (Hikosaka et al., 1988). Multisensory areas are not limited to the temporal lobe. Other brain regions showing similar sensory integration include various regions of the parietal and frontal lobes, as well as the hippocampus.

One particularly well studied multimodal site is the superior colliculus, a subcortical midbrain region. The superior colliculus participates in the control and orienting of movements. It contains orderly topographic maps of the environment in visual, auditory, and even tactile domains. These maps are integrated in the deepest layers of the colliculus (Figure 5.33).

Does the Whole Equal More Than the Sum of the Parts?

Many cells in the superior colliculus combine information from different sensory channels and integrate that information so that the sum of the multisensory input is more useful than information that could be obtained from any single modality alone. Barry Stein at Wake Forest University found that the response of individual cells in the superior colliculus was greater to a combined visual, auditory, and somatosensory stimulus than to any of the three stimuli presented alone. This phenomenon is called **multisensory integration** (N. P. Holmes & Spence, 2005).

Such enhanced responses are most effective when the unimodal stimuli fail to produce a response on their own. In this way, the combination of weak, even subthreshold unimodal signals can be detected and cause the animal to orient toward the stimulus. Integration effects require that the different stimuli be coincident in both space and time. For example, if a visual event is spatially and temporally synchronous with a loud noise, the resulting multisensory response will be enhanced. But if the sound originates from a different location than the light, or is not temporally synchronized with the light, the response of the collicular cell will be lower than if either stimulus were presented alone.

One interesting form of multimodal processing for humans is lip-reading. With practice, people are capable of learning to understand speech simply by watching the movement of the lips and face. Less appreciated but perhaps even more important for normal speech

Figure 5.33 Visual, auditory, and somatosensory spatial representations in the superior colliculus. The overlapping of the common coordinate systems can lead to a representation of multisensory space.

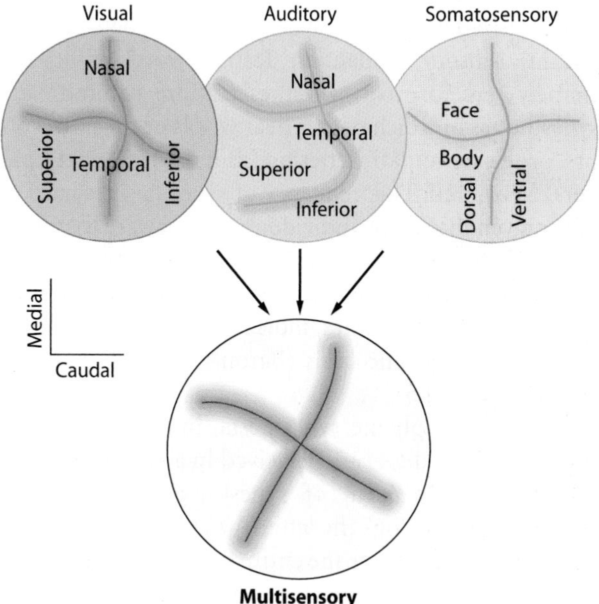

comprehension, visual cues improve our ability to understand speech. When talking with someone in a noisy café, people find it much easier to understand what is being spoken if they look directly at the speaker instead of glancing about the room.

Using fMRI, Gemma Calvert and colleagues (1997), then at Oxford University in England, discovered that silent lip-reading activated areas of the auditory cortex. To explore whether this activity reflected multisensory integration, Calvert constructed speech segments in which the sounds were either matched or mismatched with the movement of the lips. In comparison to a baseline condition in which the sounds were presented alone, a region within the superior temporal sulcus of the left hemisphere became more active when the visual and auditory segments matched and became less active when the segments mismatched. Thus, she concluded that the left STS integrates information from the two sensory channels (visual and auditory), presumably using the combined inputs to derive a stronger representation of the stimulus.

Synesthesia

J.W. experiences the world differently than most people. He tastes words. The word *exactly*, for example, tastes like yogurt; and the word *accept* tastes like eggs. Most conversations are pleasant tasting, but when J.W. is tending bar, he cringes whenever Derek, a frequent customer, shows up. For J.W. the word *Derek* tastes of earwax!

This phenomenon, in which the senses are mixed, is known as **synesthesia**, from the Greek *syn-* ("union" or "together") and *aesthesis* ("sensation"). Synesthesia is characterized by an idiosyncratic union between (or within) sensory modalities. Tasting words is an extremely rare form of synesthesia. More common are synesthesias in which people hear words or music as colors, or see achromatic lettering (as in books or newspapers) as colored. The frequency of synesthesia is hard to know given that many individuals are unaware that their multisensory percepts are odd: Estimates range from as rare as one in 2,000 to as high as one in 200. Synesthesia tends to recur in families, indicating that at least some forms have a genetic basis (Baron-Cohen et al., 1996; Smilek et al., 2005).

Colored-grapheme synesthesia, in which black or white letters or digits are perceived in assorted colors is the best-studied form of synesthesia. A synesthete might report "seeing" the letter *A* as red, the letter *B* as yellow, and so forth for the entire set of characters, as in the example shown in Figure 5.34. The appearance of

Figure 5.34 Artistic rendition of the color–letter and color–number associations for one individual with synesthesia.

color is a feature of many forms of synesthesia. In colored hearing, colors are experienced for spoken words or for sounds like musical notes. Colored touch and colored smell have also been reported. Much less common are synesthetic experiences that involve other senses. J.W. experiences taste with words; other rare cases have been reported in which touching an object induces specific tastes.

The associations are idiosyncratic for each synesthete. One person might see the letter *B* as red, another as green. Although the synesthetic associations are not consistent across individuals, they are consistent over time for an individual. A synesthete who reports the letter *B* when tested the first time in the lab will have the same percept if retested a few months later.

The sensory stimulus that triggers the synesthetic experience is referred to as the *inducer*, and the resultant synesthetic response is the *concurrent*. In colored-grapheme synesthesia, the letter is the inducer and the color the concurrent. Inducers may be real, such as an object, a printed letter, or a musical note. They can also be imagined. Just the thought of a letter or a musical note may elicit the associated concurrent. Inducers, either real or imagined, are reported as being seen either in the synesthete's "mind's eye" or projected out to a specific location in visual space. Sometimes the concurrents for different inducers are arranged in a distinct spatial pattern (Figure 5.35).

Given that synesthesia is such a personal experience, researchers have had to come up with clever methods to verify and explore this unique phenomenon. One approach with colored-grapheme synesthesia is to create modified versions of the Stroop task. As described in Chapter 4, the Stroop task requires a person to name the color of written words. For instance, if the word *green* is written in red ink, the subject is supposed to say "red." In the synesthetic variant of the Stroop task with a colored-grapheme synesthete, the stimuli are letters and the key manipulation is whether the colors of

Figure 5.35 H.B., a female subject with colored-grapheme synesthesia, sees her percepts in a specific spatial location in egocentric space. This image is an artistic representation of her percepts and was verified by H.B. to be a good likeness of her synesthetic experience.

the letters are congruent or incongruent to the individual's synesthetic palette. For the example in Figure 5.34, when the letter A is presented in red, the physical color and synesthetic color are congruent. However, if the A is presented in green, the physical and concurrent colors are incongruent. Synesthetes are faster to name the colors of the letters when the physical color matches the concurrent colors for the particular letter (Mattingley et al., 2001). People without synesthesia, of course, do not show this effect. To them, any color–letter pairing is equally acceptable.

It is interesting to consider the stage of processing at which the synesthetic experience emerges. Look at the array of numbers shown in Figure 5.36a. You have to scan the image for some time to see that the 2s, embedded among the 5s, form a rectangle. But suppose you have synesthesia and the color associated with 2 is different from that associated with 5. For these individuals, the perception of the square is immediate (as it is in Figure 5.36b for nonsynesthetes). Effects like this led Vilayanur Ramachandran of the University of California, San Diego, to argue that the inducer and the concurrent are associated at an early stage in perceptual processing (Ramachandran & Hubbard, 2001a, 2003).

Other researchers, however, propose that synesthesia arises at later processing stages. Jason Mattingley and his colleagues (Mattingley et al., 2001) at the University of Melbourne used a priming version of the synesthetic Stroop task to test this hypothesis. On each trial, the participant saw a letter followed by a color patch. The key question was this: In people with synesthesia, would seeing the letter interfere with naming the color of the color patch? For example, if the letter *A* were perceived as red, would it take longer to name a subsequent color patch that was blue? The answer was yes. When the letter was presented for 500 ms, allowing the letter to be clearly perceived, the interference effect was observed. However, when the exposure duration was reduced to 56 ms, a duration at which conscious perception was precluded, the interference effect was eliminated. Importantly, in a control task the same primes presented for the subthreshold level of 56 ms showed interference for letter naming, indicating that the letters were in fact processed. The results of this experiment suggest that the synesthetic concurrent is not associated with the inducer until the inducer has been processed *consciously.*

Further support that synesthesia arises at a late processing stage comes from the fact that attention can

Figure 5.36 When viewing a stimulus such as that shown in **(a)**, a color-letter synesthete reported seeing **(b)**. This phenomenon suggests that synesthesia arises at an early stage of processing, with the color information being used to define the shape.

(a)

(b)

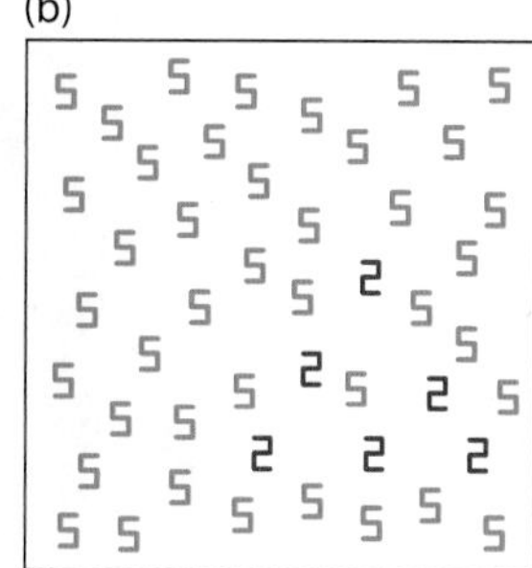

modulate the synesthetic experience. When colored-grapheme synesthetes are presented with a large letter (say, *B*) made up of different small letters (say, *A*s) (Figure 5.37), they report that the perceived color changes as attention shifts between the global form (*B*) and the local forms (*A*s). Moreover, colored-grapheme synesthetes typically experience the same color across a wide range of print forms. If *B* is seen as green, this will hold for all *B*s written in all type fonts or even if the lowercase version of the letter is used. Thus, the synesthetic bond appears to link colors to abstract representations rather than to specific shapes.

Brain-imaging studies indicate that the multisensory experience of synesthesia arises and is manifest at various stages along the visual pathway. Jeffrey Gray at King's College in London performed an fMRI study with a group of individuals who had colored-hearing synesthesia (Nunn et al., 2002). When listening to words, these individuals reported seeing specific colors; when listening to tones, they had no visual experience. Compared to control participants, the synesthetes showed increased activation in V4, similar to what we have seen in other studies of illusory color perception and in the STS, one of the brain regions associated with multimodal perception. Other studies have shown recruitment of the left medial lingual gyrus (a higher color-processing area previously implicated in color knowledge) in synesthetes during the perception of colored-grapheme synesthesia (Rich et al., 2006).

Figure 5.37 This image can be seen as either the global form (large *B*) or several local forms (small *A*s). Many synesthetes report that their synesthetic percepts (the color concurrents) change when their attention shifts between the global and local levels, indicating that the synesthetic experience arises at higher stages of processing.

Michael Esterman and his colleagues (2006) at the University of California, Berkeley, used transcranial magnetic stimulation to test the role of different neural regions in the induction of synesthesia. They reasoned that if the concurrent colors were bound to their inducers by an attentional process (see Chapter 12), then a virtual lesion of this process might reduce the synesthetic experience. Before TMS, the participants were given a synesthetic Stroop test, and as found previously, the synesthetes were slower to respond when the physical color of the letter did not match their own concurrent. Stimulating the right posterior parietal cortex with 1-Hz repetitive TMS abolished the interference effect for about 5 minutes. A similar effect was not found when the TMS was targeted to left parietal cortex or primary visual cortex. These results indicate that, even though the concurrent percepts are well established in synesthetes, their association with the inducers can be transiently disrupted by stimulation over neural regions thought to play a role in multidimensional feature integration.

Perceptual Reorganization

As we have just seen, people with synesthesia provide a dramatic example of how the brain is able to link information between distinct sensory systems. The extent of the connectivity between sensory systems is also revealed by studies on people who are deprived of input from one of their senses. When a person is blind, what happens to those regions of the brain that are usually used for visual perception? Might this unused neural tissue be able to reorganize to process other information? Is the situation for individuals who have been blind since birth different from that of individuals who became blind after having had vision?

The results of a PET study suggest a remarkable degree of functional reorganization, or what neuroscientists refer to as *cortical plasticity* (Sadato et al., 1996). The subjects for this study included people with normal vision and people who were congenitally blind—that is, blind from birth. The subjects were scanned under two experimental conditions. In one condition the subjects were simply required to sweep their fingers back and forth over a rough surface covered with dots. In the second condition they were given tactile discrimination tasks such as deciding whether two grooves in the surface were the same or different. Blood flow in the visual cortex during each of these tasks was compared to that during a rest condition in which the subjects were scanned while keeping their hands still.

Amazingly, changes in activation in the visual cortex were in opposite directions for the two groups of subjects. For the sighted subjects, a significant drop in activation was found in the primary visual cortex during the tactile discrimination tasks. Analogous decreases in the auditory or somatosensory cortex occurred during visual tasks given to normal subjects; therefore, as attention was directed to one modality, activation (as measured by blood flow) decreased in other sensory systems. In contrast, in blind subjects the activation in the primary visual cortex increased—but only during discrimination tasks, and not when they swept their fingers over the surface without having to actively use tactile information. Interestingly, a second group of subjects who had become blind early in childhood (before their fifth year) also showed the same recruitment of visual cortex when performing the tactile discrimination task.

A second experiment explored the same issue but used a task that is of great practical value to the blind: reading Braille. The subjects explored strings of eight Braille letters and had to decide whether the strings formed a word. In accord with the results of the first study, activation of the primary and secondary visual cortex increased during Braille reading in comparison with the rest state, but only in the blind subjects.

Of course the term *visual cortex* is a misnomer with blind individuals. These results indicate that tissue that, during normal development, will become sensitive to visual inputs can be exploited in a radically different manner when the environmental context is changed—for example, when all visual input is lost. At present, it is unclear how tactile information ends up activating neurons in the visual cortex of blind people. One possibility is that somatosensory projections to thalamic relays spread into the nearby lateral geniculate nucleus, exploiting the geniculostriate pathway. This hypothesis is unlikely, since the activation changes in the blind subjects' visual cortices were bilateral. Somatosensory inputs to the thalamus are strictly lateralized. Because the subjects performed the tactile tasks with the right hand, the blood flow changes should have been restricted to the left hemisphere. A more viable hypothesis is that a massive reorganization of corticocortical connections follows peripheral blindness. The sensory-deprived visual cortex is taken over, perhaps through back-projections originating in polymodal association cortical areas.

Although this study provides a dramatic demonstration of cortical plasticity, the results also suggest a neurobiological mechanism for the greater nonvisual perceptual acuity exhibited by blind people. Indeed, Louis Braille's motivation to develop his tactile reading system was spurred by his belief that vision loss was offset by heightened sensitivity in the fingertips. One account of this compensation focuses on nonperceptual mechanisms. Though the sensory representation of somatosensory information is similar for blind and sighted subjects, the former group is not distracted by vision (or visual imagery). If the focus of attention is narrowed, somatosensory information can be used more efficiently. The imaging results reviewed here, though, suggest a more perceptual account. Sensitivity increases because more cortical tissue is devoted to representing nonvisual information.

SUMMARY

The five basic sensory systems of audition, olfaction, gestation, somatosensation, and vision allow us to interpret the environment. Each sense involves unique pathways and processes to translate external stimuli into neural signals that are interpreted by the brain. Within each sense, specialized sensory mechanisms have evolved to solve computational problems to facilitate and enhance our perceptual capabilities. As shown in neuroimaging and neuropsychological studies, specialization is found across the sensory cortices of the brain; thus, people may retain the ability to see, even in the absence of cortical mechanisms for color or motion perception. In extreme situations of sensory deprivation, the cortical systems for perception may become radically reorganized. Even in people with intact sensory systems, the five senses do not work in isolation, but rather work in concert to construct a rich interpretation of the world. It is this integration that underlies much of human cognition and allows us to survive, and indeed thrive, in a multisensory world.

KEY TERMS

achromatopsia
akinetopsia
area MT
area V4
blindsight
chemical senses
cochlear nucleus
corpuscle
cortical visual areas
extrastriate visual areas
glomeruli
hemianopia
inferior colliculus
interaural time
lateral geniculate nucleus (LGN)
medial geniculate nucleus (MGN)
multisensory integration
nociceptors
odorant
photoreceptors
primary auditory cortex (A1)
primary gustatory cortex
primary olfactory cortex
primary somatosensory cortex (S1)
primary visual cortex (V1)
proprioception
retina
scotoma
secondary somatosensory cortex (S2)
superior colliculus
synesthesia
tastant
thalamus

TAKE-HOME MESSAGES

General

- Much of the brain is involved in the representation of information acquired from the different sensory receptors.

Audition

- Signal transduction from sound wave to neuronal signal begins at the eardrums. Signals are processed in the hair cells and basilar membrane of the cochlea, and the cochlea sends its information in the form of neuronal signals to the inferior colliculus and the cochlear nucleus. Information then travels to the medial geniculate nucleus of the thalamus and on to the primary auditory cortex.
- Sound localization is aided by the processing of differences in interaural time and interaural sound intensity, which are each coded separately in the brain.

Olfaction

- Signal transduction from odorant to neuronal signal begins when the odorant attaches to an odor receptor in the olfactory epithelium. The signal is then sent to the olfactory bulb through the olfactory nerve, which synapses on the primary olfactory cortex. Signals are also relayed to the orbitofrontal cortex, a secondary olfactory processing area.
- The primary olfactory cortex is important for detecting a change in external odor, and secondary olfactory cortex is important for identifying the smell itself.
- Similar to the importance of sampling sound from two ears, we use our two nostrils to obtain different olfactory samples, varying the rate of air flow through each nostril and thus altering the rate of absorption.
- The anatomical proximity and neural interactions between olfactory cortex and the limbic system likely account for why smells can trigger vivid memories.
- The olfactory pathway is the only sensory pathway that does not send information to the thalamus.

Gustation

- Gustation and olfaction are known together as the chemical senses because the initial response is to molecules (chemicals) in the environment.
- The five basic tastes are salty, sour, bitter, sweet, and umami. The perception of more complex tastes arises from the complex cortical processing of these individual tastes in areas of the brain such as the secondary gustatory cortex in the orbitofrontal region.
- Orbitofrontal cortex is also involved in processing the reward value of food and the resulting motivation to eat food.

Somatosensation

- Corpuscles located in the skin respond to somatosensory information such as touch, pressure, and temperature.
- Nociceptors (free nerve endings) respond to pain information.
- Nerve cells at the junctions of muscles and tendons provide proprioceptive information.
- Primary somatosensory cortex (S1) contains a homunculus of the body, with the more sensitive regions encompassing relatively larger areas of cortex.

- Bilateral secondary somatosensory cortex (S2) receives sensory information from both sides of the body, allowing for cross talk of sensory information.

Vision

- Photoreceptors (rods and cones) in the retina translate light into neural signals.
- The three types of cones are sensitive to different regions of the visible spectrum and are used for color perception; rods are very sensitive even under low levels of illumination but are not color sensitive.
- The fovea, at the center of the retina, is densely packed with cones; the periphery of the retina contains mostly rods.
- Light hits the retina and travels within the retina from rod or cone to bipolar cell to ganglion cell. The optic nerve is formed from the axons of the ganglion cells, some of which decussate at the optic chiasm. Axons in the optic nerve synapse on the LGN and from the LGN become the optic radiations that are sent to V1. Note that 10% of the fibers from the retina innervate non-LGN subcortical structures, including the pulvinar and superior colliculus.
- Visual cortex is made up of many distinct regions, which carry out specialized processing functions. For instance, cells in area V4 are sensitive to color information and cells in V5 are sensitive to motion information.
- Achromatopsia, the inability to perceive color results from lesions to areas in and around human V4. However, these regions do not just represent color, but also are important for shape perception. Color is one attribute that facilitates the perception of shape.
- Akinetopsia, the inability to process motion, results from lesions to area V5 (human MT).
- Superior colliculus lesions impair the ability of an animal to orient toward the position of a stimulus (which is important for spatial orientation); visual cortex lesions impair visual acuity (which is important for object identification).
- In some cases, patients with lesions of the visual cortex exhibit blindsight, the ability to locate the position of a stimulus even when they are unaware of its presence. Blindsight may occur because the information reaching the superior colliculus is sufficient to indicate position or extrastriate regions are activated without input from the primary visual cortex.

Multimodal Perception

- Some areas of the brain, such as the superior colliculus and superior temporal sulci, process information from more than one sensory modality, integrating the multimodal information to increase the sensitivity and accuracy of perception.
- When multisensory information is presented coincidently in time and space, the multisensory neural response is enhanced. The reverse is also true; that is, when multisensory information is not presented coincidently in time and space, the multisensory neural response is depressed.

Synesthesia

- People with synesthesia experience a mixing of the senses, like colored hearing, colored graphemes, or colored taste.
- The stimulus that triggers synesthesia is the inducer, and the synesthetic response is the concurrent.
- There is some debate about where along the processing stream synesthesia is processed—either early (preconsciously) or late (postconsciously).

Perceptual Reorganization

- Following sensory deprivation, the function of sensory regions of the cortex may become reorganized, or exhibit what is called plasticity. For instance, in blind individuals, areas of the brain that are usually involved in visual function may become part of the somatosensory cortex.

THOUGHT QUESTIONS

1. Imagine watching a short video segment in which a large, purple dinosaur appears briefly in the left visual field. Trace the flow of information about this stimulus and its separate features (color, shape, luminance, motion, position) from the eye through the secondary visual areas.
2. Compare and contrast the functional organization of the visual and auditory systems. What are the computational problems that each system must solve, and how are these solutions achieved in the nervous system?
3. A person arrives at the hospital in a confused state and appears to have some impairment in visual perception. As the attending neurologist, you suspect that the person has had a stroke. How would you go about examining the patient to determine the level in the visual pathways at which the damage has occurred? Emphasize the behavioral tests you would

administer, but feel free to make predictions about what you expect to see on MRI scans.

4. Define the physiological concepts of receptive field and visual area. How is the receptive field of a cell established? How are the boundaries between visual areas identified? Can either receptive fields or visual areas be studied noninvasively in humans?
5. This chapter has focused mainly on salient visual properties such as color, shape, and motion. In looking around the environment, do these properties seem to reflect the most important cues for a highly skilled visual creature? What other sources of information might an adaptive visual system exploit?

SUGGESTED READING

CHALUPA, L. M., & WARNER, J. S. (Eds.). (2004). *The visual neurosciences.* Cambridge, MA: MIT Press.

CRONER, L. J., & ALBRIGHT, T. D. (1999). Seeing the big picture: Integration of image cues in the primate visual system. *Neuron, 24,* 777–789.

LIVINGSTONE, M., & HUBEL, D. (1988). Segregation of form, color, movement, and depth: Anatomy, physiology, and perception. *Science, 240,* 740–749.

PALMER, S. E. (1999). *Vision science: Photons to phenomenology.* Cambridge, MA: MIT Press.

ZEKI, S. (1993). *A vision of the brain.* Oxford, England: Blackwell.

6

Object Recognition

Patient G.S. had a stroke while still in his 30s. Though the stroke was initially life threatening, G.S. eventually recovered most of his cognitive functions. On examination a few years after the stroke occurred, G.S.'s sensory abilities were intact. Language function was normal and there were no problems in coordination, yet G.S. had severe problems recognizing objects. When shown household objects such as a candle or a salad bowl, he was unable to name them. His deficits were even more marked when he viewed photographs of the objects.

G.S.'s problems did not seem to result from a loss of visual acuity. When presented with two lines, he had no difficulty judging which was longer. Indeed, although he could not name the household objects, he could describe their color and general shape without hesitation. The candle was long, thin, and pink; the salad bowl, curved and brown. G.S.'s deficit also did not reflect an inability to retrieve verbal labels of objects, as was demonstrated in two ways: First, if the experimenter asked G.S. the name of a round, wooden object in which lettuce, tomatoes, and cucumbers are mixed, he would respond "salad bowl"; second, G.S. could identify objects by using other senses, such as touch or smell. When presented with a candle, he reported that it was a "long object." Upon touching it, he labeled it a "crayon," but after smelling it, he corrected himself and responded "candle." Thus, G.S.'s deficit was modality specific.

Failures of perception can happen even when processes such as the analysis of color, shape, and motion are intact. Such disorders are referred to as **agnosia**. The label was coined by Sigmund Freud, derived from the Greek *a-* ("without") and *gnosis* ("knowledge"). To be *agnosic* means to experience a failure of knowledge, or recognition. When the disorder is limited to the visual modality, as with G.S., the syndrome is referred to as **visual agnosia**.

As with many neuropsychological labels, the term *visual agnosia* has been applied to a number of distinct disorders. As we will discover in this chapter, by focusing on subtypes of agnosia, cognitive neuroscientists have been able to develop detailed models of the processes involved in object recognition. In some patients, the problem is one of developing a coherent percept; in others, the agnosia reflects an inability to access knowledge of the concept of perceived objects and use this knowledge to identify them. G.S.'s problem seems to be more closely related to this latter type of agnosia. However, despite his relatively uniform difficulty in identifying visually presented objects, other aspects of his performance indicated that, in some situations, G.S. has access to this knowledge, even if it is insufficient for him to come up with the name of the object.

Consider what happened when G.S. was shown a picture of a combination lock. At first he failed to respond. Then he noted the round shape. When prompted by experimenters to provide some more details or make a guess, G.S. reported that the picture was of a telephone. Indeed, he remained adamant, insisting that the picture was of a telephone, even after the experimenter emphatically informed him that the picture did not contain a telephone. G.S.'s choice of a telephone was not random. He had perceived the numeric markings around the lock's circumference, a feature associated with many telephones in the 20th century.

G.S.'s actions also indicated that his knowledge of the stimulus went beyond his erroneous report of a telephone. While viewing the picture, he kept twirling his fingers, pantomiming the actions of opening a combination lock (Figure 6.1). When asked about this, G.S. reported that it was a nervous habit, something to do to keep his hands busy so that he would not reach out and touch the picture. Finally, the experimenter asked G.S. if the depicted object was a telephone, lock, or clock. By this time, G.S. was convinced from the experimenter's responses that the picture was not of a telephone. After a moment's hesitation, he responded "clock." And then, after a look at his fingers, he proudly announced, "It's a lock, a combination lock." G.S. had truly let his fingers do the talking!

Figure 6.1 Test demonstrating visual agnosia. When asked to name the depicted object, G.S. failed to come up with the correct answer, "combination lock," but rather continued to insist that the object was a telephone. The similar components of a lock and a traditional rotary telephone—the numbers and dial—indicate that some information is being processed. In addition, the patient's hands mimed the actions that would be required to open a combination lock.

At a fundamental level, the case of patient G.S. forces us to be precise when we use terms like *perceive* or *recognize*. Perception and recognition do not appear to be single, distinct phenomena but are manifest in many guises. This problem is one of the core issues in cognitive neuroscience. Not only will this issue be central in this chapter, but it will reappear when we turn to problems of memory, attention, and consciousness in Chapters 8 and 12.

With analytic perception, visual and auditory systems use a divide-and-conquer strategy. Features like color and motion are processed along distinct neural pathways. But perception requires more than simply perceiving the features of objects. When gazing at the coastline of San Francisco (Figure 6.2), we do not have the impression of blurs of color floating among a sea of various shapes. We perceive unified objects: the deep-blue water of the bay, the peaked towers of the Golden Gate Bridge, the silver skyscrapers, and the fog lingering over the city.

What's more, perceptual capabilities are enormously flexible and robust. The city vista looks the same whether

Figure 6.2 Our view of the world depends on our vantage point. These two photographs are taken of the same scene, but from two different positions and under two different conditions. Each vantage point reveals new views of the scene, including objects that were obscured from the other vantage point. Moreover, the colors change, depending on the time of day and weather. Despite this variability, we easily recognize that both of the photographs are of San Francisco and the Golden Gate Bridge.

we view it with both eyes or with only the left or the right eye. A change in position may reveal Golden Gate Park in the distance, but we readily recognize that we are looking at the same city. The percept remains stable even if we stand on our head. The retinal image may be inverted, but we readily attribute this change to our inverted viewing position. We do not see the world as upside down.

The product of perception is intimately interwoven with memory. Object recognition is more than linking features to form a coherent whole. That whole triggers memories. Those of us who have spent many hours roaming the hilly streets of San Francisco recognize that the pictures in Figure 6.2 were taken from the Marin headlands to the north of the city. Even if we have never been to San Francisco, there is an interplay of perception and memory. For the traveler arriving from Australia, the first view of San Francisco is likely to evoke comparisons to Sydney; for the traveler from Kansas, the vista may be so unusual that she recognizes it as such: a place unlike any other she has seen. How do shape, form, color, and other low-level visual inputs become the high-level, coherent, memory-invoking percepts of everyday life? For the answer, we turn to a discussion of the segregated functions of the visual cortex.

TWO CORTICAL PATHWAYS FOR VISUAL PERCEPTION

The pathways carrying visual information from the retina to the first few synapses in the cortex clearly segregate into multiple processing streams. Do these processing streams share any general properties? Or does information converge in a higher order region that supports object perception? One hypothesis is inspired by the fact that output from the occipital lobe is contained primarily in two major fiber bundles, or *fasciculi*. As Figure 6.3 shows, the inferior longitudinal fasciculus follows a ventral route into the temporal lobe. The superior longitudinal fasciculus takes a more dorsal path, with most of its terminations in the posterior regions of the parietal lobe.

Two researchers at the National Institutes of Health in Washington DC, Leslie Ungerleider and Mortimer Mishkin (1982), proposed that processing along these two pathways is designed to extract fundamentally different types of information. The **ventral**, or **occipitotemporal, pathway** is specialized for object perception and recognition, for determining *what* we're looking at. The **dorsal**, or **occipitoparietal, pathway** is specialized for spatial perception, for determining *where* an object is, and for analyzing the spatial configuration between different objects in a scene. What and where are the two basic questions to be answered in visual perception. Not only must we recognize what we're looking at, but also we need to know where it is in order to respond appropriately.

The initial motivation for the what–where dissociation of the ventral and dorsal pathways came from lesion studies with monkeys. Animals with lesions to the temporal lobe have great difficulty discriminating between different shapes—a "what" discrimination (Pohl, 1973). For example, they make many errors when learning that one object, such as a cylinder, is associated with a food reward when paired with another object (e.g., a cube). Interestingly, these same animals have no trouble determining where an object is in relation to other objects; this second ability depends on a "where" computation. The opposite is true for animals with parietal lobe lesions that disrupt the dorsal stream. These animals have trouble discriminating where an object is in relation to other objects ("where") but do not have trouble discriminating between two similar objects ("what").

Bear in mind that deficits in these experiments are apparent only in the presence of bilateral lesions, especially lesions in the temporal lobe. One explanation is that, although information is segregated within each hemisphere, the monkeys scan the entire visual field; thus, stimuli fall

Figure 6.3 The "what" and "where" pathways for object recognition. The outputs from the primary visual cortex (V1) follow two general pathways: The superior longitudinal fasciculus includes axons terminating in the posterior parietal cortex, a region associated with identifying the location of the object ("where"). The inferior longitudinal fasciculus contains axons terminating in the inferotemporal cortex, a region implicated in object recognition ("what").

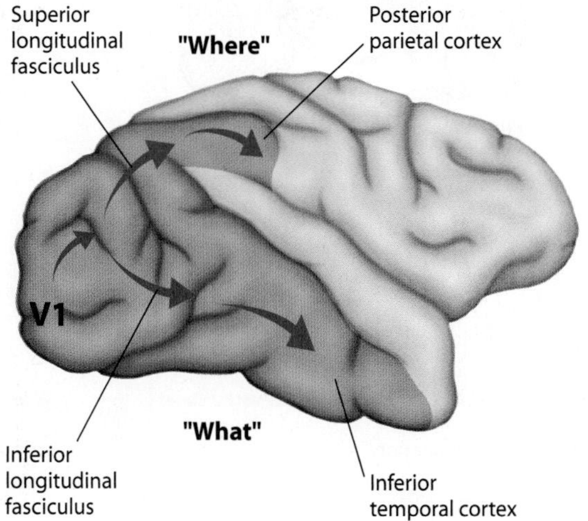

within the left and right visual fields. Alternatively, cells in the temporal cortex can respond to stimuli in either visual field, as long as those stimuli are not presented far off in the periphery. Bilateral responsiveness happens because visual areas in the temporal lobe are innervated not only by ipsilateral projections from upstream visual areas such as V2 and V4, but also by callosal projections from the contralateral hemisphere.

Experiments with combined lesions provide convincing evidence that the "what" pathway involves bilateral inputs. For example, animals were tested with an object discrimination task after lesions were created in the right striate cortex and left inferotemporal cortex. The striate lesions rendered the animals cortically blind to any stimuli falling within the left visual field. Thus, the pathway providing intrahemispheric input to the right temporal lobe was silenced. With a lesioned left temporal lobe, these animals are deprived of all temporal lobe function if all the connections are within the same hemisphere. But these combined lesions produced little or no deficit in performance. When the callosal fibers were cut, though, the animals' performance immediately fell to chance (Figure 6.4a). After combined right striate–left temporal lobe lesions were made, the intact right temporal lobe processed information received from the contralateral left striate cortex. This input was blocked after the callosal excision.

Combined lesions of the dorsal pathway revealed a slightly different situation (Figure 6.4b). Unilateral

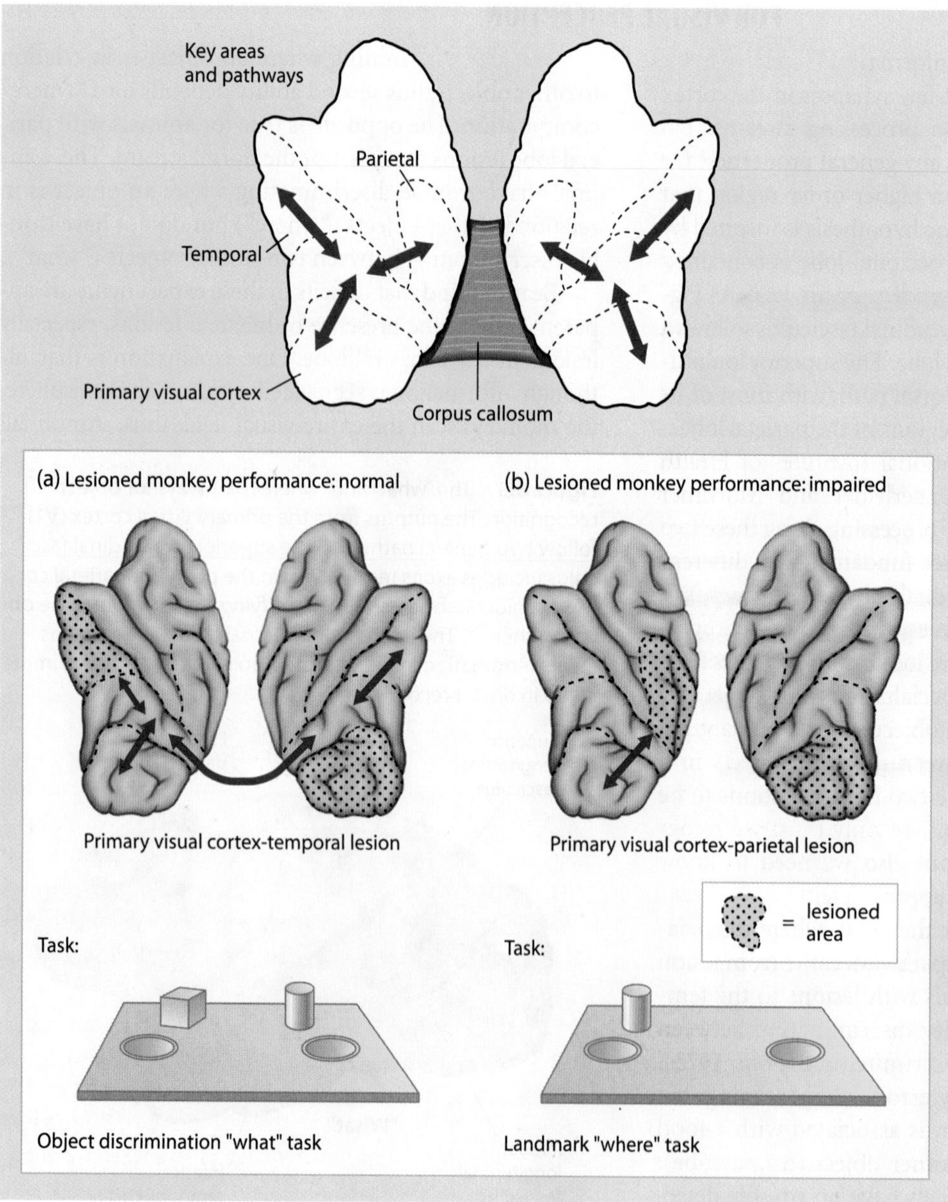

Figure 6.4 Combined-lesion studies indicated that connections via the corpus callosum are more important for transmitting information related to "what" processing. **(a)** Monkeys were given a primary visual cortex lesion on one side and a temporal lobe lesion on the other side. If each hemisphere were receiving input only from the ipsilateral visual cortex, then we would expect the animal to demonstrate severe impairment on the object discrimination task (in which the monkey must discriminate among object shapes to receive a reward) because the intact temporal lobe would be deprived of all input. However, animals with this combination of lesions showed little deficit. The importance of callosal fibers for interhemispheric "what" processing is confirmed by the fact that cutting the corpus callosum in these animals severely disrupted performance. **(b)** A combined parietal lobe and visual cortex lesion led to a severe deficit on the landmark task (in which the monkey must determine object location to receive a reward), suggesting that "where" processing is primarily intrahemispheric.

parietal lobe lesions produced only mild deficits in the landmark reversal task. When these lesions were followed by a second lesion in the contralateral striate cortex, however, performance was greatly disrupted. The animals relearned the task but needed extensive training. Sectioning the corpus callosum disrupted performance again, yet the deficit was not as marked as after striate lesions were made. Thus, although callosal fibers are essential for discriminating objects in the setting of opposite-side striate and temporal lobe lesions, these fibers are less important in transmitting location information from the contralateral hemisphere—results that agree with physiological studies showing that the majority of parietal lobe neurons have unilateral receptive fields. Processing in the "where" pathway appears to be more segregated within each hemisphere.

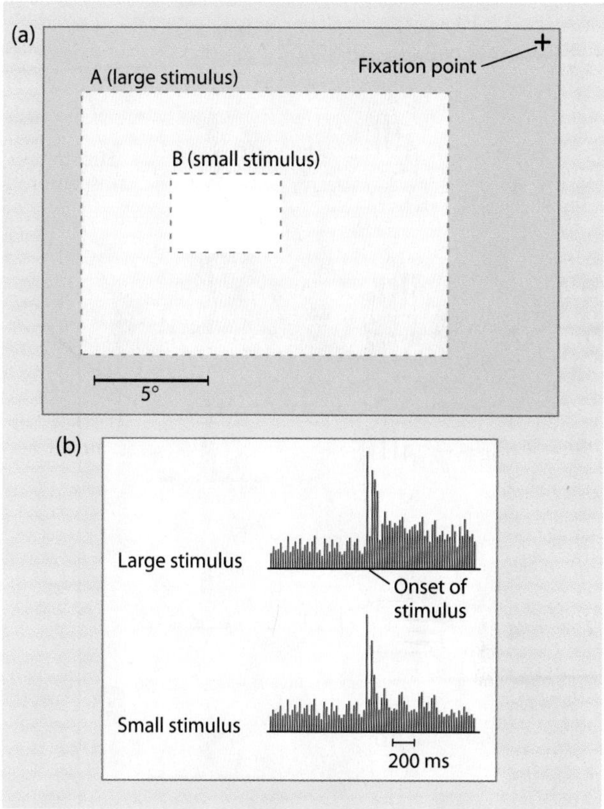

Figure 6.5 Single-cell recordings from a neuron in the posterior parietal cortex of the monkey. The receptive field of the cell was centered in the lower quadrant of the left visual field. **(a)** While fixating, the animal was presented with either a large (A) or a small (B) stimulus. **(b)** The cell responds to both stimuli, although the magnitude of activity is correlated with the size of the stimulus.

Representational Differences Between the Dorsal and Ventral Pathways

The physiological properties of neurons within the temporal and parietal lobes are quite distinct. Neurons in both lobes have large receptive fields. Neurons in the parietal lobe, however, are interesting because they can respond in a nonselective way (Robinson et al., 1978). For example, a parietal neuron recorded in an awake monkey might be activated when a stimulus such as a spot of light is restricted to a small region of space or when the stimulus is a large object that encompasses much of the hemifield (Figure 6.5). In addition, many parietal neurons are responsive to stimuli presented in the more eccentric parts of the visual field. Although 40% of these neurons have receptive fields near the central region of vision (the fovea), the remaining cells have receptive fields that exclude the foveal region.

These eccentrically tuned cells are ideally suited for detecting the presence of a stimulus, especially one that has just entered the field of view. Remember that, in examining subcortical vision, we suggested a similar role for the superior colliculus. Chapter 12 reviews the important role of the superior colliculus in visual attention.

The response of neurons in the temporal lobe is quite different (Ito et al., 1995). The receptive fields for these neurons always encompass the fovea, and the majority of these neurons can be activated by a stimulus that falls within either the left or the right visual field. The disproportionate representation of central vision appears to be ideal for a system devoted to object recognition. We usually look directly at things we wish to identify, thereby taking advantage of the greater acuity of foveal vision.

Cells within the visual areas of the temporal lobe have a diverse pattern of selectivity. Robert Desimone (1991) studied these cells in detail. One study employed a wide range of stimuli. Some stimuli were simple: edges or bars at orientations that varied in color or brightness. Others were complex, including photographs and three-dimensional models of objects like a human head, hand, apple, flower, and snake. Of the 151 cells sampled, 110 consistently responded to at least one of the stimuli. A large minority (41%) of these were similar to parietal neurons: They were activated by any of the stimuli, and their firing rates were similar across the set of stimuli. The remaining 59% of the cells exhibited some selectivity and responded more vigorously when presented with the complex stimuli.

Recordings from such a cell, located in the inferotemporal cortex, are shown in Figure 6.6. This cell is most highly activated by the human hand. The first five images in the figure show the response of the cell to various views of a hand. Activity is high regardless of the hand's orientation and is only slightly reduced

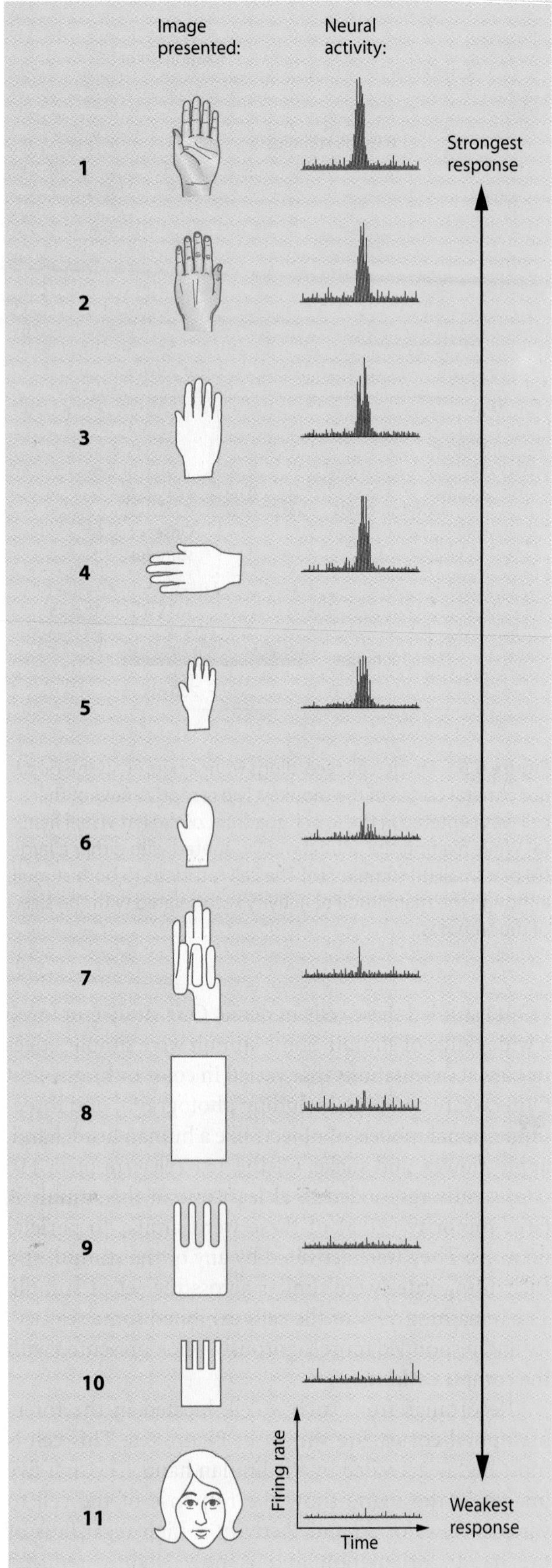

Figure 6.6 Single-cell recordings from a neuron in the inferior temporal cortex. These cells rarely respond to simple stimuli such as lines or spots of light. Rather, they respond to more complex objects, such as the hand drawings shown in the first five images. Note that the cell shows only a weak response to the mitten, indicating that its activity is not associated with the general shape of a hand. This cell does not respond to the comblike objects that contain the series of parallel lines (images 7, 9, and 10) as in the hand stimuli.

when the hand is considerably smaller. The sixth image shows that the response diminishes if the same shape lacks defining fingers.

Cells in the primary visual cortex are highly responsive to edges with a specific orientation. From the first six images in Figure 6.6 you might wonder if this inferotemporal cell is behaving similarly, preferring vertically aligned edges. But the responses of the cell to other stimuli (the last five images of Figure 6.6) argue against this hypothesis. First, nonhand stimuli with multiple vertical lines (akin to the fingers) failed to activate the cell. Second, the cell also responds to a hand rotated 90°. Neurons in the parietal lobe would not exhibit such specificity and spatial independence.

Neuroimaging studies with human subjects have provided further evidence that the dorsal and ventral streams are activated differentially by "where" and "what" tasks. In one particularly elegant study using positron emission tomography (Kohler et al., 1995), trials consisted of pairs of displays containing three objects each (Figure 6.7a and b). In the position task, the subjects had to determine if the objects were presented at the same locations in the two displays. In the object task, they had to determine if the objects remained the same across the two displays. The irrelevant factor could remain the same or change: The objects might change on the position task, even though the locations remained the same; similarly, the same objects might be presented at new locations in the object task. Thus, the stimulus displays were identical for the two conditions; the only difference was the task instruction.

The PET data for the two tasks were compared directly to identify neural regions that were selectively activated by one task or the other (Figure 6.7c). In this way, areas that are engaged similarly for both tasks—because of similar perceptual, decision, or response requirements—are masked. During the position task, regional cerebral blood flow was higher in the parietal lobe in the right hemisphere. In contrast, the object task led to increased regional cerebral blood flow bilaterally at the junction of the occipital and temporal lobes.

A number of other imaging studies have confirmed the dorsal–ventral distinction, although the studies showed

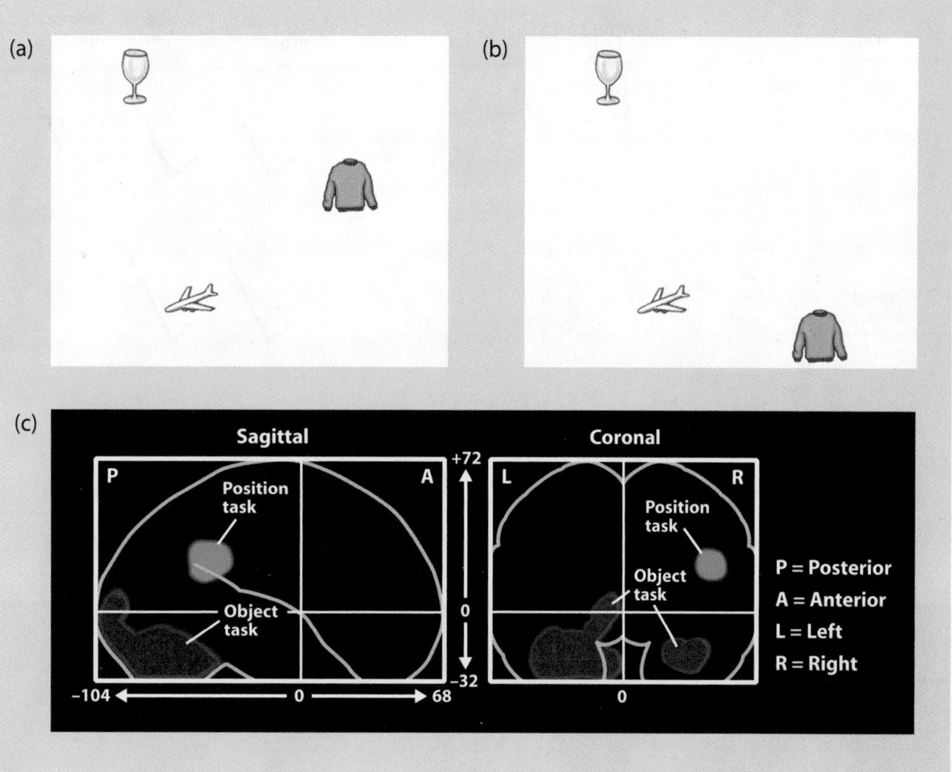

Figure 6.7 Matching task used to contrast spatial and object discrimination. **(a)** Sample stimulus. **(b)** Test stimulus for which a "same" response would be required in the object task and a "different" response would be required in the position task. **(c)** Sagittal section showing activation centers for the object task (red) and the position task (green). Although both activations are superimposed on the same slice, activation during the position task was restricted to the right hemisphere, whereas activation during the object task was bilateral.

considerable variability in the exact neural loci that were activated within the parietal and occipitotemporal cortices. Two sources likely produced this variability. First, the methods of analysis varied across the experiments. Many studies use a passive viewing condition for their baseline rather than direct comparisons between two experimental conditions. Comparisons of this type generally lead to larger areas of bilateral activation. For example, both inferior and superior regions of the parietal lobe were activated bilaterally when subjects were asked to do a spatial matching task requiring mental rotation (Haxby et al., 1994).

Second, human subjects are clever creatures and can easily adopt a variety of strategies to solve a task. Consider the object task in Figure 6.7. Do subjects make their decisions by comparing the objects in the second display with an imagined, perceptually based representation of the first display? Or do they generate the names of the objects and make their comparison on the basis of these verbal labels? Isolating specific mental operations can be a tricky business in imaging studies.

Figure 6.8 outlines the design of one study that attempted to isolate specific mental operations (Kanwisher, Woods, et al., 1997). While in the PET scanner, subjects were presented with three types of line drawings. To eliminate activations related to decision and response processes, subjects were tested only in passive viewing conditions. In one condition the lines were scrambled; in the other two conditions the line drawings formed objects that were either familiar or novel (see Figure 6.8a). All three conditions should engage processes of initial visual perception, or what is called *feature extraction*. To identify areas involved in object perception, activation during presentation of the scrambled condition was subtracted from that measured during the novel and familiar object conditions. If passive object perception also engages memory retrieval processes, then additional areas should be activated during the familiar condition compared to the novel condition. But no such differences were found. However, both the novel and the familiar object conditions led to increases in regional cerebral blood flow bilaterally in the inferior occipitotemporal areas. The center of activation was lateral and inferior to V4 (see Figure 6.8b). Many fMRI studies have similarly shown that lateral occipital cortex is a critical region for shape and object recognition (Grill-Spector et al., 2001; Figure 6.9).

Perception for Identification Versus Perception for Action

Patient studies offer even more support for a dissociation of "what" and "where" processing, although there are discrepancies between the findings from human and primate lesion studies. The parietal cortex is central to spatial attention. Lesions of this lobe can produce severe

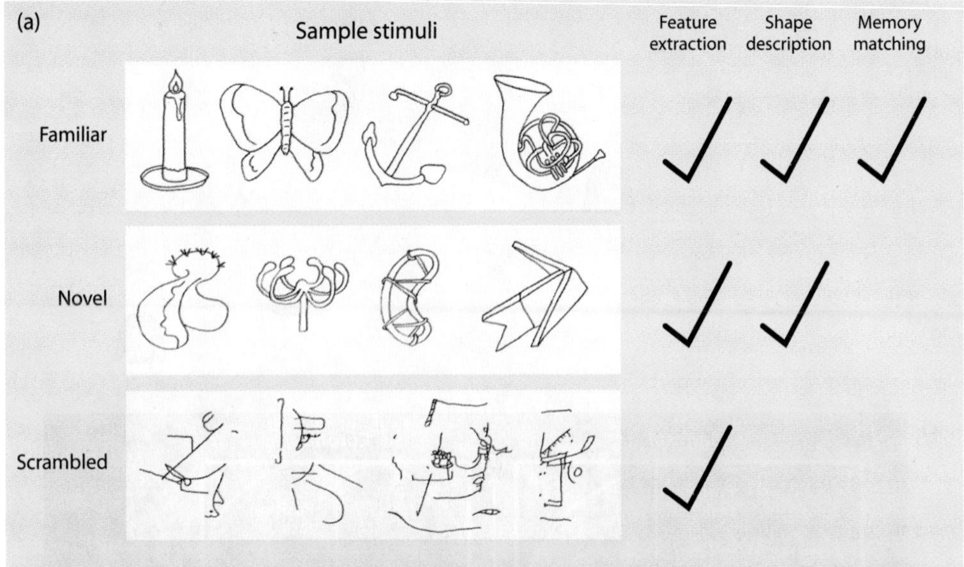

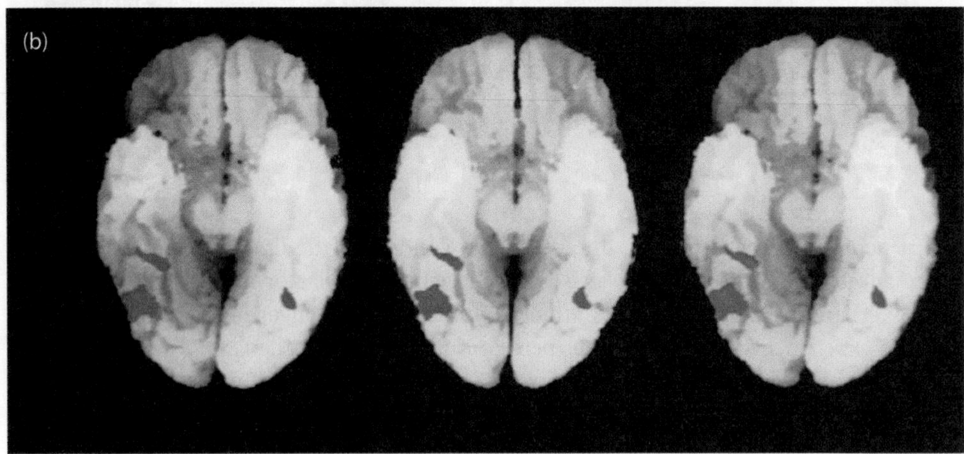

Figure 6.8 Component analysis of object recognition. **(a)** Stimuli for the three conditions and the mental operations required in each condition. Novel objects are hypothesized to engage processes involved in perception even when verbal labels do not exist. **(b)** Activation for both novel and familiar objects was bilateral along the ventral surface of the occipitotemporal cortex.

disturbances in the ability to represent the world's spatial layout and the spatial relations of objects in it. Lesions associated with agnosia do not have a clear pattern that corresponds to findings in animal studies. The lesions often fall along the ventral pathway, especially in patients with impaired face perception, or *prosopagnosia*, but they frequently extend into parietal structures (prosopagnosia is discussed in detail later in this chapter). Unlike examples from animal research, patients with severe deficits in object recognition can have unilateral lesions of either the right or the left hemisphere.

More revealing have been functional dissociations in the performance of patients with agnosia. Mel Goodale and David Milner (1992) at the University of Western Ontario described a 34-year-old patient, D.F., who suffered carbon monoxide intoxication because of a leaky propane gas heater. D.F. had a severe disorder of object recognition. When asked to name household items, she made errors such as labeling a cup an "ashtray" or a fork a "knife." She usually gave crude descriptions of a displayed object; for example, a screwdriver was "long, black, and thin." Picture recognition was even more disrupted. When shown drawings of common objects, D.F. could not identify a single one. Her deficit could not be attributed to *anomia*, a problem with naming objects, because whenever an object was placed in her hand, she identified it. Sensory testing further indicated that D.F.'s agnosia could not be attributed to a loss of visual acuity. She could detect small gray targets displayed against a black background. Although her ability to discriminate small differences in hue was abnormal, she correctly identified primary colors.

Most relevant to our concerns is the dissociation of D.F.'s performance on two tasks designed to assess her ability to perceive the orientation of a three-dimensional object. For these tasks, D.F. was asked to view a circular

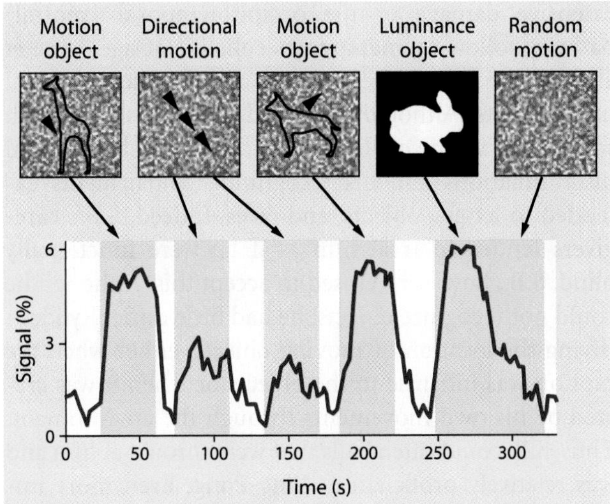

Figure 6.9 The BOLD signal in lateral occipital cortex to objects. Animals were presented in the blue regions, either formed by the motion of a subset of dots (motion object) or as static white objects on a black background (luminance object). Activity was greater during these epochs compared to when the dots either moved in a coherent direction (directional motion) or randomly (random motion).

block into which a slot had been cut. The orientation of the slot could be varied by rotation of the block. In the explicit matching task, D.F. was given a card and asked to orient her hand so that the card would fit into the slot. D.F. failed miserably, orienting the card vertically even when the slot was horizontal (Figure 6.10a). When asked to insert the card into the slot, however, D.F. quickly reached forward and inserted the card (Figure 6.10b). Her performance on this visuomotor task did not depend on tactile feedback that would result when the card contacted the slot; she simply oriented her hand prior to touching the block.

D.F.'s performance showed that processing systems make use of different sources of perceptual information. The explicit matching task showed that D.F. could not recognize the orientation of a three-dimensional object; this deficit is indicative of her severe agnosia. Yet when D.F. was asked to insert the card (the action task), her performance clearly indicated that she had processed the orientation of the slot. This dissociation suggests that the "what" and "where" systems support different aspects of cognition.

The "what" system is essential for determining the identity of an object. If the object is familiar, we will recognize it as such; if it is novel, we may compare the percept to stored representations of similarly shaped objects. The "where" system appears to be essential for more than determining the locations of different objects; it is also critical for guiding interactions with these objects. Similar to the blindsight phenomenon described in Chapter 5, D.F.'s performance provides another example of how information accessible to action systems can be dissociated from information accessible

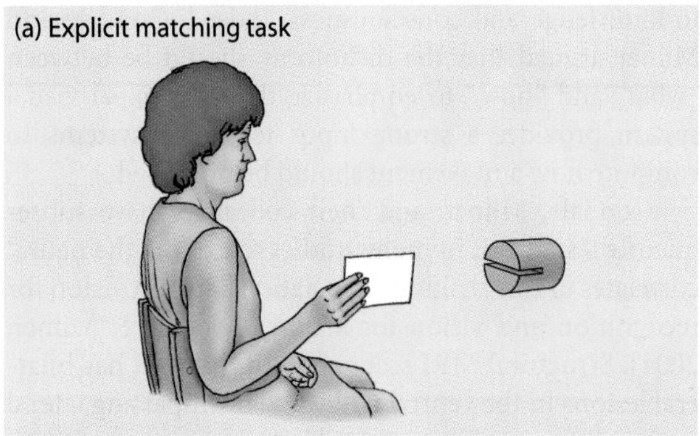

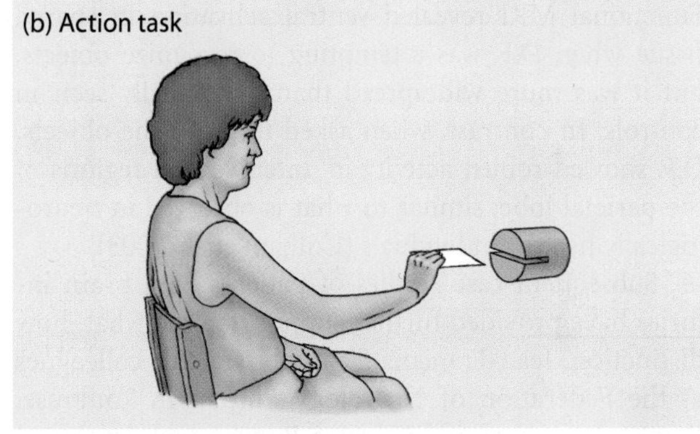

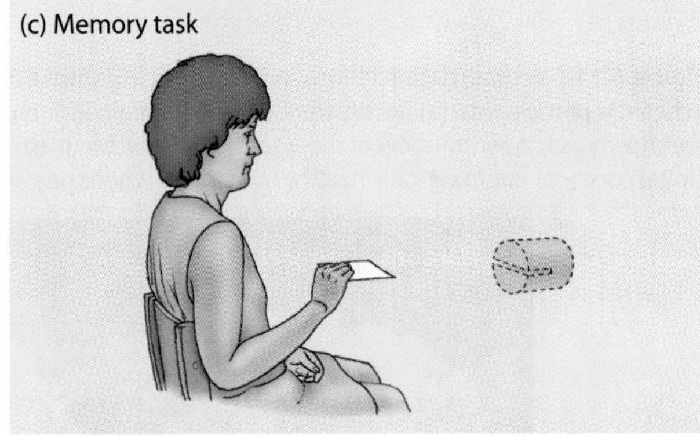

Figure 6.10 A dissociation of perception linked to awareness and perception linked to action. **(a)** In the explicit matching task (the awareness condition), D.F. was asked to match the orientation of the card to that of the slot, and she demonstrated severe impairment. **(b)** In the action task, D.F. was instructed to insert the card in the slot, and she produced the correct action without hesitation. **(c)** D.F. also showed no impairment in the memory task, verifying that her knowledge of orientation was intact.

to knowledge and consciousness. Indeed, Goodale and Milner argued that the dichotomy should be between "what" and "how," to emphasize that the dorsal visual system provides a strong input to motor systems to compute how a movement should be produced.

Goodale, Milner, and their colleagues have subsequently tested D.F. in many studies to explore the neural correlates of this striking dissociation between vision for recognition and vision for action (Goodale & Milner, 2004). Structural MRI scans showed that D.F. has bilateral lesions in the ventral pathway, encompassing lateral occipital cortex (Figure 6.11; T. W. James et al., 2003). Functional MRI revealed ventral activation in spared tissue when D.F. was attempting to recognize objects, but it was more widespread than is normally seen in controls. In contrast, when asked to grasp the objects, D.F. showed robust activity in anteroventral regions of the parietal lobe, similar to what is observed in neurologically healthy individuals (Culham et al., 2003).

Subsequent case studies of patients with brain injuries have provided further support for the what–how distinction. Jean-François Démonet and his colleagues at the Federation of Neurology Purpan in Toulouse, France, studied an individual, S.B., who had developed extensive damage of the occipitotemporal (ventral) pathway following meningoencephalitis at age 3 (Lê et al., 2002). As would be expected, S.B. had severe visual impairments. Although he could describe shapes with some accuracy, he could not perform many basic visual discriminations and his recognition impairments extended to letters, objects, and faces. Indeed, S.B.'s caregivers tended to treat him as if he were functionally blind. S.B., however, refused to accept this. Although he could not recognize objects, he had little difficulty identifying the location of moving objects, either when the motion was intrinsic to the objects or when it was created by his own movements through the environment. Thus, S.B. could catch balls that were thrown at him and was relatively proficient at Ping-Pong. Even more impressive, he loved to drive a motorcycle (although the report does not indicate if he rode on city streets)!

Patients like D.F. and S.B. offer examples of single dissociations: They show a selective (and dramatic) impairment in using vision to recognize objects while remaining proficient in using vision for action. The opposite dissociation can also be found in the clinical literature: Patients with **optic ataxia** can recognize objects yet cannot use visual information to guide their action.

Figure 6.11 Ventral-stream lesions in D.F. shown in comparison with the expected location of the lateral occipital complex (LOC) in healthy participants. **(a)** Reconstruction of D.F.'s brain lesion is shown in pale blue. Lateral views of the left and right hemispheres are shown, as is a ventral view of the underside of the brain. **(b)** The highlighted regions (yellow) indicate activation in the lateral occipital cortex of neurologically healthy individuals when they are recognizing objects.

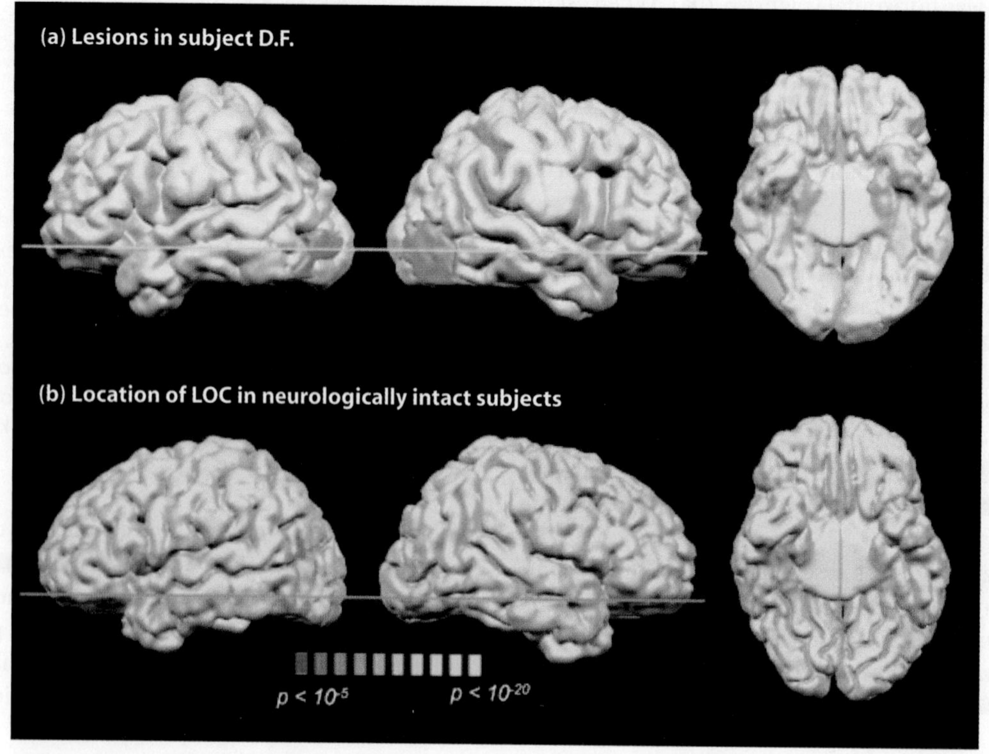

When reaching for an object, they fail to move directly toward it; rather they grope about like a person trying to find a light switch in the dark. Their eye movements present a similar loss of spatial knowledge; *saccades*, or directed eye movements, may be directed inappropriately and fail to bring the object within the fovea. When tested on the slot task used with D.F. (see Figure 6.10), these patients can report the orientation of a visual slot, even though they cannot use this information when inserting an object in the slot. In accord with what we expect on the basis of dorsal–ventral dichotomy, optic ataxia is associated with lesions of the parietal cortex.

In sum, the what–where, or what–how, dichotomy offers a functional account of two computational goals for higher visual processing. This distinction is best viewed as heuristic rather than absolute. The dorsal and ventral pathways are not isolated from one another, but rather communicate extensively. Processing within the parietal lobe, the termination of the "where" pathway, serves many purposes. We have focused here on its guiding of action; in Chapter 12 we will see that the parietal lobe plays a critical role in *selective attention*, the enhancement of processing at some locations instead of others. Moreover, spatial information can also be useful for solving "what" problems. For example, depth cues help segregate a complex scene into its component objects. The remainder of this chapter concentrates on object recognition—in particular, the visual system's assortment of strategies for perceiving and recognizing the world.

COMPUTATIONAL PROBLEMS IN OBJECT RECOGNITION

Object perception depends primarily on analysis of the shape of a visual stimulus, although cues such as color, texture, and motion certainly contribute to normal perception. For example, when we look at the surf breaking on the shore, our acuity is not sufficient to see grains of sand, and water is essentially amorphous, lacking any definable shape. Yet the textures of the sand's surface and the water's edge, and their differences in color, enable us to distinguish between the two regions. The water's motion is important too. Even if surface features like texture and color are absent or applied inappropriately, recognition is minimally affected: We can readily identify an elephant, an apple, and the human form in Figure 6.12, even though they are shown as pink, plaid, and wooden, respectively. Here object recognition is derived from a perceptual ability to match an analysis of shape and form.

To account for shape-based recognition, we need to consider two problems. The first has to do with shape encoding. How is a shape internally represented? What salient features enable us to recognize differences between a triangle and a square or between a monkey and a person? The second problem centers on how shape is processed given that the position from which an object is viewed varies. We can recognize shapes from an infinite array of positions and orientations, and our recognition system is not hampered by scale changes in the retinal image as we move close to or far away from an object.

Variability in Sensory Information

Questions about shape encoding and processing arise because our perceptual capabilities must be maintained in

Figure 6.12 Analyzing shape and form. Despite the irregularities in how these objects are depicted, we have little problem recognizing them. We may never have seen pink elephants or plaid apples, but our object recognition system can still discern the essential features that identify these objects as elephants and apples.

HOW THE BRAIN WORKS

Now You See It, Now You Don't

Gaze at the picture in Figure 1 for a couple of minutes. If you are like most people, you initially saw a vase. But surprise! After a while the vase changed to a picture of two human profiles staring at each other. With continued viewing, your perception changes back and forth, content with one interpretation until suddenly the other asserts itself and refuses to yield the floor. This is an example of *multistable perception*.

How are multistable percepts resolved in the brain? The stimulus information does not change at the points of transition. Rather, the interpretation of the pictorial cues changes. When staring at the white region, you see the vase. If you shift attention to the black regions, you see the profiles. But here we run into a chicken-and-egg question. Did the representation of individual features change first and thus cause the percept to change? Or did the percept change and lead to a reinterpretation of the features?

To explore these questions, Nikos Logothetis of the Max Planck Institute in Tübingen, Germany, turned to a different form of multistable perception: binocular rivalry (Sheinberg & Logothetis, 1997). The exquisite focusing capability of our eyes (perhaps assisted by an optometrist) makes us forget that they provide two separate snapshots of the world. These snapshots are only slightly different, and they provide important cues for depth perception. With some technological tricks, however, it is possible to present radically different inputs to the two eyes. To accomplish this while keeping the eyes fixated at a common location, researchers employ special glasses that alternately block the input to one eye and then the other at very rapid rates. Varying the stimulus in synchrony with the alternate blocking by these glasses allows a different stimulus to be presented to each eye simultaneously.

Do we see two things simultaneously at the same location? The answer is no. As with the ambiguous vase–face profiles picture, only one object or the other is seen at any single point in time, although at transitions there is sometimes a period of fuzziness in which neither object is clearly perceived. Logothetis trained his monkeys to press one of two levers to indicate which object was being perceived. To make sure the animals were not responding randomly, he included nonrivalrous trials in which only one of the objects was presented. He then recorded from single cells in various areas of the visual cortex. Within each area he selected two objects, only one of which was effective in driving the cell. In this way he could correlate the activity of the cell with the animal's perceptual experience.

As his recordings moved up the ventral pathway, Logothetis found an increase in the percentage of active cells, with activity mirroring the animals' percep-

the face of a variable world. **Object constancy** refers to our amazing ability to recognize an object in countless situations. Figure 6.13 shows four drawings of an automobile that have little in common with respect to sensory information reaching the eye. Yet we have no problem identifying the object in each picture as a car, and discerning that all four cars are the same model. Object constancy is essential for perception. Imagine how difficult life would be if we could not recognize familiar things or people unless we gazed at them from a specific point of view.

The visual information emanating from an object varies for several reasons. First, sensory information depends highly on viewing position. Viewpoint changes not only as the perceiver moves about the world but also as objects change their orientation. If we command a dog to roll over, our interpretation of the object (the dog) remains the same despite the change in our perception. The retinal projection of shape, and even the visible components of an object, can change dramatically as the object's and viewer's positions are altered. For instance, when a car is viewed from the front, the retinal projection of its width is larger than the projection of its length. Yet our percept does not reflect this distortion. We do not have the impression of a squashed car. Our perceptual system is adept at separating changes caused by shifts in viewpoint from those intrinsic to the objects themselves.

Changes in the illumination of an object introduce a second source of sensory variability (Figure 6.14). The visible parts of an object may differ depending on

tion rather than the stimulus conditions. In V1, the responses of less than 20% of the cells fluctuated as a function of whether the animal perceived the effective or ineffective stimulus. In V4, this percentage increased to over 33%. In contrast, the activity of all the cells in the visual areas of the temporal lobe was tightly correlated with the animal's perception. Here the cells would respond only when the effective stimulus, the monkey face, was perceived (Figure 2). When the animal pressed the lever indicating that it perceived the ineffective stimulus (the starburst) under rivalrous conditions, the cells were essentially silent. In both V4 and the temporal lobe, the cell activity changed in advance of the animal's response, indicating that the percept had changed. Thus, even when the stimulus did not change, an increase in activity was observed prior to the transition from a perception of the ineffective stimulus to a perception of the effective stimulus.

These results suggest a competition during the early stages of cortical processing between the two possible percepts. The activity of the cells in V1 and in V4 can be thought of as perceptual hypotheses, with the patterns across an ensemble of cells reflecting the strength of the different hypotheses. Interactions between these cells ensure that, by the time the information reaches the inferotemporal lobe, one of these hypotheses has coalesced into a stable percept. Reflecting the properties of the real world, the brain is not fooled into believing that two objects exist at the same place at the same time.

Figure 1 Does your perception change over time as you continue to stare at this drawing?

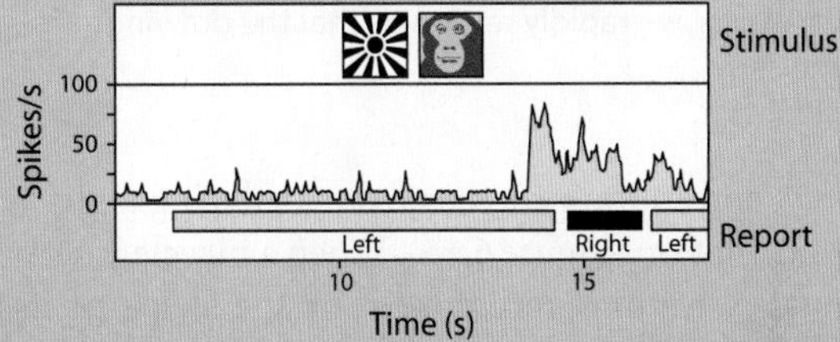

Figure 2 When the starburst or monkey face is presented alone, the cell in the temporal cortex responds vigorously to the monkey face but not to the starburst. In the rivalrous condition, the two stimuli are presented simultaneously, one to the left eye and one to the right eye. The bottom bar shows the monkey's perception, indicated by a lever press. About 1 s after the onset of the rivalrous stimulus, the animal perceives the starburst; the cell is silent during this period. About 7 s later, the cell shows a large increase in activity and, correspondingly, indicates that its perception has changed to the monkey face shortly thereafter. Then, 2 s later, the percept flips back to the starburst and the cell's activity is again reduced.

whether the object is illuminated from above or from the side. Variations in shadowing can also alter the illumination of an object's parts. Because so many visual cells are sensitive to brightness, we might expect them to have an impact on perception, but recognition is mainly insensitive to changes in illumination.

A third source of variability arises because objects are rarely seen in isolation. Although cars can be drawn on a blank page, they are usually seen on streets with pedestrians, buildings, and traffic signs—and these other objects frequently occlude part of the car. We have no trouble separating other objects from a car; our perceptual system quickly partitions the scene into components.

Object recognition must overcome these three sources of variability, but it also must accommodate the fact that changes in perceived shape can reflect changes in the object. Not only must object recognition be general enough to support object constancy, but also it must be specific enough to pick out slight differences between members of a category or class.

View-Dependent or View-Invariant Recognition?

A central debate in object recognition has to do with defining the frame of reference where recognition occurs (D. I. Perrett et al., 1994). Two general approaches have been proposed. With a **view-dependent frame of reference**, perception is assumed to depend on recognizing an object from a certain viewpoint. According to

Figure 6.13 Object constancy. The image on the retina is vastly different for these four drawings of a car. Despite this sensory variability, we rapidly recognize that the drawings are of the same car.

this theory, perception proceeds from analyzing a viewpoint's information (Figure 6.15). When a bicycle is seen from the side, we may recognize it by the shape of its frame, wheels, and seat. We may also recognize a bicycle when viewed from an aerial perspective, even though this vantage point obscures the wheels. Perhaps from this orientation the handlebar and elongated shape provide the defining components.

View-dependent theories posit that we have a cornucopia of specific representations in memory; we simply need to match a stimulus to a stored representation. The key idea is that the stored representation for recognizing a bicycle from the side is different from the one for recognizing a bicycle from above. Hence, our ability to recognize that two stimuli are depicting the same object is assumed to arise at a later stage of processing.

One shortcoming with view-dependent theories is that they seem to place a heavy burden on perceptual memory: Each object requires multiple representations

Figure 6.14 Object constancy must be achieved in spite of the many sources of variation in the sensory input, including shadows **(a)** and partial occlusion **(b)**.

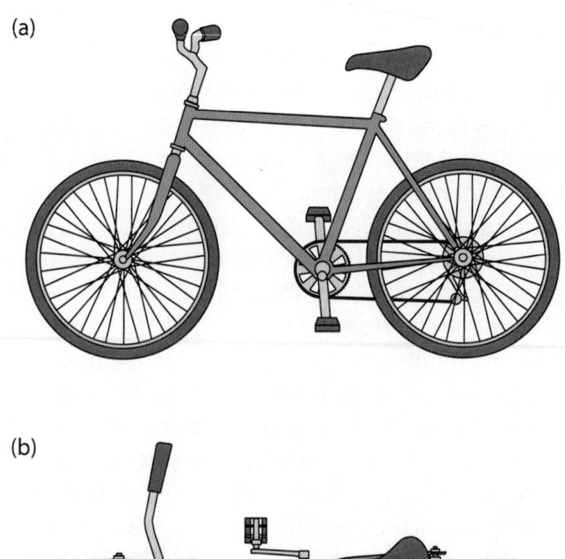

(b)

Figure 6.15 View-dependent theories of object recognition posit that recognition processes depend on the vantage point. Recognizing that both of these drawings depict a bicycle—one from a side view and the other from an aerial view—requires matching the distinct sensory inputs to view-dependent representations. For the side view **(a)**, we may include the features of the seat, chain, and spokes to match the drawing with a stored representation of a bicycle seen from this perspective. For the aerial view **(b)**, the representation would have to encompass the axis, seat, handlebar, and pedals.

in memory, each associated with a different vantage point. This problem is less daunting, however, if we assume that recognition processes are able to match the input to stored representations through an interpolation process. We recognize an object seen from a novel viewpoint by comparing the stimulus information to the stored representations and choosing the best match. This idea is supported by experiments using novel objects—an approach that minimizes the contribution of past experience and the possibility of verbal strategies. The time needed to decide if two objects are the same or different increases as the viewpoints diverge, even when each member of the object set contains a unique feature (Tarr et al., 1997).

An alternative scheme posits that recognition occurs in a **view-invariant frame of reference**. In this scheme, recognition does not happen by simple analysis of the stimulus information. Rather, sensory input defines basic properties; the object's other properties are defined with respect to these properties. David Marr of the Massachusetts Institute of Technology, in his classic book *Vision: A*

Computational Investigation Into the Human Representation and Processing of Visual Information (1982), articulated a comprehensive and influential theory of recognition based on view-invariant representations. In Marr's theory, a critical property for recognition is establishing the major and minor axes inherent to the object. The major axis of a bicycle runs along its length. The handlebar can be represented as the minor axis—its two appendages arranged perpendicularly to the primary axis. These properties generally hold across different vantage points. If viewed head-on, the minor axis produces a larger retinal image than the foreshortened major axis, but Marr would consider this a degenerate case—one that may pose a challenge for our usual effortless recognition systems. In such situations, recognition may depend on an inferential process based on a few salient features.

The brain, of course, may use both view-dependent and view-invariant operations to support object recognition. Patrick Vuilleumier and colleagues (2002) at University College London explored this hypothesis in an fMRI study. The study was motivated by the finding from various imaging studies that, when a stimulus is repeated, the BOLD response is lower in the second presentation compared to the first. This **repetition suppression effect** is hypothesized to indicate increased neural efficiency: The neural response to the stimulus is more efficient and faster when the pattern has been recently activated. To ask about view dependency, subjects were shown pictures of objects, and over the course of the scanning session, each picture was repeated. The second presentation was either in the same orientation or from a different viewpoint.

A repetition suppression effect was observed in left ventral occipital cortex regardless of whether the object was shown from the same or a different viewpoint (Figure 6.16a), consistent with a view-invariant representation. In contrast, activation in right ventral occipital cortex decreased only when the second presentation was from the original viewpoint (Figure 6.16b), consistent with a view-dependent representation. When the object was shown from a new viewpoint, the BOLD response was similar to that observed for the object in the initial presentation.

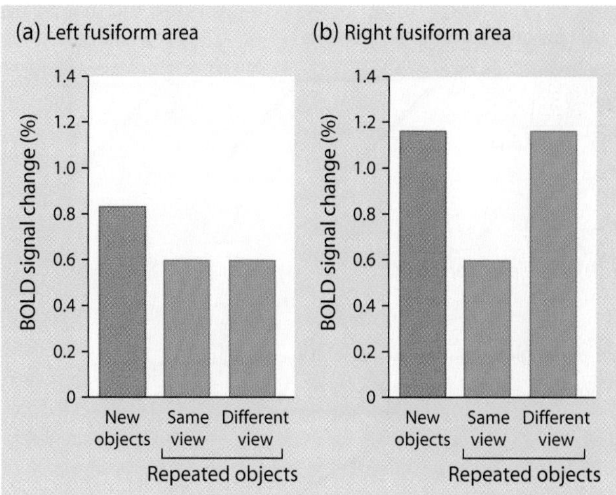

Figure 6.16 Repetition suppression effect. **(a)** A repetition suppression effect is observed in left ventral occipital cortex regardless of whether an object is shown from the same or a different viewpoint, consistent with a view-invariant representation. **(b)** In contrast, activation in right ventral occipital cortex decreased relative to activity during the presentation of novel stimuli only when the second object was presented in the original viewpoint, consistent with a view-dependent representation.

Shape Encoding

In Chapter 5 we introduced the idea that recognition may involve hierarchical representations in which each successive stage adds complexity. Features such as lines can be combined into edges, corners, and intersections to parse a visual array into component regions. These, in turn, are grouped into parts and the parts into objects.

Recognition of a triangle entails perceiving three segments that join together to form three corners, which define an enclosed region. If combined differently, these same features could define another object—for example, an arrow derived from three lines connected at their endpoints. But with the arrow there is only one point of intersection, and the lines do not enclose an area. The triangle and the arrow might activate similar representations at the lowest levels of the hierarchy, yet the combination of these features produces distinct representations at higher levels of the processing hierarchy (Figure 6.17).

What information is coded at these higher levels? We might expect the representations to include the most salient aspects of the stimulus. Each of the abstract shapes in Figure 6.18 is composed of a single, continuous curved line. In comparing the two shapes, however, we notice that some regions of curvature provide more information than others. We are not sensitive to the slight differences in curvature along the right side, but the sharp inflection point along the bottom of one of the figures is very salient. We would describe the shape in Figure 6.18a as having a flat bottom; the shape in Figure 6.18b resembles an object with two bases of support, or legs. We might use this information to guess that the object in Figure 6.18b is more mobile than the object in Figure 6.18a.

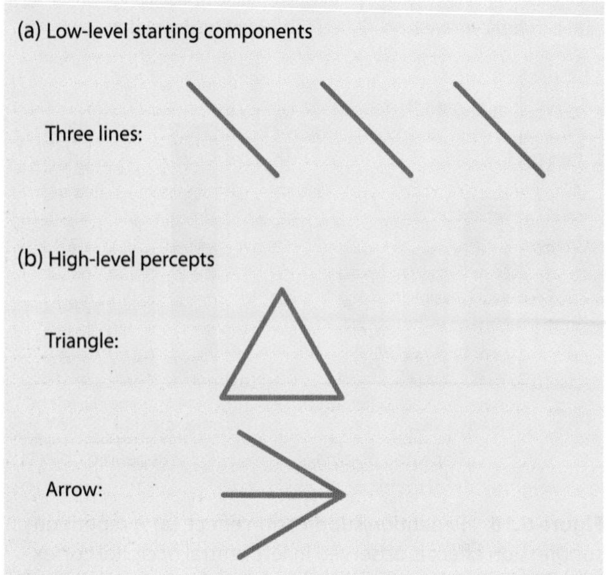

Figure 6.17 The same basic components (three lines) can form different items (e.g., a triangle or an arrow) depending on their arrangement. Although the low-level components **(a)** are the same, the high-level percepts **(b)** are distinct.

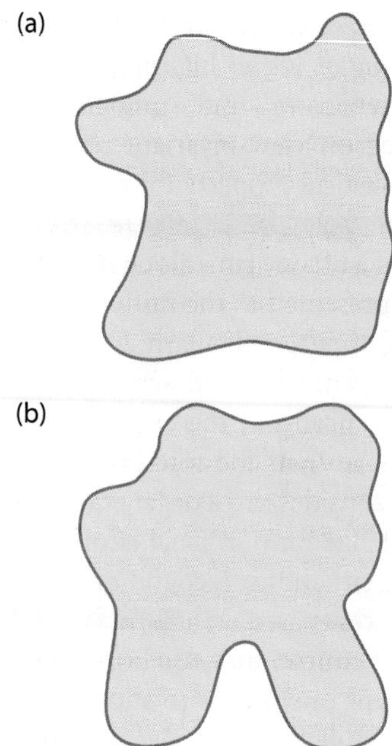

Figure 6.18 Study these two drawings for 10 s and then attempt to draw them from memory. Your drawings are likely to reflect the fact that points of greatest curvature provide the most salient sources of information. In part **(a)** the knob on the left edge is more distinctive than the wavy edge on the right edge. Reproductions of the object in part **(b)** will surely include the gap separating the two appendages at the bottom.

Although the sensory information changes from one viewpoint to another, the world has regularities that the visual system exploits—sources of information that remain constant across vantage points. Theories of object recognition have emphasized the significance of such properties. Apples can be red, green, or yellow, but they all share a basic shape. Our visual system is well tuned to exploit these properties. For example, experience teaches us that vertical parallel lines in the environment will converge in the retinal image, providing a critical cue about depth. We thus readily assume that, when two vertical lines converge in our two-dimensional image, they are parallel in the three-dimensional world. This inference can be exploited to create compelling visual illusions (Figure 6.19).

Grandmother Cells and Ensemble Coding

How are objects represented in the brain at a neural level? Do individual cells respond only to the integrated percepts that correspond to what we call *objects*, with these cells receiving inputs from other cells that code for the individual parts? Or does our perception of an object depend on the firing of an ensemble of cells?

The finding that cells in the inferotemporal lobe selectively respond to complex stimuli (objects, places, body parts, or faces) agrees with hierarchical theories of object perception. According to these theories, cells in the initial areas of the visual cortex code elementary features such as line orientation and color. The outputs from these cells are then combined to form detectors sensitive to higher order features such as corners or intersections—an idea consistent with the findings of Hubel and Wiesel (see "Milestones in Cognitive Science: Pioneers in the Visual Cortex," on p. 180). The process continues as each successive stage codes more complex combinations (Figure 6.20). The type of neuron that can recognize a complex object has been called a **gnostic unit** (from the Greek *gnostikos*, meaning "of knowledge"), referring to the idea that the cells signal the presence of a known stimulus—an object, place, or animal that has been encountered in the past.

It is tempting to conclude that the cell represented by the recordings in Figure 6.6 signals the presence of a hand, independent of viewpoint. Other cells in the inferotemporal area respond preferentially to complex stimuli such as jagged contours or fuzzy textures. The latter might be useful for a monkey, to identify that an object has a fur-covered surface and therefore might be the backside of another member of its group. Even more intriguing has been the discovery of cells in the inferotemporal gyrus and the floor of the superior temporal sulcus that are selectively activated by faces. In a tongue-in-cheek manner, the term *grandmother cell* has been

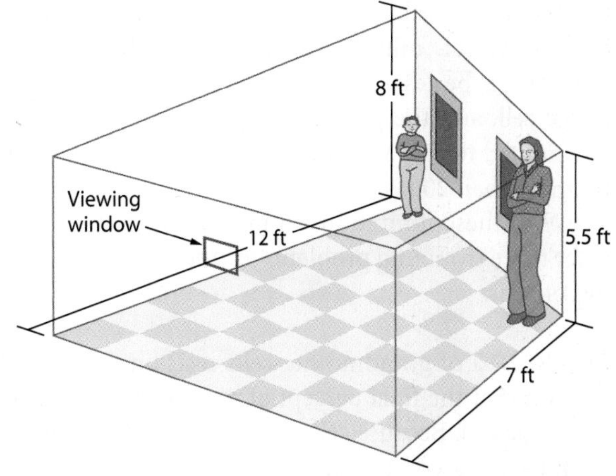

Figure 6.19 The illusory Ames room exploits the fact that, given our knowledge of rooms, we expect the back wall to be parallel with the front wall and the ceiling to be a constant height. Our perceptual system assumes that the two people are the same distance away and ends up interpreting the closer one as a giant.

coined to convey the notion that there might be gnostic units that become excited only when one's grandmother comes into view. Other gnostic units would be specialized to recognize grandpa, or a blue Volkswagen, or the Golden Gate Bridge.

How specific is the responsiveness of individual cells? Does recognition depend on the specificity of a few neurons or the aggregate behavior of large groups of neurons? A physiologist might find that a particular cell exhibits a strong preference for a hand and be tempted

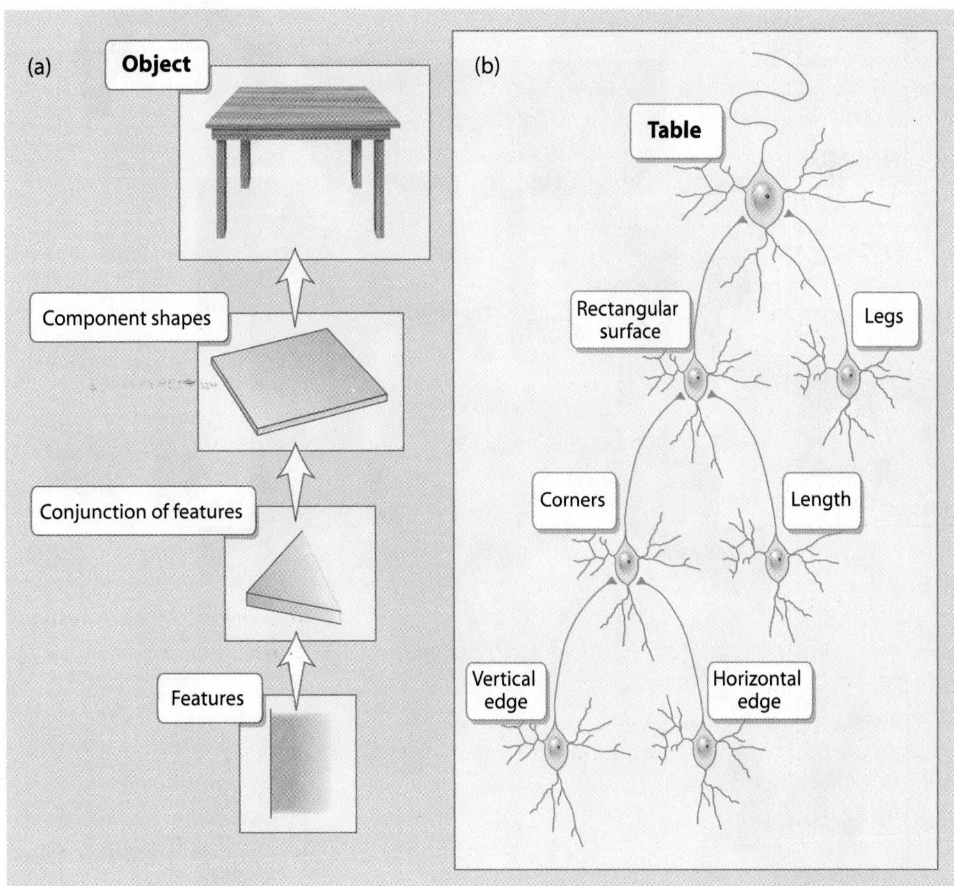

Figure 6.20 Hierarchical coding hypothesis: Elementary features are combined to create objects that can be recognized by gnostic units. At the lowest level of the hierarchy are edge detectors, units that operate similar to the way the simple cells discussed in Chapter 5 operate. These feature units combine to form corner detectors, which in turn combine to form cells that respond to even more complex stimuli, such as surfaces. **(a)** The hypothesized computational stages for hierarchical coding. **(b)** A neural implementation of the computational stages illustrated in part **(a)**, based on the idea of grandmother cells.

to conclude that this cell is the gnostic unit for that percept. However, only a limited subset of all possible objects can be tested when one is recording from any single cell, and the physiologist's explorations are usually limited to a relatively small number of cells, usually no more than 200.

With these limitations in mind, it is useful to consider three troubling problems for the grandmother cell hypothesis:

1. The idea of grandmother cells rests on the assumption that the final percept of an object is coded by a single cell. Because cells are constantly firing and refractory, a coding scheme of this nature would be highly susceptible to error. If a gnostic unit were to die, we would expect to experience a sudden loss for an object.
2. The grandmother cell hypothesis cannot adequately account for the fact that we perceive novel objects—a perception whose mechanism is unexplained.
3. Third, the gnostic theory does not account for how the grandmother cell would have to adapt as the grandmother changed over time (because of both aging and simple changes in appearance, such as altered hair length or the use of glasses).

One alternative to the grandmother cell hypothesis is to regard object recognition as resulting from activation across complex feature detectors (Figure 6.21). Granny, then, is perceived when higher order neurons are activated; some respond to her shape, others to the color of her hair, and still others to the markings on her face. According to this population, or ensemble, hypothesis, recognition is not due to one unit but to the collective activation of many units. Ensemble theories readily account for why we can confuse one visually similar object with another; both objects activate many of the same neurons. Losing some units might degrade our ability to recognize an object, but the remaining units might suffice. Ensemble theories also account for our ability to recognize novel objects. Such objects bear a similarity to familiar things, and our percept results from activating units that represent their features.

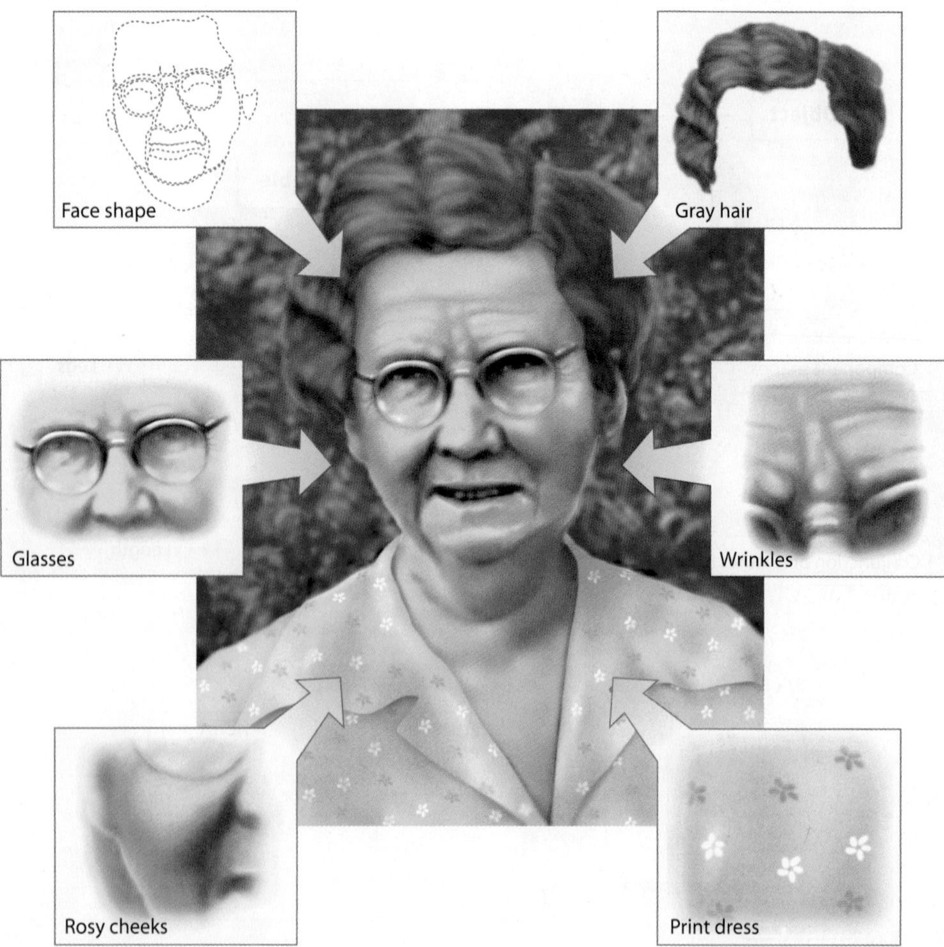

Figure 6.21 Ensemble coding hypothesis: Objects are defined by the simultaneous activation of a set of defining properties. "Granny" is recognized here by the co-occurrence of her glasses, face shape, hair color, and so on.

The results of single-cell studies of temporal lobe neurons are in accord with ensemble theories of object recognition. Although it is striking that some cells are selective for complex objects, the selectivity is almost always relative, not absolute. The cells in the inferotemporal cortex prefer certain stimuli over others, but they are also activated by visually similar stimuli. The cell represented in Figure 6.6, for instance, increases its activity when presented with a mitten-like stimulus. No cells respond to a particular individual's hand; the hand-selective cell responds equally to just about any hand. In contrast, our perceptual abilities demonstrate that we make much finer discriminations.

Summary of Computational Problems

We have considered several computational problems that must be solved by an object recognition system. Information is represented on multiple scales. Although early visual input can specify simple features, object perception involves intermediate stages of representation in which features are assembled into parts. Objects are not determined solely by their parts; they are defined by relations between parts. An arrow and the letter *Y* contain the same parts but differ in their arrangement. For object recognition to be flexible and robust, the perceived spatial relations among parts should not vary across viewing conditions.

FAILURES IN OBJECT RECOGNITION

Where does the syndrome of visual agnosia fit in with these considerations? To repeat, patients with visual agnosia have difficulty recognizing visually presented objects. A key word here is *visual*: Many people who have suffered a traumatic neurological insult or who have a degenerative disease such as Alzheimer's may experience problems recognizing things. But these problems will be generic: Whether an object is placed in their hands or described verbally, patients with Alzheimer's disease will have problems recognizing it.

For visual agnosics, the deficit is restricted to the visual domain; recognition through other sensory modalities, such as touch or audition, may be just fine. Like patient G.S., introduced at the beginning of this chapter, visual agnosics may fail to recognize a fork, but when the object is placed in their hand, they will immediately recognize it (Figure 6.22). Indeed, after touching the object, an agnosia patient may report seeing the object clearly. Because the patient can recognize the object through other modalities, and through vision with supplementary support, we know that the problem does not reflect a general loss of knowledge. Rather, it must reflect a loss of knowledge that is intimately linked to visual perception or an inability for the products of visual perception to access modality-independent knowledge stores.

Subtypes of Agnosia

Visual agnosia is differentiated from visual deficits caused by an impairment in sensory abilities. A patient who is completely blind will be unable to recognize a visually presented object. But a blind patient does not have a problem linking visual information to stored knowledge about the world; rather, a blind patient lacks the perceptual input needed to activate this internal knowledge. The label *visual agnosia* is restricted to individuals who demonstrate object

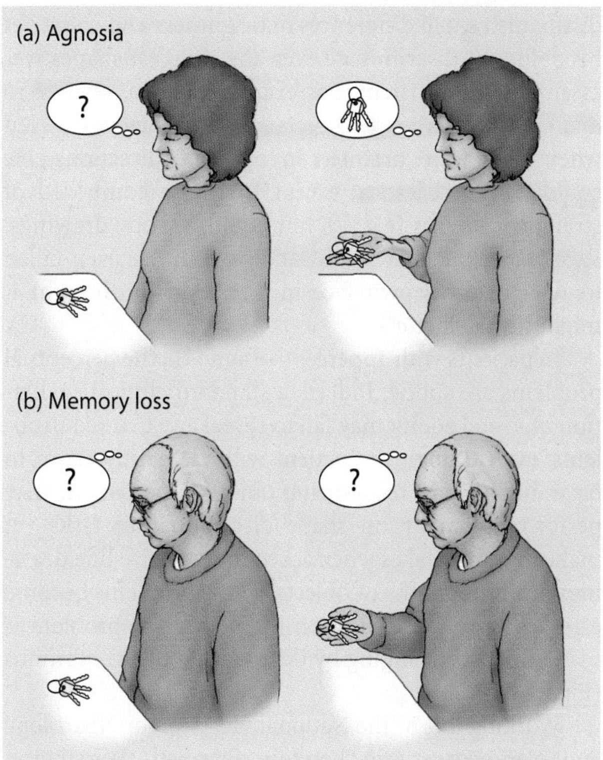

Figure 6.22 Agnosia versus memory loss. To diagnose an agnosic disorder, it is essential to rule out general memory problems. **(a)** The patient with agnosia is unable to recognize the keys by vision alone but immediately recognizes them when she picks them up. **(b)** The patient with a memory disorder is unable to recognize the keys even when he picks them up.

recognition problems even though visual information continues to be registered at the cortical level.

The 19th-century German neurologist Heinrich Lissauer first suggested the existence of two types of visual agnosia. Lissauer (1890) distinguished between recognition deficits that were primarily sensory based and those that reflected an inability to access memory visually—a disorder that he melodramatically referred to as *Seelenblindheit*, or "soul blindness." The current literature distinguishes mainly between apperceptive agnosia and associative agnosia.

Apperceptive agnosia describes failures in object recognition linked to problems in perceptual processing and is a ventral-stream disorder. **Associative agnosia**, in contrast, is reserved for patients who derive normal visual representations but cannot use this information to recognize things. Although research has led to more refined taxonomies, the distinction between apperceptive and associative agnosias continues to provide a useful classification scheme.

APPERCEPTIVE AGNOSIA

The inability to recognize objects can arise from a host of perceptual disorders. A severe case was apparent in a young man who had suffered carbon monoxide poisoning, an injury that produced widespread bilateral cortical damage. The poisoning had not produced any scotomas (visual field deficits), and the patient could distinguish small differences in brightness and color. Yet his ability to discriminate even the simplest shapes was essentially nonexistent. For example, he was unable to distinguish between two rectangles of equal area, even when they were oriented in opposite directions. He could not read letters, except for those composed of straight segments (e.g., *I*), nor could he copy drawings. Face perception was impossible for him. He even failed to recognize his own face in a mirror; he thought it might be his doctor's.

In patients with apperceptive agnosia, the perceptual problems are subtle. Indeed, a standard clinical evaluation of visual acuity may fail to reveal any marked problems, even though the patient will adamantly claim to have difficulty in recognizing objects. The patient may perform normally on shape discrimination tasks yet make many mistakes when asked to recognize line drawings or photographs of objects. These problems become especially pronounced when the perceptual problem is made more challenging by degradation of the stimulus (Figure 6.23).

Working out of the National Hospital for Neurology and Neurosurgery in London, Elizabeth Warrington (1985) has carefully investigated perceptual disabilities in patients. One of her first studies included more than 80 patients with right- or left-hemisphere lesions. Inclusion did not depend on whether the patients showed signs of agnosia; indeed, it is unlikely that many patients would have presented any clinical signs of object recognition problems. Instead, the main criterion for inclusion was evidence of a unilateral cerebral lesion (stroke or tumor). In addition, all the patients were right-handed and had normal visual acuity, either with or without glasses. This last criterion excluded patients with object recognition deficits caused by obvious sensory problems.

In the Gollin Incomplete Figures Task and the Incomplete Letters Task (Figure 6.23), patients with right-sided lesions showed poorer performance than did either control subjects or patients with left-sided lesions. Left-sided damage had little effect on performance—a result made even more impressive by the fact that many of these patients had language problems. This lateralization effect—that is, apperceptive agnosia being more apparent after right-hemisphere damage than after left-hemisphere damage—has been observed

Figure 6.23 Tests to evaluate the recognition of degraded images. Patients with agnosia following right-hemisphere lesions have more difficulty with the Incomplete Letters Task **(a)** than do patients with left-hemisphere lesions, despite the more severe language problems for the left-hemisphere group. In the Gollin Incomplete Figures Task **(b)**, subjects are presented with a series of drawings of an object, each more complete than the previous one. Patients with right-hemisphere lesions require more complete drawings in order to identify the objects correctly.

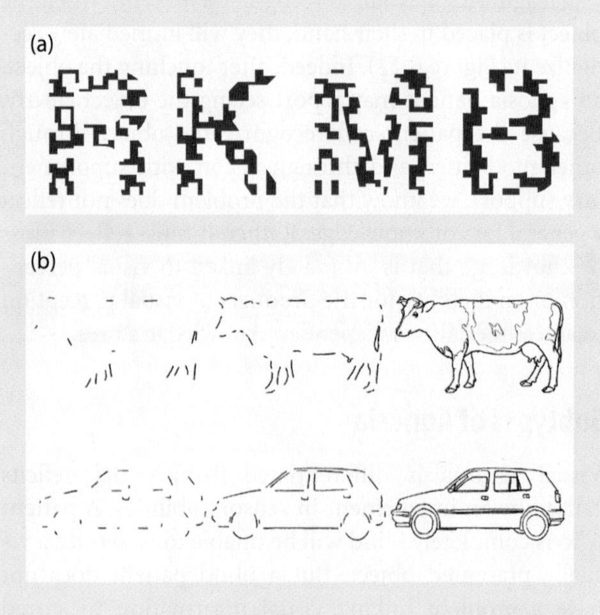

HOW THE BRAIN WORKS

Auditory Agnosia

Other sensory modalities besides visual perception surely contribute to object recognition. Distinctive odors in a grocery store enable us to determine which bunch of greens is thyme and which is basil. Using touch, we can differentiate between a cheap polyester and a fine silk garment. And we depend on sounds, both natural and human-made, to cue our actions. A siren prompts us to search for a nearby police car or ambulance. Or anxious parents immediately recognize the cries of their infant and rush to the baby's aid. Indeed, we often overlook our exquisite auditory capabilities for object recognition. Have a friend rap on a wooden tabletop, or metal filing cabinet, or glass window. You will easily distinguish between these objects.

Numerous studies have documented failures of object recognition in other sensory modalities. As with visual agnosia, a patient has to meet two criteria to be labeled *agnosic*. First, a deficit in object recognition cannot be secondary to a problem with perceptual processes. For example, to be classified as having auditory agnosia, patients must perform within normal limits on tests of tone detection; that is, the loudness of a sound that's required for the person to detect it must fall within a normal range. Second, the deficit in recognizing objects must be restricted to a single modality. For example, a patient who cannot identify environmental sounds such as the ones made by flowing water or jet engines must be able to recognize a picture of a waterfall or an airplane.

Consider a patient, C.N., reported by Isabelle Peretz and her colleagues (1994) at the University of Montreal. A 35-year-old nurse, C.N. had suffered two aneurysms—one in the right middle cerebral artery and the other in the left middle cerebral artery—over a 3-month period. Both aneurysms required surgery. Postoperatively, C.N.'s abilities to detect tones and to comprehend and produce speech were not impaired. But she immediately complained that her perception of music was deranged. Her *amusia*, or impairment in music abilities, was verified by tests. For example, she could not recognize melodies taken from her personal record collection, nor could she recall the names of 140 popular tunes, including the Canadian national anthem.

C.N.'s deficit could not be attributed to a problem with long-term memory. She also failed when asked to decide if two melodies were the same or different. That the problem was selective to auditory perception was evidenced by her excellent ability to identify these same songs when shown the lyrics. Similarly, when given the title of a musical piece such as *The Four Seasons*, C.N. responded that the composer was Vivaldi and could even recall when she had first heard the piece.

Just as interesting as C.N.'s amusia was her absence of problems with other auditory recognition tests. C.N. understood speech, and she was able to identify environmental sounds such as animal cries, transportation noises, and human voices. Even within the musical domain, C.N. did not have a generalized problem with all aspects of music comprehension. She performed as well as normal subjects when asked to judge if two tone sequences had the same rhythm. But her performance fell to a level of near chance when she had to decide if the two sequences were the same melody. This dissociation makes it less surprising that, despite her inability to recognize songs, she still enjoyed dancing!

Other cases of domain-specific auditory agnosia have been reported. Many patients have an impaired ability to recognize environmental sounds, and, as with amusia, this deficit is independent of language comprehension problems. In contrast, patients with pure word deafness cannot recognize oral speech, even though they exhibit normal auditory perception for other types of sounds and have normal reading abilities. Such category specificity suggests that auditory object recognition involves several distinct processing systems. Whether the operation of these processes should be defined by content (e.g., verbal versus nonverbal input) or by computations (e.g., words and melodies may vary with regard to the need for part-versus-whole analysis) remains to be seen … or rather heard.

during a variety of object recognition tasks. How are we to interpret these results? Do they implicate a primary role for the right hemisphere in object recognition? Or does the right hemisphere perform a special cognitive operation essential for tasks like the Gollin Incomplete Figures Task? Can we interpret this deficit within the framework of the computational problems described in the previous section?

Warrington maintained that such an analysis is possible and, indeed, provided a most cogent account of the deficit in patients with right parietal lesions. She contended that the problem is not one of contour discrimination. If patients with right parietal lesions are asked to make fine discriminations between the shapes of simple geometric figures, their performance is only slightly poorer than that of healthy subjects. The critical problem, then, is that perceptual categorization in these patients is impaired; the patient's ability to achieve object constancy is disrupted.

To test this hypothesis, Warrington devised the Unusual Views Object Test. For this test, subjects were shown photographs of 20 objects, each from two distinct views, as Figure 6.24a illustrates. In one photograph the object was oriented in a standard or prototypical view; for example, a cat was photographed with its head facing forward. The other photograph depicted an unusual or atypical view; for example, the cat was photographed from behind, without its face or feet in the picture. Subjects were asked to name the objects shown. Although normal subjects made few, if any, errors, patients with right posterior lesions had difficulty identifying the objects that had been photographed from unusual orientations. That they could name the objects when photographed in the prototypical orientation confirmed that their problem was not a deficit of lost visual knowledge.

A second task asked whether the subjects could recognize if pairs of photographs depicted the same

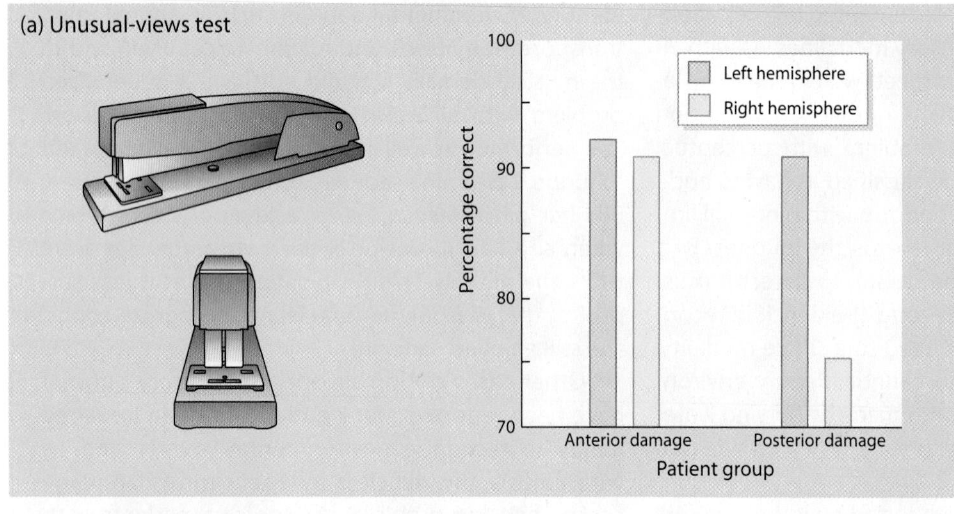

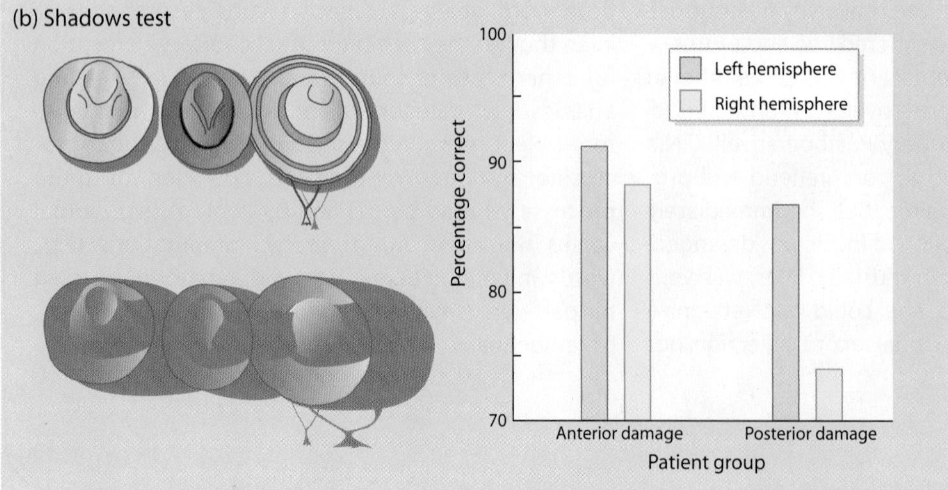

Figure 6.24 Tests used to identify apperceptive agnosia. **(a)** In the unusual-views test, subjects must judge whether two photographs taken from different vantage points show the same object. **(b)** In the shadows test, subjects must identify the object(s) when seen under normal or shadowed illumination. In both tests, patients with right-hemisphere lesions, especially in the posterior area, performed much worse than did control subjects (not shown) or patients with left-hemisphere lesions.

object. Here pairs of photographs were presented in each trial—one from the prototypical set and one from the unusual set. The two photographs were either of the same or of different objects, and the subjects' task was to judge if the objects were the same. As expected, patients with right posterior lesions showed more impairment than did healthy subjects and patient control groups. Similar results were obtained from other photographic transformations that presumably tax the object constancy mechanism. In the Shadows Test, for example, patients had problems matching an object photographed from exactly the same position but in two different lighting conditions (Figure 6.24b).

Warrington's analysis thus identified the critical deficit underlying apperceptive agnosia. Her evaluation did not simply restate the problem—that patients with right-hemisphere lesions have difficulty with object recognition because the right hemisphere is so prominent in object perception. Instead, she postulated a cognitive process associated with the posterior part of the right hemisphere, a principal player in *perceptual categorization*. People can normally recognize an object under nearly infinite orientations, distances, and illuminations. Although we see these percepts as distinct, we can identify the similarities. A cat will be identified whether it is sleeping on the couch, rolling on the floor, or prowling through the garden.

This flexibility in recognition implies that we can readily achieve object constancy; from the infinity of percepts, we extract critical features to identify the object. Patients with right parietal lobe lesions are less able to recognize objects. When presented so that the perceptual input highlights the most salient features, the object can be recognized. If these features must be inferred or extracted from a limited perceptual input, apperceptive agnosics have difficulties.

ASSOCIATIVE AGNOSIA

Associative agnosia is, by definition, a failure of visual object recognition that cannot be attributed to perceptual abilities. Associative agnosics rarely perform normally on perceptual tests, but their perceptual deficiencies are not proportional to their recognition problems. One patient, F.R.A., awoke one morning and discovered that he could not read his newspaper—a condition known as **alexia**, or *acquired alexia* (R. McCarthy & Warrington, 1986). When the problem did not subside, F.R.A. visited his local hospital. A CT scan revealed an infarct of the left posterior cerebral artery. The lesioned area was primarily in the occipital region of the left hemisphere, although the damage probably extended into the posterior temporal cortex. F.R.A.'s story is not atypical: Strokes often go unnoticed until the patient discovers an inability to perform a task.

After F.R.A.'s condition had stabilized, perceptual tests were administered. He copied geometric shapes with ease and could point to objects when they were named. Most impressive was his ability to segment a complex drawing into its parts (Figure 6.25). Apperceptive agnosia patients fail miserably when instructed to color each object differently. In contrast, F.R.A. performed the task effortlessly. Despite this ability, though, he could not name the objects that he had colored.

Further testing revealed the extent of F.R.A.'s deficits. When shown line drawings of common objects, he could name or describe the function of only half of them. If given the name verbally, he could readily generate a verbal description. In a similar manner, when presented with pictures of two animals, such as a mouse and a dog, and asked to point to the larger one, his performance was barely above what could be attributed to chance alone. If the two animal names were said aloud, F.R.A. could do the task perfectly. His problems were clearly restricted to the visual modality. The ability to recognize the meaning of visually presented objects was compromised by the stroke.

Figure 6.25 Patient F.R.A.'s drawings. Despite his inability to name visually presented objects, F.R.A. was quite successful in coloring in the components of these complex drawings. He had clearly succeeded in parsing the stimuli but still was unable to identify the objects.

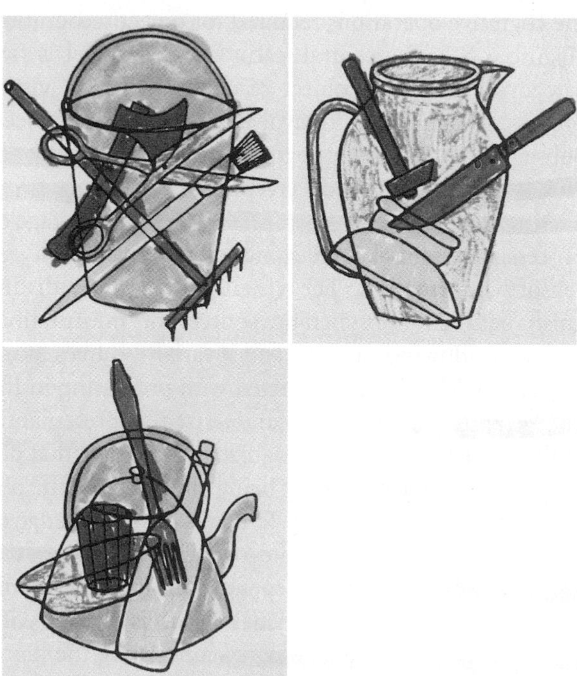

This hypothesis was explored in another test that Warrington used in her group studies. Recall that in the Unusual Views Object Test, subjects are required to judge if two pictures depict the same object from different orientations. This task requires subjects to categorize information according to perceptual qualities. In an alternative task, the Matching-by-Function Test, subjects are shown three pictures and asked to point to the two that are functionally similar. In Figure 6.26a, the correct response is to match the closed umbrella to the open umbrella, even though the former is physically more similar to the cane. The Matching-by-Function Test requires subjects to categorize stimuli on the basis of their semantic properties—that is, in relation to how they are used.

Patients with posterior lesions in either the right or the left hemisphere are impaired on this task. Yet Warrington maintained that the problems in the two groups happen for different reasons. Patients with right-sided lesions cannot do the task, because they fail to recognize many objects, especially those depicted in an unconventional manner, such as the closed umbrella. Patients with left-sided lesions can frequently recognize objects in isolation, but they cannot make the functional connection between the two visual percepts. They lack the semantic representations needed to link the functional association between the open and closed umbrellas.

Integrating Parts Into Wholes

Warrington (1985) proposed an anatomical model of the cognitive operations required for object recognition (Figure 6.27). The central feature of the model is two categorical stages of object recognition. Initial visual processing is assumed to involve both occipital cortices. Subsequently, the first categorical operation, *perceptual categorization*, is invoked. Perceptual inputs are matched with stored representations of visual objects—a stage of processing essential for dealing with the variability of sensory information. The visual system must distinguish between idiosyncratic sources of information, such as shadowing patterns, and invariant sources of information. This stage, associated with processing in the right hemisphere, can be characterized as presemantic in the sense that we may recognize two pictures that depict the same object without being able to name the object or describe its function. To access our knowledge of objects, however, a second categorization stage, *semantic categorization*—one that depends on the left hemisphere—is needed. Here visual input is linked with knowledge in long-term memory concerning the name and functions of that input.

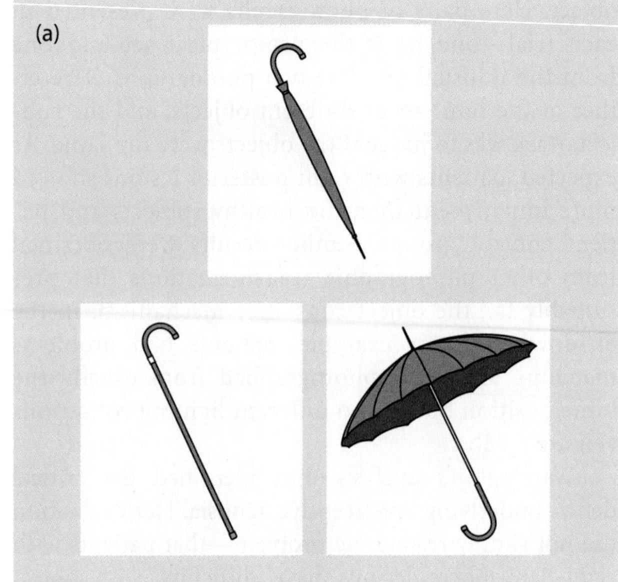

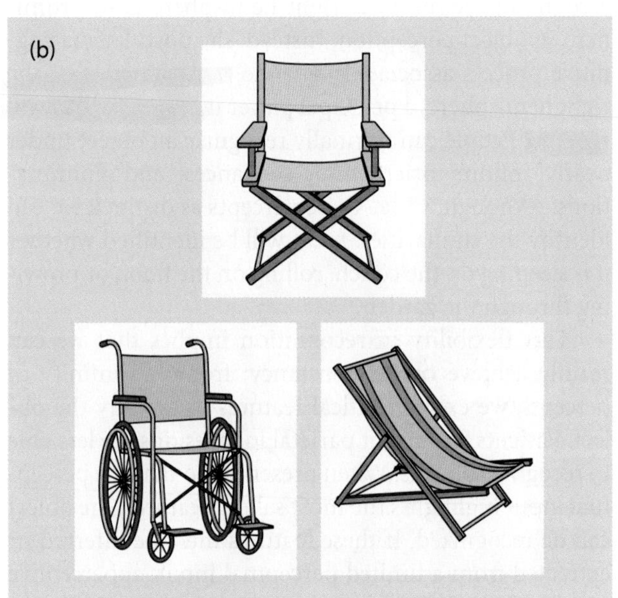

Figure 6.26 Matching-by-Function Test. Subjects are asked to choose the two objects that are most similar in terms of function. In both **(a)** and **(b)**, the object above is correctly matched with the lower-right object, despite the greater physical similarity to the lower-left object. Agnosic patients with left-hemisphere lesions demonstrate impairment on this task.

The Warrington model is a simple look at how we go about recognizing objects. The model requires elaboration, though. First, neuropathological findings have not always proved a correspondence between associative agnosia and left-hemisphere lesions. More typically, these patients usually have bilateral lesions that affect occipitotemporal regions. In addition, unilateral right-hemisphere lesions restricted to this region can

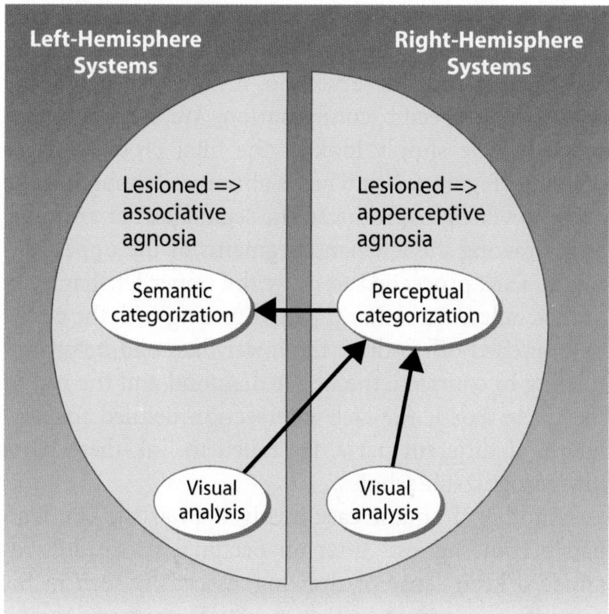

Figure 6.27 Warrington's two-stage model of object recognition. Visual analysis occurs in both hemispheres, at least when we look directly at an object. The first stage of object categorization is perceptual—the processes required to overcome the perceptual variability in the stimulus. This stage depends on the right hemisphere. The second stage is semantic categorization, in which the perceptual representation is linked to semantic knowledge. This stage depends on the left hemisphere.

produce an agnosia more similar to the associative subtype than to the apperceptive subtype.

Detailed analysis of a few case studies also pointed to the need for more refined analysis at the cognitive level of what happens in perceptual categorization. Glyn Humphreys, Jane Riddoch, and colleagues (Humphreys & Riddoch, 1987; Humphreys et al., 1994) at the University of Birmingham in England described a patient, H.J.A., who suffered a stroke while undergoing an appendectomy. The stroke resulted in bilateral lesions of the occipital lobe that extended anteriorly into the ventral part of the temporal lobe. More than 15 years of testing revealed an extensive and stable agnosia. When initially asked to name common household objects, H.J.A. succeeded on about 80% of the trials; his performance fell to 40% when line drawings were used as stimuli. As with all other visual agnosics, H.J.A.'s ability to identify objects tactilely was normal, and he demonstrated good long-term knowledge concerning the visual properties of objects (e.g., he could answer correctly when asked if the prime minister of England had a mustache).

An assessment of H.J.A.'s performance on standard measures of agnosia led to a classification of associative agnosia. He had no problem with shape-matching tasks and was able to copy accurately. He was also successful in matching photographs of objects from unusual views—Warrington's test for a perceptual categorization deficit.

It was apparent, however, that H.J.A.'s perceptual abilities were quite abnormal. When he was presented with overlapping figures, his object recognition ability failed completely; he recognized objects in isolation but had great problems when the contours of two objects overlapped. H.J.A.'s drawings offered further evidence of his limited capabilities: His renditions were produced in a piecemeal, slavish fashion. He drew each segment individually, repeatedly examining the model before progressing to the next part.

Humphreys and Riddoch proposed that H.J.A. had difficulty integrating the parts of an object into a coherent whole—a deficit they labeled **integrative agnosia**. He was unable to perceive an object "at a glance." Instead, his ability to identify objects depended on recognizing salient features or parts. To recognize a dog, H.J.A. had to independently perceive each of the legs and the characteristic shape of the body and head, and then use these part representations to identify the whole. Such a strategy runs into problems with overlapping figures, where it is necessary not only to identify the parts but also to make the correct assignment of parts to objects.

Many tests can provide evidence that H.J.A. has a deficit in grouping and integrating features. Consider the task in Figure 6.28, where subjects must determine whether a display contains an upside-down *T* among distracters that are upright or tilted *T*s. The upside-down target contains the same features (a horizontal and a vertical line) as the upright distracters. Normal subjects are much faster when the distracters form a homogeneous set (e.g., all upright *T*s) than when they are drawn from a heterogeneous set (e.g., upright and tilted *T*s). It appears that we can rapidly group homogeneous elements and detect a deviation from this consistent texture. H.J.A., though, did not have this advantage with organized displays. His reaction times were comparable in organized and random conditions, supporting the hypothesis that H.J.A. must treat each object as an independent entity, examining each pair of lines to determine whether the *T* is upright or upside down. H.J.A. also failed to identify objects when contours were well structured as opposed to being fragmented.

Riddoch, Humphrey, and their colleagues conducted a follow-up study (M. J. Riddoch et al., 1999) that looked at the changes in H.J.A. over time, comparing the initial tests in 1987 to those conducted in 1997, 10 years later. H.J.A. improved in his performance of naming real

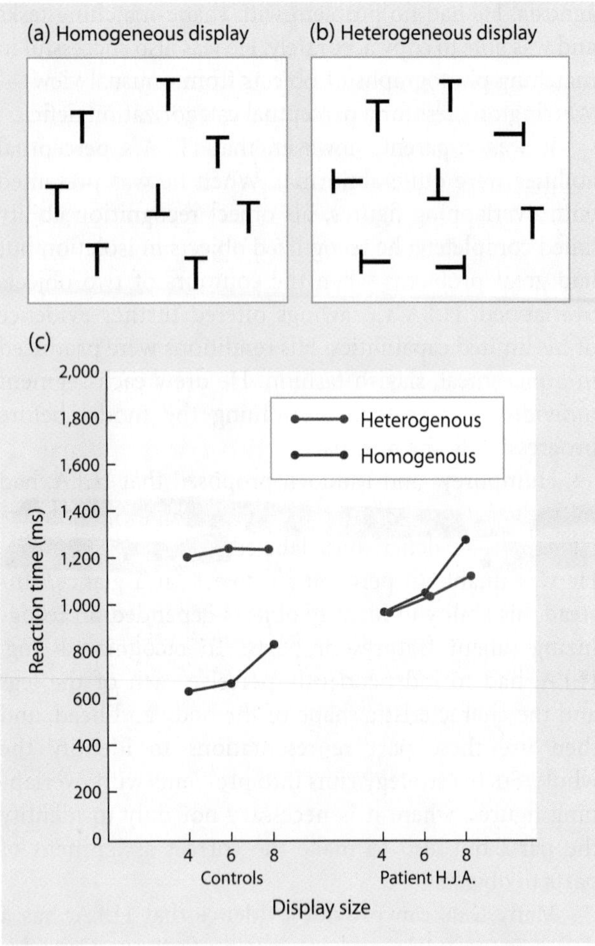

Figure 6.28 Patients with integrative agnosia have difficulty grouping common elements together. Normal subjects quickly find the upside-down *T* when all of the distracters are upright *T*s, as in **(a)**. When the distracters are heterogeneous, as in **(b)**, their reaction times are much slower. The benefit is likely due to the fact that the distracter elements group together in the homogeneous condition. **(c)** Patient H.J.A.'s reaction times are comparable in the two conditions, indicating a failure to group.

objects, even though his actual perceptual abilities remained stable. The authors contribute this change to the fact that H.J.A. was learning to compensate for his loss by using information like surface detail and depth cues in order to identify objects. Interestingly, H.J.A.'s performance deteriorated in tasks that required long-term memory for visual object components. For instance, H.J.A.'s ability to draw from memory decreased along with his ability to describe objects verbally, even though his perceptual abilities remained constant.

H.J.A. does not represent a special case of integrative agnosia. Indeed, an inability to integrate features into a coherent whole may be the hallmark of many agnosia patients. A telling example of this deficit is provided by the drawings of patient C.K., a young man who suffered a head injury in an automobile accident (Behrmann et al., 1994). C.K. was asked to draw three geometric shapes in a specific configuration. We might be impressed if we simply look at the final product of his drawing (Figure 6.29); what is abnormal, though, is the order in which he produced the segments. For example, after drawing the left-hand segments of the upper diamond, C.K. proceeded to draw the upper left-hand arc of the circle. And rather than continuing with the circle, he branched off to draw the lower diamond before returning to complete the upper diamond and the rest of the circle. For C.K., each intersection defined the segments of different parts. He failed to link these parts into recognizable wholes.

Another dramatic case involved an artist, J.R., who had become agnosic after an occipital stroke. J.R. retained a keen sense of drawing, as can be seen in his copy of a silk screen in Figure 6.30. Even after drawing the picture, though, he could not recognize the objects; he failed to identify the stove, and only after prodding was he willing to admit that the animal might be a "domestic bird."

Warrington's analysis of perceptual and semantic categorization fails to capture the integration problems faced by these patients: the inability to synthesize parts into a coherent whole. An isolated part may provide the perceiver with a hypothesis about the identity of a stimulus, perhaps even proving sufficient with unique objects (e.g., the frame of a bicycle). But in most situations, parts must be integrated into wholes. The patient described at the beginning of this chapter, G.S., fixated on the belief that the depicted combination lock was a telephone because of the circular array of numbers, a salient feature on the rotary phones of his time. He was unable

Figure 6.29 Patient C.K. was asked to copy the figure shown in **(a)**. His overall performance **(b)** was quite good; one can readily identify the two diamonds and the circle. However, the numbers indicate the order in which he produced the segments. Unlike healthy subjects, C.K. did not draw each object in its entirety, but rather followed the outer boundary, even if doing so meant switching back and forth between objects.

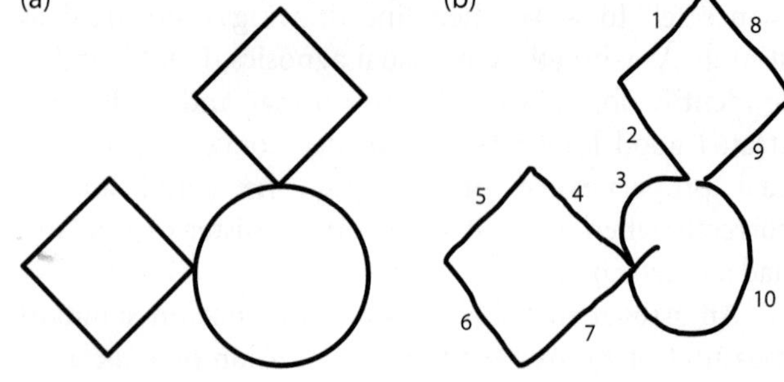

Figure 6.30 Patient J.R., a skilled artist, copied the drawing in **(a)**. Although his reproduction **(b)** is quite faithful to the original, he was not able to identify the stove or the rooster.

to integrate this part with the other components of the combination lock. In object perception, the whole truly is greater than the sum of its parts.

Category Specificity in Agnosia

Associative agnosia results from the loss of semantic knowledge regarding the visual structures or properties of objects. Early perceptual analyses proceed normally, but the long-term knowledge of visual information is lost, and thus the object cannot be recognized. Further support for the idea of a loss of visual semantics comes from bizarre reports of patients whose object recognition deficit appears to be selective for specific categories of objects (Warrington & Shallice, 1984).

Patient J.B.R. was diagnosed as having herpes simplex encephalitis in 1980. His illness left him with a complicated array of deficits, including a dense amnesia, or memory loss, and word-finding difficulties. Although his performance on tests of apperceptive agnosia was normal, J.B.R. had a severe associative agnosia. Most notable about his agnosia was that it was disproportionately worse for living objects than for inanimate ones. For drawings of common objects such as scissors, clocks, and chairs, his success rate was about 90%. In contrast, he could correctly identify only 6% of the pictures of living things. A similar dissociation of agnosia for living and nonliving things has been reported for other patients (Satori & Job, 1988).

How are we to interpret such puzzling deficits? Warrington's visual semantics hypothesis provides an answer. If we assume that associative agnosia represents a loss of knowledge about visual properties, we might suppose that a category-specific disorder results from the selective loss within this knowledge system. Semantic knowledge is structured: We recognize that birds, dogs, and dinosaurs are animals because they share common features. In a similar way, scissors, saws, and knives share characteristics. Some might be physical (e.g., they all have an elongated shape) and others functional (e.g., they all are used for cutting). Brain injuries that produce agnosia in humans do not completely destroy the connections to semantic knowledge. Even the most severely affected patient will recognize some objects. Because the damage is not total, it seems reasonable that circumscribed lesions might destroy tissue devoted to processing similar types of information. **Category-specific deficits** support this form of organization.

The lesions in the patients described in the preceding paragraphs have affected regions associated with processing information about living things. If this interpretation were valid, we might expect to find opposite results: patients whose recognition of nonliving things is disproportionately impaired. Indeed, there have been a few; for example, one patient showed much more impairment in recognizing common objects than in recognizing animals. In each trial, an array of five objects was presented. A target was then presented either visually or auditorily, and the subject's task was to choose the object in the array that was from the same category as the target (Figure 6.31). For both modalities, the patient was much slower and made more errors with the common objects than with the animals.

Thus, we do have evidence of a double dissociation between agnosia for living things and that for nonliving things. But we should be cautious: No studies have shown this double dissociation by using exactly the same stimulus materials. In the study just reviewed, no patients showed the opposite pattern of results, nor were there any control data. It may be, then, that the nonliving-object trials were simply more difficult than the living-object trials for these stimuli. Given that reports of patients with

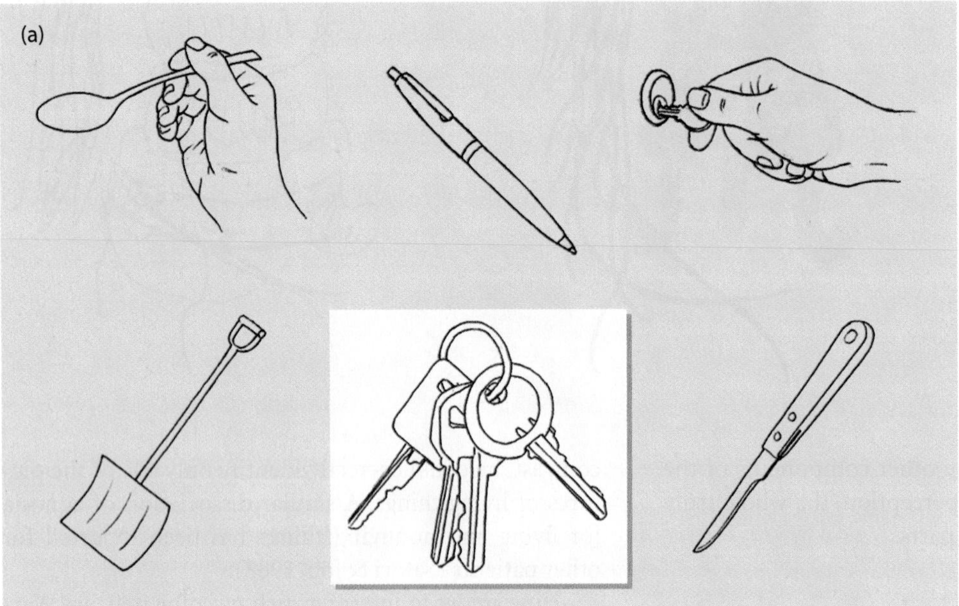

Figure 6.31 Tests to demonstrate category-specific agnosia. In each condition, the subject is asked to choose from the array of five drawings the one that goes best with the probe item in the box. A patient with a selective deficit for common objects would perform poorly in the example shown in **(a)** but normally in the example in **(b)**. The reverse would be expected in a patient with a category-specific deficit for living things.

selective deficits in recognizing nonliving objects are much rarer, we should consider alternative accounts for this pattern of category-specific agnosias.

One idea is that many nonliving things evoke representations not elicited by living things (A. R. Damasio, 1990). In particular, manufactured objects can be manipulated. As such, they are associated with kinesthetic and motoric representations. When viewing an object, we can activate a sense of how it feels or of the actions required to manipulate it (Figure 6.32). Corresponding representations will not exist for living objects. Although we may have a kinesthetic sense of how a cat's fur feels, few of us have ever stroked an elephant. And we certainly have no sense of what it feels like to pounce like a cat or fly like a bird.

According to this hypothesis, manufactured objects are easier to recognize because they activate additional forms of representation. Although brain injury can produce a common processing deficit for all categories of stimuli, these extra representations may be sufficient to recognize nonliving objects. The viability of this hypothesis can be seen in patient G.S.'s behavior. Remember that when G.S. was shown the picture of the combination lock, his first response was to call it a telephone. But even when verbalizing "telephone," his hands began to move as if they were opening a combination lock. Indeed, he was able to name the object after he looked at his hands in wonder and realized what they were trying to tell him.

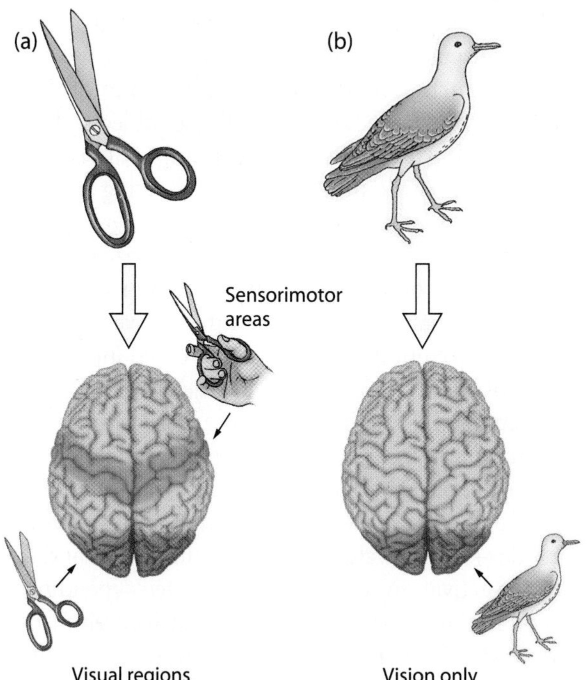

Figure 6.32 The spared ability to recognize common objects has been attributed to the fact that our visual knowledge is supplemented by kinesthetic codes developed through our interactions with these objects. **(a)** When a picture of scissors is presented, the visual code may not be sufficient for recognition. When the picture is supplemented with priming of kinesthetic codes, however, the person is able to name the object. **(b)** Kinesthetic codes are unlikely to exist for most living things.

With the advent of neuroimaging, similar studies have been conducted looking at category specificity in relation to neuronal activity. Viewing pictures of manufactured objects such as tools results in activation of the left ventral premotor cortex, a region associated with action planning. Moreover, this region is not just activated during the observation of human-made artifacts. Rather, viewing pictures of any objects that can be grasped and manipulated, for example, a rock, will result in an increase in activity in the left premotor cortex (Gerlach et. al., 2002; Kellenbach et. al., 2003). These results suggest that this area of the brain responds preferentially to action knowledge or the knowledge of how we interact with objects.

Computational Account of Category-Specific Deficits

Martha Farah and Jay McClelland (1991) used a series of computer simulations to integrate a number of these ideas. Their study was designed to contrast two ways of conceptualizing the organization of semantic memory (Figure 6.33a). One hypothesis is that semantic memory is organized by category membership. According to this hypothesis, there are distinct representational systems for living and nonliving things, and perhaps further subdivisions within these two broad categories. An alternative hypothesis is that semantic memory reflects an organization based on object properties. The idea that nonliving things are more likely to entail kinesthetic and motor representations is one variant of this view. The computer simulations were designed to demonstrate that category-specific deficits can result from lesions to a semantic memory system organized by object properties.

The architecture of Farah and McClelland's model involved a simple *connectionist network* designed to simulate performance when people are asked to associate object names with visual representations of the objects (Figure 6.33b). As with standard connectionist networks, information was distributed across a number of processing units. One set of units corresponded to peripheral input systems, divided into a verbal and visual system. Each of these was composed of 24 input units. The visual

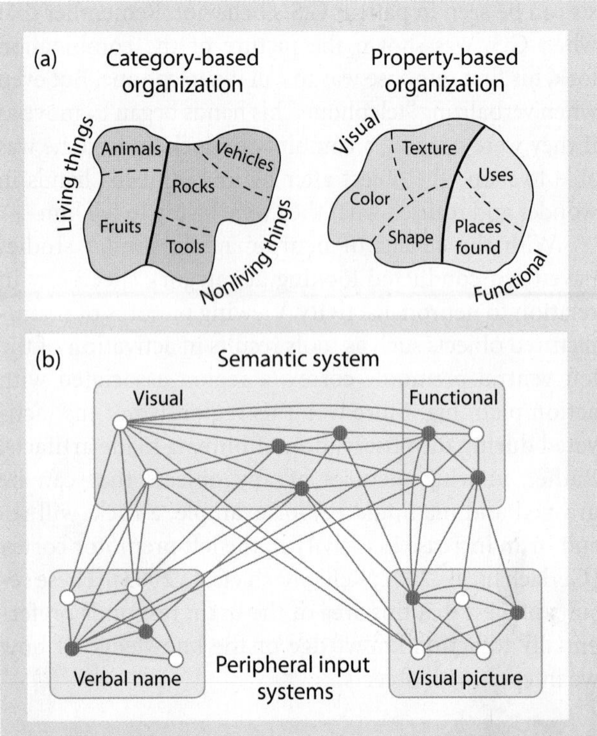

Figure 6.33 **(a)** Two hypotheses concerning the organization of semantic knowledge. A category-based hypothesis **(left)** proposes that semantic knowledge is organized according to our categories of the world. For example, one prominent division would put living things in one group and nonliving things in another. A property-based hypothesis **(right)** proposes that semantic knowledge is organized according to the properties of objects. These properties may be visual or functional. **(b)** The architecture of Farah and McClelland's connectionist model of a property-based semantic system. The initial activation for each object is represented by a unique pattern of activation in two input systems and the semantic system. In this example, the darkened units would correspond to the pattern for one object. The final activation would be determined by the initial pattern and the connection weights between the units. There are no connections between the two input systems. The names and pictures are linked through the semantic system.

representation of an object involved a unique pattern of activation across the 24 visual units. Similarly, the name of an object involved a unique pattern of activation across the 24 verbal units. In the simulations, the model was presented with 20 unique patterns representing 20 objects, half of them living objects and the other half nonliving.

Each object was also linked to a unique pattern of activation across the second type of unit in the model: the semantic memory. Within the semantic system were two types of units: visual and functional (see Figure 6.33b). Although these units did not correspond to specific types of information (e.g., colors or shapes), the idea here is that semantic knowledge consists of at least two types of information. One type of semantic knowledge is visually based, akin to Warrington's visual semantics. For example, visual semantics would embody facts, such as that a tiger has stripes or a chair has legs. The other type of semantic memory corresponds to our functional knowledge of objects. For example, functional semantics would include our knowledge that tigers are dangerous or that a chair is a type of office furniture.

The researchers imposed two constraints on the semantic memory system, intended to capture psychological differences in how visual and semantic information might be stored. The first constraint was that, of the 80 semantic units, 60 were visual and 20 were semantic. This 3:1 ratio was based on a preliminary study in which human subjects were asked to read the dictionary definitions of living and nonliving objects and indicate whether a descriptor was visual or functional. On average, 3 times as many descriptors were classified as visual. Second, the preliminary study indicated that the ratio of visual to functional descriptors differed for the two classes of objects. For living objects the ratio was 7.7:1, but for nonliving objects this ratio dropped to 1.4:1. Thus, as discussed previously, our knowledge of living objects is much more dependent on visual information than is our knowledge of nonliving objects. In the model this constraint dictated the number of visual and functional semantic units used for the living and nonliving objects being varied.

The model was trained to link the verbal and visual representations of a set of 20 objects, half of them living and the other half nonliving. Note that the verbal and visual units were not directly linked but could interact only by way of their connections with the semantic system. The strength of these connections was adjusted in a training procedure. This procedure was not intended to simulate how people acquire semantic knowledge. Rather, the experimenters would set all of the units—both input and semantic—to their values for a particular object and then allow the activation of each unit to change depending on both its initial activation and the input it received from other units. The connection weights were then adjusted to minimize the difference between the resulting pattern and the original pattern. We can test the model's object recognition capabilities by measuring the probability of correctly associating the names and pictures.

This model proved extremely adept. After 40 training trials, it was perfect when tested with both the living and the nonliving stimuli. The key question centered on how well the model did after receiving "lesions" to its semantic memory—lesions assumed to correspond to what happens in patients with visual associative agnosia. Lesions in a model consist of the deactivation of a certain percentage of the semantic units. As Figure 6.34 shows, selective lesions in either the visual or the functional semantic system produced category-specific deficits. When the damage was restricted to visual semantic memory, the model had great difficulty associating the names and pictures correctly for living objects. In contrast, when the damage was restricted to functional semantic memory, failures were limited to nonliving objects. Note that the resulting "deficit" is much more dramatic in the former simulation—the visual semantic lesion's effect on identifying living things.

This result meshes nicely with reports in the neuropsychological literature of many more instances of patients with a category-specific agnosia for living things. Even when functional semantic memory was damaged, the model remained proficient in identifying the nonliving objects, presumably because knowledge of these objects was distributed across both the visual and the functional memory units.

These simulations demonstrated how category-specific deficits might reflect the organization of semantic knowledge. The modeling work makes an important point: We need not postulate that our knowledge of objects is organized along categories such as living and nonliving. The double dissociation between living and nonliving things has been taken to suggest that we have specialized systems sensitive to these categorical distinctions. In contrast, in Farah and McClelland's model, the same system is used to recognize both living and nonliving things. Rather than assuming a partitioning of representational systems in terms of the type of object, Farah and McClelland proposed that semantic memory is organized according to the properties that define the objects.

Category-specific deficits are best viewed as an emergent property of the fact that different sources of information are needed to recognize living and nonliving objects. Our knowledge of living things is highly dependent on visual information, whereas this dependency is lessened for nonliving objects. Although stripes are the defining property of a tiger, chairs come in all shapes and sizes but have the consistent property that they are to be sat on.

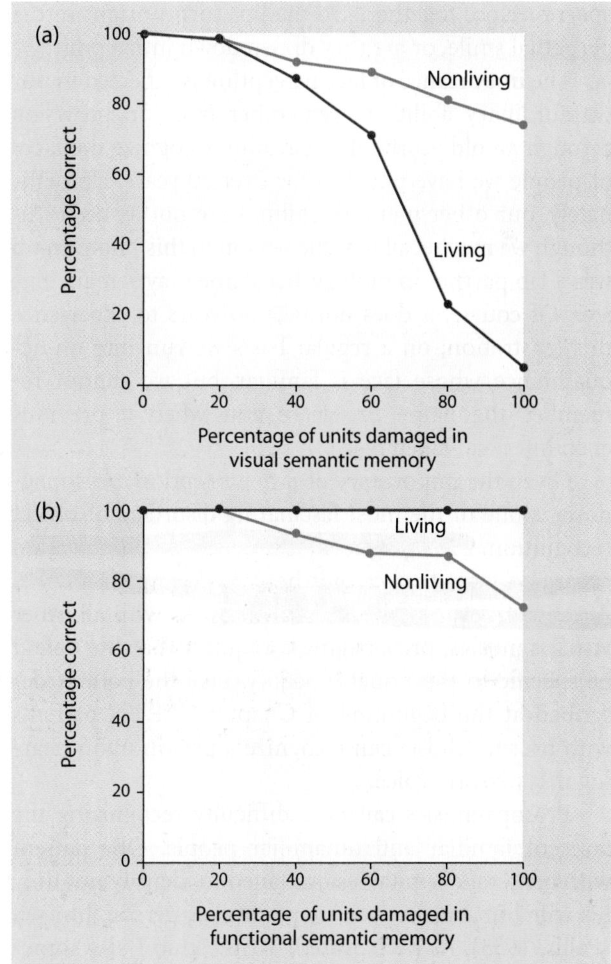

Figure 6.34 Measuring category-specific deficits. Lesions in the semantic units resulted in a double dissociation between the recognition of living and nonliving objects. After a percentage of the semantic units were eliminated, two measurements were made. In the picture-naming task, the visual input pattern for each object was activated and the resultant pattern on the verbal units was evaluated as either correct or incorrect. In the matching-to-sample test, the name pattern was activated and the resulting pattern on the picture units was evaluated. **(a)** When the lesion was restricted to the visual semantic memory units, the model showed much more impairment in correctly associating the name and picture patterns for the living things. **(b)** When the lesion was restricted to the functional semantic memory units, the model showed impairment only in associating the input patterns for nonliving things.

THE PERCEPTION OF FACES

It is hard to deny that the most important things we recognize are faces. Though people may have characteristic physiques and mannerisms, facial features provide the strongest distinctions of one person from another. Think about what you say when describing a new acquaintance to a friend. You may begin by providing information about the person's shape (e.g., large or small), but beyond that, most of the description will center on facial features: Does the person have a long or round face? Are the eyes spaced far apart or close together? Do the lips turn upright into a perpetual smile, or are they drawn down into a pout?

The importance of face perception is reflected in our extraordinary ability to remember faces. In browsing through an old yearbook, we readily recognize the faces of people we have not seen for over 30 years. Unfortunately, our other memory abilities are not as keen. Although we may recall that the person in this photograph was a lab partner in biology, her name may remain elusive. Of course, it does not take 30 years to experience this frustration; on a regular basis we run into an acquaintance whose face is familiar, but we cannot remember the name or where and when a previous encounter had taken place.

Given the importance of face perception, prosopagnosia is one of the most fascinating disorders of object recognition. **Prosopagnosia** is a deficit in the ability to recognize faces that cannot be directly attributed to a deterioration in intellectual function. As with all other visual agnosias, prosopagnosia requires that the deficit be specific to the visual modality. Like the patient described at the beginning of Chapter 5 (P.T.), patients with prosopagnosia can recognize a person upon hearing that person's voice.

Prosopagnosics can have difficulty recognizing the faces of familiar and unfamiliar people. One patient with bilateral occipital lesions failed to identify not only his wife but also an even more familiar person, himself (Pallis, 1955). As he reported, "At the club I saw someone strange staring at me, and asked the steward who it was. You'll laugh at me. I'd been looking at myself in the mirror" (Farah, 2004, p. 93). Not surprisingly, this patient was also unable to recognize pictures of famous individuals of his time, including Churchill, Hitler, Stalin, Marilyn Monroe, and Groucho Marx. This inability was particularly striking in that the patient had an excellent memory, recognized common objects with no hesitation, and could read and recognize line drawings—all tests that agnosia patients often fail.

Interestingly, brain lesions are not the only way in which prosopagnosia can develop. Recently, patients have been discovered with congenital prosopagnosia but without MRI-revealed brain damage (e.g., patient Y.T. reported by Bentin et al., 1999). These studies suggest that one or more genes are important in coding neural mechanisms essential for face perception. Indeed, genetic variations might, in part, explain why some people are much better than others at remembering faces.

Although the patient with the bilateral occipital lesions had "normal" object perception, most patients who have been studied in laboratories show abnormalities on other tests of visual perception. Nonetheless, it is clear that their recognition problems for faces are disproportionate to their ability to recognize other objects. For example, patients with severe prosopagnosia may perform perfectly on Warrington's standard perceptual categorization tasks (e.g., Unusual Views Object Test) yet fail miserably when face stimuli are substituted for the objects. Results such as these suggest that prosopagnosia is not related in a simple way to problems with recognizing nonfacial stimuli.

Are Faces Special?

Face perception may not use the same processing mechanisms as those used in object recognition—a somewhat counterintuitive hypothesis. It seems more reasonable and certainly more parsimonious to assume a single, general-purpose system for recognizing all sorts of visual inputs. Why should faces be treated differently from other objects?

One argument in favor of a specialized face-processing module is based on evolutionary theory. When we meet other individuals, we usually look at their faces rather than their bodies—a behavior that is not a newly acquired cultural convention. The tendency to focus on faces reflects behaviors deeply embedded in our evolutionary history. Across cultures, facial expressions provide the most salient cues regarding affective states. Facial gestures help us discriminate between pleasure and displeasure, friendship and antagonism, agreement and confusion.

Although evolutionary arguments can motivate a hypothesis, it is essential to develop empirical tests. Three criteria can be useful in considering whether face and other forms of object perception utilize distinct processing systems:

1. Do the processes involve physically distinct mechanisms? Do face perception and other forms of object perception depend on different regions of the brain?
2. Are the systems functionally independent? Can each operate without the other? The logic of this criterion is essentially the same as that underlying the idea of double dissociations.
3. Do the two systems process information differently?

Neural Mechanisms for Face Perception

Some patients show impairment only on tests of face perception. More often, though, the patients' performance on other object recognition tasks is below normal. This result is, in itself, inconclusive with regard to the existence of specialized brain mechanisms for face perception. Do not forget that brain injury in humans is an uncontrolled experiment! Prosopagnosia rarely occurs with single, well-circumscribed lesions. This syndrome is frequently associated with bilateral lesions caused by multiple strokes, head trauma, encephalitis, or poisoning. Even if there were a specialized face perception module, probably other visual areas would be affected. As Nancy Kanwisher (2000) writes, "The chance that a stroke or head trauma ... will obliterate all of the hypothesized face-processing region of cortex without affecting nearby cortical areas is similar to the chance that an asteroid hitting New England would obliterate all of the state of Rhode Island without affecting Massachusetts or Connecticut" (p. 760).

With this caveat in mind, we can still evaluate whether patients with prosopagnosia have a common focus of lesions. In her comprehensive monograph *Visual Agnosia: Disorders of Object Recognition and What They Tell Us About Normal Vision*, Martha Farah (1990) identified 81 patients reported to be prosopagnosic. Table 6.1 summarizes the general location of the pathology in 71 of these patients. What is most notable is that the lesions were bilateral in 46 patients (65%). The number would probably increase if the brains were examined at autopsy, since CT and MRI frequently do not detect small lesions, especially the microlesions associated with head trauma. For the remaining 25 patients (35%) with unilateral lesions, the incidence was much higher for right-sided lesions than for left-sided lesions. For bilateral and unilateral cases, the lesions generally involved occipital and temporal cortices.

Given the messiness of human neuropsychology, it is also important to look for converging evidence using the physiological tools of cognitive neuroscience. Neurophysiologists have recorded from the temporal lobes of primates to see if cells in this region respond specifically to faces. In one study (Baylis et al., 1985), recordings were made from cells in the superior temporal sulcus while a monkey was presented with stimuli like the ones in Figure 6.35. Five of these stimuli (A–E) were faces: four of other monkeys, and one of an experimenter. The other five stimuli (F–J) ranged in complexity but included the most prominent features in the facial stimuli. For example, the grating (image G) reflected the symmetry of faces, and the circle (image I) was similar to eyes. Some cells were highly selective: They responded only to the clear frontal profile of another monkey. Other cells raised their firing rate for all facial stimuli. Nonfacial stimuli hardly activated the cells. In fact, compared to spontaneous firing rates, activity decreased for some nonfacial stimuli.

Table 6.1 Summary of Lesion Foci in Patients with Prosopagnosia

Location of Lesion	Percentage of Total[a]
Bilateral ($n = 46$)	**65**
Temporal	61
Parietal	9
Occipital	91
Left only ($n = 4$)	**6**
Temporal	75
Parietal	25
Occipital	50
Right only ($n = 21$)	**29**
Temporal	67
Parietal	28
Occipital	95

[a] Within each subcategory, the percentages indicate how the lesions were distributed across the temporal, parietal, and occipital lobes. The sum of these percentages is greater than 100% because many of the lesions spanned more than one lobe. The majority of the patients had bilateral lesions.

The behavior of these cells closely resembles what would be expected of a grandmother cell in almost a literal sense.

Research of the past two decades has confirmed that cells in two distinct regions of the temporal lobe are preferentially activated by faces: one in the superior temporal sulcus, and the other in the inferotemporal gyrus (Rolls, 1992). We cannot conclude that cells like these respond only to faces; it is impossible to test all stimuli. Nonetheless, the degree of specificity is quite striking, as shown by a study that combined two neurophysiological methods in a novel manner. Monkeys were placed in an fMRI scanner and shown pictures of faces or objects. As expected, sectors of the superior temporal sulcus showed greater activation to the face stimuli; in fact, three distinct subregions in the STS responded to faces (Tsao et al., 2006; Figure 6.36).

The researchers went on to record from individual neurons, using the imaging results to position the electrodes within one of the face-sensitive subregions of the STS. Within that subregion, 97% of the neurons exhibited a strong preference for faces, showing strong responses to any face-containing stimulus and minimal responses to a wide range of other stimuli, such as body parts, food, or objects.

Various alternative ideas have been considered to account for face selectivity. For example, we might suppose that facial stimuli evoke emotional responses and it

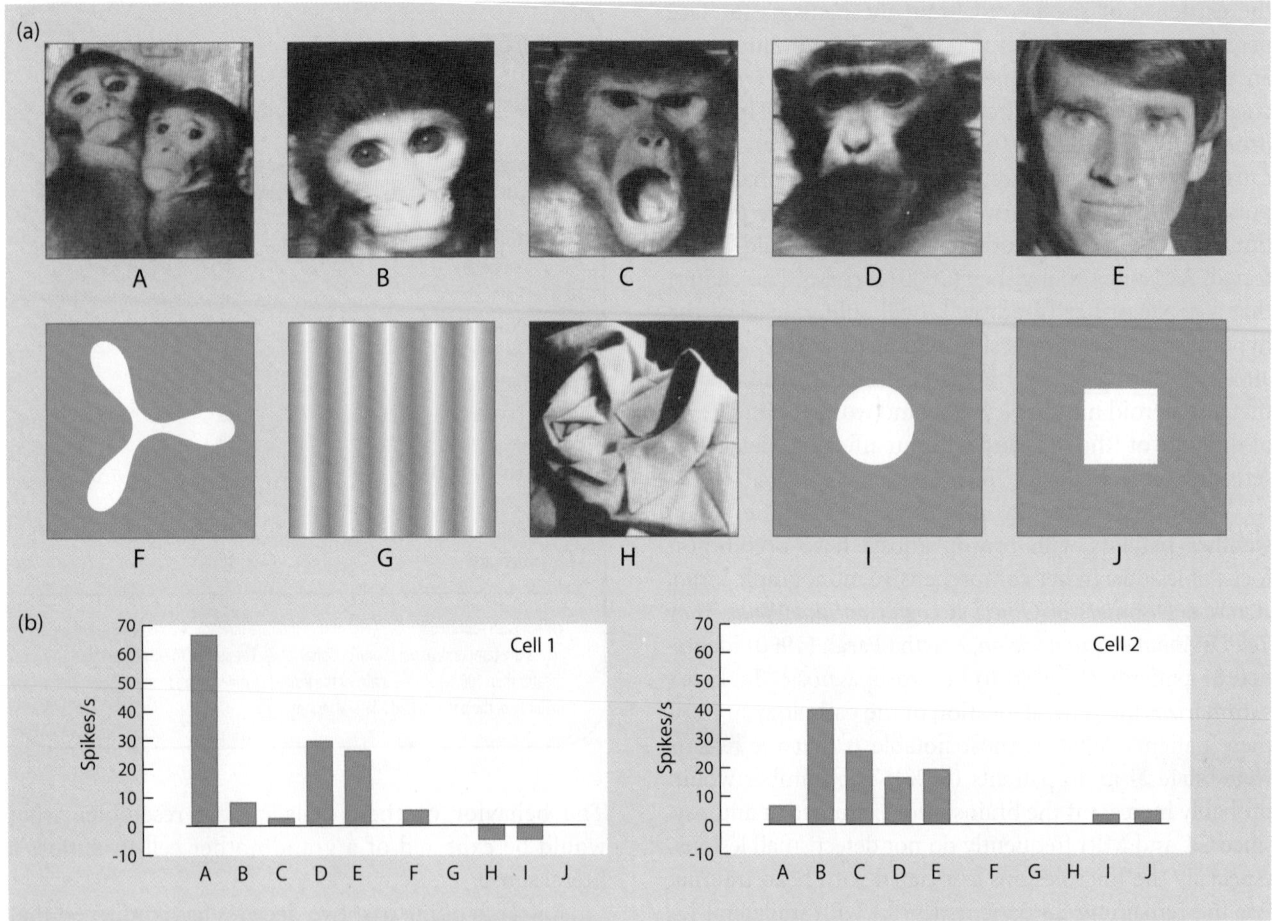

Figure 6.35 Identifying face cells in the superior temporal sulcus of the macaque monkey. The graphs in **(b)** show the responses of two cells to the 10 stimuli (labeled A–J) in **(a)**. Both cells responded vigorously to many of the facial stimuli. Either there was no change in activity when the animal looked at the objects, or, in some cases, the cells were actually inhibited relative to baseline. The firing-rate data are plotted as a change from baseline activity for that cell when no stimulus was presented.

is this property that causes a cell to respond strongly to a face and not to other, equally complex, stimuli. However, the same cells are not activated by stimuli that produce a fear response in monkeys.

The debate concerning a dedicated face perception area has sprung full bloom in the human fMRI literature. Functional MRI is well suited to investigate this problem because its spatial resolution can yield a much more precise image of face-specific areas than can be deduced from lesion studies. As in the monkey study just described, we can ask two questions by comparing conditions in which subjects view different classes of stimuli: First, what neural regions show differential activation patterns when the subject is shown faces compared to the other stimulus conditions? Second, do these "face" regions also respond when the nonfacial stimuli are presented?

In one such study (McCarthy et al., 1997), subjects were presented with pictures of faces, inanimate objects, or random texture patterns (Figure 6.37). Compared to passive viewing of the random patterns, faces led to a stronger BOLD response along the ventral surface of the temporal lobe in the **fusiform gyrus.** When the assorted-objects condition was used as the comparison, the response in the fusiform gyrus of the right hemisphere remained significant.

These results are consistent with the lesion data in that they indicate an important role for the fusiform gyrus in face perception, especially in the right hemisphere. Numerous imaging studies, using a range of different tasks and types of stimuli, have confirmed engagement of the fusiform gyrus. This region has come to be referred to as the **fusiform face area**, or **FFA**, in the literature. The activation can usually be identified on an individual basis, especially in the right hemisphere, although when the data are averaged across a group of individuals, reliable activation is also seen in the left-hemisphere FFA.

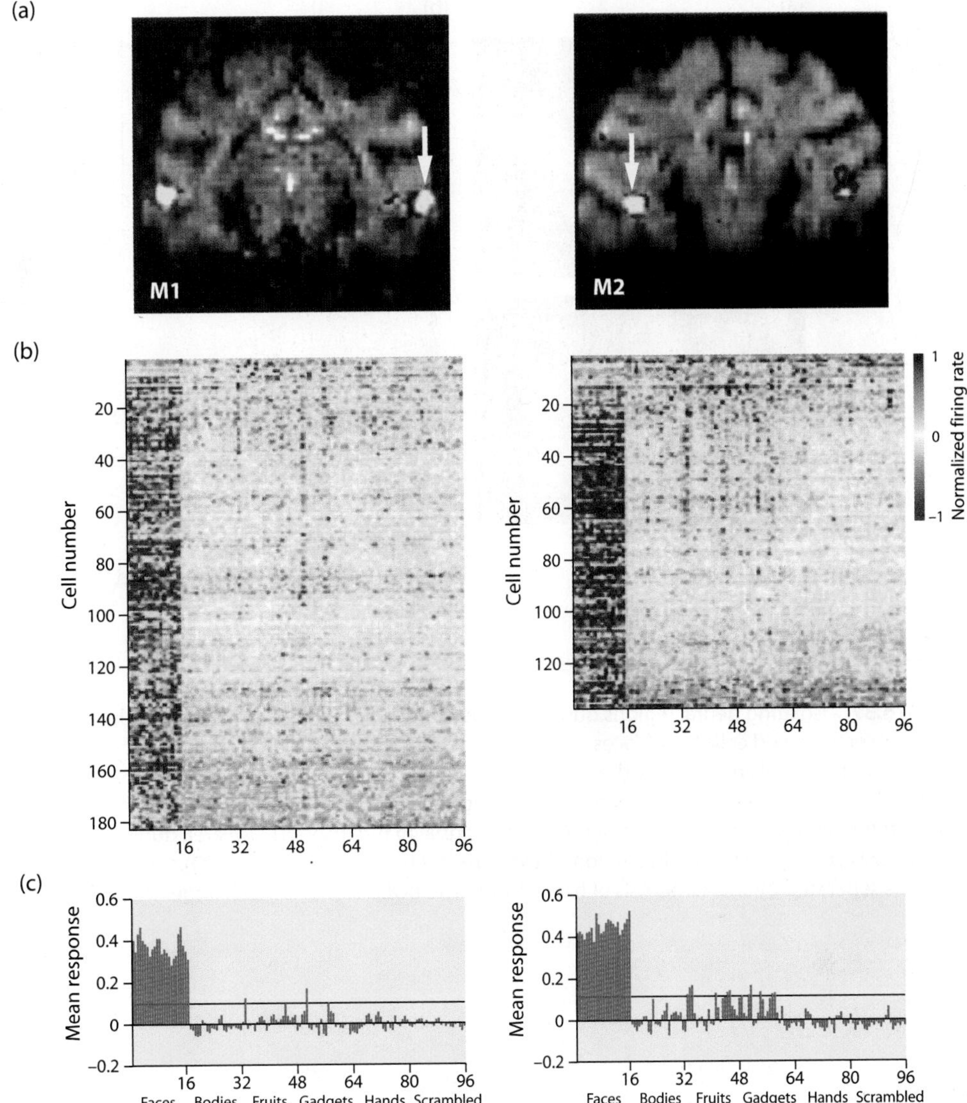

Figure 6.36 Superior temporal sulcus regions that respond to faces. **(a)** Functional-MRI activations during face perception in two macaque monkeys (M1 and M2). The white arrows indicate where subsequent neurophysiological recording was done (left STS in M1 and right STS in M2). Note that the images are displayed according to neuroradiological convention, so the right hemisphere is on the left. **(b)** The activity of each of the cells recorded from in the STS of M1 (left; 182 cells) and M2 (right; 138 cells) that responded to visual stimuli (face, bodies, fruits, gadgets, hands, or scrambled patterns). In these graphs, each row corresponds to a different cell, and each column corresponds to a different image category. **(c)** The average response size for each of the image categories across all cells. These cells were highly selective for face stimuli.

Electrophysiological methods also reveal a neural signature of face perception. Faces elicit a large negative evoked response in the EEG signal, approximately 170 ms after stimulus onset. This response is known as the **N170 response**. A similar negative deflection is found for other classes of objects, such as cars, birds, and furniture, but the magnitude of the response is much larger for humans (Carmel & Bentin, 2002; Figure 6.38). Interestingly, the stimuli need not be pictures of real human faces. The N170 response is elicited when people view faces of apes or if the facial stimuli are crude, schematic line drawings (Sagiv & Bentin, 2001).

A rather heated debate has emerged in the neuroimaging literature on the question of whether the FFA is selectively activated for faces. An alternative hypothesis is that this region is recruited when people have to make fine perceptual discriminations among highly familiar stimuli. Advocates of this hypothesis point out that imaging studies comparing face and object recognition usually entail an important, if underemphasized, confound: the level of expertise.

Consider the comparison of the perception of faces versus flowers. Although neurologically healthy individuals are all experts in perceiving faces, the same is not true for flowers. Moreover, the extent to which we analyze a face or a flower may be quite different, even at an automatic level. Face perception is essential to our social interactions. Whether or not we set out to remember someone's face, we readily encode the features that distinguish one face from another. The same is probably not true for other classes of objects. Most of us are happy to recognize that a particular picture is of a pretty flower, perhaps even to note that it is a rose. But unless we are rose enthusiasts, it is unlikely that we will

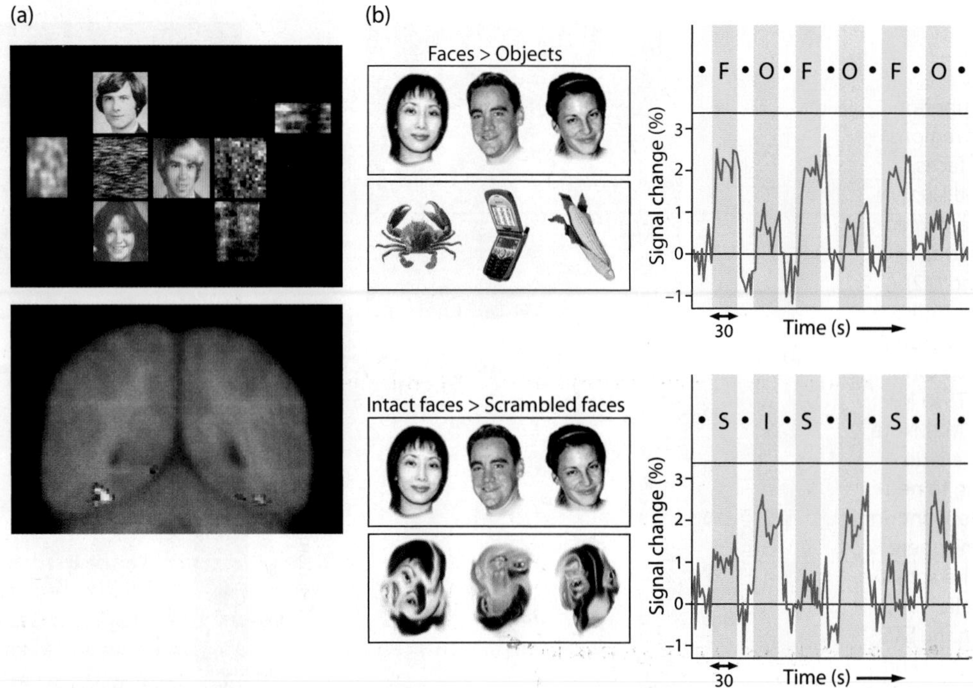

Figure 6.37 Isolating neural regions during face perception. **(a)** Bilateral activation in the fusiform gyrus was observed with fMRI when subjects viewed collages of faces and random patterns compared with collages of just the random patterns. Note that, following neuroradiological conventions, the right hemisphere is on the left. **(b)** In another fMRI study, subjects viewed alternating blocks of stimuli. In one scanning run, the stimuli alternating between faces and objects; in another run, they alternated between intact and scrambled faces. The right column shows the BOLD signal in the fusiform face area during the scanning run for the various stimuli. In each interval, the stimuli were drawn from the different sets—faces (F), objects (O), scrambled faces (S), or intact faces (I)—with these intervals separated by short intervals of fixation only. The BOLD signal is much larger during intervals in which faces were presented.

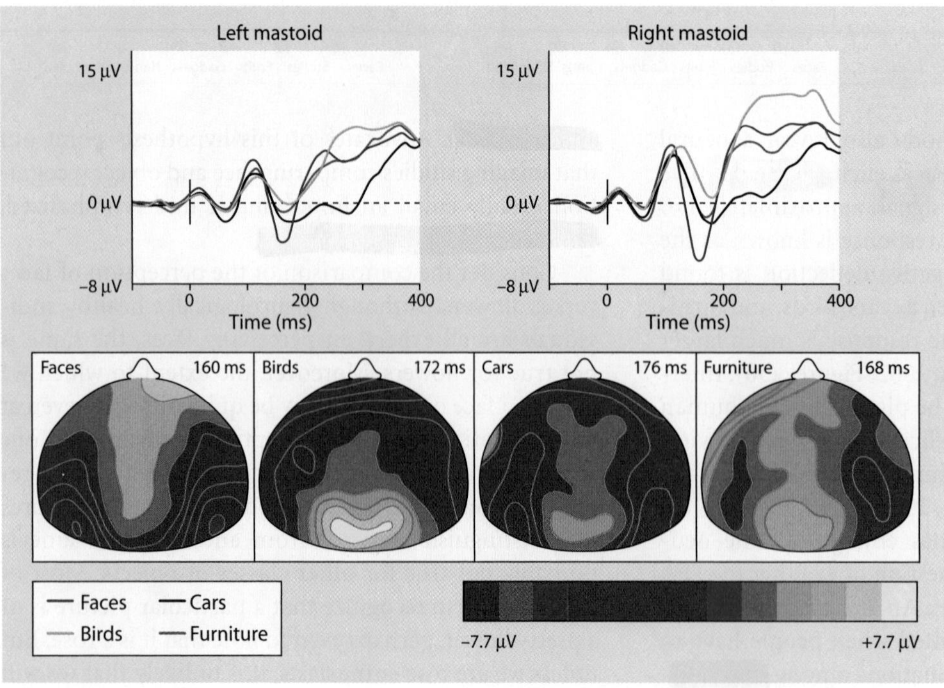

Figure 6.38 Electrophysiological response to faces: the N170 response. Subjects viewed pictures of faces, birds, furniture, and cars and were instructed to press a button whenever they saw a picture of a car. The event-related potentials shown in the graphs are from the area surrounding the back of the skull at about the level of the ears (called the *left* and *right mastoid*). Note that the N170 response, in red, occurs only during face perception.

recognize or encode the difference between a Dazzler and a Garibaldi.

To address this confound, researchers have conducted imaging studies to ask if the FFA is activated in people who are trained to be experts at discriminating objects such as cars and birds (Gauthier et al., 2000). The results are somewhat mixed. Activation in fusiform cortex is in fact greater when people view objects for which they have expertise. For example, car aficionados will respond more to cars compared to birds. Moreover, if subjects are trained to make fine discriminations between novel objects, the fusiform response increases as expertise develops (Gauthier, Tarr, et al., 1999). However, the categorization of objects by experts activates a much broader region of ventral occipitotemporal cortex, extending beyond the FFA (Grill-Spector et al., 2004; Rhodes et al., 2004).

These results suggest that the entire fusiform gyrus/ventral occipitotemporal cortex is involved in analyzing the features that allow us to recognize objects, but that the FFA may be dominated by neurons specifically tuned to face perception. The expertise argument has also been addressed with magnetoencephalography. In one study, the M170 response, the magnetic homologue of the N170 response, to nonfacial stimuli was found not to be modulated by expertise (Xu et al., 2005). Car experts did not show a larger M170 response when viewing cars compared to shoes (about which they had no particular expertise), but their M170 response to faces was much larger compared to that elicited by cars.

One face stands out among all others: our own! Given that face perception has clear neural correlates, researchers have been curious whether there is anything special about the brain response when people view pictures of themselves. Tilo Kircher and his colleagues (2001) at the University of Tübingen in Germany found that the response in the FFA was similar when subjects viewed pictures of their own faces or pictures of unknown faces. However, self-perception also led to greater activation in right limbic regions of the brain (as well as in the left prefrontal cortex and superior temporal sulcus).

A right-hemisphere role in self-perception also is supported by a particularly clever study conducted under very unusual circumstances (Keenan et al., 2001). The participants were individuals who were being evaluated for surgical intervention as a treatment for severe epilepsy. As part of the evaluation, each individual underwent a Wada test, in which a barbiturate is injected to temporarily anesthetize one hemisphere (this procedure is done to determine which hemisphere is dominant for language). During the injection, the participants were shown stimuli that constituted an "averaging" of a picture of their own face with that of a famous person. When they had recovered from the injection, they were asked to judge if they had seen their own picture or that of the famous person. Following right-hemisphere injections, the participants almost always chose the famous face; in contrast, following left-hemisphere injections they chose their own picture (Figure 6.39). On the assumption that the nonanesthetized hemisphere is encoding the face during the injection, these results also point to a role for the right hemisphere in self-perception.

Figure 6.39 Wada test for studying hemispheric involvement in face recognition. Each patient's face was morphed with that of a famous person, such as Marilyn Monroe, and the resulting picture was shown to the patient. Patients were then asked to indicate if this morphed image represented themselves or a famous person. **(a)** If the experiment was conducted when a patient's left hemisphere was anesthetized (during a Wada procedure, which is conducted on patients before they undergo surgery for epilepsy), five out of five patients indicated that a picture of their own face was presented. **(b)** In contrast, if the experiment was then conducted on the same patients when the right hemisphere was anesthetized, four out of five patients identified the famous face as the image they had viewed. This evidence suggests that the right hemisphere plays an important role in self-perception.

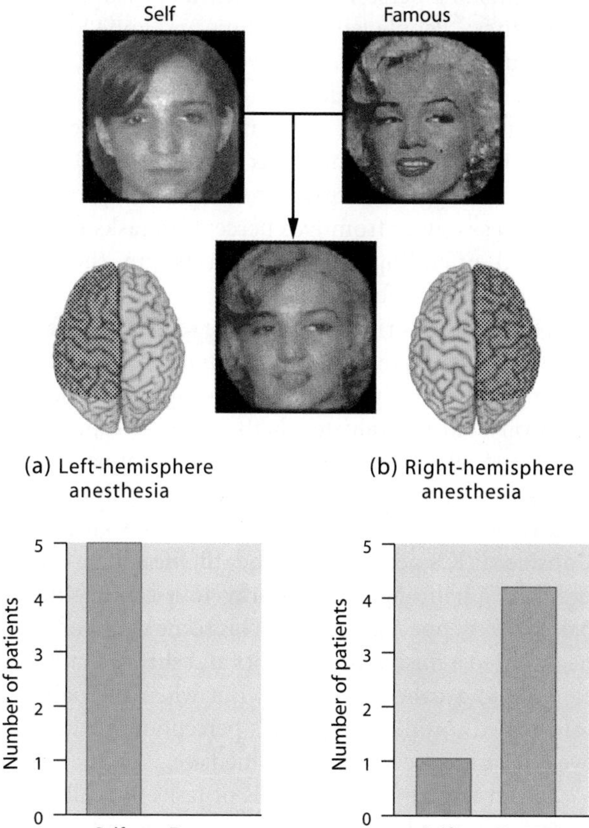

Dissociations of Face and Object Perception

Face perception appears to utilize distinct physical processing systems. But can face and object perception be dissociated? As we have discovered, many case reports describe patients who have a selective disorder in face perception: They cannot recognize faces, but they have little problem recognizing other objects. Even so, this evidence does not mandate a specialized processor for faces. Perhaps the tests that assess face perception are more sensitive to the effects of brain damage than are the tests that evaluate object recognition.

Michael Tarr of Brown University and Isabel Gauthier of Vanderbilt University (2000) have elegantly articulated this point. One concern is that neuropsychological studies tend to focus on simple measures such as overall accuracy: A person either correctly identifies an object or face, or fails to do so. As Chapter 4 emphasized, reaction time measures can provide additional insight, revealing the time course of the underlying processes. When such measures are used in face and object recognition tasks, prosopagnosia patients demonstrate impairment on both tasks; if accuracy alone had been measured, their deficit would have been selective for the face task. Why might this be? One intriguing hypothesis comes from the comments of a person with congenital prosopagnosia, who writes, "People will have come and gone long before you can identify them. So you never do. . . . People in your presence who don't know of your face blindness will be offended at your failure to recognize them" (Gauthier, Behrmann, & Tarr, 1999, p. 353). As this quote suggests, experience may teach prosopagnosics to shy away from face perception tasks in order to avoid offending anyone. Objects, on the other hand, are never offended.

Nonetheless, striking cases of the reverse situation—patients with severe object recognition problems without any evidence of prosopagnosia—support the second criterion used to evaluate whether face perception entails a specialized system. A dramatic example is C.K., the patient who could reproduce pictures only by laboriously following the outer boundaries (see Figure 6.29). Consider C.K.'s perception of the still life shown in Figure 6.40, a painting by the quirky 16th-century Italian painter Giuseppe Arcimboldo. This scene stumped C.K.; he reported a mishmash of colors and shapes that failed to gel into a coherent percept. But when the painting was turned upside down, C.K.'s perception of the face, even in caricature form, was immediate.

When we consider the kinds of tasks typically used to assess face and object perception, a different concern arises. In one important respect, face perception tests are qualitatively different from tests that evaluate the recognition of common objects. The stimuli for assessing face perception are all from the same category: faces. Subjects may be asked to decide whether two faces are the same or different, or they may be asked to identify specific individuals. When agnosic patients are tested on object perception, the stimuli cover a much broader range. Here subjects are asked to discriminate chairs from tables, or to identify common objects such as clocks and telephones. Face perception tasks involve within-category discriminations; object perception tasks typically involve between-category discriminations. Perhaps the deficits seen in prosopagnosia patients reflect not a selective problem in face perception, but a more general problem in perceiving the subtle differences that distinguish the members of a common category. This argument is similar to the expertise issue reviewed in the previous section.

Figure 6.40 The Arcimboldo painting that stumped C.K. when he viewed it right side up but became immediately recognizable as a different form when he turned it upside down. To see what C.K. saw, keep an eye on the turnip when you turn the book upside down.

The patient literature also fails to support the expertise hypothesis. A sheep farmer (W.J.) who had developed prosopagnosia was tested on a set of within-category identification tasks (Figure 6.41): one involving people, the other involving sheep (McNeil & Warrington, 1993). In the familiar-faces test W.J. performed at the level of chance. In the familiar-sheep test, by contrast, he was able to pick out photographs of sheep from his own flock. In a second experiment, recognition memory was tested. After viewing a set of pictures of sheep or faces, W.J. was shown these same stimuli mixed with new photographs. W.J.'s performance in recognizing the sheep was higher than that of other control subjects, including other sheep farmers! For faces, though, W.J.'s performance was at the level of chance, whereas the control subjects' performances were close to perfect.

Farah (1994) also argued that prosopagnosia cannot be attributed to the fact that face recognition entails a difficult within-category discrimination. Her experiments demonstrated that face perception does not involve the same processes and representations as object perception. A central figure in this work was a prosopagnosia patient, L.H., who had diffuse brain damage from a car accident. L.H. was tested with two recognition memory tests: one with face stimuli, the other with eyeglasses. Using only eyeglasses for the second set mitigates the criticism that nonfacial object recognition tests, compared to facial recognition tests, involve stimuli much more distinct from one another. In the study phase, half the stimuli from each set were presented. Then, in the memory test, all the stimuli were presented and the patient had to judge if the stimulus was old or new. Control subjects correctly recognized 85% of the faces and 69% of the eyeglasses. L.H. recognized only 64% of the faces correctly in comparison to 63% of the eyeglasses. A patient with integrative agnosia had an opposite pattern of deficits: an accuracy level of 98% for recognizing faces but performance only at the level of chance for eyeglasses.

An unusual phenomenon, the *face inversion effect* has also been taken to support the argument that faces are special. Look at the face in Figure 6.42. Try recognizing the face in its upside-down orientation and then turn your book upside down. The effect is striking. Recognition is immediate when the stimulus is viewed in its proper orientation, but difficult with inverted faces. The effect is not limited to humans. Chimpanzees also are better at recognizing other chimp faces when the faces are presented upright (Parr et al., 1998). Interestingly, chimps do not exhibit the inversion effect when shown the faces of another primate species (the capuchin) or a set of inanimate objects (automobiles).

(a)

(b)

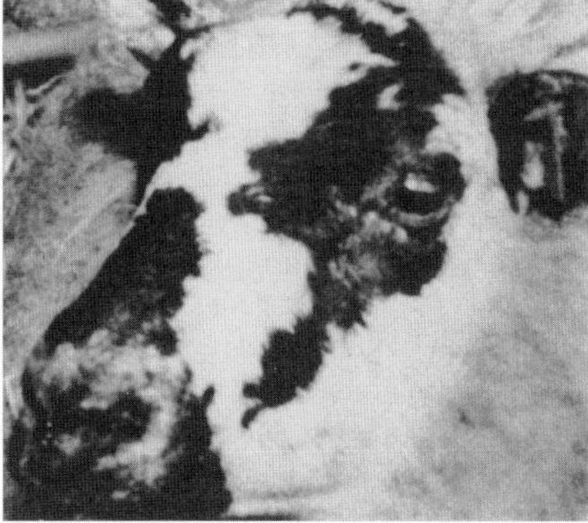

Figure 6.41 Face-specific recognition deficits cannot be attributed to the fact that faces represent a difficult within-category discrimination. In comparison to control subjects, a sheep farmer with prosopagnosia (W.J.) demonstrated impairment in recognizing famous faces **(a)**, yet was more accurate in recognizing individual sheep **(b)**. In one of the face discrimination tasks, the subjects were shown three faces and asked to point to the one familiar face. In the example illustrated in **(a)**, the familiar face is Norman Tebbit, a well-known (to the British population) politician of the Thatcher era. The faces on the left and right in **(a)** were unfamiliar to the subjects. The sheep in **(b)** were either familiar or unfamiliar to the subjects.

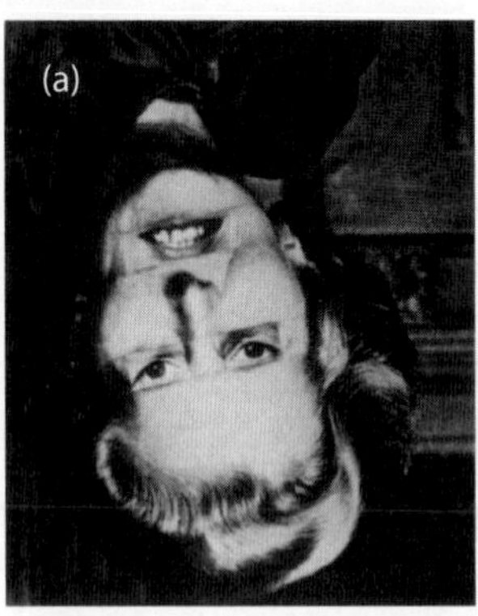

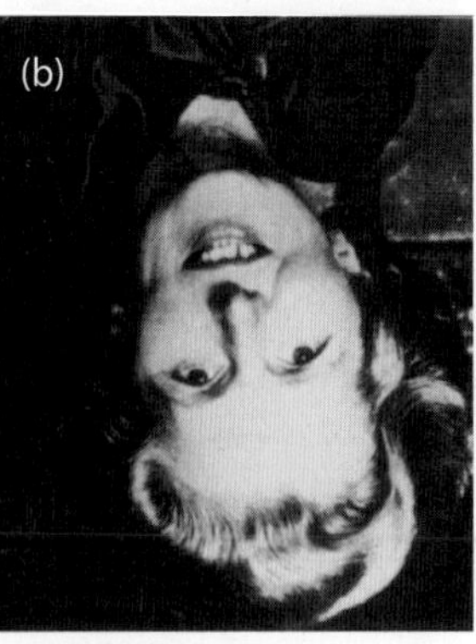

Figure 6.42 Who is this person? Is there anything unusual about the picture? Recognition can be quite difficult when faces are viewed upside down. Even more surprising, we fail to note a severe distortion in **(a)** created by inversion of the eyes and mouth—something that is immediately apparent when the image is viewed right side up. The person is former British Prime Minister Margaret Thatcher, whose face would have been widely recognized even in the United States in the late 1970s.

(a)

(b)

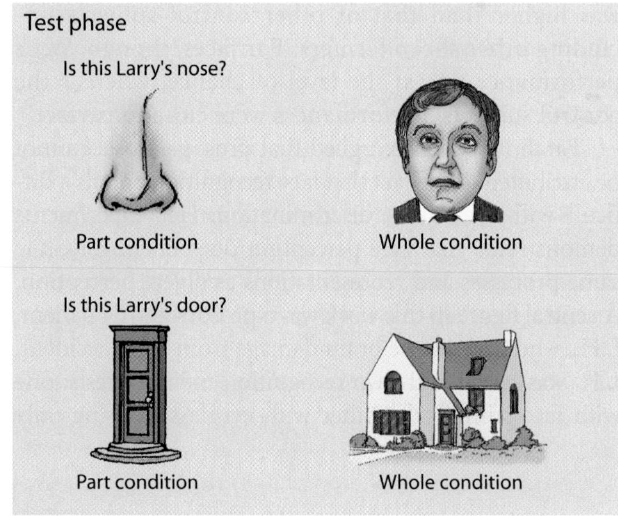

(c)

Results

Faces | Houses

Percentage correct (60, 70, 80)

Isolated-part condition

Whole-object condition

Figure 6.43 Facial features are poorly recognized in isolation. **(a)** Subjects first learned the names that correspond with a set of faces and houses. **(b)** During the recognition test, subjects were presented with a face, a house, or a single feature from the face or house. They were asked if a particular feature belonged to an individual. **(c)** When presented with the entire face, subjects were much better in identifying the facial features. Recognition of the house features was the same in both conditions.

One interpretation of the inversion effect is that we no longer can use a specialized face-processing system but must revert to a more analytic, analysis-by-parts mode of processing for an upside-down face. These faces constitute the perfect control stimulus for assessing the special status of face perception. Although stimuli in the normal and upside-down orientations contain identical information, only the normal condition should be disrupted in patients with prosopagnosia. This is exactly what was found.

In fact, L.H. had the opposite of an inversion effect. For the upright and upside-down conditions, control subjects were correct on 94% and 82% of the trials, respectively. L.H.'s performance was better with upside-down faces (72%) in comparison with upright faces (58%). One surprising finding was that, when viewing upright faces, L.H. could not bypass his damaged face recognition system. If this were so, he would have performed well with both stimuli. But he continued to utilize his face recognition system, even though it failed to produce the representations required for the recognition memory task.

Research with healthy people reinforced the notion that face perception requires a representation that is not simply a concatenation of individual parts. In one study, subjects were asked to recognize line drawings of faces and houses (Tanaka & Farah, 1993). Each stimulus was constructed of limited parts. For faces, the parts were eyes, nose, and mouth; for houses, the parts were doors, living room windows, and bedroom windows. In a study phase, subjects saw a name and either a face or a house (Figure 6.43a). For the face, they were instructed to associate the name with the face; for example, "Larry had round eyes, a pointed nose, and a narrow mouth." For the house, they were instructed to learn the name of the person who lived in the house; for example, "Larry lived in a house with a three-paneled door, shuttered living room window, and rounded bedroom windows."

After this learning period, a recognition memory test was given (Figure 6.43b). The critical manipulation was whether the probe item was presented in isolation or in context, embedded in the whole object. For example, when asked whether the stimulus matched Larry's nose, the nose was presented either by itself or in the context of Larry's eyes and mouth. As predicted, house perception did not depend on whether the test items were presented in isolation or as an entire object, but face perception did (Figure 6.43c). The subjects were much better at identifying the person when shown a face containing all three features.

TWO SYSTEMS FOR OBJECT RECOGNITION

If we accept that there is a specialized system for face perception, a natural question is whether other forms of object perception also entail specialized systems. As noted already, large sectors of the ventral occipitotemporal cortex are activated during object recognition tasks. However, the parahippocampus is consistently engaged when the stimuli contain information about spatial relations or when people are also asked to classify objects on the basis of some sort of spatial property (e.g., indoor or outdoor scene). Russell Epstein and Nancy Kanwisher (1998) named this region the *parahippocampal place area*, or *PPA*. In truth, their discovery of the PPA was serendipitous, precipitated by their inclusion of scenes as part of a large class of nonface stimuli in an early investigation on the FFA.

Nonetheless, reasonable evolutionary arguments can be made concerning why the brain might have dedicated regions devoted to recognizing faces or places, but not other types of distinctions. It is unlikely that there would be a strong adaptive advantage to individuals who could distinguish one type of apple from another (although being able to perceive color differences that cue whether a particular piece of fruit is ripe or not would be important). But our ancestors who could remember where the fruit was found would have a large advantage over their more forgetful peers. Interestingly, people with lesions to the parahippocampus become disoriented in new environments (Aguirre & D'Esposito, 1999; Habib & Sirigu, 1987).

Martha Farah has focused on a different subtype of visual agnosia—alexia—in developing a general process-based theory of object recognition. *Acquired alexia* refers to reading problems after a patient has had a stroke or head trauma. Patients with acquired alexia understand spoken speech and can speak without problems. Moreover, many patients retain the ability to write—a syndrome known as *alexia without agraphia*. But reading is painstakingly difficult. Errors usually reflect visual confusions. The word *ball* may be misread as *doll*, or *bail* as *talk*. Like prosopagnosia, alexia is a within-category deficit: the failure to discriminate between items that are a lot alike.

Anatomically, alexia and prosopagnosia are associated with different neural regions. Prosopagnosia is seen with damage that is either bilateral or unilateral in the right hemisphere (De Renzi et al., 1994) and includes ventral regions of the occipital and temporal lobes. In contrast, alexia is associated with left-hemisphere lesions, particularly lesions of the angular gyrus at the junction of the occipital, temporal, and parietal lobes or ventral occipitotemporal sulcus.

Functional-MRI scans also reveal very different patterns of activation when words are presented compared to when faces are presented. Letter strings do not activate the FFA; rather, the activation is centered more dorsally (Figure 6.44), and the magnitude of the activation increases when the letters form familiar words (L. Cohen et al., 2002). Though one may think of this area as specialized for reading, an evolutionary argument akin to what has been offered for face perception does

Figure 6.44 **(a)** Activation in response to viewing words in the visual word form area (VWFA), as indicated by the yellow circle. **(b)** Activation in response to viewing faces in the fusiform face area (FFA), as indicated by the yellow circle. In both images, the crosshairs intersect at the location of the VWFA. In **(b)** it is clear that the VWFA is dorsal, and slightly posterior to the FFA.

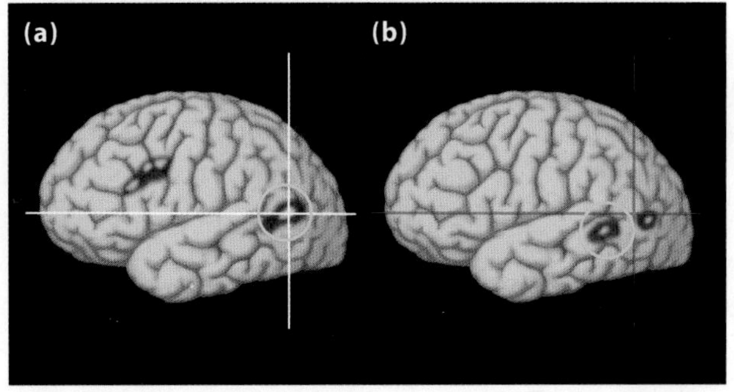

not seem tenable. Learning to read is a challenging process that is only part of our recent cultural history. Nonetheless, computations performed by this region of the brain appear to be well suited for developing the representations required for reading.

Prosopagnosia and alexia rarely occur in isolation. Both types of patients usually have problems with other types of object recognition. Importantly, a double dissociation between prosopagnosia and acquired alexia becomes evident when we consider the patterns of correlation among three types of agnosia: agnosia for faces, agnosia for objects, and agnosia for words. Table 6.2 lists the pattern of co-occurrence reported by Farah (1990) in a thorough review of the literature on visual associative agnosia. Farah did not tally the number of patients with a selective deficit in reading, because they were so numerous. She did find several patients whose ability to recognize all three types of materials was impaired. The lesions were probably extensive and affected multiple processes. More telling was the dissociation of face and word perception. Both deficits frequently occurred along with a disorder in object recognition. But, most critically, Farah could not find a single unequivocal patient in whom face perception and word perception were impaired but object perception was not. Thus, one could be prosopagnosic and agnosic without being alexic. Or one could be agnosic and alexic without being prosopagnosic.

A second significant result can be gleaned from Table 6.2. Although alexia and prosopagnosia do not occur together, it is equally telling that agnosia for objects is always accompanied by a deficit in either word or face perception, or both. Because patients with deficits in object perception also have a problem with one of the other types of stimuli, we might be tempted to conclude that object recognition involves two independent processes. It would be unparsimonious to postulate three processing subsystems. If this were so, we would expect to find three sets of patients: those with word perception deficits, those with face perception deficits, and those with object perception deficits.

Given that the neuropsychological dissociations suggest two systems for object recognition, we can now examine the third criterion for evaluating whether face perception depends on a processing system distinct from the one for other forms of object perception: Do we process information in a unique way when attempting to recognize faces? To answer this question, we need to return to the computational issues surrounding the perception of facial and nonfacial stimuli. Are there differences in the way information is represented when we recognize faces in comparison to when we recognize common objects and words?

Farah maintained that face perception is unique in one special way: Whereas object recognition decomposes a stimulus into its parts, face perception is more holistic. We recognize an individual according to the facial configuration. A person is not recognized by his or her idiosyncratic nose or eyes or chin structure. The individual parts are not sufficient for face recognition; analyzing the structure and configuration of these features is what counts—hence, integrative agnosia and prosopagnosia represent two extremes. The patient with integrative agnosia cannot identify the critical parts that form an object. The prosopagnosic patient may succeed in extracting these parts but cannot derive the holistic representation necessary for face perception.

In Chapter 11 we will see that the distinction between **analytic processing** and **holistic processing** has been important in theories of hemispheric specialization, the former associated with the left hemisphere and the latter associated with the right hemisphere. In that chapter we will review computational hypotheses that might underlie the difference between analytic and holistic processing. For our present purposes, it is useful to note that alexia and prosopagnosia are in accord with this lateralization hypothesis.

Theodor Landis and his colleagues at the University of Munich provide a nice example of how the distinction between holistic and analytic processing can be useful for understanding the representational deficits associated with prosopagnosia and alexia, respectively (Rentschler et al., 1994). When presented with various handwriting examples obtained from their friends, prosopagnosic patients could read the words but were

Table 6.2 Patterns of Co-occurrence of Prosopagnosia, Visual Agnosia, and Alexia

Pattern	Number of Patients
Deficits in all three	21
Selective deficits	
Face and objects	14
Words and objects	15
Faces and words	1 (possibly)
Faces alone	35
Words alone	Many described in literature
Objects only	1 (possibly)

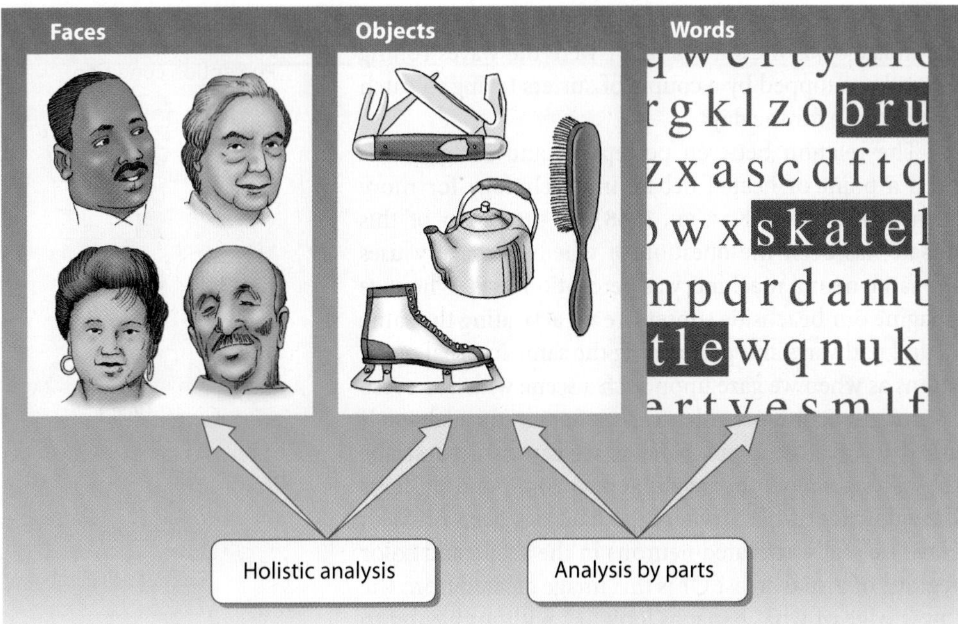

Figure 6.45 Farah's two-process model for object recognition. Recognition can be based on two forms of analysis: holistic analysis and analysis by parts. The contributions of these two systems vary for different classes of stimuli. Analysis by parts is essential for reading and is central for recognizing objects. A unique aspect of face recognition is its dependence on holistic analysis. Holistic analysis also contributes to object recognition.

unable to recognize the handwriting. Alexic patients showed the opposite pattern: They were unable to read the words, despite being able to identify the handwriting. Recognizing the unique handwriting style of an individual would depend on the overall pattern formed by the letter strings, rather than on the shapes of individual letters. Thus, the impaired holistic processing ability seen in prosopagnosia is not limited to faces.

When viewed in this way, the question of whether face perception is special has been changed in a subtle yet important way. Farah's model emphasizes that higher-level perception reflects the operation of two, distinct representational systems. The relative contribution of the analysis-by-parts and holistic systems will depend on the task (Figure 6.45). Face perception is at one extreme. Here, the critical information requires a holistic representation to capture the configuration of the defining parts. For these stimuli, discerning the parts is of little importance. Think how hard it is to notice that a casual acquaintance has shaved his mustache. Rather, recognition requires that we perceive a familiar arrangement of the parts. Faces are special, in the sense that the representation derived from an analysis by parts is not sufficient.

Words represent another special class of objects, but at the other extreme. Reading requires that the letter strings be successfully decomposed into their constituent parts. We benefit little from noting general features such as word length or handwriting. We have to recognize the individual letters in order to differentiate one word from another.

In terms of recognition, objects fall somewhere between the two extremes of words and faces. Defining features such as the number pad and receiver can identify a telephone, but recognition is also possible when we perceive the overall shape of this familiar object. If either the analytic or the holistic system is damaged, object recognition may still be possible through operation of the intact system. But performance is likely to be suboptimal. Thus, agnosia for objects can occur with either alexia or prosopagnosia.

THE RELATIONSHIPS OF VISUAL PERCEPTION, IMAGERY, AND MEMORY

Imagine walking along the beach at sunset. The glowing orange sun has kissed the water's edge and the cloud-streaked sky bursts into a palette of reds, violets, and blues. Screeching seagulls flutter over the remains of a fish washed up in the afternoon tide. The smell of the rotting carcass is pungent, adding to the saltiness of the ocean mist. Our images can be vivid. Most likely our images are of a specific place where we once enjoyed an ocean sunset. Some details may be quite salient; others may require further reflection. Were any boats passing by on the horizon in the image? Was the surf calm, or were the waves rolling in, perhaps topped by a couple of surfers trying to catch one last ride for the day?

The relation between perception and imagery has been a point of heated debate in psychology for more than two decades (Kosslyn, 1988). At the center of this debate has been the question of whether imagery uses the same neural machinery as perception uses. When we imagine our beachside sunset, are we activating the same neural pathways and performing the same internal operations as when we gaze upon such a scene with our eyes?

Introspection provides few answers to this debate. If asked to imagine a ripe banana, we can easily describe the oblong shape, the bright yellow color, and perhaps the splotches of black where the fruit has been bruised. Have we really activated neurons in the shape and color regions of visual areas? Or is this image created from the knowledge of what bananas look like without having to "see with the mind's eye"?

Experimental psychologists have devised many ways to answer these questions. Several studies demonstrated similarities in how we process images and percepts. Roger Shepard of Stanford University developed several tasks to explore the dynamics of mental processing (Podgorny & Shepard, 1978). In one task, subjects view a grid of 25 squares that contains either a block letter or one that they are to imagine as a designated letter (Figure 6.46a). The display is then turned off, and after a short delay, the grid reappears, containing a dot in one of the squares. The subjects must decide whether the dot falls on the previously seen or imagined letter. Responses are considerably slower when the dot is near an edge of the letter. Most important, this effect is as strong in the imagery condition (Figure 6.46b), as if the subjects must inspect their image in detail.

Neuropsychological research may provide the most compelling evidence of shared processing for imagery and perception. Patients with perceptual deficits have also been shown to have corresponding deficits in imagery (Farah, 1988). Strokes may isolate visual information from areas that represent more abstract knowledge, causing difficulty in both perception and imagery tasks. One patient was able to sort objects according to color, but when asked to name a color or point to a named color, her performance was impaired. With imagery tasks, the patient could not answer questions about the colors of objects. She could say that a banana is a fruit that grows in southern climates but could not name its color. Even more surprising, the patient answered metaphorical questions about colors. For example, she could answer the question "What is the color of envy?" by responding, "Green." Questions like these cannot be answered through imagery.

(a)

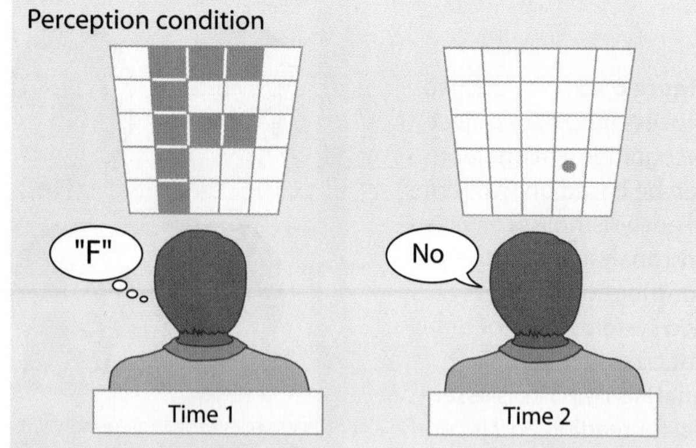

(b)

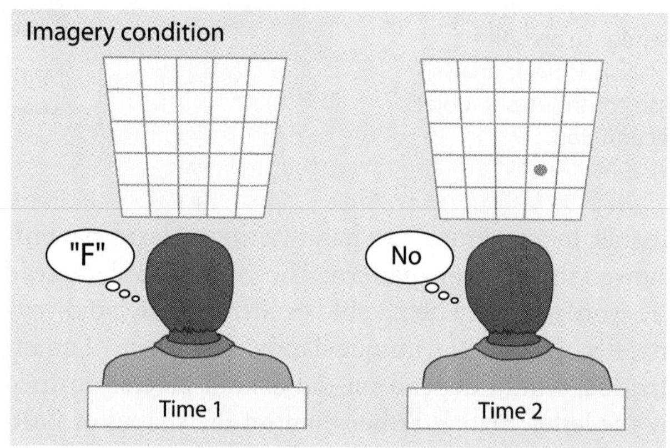

Figure 6.46 Recall processes appear to be similar for both seen and imagined objects. Subjects are shown a grid that contains a letter **(a, left)** or upon which they are to imagine the letter **(b, left)**. After a delay, a probe dot is presented **(right)** and the subjects must judge whether the probe was on the seen or imagined letter. The time required to make these judgments is quite similar in the two conditions. For example, subjects are slower to respond "no" in both conditions when the probe dot is close to the edge of the seen or imagined letter.

Patients with higher-order visual deficits have related deficits in visual imagery. Consider two patients: one with bilateral lesions of the temporal cortex and left-sided occipital involvement, and another with bilateral lesions of the parieto-occipital cortex. The patient with the more ventral, occipitotemporal lesions had difficulty imaging faces or animals. He described an elephant as having long legs and a neck that could reach the ground to pick things up, and Abraham Lincoln as having a short, round face. Despite these difficulties, this patient could readily draw a floor plan of his house and locate major cities on a map of the United States. In contrast, the patient with damage to the dorsal pathways produced vivid descriptions when he was asked to image objects, but failed spatial imagery tasks. He described the elephant as being big, with a long nose, big floppy ears, a little tail, and four thick legs. Yet this patient was unable to describe how to get around his own neighborhood or provide knowledge of more extensive geographic regions; Chicago was described as being north of Boston. Together, these patients provide evidence of a dissociation in imagery of what–where processing that closely parallels the dissociation observed in perception.

Neuropsychological evidence also comes from physiological studies of normal subjects. Farah measured evoked potentials while subjects read a list of words, or read the words and simultaneously imaged their referents. The early component of the event-related potential was identical for the two conditions. But in the imaging condition, the waveform representing the occipital electrodes increased. Although the stimuli were the same in both conditions, the imagery condition selectively enhanced activation in visual areas.

Similar findings have been reported in PET studies (Kosslyn et al., 1993). In fact, the evidence suggests that imagery not only activates visual association areas but also produces increases in regional cerebral blood flow in the primary visual cortex. As with all modern imaging studies, it is difficult to know if this activity is essential for imagery. It may be that mental images are generated in secondary visual areas and that the activation in primary visual cortex results from feedback connections.

Steven Kosslyn and his associates at Harvard University used transcranial magnetic stimulation (TMS) to assess the functional importance of visual cortex in imagery. The TMS coil was placed over primary visual cortex, and subjects received a pulse every second for 10 minutes. This procedure was hypothesized to disrupt neural activity in the target structure for about 10 minutes after the stimulation ended. As a control condition, the TMS procedure was repeated, but here the coil was reoriented such that the magnetic pulses did not reach the brain. In comparison to the sham condition, subjects were slower on making imagery-based judgments following TMS to the visual cortex. These results are consistent with the idea that representations in primary visual cortex are invoked during mental imagery, although it is possible that secondary visual areas were also disrupted by the stimulation via the feed-forward connections from the primary visual cortex.

The evidence provides a compelling case that mental imagery uses many of the same processes that are critical for perception. The sights in an image are likely to activate visual areas of the brain; the sounds, auditory areas; and the smells, olfactory areas. Indeed, the imagery research demonstrates that memory for perceptual information is not independent of perceptual processes. We need not think of perceptual processing and the memory of that processing as distinct neural entities. Perceptual memory might simply reactivate perceptual pathways.

Despite the similarities between perception and imagery, it would be premature to conclude that the two are identical. Patients frequently have corresponding deficits in perception and imagery, but there are notable exceptions. Patients with no evidence of agnosia may have imagery deficits, being unable to recall whether animals have long or short tails, or whether the letter *P* has a curved segment. By contrast, intact imagery has been observed in patients with severe agnosia. Similarly, some patients with severe achromatopsia but without corresponding deficits on tasks appear to require the use of color imagery. One such patient not only could recall the colors of familiar objects (e.g., the U.S. Postal Service's mailboxes), but also could make more subtle distinctions, such as gauging that a plum contains more red than an eggplant (Shuren et al., 1996).

We can try to account for the dissociations between imagery and perception by supposing that, although imagery and perception share forms of representation, they may achieve them in distinct ways. Consider two versions of a task that requires an observer to decide if a donkey's ears are pointed or floppy. In the imagery version, the observer must generate an internal representation. It is unlikely that the observer could do this by imaging the donkey's ears. Instead, an image of the entire animal will probably be created, and the observer will zoom in for a closer examination of the head. Imagery as such requires that the parts be generated and arranged appropriately. Now consider the perceptual version, in which an observer is shown a donkey's picture and, as with imagery, is asked to identify parts and make comparisons. In perception, the parts need not be generated but must be extracted from the representation of the stimulus. The critical process is to partition the percept into its component parts—to segment the ears from the head.

Dissociations between imagery and perception have led to models in which visual knowledge can be accessed through multiple pathways. Consider again patient C.K., the patient with severe integrative agnosia who could recognize vegetable faces. C.K. had no problems with imagery tasks. When the names of objects were read to him, C.K. produced excellent drawings (Figure 6.47). When shown the same drawings during a subsequent visit, however, he failed to identify any of them. In a similar way, although C.K. had difficulty recognizing letters, he was successful at imagery tasks that required multiple transformations.

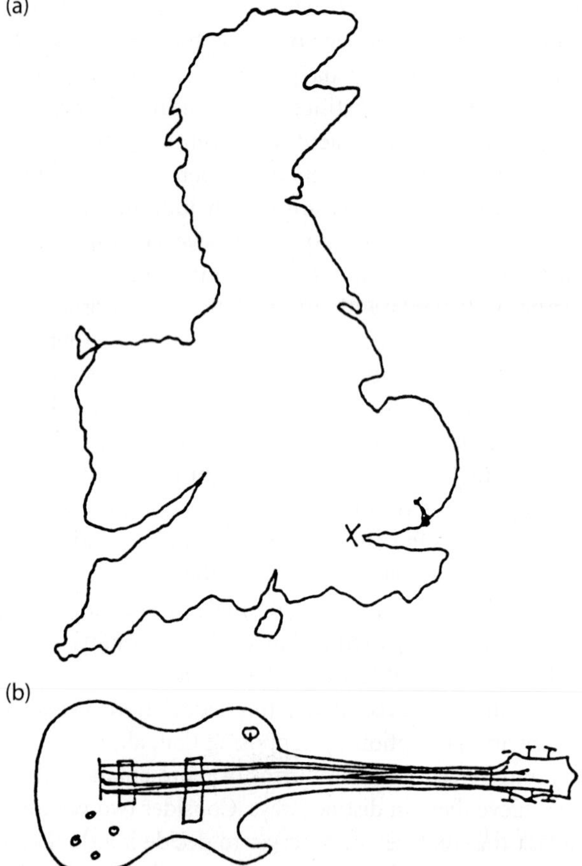

Figure 6.47 The ability to draw objects from memory may be spared in agnosia. Patient C.K.'s drawings of a map of the United Kingdom **(a)** and an electric guitar **(b)** suggest that his ability to generate an internal visual representation is intact. However, C.K. was unable to recognize the objects in his own drawings on a subsequent visit.

He readily provided the correct answer to the question "What letter do you get when you take the letter *L*, flip it from top to bottom, and add a horizontal line in the middle?" In these tasks, C.K. demonstrated that he can represent objects visually and has knowledge of visual attributes. His representations are not simply of whole objects: The letter transformation task demonstrated that he can generate and manipulate the parts. C.K. failed when he had to extract parts from the perceptual input. Without this capability, his object recognition capacity is limited.

One provocative issue that has received relatively little attention is how visual memory changes over time following damage to systems involved in visual perception. If we are deprived of consistent input, it seems reasonable to expect that our knowledge base will be reorganized. In his essay "The Case of the Colorblind Painter," Oliver Sacks (1995) described Mr. I, a successful artist who suffered complete achromatopsia following a car accident. For Mr. I, a colorless world was initially "awful, disgusting." He was horrified upon returning to his studio to discover that all of his brilliant abstract paintings, done in the most vivid colors, now appeared a morass of grays, blacks, and whites.

Mr. I's abhorrence for a colorless world extended outside of the studio. He lost interest in food because of its uniform "grayish, dead appearance," and even sex became repugnant after he viewed his wife's flesh, and indeed his own flesh, as a "rat-colored" gray. Interestingly, his shock underscores the fact that his color knowledge was still intact. Mr. I could remember with great detail the colors he expected to see in his paintings. It was the mismatch between his expectation and what he saw that was so depressing. He shunned museums because the familiar pictures just looked wrong.

During the subsequent year, however, a transition occurred. Mr. I's memory for colors started to slip away. He no longer despaired when gazing at a tomato devoid of red or a sunset drained of all color. He knew that something wasn't quite right, but his sense of the missing colors was much more vague. Indeed, he began to appreciate the subtleties of a black-and-white world. Overwhelmed by the brightness of the day, Mr. I became a night person, appreciating forms in purity, "uncluttered by color." This change can be seen in his art (Figure 6.48). Prior to the accident, Mr. I relied on color to create subtle boundaries, to evoke movement across the canvas. In his black-and-white world, geometric patterns delineated sharp boundaries.

H.J.A., the patient described previously as having integrative agnosia, experienced a similar loss of visual memory over time (M. J. Riddoch et al., 1999). Figure 6.49 shows two sets of drawings: one set drawn when he was first tested 4 years after his accident, and the other set drawn 10 years later. Although the changes might be attributed to the effects of aging, H.J.A. also showed a change over time in how he described common objects. When he was tested 15 years after his stroke, his descriptions were primarily verbal, focusing on the functions of the objects. He mentioned visual attributes less often than in his earlier test sessions. Interestingly, H.J.A.'s recognition of real objects had improved to near-normal levels by the time of the follow-up session, although he still showed impairment when he was tested on line drawings.

As H.J.A. reported, "My actual recognition has never got any worse or better. My ways of getting around it have improved—but not my recognition, at least that's what I believe." (Riddoch et al., 1999, p. 543). "Getting around" here would seem to mean a greater reliance on noting distinctive features such as the handle on a coffee

Figure 6.48 An abstract painting by Mr. I, produced 2 years after his accident. Mr. I was experimenting with colors at this time, although he was still unable to see them.

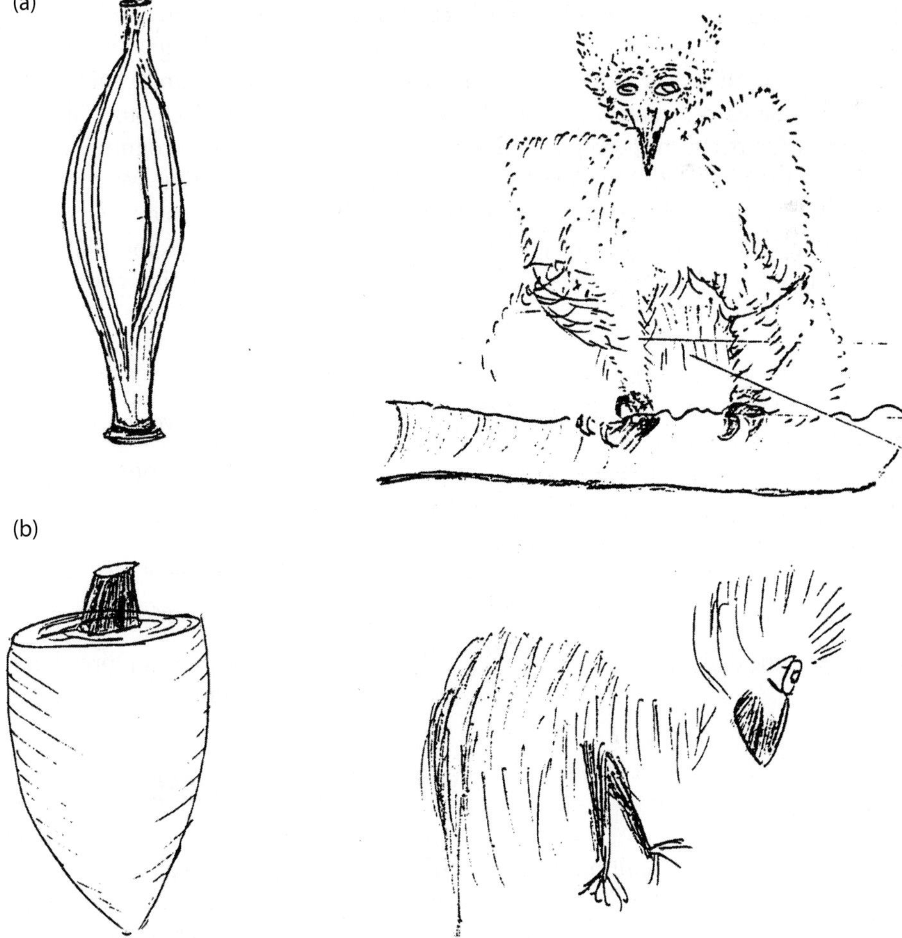

Figure 6.49 Drawings produced by H.J.A. 4 years **(a)** and 14 years **(b)** after his stroke. The left-hand drawings are of celery; the right-hand drawings, of an owl. The later drawings are much poorer, suggesting a loss of visual knowledge associated with H.J.A.'s persistent agnosia. Age-matched control subjects show little deterioration in their drawing skills over a similar period.

cup or using depth and texture information. But H.J.A.'s ability to access visual memory by integrating parts into a coherent percept has not improved. Correspondingly, the perceptual deficit has led to a decline in visual knowledge itself. We should not be surprised that a system constructed through perceptual experience would require that experience to remain intact—an issue that we discussed in Chapter 3.

SUMMARY

This chapter provided an overview of the higher level processes involved in visual perception. Like most other mammals, people are visual creatures: Most of us rely on our eyes to identify not only *what* we are looking at, but also *where* to look, to guide our actions. These processes are surely interactive. To accomplish a skilled behavior such as catching a thrown object, we have to determine the object's size and shape and track its path through space so that we can anticipate where to place our hands.

Object recognition can be achieved in a multiplicity of ways and involves many levels of representation. To recognize an object, our visual system must overcome the variability inherent in the sensory input by extracting the critical information that distinguishes one shape from another. Perceptual categorization solves only part of the recognition problem. For this information to be useful, the contents of current processing must be connected to our stored knowledge about visual objects. Semantic categorization allows us to see the similarities between percepts and recognize the unique features of objects. We do not see a meaningless array of shapes and forms. Rather, visual perception is an efficient avenue for recognizing and interacting with the world (e.g., determining what path to take across a cluttered room or which tools make our actions more efficient).

Moreover, vision provides a salient means for one of the most essential goals of perception: recognizing members of our own species. One might suppose that the importance of face perception led to the evolution of an alternative form of representation, one that analyzed the global configuration of a stimulus rather than its parts. On the other hand, multiple forms of representation may have evolved, and face perception may be highly dependent on the holistic form of representation. As Farah's model demonstrates, the evidence leads us to consider that normal perception involves part-based and holistic representations. In object recognition, these two forms of representation interact, and their relative contribution varies according to the task and the objects being perceived.

The goal-oriented aspects of perception—that we use vision to guide our movements, to manipulate tools, or to recognize faces—also underscore the selective aspects of cognition. We are not passive processors of information. We can select from the dazzling array that impinges on our senses at any one time. Depending on our goals, the relative importance of different sources of information constantly changes.

KEY TERMS

agnosia
alexia
analytic processing
apperceptive agnosia
associative agnosia
category-specific deficits
dorsal (occipitoparietal) pathway
fusiform face area (FFA)
fusiform gyrus
gnostic unit
holistic processing
integrative agnosia
N170 response
object constancy
optic ataxia
prosopagnosia
repetition suppression effect
ventral (occipitotemporal) pathway
view-dependent frame of reference
view-invariant frame of reference
visual agnosia

TAKE-HOME MESSAGES

General

- Perception and recognition are two distinct phenomena, the understanding of which is one of the core issues of cognitive neuroscience.

Agnosias and the Ventral and Dorsal Streams of Processing

- Patient G.S. suffered from visual agnosia. Even though he does not have problems with visual acuity, he is unable to recognize common objects when they are presented visually, although he can recognize them if he is allowed to touch or smell them.

- The ventral, or occipitotemporal, pathway is specialized for object perception and recognition. This is often referred to as the "what" pathway.
- The dorsal, or occipitoparietal, pathway is specialized for spatial perception and is often referred to as the "where" pathway.
- Neurons in the parietal lobe have large, nonselective receptive fields with cells representing both the fovea and the periphery. Neurons in the temporal lobe have large receptive fields that are much more selective and always represent foveal information.
- The lateral occipital cortex is an important region for shape and object recognition.
- D.F. suffered from visual agnosia as a result of bilateral lesions to the ventral pathway, encompassing the lateral occipital cortex. Despite her inability to consciously identify objects or report their properties, she performed well on a task that required her to insert a card into a slot. This example provides a dissociation between the "what" and "where" pathways. The "what" pathway is essential in determining the identity of an object; the "where" pathway is essential for determining the location of different objects and guiding interactions with these objects.
- An alternative characterization of the functional difference between the ventral and dorsal pathways focuses on "vision for recognition" versus "vision for action" to emphasize that the dorsal pathway provides strong input to the motor systems to guide action.
- Patients with optic ataxia have the opposite symptoms from those of D.F.: They can recognize objects but cannot use visual information to guide action. Optic ataxia is associated with lesions of the parietal cortex.
- Apperceptive agnosia is a ventral-stream disorder in which failures in object recognition are linked to problems in perceptual processing. A patient with apperceptive agnosia may recognize an object from a typical viewpoint, but performance will deteriorate when the patient is asked to name an object that is seen from an unusual viewpoint or is occluded by shadows.
- Associative agnosia describes patients who derive normal visual representations but cannot use this information to recognize things. A person with associative agnosia might be able to identify two pictures of the same object as being the same, but will fail to demonstrate an understanding of what the object is used for or where it is likely to be found.
- Integrative agnosia (exemplified by H.J.A.) is a deficit that results in the inability to integrate parts of an object into a coherent whole.
- Category-specific deficits are deficits of object recognition that are restricted to certain classes of objects. Evidence for category-specific deficits comes from lesion studies as well as computer modeling studies that find that virtual lesions to either visual or functional semantic systems produce category-specific deficits.
- Prosopagnosia is an inability to recognize faces that cannot be attributed to deterioration in intellectual function. Such a condition usually results from damage to the ventral "what" pathway.
- Acquired alexia is characterized by reading problems that occur after a patient has a stroke or head trauma.
- In alexia without agraphia, patients have alexia but retain the ability to write.

Theories of Object Recognition

- Object constancy is the ability we have to recognize objects in countless situations (e.g., when occluded and when shown in abnormal colors or from abnormal angles).
- There are two main theories of object recognition: one based on a view-dependent frame of reference; the other, on a view-invariant frame of reference. In view-dependent theories, perception is assumed to depend on recognition of an object from a certain viewpoint. View-invariant theories posit that recognition does not happen by simple analysis of the stimulus information.
- On the basis of her experiences with agnosias, Elizabeth Warrington proposed an anatomical model of object recognition that involved (a) initial visual processing in both occipital cortices, (b) perceptual categorization that takes place in the right hemisphere, and (c) semantic categorization that depends on the left hemisphere. This model, however, fails to address the issue of perceptual integration.
- Analytic processing is a form of perceptual analysis that emphasizes the component parts of an object and is associated with processing in the left hemisphere. Analytic-processing impairments are seen in cases of alexia.
- Holistic processing is a form of perceptual analysis that emphasizes the overall shape of an object and is associated with processing in the right hemisphere. Holistic-processing impairments are often seen with prosopagnosia.

Face Processing

- Neurophysiologists have recorded from neurons in various areas of the monkey brain, including the superior temporal sulcus, which appear to respond selectively to face stimuli.
- Functional MRI studies show that an area in the fusiform gyrus of the temporal lobe of humans is engaged during face perception. This region is referred to as the fusiform face area, or FFA.
- There is some debate as to whether the FFA is selective for faces, or whether it is activated in perceptual discrimination tasks that require fine discriminations. Such discriminations are especially important for faces. However, when fMRI evidence is combined with data from patient literature and the face inversion effect, the selectivity of the FFA for face processing appears to be the most plausible explanation for the functioning of that region.
- The face inversion effect reflects the phenomenon that, when faces are viewed in their normal orientation, they are immediately recognized. However, recognition is much more difficult when the faces being viewed are inverted. This is true in chimpanzees as well.
- Studies show that we process information about our own faces in the right hemisphere.
- Just as the FFA is specialized for processing faces, the parahippocampal place area (PPA) is specialized for processing information about spatial relations or for classifying objects based on spatial properties (e.g., an indoor versus outdoor scene).

Visual Imagery

- In general, visual imagery relies on the same neural mechanisms as visual perception does, as demonstrated by psychophysics, neuroimaging, and TMS experiments.
- Patients with higher order visual deficits have related deficits in visual imagery.

THOUGHT QUESTIONS

1. What are some of the differences between processing in the dorsal and ventral visual pathways? In what ways are these differences useful? In what ways is it misleading to imply a functional dichotomy of two distinct visual pathways?
2. Mrs. S recently suffered a brain injury. She claims to have difficulty in "seeing" as a result of her injury. Her neurologist has made a preliminary diagnosis of agnosia, but nothing more specific is noted. To determine the exact nature of her agnosia, a cognitive neuropsychologist is called in. What behavioral tests could the neuropsychologist use to make a more specific diagnosis? Remember that it is also important to conduct tests to determine if Mrs. S's deficit reflects a more general problem in visual perception or memory.
3. A scientist working with the MRI system at the hospital where Mrs. S is being treated hears about the case. Which anatomical and functional neuroimaging tests would the scientist recommend, and what specific results would support each of the possible diagnoses?
4. Review different hypotheses concerning why brain injury may produce the puzzling symptom of disproportionate impairment in recognizing living things. What sorts of evidence would support one hypothesis over another?
5. As part of a debating team, you are assigned the task of defending the hypothesis that the brain has evolved a specialized system for perceiving faces. What arguments will you use to make your case? Now change sides. Defend the argument that face perception reflects the operation of a highly experienced system that is good at making fine discriminations.

SUGGESTED READING

DESIMONE, R. (1991). Face-selective cells in the temporal cortex of monkeys. *Journal of Cognitive Neuroscience, 3,* 1–8.

FARAH, M. J. (2004). *Visual Agnosia,* 2nd ed. Cambridge, MA: MIT Press.

GOODALE, M. A., & Milner, A. D. (2004). *Sight unseen: An exploration of conscious and unconscious vision.* New York: Oxford University Press.

KANWISHER, N. (2000). Domain specificity in face perception. *Nature Neuroscience, 3,* 759–763.

RIDDOCH, M. J., & HUMPHREYS, G. W. (2001). Object recognition. In B. Repp (Ed.), *The handbook of cognitive neuropsychology: What deficits reveal about the human mind* (pp. 45–74). Philadelphia: Psychology Press.

7

The Control of Action

In July 1982, the physicians in the emergency rooms at hospitals in the San Jose, California, area were puzzled. Working in emergency rooms requires physicians to have uncommon skills. Not only do they encounter the carnage from cars and guns, but also they are generally the first point of contact for people who are suffering neurological symptoms, perhaps resulting from a stroke or from exposure to a toxic substance. Life and death decisions hinge on these doctors' ability to make an accurate diagnosis very quickly, frequently on the basis of scant information—especially when the patient is too injured or sick to provide a sufficient history. Years of medical training and experience usually provide the best guidance. But this time, none of the attending physicians could recall any precedent for what they had seen during the previous few days.

Four adults, ranging in age from 26 to 42 years, showed symptoms that did not resemble any known disease. While still conscious, the patients were essentially immobile, were unable to speak, had frozen facial expressions, and showed extreme rigidity in their arms. It was as if they had peered into Medusa's eyes and turned into stone statues. The physicians knew they had to act fast, but they could not figure out what to do. Interviews with the patients' friends and family uncovered a few clues. It was puzzling that although two of the patients were brothers, they did not know the other two. More questions revealed an important commonality among the cases: All four patients were heroin users.

The symptoms, however, bore little resemblance to those of a heroin overdose. Although heroin is a powerful central nervous system (CNS) depressant, these patients did not exhibit the typical flaccidity of a person under the influence of heroin. On the contrary, their rigidity was the opposite of what one expects from a powerful dose. No one could recall seeing a case of heroin overdose that produced these effects, nor did the symptoms resemble those of other street narcotics. A new substance was at work here. A few friends who had taken smaller doses confirmed this suspicion. When injected, this heroin had unexpectedly produced a burning sensation at the site of injection, rapidly followed by a blurring of vision, a metallic taste in the mouth, and, most troubling, an almost immediate jerking of the limbs.

It was a few days before the doctors had a breakthrough. Computed tomography (CT) and magnetic resonance imaging (MRI) revealed no structural abnormalities either in the brains of the patients, who were still rigid, or in the brains of those who had been lucky enough to have been injected with only a small dose. A neurologist at Stanford University, William Langston (1984), provided the first insight. When examining the patients, he was struck by how similar their symptoms were to those of a patient with advanced Parkinson's disease. This condition is marked by muscular rigidity and disorders of posture and volitional movement, or *akinesia*, the inability to produce volitional movement (Figure 7.1).

Everything about the patients' conditions matched this disorder. The biggest puzzles, though, were the age

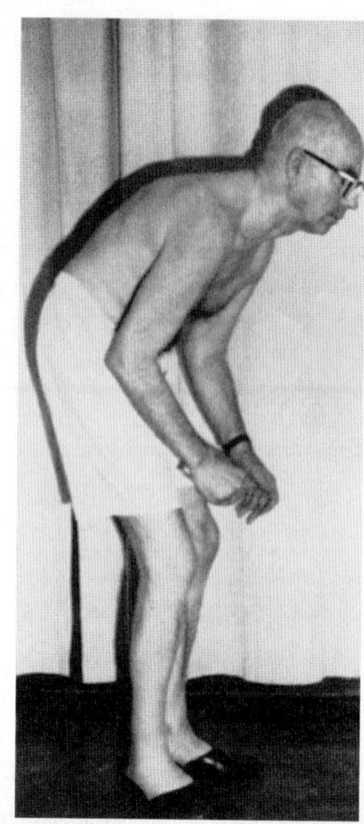

(a)

Figure 7.1 Parkinson's disease not only disrupts the production and flexibility of voluntary movement but also can distort posture. Facial expression, including blinking, is frequently absent, giving the person the appearance of being frozen. **(a)** This man has had Parkinson's disease for many years and is no longer able to maintain an upright posture. **(b)** These people developed symptoms of Parkinson's disease in their 20s and 30s, after ingesting the drug MPTP.

(b)

and history of the patients. The onset of Parkinson's disease is gradual and rarely becomes clinically evident until a person is over the age of 45. The heroin users had developed full-blown symptoms of advanced Parkinson's disease within days. Langston suspected that the drug users had come to inject a new synthetic drug being sold as heroin, and that this drug had triggered the acute onset of Parkinson's disease.

This diagnosis proved to be correct. Parkinson's disease results from cell death in the **substantia nigra**, a brainstem nucleus that is part of the basal ganglia. These cells are a primary source of the neurotransmitter dopamine. Although Langston could not see any structural damage on CT and MRI scans, subsequent positron emission tomography (PET) studies confirmed hypometabolism of dopamine in the people who had injected the toxic heroin, regardless of whether they developed Parkinson's disease. Of more immediate concern was how to treat the drug users. Langston adopted the universal treatment applied in Parkinson's disease:

He prescribed high doses of L-dopa, a synthetic cousin that is highly effective in compensating for the loss of endogenous dopamine. When Langston administered this medication to the drug abusers, they immediately showed a positive response. Their muscles relaxed and they could move, albeit in a limited form.

Although this episode was tragic for the patients involved, the incident signified a breakthrough in research on Parkinson's disease. Researchers tracked down the tainted drug and performed a chemical analysis; it turned out to be a previously unknown synthetic substance, bearing little resemblance to heroin but similar in structure to meperidine, a synthetic opioid that creates the sensations of heroin. On the basis of its chemical structure, it was given the name *MPTP*. Laboratory tests demonstrating that MPTP is selectively toxic for dopaminergic cells led to great leaps forward in medical research on the basal ganglia and on treatments for Parkinson's disease. Prior to the drug's discovery, it had been difficult to induce parkinsonism in nonhuman species. Primates do not develop Parkinson's disease naturally, perhaps because their life expectancy is short. Moreover, it is difficult to access the substantia nigra with traditional lesion methods because of its proximity to vital brainstem nuclei. By administering MPTP, researchers could now destroy the substantia nigra and create a parkinsonian animal.

Two treatment methods for Parkinson's disease have stemmed directly from research using MPTP. In the first method, parkinsonian animals are given brain grafts with fetal tissue in the hope of regenerating dopaminergic cells. This method has met with some success, not only in MPTP-treated animals (Gash et al., 1996) but also in experimental clinical trials with humans who have true Parkinson's disease. Fetal grafts can survive for extended periods of time, and PET studies indicate that the dopamine activation is enhanced in the patients (Kordower et al., 1995).

A second radical treatment method is based on the complex inhibitory and excitatory connections of the basal ganglia, a topic we will return to later in this chapter. As a result of dopamine depletion, the output from the basal ganglia ends up producing excessive inhibition on the motor structures in the cerebral cortex, thus inhibiting movement. Researchers have developed a variety of surgical methods to reduce this inhibition, either by lesioning output structures of the basal ganglia or by implanting brain stimulators within the basal ganglia. These procedures are widely practiced at many medical sites around the world, with stunning success (Krack et al., 1998; Rodriquez-Oroz et al., 2005; Samii et al., 1999).

The MPTP story exemplifies how neurological aberrations can elucidate the complicated patterns of connectivity in the motor structures of the CNS. In this chapter we review the organization of the motor system, describing how the brain produces coordinated movement and, at a higher level, selects actions to achieve our goals.

MOTOR STRUCTURES

We focus first on anatomy: the essential components of the motor system and how they are connected. Later we develop a more detailed picture from a cognitive neuroscience perspective, when we consider the computations performed by these neural systems.

Muscles, Motor Neurons, and the Spinal Cord

A part of the body that can move is referred to as an **effector**. For most actions, we think of distal effectors, those far from the body center, such as the arms, hands, and legs. But we can also produce movements with more proximal or centrally located effectors, such as the waist, neck, and head. The jaw, tongue, and vocal tract are essential effectors for producing speech, and the eyes are effectors for vision.

All forms of movement result from changes in the state of muscles that control an effector or group of effectors. Muscles are composed of elastic fibers, tissue that can change length and tension. As Figure 7.2 shows, these fibers are attached to the skeleton at joints and are usually arranged in antagonist pairs, which enable the effector either to flex or to extend. For example, the biceps and triceps form an antagonist pair that regulates the position of the forearm. Contracting or shortening the biceps muscle causes flexion about the elbow. If the biceps muscle is relaxed, or if the triceps muscle is contracted, the forearm is extended.

The primary interaction of muscles and the nervous system comes about through **alpha motor neurons**, so called because of their large size. Alpha motor neurons originate in the spinal cord, exit through the ventral root, and terminate in the muscle fibers. As with other neurons, an action potential in an alpha motor neuron releases a neurotransmitter; here the transmitter is acetylcholine. The release of transmitter does not modify downstream neurons, however. Instead, it

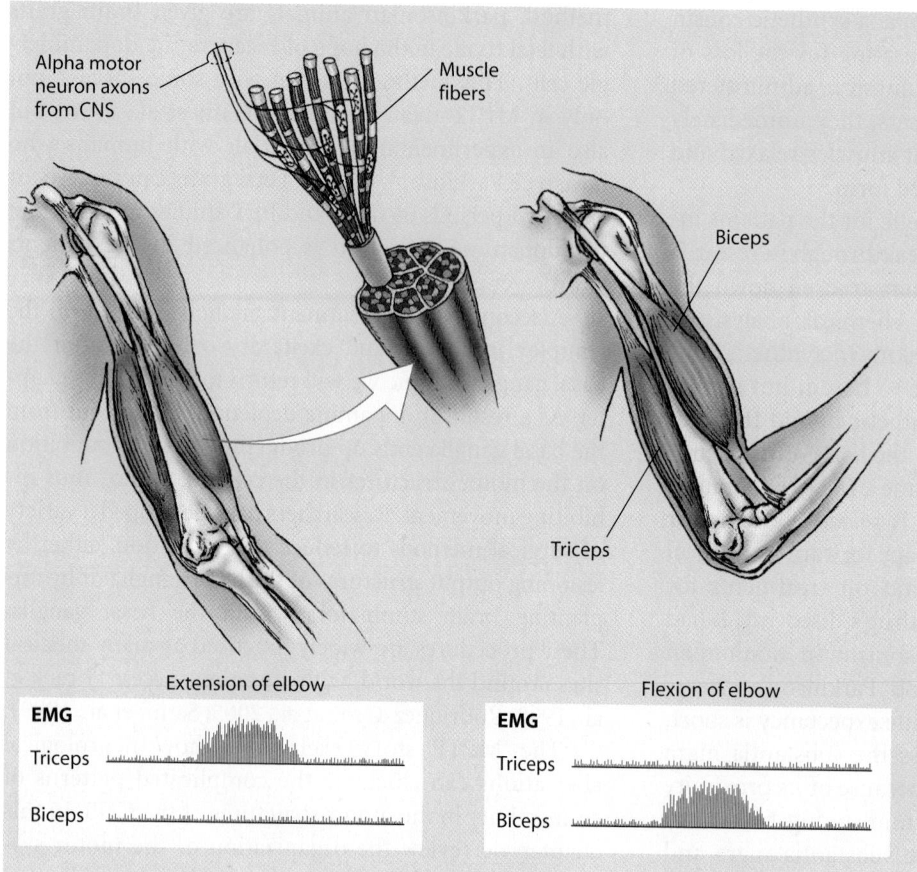

Figure 7.2 Muscles are activated by the alpha motor neurons. Electrodes placed on the skin over the muscle can measure this electrical activity, producing an electromyogram (EMG). The input from the alpha motor neurons causes the muscle fibers to contract. Antagonist pairs of muscles span many of our joints. Activation of the triceps produces extension of the elbow; activation of the biceps produces flexion of the elbow.

makes the muscle fibers contract. Thus, alpha motor neurons provide a physical basis for translating nerve signals into mechanical actions. Movement happens when the alpha motor neurons change the length and tension of muscles.

Input to the alpha motor neurons has a variety of sources. At the lowest level, alpha motor neurons receive input from sensory fibers located in the muscles themselves. When a muscle is stretched, a sensory signal is generated in the joints and muscle fibers and enters the dorsal roots of the spinal cord before synapsing directly on corresponding alpha motor neurons. If unexpected, this signal rapidly increases the output of the alpha motor neurons—a process that returns the muscle to its original length. Figure 7.3 shows the reflex chain that occurs when the family physician taps just below the kneecap. This test assesses the integrity of rapid spinal reflexes.

Alpha motor neurons also receive input from the descending fibers of the spinal cord and interneurons within the spinal segment. The descending fibers originate in several subcortical and cortical structures. These signals can be either excitatory or inhibitory and are the basis for voluntary movements. For example, descending commands that activate the biceps muscle produce flexion of the elbow. As a consequence of this flexion, the triceps stretches. If unchecked, the stretch reflex would lead to excitation of the triceps and move the limb toward its original position. Thus, to produce movement, excitatory signals to one muscle, the agonist, are accompanied by inhibitory signals to the antagonist muscle via interneurons. In this way the stretch reflex that efficiently stabilizes unexpected perturbations can be overcome to permit volitional movement.

Subcortical Motor Structures

Many neural structures of the motor system are in the brainstem, which contains the 12 cranial nerves essential for critical reflexes involving breathing, eating, eye movements, and facial expressions. In addition, many nuclei within the brainstem send direct projections down the spinal cord. These tracts are referred to collectively as the **extrapyramidal tracts**, indicating that they do not origi-

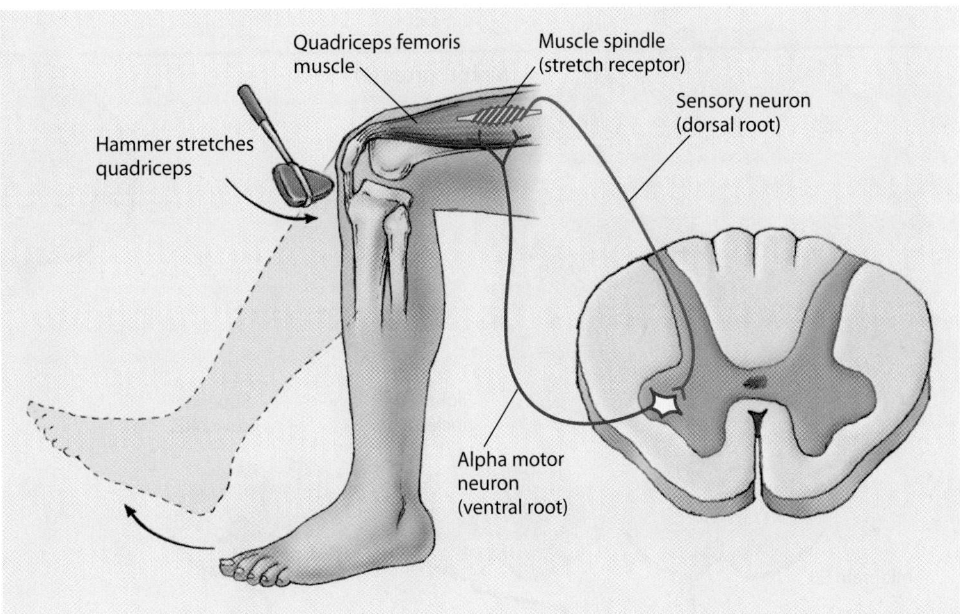

Figure 7.3 The stretch reflex. When the doctor raps your knee, the quadriceps is stretched. This stretch triggers receptors in the muscle spindle to fire. The sensory signal is transmitted through the dorsal root of the spinal cord and directly activates an alpha motor neuron to contract the quadriceps. In this manner, the stretch reflex helps maintain the stability of the limbs following unexpected perturbations.

nate in the pyramidal neurons of the motor cortex (Figure 7.4). Extrapyramidal tracts are a primary source of control over spinal activity; they receive input from subcortical and cortical structures.

Figure 7.5 shows the location of two prominent subcortical structures that play a key role in motor control: the cerebellum and the basal ganglia. The **cerebellum** is a massive structure that receives extensive sensory inputs, including information from somatosensory, vestibular, visual, and auditory channels. It also receives input from many association areas of the cortex. This input is projected primarily to the cerebellar cortex, perhaps the most densely packed neural region in the brain; indeed, more cells are in the cerebellum than in the rest of the central nervous system combined. The cerebellar cortex, though, does not send direct output to the rest of the brain. Rather, the cortex relays information to nuclei buried within the cerebellar enfolding. All cerebellar output comes from these nuclei, modulating activity in the extrapyramidal tracts or influencing motor and frontal cortical regions by way of relays in the thalamus.

The **basal ganglia** are a collection of five nuclei. Taken as a whole, the organization of the basal ganglia bears a similarity to that of the cerebellum: Input is restricted mainly to the two nuclei forming the striatum: the caudate and the putamen. Output is almost exclusively by way of the internal segment of the globus pallidus and part of the substantia nigra. The remaining components (the rest of the substantia nigra, the subthalamic nucleus, and the external segment of the globus pallidus) are in a position to modulate the output of the globus pallidus. The basal ganglia output is primarily ascending: axons of the globus pallidus terminate in the thalamus, which in turn projects to motor and frontal regions of the cerebral cortex.

Cortical Regions Involved in Motor Control

The cerebral cortex can regulate the activity of spinal neurons in direct and indirect ways. Direct connections are provided by the **corticospinal tract**. As its name implies, this tract is composed of neurons that originate in the cortex and terminate directly (monosynaptically) on alpha motor neurons or spinal interneurons. Thus, single axons of the corticospinal tract can extend for more than 1 m. The corticospinal tract is frequently referred to as the *pyramidal tract* because the giant pyramidal cells of the cortex were once believed to be the sole origin of these fibers. Now we know that corticospinal axons can arise from cells of different sizes in layer V of the cortex. Corticospinal fibers originate primarily in the **primary motor cortex** (**M1**), or Brodmann area 4 (Figure 7.6). This area is anterior to the central sulcus, the anatomical division separating the frontal and parietal cortices. Corticospinal fibers also are found in portions of somatosensory cortex and in Brodmann area 6.

Brodmann area 6 contains the secondary motor areas. Taxonomically, area 6 is divided into a lateral region (**premotor cortex**) and a medial region (the

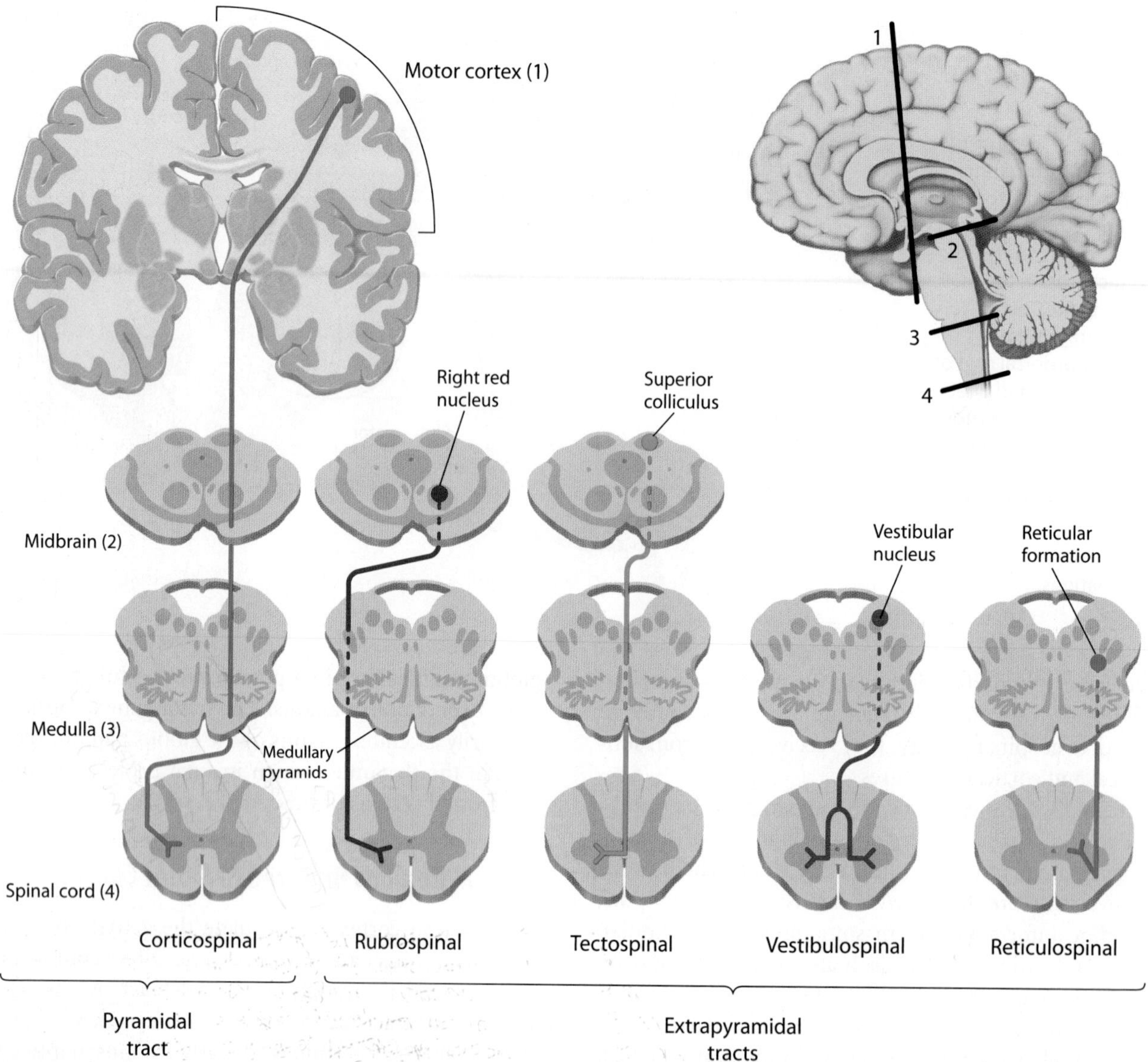

Figure 7.4 The brain innervates the spinal cord via the pyramidal and extrapyramidal tracts. The pyramidal (corticospinal) tract originates in the cortex, and almost all of the fibers cross over to the contralateral side at the pyramids. Tracts that do not travel through the medullary pyramids—the extrapyramidal tracts—originate in various subcortical nuclei and terminate in both contralateral and ipsilateral regions of the spinal cord.

supplementary motor area, or **SMA**). Multiple somatotopic maps are found within these secondary areas, similar to what has been observed in secondary sensory cortices (Dum & Strick, 2002). Thus, physiologists now make finer distinctions, such as distinguishing between dorsal and ventral premotor cortex, or between SMA and pre-SMA.

Many other association areas of the cortex are implicated in motor function. Broca's area, the insula (deep to Broca's area), and the posterior inferior frontal gyrus (Hillis et al., 2004) are involved in the production of speech movements. Area 8 includes the frontal eye fields, a region (as the name implies) that contributes to the control of eye movements. As we saw in Chapter 6, regions of the posterior parietal cortex are involved in the planning and control of actions. Along the intraparietal sulcus, neurophysiologists have identified distinct regions associated with eye movements, arm movements, and hand movements (Andersen & Buneo, 2002). Homologous regions are observed in human imaging studies, leading to functionally defined areas with names such as *posterior parietal reach area.*

Although the cerebral cortex has direct access to spinal mechanisms via the corticospinal tract, it can also

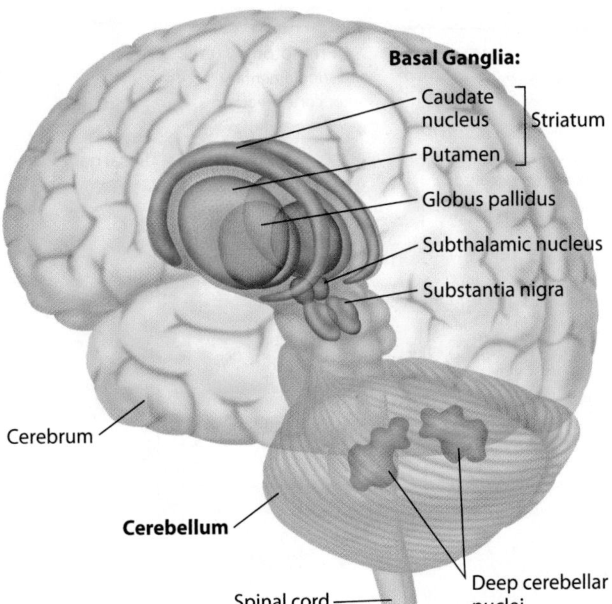

Figure 7.5 The basal ganglia and the cerebellum are two prominent subcortical components of the motor pathways. The basal ganglia proper include the caudate, putamen, and globus pallidus, three nuclei that surround the thalamus. Functionally, however, the subthalamic nuclei and substantia nigra also are considered part of the basal ganglia. The cerebellum sits below the posterior portion of the cerebral cortex. All cerebellar output originates in the deep cerebellar nuclei.

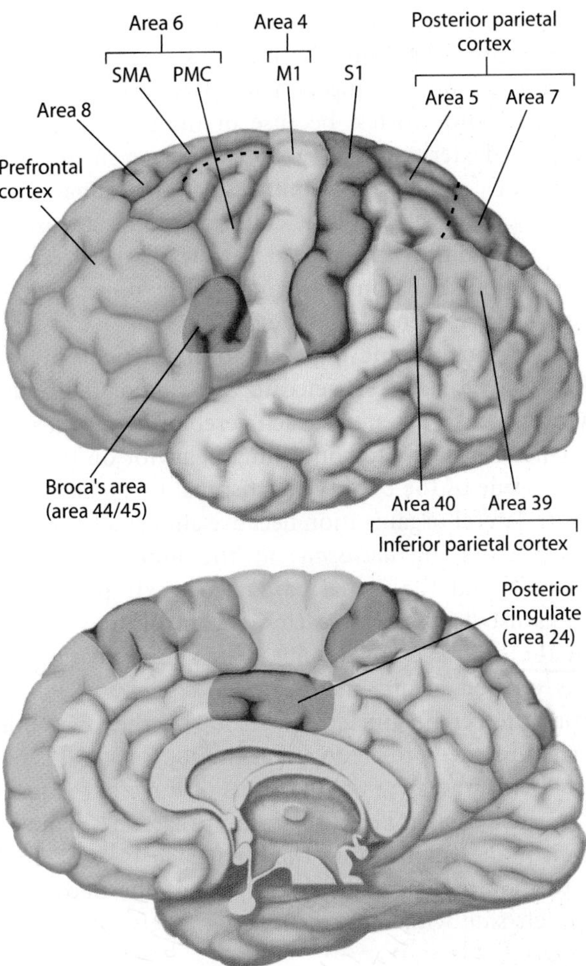

Figure 7.6 Motor areas of the cerebral cortex. Area 4 is the primary motor cortex (M1). Brodmann area 6 encompasses the *supplementary motor area* (SMA) on the medial surface and *premotor cortex* (PMC) on the lateral surface. Area 8 includes the frontal eye fields. Inferior frontal regions (area 44) are involved in speech. Regions of parietal cortex associated with the planning and control of coordinated movement include S1, the primary somatosensory cortex, secondary somatosensory areas, and posterior and inferior parietal regions.

influence movement in four other prominent ways. First, the motor cortex and premotor areas receive input from many regions of the cortex by way of corticocortical connections. Second, some cortical axons terminate on brainstem nuclei, thus cortically influencing the extrapyramidal tracts. Third, the cortex sends massive projections to the basal ganglia and cerebellum. Fourth, the corticobulbar tract is composed of cortical fibers that terminate on the cranial nerves.

Scientists studying vision are fond of claiming that over 50% of the brain is devoted to this one sensory system, but a motor control chauvinist could reasonably argue that over 50% of the brain is devoted to the control of action. We would be well over 100% without even considering the other sensory systems or functions such as memory and language! Of course, an area can be involved in both vision and motor control. A problem arises only when we stick with simple classification schemes in which brain regions are thought of as strictly motor or strictly sensory. By focusing on the kinds of computations performed by different neural regions and systems, we come to see that perception and action are intimately interwoven, a theme that will recur in this chapter.

Organization of Motor Areas

The anatomical organization of the motor areas follows two principles. First, organized, somatotopic representations of the body are found in primary and secondary motor areas (see Chapter 3). In the motor cortex, a crude somatopic representation is observed. For example, an electrical stimulus applied to the medial wall of the precentral gyrus creates movement in the foot; the same stimulus applied at a ventrolateral site elicits tongue movement. Representation of the effectors does not correspond to their actual size. Rather, the cortical area devoted to a certain effector reflects the importance of that effector for movement and the level of control required for manipulating the effector. For this reason, the fingers span a large portion of the human motor cortex, because of the significance of manual dexterity. Using TMS, we can even demonstrate this somatotopy noninvasively in humans, by varying the position of the coil over motor cortex. As the center of the coil is moved downward, the effects of stimulation shift from movement of the upper arm to the wrist and then to individual fingers.

The somatotopic representation, particularly for distal effectors, is restricted to one side of the body. As with sensory systems, each cerebral hemisphere is devoted primarily to controlling behavior on the opposite side of the body. Corticospinal tracts have this contralateral organization because almost all of these fibers cross, or *decussate*, at the junction of the medulla and the spinal cord. Most extrapyramidal fibers also decussate, so each side controls movements on the body's opposite side. The one exception to this crossed arrangement is the cerebellum. Fibers from the cerebellum cross as soon as they exit this structure; they project to either the contralateral cerebral hemisphere via the thalamus or the contralateral brainstem nuclei. The result is an ipsilateral organization of the cerebellum: The right side is associated with movements on the right side of the body and the left side with movements on the left side of the body.

The second general principle refers to the relation between motor areas. The components form a hierarchy with multiple levels of control. As Figure 7.7 illustrates, the lowest level of the hierarchy is the spinal cord. Not only do spinal mechanisms provide a point of contact between the nervous system and muscles, but also simple reflexive movements can be controlled at this level. At the highest level are premotor and association areas. Processing within these regions is critical for planning an action based on present perceptual information, past experience, and future goals. The motor cortex and brainstem structures, with the assistance of the cerebellum and the basal ganglia, translate this action goal into a movement.

Viewing the motor system as a hierarchy enables us to recognize that motor control is a distributed process. The highest levels might not be concerned with the details of a movement, but they might allow lower level mechanisms to translate motor commands into movements. Hierarchical organization also can be viewed from a phylogenetic perspective. Movement in organisms with primitive motor structures is based primarily on simple reflexive actions. An unexpected blast of water against the abdominal cavity of the sea slug automatically elicits a withdrawal response. Additional layers of control enable these reflexes to be modified, perhaps being expressed only in certain conditions. For example, a brainstem structure can inhibit spinal neurons so that a change in a muscle length does not automatically trigger a stretch reflex.

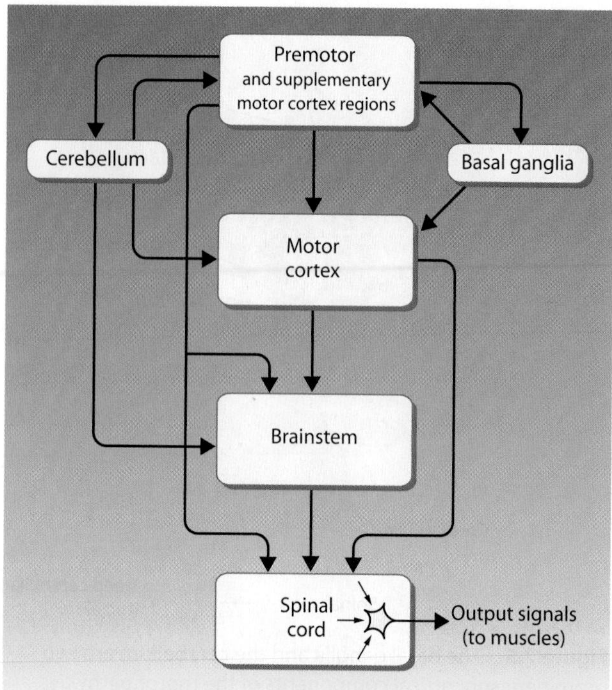

Figure 7.7 The descending pathways of the motor hierarchy. All connections to the arms and legs originate in the spinal cord. The spinal signals are influenced by inputs from the brainstem and various cortical regions, whose activity in turn is modulated by the cerebellum and basal ganglia. Thus, control is distributed across various levels of the hierarchy. Sensory information from the muscles is transmitted back to the brainstem, cerebellum, and cortex (not shown).

In an analogous fashion, the cortex can provide additional means for regulating the actions of the lower levels of the motor hierarchy. This ability offers an organism greater flexibility in its actions. We can generate any number of movements in response to a sensory signal. A tennis player can choose to hit a crosscourt forehand, go for a drop shot, or pop a defensive lob. Cortical mechanisms also enable us to generate actions that are minimally dependent on external cues. We can sing aloud, wave our hands, or pantomime a gesture. Reflecting this greater flexibility, the corticospinal tract is one of the latest evolutionary adaptations, appearing only in mammals. It affords a new pathway over which the cerebral hemispheres can activate ancient motor structures.

COMPUTATIONAL ISSUES IN MOTOR CONTROL

We have seen the panoramic view of the motor system: how muscles are activated and how this activity can be influenced by spinal, subcortical, and cortical signals. Though we identified the major anatomical components, we have yet to consider the structures' functional roles. First, however, it is useful to examine certain behavioral phenomena to understand the information processing that must take place in the motor systems. This section elucidates computational issues in motor control and sets the stage for the discussion that follows, in which physiological and neurological evidence is assessed in developing a cognitive neuroscience of action.

Peripheral Control of Movement and the Role of Feedback

The notion of hierarchical control implies that higher level systems can modulate the activity of lower level mechanisms. One implication of this view is that lower levels can produce movement. The stretch reflex is one such example. Some spinal mechanisms can maintain postural stability even in the absence of higher level processing.

Are spinal mechanisms a simple means for generating more complicated movements? In the late 1800s, Charles Sherrington, a Nobel laureate and British neurophysiologist, developed a procedure in which he severed the spinal cord in cats and dogs to disconnect peripheral motor structures such as alpha motor neurons and spinal interneurons from the cortex and subcortex (Sherrington, 1947). This procedure allowed Sherrington to observe whether the animals could produce movement in the absence of higher level commands. As expected, stretch reflexes remained intact; in fact, these reflexes were exaggerated because inhibitory influences were removed from the brain. More surprisingly, Sherrington observed that these animals could alternate the movements of their hind limbs. With the appropriate stimulus, one leg flexed while the other extended, and then the first leg extended while the other flexed. In other words, without any signals from the brain, the animal displayed movements that resembled walking.

Interestingly, although movement does not require signals from the brain, it also does not need sensory signals—a phenomenon that Thomas Graham Brown, one of Sherrington's students, first demonstrated in 1911. When Brown sectioned the spinal cord and dorsal roots, he discovered that the animal still generated rhythmic walking movements (Figure 7.8). Hence, neurons in the spinal cord can generate an entire sequence of actions without any external feedback signal.

These neurons have come to be called *central pattern generators*. They offer a powerful mechanism for the hierarchical control of movement. Consider, for instance, how the nervous system might initiate walking. Brain structures would not have to specify patterns of muscle activity. Rather, they would simply activate the appropriate pattern generators in the spinal cord, which in turn trigger muscle commands. The system is truly hierarchical, in that the highest levels need be concerned only with issuing commands to achieve an action, whereas lower level mechanisms translate the commands into a movement.

We cannot expect there to be central pattern generators for a wide range of movements. Locomotion probably represents a special situation, an action for which specialized mechanisms have evolved. But more arbitrary movements could exploit central pattern generators. When we reach to pick up an object, for example, low-level mechanisms could make the necessary postural adjustments to keep the body from tipping over as the center of gravity shifts.

Another important insight yielded by Brown's work is the observation that movements are not entirely dependent on peripheral feedback. As such, they imply internal representations of movement patterns. One influential study demonstrating the central control of movement comes from an experiment on a colony of monkeys that lived in a large, enclosed environment (Taub & Berman, 1968). Cutting the nerve fibers through the dorsal root of the spinal cord eliminates all somatosensory, or *afferent*, information from the affected limb. In this study, the deafferentation procedure was conducted in two stages. In the first stage the operation was restricted to a single arm. Following this surgery the animals showed little evidence that they could still use the limb. The affected limb hung passively by the animal's side. In the second stage, the researchers severed the dorsal root in the remaining intact limb. Paradoxically, the animals now began to use both limbs (Figure 7.9).

Indeed, after a relatively short recovery period, an outside observer would be hard-pressed to notice any abnormalities in the behavior of these animals. They move about their cages in a normal quadrupedal gait and can be coaxed into climbing the sides of their cages

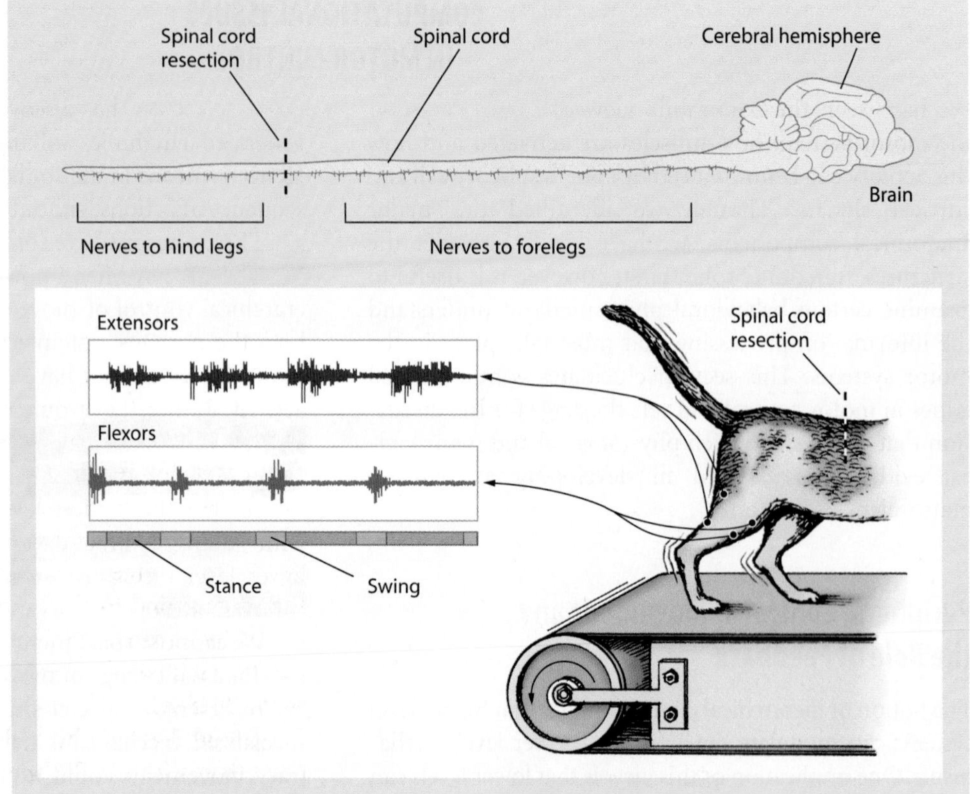

Figure 7.8 Movement is still possible following resection of the spinal cord. In Brown's classic experiment with cats, the spinal cord was severed so that the nerves to the hind legs were isolated from the brain. The cats were still able to produce stereotypical rhythmic movements with the hind legs when walking on a moving treadmill. Because all inputs from the brain had been eliminated, the motor commands must have originated in the lower portion of the spinal cord.

to fetch a reward. These results demonstrate that sensory signals are not essential for movement, although, as we might expect, an animal prefers to use a limb that has intact sensory signals.

This same sort of phenomenon has been observed in humans with severe sensory deficits, or *neuropathies.* In some patients, the large peripheral sensory fibers are destroyed or become nonfunctional; however, the motor fibers are relatively spared, perhaps because of their smaller size and reduced metabolic demands. One patient was reported to be oblivious to pinprick or even electrical stimulation of moderate intensity (Rothwell et al., 1982). Nonetheless, despite severe sensory problems, these patients can still make complicated movements.

(a)

(b)

Figure 7.9 Movement without feedback. **(a)** If the dorsal root on one side of the body is sectioned, the animal does not use the limb; it hangs limply by the animal's side. **(b)** In a second operation, the dorsal root on the other side is also sectioned, so the brain does not receive sensory information from either upper limb. Paradoxically, the monkeys now begin to use the limbs, moving about on all fours, climbing fences, and using their hands to pick up objects.

Figure 7.10 shows the tracings of one patient who was asked to draw geometric shapes in midair. In each case, the shape is drawn correctly and consistently, even though the gestures require the coordinated interplay of many muscles. It is clear that sensory feedback is not necessary for motor control. Soon, however, we will find that feedback can be useful in creating optimal motor output.

Representation of Movement Plans

Research on central pattern generators and movement without feedback highlights the importance of representations in controlling movement. Patients who are functionally deafferented must have an internal representation of the expected consequences of a motor command. For example, to trace a circle or a figure eight, they must have learned the required series of motor commands—commands that can be accessed without any sort of feedback signal. A central issue is how to characterize properties of these representations and how they translate into actions (Keele, 1986).

Figure 7.10 Movements produced by a patient with a severe sensory neuropathy. Time-lapse photography was used to record the patient's tracings of a circle **(b)**, a figure eight **(c)**, and a square **(d)**. All of the movements were made in the dark. Despite the absence of proprioceptive, kinesthetic, and visual feedback, the shapes are readily identified.

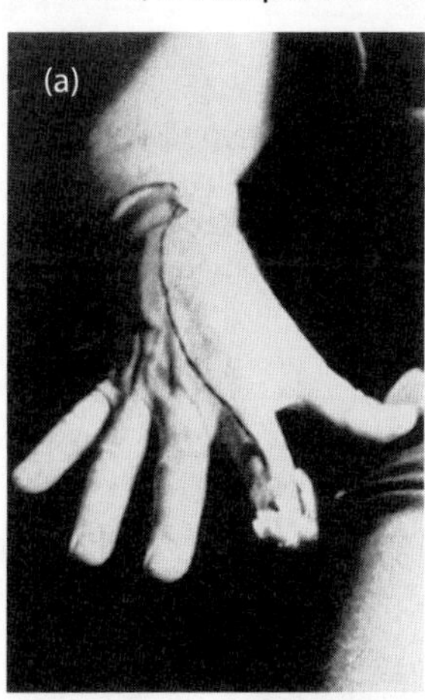

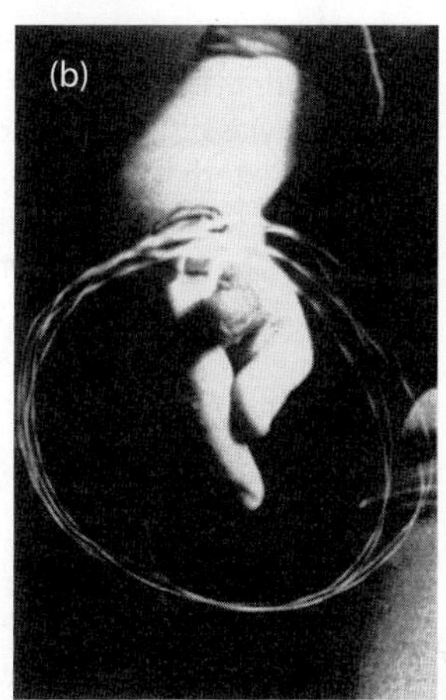

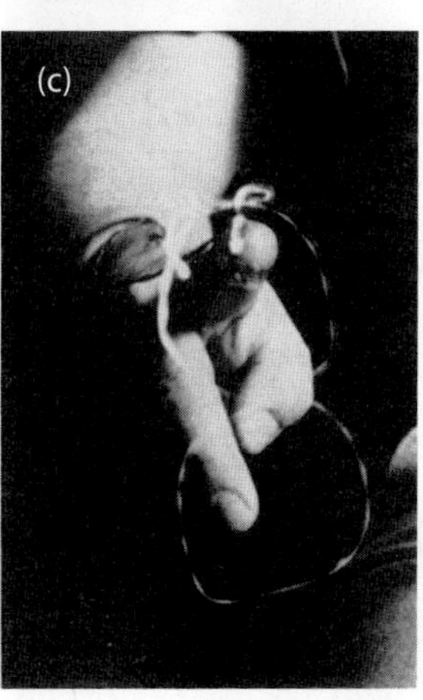

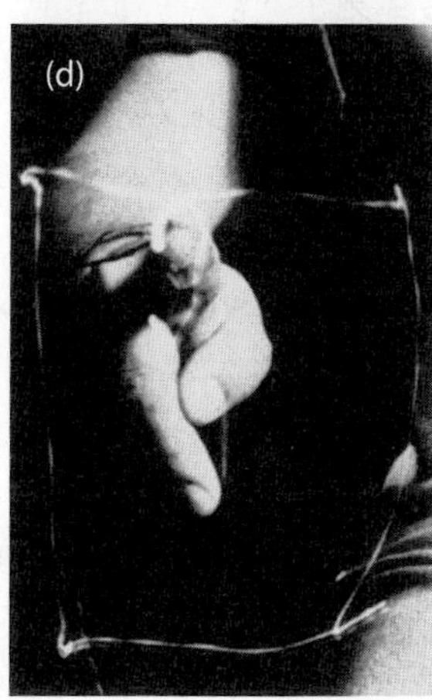

CONTENT OF MOTOR PLANS

Consider the following scenario: a writer is busily typing at the computer and decides to pause and take a sip of coffee. To accomplish this goal, she must move her hand from the keyboard to the coffee cup. This action could be represented in at least two different ways. First, by comparing the positions of the hand and the cup, our writer could plan the required movement trajectory, the path that would transport the hand from the keyboard to the cup. Alternatively, the action plan might simply specify the location of the cup and specify the motor commands that correspond to the limb being at that position. Of course, both forms of representations—trajectory based and location based—might exist at different levels of the motor hierarchy.

Emilio Bizzi and his colleagues (1984) at the Massachusetts Institute of Technology provided dramatic evidence showing that central representations can be based primarily on a location code. In their experiments, deafferented monkeys were trained in a simple pointing experiment. On each trial, a light appeared at one of several locations. After the light was turned off, the animal was required to rotate its elbow to bring its arm to the target location—the point where the light had been.

The critical manipulation included trials in which an opposing torque force was applied just when movement started. These forces were designed to keep the limb at the starting position for a short time. Because the room was dark and the animals were deafferented, they were unaware that their movements were counteracted by an opposing force. The critical question centered on where the movement ended once the torque force was removed. If the animal has learned that a muscular burst will transport its limb a certain distance, applying an opposing force should result in a movement that falls short of the target. But if the animal generates a motor command specifying the desired position, it should achieve this goal once the opposing force is removed. As Figure 7.11 shows, the results clearly favor the latter, location, hypothesis. When the torque motor was on, the limb stayed at the starting location. As soon as it was turned off, the limb rapidly moved to the correct location.

An even more dramatic demonstration of **endpoint control** occurred in a follow-up experiment. Here the

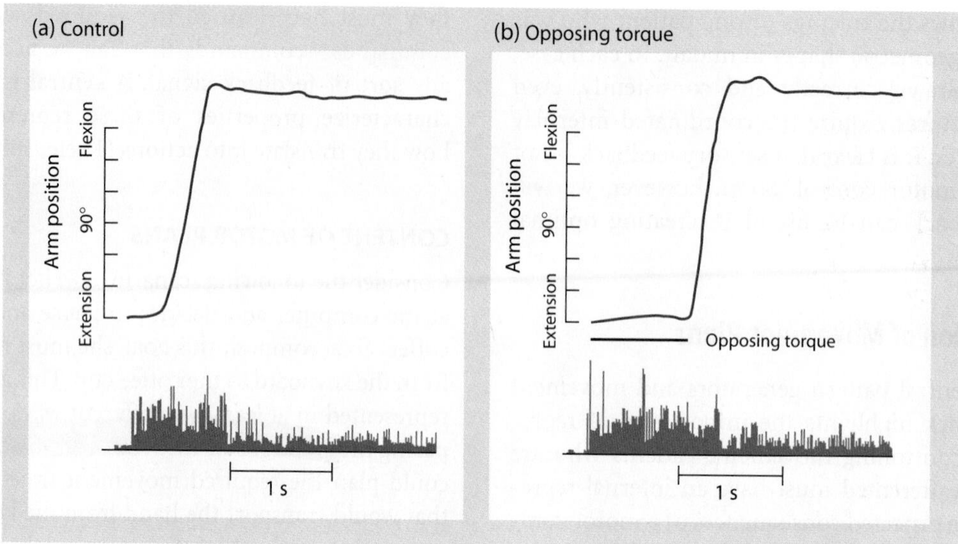

Figure 7.11 Endpoint control. Deafferented monkeys were trained to point in the dark to a target indicated by the brief illumination of a light. The top traces show the position of the arm as it goes from an initial position to the target location. The bottom traces show the EMG activity in the biceps. **(a)** In the control condition, the animals were able to make the pointing movements accurately, despite the absence of all sources of feedback. **(b)** In the experimental condition, an opposing force was applied at the onset of the movement, preventing the arm from moving (bar under the arm position trace). Once this force was removed, the limb rapidly moved to the correct target location. Because the animal could not sense the opposing force, it must have generated a motor command corresponding to the target location.

torque motor was used to transport the limb from the starting position to the final position just as the target location was illuminated. Because of the surgery, the animals were unaware of this passive displacement. Thus, the question centered on what would happen at the beginning of the movement. If the animal is programming muscular events that will result in movement of a desired distance, then the arm should be propelled well past the target. Yet if the animal is programming a desired final location, there should be no movement—the arm has already been moved to the target location.

Neither of these predictions was confirmed. When the torque was removed, the limb moved toward the original location, followed by a reversal after a few hundred milliseconds toward the final location. Indeed, a similar return toward the starting position is also seen when this manipulation is done in the monkey with intact feedback mechanisms. These results provide even more compelling support for the location hypothesis and reveal insights into the dynamics of location-based representations. At the time the target was illuminated, the monkey was still generating a motor command corresponding to the initial location (Figure 7.12). Thus, the arm began to drift toward this position once the torque force was removed. When the target's location was identified, the arm now moved toward the target location.

Figure 7.12 Pointing movements from a displaced starting location. Prior to the onset of EMG activity, the monkey's limb (solid line) was displaced mechanically to the target location. When this external force was removed, the limb began to move back to the initial location and then reversed direction to move to the target location. The central commands (dashed line) can be viewed as a step function from one posture to another, initially specifying the starting location and then abruptly shifting to the target location.

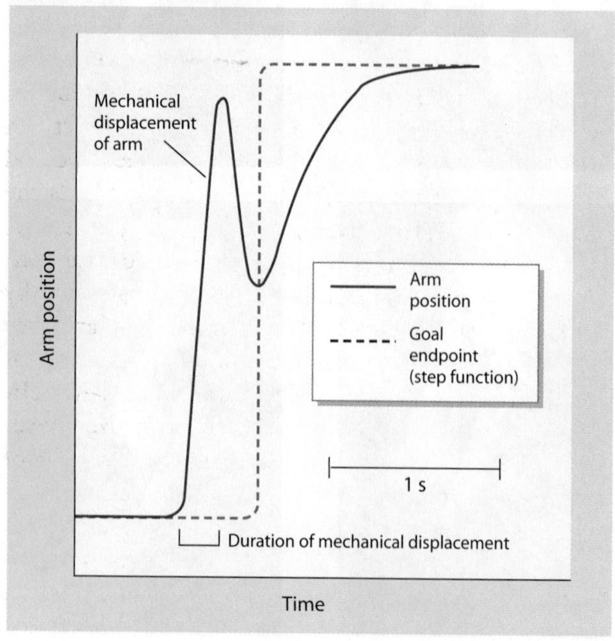

The experiment demonstrated how movement can be viewed as a shift from one postural state to another.

Although Bizzi and his colleagues provided impressive evidence in favor of location planning, it is also clear that we can represent other parameters of movement, such as distance. For example, we can reproduce a movement to a fixed distance, even when the reproduced distance is to a novel location. Moreover, when movements are made to successive locations, errors that arise in the initial movements are manifest in the final movements. If the sequence is represented as independent locations, we should not expect to observe this persistence.

We can also control the form with which a movement is executed. For example, in reaching for the coffee cup, our writer could choose to extend only her arm, or she could also rotate about her waist, thus reducing the distance that her arm has to move. In addition, we can vary how fast we execute the movement. Indeed, in many tasks the trajectory is as important as the final goal. When a skilled figure skater performs an aerial maneuver, it is essential that she land properly to maintain her balance. But it is just as important that the jump follow a certain trajectory to achieve the desired number of rotations in the most graceful manner. Viewed in this way, endpoint control reveals the fundamental capabilities of the motor control system; distance and trajectory planning demonstrate additional flexibility in the control processes.

HIERARCHICAL REPRESENTATION OF ACTION SEQUENCES

In the preceding actions, the movements entailed simple gestures such as pointing to a location in space or reaching for an object. Most of our actions are more complex, however, involving a sequence of movements. In serving a tennis ball, we have to toss the ball with one hand and swing the racquet with the other so that it strikes the ball just after the apex of rotation. In playing the piano, we must strike a sequence of keys with appropriate timing and force. Are these actions simply constructed by the linking of independent movements, or are they guided by hierarchical representational structures that govern the entire sequence? The answer is the latter. Hierarchical representational structures organize movement elements into integrated chunks. The idea of chunking was originally developed in studies of memory capacity (see "How the Brain Works: Short-Term Memory Capacity," on p. 316). Chunking is also relevant to the representation of action. In piano playing, such structure is obvious: The musical score defines measures and phrases. Similar principles apply to all skilled actions, albeit at a more implicit level.

Figure 7.13 presents a model developed by Donald MacKay (1987) of the University of California, Los Angeles, to show how the ideas of hierarchical representation can be applied to motor control. The top of the hierarchy, the conceptual level (Figure 7.13a), corresponds to a representation of the goal of the action. In this example, the man intends to accept the woman's invitation to dance. At the next level, this goal must be translated into a system (Figure 7.13b). He could make a physical gesture, such as offering his hand or starting to tap his foot. Or he could

Figure 7.13 Hierarchical control of action. Motor planning and learning can occur at multiple levels. At the lowest level are the actual commands to implement a particular action. At the highest level are abstract representations of the goal for the action. Usually multiple actions can achieve the same goal. Learning occurs at all levels. If the motor commands (lowest level) are well established, then motor learning will be limited to strengthening the more abstract representations rather than involving the muscles themselves.

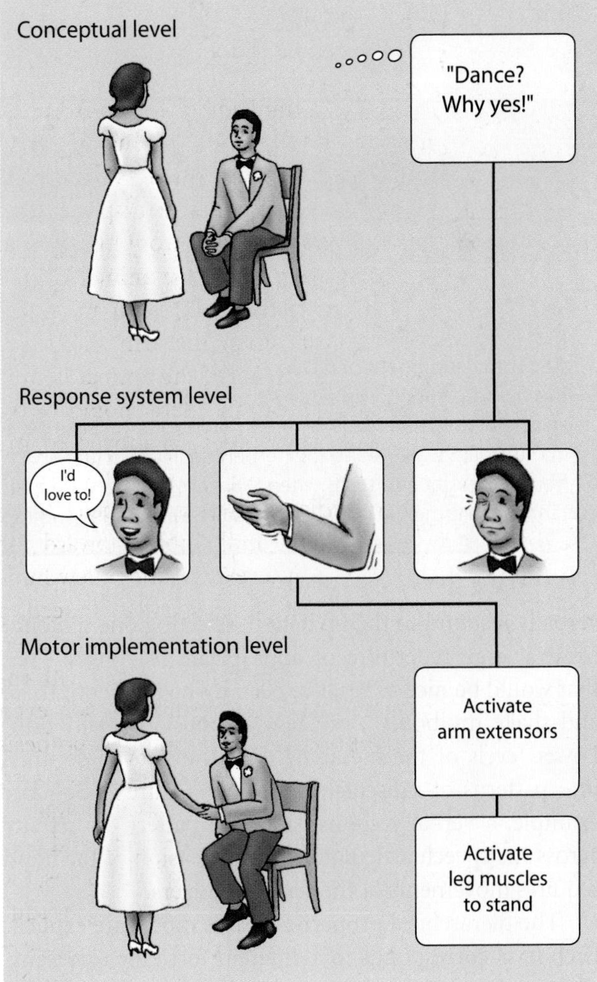

HOW THE BRAIN WORKS

Where Is It? Assessing Location Through Perception and Action

To demonstrate that spatial information can be represented differently in systems involved in conscious perception and those associated with guiding action, try the experiment outlined in the figure. While standing in an open area, have a friend place an object 6 to 12 m from you. Then have your friend move along the perpendicular direction and stop him or her when you perceive that you are both equidistant from the object. Measure your accuracy. Now have your friend place the object in a new location, again 6 to 12 m away. When ready, close your eyes and walk forward, attempting to stop right over the object. Measure your accuracy.

Assuming that your performance matches that of the average person, you will notice a striking dissociation (Loomis et al., 1992). You will probably be quite inaccurate on the first task, underestimating the distance from you to the object. Yet on the second task you should be very accurate. These results reveal a dissociation between two forms of judgment: one perceptual, the other motoric. In both situations the results suggest that separate representational systems underlie judgments of location and distance. Although location judgments are accurate, the representation of distance is subject to perceptual distortions. Our perception of distance is highly compressed: Things almost always are farther away than they appear (perhaps a "safety" mechanism to ensure that we ready ourselves for an approaching predator?). But, as this experiment demonstrates, our action systems are not similarly fooled. There is little, if any, compression of distance when we move to a target location.

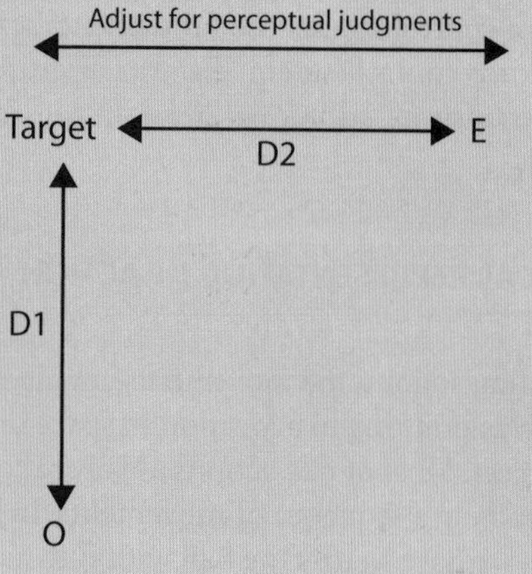

Perceptual judgment of distance. Two people are needed for this demonstration. The observer, O, stands at a fixed location in an open area. The experimenter, E, places a target at some point in the area. E walks along the perpendicular direction away from the target and stops when O judges that they are equidistant to the target (D1 = D2). The results will be quite striking.

verbally respond to the invitation, selecting one sentence from a large repertoire of appropriate responses: "Yes, that would be nice"; "Yes, I've been dying to get out there and shake my booty"; or "Yes, the music is really hot." Lower levels of the hierarchy then translate these units into patterns of muscular activation (Figure 7.13c). For example, a verbal response entails a pattern of activity across the speech articulators, and extension of the hand requires movements of the arm and fingers.

The hierarchical properties of this model are explicit. Each level corresponds to a different form for representing the action. Actions can be described in relation to the goals to be achieved, and this level need not be tied to a specific form of implementation. Whether our gentleman responds physically or vocally, the two forms of responding share a common level of representation. In a similar fashion, when we convey a linguistic message by speaking or by writing, a common level of representation is on both the conceptual and the lexical levels. Higher levels in the hierarchy need not represent all of the information.

MacKay's model also has proved useful in explaining the learning of new motor patterns. People frequently attribute motor learning to low levels of the hierarchy. We speak of "muscle memory," or our muscles having learned how to respond—for example, how to maintain balance on a bike, or how to throw a dart with fine precision. The fact that we have great difficulty verbalizing how to perform these skills reinforces the notion that the learning is noncognitive. The Olympic gymnast Peter Vidman expressed this sentiment when he said, "As I approach the apparatus … the only thing I am thinking about is … the first trick. … Then, my body takes over and hopefully everything becomes automatic" (Schmidt, 1987, p. 85).

On closer study, however, we find that some aspects of motor learning are independent of the muscular system used to perform the actions. Demonstrate this independence to yourself by taking a piece of paper and signing your name. Having done this, repeat the action but use your nondominant hand. Now do it again, holding the pen between your teeth. If you feel especially adventurous, you can take off your shoes and socks and hold the pen between your toes.

Although the atypical productions will not be as smooth as your standard signature, the more dramatic result of this demonstration is the high degree of similarity across all of the productions. Figure 7.14 shows the results of one such demonstration. This high-level representation of the action is independent of any particular muscle group. The differences in the final product reflect the fact that some muscle groups have more experience in translating an abstract representation into a concrete action.

When we view action representation in this way, we see that motor learning can take place at multiple levels. When a learned action is produced by a new set of effectors, learning is greatest at the lower level. In contrast, if we are acquiring a new action, the effects of learning are likely to be at more abstract levels of the action hierarchy.

(a)

(b)

(c)

(d)

(e)

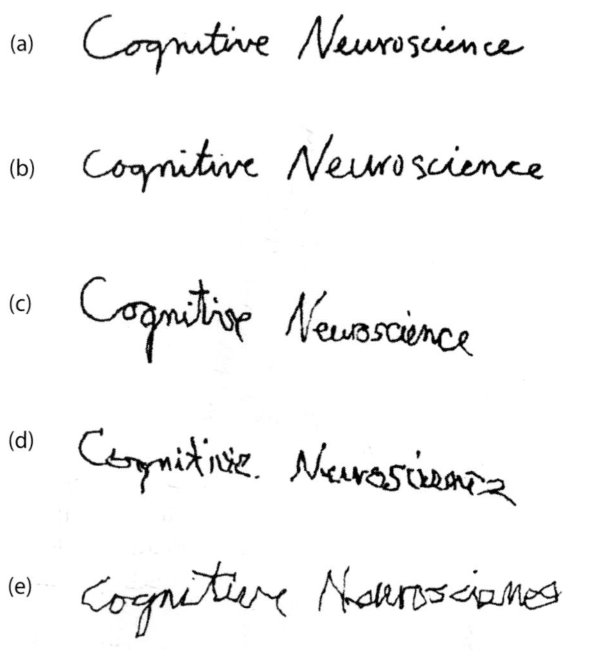

Figure 7.14 Motor representations are not linked to particular effector systems. These five productions of the words *cognitive neuroscience* were produced by the same person moving a pen with the right hand **(a)**, the right wrist **(b)**, the left hand **(c)**, the mouth **(d)**, and the right foot **(e)**. The productions show a degree of similarity, despite the vast differences in practice writing with these five body parts.

PHYSIOLOGICAL ANALYSIS OF MOTOR PATHWAYS

So far in this chapter we have stressed two critical points on movement: First, as with all complex domains, motor control depends on several distributed anatomical structures. Second, these distributed structures operate in a hierarchical fashion. We have seen that the concept of hierarchical organization also applies at the behavioral level of analysis. The highest levels of planning are best described by how an action achieves an objective; the lower levels of the motor hierarchy are dedicated to translating a goal into a movement. We now turn to the problem of relating structure to behavior: How can we best characterize the functional role of the different components of the motor system? In this section we will take a closer look at the neurophysiology of motor control. In the following section, we will address this same issue from the perspective of neurology.

Neural Coding of Movement

Neurophysiologists have long puzzled over how best to describe cellular activity in the motor structures of the CNS. Direct stimulation in primary motor cortex can produce discrete movements about single joints and has been useful for mapping the topography of the motor cortex. But this method does not provide insight into the activity of single neurons, nor can it be used to study how and when cells become active during volitional movement. To address these issues, we have to record the activity of single cells and ask what

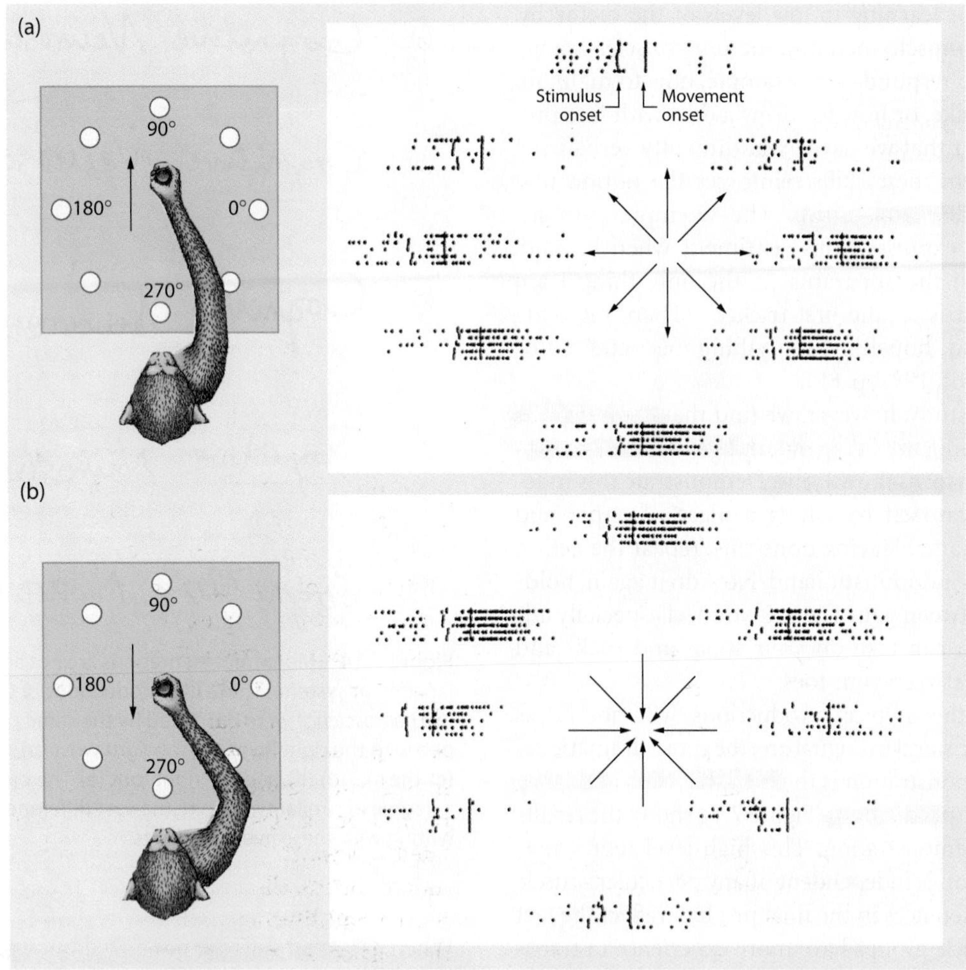

Figure 7.15 Motor cortex activity is correlated with movement direction. **(a)** The animal was trained to move a lever from the center location to one of eight surrounding locations. The activity of a motor cortex neuron is plotted next to each target location. Each row represents a single movement, and the dots correspond to action potentials. **(b)** Here, movements originated at the eight peripheral locations and always terminated at the center location. The activity for the neuron is now plotted next to the starting locations. The neuron is most active for movements in the downward direction, regardless of starting and final locations.

parameters of movement are coded by such cellular activity. For example, is cellular activity correlated with parameters of muscle activity such as force, or with more abstract entities such as movement direction or desired final location?

In a classic series of experiments, Apostolos Georgopoulos (1995) and his colleagues at Johns Hopkins University and at the Veterans Administration Medical Center in Minneapolis studied this question by recording from cells in various regions of the motor system of rhesus monkeys. The monkeys were trained with the apparatus shown in Figure 7.15 on what has come to be called, the *center-out task.* The animal initiates the trial by moving the lever to the center of the table. After a brief hold period, a light illuminates one of eight surrounding target positions and the animal moves the lever to this position to obtain a food reward. This movement is similar to a reaching action and usually involves rotating two joints, the shoulder and the elbow.

The results of these studies convincingly demonstrate that the activity of the cells in the motor cortex correlates much better with movement direction then with target location. Figure 7.15a shows a neuron's activity when movements were initiated from a center location to eight radial locations. This cell was most strongly activated when the movement was toward the animal. Figure 7.15b shows results from the same cell when movements were initiated at radial locations and always ended at the center position. In this condition the cell was most active for movements initiated from the most distant position; movement was again toward the animal.

These data suggest that motor cortex cells code movement direction and that movement in a certain direction requires activating appropriate cells. Indeed, cells within a cortical column have a common directional tuning, with that direction changing in a systematic manner across the cortex. As indicated in Figure 7.15, though, the cells' directional tuning is broad: There is significantly more activity in four of the eight directions.

Because the tuning is so broad, we should consider an alternative coding scheme. A command to move in a direction is distributed across all cells devoted to a certain limb. The response of each cell is a function of how closely the target direction corresponds to its preferred direction. If the target and preferred directions are identical, the cell will have a maximal increase in activity. If the target and preferred directions are in opposite directions, the cell will have a maximal decrease in activity. When the two axes are not parallel, the activity is a function of their difference.

This coding scheme—the summed activity over all of the cells—turns out to be the best predictor of movement direction. Georgopoulos and his colleagues called it the **population vector** because it is a way to see how a global event, a movement in a certain direction, can result from the summed activity of many small elements, each contributing its own vote (Figure 7.16). The population vector is powerful for analyzing motor neurophysiology. For example, once an experimenter has plotted the tuning curves for cells, the population vector for any movement closely agrees with the trajectory adopted by the animal—an analysis that holds for movement in three-dimensional space.

When we think about the direction of a movement, we code that action in an external reference frame. That is, we can speak of a target as being located to the left, or another as being located straight ahead. It is important to consider how a relatively abstract spatial concept such as "direction" relates to muscle activity. In the preceding example, the cell is most active when the monkey is flexing its arm, regardless of whether the animal moved its arm from the center location to the 270° target or from the 90° target to the center location. Thus, we have a confounder in this situation: The direction is the same in the two conditions (toward the body), but so is the required muscular event (flexion). We don't really know if the cell is coding movement direction or if it is coding a particular pattern of muscle activity.

To explore this question, Peter Strick and his colleagues at the Veterans Administration Medical Center in Syracuse, New York (Kakei et al., 1999), designed a clever variant of the center-out task, exploiting the fact that primates have incredibly flexible wrists or, as motor control scientists would put it, many *degrees of freedom*. Rather than using arm movements, these researchers had the animals make all of the movements with the wrist. The critical experimental manipulation was to vary the initial orientation of the wrist. It could be oriented with the palm facing down or rotated 90° (Figure 7.17). In this way, the required muscle activity for moving in a particular direction would vary considerably across the two orientations.

Consider the direction of a flexion movement. When the palm faces down, the flexion movement will be in the downward direction. In contrast, when the hand is rotated to the side, flexion will result in movement to the left. Thus, by having the animal move in eight directions with two different hand orientations, the researchers could ask if the cells were coding movement direction or muscle activity. To their surprise, both forms of coding were found in motor cortex. For the cell shown in Figure 7.17c, activity is much greater when the animal extends the wrist compared to when it flexes the wrist, regardless of movement direction. For the cell shown in Figure 7.17d, activity is greatest whenever the wrist moves to the right, even though this movement requires lateral (ulnar) rotation when the palm is facing down and extension when the hand is rotated sideways. On the basis of recordings from 88 motor cortex cells, the activity in half of the cells coded movement direction, whereas the activity in a third of the cells coded muscle activity. The coding for the remaining cells was ambiguous.

In a follow-up study (Kakei et al., 2001), this group of researchers repeated the experiment while recording from cells in premotor cortex. Here the neural activity was almost entirely coded in terms of movement direction. Thus, the neural code in different motor areas reflects a hierarchical coding in which movements are initially planned in a more abstract, direction-based form but are transformed into a form that becomes muscle based in the signals from motor cortex to the muscles.

NEURAL PROSTHETICS: USING NEUROPHYSIOLOGICAL SIGNALS FOR MOVEMENT TO CONTROL ADAPTIVE DEVICES

In cortical regions of the motor pathway, the population vector shifts in the direction of the upcoming movement before the movement is produced, indicating that the cells help to plan the movement rather than simply reflecting changes during a movement. To dissociate movement planning and movement execution, Georgopoulos provided two signals on each trial: The first indicated the movement's target direction; the second

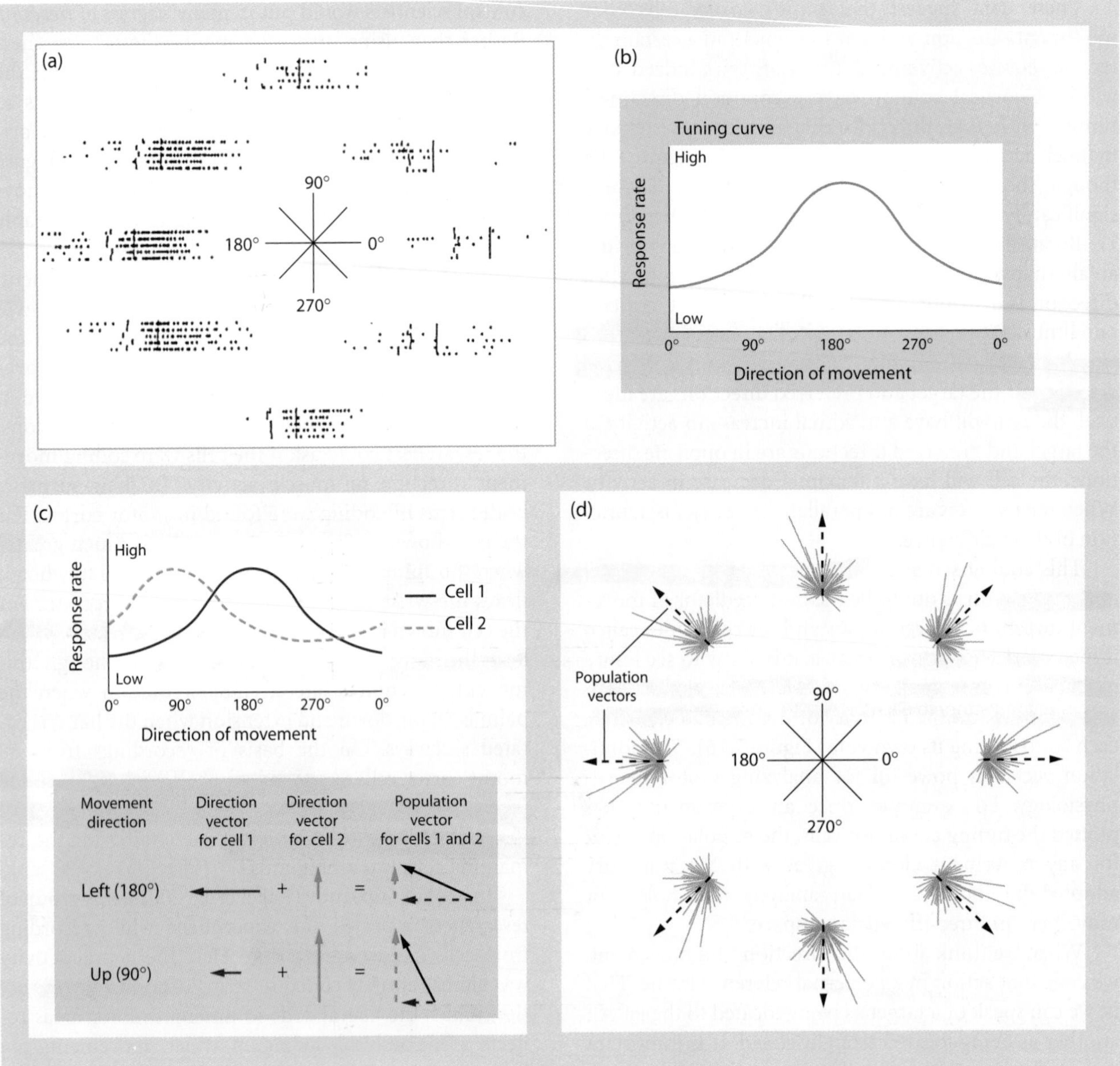

Figure 7.16 The population vector provides a cortical representation of movement. The activity of a single neuron in the motor cortex is measured for each of the eight movements **(a)** and plotted as a tuning profile **(b)**. The preferred direction for this neuron is 180°, the leftward movement. **(c)** Each neuron's contribution to a particular movement can be plotted as a vector. The direction of the vector is always plotted as the neuron's preferred direction, and the length corresponds to its firing rate for the target direction. The population vector (dashed line) is the sum of the individual vectors. **(d)** For each direction, the solid lines are the individual vectors for each of 241 motor cortex neurons; the dotted line is the population vector calculated over the entire set of neurons. Although many neurons are active during each movement, the summed activity closely corresponds to the actual movements.

served as a "go" signal indicating that the movement could now be initiated. Thus, the animals were trained to prepare the movement in advance so that they could initiate their responses as fast as possible. As the population vector in Figure 7.18 shows, cells in the motor cortex coded the intended direction well in advance of the go signal. The movement's direction could be precisely predicted when the population vector was recorded more than 300 ms prior to the movement.

The ability to predict actions from neural activity raises an intriguing possibility: Can these neural signals be used to drive a movement directly, bypassing the intermediate stage of muscles? At first glance, this question seems nonsensical. What would it mean to produce

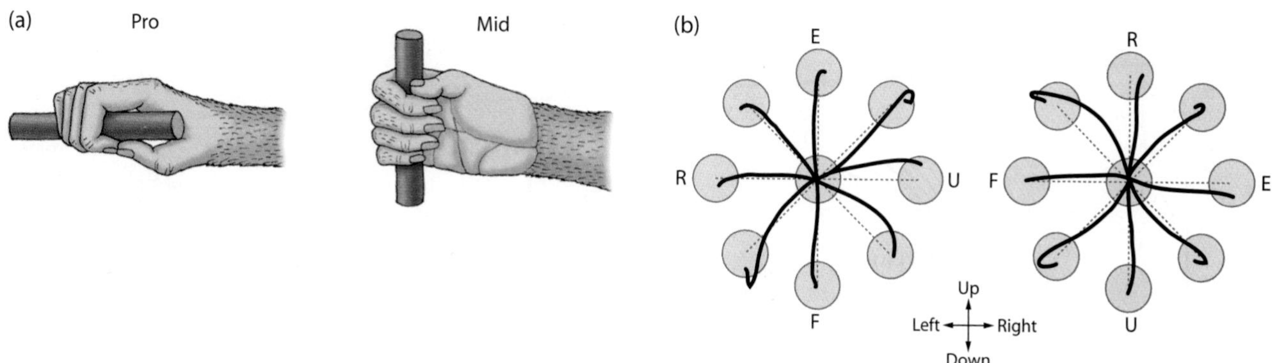

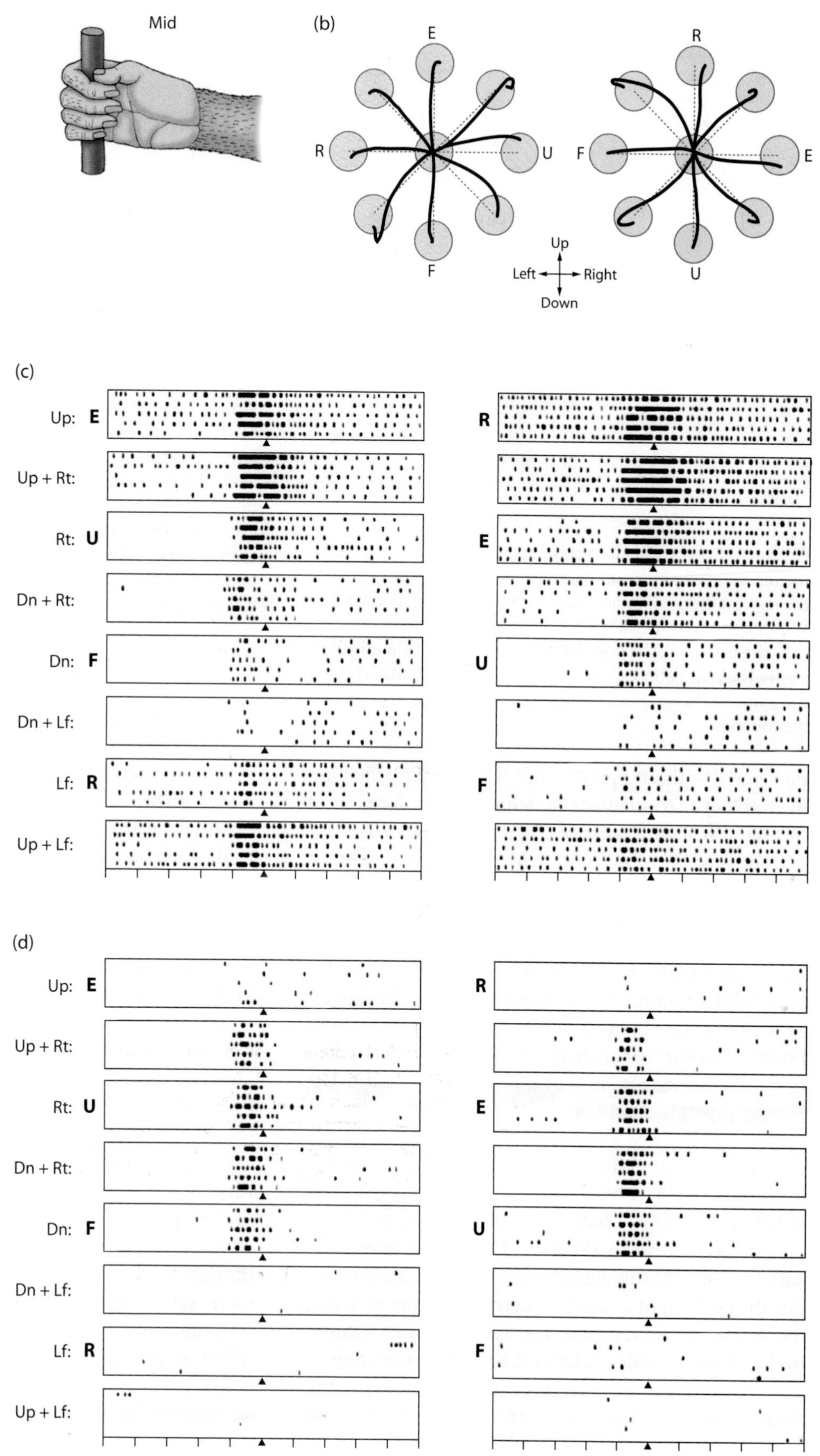

(c)

Up: E | R
Up + Rt: |
Rt: U | E
Dn + Rt: |
Dn: F | U
Dn + Lf: |
Lf: R | F
Up + Lf: |

(d)

Up: E | R
Up + Rt: |
Rt: U | E
Dn + Rt: |
Dn: F | U
Dn + Lf: |
Lf: R | F
Up + Lf: |

Figure 7.17 Exploring how direction of movement is coded. **(a)** The starting position of the monkey's hand: fully pronated (Pro) or midway (Mid). **(b)** The average movement trajectory to each of eight targets, and the type of flexion required for the movement (E = extension; F = flexion; R = radial deviation; U = ulnar deviation). **(c)** Each column indicates the activity of a neuron in primary visual cortex during each of the various muscle movements (E, F, R, U), which required a directional movement of up (Up), down (Dn), right (Rt), left (Lf), up and right (Up+Rt), down and right (Dn+Rt), up and left (Up+Lf), or down and left (Dn+Lf). The cell recorded from here shows activity related to the movement of the muscles, regardless of the direction of movement. **(d)** The activity of a different cell recorded from primary motor cortex during the same manipulations as described in **(c)**. This cell, however, is selective for the direction of wrist movement, regardless of the pattern of muscle activity necessary for the movement.

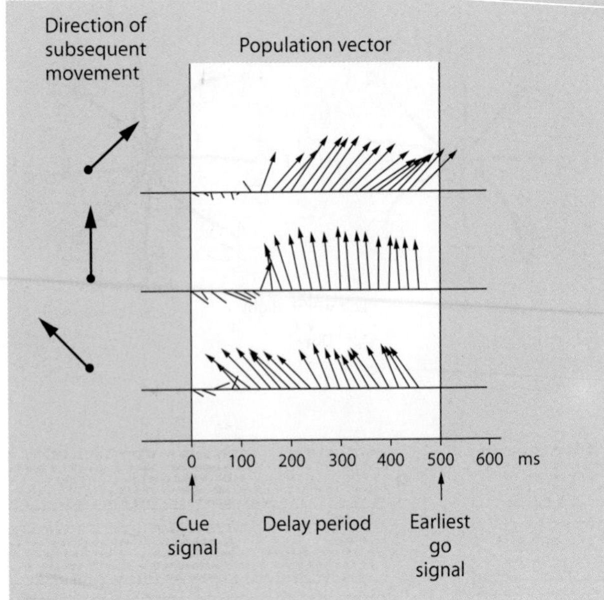

Figure 7.18 The direction of the population vector predicts the direction of a forthcoming movement. At the cue, one of the eight targets is illuminated, indicating the direction for a subsequent movement. The animal must refrain from moving until the go signal. The population vector was calculated every 20 ms. The population vector is oriented in the direction for the planned movement, even though EMG activity is silent in the muscles.

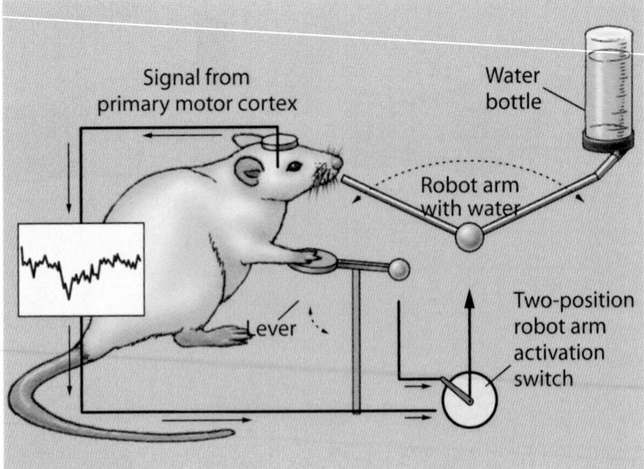

Figure 7.19 Rats can be trained to use a lever to control a robot arm that delivers them drops of water. When several neurons in the primary motor cortex of the rat are recorded while the animal presses the lever, population vectors can be discerned that correlate with the actual movement. The experimenters then change the paradigm so that lever movement doesn't control the robot arm, but rather the population vectors from the cells in the rat's brain tell the robot arm where to move. Soon, all the rat has to do is think about moving the lever and the robot arm magically delivers water!

movement without muscles? But this is exactly the kind of problem that scientists designing robots have faced for many years. All sorts of engineering solutions have been devised for robot control. Most of these have taken little inspiration from the study of motor physiology. But the work on population vectors suggests a novel approach. By combining measurements of the activity in motor cortex with fast computers, it should be possible to control a robotic device directly with neural signals. This capability would open the door to a new class of *prosthetic* devices, or artificial limbs, for individuals who have suffered amputations or injuries to the descending tracts of the motor system.

One of the first demonstrations of the viability of this idea came from the work of a group of scientists led by John Chapin at the State University of New York (Chapin et al., 1999). Rats were trained to use a lever to obtain drops of water (Figure 7.19). A computer measured the pressure on the lever and used this signal to adjust the position of a robot arm. By varying the pressure, the animals could replenish the water and then bring it to the mouth for a drink. Once the animals were trained, simultaneous activity in up to 46 neurons, mostly in the primary motor cortex, was recorded. Similar to what has been found in the primate studies, the activity of the neurons varied with the intensity of this simple movement, and population vectors could be calculated showing a strong correlation between the summed activity of the task-related neurons and the movement being produced by the rat.

It was at this point that the robot control was initiated. The connection between the lever and the robot arm was disengaged. In its place, the electrical signals driving the robot arm were controlled by the time-varying population vector. If the vector at a point in time indicated that the rat was increasing pressure on the lever, then the robot arm moved accordingly; if the vector was associated with a decrease in pressure, then the signal to the robot arm caused the device to slow down or stop. Amazingly, population vectors generated from as few as 25 neurons proved sufficient for the rats to successfully control the robot arm to obtain water.

What about the rat's paw, though? If the motor cortex is active, doesn't the paw continue to press? During the first phase of robotic control, the animals indeed did continue to generate pressing-like movements, even though these movements had no direct effect on the lever. Over time, however, these movements became sporadic, occurring only after trials in which the population vector failed to result in the water reward being delivered. The animals had learned that simply thinking about the correct movement was sufficient to move the robot arm.

Work on **brain–machine interface (BMI)** systems has proved to be one of the most exciting advances in the neurosciences over the past decade. Monkeys have been trained to control the cursor on a computer screen with amazing proficiency and speed. Even more impressive has been work using neural signals to control prosthetic devices such as artificial arms. As with Chapin's rats, the training program requires two stages. First the animals are allowed to use a limb to reach and grasp objects located at various positions. Recordings are made from cells in motor cortex to characterize the activity of each neuron and create online population vectors. Once these representations have been established, the population vectors can be used to control a robotic device directly. Thus, like the rats who learned to stop pressing the bar and receive a reward by just thinking the right thought, monkeys can be trained to control robotic devices by simply thinking about moving an arm.

With each year, the complexity of the brain-controlled actions has become more impressive. Initially BMIs were used simply to control the position of a cursor on a computer screen. With the development of more sophisticated algorithms, BMI systems have been developed in which, merely by thinking of the desired action, monkeys can control the movement of robotic arms in three-dimensional space and even perform meaningful actions. For example, Andrew Schwartz and his colleagues at the University of Pittsburgh trained monkeys to use a robot arm to grasp peanuts at arbitrary locations and then bring the device close to the mouth for a tasty reward (Figure 7.20; see also http://motorlab.neurobio.pitt.edu/videos/Direct3DRobotControl.mpg).

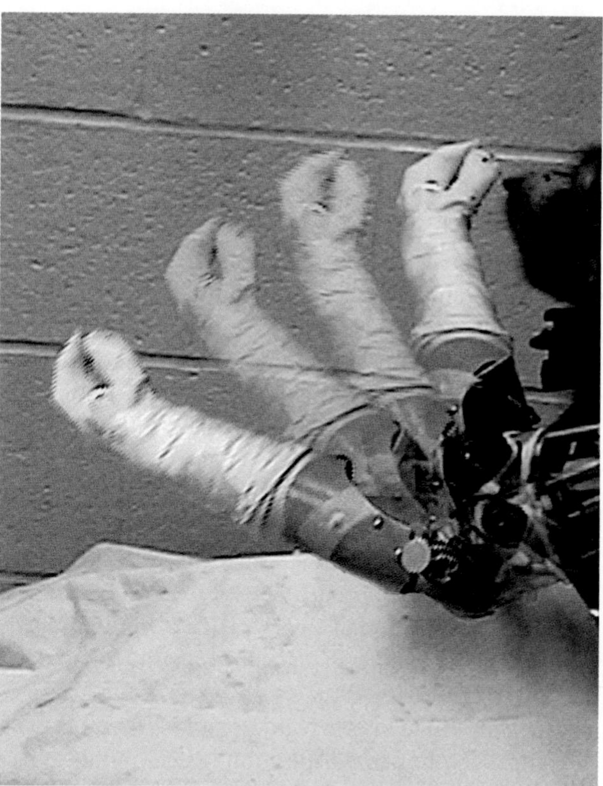

Figure 7.20 With this brain–machine interface, Andrew Schwartz and his colleagues trained monkeys to use thoughts to control a robotic arm to grasp peanuts at arbitrary locations and then move the device to the mouth to deliver the reward.

In this example, the grasping movement was crude and not under brain control; the animal simply had to position the arm above the peanut, and this movement triggered a computer command for the hand to open and close. However, Miguel Nicolelis at Duke University has developed a BMI system in which neural signals are used to control a robotic device that performs reaching and grasping movements (Carmena et al., 2003). Interestingly, in this study, recordings were made not only from primary motor cortex, but also from cells in premotor, supplementary motor, and parietal cortices. Therefore, researchers were able to compare the degree of control achieved when population vectors were based on signals from different regions of the motor system.

Overall, population vectors from primary motor cortex were most proficient for BMI control, and this result was obtained regardless of whether the analysis focused on reaching or grasping. Nonetheless, signals from other brain regions could also be used to control the robot, although here the control might be limited to certain components of the robotic action. SMA neurons could be used to control the reaching component but were quite poor for grasping. In contrast, posterior parietal neurons could control grasping but not reaching. Thus, in addition to its potential for clinical applications, BMI work can help answer basic research problems. The dissociation of SMA and parietal neurons in this study suggests that the latter may represent the final goal of an action, the grasping component, with other brain regions, such as SMA and motor cortex, translating that goal into the various movement components.

As noted already, BMI systems offer a new avenue for aiding individuals who are unable to control their limbs. Spinal injury is, unfortunately, a relatively common event, given our propensity for activities such as driving fast cars or diving into enticing swimming holes. Individuals whose injuries are below the level of the cervical nerves will become *paraplegic*, unable to use their legs. People with injuries higher up in the spinal cord—say, from a broken neck—will become *quadriplegic*, unable to use either lower or upper limbs. Now, however, clinicians recognize that, because the brain is relatively intact, the patients' neural signals contain codes that could be used to control prosthetic devices.

The use of BMI systems with humans is advancing at an incredible rate. However, one significant limitation constrains the transition from animal to human research. In the BMI work that we have reviewed, the use of neural signals to control prosthetic devices is preceded by a training phase in which the animal produces actual movements. Neural recordings made during these movements are used to decode the neural representation, which is then used to control the robotic devices. But if the person is a quadriplegic, this training period is not possible.

Nonetheless, we can achieve simple forms of control by simply linking brain activity to the control of a prosthetic device and modifying the algorithms according to performance. One approach here is to use EEG signals to control the position of a cursor on a computer screen (Wolpaw et al., 2006). An algorithm might be based on the power in different frequency regions of the EEG signal: the amplitude in one region (e.g., 5–10 Hz) is used to control the horizontal position; the amplitude in a different region (e.g., about 25 Hz) is used to control the vertical position. With feedback, people are able to regulate the EEG signal in order to control the movement of the cursor.

Interestingly, individuals typically develop idiosyncratic strategies to regulate their EEG signals. Thinking about a particular person might prove effective in moving the cursor to the right; thinking about a particular place reverses the direction. With sufficient training, people can use EEG-based systems to do things like use a computer to turn the TV on and off or control the volume. Producing each action can be pretty slow, taking a few seconds, but being able to produce the action at all, of course, can be a major step forward in providing some independence to an individual who has lost the use of all limbs.

EEG signals average the activity of millions of neurons. In principle, much finer control should be possible if the control signals are limited to the neural activity of motor structures. John Donoghue and his colleagues at Brown University and at Cyberkinetics Neurotechnology Systems have taken this radical approach in an initial clinical trial (Hochberg et al., 2006). Patient M.N., a 25-year-old quadriplegic, had suffered a complete resection of the spinal cord from a knife wound. Three years after the injury, an array of microelectrodes was implanted in his motor cortex, allowing for the simultaneous recording of many neurons. Despite 3 years of inactivity, the cells were quite active. Moreover, the firing level of the neurons varied as M.N. imagined different types of movements. Some units were active when he imagined making movements that involved the shoulder; others, when he imagined opening his hand. From this information, the researchers could generate control signals similar to those created with the population vectors in the monkey studies.

The results are simply amazing. From the activity of fewer than 100 neurons, M.N. is able to successfully move a cursor around the screen (Figure 7.21). His responses are about twice as slow as those of control participants who move the cursor directly, but in some sessions he demonstrated 90% accuracy. Using this BMI system, M.N. could control a cursor to use e-mail, draw figures using a computer graphics program, or play the popular computer game PONG. When connected to robotic devices, M.N. used his brain signals to reach and grasp objects. (Video clips of M.N. performing these tasks can be seen at http://www.nature.com/nature/journal/v442/n7099/suppinfo/nature04970.html.)

BMI systems are a compelling example of how basic findings in neuroscience—the coding of movement direction and population vector representations—can be combined with principles from bioengineering to develop new clinical therapies. Although testing with humans is still in the early stages, the promise of this approach can not be underestimated. Just 10 years ago, the notion of using thoughts to control actions would have struck most of us as pure fantasy, something to be left to Hollywood directors in movies like *The Matrix*. With pioneers such as M.N., we are now positioned to realize the potential for introducing dramatic changes for individuals who have some of the most debilitating neurological injuries.

GOAL-BASED REPRESENTATION IN MOTOR STRUCTURES

As described earlier, we can observe a hierarchical coding of movement across the motor system. In the spinal cord, the signals generated in alpha motor neurons directly correspond to the activation of specific muscles. In motor cortex, we observe a mixture of muscle- and direction-based signals. In secondary motor areas, the neural codes become more abstract, related more to the goals of an action rather than to the specific muscle patterns required to produce the movement needed to achieve the goal.

Goal-based representations have proved useful for analyzing single-unit activity in the premotor cortex. Although cells in this area may still code the movement's direction, they are not activated uniformly in move-

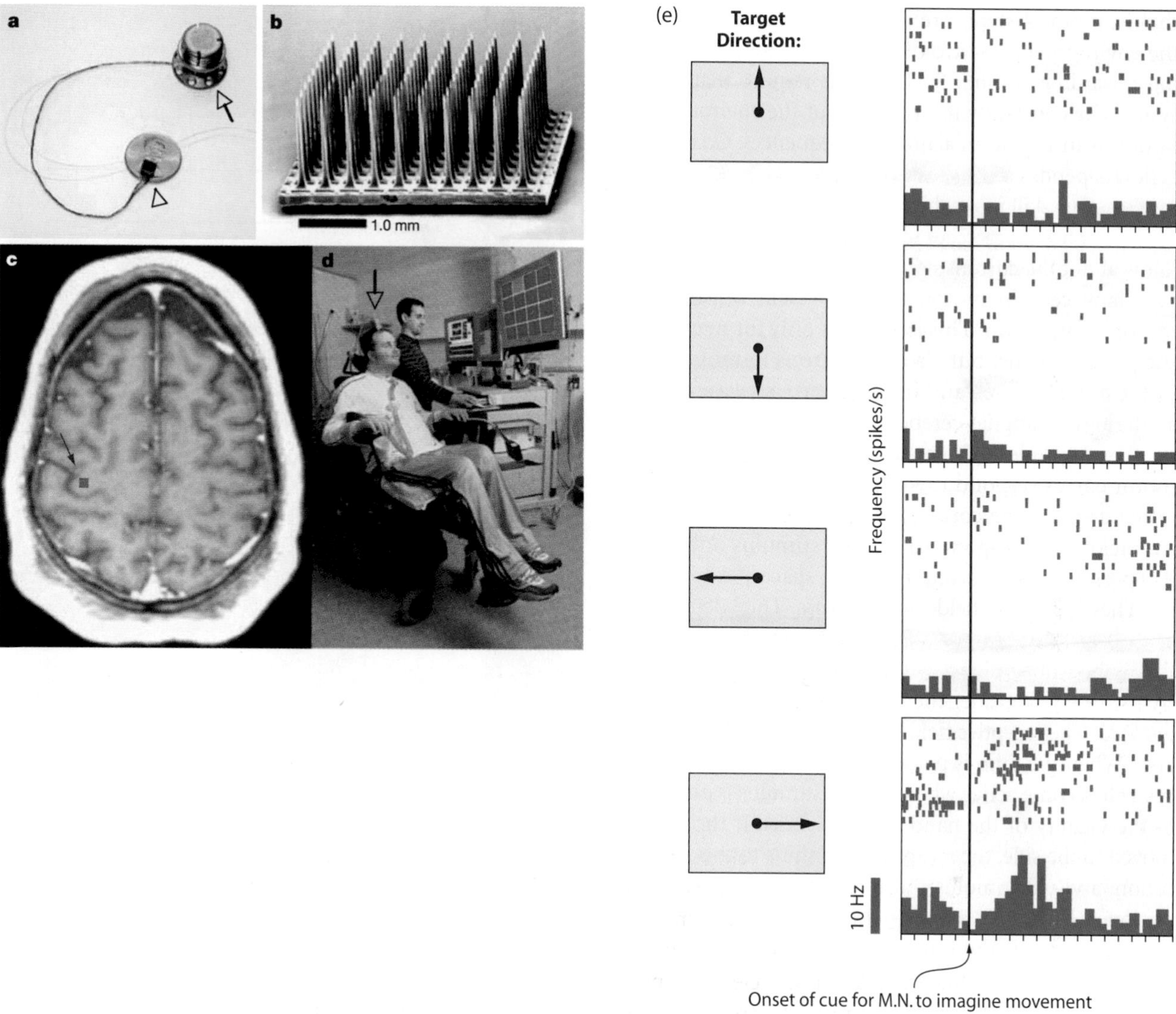

Figure 7.21 Brain–machine interface used by M.N. **(a)** The size of the implanted electrode device in relation to a U.S. penny. **(b)** A magnified image of the recording electrode array. **(c)** The location in the precentral gyrus where the electrode array was implanted. **(d)** The subject M.N. with the implanted device. He is controlling a cursor on the computer screen with his neural activity. **(e)** The firing of one cell during four different conditions in which M.N. was cued to imagine moving his hand up, down, left, or right. The cell shown here fired best when M.N. imagined moving his hand to the right; other cells fired selectively when M.N. imagined moving his hand left, up, or down. When information from all of the cells recorded from the implanted electrode were combined, the desired direction of movement could be predicted. Once the BMI device learned how the pattern of M.N.'s activity correlated with the desire to move in these directions, M.N. could begin to use his intentions to move a cursor wherever he chose. Using this technology, M.N. was also able to open simulated e-mails, operate a television, open and close a prosthetic hand, and move a robotic arm. Such technology holds great promise for people like M.N. who cannot otherwise physically interact with their environment.

ments requiring similar muscular events. Rather, the cells prefer certain motor acts. Giacomo Rizzolatti of the University of Parma, Italy, proposed that these neurons form a basic vocabulary of motor acts (Rizzolatti et al., 1988). Some cells are preferentially activated when the animal reaches for an object with its hand; others become active when the animal makes the same gesture to hold the object; and still others, when the animal attempts to tear the object—a behavior that might find its roots in the wild, where monkeys break off tree leaves. Therefore, cellular activity in this area reflects not only the trajectories of a movement but also the context in which the movement occurs.

These contextual considerations remind us that motor gestures are not made in an abstract space. Most actions are designed to manipulate an object in space;

that is, motor systems are powerful for interacting with the environment, for avoiding obstacles, and for obtaining rewarding stimuli. Such actions require that motor systems be constantly informed about the environment's layout to anticipate an action's consequences. Goal-based action depends on synthesizing sensory and motor information. Our skill in reaching for a desired object requires that we integrate perceptual information with what we know about the current state of the motor system.

Many cells in motor areas represent sensory and motor information. This is true not only for neurons in the parietal cortex but also for neurons in motor areas of the frontal cortex and in subcortical structures such as the basal ganglia, cerebellum, and superior colliculus. For example, cells in Brodmann area 6 of the premotor cortex respond to visual stimuli. As with cells in visual areas of the cortex, these neurons have a receptive field: They respond to a visual stimulus only when it is presented in a certain region of space.

These receptive fields are dynamic. They depend on how the animal has positioned its arm in space and how the limb might interact with a seen object (Graziano & Gross, 1994). Consider the cell behavior depicted in Figure 7.22. The receptive field shifts with the position of the arm. When the limb is placed in front of the animal, this cell will become active when a visual stimulus is presented in the vicinity of the hand (Figure 7.22a). If the limb is moved to the side, the receptive field shifts to this new location; a visual stimulus presented at the initial location no longer produces a change in the activity of the cell (Figure 7.22b). If the limb is positioned out of the animal's sight, the cell will not respond to any visual stimulus (Figure 7.22c). Thus the animal can use visual information to coordinate actions. The cell can represent the position of the visual stimulus with respect to the limb's current position. Perceptual knowledge has been transformed from a representation based on external space to one based on internal space. The animal represents the location of an object in the three-dimensional world and the movement that would be required to reach this object.

When we think of the motor areas of the cortex, we usually focus on areas in front of the central sulcus, the motor cortex, and secondary motor areas such as premotor cortex and the supplementary motor area. However, parts of the parietal cortex are also essential for coordinated movement. In Chapter 6 we saw that the dorsal visual stream plays an important role in visually controlled movements. Movement-related cells can be found in posterior parietal cortex. Interestingly, these cells provide a location-based code. For example, such cells will respond prior to movements to a particular location independent of the starting position of the hand.

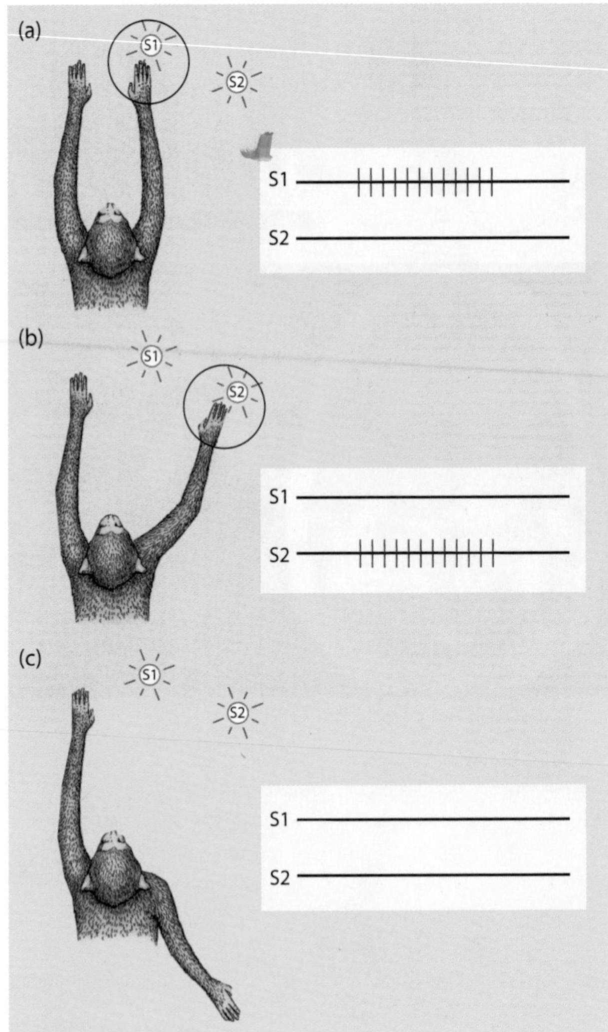

Figure 7.22 The activity of this neuron in the basal ganglia depends on the position of the hand. **(a, b)** The neuron will respond to a visual stimulus (S1 or S2) falling within the circled region. **(c)** When the hand is out of sight, the neuron does not respond to visual stimuli. Activity in this cell dynamically shifts as a function of hand position (as long as the hand is within view) and would be useful for coordinating visually guided movements.

Similar to the cell described in the preceding paragraph, this location representation is based on an internal reference frame. The internal coordinates here are defined by the position of the animal's eyes (Batista et al., 1999). In this way, the action goal is defined with respect to where the animal is currently looking.

Behavioral studies in humans further underscore the importance of the parietal cortex in representing the spatial goal for movement. Consider a particularly diabolical experiment in which the target changes position just as the person begins to reach for it. People are quite accurate under such conditions, adjusting the trajectory of an ongoing movement within 100 ms or so in order to smoothly end up near the target. These corrections can occur outside awareness, likely utilizing the same processes that are involved in normal reaching, where, as discussed previously, an initial trajectory plan is combined with a final location code to ensure that the target is reached in an efficient manner. When TMS is applied over the posterior parietal cortex, a selective disruption of the location code is observed. The trajectory of the reach is unaffected, but the person fails to make the required adjustment after the target changes location (Figure 7.23).

Figure 7.23 Transcranial magnetic stimulation over the posterior parietal cortex (PPC) disrupts rapid corrections at the end of reaching movements. **(a)** Subjects reach toward an illuminated target presented at the left side, the center, or the right side of the box. On some trials, the target jumps from the center location to one of the sides. The subjects are unaware of the target displacement because it occurs when they move their eyes just prior to the onset of the reach. **(b)** Movement paths for one subject when reaching with the right hand. On the left are trials without TMS. The solid traces show no displacement trials to the three locations. The dotted lines show the movement paths when the target jumped to the left or right. On the right are trials in which TMS was applied over the left-hemisphere PPC. Note that the reach terminates at the center position, the initial target location on all displacement trials.

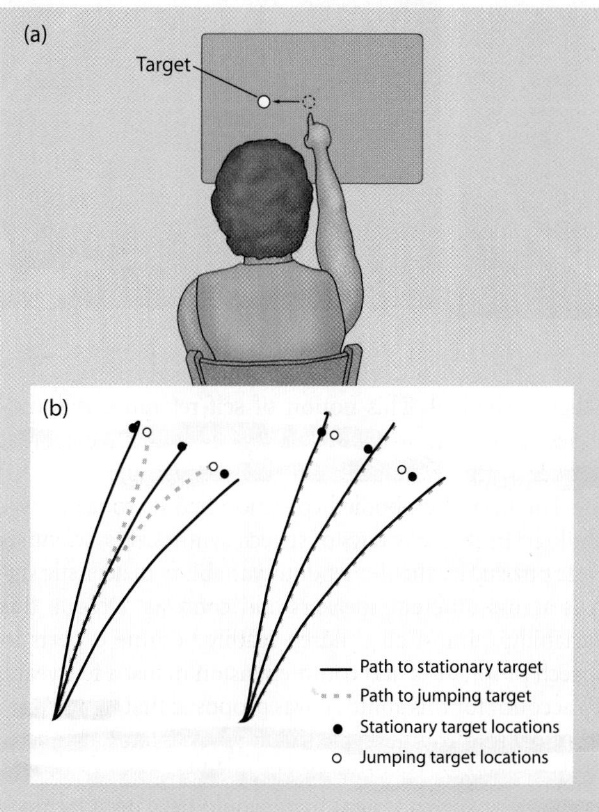

Interestingly, patients with posterior parietal lesions can move to the new position following a target displacement, but their trajectory adjustments require at least 450 ms (Pisella et al., 2000). It is as if they no longer can use an automatic location code to ensure that the movement goal is achieved. Instead, they use a slow, conscious process to plan a change in the direction code.

In thinking about how goals influence actions, it becomes clear that most movements are not simply gestures in space. They are designed to interact with the environment, and these interactions usually involve an object or a tool. We reach to pick up a coffee cup or place a hand on the mouse by the keyboard. Once the object or tool is grasped, skillful manipulation is required. With such movements, we need to learn the relationship between a movement and the consequences of that movement. For example, it takes a few minutes to adjust to the clutch of a car that we are not used to driving. Or the mouse on a new computer may be especially sensitive.

Researchers have devised nonstandard input–output relationships as a way to identify neural structures involved in representing how we learn to use these tools to achieve our goals. Reza Shadmehr of Johns Hopkins University devised an apparatus similar to that used in the population vector studies with monkeys: a device in which a two-jointed lever can be moved in any direction in a two-dimensional plane. The twist here is that a novel force field was applied to the device, perturbing the movements in a radial direction. With practice, the subjects became quite adept at adjusting to the novel field (Figure 7.24). PET scans obtained when this new skill had been acquired revealed increased activation in posterior parietal cortex, lateral premotor cortex, and cerebellum (Shadmehr & Holcomb, 1997). Later in this chapter we will see that these three areas form a network involved in visually guided movements.

Mirror Neurons

Defining where perception ends in the brain and action starts may be an impossible task. Perceptual systems have evolved to support action; likewise, actions are produced in anticipation of sensory consequences. For a monkey in the wild, seeing a ripe banana on a tree engages the action systems required to retrieve the food—movements that allow the animal to climb skillfully among the branches and that result in the satisfying taste of the fruit.

The intimate link between perception and action is underscored by the fact that our comprehension of the actions of others appears to depend on the activation of

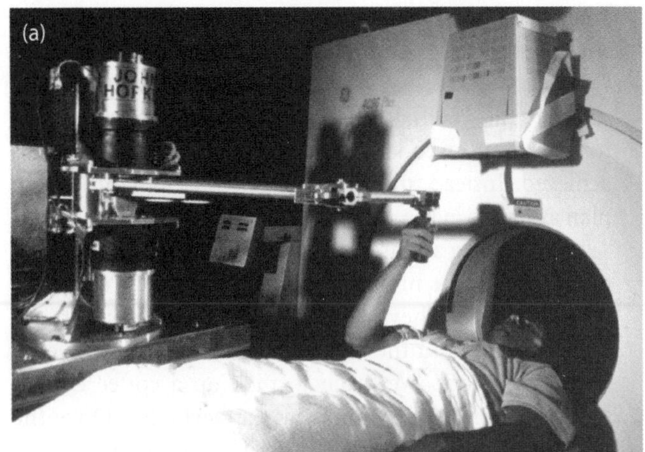

Figure 7.24 Learning to move in a novel environment. **(a)** Subjects moved the robot arm to one of eight locations. **(b)** Under normal conditions, the trajectory takes a straight path to the target. **(c)** When a radial force field is applied, the movements are initially curved. **(d)** With learning, subjects adapt to the new force field, and the trajectories become straight again. **(e)** In a PET scan session 5 hours later, subjects were tested with either the learned force field or a novel force field. For the learned environment, activity was greater in three regions: posterior parietal cortex (left), premotor cortex (center), and anterior cerebellum (right).

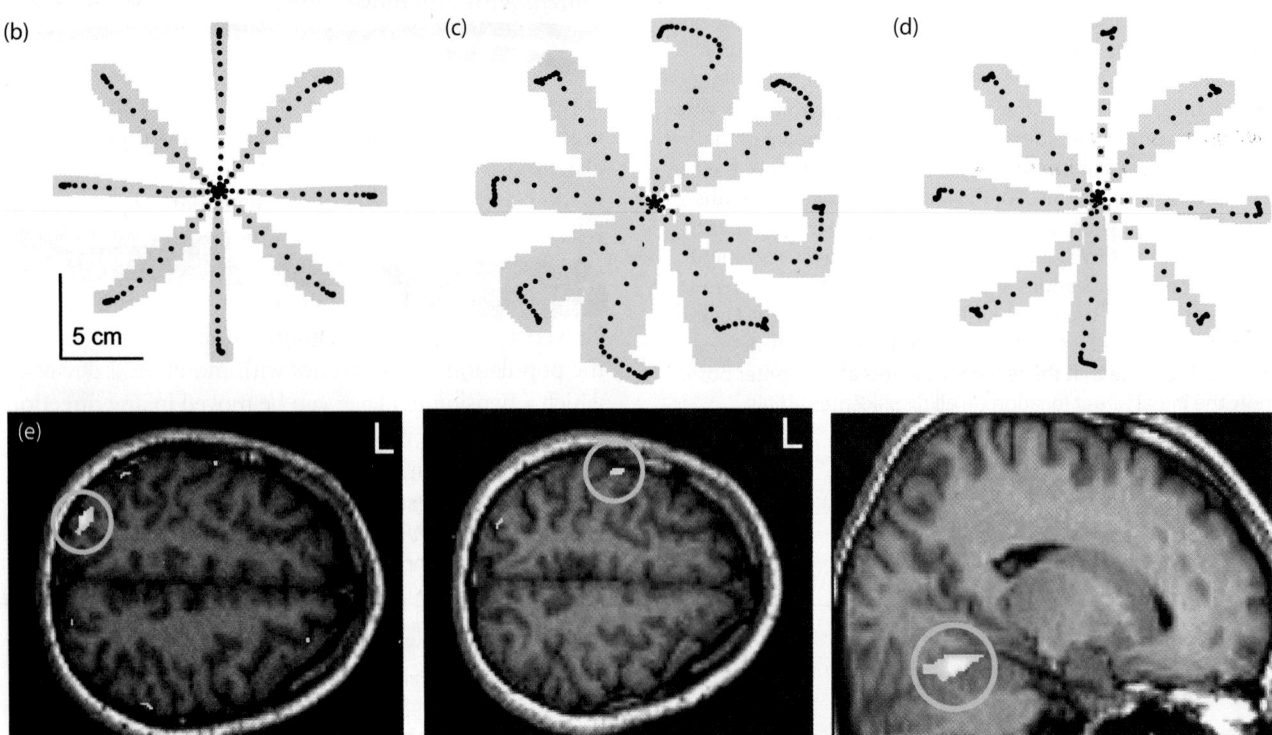

the neural structures that would be engaged if we were to produce the action ourselves. In recognition of this codependency, neuroscientists speak of a **mirror system** to describe a distributed network of neural regions involved in action production and comprehension. The term *mirror* here is intended to capture the idea that understanding the actions of another entails reference to how that action would be produced; the perceptual system is not divorced from the action system, with the brain forming abstract representations of visual patterns that conform to actions such as grasping, throwing, or dancing. Rather, our comprehension of such actions involves reference to our own ability to grasp an object or to dance with another individual. This notion of self-reference is sometimes referred to as *embodied cognition*: our conceptual knowledge is grounded in our body knowledge.

The idea of embodied cognition had its roots in psychology. In the early days of speech synthesizers, scientists were puzzled by the tremendous variability in acoustic signals across different speakers and contexts. Despite this variability, almost all children readily become experts in speech production and comprehension in just a few years. To account for this ability, it was proposed that speech perception entailed an analysis of the speech sounds in terms of the articulatory gestures that would have produced the sounds. For such a system there would have been tremendous adaptive pressure; oral communication is perhaps the most fundamental aspect of human cognition.

The motor theory of speech perception proved difficult to evaluate empirically. However, neurophysiologists pushed forward with this idea. The initial focus was on premotor cortex. As noted earlier, Rizzolatti and colleagues had demonstrated that cells in this area show an increase in activity when the monkey performs goal-based actions, such as grasping or tearing an object, independent of the specific context for that action. Rizzolatti's group then went on to show that these neurons could also be activated during action observation. In these studies the monkey viewed different objects. On some trials, the animal produced an action such as reaching or grasping the object (e.g., a peanut). On other trials, the animal observed the experimenter performing similar actions. Although some premotor neurons were active only during production trials, other neurons were also active during action perception. These latter neurons were appropriately named *mirror neurons*. A mirror neuron that was active when the animal reaches for a peanut would also respond when the animal observed the experimenter reaching for the peanut (Figure 7.25a–c).

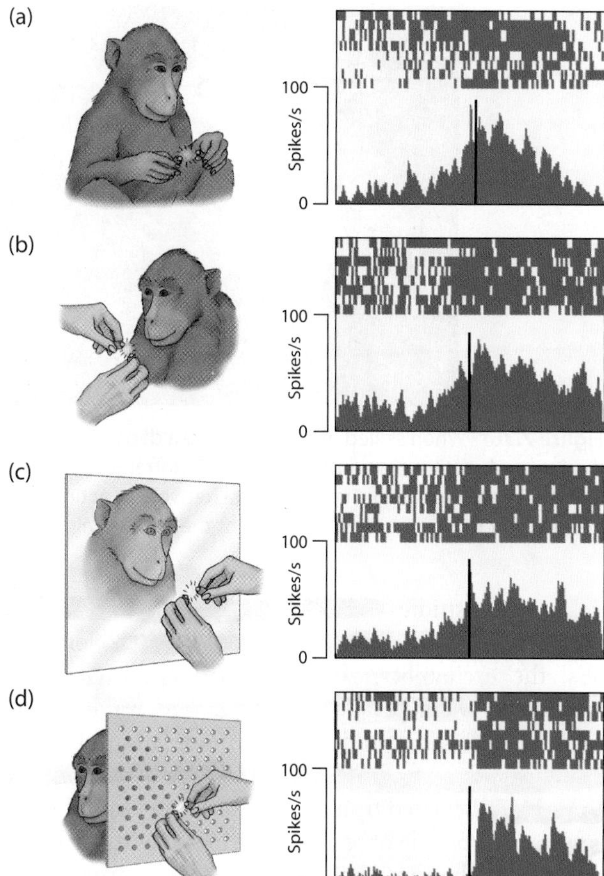

Figure 7.25 Responses of a single neuron in a monkey's ventral premotor cortex during the performance or perception of different actions: **(a)** when the monkey itself breaks a peanut and views and hears the breaking of the peanut, **(b)** when the monkey watches someone else breaking a peanut and views and hears the breaking of the peanut, **(c)** when the monkey sees someone else breaking a peanut but cannot hear the peanut breaking, and **(d)** when the monkey hears but does not see someone else breaking a peanut. This neuron can be considered a mirror neuron because it responds to actions that are undertaken by the monkey, as well as to actions that are viewed or heard by the monkey.

The activity here may be due to the similar visual properties of the action and perception conditions: A hand moves toward a peanut. Additional experiments, however, rule out this hypothesis. First, the same mirror neuron can also be activated by just the sound of a peanut being cracked (Figure 7.25d). Second, other experiments on mirror neurons have shown that these neurons are active when a monkey watches someone reach for a peanut behind a screen but cannot actually see the grasping of the peanut (and, in fact, there need not be a peanut present). However, if the monkey *knows* there is no hidden peanut behind the screen, the mirror neuron remains silent (Umilta et al., 2001). Thus, the activity of the mirror cell is correlated with a goal-oriented action—retrieving a peanut—independent of how this information is received (by the monkey's own action, by viewing another person's action, by hearing another person's action, or by viewing only a portion of another person's action but believing that the action is taking place).

Mirror neurons are not limited to the premotor cortex. Neurons in parietal and temporal lobes also show similar activity patterns during action production and comprehension, suggesting a distributed mirror system rather than a dedicated local region for linking perception and action. This point is supported by many neuroimaging studies in humans. In Chapter 6 we saw that the dorsal pathway including parietal lobe and premotor cortex was activated when people were asked to make judgments concerning the use of an object. These regions are also activated during movement execution.

Within premotor cortex, the activation patterns reveal a similar somatotopy for action production or perception. Interestingly, the extent and intensity of the activation pattern reflect the individual's motor repertoire. Skilled dancers show stronger activation in the mirror network when watching videos of familiar dance routines compared to unfamiliar dances (Figure 7.26). Unfortunately, the same study cannot be done for action production: movement is a prime source of artifact in the MRI signal, so studies of motor control in the magnet are usually limited to very simple movements.

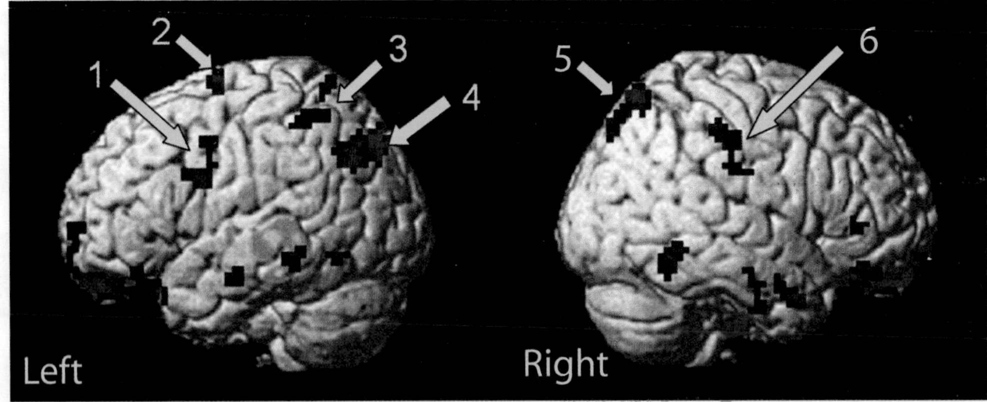

Figure 7.26 When skilled dancers observe a dance at which they are experts (versus a dance in which they have no expertise), they strongly activate premotor cortex (1, 2), intraparietal sulcus (3, 6), posterior superior temporal sulcus (4), and superior parietal lobe (5). These areas make up the neural network of action observation and include regions strongly involved in action itself, suggesting that these areas might represent the human mirror neuron system.

Imaging studies fail to show activation of the primary motor cortex during action observation. Nonetheless, the excitability of neurons in motor cortex is modulated when people observe actions produced by another individual. Indeed, this modulation shows a high degree of effector specificity. Motor evoked potentials (MEPs) elicited from hand muscles are found to be larger when people observe video clips of gestures being made with the same hand compared to videos of the same gestures being produced by the opposite hand. These effects can even be elicited with relatively abstract presentations of the actions. As evidenced by an increase in TMS-elicited MEPs, the excitability of the hand area increases when people listen to sounds associated with hand actions compared to sounds associated with foot actions.

Keep in mind that, in all of this work, we cannot draw inferences about causality. Is the activation observed in premotor cortex during action observation essential for action comprehension? Does the modulation of excitability in motor cortex indicate that understanding the actions of another requires representations in motor cortex? These are difficult questions to answer; we will turn to lesion studies in subsequent sections to gain some insight. Nonetheless, the fMRI and TMS studies are important in demonstrating the degree of overlap between neural systems involved in perception and action. They remind us that dividing the brain into perception and motor regions may be useful for pedagogical reasons (say, for defining chapters in a textbook!), but that the brain does not honor such divisions.

PLANNING AND EXECUTION OF MOVEMENT

A hierarchical organization of the motor system can be seen in studies of motor planning and execution. When people are asked to produce simple movements such as flexing or extending one finger, activation may be restricted to the contralateral sensorimotor cortex. When the task requires the production of more complex movements, the activation extends into premotor and parietal regions. This activation is frequently bilateral. This bilateral activation can be interpreted in several ways. It might correspond to the activation of an abstract motor plan—one not tied to a specific effector. Or the bilateral distribution could reflect many potential motor plans, each a viable candidate for achieving a common goal. For example, we could reach for a water glass with either the left or the right hand. With either of these hypotheses, the unilateral activation in the basal ganglia and motor cortex can be interpreted as the transformation of higher level plans into a movement linked to specific effectors.

Internal Versus External Guidance of Movement

How can we characterize the contribution of secondary and association areas for motor control? A dramatic demonstration of the role of the supplementary motor area in motor planning and execution was shown with TMS (Gerloff et al., 1997). Subjects were trained to produce a complex sequence of finger movements in a continuous fashion. When TMS was applied over the area of the motor cortex that represents the hand, the next response in the sequence was disturbed frequently, either because the movement was halted midstream or because the wrong key was pressed. Moreover, the subjects perceived the problem as a temporary loss of coordination, commenting that the finger suddenly seemed to jerk in the wrong direction.

In contrast, when the coil was repositioned to target the supplementary motor area, the effects were delayed, occurring about three key presses after the TMS pulse. Here the subjects reported that they had lost track of their place in the sequence, that they had temporarily forgotten the order of key presses. TMS over the supplementary motor area appears to disrupt the goal of the movement. Without this representation of the action plan, one can know that something is not quite right but cannot pinpoint the problem. With an error of execution such as those seen following motor cortex stimulation, the exact form of the error can be articulated because the actual response can be compared to the intended response.

Perhaps other types of actions require different types of processing. For example, to return a tennis shot a player adjusts her posture and swings according to the velocity and angle of the ball and her opponent's position. The action sequence for a successful return requires a rapid integration of external cues.

Some neuroscientists propose that the control of movement sequences depends on Brodmann area 6, but that it varies as a function of whether the action is internally or externally guided. The medial portion, supplementary motor area, will dominate when the task is internally guided, as when we drum our fingers on the tabletop. In contrast, the lateral portion, premotor area, becomes more relevant when the task depends on external cues. This area is activated when people are asked to perform movements under the guidance of visual, auditory, or somatosensory feedback. It is also activated when extrapersonal sources of feedback are removed but the action is performed with respect to an external frame of reference, such as when someone traces a path through a maze with the eyes closed. Even though the eyes are closed during the scanning sessions, it is likely that the subjects use visual imagery.

Figure 7.27 provides an overview of the anatomical basis for the internal–external control hypothesis (Goldberg, 1985). The premotor cortex is innervated extensively by the parietal cortex and the cerebellum, two areas linked not only to visuomotor function but also to rich representations extracted from other sensory channels, such as audition and touch. The supplementary motor area, by contrast, receives extensive projections from the prefrontal cortex and the basal ganglia. Because of their anatomical connections, these areas are in a position to allow limbic structures to convey information related to the animal's current motivational state and internal goals.

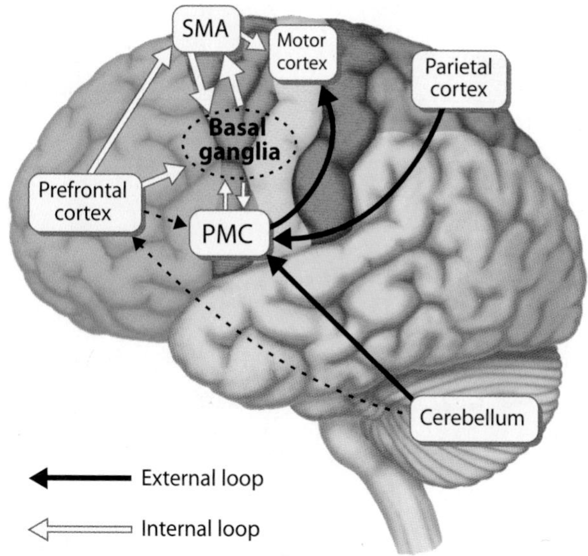

Figure 7.27 Movements may vary in terms of the contribution of internal and external sources of information. The external loop, including the cerebellum, parietal cortex, and lateral premotor cortex (PMC), dominates during visually guided movements. The internal loop, including the basal ganglia and the supplementary motor area (SMA), dominates during self-guided, well-learned movements.

To compare the roles of the supplementary motor area and the premotor cortex, monkeys were trained to generate a sequence of button presses according to two sets of instructions (Mushiake et al., 1991; Figure 7.28). In the external-guidance condition, the buttons were illuminated in succession and the animal pressed each one in turn. In the internal-guidance condition, the animal learned a sequence of button presses and then reproduced the sequence after hearing an auditory go signal. Physiological recordings were made in the supplementary motor area and the premotor cortex.

This study produced two critical results. First, in both areas, some neural activity could not be linked to specific movements but depended on the entire sequence of movements; hence, cellular activity correlated with the direction of movement, but only when that gesture was embedded in a certain sequence. When the same gesture was embedded in a different

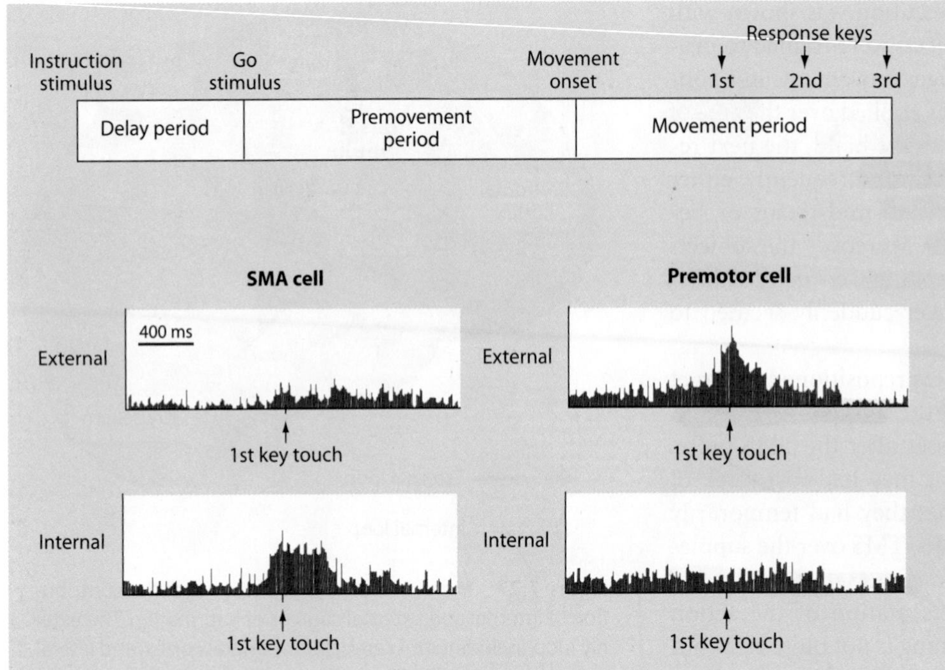

Figure 7.28 Monkeys were trained to make sequential button presses, either to a series of illuminated targets (external condition) or from memory (internal condition). Even though the movements were identical, the supplementary motor area (SMA) neuron was most active during the internal condition and the premotor neuron was most active during the external condition.

sequence, the activity of these cells showed only a slight increase compared to their baseline firing rate. This sequence specificity supports the hypothesis of a higher form of control for Brodmann area 6. The other critical result is that SMA neurons were disproportionately active during internally guided movements, whereas premotor neurons were more active during externally guided sequences. Subsequent work showed a similar dissociation in subcortical motor structures (Middleton & Strick, 2000). Activity in the basal ganglia and cerebellar neurons was linked more closely with internally generated and externally guided movements, respectively.

The distinction between internal and external control, however, is not absolute. Many cells in both cortical and subcortical motor areas were active under both types of conditions. And some SMA cells were more active in the external condition than in the internal condition, whereas the reverse held for some premotor neurons. Although these results might raise doubts about a strict dichotomy, it is also likely that movements in both conditions depend on external and internal cues. Consider the tennis player again. The decision to return a shot with a deep lob or a short drop shot depends not only on the location and velocity of the arriving ball, but also on knowing the opponent's skills. If the opponent moves slowly, the drop shot might be preferred. Coordinated actions are guided by multiple sources of information.

Shift in Cortical Control with Learning

Learning plays a critical role in producing purposeful actions. Descriptions of the processes required to serve a tennis ball are likely to be different for the novice and the skilled performer. The novice may verbalize each movement as a monk chants his mantra: "Toss the ball straight up, swing the racquet in an arc, make contact as the ball begins to descend, follow through." By contrast, the expert player's years of practice make the production of this sequence appear effortless. She ponders the finer aspects of the serve. Is her topspin serve working today? Should she serve to her opponent's forehand or backhand?

Feedback after the serve is also treated differently by the novice and the expert. After impact, the novice may have little idea where the ball is heading—in the service box, he hopes, but more likely into the net. Feedback from observing his shot helps him modify his next service. Although the expert is also concerned with the consequences of her actions, she uses feedback obtained during the course of the service to make fine adjustments. If the arm is moving too fast, the wrist can be flexed earlier to ensure an appropriate trajectory. Whereas a novice essentially uses feedback to make changes in subsequent actions, an expert uses feedback to make online changes in performance.

Motor systems invoked in the action of serving a tennis ball clearly differ for the novice and the expert.

Indeed, learning considerations have led to an alternative conceptualization of the functional difference between the lateral and the medial premotor areas. Rather than thinking that these differences reflect whether a task is guided by external or internal cues, we could consider that learning involves a transition toward greater reliance on more medial motor structures. During the early stages of learning, the lateral premotor area, with its extensive connections to the parietal cortex, would be optimal for integrating external information with a motor plan—an essential job for developing any new skill. If we learn the mapping between the movements we produce and their effects, we can anticipate the consequences of our actions, exploiting the functions of the more medial motor system.

A PET study explored metabolic changes associated with skill learning through trial and error (Jenkins et al., 1994). After hearing a tone, the subjects pressed one of four buttons. Correct responses were signaled by a high-pitched tone; incorrect responses were followed by silence. The subjects' task was to learn an eight-element pattern that was repeated cyclically. In the initial stages of training, the subjects simply had to guess the sequence. After six cycles, the subjects were averaging only one error per cycle. After one sequence was learned, the process was repeated with a new sequence. In this way, comparisons could be made between performance on new and performance on learned sequences without confounding the order of the scans with skill level. If only one sequence had been used, the earlier scan would always reflect initial learning.

The metabolic results, shown in Figure 7.29, indicate that, as learning progressed, activation shifted within Brodmann area 6. The lateral premotor area was more activated during the acquisition of a new sequence in comparison to when an old sequence was being performed skillfully. In contrast, the supplementary motor area was more active during the skilled phase. Indeed, when the subjects began to learn a new sequence, SMA activity declined.

This study further revealed that the lateral and medial regions are embedded in distinct circuits related to skill acquisition. Higher metabolism in the lateral premotor cortex was correlated with increases in the superior parietal lobe and cerebellum. Changes in SMA activity were associated with changes in the temporal lobe and limbic structures.

Remember that there is usually a high degree of correspondence between the level of learning and the extent to which a behavior depends on external cues. If prompted to serve when blindfolded, the expert tennis player most likely would succeed on a high percentage of serves. The novice would be lucky to make contact with the ball. In a similar sense, we can see a shift in the reliance on external cues and feedback in just about any skill domain. Children have to assess carefully the outcome of each stroke as they learn to write their signature. With skill, handwriting suffers little when visual feedback is removed.

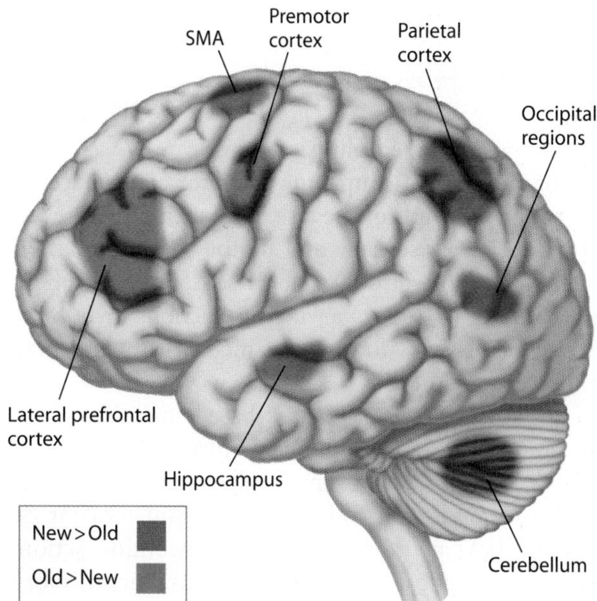

Figure 7.29 Shifts in metabolic activity during motor learning. PET scans were obtained under two conditions: while subjects performed a well-learned movement sequence (Old) and during the course of learning a movement sequence (New). Learning was associated with blood flow increases in lateral premotor and prefrontal areas; in contrast, performance of previously learned sequences was correlated with blood flow increases in the supplementary motor area (SMA) and hippocampus.

In summary, results from physiological studies using both single-cell recordings with primates and brain-imaging techniques suggest that parallel circuits may be involved in motor planning. One circuit including the parietal lobe, lateral premotor, and cerebellar pathways is essential for producing spatially directed or guided movements. These movements are likely to dominate during the early stages of skill acquisition. A second circuit, associated with the supplementary motor area, the basal ganglia, and perhaps the temporal lobe, becomes more dominant as the skill is well learned and driven by an internal representation of the desired action. Both circuits converge on the motor cortex, the primary link between the cortex and limbs for voluntary movements.

FUNCTIONAL ANALYSIS OF THE MOTOR SYSTEM AND MOVEMENT DISORDERS

So far we have emphasized how motor areas might contribute to motor control according to the demands of the task. If an action requires the coordination of sensory and motor codes, the lateral, premotor loop will dominate. If sensory requirements are reduced, either by varying instructions or by practice, control shifts toward the medial, supplementary motor area loop.

What is lacking in this task-based analysis is an explanation of the computations performed by the different motor areas. For example, the neurophysiological work on population coding is an elegant tool for describing how neurons represent forthcoming actions. But several cortical and subcortical areas share this form of representation. One might consider this homogeneity and conclude that motor systems should be viewed as distributed networks having little specialization.

Neurologists would dismiss such a hypothesis as utter foolishness. An hour in a movement disorders clinic would make it clear that the motor system is extensively specialized. Breakdowns in coordination can happen in many ways; such patterns of deficits afford clues to the contributions of the components of the motor pathways. The characteristic signatures of lesions enable neurologists to pinpoint the site and cause of pathology even in the absence of high-resolution MRI.

Before we turn to motor disorders, let's consider the computations required to perform a skilled action such as playing a difficult piano passage from Beethoven's Emperor Concerto (Figure 7.30). For one thing, the pianist must figure out the mapping between notes and fingers. A single finger might suffice for the simplest melody line, but a skillful production requires all 10 fingers. And as the context changes, the same note can be played by different fingers. Moreover, the notes must be linked in proper sequence. The popular nursery tunes "Go Tell Aunt Rhody" and "Lightly Row" share identical notes, but the different sequences of the notes create distinct tunes. Finally, for a piece to sound musical, the notes must be played with the proper timing and intensity.

Hypothetical components such as selection, sequence, force, and timing can serve as useful heuristics for analyzing disorders of the motor system. For example, if motor timing and motor selection are independent operations, then we might expect to find dissociations in the clinical problems of patients with motor disorders. A patient might select the appropriate fingers to play the notes of "Go Tell Aunt Rhody" but fail to provide the appropriate timing. Or the timing might be correct, but the notes out of order. In either case, we would fail to recognize this familiar tune. But the loss of coordination would reflect deficits in different component operations. In this way, we can develop a functional analysis of the cognitive neuroscience of motor control.

Figure 7.30 Hypothesized mental operations that must be completed in order to perform a complicated action such as playing the piano.

Possible mental operations/computations	Example: playing piano
1. Selection	Match fingers to keys, notes.
2. Sequence	Group notes into a phrase.
3. Force	Strike accented notes with greater force.
4. Timing	Establish rhythm.

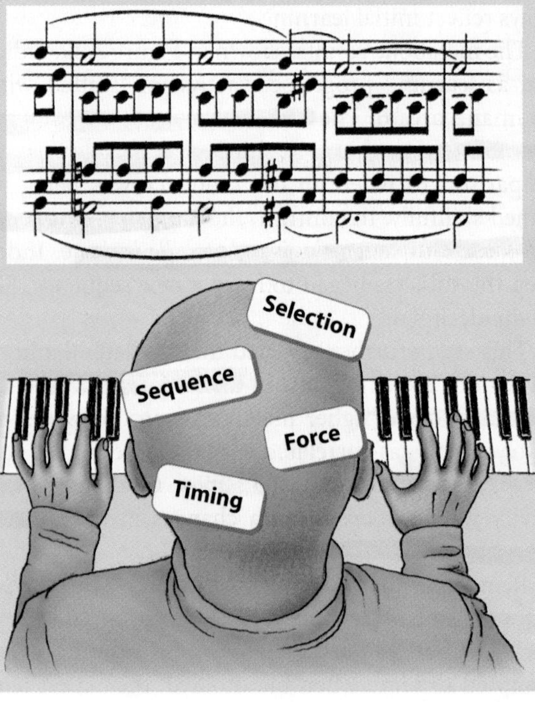

Cortical Areas

Many animals without a cerebral cortex are capable of complex actions: The fly can land with near-perfect precision; the lizard can flick its tongue at the precise moment required to snare its evening meal. Has evolution rendered a massive reorganization of the motor pathways? Or should we consider the cortex an additional piece of neural machinery superimposed on a more primitive apparatus?

HEMIPLEGIA

The primary motor cortex provides the most important signal for the production of skilled movement. This area receives input from almost all cortical areas implicated in motor control, including the parietal, premotor, and frontal cortices, and from subcortical structures such as the basal ganglia and cerebellum. In turn, the output of the motor cortex constitutes the largest signal in the corticospinal tract—not to mention its indirect influence on spinal mechanisms by way of projections to the extrapyramidal pathway.

The preeminent status of the motor cortex is underscored by the fact that lesions to this area usually result in **hemiplegia**, the loss of voluntary movements on the contralateral side of the body. Hemiplegia most frequently results from a hemorrhage in the middle cerebral artery; it is perhaps the most telling symptom of a stroke. A person who has suffered such a hemorrhage might wake up with a severe headache, or experience a sudden loss of consciousness, and notice a complete loss of control in one limb. It is not a matter of will or awareness; the hemiplegic patient may exert great effort, but his limbs will not move. The loss of movement is most evident in the distal effectors.

Reflexes are absent immediately after a stroke that produces hemiplegia; within a couple of weeks the reflexes return and may even become hyperactive. The hemiplegic patient presents a greater-than-normal reflexive response when a muscle is passively stretched. The muscles may even become spastic, reflecting the increased tone, or responsiveness, of the muscles. The spasticity is most pronounced in muscles that counteract the forces of gravity when we stand up or sit upright, leaving the patient with a contorted posture in which the arm is maintained in a flexed position at the elbow with the fingers tightly curled into the palm. The legs become hyperextended, like pillars holding up the trunk.

Hyperactive reflexes and spasticity can be understood within a hierarchical framework. Muscular activity offsetting gravitational forces and reflexes comes from a simple form of motor control, a mechanism for ensuring postural stability. The cortex provides a way to inhibit these mechanisms. By inhibiting a tendency to maintain stability, the cortex allows us to willfully impose an action. We can move an arm without having the stretch reflex counteract the gesture. When the cortical influence is removed, primitive reflexive mechanisms become manifest again.

Recovery from hemiplegia is minimal. Patients rarely regain significant control over the limbs of the contralateral side when the motor cortex has been damaged. Movement is possible, but only when carried out by gross movements that do not require the independent control and coordination of different joints. If a leg is affected, the patient may be able to walk again, but in a far-from-normal manner, perhaps by rotating the entire leg about the pelvis. The patient cannot coordinate flexion and extension about the knee and ankle. Arm movements also would be quite limited; any persisting control would be left to proximal joints like the shoulder and perhaps the elbow. Lesions of the motor cortex affect the corticospinal and extrapyramidal tracts. The loss of control over individual joints and distal extremities is attributed to damage in the corticospinal tract. Spasticity and hyperreflexivity are attributed to changes in the extrapyramidal system. When the cortical influence is removed, these more ancient systems become dominant, exerting their prominent role in maintaining postural stability. The hemiplegic patient no longer has the flexibility to generate an action based on internal goals and desires.

To date, rehabilitation methods have proved useful in reducing spasticity and thereby maximizing the effectiveness of whatever volitional control the patient has retained. However, a host of promising new methods are currently the focus of intense research. One approach is to look for ways that would promote neural recovery in the damaged hemisphere. For example, repetitive TMS over the lesioned cortex may stimulate plasticity, especially when genes associated with synaptic plasticity are elevated (Kleim et al., 2006). Another approach emphasizes rehabilitation strategies that use the unaffected limb with the hope that the training will also benefit control of the affected limb. It is unclear if this strategy helps through the development of ipsilateral pathways for control, by functional reorganization that comes about through the extensive transcallosal connections that exist between the premotor cortices of the two hemispheres, or by a combination of these factors.

APRAXIA

Many cortical lesions result in coordination deficits that cannot be attributed to hemiplegia, motoric problems of weakness, sensory loss, or motivation. This syndrome is called **apraxia**. Although the term *apraxia* technically means "no action," it is used in a more general sense to describe a loss of motor skill. For example, a patient with bilateral lesions of the parietal lobes was unable to continue her work as a fish filleter. When attempting to perform a routine that she had completed thousands of times, she correctly inserted the knife point into the head of the fish, began the first stroke, but then stopped. She claimed to know how the action should be completed but could not execute it. At home, she found herself putting the sugar bowl in the refrigerator or the coffee pot in the oven. In each case, she retained the ability to move her muscles but could no longer link gestures to a coherent act or recognize the appropriate use of an object.

The diagnosis of apraxia is mainly exclusionary: A patient is said to have apraxia if he or she has a coordination problem that cannot be linked to a deficit in controlling the muscles themselves. Moreover, it is not always clear that the problems are specific to the motor system. They may reflect a general problem in comprehension. Apraxia is observed much more frequently in patients with lesions to the left hemisphere, and almost all apraxia patients have some aphasia (Keretsz & Hooper, 1982). Perhaps the motor problems represent a failure to understand instructions or a general loss of semantic knowledge. If we forget that sugar is best stored at room temperature, it is not so surprising that, when cleaning up after a meal, a person might put the sugar bowl in the refrigerator. However, it is also true that many aphasia patients do not have apraxia.

Several standard tests for apraxia have been developed. In most such tests, patients are asked to produce goal-directed gestures. The gestures may consist of arbitrary behaviors such as saluting or following a sequence of arm gestures, or they may be actions like manipulating an external object—for example, lighting a pipe or slicing a loaf of bread. Apraxic patients are most impaired when trying to pantomime an action. When requested to slice a loaf of bread, for example, the patient may ball his hand in a fist and pound the table. If he is given a knife and a loaf of bread, his performance generally improves. Now the tool can be held appropriately, even if slicing is abnormal.

Neurologists distinguish between two general subtypes of apraxia: ideomotor and ideational. In **ideomotor apraxia**, the patient appears to have a rough sense of the desired action but has problems executing it properly. If asked to pantomime how to comb his hair, the patient might knock his fist against his head repeatedly. **Ideational apraxia** is much more severe. Here, the patient's knowledge about the intent of an action is disrupted. She may no longer comprehend the appropriate use for a tool. For example, one patient used a comb to brush his teeth, demonstrating by the action that he could make the proper gesture, but using the wrong object to do it.

At the beginning of the 20th century, one of Wernicke's students, Hugo Liepmann, made two key observations regarding apraxia: (a) The disorder was generally associated with lesions of the left hemisphere, and (b) it was most frequently observed when the lesions included the parietal cortex (Heilman et al., 1982). Liepmann proposed that the representation of a desired action was associated with the left parietal cortex (Fig-

Figure 7.31 Liepmann's model of the neural regions associated with the production of skilled actions. The premotor areas of the contralateral hemisphere are essential for skilled movements of limbs. These areas receive input from the parietal lobe of the left hemisphere, an area assumed to store the representations of the actions. Thus, a lesion in the left posterior region will lead to apraxic movements with both contralesional and ipsilesional limbs.

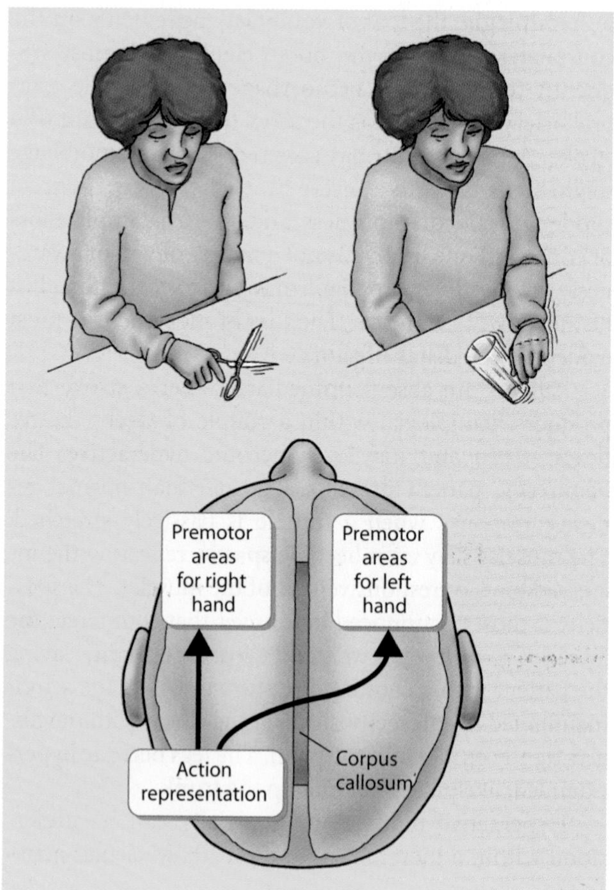

ure 7.31). This representation might specify the current spatial relationship between the environment and the actor: the changes that must be made to achieve a particular goal. The representation could then interact with secondary and primary areas of the frontal cortex, resulting in the desired movement. If that movement were executed with the right hand, processing could remain within the left hemisphere. If the desired movement were executed with the left hand, the left-hemisphere parietal representation would need to be linked to motor representations in the right hemisphere. In this manner, unilateral lesions of the left parietal region would be associated with bilateral deficits.

Liepmann's model makes two anatomical predictions. First, in terms of the anterior–posterior axis, Liepmann's model would suggest that, although lesions of left or right premotor cortex could result in impairments of skilled action production, impairments of action comprehension might be restricted to more posterior cortex. This idea has received mixed support. Kenneth Heilman and his colleagues (1982) tested two groups of apraxic patients: those with anterior lesions and those with posterior lesions. In the first part of the experiment, the patients were given a motor test in which they were asked to pantomime different gestures (Figure 7.32a). On this test, the two groups were indistinguishable, showing a similar degree of apraxia. In the second part of the experiment, the patients were given an action comprehension test (Figure 7.32b). Here they were shown short film segments in which an actor mimed a task by performing three actions. Only one of the productions was well executed, and patients were asked to identify which production correctly mimicked the intended task. On the comprehension test, the patients with posterior lesions made significantly more errors than did the patients with anterior lesions (Figure 7.32c). However, subsequent work has shown that patients with premotor lesions may not perform as well as controls on tests of action comprehension (Saygin et al., 2004).

The second prediction concerns asymmetries between the left and right hemispheres. In particular, Liepmann proposed that the left hemisphere plays a special role in praxis, or the representation of skilled movement. Although not as widely discussed as the dominant role for the left hemisphere in language or, more specifically, speech production (see Chapters 10 and 11), many lines of evidence support the idea that skilled movement involves the left hemisphere to a greater degree than the right hemisphere. Moreover, this asymmetry appears to be independent of handedness. In one study, two callosotomy patients were asked to demonstrate how to use tools with either the left or the right hand. Even though one patient was right-handed and the other left-handed, both individuals were more adept in miming tool use with the right hand (Frey et al., 2005). Imaging studies also

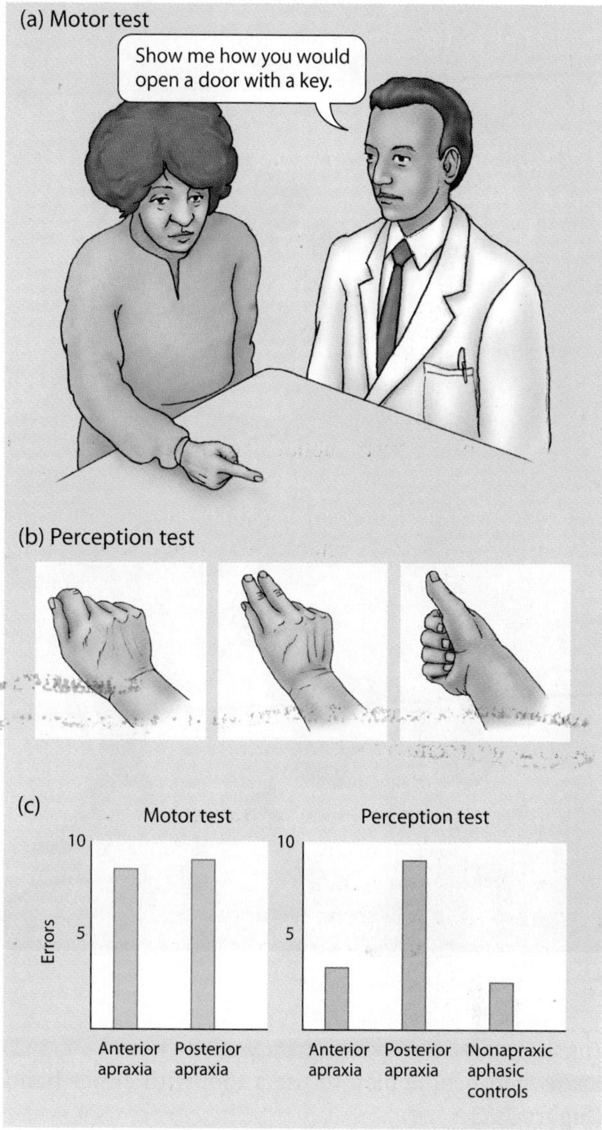

Figure 7.32 Patients with apraxia may not be able to recognize skilled movements. **(a)** In the motor test, the patient is asked to pantomime a gesture such as using a key to open a door. **(b)** In the perception test, the patient views an actor pantomiming an action in three different ways, only one of which is appropriate. The patient must choose which action is correct. **(c)** Patients with either anterior or posterior lesions who produced apraxic gestures on the motor task were selected. Only the patients with posterior lesions showed impairment on the perception test. The apraxic patients with anterior lesions performed as well as nonapraxic, aphasic control subjects on the perception test.

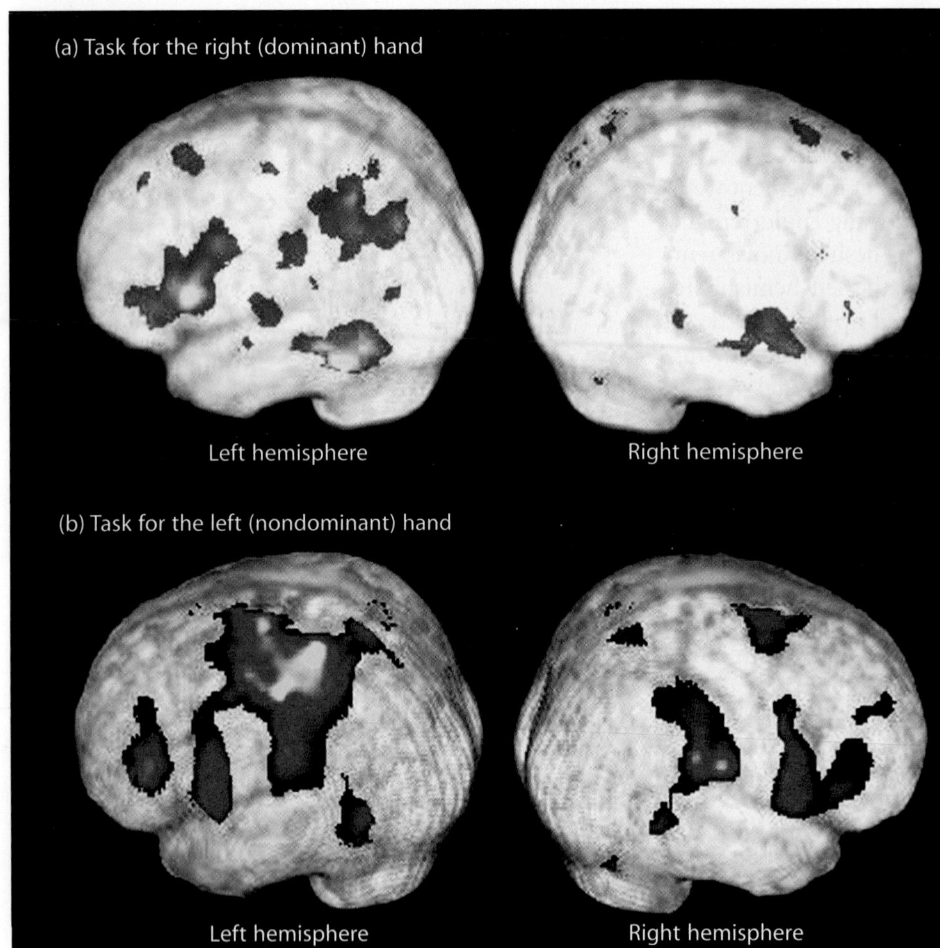

Figure 7.33 When subjects planned actions that involved tools, the left hemisphere was activated independently of which hand was to be used to carry out the task—the right, dominant, hand **(a)** or the left, nondominant hand **(b)**. Activated areas include the left posterior temporal, inferior frontal, and posterior parietal cortices, indicating that the left hemisphere is selectively activated for tool-related motor planning.

consistently show activation in the left inferior parietal lobe when people plan to use a tool with either hand (Figure 7.33).

The relationship of a left-hemisphere specialization for skilled movement and language remains unclear. Though these asymmetries could be independent of one another, they may also reflect a common computational difference between the left and right hemispheres (see Chapter 11). Language and skilled movement require temporally extended, hierarchically organized representations. Perhaps the left hemisphere is more competent in the formation of this type of representation.

THE CORTEX AND THE SELECTION OF MOVEMENT

We can hypothesize that cortical processing for motor control is concerned primarily with selecting appropriate effectors for performing a movement. In planning an action, the initial representation is abstract—a goal of what the person hopes to achieve. For example, your goal might be to drink some coffee or ask a friend to join you at the movies—goals that can be achieved in many ways. Your right or left hand could be used to reach for the coffee cup or for a pencil with which to write your friend a memo. In picking up these objects, you might grasp them with all your fingers or use a prehensile pinch of the thumb and index finger.

Translating a goal into movement might be best envisioned as a competitive process (Figure 7.34). The goal activates all movements that could produce the desired action. These candidates then compete over which movement will be selected (D. A. Rosenbaum et al., 1991). The competition can be driven by many sources, some of which reflect our internal states and past experience. For example, activation of movements with the dominant hand may be more efficient than activation of movements with the nondominant hand. Other sources can be external. Preference may be given to the hand closer to the cup or pencil because this movement requires less effort. Or, in an experiment, the task instructions might ask the subject to use one

Figure 7.34 Response selection involves a competitive process between potential responses. The writer wishes to take a swig from his coffee cup. He can achieve this goal by reaching with the left or right hand, either from his current position or by rotating his trunk. Various sources of information—the location of the cup, the current activity of the hands, experience—help resolve the competition.

hand or the other. The motor cortex can be viewed as the final tallying point of the competitive process, given that it provides the primary motor signal from the cortex. As such, the motor cortex represents a movement chosen to achieve the desired goal. If the motor cortex is lesioned, the selected movement cannot be implemented to activate the effectors.

The cortical selection hypothesis agrees with evidence that motor planning is a distributed process involving many neural regions. All these areas promote movement, but their relative contributions vary as a function of the task demands. The supplementary motor area reflects the contribution of internal sources of activation—goals and motivational states—whereas the lateral premotor area is driven more strongly by external sources, such as the positions of the effectors and objects that might be manipulated. A task is likely to encompass both sources; we should not expect only one area to be activated. The differences will be quantitative rather than qualitative.

Neurological lesions can disturb the balance between different inputs. In the acute stage after a stroke, patients with lesions of the supplementary motor area reach out and grasp objects with the affected arm, even when they have not been instructed to do so or have been told to refrain from moving. This *alien hand syndrome* reflects a dominance of externally guided lateral premotor pathways. The sight of an object within reaching distance evokes a motor plan to grasp the object. Usually we can inhibit movement if we are instructed to do so or if the movement is inappropriate. But when internal control sources are removed, the movement can be triggered by the appropriate external stimulus. The normal balance underlying movement selection is distorted.

If we view the process as competitive, we can understand why, under certain conditions, competing motor plans are activated. Consider an experiment by Steven Wise of the National Institute of Mental Health. Monkeys were trained to move a handle within one of two conditions: compatible and incompatible (S. P. Wise et al., 1996). In both conditions, a stimulus would appear at one of eight positions on a circle. For the compatible condition, the monkeys were trained to move the handle to the location of the stimulus; for the incompatible condition, the required movement was in the opposite direction of the stimulus.

Population vectors were recorded in the lateral premotor cortex. In the compatible condition, the vector immediately pointed toward the forthcoming movement; in the incompatible one, though, the vector pointed first toward the stimulus—that is, the direction away from the forthcoming movement—and with more processing time, the vector shifted toward the movement (Figure 7.35). This shift comes from two competing movement plans. Because we usually move to the location of a stimulus, the onset of a target automatically activates a motor plan toward that location. Training, however, taught these monkeys that they must move in the opposite direction. As input from this internal set became dominant, the population vector's direction shifted.

The hypothesis of widespread competition among motor plans fits in with the activation patterns observed in premotor and motor cortices. As noted already, imaging studies show that premotor activation is generally bilateral. This is surprising, given that, in most studies, all movements were performed with a single hand. Although it is possible that these areas represent both sides of the body, the bilateral activation may reflect the planning of all possible movements that could achieve an abstract goal. Activation eventually becomes lateralized over the contralateral motor cortex—the presumed outcome of a competition for one hand over the other. The transition of bilateral activation over premotor areas to unilateral activation over the motor cortex also is seen in measurements of evoked potentials (Figure 7.36).

The supplementary motor area is important in the selection process. Although the primary source of output for the supplementary motor area is the ipsilateral motor cortex, this area also has callosal projections to

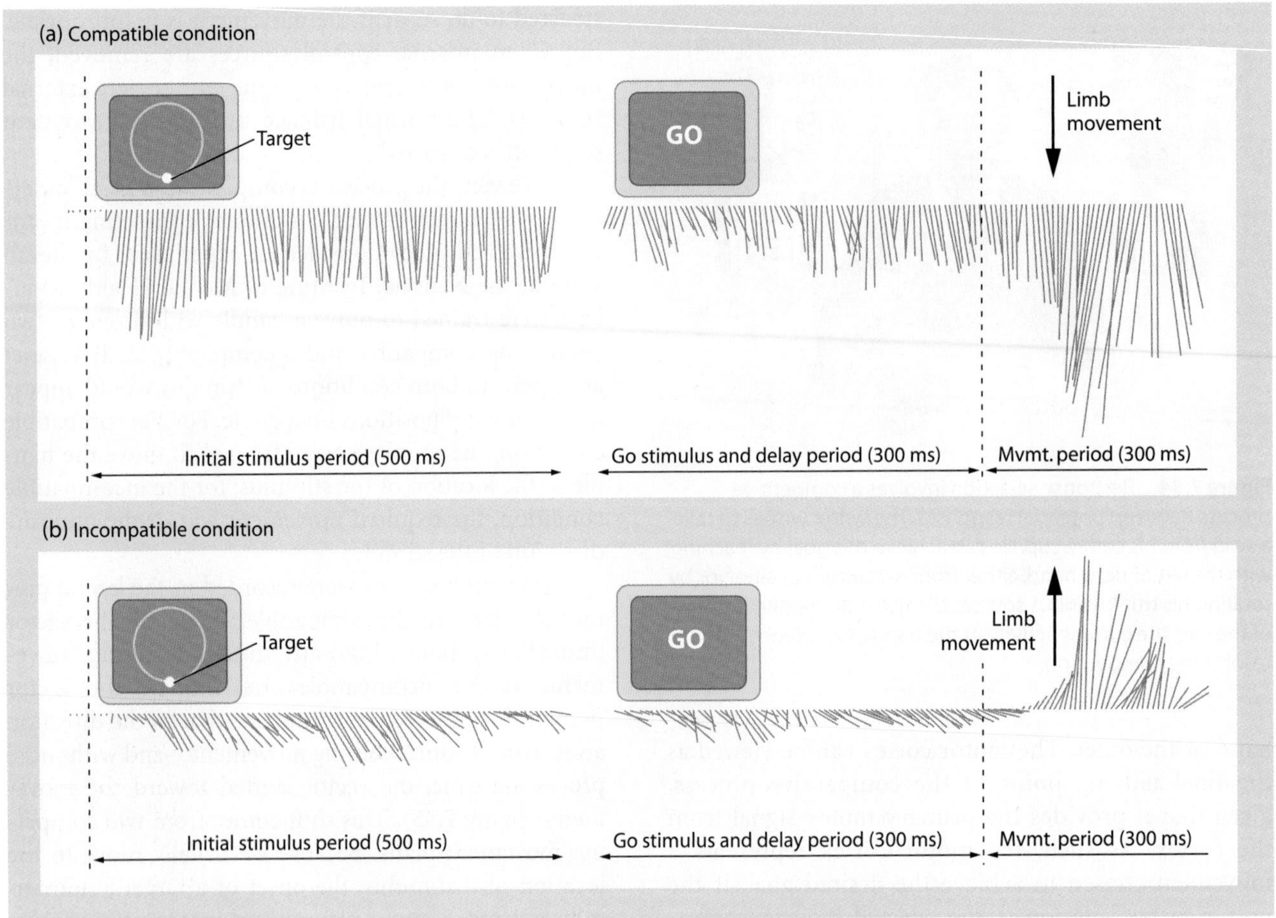

Figure 7.35 Physiological correlates of response competition. **(a)** In the compatible condition, a light comes on at a target position along the circumference of the circle. After a delay period, a go signal indicates that the monkey should move a lever to the target location. The population vectors indicate the movement direction becoming manifest during the delay period. **(b)** In the incompatible condition, the animal must move to the location opposite the one signaled by the light. During the delay period the population vector corresponds to a movement planned toward the light. The magnitude of this vector is less than that in the compatible condition, reflecting the simultaneous activation of the opposite movement. After the onset of the go signal, the population vector orients in the direction of the (correct) movement.

the contralateral SMA and motor cortex. A good number of these crossed projections are inhibitory. Thus, activation of the supplementary motor area in one hemisphere promotes the selection of a movement on the contralateral side and inhibits a similar movement on the ipsilateral side. This organization helps explain another unusual symptom associated with SMA lesions: the tendency to produce mirror movements. When a subject is asked to reach for an object with the hand contralateral to the lesion, the ipsilateral hand makes a similar gesture.

In most skilled behavior, we do not use just one hand or the other. Most motor tasks involve the coordinated use of both hands. The two hands may work in a similar fashion, as when we push a heavy object or row a boat. In other tasks, the two hands take on different, complementary roles, as when we open a jar or tie our shoes. The supplementary motor area also plays a central role in bimanual coordination. Damage to this area in both monkeys and humans can lead to impaired performance on tasks that require integrated use of the two hands, even though the individual gestures performed by either hand alone are unaffected (Wiesendanger et al., 1996). If a person is asked to pantomime opening a drawer with one hand to retrieve an object with the other, both hands may mime the opening gesture. Again, this deficit fits with the idea of a competitive process in which an abstract goal—to retrieve an object from the drawer—is activated and a competition ensues to determine how the required movements are assigned to each hand. When the supplementary motor area is damaged, the assign-

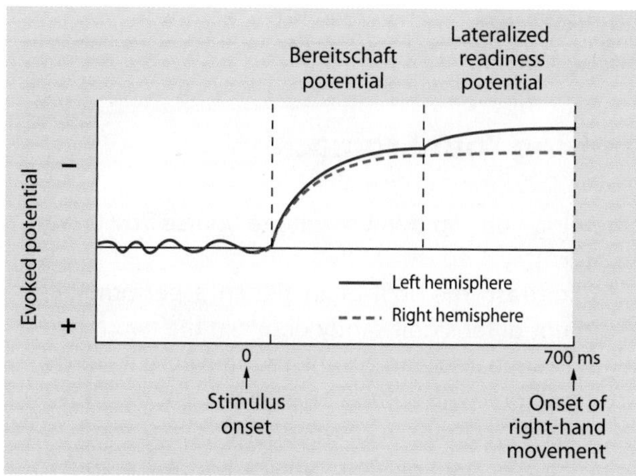

Figure 7.36 Evoked potentials recorded over the motor cortex before the right index finger presses a button. Following stimulus onset, the potential shows increased negativity, the "Bereitschaft" (readiness) potential. This potential is observed bilaterally. During the last 300 ms of the reaction time period, the potential becomes larger over the hemisphere contralateral to the hand.

ment process is disrupted and execution fails, even though the person is still able to express the general goal.

Subcortical Areas: Cerebellum and Basal Ganglia

In the preceding section we focused on how cortical motor areas select movement plans. The cortex is a vast processing network where input converges and helps an animal choose the action that achieves a goal. As such, the cortex is evolution's way of creating a flexible system. The animal need not slavishly respond to a stimulus but can modify its actions to meet current goals.

From this perspective we can expect subcortical areas to participate less in selecting motor plans. Their role may be limited to ensuring that selected movements are executed efficiently. When the areas are lesioned, we would not expect representational disorders such as the ones observed in apraxia, a disorder that generates a wrong response. Instead, we would expect the response to be poorly executed.

This hypothesis accurately describes the motor disorders observed with subcortical lesions. In this section, then, we review the motor deficits of the primary subcortical structures associated with motor control: the cerebellum and basal ganglia. In examining these disorders, we develop functional hypotheses about how the structures contribute to the coordination of skilled action.

CEREBELLUM

Lesions of the cerebellum disrupt coordination in a variety of ways—a heterogeneity reflecting the distinct regions of the cerebellum. Figure 7.37 shows the three parts of the cerebellum: vestibulocerebellum, spinocerebellum, and neocerebellum. This tripartite organization is reflected in the unique anatomical projections of these parts, as well as by the fact that lesions within each area manifest as distinct clinical symptoms. Moreover, the three regions appear to have followed different courses in phylogeny. As its name implies, the neocerebellum emerged most recently, coming after the development of the spinocerebellum and the more ancient vestibulocerebellum.

Anatomical and Functional Divisions of the Cerebellum The vestibulocerebellum is innervated by the brainstem vestibular nuclei, and output is projected back to the same region. The vestibular system is essential for controlling balance and coordinating eye movements with body movements. Lesions of this area can affect the reflexes essential for balance and stability. For example, the vestibulo-ocular reflex (VOR) ensures that the eyes remain fixed on an object despite movements of the head or body. The VOR is essential for an organism that interacts with the environment: If the eyes were displaced with each movement, it would be difficult to monitor another organism or keep track of the location of a stimulus.

The output from the spinocerebellum originates in the medial cerebellar nuclei and innervates the spinal cord and nuclei of the extrapyramidal system. Lesions of the spinocerebellum create problems for the smooth control of movement. The medial part of the spinocerebellum, the vermis, is especially important for coordination involving axial muscles, the muscles that control the body's trunk. Cells in this region are especially sensitive to the effects of alcohol. With chronic alcohol abuse, the vermis atrophies, resulting in problems with balance and walking. Even with acute alcohol use, cerebellar signs can be observed: Tests used by police on suspected drunk drivers essentially record cerebellar function.

Damage to the spinocerebellum also disrupts arm movements. Patients with lesions in this area can select the appropriate action and initiate it in a normal manner, but their gestures will be clumsy, irregular, and erratic—a condition referred to as *ataxia.* Rapid pointing movements are *hypermetric,* extending beyond the target. Moreover, the patient cannot smoothly terminate the movement. Rather, as the arm approaches the target, it begins a series of oscillations (Hore et al., 1991).

HOW THE BRAIN WORKS

Patting Your Head While Rubbing Your Stomach

Recall the childhood challenge to pat your head while rubbing your stomach. This seemingly innocent task often proves extremely frustrating. It is nearly impossible to generate the conflicting spatial trajectories, having one hand move in an up–down fashion while the other produces a circular movement. The two movements compete. We fail to map one direction for one hand and the other direction for the opposite hand. Eventually one of the movements often dominates and we end up rubbing both the head and the stomach or patting both. Within the selection hypothesis outlined in this chapter, we can think of this bimanual conflict as competition between two movement goals. Each task activates both hemispheres, and we cannot keep the cross talk from these activation patterns from interfering with one another.

If this hypothesis is correct, spatial interference should be eliminated when each movement goal is restricted to a single hemisphere and the pathways connecting the two hemispheres are severed. To test this idea, Elizabeth Franz and her colleagues (1996) at the University of California, Berkeley, tested a patient whose corpus callosum had been resected. The stimuli for this bimanual-movement study were a pair of three-sided figures, with the sides following either a common axis or perpendicular axes. The stimuli were projected briefly—one stimulus presented in the left visual field, and the other in the right visual field. After viewing the stimuli, the subjects were instructed to produce the two patterns simultaneously, using the left hand for the pattern projected in the left visual field and the right hand for the pattern in the right visual field. The brief presentation was used to ensure that each stimulus was isolated to a single hemisphere in the split-brain patient. In control subjects, rapid transfer of information via the corpus callosum was expected.

As part **(a)** of the figure shows, control subjects had little difficulty producing bilateral movements when the segments of the squares followed a common axis of movement **(a, top)**. When the segments required movements along perpendicular axes, however **(a, bottom)**, their performance deteriorated dramatically, with long pauses occurring before each segment and trajectories frequently deviating from the target—something you can demonstrate to yourself by trying this task.

In contrast, the split-brain patient's performance **(b)** did not differ significantly between the two movements. He initiated and completed movements in the two conditions with comparable speed, and the movements were accurate in both. Indeed, in a second experiment, this patient simultaneously drew a square with the left hand and a circle with the right hand. Each hemisphere produced the pattern without any signs of interference from demands presented to the opposite hemisphere.

These results indicate that the callosotomy procedure yields a spatial uncoupling in bimanual movements. Another striking observation was that, even for the split-brain patient, the actions of the two hands were not independent of one another. As with the control subjects, the two hands moved in synchrony. The segments of the squares were initiated and terminated at approximately the same time. This temporal coupling was seen more clearly when subjects were asked to produce oscillatory movements, with each hand moving along a single axis. Regardless of whether the two hands followed a common axis (e.g., both horizontal or both vertical) or perpendicular axes (e.g., one horizontal and the other vertical), the two hands reversed direction at the same time.

This study provided valuable insights to the neural structures underlying bimanual coordination. First, the spatial goals for bimanual movements are coordinated via processing across the corpus callosum. When a task requires conflicting directions of movement, interference is extensive as long as the callosal connections are intact. Second, these connections are not necessary for the temporal coupling of movement. Perhaps the initiation of movement is regulated either by a single hemisphere or by subcortical mechanisms. Third, the dissociation of spatial and temporal coupling emphasizes a distributed view of how the motor system's neural structures contribute to coordination. The neural structures that represent the spatial goals are separate from those involved in initiating the movements selected to meet these goals.

Bimanual movements following resection of the corpus callosum. While looking at a central fixation point, subjects were briefly shown the two patterns. They were instructed to simultaneously draw the pattern on the left with the left hand and the one on the right with the right hand. Normal subjects **(a)** were able to draw the patterns that shared a common axis but had severe difficulty when the orientation of the two figures differed by 90°. The split-brain patient **(b)** performed equally well in both conditions.

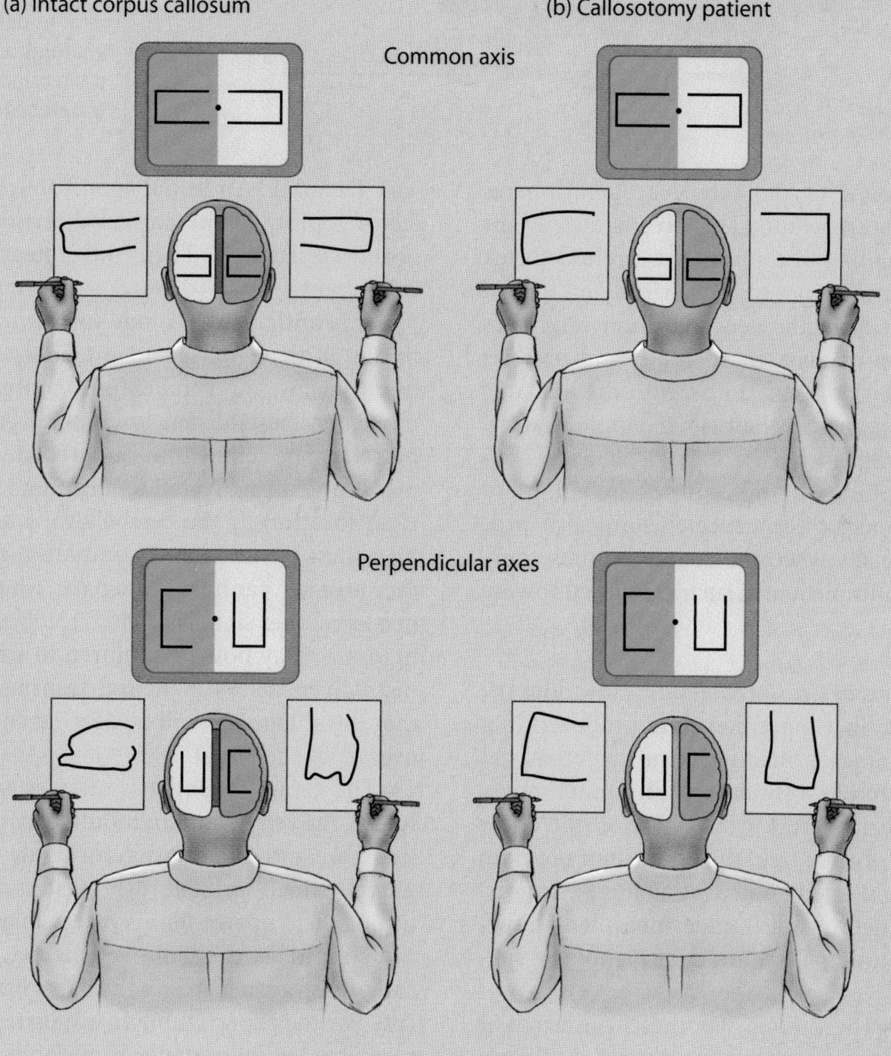

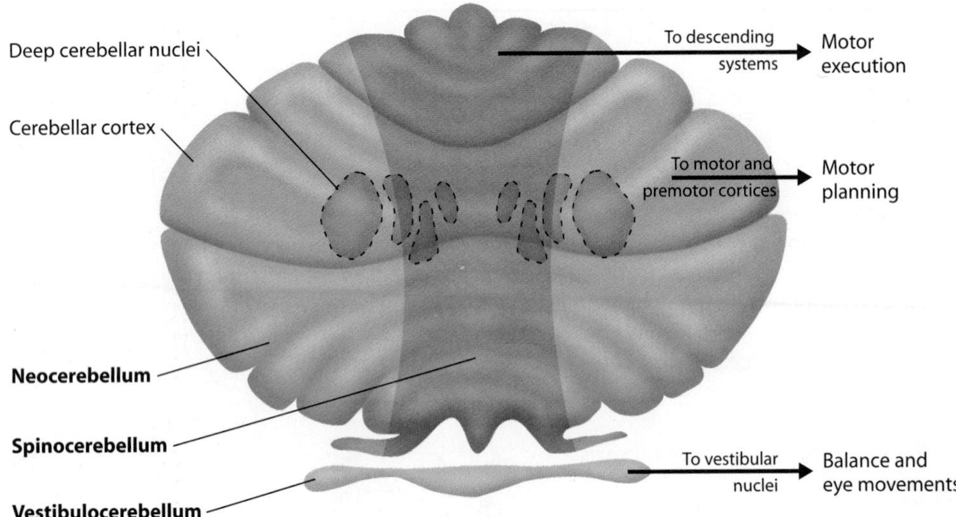

Figure 7.37 The three divisions of the cerebellum. These regions differ in terms of their anatomical projections to the deep cerebellar nuclei and extracerebellar target regions.

The lateral zones of the cerebellar hemispheres constitute the neocerebellum. This area is heavily innervated by descending fibers from the cerebral cortex originating in many regions of the parietal and frontal lobes. The output from the neocerebellum originates in the lateral deep nucleus, the dentate, and projects back to the cortex via the thalamus, with the thalamic projections terminating in the primary motor, lateral premotor, and prefrontal cortices. As such, the neocerebellum contributes to the control of voluntary movements. Lesions of the neocerebellum also produce ataxia, especially when the action requires coordination across multiple joints, such as when throwing a baseball.

Functional Analysis of the Cerebellum How does the cerebellum ensure that movements are produced in a skillful and coordinated manner? One hypothesis is that the cerebellum has a special role in timing movement. Though cortical areas primarily select the effectors needed to perform a task, the cerebellum provides the precise timing needed for activating these effectors. Thus, cerebellar neurons also code movement direction, because the timing is required for planning a specific trajectory.

Consider how the timing hypothesis can account for the cerebellar symptom of hypermetria. As Figure 7.38 shows, rapid movements require both agonist and antagonist activity. Although agonist activity is clearly needed to displace the limb, antagonist activity is, at least superficially, counterproductive. Why produce a force that counteracts a desired action? One argument for the biphasic pattern is that it enables a person to move at high speeds that do not rely on sensory feedback. An initial agonist burst propels the effector rapidly in the correct direction with little opposing resistance. Then the antagonist brakes the movement.

This anticipatory mode of control has a cost: the timing of the agonist and antagonist must be precise. In this view, the cerebellum's contribution to rapid movements establishes a temporal pattern across the muscles. The cerebellum can predict when the antagonist should be activated to terminate movement at the right location. If the cerebellum is lesioned, the agonist burst is sufficient to initiate the movement, but the animal cannot anticipate when the brake is needed. Other signals, such as feedback from the moving limb, may now be required to trigger the antagonist. Given delays in neural transmission, it is likely that the antagonist will be delayed and the animal will overshoot the target.

The timing hypothesis offers a novel slant on the role of the cerebellum in motor learning. Cerebellar lesions are most disruptive to highly practiced movements, which present the greatest need for precise timing. The novice tennis player may be pleased if he can simply get the ball over the net, and he may not care if his racquet strikes the ball a little early or a little late. For the expert, though, exquisite timing of all gestures is essential so that the ball lands in a certain place on the court.

This point is highlighted in an experiment involving a simple model of motor learning: eyeblink conditioning. When a puff of air is directed at the eye, a reflexive blink is produced—a response designed to minimize potential eye damage. If a neutral stimulus such as a tone is presented in advance of the air puff on a consistent basis,

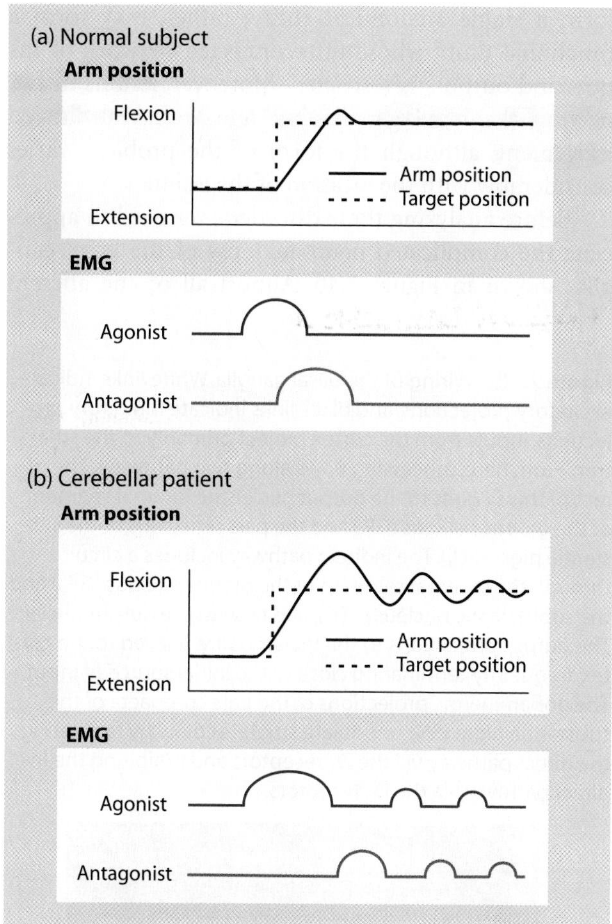

Figure 7.38 Arm position and associated EMG activity during rapid elbow movements. **(a)** During rapid elbow flexion in a normal subject, the agonist biceps muscle produces a burst to propel the limb. This movement is braked by activation of the antagonist triceps. **(b)** The fine timing of the agonist–antagonist activity is disrupted in patients with cerebellar lesions. When the onset of the antagonist is delayed, the movement ends up overshooting the target because the braking force has been lost. The oscillations seen at the end of pointing movements result from the alternation of agonist and antagonist activity.

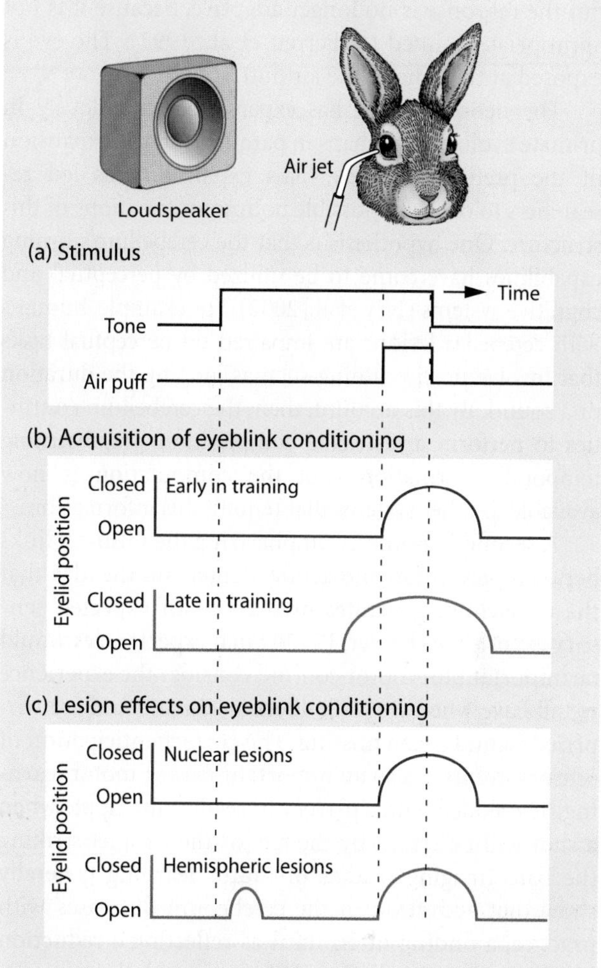

Figure 7.39 Lesions of the cerebellum disrupt the learned response in eyeblink conditioning. **(a)** A neutral tone precedes and coterminates with an aversive air puff to the eye. **(b)** Early in training, the air puff causes the animal to blink. Late in training, the animal blinks in response to the tone, thus reducing the impact of the air puff. **(c)** Lesions of the deep cerebellar nuclei abolish the learned response. The fact that the animal continues to blink reflexively in response to the air puff indicates that the lesion has produced a learning deficit and not a motor deficit. The anticipatory, learned responses are still present following lesions of the cerebellar cortex. However, they are timed inappropriately and thus are no longer adaptive.

the animal comes to blink in response to the tone (Figure 7.39). The acquired response is highly adaptive: By blinking to the tone, the animal closes its eyes before the air puff. This conditioned response is timed to reach maximal amplitude at the onset of the air puff.

Unlike lesions of the cerebral cortex or hippocampus, cerebellar lesions disrupt the acquisition and retention of a conditioned blinking response. The problem is not one of an impaired motor system, since eyeblinks to the air puffs themselves are minimally affected by cerebellar lesions. As such, the selective disruption of the conditioned response is a sensorimotor learning problem—an idea in accord with the view that the cerebellum is an important part of the motor learning system. At a computational level, the timing hypothesis helps specify how the cerebellum contributes to motor learning. It is not only important for the animal to learn that the tone and air puff co-occur; the response is adaptive only if the animal learns that the tone predicts exactly when the air puff will occur. The animal must be able to represent the temporal relationship between the two stimuli. As Figure 7.39c shows, rabbits with lesions in the cerebellar hemispheres continue to blink to the tone, but the response is no longer adaptive, because it is not appropriately timed (S. Perrett et al., 1993): The eye is exposed at the time of the air puff.

The neocerebellum has expanded tremendously in primate evolution, perhaps in parallel with the expansion of the prefrontal cortex. This expansion has led researchers to consider possible nonmotor functions of this structure. One hypothesis is that the cerebellum's timing capabilities have come to be utilized by perceptual and cognitive systems (Ivry et al., 2002). For example, humans with cerebellar lesions are impaired on perceptual tasks that involve precise timing such as judging the duration of a sound. By this account, then, the cerebellum continues to perform a restricted computation—representing temporal information—but the computation is now available to other systems that require this information.

A second hypothesis, emphasizing the intimate links between perception and action, centers on the idea that the cerebellum generates predictions of expected sensory experience (Bower, 1997). Such expectancies would be important for motor control; consider the experience we all have when we walk down a staircase and are surprised to find a step missing. The correct anticipation of sensory events is also an important part of motor learning. The skilled tennis player can readily anticipate when a shot will be errant by the feel of the racquet striking the ball. Imaging studies of motor learning generally show that activation in the cerebellum decreases with practice, a finding interpreted as reflecting a reduction in error (i.e., prediction failures) as skill improves. Against this backdrop of overall decrease in activation, however, are small areas within the cerebellum that show an increase in activity as a new skill develops. The focal increases are hypothesized to result from the generation of new predictions (Imamizu et al., 2000).

Prediction and timing are closely related. For coordinated actions, it is not only important to know the sequence of limb movements, but it is also essential that the successive movements are made at the right point in time to avoid errors. Thus, these hypotheses provide insight into nonmotor functions of the cerebellum and offer computational accounts of how the cerebellum contributes to coordination and motor learning. We see here again the links between the representational processes involved in perception and action.

BASAL GANGLIA

The basal ganglia—composed of five nuclei: caudate, putamen, globus pallidus, subthalamic nucleus, and substantia nigra (see Figure 7.5)—constitute the other major subcortical motor structure. These nuclei do not form a single anatomical entity; rather, they form a functional unity whose interconnected network of inputs and outputs is restricted. Moreover, lesions in any part of the basal ganglia interfere with coordinated movement, although the form of the problem varies considerably with the location of the lesion.

Before analyzing these disorders, we need to appreciate the complicated neuroanatomy of the basal ganglia, shown in Figure 7.40. Almost all of the afferent

Figure 7.40 Wiring of the basal ganglia. White links indicate excitatory projections, and black links indicate inhibitory projections. Inputs from the cortex project primarily to the striatum. From here, processing flows along two pathways. The direct pathway goes to the output nuclei: the internal segment of the globus pallidus (GP_i) and the pars reticularis of the substantia nigra (SN_r). The indirect pathway includes a circuit through the external segment of the globus pallidus (GP_e) and the subthalamic nucleus (STN), and then to the output nuclei. The output projections to the thalamus are relayed to the cortex, frequently terminating close to the initial source of input. The dopaminergic projections of the pars compacta of the substantia nigra (SN_c) modulate striatal activity by facilitating the direct pathway via the D_1 receptors and inhibiting the indirect pathway via the D_2 receptors.

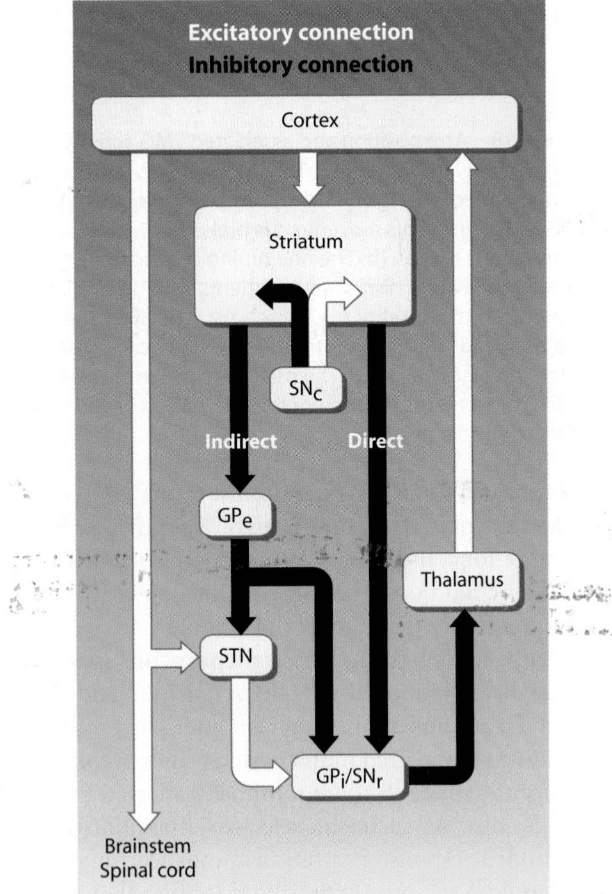

fibers to the basal ganglia terminate in the caudate and putamen, or what are collectively referred to as the *striatum*. These fibers originate across much of the cerebral cortex, including sensory, motor, and association cortices. Efferent fibers from the basal ganglia are also restricted. Output from the basal ganglia originates in the internal segment of the globus pallidus (GP_i) and the pars reticularis of the substantia nigra (SN_r). SN_r axons terminate primarily in the superior colliculus and provide a crucial signal for the initiation of eye movements. GP_i axons, on the other hand, terminate in thalamic nuclei, which in turn project to the motor cortex, supplementary motor area, and prefrontal cortex.

In terms of physiology, processing within the basal ganglia is complex. Mahlon DeLong (1990) of Emory University distinguished between direct and indirect pathways: The direct pathway consists of direct inhibitory projections from the striatum to the GP_i and SN_r; the indirect pathway also connects the striatum to these output nuclei, but only through intervening processing stages involving the external segment of the globus pallidus and the subthalamic nucleus. All of the output signals from the basal ganglia are inhibitory. Neurons in the GP_i and SN_r have high baseline firing rates that inhibit target neurons in the superior colliculus and thalamus.

The final pathway of note is the projection from the pars compacta of the substantia nigra (SN_c) to the striatum. Interestingly, this pathway has opposite effects on the direct and indirect pathways, despite a common transmitter, dopamine. The substantia nigra excites the direct pathway by acting on one type of dopamine receptor (D_1) and inhibits the indirect pathway by acting on a different type of dopamine receptor (D_2).

Functional Analysis of the Basal Ganglia Tracing what happens when cortical fibers activate the striatum can help us understand basal ganglia function. Via the direct pathway, target neurons in the output nuclei of the basal ganglia are inhibited, leading to excitation of the thalamus and cortical motor areas. On the other hand, striatal activation along the indirect pathway results in increased excitation of the output nuclei, leading to increased inhibition of the cortex. It appears, then, that the direct and indirect pathways are at odds with one another. If processing along the indirect pathway is slower, however, the basal ganglia can act as a gatekeeper of cortical activity; less inhibition from the direct pathway is followed by more inhibition from the indirect pathway. The nigrostriatal fibers enhance the direct pathway while reducing the effects of the indirect pathway. As such, this pathway is essential for promoting movement.

Seen in this light, the basal ganglia can be hypothesized to play a critical role in the initiation of actions (Figure 7.41). As we argued earlier in this chapter, processing in the cortical motor areas can be viewed as a competitive process in which candidate actions compete for control of the motor apparatus. The basal ganglia are positioned to help resolve the competition. The strong inhibitory baseline activity keeps the motor system in check, allowing cortical representations of possible movements to become activated without engaging the muscles. As a specific motor plan gains strength, the inhibitory signal is decreased for selected neurons.

Interestingly, computational analyses demonstrate that the physiology of the direct pathway in the basal ganglia is ideally designed to function as a winner-take-all system—a method for committing to one action from among the various alternatives. Greg Berns and Terry Sejnowski (1996) of the Salk Institute in La Jolla, California, evaluated the functional consequences of all pairwise connections of two synapses, either of which could be excitatory or inhibitory. By their analysis, a series of two successive inhibitory links is the most efficient way to make a selected pattern stand out from the background. With this circuit, the disinhibited signal stands out from a quiet background. In contrast, with a pair of excitatory connections the selected pattern has to raise its signal above a loud background. Similarly, a combination of inhibitory and excitatory synapses in either order is not efficient in making the selected pattern distinct from the background. Berns and Sejnowski noted that the double inhibition of the direct pathway is relatively unique to the basal ganglia. This arrangement is useful for selecting a response in a competitive system.

Dopamine has long been known to be a critical transmitter in reward pathways. One can hypothesize that, within the basal ganglia, dopamine serves to bias the system to produce certain responses over others. Dopamine release in the striatum follows successful actions—for example, a winning crosscourt forehand in tennis. This transmitter might modify the input–output channels in the basal ganglia, making it more likely that the same response will be initiated when the rewarded input pattern is reactivated in the future.

Disorders of the Basal Ganglia Several neurological disorders affect the basal ganglia; in these we see a breakdown in the delicate balance between postural stability and movement. We will concentrate on two—Huntington's disease and Parkinson's disease—since they best demonstrate how movement is disrupted by basal ganglia dysfunction. Although psychiatric conditions such

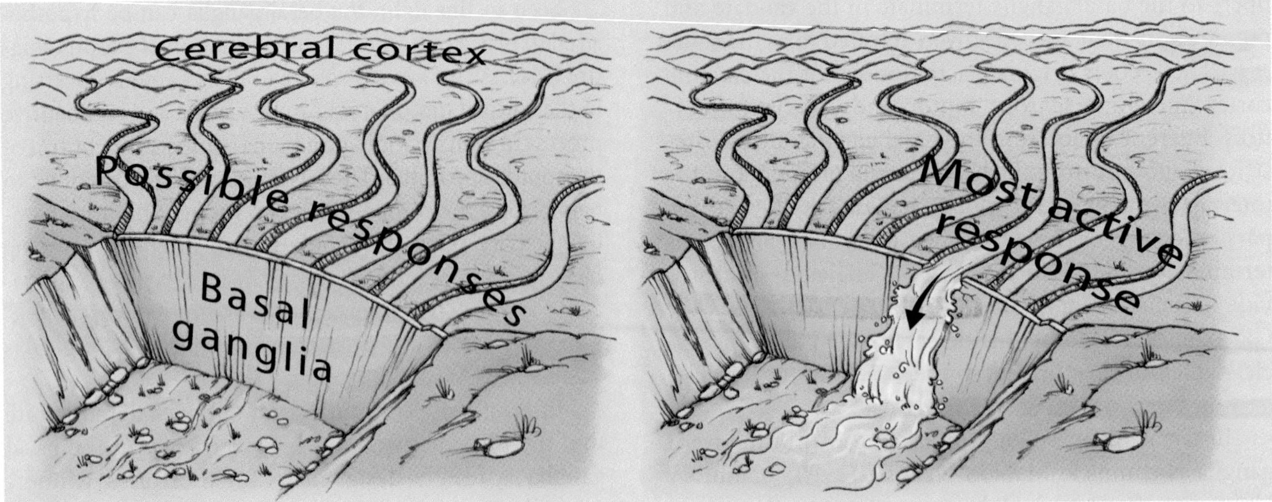

Figure 7.41 The basal ganglia play a critical role in movement initiation. Potential responses are held in check until the basal ganglia provide a triggering response.

as Tourette's syndrome and obsessive-compulsive disorder have been linked to the basal ganglia, the neuroanatomical picture is murkier.

Huntington's disease is a progressive degenerative disorder that appears in the fourth or fifth decade of life. The onset is subtle, usually a gradual change in mental attitude in which the patient is irritable, is absent-minded, and loses interest in normal activities. Within a year movement abnormalities are noticed: clumsiness, balance problems, and a general restlessness. These involuntary movements, or *chorea*, gradually dominate normal motor function. The patient may adopt contorted postures, with the arms, legs, trunk, and head in constant motion. Indeed, during the 17th century, on at least two continents, Huntington's disease patients were executed for witchcraft because their chorea made them appear possessed by an evil spirit.

Neurological deficits in Huntington's disease are not restricted to motor function. As motor problems worsen, patients develop dementia of a subcortical type, unaccompanied by apraxia, aphasia, or agnosia—common signs of a cortical dementia such as Alzheimer's disease. Even so, the patients have impaired memory, especially in acquiring novel motor skills, and become easily confused on problem-solving tasks. The disorder is also accompanied by emotional and personality changes, although it is hard to know whether these are due to the disease itself or are a reaction to the onset of such a debilitating disease.

The genetic origin of Huntington's disease is briefly reviewed in Chapter 4. Despite advances on its cause, there is no known cure; patients usually die within 12 years of onset. At autopsy, the brain of a Huntington's disease patient typically reveals widespread pathology in cortical and subcortical areas. Atrophy is most prominent in the basal ganglia, and the cell death rate is as high as 90% in the striatum. These changes are also evident from imaging studies performed as the disease unfolds.

It has been difficult to make inferences about normal motor function from studying patients with Huntington's disease. Huntington's patients frequently cannot complete experimental tasks, or they can do so with only the most labored movements. As such, selective deficits are hard to observe: The disease affects all measures of coordination. We can understand the excessive movements, or hyperkinesia, seen with Huntington's disease by considering how the pathology affects information flow through the basal ganglia.

In the early stages, striatal changes occur primarily in inhibitory neurons forming the indirect pathway. As shown in Figure 7.42a, these changes lead to a reduced output from the basal ganglia, and thus greater excitation of thalamic neurons. A second hyperkinetic disorder, *hemiballism*, is also associated with lesions of the indirect pathway, but here the lesion is centered in the subthalamic nucleus. Patients with these lesions produce violent and uncontrollable movements. These problems may persist for many years, requiring special precautions to ensure that the patients do not hurt themselves or those who come within reach.

Parkinson's disease is the most common and well-known disorder affecting the basal ganglia. It is characterized by positive and negative symptoms—

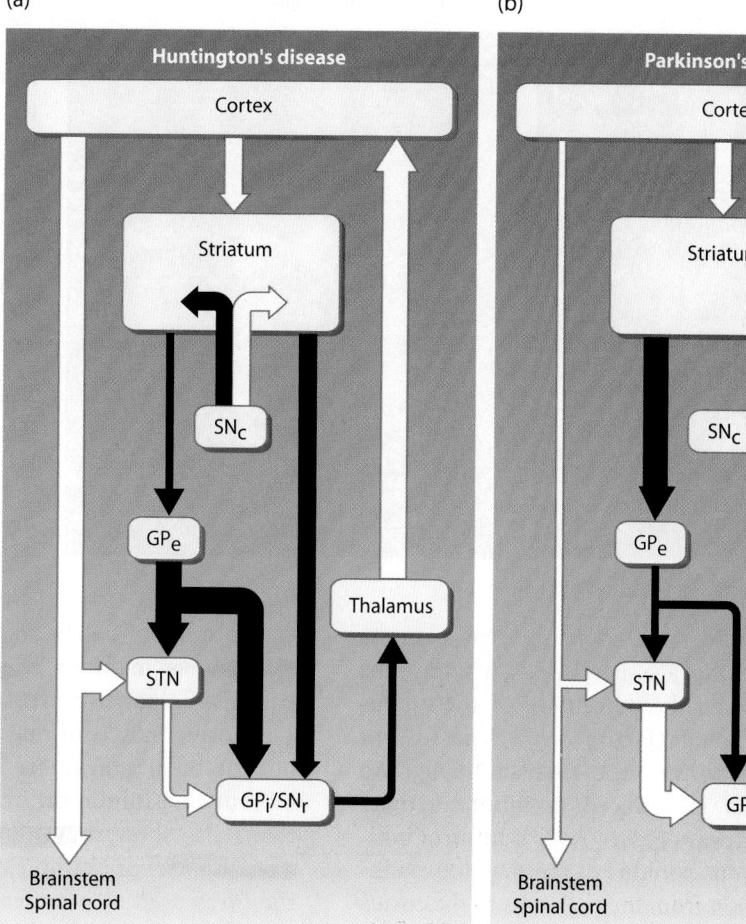

Figure 7.42 Differential neurochemical alterations in Huntington's and Parkinson's diseases. As in Figure 7.40, white links indicate excitatory projections, and black links indicate inhibitory projections. **(a)** In Huntington's disease, the inhibitory projection along the indirect pathway from the striatum to the external segment of the globus pallidus (GP_e) is reduced. The net consequence is reduced inhibitory output from the globus pallidus and thus an increase in cortical excitation and movement. **(b)** Parkinson's disease primarily reduces the inhibitory activity along the direct pathway, resulting in increased inhibition from the globus pallidus to the thalamus and thus a reduction in cortical activity and movement.

that is, motor disorders that heighten muscular activity and disorders that diminish it. Positive symptoms include resting tremor and rigidity. Resting tremor—the rapid shaking evident in distal effectors—becomes quieter, if not entirely quiescent, once the patient has initiated a volitional movement. Rigidity results when agonist and antagonist muscles are activated simultaneously. When the limb is displaced passively, the neurologist can feel alternations between resistance and relaxation—a phenomenon known as *cogwheeling.*

Negative symptoms of Parkinson's disease include disorders of posture and locomotion, hypokinesia, and **bradykinesia**. Parkinson's patients often lose their equilibrium. When the patient is sitting, the head may droop forward, or when standing, the forces of gravity will gradually pull the person forward until balance is lost. *Hypokinesia* refers to an absence or reduction in voluntary movement. Parkinson's patients act as if they are stuck in a posture and cannot change it. This problem is especially evident when patients try to initiate a new movement. Many patients develop small tricks to help them overcome the hypokinesia. For example, one patient walked with a cane, not because he needed help maintaining his balance, but because it provided him a visual target to give him a jump start. When he wanted to walk, he placed the cane in front of his right foot and kicked it—which caused him to overcome inertia and commence his walking. Once started, the movements may appear normal, although they are frequently slow, or bradykinetic. The Parkinson's patient can use his hand to reach for an object, though the entire sequence is in slow motion.

As noted at the beginning of this chapter, Parkinson's disease can develop following encephalitis or drug abuse. In most patients, however, the disease is *idiopathic,* a catchall term that neurologists use when the cause is unknown. Parkinson's is a common disorder, affecting between 1% and 2% of the elderly population. There is some evidence for a genetic origin, although the recent rise in early-onset Parkinson's disease has led researchers to suspect an increase in an environmental toxin.

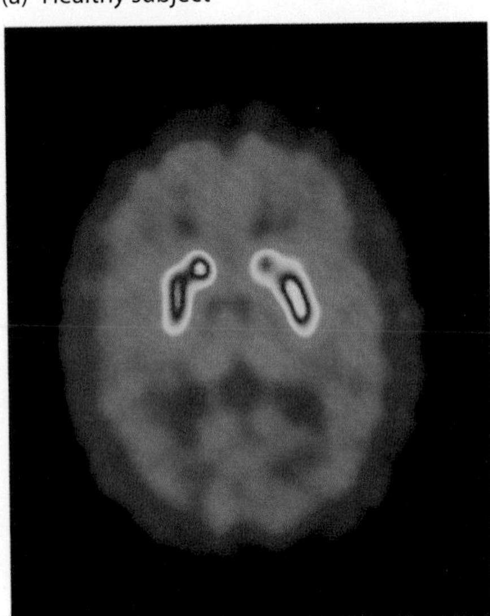

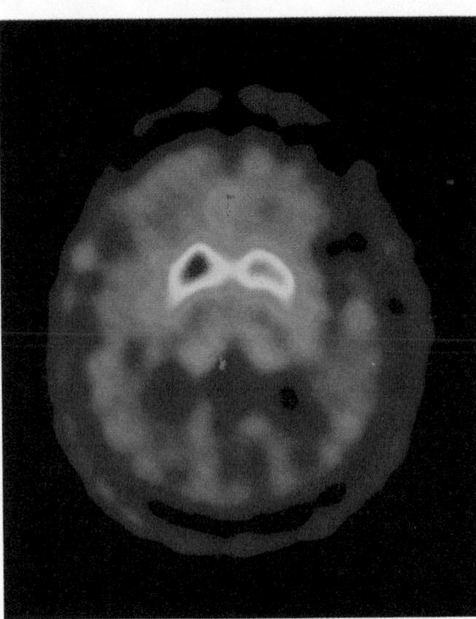

Figure 7.43 New neuroimaging techniques are able to label the distribution of specific transmitter systems. This procedure provides an opportunity to visualize reduced dopaminergic activity in patients with Parkinson's disease. Healthy subjects and Parkinson's disease patients were injected with a radioactive tracer, fluorodopa. This agent is visible in the striatum, reflecting the dopaminergic projections to this structure from the substantia nigra. Compare the reduced uptake in the scan from a healthy subject **(a)** to the uptake in a patient's scan **(b)**.

As with most brain tissue, dopaminergic neurons in the SN_c atrophy with age. Parkinsonian symptoms become manifest when the percentage of these neurons becomes too great (Figure 7.43). The loss of dopaminergic projections from the substantia nigra to the striatum results in reduced inhibitory activity along the direct pathway (Figure 7.42b). In turn, inhibition from the globus pallidus to the thalamus is increased, and excitation from the thalamus to the cortex is reduced.

In terms of behavior, the lowering of cortical excitability is manifest as a reduction in movement. Parkinson's patients are slow to initiate a movement. The cortex may continue to select a movement plan, but the basal ganglia are needed to initiate that plan by reducing inhibition of the cortex. Parkinson's patients also show reduced flexibility in their volitional movements. For example, they may not be able to vary the force used to produce a movement. Normal subjects typically produce movements of different ampli-

Figure 7.44 EMG amplitude is not scaled appropriately in Parkinson's disease. **(a)** In healthy people, the magnitude of EMG activity increases to produce larger movements. **(b)** The EMG profiles of Parkinson's disease patients tend to be more invariant. To move the limb over a large distance, a series of EMG bursts have to be generated.

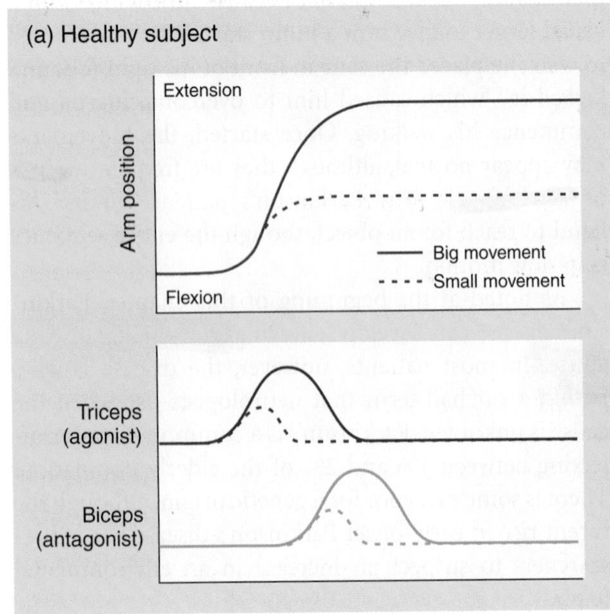

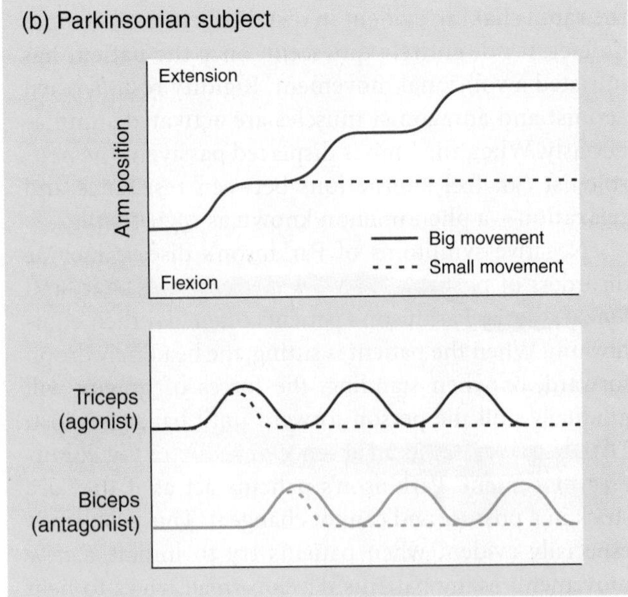

tude by scaling the magnitude of the initial agonist burst. A strong burst creates a larger force and enables one to move farther with minimal increase in the time required to complete the movement. In contrast, Parkinson's patients have to produce a series of small bursts to move a longer distance (Figure 7.44). Thus, the basal ganglia are important not only in initiating movement but also in adjusting an action's force. Both problems relate to properly energizing a movement plan. For the initiation deficit, the releasing signal is absent, preventing the muscles from becoming active; for the force deficit, the plan is implemented, but in a fixed manner.

The first evidence linking dopamine to Parkinson's disease came in the late 1950s, when postmortem examinations correlated the disease with low dopamine levels. (The observations marked the first time that a brain disease was linked to a neurotransmitter deficiency.) Treatment programs were quickly developed in which patients were provided with synthetic precursors of dopamine, L-dopa—a therapy that is of great benefit to most Parkinson's patients. Many can function with little evidence of the disease, and Parkinson's disease is no longer considered a life-threatening condition. The drug's efficacy is far from perfect, however. Over the course of a day some patients experience rapid fluctuations in the severity of their symptoms. Over time, many patients develop severe and debilitating hyperkinesias.

As the limitations of drug therapy, at least for a significant percentage of patients, have become evident, clinicians have sought to develop alternative or supplemental treatments for Parkinson's disease. Using the detailed anatomical and physiological diagrams developed by basal ganglia researchers, neurosurgeons have devised interventions that seek to restore the balance of inhibitory and excitatory circuits between the basal ganglia and the cortex. The hyperactivity of the globus pallidus that occurs when inhibitory striatal signals are attenuated by the disease can be reduced by pallidotomy, a procedure in which small lesions are made in the globus pallidus. This procedure has proved effective in many patients. However, the pallidus is quite large, and identifying the best location for the lesions is problematic. Moreover, significant risks are associated with the procedure (de Bie et al., 2002).

An alternative approach involves a relatively new technology, **deep-brain stimulation**, or **DBS** (Figure 7.45). DBS consists of surgical implantation of an electrode into the targeted neural region; for Parkinson's disease, this is usually the subthalamic nucleus (STN), although some patients receive implants in the globus pallidus and others in the thalamus. A current is then passed through the electrode at high frequencies. This stimulation alters activity in the targeted region and throughout the circuit. The net result of DBS stimulation of the STN is to reduce thalamic inhibition of the cortex.

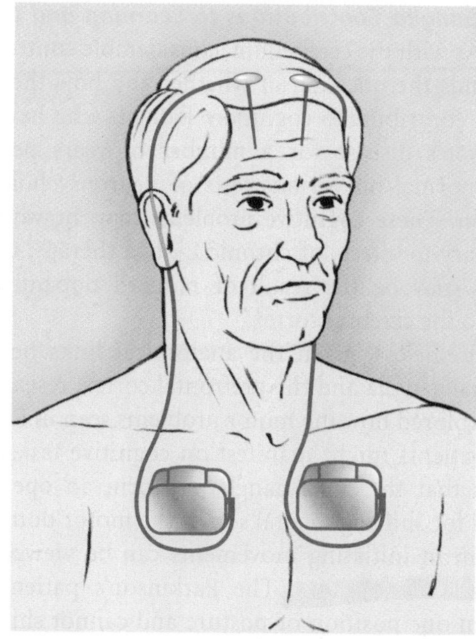

Figure 7.45 Deep-brain stimulation for Parkinson's disease is achieved by the implantation of electrodes in the basal ganglia (most commonly in the subthalamic nuclei bilaterally, or the globus pallidus bilaterally). A pacemaker-like device is connected to the electrodes and implanted subcutaneously. The electrodes can then be stimulated by the pacemaker at regular intervals to relieve many of the symptoms of Parkinson's disease.

Why DBS works remains a bit of a mystery, and the exact physiological mechanisms underlying these changes are just beginning to be unraveled (Perlmutter & Mink, 2006). The diagram in Figure 7.40 suggests that stimulation of the STN would increase excitation of the globus pallidus and result in increased inhibition of the thalamus, which would exacerbate parkinsonian symptoms. However, DBS has proved to be a very effective treatment. Indeed, in many patients the changes are quite dramatic, with simple activation of the stimulator allowing the individual to stand up and walk across the room showing little evidence of the disease. One hypothesis is that the stimulation restores a periodic, or pacemaker, signal to the cortex. By this idea, movement initiation is timed to fluctuating boosts in cortical excitability, and the DBS enhances these boosts (Hutchison et al., 2004).

Basal Ganglia Contributions to Learning and Cognition As with the cerebellum, considerable controversy surrounds the question of whether and how the basal ganglia contribute to cognition. Patients who have had Parkinson's disease for a number of years perform below normal on various tests of neuropsychological function. These cognitive problems may, however, be secondary to effects of chronic L-dopa therapy. Or the deficits may be the result of reduced dopaminergic input to the cerebral cortex.

Nonetheless, given the anatomical links between the basal ganglia and the prefrontal cortex, researchers have explored how the motor problems seen in Parkinson's patients might manifest on cognitive tasks. One idea is that the basal ganglia perform an operation critical for shifting mental set. In the motor domain, a problem in initiating movements can be viewed as a deficit in set shifting. The Parkinson's patient gets stuck in one position or posture and cannot shift to a new one. Perhaps these patients' cognitive problems can also be linked to shifting from one mental set to another.

To test this idea, Steven Keele and his colleagues at the University of Oregon (Hayes et al., 1998) developed two tasks that required a shifting operation (Figure 7.46). In the motor task, the patients were taught two short movement sequences of three elements each. After this training phase, the patients were required to produce a six-element sequence composed of either the two sequences in succession or two repetitions of one of the sequences. As predicted, the responses for the Parkinson's patients were especially slow at the switching point, the transition from the third to the fourth element, in the shifting condition. Note that, in both the repetition and the shifting condition, the fourth element requires the same response: a finger press with the index finger. The difference between the two conditions results from the hierarchical coding of these sequences. In the

Figure 7.46 Motor and cognitive tests of set shifting. **(a)** In the motor task, subjects performed two successive sequences that were either identical or different. Although the movement at the transition point was the same in both the no-shift and the shift conditions, Parkinson's patients were much slower in the latter condition. **(b)** In the cognitive task, subjects had to respond to either the color or the shape of a stimulus. Trials were paired such that the second response was either the same dimension (no shift) or the other dimension (shift). As in the motor task, Parkinson's patients were especially slow when they had to shift.

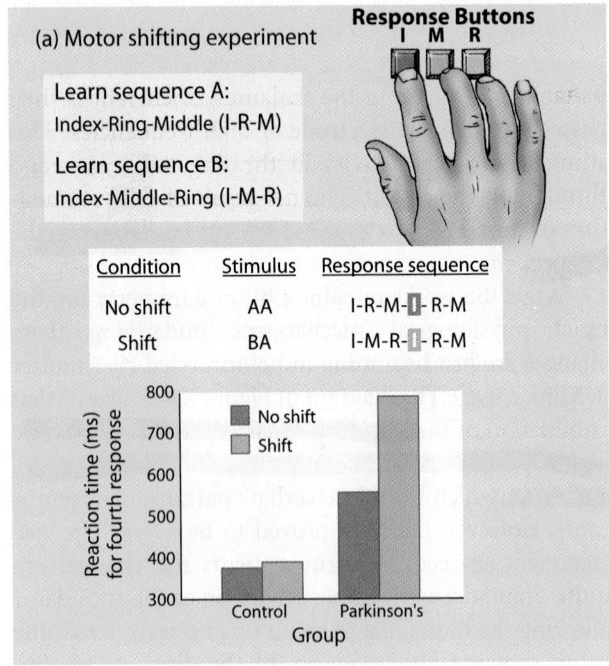

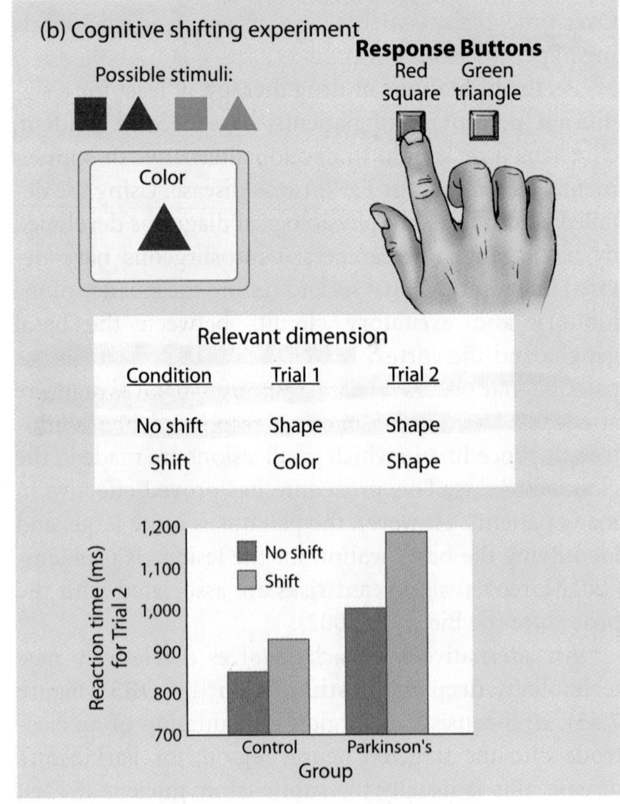

shifting condition, this response is part of a different subsequence.

For the cognitive task, the patients were trained on reaction time tasks with two responses, involving color discrimination and shape discrimination. After the patients were trained on each dimension, pairs of trials were introduced in which the two responses either were along the same dimension (e.g., color–color) or required a shift from one dimension to the other (e.g., shape–color). As in the motor task, the Parkinson's patients were significantly slower when they had to shift dimensional set. This problem cannot be attributed to a motor deficit, since the responses on the second trial were identical in all conditions (e.g., decide whether the stimulus color was red or blue).

The shifting hypothesis offers a unified framework for understanding basal ganglia function in both action and cognition. The basal ganglia are in a position to monitor activation across wide regions of the cortex, allowing a shift between different actions and mental sets by removing an inhibitory influence in selected neurons. Indeed, neurophysiological studies emphasized that the shifting operation is neither strictly motoric nor cognitive; rather, it is a necessary link between mental set and action (Brotchie et al., 1991). In this work, monkeys were trained to make a pair of movements, with a variable delay between the first and second movements. A burst in pallidal neurons observed at the end of this delay period was interpreted as a releasing signal for the cortex to switch from one plan to another.

This shifting hypothesis also may hold the key to the basal ganglia's role in learning. Dopamine is known to play a critical role in the reward systems of the brain, providing the organism with a neurochemical marker of the reinforcement contingencies that exist for different responses in the context of the current environment. Learning involves a change in behavior—either acquiring the appropriate response in an unfamiliar context or breaking a habitual response when contingencies change in a familiar context. For a rat in the wild, this might mean being sensitive to a change in the availability of food at a foraging site. For a human, it might mean recognizing that a demanding problem cannot be solved by conventional means. One can hypothesize that, within the basal ganglia, dopamine biases the system to produce certain responses over others. Dopamine release in the striatum follows successful actions. This transmitter may modify the input–output channels in the basal ganglia, making it more likely that the animal will shift to the previously rewarded action when the associated input pattern is reactivated in the future.

Viewed in this way, the ability to shift is required for producing novel behavior or for combining patterns of behavior into novel sequences. We can now see a link between basal ganglia dysfunction and psychiatric disorders such as Tourette's syndrome and obsessive-compulsive disorder. A cardinal feature in each syndrome is the repetitive production of stereotyped movement patterns. For the patient with Tourette's syndrome, such a pattern might be a simple tic, a flick of the shoulder, or a hand brushing across the face. For someone with obsessive-compulsive disorder, an entire behavioral sequence such as hand washing can be performed over and over again. A failure to shift may result in an absence of movement, the problem of the Parkinson's disease patient, or in the repeated production of a single pattern. In either case, basal ganglia dysfunction makes it difficult to select new actions that arise when sensory input or internal goals change.

Whether or not the shifting hypothesis is correct, it reveals a major feature of the cognitive neuroscience approach to brain function. Traditional neuroscience and neurology generally rely on task-based taxonomies such as motor or sensory systems. For the cognitive neuroscientist, the prime goal is to understand a neural structure's computational role, which can begin in a narrow domain but may also generalize to tasks that utilize a particular mental operation.

SUMMARY

Cognitive neuroscience has had a major impact on our conceptualization of how the brain produces skilled action. Consider the two halves of Figure 7.47. The diagram in Figure 7.47a, first introduced in 1974, shows the critical circuits of the motor pathway, emphasizing patterns of anatomical connectivity with a crude partitioning of function into motor planning, movement preparation, and movement execution. Figure 7.47b retains the basic circuitry but offers a functional decomposition of the processes involved in planning and programming.

As the figure shows, the control of action involves several distributed systems. Nonetheless, this distributed pattern does not necessarily suggest that all of the

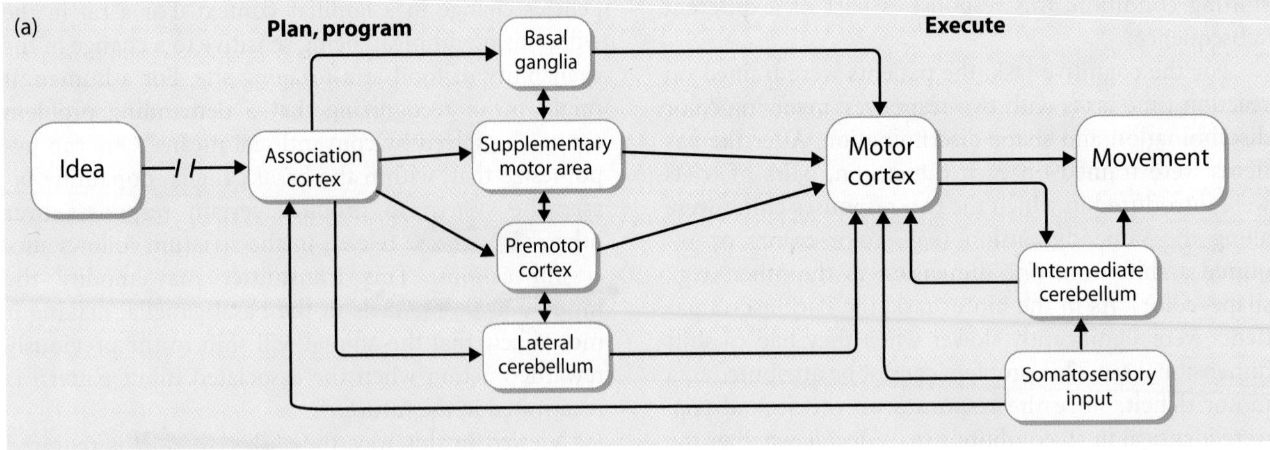

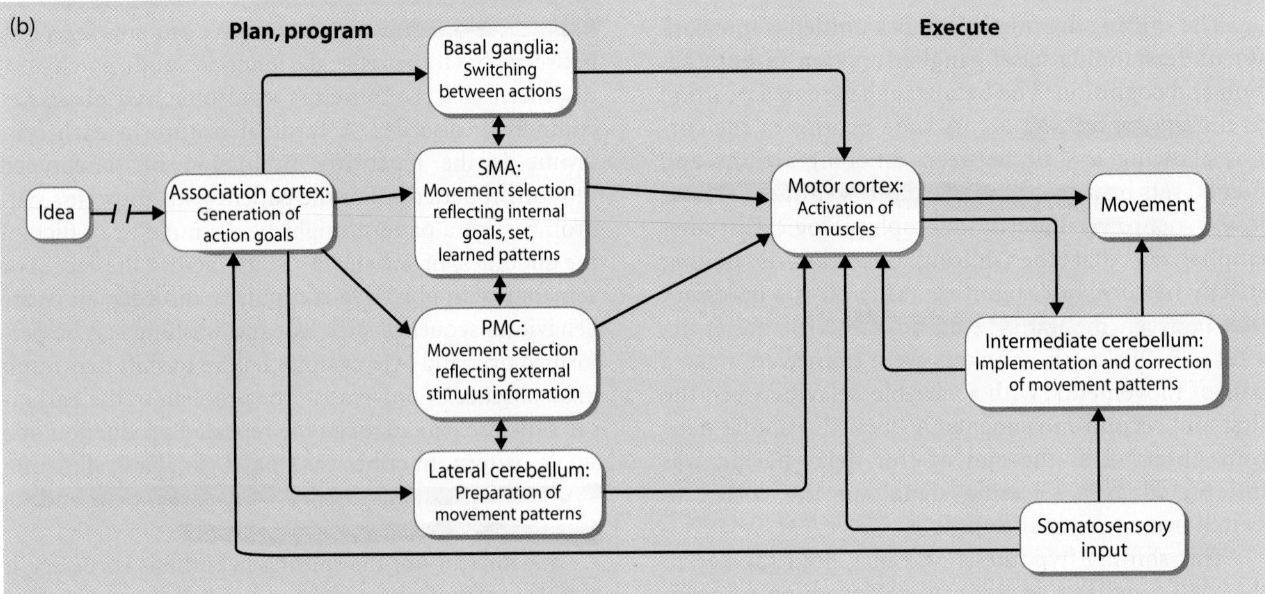

Figure 7.47 Functional architecture of the motor system. **(a)** Major neural structures, partitioned into areas associated with the planning and execution of movement. **(b)** Functional hypotheses for how these different structures contribute to actions.

systems operate in a similar manner. As with other processing domains, such as attention and memory, the different motor structures have their unique specializations. The cortical pathways for movement selection are biased to provide particular sources of information. The subcortical loops through the basal ganglia and cerebellum are essential for movement preparation, but in quite different ways.

By specifying a functional role for these structures, we can appreciate the limitations of brain theories that focus on the task rather than on the internal computations. For example, focusing on the fact that skilled movements are especially disrupted in patients with cerebellar lesions might lead us to conclude that the representation of an action shifts from one neural locus to another with practice. But when the cerebellum is viewed as a structure that is specialized to represent the temporal properties of a movement, we can see that the loss of skilled movements is a consequence of a breakdown in the fine timing. This computation would not be as important during the early phases of skill acquisition, when the person builds the representations that underlie the skill. Moreover, this functional analysis has made clear that the boundaries between perception and action are murky. In the same way that the parietal lobe is essential for both perceiving and acting in space, the timing functions of the cerebellum or shifting functions of the basal ganglia are not restricted to motor control. As noted at the beginning of this chapter, perceptual information is useful only to the extent that it facilitates behavior.

KEY TERMS

alpha motor neurons
apraxia
basal ganglia
bradykinesia
brain–machine interface (BMI)
cerebellum
corticospinal tract
deep-brain stimulation (DBS)
effector
endpoint control
extrapyramidal tracts
hemiplegia
Huntington's disease
ideational apraxia
ideomotor apraxia
mirror system
Parkinson's disease
population vector
premotor cortex
primary motor cortex (M1)
substantia nigra
supplementary motor area (SMA)

TAKE-HOME MESSAGES

General

- An important scientific breakthrough in the treatment of Parkinson's disease came from the tragic overdose of adults in San Jose, California, who thought they had taken heroin but instead had ingested MPTP, a chemical that selectively destroys dopaminergic cells. The discovery of the effect of MPTP allowed for the creation of animal models of Parkinson's disease and, thus, the massive increase in studies of Parkinson's disease treatment.

Anatomy of Action

- A part of the body that can move is referred to as an *effector.*
- Alpha motor neurons provide the primary communication between muscles and the nervous system.
- Alpha motor neurons originate in the spinal cord and terminate on the muscles, releasing the neurotransmitter acetylcholine and causing muscle contraction.
- Extrapyramidal tracts receive input from cortical and subcortical structures and send information to the spinal cord. The descending fibers originate in the brainstem.
- The corticospinal tract is also referred to as the *pyramidal tract.* These descending fibers originate in the cortex and project monosynaptically to the spinal cord.
- Primary motor cortex (Brodmann area 4) is anterior to the central sulcus. Most of the corticospinal fibers originate in this area.
- Brodmann area 6 includes secondary motor areas like the premotor cortex and the supplementary motor area.
- The primary and secondary motor cortices contain somatotopic representations.

Motor Hierarchy

- Motor areas are hierarchical: The lowest level is the spinal cord, from which motor neurons project to activate muscles. Subcortical and cortical areas, including motor cortex, can represent actions at more abstract levels corresponding to movement goals.
- Although areas higher on the motor hierarchy modulate activity, lower levels are sufficient for producing movement patterns.
- The stretch reflex is an important spinal mechanism for maintaining postural stability. It remains present in the absence of higher level commands. Descending motor signals must modulate stretch reflexes to produce voluntary movements.
- Motor plans represent the goals of motor actions. They can be location based (as in endpoint control), or they can be representations of distance or trajectory plans for an action.
- Motor learning can occur at a high level in the motor hierarchy, independent of the muscular system (as demonstrated by your ability to sign your name fairly well with your dominant hand, nondominant hand, toes, or even mouth).

Neural Coding of Movement

- A population vector is a representation of a movement formed by summation of the activity of many neurons, usually in primary or secondary motor cortex.
- Population vectors can be used to predict intended movement. When hooked up to a computer or robotic arm, the population vector can be used to control a computer cursor or robotic arm. Such brain–machine interfaces may prove useful for people who have lost mobility because of stroke or another neurological problem.

- Mirror neurons are neurons in premotor cortex and other areas (like the parietal lobe) that respond to an action, both when that action is produced by an animal and when the animal observes a similar action produced by another animal. For example, a mirror neuron might respond when the animal cracks a peanut, as well as when the animal watches someone else crack a peanut or hears the sound of a peanut cracking.
- Supplementary motor neurons tend to be active during internally guided movements; premotor neurons tend to be active during externally guided sequences. This distinction is not absolute but relative, reflecting the different sources of input to lateral and medial premotor cortex.

Motor Planning Circuits

- Parallel circuits are involved in motor planning.
- A circuit that includes the parietal lobe, lateral premotor, and cerebellar pathways is essential for producing spatially directed or guided movements. These movements dominate during the early stages of skill acquisition.
- A second circuit, associated with the supplementary motor area, basal ganglia, and perhaps the temporal lobe, becomes more dominant as the skill is well learned and driven by an internal representation of the desired action.
- Both circuits converge on the motor cortex, the primary link between the cortex and limbs for voluntary movements.

The Cerebellum

- The cerebellum is located at the base of the most posterior portion of the brain. It is divided into three parts: vestibulocerebellum, spinocerebellum, and neocerebellum.
- The vestibulocerebellum is innervated by the brainstem vestibular nuclei, and output is projected back to the same region. The output from the spinocerebellum originates in the medial cerebellar nuclei and innervates the spinal cord and nuclei of the extrapyramidal system. The neocerebellum is heavily innervated by the cerebral cortex and sends its output back to the cortex.
- One computational account of cerebellar function emphasizes a role in controlling the timing of movements. A variant of this idea is that the cerebellum provides predictions of forthcoming sensory events.

The Basal Ganglia

- The basal ganglia are a collection of five nuclei: the caudate, putamen, globus pallidus, subthalamic nucleus, and substantia nigra.
- Input to the basal ganglia is restricted primarily to the caudate and putamen, collectively called the *striatum*. Output from the basal ganglia originates in the internal segment of the globus pallidus and part of the substantia nigra.
- Motor control by the basal ganglia is cortically mediated via thalamic projections.
- There are two pathways within the basal ganglia: direct and indirect. The direct pathway consists of direct inhibitory projections from the striatum to the globus pallidus and substantia nigra; the indirect pathway also connects the striatum to these output nuclei, but only through intervening processing stages involving the external segment of the globus pallidus and the subthalamic nucleus.
- All of the output signals from the basal ganglia are inhibitory. The basal ganglia can be hypothesized as playing a critical role in the initiation of actions, or the ability to shift actions to those that are most often rewarded.

Motor Disorders

- Hemiplegia most frequently results from a hemorrhage in the middle cerebral artery and results in a loss of voluntary movements on the side of the body contralateral to the lesion.
- Apraxia is characterized by coordination deficits that cannot be attributed to hemiplegia, motoric problems of weakness, sensory loss, or motivation.
- In ideomotor apraxia, a patient appears to have a sense of what the desired action is but cannot execute the action properly.
- In ideational apraxia, the patient's knowledge about the intent of an action is disrupted. This deficit often manifests itself in the loss of knowledge of proper tool use.
- Apraxia is usually associated with left-hemisphere lesions, often in the parietal cortex.
- Damage to the cerebellum produces ataxia in which movements become uncoordinated and erratic.
- Parkinson's disease results from cell death in the substantia nigra, a brainstem nucleus that is part of the basal ganglia.
- Parkinson's disease includes disorders of posture and locomotion, hypokinesia (the absence or reduction of voluntary movement), and bradykinesia (slowness in initiating and executing movement).
- The drug L-dopa is used in treating Parkinson's disease because it is effective in compensating for the loss of endogenous dopamine.
- Deep-brain stimulation is a surgical technique in which electrodes are chronically implanted in the

brain. This procedure has become a novel treatment for Parkinson's disease with implants usually placed in the subthalamic nucleus.

- Huntington's disease is a progressive degenerative disorder that appears in the fourth or fifth decade of life. It is characterized by clumsiness, balance problems, restlessness, and involuntary movements (or chorea). Atrophy is most prominent in the basal ganglia, especially the striatum. Huntington's disease has a strong genetic component.

THOUGHT QUESTIONS

1. Viewed both from a functional perspective and from a neuroanatomical/neurophysiological perspective, motor control is organized hierarchically. Outline this hierarchy, starting with the most basic or primitive aspects of motor behavior and progressing to the highest level or most sophisticated aspects of motor behavior.
2. What is the difference between the pyramidal and extrapyramidal motor pathways? What type of movement disorder would you expect to see if the pyramidal tract were damaged? How would extrapyramidal damage differ?
3. What types of movements are possible without feedback? How might feedback be used by the motor system, both for online control and for learning?
4. Explain the concept of the population vector. How could it be used to control a prosthetic (artificial) limb?
5. Why do people with Parkinson's disease have difficulty moving? Provide an explanation based on the physiological properties of the basal ganglia. Why does dopamine replacement therapy improve their condition?

SUGGESTED READING

GEORGOPOULOS, A. P. (1995). Motor cortex and cognitive processing. In M. S. Gazzaniga (Ed.), *The cognitive neurosciences* (pp. 507–517). Cambridge, MA: MIT Press.

JEANNEROD, M. (1997). *The cognitive neuroscience of action.* Cambridge, MA: Blackwell.

LEBEDEV, M. A., & NICOLELIS, M. A. (2006). Brain-machine interfaces: Past, present, and future. *Trends in Neurosciences, 29,* 536–546.

RIZZOLATTI, G., FOGASSI, L., & GALLESE, V. (2000). Cortical mechanisms subserving object grasping and action recognition: A new view on the cortical motor functions. In M. Gazzaniga (Ed.), *The new cognitive neurosciences* (2nd ed., pp. 539–552). Cambridge, MA: MIT Press.

SHADMEHR, R., & WISE, S. P. (2005). *The computational neurobiology of reaching and pointing.* Cambridge, MA: MIT Press.

8

Learning and Memory

As a child, H.M. suffered from a form of epilepsy that was very difficult to treat. His epilepsy progressed in severity during his teenage years. He was, however, successful in completing high school, after which he worked in a factory winding wire in electrical motors. Over the years H.M.'s physicians had tried to manage his disease with the available drugs to minimize his seizures. Although these drugs worked well for some people, they were, unfortunately, largely ineffective for H.M. During his 20s, H.M.'s seizures worsened and prevented him from working, so he decided to try a then radical new therapy that involved surgery.

It was the 1950s. At that time neurologists knew that many seizures originate in the medial portions of the temporal lobe and from there can spread to other areas of the brain, leading to violent seizures and often to the loss of consciousness. It was also becoming increasingly clear that surgically removing the brain region in which the seizure activity originated, the so-called seizure focus, could help patients with epilepsy. The decision in H.M.'s case was to remove his medial temporal lobe bilaterally, in a procedure called *temporal lobectomy*.

After H.M. recovered from this major neurosurgical procedure, his epilepsy did improve. In fact, it improved enough to permit a reduction in the dosage of his epilepsy drugs. The surgery was a success, with regard to both his survival of the risks associated with any surgery of the brain and the improvement in his epilepsy. However, physicians, family, and friends soon realized that H.M. was now experiencing new difficulties. For example, H.M. could not remember meeting certain individuals, even when he had spoken with them a few minutes earlier and they merely left the room, returning after a short delay! H.M. was profoundly amnesic; that is, he suffered from a disorder of memory. However, H.M. did not have the kind of **amnesia** one usually sees depicted in television shows or movies, in which the character has lost all prior personal memories. In fact, H.M. knew who he was and could remember things about his life—but only up until a period prior to his surgery. The doctors and scientists who studied him soon realized the root of his problem: H.M. could not form *new* long-term memories.

The surgeons who performed the surgery on H.M. did not know that bilateral removal of the medial temporal lobes would lead to severe amnesia, because prior to this case, no such surgery had been performed. Ever since H.M.'s case was revealed, surgeons have taken great care to avoid removing both medial temporal lobes, and even one medial temporal lobe if the other is compromised in any way because of prior damage or disease. This adapted form of the surgery, known as *unilateral temporal lobectomy*, is still used with success today for certain patients suffering from epilepsy.

Learning and remembering information about the world around us are key cognitive abilities that we all share. Remarkably, we retain millions of pieces of information, sometimes with ease and sometimes with tremendous effort. Most people have no difficulty remembering a particular birthday party that took place during their youth. What may stand out vividly are the taste and color of the cake, the friends who attended, and some gifts. For salient events such as a birthday party, it is amazing how much we can recall about that special day. But what about the birthday party from the year before or the year after? Or what we did the next day?

Memory has the peculiar quality of being incomplete, and yet the totality of life's accumulated experiences is immense. Despite the vast stores of information contained in our brains, we continuously acquire new information and form new memories. How is it possible that we can recall the first day of school, the hair color of our best friend in first grade, or the smell of our grandmother's apple strudel as we entered her home for one of those memorable weekend visits?

We search for neural correlates of learning and memory in many ways: by developing animal models of memory in simple systems (invertebrates) and more complex systems (rodents and nonhuman primates); through studies of patients like H.M., which reveal what is and is not lost in amnesia; and with brain imaging and monitoring to investigate normal learning and memory in healthy humans. In this chapter we explore what is known about the neuroscience of learning and memory.

THEORIES OF LEARNING AND MEMORY

What is the relationship between learning and memory? Put simply, **learning** is the process of acquiring new information, the outcome of which is **memory**. That is, a memory is created when something is learned, and this learning may occur either by a single exposure to the information, or by repetition of the information. Memory is necessarily something that persists over time.

Learning and memory can be subdivided into three major hypothetical stages:

1. **Encoding** is the processing of incoming information to be stored and has two separate steps: acquisition and consolidation. **Acquisition** registers inputs in sensory buffers and sensory analysis stages; **consolidation** creates a stronger representation over time.
2. **Storage**, the result of acquisition and consolidation, represents the permanent record of the information.
3. **Retrieval** utilizes stored information to create a conscious representation or to execute a learned behavior such as a motor act.

Models of memory include distinctions among sensory memory, short-term memory, and long-term memory, which are based on how long information is retained. **Sensory memory** has a lifetime measurable in milliseconds to seconds, as when we recover what someone said to us a moment ago even though we were not paying close attention at the time. **Short-term memory** is associated with retention over seconds to minutes. This category may include remembering a phone number provided by a telephone operator as we frantically try to dial it. **Long-term memory** is measured in days or years—an event from childhood or from last week, for example. The various types of short-term and long-term memory are discussed in detail in the sections that follow and summarized in Table 8.1.

Sensory and Short-Term Memory Mechanisms

Memory, as noted, implies a temporal component. We remember things over time—short periods and long periods. This inherent characteristic of memory led University of Toronto's Endel Tulving, one of the leaders in research on memory, to describe some forms of memory as "mental time travel." By this, Tulving meant that the act of remembering something that happened in the past is to reexperience that past in the present. Hence, it is meaningful to characterize memory by how long we retain the information of interest.

SENSORY MEMORY

While you are watching the final game of the World Cup, with the score tied and seconds to go, your father enters the room and begins a soliloquy, but you're not really paying attention. Suddenly you detect an increase in the volume of his voice and hear the words, "You haven't heard a word I said!" Wisely, your response is not to admit it, but instead, in the nick of time to avoid repercussions, you metaphorically reach back and retrieve the most recent sentence with enough accuracy to say, "Sure I did, you said that the neighbor's cat is in our yard again and you want me to call her to complain."

Almost everyone you ask about this phenomenon knows what you mean. The auditory verbal information just presented to you seems to persist as a sort of echo in your head, even when you are not really paying attention to it. But if you attempt to retrieve it quickly enough, you find it is still there, and you can repeat it

Table 8.1 Types of Memory

TYPE OF MEMORY	Time Course	Capacity	Conscious Awareness?	Mechanism of Loss
	CHARACTERISTIC OF MEMORY			
Sensory	Milliseconds to seconds	High	No	Primarily Decay
Short-Term and Working	Seconds to minutes	Limited (7 ± 2 items)	Yes	Primarily Decay
Long-Term Nondeclarative	Days to years	High	No	Primarily Interference
Long-Term Declarative	Days to years	High	Yes	Primarily Interference

out loud to assuage your interrogator. We refer to this type of memory as *sensory memory*, which, for audition, we call *echoic memory*. For vision, we say *iconic memory*. What is the nature of this effect? We can begin to answer this question by considering the time course of these sensory memories.

Cognitive neuroscience approaches have been employed to investigate the time course of auditory sensory memory and to identify where in the brain it is stored. The persistence of the auditory sensory memory trace has been measured by recording of a human event-related brain potential known as the electrical *mismatch negativity* (*MMN*), or its magnetic counterpart, the *mismatch field* (*MMF*). The brain responses are recorded either by electrodes placed on the head (MMN) or with magnetic sensors placed near the scalp (MMF) (see Chapter 4 for a review of these methods). The MMN brain response is elicited by the presentation of a *deviant* stimulus, such as a high-frequency tone presented within a sequence of identical *standard* low tones. These mismatch responses are interpreted as representing sensory memory processes that hold recent auditory experience in echoic memory for comparison to new inputs because when the inputs differ, the MMN and MMF are generated. Hence, the amplitudes of these brain responses at different time intervals between the deviant and standard tones could be used to index how long the echoic memory trace persists.

Mikko Sams, Ritta Hari, and their colleagues (1993) at the Helsinki University of Technology in Finland did precisely that. They varied the interstimulus intervals between standard and deviant tones and found that the MMF could still be elicited by the deviant tone at interstimulus intervals of 9 to 10 s (Figure 8.1). After about 10 s the amplitude of the MMF declined to the point where it could no longer be distinguished reliably from noise. Because the MMN/MMF is known to be generated in the auditory cortex, these physiological studies also provide information about where sensory memories are stored: They are stored in sensory cortex as a short-lived neural trace.

What about the time course of the neural trace for a visual sensory memory? Does it also last several seconds? No, and you know this is true because when you

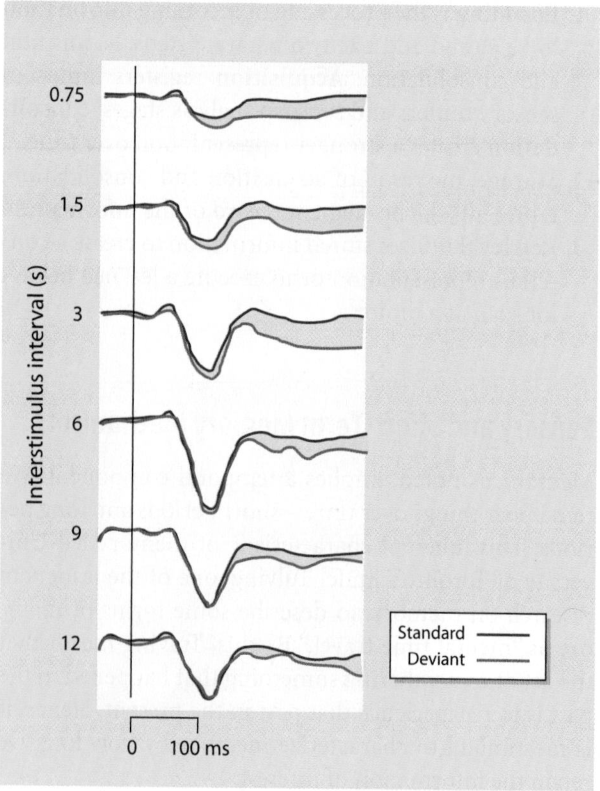

Figure 8.1 The magnetic brain response known as the *mismatch field* (*MMF*) elicited by deviant tones (blue trace) in comparison to the magnetic responses elicited by standard tones (red traces). The amplitude of the MMF (indicated by the shaded difference between the blue and red traces) declines as the time between the preceding standard tone and the deviant tone increases to 12 s. This result can be interpreted as evidence for an automatic process in auditory sensory (echoic) memory that has a time course on the order of approximately 10 s.

see your mother's face and turn away, the image does not persist very long. Most estimates of the time course of visual sensory memory suggest that the neural trace for a visual stimulus lasts only 300 to 500 ms. However, both echoic and iconic sensory memory have a relatively high capacity: A lot of information can be retained for a very short period of time.

SHORT-TERM MEMORY

In contrast to sensory memory, *short-term memory* has a longer time course—seconds to minutes—and a much more limited capacity. We will explore short-term memory in depth in the discussion of models of memory that follows.

Models of Short-Term Memory

The early data on short-term memory led to some influential models that proposed discrete stages of information processing during learning and memory. One of these, the *modal model*, represents a way of viewing data generated by studies on sensory memory, short-term memory, and long-term memory.

Cognitive psychologists Richard Atkinson and Richard Shiffrin (1968), then at Stanford University, elaborated the details of the modal model (Figure 8.2). Information is first stored in sensory memory. Items selected by attentional processes (see Chapter 12) can move into short-term storage. Once in short-term memory, if the item is rehearsed it can be moved into long-term memory. The Atkinson and Shiffrin modal model suggests that, at each stage, information can be lost by *decay* (information degrades and is lost over time), *interference* (new information displaces old information), or a combination of both. This model formalized the idea that discrete stages of memory exist and that they have different characteristics. In addition, this model has a strong serial structure: Information coming into the sensory memory can be passed to short-term memory and only then into long-term memory.

Figure 8.2 The Atkinson and Shiffrin modal model of memory. Sensory information enters the information-processing system and is first stored in a sensory register. Items that are selected via attentional processes are then moved into short-term storage. With rehearsal, the item can move from short-term to long-term storage.

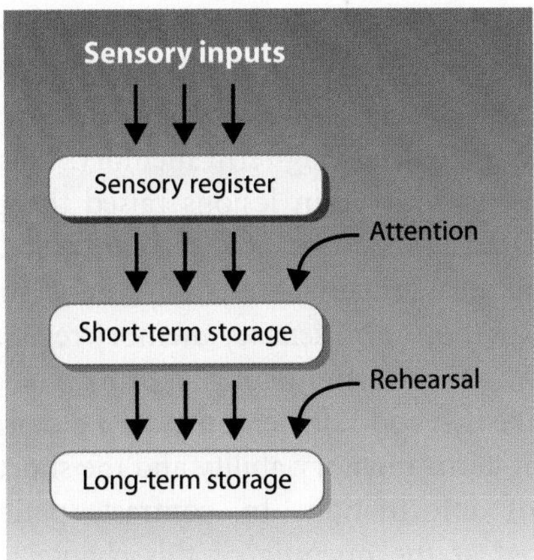

In the ensuing decades there has been intense debate in both the psychology of memory and the neuroscience of memory over this model, with data being presented to support, challenge, and extend the model. A key question is whether memories have to be encoded in short-term memory prior to being stored in long-term memory. Another way to look at this question is to ask whether the brain systems that retain information over the short term are the same or different from those that store information over the long term. Atkinson and Shiffrin pondered this themselves, writing in 1971, "Our account of short-term and long-term storage does not require that the two stores necessarily be in different parts of the brain or involve different physiological structures. One might consider the short-term store simply as being a temporary activation of some portion of the long-term store" (p. 89).

COGNITIVE NEUROSCIENCE EVIDENCE ABOUT SHORT-TERM MEMORY

Studies of patients with brain damage permit a test of the hierarchically structured modal model of memory. As introduced earlier in the chapter, in the story of H.M. (who will be described in more detail shortly), the effect of brain damage on memory function can help place constraints on cognitive models, and it is an important tool in cognitive neuroscience.

In 1969, neuropsychologists Tim Shallice and Elizabeth Warrington at University College London reported a patient (K.F.) with damage to the left perisylvian cortex (the region around the Sylvian fissure). K.F. displayed reduced digit span ability (about two items, as opposed to five to nine items for healthy persons). *Digit span* refers to how many items a person can hold in memory over a short period of time. The test is to read the subjects lists of digits to remember and repeat after a short delay of only a few seconds. The lists can be two, three, four, five, or more digits long, and the maximum number that the person can recall and report is the digit span.

Remarkably, however, K.F. still retained the ability to form certain types of new long-term memories that

HOW THE BRAIN WORKS

Short-Term Memory Capacity

Short-term memory is limited, but how limited? Precisely how much information a healthy person can retain in short-term memory varies among individuals. However, experiments have demonstrated an interesting characteristic of human memory. In the 1950s, George Miller (see Figure 1.19 in Chapter 1) investigated how much information individuals can process. Although the initial work centered on perception, the research has been extended to memory for the retention of items.

Volunteers were presented with items to be remembered, in groups of varying size. The results were amazing: Regardless of the content of the items (e.g., digits, letters, or words), the number of items that were retained typically proved to be about seven. When more than seven items were presented, volunteers were less successful at recalling all of them. Miller referred to this characteristic feature of human memory as the *span of immediate memory*, or, in the terminology we have been using up to now, the *span of short-term memory*. When digits are used, this feature is referred to as *digit span*, and it is commonly measured in neuropsychological tests.

The memory limits discovered in these studies are defined by the number of items, not the content of each item, so they tell us about the way information is coded in short-term stores. This distinction has sometimes been cast as the difference between a *bit* of information and a *chunk*—a *bit* being the elementary piece of information, and a *chunk* being a unit composed of bits. The use of words allows individual letters to be chunked into one meaningful piece of information. The word *cerebellum* is either 10 letters or one word. If 10 letters have to be remembered, the short-term memory system is taxed, but if the letters can be chunked as one word (*cerebellum*), then about seven of these chunks (or words) can be remembered. The consequence of this chunking is that, during recall of the material, the chunked information can be essentially unpacked (unchunked) to yield more bits of information than could normally be retained. That is, if we can retain in our memory 7 words of 10 letters each, we can unpack them into 70 bits of information by using knowledge about word spelling. This evidence points to the ability of humans to recode information in manageable packets, packets that can be handled within the constraints of short-term memory.

could last much longer than a few seconds, and therefore the patient displayed a very interesting dissociation between short-term and long-term memory. This finding has important implications for models of memory because the data support the idea that short-term memory might not be required in order to form long-term memory, in contrast to the flow of information in the modal model described earlier.

A more recent example of a similar patient comes from the work of Hans Markowitsch and colleagues (1999) at Bielefeld University in Germany. Their patient, E.E., had a tumor centered in the left angular gyrus, affecting the inferior parietal cortex and posterior superior temporal cortex (Figure 8.3), regions similar to but slightly different from those affected in Shallice and Warrington's patient, K.F. After the tumor was removed surgically, E.E. showed below-normal short-term memory ability but preserved long-term memory—a pattern similar to K.F.'s. E.E. showed normal speech production and comprehension and normal reading comprehension. But he had a highly selective deficit in short-term memory, which included poor short-term memory for abstract verbal material and deficits when working with numbers (transposing numbers from numerical to verbal and vice versa), although he could calculate normally. Interestingly, on tests of his visuospatial short-term memory and both verbal and nonverbal long-term memory, E.E. performed normally.

The pattern of behavior displayed by these patients demonstrates a deficit of short-term memory abilities but a preservation of long-term memory. This evidence from patients with brain lesions raised the possibility that short-term memory is not the gateway to long-term memory in the manner laid out in the modal model. Perhaps information from sensory memory registers can be encoded into long-term memory directly. The data from patients like K.F. and E.E. demonstrate a dissociation between long-term memory ability and the short-term retention of information. In contrast, patient H.M. (introduced at the opening of this chapter) had pre-

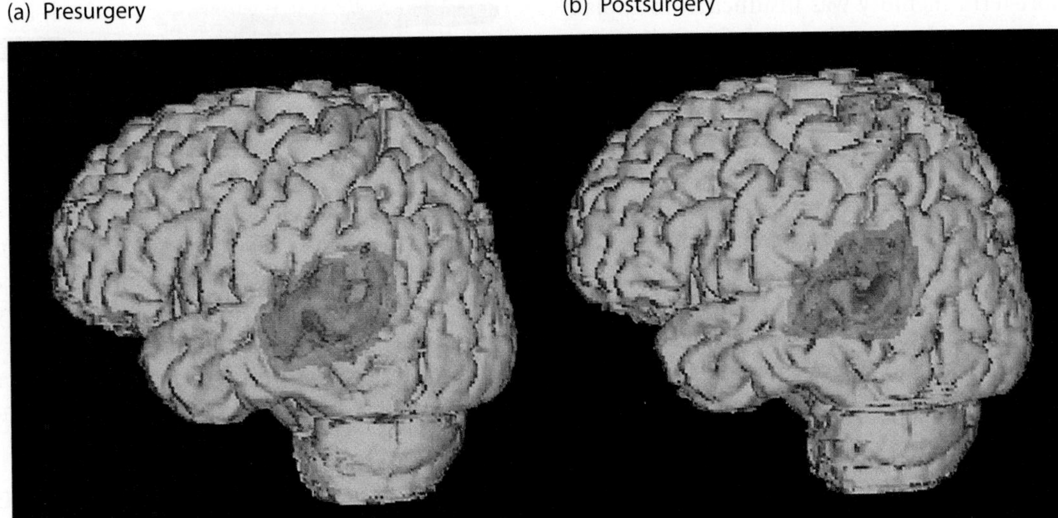

Figure 8.3 MRI scans reconstructed to provide a three-dimensional rendering of patient E.E.'s left hemisphere. E.E. had selective deficits in short-term memory. Part **(a)** shows the reconstructed scan taken prior to surgery; part **(b)**, the scan taken after surgery. The area of the tumor is indicated by shading. Positron emission tomography (PET) with a radiolabeled methionine tracer was used to identify the tumor according to its increased metabolic profile in comparison to that of surrounding brain tissue (red).

served short-term memory but lost the ability to form new long-term memories. Together, the two different patterns of memory deficit exhibited by K.F./E.E. and H.M. provide an apparent double dissociation for retention of information over the short and long term, in terms of both the memory processes and the underlying neuroanatomy (lesions of left perisylvian cortex for K.F. and E.E. versus medial temporal lobe lesions for H.M.).

As described in Chapter 4, a double dissociation is the strongest pattern of effects that can be obtained in attempts to identify and distinguish two mental processes. But whether a true double dissociation is demonstrated by these interesting patient case studies remains controversial. It has been argued that the evidence from these patient cases does not support a strong double dissociation of short- and long-term memory, because the types of memory being tested in the short-term memory tests is quite different from the types tested in the long-term memory tests. Importantly, even patients like K.F. and E.E. show deficits in long-term memory when tested carefully by means of memory tests that equate the types of information to be retained over the short term and the long term. This evidence challenges the conclusion that patients like K.F. and E.E. demonstrate the involvement of different brain systems in supporting short-term and long-term storage of information.

The emerging alternative view is that short-term memory is supported by activation of the same neural networks that are involved in storing long-term memory, but not in precisely the same fashion or to the same extent—a view foreshadowed by Atkinson and Shiffrin's proposition. These issues are clearly laid out in reviews by Zola-Morgan and Squire (1993) and Ranganath and Blumenfeld (2005); the latter source is included in the "Suggested Reading" list for this chapter.

WORKING MEMORY

The concept of working memory was developed to extend the concept of short-term memory and to elaborate the kinds of mental processes that are involved when information is retained over a period of seconds to minutes. These terms are sometimes used interchangeably in the memory literature, but here we make a distinction between short-term memory and working memory, as follows. **Working memory** represents a limited-capacity store for retaining information over the short term (*maintenance*) and for performing mental operations on the contents of this store (*manipulation*). The contents of working memory could either originate from sensory inputs by way of sensory memory (as in the modal model) or could be retrieved from long-term memory, and this latter point is an important idea. In each case, working memory contains information that can be acted on and processed, not merely maintained by rehearsal, although such maintenance is one aspect of working memory.

In their formulation of working memory in the 1970s, British psychologists Alan Baddeley and Graham Hitch (1974) at the University of York proposed that a unitary short-term memory was insufficient to explain the maintenance and processing of information over short periods. They constructed a three-part working memory system consisting of a central executive mechanism for controlling two subordinate systems involved in rehearsal of different types of information: phonological and visuospatial.

The *central executive mechanism* is a command-and-control center that presides over the interactions between two subordinate systems that are short-term memory stores (the phonological "loop" and the visuospatial "sketch pad") and long-term memory. The central executive is not specific to any one sensory modality and is a cognitive system that coordinates processes in working memory.

The *phonological loop* is a hypothesized mechanism for acoustically coding information in working memory (thus it is modality specific). The evidence for modality specificity first came from studies that asked subjects to recall strings of consonants. The letters were presented visually, but the pattern of recall errors indicated that perhaps the letters were not coded visually over the short term. The subjects were apparently using an acoustic code, because during recall they were more likely to replace a presented letter with an erroneous letter having a similar sound (e.g., *T* for *G*) rather than one with a similar shape (e.g., *Q* for *G*). The idea is that *tee* and *gee* are acoustically more similar that *kyu* and *gee*, even though the round letter *Q* is more similar to *G* in appearance. This was the first insight suggesting that an acoustic code might participate in rehearsal.

In line with this idea is evidence that immediate recall of lists of words is poorer when many words on the list sound similar than when they sound dissimilar, even when the latter are semantically related. This finding indicates that an acoustic but not a semantic code is used in working memory, because words that sound similar interfere with one another, whereas words related by meaning do not. The phonological loop might have two parts: a short-lived acoustic store for sound inputs and an articulatory component that plays a part in the subvocal rehearsal of visually presented items to be remembered over the short term.

The *visuospatial sketch pad* is a short-term memory store that parallels the phonological loop and permits information storage in either purely visual or visuospatial codes. Evidence for this system came from dissociations between verbal and visuospatial codes. The idea is that, if two codes are separate, they should not interfere with one another in working memory. If some information is coded acoustically, the introduction of a secondary visuospatial task during the retention interval should not disrupt performance. Indeed, acoustic and visuospatial codes are found to be separate; what emerges from these studies is the concept of a working memory mechanism with a central executive and two independent subsystems (the phonological loop and the visuospatial sketch pad) (Figure 8.4).

The contribution of the working memory conceptualization to models of short-term memory is that it fills in details about the relation between short-term and long-term memory. Further, the working memory concept does not assume a unitary short-term store but allows for different types of information (phonological and visuospatial) to be coded separately over the short term.

COGNITIVE NEUROSCIENCE EVIDENCE ABOUT WORKING MEMORY MECHANISMS

Deficits in short-term memory abilities, such as remembering items on a digit span test, can be correlated with damage to subcomponents of the working memory sys-

Figure 8.4 Simplified representation of the working memory model proposed by Baddeley and Hitch. This three-part working memory system has a *central executive* that controls two subordinate systems: the *phonological loop*, by which information can be phonologically (acoustically) coded in working memory; and the *visuospatial sketch pad*, by which information is visually coded in working memory.

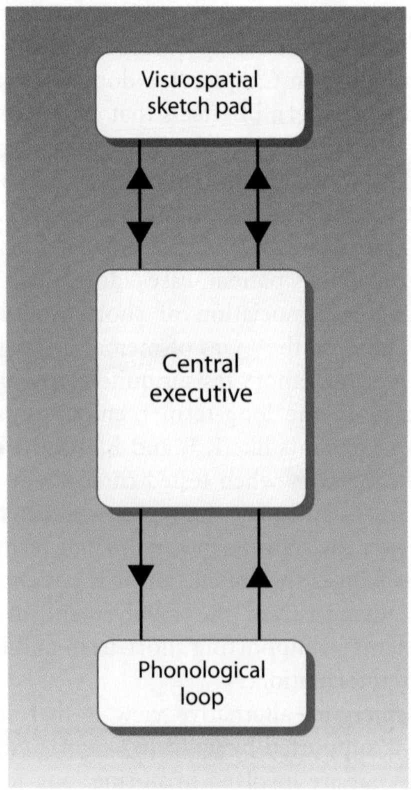

tem. Evidence about the distinct nature of these subsystems and their anatomical substrates in the human brain first came from studies of patients with specific brain lesions. Indeed, each system can be damaged selectively by different brain lesions.

Lesions of the left supramarginal gyrus (Brodmann area 40) lead to deficits in phonological working memory (Figure 8.5; see also Figure 8.3). Patients with lesions to this area have reduced auditory–verbal memory spans; they cannot hold strings of words in working memory. The rehearsal process of the phonological loop involves a region in the left premotor region (area 44). Thus, a left-hemisphere network consisting of the lateral frontal and inferior parietal lobes is involved in phonological working memory. These deficits in working memory for auditory–verbal material (digits, letters, words) have not been found to be associated with deficits in speech perception or production. This distinction between aphasia—language deficits following brain damage (see Chapter 10)—and deficits in auditory–verbal short-term memory is important to keep in mind.

The visuospatial sketch pad is compromised by damage to the parieto-occipital region of both hemispheres, but damage to the right hemisphere produces more severe deficits in visuospatial short-term memory. Patients with lesions in the right parieto-occipital region have difficulty with nonverbal visuospatial working memory tasks like retaining and repeating the sequence of blocks touched by another person. For example, if an investigator touches blocks on a table in sequences that the patient must repeat, and gradually increases the number of blocks touched, patients with parieto-occipital lesions show below-normal performance, even when their vision is otherwise normal. Similar lesions in the left hemisphere can lead to impairments in short-term memory for visually presented linguistic material.

Neuroimaging studies have helped to support this distinction. Using positron emission tomography (PET)

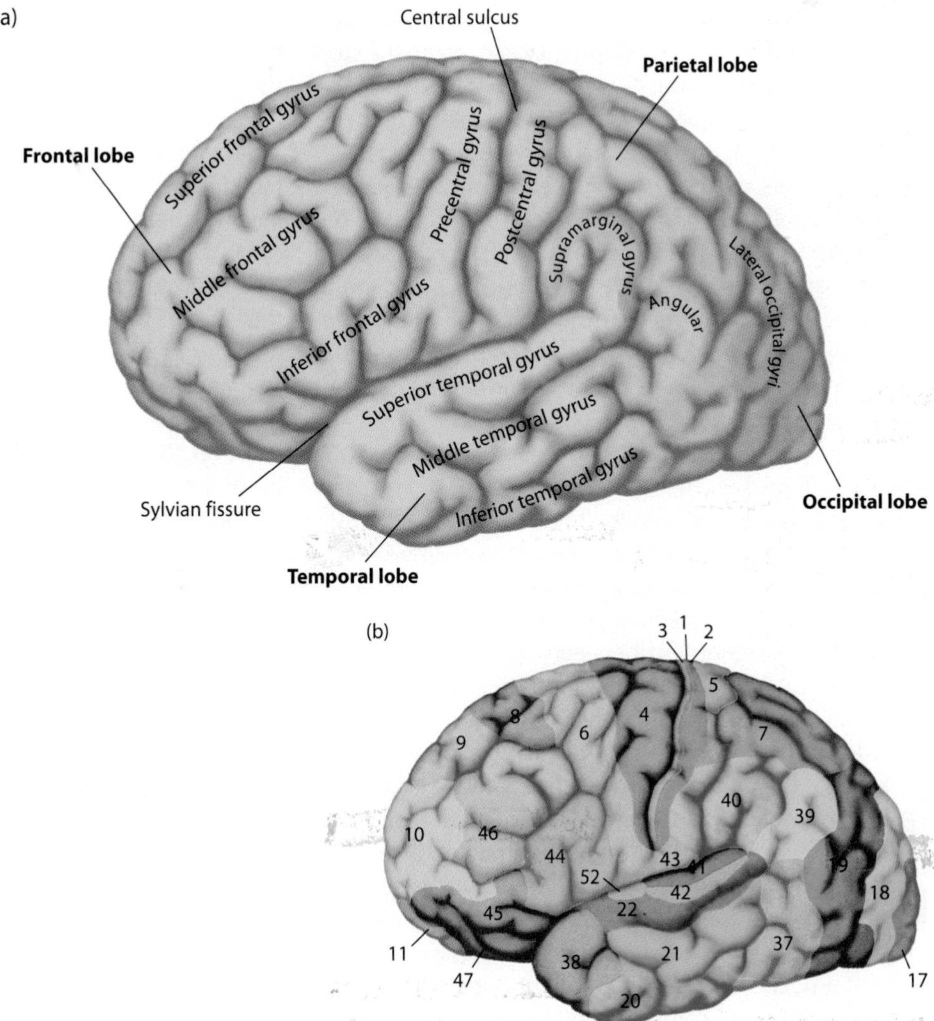

Figure 8.5 **(a)** Lateral view of the left hemisphere, indicating major sulci and gyri. **(b)** Representation of Brodmann's areas in the left hemisphere.

HOW THE BRAIN WORKS

Eyewitness Testimony

Every prosecutor in a criminal case knows that an eyewitness account is one of the most compelling types of evidence for establishing guilt. But is this type of testimony to be trusted? Elizabeth Loftus and her colleagues (Loftus & Greene, 1980; Loftus et al., 1978) illustrated the difficulty of relying on the recall of witnesses by showing subjects color slides detailing the time of an accident and, in a later test session, asking them what they saw. One of the slides showed a car at an intersection before it turned and hit a pedestrian. Half of the subjects viewed a red stop sign; the other half, a red yield sign. Subjects then answered questions about the slides: Half were presented with questions referring to the correct sign; the other half were asked questions referring to the incorrect sign. For example, a subject who was shown a yield sign might have been asked, "When the car came to the stop sign, did the driver stop?"

During subsequent recognition tests of whether a certain slide was what they had previously seen, 75% of the subjects correctly recognized a previously seen slide if the correct sign had also been mentioned in the questioning session. But when subjects previously had been questioned with the wrong sign being mentioned, only 41% correctly recognized the slides as previously seen or not seen. These findings indicate that recollections of an event can be influenced by misleading statements made during questioning.

Misinformation about things as obvious as hair color and the presence of a mustache can lead subjects to wrongly identify people they have seen previously. What does this say about the suggestibility of witnesses and the influence of misinformation on recall? Do witnesses really know the correct information but later fail to distinguish between their own memories and information supplied by another person? One line of thinking is that perhaps the information was not encoded initially, and when forced to guess, the subject provides the information given by someone else.

Not just adults are eyewitnesses in court cases. Children often are asked to testify as witnesses. Given that adults with fully developed memories have difficulty recalling what they have seen, how do young children with potentially underdeveloped memory systems behave under the pressures of authorities and courtrooms? This is a controversial issue because of situations in which children are eyewitnesses to crimes against themselves, such as child abuse or sexual abuse, in which they may be the only witnesses.

The question of how well children remember and report things that they have experienced is of special concern when the events may be traumatic. One effective way to study such conditions is to use events traumatic for children and to involve contact between them and others that can be verified. Physicians sometimes must perform genital examinations on children, which may include painful medical procedures. The children's memories of these events can be examined systematically. In one study, half of 72 girls between the ages of 5 and 7 years were given a genital examination as part of necessary medical care, and half were not. Children who received the examination were unlikely to report anything about the genital touch during free recall or when using anatomically detailed dolls. Only when asked leading questions did the majority of girls reveal that they had been so examined. The control group made no false reports during free recall or with the dolls, but with leading questions, three children made false reports.

Psychologist Gail Goodman and her colleagues (1994) at the University of California, Davis, emphasized that one of the most important predictors of accurate memory performance is age. Memory performance for traumatic events is significantly worse in children 3 to 4 years old than in older children. Dr. Goodman also noted, however, that other factors influence memory accuracy in children. Such factors include how well the traumatic episode is actually understood, the degree of parental emotional support and communication, and the children's emotional (positive versus negative) feelings.

The goal of this research is to determine the validity of children's reports on events—including negative ones such as abuse—that may have happened to them, and how they might invent stories. Of special interest is whether leading questions can induce children to fabricate testimony. We need to know this when interpreting children's testimony that involves other persons, such as therapists or members of the legal system. From the cognitive neuroscience perspective, it is important to know whether the neural signature of real and false memories might be different (see "How the Brain Works: False Memories and the Medial Temporal Lobes" on p. 350).

imaging (see Chapter 4), Edward Smith and his colleagues (1996) at Columbia University provided evidence for dissociations in the brain regions activated in healthy volunteers performing spatial versus verbal working memory tasks. They presented subjects with either an array of locations marked on a computer screen or an array of letters, and asked them to remember the locations or the letters during a delay period of 3 s. They then presented a location marker for the spatial memory task or a letter at fixation for the verbal memory task and asked subjects whether the location or letter had been in the original array. They found activation (increasing blood flow coupled to increased neural activity) in left-hemisphere sites in inferolateral frontal cortex, but activation primarily in right-hemisphere regions (inferior frontal, posterior parietal, and extrastriate cortex in the occipital lobe) for the spatial working memory task (Figure 8.6).

Impairments in working memory for phonological and visuospatial information, then, are associated with discrete lesions in distinct brain areas. However, the extent to which this can be taken as evidence that working memory and long-term memory are supported by wholly different brain systems is limited. In part, the same types of reasoning that we brought up earlier in this chapter when reviewing the patient lesion evidence regarding short-term memory apply here: Patients with lesions in perisylvian cortex or parieto-occipital regions that result in deficient working memory ability will also show deficits in long-term memory when tested appropriately. Further, as we will learn in the following sections, these areas are largely distinct from the areas associated with deficits in long-term memory. We will return to further discussion of the cognitive neuroscience of working memory in Chapter 13.

Models of Long-Term Memory

Information retained for a significant time is referred to as *long-term memory*. Theorists have tended to split long-term memory into two major divisions that reflect the characteristics of the information stored, and that take into account the observable fact that not all stored knowledge is the same. The key distinction is between declarative and nondeclarative memories.

Declarative memory is knowledge to which we have conscious access, including personal and world knowledge. In contrast, **nondeclarative memory** is knowledge to which we have no conscious access, such as motor and cognitive skills (procedural knowledge), perceptual priming, and simple learned behaviors that derive from conditioning, habituation, or sensitization. Figure 8.7 summarizes the essential relations of these forms of long-term memory.

DECLARATIVE MEMORY

Declarative memory can be broken down further into things that we recall about our own lives (*episodic memory*—i.e., the recall of events in our lives) and world knowledge (*semantic memory*) that does not relate to events in our lives, but is factual in nature. In the 1970s, psychologist Endel Tulving introduced this distinction between episodic and semantic memory. Examples of

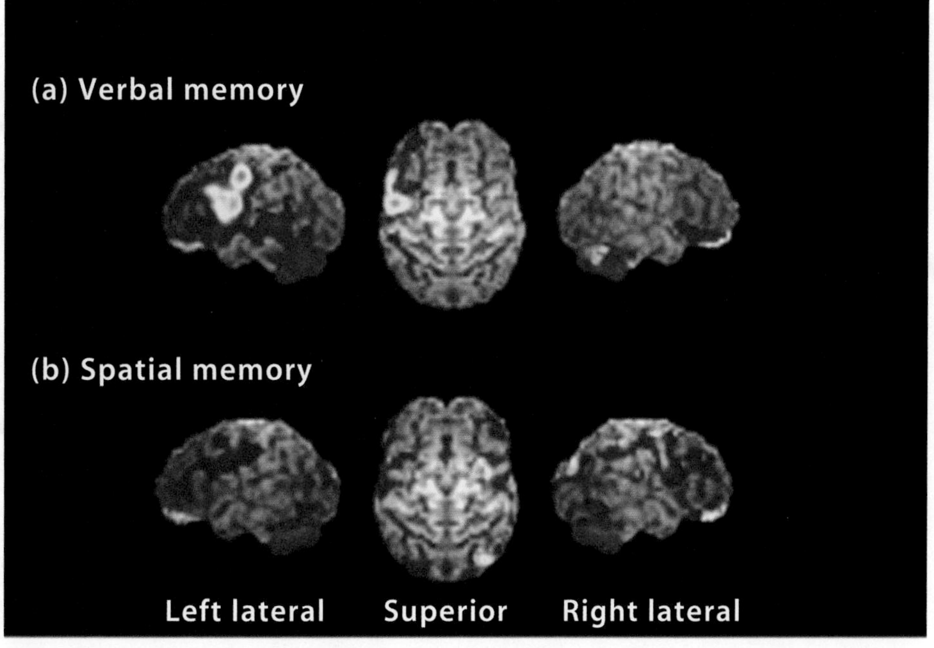

Figure 8.6 Changes in local cerebral blood flow, measured with positron emission tomography for verbal **(a)** and spatial **(b)** working memory tasks in healthy volunteers. In each part the views of the cortical surface show the left hemisphere **(left)**; superior (dorsal) surface of both hemispheres, with the frontal lobe at the top **(middle)**; and right hemisphere **(right)**. See text for details.

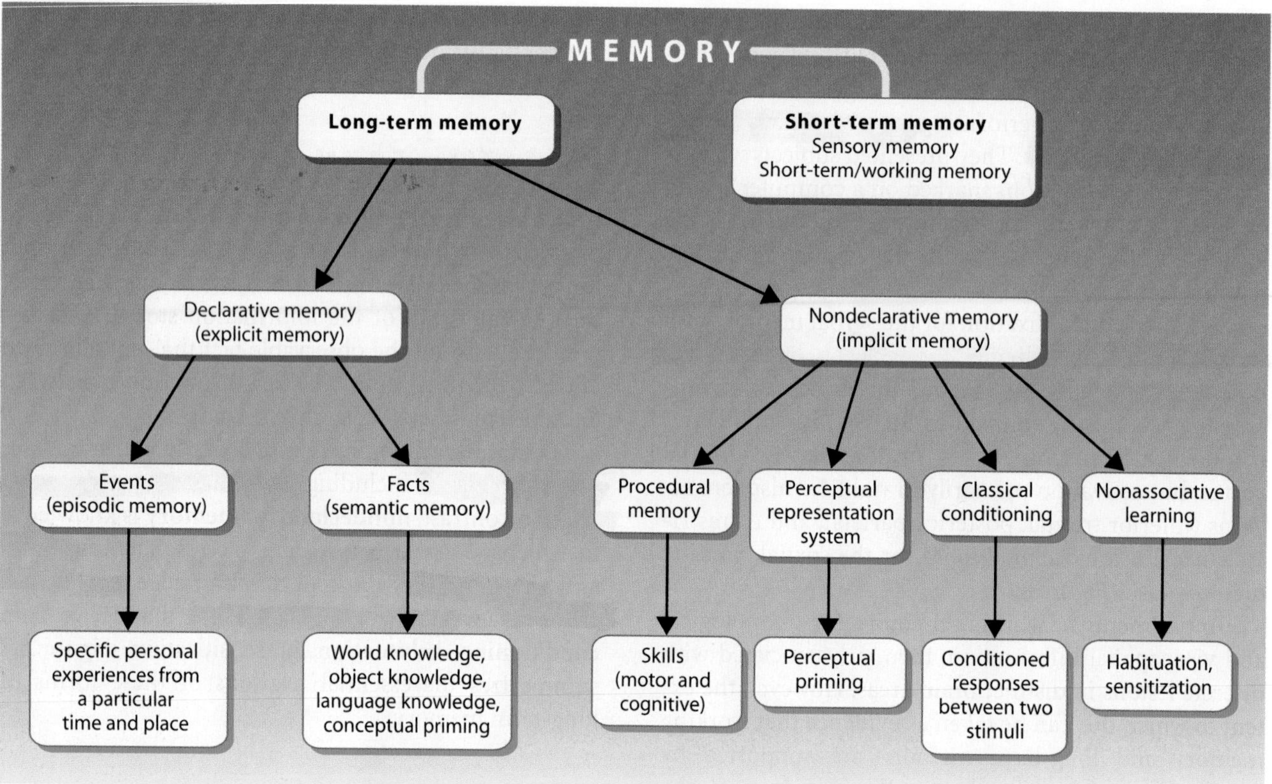

Figure 8.7 The hypothesized structure of human memory, diagramming the relationships among different forms of memory.

episodic memory include events in our personal history, such as meeting a friend for the first time, our 18th birthday party, or the time we fell off a new bicycle, badly skinning an elbow and scratching some of that beautiful red paint off the bike. Episodic memory involves conscious awareness of past events; it is our personal, autobiographical memory (Figure 8.8).

Semantic memory, in contrast, reflects knowing things such as how to tell time, who the 21st president was, how to cook an omelet, how to subtract two numbers, that rocks and animals are fundamentally different, that things we can sit on may (or may not) be chairs even if they look very different, and other similar facts and concepts. Semantic memory is world knowledge that we remember in the absence of any recollection of the specific circumstances surrounding its learning. That is, in the vast majority of cases, no episodic memory is associated with the semantic information. The take-home message is that world knowledge is fundamentally different from our recollection of events in our own lives.

When Tulving introduced this idea decades ago, the dominant thinking was that there is a unitary memory system, so if Tulving was right, which seems intuitively correct, then perhaps different underlying brain systems support these two different flavors of declarative long-term memory. We will turn to the cognitive neuroscience of long-term memory shortly, but first, let's take a look at the other major division of long-term memory.

NONDECLARATIVE MEMORY

One of the most exciting areas of memory research in the past decade or so has been nondeclarative memory. This form of memory is revealed when previous experiences facilitate performance on a task that does not require intentional recollection of the experiences.

Nondeclarative memory encompasses several forms of knowledge that we can observe on a day-to-day basis and that can be revealed with appropriately designed experimental testing. In Figure 8.7, which presents a taxonomy of memory, nondeclarative memory includes forms of memory that are learned and retained even when explicit memory for that knowledge does not exist. **Procedural memory** is one form of nondeclarative memory that involves the learning of a variety of motor skills (e.g., how to ride a bike) and cognitive skills (e.g., how to read).

One form of nondeclarative memory that acts within the perceptual system is known as the **perceptual representation system** (**PRS**). In the PRS, the structure

Figure 8.8 According to Tulving, animals like his cat have no episodic memory, although they have knowledge of many things. Tulving argues that they therefore do not remember past experiences the same way we do; they can merely know about such experiences.

and form of objects and words can be primed by prior experience. *Priming* refers to a change in the response to a stimulus or in the ability to identify a stimulus as the result of prior exposure to that stimulus. Forms of objects or words that have been presented previously (i.e., primed) are more easily recognizable (we are faster at identifying them) than are forms that have not previously been presented (not primed).

Two other domains of nondeclarative memory include *classical conditioning* and *nonassociative learning.* In classical conditioning, sometimes referred to as *Pavlovian conditioning*, a conditioned stimulus (CS; an otherwise neutral stimulus to the organism) is paired with an unconditioned stimulus (US; one that elicits an established response from the organism). Following this pairing, the conditioned stimulus can evoke a conditioned response (CR) similar to that typically evoked by the unconditioned stimulus (the unconditioned response, UR), as in the Nobel Prize–winning experiments of the Russian Ivan Pavlov (1849–1936) with his dogs, which started to salivate at the sound of a bell that Pavlov rang before he gave them food (Figure 8.9). Before conditioning, the bell was not associated with food and did not cause salivation. After conditioning in which the bell and the food were presented together, the bell (CS) caused salivation even in the absence of the food (US).

Nonassociative learning, as its name implies, does not involve the association of two stimuli to elicit a behavioral change. Rather it consists of forms of simple learning such as *habituation* (decrease in a response with repeated presentations of the stimulus) and *sensitization* (increase in a response with repeated presentations of the stimulus). We will not consider classical conditioning or nonassociative memory further in this chapter but instead will focus on the neural substrates of declarative (episodic and semantic memory) and nondeclarative memory (procedural memory and the perceptual representation system).

Summary of Memory Models

Memory theories include two main distinctions about how we learn and retain knowledge. The first is that different forms of memory can be defined by how long the information is retained. Thus, we have identified sensory memory, short-term memory (including working memory), and long-term memory. The second distinction is that memories can be characterized by their content and

Figure 8.9 Classical (Pavlovian) conditioning. When a stimulus is presented that has no meaning to an animal, such as the sound of a bell (CS), there is no response (NR) **(a)**. In contrast, presentation of a meaningful stimulus like food (US) generates an unconditioned response (UR) **(b)**. When the sound is paired with the food, however, the animal learns the association **(c)**; and later the now conditioned stimulus (CS) alone can elicit the response, which is now termed a conditioned response (CR) **(d)**.

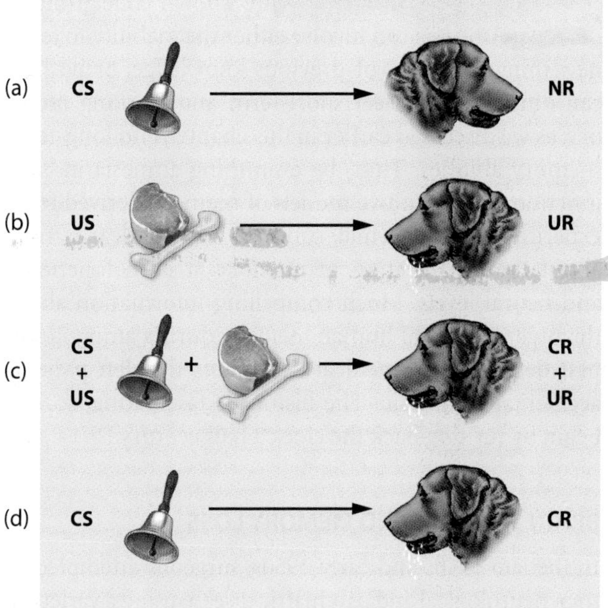

that different types of information may be retained in partially or wholly distinct memory systems.

For example, we have identified subtypes of long-term memory. The main distinction is the dichotomy between declarative and nondeclarative. Knowledge may be stored as declarative memories, which are memories about events from our lives (episodic memory), and world knowledge (semantic memory) to which we have conscious access and about which we can make declarations. Other forms of knowledge can be said to be nondeclarative, including procedural knowledge (e.g., how to ride a bike), perceptual priming, conditioned responses, and nonassociative learning. The information stored as nondeclarative memory is typically out of the reach of our conscious awareness.

A key question that remains is whether these various different types of memory are supported by different neural circuits and systems in the brain. If they were, then we would have converging evidence for the idea that these qualitatively different forms of learning and memory are reflections of distinct memory mechanisms—a view that remains controversial. Hence, in the next section we focus on the cognitive neuroscience of memory with a look at amnesia, including a detailed look at patient H.M., whom we met briefly at the opening of this chapter.

MEMORY AND BRAIN

The field of the cognitive and experimental psychology of memory is rich with theory and data and has produced a set of concepts about the organization of human memory. In the foregoing discussion we crystallized a vast literature into a few general concepts. In this section we turn to neuroscientific studies of memory, both to understand how they have contributed to general theories of memory and to investigate whether specific neural circuits and systems enable the learning and retention of specific forms of knowledge. The story is unfolding as we write and is one of the great challenges of cognitive neuroscience, and an enduring question facing humanity.

Human Memory, Brain Damage, and Amnesia

Deficits in memory as a function of brain damage, disease, or psychological trauma are known collectively as *amnesia.* Amnesia can involve either the inability to learn new things or a loss of previous knowledge, or both. It can differentially affect short-term and working memory, as we discussed earlier in this chapter, and long-term memory abilities. Thus, by examining amnesia in conjunction with cognitive models of memory derived from experiments on normal subjects, we can learn more about the organization of memory at both functional and neural levels. Much compelling information about the organization of human memory during amnesia was first derived from medical treatments that left patients accidentally amnesic. The history is fascinating, so let's begin by turning back the clock a half century.

BRAIN SURGERY AND MEMORY LOSS

In the late 1940s and early 1950s, surgeons attempted to treat neurological and psychiatric disease using a variety of neurosurgical procedures, including prefrontal lobotomy (removing or disconnecting the prefrontal lobe), corpus callosotomy (surgically sectioning the corpus callosum that connects the two hemispheres of the brain), amygdalectomy (removal of the amygdala), and temporal lobe resection (removal of the temporal lobe). These surgical procedures opened a new window on human brain function as they revealed, usually quite by accident, fundamentally important principles of the organization of human cognition. One surgical procedure relevant to memory was removal of the medial portion of the temporal lobe, including the hippocampal formation, so we return now to the story of H.M.

In 1953, at a meeting of the Harvey Cushing Society, a medical society, neurosurgeon William Beecher Scoville from the Hartford Hospital in Connecticut, reported on bilateral removal of the medial temporal lobe in one epileptic patient and several schizophrenic patients. Shortly thereafter he wrote this:

> Bilateral resection of the uncus, and amygdalum alone, or in conjunction with the entire pyriform amygdaloid hippocampal complex, has resulted in no marked physiologic or behavioral changes with the one exception of a very grave, recent memory loss, so severe as to prevent the patient from remembering the locations of the rooms in which he lives, the names of his close associates, or even the way to the toilet. (Scoville, 1954)

At the time, prefrontal lobotomy and orbitofrontal undercutting—a less radical method than lobotomy for treating severe mental disorders—had shown promise for treating severely psychotic patients. These procedures, confined to the prefrontal cortex, showed no other major side effects according to simple medical examination—patients did not lose memory, speech, motor skills, or other abilities. Because of the links between the orbitofrontal cortex and the medial temporal lobe, surgeons reasoned that further resections of the medial temporal lobe might ameliorate certain mental illnesses. As indicated in the quote from Scoville's work, however, the epileptic patient that he treated underwent similar surgery (without the orbitofrontal undercutting)—removal of the presumably abnormal brain tissue in the medial temporal lobe—to control his severe epilepsy. This patient, unfortunately, was not entirely unscathed following his surgery.

Together with psychologist Brenda Milner, Scoville began neuropsychological examination of his patients in earnest. The findings from 10 patients were reported by Scoville and Milner in 1957; the findings from two of these patients had been reported in Scoville's earlier publication. What Milner revealed was that, of the patients having medial temporal lobe resections as part of their treatment, the extent of the deficit in patients showing memory impairment depended on how much of the medial temporal lobe had been removed. The farther posterior along the medial temporal lobe the resection was made, the worse was the amnesia. Strikingly, however, only *bilateral* resection of the hippocampus resulted in severe amnesia. In comparison, in one patient whose entire right medial temporal lobe (hippocampus and hippocampal gyrus) was removed, no residual memory deficit was reported by Scoville and Milner, although today more sensitive tests would reveal some memory deficits. The most interesting patient was the young man who had had bilateral medial temporal resection.

The Story of Patient H.M. Patients who underwent bilateral medial temporal lobe resection developed dense amnesia. H.M. was the most famous such patient. H.M.'s case holds a prominent position in the history of memory research because, as we described at the beginning of the chapter, although he had epilepsy, was of normal intelligence, and had no psychological or mental illness, as a result of the surgery he developed a severe and permanent inability to acquire new information (Scoville & Milner, 1957; Milner et al., 1968).

After the surgery, H.M. had normal short-term memory (sensory registers and working memory). Like many other amnesics (Figure 8.10), H.M. had normal digit span abilities, performing well at holding strings of digits in working memory. But unlike normal subjects, he performed poorly on digit span tests that required the acquisition of new long-term memories; that is, his digit span ability hardly improved with practice. What appeared to be disrupted was the transfer of information from short-term storage to long-term memory. Recall the case of Shallice and Warrington's patient K.F., described in the section on short-term memory earlier in the chapter. K.F. had below-normal digit span ability (short-term and working memory) but normal long-term memory ability. H.M., however, showed the inverse pattern. Recall also that patient K.F. had damage to the perisylvian cortex but not the medial temporal lobe. In H.M.'s case, the surgical lesion is confined to the medial temporal lobe.

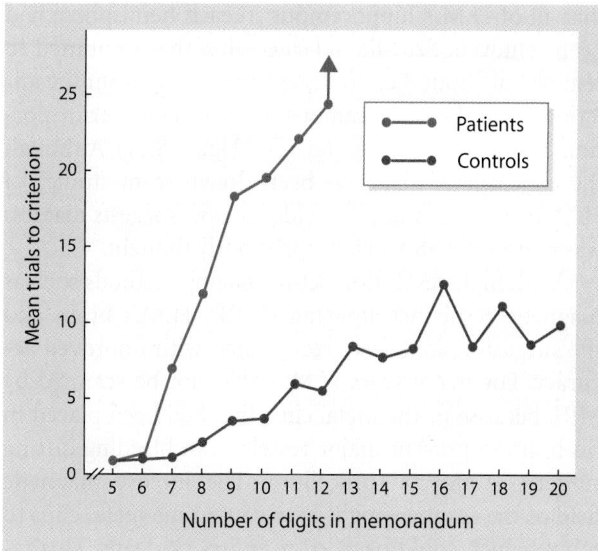

Figure 8.10 Digit span for amnesic patients and control subjects. A sequence of five digits was read to the subjects, who were then asked to repeat the digits back to the experimenter. If the digits were repeated correctly, one more digit was added to the next sequence presented. If the digits in a sequence were reported incorrectly, that sequence was repeated until the subject reported it correctly. Amnesic patients had relatively normal digit span ability but required more trials to learn strings of digits. At the point where control subjects begin to rely on long-term memory to retain the longer digit sequences (with a dozen or so items requiring 5 to 10 trials to perform correctly), the patients begin to fail in this task.

AMNESIA AND THE MEDIAL TEMPORAL LOBE

Which region or regions of the medial temporal lobe were critical for supporting the long-term memory ability lost in H.M.? The medial temporal area includes the amygdala, the hippocampus, the entorhinal cortex, and the surrounding parahippocampal and perirhinal cortical areas (see Chapter 3). We will return to a more detailed analysis of these areas based on work in animals later in this chapter. Here we focus on the story as it has emerged from work in amnesic patients.

For the past 55 years, scientists studying H.M. have used surgical reports of his lesions to guide theories of memory and amnesia and their neural bases. Original reports by Scoville, who performed the surgery, indicated that all of H.M.'s hippocampus in each hemisphere had been removed. Scoville indicated that this amounted to removal of about 8 cm of tissue, measuring from the anterior tip of the hippocampus toward the posterior portions of the medial temporal lobe (Figure 8.11). Although the conclusions that have been drawn from studies of H.M. may not change, the evidence now suggests that less was removed than had been previously thought.

With high-resolution neuroimaging methods such as magnetic resonance imaging (MRI), H.M.'s brain and the surgical lesions were reevaluated with improved accuracy. For many years H.M. could not be scanned by MRI, because of the metal clips that had been placed in his brain to prevent major vessels from bleeding during surgery—a normal procedure. The intense magnetic field of the scanner might have caused the metal clips to move, which could have led to injury or death. This restriction applies only to ferromagnetic items affected by magnetic fields; many metals are not ferromagnetic. It was not known whether H.M.'s clips were ferromagnetic. His surgery had been performed long before MRI was developed, and clips developed for surgery at that time might or might not have been ferromagnetic. Thus, it was possible that MRI scanning would endanger H.M.

In an unusual detective story, Suzanne Corkin of the Massachusetts Institute of Technology and journalist-author Philip Hilts (1995) tracked the history of H.M.'s surgery. They determined that the clips used were not ferromagnetic, and that it would be safe to scan H.M. using MRI. As a result, in 1997, more than 40 years after his surgery, H.M.'s surgical lesion was investigated with modern neuroimaging techniques (Figure 8.12).

Data gathered by Corkin and her colleagues were analyzed by neuroanatomist David Amaral of the University of California, Davis (Corkin et al., 1997). This analysis, shown in Figure 8.13, is an example of remarkable scientific and historical revisionism. Contrary to Scoville's reports, approximately half of the posterior region of H.M.'s hippocampus was intact. And only 5 cm, not 8 cm, of the medial temporal lobe had been removed. However, the remaining portions of H.M.'s hippocampi were atrophied, probably because of the loss of inputs from the surrounding perihippocampal cortex that had been removed in the 1953 surgery. Thus, despite the original error in our knowledge about H.M.'s lesion, it may be that no functional hippocampal tissue remains. Bear in mind that, in addition to the hippocampus, some of H.M.'s surrounding cortex was also removed—a point that will become relevant later in this chapter, when we consider the role of the hippocampus versus parahippocampal cortex in memory.

Is damage to the hippocampus sufficient to block the formation of new long-term memories? Consider

Figure 8.11 Anatomy of the medial temporal lobe and areas believed to have been removed from H.M. (in red) as reported by the surgeon. (Note that the resection is shown here on one side only, to permit a comparison of the resected region with an intact brain at the same level. H.M.'s actual lesion was bilateral.) At the top is a ventral view of the brain showing both hemispheres and the details of the right medial temporal area (at left). The four anterior-to-posterior levels (A–D) shown in this ventral view correspond to the four coronal sections below.

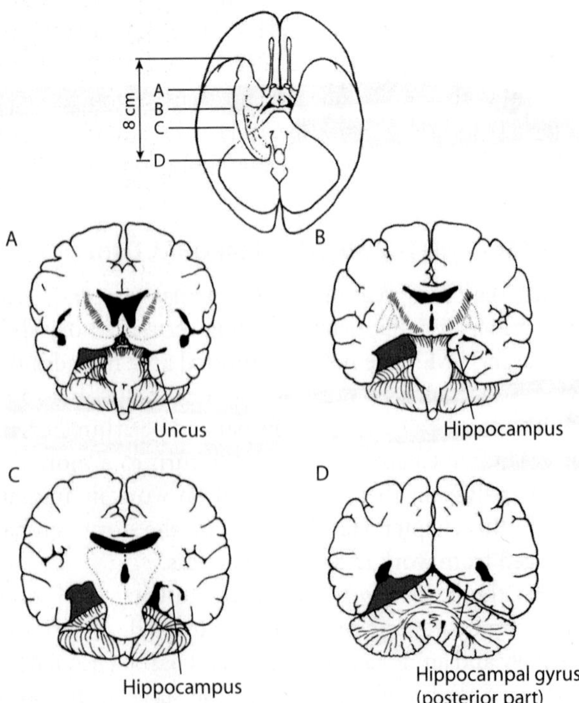

Figure 8.12 Coronal MRI scans of H.M.'s brain. **(a)** This anterior slice shows that the hippocampus has been removed bilaterally. **(b)** In this more posterior slice, however, the hippocampus is still intact in both hemispheres! This finding is in marked contrast to the belief that H.M. has no hippocampus—a view that had been held by the scientific community for the prior 40 years and that was based on the surgeon's report.

(a) Anterior

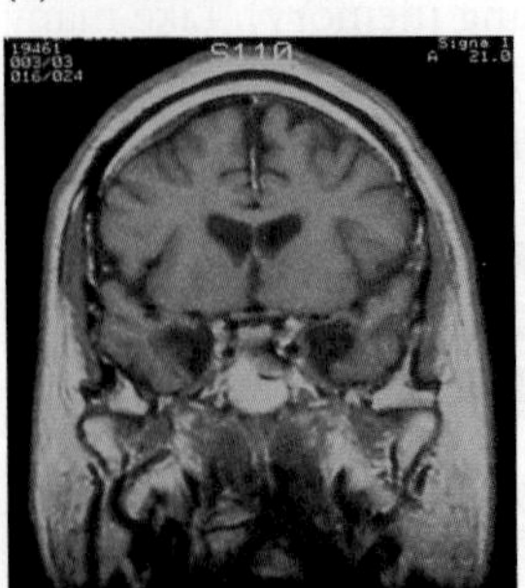

(b) Posterior

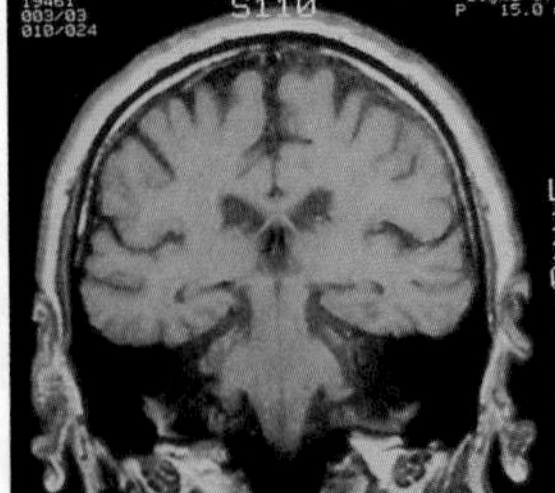

HOW THE BRAIN WORKS

Temporary Losses of Memory

A common theme in novels and movies is the temporary loss of memory after a bump on the head or psychological trauma. Such things do happen outside of Hollywood and might have many causes, including head injury or epilepsy. However, sometimes temporary memory loss occurs for other reasons, and one such syndrome is known as *transient global amnesia*, or *TGA*. Most clinicians consider TGA to be distinct from the temporary memory loss caused by head injury, epileptic activity, or stroke. Vascular effects are suspected as the main cause of TGA, but they are limited to transient ischemia (reduced blood flow to a brain area) that does not lead to cerebral infarct (permanent damage to brain tissue). The tissue recovers, and so does the patient's memory. The prime candidates for affected brain areas are the medial temporal lobe and diencephalic areas. The patients have symptoms similar to those of persons with permanent damage to the medial temporal lobe, such as H.M.

Here's a simple scenario common for TGA: An otherwise healthy person over 50 years old is taken (or goes) to the hospital after experiencing some problems with memory. During questioning by a physician, the person is not sure why he is there and may not be sure how he got there or where he is. He does know his name, birth date, job, and perhaps address, but he has retrograde amnesia pertaining to a period of weeks or months—perhaps even years. Thus, if he had recently moved, he would have supplied his past address and circumstances. He has normal short-term memory and thus can repeat lists of words told to him. But his ability to form new episodic memories is impaired, and when told to remember a list of words, he forgets it within a couple of minutes if he is prevented from rehearsing it. He continually asks who the physician is and why he is there. He does show an awareness that he *should* know the answer to some questions, which worries him. He performs normally on most neuropsychological tests, except for the ones indexing memory. He manifests a loss of time sense, and so responds incorrectly to questions asking how long he has been in the hospital. He also might have reduced verbal fluency and show impairment in generating words that begin with a certain letter, such as *A*, when asked to do so. However, he does not have deficits in producing category names—for example, general names for fruits. This latter pattern is typical of frontal lobe problems. During the hours following the amnesia-inducing event, distant memories return, and his anterograde memory deficit resolves. Within 24 to 48 hours he is essentially back to normal, although mild deficits may persist for days or even weeks.

Persons having one such attack are more likely to experience TGA again, but it does not usually occur often. Some people may never have another episode. The recurrence rate is about 18% within a 20-year period. Men are more likely to experience TGA.

The physiological cause is thought to be ischemia due to a disruption of normal blood flow in the vertebral-basilar artery system, which supplies blood to the medial temporal lobe and the diencephalon. TGA most often is triggered by physical exertion. Unlike patient R.B. described in the text, who had such a severe ischemic attack that it caused neurons in his hippocampus to die, TGA patients suffer only a transient deficit in the medial temporal lobe or in thalamic functioning. PET and single-photon-emission computed tomography (SPECT) studies in a few patients have demonstrated this transient deficit: Blood flow in the medial temporal lobe decreases during a TGA attack but later returns to normal. So far, we do not know whether these patients have normal implicit learning or memory, in part because their impairment does not last long enough for researchers to adequately index things like procedural learning. The answer to this question would improve our understanding of human memory and of a form of amnesia that could happen to any of us later in life.

another patient, R.B., who in 1978 lost his memory after an ischemic episode (reduction of blood to the brain) during heart bypass surgery and whose memory performance was studied by Stuart Zola, Larry Squire, and David Amaral at the University of California, San Diego. R.B. developed dense **anterograde amnesia** similar to H.M.'s: He could not form new long-term memories. He also had **retrograde amnesia** that extended back about 1 or 2 years—slightly less severe than H.M.'s retrograde loss.

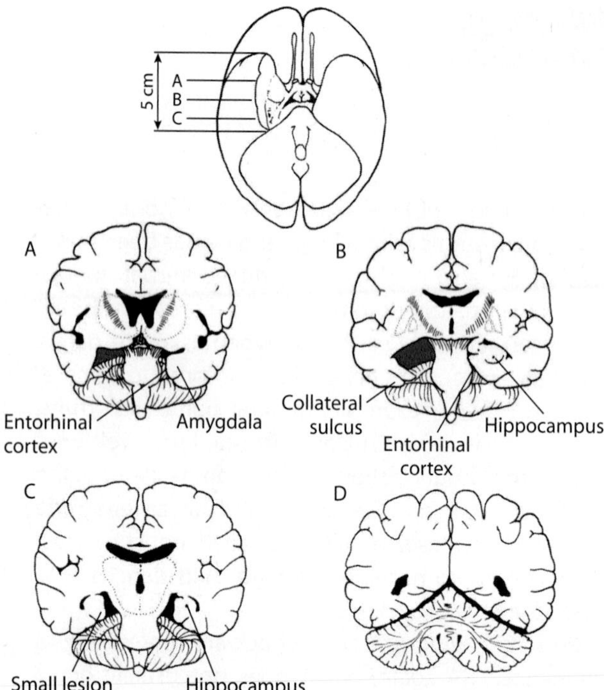

Figure 8.13 Modern reconstruction by Amaral and colleagues showing that portions of H.M.'s posterior hippocampus were not removed during surgery. However, this tissue does show signs of atrophy and may no longer be functioning normally. Compare with Figure 8.11.

R.B.'s case is remarkable because his lesions were found to be restricted to his hippocampus. The limited extent of his lesion was learned when he died a few years after surgery. After his death his brain was donated for study, permitting a detailed analysis of the extent of his neuroanatomical damage. Because R.B.'s memory had been tested extensively after his amnesia began and until his death, much that was known about his memory capacities could then be related to the precise information about the extent of his lesions from postmortem analysis.

On gross examination of R.B.'s medial temporal lobe, the hippocampus appeared to be intact (Figure 8.14a). But histological analysis revealed that, within each hippocampus, R.B. had sustained a specific lesion restricted to the CA1 pyramidal cells (Figure 8.14b). Compare his hippocampus (Figure 8.14b) with that of a normal person after death (Figure 8.14c).

These findings in patient R.B. support the idea that the hippocampus is crucial for the formation of new long-term memories. R.B.'s case also supports the distinction between areas that store long-term memories and the role of the hippocampus in forming new memories. Even though retrograde amnesia is associated with damage to the medial temporal lobe, it is temporally limited and does not affect long-term memories of events that happened more than a few years prior to the amnesia-inducing event. Subsequently, several patients with similar medial temporal lobe lesions have also been identified and studied, showing highly similar patterns of memory loss. In addition, other diseases that involve damage to the medial temporal lobe and its connections also lead to amnesia, providing converging evidence for the role of the medial temporal lobe in long-term memory.

Alcoholic Korsakoff's Syndrome and Diencephalic Amnesia The medial temporal lobe is not the only area of interest in human memory. Amnesia emerges from brain damage in other regions too. For example, damage to midline structures of the diencephalon is also associated with amnesia. The prime structures are the dorsomedial nucleus of the thalamus and the mammillary bodies (Figure 8.15). Damage to these midline subcortical regions can be caused by stroke, tumors, and metabolic problems like those brought on by chronic alcoholism, as well as by trauma.

In the last half of the 19th century, the Russian neuropsychiatrist Sergei Korsakoff reported an anterograde and retrograde amnesia associated with alcoholism. Long-term alcohol abuse can lead to vitamin deficiencies (vitamin B_1, also known as thiamine) that cause brain damage. Patients suffering from alcoholic Korsakoff's syndrome have degeneration in the diencephalon, especially the dorsomedial nucleus of the thalamus and the mammillary bodies. It remains unclear whether the dorsomedial thalamic nucleus, the mammillary bodies, or both are necessary for the patients' amnesia. Nonetheless, damage to the diencephalon can produce amnesia.

The symptoms of amnesia resulting from Korsakoff's syndrome resemble those that accompany damage to the medial temporal lobe. Both types of amnesics lose declarative memory and preserve nondeclarative memory. Because patients with Korsakoff's syndrome initially have no damage to the medial temporal lobe, it is likely that connections between the midline diencephalon and medial temporal lobe are disrupted, giving rise to the deficit by compromising the circuitry that involves the hippocampus.

Alzheimer's Disease At the start of the 20th century, German psychiatrist Aloysius Alzheimer described a 51-year-old female patient in Frankfurt who had a significant short-term memory loss and who deteriorated cognitively over the period of the next 5 years until her death in 1906. Alzheimer was able to perform postmortem histological studies of this patient's brain with

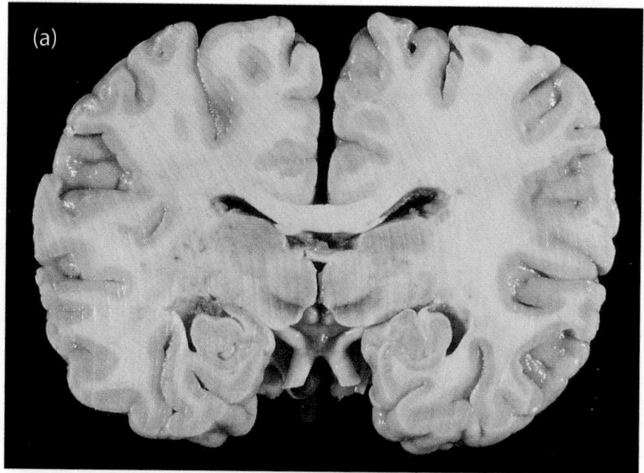

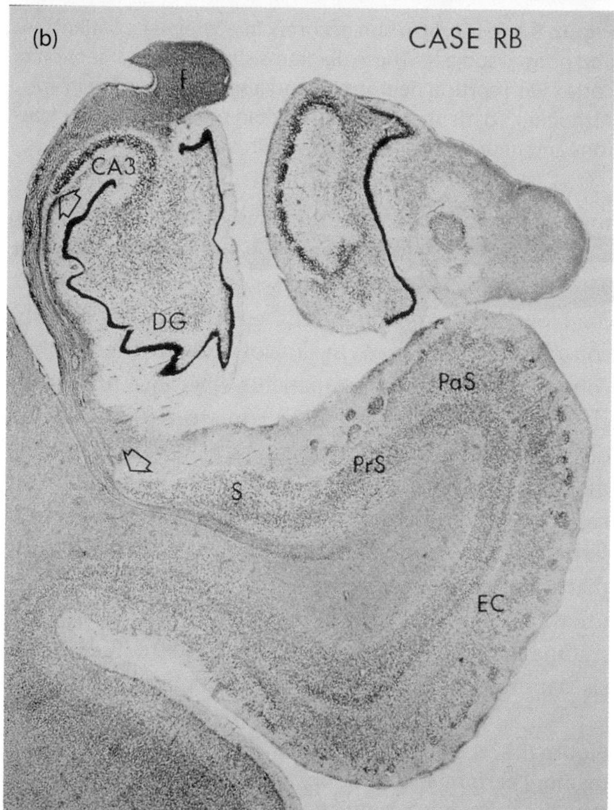

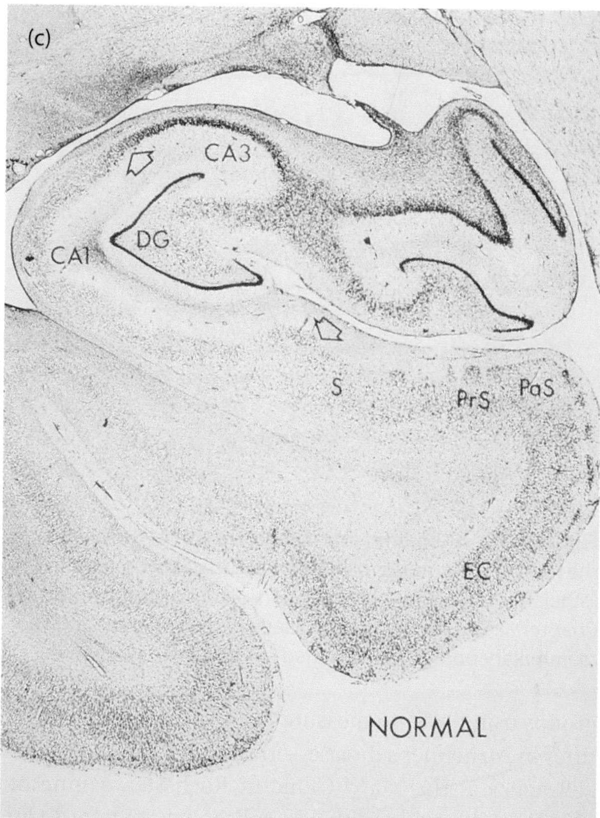

Figure 8.14 Comparison of R.B.'s brain with that of a normal subject. **(a)** This section is from R.B.'s brain following his death. In contrast to the MRI sections from H.M. in Figure 8.12, which show an absence of the anterior and middle portions of the hippocampus, R.B.'s medial temporal lobe appeared intact on gross examination. **(b)** Careful histological examination, however, revealed that cells in the CA1 region of the hippocampus were absent (see the region between the arrows). The absence of cells was the result of an ischemic episode following surgery. Cells of the CA1 region are particularly sensitive to transient ischemia (temporary loss of blood supply to a brain region). **(c)** This histological section from the brain of a normal subject shows an intact CA1 region (labeled "CA1" and delimited as the region between the arrows).

his German and Italian colleagues in Munich. They observed that her brain contained the now infamous amyloid plaques (clumps of insoluble protein between neurons) and neurofibrillary tangles (tangles of protein fibers within cortical neurons) that are characteristic of Alzheimer's disease (Figure 8.16).

Alzheimer's disease affects as many as a million Americans. On average, one out of every four Americans over the age of 85 has Alzheimer's, and with the increasing number of elderly people, the disease is becoming a sort of "old-age epidemic." Indeed, the incidence of Alzheimer's disease goes up rapidly after age 65, with the percentage of affected persons roughly doubling for each 5 years of aging, so that by age 95, the incidence may be as high as 30% of the population. Alzheimer's disease should not be considered part of normal aging, but rather a disease that increases in risk with age.

Although Alzheimer's disease causes widespread neuronal deterioration, it is now widely believed that the hippocampus deteriorates more rapidly in Alzheimer's patients than in people undergoing the normal aging process, and that the plaques and tangles that are anatomical hallmarks of Alzheimer's disease congregate in this medial temporal area. In the early 1990s, research

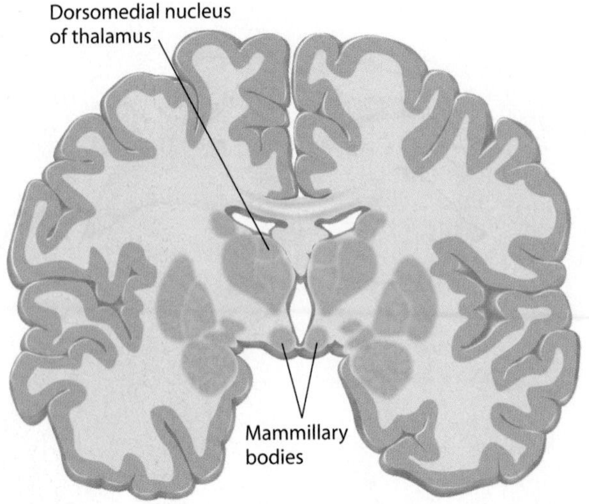

Figure 8.15 Diagrammatic coronal section of the brain at the level of the anterior nucleus of the thalamus, mammillothalamic tract, and the rostral portion of the crus cerebri (see Chapter 3). The dorsomedial nucleus of the thalamus and the mammillary bodies are damaged in Korsakoff's syndrome.

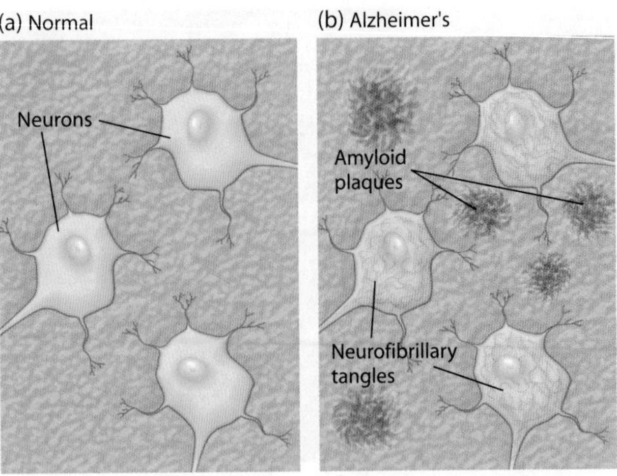

Figure 8.16 Comparison of cortex in Alzheimer's patients and normal subjects. These diagrams show a normal section of cortex with cortical neurons **(a)** and a section of cortex in an Alzheimer's patient containing amyloid plaques between neurons and neurofibrillary tangles within neurons **(b)**.

groups using MRI to measure the volume of brain structures in Alzheimer's disease—including Clifford Jack and colleagues at the Mayo Clinic in Rochester, Minnesota (2002), and David Smith and colleagues at Oxford University in the United Kingdom (Jobst et al., 1994)—were able to show that the size of the hippocampus changes with the progression of Alz-heimer's disease and that people with thicker hippocampi develop dementia to a lesser extent.

Morris Moscovitch and colleagues at the Rotman Research Institute and the University of Toronto, Canada, have recently demonstrated that the extent of atrophy in the medial temporal lobe in Alzheimer's patients is most closely related to their deficits in episodic memory. In addition, there is a large loss of acetylcholine (ACh) cells that connect to the hippocampus and prefrontal cortex in Alzheimer's disease. This dysfunctional connectivity between the hippocampus and prefrontal cortex due to the loss of Ach appears to play a role in the progressive loss of ability to form new episodic memories in Alzheimer's patients.

MEMORY CONSOLIDATION, THE HIPPOCAMPUS, AND THE NEOCORTEX

Memories are solidified in long-term stores over days, weeks, months, and years. As defined earlier in this chapter, this process is called *consolidation*, an old concept that refers to how long-term memory develops over time after initial acquisition. In most current models, the idea is that consolidation has different phases: an initial rapid consolidation process, followed by a slower permanent consolidation process.

How do we know that long-term memories must be consolidated over time? One line of evidence for temporal consolidation comes from patients who have undergone electroconvulsive therapy (ECT) to treat psycho-logical disorders. In ECT, an electrical current is passed through the brain by electrodes placed on the scalp—a useful treatment for conditions such as severe depression. In patients so treated, retrograde amnesia is more likely to affect items that were learned close to the time of the treatment (Figure 8.17). A similar pattern is observed with severe head trauma that leads to closed-head injury. Retrograde amnesia is more likely for recent events, and even as the amnesia

Figure 8.17 Effects of electroconvulsive therapy (ECT) on memory performance. Memory apparently changes for a long time after initial learning, with some material being forgotten and the material that remains becoming more resistant to disruption.

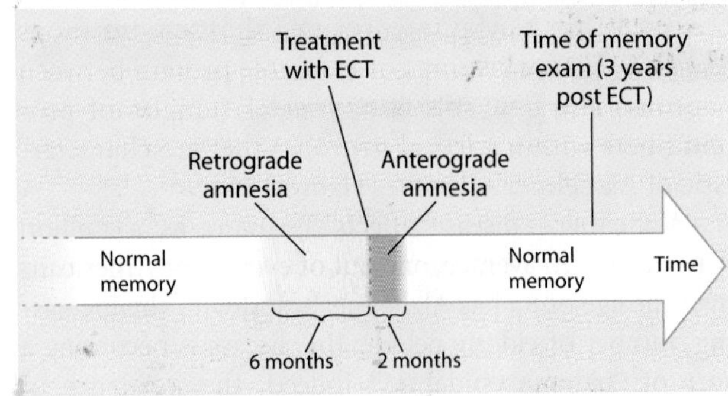

HOW THE BRAIN WORKS

Stress and Memory

Stress, both physical and psychological, triggers the release of cortisol, a hormone produced by the adrenal cortex in the adrenal glands, which are located above the kidneys. In small quantities, cortisol can aid learning and increase attentiveness. Chronic high stress, however, has detrimental effects on cognitive functions, including memory. The receptors in the brain that are activated by cortisol are called *glucocorticoid receptors* and are found at concentrated levels in the hippocampus (especially in the dentate gyrus and CA1 region; see Figure 8.14c).

The CA1 region of the hippocampus is the origin of connections from the hippocampus to the neocortex that are important in the consolidation of episodic memory. The functions of this circuitry can be disrupted by high levels of cortisol, perhaps by impairment of long-term potentiation (LTP); LTP is discussed in the final section of this chapter. Researchers have discovered that episodic memory (but not procedural memory) is impaired by high levels of cortisol. Clemens Kirschbaum at the Technical University of Dresden in Germany and his colleagues (1996) showed that a single dose of hydrocortisone (10 mg) had a detrimental effect on verbal episodic memory. Subjects were given a list of words to study, after which they were given either a dose of hydrocortisone or a placebo. Subjects who received the hydrocortisone recalled significantly fewer words in a cued recall test given an hour after administration of the drug than did the control subjects who received a placebo.

Clinical evidence from all disorders characterized by high levels of cortisol—including Cushing's syndrome, major depression, and asthma treated with the glucocorticoid prednisone—show impaired memory function (Payne & Nadel, 2004). Furthermore, Sonia Lupien of McGill University and her colleagues (2005) found that elderly individuals who have experienced chronic stress and have prolonged high levels of cortisol have a 14% reduction in hippocampal volume as compared to age-matched individuals without chronic stress and with normal levels of cortisol, indicating a long-term deleterious effect of cortisol on the hippocampus. These individuals also show marked impairment of episodic memory.

Interestingly, cortisol levels normally rise gradually during the night as we sleep, from low levels at the beginning of sleep to the highest levels before awaking. In concert with this knowledge is the finding that dreams rich in episodic material are concentrated at the beginning of sleep, and episodic memory consolidation is most likely to occur early in the sleep process. Jessica Payne and Lynn Nadel (2004) at the University of Arizona propose that "variations in cortisol . . . determine the functional status of hippocampal/neocortical circuits, thereby influencing the memory consolidation processes that transpire during sleep" (p. 671). Sleep research is a hot topic in neuroscience (see "How the Brain Works: Sleep and Memory Consolidation," on p. 336), and new studies should elucidate whether Payne and Nadel's appealing theory is correct.

remits over time, the most recent events are affected longest, and sometimes permanently. It is as if items that have undergone initial rapid consolidation but have not completed the slow permanent consolidation process are the ones that are lost.

One important question is how new information is consolidated in the brain. That is, what is the role of the medial temporal lobe and related structures, as well as the neocortex, in this process. In some models of memory formation, the neocortex is considered crucial for the storage of fully consolidated long-term memories.

As we are learning, the medial temporal lobes, particularly the hippocampi, are essential for the rapid consolidation and initial storage of information for episodic and semantic memories. The mechanisms of the slow consolidation process, however, remain rather more controversial. Larry Squire and his colleagues have proposed that rapid consolidation in the medial temporal lobe is replaced by a permanent memory trace in the neocortex that arises from some sort of medial temporal lobe interaction with neocortex. Others, such as Lynn Nadel in Arizona and Morris Moscovitch in Toronto, have suggested that only the long-term stores for semantic information rely on the neocortex, but that some aspects of episodic memory continue to rely on medial temporal lobe structures.

HOW THE BRAIN WORKS

Sleep and Memory Consolidation

Recent evidence suggests that sleep plays a crucial role in memory consolidation after learning. Matt Wilson and his colleagues at the Massachusetts Institute of Technology have studied the relationship between sleep and memory in the rat. They recorded from ensembles of neurons in the rat hippocampus that fire when an animal is in a specific place in its environment (in relation to a landmark cue). These cells are called *place cells*. In the initial study, Matt Wilson and Bruce McNaughton (1994) of the University of Arizona found that the place cells that fired together during the learning of spatial behavioral tasks were more likely to fire together during postlearning sleep than they had been before the task was learned, indicating that the neurons might be "replaying" the learned tasks during sleep.

Further studies of a similar nature have shown that hippocampal cells tended to replay not only with spatial coordination, but also in the same temporal sequence of neuronal firing in which they were learned. Activities (and resulting neuronal firing patterns) that took place over minutes were replayed during sleep in a sequential pattern corresponding to that of the awake activity. These studies implicate the hippocampus in the consolidation of memory via "replaying" of the neuronal firing of spatial and temporal patterns that were first activated during awake learning. Replay of this type is not limited to sleep.

Foster and Wilson (2006) recently reported that sequential replay also takes place in the rat hippocampus when the animal is awake, in the period just after the rat experiences a pattern of spatial activity. Interestingly, replay during waking has the unusual property of taking place in the reverse temporal order of the original experience (e.g., running in a maze). One hypothesis is that this sort of waking replay of neural activity represents a basic mechanism for learning and memory.

Thus there are two mechanisms: the reverse waking replay of neural activity, and the sleep-related replay, in which activity is replayed in the same temporal order as it was experienced. Something about the sleep-related forward replay is apparently related to memory consolidation. But the reverse waking replay must be doing something different. Foster and Wilson propose that it reflects a mechanism that permits recently experienced events to be compared to their "memory trace" and may, potentially, reinforce learning.

One region of special interest to the permanent consolidation of semantic information is the temporal neocortex outside the medial temporal lobe. Lesions that damage the lateral cortex of the anterior temporal lobe, near the anterior pole, lead to a dense amnesia that includes severe *retrograde* amnesia; in such cases the entorhinal cortex and parahippocampal cortex may be involved. The retrograde amnesia may be severe, extending back many decades before the amnesia-inducing event occurred or encompassing the patient's entire life. Various forms of damage can lead to this condition. Progressive neurological diseases like Alzheimer's (in its later stages) and herpes simplex encephalitis involving viral infection of the brain are two such conditions.

Some patients with dense retrograde amnesia might still form new long-term memories. This type of amnesia is called *isolated* retrograde amnesia. It is particularly related to damage of the anterior temporal lobe. This portion of the temporal lobe is not, therefore, essential for acquiring new information.

Are these lateral and anterior regions of the temporal lobe the sites where long-term declarative memories are stored? The answer is maybe, but another view is that these regions may be particularly important for the retrieval of information from long-term stores. Where, then, are memories stored? More recent evidence from neuroimaging studies suggests that memories are stored as distributed representations throughout the neocortex (see "The Cognitive Neuroscientist's Toolkit: Connectionist Modeling of Memory" on p. 336), involving the regions that originally encoded the perceptual information and regions representing information that was associated with this incoming information (as noted in the previous section, the medial temporal lobe may coordinate the consolidation of this information over time). Why do we not believe that the lateral and anterior areas of the temporal lobe are where the brain stores all long-term memories? If these sites were the sole repository of declarative memories, we would not find patients who had lost all previously acquired memories but still acquired new ones, yet such patients have been identified.

AMNESIA AND THE ACQUISITION OF NEW DECLARATIVE INFORMATION

The insights derived from H.M. and other amnesic patients with medial temporal lobe or diencephalic damage indicate that a core problem with this form of amnesia is the inability to learn and retain new information. That is, as noted previously, damage to the medial temporal lobe generally is associated with the inability to learn new information, as opposed to losses of older memories obtained prior to the damage (except for a time-limited retrograde amnesia). The inability to learn new information often was considered to be equally true for episodic and semantic information; we will return to consider procedural learning shortly. But is it true that damage to the medial temporal lobe (and diencephalic) memory systems affects both episodic and semantic memory? Let's consider whether new learning of semantic information (world knowledge) can take place in amnesia patients even though the ability to form new episodic memories is clearly lost.

H.M. had severe anterograde amnesia; nonetheless, he was still able to learn some new information. Since his surgery, H.M. has been able to form some new memories. For example, he can fairly accurately draw a floor plan of the home in which he lived for a period of years after recovery from surgery (Figure 8.18). H.M. also knows the names and faces of some famous people learned after his surgery, but overall he is severely impaired in tests of famous faces. As described by Suzanne Corkin (2002), who has studied H.M. extensively, "These results indicate that H.M.'s public semantic knowledge, although inferior to that of control

(a) H.M.'s 1966 drawing

(c) Current owner's floor plan

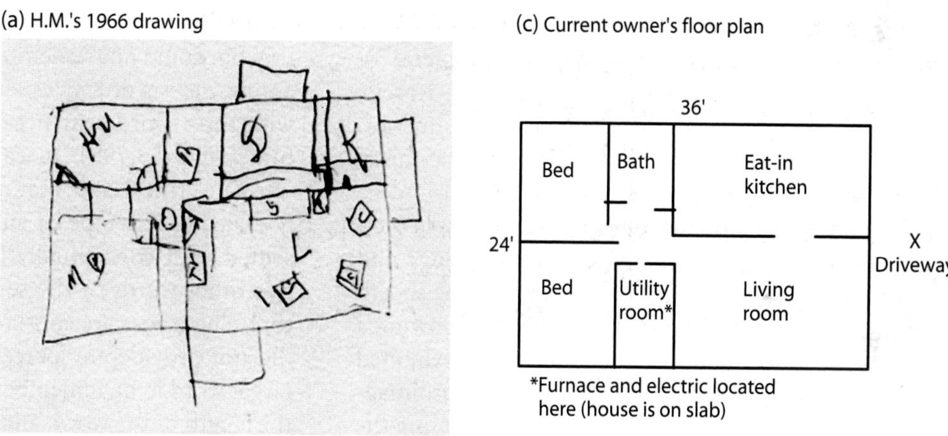

(b) H.M.'s 1977 drawing

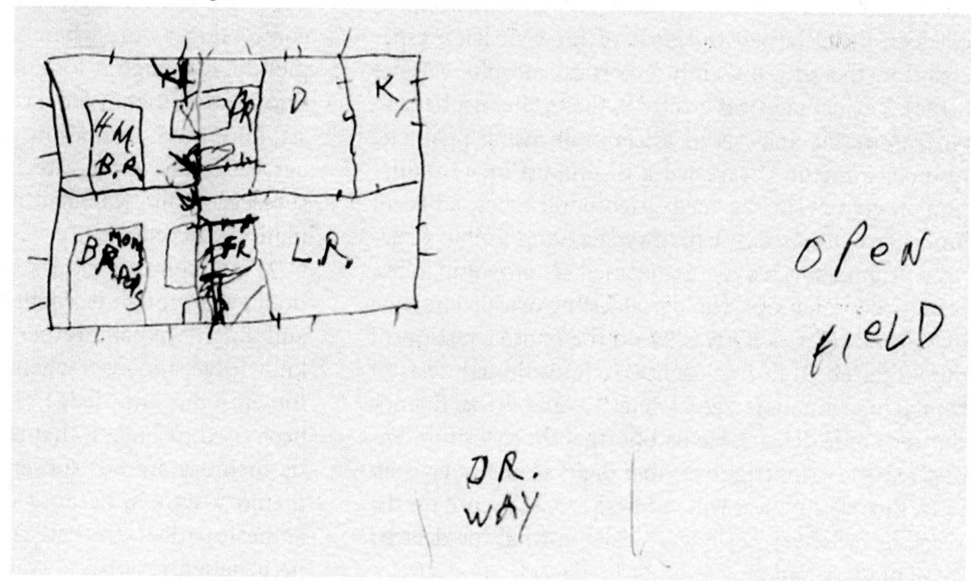

Figure 8.18 Drawings from memory by patient H.M. of the house where he lived beginning 5 years after his surgery. He lived in the house for 16 years, from 1958 to 1974, and the drawing in **(a)** was made in 1966 while he still lived in the house. Three years after moving from the house in 1974, he drew the floor plan shown in **(b)**. The accuracy of these drawings can be compared to the actual floor plan of the home **(c)**, obtained more recently from the owner, who removed a wall in the kitchen after H.M. lived there.

participants, does include some information from the decades after the onset of his amnesia. Nevertheless, the traces of information that are stored in H.M.'s brain are fragmented and lacking in detail, so that they give rise to incomplete representations of, for example, public figures" (p. 158).

Thus, amnesics with lesions of the medial temporal lobe memory system who experience profound deficits in acquiring new episodic memories may nonetheless learn some new information. Semantic memories such as details related to other people (e.g., John F. Kennedy was a president), new vocabulary for technical terms (e.g., a *laptop* is a portable computer), and novel, one-word descriptions of usual circumstances (e.g., a "jowend" is the celebration of one's 39th birthday), have been reported to be learned by amnesic patients. In line with their episodic memory deficits, this acquisition of new knowledge typically happens in amnesics who do not remember the source of the knowledge; that is, they do not know about the episode in which the information was learned—a condition sometimes termed *source amnesia* (we will return to this topic in Chapter 13). Endel Tulving and his colleagues (1991; R. S. Rosenbaum et al., 2005) have been studying this phenomenon for more than 20 years in one very interesting amnesic patient, K.C.

K.C. developed amnesia following a motorcycle accident at the age of 30. He suffered severe head injury, and a subdural hematoma (a pool of blood under the sheath covering his brain) was surgically removed. Following a long convalescence and rehabilitation, K.C. exhibited several residual neurological complications. Neuroimaging revealed damage in several brain areas, including the medial temporal lobe; the left dorsolateral prefrontal cortex and premotor cortex; the parietal and occipital cortices, including enlargement of his ventricles, especially on the left; and diffuse cortical atrophy (Figure 8.19a). The damage was greater in the left hemisphere.

Volumetric analysis of K.C.'s brain using magnetic resonance methods revealed a disproportionate reduction in volume in the medial temporal lobes, adjacent limbic structures (e.g., left amygdala), and limbic structures interconnected with the medial temporal lobes. Nonetheless, neuropsychological testing revealed normal intelligence (K.C.'s IQ was 94 on the revised version of the Wechsler Adult Intelligence Scale), although tests of frontal lobe function (see Chapter 13) and verbal fluency showed some deficits. He had normal short-term memory, remembering eight or nine digits in memory span tests. But, as is typical with amnesics, K.C.'s score on the Wechsler Memory Scale was below normal for delayed recall of information.

Of particular note, K.C. had severe anterograde *and* retrograde amnesia. Curiously, his retrograde amnesia involved episodic information from his entire life! He did not remember a single event in his personal history, although he had factual knowledge of things that pertained to his life—for example, that he went to high school at a particular place, that he had certain talents, that his family consisted of a particular number of people, who his family members were, and so on. If shown pictures of family and friends taken before his accident, however, K.C. was not able to relate the circumstance or tie the immediate percept of the photographs to other events, their time of occurrence, or their personal emotional meaning; it was as if he were seeing them for the first time.

Despite K.C.'s dense episodic and source amnesia, he had intact semantic memory for general world knowledge acquired prior to his accident. K.C. had not forgotten how to use implements common to daily life, nor had he lost knowledge about the structure of the world around him. He was able to learn some new information but could not remember how he acquired it. For example, in tests of K.C.'s memory skills, he was presented with three-word sentences together with a related picture (Figure 8.19b). In each sentence the final words were the critical ones that he was to be tested on later.

During one type of subsequent test, K.C. was presented with conceptually based cues consisting of the two other words of the sentence or the associated picture. These cues are considered conceptual because they did not provide any perceptual information about the target word to be remembered—that is, any of its letters, the length of the word, and so on. Remarkably, K.C. displayed an ability to learn new facts (semantic knowledge). He showed a greater likelihood of generating the correct target word when he saw the associated words or picture. Although it took K.C. longer to learn semantic information than it did a control person without amnesia, once the information was learned, forgetting it occurred at the same rate in K.C. as it did in control subjects. Again, K.C. had no inkling of how this information was acquired.

Thus, some amnesics can learn semantic information, even though it might be more difficult to acquire and might remain rather unrelated to more general knowledge, and even when such learning is not possible for episodic knowledge. These sorts of findings have been used to suggest that episodic memory and semantic memory are not subserved by the same underlying memory system, because they could be dissociated in amnesic patients. Is there converging evidence from amnesic patients for this distinction?

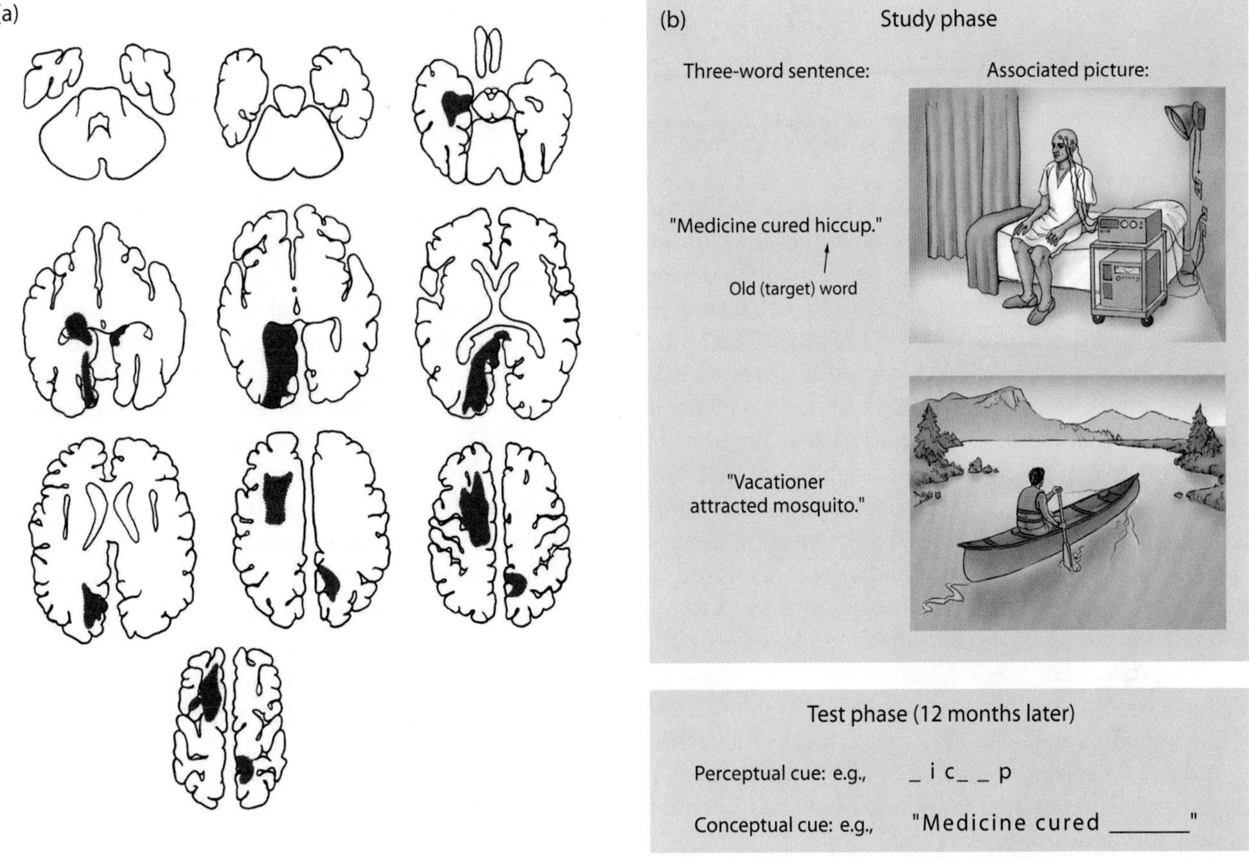

Figure 8.19 **(a)** K.C.'s major lesions, identified by the use of MRI scans, are represented in outline drawings of horizontal sections of a template brain as reported in Tulving et al., 1991. In these drawings, the left hemisphere is shown on the left of each section. The red areas indicate the major sites of lesions due to trauma. Note that, because these are template brains, they do not reveal the enlarged ventricles, especially on the left, that are evident on K.C.'s scans. For the most comprehensive evaluation of K.C.'s amnesia and brain damage, and to view more recent MRI scans of his brain, see R. S. Rosenbaum et al., 2005. **(b)** To test K.C.'s memory skills, Tulving and colleagues presented him with three-word sentences together with a related picture. In each sentence, the final word was the critical (target) word tested for later. During subsequent test sessions, K.C. was presented with word fragments (a few letters forming a perceptual cue) or conceptually based cues consisting of the other two words of the sentence or the associated picture. K.C. showed priming effects (improved performance) with the word fragments for words he had seen previously (old words) as compared to words he had not seen (new words), and these priming effects remained 12 months later.

In 1997, Faraneh Vargha-Khadem and her colleagues at University College London, with Mortimer Mishkin from the National Institute of Mental Health, reported on memory deficits suffered by three young patients who had sustained bilateral injury to the hippocampus, sparing the perirhinal, entorhinal, and parahippocampal cortices. The brain damage in these three occurred when they were children: one at birth (Beth), another at 4 years of age (Jon), and the third at 9 years old (Kate). These patients were interesting because their hippocampal damage happened before they could have acquired much semantic knowledge.

The patients were tested at ages 14, 19, and 22, respectively. All three patients attended mainstream schools and had good semantic memory abilities (they could learn new world knowledge), but they had many problems with episodic memory, which created difficulty for them at home and in school. These three cases tend to support the idea that episodic and semantic memory are, to an extent, dissociable. Vargha-Khadem and colleagues (1997) interpreted their findings as evidence that "the episodic and semantic components of cognitive memory are partly dissociable, with only the episodic component being fully dependent on the hippocampus" (p. 376).

Despite the interesting evidence from patients like K.C. and the children described in the foregoing paragraphs, not all evidence supports the idea that episodic and semantic memory are completely separate, with episodic memory being dependent on the hippocampus,

THE COGNITIVE NEUROSCIENTIST'S TOOLKIT

Connectionist Modeling of Memory

How are memories stored in the brain? We do not really know the answer to this question, but there are a lot of ideas. Some models consider memories to be stored as items: Once created, they are filed in neat order somewhere in the brain. Other models propose that networks consisting of discrete nodes are formed. The nodes are interconnected via associative links that relate bits of information together for storage; the basic organizing principles are that symbolic nodes and associated nodes become more tightly interconnected during learning. In contrast, connectionist models hold that memories are stored as changes in the instructions that neurons send to one another. New incoming information induces a specific pattern of activity over a population of neurons, and this pattern is the representation of that information. Such models, then, embody the concept of a **distributed representation**, and they bear resemblance to concepts such as sparse coding, which has been observed in sensory systems and in the hippocampus in neuronal recordings in animals.

Connectionist models also rely on concepts such as Hebbian learning (see the text), in which the interconnections between units in the population can change their strength (weight) to reflect the changing patterns of instructions that the units send to one another. These weights change as learning occurs, and connectionist models use training algorithms such as "back propagation" to accomplish this learning and to adjust the weights in the network. The figure demonstrates a simple model in which the visual inputs and olfactory inputs from a rose can be stored in the same network by the pattern of weights between the units. The four-by-four matrices in part (b) show the pattern of weights from the visual inputs (left matrix) summed with those from the olfactory inputs (middle matrix) to yield the final matrix, which reflects the stored representation of the multimodal features of the rose. The key point is that the visual and olfactory features need not be stored separately but can be represented across the same network of units. Hence, it is the pattern of activity across the same units, not activity in distinct groups of units (neurons), that accounts for the storage of visual or olfactory information.

Connectionist models vary from very simple ones, like the one shown in the figure, to complex models that are built from detailed knowledge of the neuronal connectivity in well-studied neural systems. These models, like all other models, are formalizations of concepts that were derived from experimental work. They provide a powerful method for testing cognitive and biological theories because they can be implemented in computer simulations. In addition, such models might reveal new ways of thinking about old data, by demonstrating the consequences of one or another model through direct tests in the simulations and by making explicit predictions that can be tested experimentally.

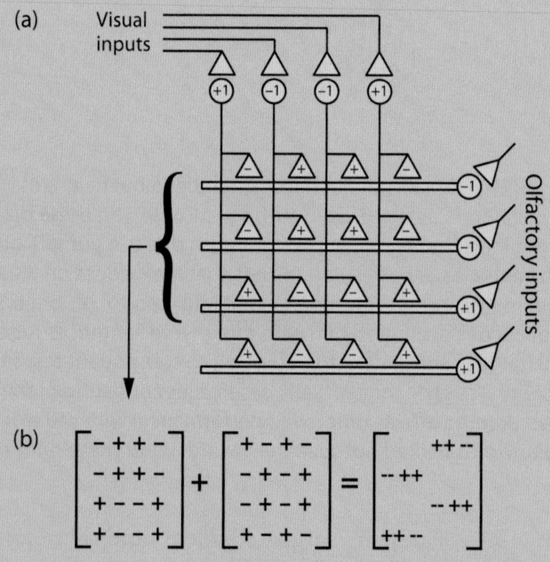

(a) This associative network demonstrates how information from two sources can be stored as different sets of weights across the same population of neurons within the network. **(b)** The left-hand matrix represents the weights in the network induced by the visual inputs—the weights shown in **(a)**—and the middle matrix represents the olfactory inputs. These can be summed to yield the right-hand matrix, representing the network of combined visual and olfactory inputs. Note that the middle matrix is not represented in connections in **(a)**. In both **(a)** and **(b)**, + = +0.25 and – = –0.25, except where noted (i.e., +1 or –1); ++ = +0.50 and – – = –0.50 in the summed matrix at lower right.

and semantic memory relying less on the hippocampus. Larry Squire and colleagues (Hamann & Squire, 1995) at the University of California, San Diego reported findings from E.P., an amnesic patient. E.P. was a 73-year-old man who, in 1992, developed severe amnesia following herpes simplex encephalitis that severely damaged his medial temporal lobes bilaterally. Squire and colleagues used methods similar to that employed by Tulving and colleagues to train patient K.C., but patient E.P. exhibited no evidence of semantic memory ability whatsoever. So, unlike K.C., or the three children described by Vargha-Khadem and colleagues, E.P. could not acquire new episodic or semantic information. Interestingly, as reported in a separate study (1995) by Larry Squire and Barbara Knowlton, E.P. could learn to make category judgments. That is, when shown items or words from one category (e.g., foods) he could classify those items presented to him later as having belonged to the previously viewed category or not—even though he could not form new episodic or semantic memories.

Psychologists Andrew Yonelinas, Neal Kroll, and their colleagues (1998) at the University of California, Davis, believe that this ability for some amnesics to learn new information can be conceptualized as a preservation of their ability to *recognize* prior events on the basis of a kind of strength signal. In their studies of amnesics who had damage in the left medial temporal lobe following stroke, they quantified the patients' ability to recognize words that they had heard previously. A strength score was assigned that indicated how well the amnesics could distinguish a true signal (the words presented to them an hour before) from noise (distracter words not presented previously). The amnesics reliably indicated that they had heard a word before, even though they had no episodic memory for its prior presentation (Figure 8.20). Similar approaches are difficult to apply in persons with normal memory because the memory for items is aided by their intact episodic knowledge of the prior events.

Figure 8.20 Testing amnesia patients for ability to learn new information. Investigators read lists of words to amnesic patients. Then, one hour later, the words were read again together with new words that had not been in the previous reading. The patients were asked to indicate their confidence that the words had been presented previously. Their answers were used to compute quantitative metrics of their memory ability using signal detection theory—a method borrowed from perceptual sciences and adapted to studies of memory.

AMNESIA AND THE ACQUISITION OF NEW NONDECLARATIVE KNOWLEDGE

Studies of amnesia have revealed that fundamental distinctions between long- and short-term memory have neural correlates and that, to an extent, episodic and semantic memory can be distinguished from one another by their relative sensitivity to brain damage. However, learning with amnesia is not limited to semantic knowledge. Amnesics can show implicit learning and nondeclarative memory. In this section we will consider how amnesic patients can learn new nondeclarative information via procedural learning and perceptual priming.

Procedural Learning in Amnesia One test of procedural learning is the *serial reaction-time task.* Subjects press buttons that correspond to locations of stimuli in front of them. For example, the subject might be presented with four buttons located under each of the fingers on one hand. Each button corresponds to one of four lights; the mapping between button and light can be based on spatial relationships (i.e., the left light maps to the left button). The task given the subjects is to press the button with the finger that corresponds to the light that is illuminated (Figure 8.21a). The lights can be flashed in different sequences: A totally random sequence can be flashed, or a pseudorandom sequence might be presented in which the lights seem to be flashing randomly to the participant, but in reality they are flashing in a complex repetitive sequence.

Over time, healthy subjects increase their speed of responding to the pseudorandom sequences in comparison to their responses to a totally random sequence. Thus, with practice on the pseudorandom sequence, the healthy subjects show improved (faster) performance. The key point, however, is that, when the subjects are questioned about whether the sequences were random, most report that they were completely random as far as they could tell, and they express no knowledge that any pattern existed (if the pseudorandom sequence is constructed properly, of course). Yet they learn the skill, which demonstrates procedural learning independent of any explicit knowledge about what was learned. This kind of evidence has

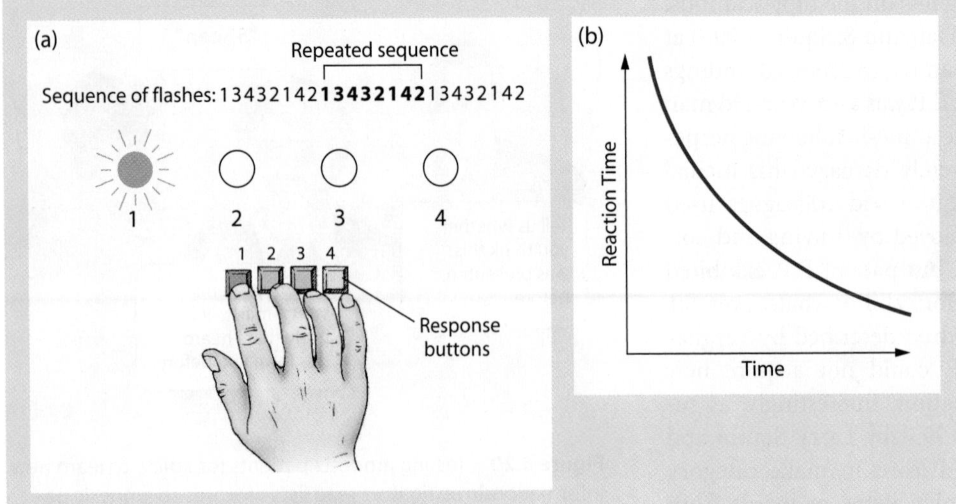

Figure 8.21 Procedural learning of sequences in the serial reaction-time task. **(a)** Using their fingers, subjects are asked to push buttons corresponding to flashes of lights in a complex sequence that is repeated but not obvious to the subjects. **(b)** Over time, subjects' reaction time to the repeating sequence becomes faster as compared to a sequence that is totally random, although they apparently have no knowledge that any pattern exists.

been used to argue for the distinction between declarative and procedural knowledge, because subjects appear to acquire one (procedural knowledge) in the absence of the other (declarative knowledge).

Some investigators have challenged the idea that healthy subjects learn in the absence of any explicit knowledge of what was learned. For example, sometimes the investigators ask healthy volunteers about the sequences and find that, in fact, some can describe explicitly the learned material. So perhaps the subjects who deny any such knowledge have low confidence and therefore do not state the declarative memory that they have about the repeating sequence. Given this possibility, if we do not find evidence for explicit knowledge during skill acquisition, how can we be sure that it's not there?

An answer comes from studies of procedural learning in amnesics like H.M. and others who have anterograde amnesia and cannot form new declarative memories. The logic is that, if amnesics cannot form new episodic memories for newly learned material but can learn procedural tasks, then explicit knowledge is not required for acquiring procedural knowledge. When tasks such as that in Figure 8.21a are presented to amnesic patients, those with dense anterograde amnesia (i.e., with loss of episodic learning) can still improve their performance by repeating the task. This result is shown as a speeding of reaction time for repeated sequences compared to random sequences over time. Typically, amnesic patients practice the task on one day and are tested on separate days. Even though they state that they have never performed the task before, they show a similar improvement on the repeated sequences; that is, they have learned the procedure. Therefore, procedural learning can proceed independently of the brain systems required for episodic memory.

This type of dissociation of declarative and nondeclarative learning and memory for procedural learning also happens in patients with diencephalic amnesia such as Korsakoff's syndrome. In addition, normal subjects taking drugs like benzodiazepines (tranquilizers) and scopolamine, an anticholinergic agent that acts on the muscarinic acetylcholine receptor (used to prevent motion sickness), also show this dissociation. These drugs cause deficits in declarative memory but do not affect procedural learning.

What brain systems support procedural memory? For motor skill learning, the basal ganglia have been implicated. When patients with disorders of the basal ganglia or inputs to these subcortical structures are tested on a variety of procedural learning tasks, they perform poorly. These disorders include Parkinson's disease, in which cell death in the substantia nigra disrupts dopaminergic projections into the basal ganglia; and Huntington's disease, in which neurons in the basal ganglia degenerate. Affected patients, who are not amnesic per se, have impairments in their ability to acquire and retain motor skills as assessed by a variety of tests involving motor skill learning.

Perceptual Priming in Amnesia Another exciting area of memory research has been the topic of *implicit learning and memory*, a term that Daniel Schacter (1987) coined. In most formulations, implicit memory and nondeclarative memory are essentially the same, and for simplicity we will consider them so here. In this section we will focus on perceptual priming studies.

Priming tasks have been used extensively to demonstrate information storage in brain systems involved in perceptual processing. *Priming* is the improvement in identifying or processing a stimulus as a result of its having been observed previously. For example, subjects can be presented with lists of words, and then in a test phase their memory of those words can be evaluated by either an explicit or an implicit test. In explicit memory tests, subjects consciously attempt to recognize previously seen material: Subjects are presented with a second word list (after a delay of hours or days) composed of new words plus words from the previous list (old words) and asked to identify words that they were shown in the initial presentation. In contrast, an implicit memory test might use a word fragment completion task: During the later test phase, subjects view only some letters—for example, "t_ou_h_s" for *thoughts* (Figure 8.22). The fragments can be from either new words or old words; the task is to complete the fragment. Subjects are not told that some words might have been in the initial list; thus, there is no attempt to recall whether the words were part of the initial list, and that knowledge is not relevant to the task.

Subjects are significantly better at correctly completing fragments for words presented in the initial list. Subjects benefit from having seen the words before, even if they are not told that the words were in the previous list. Priming for fragment completion does not lessen over time (hours versus days). In contrast, performance in the recognition task (explicit test) does decrease over time. The evidence suggesting that priming effects do not depend on explicit memory is simple: There is no relation between the ability to recognize old words (e.g., answering the question, "Did we show you this word before?") and the ability to complete fragments of those same words. Is this form of learning—perceptual priming—also damaged in amnesia? The answer is no for amnesia patients who have medial temporal damage and anterograde amnesia.

Recall patient K.C., who showed the ability to learn new semantic information when shown novel three-word sentences (e.g., "Medicine cured hiccup.") even though he had no episodic memory of being shown the sentences before (see Figure 8.19). In word fragment completion tests, K.C. was also tested for perceptual priming. In these tests, performed at varying times after the presentation of the word triplets, K.C. was presented with word fragments such as "_ic_ _p" (perceptual cues). K.C. demonstrated perceptual priming effects with the word fragments that remained even when tested 12 months later; *priming* here means that K.C. was better at generating words from fragments with words that he had seen previously, in comparison to words that he had not seen previously. This is a key pattern of results because it demonstrates that a form of nondeclarative memory—perceptual priming (see Figure 8.7)—was intact in K.C., even though he had no episodic memory of having seen the words before in the test setting.

Patient H.M. also shows this interesting preserved ability to benefit from repetition priming. It has been demonstrated many times that he shows perceptual priming of the same type that patient K.C. exhibits. An example comes from a study reported in 1998 by Bradley Postle and Suzanne Corkin. They showed H.M. words one at a time on a computer screen at short durations followed by a mask (a stimulus that appeared at the offset of the word and made reading the word

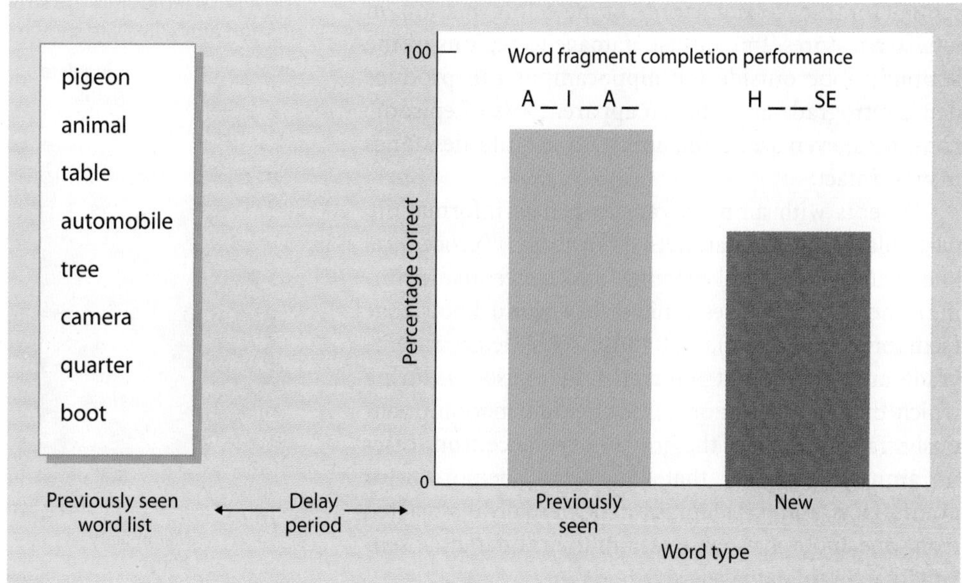

Figure 8.22 A typical word-priming study. Subjects are shown lists of words and then wait varying amounts of time to perform a fragment completion task. Tulving and Schacter (1990) showed that subjects are better at completing fragments of words that were previously shown to them.

harder) and asked him to say them out loud. They adjusted the duration of word presentation such that H.M. was correct on only about 50% of the words. One minute after the study session, H.M. was shown (for longer periods) word stems consisting of three letters of words and asked to complete the fragment with the first word that came to mind (e.g., "fra____" could be a stem for the word *fragrance*).

H.M. showed priming for the words that he had previously been shown in comparison to those not in the prior study list; that is, he showed perceptual priming. This work demonstrates that patients with medial temporal lobe damage and severe anterograde amnesia do show perceptual priming, in line with the idea that perceptual priming relies on information in perceptual brain systems located outside the medial temporal lobe.

SUMMARY OF AMNESIA AND MEMORY

The special cases that we have reviewed have implicated specific brain regions in distinct forms of memory impairment. The learning and retention of new information about one's autobiographical history (episodic memory) require an intact medial temporal lobe (primarily hippocampus) and related structures, such as the midline diencephalon. Damage to these areas impedes the formation of *new* declarative memories (anterograde amnesia). Damage to these areas also leads to difficulties in remembering events in the years immediately prior to the injury (time-limited retrograde amnesia) but leaves intact most previous episodic and semantic memories acquired during life. Therefore, these structures are not likely to be the storage sites of information in long-term memory but appear to be essential for the consolidation of new information in long-term stores. In contrast, damage to regions of the temporal lobe outside the hippocampus can produce dense retrograde amnesia, an apparent loss of episodic memories, even while the ability to acquire new ones may be intact.

Patients with amnesia can learn new information, particularly nondeclarative knowledge (procedural knowledge, perceptual priming, and conceptual priming) and in some cases limited new world knowledge (semantic knowledge), but those with dense anterograde amnesia do not remember the episodes during which they learned or observed the information previously. Taken together, the growing evidence from cases of amnesia suggests that long-term memories for events, facts, and procedures can be partially dissociated from one another, as expressed in their differential sensitivity to brain damage.

Animal Models of Memory and the Medial Temporal Lobe

Studies in animals with lesions to the hippocampus and surrounding cortex have been invaluable to improving our understanding about the contributions of the medial temporal lobe to memory. This field of study is immense and includes investigations in invertebrates (briefly touched on later in the chapter), as well as studies in various mammalian species, including nonhuman primates. A comprehensive review of this field of work is much beyond the scope of this textbook, but a few of the most important findings from animal studies are essential for understanding memory mechanisms. Hence, we will turn for a moment to look at studies in animals aimed at elucidating the role of the medial temporal lobe in long-term memory.

One of the key questions in memory research has been how much the hippocampus alone, as compared with surrounding structures in the medial temporal lobe, participates in the memory deficits of patients like H.M. In other words, what structures of the medial temporal lobe system are involved in episodic memory? For example, does the amygdala influence memory deficits in amnesics (Figure 8.23)? Data from amnesic patients indicate that the amygdala is not part of the brain's episodic memory system, although, as we will learn in Chapter 9, it has a role in emotion and emotional memories.

To test the idea that the amygdala is not essential in memory formation, surgical lesions were created in the

Figure 8.23 Medial view of the human right hemisphere. The medial temporal lobe structures, including the hippocampus and amygdala, are shown in red.

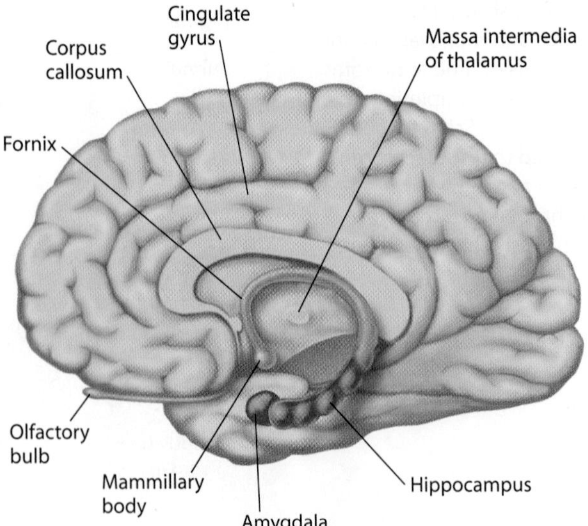

medial temporal lobe and amygdala of monkeys, to cause memory impairment. In classic work on monkeys conducted by Mortimer Mishkin (1978) at the National Institute of Mental Health, the hippocampus, the amygdala, or both were removed surgically. Mishkin found that the resulting amount of impairment, as measured on tests, varied according to what had been lesioned.

The brain-lesioned monkeys were tested with a popular behavioral task known as the *delayed nonmatch-to-sample task* that Mishkin developed. A monkey is placed in a box with a retractable door in the front (Figure 8.24). When the door is closed, the monkey cannot see out. With the door closed, a food reward is placed under an object (Figure 8.24a). The door is opened and the monkey is allowed to pick up the object to get the food (Figure 8.24b). The door is closed again and the same object plus a new object are put in position (Figure 8.24c). The new object now covers the food reward, and after a delay that can be varied, the door is reopened and the monkey must pick up the new object to get the food reward. If the monkey picks up the old object, as in Figure 8.24d, there is no reward. With training, the monkey picks the new, or nonmatching, object; hence, learning and memory are measured by observation of the monkey's performance.

In his early work, Mishkin found that, in the monkey, memory was impaired only if the lesion included both the hippocampus and the amygdala. This finding led to the (incorrect) idea that the amygdala is a key structure in memory. That idea, however, does not fit well with data from amnesics like R.B. (described earlier), who had anterograde amnesia caused by a lesion restricted to CA1 neurons of the hippocampus and no damage to the amygdala.

Stuart Zola, Larry Squire, and colleagues (Zola-Morgan et al., 1993) at the University of California, San Diego, investigated this dilemma. They performed more selective lesions of the brains of monkeys by distinguishing between the amygdala and the hippocampus, as well as the surrounding cortex near each structure. They surgically created lesions of the amygdala, the entorhinal cortex (Brodmann areas 28 and 34), or the surrounding

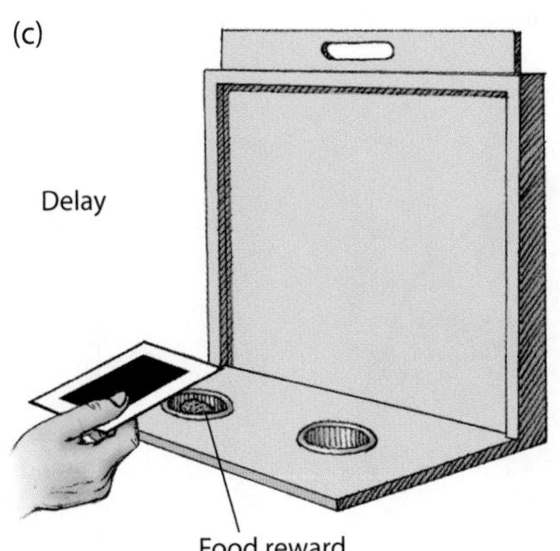

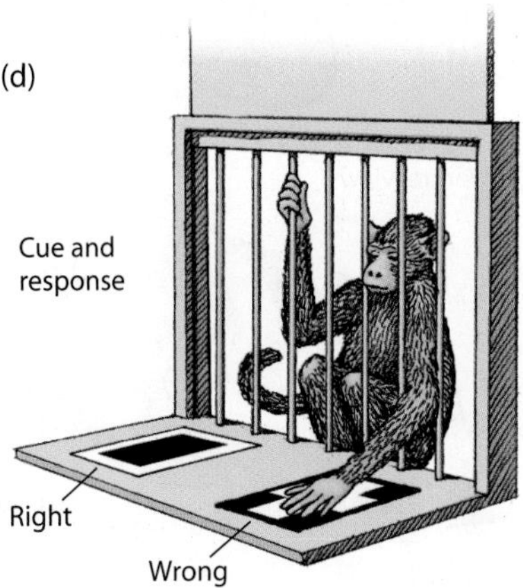

Figure 8.24 Delayed nonmatch-to-sample task. **(a)** The correct response has a food reward located under it. **(b)** The monkey is shown the correct response, which will yield a reward for the monkey. **(c)** The door is closed, and the reward is placed under a second response option. **(d)** The monkey is then shown two options and must pick the correct response (the one that does *not* match the original sample item) to get the reward. Here the monkey is shown making an error.

neocortex of the parahippocampal gyrus and the perirhinal cortex (Brodmann areas 35 and 36) (Figure 8.25). They wanted to extend Mishkin's work, which always involved lesions of the neocortex surrounding the amygdala or hippocampus, owing to the way the surgery was performed.

The results indicated that lesions of the hippocampus and amygdala produced the most severe memory deficits only when the cortex surrounding these regions was also lesioned. When lesions of the hippocampus and amygdala were made but the surrounding cortex was spared, the presence or absence of the amygdala lesion did not affect the monkey's memory. The amygdala, then, could not be part of the system that supported the acquisition of long-term memory.

In subsequent investigations, Zola and his colleagues selectively created lesions of the surrounding cortex in the perirhinal, entorhinal, and parahippocampal regions. The parahippocampal and perirhinal areas receive information from the visual, auditory, and somatosensory association cortex and send these inputs to the hippocampus (Figure 8.26), and from there to other cortical regions. These selective lesions worsened memory performance in delayed nonmatch-to-sample tests (Figure 8.27). Follow-up work showed that lesions of only the parahippocampal and perirhinal cortices also produced significant memory deficits.

How does this make sense in relation to R.B.'s profound anterograde amnesia with damage limited to the hippocampus and not involving the surrounding parahippocampal or perirhinal cortex? The answer is that the hippocampus cannot function properly if these vital connections are damaged. But more than this, we now also know that these regions are involved in much processing themselves, and hence lesions restricted to the hippocampus do not produce as severe a form of amnesia as do lesions that include surrounding cortex.

In summary, the data from animals are highly consistent with evidence from amnesic patients such as R.B. and H.M. implicating the hippocampal system in the medial temporal lobe and the associated cortex as critical for forming long-term memories. Lesions that damage the hippocampus directly, or damage the input–output relations of the hippocampus with the neocortex (Figure 8.28), produce severe memory impairments. The amygdala is not a crucial part of the system for episodic memory but is important for emotional memory (see Chapter 9).

Figure 8.25 Gross anatomy of the medial temporal lobe. **(a)** This lateral, see-through view of the left hemisphere shows the amygdala (green) and hippocampus (purple) within the temporal lobe. **(b)** This view from the ventral surface of the same hemisphere shows the amygdala and hippocampus, and indicates the locations of the parahippocampal gyrus and the entorhinal area (consisting of Brodmann areas 28 and typically also 34, being located in the most anterior portion of the parahippocampal gyrus).

(a) Lateral view

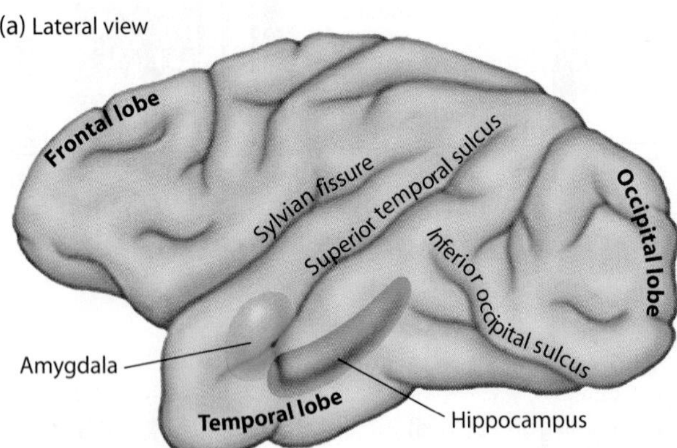

(b) Ventral view

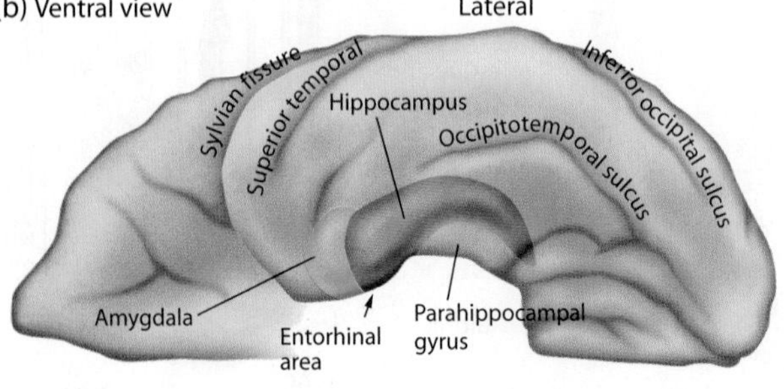

Figure 8.26 Flow of information between the neocortex and the hippocampal system. CA = cornu ammonis neuronal fields (CA1–CA3); DG = dentate gyrus; EC = entorhinal cortex; Sub = subiculum.

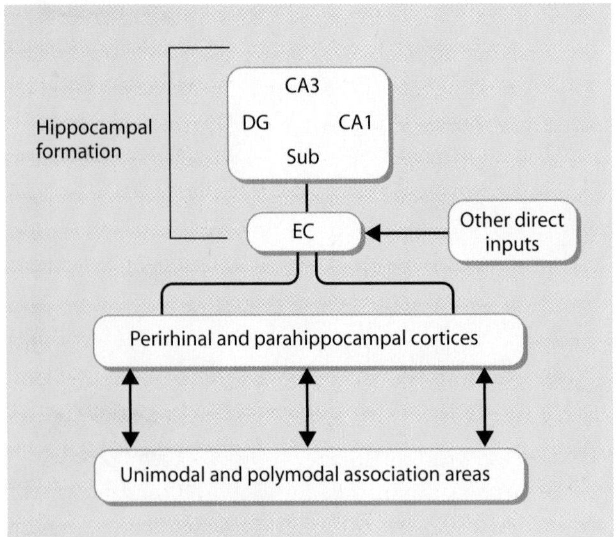

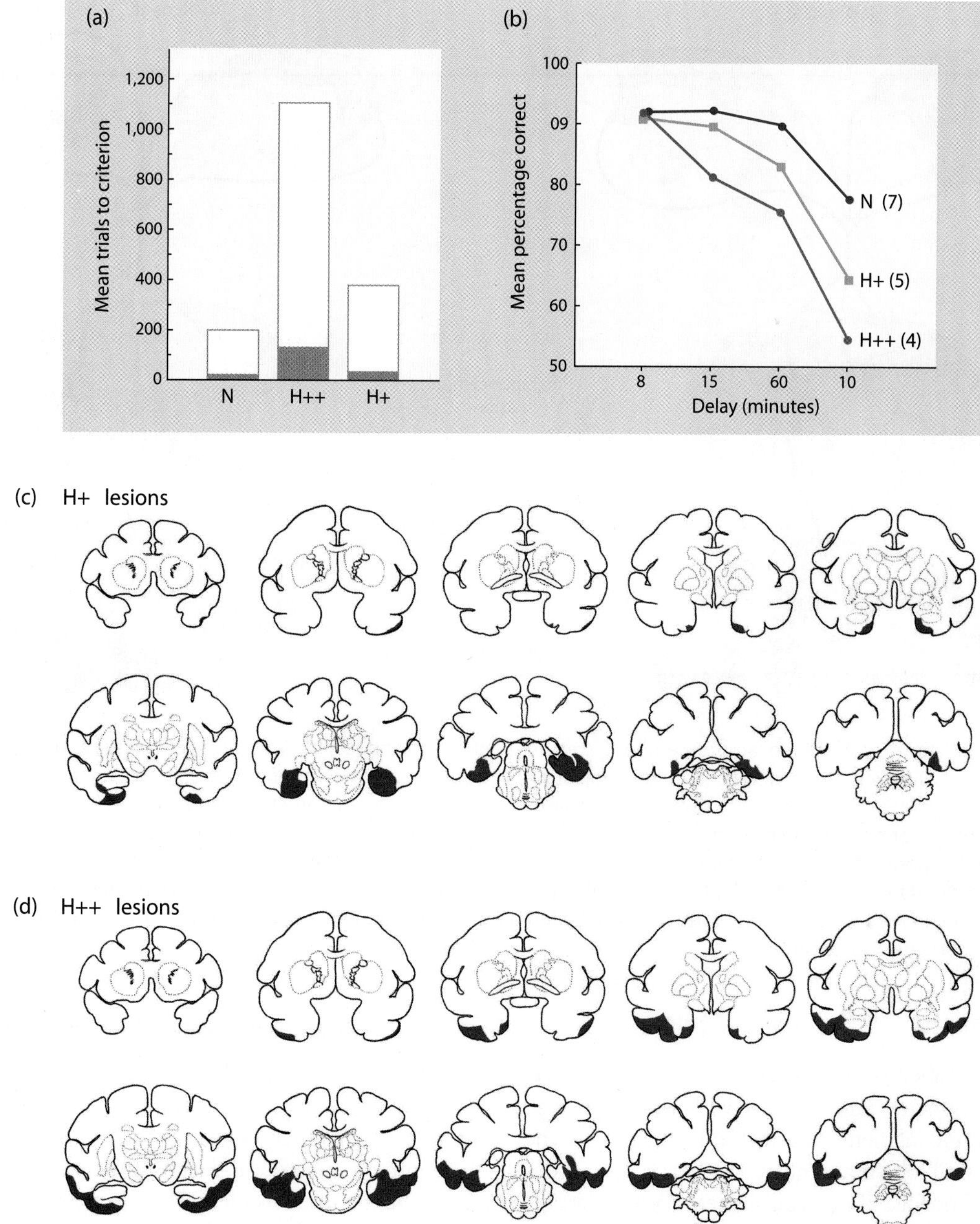

Figure 8.27 Performance on the delayed nonmatch-to-sample task at two different test sessions for normal monkeys (N); monkeys with lesions of the hippocampal formation, parahippocampal cortex, and perirhinal cortex (H++); and monkeys with lesions of the hippocampal formation and the parahippocampal cortex (H+). **(a)** Initial learning of the task with a delay of 8 s: Open bars = test 1; filled bars = test 2. **(b)** Performance across delays for the same groups. Lesions (red) in H+ **(c)** and H++ **(d)** are shown in coronal sections.

Moreover, the animal data match well the data from amnesic patients with regard to the preservation of short-term memory processes after the medial temporal lobe has been damaged; monkeys' memory deficits in the delayed nonmatch-to-sample task became more pronounced as the interval between the sample and the test increased. The medial temporal lobe, then, is not essential for short-term or working memory processes. As we noted earlier, the medial temporal lobe is likely not the locus of long-term storage, because retrograde amnesia is not total after damage to this area; rather, the medial temporal lobe is a key component in organizing and consolidating long-term memory that is permanently stored in a distributed fashion in the neocortex.

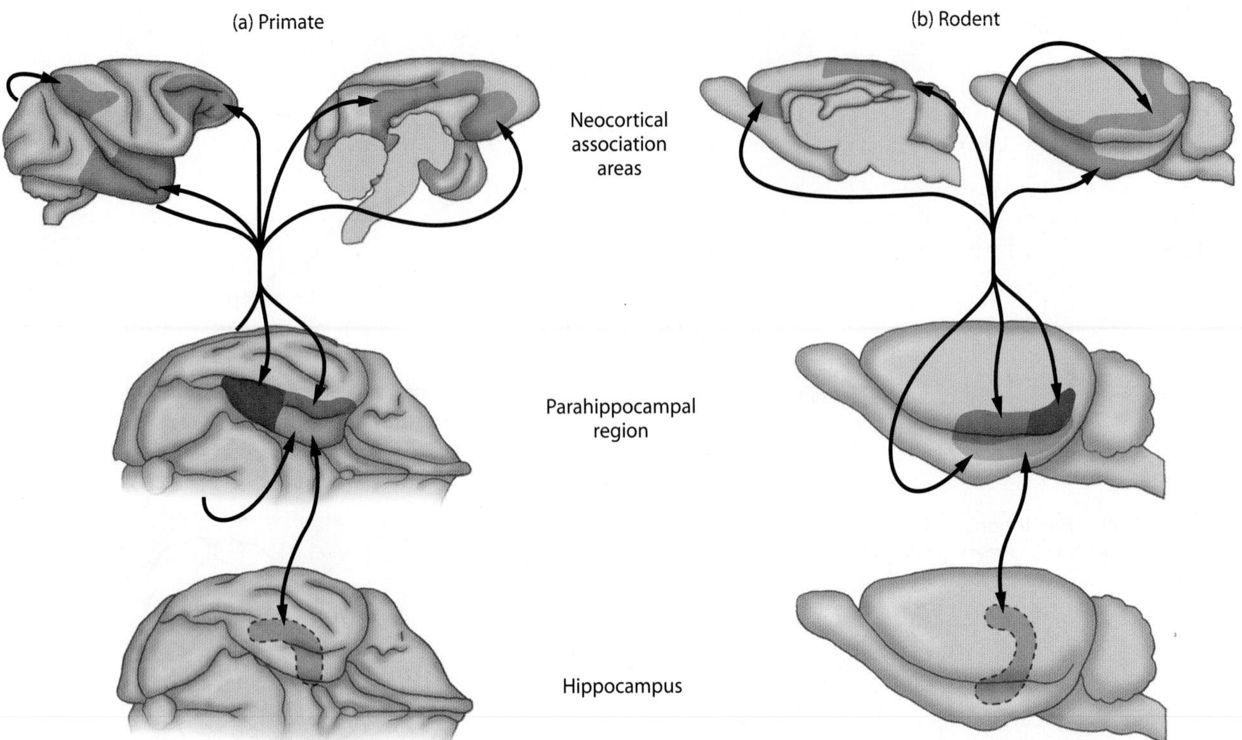

Figure 8.28 Anatomy of the hippocampal memory system in monkeys **(a)** and rats **(b)**. Most areas of cortex send information to the hippocampus. Different neocortical zones (blue) project to one or more subdivisions of the parahippocampal region. These subdivisions are the perirhinal cortex (purple), the parahippocampal cortex (dark purple), and the entorhinal cortex (light purple). These latter areas are interconnected and project to different regions of the hippocampus (green), including the dentate gyrus, CA3 and CA1 fields of the hippocampus, and the subiculum. As a result, the parahippocampal region serves as a site for the convergence of various cortical inputs. In addition, the parahippocampal region passes this information from the cortex to the hippocampus. Following processing in the hippocampus, information can be fed back via the parahippocampal region to the same areas of the cortex from which the original inputs came.

Imaging the Human Brain and Memory

The work described so far has dealt primarily with evidence from humans and animals with brain damage. These data are consistent with regard to the role of the medial temporal lobe in memory, and they suggest a degree of independence of procedural memory and perceptual priming (as well as conditioning and nonassociative learning) from the medial temporal lobe system. Over the past 15 years the number of studies of normal subjects using functional brain-imaging methods (both magnetic resonance methods and electromagnetic recording methods) to investigate memory mechanisms has increased exponentially. When considered together with evidence from work on animals and studies of brain damage in humans, neuroimaging is helping to clarify the role of various brain structures and systems in memory processes. Next we will consider key studies of the brain organization of episodic memory, semantic memory, procedural memory, and perceptual priming using methods of imaging and recording the function of the brain.

LONG-TERM MEMORY ENCODING AND RETRIEVAL

We started this chapter by defining different components of long-term memory, including *encoding* of new information that, after consolidation, creates a long-term memory; and *retrieval* that uses the stored information to create a conscious memory or to produce an action.

Given the role of the hippocampal system in forming long-term memories, researchers have eagerly tested this idea using functional brain-imaging methods in healthy human volunteers with intact memory ability. As described in Chapter 4, tools such as functional magnetic resonance imaging (fMRI) have provided significant new insights into human brain functions, including memory.

A key question has been whether the hippocampus becomes active during the encoding of new information, during the retrieval of information, or both. In this section we will review evidence demonstrating that the hippocampus is involved in both the encoding and the retrieval of information, but that different types of memory differentially rely on subregions of the medial

THE COGNITIVE NEUROSCIENTIST'S TOOLKIT

Monitoring Recollection Using Human Brain Electrophysiology

An invaluable criterion for ascertaining whether explicit and implicit processes are subserved by separate brain systems is to demonstrate that they are independent. What we want to show is that performance on implicit tests is not correlated with explicit recollections about test items. One problem in memory research has been the difficulty of revealing how much recollective experience patients might have for previously viewed information, even though they are not required to recollect anything about that information. It would be tremendously helpful to distinguish between normal subjects who do have and those who do not have recollective experiences. Ken Paller, Marta Kutas, and Heather McIsaac (1995) provided a means of doing this through electrical recordings (event-related potentials, or ERPs) of brain activity in healthy persons.

They varied the depth of encoding words by having subjects generate a mental image corresponding to the word or merely indicate whether the word contained more than one syllable. Later the subjects were asked to make a lexical decision (is it a word?) about a list of words and nonword letter strings. The words were a mixture of those from the prior image task list, those from the prior syllable task list, and new words that they had not seen. In a second experiment, the researchers asked subjects to perform the lexical decision task and give a recognition judgment about whether they had seen the words before. In each experiment, the researchers performed separate recognition posttests to assess the extent to which subjects could recollect the words.

The behavioral measures revealed priming in the lexical decision task (previously seen words were classified as words faster than were new words). Priming was not affected by whether subjects had studied the words in the image versus the syllable condition. Recognition scores from the posttest, though, differed significantly according to the study task: Subjects were better at recognizing previously seen words if, at the time of the study, they had generated an image corresponding to the word. Thus, the behavioral data differed in how the task affected implicit (lexical decision) versus explicit (recognition) processes. Were there any electrophysiological signs of recollection? Yes, as the figure shows, the voltage of ERPs elicited by words was more positive 500 to 900 ms after the onset of words that had been seen previously in the image condition than for words in the syllable condition. Because this ERP mirrored the effect of the study task on recognition performance, it is a physiological sign of recollection. This is especially true because recollection was not necessary for the implicit memory test. The researchers noted that the ERPs permitted a view of human subjective experience that was not contaminated by introspective reports, which are notoriously unreliable.

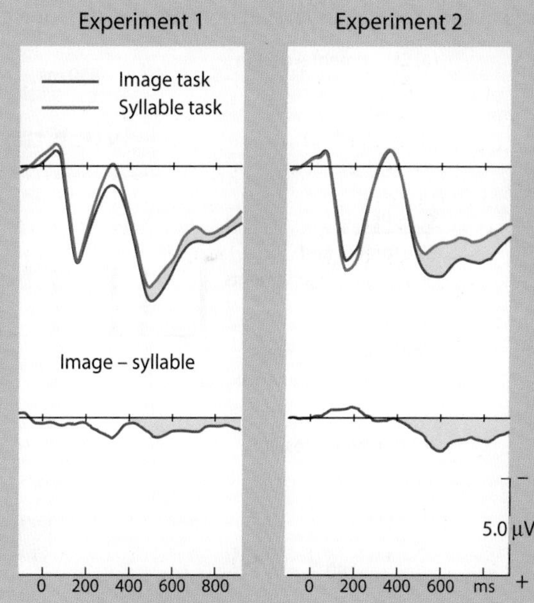

At the top, ERPs from two experiments by Paller, Kutas, and McIsaac (1995) showing responses for words that had been seen previously in one of two conditions: when the words were used to generate images (red line), and when the subjects decided how many syllables were present in the word (blue line). At the bottom, the difference between these two conditions is plotted as the subtraction waveform (image condition minus syllable condition). Words that had been encoded during the image task elicited more positivity between latencies of 500 to 900 ms (shaded pink), and this effect was larger when, on the test, the subjects were required to include recognition judgments (bottom right).

temporal lobe during encoding and retrieval, and that during retrieval the medial temporal lobe memory systems reactivate cortical regions that were important during the original encoding of information. We will follow this with a discussion of the role of the frontal cortex in long-term memory encoding and retrieval.

Encoding and the Hippocampus Functional-MRI studies have shown that the human hippocampus is active when new information is encoded. This kind of work typically involves the subsequent-memory paradigm. In this type of paradigm, subjects are presented with items that they are asked to remember, and their brain activity is measured with fMRI while they are encoding the information. Then, during a later test, memory for the items can be assessed in different ways, such as by asking subjects whether they have seen the item previously when the items are embedded in new lists that contain things not included in the original encoding session. Using event-related fMRI methods, it is then possible to sort and analyze the original data gathered during encoding as a function of whether the items were later remembered or forgotten. That is, data for the brain responses to the items that were later remembered are col-

Figure 8.29 Experimental design and behavioral results of testing for involvement of the hippocampus in information encoding. **(a)** The sequence of events in one scanning run. At encoding, subjects viewed a series of words and made either an animacy (animate versus not animate) or size (large versus small) judgment for each, depending on the color in which the word was shown (e.g., red font meant to perform a size judgment, so for the word *NICKEL* in green ink, the correct response would be "inanimate"). Later, in a test at retrieval after the scan session, subjects made two decisions about the items presented, which included the old items and new items never seen before. First, subjects were asked to indicate whether and how well (how confidently) they recognized the items (e.g., on a scale of 1 to 6, from definitely new to definitely old). Second, they had to make a source memory judgment (had it previously been presented in red or in green?) for each word. **(b)** Mean proportions of studied ("old") and unstudied ("new") items endorsed at each confidence level. Performance on the source memory judgment (red or green) is not shown.

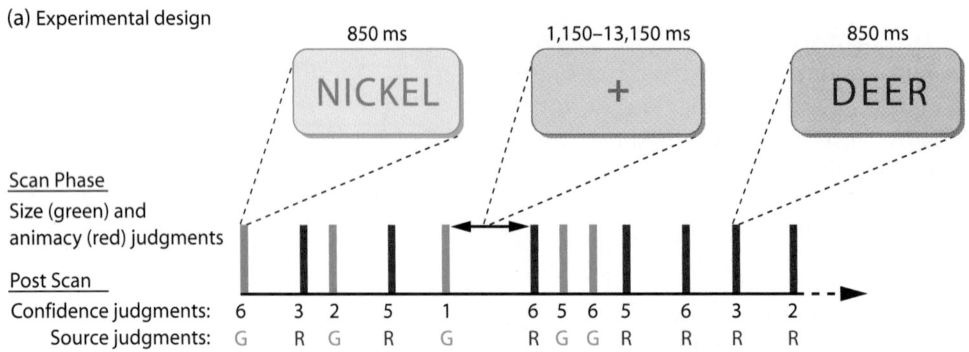

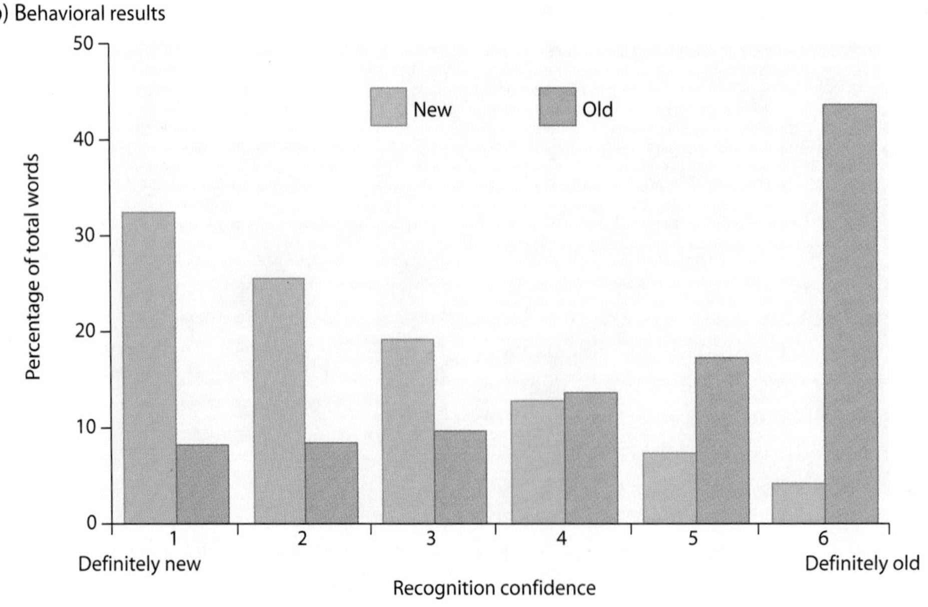

lapsed together, and the same is done separately for data for the responses to the items that were forgotten.

Such analysis made it possible to demonstrate that the hippocampus was active during encoding of the information that was later remembered. Charan Ranganath and Andrew Yonelinas at the University of California, Davis; Mark D'Esposito at the University of California, Berkeley; and their colleagues (2004) performed this type of analysis using the paradigm shown in Figure 8.29. They presented healthy volunteers with words on a screen at a rate of about one word every 2 s. The words (360 in total) consisted of animate and inanimate items that were either large or small, and either red or green. Depending on the color, the subjects were required to make either an animacy judgment or a size judgment for each item.

While viewing and making these decisions (the encoding phase of the experiment), the subjects' brains were scanned in an MRI scanner. Later, outside the scanner, the subjects were tested on their memory for the items that they had been shown; the 360 "old" items were mixed with 360 "new" items not shown earlier. Subjects were asked to rate each item (now shown in black) on a scale of 1 to 6 to indicate whether they recalled having seen the word before, and also to specify whether the item had been presented in green or red (a source memory judgment—the source being the context in which the item had been previously viewed). The trick then was to sort and separately analyze the old items as a function of (a) whether they were properly recollected and (b) whether the source was correctly identified. First we will consider the brain regions that were active at *encoding* for correctly recollected items (those that the subject had seen, reported having seen before, and correctly indicated the color of their presentation).

Ranganath and his coworkers found that correctly recollected words activated regions of both the hippocampus and the posterior parahippocampal cortex (Figure 8.30a). This evidence that the medial temporal lobe, including the hippocampus proper, was activated

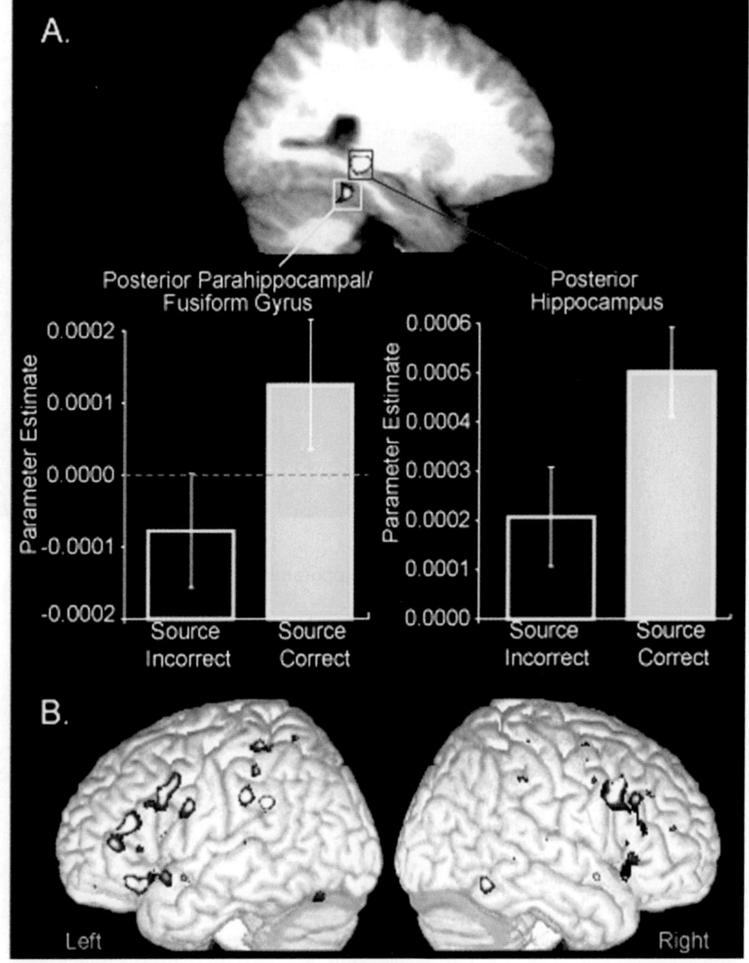

Figure 8.30 Subsequent memory effects: activity at encoding that correlates with better recollection of words at testing—that is, those for which the source memory judgment of red or green (see Figure 8.29) was correct. **(a)** Sagittal section through the right medial temporal lobe. Two regions in the medial temporal lobe that exhibited subsequent recollection effects were the posterior hippocampus (shown within the red square) and the posterior parahippocampal cortex (yellow square). The plots for the parahippocampal cortex and the hippocampus show the statistical parameter estimates (indexing response amplitude) for recognized items eliciting correct (filled bars) versus incorrect (open bars) source judgments. **(b)** Surface renderings of the left and right hemispheres show additional regions of cortical activation at encoding for items recollected correctly later.

during encoding fits well with evidence from studies in animals and patients with amnesia suggesting that the hippocampus is important for the formation of new long-term memories. Therefore, one problem with hippocampal damage may be an inability to encode the information properly in the first place. These researchers also observed regions of the frontal cortex that were activated during encoding (Figure 8.30b), a topic that we will return to later in the chapter.

Retrieval and the Hippocampus The hippocampus is also involved in the retrieval of information from long-term memory. In one study similar to that described in the preceding section, event-related fMRI methods were used to reveal that the hippocampus is activated when information is correctly recollected. Laura Eldridge and her colleagues at the University of California, Los Angeles (2000), presented subjects with lists of words that they were told to memorize. No other task was involved at the encoding stage, and no memory strategy was suggested. Twenty minutes later, in a retrieval task, the subjects were presented with the previously presented (old) words intermingled with new words and asked to respond whether they had seen the word during the prior encoding phase, and if they indicated "yes," then to make a decision about whether they actually remembered (recollected) seeing it before or whether the item merely seemed familiar to them.

The interesting part of this study was that neuroimaging data were collected during the retrieval phase of the study, and brain responses measured with fMRI could be sorted according to whether the subjects actually recollected the item, were only familiar with the item, were sure they had not seen the word before, or

Figure 8.31 Retrieval in the hippocampus. **(a)** Horizontal sections through the brain at the level of the inferior (left), middle (center), and superior (right) hippocampus. The red outline of the region of interest in the left hippocampus is based on anatomical landmarks. **(b)** Hemodynamic responses from event-related fMRI measures taken during the retrieval of previously studied words (see text for paradigm). The hippocampus was activated by correctly recollected words (solid red line) but not by words that the subjects had previously seen but could not recollect, indicating that the words merely seemed familiar (solid black line); there was no hippocampal activity for words that were correctly identified as new (not seen previously; dashed red line) or for errors in which the subject did not remember the words (dashed black line), despite having seen them previously.

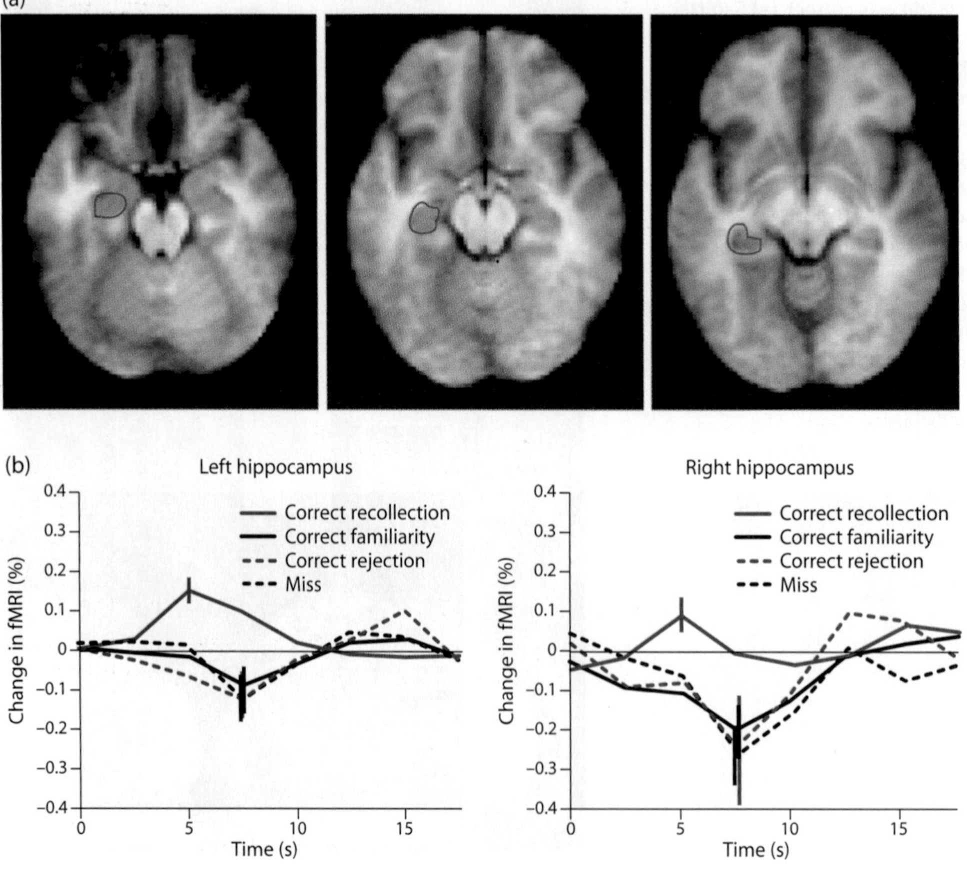

were mistaken about whether they had seen the word. The neuroimaging results were clear: During retrieval the hippocampus was selectively active only for items that were actually correctly recollected (Figure 8.31). This finding strongly suggests that the hippocampus is involved in retrieval for episodic memories.

Does this make sense with respect to the amnesia literature reporting that patients with damage to the hippocampus show an intact ability to retrieve episodic memories from most of their lives prior to the hippocampal damage? Yes, if one considers the experimental paradigm used here. The subjects had retained the new memories in this study for only 20 minutes before the retrieval test was administered. Therefore, combining this information from neuroimaging with the amnesia findings supports the idea that, over time, memories are consolidated and eventually become independent of the hippocampus for retrieval, as in the case of patient H.M., who could remember most of his life before a period of months prior to the surgery on his bilateral medial temporal lobes.

Encoding, Retrieval, and the Medial Temporal Lobe Of increasing interest are the roles of different subdivisions of the medial temporal lobe in long-term memory. For example, in the study of retrieval described in the previous section and illustrated in Figure 8.31, the hippocampus was activated only for episodic recollections and not for memory that did not contain awareness of the prior event; that is, the items recollected were familiar to the subjects and were recognized by their **familiarity** alone. This and related data raise the question of what brain regions are involved in nonepisodic, familiarity-based memory encoding and retrieval.

To begin to answer this question, we return to the encoding study of Ranganath and his colleagues described in Figure 8.29, in which subjects were required to make source memory judgments related to episodic memory (see Figure 8.30) and also to rate their confidence about whether they had seen the item before—a measure that taps familiarity. Figure 8.32 contains the neuroimaging results from this analysis of confidence ratings and shows that regions of the anterior parahippocampal gyrus, in and around the entorhinal cortex, were activated during recognition based on familiarity. Under these conditions, however, the hippocampus itself was not activated. Taken together, the work of these researchers demonstrates a double dissociation in the medial temporal lobe for encoding different forms of memory: one for recognition based on the recollection of episodic (source) information involving the hippocampus and posterior parahippocampal cortex, and the other for supporting familiarity-based recognition memory in the entorhinal cortex.

Does a similar distinction between recollection and familiarity hold for retrieval of long-term memories? Yes. Studies investigating recollection and familiarity using fMRI measures during retrieval have shown that

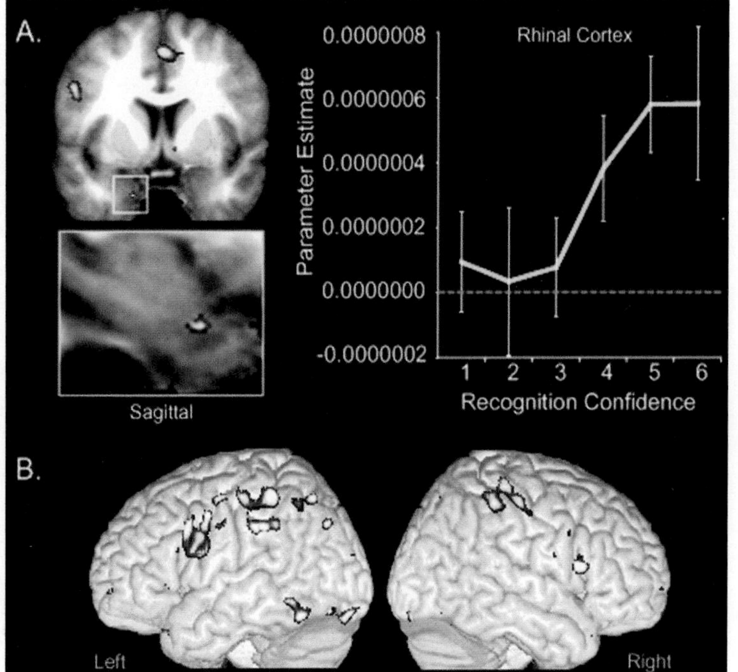

Figure 8.32 Familiarity-based recognition memory: activity during encoding that correlates with the confidence of recognizing an item as having been seen before. **(a)** Coronal section through the brain at the level of the anterior medial temporal lobe. Functional-MRI activations that correlated with confidence ratings can be seen in the entorhinal cortex (yellow box and in an expanded view below the coronal section). **(b)** These images of the left and right hemispheres show other regions of cortical activation.

HOW THE BRAIN WORKS

False Memories and the Medial Temporal Lobes

When our memory fails, we usually forget events that happened in the past. Sometimes, however, something more surprising occurs: We remember events that never happened. Whereas forgetting has been a topic of research for more than a century, memory researchers did not have a good method to investigate false memories in the laboratory until Henry Roediger and Kathleen McDermott at Washington University rediscovered an old technique in 1995. In this technique subjects are presented with a list of words (e.g., *thread, pin, eye, sewing, sharp, point, haystack, pain, injection*, etc.) in which all the words are highly associated to a word that is not presented (in this case, *needle*; did you have to go back and recheck the list?). When subjects are asked subsequently to recall or recognize the words in the list, they show a strong tendency to falsely remember the associated word that was not presented. The memory illusion is so powerful that participants are willing to claim that they vividly remember seeing the nonpresented critical word in the study list.

However, when participants are interrogated carefully about the conscious experience associated with remembering items from the list (true items) and the critical nonpresented words (false items), they tend to rate true items higher than false items in terms of sensory details (Mather et al., 1997; K. A. Norman & Schacter, 1997). This finding introduced a conundrum in false-memory research: How can human participants believe in their illusory recollections, and at the same time be able to differentiate them from genuine recollections in terms of sensory detail?

Roberto Cabeza at Duke University and collaborators (2001) provided a possible answer to this conundrum. In their study, subjects watched a videotape segment in which two speakers alternatively presented lists of associated words. The subjects then were required to perform an old/new recognition test that included true items, false items, and unrelated new words (new items), while their brains were scanned with functional MRI. Changes in blood flow in the brain that indicated changing patterns of neural activity were measured separately for each kind of item. Memory performance showed the same pattern as in previous studies: Participants were able to reject new items but showed a strong tendency to falsely recognize false items.

The researchers found a dissociation between two medial temporal lobe regions, as the figure illustrates. In the hippocampus bilaterally, false items elicited

the hippocampus is activated during the recognition of items based on recollection of having seen them before, whereas regions of the entorhinal cortex are influenced by the familiarity engendered by items during retrieval. One study nicely making this point is the work of Daniela Montaldi and her colleagues at the University of Oxford (2006). They showed subjects pictures of scenes during an encoding session, and then 2 days later tested them on their recognition of the scenes among new scenes they had not seen before; fMRI measures of brain activity were obtained during this retrieval session.

Montaldi and colleagues asked subjects to rate the pictures of scenes as new, slightly familiar, moderately familiar, very familiar, or recollected. The results showed the same pattern as in the encoding study already described. The hippocampus was activated only for pictures of scenes that the subjects could recollect having seen before, whereas regions of the medial temporal lobe outside the hippocampus, including the entorhinal cortex, were correlated in activity with the strength of subjects' familiarity with the scenes when not actually recollected (Figure 8.33).

In sum, evidence from several sources converges to indicate that the medial temporal lobe supports different forms of memory, and these different forms of memory (recollective experience versus familiarity) are

more neural activity than did new items, and as much activity as true items; whereas in the left parahippocampal gyrus—a region surrounding the hippocampus—false items elicited about the same amount of activity as new items and significantly less activity than true items. In other words, the hippocampus responded similarly to true and false items, and the parahippocampal gyrus responded more strongly to true than to false items. Because true and false items were similar in terms of semantic content but differed in terms of sensory content, these results suggest that the hippocampus is involved in the retrieval of semantic information, whereas the parahippocampal gyrus is involved in the retrieval of sensory information.

This dissociation provides a possible solution for the aforementioned conundrum: The memory system in the medial temporal lobes can generate two different types of messages when information is presented. Whereas anterior hippocampal activity suggests that false items are like true items, posterior parahippocampal activity suggests that false items are like new items. These two messages are not contradictory: False items are like true items in terms of their semantic properties, but they are like new items in terms of their sensory properties.

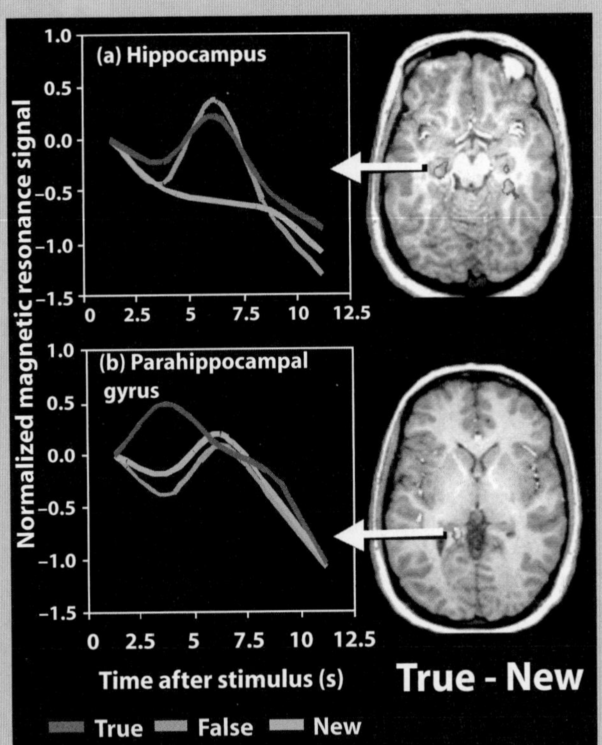

Significant increases in blood flow in regions of the medial temporal lobes (right side of figure), and their corresponding hemodynamic response functions (left side of figure). **(a)** Bilateral hippocampal regions were more activated for true and false items than for new items. There was no difference between activations for true and false items. **(b)** A left posterior parahippocampal region was more activated for true items than for false and new items. There was no difference between activations for false and new items. The hemodynamic response functions at left were taken from the regions of interest defined by the statistical contrast of true activations minus new activations, which is shown at right in the brain sections.

supported by different subdivisions of this brain region. The hippocampus is involved in encoding and retrieval for episodic memories that are recollected, and areas outside the hippocampus, especially the entorhinal cortex, support recognition based on familiarity.

Relational Memory, Recollection, Familiarity, and the Medial Temporal Lobe Why are recollective processes and familiarity-based recognition processes supported by different parts of the medial temporal lobe? The answer is in the anatomy. The neocortex provides different types of information to different subregions of the medial temporal lobe. Information from unimodal sensory regions of neocortex about "what" an item is enters the entorhinal cortex via the anterior parts of the parahippocampal region through what is referred to as *perirhinal cortex.* In contrast, information from polymodal neocortical areas about "where" something is located enters a different part of the entorhinal cortex via the more posterior parts of the parahippocampal cortex. These two streams of information about something that is perceived remain segregated in entorhinal cortex but then converge in the hippocampus. As a result, the hippocampus is able to relate the two types of information about something that the individual encounters; we can refer to this as *relational memory.*

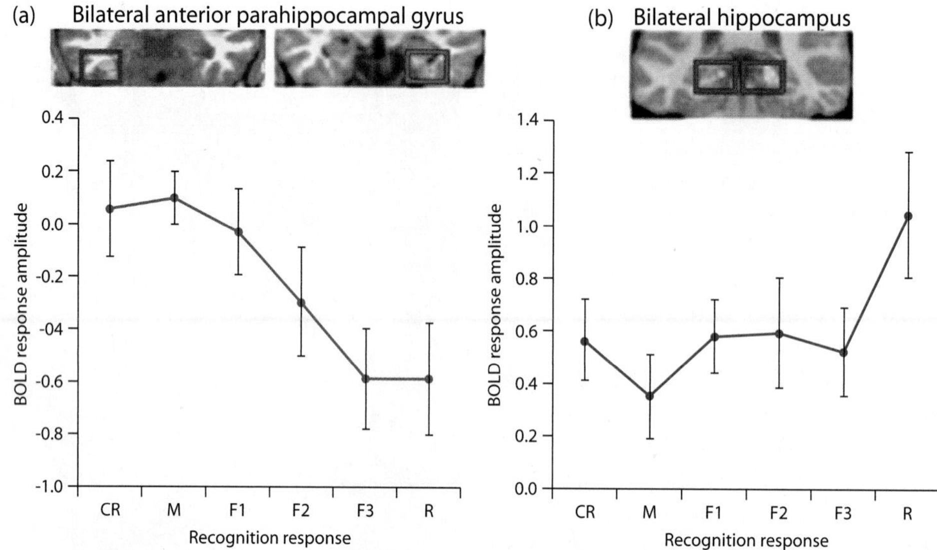

Figure 8.33 Recollection (R) and familiarity (F) during retrieval. Coronal sections through the hippocampus. Participants studied scenes and were scanned during recognition testing. Activation in bilateral anterior parahippocampal regions **(a)** monotonically decreased with increasing confidence. In contrast, activations in bilateral hippocampal regions **(b)** increased only for recollected items, as compared with nonrecollected items. CR = correct rejection (an item that was correctly identified as new); M = miss (an item that was seen before but the subject reported as not having seen previously; F1 = weak familiarity, F2 = moderate familiarity, F3 = strong familiarity.

In general, what we have been referring to as *episodic information* that leads to recollective experiences is relational memory because not only can we indicate that something has been encountered previously, but we can also retrieve the relational context (sources) in which it was encountered before. Neal Cohen and his colleagues (Ryan et al., 2002) at the University of Illinois have investigated relational memory using measures of eye fixation in complex scenes whose object and spatial relationships they manipulate experimentally. They found that healthy subjects were sensitive to changing relationships in the scenes, even when not aware of them, as demonstrated by their altered patterns of eye movements (Figure 8.34), but amnesic subjects with hippocampal damage were not. These researchers have therefore argued that medial temporal amnesia is a disorder of relational memory.

Taken together with the dissociations in recollection and familiarity for encoding and retrieval reviewed in the preceding discussion, this line of reasoning suggests a model for the medial temporal lobe in long-term memory that helps us understand why different regions of the medial temporal lobe are more sensitive for recollective experience (relational memory) while others are more involved in familiarity-based recognition that does not require the recollection of episodic information. If this is so, we can ask whether the hippocampus is the store for information that has been related from the "what" and "where" inputs to the medial temporal lobe. The answer is no, as might be expected from studies that have shown intact remote memories in amnesia. But then what is the mechanism? We describe a possible mechanism next.

Retrieval and Reactivation in Long-Term Memory

The anatomy of the projections of "what" and "where" information into the hippocampus described in the previous section is matched by a similar outflow from the hippocampus to the neocortex. Feedback projections from the hippocampus go to the entorhinal cortex, then to the perirhinal and parahippocampal cortices, and then back to the neocortical areas that provided the inputs to the neocortex in the first place. What is the role of this feedback system? Evidence to answer this question comes from neuroimaging studies during retrieval.

Mark Wheeler and his colleagues at Washington University in St. Louis (2000) investigated the brain regions that were involved in the retrieval of different types of information. They asked subjects to learn a set of sounds or pictures (visual stimuli) during an encoding period over 2 days. Each sound or picture was paired with a written label describing the item (e.g., the word *BELL*, followed by the sound of a bell). On the third day the subjects were given perceptual and memory tests while being scanned with fMRI. The perceptual test was the presentation of the stimuli (label plus sound or picture) to identify brain regions involved in the perceptual processing of the items. The memory retrieval test presented the word label and asked each subject to retrieve the associated picture

(a)

(b)

Figure 8.34 Scenes with changing relational information used to test for relational memory. Eye movements (red lines) and fixations (white crosses) for two healthy subjects are shown superimposed on the same scene with different viewing histories. A critical region is outlined by the rectangle. **(a)** When the scene was viewed as a repeated scene and nothing changed in the critical area, it did not attract eye fixations. **(b)** However, when the scene was viewed as a manipulated scene (two girls present during the first showing were removed in the subsequent test block, the latter is shown here), many eye fixations focusing on that region were observed (i.e., white crosses in the critical region).

or sound from memory and then indicate with a press of a button whether the item was a sound or a picture.

Wheeler and coworkers found that, during retrieval of pictures, regions of neocortex that had been activated during perception of the pictures were reactivated. Similarly, during retrieval of sounds, different areas of the neocortex that had been activated during the perception of sounds were reactivated. In each case, during memory retrieval the modality-specific regions of activity in the neocortex were subsets of the areas activated by presentation of the perceptual information alone, when no memory task was required (Figure 8.35). Interestingly, the activated areas of sensory-specific neocortex were not lower level sensory cortical regions, but later stages of visual and auditory association cortex, at a stage where the incoming signals would have been perceptually well processed (e.g., to the point where identity was coded).

This finding suggests that the specific relational information for items stored in long-term memory may be coded during retrieval by *reactivation* of the original neocortical areas that provide input to the hippocampus during encoding. In subsequent work, Wheeler and colleagues (2006) showed that visual processing regions in inferotemporal cortex were involved in the preparation to retrieve visual information, whereas the more dorsal parietal and superior occipital activity was related to the process of searching memory for the relevant item. These findings help refine the role of different brain regions in reactivation during long-term memory retrieval.

Encoding, Retrieval, and the Frontal Cortex In both the neuroimaging research into memory and the studies of amnesia caused by brain damage or disease, the frontal cortex is consistently found to be involved in both short-term and long-term memory processes. In particular, across many studies of memory the role of the frontal cortex in encoding and retrieval in long-term memory has been a key point of debate. In a meta-analysis of the literature, Roberto Cabeza, Lars Nyberg, Endel Tulving, and their colleagues have investigated the way in which frontal cortex contributes to encoding and retrieval (Nyberg et al., 1996).

As Figure 8.36 shows, the left frontal cortex is often found to be involved in encoding of episodic information, whereas the right frontal cortex is often found to be activated in episodic retrieval. These findings led Cabeza and colleagues to develop a model proposing that contributions to encoding (left frontal) and retrieval (right frontal) were lateralized within frontal cortex. However, as Figure 8.36 also shows, semantic *retrieval* tends to involve the left frontal cortex, as does encoding. The same is true of regions including Broca's area (Brodmann area 44 extending into area 46) and the ventral lateral region (Brodmann areas 44 and 45). This lateralization to the left hemisphere for semantic information remains regardless of whether the memories being retrieved are of objects or of words.

Others, including William Kelley at Dartmouth College and his colleagues have argued that lateralization of

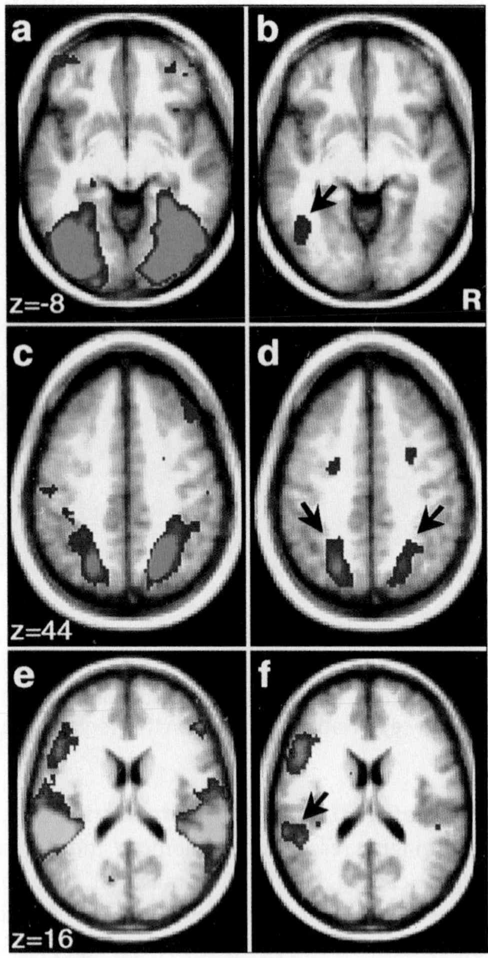

Figure 8.35 Reactivation of modality-specific cortex during long-term memory retrieval. **(a, c, e)** Areas activated by viewing pictures **(a and c)** and hearing sounds **(e)**. **(b, d, f)** Areas activated during the retrieval of pictures or sounds from memory. Arrows indicate regions of overlap between memory and perceptual activations. The right hemisphere of the brain is on the right of each image.

frontal cortex activity during long-term memory retrieval is more related to the nature of the material to be processed than to a distinction between encoding and retrieval (Buckner et al., 1999). The idea is that the left hemisphere is more involved in processes coded by linguistic representations, whereas the right frontal cortex is more involved in object and spatial memory information (Figure 8.37). Much work remains to establish the probably many roles of the frontal cortex in memory processing, since various competing models remain viable to explain the patterns of deficits in amnesia and activations in functional imaging that have been reported.

ENCODING AND RETRIEVAL OF PROCEDURAL MEMORY

Earlier we learned that amnesic patients demonstrate implicit learning of motor sequences, acquiring new procedural knowledge even when they cannot form explicit memories about the stimulus sequence (see Figure 8.21). Amnesics provide powerful evidence that implicit learning need not be mediated by explicit knowledge about the material—a point that is difficult to demonstrate behaviorally in healthy subjects because of the possibility that some explicit knowledge of the sequences contributed to sequence learning.

Scott Grafton of the University of California, Santa Barbara, and his colleagues, including one of the authors, R.B.I. (1995), used neuroimaging to investigate the brain basis of procedural motor learning in normal subjects. They compared conditions in which the subjects learned motor sequences implicitly during dual-task conditions, which helped to prevent subjects from explicitly noticing and learning the sequence. The subjects responded to stimulus sequences by pushing a button with the right hand while also monitoring a

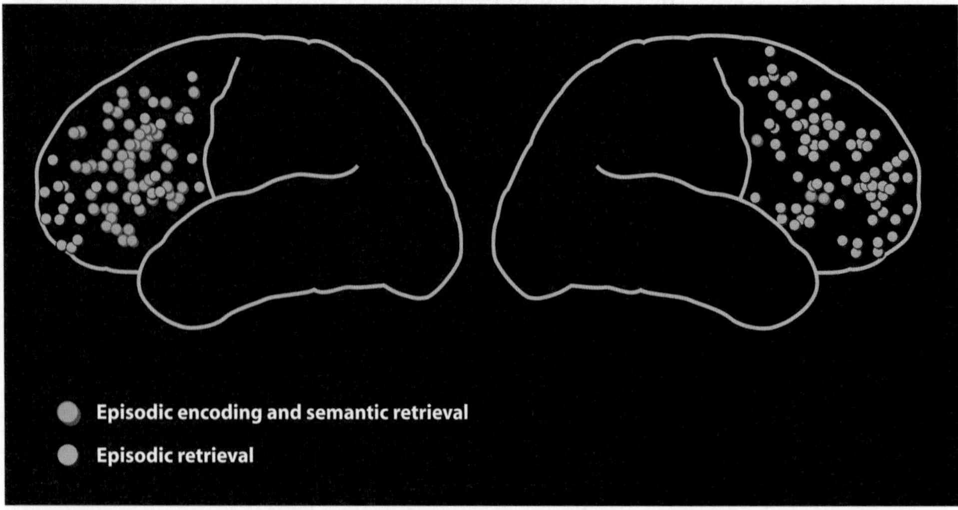

Figure 8.36 Summary of regions in the prefrontal cortex that showed activation for episodic encoding and semantic retrieval (blue) or episodic retrieval (red). The data are from many studies, reported in Nyberg, Cabeza, & Tulving, 1996, 1998; and Tulving et al., 1994.

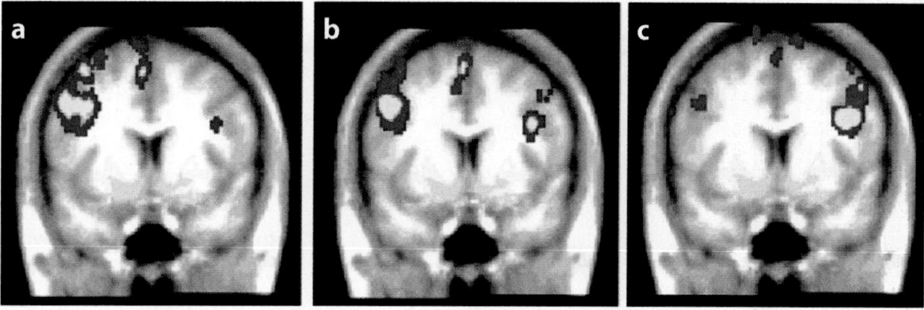

Figure 8.37 Material-specific frontal cortex activation during memory encoding. **(a)** Words activate left frontal cortex during encoding. **(b)** Nameable objects activate both left and right frontal cortex during encoding. **(c)** Encoding of faces activates primarily right frontal cortex.

sequence of tones and counting the tones of lower frequency. The investigators compared this scenario to the condition in which subjects performed only the sequence-learning task and thus might become explicitly aware of the sequence.

PET scanning conducted during the dual-task condition demonstrated activation of the motor cortex and the supplementary motor area of the left hemisphere, as well as the putamen in the basal ganglia bilaterally—all part of the motor system. Also activated were the rostral prefrontal cortex and the parietal cortex, which also play roles in motor control. Therefore, when subjects were implicitly learning the task, brain areas that control limb movements were activated (Figure 8.38a). When the distracting auditory task was removed, the right dorsolateral prefrontal cortex, right premotor cortex, right putamen, and parieto-occipital cortex were activated bilaterally (Figure 8.38b). Under these conditions, 7 of the 12 subjects became aware of the sequence. The differences in activations for the seven aware and five unaware subjects are presented in Figure 8.38c. The awareness effects were correlated with activity in the right temporal lobe, left and right inferior parietal cortex, right premotor cortex, and anterior cingulate cortex.

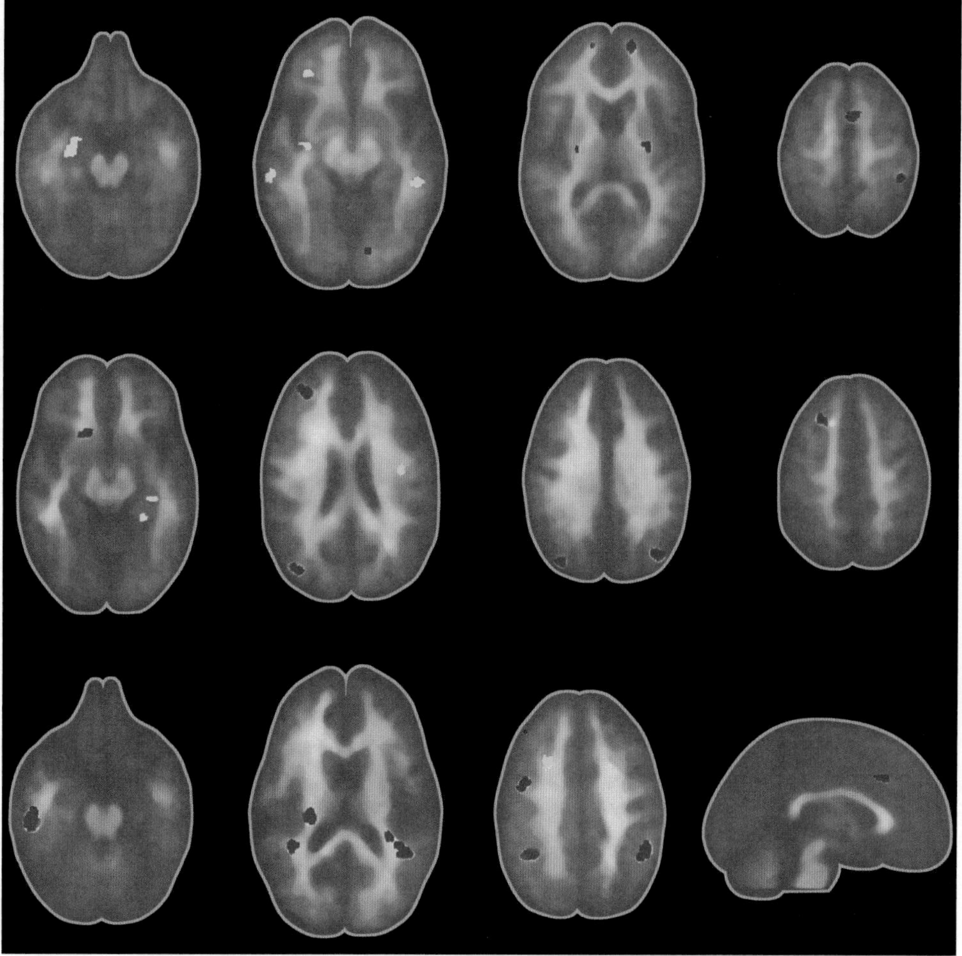

Figure 8.38 Activations corresponding to implicit learning of motor sequences in normal subjects. Scans showing areas of activation (yellow-orange) are overlaid onto MRI scans. The right hemisphere is on the left. Different brain areas were activated when subjects performed the task under dual-task conditions designed to emphasize implicit learning **(a)** than when they performed the task under single-task conditions, during which the subject might develop explicit awareness **(b)**. The images in part **(c)** show the differences between the seven subjects who reported awareness of the sequence in the single-task condition and the five subjects who did not.

(a) Dual task

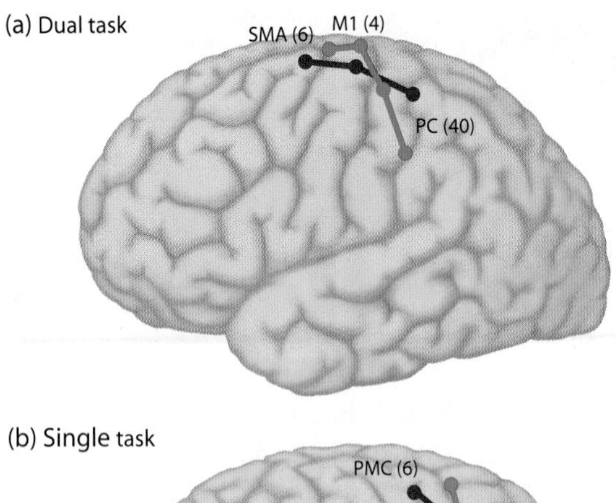

(b) Single task

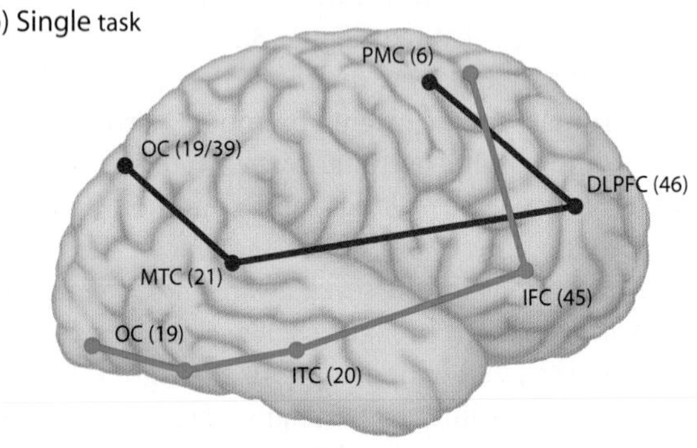

Figure 8.39 Model of two systems for motor sequence learning. Major cortical regions showing increased blood flow correlated with dual-task sequence learning **(a)** and single-task learning **(b)**. Red lines refer to learning of visuospatial sequences based on Grafton et al., 1995; green lines refer to learning of color sequences based on Hazeltine et al., 1997. Under dual-task conditions, where learning of sequences is implicit, increased neural activity was observed in the parietal cortex (PC), supplementary motor area (SMA), and primary motor cortex (M1), and is referred to in the theory as the *dorsal pathway* for sequence learning. Under single-task conditions, where either implicit or explicit learning may be involved, activity was restricted to the occipital cortex (OC), temporal cortex (medial temporal [MTC] and inferior temporal [ITC]), prefrontal cortex (inferior frontal [IFC] and dorsolateral prefrontal [DLPFC]), and lateral premotor cortex (PMC). This network is referred to as the *ventral pathway* for sequence learning. The numbers in parentheses refer to Brodmann's areas.

These PET data, as well as convergent evidence from transcranial magnetic stimulation and animal studies that we do not discuss here, indicate that the motor cortex is critical for implicit procedural learning of movement patterns. Activations in the putamen would be expected, given that patients with Huntington's disease (a disease of the basal ganglia) have deficits in sequence-learning tasks. Because the supplementary motor cortex was also activated during implicit learning, it might be part of a network of subcortical and cortical areas collectively known as the *cortical–subcortical motor loop*, which regulates voluntary movements. Explicit learning and awareness of the sequences required increased activity in the right premotor cortex, the dorsolateral prefrontal cortex associated with working memory, the anterior cingulate, areas in the parietal cortex concerned with voluntary attention, and the lateral temporal cortical areas that store explicit memories. Demonstrated here are clear dissociations between brain systems involved in explicit and implicit learning and memory in healthy humans.

These and related findings have led to the development of a theory of sequential motor learning. Richard Ivry of the University of California, Berkeley, and his colleagues articulated this model in 2003 (Keele et al., 2003). They proposed that there are two neurocognitive systems for sequence learning (Figure 8.39): a dorsal system in which learning is implicit, and a ventral system in which learning can be implicit or explicit.

SUMMARY OF NEUROIMAGING OF MEMORY

Neuroimaging studies have demonstrated patterns of neuronal activation that are consistent with memory systems derived from cognitive research consisting of studies in both human amnesia patients and animal models. Neuroimaging also has provided some notable new findings in the cognitive neuroscience of memory, including, for example, the evidence that hippocampus and surrounding parahippocampal and entorhinal cortices may play different roles in memory, supporting different forms of recognition memory. In the years to come, functional neuroimaging clearly will continue to provide invaluable information about human memory and its neural substrates in the healthy human.

CELLULAR BASES OF LEARNING AND MEMORY

Most models of the cellular bases of memory hold that memory is the result of changes in the strength of synaptic interactions among neurons in neural networks. How would synaptic strength be altered to enable learning and memory? Hebb (1949) proposed one possibility: Hebb's law states that, if a synapse is active when a postsynaptic neuron is active, the synapse will be strengthened; this phenomenon is known as **Hebbian learning.**

Long-Term Potentiation and the Hippocampus

Because of the role of the hippocampal formation in memory, it has long been hypothesized that neurons in the hippocampus must be plastic—that is, able to change their synaptic interactions. Since the late 1960s, researchers have sought the mechanisms behind this type of plasticity in learning and memory storage. Although it is now clear that storage itself is not in the hippocampus, this was not understood when work on hippocampal cell physiology first began. This fact does not invalidate the hippocampal models that we will examine, because the same cellular mechanisms can operate in various cortical and subcortical areas.

First, let's quickly review the major excitatory neural components of the hippocampus (Figure 8.40): Neocortical association areas project to the entorhinal cortex via the parahippocampal cortex or perirhinal cortex. The entorhinal cortex projects via the *perforant pathway* onto the granule cells of the dentate gyrus with excitatory inputs. The *mossy fibers* connect the granule cells of the dentate gyrus to the hippocampal CA3 pyramidal cells (on their dendritic spines), and then the *Schaffer collaterals* connect the CA3 pyramidal cells to the CA1 pyramidal cells. This system provides an opportunity for researchers to examine synaptic plasticity as the mechanism of learning at the cellular level.

In studies by Bliss and Lømo (1973), stimulation of axons of the perforant pathway of the rabbit resulted in a long-term increase in the magnitude of excitatory postsynaptic potentials (EPSPs). That is, stimulation led to greater synaptic strength in the perforant pathway such that later stimulation created larger postsynaptic responses in the granule cells of the dentate gyrus. This phenomenon, named *long-term potentiation* (*LTP*) (*potentiate* means "to strengthen or make more potent"), was later extended to the other two excitatory projection pathways of the hippocampus. The changes could last for hours in isolated slices of hippocampal tissue placed in dishes, where recording was easier. LTP can even last days or weeks in living animals. It has since been found that the LTP in the three pathways varies. Nonetheless, Hebb's (1949) law is confirmed physiologically by the discovery of LTP.

One way that we can record LTP is by placing stimulating electrodes on the perforant pathway and a recording electrode in a granule cell of the dentate gyrus (Figure 8.41). First a single pulse is presented, and the resulting EPSP is measured. The size of this first recording is the strength of the connection before the LTP is induced. Then the perforant pathway is stimulated with a burst of pulses; early studies used approximately 100 pulses/s but more recent studies have used as few as 5 pulses/s. After LTP is induced, a single pulse is sent again, and the magnitude of the EPSP in the postsynaptic cell is measured. The magnitude of the EPSP increases after LTP is induced, signaling the greater strength of the synaptic effect (Figure 8.41a). A fascinating finding is that, when the pulses are presented slowly, the opposite effect, long-term depression (LTD), develops (Figure 8.41b).

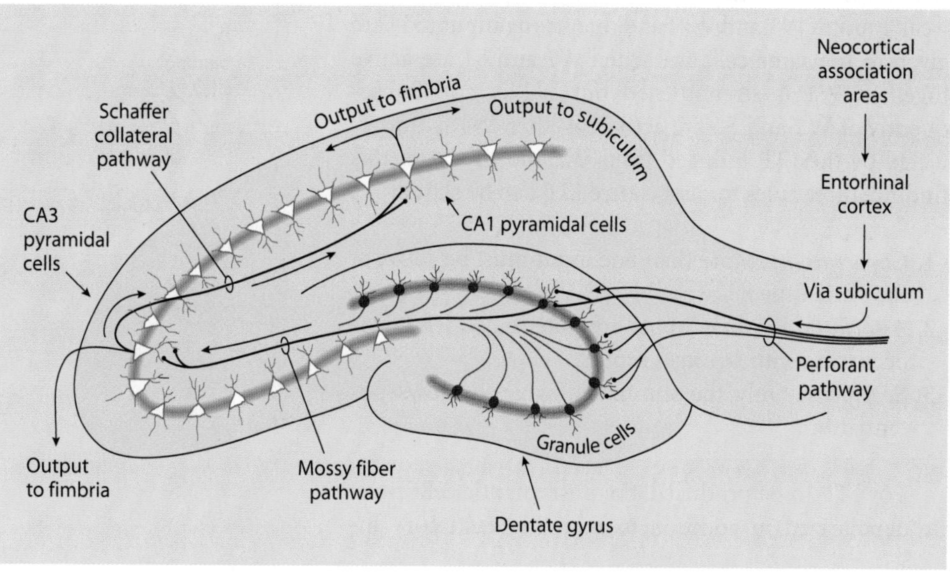

Figure 8.40 Synaptic organization of the rat hippocampus. See text for description of the major projection pathways.

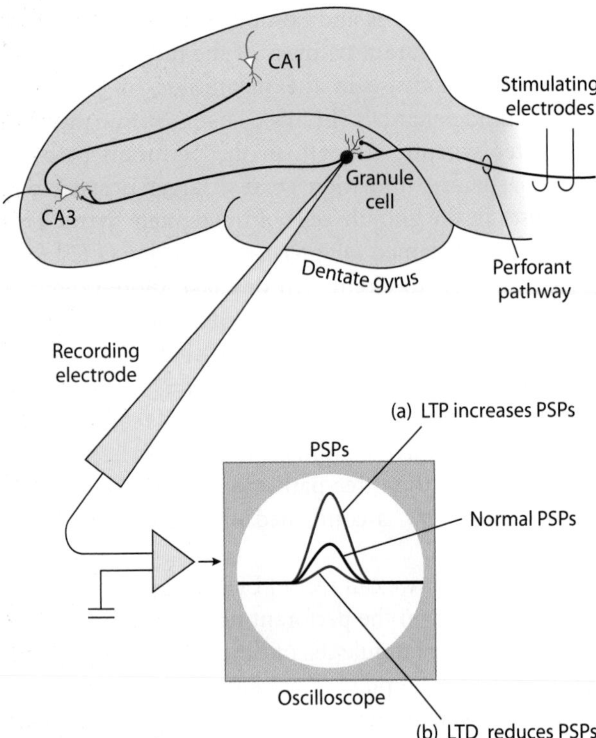

Figure 8.41 Stimulus and recording setup for the study of long-term potentiation (LTP) in perforant pathways. **(a)** The pattern of responses (in microvolts) before and after the induction of LTP. **(b)** The pattern of responses in long-term depression (LTD). PSPs = postsynaptic potentials.

HEBBIAN LEARNING

Associative LTP is an extension of Hebb's law and asserts that, if a weak and a strong input act on a cell at the same time, the weak synapse becomes stronger. This association has been tested directly by the manipulation of LTP in the CA1 neurons of the hippocampus. When two weak inputs (W1 and W2) and one strong input (S1) are given to the same cell, and when W1 and S1 are active together, W1 is strengthened but W2 is not. Subsequently, if W2 and S1 are active together, W1 is not affected by the LTP induced from W2 and S1. From this finding, three rules for associative LTP can be stated:

1. *Cooperativity.* More than one input must be active at the same time.
2. *Associativity.* Weak inputs are potentiated when co-occurring with stronger inputs.
3. *Specificity.* Only the stimulated synapse shows potentiation.

For LTP to be produced, the postsynaptic cells must be depolarized in addition to receiving excitatory inputs; in fact, LTP is reduced by inhibitory inputs to postsynaptic cells. In addition, when postsynaptic cells are hyperpolarized, LTP is prevented. Conversely, when postsynaptic inhibition is prevented, LTP is facilitated. If an input that is normally not strong enough to induce LTP is paired with a depolarizing current to the postsynaptic cell, LTP can be induced.

THE NMDA RECEPTOR

That an excitatory input and postsynaptic depolarization are needed to produce LTP is explained by the properties of the doubly gated *N*-methyl-D-aspartate (NMDA) receptor (Figure 8.42) located on the dendritic spines of postsynaptic neurons that show LTP. Glutamate is the major excitatory transmitter in the hippocampus, and it can bind with NMDA and non-NMDA receptors. When 2-amino-5-phosphonopentanoate (AP5) is introduced by experimenters to CA1 neurons, NMDA receptors are chemically blocked and LTP induction is prevented. But the AP5 treatment produces no effect on previously established LTP in these cells. Therefore, NMDA receptors are central to producing LTP but not to maintaining it. It turns out that maintenance of LTP probably depends on the non-NMDA receptors.

What cellular mechanism permits LTP to develop via the NMDA receptors, and why does blocking those receptors with AP5 prevent LTP? NMDA receptors are

Figure 8.42 NMDA receptor. As this simplified cross-sectional schematic shows, the NMDA receptor is naturally blocked by the Mg^{2+} molecule. Unblocking (channel opening) occurs when the proteins that form the channel shift following the binding of glutamate to the glutamate binding site.

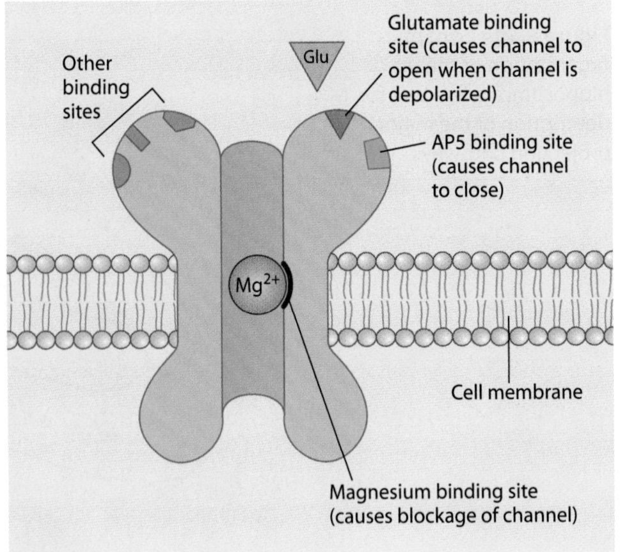

naturally blocked by magnesium ions (Mg^{2+}). The Mg^{2+} ions can be ejected from the NMDA receptors only when the neurotransmitter glutamate binds to the receptors and when the membrane is depolarized; that is, the NMDA receptors are transmitter and voltage dependent (gated). When these two conditions are met, Mg^{2+} is ejected and calcium (Ca^{2+}) can enter the cell (Figure 8.43).

The effect of Ca^{2+} influx via the NMDA receptor is critical in the formation of LTP. Ca^{2+} acts as an intracellular messenger conveying the signal, which changes enzyme activities that influence synaptic strength. Despite rapid advances in understanding the mechanisms of LTP at physiological and biochemical levels, the molecular mechanisms of synaptic strengthening in LTP are still subject to extensive debate.

The synaptic changes that create a stronger synapse after LTP induction likely include presynaptic and postsynaptic mechanisms. One hypothesis is that LTP raises the sensitivity of postsynaptic non-NMDA glutamate receptors and prompts more glutamate to be released presynaptically. Or perhaps changes in the physical characteristics of the dendritic spines transmit EPSPs more effectively to the dendrites. Finally, via a message from the postsynaptic cell to the presynaptic cell, the efficiency of presynaptic neurotransmitter release is increased.

LONG-TERM POTENTIATION AND MEMORY PERFORMANCE

With a candidate cellular mechanism for long-term plastic changes in synaptic strength identified, it should be possible to produce deficits in learning and memory by eliminating LTP. Chemically blocking LTP in the hippocampus of normal mice impairs their ability to demonstrate normal place learning; thus, blocking LTP prevents normal spatial memory. In a similar way, genetic manipulations that block the cascade of molecular triggers for LTP also impair spatial learning. These experiments provide strong evidence that blocking NMDA receptors and preventing LTP impairs spatial learning.

Two studies with different results cast doubt on the role of LTP in learning and memory, however (Bannerman et al., 1995; Saucier & Cain, 1995). Both experiments found that pharmacological NMDA receptor blockers did not stop rodents from learning how to navigate in a water maze; the animals were able to develop a

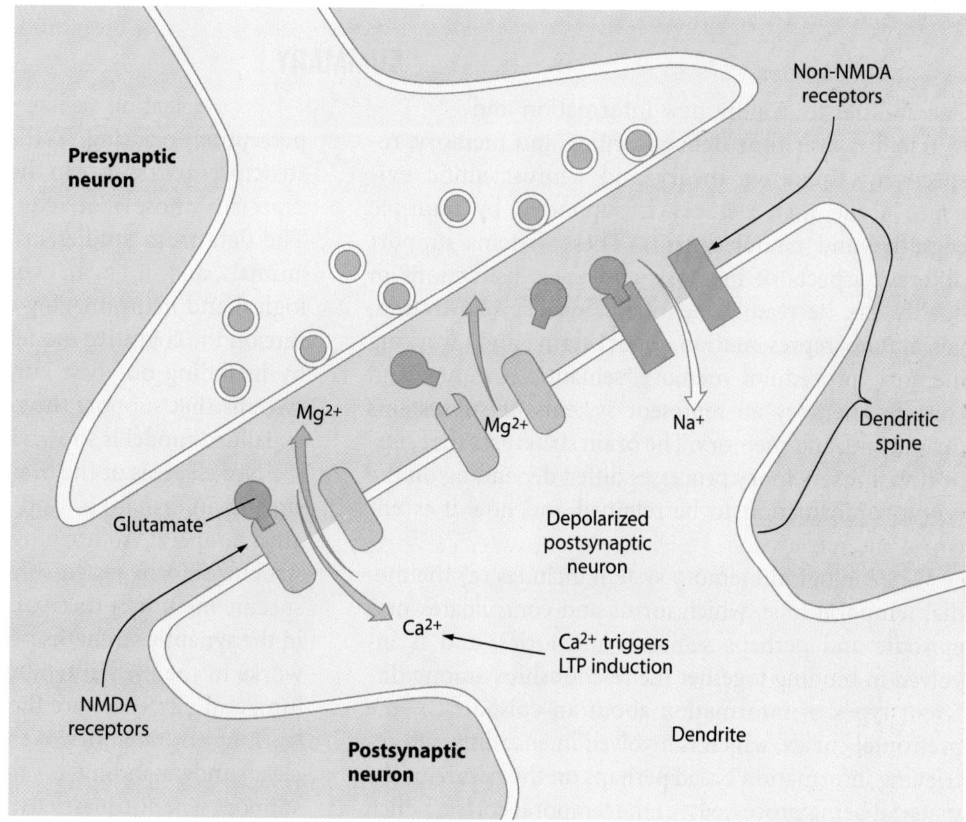

Figure 8.43 The role of Mg^{2+} and Ca^{2+} in the functioning of the NMDA receptor. See text for details.

new spatial map even when LTP was prevented. Unlike previous studies, these studies pretrained the rodents to swim to a platform, which prevented the impairment of new spatial learning when the NMDA receptors were blocked. When mice were pretrained by either a water maze task or a nonspatial task, the introduction of AP5 (the NMDA receptor blocker) in the hippocampus prevented new learning in mice pretrained for the nonspatial task, but it did not affect mice pretrained for the spatial task. The conclusion is that NMDA receptors may be needed to learn a spatial strategy but not to encode a new map.

Another experiment also revealed that blocking LTP did not affect behavior, but the pattern was slightly different. When mice were pretrained with a nonspatial task, spatial memory was not interrupted by the introduction of an NMDA antagonist. The conclusion is that the pretraining merely allowed the motor-related side effects of NMDA receptor blockage to be avoided. Although these two studies did not exclude the possibility that new spatial learning involves NMDA receptors, they do point to the possibility that at least two memory systems could utilize NMDA receptors. These systems participate in the water maze task but possibly could be consolidated by pretraining.

The role of LTP in memory on the cellular and behavioral levels is still being unraveled. Whether the maintenance of LTP is located presynaptically or postsynaptically, and even whether LTP is necessary for spatial memory, is the subject of much debate. Daniel Zamanillo and his colleagues (1999) at the Max Planck Institute in Heidelberg, Germany used gene knockout protocols to study mice that could not produce LTP in the synapses of neurons between the CA3 and CA1 regions of the hippocampus. Behaviorally, however, these mice could learn spatial tasks just as easily as normal control mice could. In a similar manner, mice with enhanced LTP were studied by Martine Migaud and colleagues (1998) at the University of Edinburgh and found to have severe impairment in spatial learning. We hope that much more research into the importance of LTP for spatial and other forms of learning will elucidate this debate in the coming years.

Two points of agreement are (a) that LTP does exist at the cellular level and (b) that NMDA receptors play a crucial role in LTP induction in many pathways of the brain. Because LTP is also in brain areas outside the hippocampal system, the possibility that LTP forms the basis for long-term modification within synaptic networks remains promising.

SUMMARY

The abilities to acquire new information and to retain it over time define learning and memory, respectively. Cognitive theory and neuroscientific evidence argue that memory is supported by multiple cognitive and neural systems. These systems support different aspects of memory, and their distinctions in quality can be readily identified. Sensory registration, perceptual representation, short-term and working memory, procedural memory, semantic memory, and episodic memory all represent systems or subsystems for learning and memory. The brain structures that support various memory processes differ, depending on the type of information to be retained and how it is encoded and retrieved.

The biological memory system includes (a) the medial temporal lobe, which forms and consolidates new episodic and perhaps semantic memories, and is involved in binding together the relationships among different types of information about an episode; (b) the prefrontal cortex, which is involved in encoding and retrieving information based perhaps on the nature of the material being processed; (c) the temporal cortex, which stores episodic and semantic knowledge; and (d) the association sensory cortices for the effects of perceptual priming. Other cortical and subcortical structures participate in the learning of skills and habits, especially those that require implicit motor learning. The data from studies in human amnesic patients, in animals, and in normal volunteers using electrophysiological and neuroimaging methods permit us to elaborate on the cognitive model first presented in Figure 8.7, by including our best current estimates of the neural systems that support the memory functions listed; this expanded model is shown in Figure 8.44.

Not all areas of the brain have the same potential for storing information, and although widespread brain areas cooperate in learning and memory, the individual structures form systems that support and enable rather specific memory processes. At the cellular level, changes in the synaptic strengths between neurons in neural networks in the medial temporal lobe, neocortex, cerebellum, and elsewhere are the most likely mechanisms for learning and memory. We are rapidly developing a very clear understanding of the molecular processes that support synaptic plasticity, and thus learning and memory, in the brain.

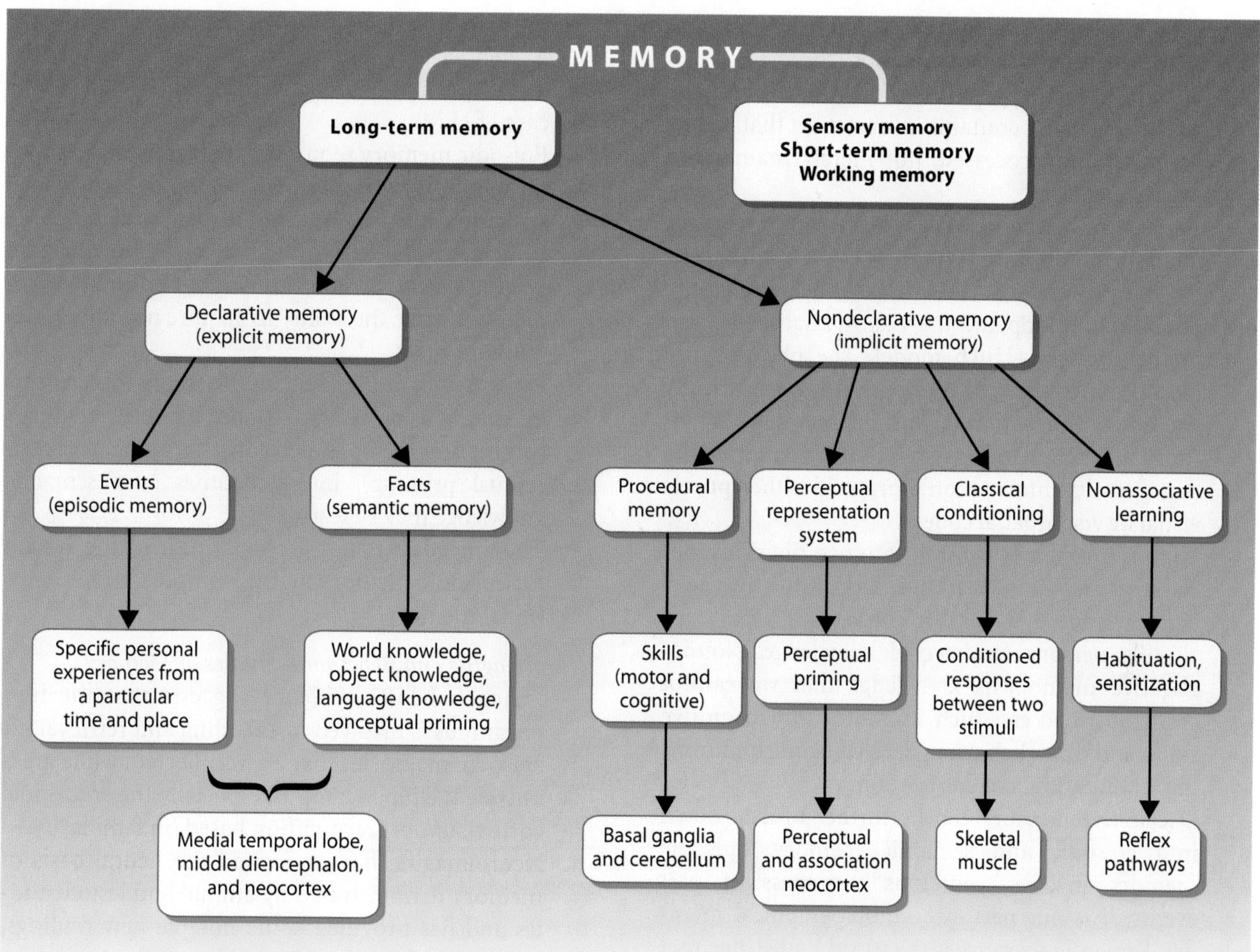

Figure 8.44 Generalized diagram of the relationships of long-term memory systems to the underlying brain systems. This figure elaborates on Figure 8.7 to include candidate brain areas.

KEY TERMS

acquisition
amnesia
anterograde amnesia
consolidation
declarative memory
distributed representation
encoding
familiarity
Hebbian learning
learning
long-term memory
memory
nondeclarative memory
perceptual representation system (PRS)
procedural memory
retrieval
retrograde amnesia
sensory memory
short-term memory
storage
working memory

TAKE-HOME MESSAGES

General

- H.M. received a bilateral temporal lobectomy for treatment of chronic epilepsy. The surgery left him unable to form new long-term memories.
- Learning is the process of acquiring new information, the outcome of which is memory.
- Learning has many stages, including encoding (acquisition and consolidation), storage, and retrieval.

Types of Memory

- Sensory memory lasts only seconds at most, short-term memory lasts seconds to minutes, and long-term memory lasts days to years.

- Echoic memory is sensory memory for audition; iconic memory is sensory memory for vision.
- Working memory extends the concept of short-term memory: it contains information that can be acted on and processed, not merely maintained by rehearsal.
- The central executive mechanism of the working memory system is the command-and-control center that presides over the interactions between the phonological loop and the visuospatial sketch pad in the Baddeley–Hitch model. The phonological loop is a hypothesized mechanism for acoustically encoding information in working memory; the visuospatial sketch pad is a short-term memory store that permits information storage in either purely visual or visuospatial codes.
- Long-term memory is split into two divisions: declarative and nondeclarative. Declarative memory is knowledge that we can consciously access, including personal and world knowledge. Nondeclarative memory is knowledge that we cannot consciously access, such as motor and cognitive skills, and other behaviors derived from conditioning, habituation, or sensitization.
- Declarative memory can be further broken down into episodic and semantic memory. Episodic memory involves conscious awareness of past events; it is our personal, autobiographical memory. Semantic memory is the world knowledge that we remember in the absence of any recollection of the specific circumstances surrounding its learning.
- Procedural memory is a form of nondeclarative memory that involves the learning of a variety of motor and cognitive skills. Other forms of nondeclarative memory include perceptual priming, conditioned responses, and nonassociative learning.

Amnesia

- Retrograde amnesia is the loss of memory for events that happened in the past (episodic memory) and is one of the hallmarks of late-stage Alzheimer's disease. Anterograde amnesia is the loss of the ability to form new memories, as in the case of H.M.
- Episodic memory requires an intact medial temporal lobe (primarily the hippocampus) and related structures, such as the midline diencephalon.
- Damage to the temporal lobe outside of the hippocampus can produce the loss of episodic memory even while the ability to acquire new memories remains intact.
- Patients with amnesia retain the ability to learn new information, particularly nondeclarative memories (procedural memory, perceptual priming, and conceptual priming), but sometimes even semantic knowledge may be learned.
- The amygdala is not a crucial part of the system for episodic memory, but it is important for emotional memory.

Neuroimaging and Behavioral Studies of Memory

- Functional-MRI evidence suggests that the hippocampus is involved in encoding and retrieval for episodic memories that are recollected, while areas outside the hippocampus, especially the entorhinal cortex, support recognition based on familiarity.
- Neuroimaging has confirmed the neural basis of memory demonstrated by animal and lesion studies and has provided some notable new findings, including, for example, evidence that the hippocampus and surrounding parahippocampal and entorhinal cortices may play different roles in memory, supporting different forms of recognition memory.
- In Hebbian learning, if a synapse is active when a postsynaptic neuron is active, the synapse will be strengthened. Long-term potentiation is the long-term strengthening of a synapse.
- NMDA receptors are central to producing LTP but not to maintaining it.

THOUGHT QUESTIONS

1. Compare and contrast the different forms of memory on the basis of their time course. Does the fact that some memories last seconds while some last a lifetime necessarily imply that different neural systems mediate the two forms of memory?
2. Patient H.M. and others with damage to the medial temporal lobe develop amnesia. What form of amnesia do they develop? For example, is it like the amnesia most often shown in Hollywood movies? What information can such amnesia patients retain, what can they learn, and what does this tell us about how memories are encoded in the brain?
3. Can you ride a bike? Do you remember learning to ride a two-wheeler? Can you describe to others the principles of riding a bike? Do you think that, if you gave a detailed set of instructions to another person who had never ridden a bike, he or she could carefully study your instructions and then hop on a bike

and ride happily off into the sunset? If not, why not?

4. Describe the subdivisions of the medial temporal lobe and how they contribute to long-term memory. Consider both encoding and retrieval.
5. Relate models of long-term potentiation (LTP) to changing weights in connectionist networks. What constraints do cognitive neuroscience findings place on connectionist models of memory?

SUGGESTED READING

AGGLETON, J. P., & BROWN, M. W. (2006). Interleaving brain systems for episodic and recognition memory. *Trends in Cognitive Sciences, 10,* 455–463.

CLARK, R. E., MANNS, J. R., & SQUIRE L. R. (2002). Classical conditioning, awareness, and brain systems. *Trends in Cognitive Sciences, 6,* 524–531.

COLLINGRIDGE, G. L., & BLISS, T. V. P. (1995). Memories of NMDA receptors and LTP. *Trends in Neurosciences, 18,* 54–56.

CORKIN, S. (2002). What's new with the amnesic patient H.M.? *Nature Reviews Neuroscience, 3,* 153–160.

EICHENBAUM, H., YONELINAS, A. P., & RANGANATH, C. (In press). The medial temporal lobe and recognition memory. *Annual Review of Neuroscience.*

MCCLELLAND, J. L. (2000). Connectionist models of memory. In E. Tulving and F. I. M. Craik (Eds.), *The Oxford handbook of memory* (pp. 583–596). New York: Oxford University Press.

MILLER, G. (2003). The cognitive revolution: A historical perspective. *Trends in Cognitive Sciences, 7,* 141–144.

PALLER, K., KUTAS, M., & MCISAAC, H. (1995). Monitoring conscious recollection via the electrical activity of the brain. *Psychological Science, 6,* 107–111.

RANGANATH, C., & BLUMENFELD, R. S. (2005). Doubts about double dissociations between short- and long-term memory. *Trends in Cognitive Sciences, 9,* 374–380.

SQUIRE, L. (2006). Lost forever or temporarily misplaced? The long debate about the nature of memory impairment. *Learning and Memory, 13,* 522–529.

9

Emotion

S.M. was a 20-year old woman living an active, if perhaps hectic, life. In addition to taking some college courses, she was working part-time jobs and starting a family. However, something was amiss. Over the past few months, S.M. had been experiencing what appeared to be seizures. Her neurologist ordered a CT scan and an MRI, concerned that S.M. might have a brain tumor. While the scans did not show evidence of a tumor, they did reveal the cause of the seizures. S.M.'s amygdala, an almond-shaped area of the brain located in the medial temporal region, was severely atrophied. Moreover, the damage was bilateral (Figure 9.1). Further tests revealed that S.M. had a rare autosomal recessive genetic disorder, Urbach-Wiethe disease, which caused an accumulation of glycoprotein calcium in the medial temporal lobe and led to degeneration of the amygdalae (Adolphs et al., 1994, 1995; Tranel & Hyman, 1990). The deterioration of the amygdala was highly specific. The scans revealed no additional structural abnormalities.

On standard neuropsychological tests of cognitive function, S.M. did quite well. Her intelligence scores were in the normal range, and she didn't show any evidence of perceptual or motor problems. Despite her seemingly normal cognitive function, researchers at the University of Iowa recruited S.M. to participate in studies on emotional knowledge, using a set of tests that are not typically included in standard neurological assessment batteries. For one of these tests, S.M. was shown a large set of photographs and asked to judge the emotion being expressed by the individuals in the pictures. For most of the photographs, S.M. performed similar to neurologically healthy individuals: she reported that the person was sad when shown a picture of a woman crying whereas she described someone with a beaming smile as ecstatic. She also accurately identified expressions conveying anger, disgust, and surprise. However, there was one facial expression that seemed to baffle S.M. She did not appear to be able to comprehend fear. If shown a fearful face (look ahead to the bottom right photo of Figure 9.4, for a similar example), S.M. would report that the face was expressing surprise, anger, or some other emotion. She seemed to know that some emotion was being expressed, but she could not correctly identify it. Her inability to sense fear was especially striking when considering that her perception of many other, more subtle emotions was essentially intact (Figure 9.2).

Faced with this puzzling dissociation, the researchers then went on to explore the basis of S.M.'s problem in recognizing fear. A tantalizing possibility was that she was unable to process the concept of fear. However, she was able to describe situations that would elicit fear and used words describing fear properly (Adolphs et al., 1995). Also, her performance on a task that required identification of emotional prosody (the speech sounds

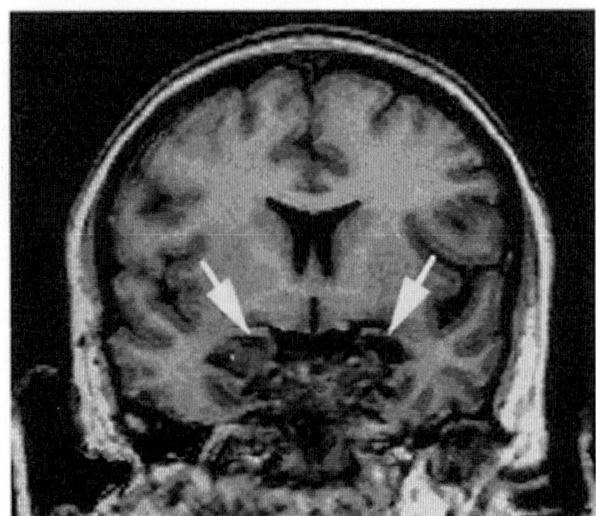

Figure 9.1 Bilateral amygdala damage in Patient S.M. The white arrows indicate where the amygdala are located in the right and left hemispheres. Patient S.M. has severe atrophy of the amygdala, with the brain tissue now replaced by cerebrospinal fluid (black).

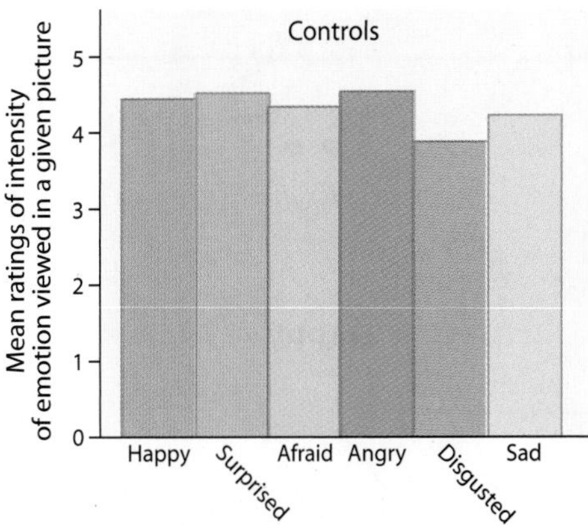

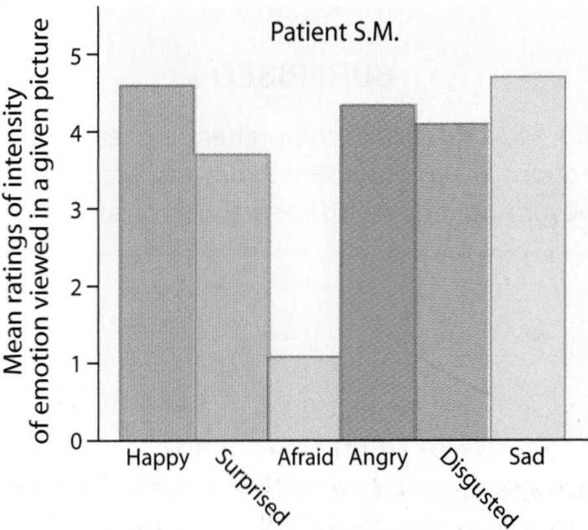

Figure 9.2 Ratings of emotional intensity of facial expressions by controls (top) and S.M. (bottom). S.M. shows a selective attenuation of her rating for a face depicting someone who is afraid.

that indicate emotion) was the same as that of controls. She had no trouble labeling fearful prosody (Adolphs & Tranel, 1999). These observations appeared to rule out a generalized conceptual deficit.

But investigators noticed that S.M. had another baffling deficit when they asked her to draw pictures depicting different emotions. She was able to provide reasonable cartoons of a range of states; however, she again failed when asked to depict fear. At first she was hesitant to draw, commenting that she was at a loss to come up with an idea. When prodded, she scribbled for a few minutes, only to reveal a picture of a baby crawling! Perhaps a Freudian might interpret that the image came from a scary moment in S.M.'s distant childhood. S.M. certainly couldn't say why she had produced this image. Her inability to recognize fearful facial expressions extended to an inability to replicate them on paper, a striking contrast to her intact abilities to recognize and replicate all other emotions tested (Figure 9.3).

The mystery of S.M.'s deficits was only recently solved. We will reveal the solution later in the chapter. However, before we get there, it is worth examining some useful lessons from this case study. Two important lessons can be drawn. First, the amygdala must play a critical role in the identification of facial expressions of fear. It is not altogether surprising that this would be the case, since previous research has indicated that the amygdala is important for other forms of emotional processing, including affective aspects of memory. While there may indeed be some general role of the amygdala in processing or even storing emotional memories, it is also clear that this brain region is especially important for representing fear.

Second, the fact that people could fail to comprehend one emotion with little impairment in their knowledge of other emotions helped inspire new views in thinking about the neural bases of emotion. Similar to how vision researchers have emphasized that there are multiple areas and pathways for representing objects, researchers interested in emotion began to emphasize the distributed nature of emotional processing and representations.

We begin this chapter with a review of some basic concepts in the study of emotion. We then turn to a discussion of the role of emotion in learning, asking how affective states influence our memories. Next, we proceed to look at how emotions can influence behavior. We conclude with a survey of recent research regarding the brain structures associated with various emotions.

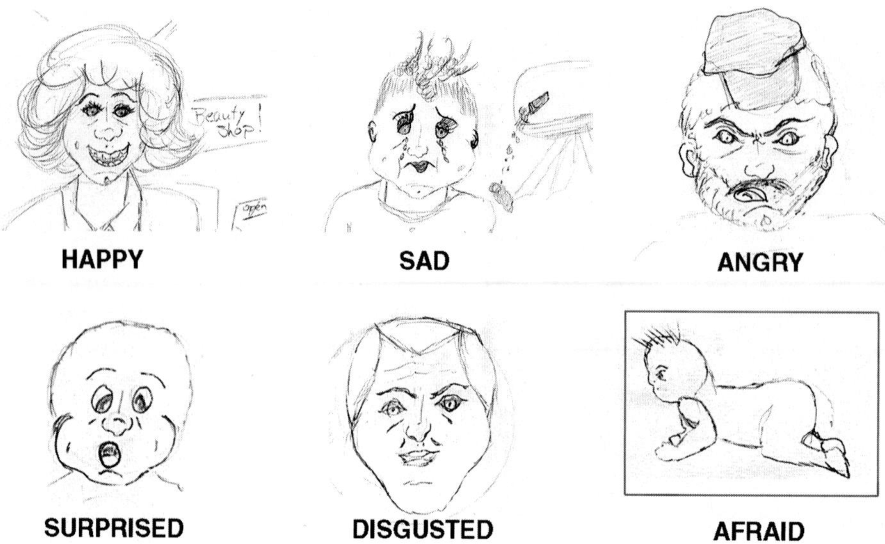

Figure 9.3 S.M.'s deficit in comprehending fear is also observed on a production task. She was asked to draw faces that depicted basic emotions. When prompted to draw a person who was afraid, S.M. hesitated and then produced the picture of the baby. She was, however, not happy with her drawing of "afraid."

THE COGNITIVE NEUROSCIENCE OF EMOTION

It is not possible to understand who we are or how we interact with the world without considering our emotional lives. The cognitive neuroscience of **emotion** has been slow to emerge because emotion is a behavior that is difficult to study systematically. Nevertheless, researchers have been taking on the challenge, and emotion is emerging as a critical research topic.

Issues in the Cognitive Neuroscience of Emotion

Happy, sad, fearful, anxious, elated, smitten, disappointed, angry, pleased, disgusted, excited, shameful, guilty, and *infatuated* are just some of the terms we use to describe our emotional lives. Unfortunately, our rich language of emotion is difficult to translate into discrete states and variables that can be studied in the laboratory. In an effort to apply some order and uniformity to our definition of emotion, researchers have focused on two primary categories of emotion: (a) basic emotions, as seen through facial expression; and (b) dimensions of emotion, seen as reactions to events.

BASIC EMOTIONS

Although we may use words like *elated, joyful,* and *gleeful* to describe how we feel, most people would agree that all of these terms represent a variation of feeling happy. Since Darwin's work on the evolutionary basis of human behavior, investigators have been proposing that we define a finite set of universal, basic emotions. Darwin approached this problem by questioning people who were familiar with a variety of different cultures around the world about the emotional lives of these varied cultures. From these discussions Darwin determined that humans have evolved to have a finite set of basic emotional states, each of which is unique in its adaptive significance and physiological expression.

One of the more recent attempts to characterize basic emotions examined the universality of **facial expression** (Ekman & Friesen, 1971). By studying different cultures around the world, Paul Ekman of the University of California, San Francisco, discovered that the means by which emotion is conveyed through facial expression does not vary from culture to culture. Whether we are from the Bronx, Beijing, or Papua New Guinea, how we show with facial expression that we are happy, sad, fearful, disgusted, angry, or surprised is pretty much the same (Figure 9.4). From this work, Ekman and others suggested that *anger, fear, disgust, happiness, sadness,* and *surprise* are the six basic human facial expressions representing emotional states.

Although there is still considerable debate as to whether any single list is adequate to capture our full range of emotional experiences, most people accept the idea that there are basic, universal human emotions. Basic emotions such as fear and rage have been largely confirmed in animals, which show dedicated subcortical circuitry for such emotions. Consequently, scientists have adopted the notion of basic emotions in order to investigate the different neural systems underlying reported emotional states or moods, as well as the neural and developmental basis of facial expression and evaluation.

DIMENSIONS OF EMOTION

Another way of approaching the categorization of emotions is to describe them not as discrete states but rather as reactions to events in the world that vary along a continuum. For instance, most would agree that being happy is a pleasant feeling and being angry is an unpleasant feeling. However, we are happy when we find a penny on the sidewalk. We are also happy when we win $10 million in a lottery. Although in both situations we experience something that is pleasant, the intensity of that feeling is certainly different. One type of dimensional approach to categorization proposes that emotional reactions to stimuli and events can be characterized by two factors: *valence* (pleasant–unpleasant or good–bad) and *arousal* (the intensity of the internal emotional response, high–low; Osgood et al., 1957; Russell, 1979). We might be pleasantly surprised at finding a penny on the street, but most people would not describe their reaction to this event as intense or arousing. Winning the lottery, however, likely would lead to a very intense, arousing, and elated state. By using this dimensional approach—tracking valence and arousal—researchers can achieve a more concrete assessment of the emotional reactions elicited by stimuli.

A second dimensional approach that has been used in cognitive neuroscience is to characterize emotions by the actions and goals that they motivate. Richard Davidson and colleagues (1990) at the University of Wisconsin–Madison suggested that different emotional reactions or states can motivate us either to approach or to withdraw from a situation. For example, happiness and surprise may excite a tendency to *approach* or engage in the eliciting situations, whereas fear and disgust may motivate us to *withdraw* from the eliciting situations.

Figure 9.4 The universal emotional expressions. The meaning of these facial expressions is similar across all cultures. Can you match the faces to the emotional states of anger, disgust, fear, happiness, sadness, and surprise?

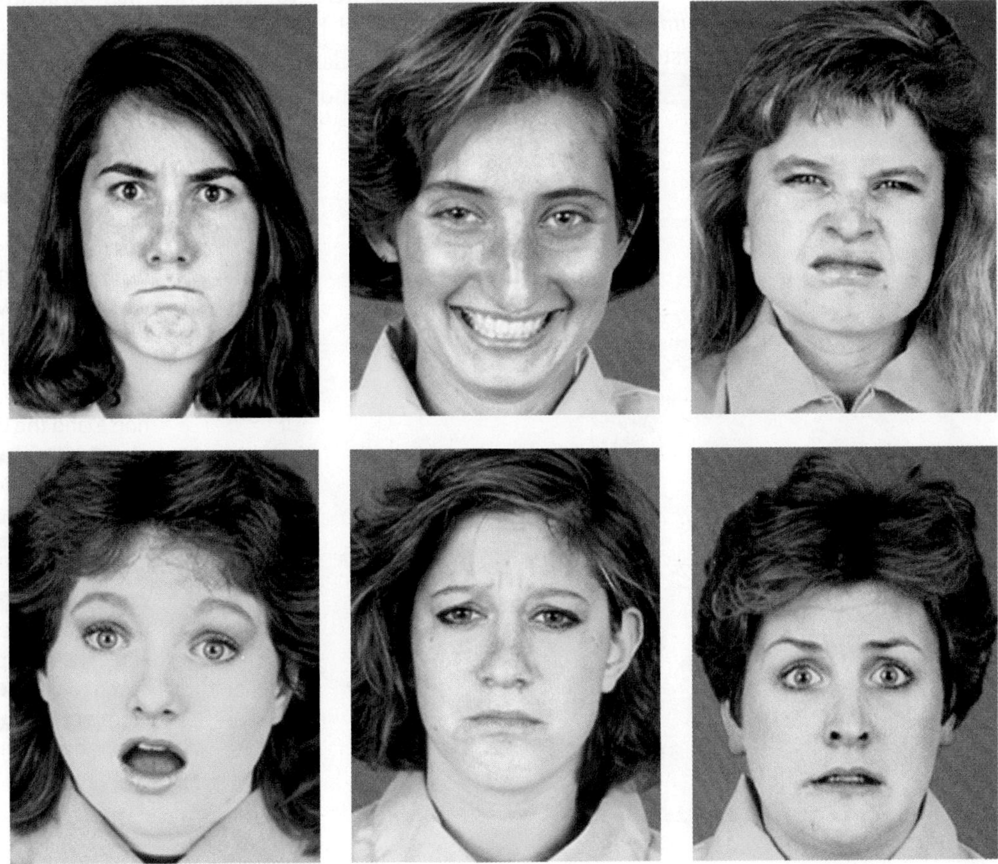

Clearly, the basic and dimensional approaches to defining emotions are not adequate to capture all of our emotional experience. However, they provide a beginning framework that we can use in our scientific investigations of emotion. No single approach is correct. It is essential though that we are clear in our research about how we define *emotion* so that accurate consensus can emerge from a range of results.

NEURAL SYSTEMS IN EMOTIONAL PROCESSING

Early Concepts: The Limbic System

One goal of research on the cognitive neuroscience of emotion, as demonstrated in the earlier example of S.M., is to identify and understand the neural systems underlying different emotional states and processes. Actually, the notion of a network of brain structures underlying emotional behavior in general is not new. In 1937, James Papez (pronounced "payps") proposed a circuit theory of the brain and emotion, suggesting that emotional responses involve a network of brain regions including the hypothalamus, anterior thalamus, cingulate gyrus, and hippocampus. Paul MacLean (1949, 1952) later named these structures the *Papez circuit*. He then extended this emotional network to include the amygdala, orbitofrontal cortex, and portions of the basal ganglia. He called this extended neural circuit of emotion the limbic system from the Latin *limbus*, meaning "rim." The structures of the limbic system roughly form a rim around the corpus callosum (Figure 9.5).

MacLean's early work identifying the limbic system as the "emotional" brain was very influential. To this day, it is not uncommon to see references to the "limbic system" or "limbic" structures in studies on the neural basis of emotion. The continued popularity of the term *limbic system* in more recent work is due primarily to the inclusion of the orbitofrontal cortex and amygdala in that system, two areas which, as we shall see, have been the focus of investigation into the neural basis of emotion (Figure 9.6; Damasio, 1994; LeDoux, 1992). However, the limbic system concept as strictly outlined by MacLean has not been supported over the years (Brodal, 1982; Kotter & Meyer, 1992; LeDoux, 1991; Swanson, 1983).

Although several of the limbic structures are known to play a role in emotion, it has been impossible to determine criteria for defining which structures and pathways should be included in the limbic system. At the same time, classic limbic areas such as the hippocampus have been shown to be more important for other, non-

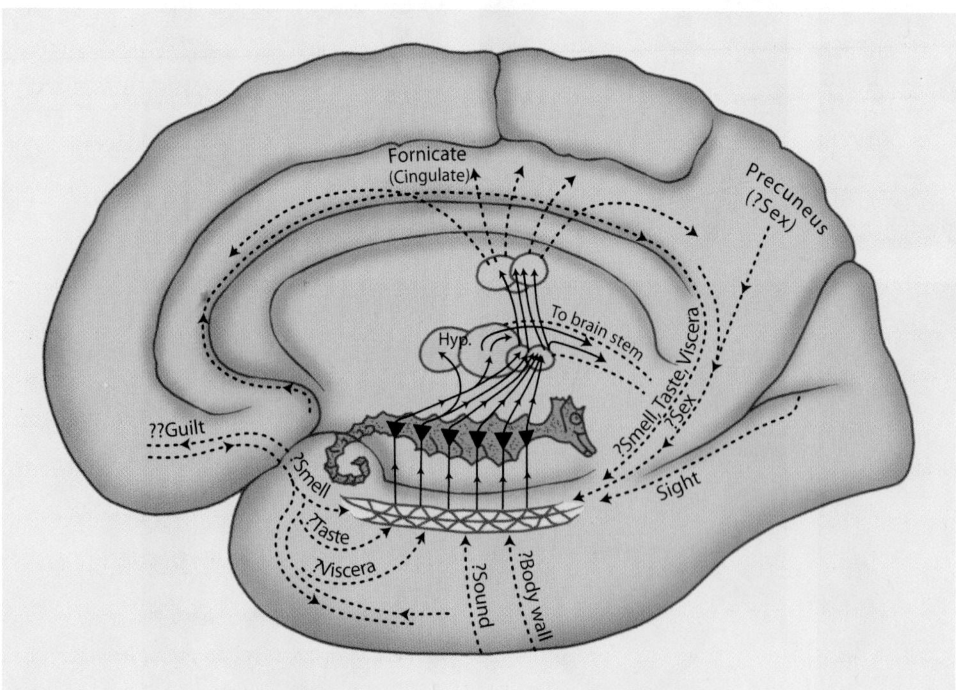

Figure 9.5 MacLean's limbic system. The hippocampus (Greek for "seahorse") was named for its anatomical shape and was the centerpiece of the limbic system. The structure is represented here by a seahorse, and the black triangles represent pyramidal cells. The hippocampus was believed to receive inputs from external sensations, as well as from the internal and visceral environment. The integration of these internal and external inputs was believed to be the basis for emotional experience. Hyp. = hypothalamus.

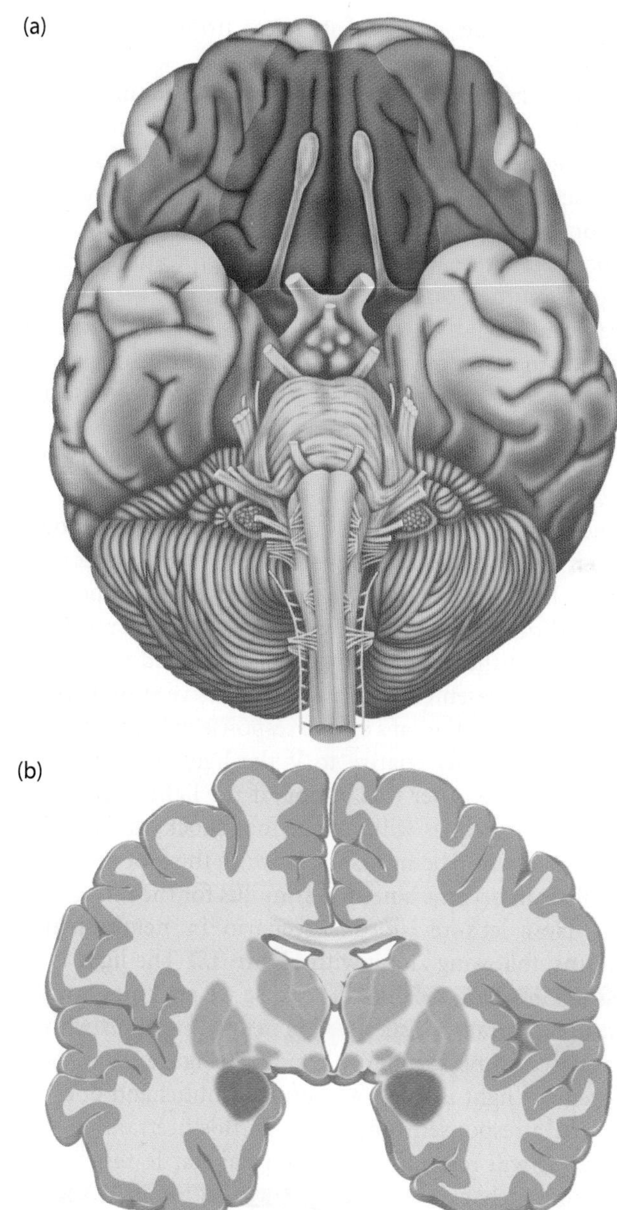

Figure 9.6 Neural regions central to the processing of emotion include **(a)** the orbitofrontal cortex and **(b)** the amygdala. Within the OFC, distinctions are frequently made between the ventromedial prefrontal cortex (red) and lateral orbitofrontal cortex (green).

emotional processes, such as memory (see Chapter 8). Without any clear understanding as to why some brain regions and not others are part of the limbic system, MacLean's concept has proved to be more descriptive and historical than functional in our current understanding of the neural basis of emotion.

These early attempts to identify neural circuits of emotion tended to view emotion as a unitary concept that could be localized to one specific circuit, such as the limbic system, thus separating this "emotional brain" from the rest of the brain. Over the years our investigations of emotion have become more detailed and complex. We acknowledge that emotion is a multifaceted behavior that may not be captured by a single definition or captured in a single neural circuit or brain system. Indeed, S.M.'s isolated emotional deficit in fear recognition following bilateral amygdala damage supports this idea.

Research now focuses on specific types of emotional tasks and on identifying the neural systems underlying specific emotional behaviors. We no longer think there is only one neural circuit of emotion. Rather, depending on the emotional task or situation, we can expect different neural systems to be involved. These systems might involve some brain regions that are more or less specialized for emotional processing, along with others that serve many functions depending on what role a particular emotion plays. For example, brain regions that support attentional vigilance are recruited to detect threat signals.

Note that the amygdala is not the only region important in emotional processing. Other brain regions involved in emotion are discussed in "How the Brain Works: To Approach or Withdraw," in Chapter 11. For instance, studies of the cognitive neuroscience of emotion focus on a number of brain regions that play a role in different emotional tasks (e.g., orbitofrontal cortex, anterior cingulate gyrus, hypothalamus, basal ganglia, insular cortex, somatosensory cortex). We will return to these areas later in the chapter. For now, let's focus on the amygdala (Figure 9.6b), which, through studies like those on S.M., has emerged as a brain region with primary functions related to the processing of emotion. Understanding this region is crucial to our investigation into the cognitive neuroscience of emotion.

Amygdala

As mentioned earlier, the **amygdala** is a small, almond-shaped structure in the medial temporal lobe adjacent to the anterior portion of the hippocampus. Structures in the medial temporal lobe were first proposed to be important for emotion in the early 20th century, when Heinrich Klüver and Paul Bucy at the University of Chicago (1939) documented unusual emotional responses in monkeys following damage to this region. The observed deficit was called *psychic blindness*, and one of the prominent characteristics was a lack of fear as demonstrated by a tendency to approach objects that would normally elicit a fear response. Not until the 1950s was the amygdala identified as the primary medial temporal lobe structure underlying the fear-related deficits observed with what became known as *Klüver–Bucy syndrome* (Weiskrantz, 1956). Since that time, the amygdala has been a focus of research on emotional processing in the brain.

Although humans with amygdala damage do not show the classic signs of Klüver–Bucy syndrome, they do, as S.M. demonstrates, show more subtle deficits in fear processing. We will return to patients with bilateral amygdala damage in a moment and discuss more recent studies revealing deficits in emotional memory, but first let's discuss what is known about the amygdala from studies of nonhuman primates indicating a strong role for the amygdala in implicit emotional learning.

IMPLICIT EMOTIONAL LEARNING

Imagine that a young man is taking the train to work one day and starts a conversation with another commuter, whom he has not met before. After they have been conversing for a few minutes, a terrible accident occurs: The train hits a car. Everyone on the train is thrown, several passengers on the train are injured, and the driver of the car is killed. Immediately after the accident, the frightened young man, who has sustained only minor cuts and bruises, leaves the train. He decides to go home to try to calm down. A few months later the young man is invited to a cocktail party. At the party is a guest whom he does not immediately recognize but who looks familiar. This guest starts talking to him, and for some reason the young man becomes immediately uneasy and nervous and excuses himself. Later he asks the host who this person is, and he realizes it is the fellow commuter from the train on the day of the horrible accident.

Although the young man at first could not consciously identify the party guest as the fellow commuter, when the party guest started talking to him, his emotional response indicated that he had some memory of this person. He showed signs of physiological arousal that left him feeling uneasy and nervous. His body's response indicated that the image of this fellow commuter/party guest was linked to the train on that fateful day and the aversive consequences of the accident.

This type of learning, in which a neutral stimulus acquires aversive properties by virtue of being paired with an aversive event, is an example of fear conditioning, and it is a primary paradigm used to investigate the amygdala's role in emotional learning. **Fear conditioning** is a form of classical conditioning in which the unconditioned stimulus is aversive. One advantage of using the fear-conditioning paradigm to investigate emotional learning is that it works essentially the same across a wide range of species, from fruit flies to humans.

One laboratory version of fear conditioning is illustrated in Figure 9.7. Before bringing in the neuroscientific nomenclature, however, we'll explain the paradigm in descriptive terms. This experiment tests a rat's response to specific stimuli and tracks how those responses change after learning. In the pretraining stage, a light is turned on in the rat's cage and the rat does not respond fearfully, because the light is a neutral stimulus. When the rat receives a foot shock, on the other hand, it responds by jumping (this is called a *startle response*) because a shock is an innately aversive stimulus.

If the rat then receives training whereby the light is always paired with the foot shock (the light comes on, and just before it goes off the rat receives the shock), then the light will become associated with the upcoming foot shock. In fact, the light presented alone, without the foot shock, will eventually come to startle the rat. Additionally, if the light (having been associated with a foot shock) is presented with another aversive stimulus (say, a loud noise), the rat's startle response will be enhanced (or potentiated) relative to if the light were just presented alone. After this testing, if the light is presented again many times without the foot shock, the light will eventually stop being associated with the foot shock and will again become a neutral stimulus for the rat.

Now let's revisit this scenario in neuroscientific terms, following along with Figure 9.7. The light is the *conditioned stimulus* (*CS*) because we are going to condition the rat to associate this neutral stimulus with an aversive stimulus. Before training (Figure 9.7a), however, the light is solely a neutral stimulus and does not evoke a response from the rat. In this pretraining stage the rat will respond with a normal startle response to any innately aversive *unconditioned stimulus* (*US*)—for example, a foot shock or a loud noise—that invokes an innate fear response. During training (Figure 9.7b), the light is paired with a shock that is delivered immediately before the light is turned off. The rat has a natural fear response to the shock (usually startle or jump), called the *unconditioned response* (*UR*). This stage is referred to as *acquisition*. After a few pairings of the light (CS) and the shock (US), the rat learns that the light predicts the shock, and eventually the rat exhibits a fear response to the light alone (Figure 9.7c). This anticipatory fear response is the *conditioned response* (*CR*).

The CR can be enhanced in the presence of another fearful stimulus or an anxious state, as is illustrated by the potentiated startle reflex exhibited by a rat when it sees the light (the CS) at the same time that it experiences a loud noise (a different US). The CS and resulting

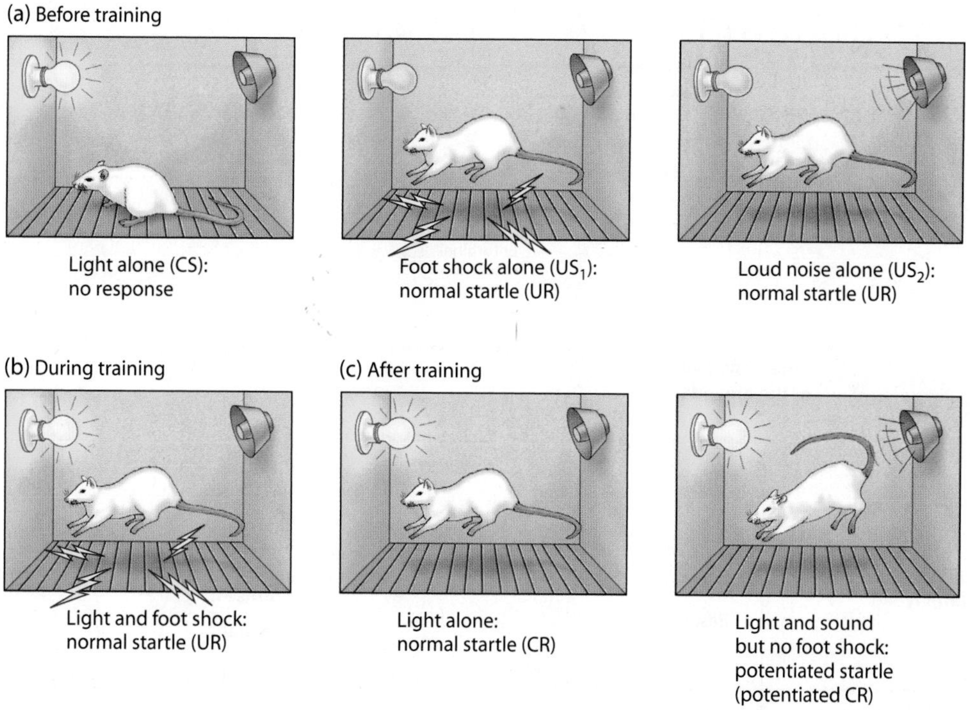

(a) Before training

Light alone (CS): no response

Foot shock alone (US_1): normal startle (UR)

Loud noise alone (US_2): normal startle (UR)

(b) During training

Light and foot shock: normal startle (UR)

(c) After training

Light alone: normal startle (CR)

Light and sound but no foot shock: potentiated startle (potentiated CR)

Figure 9.7 Fear conditioning. **(a)** Before training, three different stimuli—light (CS), foot shock (US_1), and loud noise (US_2)—are presented alone, and both the foot shock and the noise elicit a normal startle response in rats. **(b)** During training, light (CS) and foot shock (US_1) are paired to elicit a normal startle response (UR). **(c)** In tests following training, presentation of light alone now elicits a response (CR), and presentation of the light together with a loud noise but no foot shock elicits a potentiated startle (potentiated CR) because the rat is startled by the loud noise and has associated the light (CS) with the startling foot shock (US).

CR can become unpaired again if the light (CS) is presented alone, without the shock, for many trials. This phenomenon is called *extinction* because at this point the CR is considered extinguished (and the rat will again display the same response to light as in Figure 9.7a).

Many responses can be assessed as the CR in this type of fear-learning paradigm. To illustrate this point, let's apply the above definitions to the earlier example of the young man on the train. The CS is the fellow commuter, the US is the accident, the UR is the fear and pain during the accident, and the CR is the uneasy and nervous feeling that the young man experienced later in the presence of the commuter at the party. The man at the party and the rat receiving foot shocks are just two examples that demonstrate the range of potential CRs that can be acquired. Generally, measures of autonomic nervous system arousal, such as a change in heart rate or skin conductance response, are quite useful in detecting a CR.

Regardless of the stimulus used or the response evoked, one consistent finding has emerged in rats (and we will soon see that this also holds true in humans): Damage to the amygdala impairs conditioned fear responses. Lesions to the amygdala do not usually block the UR to the aversive event, indicating that the amygdala is not necessary to exhibit a fear response. However, amygdala lesions block the ability to acquire and express a CR to the neutral CS that is paired with the aversive US.

Using the fear-conditioning paradigm, researchers such as Joe LeDoux (1996) of New York University, Mike Davis (1992) of Emory University, and Bruce Kapp and his colleagues (1984) of the University of Vermont have been able to map out the neural circuits of fear learning from stimulus perception to emotional response. From these studies it has become clear that the amygdala is a complex structure consisting of several subnuclei. As Figure 9.8 shows, the lateral nucleus of the amygdala serves as a convergence area for information from multiple brain regions, allowing for the formation of associations underlying fear conditioning. The lateral nucleus then projects to the central nucleus of the amygdala. These projections to the central nucleus initiate an emotional response if a stimulus, after being analyzed and placed in the appropriate context, is determined to represent something threatening or potentially dangerous.

An important aspect of this circuitry of fear conditioning is that information about a US or a CS can reach

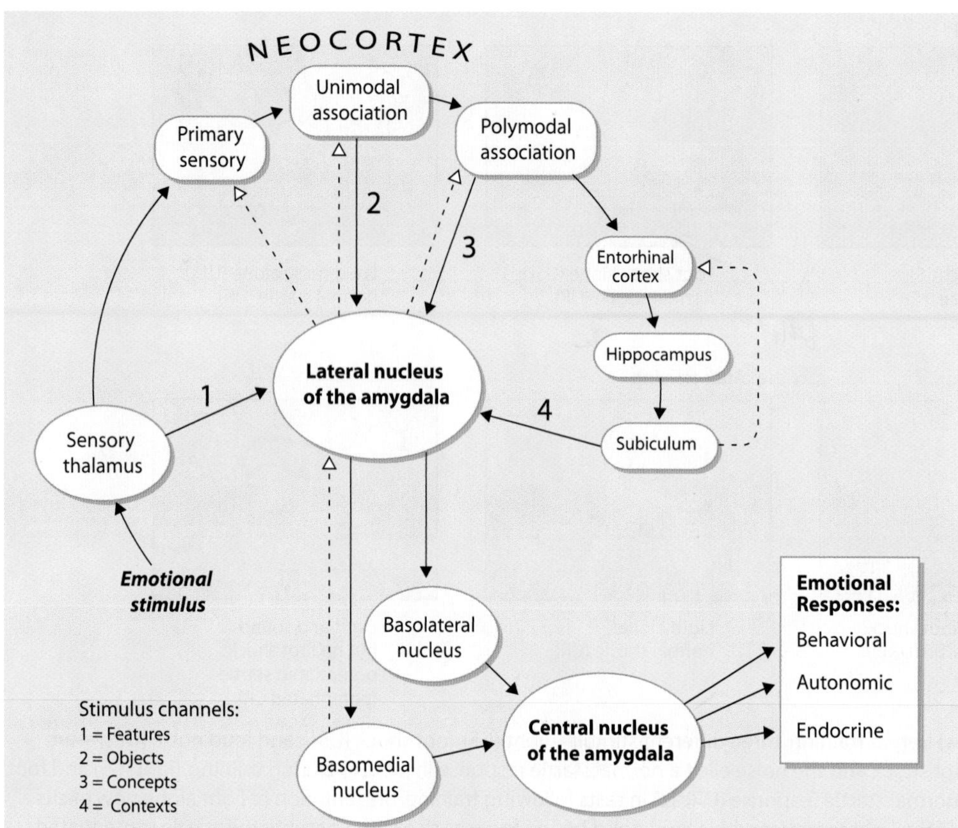

Figure 9.8 Amygdala pathways and fear conditioning.

the amygdala through two separate and simultaneous pathways (LeDoux, 1996). One is sometimes called the *low road*; it is quick but dirty. This is a subcortical pathway in which sensory information about a stimulus projects to the thalamus, which in turn sends a signal directly to the amygdala. The thalamus does not produce a sophisticated analysis of this sensory information, but it can send a crude signal to the amygdala indicating whether this stimulus roughly resembles the CS.

At the same time, sensory information about the stimulus is being projected to the amygdala via another, cortical pathway, sometimes referred to as the *high road*. The high road is somewhat slower, but the analysis of the stimulus is more thorough and complete. The sensory information projects to the thalamus; then the thalamus sends this information to the sensory cortex for a finer analysis. The sensory cortex projects the results of this analysis to the amygdala. The low road allows for the amygdala to receive information quickly in order to prime, or ready, the amygdala so that it can respond right away if the information from the high road confirms that the sensory stimulus is the CS. Although it may seem redundant to have two pathways to send information to the amygdala, when it comes to responding to a threatening stimulus, it is adaptive to be both fast and sure. Figure 9.9 shows an example of the neural circuits involved in the amygdala's response to a threatening stimulus.

The role of the amygdala in learning to respond to stimuli that have come to represent aversive events through fear conditioning is said to be *implicit*. This term is used because the learning is expressed indirectly through a behavioral or physiological response, such as autonomic nervous system arousal or potentiated startle. When studying nonhuman animals, we can assess the CR only through indirect, or implicit, means of expression. In humans, however, we can also assess the response directly, by asking the subjects to report if they know that the CS represents a potential aversive consequence (the US). Although patients with amygdala damage fail to demonstrate an indirect CR, when they are asked to report the parameters of fear conditioning explicitly or consciously, they demonstrate no deficit. Damage to the amygdala appears to leave this latter ability intact.

This concept is illustrated by the study of a patient very much like S.M. This patient, called S.P., also has bilateral amygdala damage (Figure 9.10). To relieve epilepsy, at age 48 S.P. underwent a lobectomy that re-

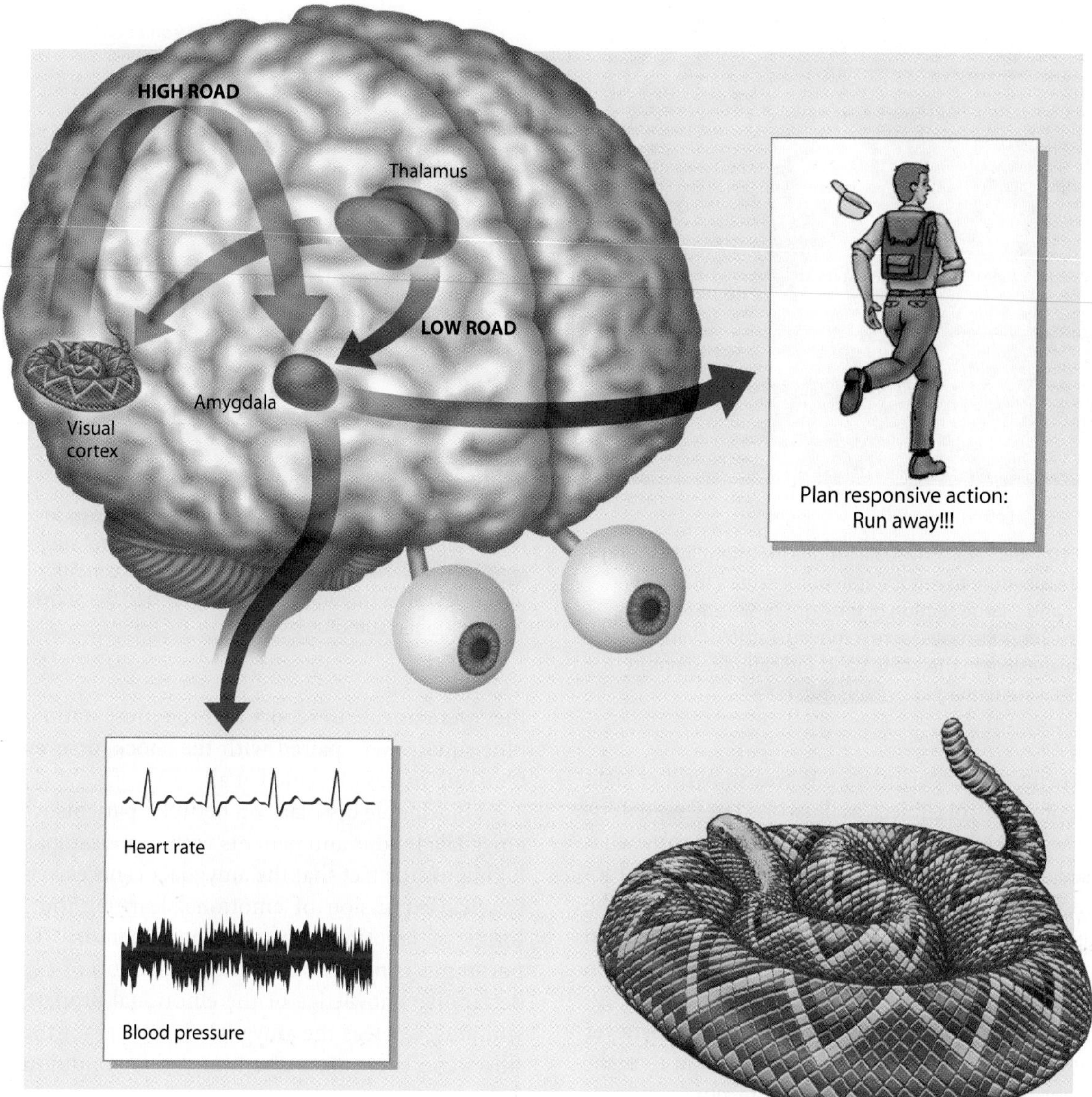

Figure 9.9 The amygdala receives visual information along two pathways. When a hiker chances upon a rattlesnake, the visual information activates affective memories through the cortical "high road" and subcortical "low road" projections to the amygdala. These memories not only produce autonomic changes, such as an increase in heart rate and blood pressure, but also can influence subsequent actions through the projections to the frontal cortex. The hiker will use this emotion-laden information in choosing his next action: Turn and run, or slowly move around the snake?

moved her right amygdala. MRI at that time revealed that her left amygdala was already damaged, most likely from mesial temporal sclerosis, a syndrome that causes neuronal loss in the medial temporal regions of the brain (Anderson & Phelps, 2001; Phelps et al., 1998). Like S.M., S.P. is unable to recognize fear in the faces of others (Adolphs et al., 1999).

In a study on the role of the amygdala in human fear conditioning, S.P. was shown a picture of a blue square (the CS), which was periodically presented for 10 s. During the acquisition phase, S.P. was given a mild electrical shock to the wrist (the US) at the end of the 10-s presentation of the blue square (the CS). In measures of skin conductance response (Figure 9.11), S.P.'s performance was as predicted: She showed a normal fear response to the shock (the UR), but no change in response when the blue square (the CS) was presented, even after several acquisition trials. This lack of change in the skin conductance response to the blue square demonstrates that she failed to acquire a CR.

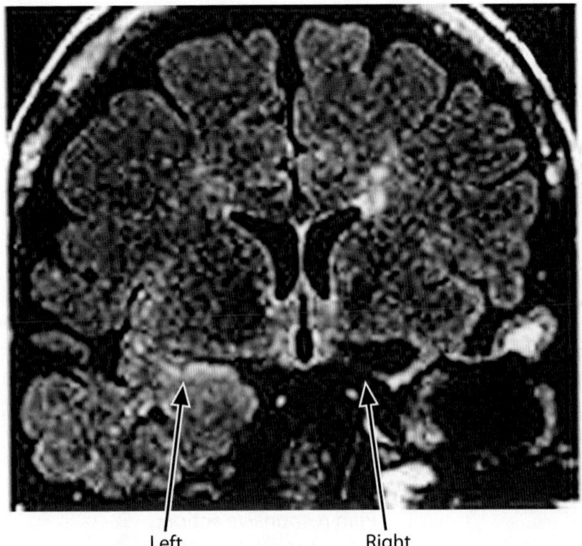

Figure 9.10 Bilateral amygdala lesions in Patient S.P. During a surgical procedure to reduce epileptic seizures, the right amygdala and a large section of the right temporal lobe, including the hippocampus were removed. Pathology in the left amygdala is visible in the white band, indicating regions in which cells were damaged by neural disease.

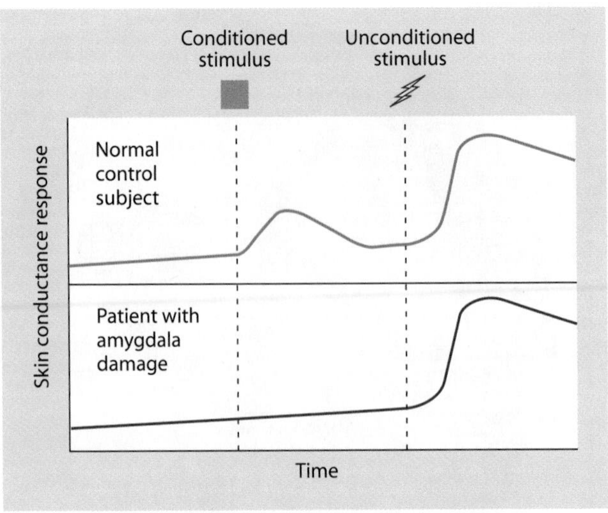

Figure 9.11 Increase in skin conductance response to conditioned and unconditioned stimuli. Unlike control subjects, S.P. showed no response to the blue square (the conditioned stimulus, or CS) after training. She did respond to the shock (the unconditioned stimulus, or US).

Following the experiment, S.P. was shown her data and that of a control subject, as illustrated in Figure 9.11, and she was asked what she thought. She was somewhat surprised that she showed no change in skin conductance response (the CR) to the blue square (the CS). She reported that she knew after the very first acquisition trial that she was going to get a shock to the wrist when the blue square was presented. She claimed to have figured this out early on and expected the shock whenever she saw the blue square. She was not sure what to make of the fact that her skin conductance response did not reflect what she consciously knew to be true.

This dissociation between intact explicit knowledge of the events that occurred during fear conditioning and impaired conditioned responses has been shown also in other patients with amygdala damage (Bechara et al., 1995; LaBar et al., 1995). As discussed in Chapter 8, explicit or declarative memory for events depends on another medial temporal lobe structure, the hippocampus. Damage to the hippocampus impairs the ability to explicitly report memory for an event. When the conditioning paradigm described for S.P. was conducted with patients who had bilateral damage to the hippocampus but an intact amygdala, the opposite pattern of performance emerged. These patients showed a normal skin conductance response to the blue square (the CS), indicating acquisition of the conditioned response. When asked what had occurred during conditioning, however, they were unable to report that the presentations of the blue square were paired with the shock, or even that a blue square was presented at all.

This double dissociation between patients who have amygdala lesions and patients with hippocampal lesions highlights the fact that the amygdala is necessary for the implicit expression of emotional learning, but not all forms of emotional learning and memory. The hippocampus is necessary for the acquisition of explicit or declarative knowledge of the emotional properties of a stimulus, whereas the amygdala is critical for the acquisition and expression of an implicitly conditioned fear response.

EXPLICIT EMOTIONAL LEARNING AND MEMORY

Though the double dissociation described above clearly indicates the necessity of the amygdala for implicit emotional learning but not explicit emotional learning, it does not force us to conclude that the amygdala is entirely uninvolved with explicit learning and memory. Indeed, the amygdala interacts with other memory systems, particularly the hippocampal memory system, when there are emotional events or information. The amygdala interacts with hippocampus-dependent declarative (conscious) memories in two primary ways: First, the amygdala is necessary for normal indirect emotional responses to stimuli whose emotional properties are learned explicitly, by means other than fear conditioning. Second, the amygdala can enhance the strength of explicit or declarative memories for emotional events by modulating the storage of these memories.

Imagine that a young woman is walking down the street in her neighborhood and sees a neighbor's dog on the sidewalk. Even though this woman is a dog owner herself, she is afraid of this particular dog. When she encounters it, she becomes nervous and fearful, so she decides to walk on the other side of the street. Why might this woman, who likes most dogs, be afraid of this particular dog? There are a few possible reasons: For example, perhaps this dog once bit her. In this case her fear response to the dog was acquired through fear conditioning. The dog (the CS) was paired with the dog bite (the US), resulting in pain and fear (the UR) and an acquired fear response to the dog (the CR).

However, the woman may fear this dog for another reason—because she has heard from her neighbor that this is a mean dog that *might* bite her. In this case she has no aversive experience linked to this particular dog. Instead, she learned about the aversive properties of the dog explicitly. Her ability to learn and remember this type of information depends on her hippocampal memory system. It is unlikely that she experienced a fear response when she learned this information during a conversation with her neighbor. She did not experience a fear response until she actually encountered the dog. Her fear response is not based on actual experience with the dog, but rather is anticipatory, on the basis of her explicit knowledge of the potential aversive properties of this dog. This type of learning, in which we learn to fear or avoid a stimulus because of what we are told as opposed to actual experience, is a common example of emotional learning in humans.

This explicit learning of the emotional properties of a stimulus, in the absence of aversive experience, is modeled in the instructed-fear paradigm illustrated in Figure 9.12. There are two means by which a person can

Figure 9.12 Two methods by which humans can learn about the aversive properties of an event. **(a)** In fear conditioning, the aversive properties of the blue square are learned by the pairing of the square and shock. **(b)** In instructed fear, the blue square is linked to the shock by verbal instruction. In both cases the amygdala plays a role in the expression of the fear response.

learn that the presentation of a blue square predicts a shock to the wrist. Figure 9.12a shows an example of fear conditioning, in which a person fears the presentation of a blue square because it was previously paired with a shock. Figure 9.12b shows an example of instructed fear, in which a person fears a blue square because he was told it might be paired with a shock. As mentioned earlier, we know that the amygdala is critical to the ability to show a conditioned fear response during fear conditioning. The question is this: Does the amygdala play a role in the indirect expression of the fear response in instructed fear?

Elizabeth Phelps of New York University and her colleagues (Funayama et al., 2001; Phelps et al., 2001) addressed this question. They found that, even though explicit learning of the emotional properties of the blue square depends on the hippocampal memory system, the amygdala is critical for the expression of some fear responses to the blue square. During the instructed-fear paradigm, patients with amygdala damage (including S.P.) were able to learn and explicitly report that some presentations of the blue square might be paired with a shock to the wrist, even though none of the subjects ever received a shock. Unlike normal control subjects, however, they did not show a potentiated startle response when the blue square was presented. In addition, normal control subjects showed an increase in skin conductance response to the blue square that was correlated with amygdala activity. These results suggest that, in humans, the amygdala is sometimes critical for the indirect expression of a fear response when the emotional learning occurs explicitly, by means other than fear conditioning. Similar deficits have been observed when patients with amygdala lesions respond to emotional scenes (Angrilli et al., 1996; Funayama et al., 2001).

Although animal models of emotional learning highlight the role of the amygdala in fear conditioning and the indirect expression of the conditioned fear response, human emotional learning can be much more complex. We can learn that stimuli in the world are linked to potentially aversive consequences in a variety of ways, including instruction, observation, and experience. Whatever is the manner by which we learn the aversive or threatening nature of stimuli—whether explicit and declarative, implicit, or both—the amygdala may play a role in the indirect expression of the fear response to those stimuli.

The instructed-fear studies indicate that a hippocampal-dependent, declarative representation about the emotional properties of stimuli can influence amygdala activity, which then modulates some indirect emotional responses. But is it possible for the reverse to occur? Can the amygdala modulate the activity of the hippocampus? James McGaugh (1992) of the University of California, Irvine, and his colleagues (Ferry & McGaugh, 2000) demonstrated that this is indeed the case. They found that the amygdala modulates the strength of declarative memories for emotional events.

How do we use declarative memory in everyday life? The types of things we recollect on a daily basis are things like where we left the keys, what we said to a friend the night before, or whether we turned the iron off before leaving the house. But when we look back on our lives, we do not remember these mundane events. We remember a first kiss, being teased by a friend in school, the pride of our family at graduation, or hearing about a horrible accident. The memories that last over time are those of emotional or important events. These memories seem to have a persistent vividness that other memories lack. One reason for this persistence may be related to the action of the amygdala.

In his autobiography *My Early Life: A Roving Commission* (1930), Winston Churchill described in great detail an exam that he took to gain admittance to secondary school: "I wrote my name at the top of the page. I wrote down the number of the question 'I'. After much reflection I put a bracket around it thus '(I)'. But thereafter I could not think of anything connected with it that was either relevant or true. Incidentally there arrived from nowhere in particular a blot and several smudges. I gazed for two whole hours at this sad spectacle: and then merciful ushers collected my piece of foolscap with all the others and carried it up to the Headmaster's table."

Although this event occurred decades before Churchill wrote about it, he still remembered very specific details. What was it about this particular event that made it stand out in Churchill's memory? It was not the first exam he had taken or the first exam he had failed. Given the circumstances (an admittance exam for a prestigious school), however, it was a particularly important and embarrassing event. He was nervous about taking the exam and especially aroused when he discovered that he was unable to answer the questions.

An arousal response can influence the ability to store declarative or explicit memories, which may partially explain Churchill's detailed recollection of the events that occurred during the exam. This effect has been demonstrated in studies across species. For example, creating an arousal response is known to enhance performance on declarative, hippocampal-dependent memory tasks in rats. In a series of studies, McGaugh and colleagues (1996) demonstrated that this memory enhancement effect of arousal is blocked by lesions to the amygdala.

Two important aspects of this work help us understand the mechanism underlying the role of the amygdala in enhancing declarative memory that has been observed with arousal. The first is that the amygdala's role is modulatory. The tasks used in these studies depend on the hippocampus for acquisition. For example, investigators frequently use the Morris water maze task to test a rat's spatial abilities and memory. A lesion to the amygdala does not impair the ability of rats to learn this task under ordinary circumstances. However, if the rat is aroused immediately after training, by either a physical stressor or the administration of drugs that mimic an arousal response, then the rat will show improved retention of this task. The memory is *enhanced* by arousal. It is this arousal-induced enhancement of memory, rather than memory acquisition itself, that is blocked by lesions to the amygdala. In other words, the amygdala is not necessary for learning this hippocampal-dependent task, but it is necessary for the arousal-dependent modulation of memory for this task.

The second important facet of this work is that this effect of modulation with arousal can occur *after* initial encoding of the task, during the retention interval. The administration of drugs that mimic an arousal response immediately after learning leads to enhanced memory for the task. The same is true if the rat is physically stressed after learning. Using pharmacological lesions to temporarily disable the amygdala immediately after learning eliminates any arousal-enhanced memory effect (Teather et al., 1998). All of these studies point to the conclusion that the amygdala modulates hippocampal, declarative memory by enhancing retention, rather than by altering the initial encoding of the stimulus. Because this effect occurs during retention, the amygdala is thought to enhance hippocampal consolidation. As described in Chapter 8, *consolidation* occurs over time, after initial encoding, and leads to memories becoming more or less stable. When there is an arousal response, the amygdala alters hippocampal processing by strengthening the consolidation of memories. McGaugh and colleagues (1996) showed that the basolateral nucleus of the amygdala is important for this effect. Recent evidence, however, also suggests that the amygdala can interact directly with the hippocampus during the *initial* encoding phase (not just the consolidation phase) of an experience, which in turn also positively affects the long-term consolidation (Dolcos et al., 2004). Thus, the amygdala can modulate hippocampus-dependent declarative memory at multiple stages, leading to a net effect of enhanced retention.

This role for the amygdala in enhancing emotional, declarative memory has also been demonstrated in humans. Various studies over the years have indicated that a mild arousal response can enhance declarative memory for emotional events (e.g., see Christianson, 1992). This effect of arousal on declarative memory is blocked in patients with bilateral amygdala damage (Cahill et al., 1995). Interestingly, studies on patients with unilateral amygdala damage reveal that it is the right, and not the left, amygdala that is most important for the retrieval of autobiographical emotional memories relating to negative valence and high arousal (Buchanan et al., 2006). In addition, functional neuroimaging studies have shown that activity observed in the human amygdala during the presentation of emotional stimuli is correlated with the arousal-enhanced recollection of these stimuli (Cahill et al., 1996; Hamann et al., 1999). There is also increased effective connectivity bidirectionally between the amygdala and hippocampus during recall of emotional information that is relative to current behavior (Smith et al., 2006). These studies indicate that normal amygdala function plays a role in the enhanced declarative memory observed with arousal in humans.

The mechanism for this effect of arousal appears to be related to the amygdala's role in modifying the rate of forgetting for arousing stimuli. In other words, arousal may alter how quickly we forget. This is consistent with the notion of a postencoding effect on memory, such as enhancing hippocampal storage or consolidation. Although the ability to recollect arousing and nonarousing events may be similar immediately after they occur, arousing events are not forgotten as quickly as nonarousing events are (Kleinsmith & Kaplan, 1963). Unlike normal control subjects, who show less forgetting over time for arousing compared to nonarousing stimuli, patients with amygdala lesions forget arousing and nonarousing stimuli at the same rate (LaBar & Phelps, 1998).

Studies on both animal models and human populations converge on the conclusion that the amygdala acts to modulate hippocampal consolidation for arousing events. However, this mechanism does not underlie all of the effects of emotion on human declarative memory. Emotional events are more distinctive and unusual than are everyday life events. They also form a specific class of events. These and other factors may enhance declarative or explicit memory for emotional events in ways that do not depend on the amygdala (Phelps et al., 1998).

For example, it appears that acute stress can facilitate memory. Kevin LaBar and his colleagues at Duke University (Zorawski et al., 2006) have found that the amount of endogenous stress hormone (cortisol) released during the acquisition of a conditioned fear accurately predicts how well fear memories are retained one day later in humans. However, Robert Sapolsky of Stanford University (1992) and his colleagues demonstrated that extreme arousal or chronic stress may actually *impair* performance of the hippocampal memory system. This memory impairment is due to the effect of excessive stress hormones, such as glucocorticoids, on the hippocampus. The precise role of the amygdala in this impairment of hippocampal memory during chronic or excessive stress is not fully understood.

The amygdala's interactions with the hippocampal memory system and explicit memory are specific and complex. The amygdala acts to modulate the storage of arousing events, thus ensuring that they will not be forgotten over time. In addition, we can learn explicitly that stimuli in the environment are linked to potential aversive consequences, without having to experience these consequences. This explicit, hippocampal-dependent representation of the emotional properties of events can affect amygdala activity and certain indirect fear responses. The interactions of the amygdala and hippocampus help ensure that we remember important and emotionally charged information and events for a long time. This ultimately ensures that our bodily response to threatening events is appropriate and adaptive.

SOCIAL RESPONSES

The human amygdala does not appear to be important for most forms of explicit evaluation. That is, the ability to consciously label a stimulus as *good, bad, arousing*, or *neutral* does not depend on the amygdala. However, there are a couple of exceptions: The human amygdala is important for normal responses to a subset of social stimuli—for instance, facial expressions. It also appears to play a role in social grouping.

Facial Expression and the Amygdala We first came across the idea that the amygdala is involved in processing of the facial expression of fear with the study of S.M. at the beginning of the chapter. This idea is also supported by functional neuroimaging. Activity in the amygdala increases in response to brief presentations of faces with fearful expressions compared to faces with neutral expressions (Breiter et al., 1996). Although the amygdala will show an activation response to other emotional expressions, such as happy or angry, the activation response to fear is significantly greater.

One interesting aspect of the amygdala's response to fearful facial expressions is that the subject does not have to be aware of seeing the fearful face for the amygdala to respond. Fearful facial expressions that are presented subliminally—so quickly that the subject is unaware of their presentation—and then masked with neutral expressions will still result in activation of the amygdala. The activation to subliminal fearful faces is as strong as the response to fearful faces that the subject is aware of seeing (Whalen et al., 1998).

This critical role for the amygdala in explicitly evaluating fearful faces also extends to other social judgments about faces, such as indicating from a picture of a face whether or not the person appears trustworthy or approachable (Adolphs et al., 2000). However, the amygdala does not appear to be critical for all types of social communication. Unlike patients with damage to the orbitofrontal cortex, patients with amygdala lesions do not show gross impairment in their ability to respond to social stimuli. They can interpret descriptions of emotional situations correctly, and they can give normal ratings to emotional prosody (the speech sounds that indicate emotion), even when a person is speaking in a fearful tone of voice (Anderson & Phelps, 1998; Scott et al., 1997; Adolphs et al., 1999). They do not show other, nonemotional face recognition deficits and are even able to recognize the perceptual similarity between facial expressions whose emotional content they label incorrectly. In addition, their deficit appears to be restricted to the *recognition* of facial expressions; they are able to generate and communicate a full range of facial expressions (Anderson & Phelps, 2000).

Recall that this is the unusual deficit exhibited by S.M. After nearly a decade of testing S.M., Ralph Adolphs and colleagues (2005) discovered an explanation for the intriguing impairment. They used computer software that exposed only parts of either a fearful or happy facial expression in order to find out what regions of the face the subjects relied on to discriminate between expressions. They found that control subjects consistently relied on eyes to make decisions about expression. S.M., on the other hand, did not derive information from the eyes. Indeed, a subsequent experiment using eye-tracking technology confirmed that she did not even look at the eyes of *any* face, regardless of the emotion it conveyed (Figure 9.13a).

So if, unlike controls, S.M. did not automatically use eyes to derive information from faces, why did she only have trouble with identifying fear? Most expressions contain other cues that can be used for identification.

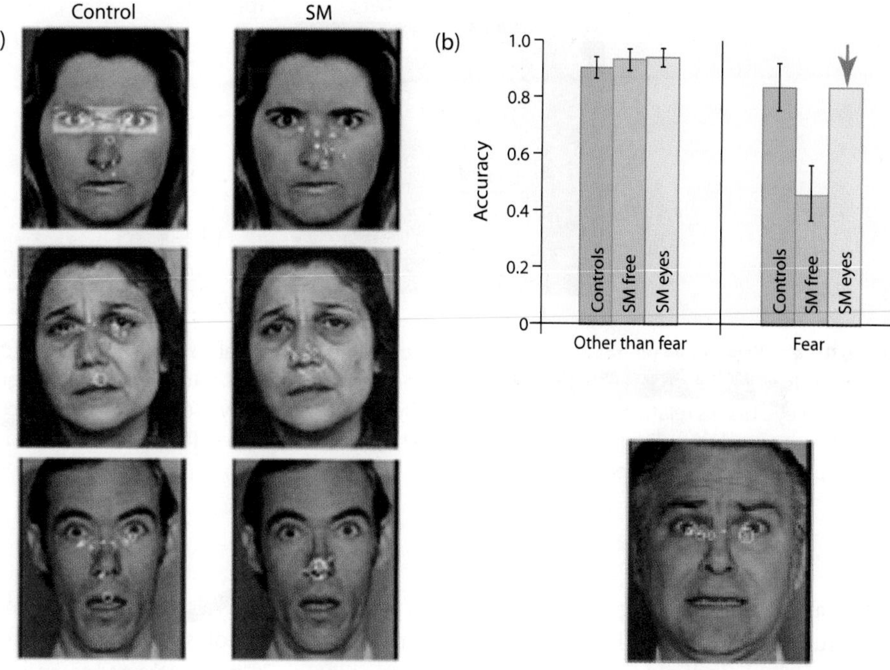

Figure 9.13 Abnormal eye movement patterns during face perception following amygdala lesions. **(a)** Unlike control participants, S.M.'s eye movements do not target the eyes of other faces. **(b)** However, when instructed to focus on the eyes, S.M. is able to identify fearful expressions as well as controls. The bottom panel shows that, when instructed, S.M. is able to look at the eyes. Red lines indicate eye movements and white circles indicate points of fixation.

For instance, an expression of happiness reliably contains a smile. But the identifying feature of a fearful expression is the increase in size of the white region (sclera) of the eyes (Figure 9.14). This prominent characteristic is captured by the frequently used phrase "I could see the fear in his eyes." More empirically, one study found that viewing sclera from a fearful face without any other accompanying facial information is sufficient to increase amygdala activity in normal subjects (relative to sclera from facial expressions of happiness; Whalen et al., 2004).

Stunningly, the investigators could induce S.M. to overcome her deficit by providing her with a simple instruction: "Focus on the eyes." If told to do so, she no longer had any difficulty identifying fearful faces (Figure 9.13b). Consequently, the amygdala appears to be an integral part of a system that automatically directs visual attention to the eyes when encountering *any* facial expressions. This novel function of the amygdala is still not fully understood and is just one example of the diverse topics on the frontier of emotion research.

Social Group Evaluation The amygdala also appears to be activated during the categorization of people into groups. Although such implicit behavior might sometimes be helpful (separating people within a social group from people outside of the group or identifying the trustworthiness of a person), it can also lead to negative behaviors, such as racial stereotyping. A variety of research has looked at racial stereotyping, from both a behavioral and a functional imaging perspective.

Behavioral research has gone beyond simple, explicit measures of racial bias, as obtained through simple self-report, to implicit measures that examine indirect behavioral responses demonstrating a preference for one group over another. One common indirect measure for examining bias is the Implicit Association Test (IAT). Devised by Greenwald and colleagues (1998), the IAT measures the degree to which social groups (black versus white, old versus young, etc.) are automatically associated with positive and negative evaluations (see https://implicit.harvard.edu/implicit to take the test yourself). Subjects are asked to categorize faces from each group while simultaneously categorizing words as either good or bad. For example, for one set of trials the subject responds to "good" words and black faces with one hand, and to "bad" words and white faces with the other hand. In another set of trials the pairings are switched. The measure of bias is computed by the difference in the response latency between the black-and-good/white-and-bad trials versus the black-and-bad/white-and-good trials.

To study the neural basis of this racial bias, Elizabeth Phelps and her colleagues (2000) used functional MRI to examine amygdala activation in white subjects viewing black and white faces. They found that the amygdala was activated when white Americans viewed unfamiliar black faces (but not faces of familiar, positively regarded blacks like Michael Jordan, Will Smith,

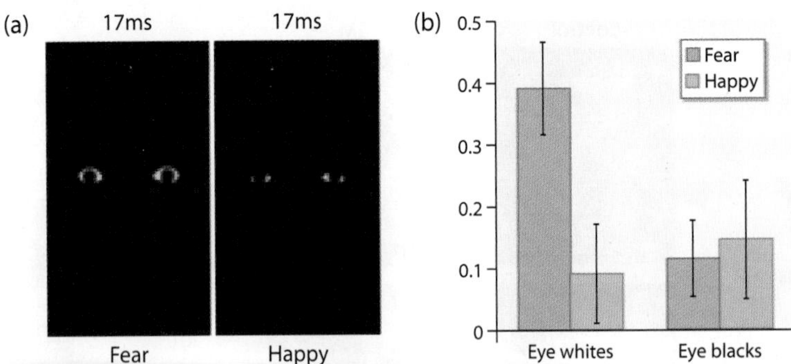

Figure 9.14 Size of eye whites alone is sufficient to induce differential amygdala response to fearful expressions. **(a)** Volume of eye whites is greater in fearful expressions than in happy expressions. **(b)** Activity in the left ventral amygdala in response to eye whites and eye blacks relative to fixation demonstrate that fearful eye whites alone induce increased response above baseline. Eye blacks were control stimuli, which were identical in shape to the stimuli in **(a)** but had inverted colors, such that the eye whites were actually black on a white screen.

and Martin Luther King, Jr.). More important, the magnitude of the amygdala activation was significantly correlated with indirect measures of racial bias as determined by the IAT. Subjects who showed more racial bias as measured by the IAT showed greater amygdala activity during the presentation of black faces. The researchers concluded that the amygdala responses and behavioral responses to black versus white faces in white subjects reflected cultural evaluations of social groups as modified by experience.

Although the amygdala does appear to be activated during these tasks, is it necessary for such evaluation? Phelps and colleagues (2003) compared the performance of the patient S.P., who had bilateral amygdala damage, to the performance of control subjects on explicit and implicit measures of racial bias. They found no significant differences between the patient and controls on either measure and were forced to conclude that the amygdala is not a critical structure for the indirect evaluation of race, suggesting instead that it might be important for differences in the perceptual processing of "same" versus "other" race faces.

More recent studies have expanded our understanding of the role that the amygdala plays in social group evaluations. William Cunningham and colleagues (2004) compared areas of brain activation in white subjects using functional MRI for brief and more prolonged presentation of faces of black and white males. Their findings led them to propose two separate systems for social evaluation processing (Figure 9.15). For brief presentations, where the evaluation must be made quickly and automatically, the amygdala is activated, and the activation is greater for black faces than for white faces. With longer presentations, when controlled processing can take place, amygdala activation is not significantly different between races. Instead, significantly more activity in the right ventrolateral prefrontal cortex was found during viewing of black faces than of white faces. Cunningham's team proposed that there are distinct neural differences between automatic and more controlled processing of social groups and that the controlled processing may modulate the automatic evaluation.

We must be careful in drawing sweeping conclusions about racial stereotypes from this data. It does appear that certain processes in the brain make it likely that people will categorize others on the basis of race. However, this is not the same thing as determining whether someone is a racist. The ability to use such a categorization strategy may lead to racism, but it does not do so necessarily. Kurzban and colleagues (2001) offer a promising finding: Even though people encode the race of each individual they encounter, when categorization cues stronger than race are present (e.g., groups of people of both races wearing red clothing versus groups of people of both races wearing green clothing), the categorization based on race is diminished.

FUTURE AMYGDALA-BASED RESEARCH

The amygdala is involved in a variety of emotional tasks, ranging from fear conditioning to social responses. We have focused on its role in responding to fear or threatening emotional events. However, it would be misleading to suggest that the amygdala responds only to negative stimuli. The amygdala also plays a role in responding to positive stimuli in somewhat more limited circumstances. For instance, the ef-

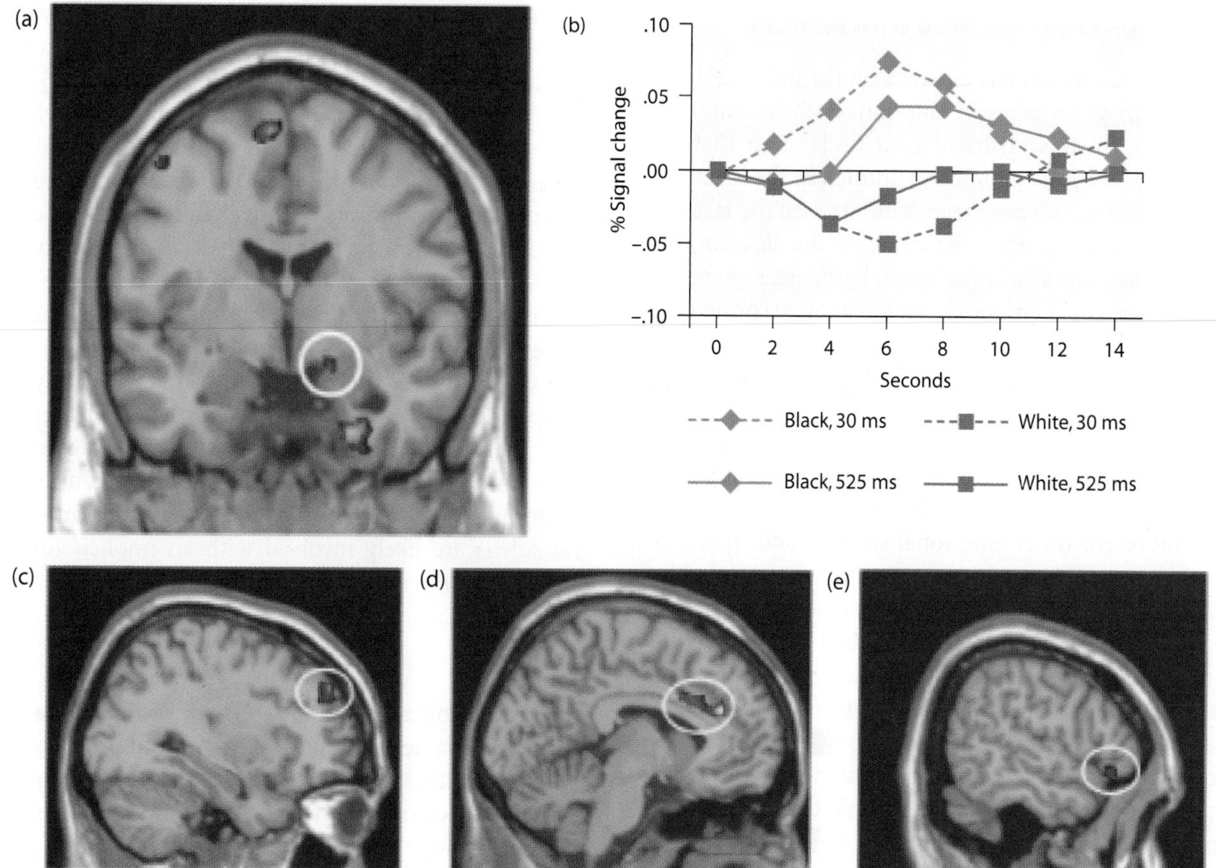

Figure 9.15 Differential neural response to masked and unmasked black and white faces. Black and white faces were presented for either 30 ms (masked) or for 525 ms (unmasked). **(a)** The right amygdala is more active for black versus white faces when faces are presented for 30 ms. **(b)** The pattern of amygdala activity is similar at 525 ms though the effect is attenuated. Also during the longer stimulus presentation, activity in the **(c)** dorsolateral prefrontal cortex, **(d)** anterior cingulate cortex, and **(e)** ventrolateral prefrontal cortex was greater for black faces relative to white faces. Activity in one or more of these areas may be responsible for the attenuation of amygdala activity at 525 ms.

fects of the amygdala modulating hippocampal consolidation appear to be mediated by arousal, a response to positive or negative events (Hamann et al., 1999). In addition, the amygdala plays a role in some learning tasks in which a rewarding stimulus is associated with a neutral stimulus (Gaffan & Harrison, 1987; Johnsrude et al., 2000; Gallagher & Holland, 1992; Hampton et al., 2007). It would be inaccurate to say that the amygdala is involved in responding only to negative or fear stimuli, although it does appear to be particularly sensitive to these types of stimuli. Such a preference is clearly evolutionarily advantageous for an organism.

Our discussion of the amygdala has focused on how this structure operates independently. However, some of the more exciting current research in the cognitive neuroscience of emotion is starting to outline how this region works together with other brain areas to produce normal emotional responses. For example, although acquisition of fear conditioning requires the amygdala, normal extinction of a conditioned response involves interactions of the amygdala and the prefrontal cortex (Morgan & LeDoux, 1999). Studies examining the ability to associate a reward with a stimulus found that the amygdala and orbitofrontal cortex may act together on this type of task (Baxter et al., 2000; Hampton et al., 2007). A neuroanatomical model of depression suggests that a circuit of structures (amygdala, orbitofrontal cortex, and thalamus) is overactive in depressed patients and that the structures in this circuit, working in concert, lead to some of the symptoms of depression (Drevets, 1998). Finally, Damasio's somatic marker hypothesis (see Chapter 14) proposes that the amygdala and orbitofrontal cortex interact and make unique contributions to emotional decision making.

Other Brain Areas Involved with Emotion

So far, our discussion has centered on the important role that the amygdala plays in emotion. Such an emphasis should not be misconstrued as a declaration that the amygdala is the lone neural area studied in the investigation of emotion. We have repeatedly stressed the fact that the amygdala is important for some, but *not all*, emotions. This then leads us to wonder which brain areas are necessary for these other emotions, a topic we now consider.

ANGER

The elucidation of the neural basis of various emotions has benefited greatly from functional brain imaging. Investigators can expose subjects to different facial expressions (or other emotional stimuli) and then analyze the areas of the brain that are uniquely activated for different emotions (Figure 9.16). James Blair and colleagues (1999) applied this strategy in a landmark study of the neural basis of anger. They used a computer program to manipulate a neutral facial expression into one that looked increasingly angry (Figure 9.16a) and searched for brain activation associated with the gradient of expression intensity. They found that the right **orbitofrontal cortex** (OFC; refer back to Figure 9.6a) was increasingly active when subjects viewed increasingly expressive angry, but not sad, faces (Figure 9.17). These results indicate a role for the OFC in explicit emotional labeling of angry faces.

The role of the OFC in anger was further characterized by a study that employed the dichoptic listening task, described in Chapter 12 (Sander et al., 2005). Researchers presented one ear with meaningless phrases pronounced with neutral prosody and the other ear with meaningless phrases pronounced with angry prosody. Then they had subjects selectively attend to one ear or the other. They found that activity in the right amygdala and superior temporal sulcus (involved in high level auditory processing) was modulated by angry prosody independent of attention. The OFC, on the other hand, was only activated by angry prosody that was attended to (implying that it was heard). This provides further support that the OFC is important for explicit processing of anger and suggests that it responds to anger conveyed by multiple modalities. The amygdala and superior temporal sulcus are likely involved with an implicit form of anger detection and processing.

SADNESS

Blair and colleagues (1999) also investigated sadness using the same paradigm. They found that the left amygdala and the right temporal pole both exhibited activity associated with the intensity of sad expressions. However, these findings are at odds with other recent findings. For example, Adolphs and Tranel (2004) found that damage to the right amygdala produced a greater deficit in identifying sad faces than damage to the left amygdala. The former conclusions were based on per-

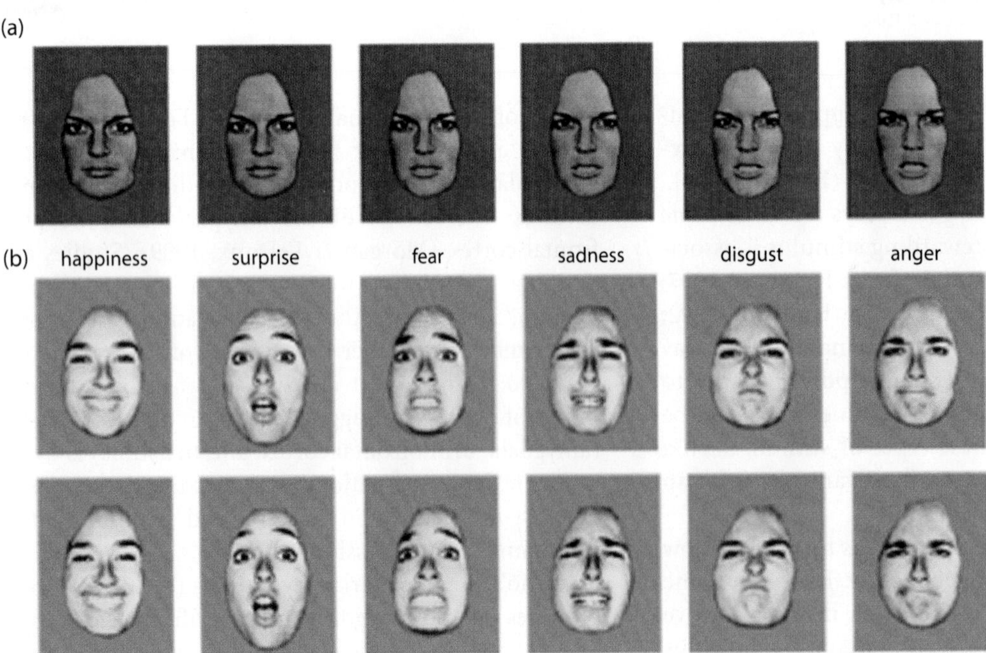

Figure 9.16 Examples of morphed facial expressions. **(a)** Transition from a neutral expression (far left) to an angry expression (far right) in increments of 20% increased intensity. **(b)** Exaggeration of various facial expressions from 100% (top row) to 150% (bottom row). Facial expressions produced by morphing software have proven to be very useful stimuli in the investigation of the neural correlates of facial expression identification.

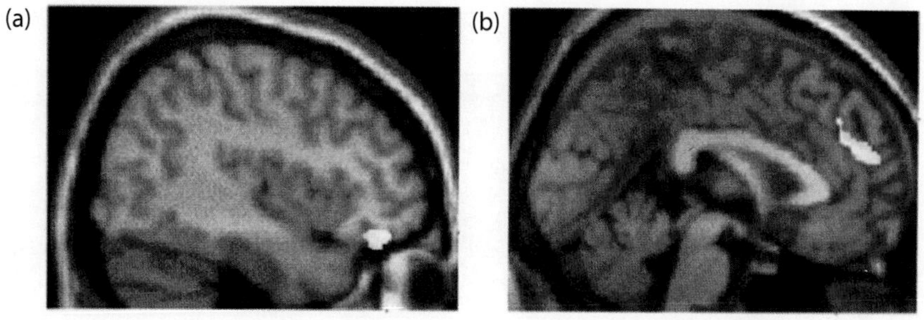

(a) (b)

Figure 9.17 Neural correlates of the perception of anger. Activity in the **(a)** right orbitofrontal cortex and **(b)** anterior cingulate increased as the intensity of an angry facial expression increased.

formance of a task that involved rating intensity of an emotion rather than just labeling it as "happy" or "sad." The authors argue that this is a more sensitive approach, which may be why it yielded different conclusions.

In another study, investigators masked expressions of happiness or sadness in order to find brain areas associated with automatic, implicit analysis of emotion (Killgore & Yurgelun-Todd, 2004). These investigators found amygdala activity associated with analysis of happy but not sad faces, further convoluting an already complicated topic. However, it is important to keep in mind that these varying results are hard to directly compare because they are derived from different tasks. It does appear that the amygdala is involved in the processing of sad faces, though there is no consensus on the extent to which it is necessary. At the very least, these varying results appear to mirror the results from studies of anger processing that indicate the existence of different systems for explicit and implicit detection of emotion.

DISGUST

Unlike the study of sadness, investigation of disgust has not been plagued by contradicting results. Indeed, there is consensus that at least one area, the anterior **insula**, is essential to both detection and experience of disgust (Philips et al., 1997, 1998). This conclusion, based on imaging studies, is consistent with a report of a patient with insula damage who is unable to detect disgust conveyed in various modalities (Calder et al., 2000).

A recent study by Giacomo Rizzolatti (the brilliant neuroscientist who studies mirror neurons, discussed in Chapter 7) and colleagues (Wicker et al., 2003) confirmed these findings and went a step further. They analyzed the neural response during observation of others experiencing disgust and firsthand experience of disgust. They observed that the same portion of the anterior insula was activated both when subjects viewed expressions of disgust in others and when they smelled unpleasant odors (a firsthand experience of disgust). These results are significant for two reasons. First, they provide additional evidence that the insula is a neural correlate of disgust identification in others and of experiencing disgust directly. Second, they suggest that understanding the emotions of others may require simulating, and thus mildly experiencing, these emotions ourselves. This latter conclusion implies a role for emotion in empathy and theory of mind (discussed in Chapter 14).

UNIQUE SYSTEMS, COMMON COMPONENTS

It is perhaps an oversimplification to associate each of the emotions we have addressed with a single brain structure. However, by revealing the various locations in the brain that different emotions are associated with, we have made it clear that there is no single brain area responsible for emotion (Figure 9.18). The challenge has shifted from identifying areas that specialize in a specific emotion to characterizing how these areas interact and determining if there are any interactions common to different flavors of emotional experience.

To this end, there is promising evidence that suggests the anterior cingulate cortex (ACC) could be essential for emotional processing more generally. One study found that emotional arousal while watching films and recalling various emotional experiences was associated with activity increase in the ACC (Lane et al., 1997). Furthermore, the ACC is known to receive projections from the amygdala, the OFC, and the anterior insula (Devinsky et al., 1995) making it plausible that it is an essential component of common emotional circuitry. The ACC was also activated during recognition of facial expressions of disgust (Wicker et al., 2003) and anger (Blair et al., 1999). These observations are suggestive but are far from conclusive. As the study of emotion progresses, it will be essential to develop an understanding of how distant areas of the brain interact to facilitate the detection and experience of emotion.

(a)

Emotion	Associated Brain Area	Functional Role
Fear	Amygdala	Learning, Avoidance
Anger	Orbitofrontal Cortex, Anterior Cingulate Cortex	Indicate Social Violations
Sadness	Amygdala, Right Temporal Pole	Withdraw
Disgust	Anterior Insula, Anterior Cingulate Cortex	Avoidance

(b)

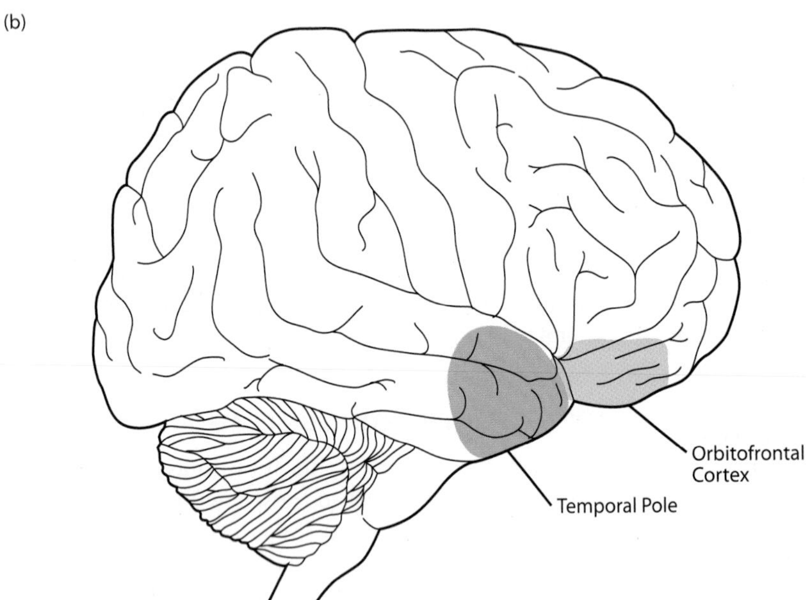

(c)

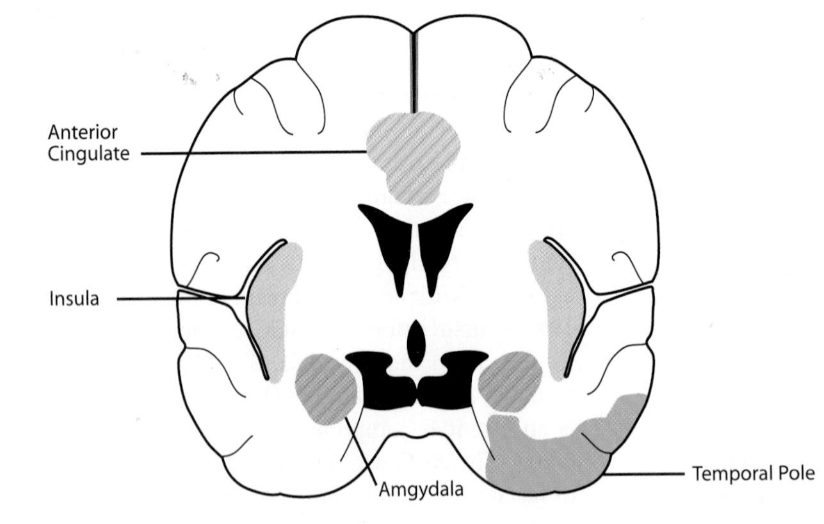

Figure 9.18 Brain areas associated with various emotions.

SUMMARY

Scientists have attributed emotional states to brain processing for almost a century, but recently, with case studies on intriguing impairments following bilateral amygdala damage and functional-imaging studies indicating how and where emotions are processed in the brain, we have made great strides toward characterizing the functional neuroanatomy of emotion.

Scientists face many challenges in studying emotion, a behavior that is often difficult to define and therefore difficult to manipulate and study in a scientific manner. One challenge has been establishing a proper place for studies of emotion in cognitive neuroscience. Earlier research and theories tended to view emotion as separate from cognition, implying that they could be studied and understood separately. As research in the neuroscience of emotion proceeded, however, it became clear that emotion could not be considered independently from other, more "cognitive" abilities or vice versa. The neural systems of emotion and other cognitive functions are interdependent. Although emotion, like all other behaviors, has unique and defining characteristics, current research strongly argues against a concrete emotion–cognition dichotomy.

Studies in the cognitive neuroscience of emotion have tended to emphasize the importance of the amygdala. Our understanding of the role of the amygdala in emotion has been influenced significantly by research with nonhuman animals. In both humans and other species, the amygdala plays a critical role in implicit emotional learning as demonstrated by fear conditioning. In addition, through interactions with the hippocampus, the amygdala is involved in explicit emotional learning and memory. It is also prominently involved in social interactions, enabling us to automatically derive information from the eyes of other people when assessing facial expression and facilitating categorization of other individuals.

The amygdala is no longer the sole focus of research seeking to characterize the neural correlates of emotion. Indeed, different emotions are associated with other neural structures, including the orbitofrontal cortex (anger) and the insula (disgust). Despite the success of relating these structures to various emotions, an emerging shift in our approach to studying the cognitive neuroscience of emotion is transferring the emphasis from the study of isolated neural structures to the investigation of neural systems. Certainly the amygdala, orbitofrontal cortex, and insula are critical for different forms of emotional processing, but it is now clear that in order to understand how the brain produces normal and adaptive emotional responses we need to understand how these structures interact with each other and with other brain regions.

KEY TERMS

amygdala
emotion
facial expression
fear conditioning
orbitofrontal cortex (OFC)
insula

TAKE-HOME MESSAGES

General

- In S.M., bilateral damage to the amygdala caused a deficit in identifying facial expressions conveying fear. This deficit was later shown to be the result of an inability to automatically use information from others' eyes to evaluate facial expressions.
- Six basic human facial expressions represent emotional states: anger, fear, disgust, happiness, sadness, and surprise.
- Another way to describe emotions is the dimensional approach, which, instead of describing discrete states of emotion, describes emotions as reactions that vary along a continuum.

Brain Areas Involved in Emotion

- The Papez circuit describes the brain areas that James Papez believed were involved in emotion. They include the hypothalamus, anterior thalamus, cingulate gyrus, and hippocampus (and sometimes the amygdala, orbitofrontal cortex, and portions of the basal ganglia). We no longer think there is only one neural circuit of emotion. Rather, depending on the emotional task or situation, we can expect different neural systems to be involved.
- The amygdala is heavily involved in fear conditioning (a form of implicit memory).

- Information can reach the amygdala via two separate pathways: The "low road" goes directly from the thalamus to the amygdala; the "high road" goes from the cortex to the amygdala.
- The amygdala is also important for explicit memory of emotional events. First, the amygdala is necessary for normal indirect emotional responses to stimuli whose emotional properties are learned explicitly, by means other than fear conditioning. Second, the amygdala can enhance the strength of explicit (or declarative) memories for emotional events by modulating the storage of these memories.
- The amygdala appears to be necessary for automatically deriving information from the eyes of others when identifying emotional facial expressions. This ability is especially critical for the proper identification of fear because the defining characteristic of fear is an increase in the volume of the eye whites.
- The amygdala is also activated during the categorization of people into groups. Research into this phenomenon has elucidated how our brains participate in implicit stereotyping.
- The amygdala may also participate in the processing of sad facial expressions.
- Other brain areas are associated with the processing of different emotions. The orbitofrontal cortex is activated when identifying angry facial expressions and hearing angry prosody, and the anterior insula is linked to identification and experience of disgust.
- Ultimately, understanding how we perceive and experience emotion will require studying the interactions of a diverse set of neural structures.

Fear Conditioning

- Fear conditioning is a form of classical conditioning in which the unconditioned stimulus is aversive. It is a form of implicit learning.
- The conditioned stimulus is a neutral stimulus that, through classical conditioning, will eventually evoke a response. The unconditioned stimulus is the stimulus that, even without training, evokes a response.
- The unconditioned response is the response naturally elicited (without training) by the unconditioned stimulus. The conditioned response is the response that is elicited (with training) by the conditioned stimulus. Usually the unconditioned response and the conditioned response are the same (e.g., the startle response in the rat), but they have different names depending on what elicits the response.
- S.P., who, like S.M., had bilateral amygdala damage, failed to acquire a conditioned response during fear conditioning, indicating that the amygdala is necessary for such conditioning to occur.

THOUGHT QUESTIONS

1. Briefly describe the limbic system hypothesis and its historical role in the cognitive neuroscience of emotion.
2. Explain the amygdala's role in fear conditioning. Be sure to cover what is known about the neural pathways for emotional learning based on nonhuman animal models, and also explain why the amygdala's role in emotional learning is said to be implicit.
3. In what two ways do the amygdala and hippocampus interact in emotional learning and memory?
4. What evidence is there for different levels (i.e., implicit, explicit) of emotion processing? What are the potential benefits of having neural circuitry devoted to each type of processing?

SUGGESTED READING

ADOLPHS, R., GOSSELIN, F., BUCHANAN, T. W., TRANEL, D., SCHYNS, P., & DAMASIO, A. R. (2005). A mechanism for impaired fear recognition after amygdala damage. *Nature, 433,* 68–72.

BLAIR, R. J. R., MORRIS, J. S., FRITH, C. D., PERRETT, D. I., & DOLAN, R. J. (1999). Dissociable neural responses to facial expressions of sadness and anger. *Brain, 122,* 883–893.

DAMASIO, A. R. (1994). *Descartes' error: Emotion, reason, and the human brain.* New York: Putnam.

DAVIDSON, R. J., JACKSON, D. C., & KALIN, N. H. (2000). Emotion, plasticity, context, and regulation: Perspectives from affective neuroscience. *Psychological Bulletin, 126,* 890–909.

LEDOUX, J. E. (1996). *The emotional brain: The mysterious underpinnings of emotional life.* New York: Simon and Schuster.

ROLLS, E. T. (1999). *The brain and emotion.* Oxford, England: Oxford University Press.

SAPOLSKY, R. M. (1992). *Stress, the aging brain, and the mechanisms of neuron death.* Cambridge, MA: MIT Press.

WHALEN, P. J. (1998). Fear, vigilance, and ambiguity: Initial neuroimaging studies of the human amygdala. *Current Directions in Psychological Science, 7,* 177–188.

10

Language

It had been an otherwise uneventful day at the major U.S. airport where Flight 301 was preparing to depart. The cabin crew was completing all preflight preparations. In the meantime, the flight attendants and gate personnel had finished boarding all the passengers. The passengers were waiting for the plane to leave so that all manner of electronic devices could be retrieved, activated, and set into the usual frenzy of beeping, chirping, and flashing. Soon they were rewarded as the plane was pushed back from the gate and began to taxi toward the runway. Suddenly, though, the plane turned around and started to head back to the gate, naturally accompanied by the groans and sighs of now wary and unhappy passengers: "Yet another delay? What's wrong? Hopefully it's just another indicator light in the cockpit that burned out."

Back in the control tower, however, air traffic controllers looked tense and were frantically searching through airport procedure manuals, following every guideline for the emergency now facing them. Prepared and on alert, airport security personnel were rushing toward Flight 301 from every direction, while the Federal Aviation Administration, the FBI, and local law enforcement were mobilizing their resources to aid the passengers and crew of the airplane. What had happened? What was wrong with the airplane? What imminent danger elicited this massive response?

The controller in the tower who was in charge of guiding Flight 301 to a safe takeoff had been communicating with the pilots over the radio, as is normal during the preflight period. A checklist of details had to be dealt with before the plane could be cleared to depart the gate and begin takeoff. As the plane was pushing away from the gate, the controller in the tower heard the fateful word from the cockpit that everybody in aviation fears: "Hijack!" This simple word called for immediate action, and the controller engaged a well-prepared plan developed for just such a situation. He notified authorities and then ordered the plane back to the gate. The pilots did as they were instructed and turned the plane around and headed to the gate, only to be met by a swarm of armed and nervous officers.

After some initial tense moments and an investigation on the scene, the security officers decided that Flight 301 was not being hijacked, and gave the green light for departure; none of the passengers even had to leave the plane. What had happened? Because of a heightened sensitivity for such situations and a need for extreme caution, a simple matter of human language had gotten in the way. One of the last passengers to board the plane had recognized the pilot, his friend Jack, and had greeted him with the carefree words, "Hi, Jack!" which the tower personnel had heard over the radio and had taken to mean something entirely different.

The misinterpretation of the simple phrase "Hi, Jack" by the air traffic controller in the tower illustrates one of the many complexities that we encounter in everyday language. Language is indeed one of the most complex of the human brain's feats. The meanings of words; their organization into sentences; how they are produced as speech, sign language, or in written form; and perhaps most important, how they are understood by the listener, viewer, or reader contribute to one of the most fascinating ongoing detective stories in cognitive neuroscience.

Communication and brain complexity took a monumental leap from the most intelligent of the nonhuman primates to humans, for whom communication includes language. Speech and symbolic language, being uniquely human, mark a dramatic shift between monkey brains and human brains. It has been surprisingly difficult, though, to identify human brain systems and specializations that support language. Some brain regions have long been known to be critical for normal speech and comprehension, but these 100-year-old clues from neurology, although foundational, have provided only modest insights into the neural organization of language. Today, however, a growing body of work on brain and language processes, guided by careful psycholinguistic models and aided by modern tools, is providing remarkable new data for cognitive neuroscientists to ponder. This chapter introduces a cognitive neuroscience perspective on the human language system, a system so complex that the smallest misinterpretation, such as the one in the story of Flight 301, can have sometimes dire or, at the very least, interesting consequences.

THEORIES OF LANGUAGE

How does the brain cope with spoken and written input to derive meaning? To answer this question we have to know how words are represented in the brain. This question turns out to be difficult to answer, but cognitive neuroscience has elucidated a number of key principles. We will begin by tackling the question of how the brain stores words by reviewing data from the perspective of theoretical–experimental models and neurophysiological data.

Storage of Words and Concepts: The Mental Lexicon

One of the central concepts in word representation is the **mental lexicon**—a mental store of information about words that includes *semantic* information (the words' meanings), *syntactic* information (how the words are combined to form sentences), and the details of *word forms* (their spellings and sound patterns). Most psycholinguistic theories agree on the central role for a mental lexicon in language. But some theories propose one mental lexicon for both language comprehension and production, whereas other models distinguish between input and output lexica. In addition, the representation of *orthographic* (vision-based) and *phonological* (sound-based) forms must be considered in any model. The principal concept, though, is that a store (or stores) of information about words exists in the brain, and we have some, albeit limited, ideas about how it must be organized conceptually.

A normal adult speaker has passive knowledge of about 50,000 words and yet can recognize and produce about three words per second without any difficulty. Given this speed and the size of the database, the mental lexicon must be organized in a highly efficient manner. It cannot be merely the equivalent of a dictionary. If, for example, the mental lexicon were organized in simple alphabetical order, it might take longer to find words in the middle of the alphabet, such as the ones starting with *K*, *L*, *O*, or *U*, than to find a word starting with an *A* or a *Z*. Fortunately, this is not the case.

The mental lexicon differs in other respects from a dictionary on the shelf. For one thing, it has no fixed content: Words can be forgotten and new words can be learned (when was the last time you picked up a dictionary, excluding new editions, to see that new words had miraculously appeared)? Another significant difference is that in the mental lexicon, more frequently used words are accessed more quickly; for instance, the word *table* is more readily available than the word *snail*. In addition, the process of accessing lexical (word) representations in the mental lexicon is influenced by the so-called neighborhood effect. Let's consider this phenomenon from the perspective of understanding spoken words.

The *auditory neighborhood* of a word is defined as the number of words that differ from the target word by only one phoneme. A *phoneme* is the smallest unit of sound that makes a difference to meaning. In English, the sounds for the letters *L* and *R* are two phonemes (the words *late* and *rate* mean different things), but in the Japanese language, no meaningful distinction is made between *L* and *R*, so they are represented by only one phoneme. Auditory neighbors for the word *hate* are *late*, *rate*, and *eight*. Words having more neighbors are identified more slowly. The idea is that there may be competition between activations of different words during recognition of speech, and this phenomenon tells us something about the organization of our mental lexicon.

The mental lexicon, then, is quite dissimilar from the average college dictionary. It is thought to be organized as information-specific networks. The example in Figure 10.1 is taken from a model proposed by Willem Levelt from the Max Planck Institute for Psycholinguistics in the Netherlands (this model will be discussed in more detail later in the chapter, in the section on speech production). As this fragment of a lexical network shows, information-specific networks exist for the word forms at the so-called *lexeme* level, and for the grammatical properties of words at the *lemma* level. At the lemma level the semantic specifications of words are represented as well. This semantic information defines the conceptual conditions under which it is appropriate to use a certain word—for example, whether the word represents an animate object (living thing) or an inanimate object (nonliving thing). These specifications are communicated by the "sense" connections between the lemma level and the conceptual level; the semantic knowledge of words is represented at the conceptual level. As Figure 10.1 also shows, the organization of the representations in the mental lexicon involves the relations between words; that is, words that are related in meaning are connected and tend to be close together in the network (e.g., *sheep* and *goat*).

Support for the idea that representations in the mental lexicon are organized according to meaningful relationships between words comes from semantic priming studies that utilize a lexical (word) decision task. In a semantic priming task, subjects are presented with pairs of words. The first member of the pair, the *prime*, is a word; the second member, the *target*, can be a real word or a nonword (like *sfhsi*) or a pseudoword (like *fisch*). If the target is a real word, it can be related or unrelated in meaning to the prime. For the lexical decision task in such a design, the subjects must decide as quickly and accurately as possible whether the target is a word, pressing a button indicating their decision. Subjects are faster and more accurate at making the lexical decisions when the target is preceded by a related prime (e.g., the prime *car* for the target *truck*) than an unrelated prime (e.g., *tulip* for *truck*). Related patterns are found when the subject is asked to pronounce the target (under conditions when it is always a word but is either related or unrelated to the prime). Here, naming latencies are faster for related words than for unrelated ones.

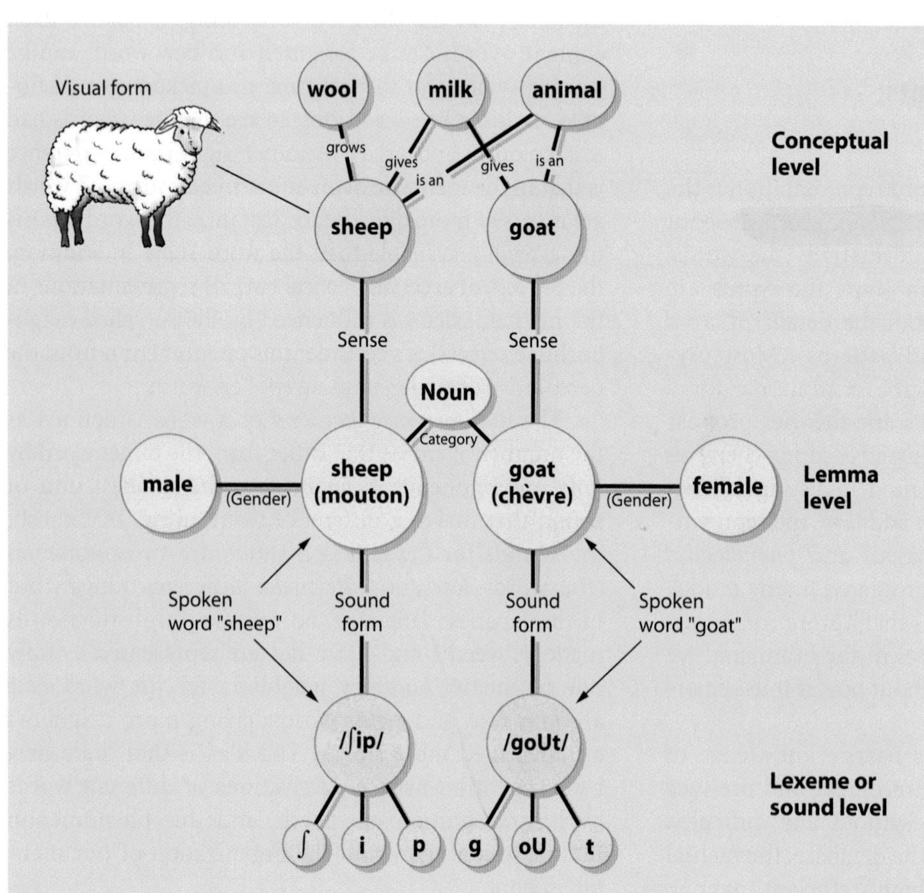

Figure 10.1 Fragment of a lexical network according to the Levelt model. See text for description. This model describes the processes for spoken-word input; a similar model applies to written-word input.

What does this pattern of facilitated response speed tell us about the organization of the mental lexicon?

Initially, these effects of priming were thought to result exclusively from an automatic spread of activation between the nodes in the word network. But over many years of research on priming with lexical (word) decision tasks, it has become clear that priming can result from more than these implicit or automatic types of processes. *Expectancy-induced priming* might occur if the time between the presentation of primes and targets is long (e.g., >500 ms) and the proportion of related word pairs in a list is large (e.g., when 50% or more of the pairs consist of related words, such as *car* and *truck*, *cat* and *dog*, etc.). Subjects may then expect some possible target words after hearing the prime. Thus, if they hear the word *cat*, for example, they may generate an expectancy set consisting of words that are related, such as *dog* and *mouse*. If the target word matches one of the words in the expectancy set (*dog* or *mouse*), then reaction times to this word will be faster or facilitated. In contrast, when the target word does not match the expectancy set, the response will be slower or inhibited.

In another process, *semantic matching*, subjects actively try to match the meaning of the target word with the meaning of the prime. In a lexical decision task, semantic matching leads to faster "yes" responses to words that match the preceding context word in meaning than to words that do not match. This process of semantic matching is postlexical; it happens after the representations in the mental lexicon have been accessed.

Let's now consider a bit more about the conceptual level as represented in Figure 10.1. The conceptual level goes beyond our linguistic knowledge of words. Semantic knowledge of words can be distinguished from pure linguistic knowledge. This distinction becomes clear when we consider words that have one form of representation but two or more unrelated meanings—for example, the word *bank*. In order to arrive at the meaning of the word *bank*, contextual information is needed to decide whether the intended meaning is the "side of a river" (which is sandy; trees can grow there) or a "money institution" (which is a building; people can work there).

As we saw in Chapter 8, Endel Tulving proposed in the early 1970s that a distinction be made between episodic memory (our memory for personal events) and semantic memory (our memory for facts and general knowledge). Semantic memory is important for language comprehension and production and is therefore clearly connected to our mental lexicon, as can be seen in Figure 10.1, but semantic memory and the mental lexicon are not necessarily the same thing. In general, we can say that conceptual, or semantic, representations reflect our knowledge of the real world. These representations can become activated through our own thoughts and intentions or through our perceptions of words and sentences, of pictures and photographs, and of events, objects, and states in the real world. Many investigations have studied the nature of conceptual or semantic representations, but the issues of how and where in the brain concepts are represented are still very much disputed.

First is the matter of how many conceptual or semantic systems there are. Some investigators have argued for a unitary semantic system that utilizes a verbal or proposition-based format, or a unitary perception-based format. Others favor the idea that different types of information can be stored on the basis of perceptual *and* verbal codes. The question of unitary or multiple conceptual systems is related but not identical to the question of whether our conceptual or semantic system is amodal or modality-specific and independent meaning systems exist. Is the same conceptual representation of a robin activated regardless of whether one hears the word *robin* or sees a robin flying?

This question highlights some of the ongoing uncertainty about how conceptual information is represented, and indeed, many organizational structures, such as feature lists, schemas, exemplars, and connectionist networks, have been proposed. In one very influential model, proposed by Collins and Loftus (1975), word meanings are represented in a semantic network in which words, represented by conceptual nodes, are connected with each other. Figure 10.2 shows an example of a semantic network. The strength of the connection and the distance between the nodes are determined by the semantic relations or associative relations between the words. For example, the node that represents the word *car* will be close to and have a strong connection with the node that represents the word *truck*.

A major component of this model is the assumption that activation spreads from one conceptual node to others, and nodes that are closer together will benefit more from this spreading activation than will distant nodes. If we hear "car," the node that represents the word *car* in the semantic network will be activated. In addition, words like *truck* and *bus* that are closely related to the meaning of *car*, and are therefore nearby and well connected in the semantic network, will receive a considerable amount of activation. In contrast, a word like *rose* most likely will receive no activation at all when we hear "car." This model predicts that hearing "car" should facilitate recognition of the word *truck* but not *rose*.

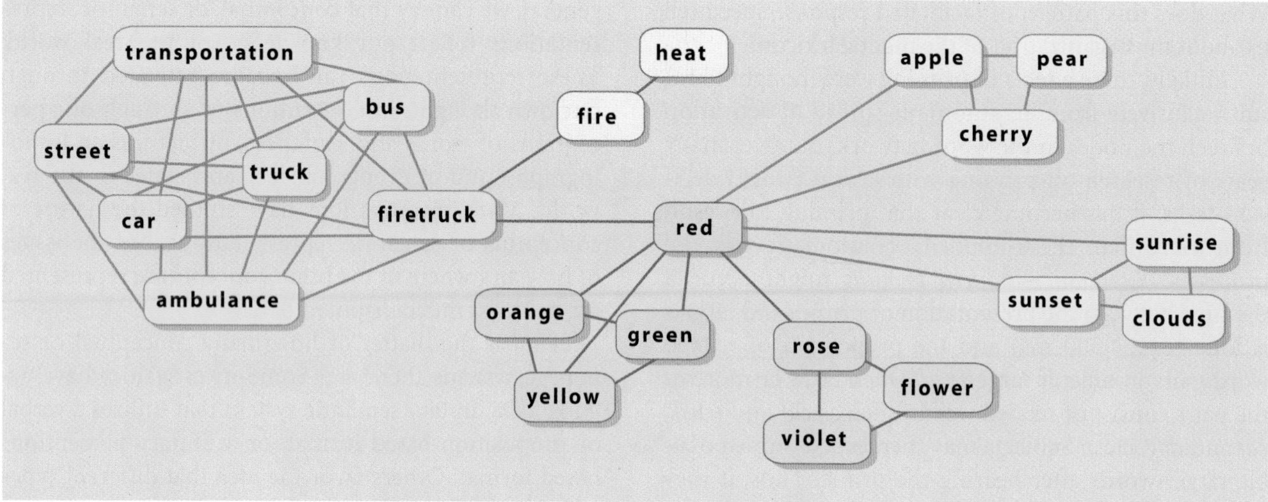

Figure 10.2 Semantic network. Words that have strong associative or semantic relations are closer together in the network (e.g., *car* and *truck*) than are words that have no such relation (e.g., *car* and *clouds*). Semantically related words are colored similarly in the figure, and associatively related word (e.g., *firetruck–fire*) are closely connected.

Although the semantic-network model that Collins and Loftus proposed has been extremely influential, the way that word meanings are organized is still a matter of dispute. There are many other models and ideas of how conceptual knowledge is represented. Some models propose that concepts are represented by their semantic features or semantic properties. For example, the word *dog* has several semantic features, such as "is animate," "has four legs," and "barks," and they are assumed to be represented in the conceptual network. Such models are confronted with the problem of activation: How many features have to be activated in order for a person to recognize a dog? For example, it is possible to train dogs not to bark, yet we can recognize a dog even when it does not bark, and we can identify a barking dog that we cannot see. Furthermore, it is not exactly clear how many features would have to be stored. For example, a table could be made of wood or glass, and in both cases we would recognize it as a table. Does this mean that we have to store the features "is of wood/glass" with the table concept? In addition, some words are more "prototypical" examples of a semantic category than others, as reflected in our recognition and production of these words. When we are asked to generate bird names, for example, the word *robin* comes to mind as one of the first examples, but a word like *ostrich* might not come up at all, depending on where we grew up or have lived.

In sum, it is a matter of debate how word meanings are represented. No matter how, though, everyone agrees that a mental store of word meanings is crucial to normal language comprehension and production. Evidence from brain-lesioned patients and from functional brain-imaging studies is revealing how the mental lexicon and conceptual knowledge may be organized.

NEURAL SUBSTRATES OF THE MENTAL LEXICON AND CONCEPTUAL KNOWLEDGE

Through observations of deficits in patients' language ability, we can infer a number of things about the functional organization of the mental lexicon. Different types of neurological problems create deficits in understanding and producing the appropriate meaning of a word or concept. Patients with **Wernicke's aphasia**, a language deficit usually due to brain lesions in the posterior parts of the left hemisphere (we will discuss aphasia in detail later), make errors in speech production that are known as **semantic paraphasias**. For example, they might use the word *horse* when they mean *cow*. Patients with *deep dyslexia* make similar errors in reading: They might read the word *horse* where *cow* is written (see "How the Brain Works: From Written Text to Word Representation" on p. 406).

Patients with *progressive semantic dementia* initially show impairments in the conceptual system, but other mental and language abilities are spared. For example, these patients can still understand and produce the syntactic structure of sentences. This impairment has been associated with progressive damage to the temporal lobes, mostly on the left side of the brain. But the superior regions of the temporal lobe that are important for hearing and speech processing are spared (these areas will be discussed later in this chapter, in the section on spoken input). Patients with semantic dementia have difficulty assigning objects to a semantic category. In addition, they often name a category when asked to name a picture; when viewing a picture of a horse, they will say "animal," and a picture of a robin will produce "bird." This neurological evidence provides support for the semantic-network idea because related meanings are substituted, confused, or lumped together, as we could predict from the degrading of a system interconnected by nodes that specify information.

In the 1970s and early 1980s, Elizabeth Warrington and her colleagues performed groundbreaking studies on the organization of conceptual knowledge in the brain. Some of these studies were done on patients who would now be classified as suffering from semantic dementia, as just described. These researchers found that semantic problems can be localized specifically to certain semantic categories, such as animals versus objects. They reported studies of patients who had great difficulties *pointing* to pictures of food or living things when presented with a word, but who performed much better with man-made objects like tools. These difficulties were also found when the patients were asked to *name* foods or living things when presented with a picture, though their naming of man-made things was spared. The reverse pattern was found in another group of patients: Their ability to identify foods and living things was preserved, but their ability to identify man-made objects was impaired.

Since these original observations by Warrington, many cases of patients with category-specific deficits have been reported, and there appears to be a striking correspondence between the sites of lesions and the type of semantic deficit. The patients whose impairment involved living things had lesions that included the inferior and medial temporal cortex, and often these lesions were located anteriorly. The anterior inferotemporal cortex is located close to areas of the brain that are crucial for visual object perception, and the medial temporal lobe contains important relay projections from association cortex to the hippocampus, a structure that, as you might remember from Chapter 8, has an important function in the encoding of information in long-term stores. Furthermore, the inferotemporal lobe is the end station for "what" information, or the object recognition stream, in vision (see Chapter 6).

Less is known about the localization of lesions in patients who show greater impairment for man-made things, simply because fewer patients have been observed. But left frontal and parietal areas appear to be involved in this kind of semantic deficit. These areas are close to or overlap with areas of the brain that are important for sensorimotor functions, and therefore they are likely to be involved in the representation of actions that can be undertaken when man-made artifacts such as tools are being used.

The observed correlations between type of semantic deficit and area of lesion are consistent with a hypothesis by Warrington and her colleagues about the organization of semantic information. They suggested that the patients' problems are reflections of the types of information stored with different words in the semantic network. Whereas the biological categories (fruits, foods, animals) rely more on physical properties or visual features (e.g., what is the color of an apple?), man-made objects are identified by their functional properties (e.g., how do we use a hammer?).

This idea has been both tested and challenged. An example of evidence in favor of the idea of a modality-specific organization of the semantic network comes from a computational model by Martha Farah and James McClelland (1991). Computational models can provide important tests of the plausibility of particular hypotheses. In this specific case, Farah and McClelland modeled semantic memory as consisting of separate visual and functional subsystems, and further, they included the idea that living things must include representations based on visual attributes, whereas nonliving things include information about functional attributes. They found, as predicted by the hypothesis of Warrington, that if they "lesioned" visual properties in their model (by removing nodes in their network in the computer simulation) the model was especially "impaired" in dealing with living things, whereas "lesioning" of functional properties led to "impairments" with nonliving things.

The challenge for Warrington's proposal comes from observations by Alfonso Caramazza and others (e.g., Caramazza & Shelton, 1998) that the studies in patients did not always use well-controlled linguistic materials. For example, when comparing living things versus man-made things, some studies did not control the stimulus materials to ensure that the objects tested in either category were matched on visual complexity, visual similarity across objects, the frequency of use, and the familiarity of objects. If these variables vary widely between the categories, then clear-cut conclusions about differences in their representation in a semantic network cannot be drawn. Caramazza has proposed an alternative theory in which the semantic network is organized along lines of the conceptual categories of animacy and inanimacy. He argues that the selective damage that has been observed in brain-damaged patients, as in the studies of Warrington and others, genuinely reflects "evolutionarily adapted domain-specific knowledge systems that are subserved by distinct neural mechanisms" (Caramazza & Shelton, 1998, p. 1).

Recent studies using imaging techniques in neurologically unimpaired human participants have looked further into the problem of the organization of semantic representations. Alex Martin and his colleagues (1996) at the National Institute of Mental Health (NIMH) conducted studies using positron emission tomography (PET) and functional magnetic resonance imaging (fMRI). Their findings reveal how the intriguing dissociations in neurological patients that we just described can be identified in neurologically normal brains. When subjects read the names of or answered questions about animals, or when they named pictures of animals, the more lateral aspects of the fusiform gyrus (on the brain's ventral surface) and the superior temporal sulcus were found to be active. But naming of animals also activated a brain area associated with the early stages of visual processing—namely, the left medial occipital lobe. In contrast, identifying and naming tools were associated with activation in the more medial aspect of the fusiform gyrus, the left middle temporal gyrus, and the left premotor area, a region that is also activated by imagining hand movements. These findings are consistent with the idea that conceptual representations in our brains of living things versus man-made tools rely on separable neuronal circuits engaged in processing of perceptual versus functional information.

One of the most compelling pieces of evidence for category-specific deficits comes from Hanna Damasio and her colleagues (1996) at the University of Iowa, who investigated a large population of patients with brain lesions. These patients had to perform a naming task in three different conditions: (a) naming famous faces, (b) naming animals, and (c) naming tools. To dissociate conceptual problems (damage to the conceptual representations of objects themselves) from problems at the level of word retrieval (accessing the name of an object), the following procedure was used: If a subject was able to describe many of the features of the picture but was unable to name it, a naming error was recorded. For example, when the subject was asked to name the picture of a skunk, the following answer showed that the subject recognized it but could not name it: "Oh, that animal makes a terrible smell if you get too close to it; it is black and white, and gets squashed on the road by cars sometimes." But if the subject was not specific in describing the picture, the answer was not included in the naming score (e.g., "Some kind of animal; I don't know what . . . just an animal"). The naming response was scored correct when it was the same as that of healthy subjects.

Thirty patients, 29 of whom each had a lesion in the left hemisphere, showed impairments on this task. The naming deficit was very selective in 19 patients: Of these, 7 demonstrated impairment in naming faces; 5 patients, in naming animals; and 7, in naming tools. The remaining 11 patients had a combination of problems in word retrieval for faces, animals, and tools; or faces and animals; or animals and tools—but never for the combination of faces and tools together without also a deficit in animals. When the researchers examined where the patients had their brain lesions, they were able to correlate naming deficits with specific regions (Figure 10.3).

Damasio discovered that brain damage in the left temporal pole (TP) correlated with problems in retrieving the names of persons, whereas lesions in the anterior part of the left inferotemporal (IT) lobe correlated with problems in naming animals; and finally, damage to the posterolateral part of the left inferotemporal lobe, along with the lateral temporo-occipitoparietal junction (IT+), was correlated with problems in retrieving the names of tools. In a coordinated PET scan study of neurologically normal subjects, these same brain areas were activated when subjects engaged in naming persons (TP), animals (IT), and tools (IT+), as illustrated in Figure 10.4.

Damasio and her colleagues concluded that, since they had made sure that patients with problems retrieving the names of words could still activate many of the conceptual properties relevant to the word (e.g., saying, in response to a picture of a skunk, "Oh, that animal makes a terrible smell if you get too close to it; it is black and white, and gets squashed on the road by cars sometimes"), the correlated brain areas that were lesioned in these patients must play a role in word retrieval. They therefore did not assume that their findings reflect the organization of a conceptual network in the brain, but rather proposed that their findings reflect the organization at the word (lexical) level. They argued that their results indicate that the brain has three levels of representation for word knowledge, as illustrated in Figure 10.5. These representational levels were predicted by cognitive models of word production.

The top level in Figure 10.5 represents the conceptual level, a preverbal level that contains the semantic features about words (e.g., four legs, furry, tail). At the lexical level the word form that matches the concept is represented (*cat*). Finally, at the phonological level the sound information that corresponds to the word is represented. (Note that this model of word representation is different from what we have discussed thus far be-

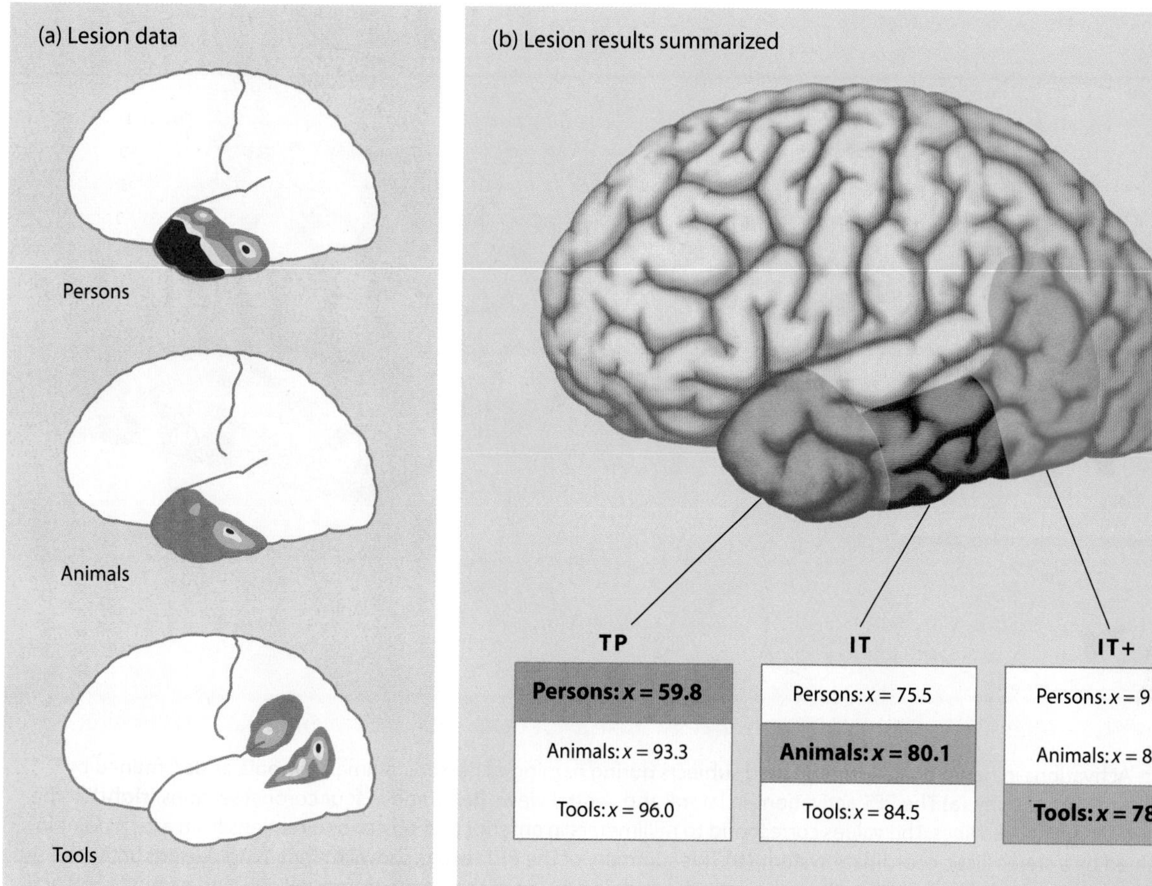

Figure 10.3 Locations of brain lesions that are correlated with selective deficits in naming persons, animals, or tools. **(a)** Actual averaged lesion data are displayed for patients that had person-naming **(top)**, animal-naming **(middle)**, or tool-naming **(bottom)** deficits. The colors indicate the percentage of patients with a given deficit whose lesion is located in the indicated area. Red indicates that most patients had a lesion in that area; purple indicates that few had a lesion in that area. **(b)** In this summary of the lesion results, the blue area corresponds to the temporal pole (TP); the red area, to the inferotemporal region (IT); and the green area, to the posterior part of the inferotemporal lobe extending to the anterior part of the lateral occipital region (IT+). Scores in the boxes indicate the percentage of recognized items that were correctly named. Patients with TP lesions scored lowest on naming persons (59.8%), patients with IT lesions scored lowest on naming animals (80.1%), and patients with IT+ lesions scored lowest on naming tools (78.5%).

cause there is no representation of the lemma level; see Figure 10.1.) Damasio and her colleagues proposed that the brain's conceptual networks involve several neuronal structures in the left and the right hemispheres. These conceptual networks are connected to the lexical networks in the left temporal lobe and might contain specialized information for persons, animals, or tools. These areas in turn activate the phonological network that touches off the sound patterns needed to pronounce the word.

Perceptual Analyses of the Linguistic Input

All models of normal language comprehension have to begin with the problem of how words are represented. The next step is to identify what enables understanding of the linguistic input; Figure 10.6 depicts the processes and representations that are important to normal language comprehension.

As we will see, understanding spoken language and understanding written language share some processes, but there are also some striking differences in how spoken and written inputs are analyzed. When attempting to understand spoken words (see Figure 10.6), the listener has to decode the acoustic input. The result of this acoustic analysis is translated into a phonological code because that is how the lexical representations of auditory word forms are stored in the mental lexicon. Both of these processing steps are prelexical and do not involve the mental lexicon. After the acoustic input has

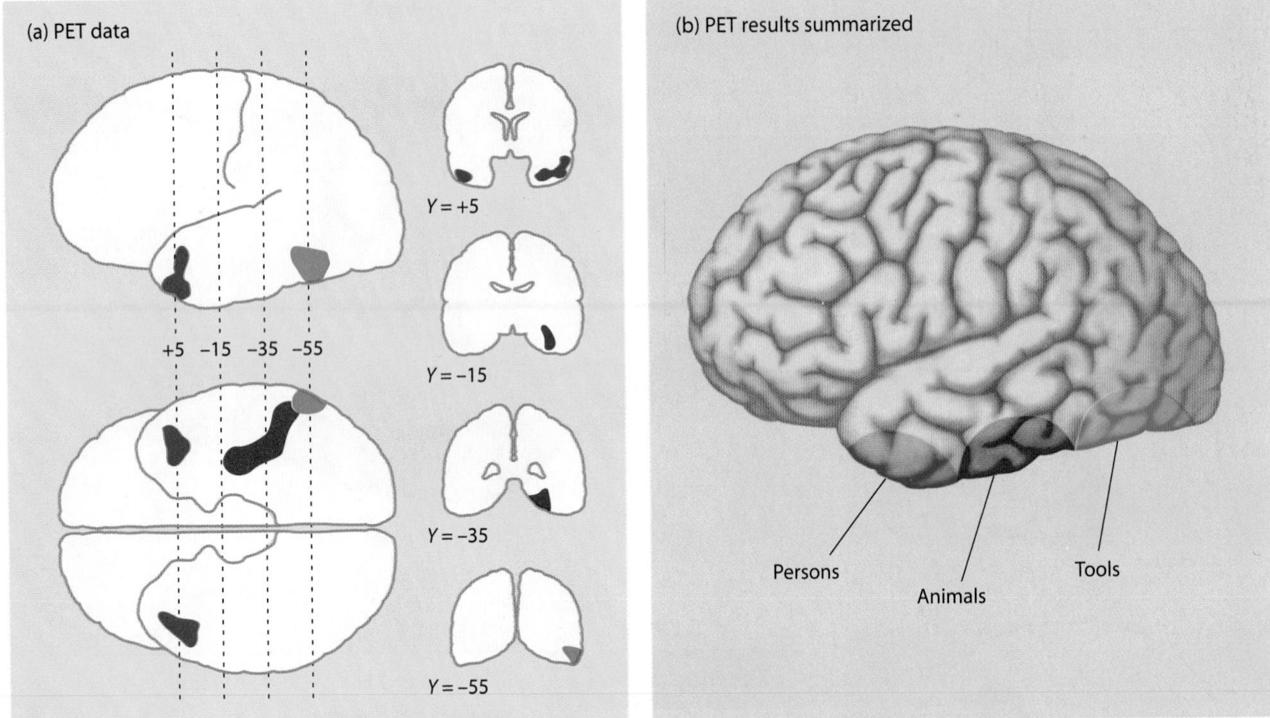

Figure 10.4 Activations in neurologically unimpaired subjects during naming of persons, animals, or tools, as determined by positron emission tomography. **(a)** The PET activations in lateral and ventral views **(left)**, and in four coronal sections **(right)** at the levels indicated by the dashed lines. The values correspond to millimeters in anterior and posterior directions from a zero point in the brain defined by a stereotactic coordinate system. **(b)** This summary of the PET results shows that naming persons activated mostly the temporal pole, naming animals activated mostly the middle portion of the inferior temporal gyri, and naming tools activated mostly the posterior portions of the inferior temporal gyrus.

Figure 10.5 Three levels of representation that are needed in speech production: semantic features, lexical nodes, and phonological segments. **(a)** The semantic features of the word *cat* (four legs, furry) activate the lexical node of the word *cat*, which in turn activates the phonological segments of that word. **(b)** A model that fits the data of Damasio and colleagues shown in Figures 10.3 and 10.4. The information at the lexical level is organized according to specific semantic categories (e.g., animals versus tools).

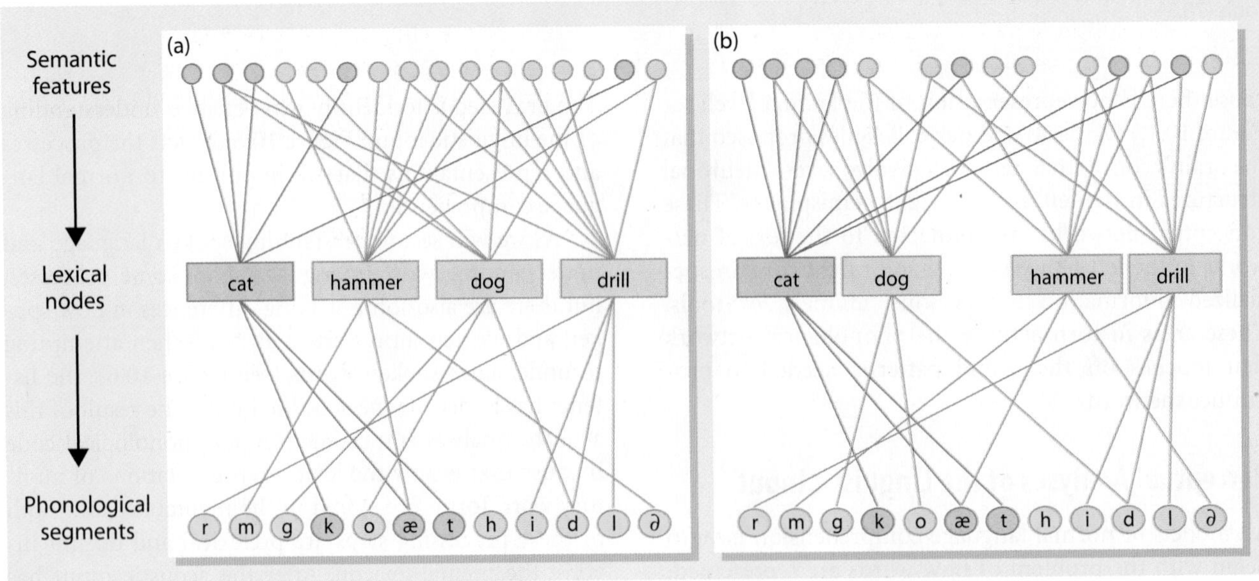

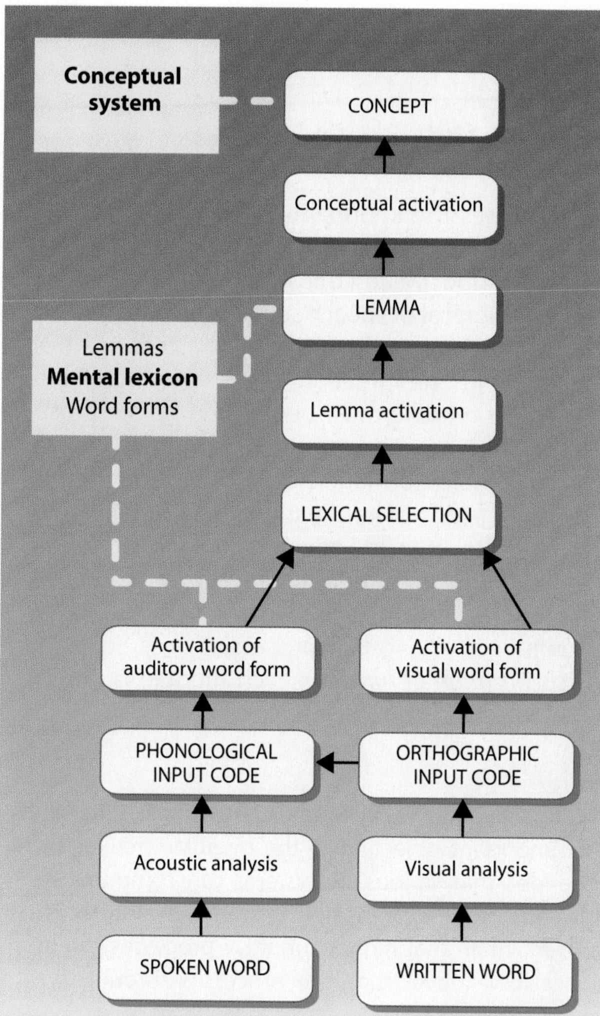

Figure 10.6 Schematic representation of the components involved in spoken and written language comprehension. Inputs can enter via either auditory (spoken word) or visual (written word) modalities. Notice that the information flows from the bottom up, from perceptual identification to "higher level" word and lemma activation. Interactive models of language understanding would predict top-down influence to play a role as well. For example, activation at the word form level in this case would be able to influence earlier perceptual processes. We could introduce this type of feedback into this schematic representation by making the arrows bidirectional.

been translated into a phonological format, the lexical representation in the mental lexicon that best matches the auditory input can be selected; this process is known as **lexical selection**. The selected word form, in turn, activates the lemma (store of grammatical information) and then the word's meaning (store of the lexical-semantic information).

The process of reading words shares with auditory comprehension at least the last two steps of linguistic analysis (i.e., lemma and meaning activation), but it differs at the earlier processing steps, owing to the different modality of the input. Given that the perceptual input is different (see Figure 10.6), what are these earlier stages in reading? The first analysis step requires that the reader identify orthographic units from the visual input. These orthographic units may then be directly mapped onto orthographic word forms in the mental lexicon, or alternatively, the identified orthographic units might be translated into phonological units, which in turn activate the phonological word form in the mental lexicon as described for auditory comprehension.

Notice that in Figure 10.6 information flows strictly from the bottom up. But according to some interactive models (see "How the Brain Works: Modularity Versus Interactivity"), feedback of information from higher to lower representational levels is possible. We could easily adapt Figure 10.6 to this type of architecture by making the arrows bidirectional. Another important point is that some models of language comprehension, in contrast to what we have discussed thus far, do not assume that words are represented permanently in the brain (in which case there would be no word form or lemma representations), but rather that they emerge as a pattern of activation in a distributed network. Which type of model fits better will have to be determined in future experiments by clever scientists (possibly you!).

In the next few sections we will delve into the processes involved in the understanding of spoken and written inputs of words. Then we will consider the understanding of sentences. First, though, let's take a closer look at the perceptual analyses of the linguistic input. The first task that faces a listener or reader is to identify individual words in a spoken utterance or in a written text. The input must be perceptually analyzed, which is a prelexical process that does not involve the mental lexicon. Naturally, the perceptual analyses required for spoken and written input are quite different.

SPOKEN INPUT

The input signal in spoken language is very different from that in written language. Whereas for a reader it is immediately clear that the letters on a page are the physical signals of importance, a listener is confronted with a variety of sounds in the environment and has to identify and distinguish the relevant speech signals from other "noise." Let's begin with some of the basic units that constitute the speech signal.

As introduced earlier, important building blocks of spoken language are *phonemes*. These are the smallest

HOW THE BRAIN WORKS

Modularity Versus Interactivity

Two major questions that have puzzled cognitive psychologists and cognitive neuroscientists are, (a) Do the different component processes involved in remembering, or paying attention, or understanding and producing language, interact? and (b) If so, at what level of processing? In reading a text, for example, we need to analyze the features that make up the letters, and the letters have to be grouped such that they form a word that we can understand. As we have seen in the text, scientists differ in their view of how these processes take place. Some (like Selfridge; see Figure 10.11) argue that the analysis process works purely from the bottom up, from sensory input to higher level representations of words. Others (like McClelland and Rumelhart; see Figure 10.12) think that higher level processes can influence lower level perceptual analyses.

These different views can be recognized in the literature as modular or interactive. The best-known proposal for modularity of cognitive processes comes from Jerry Fodor in his book *The Modularity of Mind* (1983). His proposal consists of two central ideas: (a) Language is an input system rather than part of a central system, where a central system can influence different knowledge domains; and (b) input systems have a modular architecture.

Fodor argued that input systems with a modular architecture should have the following characteristics:

- *Domain specificity.* The input system receives information from several sensory systems, but processes the information with codes that are specific to the system. For example, the language input system translates visual input into a phonological or speech sound representation.
- *Information encapsulation.* The processing goes strictly in one direction. The processing of the earliest module must be finished before it can send its information to the next module, and so on. Partial information cannot be transmitted. This direction of information flow is strictly from the bottom up. In Fodor's model higher cognitive modules cannot influence lower cognitive modules. In other words, there is no top-down influence in language processing.
- *Localization of function.* Each module is implemented in a particular brain region.

Interactive views challenge all these premises. But the most important objection to the modular architecture is the idea that various subsystems can communicate with each other only in a bottom-up way. Interactive views maintain that higher cognitive processes can influence lower level cognitive processes through systems of feedback.

In many aspects of language comprehension and production, the question of modularity versus interactivity is relevant, and debates on this issue pertain to all of the component processes discussed in this chapter.

units of sound that make a difference to meaning; for example, in the words *cap* and *tap* the only difference is the first phoneme (/c/ versus /t/). To describe the phonemes of our language, we make use of the phonetic alphabet, which is not the same as our orthographic, or letter, alphabet. For example, [i] is the phonetic symbol for the phoneme /ee/ as in *meet*, but [I] is the phonetic symbol for the phoneme /i/ as in *it*. The English language uses 40 phonemes; other languages may use more or less.

To get a feel for what a listener has to deal with when listening to spoken input, it is useful to know how different speech sounds are produced. We can produce different speech sounds by making use of different features of the vocal apparatus. Three main factors determine the actual speech sound that we produce. The first one is *voicing*, or whether we use our vocal cords to produce a speech sound. All vowels are voiced (*A, E, I, O, U, Y*), but not all consonants are. Examples of voiced consonants are *B* and *M*; of unvoiced consonants, *S* and *T*. For consonants there are two other ways to modify the speech sound. One has to do with the part of the speech apparatus used to produce the sound (*point of articulation*)—for example, whether we use both lips ([b]), or the lips and the mouth ([f]). The other has to do with the manner in which the airstream is changed (*manner of articulation*); for example, we make a [p] sound by blocking the airstream, whereas [l] hardly obstructs airflow at all. For vowels there is another way to modify speech sounds: via placement of the tongue in the mouth. The tongue can be placed high or low, and front or back.

Having recognized that phonemes are important building blocks of spoken language by no means simplifies the task of the listener. The listener's brain must resolve a number of additional difficulties with the speech signal; some of these have to do with the variability of the signal. For example, speech sounds vary on the basis of the context in which they are spoken (lack of invariance). So even though they start with the same phoneme, the speech signal of the syllable "bo" is very different from the speech signal of the syllable "bi," whereas "bi" greatly resembles "di," even though they start with a different phoneme. So pronunciation of a phoneme is modified dramatically as a function of whether it is followed by an *O* or an *I*. Yet a listener will still be able to perceive a *B* and distinguish it from a *D*. Another problem a listener faces is that variability in the production of the *same* speech sound is introduced when it is pronounced by different speakers—for example, by a male or a female.

Additional problems for the listener emerge because the phonemes often do not appear as separate little chunks of information; in other words, they lack segmentation. Whereas physical boundaries divide words and sentences in written language, these boundaries are mostly absent in speech. As you read this text, you see each word separated by a blank space and each sentence terminated by a period. These physical cues help you discriminate between words and sentences. By contrast, the word boundaries of speech are murky, as illustrated in Figure 10.7, where the speech waveform of the word *captain* looks as though the signal represents two words because of a "silence" within the word.

In addition to silences within words, spoken sentences also typically lack a clear silence between words because they become *coarticulated*. Their ends and beginnings are united, as in "I dunno" instead of "I don't know." As Figure 10.8 shows, no clear boundaries fall between the words *do you mean* when they are uttered at normal conversational speed (i.e., as *connected speech*). This problem of unclear boundaries within and between words in spoken language has been labeled the *segmentation problem*.

We have now established that the listener is confronted with enormous variability in input. In spoken language there cannot be a one-to-one relation between a physical signal and representations in memory, so the perceptual analysis of auditory input must account for this fact. How the brain is able to extract meaning from

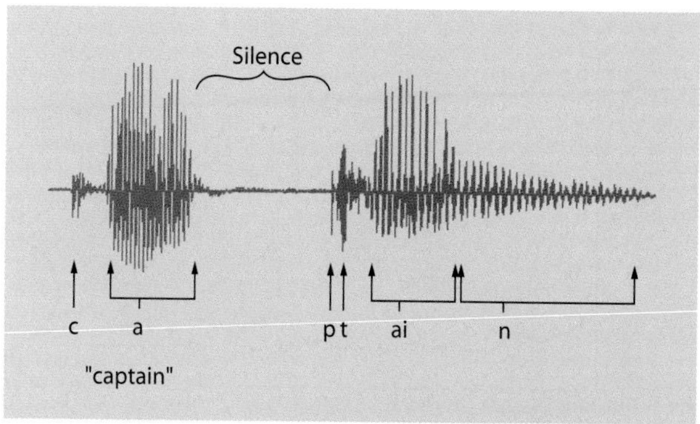

Figure 10.7 Speech waveform for the word "captain." Note the silence within the word. Time progresses from left to right, and amplitude is registered in the vertical dimension.

speech in the face of this variability in the physical signals has puzzled researchers and has led to the question of what the abstract units of representation might be for spoken inputs.

Some researchers have proposed that these representations are built on spectral properties (frequency content) of the incoming signal. These spectral properties vary according to different sounds, as Figure 10.9 shows. The features derived from spectral analysis might form a phonetic representation, which might be the access code to phonological representations. But other units of representation have been proposed, such as the phoneme itself, syllables, and the way the speaker has intended to pronounce the phoneme. Other theorists have altogether rejected the idea that there are discrete units of representation for the speech signal.

Figure 10.8 Speech waveform for the question, "What do you mean?" Note that the words "do you mean" are not physically separated. Even though the physical signal provides few cues to where the spoken words begin and end, the language system is able to parse them into the individual words for comprehension.

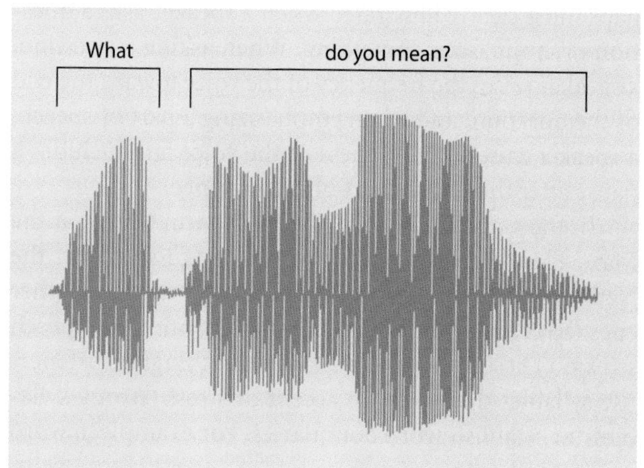

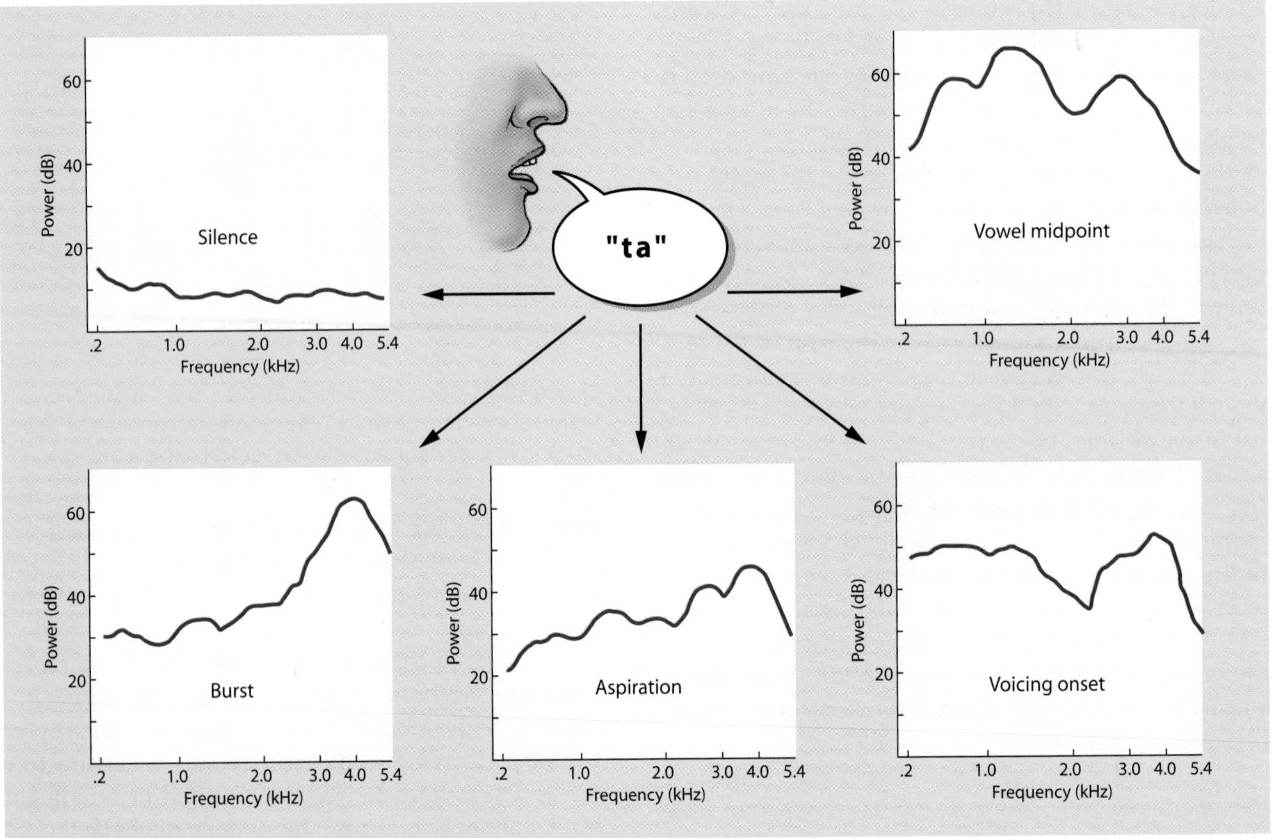

Figure 10.9 Spectral properties vary according to sounds. The sound "ta" can be analyzed to yield five different critical-band spectra. Each critical band has a particular frequency content (horizontal axis). For example, the "burst" portions of the sound have a lot of power in the higher frequencies (4- to 5-kHz range).

So how do we break up the spoken input? Fortunately, some other clues—namely, *prosodic* information, which is what the listener derives from the speech rhythm and the pitch of the speaker's voice—help us divide the speech stream into meaningful segments. The speech rhythm comes from variation in the duration of words and the placement of pauses between them. Prosody is apparent in all spoken utterances, but it is perhaps most clearly illustrated when a speaker asks a question or emphasizes something. When asking a question, a speaker raises the frequency of the voice toward the end of the question; and when emphasizing a part of speech, a speaker raises the loudness of the voice and includes a pause after the critical part of the sentence.

In their psycholinguistic research, Ann Cutler, at the Max Planck Institute for Psycholinguistics in the Netherlands, and her colleagues have revealed other cues that can be used to segment the continuous speech stream. These researchers showed that English listeners use syllables that carry an accent or stress (strong syllables) to establish word boundaries. For example, a word like *lettuce*, with stress on the first syllable, is usually heard as a single word and not as two words ("let us"). In contrast, words such as *invests*, with stress on the last syllable, are usually heard as two words ("in vests") and not as one word (although we know it is one word).

Interestingly, in other languages, such as Dutch and French, syllables themselves seem more important than stress in helping the listener to segment the continuous speech stream. When listeners in these languages are asked to detect a string of letters in a word, they are faster when the string exactly corresponds to a syllable in a heard word, and they have more difficulty when the string is longer or shorter than a syllable. For example, Dutch listeners would be very fast to detect the first syllable "bak" in the word *bakker* (which means "baker") but slow at this task with the word *baken* (beacon"), where "ba" and not "bak" is the first syllable.

Neural Substrates of Spoken-Word Processing Now that we have identified the initial steps in understanding speech from the perspective of psycholinguistic theory and research, we turn to the question of where in the brain these processes may take place and what neural circuits and systems support them. From animal studies, studies in patients with brain lesions, and PET and fMRI studies in humans, we know that the superior temporal cortex is important to sound perception. At the beginning of the 20th century, it was already well understood that patients with bilateral lesions restricted to the superior parts of the temporal lobe had the syndrome of "pure word deafness." Although they could process other sounds relatively normally, these patients had specific difficulties recognizing speech sounds. Because there was no difficulty in other aspects of language processing, the problem seemed to be restricted primarily to auditory or phonemic deficits—hence the term *pure word deafness.* With evidence from more recent studies in hand, however, we can begin to determine where in the brain speech and nonspeech sounds are first distinguished.

When the speech signal hits the ear, it is first processed by pathways in the brain that are not specialized for speech but that are used for hearing in general. Heschl's gyri, which are located on the supratemporal plane, superior and medial to the superior temporal gyrus (STG) in each hemisphere, contain the primary auditory cortex, or the area of cortex that processes the auditory input first (see Chapter 3). The areas that surround Heschl's gyri and extend into the STG are auditory association cortex. PET and fMRI studies in humans have shown that Heschl's gyri and the STG of both hemispheres are activated by speech and nonspeech sounds (e.g., tones) alike, but that this activation is not particularly selective for one of the two. This pattern of activity in response to sounds suggests that the STG is important for sound perception but not necessarily specialized for linguistic processes.

As we will see later in this chapter (in the discussion of aphasia), this finding is a big surprise. More than a century ago, the famous neurologist Carl Wernicke found that patients with lesions in the left temporoparietal region that included the STG had difficulty understanding spoken and written language. This observation led to the now-century-old notion that this area—which was christened *Wernicke's area*—is crucial to word comprehension. But even in Wernicke's original observations, the lesions were not restricted to the STG. And we can now conclude that the STG alone is probably not the seat of word comprehension.

If not in the STG, where else in the brain do we distinguish speech from other sounds? Some strong indications suggest that the midsection of the superior temporal sulcus, of both hemispheres (but mostly of the left hemisphere), plays an important role in this process. These regions are ventral to the STG, which is important for acoustic analyses, as we just described. In one fMRI study, Jeffrey Binder and colleagues (2000) at the Medical College of Wisconsin compared different types of nonspeech sounds. The nonspeech sounds consisted of noise that contained no systematic frequency or amplitude modulations, or tones that were frequency modulated between 50 and 2400 Hz; the speech sounds consisted of reversed speech sounds (real words that were played backward), pseudowords (pronounceable strings that are not real words but that contain the same letters as the real word—for example, *sked* from *desk*), and real words.

Figure 10.10 shows the results of the Binder study. Relative to noise, the frequency-modulated tones activated posterior portions of the STG bilaterally. Areas that were more sensitive to the speech sounds than to tones were more ventrolateral, in or near the superior temporal sulcus. In the same study, Binder and colleagues also showed that these areas are most likely not involved in lexical-semantic aspects of word processing (i.e., the processing of word forms and word meaning), because they were equally activated for words, pseudowords, and reversed speech. Recall that the results of the studies we discussed earlier (in the section titled "Neural Substrates of the Mental Lexicon and Conceptual Knowledge") showed that the areas implicated in the processing of lexical-semantic information are lateralized much more to the left and are mostly ventral to the superior temporal areas associated with speech perception per se.

Researchers also have tried to identify areas in the brain that are particularly important for the processing of phonemes. This investigation has proved difficult because it is very hard to find ways to activate only phonemes, since hearing a word also automatically activates its meaning. So the definitive answer is not in yet, but some PET and fMRI studies have looked at reading of words or at listening to spoken words and pseudowords and have found middle temporal gyrus activations, sometimes lateralized to the left hemisphere—evidence, perhaps, that reading can and often does activate phonological information (see "How the Brain Works: From Written Text to Word Representation" on p. 406).

WRITTEN INPUT

For written input, readers must recognize a visual pattern. These visual patterns vary across different writing

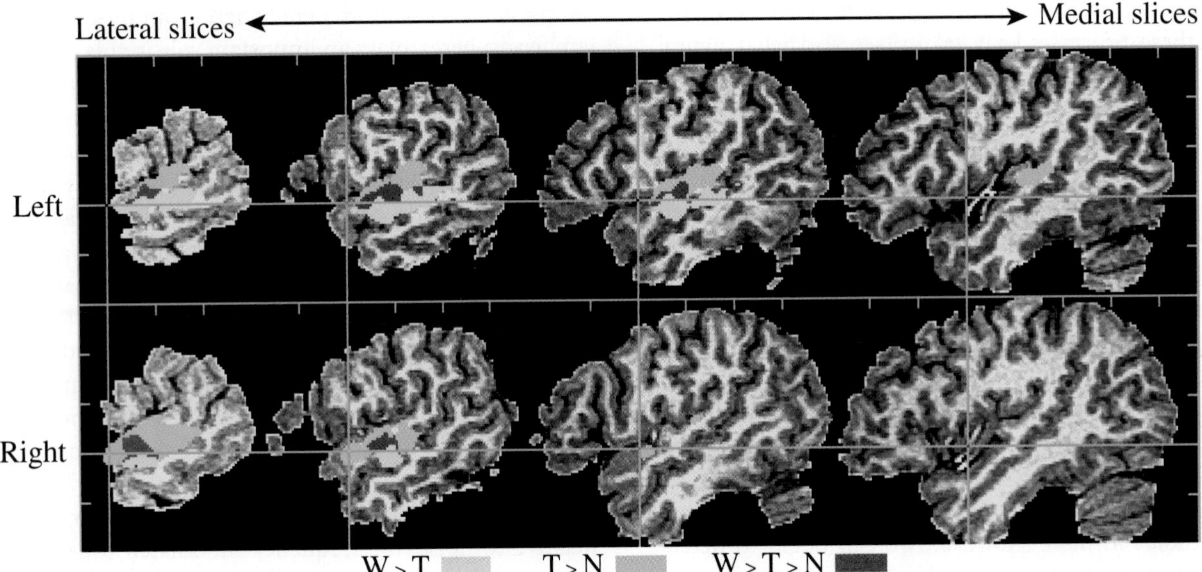

Figure 10.10 Superior temporal cortex activations to speech and nonspeech sounds. Four sagittal slices are shown for each hemisphere. The posterior areas of the superior temporal gyrus are more active bilaterally for frequency-modulated tones (T) than for simple noise (N) (in blue), whereas areas that are more sensitive to speech sounds (W) are located ventrolateral to this area (in yellow), in or near the superior temporal sulcus. This latter activation is somewhat lateralized to the left hemisphere (top row). Areas that are more active for words (W) and tones (T) than for noise (N) are also indicated (in red).

systems. There are three different ways in which words can be symbolized in writing: alphabetic, syllabic, and logographic. Many Western languages (e.g., English) use the *alphabetic system*, in which the symbols approximate the phonemes. However, languages that use the alphabetic system differ in how close the correspondence between letters and sounds is. Some languages, such as Finnish and Spanish, have a close correspondence (shallow orthography). In contrast, English often lacks a correspondence between letter and sound, which means that English has a relatively *deep orthography*.

Compare, for example, the differences in the pronunciation of the following three words, even though they start with the same four letters: *sign*, *signal*, and *signing*. The lack of correspondence between letter and sound makes it harder to learn to spell (and it might also have consequences for reading; see "How the Brain Works: From Written Text to Word Representation"). Luckily, at the next level of organization is the *morpheme*, the smallest unit of language that has meaning—that is, a word and the existing variations on a word (e.g., with prefixes or suffixes added, as in *signing* from *sign*). There tends to be slightly more correspondence in the spelling of morphologically related words.

Other languages, such as Chinese and Japanese, have different writing systems. The Japanese writing system kana uses the *syllabic system*, in which each symbol reflects a syllable. A syllabic system is possible in this case because Japanese has only about 100 unique syllables, whereas English has close to 1,000.

In the third writing system, the *logographic system*, a unique symbol is used for each word or each morpheme. An example of a living language that uses something close to a logographic system is Chinese, in which characters can symbolize whole morphemes. However, the characters also represent phonemes, so Chinese is not a pure logographic system. The reason for this representation system in writing is that Chinese is a tonal language. The same words can mean different things, depending on the rise and fall in the pitch or tone of the vowels. Such tonal variation would be difficult to represent in a system that symbolized only speech sounds or phonemes.

The three writing systems symbolize different aspects of speech (phonemes, syllables, and morphemes or words), but they all use arbitrary symbols. In other words, the symbols used are abstract representations that do not resemble what they represent. So the written word *dog* in English does not resemble in any way the real-life Fluffy who wags his tail and barks when he sees the mailman.

Regardless of the writing system used, readers must be able to analyze the primitive features, or the shapes of the symbols. In the alphabetic system, our focus here, this process would amount to the visual analysis of horizontal lines, vertical lines, closed curves, open curves, intersections, and other elementary shapes.

A model for letter recognition, the *pandemonium model* proposed by O. G. Selfridge in 1959, is displayed in Figure 10.11. In this model the sensory input ("R") is temporarily stored as an iconic memory by the so-called *image demon.* (Selfridge used the term *demon* to refer to a discrete stage or substage of information processing.) Then 28 *feature demons* sensitive to features like curves, horizontal lines, and so forth start to decode features in the iconic representation of the sensory input. Figure 10.11 indicates where all the feature demons are located. In the next step, all representations of letters with these features are activated by *cognitive demons.* Finally, the representation that best matches the input is selected by the *decision demon.*

In 1981, James McClelland and David Rumelhart proposed another model that has been very important for visual letter recognition. This model is a computational model that assumes three levels of representation: (a) a layer for the features of the letters of words, (b) a layer for letters, and (c) a layer for the representation of words. A very important characteristic of this model is that it allows for top-down information (i.e., information from the higher cognitive levels, such as the word layer) to influence earlier processes that happen at lower levels of representation (the letter layer and/or the feature layer). This model contrasts sharply with the model of Selfridge, where the flow of information is strictly bottom-up (from the image demon, to the feature demons, to the cognitive demons, and finally to the decision demon). This difference between these models provides an example of a crucial theoretical distinction between modularity and interactivity, of which we will see more examples later in this chapter (see "How the Brain Works: Modularity Versus Interactivity," on p. 398).

Another important difference between the two models is that, in the McClelland and Rumelhart

Figure 10.11 Selfridge's (1959) pandemonium model of letter recognition. For written input, the reader must recognize a pattern that starts with the analysis of the sensory input. The sensory input is stored temporarily in iconic memory by the image demon, and a set of 28 feature demons decodes the iconic representations. The cognitive demons are activated by the representations of letters with these features, and the representation that best matches the input is then selected by the decision demon.

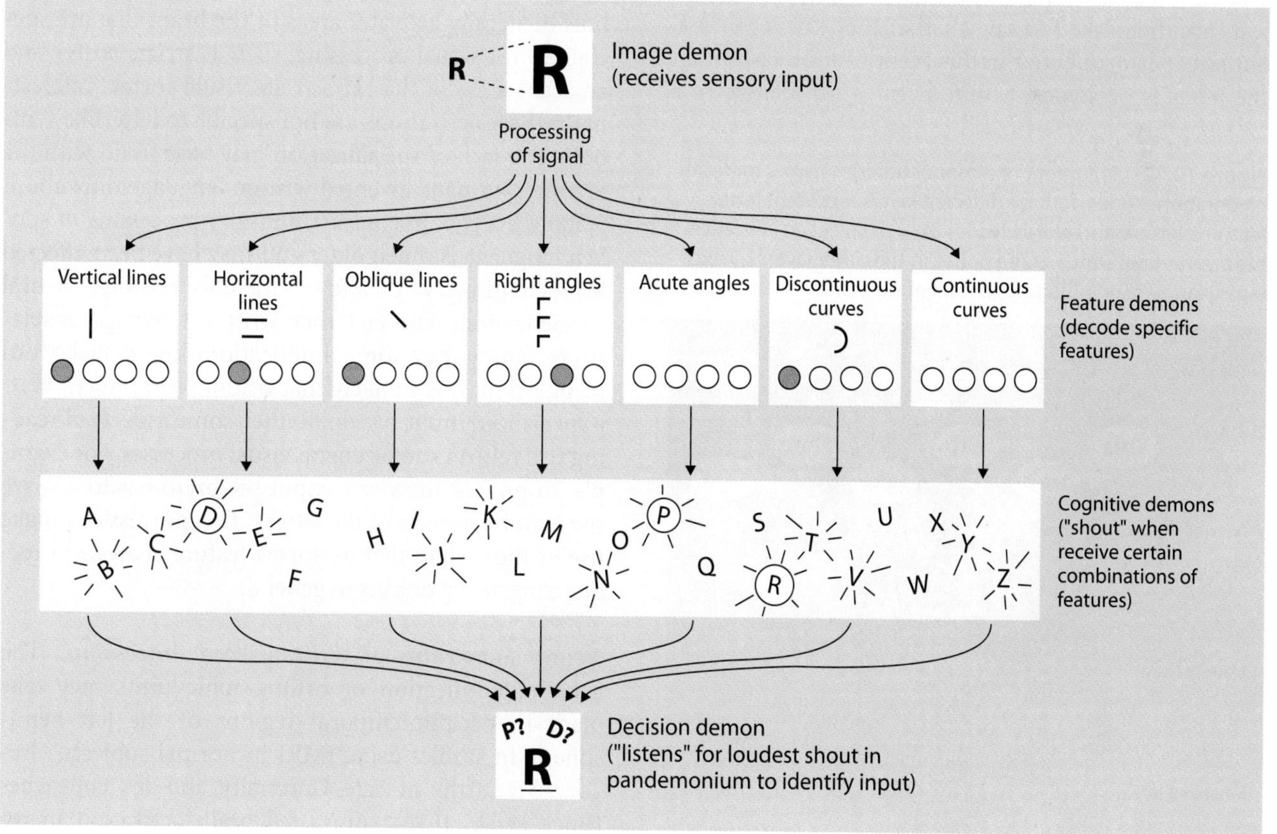

model, processes can take place in parallel such that several letters can be processed at the same time, whereas in Selfridge's model, one letter is processed at a time in a serial manner. Figure 10.12 shows that the model of McClelland and Rumelhart permits both excitatory and inhibitory links between all the layers. If a reader reads the word *trip*, for example, then activations will ensue in all representational layers that match with the features and letters of the word *trip*, as well as with the word *trip* itself. But when the word node *trip* is activated, it will send out inhibitory signals to lower layers, and letters and features that do not match the word *trip* will be inhibited.

Computational models are very important in cognitive neuroscience because they enable scientists to precisely formalize which components are essential to a given cognitive process, as well as how these components might interact. The empirical validity of a model can be tested on real-life behavioral phenomena or against physiological data. The connectionist model of McClelland and Rumelhart does an excellent job of mimicking reality for a phenomenon that has been labeled the *word superiority effect*. Experimentally, this effect can be observed when three types of visual stimuli are briefly flashed to the subjects. The stimulus may be a word (*trip*), a nonword (*pirt*), or a letter (*t*). The subjects are then asked to say whether they saw a *t* or a *k*. Subjects perform better in this identification task when the letter is presented within a real word relative to a nonword, but interestingly, they are also better at identifying the letter when it is presented in the word than when it is presented as the individual letter. This remarkable result indicates that words are probably not perceived on a letter-by-letter basis. The word superiority effect can be explained in terms of the McClelland and Rumelhart model, because the model proposes that top-down information of the words can either activate or inhibit letter activations, thereby helping the recognition of letters.

Figure 10.12 Fragment of a connectionist network for letter recognition. Nodes at three different layers represent letter features, letters, and words. Nodes in each layer can influence the activational status of the nodes in the other layers by excitatory (arrows) or inhibitory (lines) connections.

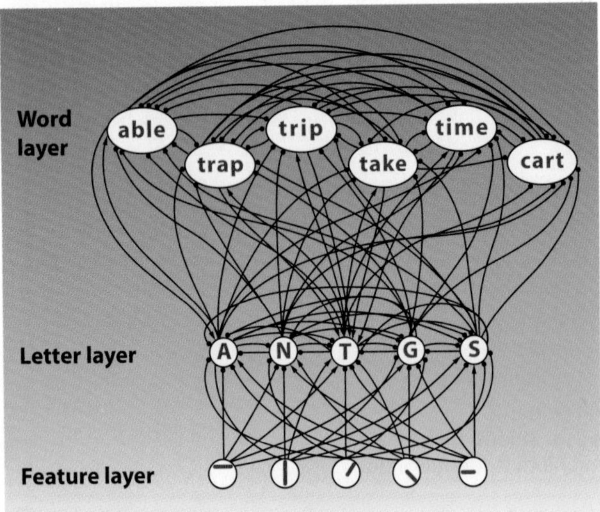

As we learned in earlier chapters, the brain is well equipped for pattern recognition, so let's fill in the lower levels of the letter recognition models with physiological details. Single-cell recording techniques, for example, have enlightened us about some of the basics of visual feature analysis. We know how the brain analyzes edges, curves, and so on. But unresolved questions remain because letter and word recognition are not really understood at the cellular level, and recordings in monkeys are not likely to enlighten us about letter and word recognition in humans. Recent studies using PET and fMRI in humans have started to shed some light on where humans may process letters in the brain.

If subjects are presented with letters or letterlike symbols, the initial perceptual analysis of written symbols bilaterally activates areas of the brain that are specialized for visual processing, such as striate cortex and adjacent areas of the extrastriate visual cortex. Interestingly, these activations are not specific to letterlike symbols. The lack of specialization may have to do with the fact that humans invented written language only about 5,500 years ago. In contrast, auditory processing of spoken language is much older and may have been affected by evolutionary pressures, thereby creating neural specialization. The fact that written language is relatively young has some implications for visual word recognition: It is unlikely that reading is represented by a specialized input system. Rather, some aspects of reading will rely on some general visual processes. For example, to process the visual input the brain has to analyze the featural aspects of the letters. This process can make use of the system that performs feature analysis in recognizing visual objects in general.

Neural Substrates of Written-Word Processing The actual identification of orthographic units may take place in occipitotemporal regions of the left hemisphere. In studies using fMRI in normal subjects, Gregory McCarthy at Yale University and his colleagues (Puce et al., 1996) contrasted brain activation in response to letters with activation in response to faces and visual textures. They found that regions of the occipitotemporal cortex were activated preferentially in response to unpronounceable letter strings (Figure 10.13). Interestingly, this finding confirmed results from an earlier study by the same group (Nobre et al., 1994), in which intracranial electrical recordings were made from this brain region in patients who later underwent surgery for intractable epilepsy. In this study they found a large negative polarity potential at about 200 ms in occipitotemporal regions, in response to the visual presentation of letter strings. This area was not sensitive to other visual stimuli, such as faces, and importantly, it also appeared to be insensitive to lexical or semantic features of words. Finally, lesions of this area can give rise to *pure alexia*, a condition in which patients cannot read words, even though other aspects of language are normal. This convergent neurological and neuroimaging evidence gives clues as to how the human brain solves the perceptual problems of letter recognition.

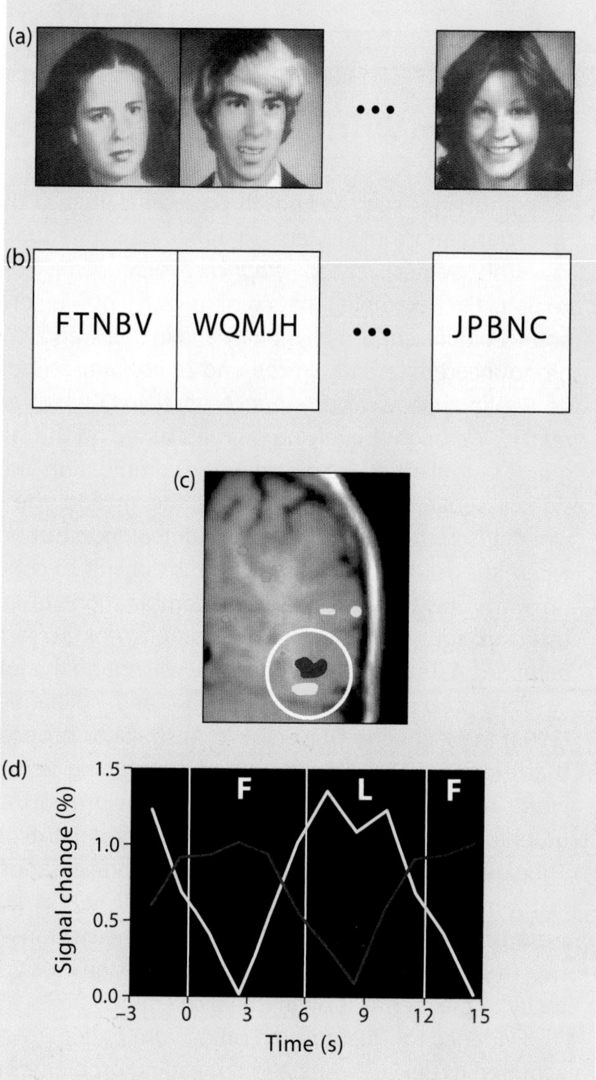

Figure 10.13 Brain activations by faces (F; example in **(a)**) compared to activation by letters (L; example in **(b)**) in the ventral part of the left hemisphere (white circle in the brain scan shown in **(c)**). The scan presented is a slice in the coronal plane (medial is on the left of the image) and shows only the left hemisphere at the level of the anterior occipital cortex. The scan shows activated voxels superimposed on the corresponding anatomical image. Faces activated a region of the lateral fusiform gyrus (yellow); letter strings activated a region of the occipitotemporal sulcus (pink). **(d)** These graphs show the corresponding time course of fMRI activations averaged over all alternation cycles for faces (yellow lines) and letter strings (pink lines).

Recognition of Words

Word, or lexical, processing is a well-investigated phenomenon in psycholinguistics. Most scientists agree on its main components: lexical access, lexical selection, and lexical integration. **Lexical access** refers to the stage(s) of processing in which the output of perceptual analysis activates word form representations in the mental lexicon, including their semantic and syntactic attributes.

Lexical access differs, in most cases, for the visual and auditory modalities, and decoding the input signal such that it can make contact with word form representations in the mental lexicon presents the language comprehender with a distinct set of challenges in either case. For the written input there is the question of how we can read not only words with a spelling that does not directly translate into sound (e.g., the word *colonel*) but also pseudowords that have no matching word form (e.g., *lonocel*). Reading pseudowords cannot be the result of direct mapping of the orthographic output onto a word form, because there is none.

Therefore, researchers have suggested that we need to translate the letters into their corresponding phonemes to be able to read *lonocel*. On the other hand, if we wanted to read aloud the word *colonel*, we would mispronounce it if we directly translated it into the corresponding phonemes, and to prevent such errors we might use a direct route from the orthographic units to the word form representation. This observation has led researchers to propose dual-route reading models, with one direct route from orthography to word form, and one indirect route (or assembled route) where the written input is translated into phonology before it is mapped onto the word form (for more details, see "How

HOW THE BRAIN WORKS

From Written Text to Word Representation: One or Two Pathways?

Languages such as English pose difficulties in the translation of letters (graphemes) to sounds (phonemes), called *grapheme-to-phoneme conversion*. For example, the combination "ph" is pronounced differently in *physiology* and in *uphill*, and "c" is pronounced differently in *cop* and *cerebellum*. So how do we know how to pronounce *physiology* when we read it? We might be relying on rules based on the language's regularities. For example, the combination "mb" signals separate pronunciation of the *m* and the *b* when it is in the middle of a word (*ambulance*) but not when it is at the end (*bomb*). But it is difficult to come up with rules that will predict all combinations of letters and sounds; consider, for example, *bomber* and *bombard*. A rule-based system alone will not do the job.

This problem led Max Coltheart and colleagues (1993) at Macquarie University in Australia to propose that there must be a direct route from reading text to word representation: from the whole-word orthographic input to representations in the mental lexicon. Thus, getting from written text to word representations in the mental lexicon might be accomplished in two ways, or by dual routes: grapheme-to-phoneme translation (the so-called *assembled route*), or written input directly to the mental lexicon (the *direct route*).

Evidence for dual routes comes from patients with acquired dyslexia. These patients' reading problems are due to brain damage. The deficit is modality specific; that is, the patients can comprehend spoken language and may even be able to produce written language (alexia without agraphia). Two types of acquired dyslexia have been found. Patients with deep, or phonological, dyslexia are unable to read pseudowords like *grimp* aloud, but have no problem reading irregular words like *broad* or difficult ones like *chrysanthemum*. That is, they cannot read aloud words that do not have a representation in the mental lexicon, but they have no difficulty with words in the lexicon. In addition, the patients make semantic errors (e.g., *rose* for *iris*).

Such problems cannot be explained as a loss of phonological representations, because patients with deep dyslexia usually perform well on a rhyming task if the stimuli are presented auditorily. Instead, the patients rely exclusively on the direct lexical route when reading. In contrast, patients with surface dyslexia rely only on rules based on regularity. They overregularize the pronunciation of irregular words (e.g., they might read "heed" for *head*) and thereby show a propensity for a direct translation from the letter to the sound representations. These forms of dyslexia provide a powerful double dissociation that tells us there might be two routes by which text that we read can be converted into verbal output.

However, a computational model has been proposed to explain these data by assuming a single route that always makes use of phonological information; it just uses more in some cases than in others (Seidenberg & McClelland, 1989). In this model there is a continuous interaction between written input units and phonological units, and feedback allows the model to learn about correct pronunciations of words. This model has been successful in reproducing some of the phenomena that we just described, but the model is not very good at reading pseudowords (words that sound and look like real words but are not—for example, *fisch*), something that generally poses no difficulty for humans.

the Brain Works: From Written Text to Word Representation" above).

As noted earlier, the continuity of the speech signal in spoken input is different from the clear boundaries in written input. A listener is challenged to segment speech and to control the speed of its input. When we read text in a book, we can go back and reread it. But when we are trying to understand what someone is saying, we can lose track of the conversational flow. Spoken language, then, has a temporal dimension that should be factored into any model of spoken-language comprehension.

An influential model in this respect is the cohort model of British psychologist William Marslen-Wilson (Marslen-Wilson & Tyler, 1980). This model (Figure 10.14) assumes that processing in speech starts with the very first sound or phoneme that the listener has identified as the onset of a word. It is clear that initially, when not all the perceptual information is yet available, more than one representation will be activated because more

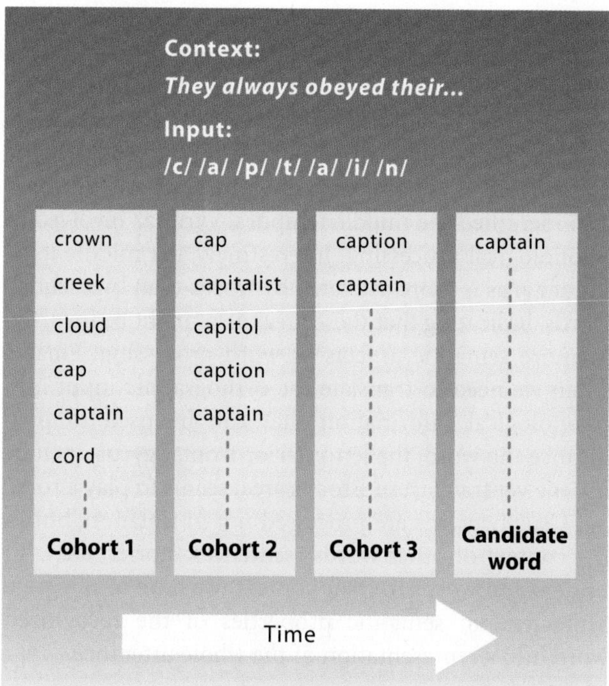

Figure 10.14 Cohort model of spoken-word recognition. At first, all words that start with the same initial sound are activated, forming the word initial cohort (Cohort 1). As time progresses, fewer competitors match with the actual speech signal and are eliminated from the cohort, until only the actual candidate word remains (see text for further explanation).

than one representation will fit the first part of the output of the perceptual system. This means that, of the activated word form representations, the one that best matches the sensory input has to be selected—a process labeled *lexical selection*, mentioned earlier.

Here is an example of how lexical selection plays a role in understanding words: The initial sound [ca] of the word *captain* fits *captain*, but also fits words like *cap*, *capital*, *capitalist*, *caption*, and *capitol*. When we hear [ca], all the word forms that match this sound will become activated in what is called a *word initial cohort*. When more perceptual information becomes available, the number of activated representations narrows to the element that best matches the input, resulting in selection of the word *captain*, and deactivation of the other, nonmatching word forms. In this model, selecting the appropriate word form depends on the incoming sensory information and the number of competitors in the word initial cohort. A word is selected at its uniqueness point, the time when a word is uniquely distinguishable from all its competitors.

This model clearly takes into account the temporal aspects of speech perception. However, another difficulty faces the listener: We have only 30 to 40 phonemes to represent words in our language, but our mental lexicon contains tens of thousands of words. Therefore, many words resemble each other, and they have other words embedded within them. For example, a word such as *strange* contains the words *strain* and *range*, and it resembles the words *straight* and *change*. The listener has the difficult job of identifying what the actual words in the input stream are. As we noted previously, this task can be accomplished by the use of sublexical cues such as stress patterns in the words.

In addition, to address the problem of identifying words, recent models for auditory word recognition propose that the competition between word candidates is not limited to words that have the same word initial cohort (as in the cohort model just described). Instead, all lexical forms that partially overlap with the speech input become activated. Let's illustrate this with our previous example. If we hear the word *strange*, all word forms that partially match this input are activated, such as *strain*, *range*, *straight*, and *change*. Because only the word form *strange* completely matches the actual input signal, it will win the competition against all the word forms that do not match the input signal completely, and it will do so by inhibiting the competitors.

An example of a study from Anne Cutler's group (e.g., Norris et al., 1995) provides evidence for the idea that competition plays a role in word recognition. These researchers showed that subjects were *slower* to recognize real words embedded in nonsense strings that can activate competing words (e.g., *mess* in *domess*, which could activate the real word *domestic*), than to recognize real words embedded in nonsense strings that have no overlap with real words (e.g., *mess* in *bemess*, which could not activate any real words).

We have now sketched the ingredients important to understanding written and spoken words. We started the chapter with a description of the mental representations of words and their meanings, and then surveyed the perception of speech and written input. In this section we described how this perceptual information translates into the activation of word forms in the mental lexicon. Throughout, we have provided some hints of where these processes and representations may be localized in the brain. This functional neuroanatomical story is based on convergent evidence from specific functional losses in some patients, the relationship between patient brain lesion data and their language deficits, and some imaging and intracranial recording data. More recently, some cognitive neuroscience studies have been tackling this organization directly using neuroimaging tools to study the brain circuits and systems involved in reading and listening to words.

BRAIN SYSTEMS FOR WORD RECOGNITION

For auditory word perception, Jeffrey Binder and colleagues (2000) proposed a hierarchical model of speech processing in the brain that is illustrated in Figure 10.15. This model is based on studies that used fMRI to identify brain regions that become activated in relation to subcomponents of speech processing. First, the stream of auditory information proceeds from auditory cortex in Heschl's gyri to the superior temporal gyrus. In these parts of the brain, no distinction is made between speech and nonspeech sounds, as noted earlier.

The first evidence of such a distinction is in the adjacent superior temporal sulcus, but no lexical-semantic information is processed in this area. From the superior temporal sulcus, the information proceeds to the middle temporal gyrus and the inferior temporal gyrus, where phonological and lexical-semantic aspects of words may be processed. The next stage involves analysis in the angular gyrus, posterior to the temporal areas just described (see Chapter 3), but then in more anterior regions in the temporal pole. Only these latter four areas seem to be lateralized more to the left hemisphere.

For written input we have seen that the initial perceptual analysis of letters takes place in the primary and secondary visual cortex of both hemispheres, areas of the brain that are specialized for visual processing but not specific to letters. Occipitotemporal regions of the left hemisphere may be specialized for the identification of orthographic units (see Figure 10.13). Reading studies that compared areas of the brain that become activated during the processing of words and pseudowords also identified the middle temporal gyrus as involved in phonological processing. Interestingly, the middle temporal gyrus is more activated by words than by pseudowords, indicating that these areas also might be involved in more semantic aspects of word processing. Finally, when we need to translate the orthographic input into phonological information that can be used to pronounce the word, the left inferior frontal gyrus, including the ventral part of Broca's area, seems to play a role.

Usually words are processed not in isolation, but in the context of other words (sentences, stories, etc.). To understand words in their context, we have to integrate syntactic and semantic properties of the recognized word into a representation of the whole utterance.

THE ROLE OF CONTEXT IN WORD RECOGNITION

One question that puzzles psycholinguistic researchers is this: At what point during language comprehension does linguistic context influence word processing? More

Figure 10.15 A hierarchical processing stream for speech processing (see text for explanation). Four slices are shown for the left **(a)** and right **(b)** hemispheres. Heschl's gyri, which contain the primary auditory cortex, are indicated in purple. Indicated in blue are areas of the dorsal superior temporal gyri that are activated more by frequency-modulated tones than by random noise. Yellow areas are clustered in the superior temporal sulcus and are speech specific; that is, they show more activation for speech sounds (words, pseudowords, or reversed speech) than for nonspeech sounds. Finally, red areas include regions of the middle temporal gyrus, inferior temporal gyrus, angular gyrus, and temporal pole and are more active for words than for pseudowords or nonwords. Note that these "word" areas are lateralized mostly to the left. The latter areas were identified in several studies (Démonet et al., 1992, 1994; Perani et al., 1996; Binder et al., 1999, 2000).

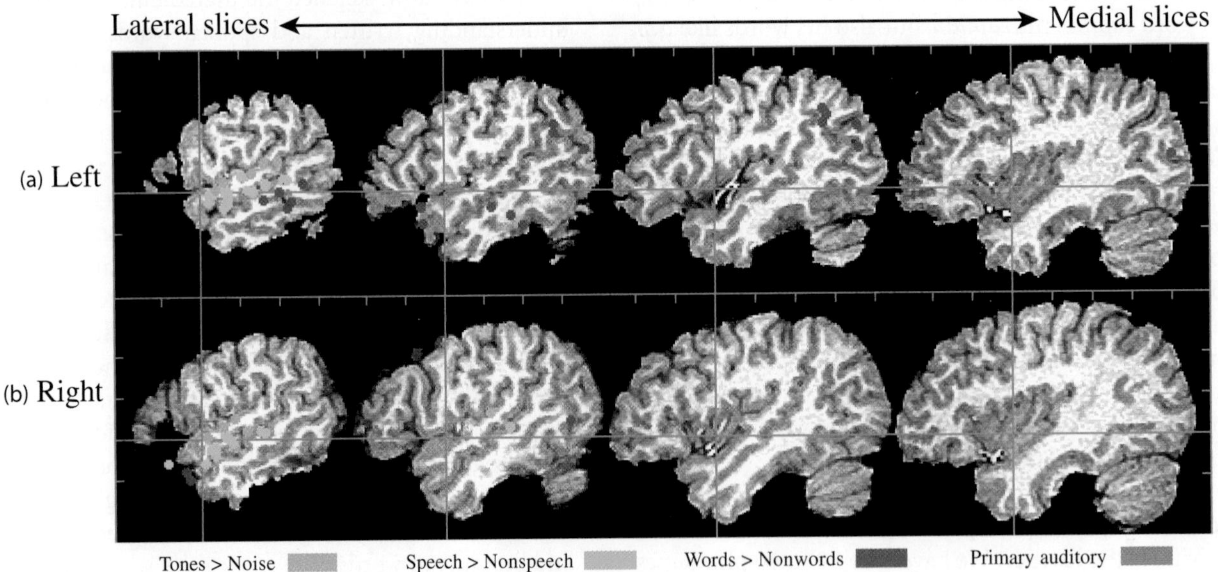

specifically, does context influence word processing before or after lexical access and lexical selection are complete? This question has to do with the issue of modularity versus interactivity (see "How the Brain Works: Modularity Versus Interactivity," on p. 398).

Consider the following sentence, which ends in an ambiguous word having more than one meaning: "The tall man planted a tree on the bank." *Bank* can mean both "money institution" and "side of the river." Semantic integration of the meaning of the final word *bank* into the context of the sentence allows us to interpret *bank* as the "side of the river" and not as a "money institution." The relevant question is, When does the sentence's context influence the activation of the multiple meanings of the word *bank*? Do both the contextually appropriate meaning of *bank* (in this case "side of the river") and the contextually inappropriate meaning (in this case "monetary institution") become briefly activated regardless of the context of the sentence? Or does the sentence context immediately constrain the activation to the contextually appropriate meaning of the word *bank*?

From this example we can already see that two types of representations play a role in word processing in the context of other words: lower level representations, those constructed from sensory input (in our example, the word *bank* itself); and higher level representations, those constructed from the context preceding the word to be processed (in our example, the sentence preceding the word *bank*). Contextual representations are crucial to determine in what sense or what grammatical form a word should be used. But without sensory analysis, no message representation can take place. The information has to interact at some point. The point at which this interaction occurs differs in competing models.

As alluded to previously, models of word recognition also vary in the amount of interactivity that they propose. In general, three types of models attempt to explain word comprehension. *Modular models* (also called *autonomous models*) claim that normal language comprehension is executed within separate and independent modules. Thus, higher level representations cannot influence lower level ones, and therefore the flow is strictly data driven, or bottom-up. In modular models the representation of the context information cannot affect lexical access and lexical selection processes. For our *bank* example, an autonomous model of word recognition would predict the activation of both the "side of the river" meaning and the "monetary institution" meaning, even if we have a context such as "The tall man planted a tree on the bank." Only after lexical access, selection of the word form, and activation of both meanings can context play a role in selection of the contextually appropriate meaning of the word—in our example, the "side of the river" meaning.

In contrast, *interactive models* maintain that all types of information can participate in word recognition. In these models, context can have its influence even before the sensory information is available, by changing the activational status of the word form representations in the mental lexicon. McClelland and colleagues (1989) have proposed this type of interactivity model. Many of these models also do not suggest that words forms are represented as whole units. A certain word is recognized when particular nodes in a distributed network become activated together. For our *bank* example, this would mean that the context of the sentence can guide the selection of the contextually appropriate meaning, and therefore we would find no activation of the "monetary institution" meaning of the word *bank* in our example.

Between these two extreme views is the notion that lexical access is autonomous and not influenced by higher level information, but that lexical selection can be influenced by sensory and higher level contextual information. In these *hybrid models*, information is provided about word forms that are possible given the preceding context, thereby reducing the number of activated candidates. The version of Marslen-Wilson's model of auditory word recognition that we discussed earlier is an example of such a hybrid model.

A elegant example of a study that addressed the question of modularity versus interactivity in word processing is one that Pienie Zwitserlood of the University of Münster in Germany performed while at the Max Planck Institute for Psycholinguistics in the Netherlands (Zwitserlood, 1989). She asked subjects to listen to short texts such as this: "With dampened spirits the men stood around the grave. They mourned the loss of their *captain*." At different points during the auditory presentation of the word *captain* (e.g., when only [c] or only [ca] or only [cap], etc., could be heard), a visual target stimulus was presented. This target stimulus could be related to the actual word *captain*, or to an auditory competitor—for example, *capital*. In this example, target words could be words like *ship* (related) or *money* (unrelated). In other cases a pseudoword would be presented. The task was to decide whether the target stimulus was a word or not (lexical decision task).

The results of this study showed that subjects were faster to decide that *ship* was a word in the context of the story about the men mourning their captain, and slower to decide that *money* was a word, even when only partial sensory information of the stimulus word *captain* was available (i.e., before the whole word was spoken). Apparently the lexical selection process was influenced by the contextual information that was available from the text that the subjects had heard before the whole word *captain* was spoken. However, some sensory information of the word *captain* had to be heard, or the reaction time benefit was not found.

This result is consistent with the ideas that the process of lexical access can be guided by the sensory input and not much by the higher order contextual information alone, and importantly, that lexical selection can be influenced by sentence context. We do not know for certain which type of model fits word comprehension the best, but there is growing evidence from studies like that of Zwitserlood and others that at least lexical selection is influenced by higher level contextual information.

Integration of Words in Sentences

In the foregoing discussion we examined processes dedicated to recognizing a word in the linguistic input. But normal language comprehension requires more than just recognizing individual words. To understand the message conveyed by a speaker or a writer, we have to integrate the syntactic and semantic properties of the recognized word into a representation of the whole sentence or utterance. Let's consider again the following sentence: "The tall man planted a tree on the bank." Why do we read *bank* to mean "side of the river" instead of "monetary institution"? The reason is that the rest of the sentence has created a context that is compatible with one meaning and not the other. Let's consider another example: "The pianist rose to the applause of the audience." Once again, there is more than one way to interpret the sentence, and integration processes help us interpret *rose* as a verb ("to stand") and not a noun ("a flower"). This integration process has to be executed in real time—as soon as we are confronted with the linguistic input. If we come upon a word like *bank* in a sentence, usually we are not aware that this word has an alternative meaning, because the appropriate meaning of this word has been rapidly integrated into the context.

Understanding a word with respect to the higher order representation of sentence meaning involves semantic and syntactic integration processes. Higher order semantic processing is important to determine the right sense or meaning of words in the context of a sentence, as with ambiguous words such as *bank*, which have the same form but more than one meaning. Semantic analysis is also needed for making sense of nonambiguous words such as *piano*, whose meanings can be emphasized in different contexts (as in "the piano is a heavy instrument" versus "the piano is a beautiful instrument").

For a full interpretation of linguistic input, though, we also have to assign a grammatical structure. Semantic information in words alone is not enough to understand the message, as is clear from the following sentence: "The little old lady bites the gigantic dog." Syntactic analysis of this sentence reveals its structure: Who was the actor, what was the theme or action, and what was the subject? The syntax of the sentence demands that we imagine an implausible situation in which an old lady is biting and not being bitten.

Syntactic analysis goes on even in the absence of real meaning. Normal subjects are faster at detecting a target word in a sentence when it makes no sense but is grammatically correct, than when the grammar is locally disrupted. Typically, subjects in such studies are asked to listen to sentences in different conditions and are instructed to press a button as soon as they hear a target word, such as *kitchen*. In a baseline condition, normal sentences would be presented. A normal sentence might be, "The maid was carefully peeling the potatoes in the garden because during the summer the very hot kitchen is unbearable to work in." In this baseline condition, subjects take about 300 ms to press a button (from the onset of the target word *kitchen*).

These reaction times can be compared with reaction times to sentences that are semantically absurd but grammatically normal, such as, "An orange dream was loudly watching the house during smelly nights because within these signs a very slow kitchen snored with crashing leaves." Here the subjects' mean response to the target word is slowed by about 60 ms. Yet when the syntax of the sentence is also disrupted, the response times are even slower (by another 45 ms). An example of such a sentence is, "An orange dream was loudly watching the house during smelly nights because within these signs a slow very kitchen snored with crashing leaves." The word order of the phrase *a slow very kitchen* is grammatically incorrect. These types of findings inform us that syntactic analysis proceeds even when sentences are meaningless.

From a psycholinguistic point of view, how do we process the structure of sentences? When we hear or read sentences, we activate word forms (*lexemes*) that in turn activate the lemma information. As we discussed earlier, the lemma is hypothesized to contain not only information about syntactic properties of the word (e.g., whether it is a noun or a verb) but also information about the possible sentence structures that can be generated, given a certain verb. For example, a verb such as *eat* requires a subject and an object, as in "The cat (subject; the eater) *eats* the food (object; the eatee)."

As soon as the appropriate lemma information is retrieved, structure building can start. This means that words in a sentence are assigned their syntactic roles and clustered into groups or syntactic phrases. For example, "The cat eats the food" consists of a noun phrase (*The cat*), a verb phrase (*eats*), and another noun phrase (*the food*). This process is incremental: As soon as the information for a lemma is retrieved, it is inserted into the constituent structure that has already been built. This immediate assignment of syntactic structure to incoming words has been labeled **parsing**, and the processor that does the parsing is called the *parser*. Unlike the representation of words and their syntactic properties (lexemes and lemmas) that are stored in a mental lexicon, representations of whole sentences are not stored in the brain. It is just not feasible for the brain to store the incredible number of different sentences that can be written and produced. Parsing is therefore a building process that does not, and cannot, rely on the retrieval of representations of sentences.

How does parsing work? A very influential theory on how syntactic analysis takes place is the *garden path model*, championed by Lynn Frazier (1987). The essence of the model is that sentences have a preferred interpretation. This preference could lead to garden path effects, which means being led to believe something that seems correct at first but is not. To understand this model, we must introduce the idea of sentence structure.

A sentence consists of a linear arrangement of phrases and words, which can be represented by a hierarchical tree that reflects the sentence's structure. An example of a hierarchical tree for the sentence "The spy saw the cop with binoculars" is presented in Figure 10.16, where the sentence consists of two large phrases, a noun phrase and a verb phrase. The noun phrase has an article (*the*) and a noun (*spy*). The verb phrase is divided into the main verb (*saw*); a noun phrase (*the cop*), which has an article (*the*) and a noun (*cop*); and a prepositional phrase (*with binoculars*), which has a preposition (*with*) and a noun (*binoculars*). Mental representations of the tree's components are labeled *syntactic nodes.*

The formation of constituent structures plays a central role in the garden path model (but also in other models of parsing). The garden path model assumes that we process syntactic information in a way that minimizes what we have to do to meet the demanding time pressure of normal comprehension. Two mechanisms that would help this economy principle are postulated: *minimal attachment* and *late closure.* The minimal-attachment mechanism makes sure that syntactic analysis is done in such a way that the minimum number of additional syntactic nodes must be computed. The late-closure mechanism tries to assign incoming words to the syntactic phrase or clause currently being processed.

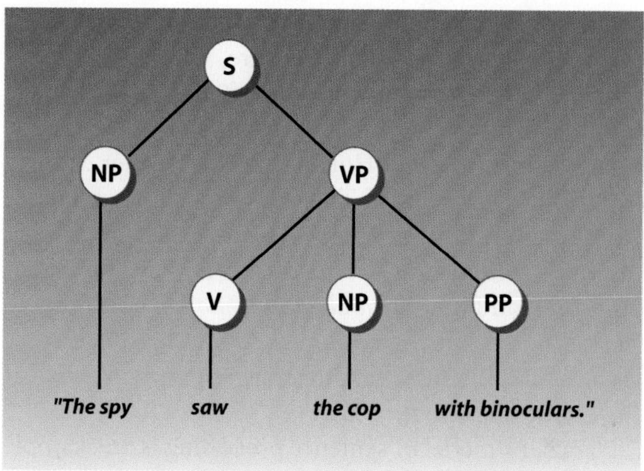

Figure 10.16 Constituent structure of a sentence. As explained in the text, this structure is based on the principles of minimal attachment. S = sentence; NP = noun phrase; V = verb; VP = verb phrase; PP = prepositional phrase.

Let's consider another possibility for the sample sentence represented by the hierarchical tree shown in Figure 10.16. In the example in Figure 10.17, the meaning of the sentence is changed because a different syntactic structure is assigned. This tree leads to the interpretation that the cop rather than the spy was equipped with binoculars. The interpretation in the tree in Figure 10.16 is preferred over that in Figure 10.17 because it has fewer and less complex nodes. The minimal-attachment and late-closure principles were proposed for reasons of

Figure 10.17 Alternative constituent structure of the same sentence as in Figure 10.16. The hierarchical tree shown here presents an example of nonminimal attachment. See the text for further explanation. S = sentence; NP = noun phrase; V = verb; VP = verb phrase; PP = prepositional phrase.

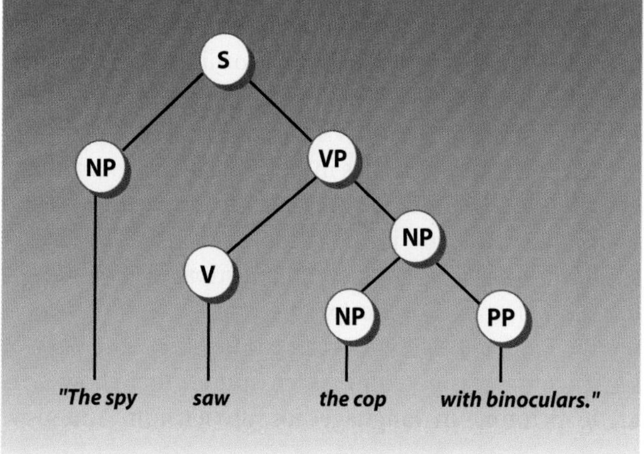

economy. Because the language processor must work under an enormous time pressure, the less time required for syntactic analysis, the better. Sometimes the minimal-attachment principle leads to mistakes, as, for example, in "Ron loves Holland and his mother enjoyed her trip to Amsterdam." This is a garden path sentence whose preferred interpretation leads to a wrong solution and hence must be reanalyzed. That is, the reader tends to read both *Holland* and *his mother* as objects of the verb *loves* but then, upon encountering the second verb (*enjoyed*), must reevaluate the sentence to arrive at the correct meaning.

Frazier's model of sentence processing is an example of a modular model (see "How the Brain Works: Modularity Versus Interactivity," on p. 398). Syntactic processing is encapsulated, and the first analysis of the sentence is based on its syntactic structure alone and is not influenced by other sources of information, such as the meaning of words or more general knowledge of the world. Let's illustrate this with the following example: "The manager sold the couch and the employee sold the desk." In this example, the meaning of the verb *sold* would make it easier to construct a syntactic structure in which the noun *employee* starts a second clause, because employees usually are not sold by managers. In linguistic terms, *sold* can go together easily with an inanimate object (e.g., *couch*) but not very easily with an animate object (e.g., *employee*). However, Frazier's modular model claims that, independent of this type of contextual information, in the first instance a structure is assigned on the basis of syntactic structure and the principles of minimal attachment and late closure alone. So even in this example, we would be led down the garden path, and we would structure the sentence first as if the manager sold both the couch and the employee. Only at a later stage, when semantic information is evaluated by a so-called semantic interpreter, can we revise the structure of the sentence to reflect its actual meaning.

More interactive views of sentence processing propose that other sources of information can immediately influence syntactic processing. According to these models, the semantic information of the verb *sold* in our example would prevent us from being led down the garden path. Many studies indicate that we can immediately use meaning information, our knowledge of the world, and syntactic information to determine the correct structure of a sentence, which supports a more interactive view of sentence processing.

One piece of evidence for a more interactive view of sentence processing comes from studies that show syntactic priming in language comprehension. You now know that a word preceded by an identical or semantically related prime word is processed more easily. But can the structure of language be primed as well? Does recent exposure to a difficult sentence structure help subsequent understanding or production of a sentence with the same difficult structure, or, in other words, can syntactic structures be primed?

As illustration, consider the following difficult syntactic structure: "The man watched by the woman was tall and handsome." In this sentence the syntactically preferred and easiest first analysis would lead us down the garden path. That is, in the easiest syntactic analysis the man would be the subject of the sentence—the person who is doing the watching. But as we come to the word *by* in the sentence, we realize that our initial structural analysis was incorrect, and that the woman in this sentence is the one doing the watching. The question, then, is this: What if we read a sentence that has the same structure as in the example after very recently being exposed to this difficult syntactic structure—for example, "The child watched by the parent was playing quietly." This sentence has the same syntactic structure as in the previous example, and the only word that is exactly repeated from the previous example is the verb. Syntactic priming would be suggested if the more difficult structures represented with the verb were easier to process upon subsequent encounters.

In a series of experiments, Kristen Tooley, Matt Traxler, and Tamara Swaab at the University of California, Davis, found that syntactic priming does indeed occur in language comprehension. In one experiment they measured event-related potential (ERPs) to the word *by* in sentences with the same structure as in the preceding examples, both when the sentence was presented for the first time (the *prime* sentence), and when the structure of the sentence was repeated (the *target* sentence; Tooley et al., 2007). The word *by* is the earliest possible disambiguating critical word in these types of sentences. The response to the word *by* in the target sentences showed a smaller syntactic ERP (P600; see the later section titled "Electrophysiology of Language") than to *by* when encountered in the first presentation of the sentence (the prime sentence). This reduction in the amplitude of the ERP to the second presentation of *by* can be interpreted as evidence that it was easier to understand the difficult syntactic structure when it had been primed by an identical structure (Figure 10.18).

These scientists have thus shown that repetition of the verb between prime and target structures is essential to syntactic priming. The fact that lexical repetition is

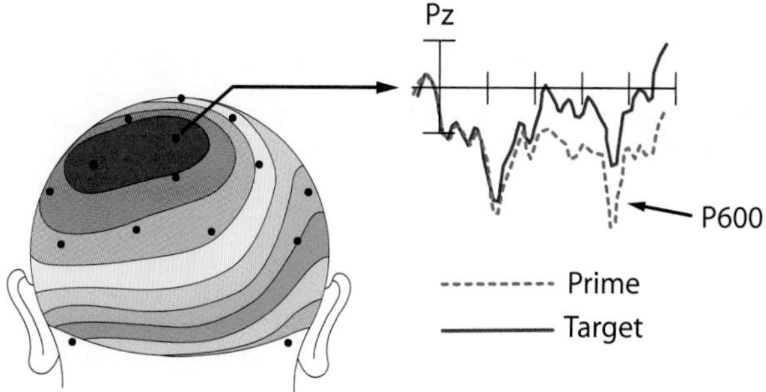

Figure 10.18 Syntactic priming effects demonstrated with ERPs. Topographic ERP voltage map **(left)** showing a rear view of the head and plotting the P600 difference effect (shown in waveforms, **right**) in a study of syntactic priming. On the topographic map, red represents more positive voltage to the prime than to the target sentence. The arrows from the topographic map indicate the site on the scalp (the midline parietal scalp electrode site, Pz) where the waveforms were recorded. The waveforms show that the response to the prime sentence was larger than to the target sentence, which reflects the effect of syntactic priming.

crucial to this syntactic priming effect is important to help distinguish between modular and interactive models of normal language comprehension. As we have seen already, modular *context-free* grammars suggest that an initial syntactic tree is built without the influence of other types of information, such as the identity of the verb. In addition, in these types of models lexical representations in our mental lexicon do not include information about possible sentence structures. By contrast, interactive, constraint-based *lexicalist* grammars suggest that information about possible syntactic structures is actually stored with lexical representations of verbs in our mental lexicon, and when these representations are activated the structural information becomes activated as well. Effects of syntactic priming that depend on verb repetition can be explained in lexicalist frameworks, but not in context-free grammars.

Other studies have shown that "nonlinguistic" sources of information can be taken into account immediately during normal sentence comprehension. One study that illustrates this phenomenon was performed by Thomas Münte and colleagues (1998) at the University of Magdeburg in Germany. These researchers asked the following question: Can the way we process sentences be influenced immediately by our conceptual knowledge of how events are temporally organized? To test this idea, they asked subjects to read sentences that differed only in the first word, such as "After/Before the scientist submitted the paper, the journal changed its policy." According to our knowledge of the world, a more "logical" sequence of events would be that the journal changed its policy *after* the scientist had submitted the paper, because this sequence follows the actual order of events. In contrast, the *before* sentences signal a reverse order of events and are therefore more difficult to understand.

ERPs were recorded while the subjects read the sentences. The issues the researchers addressed were (a) if and when there would be any difference in the brain's response to the words *after* and *before* and (b) if such a difference would influence the processing of the rest of the sentence. Interactive models would predict that our conceptual knowledge of the order of events can immediately influence the processing of the sentence; modular models would predict that this influence does not occur until later. The results are more in line with an interactive view. As Figure 10.19 shows, beginning almost immediately the ERPs in response to the word *before* are more negative in polarity than they are in response to the word *after*, and this effect lasts over the course of the sentence. These findings indicate that conceptual knowledge of the temporal order of events can indeed influence the processing of sentences almost from the onset, and moreover, this knowledge has lasting consequences for the processing of the rest of the sentence.

In a fascinating new study, Peter Hagoort and his colleagues at the F. C. Donders Centre for Cognitive Neuroimaging in the Netherlands also found evidence for an immediate influence of world knowledge on the comprehension of words in sentences. They addressed a question that has puzzled philosophers and language researchers alike: whether knowledge of the world and knowledge of words are accessed and processed in parallel and by the same neural circuits in the brain. The traditional view on this conundrum has been that language comprehenders access the knowledge of words or semantic information before knowledge of the world (pragmatic knowledge) can be accessed and used.

Consider, for example, the following statement: "The president of the United Stated is divorced and very unhappy." Even though this statement is semantically perfectly normal—presidents, in principle, can be divorced—our knowledge of the world tells us that it is not a true statement of any of the presidents of the United States in recent history. The traditional view would predict that, at some moment, our brains would process the word *divorced* in the example above as if normal because it does not violate any semantic information, and only at a later stage would the truth value of the statement influence comprehension.

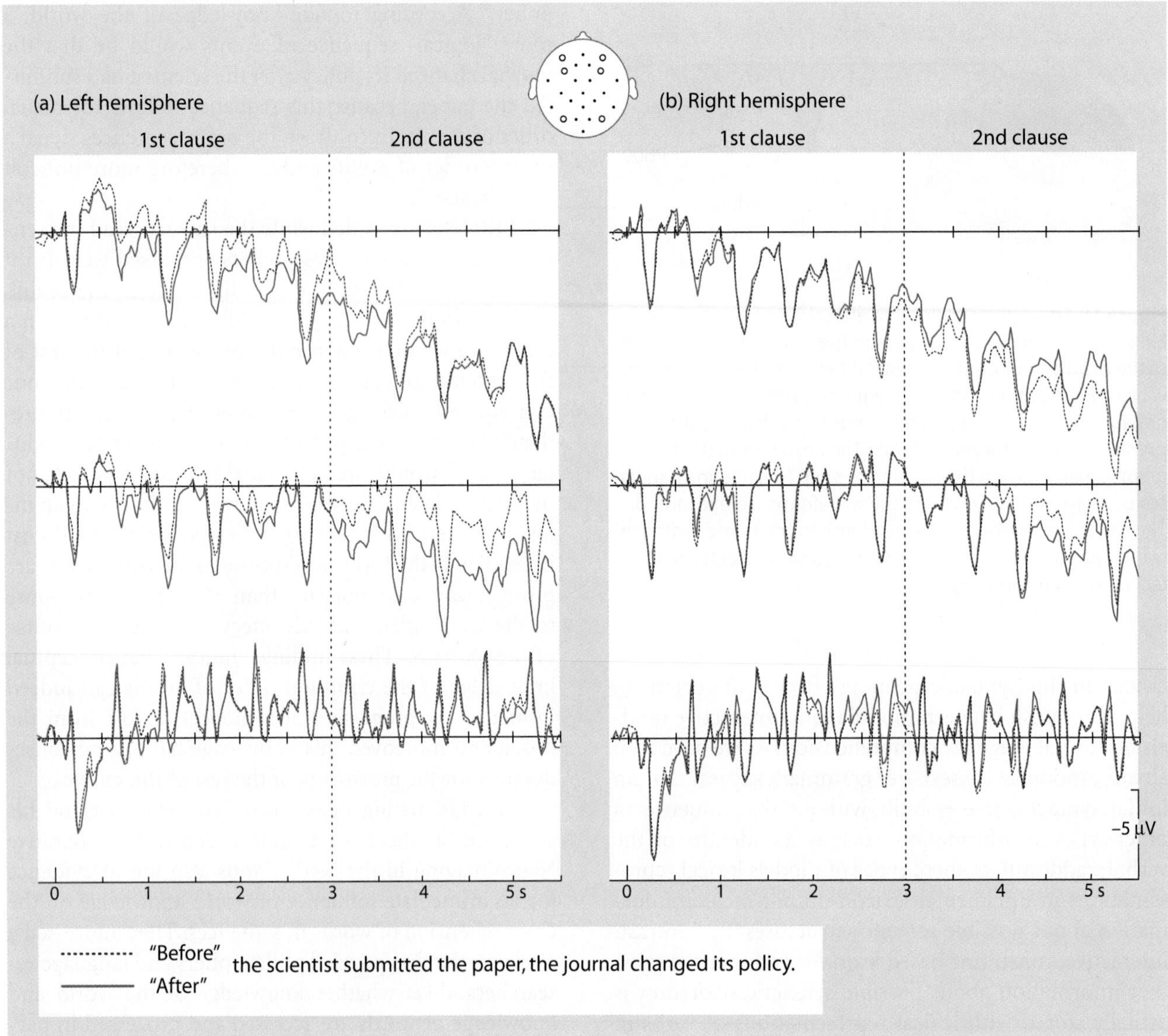

Figure 10.19 Event-related potentials (ERPs) recorded in response to sentences that start with *before* (dashed red line) or *after* (solid blue line). These ERPs are recorded from prefrontal **(top)**, frontal **(middle)**, and occipital **(bottom)** scalp sites of the left **(a)** and right **(b)** hemispheres. At the left prefrontal site (upper-left traces), the waveforms for *before* and *after* start to diverge almost immediately (at 300 ms). At the prefrontal and frontal sites, this effect lasts throughout the sentence and is largest during the second clause. See text for further explanation.

Hagoort and his team addressed this question of when and where our brains integrate semantic and pragmatic information during sentence comprehension by presenting Dutch speakers with sentences in three conditions, such as in the following example:

- *Condition 1: Correct.* "Trains in the Netherlands are *yellow* and very crowded."
- *Condition 2: World knowledge violation.* "Trains in the Netherlands are *white* and very crowded."
- *Condition 3: Semantic violation.* "Trains in the Netherlands are *sour* and very crowded."

The critical word in each of the three sentences (italicized in each example) was manipulated such that, in comparison to the correct sentence in Condition 1, either a semantic violation was created (see Condition 3; sour is generally a feature of food items and not trains), or a world knowledge violation was introduced (see Condition 2; trains in the Netherlands are yellow and not white, and all Dutch people know this).

ERPs and fMRI activation were measured for the critical words in the three conditions. As Figure 10.20 shows, a response (N400; see the later section titled "Electrophysiology of Language") with very similar onset latency, am-

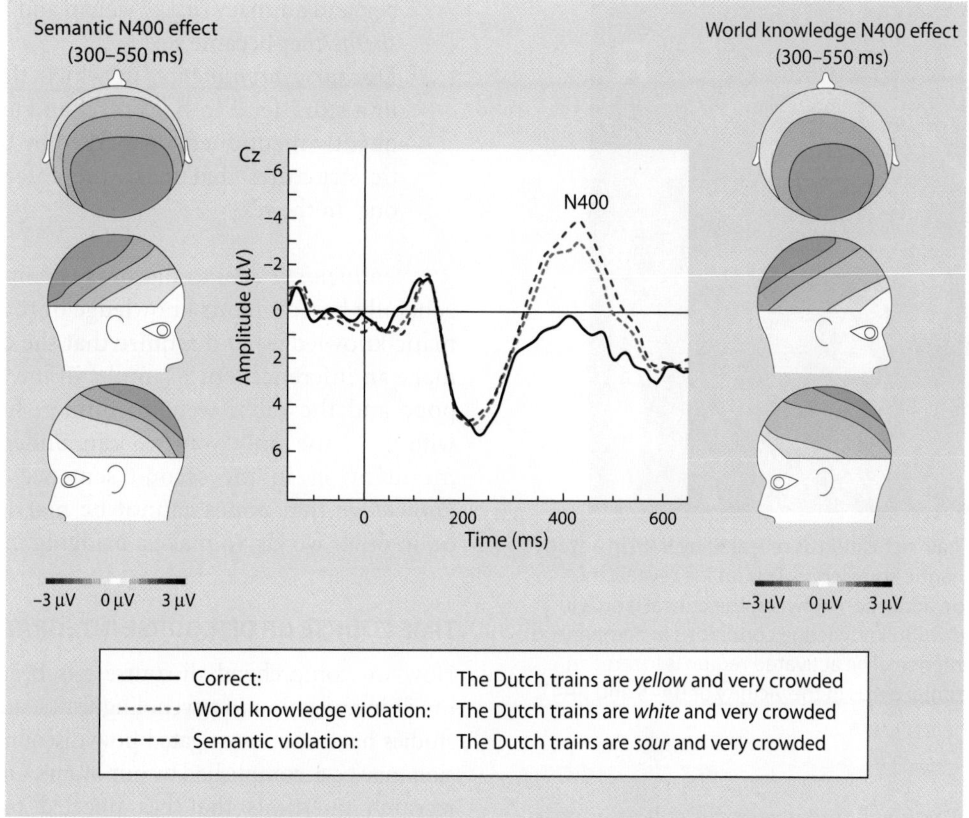

Figure 10.20 ERPs in the study of world and semantic knowledge. Plotted here is an average from 30 volunteers of the ERPs measured at the midline central scalp site, Cz, for the correct condition (black line), the world knowledge violation condition (blue dotted line), and the semantic violation condition (red dashed line). Semantic and world knowledge violations resulted in a larger response amplitude between 300 and 550 ms than did the control, the correct condition. Topographic maps for this latency range are shown for semantic **(left)** and world knowledge **(right)** conditions, which did not differ, in both cases peaking at the central parietal scalp.

plitude, and topographic distribution was found for both the semantic and the world knowledge violations, indicating that the two types of information have been accessed and integrated in the sentence context in parallel, not sequentially. The fMRI data showed activation of BA45 and BA47 in the left inferior frontal gyrus of the left hemisphere, indicating that the same brain structure was used when word and world knowledge violations occurred (Figure 10.21). The researchers concluded that "it does not take longer to discover that a sentence is untrue than to detect that it is semantically anomalous" (Hagoort et al., 2004, p. 441).

Lexical Integration in Discourse

You have now learned a great deal about language, but we still have not talked at all about language as we use it in our daily lives—for example, when we read a good book or converse with other people. This type of language comprehension goes beyond single words and single sentences and takes us to the level of discourse. Discourse is more than just the sum of the meaning of individual sentences. To illustrate this point, try reading the following passage for comprehension:

> This is very rewarding but tends to be quite expensive even if you own all that you need. The outfit does not really matter. One can get seriously injured without proper instruction even if it comes more naturally to some people than others. Some don't like the smell or the lack of control. So some people are scared to try even if they've dreamed of it since they were a kid reading about it in books and watching it on television. A running start is uncommon, although there are some who do it. Typically, success requires that you start with your left leg, and make sure it is securely in place. Then swing your body high into the air. The direction matters. Once you are settled, your thumbs should be pointing up. Sometimes there is no security but the animal's hair. Other times you can hang off the side. In any case you will be sore if this is your first time.

Do you find this paragraph hard to understand? Do you have any idea what it is about? If you are like most of the people in the study conducted by Bransford and

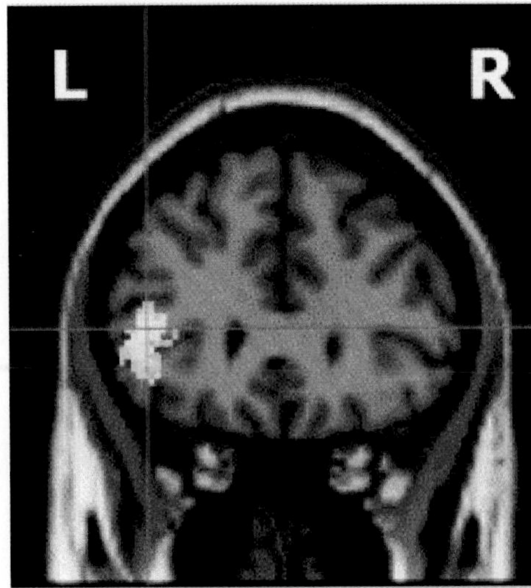

Figure 10.21 Brain activation as revealed by fMRI in a study of world and semantic knowledge. This image reveals the region of common activation between the critical words in the semantic and world knowledge conditions in comparison to the correct sentences. The activated region is located in the left inferior frontal gyrus in the vicinity of BA45 and BA47. See text.

Johnson (1972), you will find it very difficult or impossible to read this passage as a meaningful and cohesive story, even though each individual sentence is perfectly grammatical, and none of the words used in the passage are difficult to comprehend. But if we give you the title of the story, "Horseback Riding," then all of a sudden you can comprehend the meaning of the passage.

CUES IN DISCOURSE COMPREHENSION

In contrast to the preceding example, the aim of the writer or speaker is to make a text understandable. Fortunately, a number of cues can make a text cohesive. One of the main tasks of discourse comprehenders is to link the current text to the larger discourse. For example, in the sentence "Mary enjoyed the movie yesterday; it was about an opera star," the comprehender has to understand that the pronoun *it* in the second clause refers to *movie* in the first clause, or, in other words, the reader or listener has to find in memory an antecedent (i.e., movie) for an anaphor (i.e., it). He or she can use linguistic and nonlinguistic cues to do so. The *linguistic cues* include

- *Repetition and synonyms* (e.g., "Mary enjoyed the movie yesterday; the *movie/film* was about an opera star")
- *Pronoun morphology,* in which the pronoun anaphor matches its antecedent in gender, number, and animacy (e.g., "Melvin and Susie left when *she/he/they* became sleepy")
- *Discourse prominence,* in which the antecedents in a story tend to be central and are first or frequently mentioned, or marked by certain syntactic structures that make the antecedents "stand out" in the text

Nonlinguistic cues to discourse comprehension are generally based on our knowledge of the world (pragmatic knowledge) and require that the comprehender make an inference. For example, in the sentence "The pope and the rabbi went to dinner; he brought his wife . . ." the only way we can understand who is meant by *he* in the second sentence is to tap our knowledge that popes cannot be married in real life or, in other words, to make a bridging inference.

TIME COURSE OF DISCOURSE INTEGRATION

How we comprehend discourse has been the topic of much investigation in psycholinguistics, and more recent studies have also investigated how discourse comprehension may be accomplished by our brains. One of the major research questions that has puzzled psycholinguistic researchers is the time at which the overall meaning of the larger discourse can influence processing of the meaning of the local sentence. So, for example, there is nothing wrong with the meaning of the sentence "My uncle ate a big juicy steak." But if we consider the local context of the sentence in light of the global context of a larger discourse in which it was made clear that the uncle has been a vegetarian for years, then the final word *steak* does not make much sense.

For some time it has been argued that a comprehender first computes the meaning of the words in the local sentence context, regardless of what he or she has read or heard in the previous discourse. Only after the lexical, syntactic, and semantic properties of a word have been integrated with the meaning of the local sentence context can the meaning of the wider discourse start to exert its influence. This view is consistent with a more modular architecture of language processing. Constraint-based architectures, on the other hand, would predict that there is no delay in the influence of discourse meaning on the processing of words in local sentences. There are now several studies that seem more consistent with this latter view. In other words, when we go back to our example, a comprehender would immediately, without any measurable delay, use the information from the discourse that the uncle is a vegetarian to compute that *steak* is inappropriate in the larger context, even though it is consistent with the local sentence context.

COMPREHENSION OF WORDS IN DISCOURSE

In recent years, researchers interested in discourse comprehension have also investigated how precisely each word is processed when we are reading or listening to passages. And studies show that language comprehenders are, in general, remarkably skilled at arriving at a precise interpretation of the discourse. But in some instances a seemingly clear semantic error in the text goes unnoticed. An example is the following question: "After an air crash, where should the survivors be buried?" Even though you were forewarned, you may not have noticed anything strange in this sentence, but there is: Nobody would want to bury survivors!

If you noticed nothing strange in this sentence, you are like half of the participants in a study conducted by Anthony Sanford and colleagues at the University of Glasgow in Scotland. When asked this question, participants had answers like, "Bury them where their relatives want." This phenomenon has been labeled a *semantic illusion*, and it illustrates that sometimes comprehenders interpret discourse without taking into full account the semantic information of each individual word. Sanford and his collaborators noticed that this semantic illusion effect, or "not noticing the evidence," is especially apparent when the unnoticed word is related in meaning to the overall message of the text. So in this example the word *survivors* is clearly related to the air crash scenario.

Does this semantic illusion effect occur immediately when the meaning of the "unnoticed" word in the text is retrieved, or when the meaning of this word is integrated into an overall representation of the discourse context? This question has, in part, been answered by Jos van Berkum and his colleagues at the University of Amsterdam and the Max Planck Institute for Psycholinguistics in the Netherlands.

In an experiment on semantic illusions, they presented participants with stories like the following:

> A tourist wanted to bring his huge suitcase onto the airplane. However, because the suitcase was so heavy, the woman behind the check-in counter decided to charge the tourist extra. In response, the tourist opened his suitcase and threw some stuff out. So now, the suitcase of the resourceful tourist weighed less than the maximum twenty kilos. (Nieuwland & Van Berkum, 2005, p. 692)

Then the story continued in either a coherent or anomalous way as in the following:

> *Coherent:* Next, the woman told the tourist that she thought he looked really trendy. The tourist grabbed the woman's hand and eagerly asked her for a date. But the woman reprimanded the tourist for being pushy and told him to just get on the plane right away.

> *Anomalous:* Next, the woman told the suitcase that she thought he looked really trendy. The suitcase grabbed the woman's hand and eagerly asked her for a date. But the woman reprimanded the suitcase for being pushy and told him to just get on the plane right away.

ERPs to the critical word were measured in both anomalous and congruent conditions (Figure 10.22). Interestingly, the anomalous continuation did not elicit a semantic effect in the ERPs (i.e., an N400 effect, described later in the chapter), but instead a different brain response was observed; it was a late positive-voltage ERP that had its onset about 500 to 600 ms after the violating word had been presented: The absence of a semantic (N400) effect showed that readers of these stories did not immediately notice the presence of a semantic violation. In other words, they did not notice the evidence when they retrieved the meaning of the word *suitcase*. But the presence of this late positive effect shows that they did notice that they had made an incorrect semantic analysis relatively quickly, when they attempted to integrate the meaning of suitcase into the larger preceding context: Women generally do not tell a suitcase anything!

NEURAL SUBSTRATES OF SYNTACTIC PROCESSING

What do we know about the brain circuitry involved in syntactic processing? To try to answer this question, let's consider evidence from brain-damaged patients and brain-imaging studies. Some brain-damaged patients have severe difficulty producing sentences and also understanding complex sentences. These deficits are apparent in patients with **agrammatic aphasia**, who generally

Figure 10.22 Grand-average ERPs elicited by the critical words in the coherent (solid) and anomalous (dashed) conditions recorded from the midline parietal scalp site, Pz. See text for further explanation.

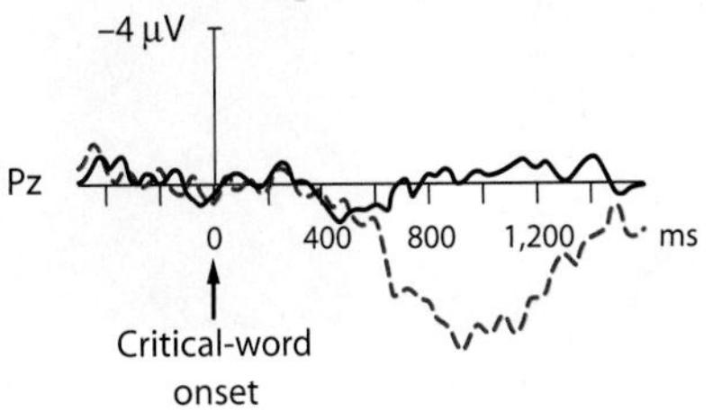

produce two- or three-word sentences consisting exclusively of content words and hardly any function words (*and, then, the, a,* etc.), or grammatical or morphological markers and inflections (e.g., *was pushing*). An example of such an impoverished sentence is "Son . . . university" instead of "My son is at the university."

In language comprehension, agrammatic aphasic patients often have great difficulty understanding complex syntactic structures. So when they hear the sentence "The gigantic dog was bitten by the little old lady," they will most likely understand it to mean that the lady was bitten by the dog. This problem in assigning syntactic structures to sentences traditionally has been associated with lesions that include Broca's area of the left hemisphere, a region that we will describe later. Much variability has been observed in the functional anatomy that has been described, and some agrammatic aphasic patients do not have lesions in Broca's area as it is classically defined.

Other evidence that Broca's area may be important for processing syntactic information comes from PET studies by David Caplan and colleagues (2000) at Harvard Medical School. In these studies, PET scans were made while subjects read sentences varying in syntactic complexity. For example, sentences with a relatively simple syntactic structure, such as "The child enjoyed the juice that stained the rug," were compared to sentences with a more complex syntactic structure, such as "The juice that the child enjoyed stained the rug." The second sentence is more complex because the main sentence ("the juice stained the rug") is interrupted by a *relative clause* ("that the child enjoyed"). Therefore, the thematic role (subject? object?) of the first noun (*juice*) cannot be assigned until the verb that follows the relative clause (*stained*) is encountered. The first noun phrase (*the juice*) has to be kept in some kind of working memory buffer. This type of working memory is not taxed as much in the first sentence because there the thematic roles can be assigned almost immediately. Caplan and colleagues found increased activation in Broca's area for the more complex syntactic structures (Figure 10.23).

However, the specificity of Broca's area for syntactic comprehension has been questioned. Sentence complexity manipulations in other studies led to activations of more than Broca's area alone. Marcel Just and colleagues (1996) reported activation in Broca's and Wernicke's areas (lateral frontal and posterior superior temporal cortex, respectively, as discussed later in the chapter) and in the homologous areas in the right hemisphere. In addition, activations of Broca's area have been found in sentence production studies and in studies that did not look at sentence processing at all, but, for example, at memorizing, maintaining, and retrieving lists of items. In general, then, the question of whether Broca's area is specific to syntactic processing remains a matter of debate. Some have argued that this area has a more general role in working memory operations that are not specific to syntax.

Another candidate for syntactic processing in the brain has been identified by PET as being located in the anterior portions of the superior temporal gyrus, in the vicinity of area 22 (Figure 10.24a). Nina Dronkers at the University of California, Davis, and colleagues (1994) also implicated this area in aphasics' syntactic processing deficits (Figure 10.24b). Since parsing is such a complex process, it is not at all surprising that more than one area in the brain would subserve it (see also Dronkers et al., 2004, in the "Suggested Reading" list for this chapter). Future research will have to elucidate which aspects of the parsing process are subserved by which areas in the brain, but scientists are narrowing in on the answer using a variety of methods.

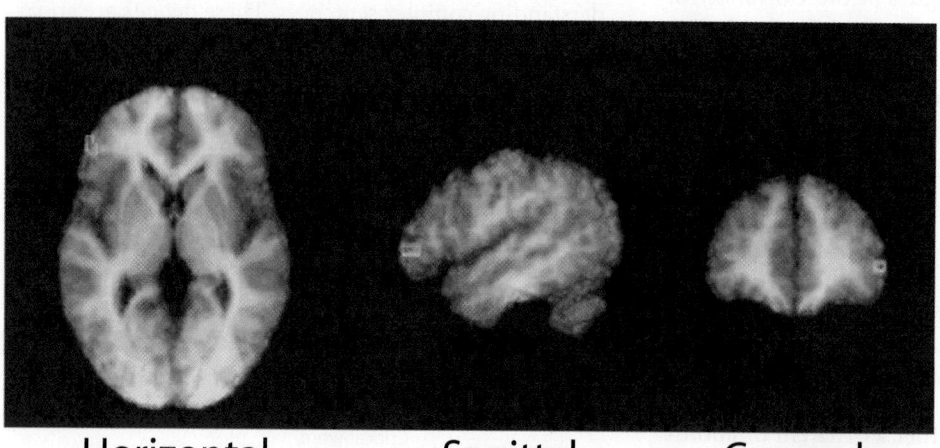

Figure 10.23 Increase in blood flow in Broca's area when subjects are processing complex relative to simple syntactic structures. See text for further explanation.

(a)

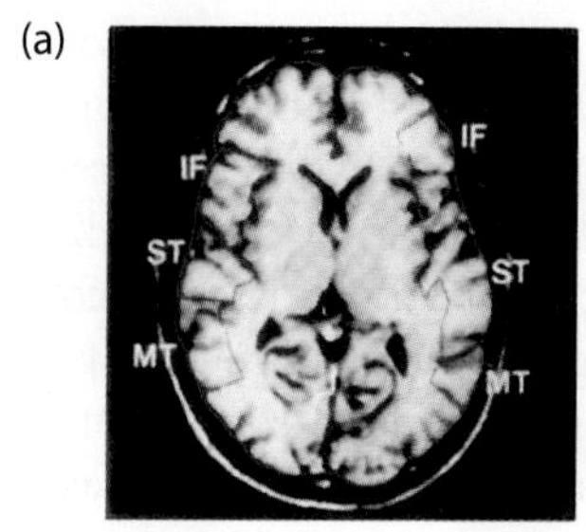

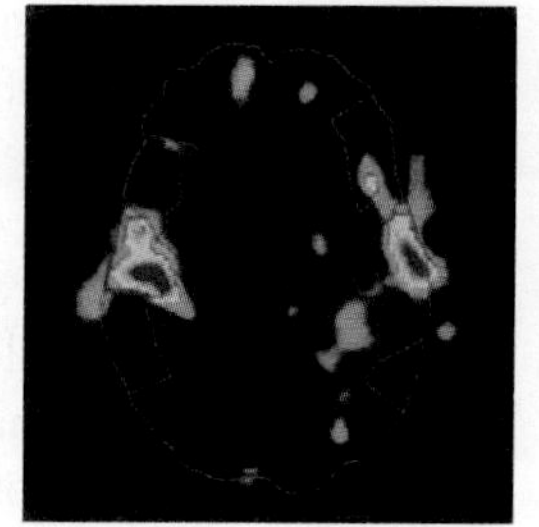

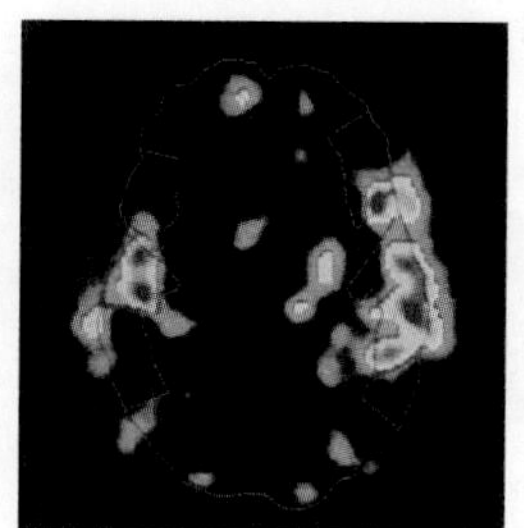

(b)

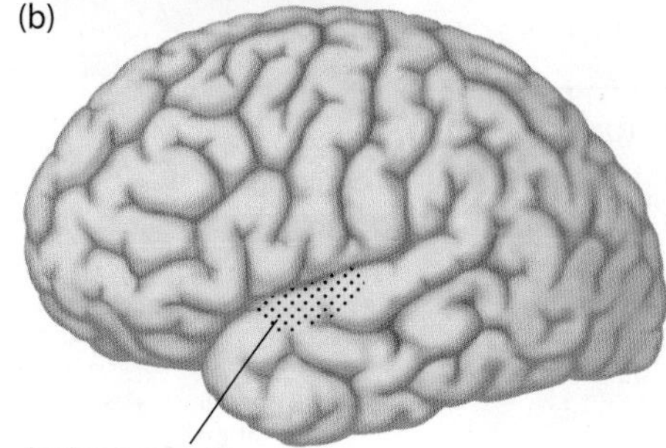

Figure 10.24 Localization of syntactic processing in the brain. **(a)** PET activations in the anterior portion of the superior temporal gyrus related to syntactic processing. IF = inferior frontal; MT = middle temporal; ST = superior temporal. **(b)** Summary of lesions in the anterior superior temporal cortex that lead to deficits in syntactic processing.

Speech Production

Up to now we have focused mainly on language comprehension; now we turn our attention to language production. To provide a framework for discussion, we will concentrate mostly on one influential model for language production, proposed by Willem Levelt (1989) of the Max Planck Institute for Psycholinguistics in the Netherlands. Figure 10.25 illustrates this model.

A seemingly trivial but nonetheless important difference between comprehension and production is our starting point. Whereas language comprehension starts with spoken or written input that has to be transformed into a concept, language production starts with a concept for which we have to find the appropriate words.

The first step in speech production is to prepare the message. Levelt maintains that there are two crucial aspects to message preparation: *macroplanning* and *microplanning*. The speaker must determine what she wants to express in her message to the listener.

A message directing someone to our home will be formulated differently from a message instructing someone to close the door. This communicative intention is represented by goals and subgoals expressed in an order that best serves the communicative plan. This aspect of message planning is macroplanning.

Microplanning, in contrast, proposes how the information is expressed, which means taking perspective. If we describe a scene in which a house and a park are situated side by side, we must decide whether to say, "The park is next to the house" or "The house is next to the park." The microplan determines word choice and the grammatical roles that the words play (e.g., subject, object).

The output of the macroplanning and microplanning is a conceptual message that constitutes the input for the hypothetical *formulator*, which puts the message in a grammatically and phonologically correct form. During grammatical encoding, a message's surface structure—its syntactic but not conceptual representation, including information such as "is subject of," "is object of," the grammatically correct word order, and so on—is computed. The lowest level elements of surface structure are the lemmas. These are stored in the mental lexicon and, as introduced earlier, contain information about a word's syntactic properties (e.g., whether the word is a noun or a verb, gender information, and other grammatical features) and its semantic specifications, and/or the conceptual conditions where it is appropriate to use a certain word. Lemmas in the mental lexicon are organized in a network that links them by meaning, as you might remember from the beginning of this chapter (see Figure 10.1), which is a fragment of a lexical network.

Imagine that a subject is presented with a picture of a sheep and her task is to name the picture. Levelt's model predicts the following result: First the concept that represents sheep is activated, but concepts related to the meaning of sheep are also activated—for example, goat, wool, milk. Evidence for the idea that related concepts are activated on seeing the picture representing a word like *sheep* comes from the picture–word interference paradigm, in which subjects are asked to name pictures as fast and as accurately as they can. Soon after the

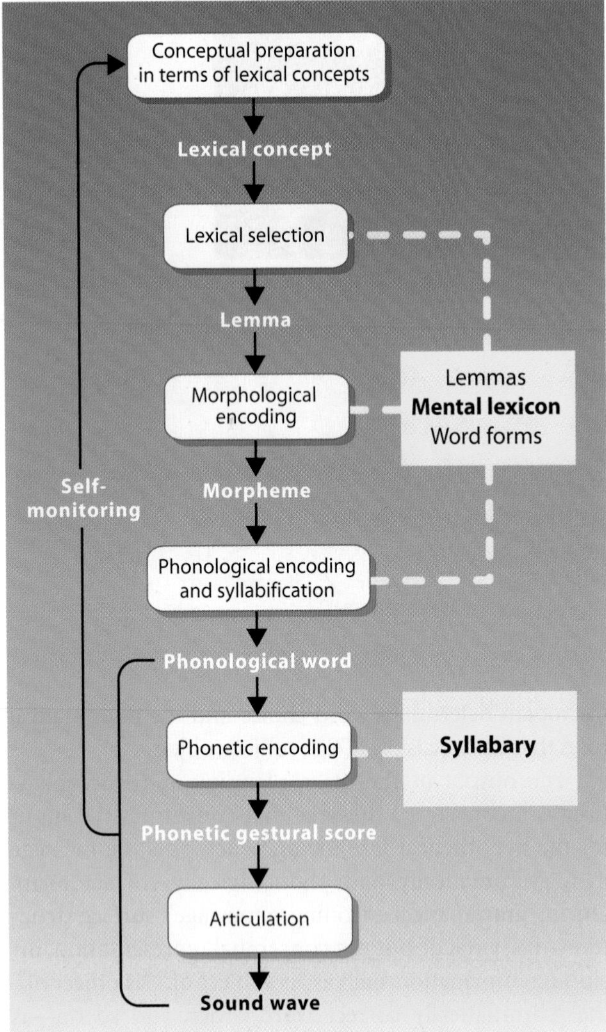

Figure 10.25 Outline of the theory of speech production developed by Willem Levelt. The processing components in language production are displayed schematically. Word production proceeds through stages of conceptual preparation, lexical selection, morphological and phonological encoding, phonetic encoding, and articulation. Speakers monitor their own speech by making use of their comprehension system.

picture is presented, an interfering auditory word is presented. The naming latency for the word *sheep* will increase if the interfering stimulus is the word *goat*, but not if the interfering stimulus is the word *house*.

Activated concepts, in turn, activate representations in the mental lexicon, starting with nodes at the lemma level to access syntactic information such as word class (in our example, *sheep* is a noun, not a verb). At this point, the lemma appropriate to the presented picture must be retrieved—a process that is called *lexical selection* in word production. The selected lemma (or the lemma that is most highly activated, in our example, *sheep*) activates the lexeme or word form. This lexeme contains both phonological information and *metrical information*, which is information about the number of syllables in the word and the stress pattern (in our example, *sheep* consists of one syllable that is stressed). The process of phonological encoding ensures that the phonological information is mapped onto the metrical information. Sometimes we cannot activate the sound form of a word; this is known as the *tip of the tongue* (*TOT*) state. You most likely have experienced a TOT state: You know a lot about the thing (i.e., a sheep) that you are trying to name, you can say that it has four legs and white curly hair, you can visualize it in your mind, you can also reject words that do not match the concept (e.g., *goat*), and if someone tells you the word's first letter (*s*), you probably say, "Oh yes, 'sheep.'"

In addition to mental blocking on a word, speech errors might happen during the transition from the lemma level to the lexeme level. Sometimes we mix up speech sounds or exchange words in a sentence. But if all goes well, the appropriate word form is selected, and phonetic and articulatory programs are matched. In the last phase of speech production, we plan our articulation: The word's syllables are mapped onto motor patterns that move the tongue, mouth, and vocal apparatus to generate the word. At this stage we can repair any errors in our speech—for example, by saying "um" and gaining more time to generate the appropriate term.

Not only do production errors happen in normal speech, but brain damage can also affect each of the processing stages. Some anomic patients (impaired in naming) are afflicted with an extreme TOT state. When asked to name a picture, often they can give a fairly accurate description but cannot name the word. Their problem is not one of articulation, because they can readily repeat the word aloud; these patients' problems are on the lexeme level. Patients with Wernicke's aphasia produce *semantic paraphasias*; they generate words related in meaning to the intended word. This problem can be one of inappropriate selection of concepts or lemmas or lexemes. Patients with Wernicke's aphasia also might make errors at the phoneme level by incorrectly substituting one sound for another. Finally, Broca's aphasia is often accompanied by dysarthria, which hinders articulation and results in effortful speech, because the muscles that articulate the utterance cannot be properly controlled.

So it appears that the distinctions made in Levelt's model with respect to the different levels in speech production are adequate, and in the literature there is general agreement on the distinctions among conceptual, syntactic, and phonological processing levels. However, the claim that the selection of the lemma of a word has to precede phonological encoding is under discussion. If this claim is correct, *only* the word form that matches the selected lemma information will become activated. According to this view, phonological information cannot influence the selection of lemma information.

In contrast to this modular view, interactive models such as the one proposed by Gary Dell (1986) at the University of Illinois suggest that phonological activation begins shortly after the semantic and syntactic information of words has been activated, and actually overlaps in time. Another big difference between modular and interactive models for speech production is that interactive models allow for feedback from the phonological activation to the semantic and syntactic properties of the word, thereby enhancing the activation of certain syntactic and semantic information.

One study by Miranda van Turennout and her colleagues (1999) at the Max Planck Institute for Psycholinguistics in the Netherlands tested whether lemma selection indeed precedes activation of the appropriate lexeme (as in Levelt's model), or whether phonological information can feed back and change the activation levels of the lemma nodes (as in Dell's model). These researchers presented subjects with pictures of animals and objects whose names started with either an [s] or a [b] sound (e.g., pictures of a sheep, bear, shoe, and book). The study was done in Dutch, where, in addition to word class, lemmas represent the syntactic gender of a word—either common or neuter. The syntactic gender determines which article to use in Dutch (so *the* has two translations from English to Dutch: *de* is used for common gender, and *het* for neuter), and it also modifies the adjectives that precede the common-gender or neuter-gender noun. In our example, *sheep* and *book* are neuter-gender words; and *bear* and *shoe* are common-gender words.

In one task (Figure 10.26), subjects were asked to press a button *only* when the picture represented a word that started with a *b*. Furthermore, they had to respond with the left hand when the picture represented a common-gender word starting with a *b* but with the right hand

Figure 10.26 Examples of stimuli used in an ERP study of word production in Dutch. Below each picture is the Dutch name for it, and the adjective meaning "red" inflected for common (*rode*) or neuter (*rood*) gender. Subjects were asked to respond only when the words representing the picture started with a *b* (go trials), and to refrain from responding when the word started with an *s* (no-go trials). On go trials, they were instructed to respond with the left hand for common-gender words and with the right hand for neuter-gender words. In addition, subjects had to respond by naming the word for all trials. See text for further explanation.

when it represented a neuter-gender word starting with a *b*. In this experimental design the decision of whether to respond was based on the phonological information at the lexeme level (initial letter *s* or *b*), and choice of response hand was based on lemma information (syntactic gender).

The researchers in this study made use of an ERP component that is sensitive to response preparation: the *lateralized readiness potential*, or *LRP*. The LRP is a brain wave recorded from the scalp over motor cortex and starts to appear when a person plans to make a movement, and hence before the actual movement is carried out. This brain potential is a sensitive measure of motor activation because even when the button ultimately is not pressed, the LRP can signal that a response was being prepared (sort of like spying on the subjects' momentary intent). Van Turennout and her colleagues found that the correct LRP (i.e., corresponding to left or right hand motor activation) started to develop even when the subjects were not supposed to respond—that is, when the picture represented a word that started with an *s* (Figure 10.27). What does this mean? The subjects must have had the lemma information available before they had access to the phonological information that could tell them not to respond. These findings therefore indicate that lemma selection might occur before the phonological information at the lexeme level is activated.

What do we know about language production in the brain? We will return to this topic later when considering the role of brain damage in language deficits. But for now, we note that imaging studies of the brain during picture naming and word generation found activation in the basal temporal regions of the left hemisphere and in the left frontal operculum (Broca's area). The activation in the frontal operculum might be specific to phonological encoding in speech production. The articulation of words likely involves the posterior parts of Broca's area (area 44), but in addition, studies showed bilateral activation of motor cortex, the supplementary motor area (SMA), and the insula. A lesion in the insula leads to **apraxia of speech** (a difficulty in pronouncing words) in patients with Broca's aphasia. In addition, cortical stimulation (which disrupts neural processing) of the basal temporal region of the left hemisphere in epileptic patients produces a temporary inability to produce words. It is clear that a widespread network of brain regions, predominantly in the left hemisphere in most people, is involved in producing speech.

Summary of Language Theories

To summarize, language processing involves representing, comprehending, and communicating symbolic information, either written or spoken. During reading and listening, the most important issues are how the meanings of words are stored in the brain and how they are accessed by visual or auditory inputs. Specializations in the brain support the analysis of language inputs and produce outputs, but the richness of linguistic capacity escapes simple analysis of language's organization. The most significant features of language are its amazingly rapid time course and vast store. Where is language hiding in the uncharted reaches of the human brain? We have reviewed some tentative answers from research in patients with brain lesions and also from imaging studies in neurologically unimpaired subjects. In the next section we will examine further which complex cortical networks may be involved in language comprehension and production.

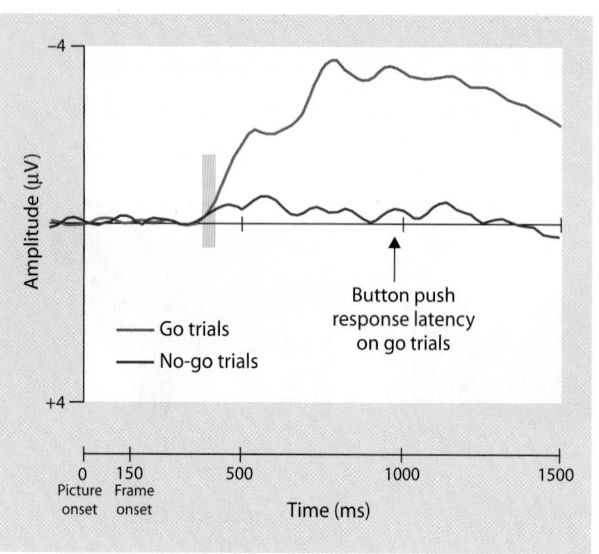

Figure 10.27 LRP response to go trials (blue line) and no-go trials (red line). The shaded area indicates the time period in which the brain's response to no-go trials is the same as to go trials. This period represents preparation of the response for no-go trials, even when no overt response is given. See text for further explanation.

NEUROPSYCHOLOGY OF LANGUAGE AND LANGUAGE DISORDERS

Investigators of brain function have struggled with the concept of localization, as we noted at the beginning of this book. The opportunity for research on relationships between brain structure and function that arises in brain-damaged or brain-diseased subjects has provided numerous insights into perception, attention, and memory, and the same holds for language. The complexity of the language system, as well as the absence of an animal model of language, however, hampers the elucidation of its structure and neural mechanisms, so the struggle to clarify the neural mechanisms of language remains one of the great scientific challenges facing cognitive neuroscience.

We are unable to describe how the detailed psycholinguistically defined functions of the language system map directly onto the brain's complex anatomical structures. However, as we saw earlier in the chapter, we do have clues to the language–brain puzzle, many coming from patients with aphasia—language problems following brain damage or disease. In this section we will begin by reviewing the contributions of aphasia research to our knowledge of language and the brain. We will start with the history of aphasia and research on language and the brain, presenting the classic models that have dominated brain and language research for more than a century.

Even though current evidence about the brain organization of language functions has gone much beyond the classic models, these models still influence modern-day thinking to a great degree, and the terms and concepts developed in the history of aphasia research are crucial to our understanding of current ideas and concepts about the representation of language in the brain. So we will take a short step back to tell the whole tale. Then, after considering classic models, we will return to ponder what the current studies of aphasia are revealing about the organization of language in the brain.

Aphasia

Brain injury can lead to language disorders called **aphasia**—a term that refers to the collective deficits in language comprehension and production that accompany neurological damage. Aphasia is extremely common. Approximately 40% of all strokes produce some aphasia, at least in the acute period during the first few months after the stroke occurred. In many patients, however, the aphasic symptoms persist, causing lasting problems in understanding or producing spoken and written language. Primary and secondary aphasic impairments are distinct. *Primary aphasia* is due to problems with the language-processing mechanisms themselves. *Secondary aphasia* results from memory impairments, attention disorders, or perceptual problems. Some investigators classify patients as aphasic only when their problems are caused by impairment to the language system (i.e., only when they exhibit primary aphasia).

History of Aphasia

The most useful way to understand classification schemes of aphasia is to review the history of the brain and language that emerged from studies of aphasic patients. Investigators in the 19th century held that localized brain lesions should lead to specific functional losses. One such person, the Frenchman Jean-Baptiste Bouillaud, collected evidence from hundreds of brain-injured patients who displayed language problems. On the basis of the side (left or right hemisphere) and position of the damage, he concluded that language resided in the frontal lobe. This line of thinking was dominant during the period when Paul Broca began his observations of language and the brain, and indeed, it was not entirely incorrect.

Broca treated a patient with a leg infection. The patient had already been hospitalized for many years, having lost speech more than 20 years earlier. Ten years before coming to Broca's clinic, the patient had lost the use of his right arm. His name was Leborgne, but other patients called him "Tan" because for many years he had been unable to utter anything but the nonsense word *tan* ("Tan tan tan, tan tan, tan tan tan . . .") and an occasional curse word. Leborgne died only a few days after being transferred to Broca's clinic.

Upon autopsy, Broca observed that the patient had a brain lesion in the posterior portion of the left inferior frontal gyrus. This region, which includes the subdivisions of the inferior frontal gyrus known as the *pars triangularis* and *pars opercularis*, is referred to as *Broca's area* (Figure 10.28). During the autopsy, only a superficial anatomical analysis was performed, and the brain was not sectioned or studied with microanatomical techniques. However, the patient's brain tissue was tested for signs of softening, a clue to damage. Broca found softening from the frontal lobe, where the lesion was noticeable on visual inspection, to the operculum, which included the most inferior portions of the precentral gyrus and adjoining regions.

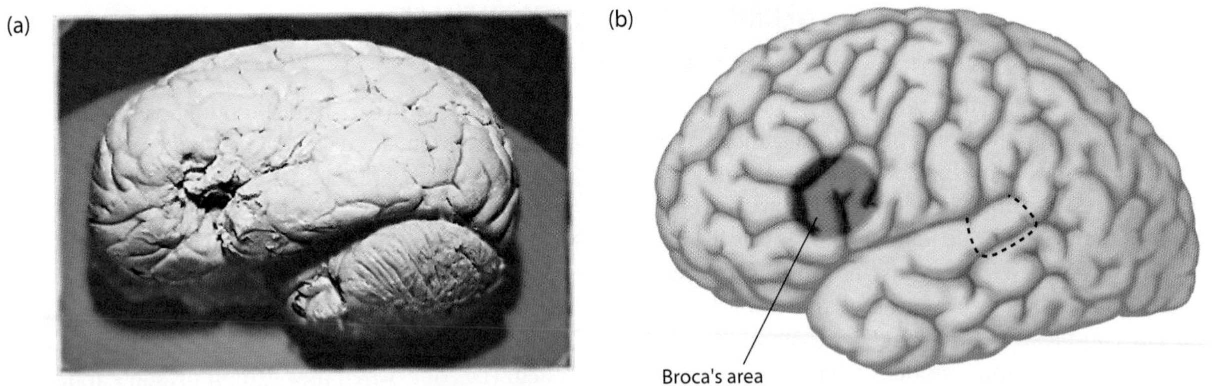

Figure 10.28 Broca's area. **(a)** The preserved brain of Leborgne (Broca's patient "Tan") which is maintained in a Paris museum. **(b)** Red shading identifies the area in the left hemisphere lesioned in Leborgne's brain and now known as *Broca's area*. The dotted lines indicate the location of Wernicke's area.

After this patient, Broca studied other patients with language deficits associated with brain damage. They generally had right hemiparesis (weakness of the right arm and leg) in conjunction with language disorders. Because these persons were right-handed, Broca concluded that brain areas that produce speech were localized in the inferior frontal lobe of the left hemisphere. This deduction was based on the fact that damage to the right hemisphere led to the most severe deficits in sensation and motor control for the left side of the body, and vice versa. Thus, if the right side is hemiparetic, the left hemisphere is damaged. If language disorders are present, they must also result from left-hemisphere damage.

A second brain region involved in language was found in posterior areas, as opposed to the frontal region described by Broca. In Germany in the 1870s, another physician, Carl Wernicke, described two patients who had problems understanding spoken language after having a stroke. Unlike the aphasics described by Broca, these patients had fluent speech but spoke nonsensical sounds, words, and sentences. Moreover, they had severe deficits in comprehending what was spoken to them. Later Wernicke performed an autopsy on one patient's brain and discovered damage in the posterior regions of the superior temporal gyrus. Since auditory processing occurs nearby (anteriorly) in the superior temporal cortex within Heschl's gyri, Wernicke deduced that this more posterior region participates in the auditory storage of words—that is, as an auditory memory area for words. This area later became known as *Wernicke's area* (Figure 10.29). According to Wernicke, damage to this area produced poor language comprehension because it had lost word-related memories, whereas nonsense speech, he posited, resulted from patients' inability to monitor their own verbal output.

Although Wernicke was not entirely correct with respect to the nature of the functional loss that he observed in language, his discovery was the second key piece of information derived from observations of language deficits following brain injury. It established the dominant view of the brain and language for almost 100 years: Damage to Broca's area of the inferolateral left frontal lobe created difficulties in producing speech (*expressive aphasia*), and damage to the posterior inferolateral left parietal and supratemporal areas (including the supramarginal gyrus, angular gyrus, and posterior regions of the superior temporal gyrus) hampered the comprehension of language (*receptive aphasia*).

Figure 10.29 Lateral view of the left hemisphere language areas and connections. Wernicke's area is shown shaded in red. The arcuate fasciculus is the bundle of axons that connects Wernicke's and Broca's areas. It originates in Wernicke's area, goes through the angular gyrus, and terminates on neurons in Broca's area (dotted circle).

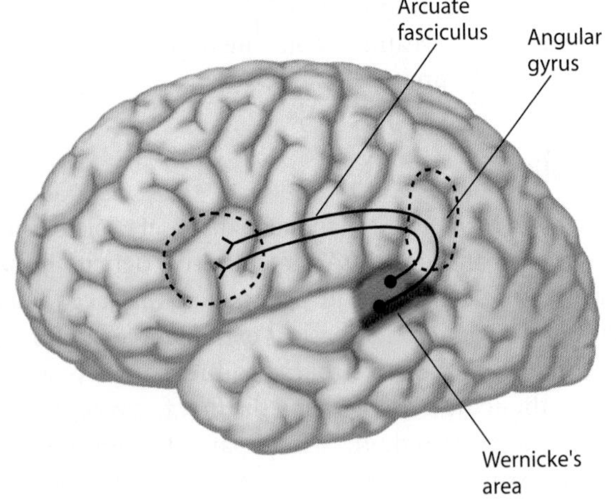

HOW THE BRAIN WORKS

Does the Right Hemisphere Understand Language?

That the left hemisphere is dominant for language processing does not mean that the right hemisphere is completely without language function or is unable to understand language. One bit of evidence that the right hemisphere has some ability to understand language comes from patients with surgically isolated hemispheres. In these split-brain patients, the fiber tracts that connect the right and the left hemisphere (the corpus callosum) have been cut to relieve severe epilepsy. In other words, the right and the left hemispheres can no longer communicate with each other at the cortical level; therefore, when visual information is presented to the left visual hemifield, it goes exclusively to the right hemisphere and vice versa, as discovered by Michael Gazzaniga and Roger Sperry in the 1960s. Such patients open the possibility to study the language capabilities of the isolated right hemisphere because there can be no transfer of information from the perceptual areas of the right hemisphere to the language areas in the left.

Split-brain patients with a disconnected right hemisphere can make simple semantic judgments and can read material presented to the right hemisphere. However, only grammatically simple sentences can be managed well by the isolated right hemisphere; thus, such patients can misunderstand sentences like "The boy that was hit by the girl cried."

Other evidence for the right hemisphere's role in linguistic processing comes from patients with lesions in the right hemisphere. Although these patients are generally nonaphasic, they do have subtle language deficits. Peter Hagoort and his colleagues (1996) found that patients with right-hemisphere lesions have normal priming effects for words that are associatively related (e.g., *cottage cheese*). In contrast, these patients do not show priming effects for words that are not associatively related but are from the same semantic category (e.g., *dog* and *horse*). These findings could mean that the left hemisphere is not very good at processing distant semantic relations but that the right hemisphere is—an idea supported by experimental research in healthy subjects. Christine Chiarello (1991) found a left-visual-field/right-hemisphere advantage for the processing of words that come from the same semantic category but that have no associative relation—for example, *dog* and *horse*. In short, the right hemisphere does have language abilities that might play an important role in the processing of meaning.

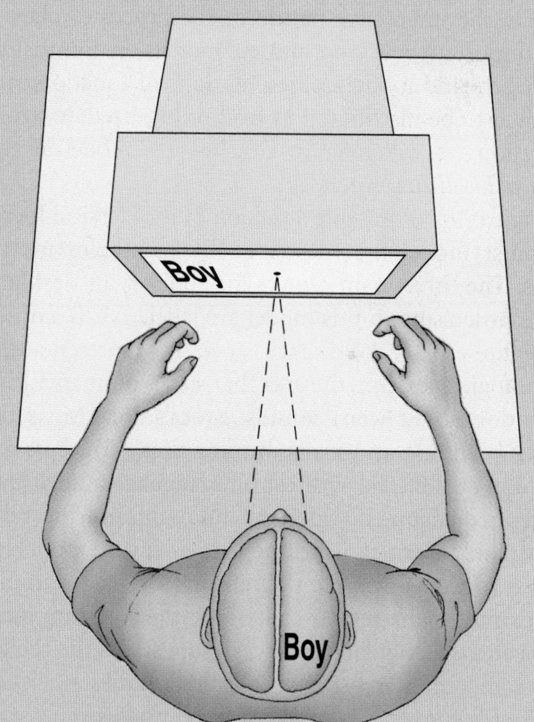

Stimuli entering the left visual field are transmitted to the right hemisphere. In split-brain patients, the absence of the corpus callosum means that the information (in this case the word *Boy*) cannot reach the language-dominant left hemisphere. Thus, such individuals offer the opportunity for investigation into the language capacity of the right hemisphere.

During Broca's time, most emphasis was on word-level analysis; hence, little consideration was given to processing losses at the sentence level. This focus was reflected in the prevailing view of language, in which word memory was taken to be the key: Broca's area was considered the locus of motor memory for words; Wernicke's area was the region concerned with the sensory memory for words. These ideas led to a view of language in which three brain centers interacted as the foundations of language: a production area, a comprehension area, and a conceptual area.

EARLY MODEL OF LANGUAGE ORGANIZATION

Wernicke, Broca, and their contemporaries fueled the idea that language was localized in structures interconnected anatomically to create the brain's total language system. Sometimes referred to as the *classical localizationist model* or the *connectionist model of language*, this idea dominated through the 1970s after being revived in the 1960s by the American neuropsychologist Norman Geschwind (1967). Note that the "connectionist" model of Geschwind is not the same as the interactive or connectionist models that were developed later by researchers such as McClelland and Rumelhart, and implemented in computer simulations. In the latter models, the interactive nature of the processes plays a very important role, and in these models, in contrast to the Geschwind model, representations of functions are assumed to be distributed instead of localized; to avoid confusion we will refer to Geschwind's model as the *classical localizationist model.*

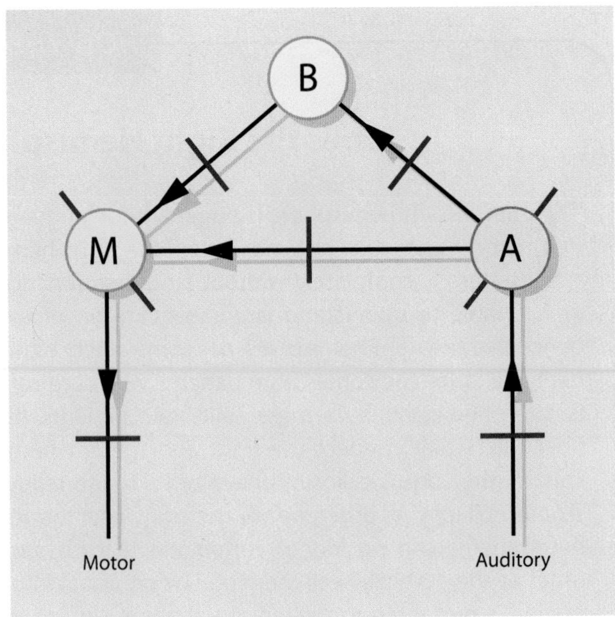

Figure 10.30 Lichtheim's classic model of language processing. The area that stores permanent information about word sounds is represented by A. The speech planning and programming area is represented by M. Conceptual information is stored in area B. The arrows indicate the direction of information flow. This model formed the basis of predictions that lesions in the three main areas, or in the connections between the areas, or the inputs to or outputs from these areas, could account for seven main aphasic syndromes. The locations of possible lesions are indicated by the line segments transecting the connections between A, B, and M.

Figure 10.30 presents a version of the classical localizationist model first described by Lichtheim in the 1880s. The three main centers for auditory or oral language processing in this model are labeled A, B, and M in Figure 10.30. Wernicke's area, A, represents the phonological lexicon, the area that stores permanent information about word sounds. Broca's area, M, is the speech planning and programming area. Concepts are stored in area B. The 19th-century language models had concepts distributed widely in the brain, but the relatively newer Wernicke–Lichtheim–Geschwind model localized concepts in more discrete areas. As an example, in this model the region containing the supramarginal gyrus and the angular gyrus was proposed as the region where incoming sensory properties (auditory, visual, and tactile) or features of words were processed.

This classical localizationist model of language represents linguistic information as being localized to discrete brain regions interconnected by white matter tracts. Language processing was thought to activate these linguistic representations and involve their transfer between language areas. The idea is simple. According to the classical localizationist model, in auditory language the flow of information is as follows: Auditory inputs are transduced in the auditory sensory system, which then passes the information to the parieto-temporo-occipital association cortex (centered on the angular gyrus), and then to Wernicke's area, where representations of words can be accessed from phonological information. From Wernicke's area, information flows through the arcuate fasciculus (a white matter tract) to Broca's area, where the grammatical properties are stored and phrase structure can be assigned. Word representations, in turn, activate related concepts in the concept centers, and voilà, auditory comprehension occurs. In speech production, a similar process occurs, except concepts activated in the concept areas generate phonological representations of words in Wernicke's area and then are sent to Broca's area to program motor actions for speech articulation.

In Figure 10.30, lines connecting areas A, B, and M are transected. These lines represent white matter fibers in the brain that interconnect Wernicke's area, Broca's area, and the conceptual centers; lesions of these fibers, hypothetically, would disconnect the areas. Lesions in centers A, B, and M themselves would reflect damage to specific language areas. Thus, if the Wernicke–Lichtheim–Geschwind model were correct, we would expect forms of language deficits from brain damage that had symptoms and signs corresponding to the ones predicted by the model. Indeed, various aphasias correspond to what would be predicted by the model, so the model was actually pretty good.

Lichtheim reported cases of the aphasias predicted by the model in pure form, but it remains unclear how distinct they really were. Some extant data support the basic tenets of the Wernicke–Lichtheim–Geschwind model, yet the model still has significant shortcomings. For one thing, prior to the advent of neuroimaging with computed tomography (CT) and magnetic resonance imaging (MRI), lesion localization was poor and relied on sometimes inaccessible autopsy information, or guesses based on the co-occurrence of other, better defined symptoms (e.g., hemiparesis). Second, the way lesions are defined in autopsy studies (as well as in neuroimaging data) varies greatly. Third, the lesions themselves vary greatly; as an example, sometimes anterior brain lesions produce Wernicke's aphasia! Finally, when classified, patients often fall into more than one diagnostic category. Broca's aphasia has several components, for instance. In light of all this, it is worth reviewing the major aphasic syndromes and considering the interpretational difficulties in the literature on brain and language. The goal is to provide insights to aphasic syndromes and their relation to brain structures in classical models and modern ones. Before reviewing the syndromes, though, we should briefly consider how aphasia is diagnosed and classified in the clinic.

Classification of Aphasia

Speech pathologists and aphasiologists have elaborate criteria for diagnosing and characterizing language disorders such as aphasia. Diagnostic classifications might exclude neuropathologies that may be treatable or require special management, care, and rehabilitation of aphasic patients. The schemes also vary in their ability to distinguish language deficits. This variability is partly because a brain lesion in one patient rarely, if ever, has the same pattern as that in another patient. Nonetheless, the classification of aphasic patients into subtypes is successful, given its goal clinically. The three main test parameters for language disorders are spontaneous speech, auditory comprehension, and verbal repetition (see Figure 10.31). The patients' performance permits a trained clinician to classify aphasics into general groups.

CLASSIFYING BROCA'S APHASIA

Broca's aphasia is the oldest and perhaps best-studied form of aphasia. Characterized by speech difficulties, it includes a wide range of symptoms (Figure 10.31). In the most severe forms of Broca's aphasia, single-utterance patterns of speech such as that of Broca's original patient are often observed (Figure 10.31a). But the variability is large and may include unintelligible mutterings, single syllables or words ("tan," "yes," "no"), short simple phrases or sentences that mostly lack function words or grammatical markers, or idioms such as "Fit as a fiddle and ready for love." Sometimes the ability to sing normally is undisturbed, as might be the ability to recite phrases and prose, or to count.

Figure 10.31 Speech problems in Broca's aphasia. Broca's aphasics can have various problems when they speak or when they try to comprehend or repeat the linguistic input provided by the clinician (here, the woman at left). **(a)** The speech output of this patient is slow and effortful, and it lacks function words: It resembles a telegram. **(b)** Broca's aphasics also may have problems with speech articulation because of deficits in regulation of the articulatory apparatus (e.g., muscles of the tongue). **(c)** Finally, these patients sometimes have a hard time understanding reversible sentences, where a full understanding of the sentence depends on correct syntactic assignment of the thematic roles (e.g., who hit whom?).

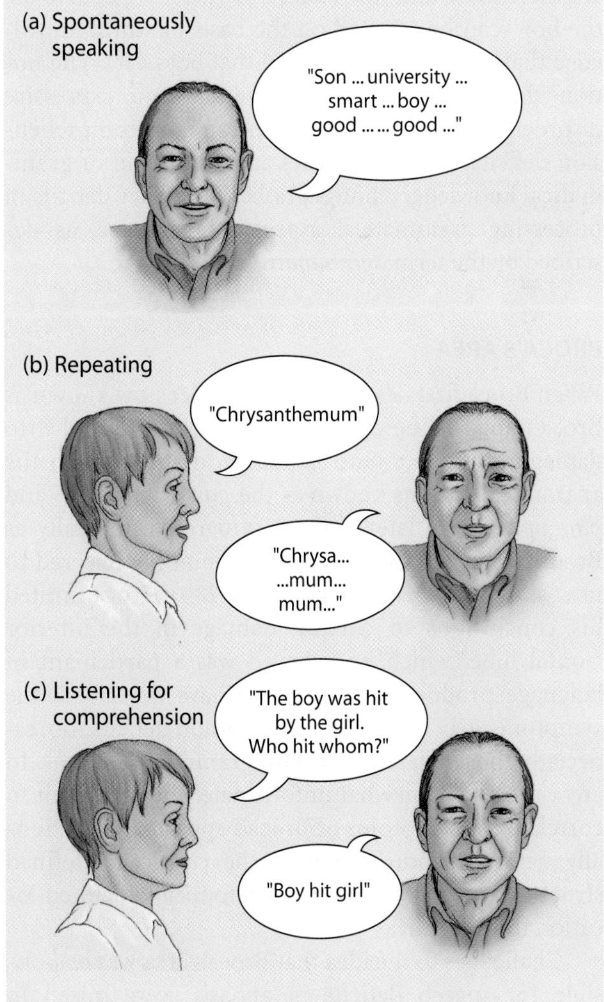

The speech of Broca's aphasics is often telegraphic and very effortful, coming in uneven bursts. The ability to find the appropriate word or combination of words and to execute pronunciation is compromised in Broca's aphasics. Some problems are derived from speech deficits such as dysarthria (loss of control over articulatory muscles; Figure 10.31b) and speech apraxia (deficits in the ability to program articulations).

The extent to which Broca's aphasia is limited to language production, especially spoken language, depends on whether any comprehension deficits are also present. These deficits are easiest to observe when the meaning of a sentence requires precise interpretation of its grammatical structure and cannot be derived simply from the sentence's individual words. Consider the following examples: "The boy ate the cookie" and "The boy was hit by the girl" (Figure 10.31c). The second sentence is more complex and could be misunderstood by the listener, except that grammatical rules determine who kicked whom; such rules are not needed for the aphasic to understand in the first example that the boy ate the cookie and not vice versa (i.e., "the cookie ate the boy" can be rejected on the basis of world knowledge that cookies are eaten and that boys eat). The notion that Broca's aphasics have only an expressive disorder is not correct; they also can have comprehension deficits. Broca's aphasics are not devoid of grammatical knowledge, though; rather, they have deficits in processing grammatical aspects of language, as described by the term *agrammatism.*

BROCA'S AREA

When Broca first described the disorder now known as Broca's aphasia, he called it *aphemia* and related it to damage in the left ventrolateral frontal cortex, in the anatomical regions known as the *pars triangularis* and *pars opercularis,* later defined cytoarchitectonically as Brodmann areas 44 and 45 and commonly referred to now as *Broca's area* (see Figure 10.28b). Broca limited his conclusions to cortical damage in the inferior frontal lobe, which he believed was a participant in language production, but as we have described, the symptoms may include comprehension deficits too, especially those related to certain grammatical forms. In any case, and somewhat unfortunately, it is difficult to correlate the symptoms of Broca's aphasia (a functionally defined syndrome) with the classically defined structures in Broca's area (an anatomically defined location in the brain).

Challenges to the idea that Broca's area was responsible for speech deficits in aphasia were raised in Broca's time. Some reports noted damage to Broca's area without deficits in speech; others noted speech deficits when damage was limited to more posterior brain regions, outside Broca's area. Researchers continue to question the relation between Broca's area and Broca's aphasia. For example, aphasiologist Nina Dronkers (1996) at the University of California, Davis, reported 22 patients with lesions in Broca's area, as defined by neuroimaging, but only 10 of these patients had Broca's aphasia.

The regions classically defined as Broca's area are generally limited to the gray matter in the ventrolateral frontal cortex of the left hemisphere. Broca did not consider the underlying white matter, deep cortex, and subcortical structures as potential contributors to the syndrome he observed. By the start of the 20th century, however, scientists were proposing that structures deep to Broca's area were involved in the deficits of Broca's aphasia. Brain areas including the insular cortex, the lenticular nucleus of the basal ganglia, and fibers of passage have been implicated in Broca's aphasia. Research by Dronkers (1996) found that all patients with Broca's aphasia and apraxia of speech (difficulty in the pronunciation of words), including those studied by autopsy or neuroimaging, have damage in the insula.

This was the case even for Broca's original patient. His brain is now housed in a French museum, and recent CT scans showed that his lesions extended into regions underlying the superficial cortical zone of Broca's area, and thus included the insular cortex and portions of the basal ganglia. Damage to the classic regions of the frontal cortex known as *Broca's area* is not, therefore, solely responsible for the deficits of Broca's aphasics.

CLASSIFYING WERNICKE'S APHASIA

Wernicke's aphasia is primarily a disorder of language comprehension. Patients with this syndrome have problems understanding spoken or written language, and sometimes they cannot understand at all. They are cut off from communication with others by their comprehension problems, and they cannot speak meaningful sentences. Wernicke's patients can produce fluent-sounding speech, in contrast to the broken speech patterns of Broca's aphasics, but the speech is meaningless. To provide insight to what it means for a person to be fluent and to have Wernicke's aphasia, imagine you are listening to someone speaking a language you do not know. You would probably not detect any deficits. And as might be expected, the speech sounds fine but is composed of meaningless strings of words, sounds, and jargon. Figure 10.32 shows the speech of two patients with

Figure 10.32 Wernicke's aphasics can speak fluently. If one is not a native speaker of a language, one might not detect that there is anything wrong with the speech of a patient with Wernicke's aphasia. For example, to most people in the United States, the message in Dutch in **(b)** might sound perfectly normal (unless you speak Dutch) because it flows smoothly. However, as the English translation in **(a)** indicates, the speech output of Wernicke's aphasics is often meaningless. They also make semantic errors. For example, they might say "television" for *telephone*. Sometimes these patients produce utterances that do not exist in their language (jargon), as is the case with "romer" in both of these examples.

Wernicke's aphasia—one in English and the other in Dutch. Unless you speak Dutch, it is unlikely that you can discriminate this passage from that of normal Dutch prose.

WERNICKE'S AREA

The syndrome known as *Wernicke's aphasia* was first related to what is now called *Wernicke's area* in classic studies of the 19th century. Wernicke's area includes the posterior third of the superior temporal gyrus. However, language comprehension deficits also arise from damage to the junction between the parietal and temporal lobes, including the supramarginal and angular gyri. How well do language comprehension deficits relate to Wernicke's area, and how much can be attributed to damage in the surrounding cortex and white matter?

As with Broca's aphasia and Broca's area, sometimes lesions that spare Wernicke's area still lead to comprehension deficits. In one study of 70 patients with Wernicke's aphasia, 7 had damage confined to regions outside of Wernicke's area. In contrast, some patients who have Wernicke's aphasia with damage in Wernicke's area may be able to comprehend more as their aphasia improves over time, leaving a milder aphasia or even only an anomic syndrome (see "How the Brain Works: The Man Without Nouns," on p. 430).

Recent studies support this picture. Dense and persistent Wernicke's aphasia is ensured only if there is damage in Wernicke's area and in the surrounding cortex of the posterior temporal lobe, or damage to the underlying white matter that connects temporal lobe language areas to other brain regions. Thus, Wernicke's area remains in the center of a posterior region of the brain whose functioning is required for normal comprehension. Lesions confined to Wernicke's area lead to only temporary Wernicke's aphasia because the damage to this area does not actually cause the syndrome; instead, secondary damage due to tissue swelling contributes to the most severe problems. When swelling around the lesioned cortex goes away, comprehension improves. Some researchers, such as Dronkers, have suggested that the white matter underlying Wernicke's area may hold the key. Cortical damage that temporarily compromises white matter tracts below the cortex may explain much of the "here and gone again" characteristics of Wernicke's aphasia. More functional analyses are clearly needed.

Damage to Connections Between Language Areas

In describing the Wernicke–Lichtheim–Geschwind model, we alluded to strong links between anterior and posterior regions of the brain involved in speech production and comprehension, respectively. In the context of the model, as presented in Figure 10.30, systematic syndromes were implied to result from damage to these white matter tracts. Wernicke predicted that a certain type of aphasia should result from damage to fibers projecting from Wernicke's to Broca's areas. Indeed, a disconnection syndrome, now known as **conduction aphasia**, can occur when the **arcuate fasciculus**, the pathway from Wernicke's to Broca's area, is damaged (see Figure 10.29).

Conduction aphasics have problems producing spontaneous speech as well as repeating speech, and sometimes they use words incorrectly. They can understand words that they hear or see and can hear their own speech errors, but they cannot repair them. Hence, conduction aphasia arises from damage to connections between posterior and anterior language areas. But similar symptoms are evident with lesions to the insula and

HOW THE BRAIN WORKS

The Man Without Nouns

Damage to Wernicke's area or surrounding cortex can sometimes produce a disorder called *anomia*, the inability to name things in the world. Patients with anomia have difficulty finding the words that label objects. This disorder can be strikingly discrete; the language deficit is limited to the inability to name objects, but comprehension is intact and speech is unaffected. One such patient is H.W., an intelligent businessman who headed his own company. He was studied by cognitive neuroscientist Kathleen Baynes of the University of California, Davis. After suffering a stroke in his left hemisphere, H.W. was left with anomia and almost no other deficits of note except a slight right-side hemiparesis (which was actually quite minor; he was a physically robust individual) and a slight deficit in face recognition. But his anomia was extraordinary. Here is a passage of H.W.'s speech as he described the contents of a picture of a boy falling off a stool while reaching for cookies in a jar on the shelf and handing one to his sister:

> First of all this is falling down, just about, and is gonna fall down and they're both getting something to eat . . . but the trouble is this is gonna let go and they're both gonna fall down . . . I can't see well enough but I believe that either she will have some food that's not good for you and she's to get some for her, too . . . and that you get it there because they shouldn't go up there and get it unless you tell them that they could have it. And so this is falling down and for sure there's one they're going to have for food and, and this didn't come out right, the, uh, the stuff that's uh, good for, it's not good for you but it, but you love, um mum mum [H.W. intentionally smacks lips] . . . and so they've . . . see that, I can't see whether it's in there or not . . . I think she's saying, I want two or three, I want one, I think, I think so, and so, so she's gonna get this one for sure it's gonna fall down there or whatever, she's gonna get that one and, and there, he's gonna get one himself or more, it all depends with this when they fall down . . . and when it falls down there's no problem, all they got to do is fix it and go right back up and get some more.

H.W. was able to describe aspects of the scene, but without the ability to say nouns the information was minimal. Nonetheless, H.W. used proper grammatical structures, such as noun phrases; they simply lacked a noun. For example, H.W. would say "this" instead of "the chair." He substituted generic nouns such as "food" for "cookie" although he knew it was a cookie, that it tasted good, and that adults consider this food bad for children. The location of his lesion is enlightening and disappointing: He had a large left-hemisphere lesion that included large regions of the posterior language areas. Yet his functional deficit was discrete: He had no nouns.

Picture similar to that shown to H.W. by cognitive neuroscientist Kathleen Baynes.

portions of the auditory cortex. One explanation for this similarity may be that damage to other nerve fibers is not detected, or that connections between Wernicke's area and Broca's area are not as strong as connections between the more widely spread anterior and posterior language areas. Indeed, the emphasis should not really be on Broca's and Wernicke's areas but on the brain regions better correlated with the syndromes of Broca's aphasia and Wernicke's aphasia. Considered in this way, a lesion to the area surrounding the insula could disconnect comprehension from production areas.

The Wernicke–Lichtheim–Geschwind model also predicted that damage to the connections between conceptual representation areas (area B in Figure 10.30, perhaps in the supramarginal and angular gyri) and Wernicke's area would harm the ability to comprehend spoken inputs but not the ability to repeat what was heard (*transcortical sensory aphasia*). Indeed, patients with lesions in the supramarginal and angular gyri regions display such problems. Further, they have the unique ability to repeat what they heard and to correct grammatical errors in what they heard when they repeat it. These findings have been interpreted as evidence that this aphasia may come from losing the ability to access semantic information without losing syntactic or phonological abilities.

The picture that emerges from these classifications of major aphasic syndromes is not unlike the one that was put forward by the classical Wernicke–Lichtheim–Geschwind model. As we have seen, however, studies in patients with specific aphasic syndromes have revealed the classical model's assumption that only Broca's and Wernicke's areas are associated with Broca's aphasia and Wernicke's aphasia, respectively, is most likely incorrect. Part of the problem is that the original lesion localizations were not very sophisticated. But another part of the problem lies in the classification of the syndromes themselves, because Broca's and Wernicke's aphasias are associated with a conglomerate of symptoms that together constitute each syndrome. As we now know, Broca's aphasics, for example, may have apraxia of speech and agrammatic comprehension. From our discussion of psycholinguistic models of normal language comprehension and production, it should be clear that these are very different linguistic processes, and it is not at all surprising that this variety of language functions is supported by more than Broca's area alone.

Mechanisms of Aphasic Deficits

We have reviewed numerous language deficits associated with major classes of aphasia and implied that these represent problems in the underlying language systems of the brain. But what form would these problems take? Are aphasic deficits the result of selective losses of parts of the language system, like damage isolated to the second gear in an automobile transmission while the other gears are intact? Or is the problem in aphasia more like losing the ability to use the linguistic information properly, like having a perfectly good set of gears but a burned-out clutch?

These questions reflect a pivotal issue in aphasia research: Do comprehension deficits in aphasic patients result from losses of stored linguistic information (e.g., words in the mental lexicon), or from disruption of the computational language processes that act on representations of the linguistic inputs? Aphasic deficits have classically been attributed to losses of semantic or syntactic knowledge structures. In recent years, however, many deficits in aphasia have been attributed to processing impairments rather than to true losses of knowledge. Two results are central to this change in perspective.

Broca's aphasics with severe problems in syntactic understanding were tested in a sentence–picture matching task. Often they were unable to point to a picture that matched the meaning of the sentence they had to read, especially when more complex sentence constructions were used. For example, Broca's aphasics might not understand who is kicking whom in the sentence "The boy was kicked by the girl." If they have to choose from two pictures—one in which a girl is kicking a boy and one in which a boy is kicking a girl—they often select the wrong picture. But in one seminal study (Linebarger et al., 1983), Broca's aphasics who were impaired in their ability to match pictures to reversible sentences, as in the preceding example, performed considerably above chance when they had to distinguish syntactically well-formed sentences from incorrect ones in a grammar judgment task, even when they had to cope with numerous syntactic structures.

The task that one uses, then, directly influences the aphasic patient's performance. Moreover, sometimes Broca's aphasics also can access and exploit structural knowledge. Variable performance across linguistic tasks supports the notion that agrammatic comprehension results from a processing deficit rather than a representational deficit; patients still have syntactic knowledge, but sometimes they cannot use it while at other times they can.

The classic notion of loss of semantic knowledge in Wernicke's aphasics also has been challenged by experiments in which aphasic patients were required to make speedy decisions about target words. In this lexical decision task, aphasics had to decide as quickly as possible whether a letter string or a sound sequence was a word. Neurologically normal persons made faster lexical decisions on words primed by a semantically or associatively related word than when preceding words were unrelated. Wernicke's aphasics consistently displayed the normal pattern of priming for semantically or associatively related word pairs in this task. They showed this effect even though they demonstrated severe impairment when asked to make judgments on word meaning. Thus, despite problems in comprehension, when lexical-semantic processing is tested in an implicit test (such as in the lexical decision task), patients do not show impairment. This finding suggests that, although lexical-semantic knowledge might be preserved, aphasics sometimes cannot access or exploit it to achieve normal comprehension. How might this work?

An alternative to the idea that linguistic information is lost is the idea that real-time mental processes that act on linguistic information might be compromised in aphasia. One view is that these patients' brains cannot keep up with the time challenges of language comprehension or production, because the processes of accessing and exploiting stored linguistic information no longer operate at normal speeds. Consider the following analogy: A soccer player kicks the ball to a teammate who is charging the goal. In the nick of time, with perfect coordination, the teammate receives the ball and, with a punishing kick, sends it past the goalkeeper for a score! In this normal situation all players are on the field and are healthy, and their interactions are temporally coordinated in a fast-paced setting.

What would happen if no player were charging toward the goal to receive and relay the ball into the net? No goal, of course! This situation would be analogous to the case in which stored linguistic information in the brain is actually lost owing to aphasia and therefore could not be used in the service of language comprehension and production. But consider another situation, in which the player receiving the ball is merely injured and slow, making it hard to manage the pass from the teammate and leading to the ball being lost and, therefore, no goal. In both situations the outcome is the same—no goal—but the underlying causes for the failure are very different. In the first situation a player is absent; in the second, the player is still on the field, still knows what to do, and can still receive passes and kick the ball, but simply cannot do so with the facility necessary to compete in a rapidly moving soccer match. Language processing is also a rapidly moving game, and deficits that undermine normal real-time processing could lead to aphasia. We can refer to this general idea as the *processing-impairment model* of comprehension deficits in aphasia.

A central question about the processing-impairment model of comprehension deficits in aphasics is this: When is the impairment manifested during language processing? Two suggestions have been put forward: One is that the dynamics of lexical access are affected in aphasic comprehenders; an alternative proposal is that automatic lexical access might be largely intact but problems arise later, during lexical integration.

The claim for impaired lexical access has been derived, for example, from word-priming experiments. Some studies found that Broca's aphasics lack semantic priming in lexical decision tasks, even though normal control subjects and Wernicke's aphasics show faster reaction times to words related to the prime. Yet support for this claim is not decisive, for two reasons: First, in other semantic priming studies, Broca's aphasics actually demonstrated an effect of semantic priming. Second, to make claims about automatic access, the time between the onset of the priming word and that of the target (stimulus onset asynchrony, or SOA) should be short (approximately 200 ms). In normal subjects, semantic priming at long SOAs does not result only from automatic lexical activation but may involve other postlexical processes. In line with this idea, studies using long SOAs between prime and target words in aphasics failed to find priming, whereas those using shorter SOAs revealed semantic priming.

What emerges is more compatible with the idea that lexical integration rather than lexical access is impaired in these patients. The patients have difficulty integrating the meaning of words into the current context established by the preceding words in the sentence; that is, they cannot use the contextual information to select the appropriate meaning of a word quickly enough for normal comprehension. Thus, in the sentence "The man planted a tree on the bank," under normal conditions the context tells us that *bank* refers to the "side of a river" and not a "monetary institution." One can readily appreciate the comprehension problems that would ensue if such processes were disrupted as with aphasia (see "The Cognitive Neuroscientist's Toolkit: Aphasia and Electrophysiology," on p. 441).

NEUROPHYSIOLOGY OF LANGUAGE

The neuropsychological lesion approach epitomized by research on aphasia and other language disorders represents only one way to investigate the biological bases of language. In this section we briefly review some additional evidence from neurophysiological studies of language, including functional neuroimaging, studies involving stimulation of the human cortex during neurosurgical procedures, and recordings of language-related brain potentials (i.e., ERPs) from healthy and aphasic persons. These approaches yield information about the normal language system that may not be obvious from observations of the performance of damaged brains alone. Further, the neurophysiological approach can provide measures of brain activity and functional processing in persons with language disorders that are not possible to infer from behavior or anatomical imaging alone.

Functional Neuroimaging of Language

As we have reviewed throughout the chapter, PET and fMRI can be used to identify areas in the brain that are active during specific psycholinguistic processes, or to identify linguistic and conceptual representations in normal, neurologically unimpaired volunteers. But these methods also can be used passively to investigate the metabolic correlates of language disorders such as Broca's aphasia during rest. The goal is to identify the extent of the functional lesion beyond the structural lesion on which most neuropsychological investigation is based. Anterograde and retrograde degeneration of neurons occurs when part of the neuron is damaged, and transneuronal degeneration for neurons projecting to or receiving inputs from the lesioned region may also occur. As a result, sites interconnected with a lesioned area also may be affected adversely, and these effects cannot be seen if we use structural imaging with CT or MRI, because they may manifest only as regions of lowered metabolism.

The ^{18}F-deoxyglucose PET method measures neuronal metabolism by using radioactively labeled glucose analogues that are taken up by active cells and trapped within them. The radioactivity can then be imaged with a PET scanner. The advantage of this technique is that we can learn about the functional consequences of lesions that extend beyond the structurally damaged region.

METABOLIC CORRELATES OF APHASIA

Research on resting brain metabolism has revealed a complex picture of the effects of aphasia. Focal brain lesions from stroke can lead to widespread changes in metabolism; that is, the effects of stroke extend to regions outside the lesioned areas (Figure 10.33). Remote metabolic changes typically are observed in stroke victims who have observable symptoms, but not when they do not show neurological symptoms.

In 100% of the aphasic patients studied, PET measures obtained during a resting state revealed hypometabolism (lower glucose utilization) in the temporoparietal region, regardless of the type of aphasia. Of these patients, 97% had metabolic changes in the angular gyrus and 89% had such changes in the supramarginal gyrus; 87% showed hypometabolism in the superior temporal gyrus. These PET-defined hypometabolic regions were then compared to the anatomically defined lesions. Such comparisons showed that 67% of the patients had parietal lesions, 67% had damage in Wernicke's area, and 58% had damage in the posterior middle temporal region. Even when the anatomically defined damage did not include the supramarginal and angular gyri, these brain areas had reduced neuronal metabolism during a resting state. The lesson here is that correlating the behavioral

Figure 10.33 Measuring the extent of neural dysfunction caused by a stroke. **(a)** Diagram of lesions and **(b)** PET scan showing regions of lowered metabolism in the brain of a stroke patient. The regions showing decreased metabolic activity include those that were damaged by the stroke and have cell loss. The regions connected to the damaged areas experience changes in activity and, hence, possible function, but are not themselves damaged by the stroke. These areas can be thought of as functionally lesioned and may contribute to deficits seen in the patients, thereby making it difficult to infer a structure–function correlation from CT or structural MRI scans, which reveal only the areas of physical damage.

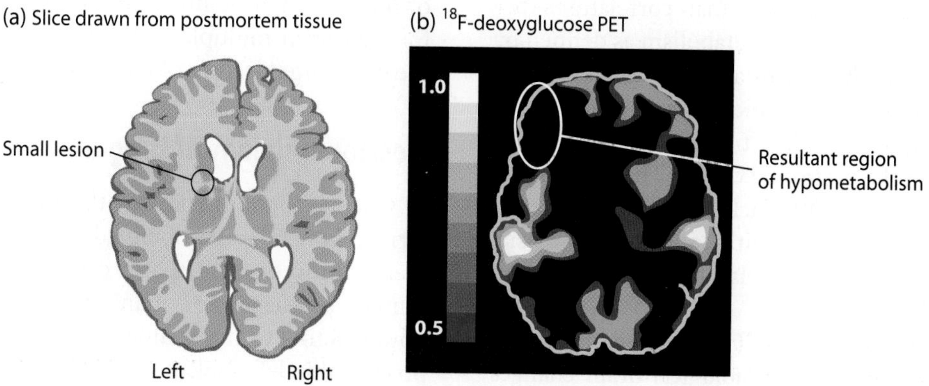

THE COGNITIVE NEUROSCIENTIST'S TOOLKIT

Stimulation Mapping of the Human Brain

The scene is out of a Walt Disney or Steven Spielberg film. A young man lies on a table covered with clean, light-green sheets. He is lying on his side and is awake. His head is partially covered by a sheet of cloth, so we can see his face if we wish. On the other side of the cloth is a woman wearing a surgical gown and mask. The man is a patient; the woman is his surgeon. His skull has been cut through, and his left hemisphere is exposed. Yes, he is awake; no, this is not another time or another place. This is here and now at the University of Washington Medical School, where George Ojemann and his colleagues (1989) have been using direct cortical stimulation and recording methods to map the brain's language areas.

The patient suffers from epilepsy and is about to undergo a surgical procedure to remove the epileptic tissue. But first, because this epileptic focus is in the left, language-dominant hemisphere, it is essential to determine where language processes are localized in the patient's brain. Such localization can be done by electrical stimulation mapping. Electrodes are used to pass a small electrical current through the cortex, momentarily disrupting activity; thus, electrical stimulation can probe where a language process is localized. The patient has to be awake for this test. Language-related areas vary among patients, so these areas must be mapped carefully. During surgery, it is essential to leave the critical language areas intact.

One benefit of this work is that we can learn more about the organization of the human language system. Patients are shown line drawings of everyday objects and are asked to name those objects. During naming, regions of the left perisylvian cortex are stimulated with low amounts of electricity. When the patient makes an error in naming or is unable to name the object, the deficit is correlated with the region being stimulated during that trial, so that area of cortex is assumed to be critical for language production and comprehension.

Stimulation of between 100 and 200 patients revealed that aspects of language representation in the brain are organized in mosaic-like areas of 1 to 2 cm^2. These mosaics usually include regions in the frontal cortex and posterior temporal cortex. In some patients, however, only frontal or posterior temporal areas were observed. The correlation between these effects in either Broca's area or Wernicke's area was weak; some patients had naming disruption in the classic areas, and others did not. Perhaps the single most intriguing fact is how much the anatomical localizations vary across patients, a point that has implications for how across-subject averaging methods, such as PET activation studies, reveal significant effects.

deficits in aphasia with only the visible anatomical lesions may not provide a complete picture and may even lead to confusion.

Some researchers maintain that correlations between aphasic symptoms and metabolism as defined by PET are better than those with anatomical lesion data. Broca's aphasics with anatomical damage to Broca's area and perhaps surrounding tissue show marked hypometabolism in the prefrontal cortex. This effect is reduced in patients with Wernicke's aphasia and even further diminished in those with conduction aphasia, but half of these patients display hypometabolism in Broca's areas.

Anatomically defined correlates of aphasia, therefore, may not capture the physiological brain changes that accompany the aphasic syndrome. These findings remind us of the shortcomings of the anatomical correlation method for determining the functional anatomy of human language function. One certainty is the need for data from multiple methods in trying to pin down the brain organization of language.

Electrophysiology of Language

In Chapter 4 we introduced the ERP method and described how ERPs are obtained for different stimuli and mental processes. ERPs also can be used to investigate human language. For many reasons, they provide a powerful tool to study language comprehension. To appreciate this, let's look at some brain waves or ERP com-

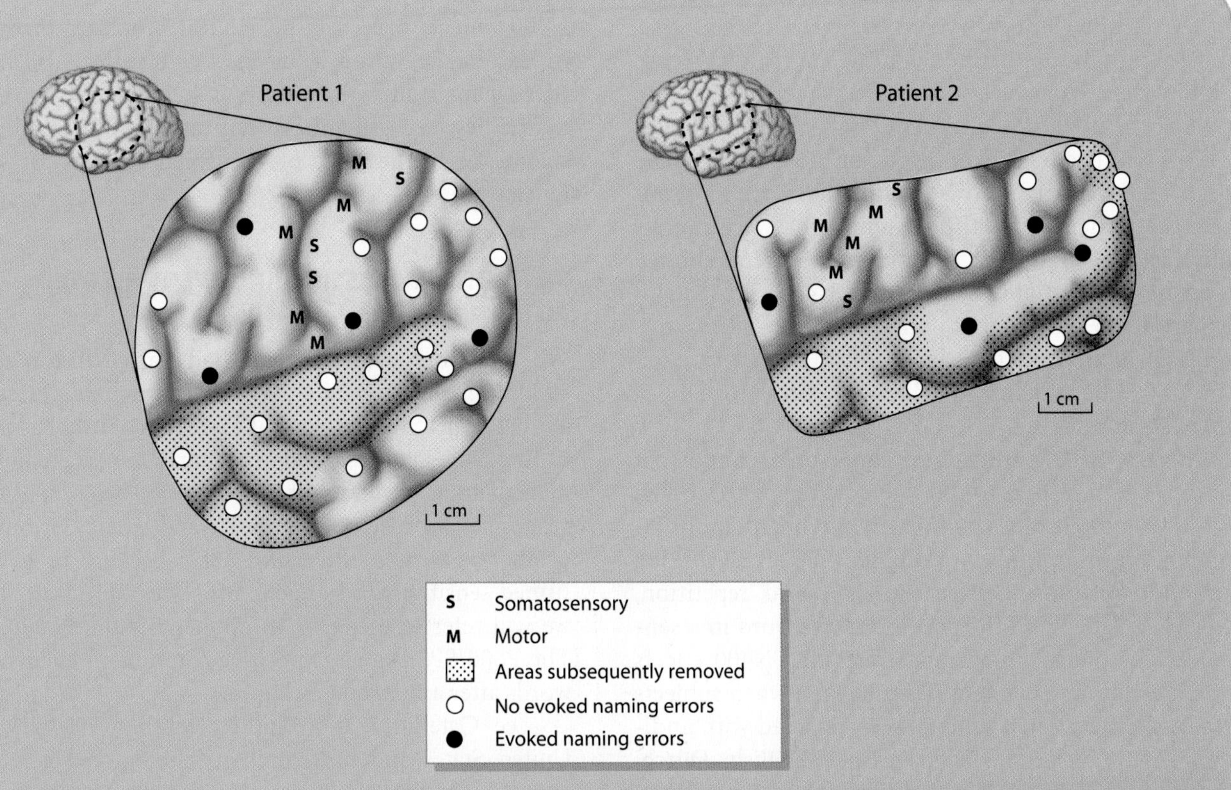

Regions of the brain of two patients studied with cortical stimulation mapping. During surgery, with the patient awake and lightly anesthetized, the surgeon maps the somatosensory and motor areas by stimulating the cortex and observing the responses. The patient is shown pictures and asked to verbally name them. Discrete regions of the cortex are stimulated with electrical current during the task. Areas that induce errors in naming when they are stimulated are mapped, and those regions are implicated as being involved in language. The surgeon uses this mapping to avoid removing any brain tissue associated with language. The procedure thus not only treats brain tumors or epilepsy, but also enlightens us about the cortical organization of language functions.

ponents that index aspects of semantic and syntactic processing during language comprehension.

SEMANTIC PROCESSING AND THE N400 WAVE

The **N400 response** is a brain wave related to linguistic processes. It was named *N400* because it is a negative-polarity voltage peak in brain waves for words that usually reaches maximum amplitude about 400 ms after onset of the word stimulus. This brain wave is especially sensitive to semantic aspects of linguistic input.

Marta Kutas and Steven Hillyard (1980) at the University of California, San Diego, discovered the N400 wave. They compared the processing of the last word of sentences in three conditions:

1. Normal sentences that ended with a word congruent with the preceding context, such as "It was his first day at work"
2. Sentences that ended with a word anomalous to the preceding context, such as "He spread the warm bread with socks"
3. Sentences that ended with a word semantically congruent with the preceding context but physically deviant, such as "She put on her high-heeled shoes"

The sentences were presented on a computer screen, one word at a time. The subjects were asked to read the sentences attentively, knowing that questions about the sentences would be asked at the end of the experiment. The electroencephalograms (EEGs) were averaged for the sentences in each condition, and the ERPs were extracted by averaging data for the last word of the sentences separately for each sentence type.

The amplitude of the N400 to anomalous words ending the sentence was increased when compared to that of the N400 to congruent words (Figure 10.34). This difference in the amplitude of the N400 is called the *N400 effect.* In contrast, words that were semantically congruent with the sentence but were merely physically deviant (e.g., having larger letters) elicited a positive potential rather than an N400. Subsequent experiments showed that nonsemantic deviations like musical or grammatical violations also fail to elicit the N400 effect. Thus, the N400 is specific to semantic analysis.

Figure 10.35 summarizes some other important findings with respect to the N400. As the figure shows, the N400 amplitude is modulated as a function of manipulation of a number of different factors, including semantic relations between words, word repetition, word frequency, and the position of the word in a sentence. The figure also demonstrates that N400 effects are modality independent. They happen when subjects read sentences; when subjects are presented with auditory input, including languages like English, Dutch, French, and Japanese (for speakers of those languages); and even when congenitally deaf subjects are presented with American Sign Language (not shown in the figure). With respect to linguistic neural processing, the N400 reflects primarily postlexical processes involved in lexical integration. Hence, an N400 effect will happen when lexical integration is hampered by a mismatch between semantic specifications of a word and semantic specifications of its preceding word or sentence context.

SYNTACTIC PROCESSING AND EVENT-RELATED POTENTIALS

Whereas work with the N400 had started in the early 1980s, only in the last decade have researchers started to study the electrophysiological correlates of other aspects of linguistic analysis, such as syntax. One ERP component that has been identified has been labeled the **P600 response** (because of its polarity and latency of onset) or the *syntactic positive shift* (*SPS,* because of its assumed sensitivity to syntactic processes). From now on we will refer to this ERP component as the P600/SPS. The P600/SPS is a large positive component elicited by words after a syntactic violation.

Lee Osterhout and Phil Holcomb (1992) in the United States and the Dutch psychologists Peter Hagoort, Colin Brown, and their colleagues (1993) at the Max Planck Institute for Psycholinguistics in the Nether-

Figure 10.34 ERP waveforms differentiate between congruent words at the end of sentences (*work* in the first sentence) and anomalous last words that do not fit the semantic specifications of the preceding context (*socks* in the second sentence). The anomalous words elicit a large negative deflection (plotted upward) in the ERP called the *N400.* Words that fit into the context but are printed with a larger font (*shoes* in the third sentence) elicit a positive wave (P560) and not the N400, indicating that the N400 is not generated only by surprises at the end of the sentence.

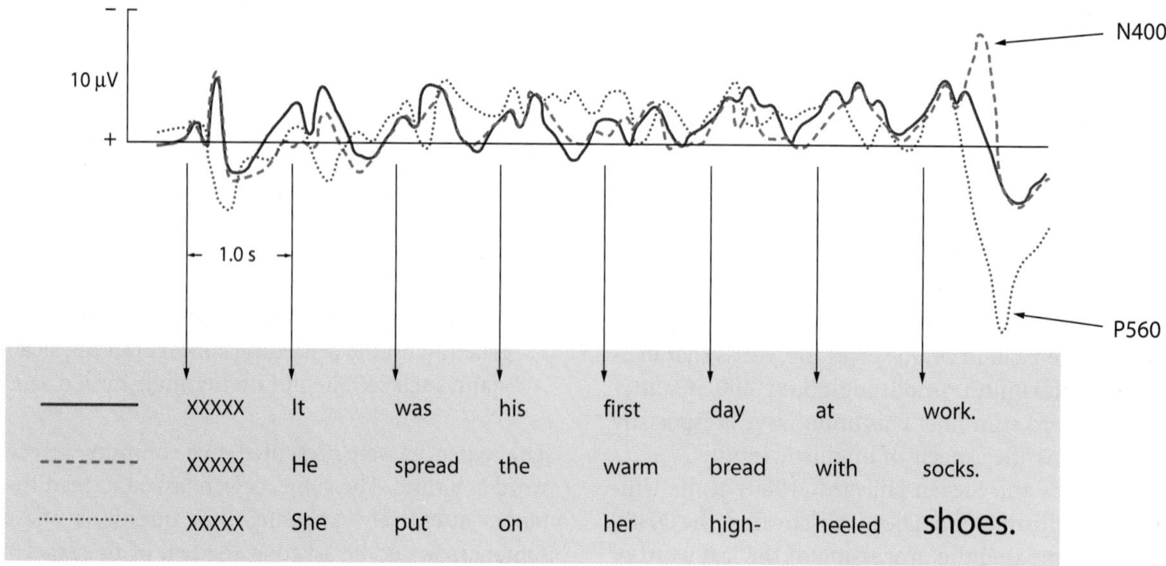

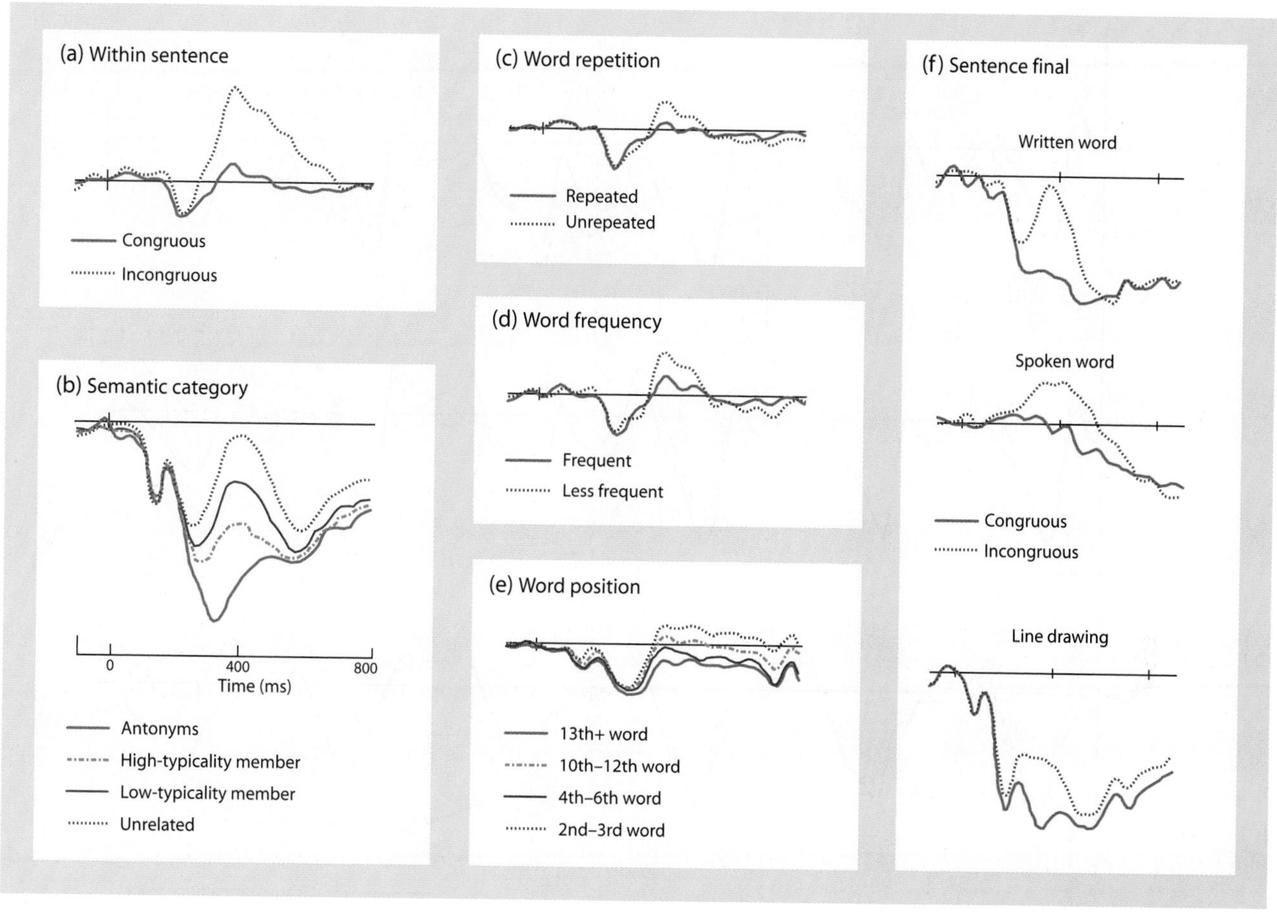

Figure 10.35 The N400 response to various language manipulations. The N400 is modulated as a function of congruency with the context **(a)**, degree of semantic relations between words **(b)**, word repetition **(c)**, word frequency **(d)**, and position of the word in a sentence **(e)**. These effects are modality independent **(f)**.

lands discovered this component. To illustrate the sensitivity of the P600/SPS to syntactic violations, we will concentrate here on a study in which Hagoort and Brown asked subjects to silently read sentences that were presented one word at a time on a video monitor. Brain responses to normal sentences were compared with those to sentences containing a grammatical violation. Figure 10.36 shows the results. As the figure illustrates, there is a large positive shift to the syntactic violation in the sentence (labeled SPS), and the onset of this effect is approximately 600 ms after the violating word (*throw* in the example). The P600/SPS shows up in response to a number of other syntactic violations as well, and it occurs both when subjects have to read sentences and when they have to listen to them. As with the N400, the P600/SPS has now been reported for a number of different languages.

However, the P600/SPS is sensitive to more than syntactic violations alone. Researchers have found that the P600/SPS also shows up when subjects read syntactically correct but dispreferred continuations, or garden path sentences. As you might remember from the section on syntactic processing earlier in this chapter, garden path sentences are sentences that are misleading and require revision after a first, incorrect structural assignment has been made (for an example, see the section titled "Integration of Words in Sentences"). Recent studies also showed that the P600/SPS is sensitive to this revision process.

Syntactic processing is reflected in other types of brain waves as well. Cognitive neuroscientists Thomas Münte and colleagues (1993), and Angela Friederici and colleagues (1993), in Germany, described a negative wave over the left frontal areas of the brain. This brain wave has been labeled the *left anterior negativity* (*LAN*) and has been observed when words violate the required word category in a sentence (e.g., as in "the red eats," where a noun instead of a verb lemma is required), or

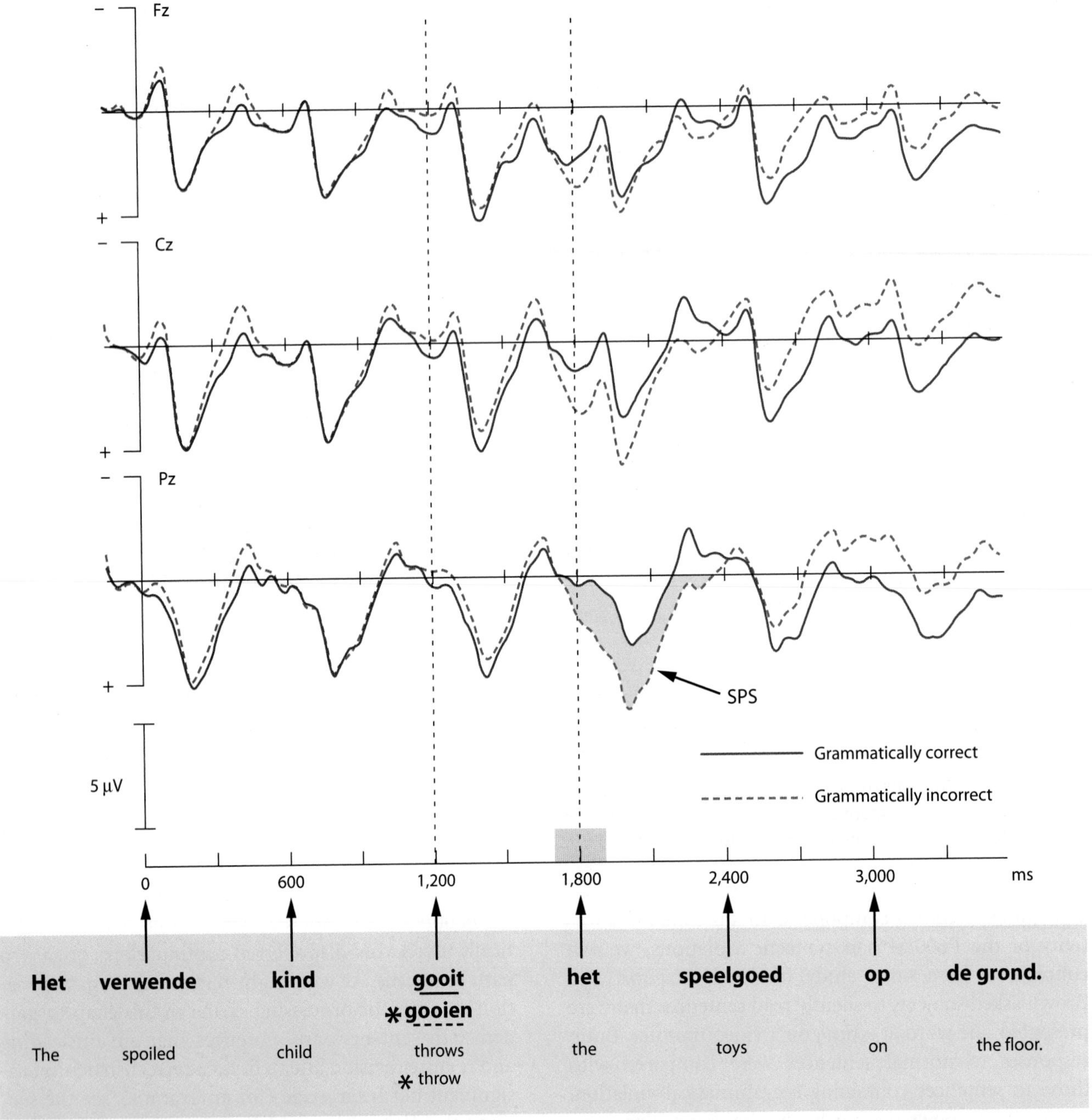

Figure 10.36 ERPs from frontal (Fz), central (Cz), and parietal (Pz) scalp recording sites elicited in response to each word of sentences that are syntactically anomalous (dashed waveforms) versus those that are syntactically correct (solid waveforms). In the violated sentence, a positive shift emerges in the ERP waveform at about 600 ms after the syntactic violation (shaded). It is called the *syntactic positive shift* (*SPS*) or P600.

when morphosyntactic features are violated (e.g., as in "he mow"). The LAN has about the same latency as the N400 but a different voltage distribution over the scalp, as Figure 10.37 illustrates.

One issue that has long intrigued psycholinguistic researchers is whether semantic and syntactic processes are modular or interactive. The distinct electrophysiological signatures of these processes enable us to address this question physiologically. In addition, now that clearly defined electrical activity has been linked to semantic and syntactic processing, these waves can be used as tools to probe human language in persons with deficits due to

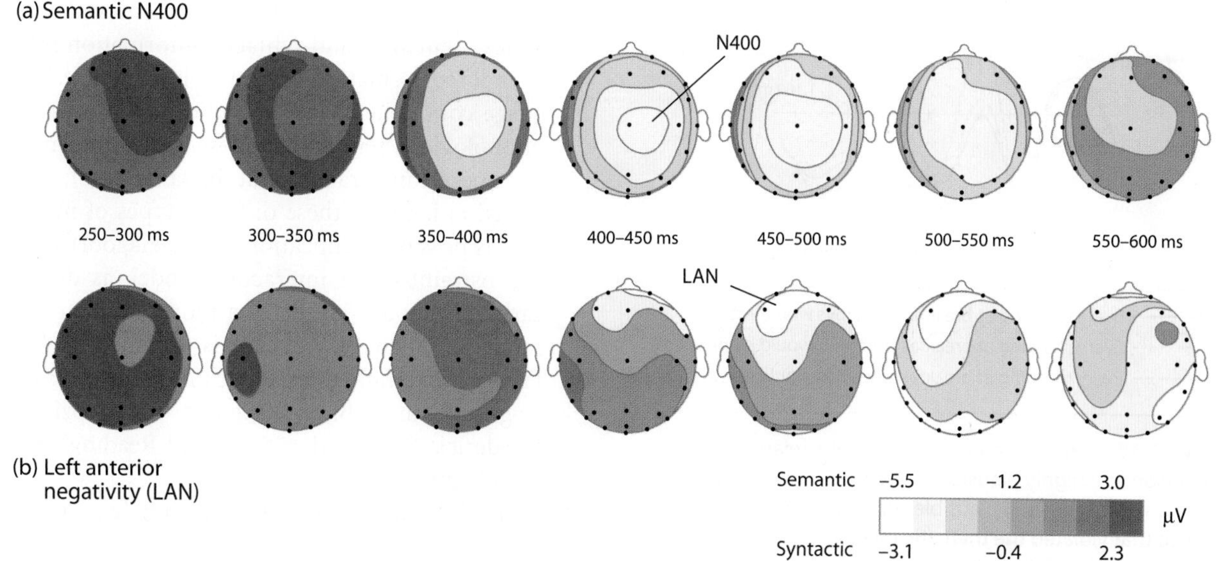

Figure 10.37 ERPs related to semantic and syntactic processing. The voltage recorded at multiple locations on the scalp at specific time periods can be displayed as a topographic voltage map. These maps show views of the topographies of **(a)** the N400 to semantic violations (see Figure 10.34 for equivalent waveforms) and **(b)** a left anterior negativity (LAN) to syntactic violations. The maps are read in a manner similar to the way elevation maps of mountain ranges are read, except here the topography shows "mountains" and "valleys" of voltage. The N400 and LAN have different scalp topographies, implying that they are generated in different neural structures in the brain.

neurological disease and damage (see "The Cognitive Neuroscientist's Toolkit: Aphasia and Electrophysiology," on p. 441). Such approaches to investigating the human language system are powerful tools for understanding language structure.

In order to understand sentences, a language comprehender not only has to parse the syntactic structure and understand the semantics of each word in the sentence, but she also has to compute the thematic relationships of the verb with its arguments. Assignment of thematic roles is one of the core processes of language comprehension. It requires the rapid integration of syntactic, semantic, and pragmatic (knowledge of the world) information.

Compare, for example, the following three sentences: (a) "The dog is biting the mailman," (b) "The poet is biting the mailman," and (c) "The box is biting the mailman." All three sentences are syntactically unambiguous, but they vary in the plausibility of the conceptual relationship between the verb and its preceding subject noun phrase. In (a), the subject noun *dog* is a perfectly legitimate agent of the verb *bite*. In (b), a pragmatic violation occurs; even though the poet is capable of biting a mailman, such an event is not consistent with our common understanding of the world, and the incongruity makes thematic integration more difficult. And in (c), a violation of thematic roles occurs: The subject noun *box* cannot serve as the agent of the verb *bite*, because the action of biting requires an animate agent. Biting a box constitutes what is known as a *selection restriction violation*, and in such cases thematic integration cannot be achieved. Given what we now know about the N400 and the P600, we would expect an N400 to the word *biting* in examples (b) and (c)—that is, when the poet and the box are biting the mailman. Right? Wrong.

A study by Gina Kuperberg and colleagues (2003) at Tufts University and Massachusetts General Hospital, for example, showed a surprising effect when the thematic relationship between the verb and its argument was violated—that is, when the box was biting the mailman. Instead of the expected N400 effect, they found a P600, which, as we have seen before, had previously been associated only with syntactic violations and syntactic-processing difficulty (Figure 10.38). So what does this mean for our understanding of normal language comprehension? Is the distinction between syntax and semantics no longer valid? Or is the P600 really not a syntax-specific ERP component?

Kuperberg suggests that normal language comprehension relies on both a system based on semantic memory and a system that structures language according to both syntactic rules and semantic and thematic constraints (e.g., a box cannot bite). Both systems output a

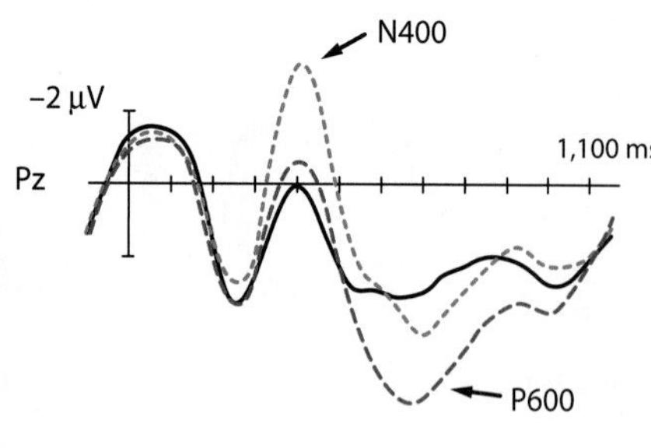

Figure 10.38 ERPs to violations of thematic relationships. In comparison to a highly plausible sentence (solid line) or a slightly less likely but still plausible sentence (dotted line), a sentence that violated the thematic relationships (i.e., in which the eggs were doing the eating) produced a P600 response (dashed line). Recordings from the midline parietal site, Pz. See text.

representation, and when these representations are in conflict, a P600 results. This model is different from the syntax-first garden path models proposed by Frazier and others (discussed elsewhere in this chapter) because syntax-first models posit that the initial processing of sentences occurs on the basis of syntax alone.

Neural Models of Language Comprehension

New neural models of language have emerged that are different from the classical Wernicke–Lichtheim–Geschwind model, and that connect findings from psycholinguistics to a possible neural circuitry in the brain. In these models, the neural circuitry of language is still thought to include the traditional language areas that had been identified by Paul Broca and Carl Wernicke, but these areas are no longer always considered language specific, nor do they have only the roles in language processing that were proposed in the classical model. Moreover, additional areas in the brain have been found to be part of the circuitry that is used for, but is not necessarily specific to, normal language processing.

One new neural model of language that combines recent work in brain and language has been proposed by Peter Hagoort. He suggests three functional components of language processing and their possible representation in the brain (Figure 10.39):

1. *Memory.* Storage and retrieval from the mental lexicon or the long-term memory store for word information, as defined earlier in this chapter.
2. *Unification.* Integration of lexically retrieved phonological, semantic, and syntactic information into an overall representation of the whole utterance. In language comprehension the unification processes for phonological, semantic, and syntactic information can operate in parallel (or at the same time); and interaction between these different types of information is possible. Unification makes Hagoort's model a constraint-based interactive model, as discussed earlier. A good example of a more modular neural model of language processes is provided by Angela Friederici from the Max Planck Institute for Human Cognitive and Brain Sciences in Leipzig (see Friederici, 2002, in the "Suggested Reading" list for this chapter).
3. *Control.* Relating language to action (e.g., in bilingualism and turn taking).

As Figure 10.39 shows, the temporal lobes are especially important for the storage and retrieval of word representations. Phonological and phonetic properties of words are stored in the central to posterior superior temporal gyrus (STG, which includes Wernicke's area) extending into the superior temporal sulcus (STS), and semantic information is distributed over different parts of the left middle and inferior temporal gyri. This part of the model is very similar to what we have seen before in Binder's neural model of spoken-word comprehension (see Figure 10.10).

The processes that combine and integrate (unify) phonological, lexical–semantic, and syntactic informa-

Figure 10.39 Memory–unification–control model. The three components of the model are shown in colors overlaid onto a drawing of the left hemisphere containing Brodmann's areas: the memory component in yellow in the left temporal lobe, the unification component in blue in the left inferior frontal gyrus, and the control component in gray in the lateral frontal cortex.

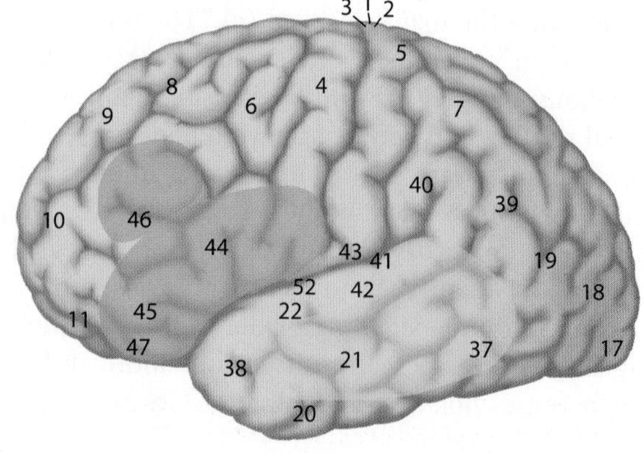

THE COGNITIVE NEUROSCIENTIST'S TOOLKIT

Aphasia and Electrophysiology

Since investigators have been struggling with the question of whether aphasic symptoms reflect processing versus representational losses, interest in online measures of language processing has grown. Such measures include the ERPs elicited by language processing. The idea is to investigate the processing of spoken language and observe how the patient's brain responds to linguistic inputs, and to compare these responses to those in healthy control subjects. One study used the N400 component of the ERP to investigate spoken-sentence understanding in Broca's and Wernicke's aphasics. Tamara Swaab (now at the University of California, Davis), Colin Brown, and Peter Hagoort at the Max Planck Institute for Psycholinguistics in the Netherlands (1997) tried to determine whether spoken-sentence comprehension might be hampered by a deficit in the online integration of lexical information.

The patients listened to sentences spoken at a normal rate. In half of the sentences, the meaning of the final word of the sentence matched the semantic meaning building up from the sentence context. In the other half of the sentences, the final word was anomalous with respect to the preceding context. As in Kutas and Hillyard's (1980) study, the N400 amplitude should be larger to the anomalous final words than to the congruent final words. This result was obtained for normal age-matched control subjects. In comparison to the controls, nonaphasic brain-damaged patients (controls with right-hemisphere damage) and aphasic patients with a light comprehension deficit (high comprehenders) had an N400 effect comparable to that of neurologically unimpaired subjects. In aphasics with moderate to severe comprehension deficits (low comprehenders), the N400 effect was reduced and delayed.

The results are compatible with the idea that aphasics with moderate to severe comprehension problems have an impaired ability to integrate lexical information into a higher order representation of the sentence context because the N400 component indexes the process of lexical integration. The incorporation of electrical recordings into studies of neurological patients with behavioral deficits such as aphasia permits scientists to track the processing of information in real time as it occurs in the brain. Observations from this tracking can be combined with analysis by means of traditional approaches such as reaction time measures in, for example, lexical decision tasks. Importantly, ERPs can also provide measures of processing in patients whose neurobehavioral deficit is too severe to use behavior alone because their comprehension is too low to understand the task instructions.

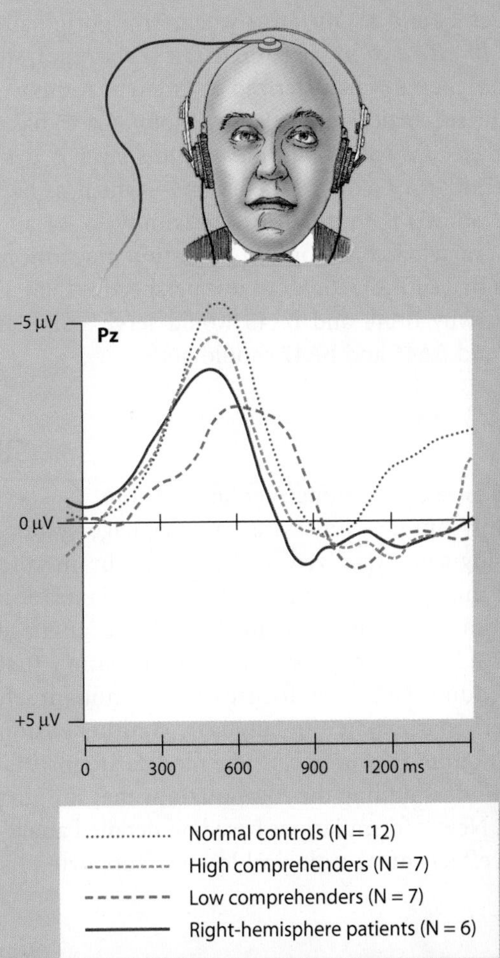

The N400 effect to different anomalous words at the end of a sentence in different groups of patients and healthy control subjects. The recording is from a single electrode located at the midline parietal scalp site, Pz, in elderly healthy control subjects, aphasics with high comprehension scores, aphasics with low comprehension scores, and patients with right-hemisphere lesions (control patients). The waveform for the low comprehenders is clearly delayed and somewhat reduced compared to that for the other groups. The waveforms for the normal control subjects, the high comprehenders, and the patients with right-hemisphere lesions are comparable in size and do not differ in latency. This pattern implies a delay in time course of language processing in the patients with low comprehension.

tion recruit frontal areas of the brain, including our old friend Broca's area or the left inferior frontal gyrus (LIFG). But, as Hagoort's neural model reveals, Broca's area is certainly not a language production module, nor is it the seat of syntax. And it is not likely that Broca's area as it was originally defined should serve one function to begin with.

You may remember from Chapter 4 that Brodmann's cytoarchitectonic organization was determined by the organization of the cells in the six cortical layers. When we look at the cytoarchitechtonic nature of Brodmann areas 44 and 45, the areas where Broca originally localized *Broca's area* in his patient Tan (Leborgne), we can see that they are characterized by different compositions of the six cortical layers. For example, area 45 has a granular layer IV, whereas in area 44 this layer is dysgranular. But area 47, on the other hand—which, as Figure 10.39 shows, is in very close proximity to 44 and 45—shows a cytoarchitectonic organization much more similar to that of BA45. So from this perspective there is no reason why BA44 and BA45 would serve a similar function and BA45 and BA47 should not.

Thus, it may not come as a big surprise that neuroimaging studies have started to highlight a functional anatomy different from Broca's area per se, and extending into other areas of the prefrontal cortex (for a review of fMRI findings, see Kaan & Swaab, 2002, in the "Suggested Readings" list for this chapter). With this in mind, let us return to our discussion of the areas in frontal cortex that may be crucial to the unification processes. LIFG now appears to be involved in all three unification processes, with semantic unification in BA47 and BA45, syntactic unification in BA45 and BA44, and phonological unification in BA44 and parts of BA6.

The control component of the model becomes important when people are actually involved in communication—for example, when they have to take turns during a conversation. Cognitive control in language comprehension has not been studied very much, but areas that are involved in cognitive control during other tasks, such as the anterior cingulate cortex (ACC) and the dorsolateral prefrontal cortex (DLPC, BA46/9), also play a role during cognitive control in language comprehension.

SUMMARY

Language is unique among mental functions in that only humans possess a true language system. How is language organized in the human brain, and what can this functional and anatomical organization tell us about the cognitive architecture of the language system? We have known for more than a century that regions around the Sylvian fissure of the dominant left hemisphere participate in language comprehension and production. However, classical models are insufficient for understanding the computations that support language. Newer formulations based on detailed analysis of the effects of neurological lesions (supported by improvements in structural imaging), functional neuroimaging, human electrophysiology, transcranial magnetic stimulation, and computational modeling now provide some surprising modifications of older models. But the human language system is complex, and much remains to be learned about how the biology of the brain enables the rich speech and language comprehension that characterize our daily lives. The future of language research is promising as psycholinguistic models combine with neuroscience to elucidate the neural code for this uniquely human mental faculty.

KEY TERMS

agrammatic aphasia	Broca's aphasia	mental lexicon	parsing
aphasia	conduction aphasia	N400 response	semantic paraphasia
apraxia of speech	lexical access	P600 response	Wernicke's aphasia
arcuate fasciculus	lexical selection		

TAKE-HOME MESSAGES

General

- The mental lexicon is a repository of information about words that includes semantic and syntactic information, as well as the details of word forms.
- Semantic information describes meaning of the

world; syntactic information describes how words are combined to form a sentence; word forms describe information about how words are spelled and their sound patterns.
- Word representations can be either orthographic (vision based) or phonological (sound based).

Language Theories
- Collins and Loftus proposed one very influential model in which word meanings are represented in a semantic network where words, represented by conceptual nodes, are connected with each other.
- Warrington and her colleagues used data from their patients who had language difficulties isolated to living things (as opposed to man-made objects) to theorize about the organization of semantic information. They suggested that the patients' problems are reflections of the types of information stored with different words in the semantic network. Whereas the biological categories rely more on physical properties or visual features, man-made objects are identified by their functional properties.
- On the basis of work with lesion patients, Damasio and her colleagues similarly proposed that the brain's conceptual networks involve several neuronal structures in the left and right hemispheres. These conceptual networks are connected to the lexical networks in the left temporal lobe and might contain specialized information for persons, animals, or tools.

Speech Comprehension
- A phoneme is the smallest unit of sound that makes a difference to meaning.
- The sound of phonemes in spoken words is influenced by voicing, the point of articulation, and the manner of articulation.
- The prosody of speech is the rhythm and the pitch of the speaker's voice.
- Sound comprehension involves the superior temporal cortex. People with damage to this area have pure word deafness.

Written Comprehension
- A morpheme is the smallest unit of language that has meaning.
- Written-word processing takes place in occipitotemporal regions of the left hemisphere. Damage to this area can cause pure alexia, a condition in which patients cannot read words, even though other aspects of language are normal.
- The main components of word recognition are lexical access, lexical selection, and lexical integration. Lexical access is the process by which perceptual inputs activate word information in the mental lexicon, including semantic and syntactic information about the word. In lexical selection of the activated word form representations, the one that best matches the sensory input will be selected. Lexical integration is the process by which linguistic information is combined with contextual and background knowledge in order to arrive at a representation and understanding of the overall message.
- Occipitotemporal regions of the left hemisphere may be specialized for the identification of orthographic units.
- When we need to translate the orthographic input into phonological information that can be used to pronounce the word, the left inferior frontal gyrus, including the ventral part of Broca's area, seems to play a role.
- Modular (autonomous) models claim that normal language comprehension is executed within separate and independent modules. In contrast, interactive models maintain that all types of information can participate in word recognition. In these models, context can have its influence even before the sensory information is available, by changing the activational status of the word form representations in the mental lexicon.

Aphasia
- Language disorders, generally called aphasias, can include deficits in comprehension or production of language resulting from neurological damage.
- Agrammatic aphasic patients have difficulty producing or understanding the structure of sentences.
- Patients with Broca's aphasia have damage to the area of the brain (Broca's area) responsible for planning speech production and thus have marked difficulty producing speech.
- Wernicke's aphasia results from damage to the area of the brain responsible for speech comprehension (Wernicke's area in the posterior third of the superior temporal gyrus).
- Aphasia can also result from damage to the connection between Wernicke's and Broca's areas (the arcuate fasciculus). Conduction aphasia is the disorder that results from such damage, and people with this type of aphasia have problems producing spontaneous speech, as well as repeating speech.
- Apraxia, or difficulty pronouncing words, results from a lesion to the insula.

Neuroimaging

- In aphasic patients, PET measures obtained during a resting state revealed hypometabolism (lower glucose utilization) in the temporoparietal region, regardless of the type of aphasia.
- In the ERP method, the N400 is a negative-polarity brain wave related to semantic processes in language, and the P600/SPS is a large positive component elicited after a syntactic violation.

New Model

- Peter Hagoort proposes a new neural model of language that suggests three functional components to language processing: memory (storage and retrieval of words), unification (the integration of phonological, semantic, and syntactic information into an overall representation of the whole utterance), and control (relating language to action).

THOUGHT QUESTIONS

1. How might the mental lexicon be organized in the brain? Would we expect to find it localized in a particular spot in cortex? If not, why not?
2. At what stage of input processing are the comprehension of spoken and of written language the same, and where must they be different? Are there any exceptions to this rule?
3. Describe the route that an auditory speech signal might take in the cortex, from perceptual analysis to comprehension.
4. What evidence exists for the role of the right hemisphere in language processing? If the right hemisphere has a role in language, what might that role be?
5. Can knowledge of the world around you affect the way you process and understand words?

SUGGESTED READING

CARAMAZZA, A. (1996). The brain's dictionary. *Nature, 380,* 485–486.

DRONKERS, N. F., WILKINS, D. P., VAN VALIN, R. D., JR., REDFERN, B. B., & JAEGER, J. J. (2004). Lesion analysis of the brain areas involved in language comprehension. *Cognition, 92,* 145–177.

FRIEDERICI, A. D. (2002). Towards a neural basis of auditory sentence processing. *Trends in Cognitive Sciences, 6,* 78–84.

HAGOORT, P. (2005). On Broca, brain, and binding: A new framework. *Trends in Cognitive Sciences, 9,* 416–423.

KAAN, E., & SWAAB, T. (2002). The brain circuitry of syntactic comprehension. *Trends in Cognitive Sciences, 6,* 350–356.

LEVELT, W. J. M. (2001). Spoken word production: A theory of lexical access. *Proceedings of the National Academy of Sciences, USA, 98,* 13464–13471.

MARTIN, A., HAXBY, J. V., LALONDE, F. M., WIGGS, C. L., & UNGERLEIDER, L. G. (1995). Discrete cortical regions associated with knowledge of color and knowledge of action. *Science, 270,* 102–105.

PINKER, S. (1994). *The language instinct.* New York: Morrow.

SIGNORET, J.-L., CASTAINE, P., LHERMITTE, F., ABELANET, R., & LAVOREL, P. (1984). Rediscovery of Leborgne's brain: Anatomical description with CT scan. *Brain and Language, 22,* 303–319.

11

Hemispheric Specialization

We live in a society that treasures the individual. Unique twists and interpretations of life's events are a marvel, and friends who offer other ways of looking at the world are a delight. So imagine how intriguing the world might be if our brain's two hemispheres were disconnected. Surgeons have done this, in a procedure called a *callosotomy*, or *split-brain surgery*, mainly in an effort to treat epilepsy, and their patients have been studied extensively. Each hemisphere is evaluated as to whether it, and only it, possesses specific functions. The big question is this: Could each half of the brain provide a different view of the world?

W.J. was the first patient to have his brain split in recent years. A charismatic war veteran, W.J. appeared perfectly normal, possessed a sharp sense of humor, and charmed all those whom he met in life. Following his surgery to relieve intractable epilepsy in 1961, his delightful personality remained unchanged, but W.J. exhibited a most remarkable phenomenon: He was able to name and describe visual information presented to his left dominant hemisphere, but when the same information was presented to the right hemisphere, W.J. claimed he saw nothing. How could that be?

Such questions gave birth to human **split-brain research**. The phenomenon seen in W.J. has been observed repeatedly in other patients. Even so, much of the split-brain story was revealed in this one study. What was so remarkable was that this patient's right hemisphere could do things that the left could not do. For example, the two hemispheres were strikingly different in performance on the block design task shown in Figure 11.1. Previously he had been able to write dictated sentences and carry out any kind of command, such as making a fist or drawing geometric shapes with his right hand. After surgery, though, he could not arrange four red and white blocks in a simple pattern with his right hand. The surgery had disconnected specialized systems in the right hemisphere from the motor apparatus in the left hemisphere, which in turn controls the right hand. Even when given as much time as needed, W.J. was unable to perform tasks with his right hand, because motor commands specific to the tasks could not be communicated from the isolated left hemisphere.

At the same time, W.J.'s right hemisphere was a whiz. When blocks were presented to his left hand (controlled by his right hemisphere), he quickly and adeptly arranged them into the correct pattern. This simple observation gave birth to the idea that "Mind Left" and "Mind Right" do different things, supporting the idea that the central nervous system is laterally specialized. Each of the two cerebral hemispheres has processes that the other does not have—hence, W.J.'s unique perspective on the world.

After the first testing session revealed this separation so clearly, investigators arranged to film W.J. carrying out tasks. The scientists knew a young fashion photographer, Baron Wolman, who dabbled in filmmaking (and would later help found *Rolling Stone* magazine); he was invited to come to a session during which the whole test was carried out again. Wolman could not believe his

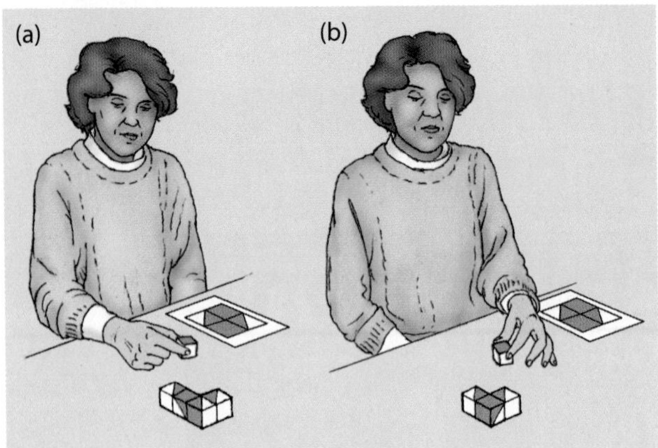

Figure 11.1 The pattern in red on the right is the shape that the patient is trying to create with the blocks given to her. **(a)** With her right hand (left hemisphere), she is unable to duplicate the pattern. **(b)** With her left hand (right hemisphere), she is able to perform the task correctly.

eyes. During filming, W.J.'s right hand attempted to arrange the blocks, and his left hand kept trying to intervene. Mind Right saw the problem, knew the solution, and tried to help out just like a good friend. W.J. had to sit on his left hand so that the inadequate but dominant right hand could at least try.

It was all to no avail. For the film's final scene, everyone decided to see what would happen if both hands were allowed to arrange the blocks. Here we witnessed the beginning of the idea that Mind Left can have its own view of the world with its own desires and aspirations, and Mind Right can have another view. As soon as Mind Right, working through the left hand, began to arrange the blocks correctly, Mind Left would undo the good work. The hands were in competition. The specializations of each hemisphere were different, and growing out of that difference were the behaviors of each half of the brain.

The perspective of natural selection, by which organisms acquire specific adaptations, would suggest that the two hemispheres do not function identically. After all, one does not need two speech production systems or two places to store the memory of faces. Once a brain region has evolved a functional specialization, there would seem to be no need to duplicate it in a second region. Be that as it may, the organization of the cerebral cortex suggests that duplication, rather than unilateral specialization, is the rule.

The two hemispheres are much more similar to one another in function than you might think; differences surface at a more subtle level of analysis. Each hemisphere's visual areas are devoted to representing the shapes and colors of objects, and their primary specializations relate to the objects' positions—that is, whether the objects are on the left side of space or the right side. Furthermore, the motor cortices are roughly mirror images of one another, both in structure and in function. Although each cortex can be represented by a motor homunculus of the body, it is dominated by fibers that project to muscles on the opposite side of the body.

Evolution could have utilized the available cerebral space in a completely different way. Visual functions could have been isolated in the left hemisphere, and motor projections to both limbs could have originated in the right hemisphere. Yet selective pressures appear to have favored a cerebral organization that reflects structural properties of the world and the organism. The world's spatial structure is reflected in our biology.

Hemispheric specializations are best conceived as superimposed on this fundamental symmetry. In some instances, specializations may have evolved because there was an advantage in having a single system devoted to a certain process. For example, one hypothesis postulates that speech production became strongly lateralized because of the need to communicate at rapid rates. **Transcortical** processing and integration take time and might slow down complicated articulatory gestures. Indeed, lateralization may underlie stuttering, because two parallel systems compete for control of speech output.

Others argue that hemispheric specializations evolved because of the inherent advantages in having nonidentical forms of representation. Homologous visual areas perform related operations, but differently enough that the resultant nonidentical representations are imbued with unique advantages in performing certain tasks. This does not mean that these tasks are strictly localized—that language functions are restricted to the left hemisphere or that spatial behavior emanates from the right hemisphere. Not only does the normal performance of these tasks require distributed operations that might span both hemispheres, but also usually both hemispheres contain the essential machinery for performing the task. This organization helps explain why patients with large unilateral lesions that damage 25% of the cortical tissue on one side still have an amazing capacity for recovery. Even more dramatic evidence comes from patients with isolated cerebral hemispheres—a condition that arises after a split-brain operation. Because this radical operation remarkably preserves function, such patients are invaluable for giving us clues to subtle **functional asymmetries** and basic capabilities of each cerebral hemisphere.

The study of **cerebral specialization** has a long and storied tradition in the behavioral and biomedical sciences. Today, left-brain/right-brain claims are everywhere. They are popular, and on the surface they are entertaining accounts of how the human brain might be organized. But how much of it is true, and where do these stories come from? What are the facts about the left and right sides of the brain? These and other issues concerning a broad range of human cognitive processes, from perception and attention to language and emotions, are considered in this chapter.

We will find that research on laterality has provided extensive insights into the organization of the human brain, and that the simplistic left-brain/right-brain claims that permeate popular culture distort the complex mosaic of mental processes that contribute to cognition. Split-brain studies profoundly demonstrate that the two hemispheres do not represent information in an identical manner. Complementary studies on patients with focal brain lesions underscore the crucial role played by lateralized processes in cognition. This research, and recent computational investigations of lateralization and specialization, have advanced the field far beyond the popular interpretations of left-brain/right-brain processes, and they provide the scientific basis for future explorations of many fascinating issues concerning cerebral lateralization and specialization.

In this chapter we examine the differences between the right and left cerebral hemispheres. Research on the human brain has revealed marked differences between the two halves. We begin at the beginning: the anatomy and physiology of the two halves and their interconnections.

PRINCIPLES OF CEREBRAL ORGANIZATION

The two cerebral cortices of the human brain are of equal size and surface area. The major lobes (occipital, parietal, temporal, and frontal) appear, at least superficially, to be symmetrical. Nonetheless, for centuries the effects of unilateral brain damage have revealed major functional differences between the two hemispheres. Most dramatic has been the effect of left-hemisphere damage on language functions. The dominant role of the left hemisphere in language has been confirmed by various behavioral methods in normal humans, including stimulation techniques in which the input is directed to one hemisphere or the other, and injections of **amobarbital** (Amytal) into the carotid artery to produce a rapid and brief anesthesia of the ipsilateral hemisphere (i.e., the hemisphere on the same side as the injection; Figure 11.2).

This latter approach is called the *Wada test* and was pioneered by Juhn A. Wada and Theodore Rasmussen in the late 1950s as a way of determining, prior to elective surgery for the treatment of disorders such as epilepsy, which hemisphere possesses language. A patient is given an injection of amobarbital into the two hemispheres on separate days. When the injection is delivered to the hemisphere that possesses language, the ability of the patient to speak, or to comprehend speech, is disrupted for up to several minutes. Thus, this procedure unequivocally localizes language, and like the stimulation techniques, it has revealed an extremely strong bias for language to be lateralized to the left hemisphere. Similarly, functional neuroimaging techniques, such as PET and fMRI, have further confirmed that language processing is preferentially biased to the left hemisphere (Binder & Price, 2001), although right-hemisphere regions are also engaged, especially for language tasks that require higher level comprehension (Bookheimer, 2002).

Anatomical Correlates of Hemispheric Specialization

The dominant role of the left hemisphere in language is not strongly correlated with **handedness**. About 96% of all right-handers are left-hemisphere dominant for speech, and a majority of left-handers (approximately 60%) are also left-hemisphere dominant for speech (Risse et al., 1997). Because left-handers constitute only 7% to 8% of the total population, this means that 96% of humans, regardless of which hand is dominant, have a left-hemisphere specialization for language. This dramatic functional asymmetry has led to the search for structural asymmetries in regions of the brain associated with language functions.

Anatomists in the 19th century could see that the **Sylvian fissure** (also called the *lateral fissure*)—the large sulcus that defines the superior border of the temporal lobe—has a more prominent upward curl in the right hemisphere in comparison to the left hemisphere, which is relatively flat. This difference in shape of the Sylvian fissure between the two cerebral hemispheres is directly related to subsequent reports of size differences in adjacent cortical regions buried within the lateral fissure. In the 1960s Norman Geschwind, of

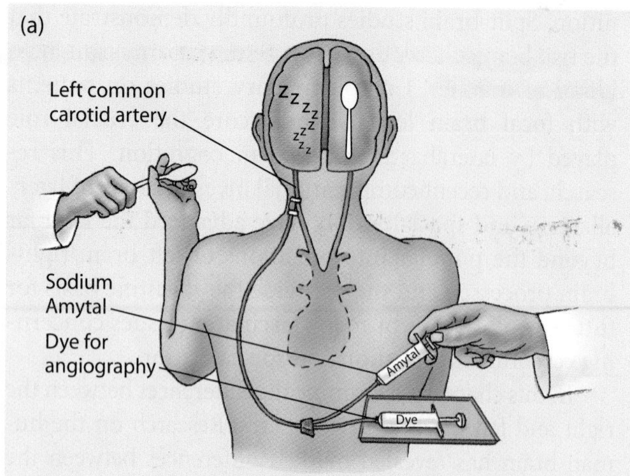

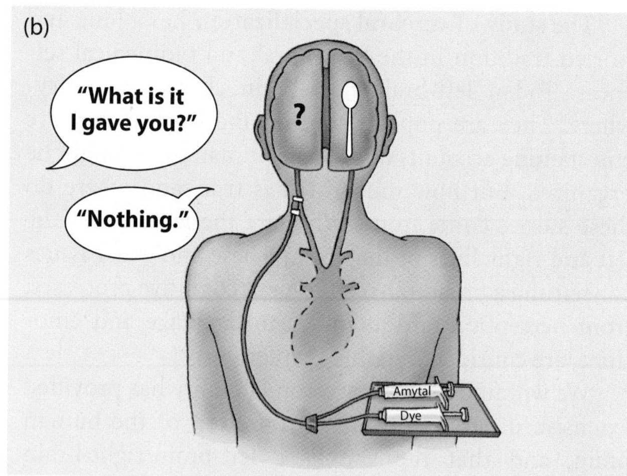

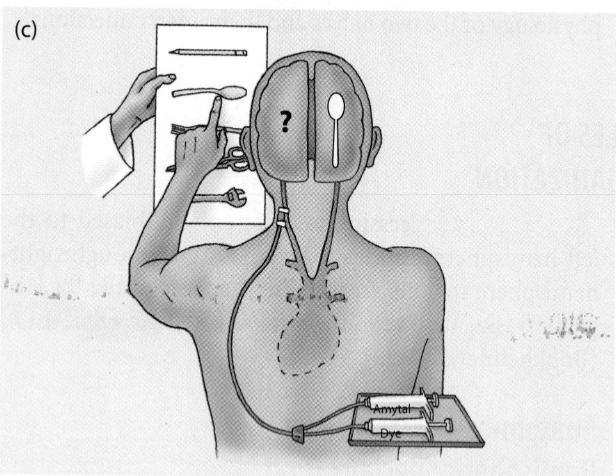

Figure 11.2 Methods used in amobarbital (Amytal) testing. **(a)** Subsequent to angiography, amobarbital is administered to the left hemisphere, anesthetizing the language and speech systems. A spoon is placed in the left hand, and the right hemisphere takes note. **(b)** When the left hemisphere regains consciousness, the subject is asked what was placed in his left hand, and he responds, "Nothing." **(c)** Showing the patient a board with a variety of objects pinned to it reveals that the patient can easily point to the appropriate object, because the right hemisphere directs the left hand during the match-to-sample task.

the Harvard Medical School, examined brains obtained from 100 people known to be right-handed (Geschwind & Levitsky, 1968). After slicing through the lateral fissure, Geschwind measured the temporal lobe's surface area and discovered that the **planum temporale**, which encompasses Wernicke's area, was larger in the left hemisphere—a pattern found in 65% of the brains. Of the remaining brains, 11% had a larger surface area in the right hemisphere and 24% had no asymmetry.

The asymmetry in this region of the temporal lobe may extend to subcortical structures connected to these areas. For example, the lateral posterior nucleus of the thalamus also tends to be larger on the left. Because these temporal lobe asymmetries seem to be a characteristic of the normally lateralized brain, other investigations have explored whether the asymmetry is absent in individuals with developmental language disorders. Interestingly, MRI studies reveal that the area of the planum temporale is approximately symmetrical in children with dyslexia—a clue that their language difficulties may stem from the lack of a specialized left hemisphere.

The asymmetry of the planum temporale is one of the few examples in which an anatomical index is correlated with a well-defined functional asymmetry. The complex functions of language comprehension presumably require more cortical surface. However, a number of questions remain concerning both the validity and the explanatory power of this asymmetry. First, although the left-hemisphere planum temporale is larger in 65% of right-handers, functional measures indicate that over 95% of right-handers show left-hemisphere language dominance. Second, recent work has suggested that the apparent asymmetries in the planum temporale result from the techniques and criteria used to identify this region. When new three-dimensional imaging techniques—techniques that take into account asymmetries in curvature patterns of the lateral fissures—are applied, hemispheric asymmetries become negligible (Figure 11.3). If this new view is correct, then the anatomical

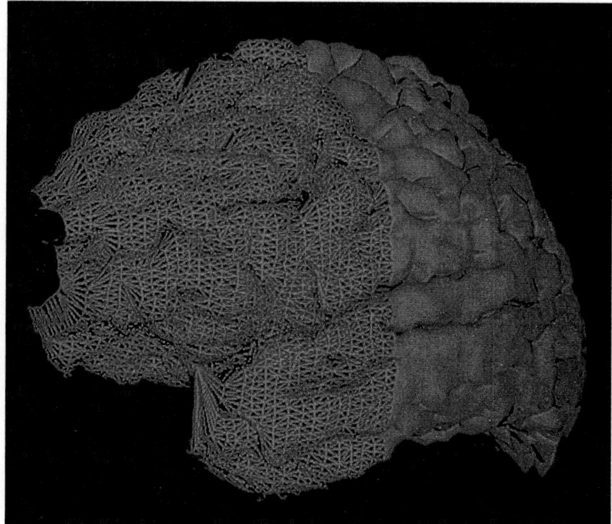

Figure 11.3 Three-dimensional computer reconstructions such as this one can be used to model the cortical surface as a folded mesh composed of many small polygons. These models, which are derived from magnetic resonance images (MRIs), permit the measurement of specific regions of the cortex, such as the planum temporale located on the dorsal surface of the temporal lobe. Measurements in both hemispheres can be used to assess left–right anatomical asymmetry in living subjects. Investigations of the planum temporale based on these models have revealed that it may not be as asymmetrical as was previously thought.

basis for left-hemisphere dominance in language may not be reflected in gross morphology; instead it would require an analysis of the neural circuits within these cortical locations.

Microanatomical Investigations of Anatomical Asymmetries

The cellular basis of hemispheric specialization is an exciting new field of investigation that seeks to understand whether differences in neural circuits between the hemispheres might underlie functional asymmetries in such tasks as language. Although many investigators have examined gross size differences between the two hemispheres, only a few studies have explored whether there are differences in neural connectivity and organization that underlie these gross hemispheric asymmetries. One possibility is that specific organizational characteristics of local neuronal networks—for example, the number of synaptic connections—may be responsible for the unique functions of different cortical areas. Current knowledge of local cortical organization is based primarily on studies of visual cortex, but one promising place to look for specializations in cortical circuitry is within homotopic areas of the two cerebral hemispheres that are known to be functionally asymmetrical.

Differences have been found in the specifics of cortical microcircuitry between the two hemispheres in both anterior (Broca's) and posterior (Wernicke's) language-associated cortex. The cortex is a sheet of tightly spaced columns of cells, each of which comprises a circuit of neurons that is repeated over and over across the cortical surface. From studies of visual cortex we know that cells in an individual column act together to encode relatively small features of the visual world. Individual columns connect with adjacent and distant columns to form ensembles of neurons that can encode more complex features.

In language-associated regions, several types of asymmetries between the hemispheres have been identified. Some of these asymmetries occur at the level of the individual neurons that make up a single cortical column, some are found in the relationships between adjacent neuronal columns, and some are found in larger ensembles of more distant cortical columns (Hutsler & Galuske, 2003). Within Wernicke's area in the left hemisphere, for example, columns are spaced farther from each other, possibly to accommodate additional connectional fibers between the columns. Individual cells within a column of the left primary auditory cortex have a tangential dendritic spread that accommodates the greater distance between cell columns; but secondary auditory areas that show the same increase in distance between the columns do not have longer dendrites in the left hemisphere. The cells in these columns contact fewer adjacent cell columns than do those in the right hemisphere.

Additional structural differences also have been documented in both anterior and posterior language cortex. These asymmetries include cell size differences between the hemispheres, such as those shown in Figure 11.4, and may suggest a greater long-range connectivity in the left-hemisphere language-associated regions. Asymmetries in connectivity between the two hemispheres have been directly demonstrated by tracing of the neuronal connections within posterior language-associated regions using dyes that diffuse through postmortem tissue. Such dyes show a patchy pattern of connectivity within these regions of each hemisphere, but within the left hemisphere these patches are spaced farther apart than those in the right hemisphere (Galuske et al., 2000).

What is the functional significance of these various findings of asymmetries within cortical circuitry, and

(a) Right hemisphere

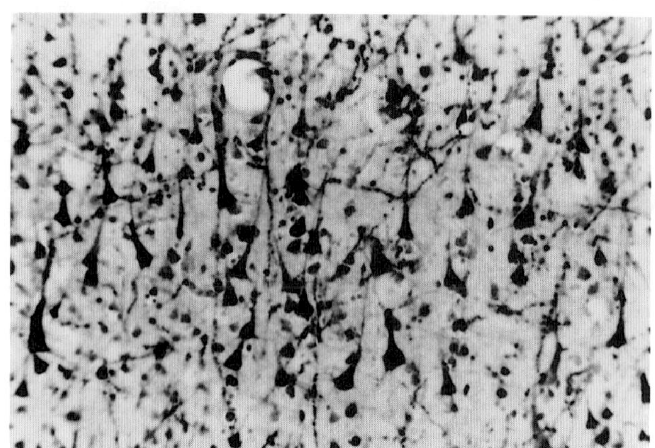

(b) Left hemisphere

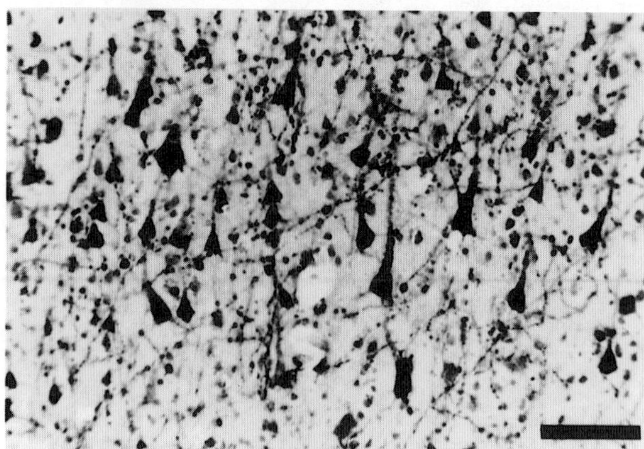

Figure 11.4 Visual examination reveals a subtle difference in the sizes of the largest subgroups of layer III pyramidal cells (stained here with acetylthiocholinesterase) in the left hemisphere **(b)** compared to the right **(a)**.

how might these changes specifically alter information processing in the language-dominant hemisphere? Most interpretations of these findings have focused on the relationship between adjacent neurons and adjacent columns, highlighting the fact that differences in both columnar spacing and dendritic tree size would cause cells in the left hemisphere to connect to fewer neurons. This structural specialization might underlie more elaborate and less redundant patterns of connectivity, which in turn might give rise to better separation between local processing streams. Further refinement of this type could also be driving the larger distance between patches in the left hemisphere, since this larger spacing might also imply more refined connections.

A thorough understanding of the anatomy and physiology of language-associated cortices could shed considerable light on the cortical mechanisms that facilitate linguistic analysis and production. Because cortical areas have a basic underlying organization, documenting cortical locations involved in certain functions should distinguish, in terms of form and variety, between the neural structures common to all regions and the structures critical for a region to carry out particular cognitive functions. These questions hold importance not only for the greater understanding of species-specific adaptations such as language, but also for understanding how evolution may build functional specialization into the framework of cortical organization.

HOW THE TWO HEMISPHERES COMMUNICATE

The cerebral cortices are interconnected by the largest fiber system in the brain, the **corpus callosum**. In humans, this bundle of white matter includes more than 200 million axons. As Figure 11.5 shows, many of the callosal projections link **homotopic areas**, areas in corresponding locations in the two hemispheres. For example, regions in the left prefrontal cortex project to homotopic regions in the right prefrontal cortex. Although this pattern holds for most areas of the association cortex, it is not always seen in primary cortices. Callosal projections connecting the two halves of the primary visual cortex link only those areas that represent the most eccentric regions of space, and in both the primary motor and the somatosensory cortices, homotopic callosal projections are sparse.

Callosal fibers also connect to **heterotopic areas.** These projections generally mirror the ones found within a hemisphere. A prefrontal area sending projections to premotor areas in the same hemisphere is also likely to send projections to the same premotor area in the contralateral hemisphere. Yet, heterotopic projections are usually less extensive than are projections within the same hemisphere.

Several functional roles have been proposed for callosal connections. Some researchers point out that, in the visual association cortex, receptive fields can span both visual fields. Communication across the callosum

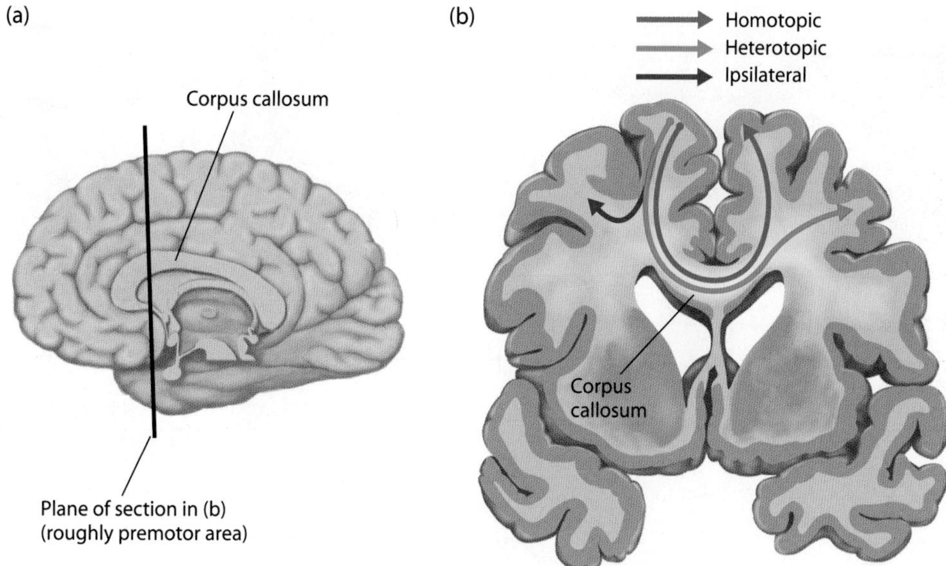

Figure 11.5 Tracing connections between and within the cerebral cortices. **(a)** Midsagittal view of the right cerebral hemisphere, with the large corpus callosum labeled. **(b)** The caudal surface of a coronal section of brain roughly through the premotor cortical area. Homotopic callosal fibers (blue) connect corresponding sections of the two hemispheres via the corpus callosum; heterotopic connections (green) link different areas of the two hemispheres of the brain. In primates, both types of contralateral connections (blue and green), as well as ipsilateral connections (red), start and finish at the same layer of neocortex.

enables information from both visual fields to contribute to the activity of these cells. Indeed, the callosal connections could play a role in synchronizing oscillatory activity in cortical neurons as an object passes through these receptive fields (Figure 11.6). In this view, callosal connections facilitate processing by pooling diverse inputs. Other researchers take a more competitive view of callosal function. If the callosal fibers were inhibitory, they would provide a means for each hemisphere to compete for control of current processing. For example, multiple movements might be activated, all geared to a common goal; later processing would select one of these candidate movements (see Chapter 7). Inhibitory connections across the corpus callosum might be one contributor to this selection.

In developing animals, callosal projections are diffuse, more evenly distributed across the cortical surface. Cats and monkeys lose approximately 70% of their callosal axons during development; some of these transient projections are between areas (portions of the primary sensory cortex) that, in adults, are not connected by the callosum. Yet this loss of axons does not produce cell death in each cortical hemisphere, because a single cell body can send out more than one axon terminal: one to cortical areas on the same side of the brain, and one to the other side of the brain. Thus, loss of a callosal axon may well leave its cell body alive, with its secondary collateral connection to the same hemisphere intact. The refinement of connections is a hallmark of callosal development, just as such refinement characterizes intrahemispheric development (see Chapter 3).

In general terms, hemispheric specialization must have been influenced and constrained by callosal evolution. The appearance of new cortical areas might be expected to require more connections across the callosum (expansion). In contrast, lateralization might have been facilitated by a lack of callosal connections. The resultant isolation would promote divergence among the functional capabilities of homotopic regions.

As with the cerebral hemispheres, researchers have investigated functional correlates of anatomical differences in the corpus callosum. Usually investigators measure gross aspects like the cross-sectional area or shape of the callosum. Variations in these measures are linked to gender, handedness, mental retardation, autism, and schizophrenia. Interpretation of these data, however, is complicated by methodological disagreements and by contradictory results. The underlying logic of measuring the corpus callosum's cross-sectional area relies on the relation of area to structural organization. Callosal size could be related to the number and diameter of axons, the proportion of myelinated axons, the thickness of myelin sheaths, and measures of nonneural structures

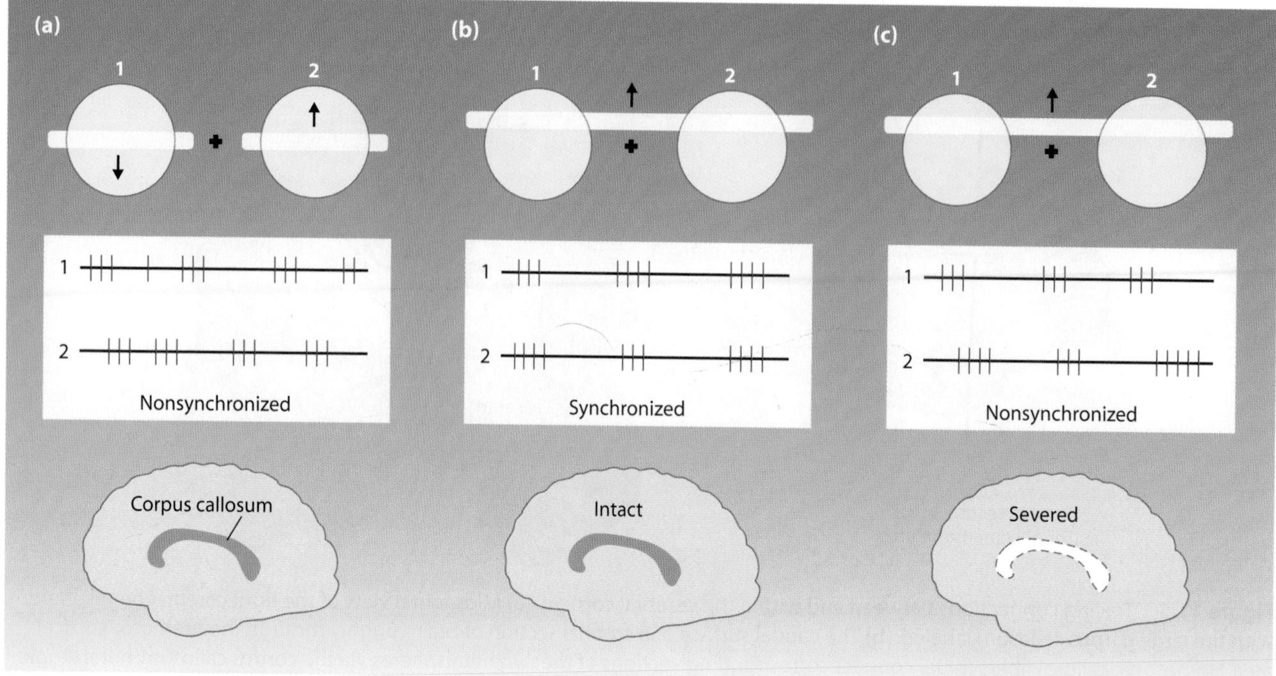

Figure 11.6 Synchrony in cortical neurons. **(a)** When receptive fields (1 and 2) on either side of fixation are stimulated by two separate light bars moving in different directions (as indicated by the arrows), the firing rates of the two cells are not correlated. **(b)** In animals with an intact corpus callosum, cells with spatially separate receptive fields fire synchronously when they are stimulated by a common object, such as a long light bar spanning both fields. **(c)** In animals whose corpus callosum has been severed, synchrony is rarely observed.

such as the size of blood vessels or the volume of extracellular space. With large samples of callosal measures from age-matched control subjects, sex-based differences are seen in the shape of the callosum but not in its size. Handedness may be associated with the size of the callosum's subregions, but parsing the callosum into distinct subregions is artificial, at best.

Cortical Disconnection

Because the corpus callosum is the primary means of communication between the two cerebral hemispheres, we learn a great deal when we sever the callosal fibers. This approach was most successfully used in the pioneering animal studies of Ronald Myers and Roger Sperry at the California Institute of Technology. They showed that the corpus callosum is crucial for unified cortical function. Myers and Sperry demonstrated that visual discrimination learned by one hemisphere did not transfer to the other hemisphere. In this study, cats were trained to choose a "plus" stimulus versus a "circle" stimulus randomly alternated between two doors. If the cats chose correctly, they were rewarded with food. Myers and Sperry made the startling discovery that, when the callosum and anterior commissure were sectioned, such visual discriminations trained to one half of the brain were not known to the other half.

This important research laid the groundwork for comparable human studies initiated by Sperry and Michael Gazzaniga in the 1960s (Sperry et al., 1969). Unlike lesion studies, the split-brain operation does not destroy any cortical tissue; instead, it eliminates the connections between the two hemispheres. With split-brain patients, functional inferences are not based on how behavior changes after a cortical area is eliminated. Rather, it becomes possible to see how each hemisphere operates in relative isolation.

Split-brain surgery is used to treat intractable epilepsy. As with all other forms of neurosurgery, the procedure is undertaken only when other forms of treatment, such as medication, fail. By severing the transcortical connections, surgeons are attempting to hold the epileptogenic activity in check. Remarkably, the operation is almost always successful. Seizures generally subside immediately, even in patients who, prior to the operation, experienced up to 15 seizures per day. The operation enables the resumption of a normal life with no obvious side effects.

Many methodological issues arise in evaluations of the performance of split-brain patients. First, bear in mind that these patients were not neurologically normal prior to the operation; they were all chronic epileptics. Therefore, it is reasonable to ask whether they provide an appropriate barometer of normal hemispheric function after the operation. There is no easy answer to this question. Several patients do display abnormal performance on neuropsychological assessments, and they may even be mentally retarded. But in some patients the cognitive impairments are negligible; these are the patients studied in closest detail.

Second, it is important to consider whether the transcortical connections were completely sectioned, or whether some fibers remain intact. In the original California operations, reviewing surgical notes was the only way to determine the completeness of the surgical sections, but in recent years MRIs, such as in Figure 11.7b, and electrical brain-mapping techniques have provided a more accurate representation of the extent of surgical sections. Accurate documentation of a callosal section is crucial for learning about the organization of the cerebral commissure.

The main methods of testing the perceptual and cognitive functions of each hemisphere have changed little over the past 30 years. Researchers use mainly visual stimulation, not only because of the preeminent status of this modality for humans but also because the visual system is more strictly lateralized than are other sensory modalities, such as the auditory and olfactory systems.

We can restrict the visual stimulus to a single hemisphere by quickly flashing the stimulus in one visual field or the other (Figure 11.8). Prior to stimulation, the patient is required to fixate on a point in space. The brevity of stimulation is necessary to prevent eye movements, which would redirect the information into the unwanted hemisphere. Eye movements take roughly 200 ms, so if the stimulus is presented for a briefer period of time, the experimenter can be confident that the stimulus was lateralized. More recent image stabilization tools—tools that move in correspondence with the subject's eye movements—allow a more prolonged, naturalistic form of stimulation. This technological development has opened the way for new discoveries in the neurological and psychological aspects of hemisphere disconnection.

Functional Consequences of the Split-Brain Procedure

Reports on the California patients dealt with several fundamental issues concerning the psychological properties of the separated cerebral hemispheres, as well as the basic aspects of neurological organization. In many respects, the issues raised in the original studies still drive current research efforts, so let's review the neurological consequences of callosum sectioning before we investigate the separate psychological properties of the two cerebral hemispheres.

Humans were initially studied in the context of new animal evidence that a division of the cerebral commissure produces a profound deficit in the interhemispheric transfer of sensory and motor information. Following operations on cats, monkeys, and chimpanzees that severed both the corpus callosum and the anterior commissure, researchers discovered that visual

Figure 11.7 Sagittal views of the human brain. **(a)** The corpus callosum is the large fiber tract that is sectioned by a neurosurgeon seeking to control otherwise intractable epilepsy. **(b)** This MRI shows a corpus callosum that has been entirely sectioned, with the result that information is no longer transferred between the cerebral hemispheres.

(a)

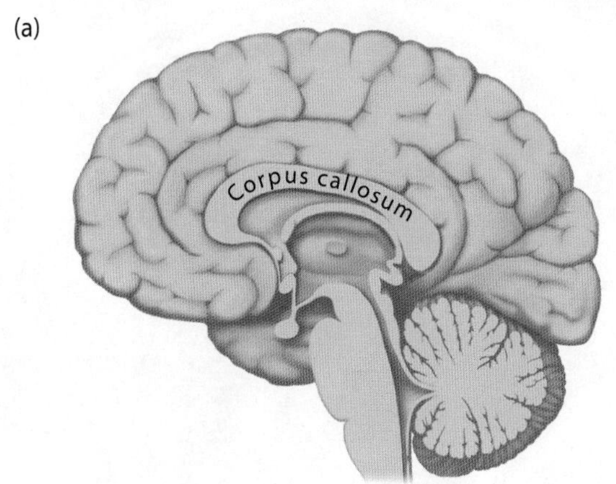

(b)

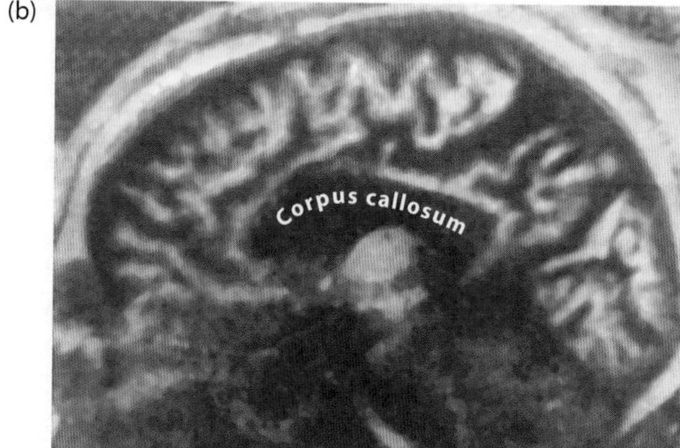

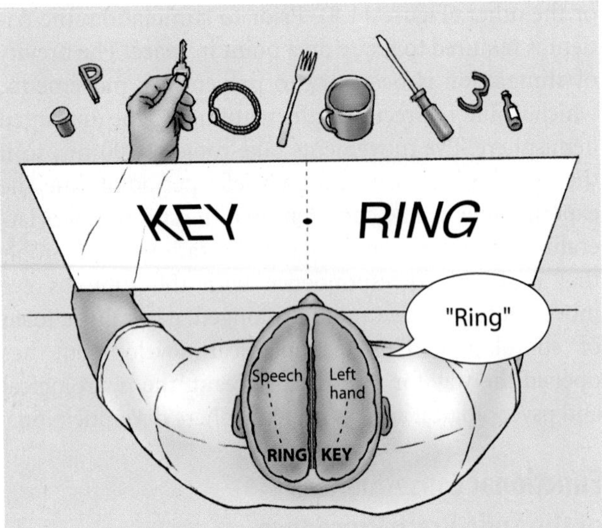

Figure 11.8 Restricting visual stimuli to one hemisphere. The split-brain patient reports through the speaking hemisphere only the items flashed to the right half of the screen and denies seeing left-field stimuli or recognizing objects presented to the left hand. Nevertheless, the left hand correctly retrieves objects presented in the left visual field, about which the subject verbally denies knowing anything.

and tactile information that was lateralized to one hemisphere did not transfer to the opposite hemisphere—hence, the split-brain animal. This startling discovery was completely contrary to earlier reports on the effects of human commissure section reported by A. J. Akelaitis (1941) of the University of Rochester. He claimed that no significant neurological and psychological effects were seen after the callosum was sectioned.

Careful testing with the California patients, however, revealed behavioral changes similar to those seen in split-brain primates. Visual information presented to one half of the brain was not available to the other half. The same principle applied to touch. Patients were able to name and describe objects placed in the right hand but not objects presented in the left hand. Sensory information restricted to one hemisphere was not available to accurately guide movements with the ipsilateral hand. For example, when a picture of a hand portraying the "OK" sign was presented to the left hemisphere, the patient was able to make the gesture with the right hand, which is controlled from the left half of the brain. However, the patient was unable to make the same gesture with the left hand, which is controlled from the disconnected right hemisphere.

From a cognitive point of view, these initial studies confirmed long-standing neurological knowledge about the nature of the two cerebral hemispheres: The left hemisphere is dominant for language, speech, and major problem solving; the right hemisphere appears specialized for visuospatial tasks such as drawing cubes and other three-dimensional patterns. Thus, split-brain patients cannot name or describe visual and tactile stimuli presented to the right hemisphere, because the sensory information is disconnected from the dominant left (speech) hemisphere. But this does not mean that knowledge about the stimuli is absent in the right hemisphere. Nonverbal response techniques are required to demonstrate the competence of the right hemisphere. For example, the left hand can be used to point to named objects or to demonstrate the function of depicted objects presented in the left visual field.

Specificity of Callosal Function

When the corpus callosum is fully sectioned, little or no perceptual or cognitive interaction occurs between the hemispheres. Surgical cases in which callosal section is limited or part of the callosum is inadvertently spared have enabled investigators to examine specific functions of the callosum by region. For example, when the **splenium**, the posterior area of the callosum that interconnects the occipital lobe, is spared, visual information is transferred normally between the two cerebral hemispheres (Figure 11.9). In these instances, pattern, color, and linguistic information presented anywhere in either visual field can be matched with information presented to the other half of the brain. Even so, the patients show

Figure 11.9 MRI scan showing that the splenium (arrow) was spared in the split-brain procedure performed on this patient. As a result, visual information can still be transferred between the cerebral hemispheres.

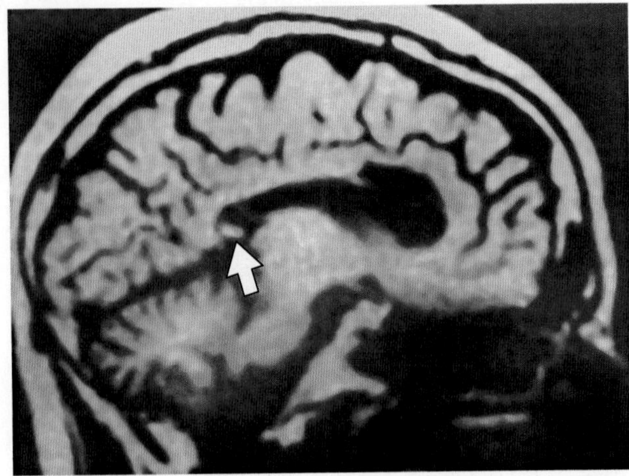

no evidence of interhemispheric transfer of tactile information from touched objects.

A recent investigation of the connectivity of the human splenium is based on a new neuroimaging technique: diffusion tensor imaging (DTI; see Chapter 4). This track-tracing method was used to identify the connections between the splenium of the corpus callosum and every major Brodmann area of cortex in neurologically healthy individuals. The results showed homotopic and heterotopic connections between the splenium and posterior visual areas, including the occipital and posterior parietal cortices. Surprisingly, in nearly a third of the participants, homotopic fibers also connected primary visual cortices—a result at odds with the long-standing belief that V1 does not contain interhemispheric connections. Across all participants, there were more instances of splenial connections with the right hemisphere than with the left hemisphere. This asymmetrical cortical projection pattern may be the anatomical basis for the well-established behavioral observation that interhemispheric transfer of visual information is faster from the right to the left hemisphere than vice versa (Steven et al., 2006).

The anterior part of the callosum is involved in the higher order transfer of semantic information. Surgeons sometimes prefer to perform the split-brain procedure in stages, restricting the initial operation to the front (anterior) or back (posterior) half of the callosum. The remaining fibers are sectioned in a second operation only if the seizures continue to persist. This two-stage procedure offers a unique glimpse into what the anterior callosal regions transfer between the cerebral hemisphere. When the posterior half of the callosum is sectioned, transfer of visual, tactile, and auditory sensory information is severely disrupted. Yet the remaining intact anterior region of the callosum is able to transfer higher order information. For example, one patient (J.W.) was able to name stimuli presented in the left visual field following a resection limited to the posterior callosal region. Close examination revealed that the left hemisphere was receiving higher order cues about the stimulus without having access to the sensory information about the stimulus itself (Figure 11.10). In short, the anterior part of the callosum transfers semantic information about the stimulus but not the stimulus itself. After the anterior callosal region was sectioned in this patient, this capacity was lost.

Recently, new light has been shed on the importance of information transfer between the hemispheres by the combination of several methodological approaches to studying the naming of visual objects presented in an unfamiliar or unusual orientation. Previously it was demonstrated that this tasks relies on both the left inferior frontal cortex (for naming) and the right parietal lobe (for object recognition). For successful task completion, these two regions must communicate across the corpus callosum. By a combination of fMRI and DTI, it has been demonstrated that the strength of activation in these two locations is directly associated with measures of the integrity and organization of white matter within the corpus callosum. Furthermore, the relationship between functional activation and white matter structure actually predicts the reaction times of individual subjects performing the task (Figure 11.11; Baird et al., 2005). This remarkable confluence of methods further underscores the important links between structural organization, functional activation, and behavior.

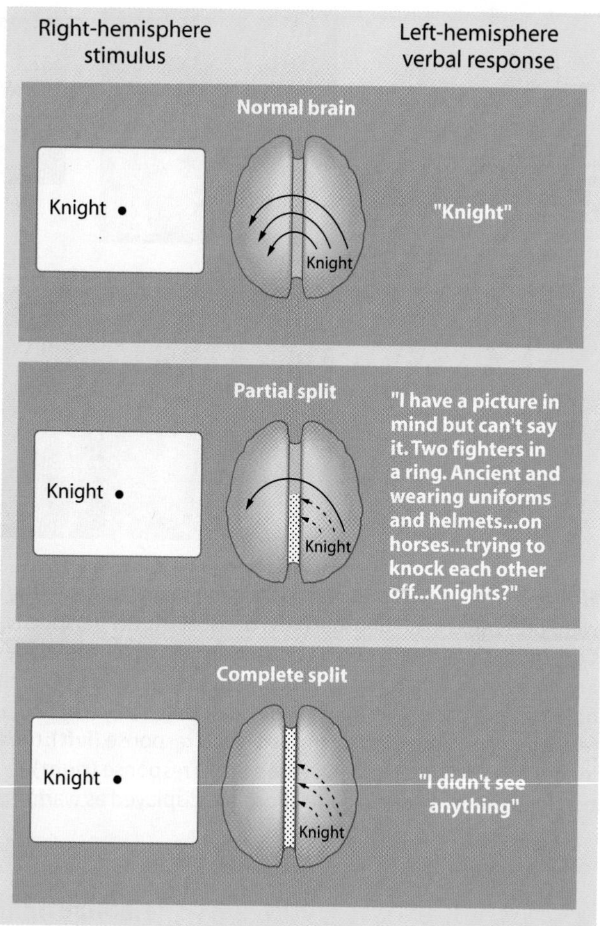

Figure 11.10 Schematic representation of split-brain patient J.W.'s naming ability for objects in the left visual field at each operative stage.

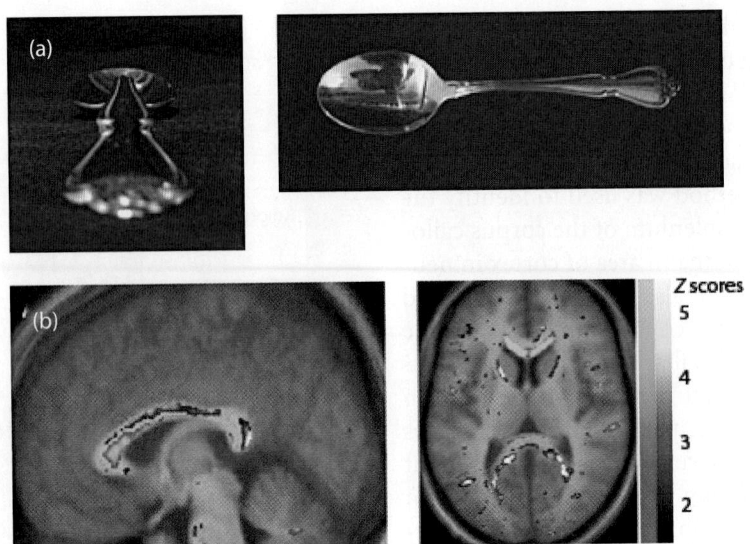

Figure 11.11 BOLD and reaction time differences across the corpus callosum. **(a)** Common objects such as the spoon shown here were presented in an unusual **(left)** or usual **(right)** perspective, and the participants had to name the objects as fast as possible. Correlations were performed between structural MRI measures using diffusion tensor imaging (fractional anisotropy values, indicating the level of coherence of white matter fibers) and fMRI activity during the naming task, as well as the reaction times when the objects were presented from an unusual perspective. **(b)** The posterior portion of the corpus callosum (splenium) is associated with faster reaction times and decreased BOLD response **(left)**; the frontal portion of the corpus callosum (genu) is associated with longer reaction times and increased BOLD response **(right)**. Note that the color coding of these images does not represent activation level; rather, positive correlations are displayed as warm colors and negative correlations as cool colors.

HEMISPHERIC SPECIALIZATION

One of the cardinal features of behavioral studies of human and animal brains has been the realization that specific brain areas appear to be involved with specific perceptual and cognitive functions. The split-brain approach to this issue has been straightforward. By testing each disconnected hemisphere, one can assess the different capacities that each might possess. Although some claims are exaggerated, there are marked differences between the two halves of the brain. The most prominent lateralized function in the human brain is the left hemisphere's capacity for language and speech.

Language and Speech

A useful dichotomy when we're trying to understand the neural bases of language is the distinction between grammatical and lexical functions. The grammar–lexicon distinction is different from the more traditional syntax–semantics distinction commonly invoked to improve understanding of the differential effects of brain lesions on language processes (see Chapter 10). In general terms, *grammar* is the rule-based system that humans have for ordering words to facilitate communication. The *lexicon*, by contrast, is the mind's dictionary, where words are associated with specific meanings.

The reason for the distinction is that it takes into account factors such as memory, since, with memory, word strings as idioms can be learned by rote. For example, the cliché "you can't teach an old dog new tricks" is most likely a single lexical entry. Although the lexicon cannot possibly encompass the infinite number of unique phrases and sentences that humans can generate—such as the one you are now reading—memory does play a role in many short phrases. When uttered, such word strings do not reflect an underlying interaction of syntax and semantic systems; they are, instead, essentially an entry from the lexicon. A modern view would predict that there ought to be brain areas wholly responsible for grammar, whereas the lexicon's location ought to be more elusive, since it reflects learned information and thus is part of the brain's general memory and knowledge systems. The grammar system, then, ought to be discrete and hence localizable, and the lexicon should be distributed and hence more difficult to damage completely.

Language and speech processes are rarely present in both hemispheres. Although the separated left hemisphere normally comprehends all aspects of language, the linguistic capabilities of the right hemisphere are not necessarily nonexistent. Indeed, out of dozens of split-brain patients who have been carefully examined, only six showed clear evidence of residual linguistic functions in the right hemisphere. And even in these patients, the extent of right-hemisphere language functions is severely limited and restricted to the lexical aspects of comprehension.

The left and right lexicons of these special patients can be near equal in their capacity, but they are organized quite differently. For example, both hemispheres show a phenomenon called the *word superiority effect* (see Chapter 4). Normal readers are better able to identify letters (e.g., *L*) in the context of real English words (e.g., *belt*) than when the same letters appear in pseudowords (e.g., *kelt*) or nonsense letter strings (e.g., *ktle*). Because pseudowords and nonwords do not have lexical entries, letters occurring in such strings do not receive the additional processing benefit bestowed on words. Thus, the word superiority effect emerges.

The word superiority effect may be a useful measure of the integrity of the visual lexicon. When these effects are assessed for each hemisphere, the patients with right-hemisphere language exhibit a visual lexicon, as evidenced by a word superiority effect. Yet it may be that each hemisphere accesses this lexicon in a different way. Investigators evaluated this possibility by using a letter-priming task. Subjects were asked simply to indicate whether a briefly flashed uppercase letter was an *H* or a *T*. On each trial the uppercase letter was preceded by a lowercase letter that was either an *h* or a *t*. Normally subjects are significantly faster, or primed, when an uppercase *H* is preceded by a lowercase *h* than when it is preceded by a lowercase *t*.

The difference between response latency on compatible (*h–H*) versus incompatible (*t–H*) trials is taken to be a measure of letter priming. J.W., a split-brain participant, performed a lateralized version of this task in which the prime was displayed for 100 ms to either the right or the left visual field, and 400 ms later the target letter appeared in either the right or the left visual field. The results, shown in Figure 11.12, provide no evidence of letter priming for left-visual-field trials but clear evidence of priming for right-visual-field trials. Thus, the lack of a priming phenomenon in the disconnected right hemisphere suggests a deficit in letter recognition, prohibiting access to parallel processing mechanisms. J.W. exhibited a variety of other deficiencies in right-hemisphere function as well. For example, he was unable to judge whether one word was superordinate to another (e.g., *furniture* and *chair*), or whether two words were antonyms (e.g., *love* and *hate*).

In sum, there appear to be two lexicons, one in each hemisphere. The right hemisphere's lexicon seems organized differently from the left hemisphere's lexicon, and these lexicons are accessed in different ways. These observations are consistent with the view that lexicons reflect learning processes and, as such, are more widely distributed in the cerebral cortex. Although it has been a long-held belief that in the general population the lexicon appears to be in the left hemisphere, recent evidence from functional-imaging studies suggests a broader role for the right hemisphere in language processing, although the precise nature of that role remains to be defined.

In contrast, generative syntax is present in only one hemisphere. Although the right hemisphere of some patients clearly has a lexicon, the hemispheres perform erratically on other aspects of language, such as understanding verbs, pluralizations, the possessive, or active–passive differences. In patients who possess some language, the right hemisphere also fails to use word order to disambiguate stimuli for correct meaning. Yet these right hemispheres can indicate when a sentence ends with a semantically odd word! In addition, right hemispheres with language capacities can make grammar judgments. For some peculiar reason, they cannot use syntax to disambiguate stimuli, but they can judge that one set of utterances is grammatical while another set is not. This startling finding suggests that patterns of speech are learned by rote. Yet recognizing the pattern of acceptable utterances does not mean that a neural system can use this information to understand word strings (Figure 11.13).

Figure 11.12 Letter priming as a function of visual field in split-brain patients. The graph shows the response latencies for compatible and incompatible words in the right and left visual fields (RVF and LVF, respectively). The latencies for both types of words are much longer for the left visual field (right hemisphere).

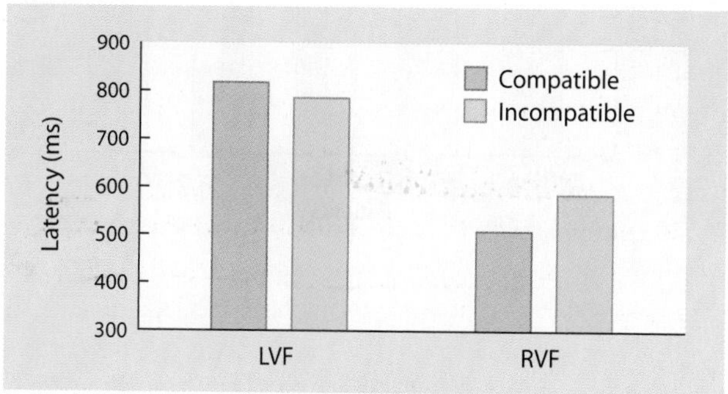

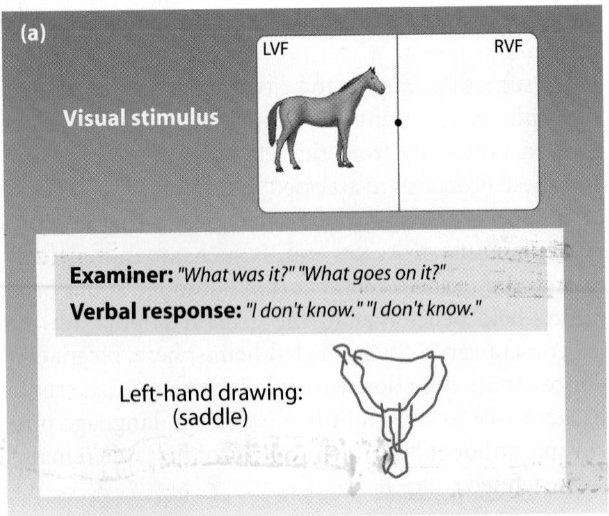

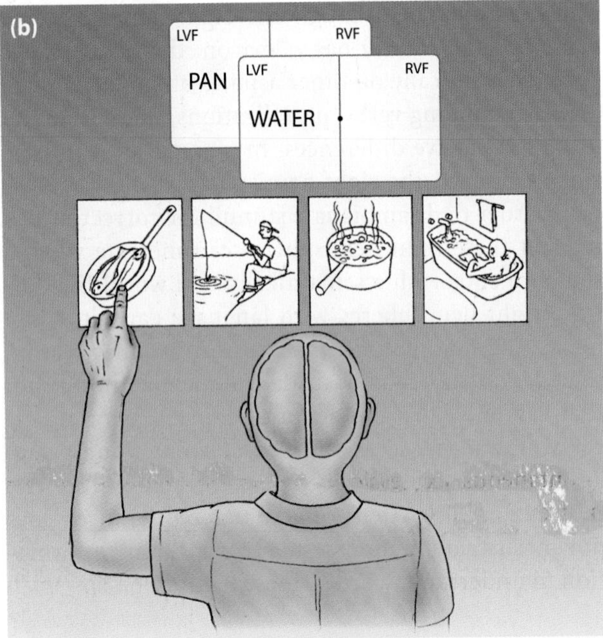

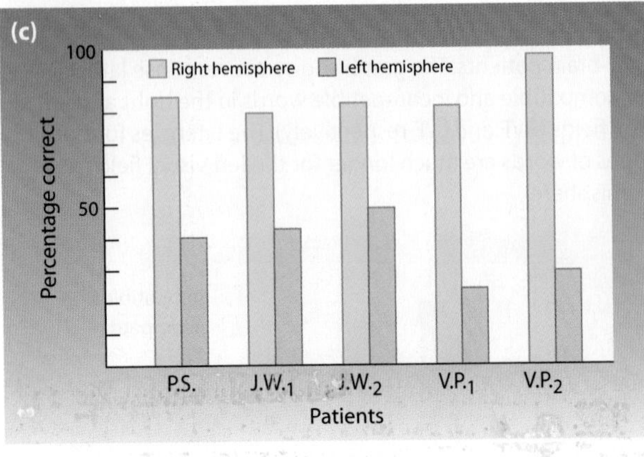

Figure 11.13 Cognitive abilities of the right hemisphere. **(a)** The right hemisphere is capable of understanding language but not syntax. When presented with a horse stimulus to the left visual field (right hemisphere), the subjects maintain through the left hemisphere that they saw nothing. When asked to draw what goes on the object, the left hand (right hemisphere) is able to draw a saddle. **(b)** The capacity of the right hemisphere to make inferences is extremely limited. Two words are presented in serial order, and the right hemisphere (left hand) is simply required to point to a picture that best depicts what happens when the words are causally related. The left hemisphere finds these tasks trivial, but the right cannot perform the task. **(c)** Data from three patients show that the right hemisphere is more accurate than the left in recognizing unfamiliar faces.

One of the hallmarks of most split-brain patients is that their speech is produced in the left hemisphere and not the right. This observation, consistent with the literature and with amobarbital studies, shows that the left hemisphere is the dominant hemisphere for speech production. Nonetheless, there are now a handful of documented cases of split-brain patients who can produce speech from both the left and the right hemispheres. Although speech is restricted to the left hemisphere following callosal bisection, in these rare patients the capacity to make one-word utterances from the disconnected right hemisphere has emerged over time.

This intriguing development raises the question of whether information is somehow transferring to the dominant hemisphere for speech output or whether the right hemisphere itself is capable of developing speech production. After extensive testing, it became apparent that the latter hypothesis is correct. For example, the patients were able to name an object presented in the left field and in the right field but were not able to judge whether the two objects were the same! Or, when words like *father* were presented such that the fixation point fell between the *t* and the *h*, the patients said either "fat" or "her," depending on which hemisphere controlled speech production. These findings illustrate that an extraordinary plasticity lasts sometimes as long as 10 years after callosal surgery. In one patient, in fact, the right hemisphere had no speech production capability for approximately 13 years before it "spoke."

Finally, note that although most language capabilities are left lateralized, the processing of the emotional content of language appears to be right lateralized. It is well known that patients with damage to certain regions of the left hemisphere have language comprehension difficulties. Speech, however, can communicate emotion information beyond the meanings and structures of the words. A statement such as "John, come here" can be interpreted in different ways if it is said in an angry tone, a fearful tone, a seductive tone, or a surprised tone. This nonlinguistic, emotional component of speech is called *emotional prosody*. One patient with left-hemisphere damage reportedly has difficulty comprehending words but shows little deficit in interpreting the meaning of emotional prosody (Barrett et al., 1999). At the same time, several patients with damage to the temporoparietal lobe in the right hemisphere have been shown to comprehend the meaning of language perfectly but have difficulty interpreting phrases when emotional prosody plays a role (Heilman et al., 1975). This double dissociation between language and emotional prosody in the comprehension of meaning suggests that the right hemisphere is specialized for comprehending emotional expressions of speech.

Visuospatial Processing

The second primary task domain that has been studied in split-brain patients is visuospatial processing. As Figure 11.1 shows, the isolated right hemisphere is frequently found to be superior on neuropsychological tests such as the block design task, a subtest of the Wechsler Adult Intelligence Scale. Here the simple task of arranging some red and white blocks to match those of a given pattern can find the left hemisphere performing poorly while the right triumphs. However, asymmetries with tasks such as these have proved to be inconsistent. In some patients, performance is impaired with either hand; in others, the left hemisphere is quite adept at this task.

This inconsistency is, at least in part, due to the fact that the component operations required for the block design task have not been identified. Patients who demonstrate a right-hemisphere superiority for this task exhibit no superiority on the perceptual aspects of the task. If a picture of the block design pattern is lateralized, either hemisphere can easily find the match from a series of pictures. And since each hand is sufficiently dexterous, the crucial link must be in the mapping of the sensory message onto the capable motor system.

Monitoring and producing facial expressions are also managed by different hemispheres. In the perceptual domain, the right hemisphere appears to have special processes devoted to the efficient detection of upright faces. The left hemisphere can also perceive and recognize faces, although it is generally not as adept as the right hemisphere, at least when the faces are unfamiliar. This pattern of asymmetry also has been shown in the rhesus monkey. In addition, split-brain studies have been conducted to examine laterality patterns for a special recognition ability: that of recognizing one's own face. These patients can recognize pictures of the self in *both* visual hemispheres. As with the recognition of familiar faces in general, however, the left hemisphere outperforms the right hemisphere in this task (Gazzaniga, 2005).

Finally, studies of the production and management of facial expressions show that, although both hemispheres can generate spontaneous facial expressions, only the dominant left hemisphere can generate voluntary facial expressions. Indeed there appear to be two neural systems for controlling facial expressions (Figure 11.14). The system that controls voluntary expression is managed by the left hemisphere (Gazzaniga & Smylie, 1990). It sends its messages to the contralateral facial nucleus (cranial nerve VII), which in turn innervates the right facial muscles. At the same time, the left hemisphere sends a command over the corpus callosum to the right half of the brain. The right hemisphere sends the message down to the left facial nucleus, which in turn innervates the left half of the face. The result is that one can make a symmetrical facial response such as a smile or frown.

Spontaneous facial expression is managed by a different neural pathway. First, unlike voluntary expressions, which only the left hemisphere can trigger, spontaneous expressions can be managed by either half of the brain. When either half triggers a spontaneous response, the pathways that activate the brainstem nuclei are signaled through another pathway—one that does not course through the cortex. Each hemisphere sends signals straight down through the midbrain and out to the brainstem nuclei. Clinical neurologists know of the distinction between these two ways of controlling facial muscles. For example, a patient with a lesion in the part of the right hemisphere that participates in voluntary expressions is unable to move the left half of the face when the subject is told to smile. At the same time, the very same patient can easily move the left half of the face when spontaneously smiling because those pathways are unaffected by right-hemisphere damage. In addition, with Parkinson's disease the pathways supporting spontaneous facial expressions do not work, whereas the pathways that support voluntary expressions do work. Such patients can lose their masked-face appearance when told to smile (Figure 11.15).

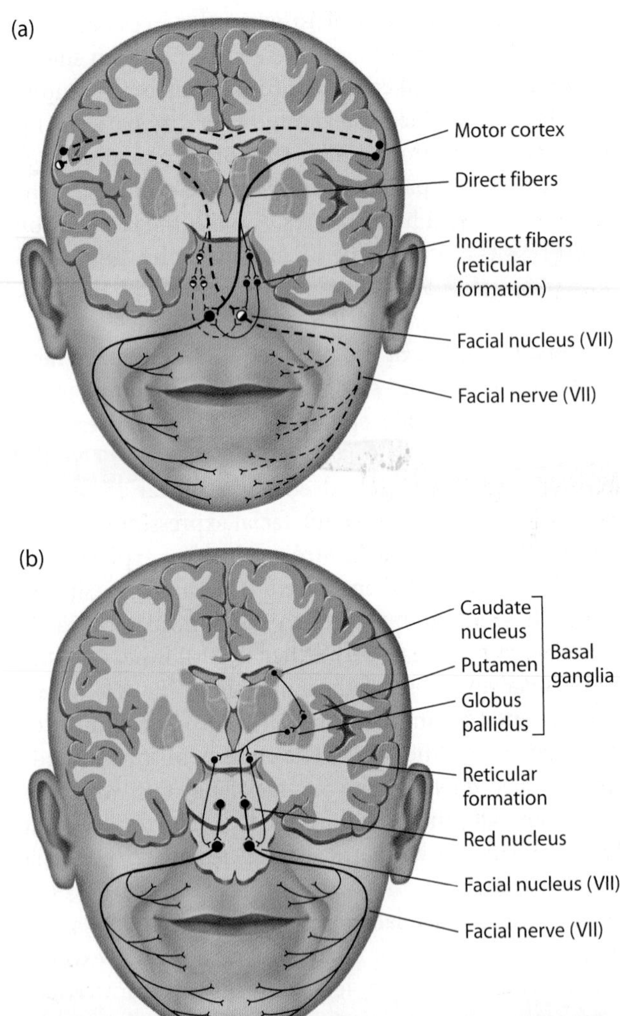

Figure 11.14 The neural pathways that control voluntary and spontaneous facial expression are different. **(a)** Voluntary expressions that can signal intention have their own cortical networks in humans. **(b)** The neural networks for spontaneous expressions involve older brain circuits and appear to be the same as those in chimpanzees.

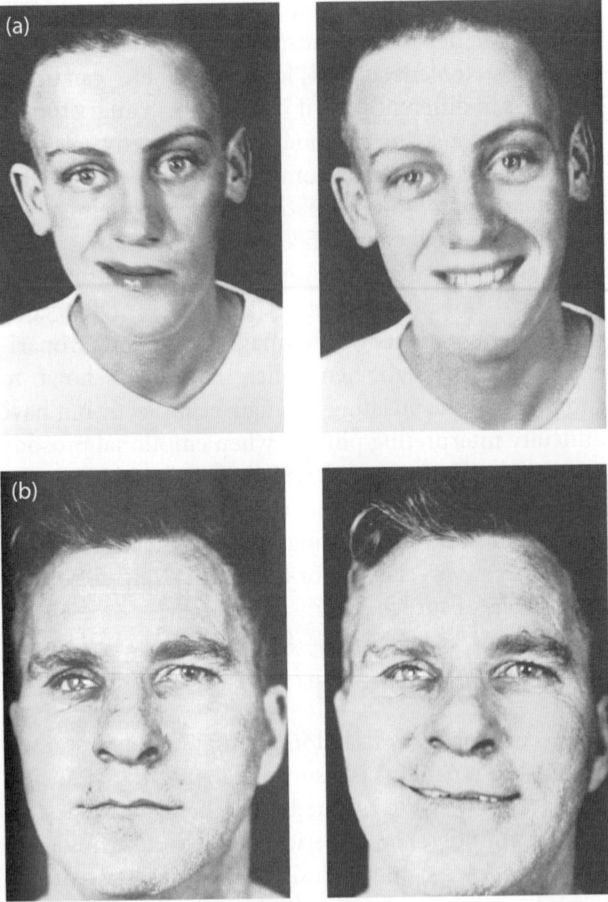

Figure 11.15 Facial expressions of two kinds of patients. **(a)** This patient suffered brain damage to the right hemisphere; the lesion interfered with voluntary facial expression. **(b)** This Parkinson's disease patient has a typical masked face. Because Parkinson's disease involves the part of the brain that controls spontaneous facial expression, the faces of these patients, when they are told to smile, light up because the other pathway is still intact.

Attention and Perception

The attentional and perceptual abilities of split-brain patients have been explored extensively. Visual perception is the easiest to study. After cortical disconnection, perceptual information does not interact between the two cerebral hemispheres, but the supporting cognitive processes of attentional mechanisms do sometimes interact.

Split-brain patients cannot integrate visual information between the two visual fields. When visual information is lateralized to either the left or the right disconnected hemisphere, the unstimulated hemisphere cannot use the information for perceptual analysis. This is also true for certain types of somatosensory information presented to each hand. Although touching any part of the body is noted by either hemisphere, patterned somatosensory information is lateralized. Thus, when holding an object in the left hand, a split-brain patient is unable to find an identical object with the right hand. Although some investigators argue that higher order perceptual information is integrated by way of subcortical structures, others have not replicated these results.

In one study, for example, split-brain patients sometimes drew pictures that combine word information presented to the two hemispheres (e.g., *ten* + *clock* = a picture of a clock set at 10). Although this outcome initially seemed to imply the subcortical transfer of higher

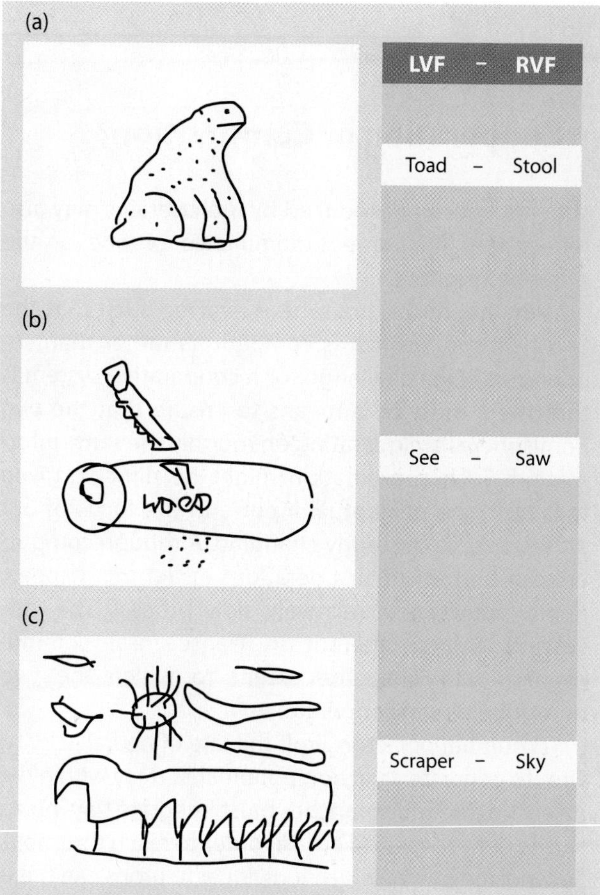

Figure 11.16 Pictures drawn by split-brain participant J.W.'s left hand in response to stimuli presented to the left and right visual fields (LVF and RVF). **(a)** Drawing of the left-visual-field word *Toad* (ipsilateral to the drawing hand). **(b)** Drawing of the right-visual-field word *Saw* (contralateral to the drawing hand). **(c)** Drawing combining both words: *Scraper* and *Sky* (ipsilateral + contralateral).

order information between the hemispheres, subsequent observations (Figure 11.16; Kingstone & Gazzaniga, 1995) suggested that it actually reflects dual hemispheric control of the drawing hand (with control biased to the left hemisphere). Conceptually ambiguous word pairs, such as *hot dog*, were always depicted literally (e.g., a dog panting in the heat) and never as emergent objects (e.g., a frankfurter). Moreover, right- and left-hand drawings often depicted only the words presented to the left hemisphere.

Whereas the previous work with split-brain patients showed that object identification occurs in isolation in each hemisphere, the evidence does suggest that crude information concerning spatial locations can be cross-integrated. In one set of experiments, a four-point grid was presented to each visual field. On a given trial, one of the positions on the grid was highlighted, and one condition of the task required the subject to move her eyes to the highlighted point within the visual field with the highlighted stimulus (Figure 11.17a). In the second condition the subject was required to move her eyes to the relative point in the visual field opposite to the one with the highlighted stimulus (Figure 11.17b). Split-brain subjects did this easily, raising the possibility of crude cross-integration of spatial information. The ability remained intact even when the grid was randomly positioned in the test field.

The finding that some type of spatial information remains integrated between the two halves of the brain raises this question: Are the attentional processes associated with spatial information affected by cortical disconnection?

Surprisingly, split-brain patients can use either hemisphere to direct attention to positions in either the left or the right visual field. This conclusion was based on studies using a modified version of the spatial cuing task (see Chapter 12). As Figure 12.8 will illustrate, in this task subjects respond as quickly as possible upon detecting a target that appears at one of several possible locations. The target is preceded by a cue, either at the target location (a valid cue) or at another location (an invalid cue). Responses are faster on valid trials, indicating spatial orienting to the cued location. In split-brain patients, as with normal subjects, a cue to direct attention to a particular point in the visual field was honored no matter which half of the brain was presented with the critical stimulus. These results suggest that the two

Figure 11.17 Cross-integration of spatial information. **(a)** On within-field trials, the eye moved to the stimulus that was surrounded by the probe. **(b)** On between-field trials, the eye moved to the corresponding stimulus in the other hemifield.

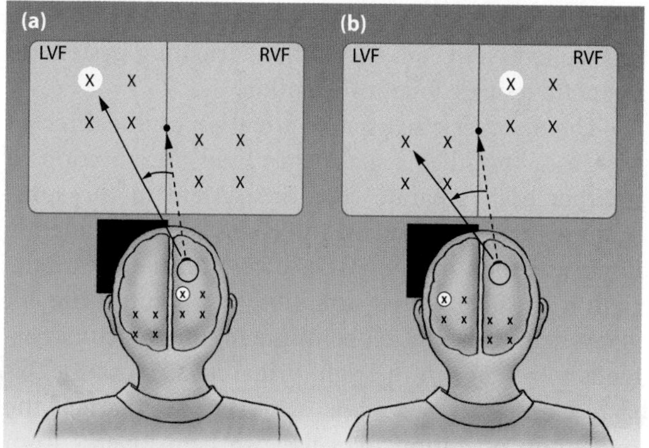

HOW THE BRAIN WORKS

Interhemispheric Communication: Cooperation or Competition?

Theories of callosal function generally have focused on the idea that this massive bundle of axonal fibers provides the primary pathway for interhemispheric transfer. For example, in Chapter 6 we discussed Warrington's model of object recognition. In her view, the right hemisphere performs a specialized operation essential for perceptual categorization. This operation is followed by a left-hemisphere operation for semantic categorization. Interhemispheric communication is essential in this model for shuttling the information through these two processing stages. Even in less serially oriented models, interhemispheric transfer frequently is assumed to allow each hemisphere to access the information that might have been lateralized initially.

On the other hand, interhemispheric communication need not be conceptualized as a cooperative process. Connections across the corpus callosum may actually underlie a competition between the hemispheres. Indeed, the primary mode of callosal communication may be inhibitory rather than excitatory: As activation built in a region within a hemisphere, the homologous, corresponding region in the other hemisphere would be inhibited. By this view, we need not assume that interhemispheric communication is designed to share information processing within the two hemispheres to facilitate concurrent, and roughly identical, activity in homologous regions. Similar to the way in which split-brain behavior is assumed to reflect the independent operation of the two hemispheres, behavior produced by intact brains may also reflect the (fluctuating) dominance of one or the other hemisphere.

Why might the brain have evolved such that the two hemispheres act as competitors rather than cooperators? One challenge for a cooperative system is that there must be a means to ensure that the two hemispheres are operating on roughly the same information. Such coordination might be difficult, given that both the perceptual input and the focus of our attention are constantly changing. Although computers can perform their operations at lightning speed, neural activity is a relatively slow process. The processing delays inherent in transcallosal communication may limit the extent to which the two hemispheres can cooperate.

A number of factors limit the rate of neural activity. First, to generate an action potential, activity within the receiving dendritic branches must integrate tiny inputs across both space and time in order to reach threshold. Second, the rate at which individual neurons can fire is limited, owing to intrinsic differences in membrane properties, tonic sources of excitation and inhibition, and refractory periods between spike-generating events. Third, and most important, neural signals need to be propagated along axons. These conduction times can be quite substantial, especially for the relatively long fibers of the corpus callosum.

James Ringo and his colleagues (1994) at the University of Rochester provided an interesting analysis

hemispheres rely on a common orienting system to maintain a single focus of attention.

The discovery that spatial attention can be directed with ease to either visual field raised the question of whether each separate cognitive system in the split-brain patient, if instructed to do so, can independently direct attention to a part of its own visual field. Can the right hemisphere direct attention to a point in the left visual field while the left hemisphere simultaneously attends to a point in the right visual field? Normal subjects cannot so divide their attention, but perhaps the split-brain operation frees the two hemispheres from this constraint.

As it turns out, the split-brain patient cannot divide spatial attention between the two halves. It appears that only one integrated spatial attention system remains intact following cortical disconnection. Thus, as in neurologically intact observers, the attentional system of split-brain patients is unifocal. They are unable to prepare for events in two spatially disparate locations.

The dramatic effects of disconnecting the cerebral hemispheres on perception and cognition might suggest that each half has its own attentional resources (Kinsbourne, 1982). If that is true, the cognitive operations of one half, no matter what the difficulty, would have scant influence on the cognitive activities of the

of this problem. They began by calculating estimates of transcallosal conduction delays. Two essential numbers were needed: the distance to be traveled, and the speed at which the signal would be transmitted. If the distances were direct, the average distance of the callosal fibers would be short. However, most axons follow a circuitous route. Taking this point into consideration, a value of 175 mm was used as representative of the average length of a callosal fiber in humans. The speed at which myelinated neural impulses travel is a function of the diameter of the fibers. Using the limited data available from humans, in combination with more thorough measures in the monkey, the average conduction speed was estimated to be about 6.5 m/s. Thus, to travel a distance of 175 mm would take almost 30 ms. Single-cell studies in primates have confirmed that interhemispheric processing entails relatively substantial delays.

Ringo used a neural network to demonstrate the consequences of slow interhemispheric conduction times. The network consisted of two identical sets of processing modules, each representing a cerebral hemisphere. It included both intrahemispheric and interhemispheric connections, with the latter much more sparse to reflect the known anatomy of the human brain. This network was trained to perform a pattern recognition task. After it had learned to classify all of the patterns correctly, the interhemispheric connections were disconnected. Thus, performance could now be assessed when each hemisphere had to operate in isolation.

The critical comparison was between networks in which the interhemispheric conduction times during learning had been either slow or fast. The results showed that, for the network trained with fast interhemispheric connections, the disconnection procedure led to a substantial deterioration in performance. Thus, object recognition was dependent on cooperative processing for the network with fast interhemispheric connections. In contrast, for the network trained with slow interhemispheric connections, performance was minimally affected by the disconnection procedure. For this network, recognition was essentially dependent only on intrahemispheric processing. These results led Ringo to conclude that a system with slow interhemispheric conduction delays—for example, the human brain—ends up with each hemisphere operating in a relatively independent manner.

Interestingly, these delays could be reduced if the callosal fibers were larger because the larger size would increase conduction speed. However, larger fibers would require a corresponding increase in brain volume. For example, to reduce the conduction delay by a factor of 2 would lead to a 50% increase in brain volume. Such an increase would have severe consequences in terms of metabolic demands and for childbirth. The brain appears to have evolved such that each hemisphere can have rapid access to information from either side of space, but with limited capability for tasks that would require extensive communication back and forth across the corpus callosum. The delays associated with transcallosal communication not only might limit the degree of cooperation between two hemispheres but also might have provided an impetus for the development of hemispheric specialization. Independent processing systems would be more likely to evolve nonidentical computational capabilities.

other. The competing view is that the brain has limited resources that manage such processes; if they are being applied to Task A, fewer are available for Task B. According to this model, the harder Hemisphere A worked on a task, the worse Hemisphere B would do on a task of equivalent complexity.

Many have investigated this phenomenon, and all studies have confirmed that the central resources are limited. Consider the following experiment: In what was called the *mixed*, or *hard, condition*, two series of three different geometric shapes were displayed concurrently to the left and right of the central fixation point and thus were lateralized to the right and left hemispheres, respectively. In the *redundant*, or *easy*, *condition* (illustrated in Figure 11.18), the three geometric shapes were presented to only one hemisphere while three identical geometric shapes were presented to the other. To test recognition memory, a single shape was then presented in either the left or the right visual field. The observer indicated with a forced-choice key press whether this probe matched any of the shapes that had been presented in the same hemifield. When the shapes in both hemifields had been identical in every trial (redundant condition), performance was better than when three different shapes had been presented in the other hemifield (mixed condition). Indeed, in the mixed condition,

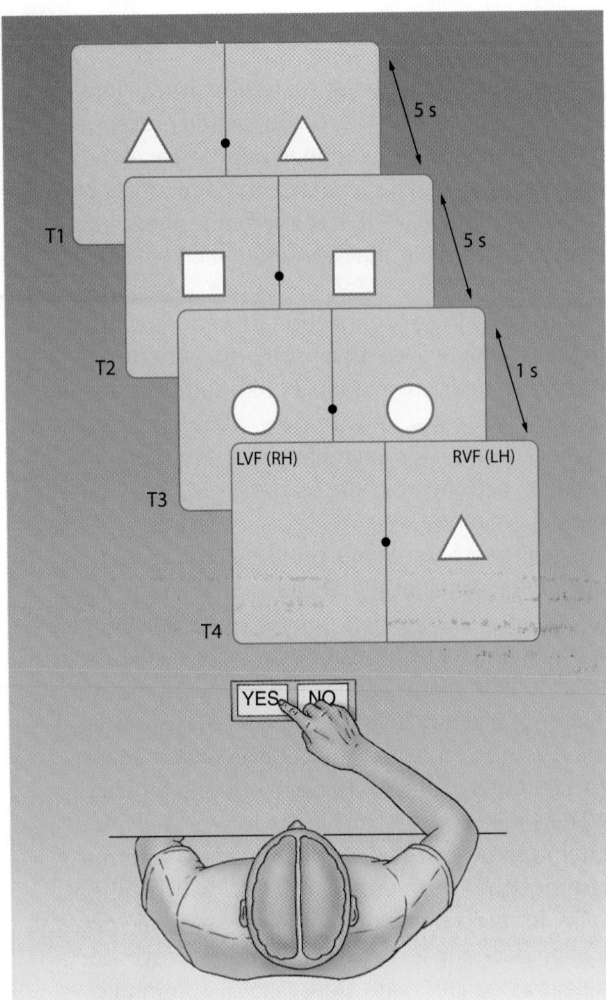

Figure 11.18 Sequence of events for a redundant three-condition trial. Stimuli were selected from a set of seven geometric forms. Each stimulus appeared for 150 ms. A delay followed presentation of the last stimulus, and the unilateral probe stimulus was presented for 150 ms. The subject then had to decide whether the probe stimulus had been shown previously in the corresponding visual field. T1–T4 = Time 1 through Time 4.

in which six distinct shapes had been presented, performance was poor with either hemisphere.

This concept of resources should be distinguished from other properties of sensory systems associated with information processing. The limits to information processing captured by the concept of resource limitations are more general than the limits and mechanisms now studied in such phenomena as searching a visual scene for information. For example, although the overall resources that a brain commits to a task appear constant, the method by which they are deployed can vary. The time needed to detect a complex object increases as more items are added to the display. For example, normal control subjects require about an extra 70 ms to detect the target when two extra items are added to the display, and another 70 ms for each additional pair of items. In split-brain patients, when the items are distributed across the midline of the visual field, as opposed to all being in one visual field, the reaction time to added stimuli is cut almost in half.

This finding was recently qualified: The strategy differed in how each hemisphere examined the contents of its visual field. The left, dominant hemisphere utilized a "guided" or "smart" strategy, and the right hemisphere did not. Hence, the left hemisphere adopts a helpful cognitive strategy in problem solving, but the right hemisphere does not have extra cognitive skills (Kingstone et al., 1995).

The concept of resources in many ways refers to processes engaged when attention to an information-processing task is allocated voluntarily. Searching a visual scene, however, calls upon more automatic processes that may well be built-in properties of the visual system itself. That these systems are distinct is reflected in the discovery that splitting brains has a different effect on the processes.

Complex Cognition

People are natural scientists, interested in explaining how the world works. Consider the American traveler witnessing her first cricket match while wandering about New Zealand. She notes the strange movement of the ball as it is thrown by the bowler toward the batsman. The ball appears to have an unusual spin, sometimes even eluding the large bat used to strike the ball. Indeed, following some of these misses the ball hits a post, leading to celebrations around the field. Although the rules of the game may elude our new fan, she can still infer certain causal relationships. For example, she can assume that the spin on the ball is caused by the unusual movement and delivery of the bowler. The fact that these events are visible leads to the notion that the observer is engaging in *causal perception*. On the other hand, the observer may, on the basis of her familiarity with baseball, infer that when the ball knocks over the post, the batsman is out (or, more technically, a "wicket" is scored). Here our observer is making a *causal inference*.

Studies of split-brain patients suggest that these two types of causal reasoning may be lateralized in different ways (Roser et al., 2005). Judgments of causal perception are better when the information is presented in the left visual field. In contrast, judgments of causal inference are best when the information is presented in the right visual field. These results suggest that the right hemisphere is more adept at detecting that one object is influencing another object in both time and space—computations essential for causal perception. The left-hemisphere role in causal inference may arise because of the need to apply logical rules and conceptual knowledge in order to correctly interpret complex stimuli and events to assemble them into a cohesive whole. These skills are critical to inferring the relationship between events that may not be perceptually related.

George Wolford and his colleagues at Dartmouth College (2000) have proposed an intriguing idea concerning asymmetrical biases in the two hemispheres with respect to problem solving. Subjects were presented with a simple task of trying to guess which of two events would happen next. Each event had a different probability of occurrence (e.g., a red stimulus might appear 75% of the time and a green one 25% of the time), but the order of occurrence of the events was entirely random. There are two possible strategies for responding in this task: *matching* and *maximizing*. In the red–green example, frequency matching would involve guessing red 75% of the time and guessing green 25% of the time. Because the order of occurrence was random, this strategy potentially would result in a great number of errors. The second strategy, maximizing, involves simply guessing red every time. That approach ensures an accuracy rate of 75% because red appeared 75% of the time. Animals such as rats and goldfish maximize. Humans match. The result is that nonhuman animals perform better than humans in this task! The humans' use of this suboptimal strategy has been attributed to a propensity to try to find patterns in sequences of events, even when told that the sequences are random.

Wolford and colleagues tested the two hemispheres of split-brain patients in this type of probability-guessing paradigm. They found that the left hemisphere used the frequency-matching strategy, whereas the right hemisphere maximized. When patients with unilateral damage to the left or right hemisphere were tested on the probability-guessing paradigm, the findings indicated that damage to the left hemisphere resulted in use of the maximizing strategy, whereas damage to the right hemisphere resulted in use of the suboptimal frequency-matching strategy (Figure 11.19).

Together, these findings suggest that the right hemisphere outperforms the left hemisphere because the right hemisphere approaches the task in the simplest possible manner, with no attempt to form complicated hypotheses about the task. The left hemisphere, on the other hand, engages in the human tendency to find order in chaos. The left hemisphere persists in forming hypotheses about the sequence of events, even in the face of evidence that no pattern exists. Although this tendency to search for causal relationships has many potential benefits, it can lead to suboptimal behavior when there is no simple causal relationship. Some of the common errors in decision making are consistent with the notion that we are prone to search for and posit causal relationships, even when the evidence is insufficient or even random. This search for causal explanations appears to be a left-hemisphere activity and is consistent with previous work on the **interpreter** (a term coined for this use by Michael Gazzaniga), the left-lateralized system that seeks explanations for internal and external events in order to produce appropriate response behaviors.

A reconsideration of hemispheric memory differences suggests why this dichotomy between a left hemisphere that seems driven to interpret events, and a right hemisphere that does not, might be adaptive. When split-brain patients are asked to decide whether a series of stimuli appeared in a study set, the right hemisphere is able to correctly identify previously seen items and reject new items. The left hemisphere, however, tends to falsely recognize new items as having occurred previously when they are merely similar to previously presented items, presumably because they fit into the schema that it has constructed (Metcalfe et al., 1995; Phelps & Gazzaniga, 1992).

This finding is consistent with the hypothesis that the left-hemisphere interpreter constructs theories to assimilate perceived information into a comprehensible whole. By going beyond simply observing events to asking why they happened, a brain can cope with such events more effectively, should they happen again. In doing so, however, the process of elaborating (story making) has a deleterious effect on the accuracy of perceptual recognition, as it does with verbal and visual material. But accuracy remains high in the right hemisphere because it does not engage in these interpretive processes. The advantage of having such a dual system is obvious. The right hemisphere maintains an accurate record of events, leaving the left hemisphere free to elaborate and make inferences and predictions about the presented material. In an intact brain, the two systems complement each other, allowing for elaborative processing without sacrificing veracity.

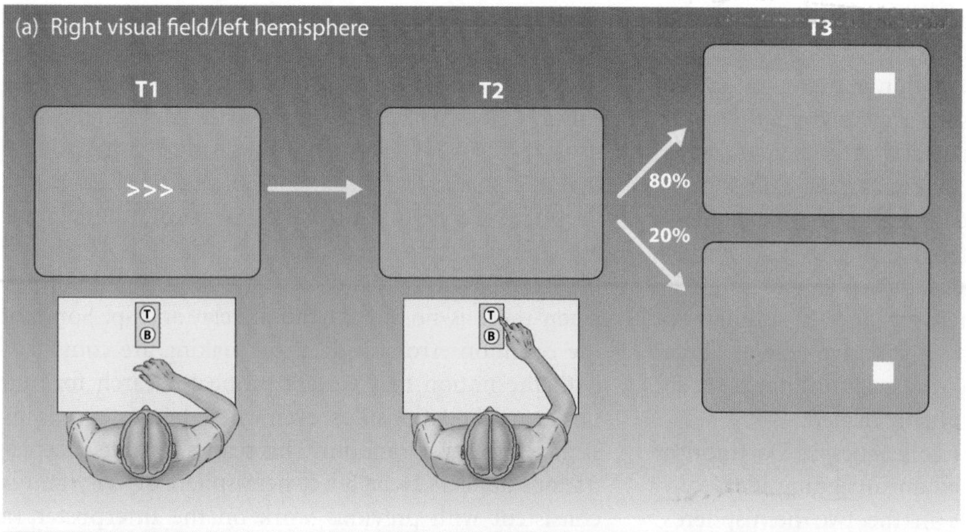

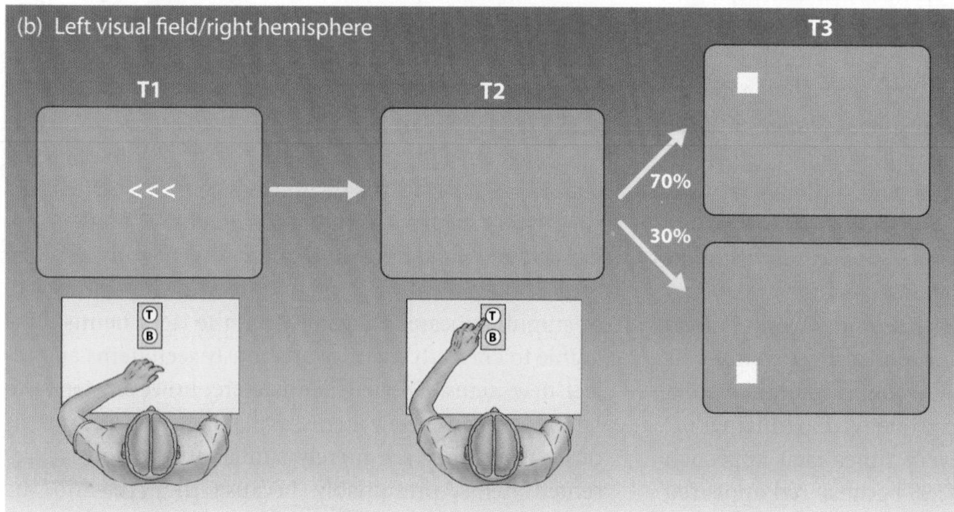

Figure 11.19 The two hemispheres respond differently when trying to predict where a stimulus will appear. At time 1 (T1), arrows indicate the side of the forthcoming stimulus. After a blank interval (T2), a light appears on the cued side. The light is presented either above or below the horizontal meridian. The position of the light is determined randomly on each trial, subject to the constraint that it will appear in the upper quadrant on 80% of the trials when presented in the right visual field **(a)** and on 70% of the trials when presented in the left visual field **(b)**. Over time, each hemisphere learns that the light is more likely to appear in the upper quadrant. However, different decision-making strategies are adopted. The left hemisphere responds by matching the probabilities, predicting the upper quadrant on about 80% of the trials for right-visual-field trials. The right hemisphere responds by maximizing, predicting the upper quadrant on almost every trial for the left visual field. Interestingly, the maximizing strategy is better.

CONVERGING EVIDENCE OF HEMISPHERIC SPECIALIZATION

Studies of split-brain patients have given us the most dramatic evidence of hemispheric specialization (Gazzaniga, 1995c). Many cognitive neuroscientists concentrate on identifying the capabilities of the two hemispheres when forced to act in isolation: Can the right hemisphere produce speech? Do the two hemispheres share common attentional resources? Can information be integrated at the subcortical level?

Functional Asymmetries in Patients with Unilateral Cortical Lesions

Research on hemispheric specialization has not been limited to split-brain studies. Two other prominent methodologies have come into play. First, many researchers have examined the performance of patients with unilateral, focal brain lesions. The basic idea has been to compare how patients perform when their lesions are restricted to either the right or the left hemisphere. An appealing feature of this approach is that there is no need to lateralize the stimuli to one side or the other; stimuli can be presented without restriction. Laterality effects are assumed to arise because of the unilateral lesions. If lesions to the left hemisphere result in more disruption in reading tasks, the deficit is attributed to the hemisphere's specialization in reading processes. Of course, it is necessary to show that similar lesions to the right hemisphere do not produce a similar deficit.

This approach, called the *double dissociation method*, provides strong evidence that many cognitive functions are lateralized to the left or right hemisphere (see Chapter 4). The logic is straightforward: If damage to one region affects Process A (e.g., language) without affecting Process B (e.g., spatial orientation), and a similar lesion to a different area affects Process B without affecting Process A, evidence for functional separation receives strong support. For instance, it has been demonstrated consistently that lesions in the left hemisphere can produce deficits in language function (such as speaking and reading) that do not follow comparable lesions to the right hemisphere. Similarly, lesions to the right hemisphere can disrupt spatial orientation (such as the ability to accurately locate visually presented items) that do not follow from comparable lesions to the left hemisphere.

To illustrate the nature of lateralized functions in patients suffering from unilateral brain lesions, consider the stimulus in Figure 11.20. If asked to describe the stimulus, your first response might be to say that it is a house. When prodded for more description, you might note the intricate detailing on the front door, the windows running across the front facade, and the roof made of asphalt shingles. In recounting the picture, you would have provided a hierarchical description. The house can be described on multiple levels: In terms of its shape and attributes, it is a house. But it is also a specific house, with a specific configuration of doors, windows, and materials. This description is hierarchical in that the finer levels of description are embedded in the higher levels. The shape of the house evolves from the configuration of its component parts—an idea that was developed in Chapter 6.

David Navon (1977) of the University of Haifa introduced a model task for studying **hierarchical structure**. He created stimuli that could be identified on one of two levels, an example of which is given in Figure 11.21. At each level, the stimulus contains an identifiable letter. The critical feature is that the letter defined by the global shape is composed of smaller letters. In Figure 11.21a, for example, the global *H* is composed of local *F*s.

Navon was interested in how we perceive hierarchical stimuli. He initially found that the perceptual system first extracted the global shape. Not only were reaction times slower when subjects had to identify local elements, but there was considerable interference when the global shape and local elements were discordant. The interference was not symmetrical. The time required to identify the global letter was independent of the identity of the constituent elements. Subsequent research has qualified these conclusions. Global precedence depends on factors like object size and number of local elements. Although Navon had assumed that a

Figure 11.20 We represent information at multiple scales. At its most global scale, this drawing is of a house. We can also recognize and focus on the component parts of the house.

Figure 11.21 Local and global stimuli used to investigate hierarchical representation. Each stimulus is composed of a series of identical letters whose global arrangement forms a larger letter. The subjects' task is to indicate whether the stimulus contained an *H* or an *L*. When the stimulus set included competing targets at both levels **(b)**, the subjects were instructed to respond either only to local targets or only to global targets. Neither target is present in **(e)**.

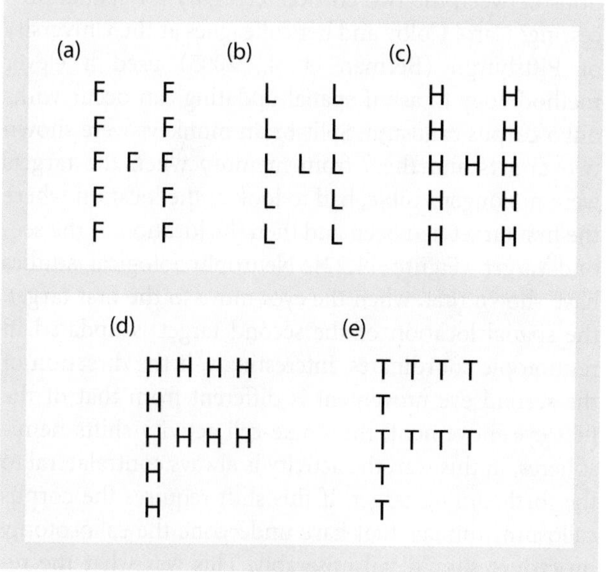

```
(a)          (b)          (c)
F   F        L   L        H   H
F   F        L   L        H   H
F F F        L L L        H H H
F   F        L   L        H   H
F   F        L   L        H   H

(d)               (e)
H H H H           T T T T
H                 T
H H H H           T T T T
H                 T
H                 T
```

single system processes hierarchical stimuli, the lack of invariance suggested otherwise. Perhaps different processing systems were essential for representing local and global information.

Experiments with patients who have suffered a unilateral lesion to the left or right hemisphere support this proposal. After carefully determining the focus of patients' lesions, Lynn Robertson and her colleagues (1988) at the Veterans' Administration medical center in Martinez, California, presented the patients with local and global stimuli to the center of view (the critical laterality factor was the side of the lesion). Patients with left-side lesions were slow to identify local targets, and patients with right-side lesions were slow with global targets, demonstrating that the left hemisphere is more adept at representing local information and the right hemisphere is better with global information.

It is important to keep in mind, however, that both hemispheres can abstract either level of representation. How they differ is in the efficiency with which they represent local or global information. Thus, patients with left-hemisphere lesions are still able to analyze the local structure of a hierarchical stimulus, but they must rely on an intact right hemisphere, and this hemisphere is inefficient at abstracting local information. Further confirmation of this idea comes from studies of local and global stimuli with split-brain patients (Robertson, Lamb, & Zaidel, 1993). Here, too, patients generally identify targets at either level, regardless of the side of presentation. But, as with normal subjects and patients with unilateral lesions, split-brain patients are faster at identifying local targets presented to the right visual field and global targets presented to the left visual field.

The question is this: Are interhemispheric connections between the two cortices *necessary* for spatial processing? Carol Colby and her colleagues at the University of Pittsburgh (Berman et al., 2005) used a clever methodology to ask if spatial updating can occur without a corpus callosum. Split-brain monkeys were shown two targets and then, from memory when the targets were no longer visible, had to look at the location where the first target had been and then the location of the second target (Figure 11.22). Neurophysiological studies have shown that, when the eyes move to the first target, the spatial location of the second target is updated in retinotopic coordinates. Interestingly, if the direction of the second eye movement is different from that of the first eye movement, the single-cell activity shifts hemispheres; in this way, the activity is always contralateral to the forthcoming target. If this shift requires the corpus callosum, animals that have undergone the callosotomy procedure should fail miserably. This was what the researchers observed when the reversal trials were first introduced. Surprisingly, though, the animals quickly mastered the task. One account of this finding is that, in the absence of transcallosal connections, subcortical pathways may be sufficient to support the transfer of visuospatial information.

In extreme cases in humans, however, the hemispheric biases for one level of representation can completely override other levels. In the case study at the beginning of this chapter, W.J. was unable to manipulate blocks into their global configuration when he was restricted to using his right hand. Similar dramatic things happen with stroke victims. Figure 11.23 displays drawings made by patients who *recently* had strokes in either the right or the left hemisphere. They were shown a hierarchical stimulus and asked to reproduce it from memory. Drawings from patients with left-hemisphere lesions faithfully followed the contour, but without any hints of local elements. In contrast, patients with right-hemisphere lesions produced only local elements. Note that this pattern was consistent with both linguistic and nonlinguistic stimuli; hence, the representational deficits were not restricted to certain stimuli. Note also that, because of the plasticity of the brain, such stark differences might not be seen months after the stroke.

Functional Asymmetries in the Normal Brain

The second important alternative methodology tests people with intact brains. Here the emphasis is on designing experiments that differentially require processing in either the right or the left hemisphere—similar to the procedures used in split-brain studies. In the visual domain, comparisons are made between presentations of stimuli to the left or right visual field. Although this procedure ensures that information will be projected initially to the contralateral hemisphere, the potential for rapid transcortical transfer is high. Even so, we find consistent differences from various sides of stimulation. For example, subjects are more adept at recognizing whether a briefly presented string of letters forms a word when the stimulus is shown in the right visual field than in the left visual field. Results like these lead to the conclusion that transfer is of limited functional utility, or that the information becomes degraded during the transfer. Thus, we assume that performance is dominated by the contralateral hemisphere with peripheral visual input.

Studies of auditory perception similarly attempt to isolate the input to one hemisphere. As in vision work, the stimuli can be presented monaurally—that is, restricted to one ear. But because auditory pathways are not as strictly lateralized as visual pathways, an alterna-

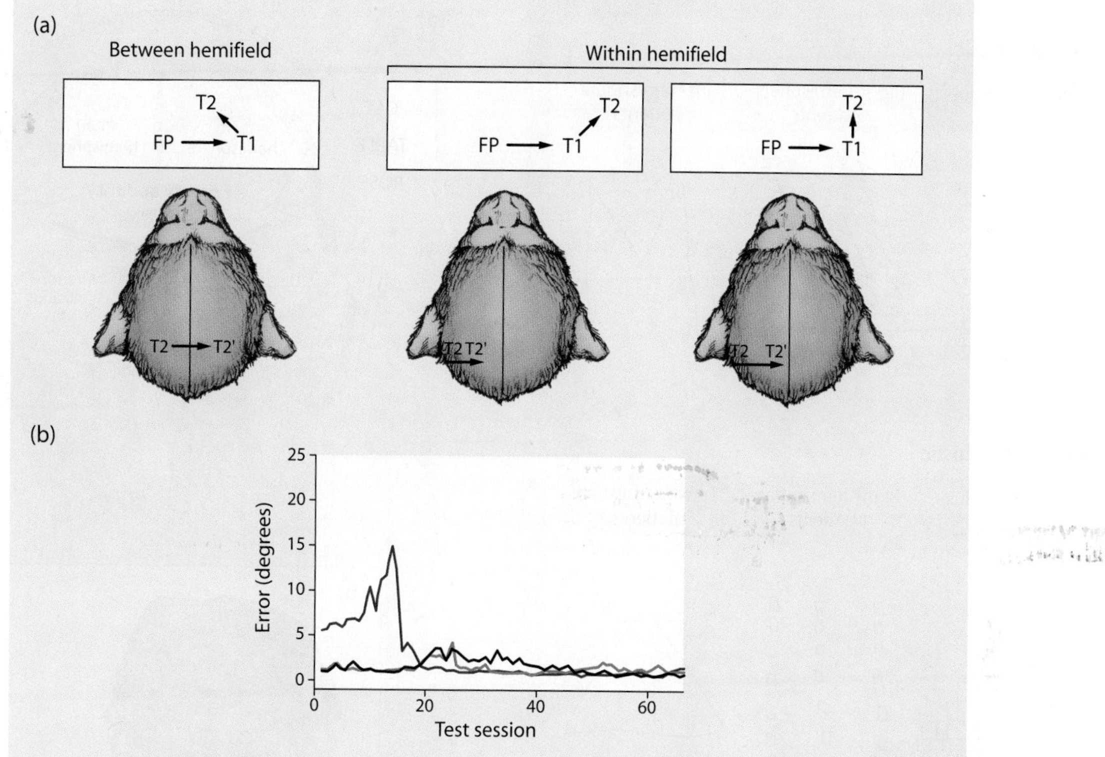

Figure 11.22 Interhemispheric communication in split-brain monkeys. **(a)** While the monkeys maintained fixation (FP), two targets appeared in succession. When the second target was turned off, the monkeys moved their eyes to the first location (T1) and then to the second location (T2). In the across-hemifield condition, the direction of the second eye movement is opposite that of the first eye movement. Assuming that spatial representations are updated in the parietal lobe, the location of the target would now be maintained in the other hemisphere (T2′). **(b)** Spatial error was measured by the difference between the end of the second eye movement and the target location. Accuracy was near perfect in the two conditions in which the second eye movement was either in the same direction as the first (green) or to straight above the end of the first eye movement (black). During the initial test sessions, the monkey failed to move its eyes to the second location in the across-hemifield condition (red) and generally moved the eyes straight above the end of the first eye movement. The increase in error starting around the fifth session occurred when the animal generated large eye movements, attempting to locate the second target. With subsequent sessions, performance quickly improved, and eventually the monkey was equally accurate in all three conditions, suggesting that interhemispheric transfer could be accomplished by intact subcortical pathways.

tive methodology for isolating the input is the dichotic listening task shown in Figure 11.24. In this task, two competing messages are presented simultaneously, one to each ear, and the subject tries to report both messages. The ipsilateral projections from each ear presumably are suppressed when a message comes over the contralateral pathway from the other ear.

The **dichotic listening task** was introduced in the early 1970s by Doreen Kimura (1973) while she was at the Montreal Neurological Institute. In a typical study, subjects heard a series of dichotically presented words. When asked to repeat as many words as possible, they consistently produced words that had been presented to the right ear—an effect dubbed the *right-ear advantage*. Results like these mesh well with expectations that the left hemisphere is dominant for language.

In vision and audition, the demonstration of performance asymmetries with lateralized stimuli generated great excitement. Here at last was a simple method for learning about hemispheric specialization in neurologically healthy people! It is not surprising that thousands of laterality studies on healthy subjects have been conducted using almost any imaginable stimulus manipulations.

However, the limitations of this kind of laterality research should be kept in mind (Efron, 1990):

- The effects are small and inconsistent, perhaps because healthy people have two functioning hemispheres connected by an intact corpus callosum.
- There is a bias in the scientific review process to publish papers that find significant differences over papers

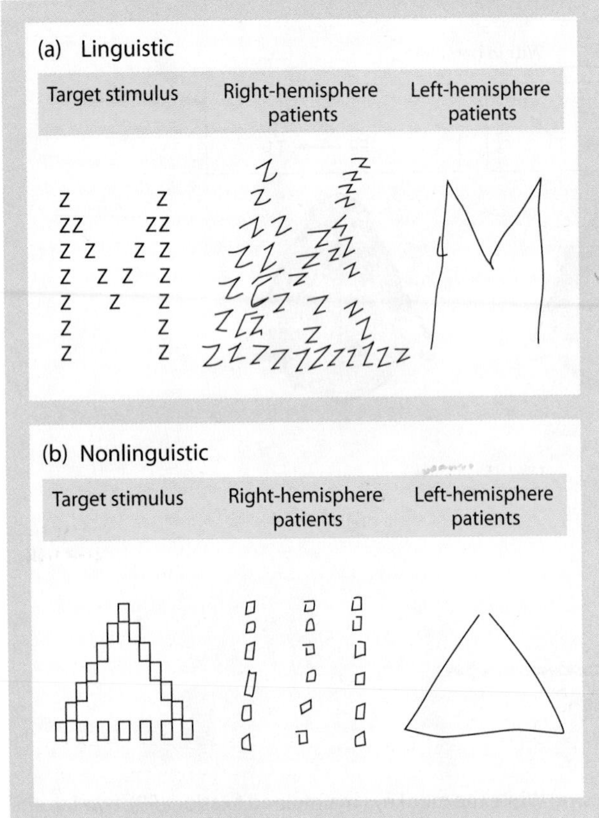

Figure 11.23 Extreme failures of hierarchical processing following brain damage. Two patients were asked to draw the two figures shown in the left column. The patient with right-hemisphere damage was quite accurate in producing the local element—the *Z* in **(a)** or the square in **(b)**—but failed to arrange these elements into the correct global configuration. The patient with left-hemisphere damage drew the overall shapes but left out all of the local elements. Note that the drawings for both patients were quite consistent for both the linguistic **(a)** and the nonlinguistic **(b)** stimuli, suggesting a task-independent representational deficit.

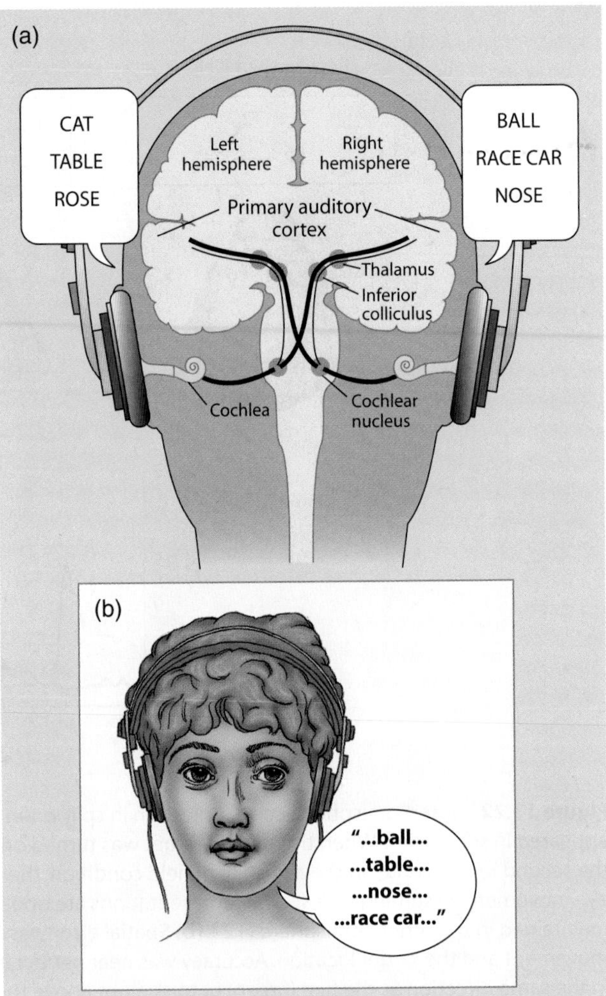

Figure 11.24 The dichotic listening task is used to compare hemispheric specialization in auditory perception. **(a)** Competing messages are presented, one to the left ear and one to the right ear. Auditory information is projected bilaterally. Although the majority of ascending fibers from the cochlear nucleus project to the contralateral thalamus, some fibers ascend on the ipsilateral side. **(b)** The subject is asked either to report the stimuli or to judge whether a probe stimulus was part of the dichotic message. Comparisons focus on whether the reported information had been heard in the right or left ear, with the assumption that the predominant processing occurred in the contralateral hemisphere. With linguistic stimuli, subjects are more accurate in reporting the information presented to the right ear.

that report no differences. It is much more exciting to report asymmetries in the way we remember lateralized pictures of faces than to report that effects are similar for right- and left-visual-field presentations.

- Interpretation is problematic. What can be inferred from an observed asymmetry in performance with lateralized stimuli? In the preceding examples, the right-visual-field and right-ear advantages were assumed to reflect the fact that these inputs had better access to the language processes of the left hemisphere. But perhaps people are just better at identifying information in the right visual field.

To rule out this last possibility, one must identify tasks that produce a left-ear or left-visual-field advantage. For example, shortly after Kimura's initial work, scientists discovered that people are better at recognizing the left-ear member of dichotic melody pairs; indeed, a double dissociation happens when subjects are presented with dichotic pairs of sung melodies (Bartholomeus, 1974). We find a right-ear advantage for the song's words but a left-ear advantage for its melodies (Figure 11.25).

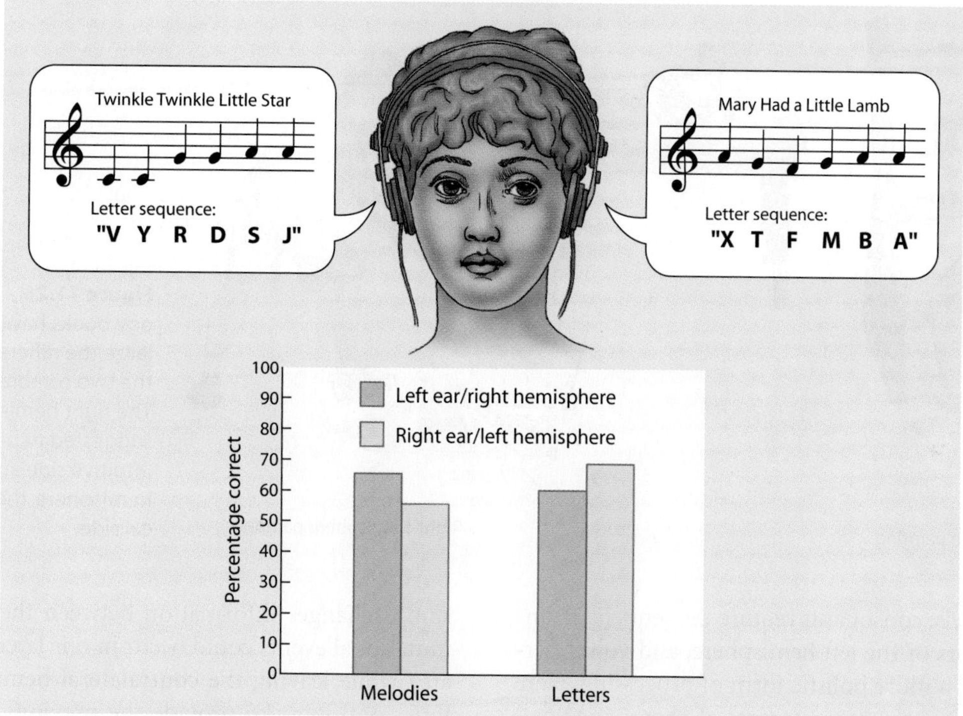

Figure 11.25 A right-ear advantage is not found on all tasks. Subjects listened to a dichotic message in which each ear was presented with a series of letters sung to short melodies. When given a recognition memory test, subjects were more accurate on the letter task for stimuli heard in the right ear. In contrast, a left-ear advantage was observed when the subjects were tested on the melodies.

WHAT BRAIN FUNCTIONS ARE LATERALIZED?

Laterality researchers continually grapple with appropriate ways to describe asymmetries in the function of the two hemispheres (Allen, 1983; Bradshaw & Nettleton, 1981; Bryden, 1982). Early hypotheses fixed on the stimuli's properties and the tasks employed. For example, the left hemisphere was described as verbal and the right hemisphere as spatial. By this view, one might suppose that the left hemisphere has sole province over all language functions. In the dichotic listening task, words presented to the left ear are recognized only when they succeed in being transferred to the left hemisphere. But, as seen in split-brain and stroke research, such absolutes are rare. Many tasks can be performed successfully by either hemisphere, although they may differ in efficiency.

An alternative approach for characterizing hemispheric specialization is to look for differences in processing style. From this perspective the left hemisphere has been described as analytic and sequential, and the right hemisphere is viewed as holistic and parallel. The popular press has promoted such descriptions, triggering industries devoted to helping people learn to "think" with the right hemisphere or improve the "power" of the left hemisphere (Figure 11.26).

Hypotheses about modes of processing are not restricted to specific task domains; instead they describe general processing styles. Hemispheric specializations may emerge because certain tasks benefit from one processing style or another. Language, for example, is seen as sequential: We hear speech as a continuous stream that requires rapid dissection and analysis of its component parts. Spatial representations, in contrast, call for not only perceiving the component parts but also seeing them as a coherent whole.

Although this analytic–holistic dichotomy has intuitive appeal, it is difficult to know whether a particular cognitive task would benefit most from analytic or holistic processing. In many cases the theoretical interpretation disintegrates into a circular redescription of results. For example, although a right-ear advantage exists in the perception of consonants, no asymmetry is

Figure 11.26 Pop psychology books have tended to trivialize the differences between the two cerebral hemispheres. The right hemisphere has been suggested to be the creative, intuitive side and the left hemisphere, the analytic, logical side.

found for vowels; consonants require the sequential, analytic processors of the left hemisphere, and vowel perception entails a more holistic form of processing. Here we have redefined the requirements of processing vowels and consonants according to our theoretical framework, rather than using the data to establish and modify that theoretical framework.

With verbal–spatial and analytic–holistic hypotheses, we assume that a single fundamental dichotomy can characterize the differences in function between the two hemispheres. The appeal of "dichotomania" is one of parsimony: The simplest account of hemispheric specialization rests on a single difference. Current dichotomies all have their limitations.

It is also reasonable, however, to suppose that a fundamental dichotomy between the two hemispheres is a fiction. Hemispheric asymmetries have been observed in many task domains: language, motor control, attention, object recognition. Perhaps specializations are specific to particular task domains. There need not be a causal connection between hemispheric specialization in motor control (e.g., why people are right- or left-handed) and hemispheric differences in representing language or visuospatial information. Maybe the commonality across task domains is their evolution: As the two hemispheres became segregated, they shared an impetus for the evolution of systems that were nonidentical.

Asymmetry in how information is processed, represented, and utilized may be a more efficient and flexible design principle than redundancy across the hemispheres. With a growing demand for cortical space, perhaps the forces of natural selection began to modify one hemisphere but not the other. Because the corpus callosum exchanges information between the hemispheres, mutational events could occur in one lateralized cortical area while leaving the contralateral hemisphere intact, thus continuing to provide the previous cortical function to the entire cognitive system. In short, asymmetrical development allowed for no-cost extensions; cortical capacity could expand by reducing redundancy and extending its space for new cortical zones. Support for this idea is provided by the fascinating work of Galuske and colleagues, which has revealed that differences in the neuronal organization of the left and right brain areas are related to the processing of auditory signals associated with human speech (Galuske et al., 2000; Gazzaniga, 2000).

The idea of asymmetrical processing also underscores an important point in modern conceptualizations of hemispheric specialization—namely, that the two hemispheres may work in concert to perform a task, even though their contributions may vary. There is no need to suppose some sort of master director that decides which hemisphere is needed for a task. Language is not the exclusive domain of the left hemisphere. The right hemisphere also might contribute, although the types of representations it derives may not be efficient for certain tasks. And the left hemisphere does not defer to the right hemisphere on visuospatial tasks but processes this information in a different way. Seeing the brain organized in this way, we begin to realize that much of what we learn from clinical tests of hemispheric specialization tells us more about our tasks rather than the computations performed by each hemisphere. This point is also evident in split-brain research. With the notable exception of speech production, each hemisphere has competence in every cognitive domain.

Asymmetries in Perceptual Representations

Objects that we attend to in our environment are rarely restricted to a single visual field. If we notice a fast car approaching from the left, we quickly shift our gaze to its direction. Given that foveal input is projected bilaterally, coupled with the fact that we make many small eye movements, stimuli reach both hemispheres directly. But this does not mean that the two hemispheres derive identical representations from this common input.

An excellent illustration of this point was provided in the preceding section when we considered how hierarchical (local and global) stimuli are represented by the human brain. Inspired by laterality dichotomies in analytic–holistic processing, Justine Sergent (1982) of the Montreal Neurological Institute modified the global–local task developed by Navon to look for hemispheric asymmetries. On each trial, a hierarchical pattern was presented for 150 ms in either the left or the right visual field (or at a central viewing location—a condition we will not consider here). As with split-brain studies, brief exposures ensured that subjects could not move their eyes and look directly at the peripheral stimuli, thus allowing the information to be projected to both hemispheres. The subjects were asked to press one button if the stimulus contained an *H* or *L*, and the other button if neither of these targets was present. The target could be at both the local and the global level (one *H* and one *L*), at one level only, or at neither level. The letters *F* and *T* were shown at levels that did not contain a target.

Figure 11.27 shows the intriguing interaction between the target level and the side of presentation. When both the global and local levels contained a target, subjects responded faster when the stimulus was presented in the left visual field. Even though this response time might reflect heightened arousal for the right hemisphere or a generalized advantage on visual tasks, the local-only results suggest otherwise; here reaction times were fastest when the stimulus was in the right visual field. The asymmetries between the two target conditions were tied to the type of analysis required. The left hemisphere was more adept at representing local information, and the right hemisphere was better with global information. And, as we have discovered, experiments with neurologically impaired patients confirm that this interaction stems from the asymmetrical functions of the two hemispheres.

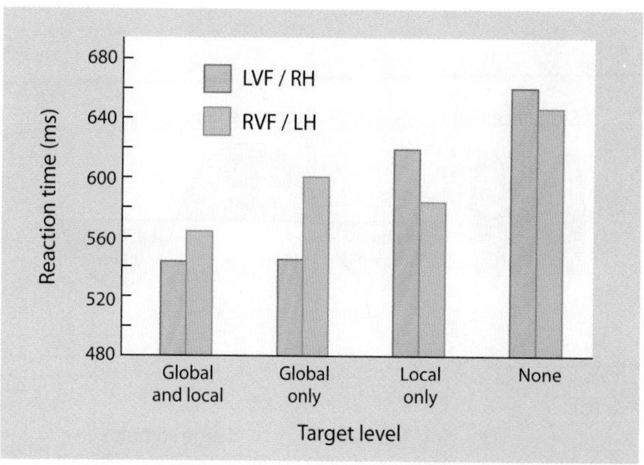

Figure 11.27 Reaction times to hierarchical letter stimuli, presented in either the left or the right visual field. Subjects judged whether the stimulus contained (at least) one of two letters: *H* or *L*. Reaction times were faster for left-visual-field (right-hemisphere) stimuli when the target was defined at the global level or at both levels. In contrast, reaction times were faster for the right-visual-field (left-hemisphere) stimuli when the target was defined at the local level.

COMPUTATIONAL BASIS OF LOCAL AND GLOBAL ASYMMETRIES

What defines the local and global structures of a stimulus? An obvious answer is that they differ in size: Global structure is larger than local structure. But how does the visual system process differences in size? To answer this question, consider the receptive-field properties of neurons involved in the analysis of shape.

A notable feature of visual receptive fields is that they are tuned to detect changes in contrast, or lightness. Most visual neurons respond weakly to a uniform field of light. Instead, as we saw in Chapter 5 (see "Milestones in Cognitive Neuroscience: Pioneers in the Visual Cortex"), they are most sensitive to changes in lightness because the neurons have a center–surround structure in which one region is excited by light and flanking regions are inhibited by it. In an on–off (on center–off surround) cell, the center region is excited by light; in an off–on (off center–on surround) cell, the center is inhibited by it (Figure 11.28). Moreover, the sizes of the center and surround regions vary. Such a computational device is sensitive to an object's size. The narrow receptive field fails to respond to the large bar because the bar spans the excitatory and inhibitory regions; the net result is that the excitation is canceled by the inhibition. In contrast, the same receptive field is maximally activated by the narrow bar.

The center–surround structure has led some theorists to conceptualize visual neurons as *spatial-frequency*

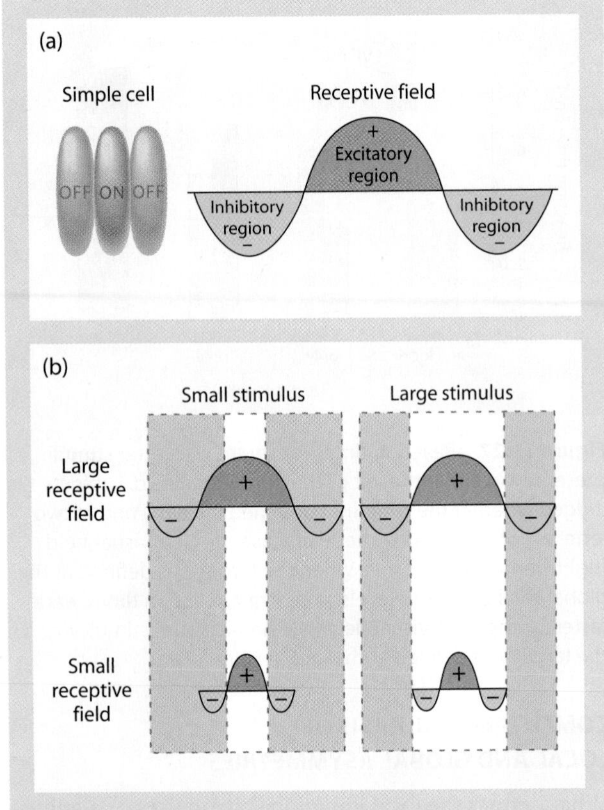

Figure 11.28 Stimulus size is encoded by the spatial extent of a neuron's receptive field. **(a)** Striate-cortex neurons not only have a preferred orientation but also are sensitive to the size of a stimulus. Size sensitivity is determined by the width of the excitatory and inhibitory regions of the cell's receptive field. An on–off cell responds when a light stimulus falls in the excitatory region and a dark stimulus falls in the inhibitory region. **(b)** A small stimulus produces a high response rate in the neuron with the smaller receptive field. This stimulus produces little activity in the neuron with the large receptive field because the excitatory center region is also stimulated by the dark background. The opposite occurs with the large stimulus. The larger receptive field is maximally responsive to this stimulus. The smaller receptive field does not respond, because the stimulus spans both the excitatory and the inhibitory regions.

Figure 11.29 Three sinusoidal gratings. Intensity varies in a sinusoidal manner across the horizontal dimension. The frequency of the sinusoids varies, being lowest for the stimulus at the **top** and highest for the stimulus at the **bottom**. The firing rate of a visual cortex neuron to these stimuli varies according to the width of the neuron's receptive field. In this way, visual neurons operate as spatial-frequency filters.

filters, referring to how the brightness of a visual pattern varies as a function of space. Consider the simple patterns in Figure 11.29, in which brightness varies in a sinusoidal manner along the horizontal axis. In the top pattern the variation is slow: The transition from light to dark and back to light again spans most of the page. The variation is much faster in the bottom pattern; hence, the transition between the contrasting stripes is more rapid. The transition rate can be described by its periodicity with respect to a unit of space. For example, the top pattern has a frequency of 2 cycles/page; the bottom pattern, a frequency of 8 cycles/page. In visual perception, units are expressed as cycles per degree, where the unit corresponds to 1 degree of visual angle (about the size subtended by a thumb held at arm's length).

A cell with narrow center–surround regions operates like a high-frequency spatial filter that responds vigorously to high-frequency patterns. A cell with a wide center–surround region operates as a low-frequency filter, responding only to low-frequency patterns.

An appealing feature of the **spatial-frequency hypothesis** is that any complex visual pattern can be described by its component spatial frequencies (Figure 11.30). Sergent (1982) conjectured that the spatial-frequency hypothesis might be the computational basis for hemispheric asymmetries in visual perception. She proposed that the left hemisphere is more adept at representing high-spatial-frequency information and that the right hemisphere is better with low-frequency information. Sergent assumed that the local structure of a hierarchical pattern would be carried by neural systems that respond to higher frequencies, while the global structure of a hierarchical pattern would be carried by neural systems that respond to lower frequencies.

As illustrated in Figure 11.31, computer algorithms were used to re-create a hierarchical stimulus after either the high- or the low-frequency information was removed. In a low-pass stimulus (from which high frequencies are removed) the identity of local elements cannot be distinguished, even though the global shape persists (see Figure 11.31b). In a high-pass stimulus (from which low frequencies are removed), both levels can be identified, but much of the contrast is absent (see Figure 11.31c). The advantage of identifying global targets is abolished with high-pass filtered patterns, presumably because the same units—such as receptive fields with narrow center–surround regions—are required for both kinds of stimuli.

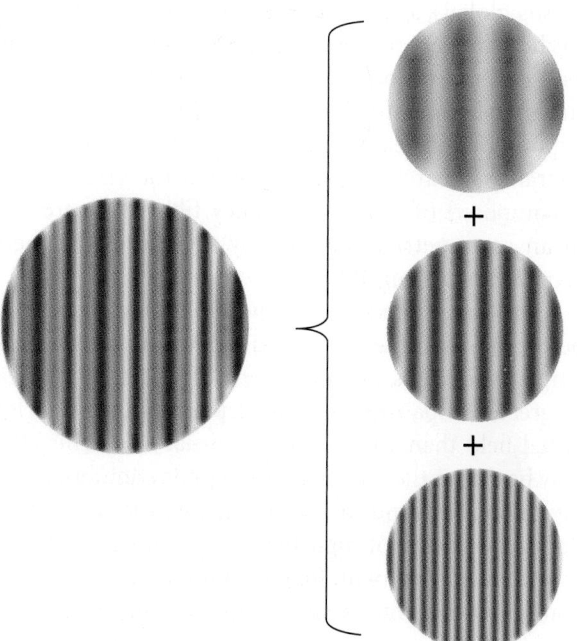

Figure 11.30 Any complex pattern can be described as the composite of sinusoids that vary in power and phase (starting position). The grating pattern on the left is created by combination of the three sinusoids on the right. For each position along the horizontal axis, the brightness in the compound grating is determined by averaging the brightness at the corresponding points in the sinusoids. In an identical manner, any complex pattern could be decomposed into a set of sinusoids. The set would have to include a large range of component frequencies oriented in all possible directions.

Fred Kitterle and his colleagues (1990) at the University of Toledo provided more direct support for the spatial-frequency hypothesis. They used sinusoidal gratings rather than hierarchical patterns. An advantage with sinusoids is their simplicity: Any complex pattern has many component frequencies, but sinusoids have

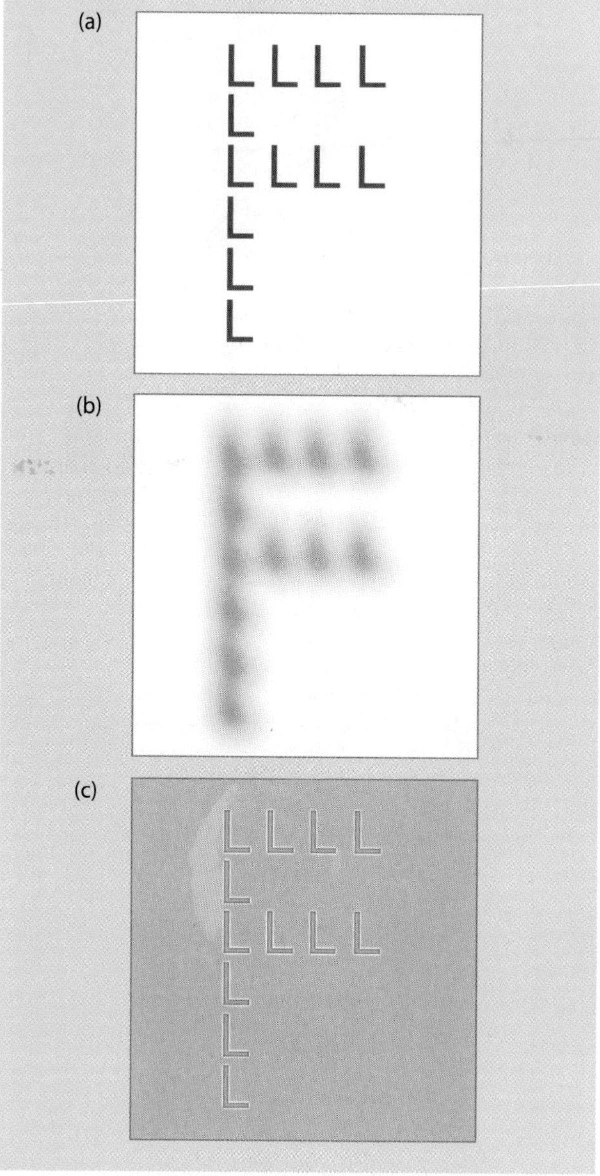

Figure 11.31 A hierarchical letter stimulus, before and after low- and high-pass frequency filtering. **(a)** The unfiltered stimulus. **(b)** The same stimulus after all of the high frequencies have been removed (low pass). Neurons sensitive only to these low frequencies would not be able to represent the local elements. **(c)** The stimulus after all of the low frequencies have been removed (high pass). High frequencies can still support local and global identification. However, the contrast of the stimulus is reduced.

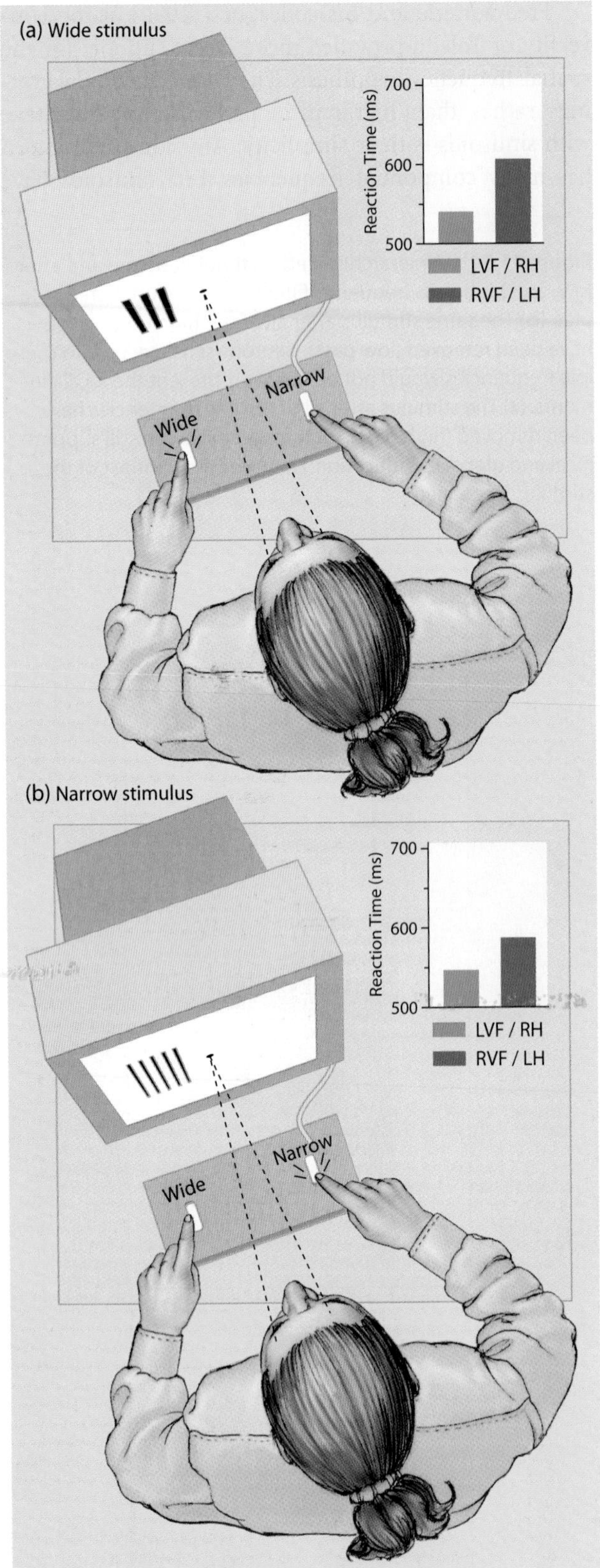

Figure 11.32 Asymmetries in how frequency information is represented in the two hemispheres may account for laterality effects in visual perception. A low-frequency (1 cycle/degree) or high-frequency (3 cycles/degree) stimulus was presented in either the left or the right visual field. Subjects judged whether the pattern was wide or narrow. Reaction times to the low-frequency stimuli presented in the left visual field (right hemisphere) were much faster. This side also showed an advantage for the high-frequency stimulus, but the magnitude of the asymmetry was reduced.

only one. Sinusoids of 1 cycle/degree or 3 cycles/degree were presented in either the left or the right visual field. Subjects were asked to respond as quickly as possible, pressing one key if the stimulus had "wide" stripes (1 cycle/degree) and the other key for "narrow" stripes (3 cycles/degree). Although subjects were always faster when responding to the wide pattern, the results also showed the predicted side-by-size interaction. The reaction times for wide-striped, low-frequency patterns were faster when the stimulus was presented to the left visual field; narrow-striped, high-frequency patterns were identified fastest when presented to the right visual field (Figure 11.32).

APPLYING THE SPATIAL-FREQUENCY HYPOTHESIS

The spatial-frequency hypothesis offers a powerful account of hemispheric asymmetries in visual perception because it focuses on an explicit source of information in the stimulus, rather than emphasizing difficult-to-define stimulus characteristics (e.g., local versus global) or processing modes (e.g., analytic versus holistic). Moreover, the hypothesis is grounded in a well-developed computational theory of how the visual system operates. In addition, the spatial-frequency hypothesis may explain a great number of findings in laterality research by proposing that the visual system is composed of spatial-frequency filters that are used in an asymmetrical manner by the two hemispheres (Ivry & Robertson, 1998).

The spatial-frequency hypothesis may account for perceptual asymmetries across a range of tasks. For example, numerous manipulations of visual stimuli lead to greater impairments in perception within the right visual field than within the left visual field. This effect may be due to the fact that blurring the stimulus, reducing its contrast, and/or restricting the exposure time reduces the fidelity of high-frequency content more than low-frequency content. Reducing high-frequency information in a stimulus should interfere disproportionately with left-hemisphere representations that are better suited to analyzing the high frequencies.

The spatial-frequency hypothesis may even offer a parsimonious interpretation of experiments that show reversals in visual field advantages even when stimuli remain unchanged. Sergent (1985) presented 16 photographs of familiar faces—each one shown in either the left or the right visual field. In one condition, subjects judged whether the person was male or female. In another condition, subjects had to identify the person shown. Whereas performance on the male–female task revealed a left-visual-field advantage, performance on the identification task showed a right-visual-field advantage.

Sergent maintained that this reversal reflected the fact that the critical information for performing each task was contained in different portions of the frequency spectrum. Determining whether a person is male or female could be done with low-spatial-frequency information. Identifying a specific person, however, requires the more detailed information in higher spatial frequencies. This hypothesis was tested in a second experiment, using the same photographs, but with the high-frequency information removed (Figure 11.33). This manipulation had little effect on the male–female task but was very disruptive to the identification task. A processing-mode hypothesis would have to account for this finding by assuming that the two tasks required subjects to shift between analytic and holistic processing modes. The spatial-frequency hypothesis assumes that the processing remains unchanged. The laterality effects reverse simply because the critical information is different for the two tasks.

A similar asymmetry may hold in auditory perception, but here the distinction is based on sound frequencies rather than spatial frequencies (Ivry & Lebby, 1993). For instance, consider speech perception, which depends largely on high sound frequencies and for which the left hemisphere is clearly dominant. Patients with left-hemisphere lesions may be unable to discriminate simple consonant contrasts that depend on high-frequency information, such as "ba" and "da," whereas the problem is rare in patients with right-hemisphere lesions.

Nevertheless, the right hemisphere has been linked to one aspect of speech perception: prosody, which is carried primarily by fluctuations in the low-frequency portion of the speech signal. *Prosody* refers to the connotative aspects of oral language, the way we vary articulation to convey affect or intonation. The statement "we need to talk" can be perceived either as an encouraging solicitation or as a stern warning, depending on intonation. The importance of low-frequency information is evident from the way people can still make prosodic judgments even when high sound frequencies are eliminated. For example, consider a conversation overheard from the office next door. Though we may fail to recognize the words because the walls effectively filter out the relatively high frequencies, the low-frequency information is sufficient to alert us when the voices have taken on an angry tone.

Lesions of the right hemisphere disrupt prosody much more than do lesions of the left hemisphere (Blonders et al., 1991; Ley & Bryden, 1982). A task-based account of laterality must assume that the left hemisphere is activated for linguistic tasks and the right

Figure 11.33 Tasks vary in terms of which spectral cues are most informative. When shown pictures of faces that contain the full spectrum of frequency information **(a)**, subjects can state whether the person is male or female and, if familiar, the person's identity. Gender can still be determined when only the low frequencies are left intact **(b)** but the person's identity is obscured.

for paralinguistic tasks such as prosody. A frequency hypothesis assumes that the speech signal is projected to both hemispheres, but that the two hemispheres produce representations that amplify different frequency regions of the stimulus. Identifying words requires an analysis of the signal's high-frequency portion. Prosodic analysis can be performed on low-frequency portions of speech.

Asymmetries in Representing Spatial Relations

In the preceding section we focused on hemispheric differences in how stimuli are identified. The central message is that different sources of information identify the attributes of a stimulus. In vision, high-frequency information is critical for identifying the local structure, or details; low-frequency information is more efficient for abstracting the global structure, or shape. In a similar fashion, if we extend the model to sound and speech, lexical analysis depends on the higher sound frequency components of the speech signal; prosodic information is carried in lower frequencies.

In Chapter 5 we noted an important distinction between cortical pathways involved in identification and those involved in localization (the what–where distinction). Studies of hemispheric asymmetries have not been limited to "what" problems; they also have been applied to "where" problems.

CATEGORICAL AND COORDINATE SPATIAL RELATIONSHIPS IN MEMORY

Stephen Kosslyn (1987) of Harvard University contended that a distinction can be made between two types of spatial representations. One type is essential for specifying the positions of objects or parts of objects. For example, when a guest begins to search the kitchen drawers to locate the silverware, the host might instruct her to look "to the left" or "just under that drawer." Here the emphasis is on the relative spatial position between two objects: the drawer being searched and the drawer containing the silverware. Kosslyn termed this spatial relationship *categorical* because it assigns the relation to a broad equivalence class. With respect to a referent, an object is to the left or right, above or below, inside or outside. **Categorical spatial relationships** capture general properties in abstract terms.

Though categorical spatial relationships are usually sufficient, sometimes precise spatial information is needed. Consider the scene in Figure 11.34. We would know where to go if we were told to sit on the couch behind the coffee table, but to accomplish this action we need to represent the exact locations of the couch, the coffee table, and any other obstacles that clutter up the living room. So we need coordinate, or metrical, spatial representations. **Coordinate spatial relationships** specify the exact locations of objects, with respect either to one another or to the perceiver's position. A coordinate spatial relationship not only gives the relative position of the couch and coffee table but also specifies the exact location of the couch.

Kosslyn maintained that categorical and coordinate spatial relationships have distinct purposes. A primary purpose of categorical spatial relationship is to classify objects by using spatial information. For example, the letters *b*, *d*, *q*, *p*, and *P* have the same component parts but differ in terms of the relative position of the line and circle. Within a wide range of sizes and handwriting styles, we can make the appropriate classification once

Figure 11.34 Spatial information can be represented in abstract, categorical terms or in a precise, coordinate manner. Categorical spatial relationships **(a)** capture basic relational information such as the relative position of two objects from a particular point of view. Coordinate spatial relationships **(b)** specify the exact positions of the objects and the distances between the objects.

(a) Categorical representation

Rocking chair LEFT of couch

Wine glass on TOP of table, candy INSIDE candy dish

(b) Coordinate representation

Rocking chair is CLOSER than the dining chair to the couch

we learn the invariant categorical relations. For example, "the circle is to the left and at the base of the line for *d*." These spatial relations provide valuable cues to an object's *identity*.

Coordinate relations, by contrast, are essential for *action*. If we need to pick up a wine glass on a coffee table, we do not rely solely on the categorical relationship that it is on top of the table and grope about for it. Instead we use its coordinate relations to target the glass for the specific action that we wish to perform on it.

Kosslyn hypothesized that the two hemispheres might differ in their contribution to categorical and coordinate spatial relationships. He proposed that the left hemisphere forms categorical spatial relationships and the right hemisphere forms coordinate spatial relationships. This hypothesis is motivated by consideration of the similarity between categorical spatial relationships and language. The general equivalences given by categorical relations are captured by linguistic terms (e.g., *up, down, inside*), and categorical encoding is a prominent feature of language. For example, despite the many variations in how a word can be articulated, the cardinal feature of speech perception is that the surface attributes of an utterance are stripped away to identify the phonemes that form the word. In a similar sense the precise specification of an object's location might rely on, or underlie, the dominant role of the right hemisphere in perceiving spatial information.

To test this hypothesis, Kosslyn and his associates devised tasks that require judgments based on either categorical or coordinate spatial relations (Kosslyn et al., 1989). In one study, the stimulus consisted of a bar and a dot, presented to either the left or the right visual field. In the categorical condition, the subjects had to decide whether the dot was located above or below the line. In the coordinate condition, the judgment required metrical information: Here the subject was required to judge the distance between the line and the dot, discriminating between distances that were near and those that were far. The clever twist in this experiment is that the same set of stimuli was used in both conditions. However, the assignment of stimuli to response categories differed as a function of the instruction (Figure 11.35).

Responses on the near–far task were faster when stimuli were presented to the left visual field—a result consistent with the hypothesis that the right hemisphere is more adept in making metrical judgments. The opposite trend was found for the above–below task. These categorical judgments were made more rapidly when the stimuli were presented in the right visual field.

These results call for a few caveats. First, as with many laterality studies, there have been problems with replication. Tasks such as the line–dot task appear to be especially problematic. Even in the original study, the effects disappeared after a few blocks of practice. Kosslyn suggested that subjects quickly form new categories that can be applied in the near–far task because the stimulus set is relatively small.

Second, it is important to ask whether the observed differences can be accounted for by alternative hypotheses, such as the spatial-frequency hypothesis. It turns out that the critical frequencies required for the two tasks

Figure 11.35 Hemispheric asymmetries on categorical and coordinate spatial judgments. **(a)** On each trial, the stimulus consisted of the bar and one of the 12 dots. For the categorical task, subjects judged whether the dot was above or below the bar. For the coordinate task, subjects judged whether the dot was near to or far from the bar. **(b)** The reaction time data show a task by visual field interaction. Categorical judgments were faster when the stimuli were shown in the right visual field (left hemisphere). Coordinate judgments were faster when the stimuli were shown in the left visual field (right hemisphere).

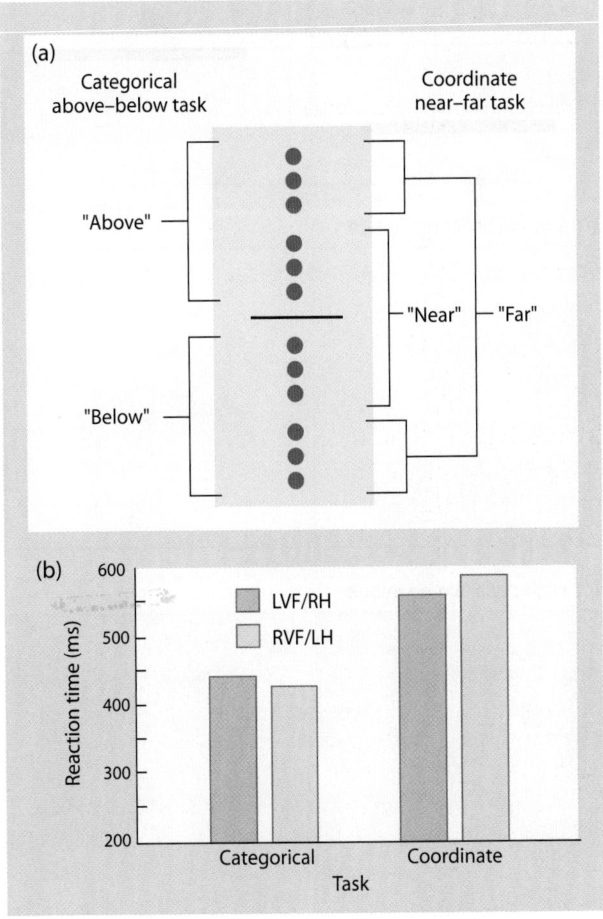

may differ. As shown in the low-pass filtered image in Figure 11.36b, low-frequency information may be insufficient for determining whether dots at the closest locations are above or below the line. Thus, the above–below task may depend on the left hemisphere—not because of the categorical nature of the judgment but because of the need for examining high-frequency information.

These problems alert us to seek converging evidence. Bruno Laeng (1994) of the University of Michigan studied a group of neurologically impaired patients that support the categorical–coordinate dichotomy. At the beginning of each trial, the patients were shown a drawing of a pair of items, such as two cats. After a 5-s delay, two drawings were shown, one that matched the original drawing and one that was a transformed version of the original. The transformations were of two types, as shown in Figure 11.37. In categorical transformations, the relationship between the two items was changed; for example, the left–right position of the cats was reversed. In coordinate transformations, a metrical property was changed; for example, the distance between the two cats was increased. In both tasks participants were asked to choose the drawing identical to the original drawing.

Compared to control subjects, the patient groups made more errors with both types of transformations. For patients with left-hemisphere impairment, how-

Figure 11.36 Frequency-based interpretation of the categorical–coordinate dissociation. **(a)** Two of the stimuli. **(b)** Low-pass filtered representation of the stimuli. **(c)** High-pass filtered representation of the stimuli. The categorical, above–below task distinction is difficult to make from the low-frequency information alone, suggesting an alternative reason for the left-hemisphere advantage on this task.

(a) Actual stimulus

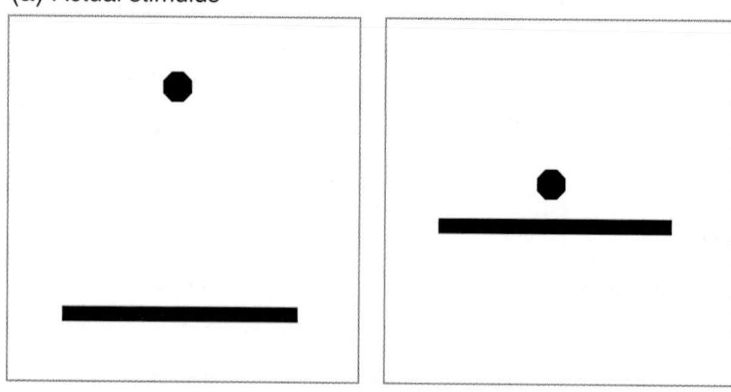

(b) Low-pass filtered image

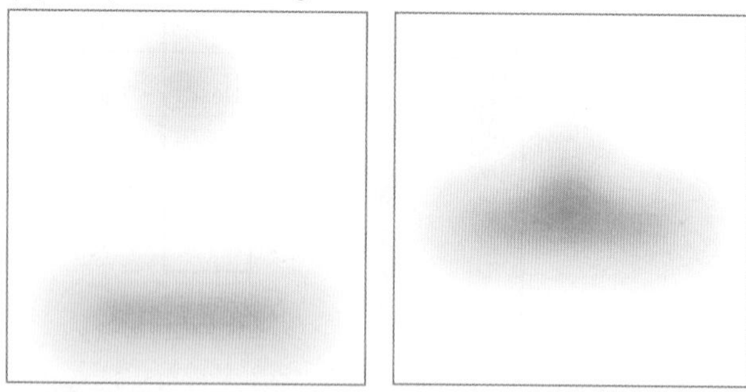

(c) High-pass filtered image

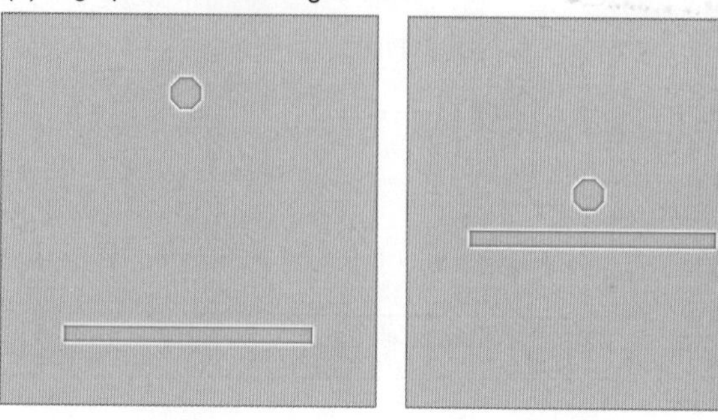

Figure 11.37 Memory test of spatial relations. **(a)** Subjects were presented with a target stimulus consisting of a pair of objects such as the two cats shown here. **(b, c)** After a 5-s delay, a probe stimulus appeared and the subjects judged whether it was the same as the target. In these two examples, the correct answer would be no. The left–right reversal **(b)** alters categorical relations; increasing the distance between the cats **(c)** constitutes a coordinate transformation.

ever, most errors involved selecting a drawing that required a categorical transformation. For the patients with right-hemisphere lesions, most errors involved coordinate transformations.

This experiment emphasized two advantages of patient studies in laterality research. First, because the stimuli were presented centrally, we do not need to make assumptions about the projection of visual information to the contralateral hemisphere. Second, effects that may be small and transient with normal subjects are frequently amplified when explored in people with neurological disorders.

GENERALIZING CATEGORICAL AND COORDINATE DISTINCTIONS TO OTHER PROCESSING DOMAINS

Laeng's task represents an interesting intersection of perception and memory. Subjects first encoded a target item and, after a short delay, were asked to match it to one of two probe items. The tendency for patients with left-hemisphere lesions to select probes in which categorical relations were transformed may reflect an encoding problem (an inability to represent the information) or a memory problem (an inability to retain the information). And the difficulty that patients with right-hemisphere lesions have with coordinate relations could be attributed to either an encoding or a memory problem.

Although the parietal lobes are critical for abstracting spatial relations, the inferior part of the temporal lobe is the neural locus for memories of visual representations of shape. The format of the representations appears to differ for the two hemispheres: Whereas left-hemisphere memories appear to be abstract or categorical, right-hemisphere representations retain the specific metrics of the stimulus.

Think about what a dog looks like. Your image might be of a small animal with four legs, covered with shaggy fur, floppy ears, and a long, wagging tail. Of course, this picture does not describe all dogs. It might be apt for an Irish setter but not a boxer, which has short fur and a short, stubby tail (Figure 11.38). The initial

Figure 11.38 Knowledge may be represented in an exemplar or prototype format. Exemplars are particular dog breeds such as the Irish setter or Chesapeake Bay retriever. The prototypical dog is a composite blend, the "average" dog.

image is not necessarily of a particular species; rather, it reflects a *prototype*, a composite melded by combining features from lots of dogs. The dogs you are familiar with are *exemplars*, or specific examples of dogs. A long and contentious debate rages as to whether memory contains prototypes or exemplars. Results of recent laterality studies suggest that both views may be correct. The left hemisphere may rely on prototypes, or representations that categorize information into general equivalence classes. The right hemisphere may use an exemplar representational format.

This distinction is made clear in a study by Chad Marsolek of the University of Minnesota (1995). The components of an initial set of prototypes were shifted to create distinct sets of abstract line drawings (Figure 11.39). During a training phase, subjects viewed a subset of the drawings and were trained to categorize them. After training, the subjects were given an accelerated classification task in which they categorized the drawings as quickly as possible. In this test phase, the stimuli were presented in either the left or the right visual field. When judging the studied subset, the subjects were faster when the stimuli were presented in the left visual field (right hemisphere). In contrast, when judging the previously unseen prototypes, the subjects were faster when the stimuli were presented in the right visual field (left hemisphere).

Kosslyn used the metaphor of a rolling snowball to account for the generalization of the categorical–coordinate distinction to multiple task domains. In his view, a fundamental asymmetry appears as a specialization to solve a problem. But this asymmetry then cascades into secondary specializations that build on the initial functional difference. Although it is difficult to trace the evolutionary development of hemispheric specialization, Kosslyn conjectured that the key event was the establishment of a left-hemisphere specialization for language production.

Unlike manual gestures that can be performed by one hand or the other, speech production requires bilateral coordination of the muscles required for articulation. Thus it became important to localize control in a single focus, since interhemispheric communication requires time and might limit how fast we can vocalize. A left-hemisphere specialization for language followed because this hemisphere had primary access to the speech production system. As we have noted, language is categorical in nature, with its emphasis on mapping percepts to broad semantic classes. The tendency for the left hemisphere to categorize is now found in many processing systems, including language, perception, and memory.

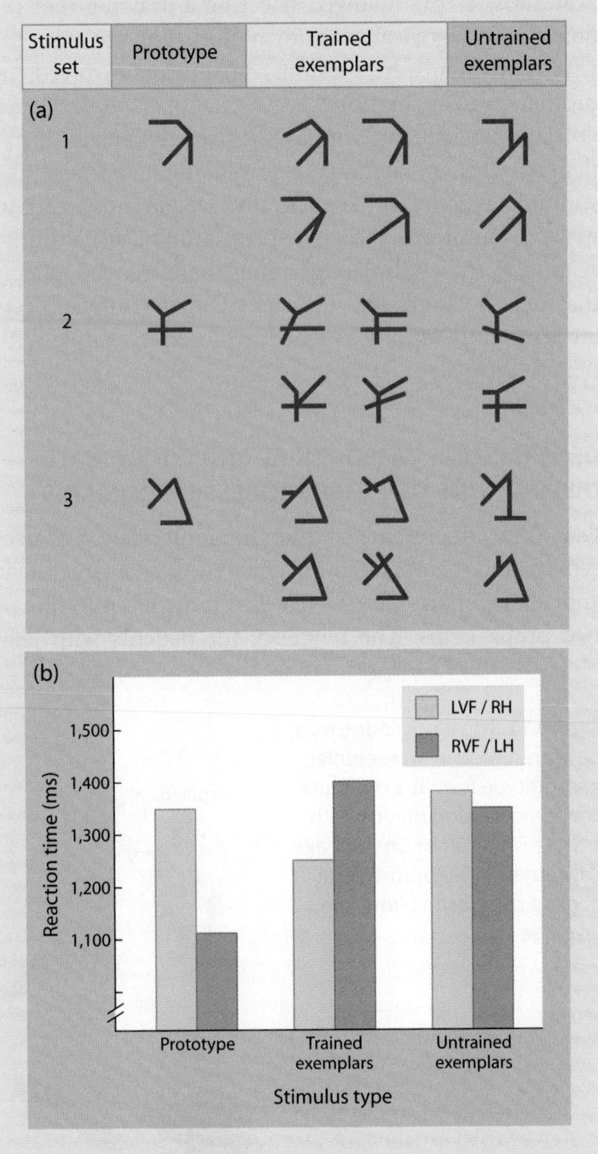

Figure 11.39 Hemispheric asymmetries in exemplar and prototype memory tasks. **(a)** Stimulus sets were constructed by distortion of a prototype pattern to create six exemplars. During the study phase, subjects were presented with a subset of the exemplars and learned to categorize them using the arbitrary numbers assigned to each set. In the test, they performed the categorization task with the prototype, the trained exemplars, and the untrained exemplars. **(b)** The prototype was more rapidly classified when it was presented in the right visual field, supporting the idea that this form of representation is characteristic of left-hemisphere processing. The trained exemplars, in contrast, were more rapidly classified when presented in the left visual field.

VARIATIONS IN HEMISPHERIC SPECIALIZATION

In this chapter we have reviewed general principles of hemispheric asymmetry in humans. The research showing asymmetries in how perceptual information is processed or in how spatial relations are represented has focused on differences that characterize the typical person. Most of us are right-handed and rely on the left hemisphere for speech production, but a significant percentage of the population is left-handed and may have a different organization of hemispheric specialization. Even within the right-handed population, lateralization profiles show significant individual differences. A complete understanding of hemispheric specialization must account for these differences, as well as for the prototypical organization.

The Relation Between Handedness and Left-Hemisphere Language Dominance

An ongoing debate in the laterality literature centers on whether there is a causal relationship between the predominance of right-handedness and left-hemisphere specialization for language. Some theorists point to the need for a single motor center as the critical factor. Though there may be benefits to perceiving information in parallel, our response to these stimuli must be unified. We cannot allow the left hemisphere to choose one course of action while the right hemisphere opts for another. Our brains may have two halves, but we have only one body. By localizing action planning in one hemisphere, the brain can achieve unification.

One hypothesis is that the left hemisphere is specialized for the production of sequential movements. Speech obviously depends on such movements. Our ability to produce speech is the result of many evolutionary changes in the shape of the vocal tract and articulatory apparatus. These adaptations make it possible for us to communicate at phenomenally high rates; the official record is 637 words/minute, set on the late-1980s British television show *Motormouth.* Such competence requires an exquisite control of the sequential gestures of the vocal cords, jaw, tongue, and other articulators.

Similarly, the left hemisphere has been linked to sequential movements in nonlinguistic domains. Left-hemisphere lesions are more likely to cause apraxia, a deficit in the ability to produce coherent actions that cannot be attributed to weakness or a problem controlling the muscles (see Chapter 7). This deficit can manifest in movements with either hand. Oral movements also have a left-hemisphere dominance, regardless of whether the movements create speech sounds or nonverbal facial gestures. In both domains, the gestures are more pronounced on the right side of the face, and activation of the right facial muscles is quicker than that of the corresponding muscles on the left. Hence, the left hemisphere may have a specialized role in the control of sequential actions, and this role may underlie hemispheric asymmetries in both language and motor functions.

In his book *The Lopsided Ape: Evolution of the Generative Mind* (1991), Michael Corballis of the University of Auckland eloquently articulates this hypothesis. He takes an evolutionary perspective to account for the emergence of language and handedness. To Corballis, the main characteristic of human cognition is that we act and think in a generative manner. Thousands of human languages are based on a limited set of phonemes, or basic articulatory gestures. From these 16 to 44 elements (the number of basic speech sounds varies across languages), we have created vocabularies of over a million words and can combine these words to generate an infinity of sentences expressing perceptions, intentions, and desires. Corballis believes that the left hemisphere is uniquely equipped with a **generative assembling device (GAD)**, a device that generates complex representations from a small vocabulary of primitive units (Figure 11.40).

Corballis assumes that the processing capabilities of the GAD are available to other left-hemisphere functions, including control of the right hand. With bipedalism, the hands are free to operate independently. In quadrupeds, the forelimbs and hind limbs are used primarily for locomotion. Symmetry is favored here: The animal moves along a linear trajectory. If the limbs on one side of the body were longer than the other, an animal would circle about. As our ancestors adopted an upright posture, however, the hands were no longer required to move symmetrically. One hand could hold a carcass while the other reached inside to extract morsels of meat.

The generative aspects of an emerging communication system could have been applied to the way hands manipulated objects, and the lateralization of GAD would have favored the right hand. The favoring of one hand over another would be most evident in tool use. Although nonhuman primates and birds can fashion primitive tools to gain access to foods that are out of

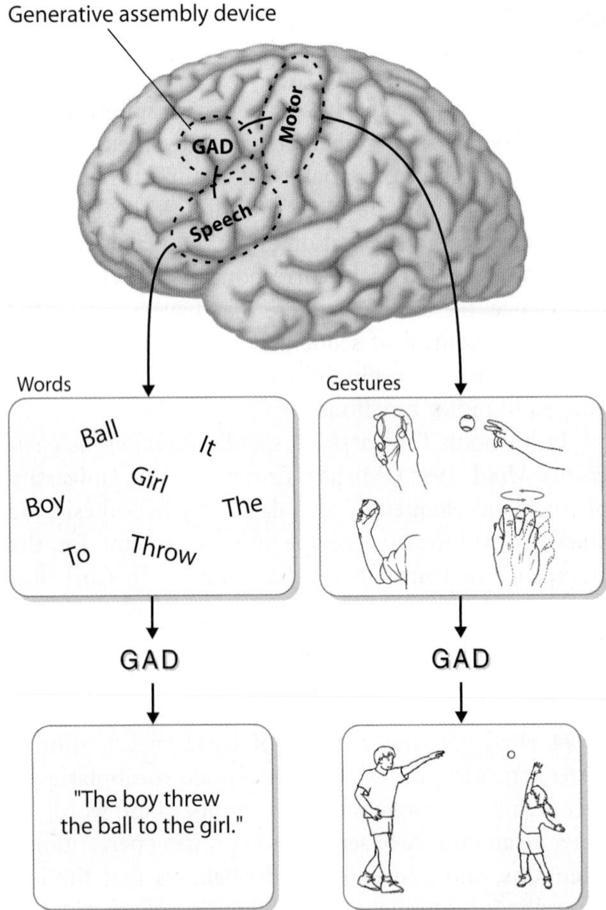

Figure 11.40 Corballis hypothesized that the left hemisphere has evolved a generative assembly device (GAD). This mechanism is thought to underlie the production of an infinite set of sequences from a relatively small set of units such as words or gestures.

reach or encased in hard shells, humans manufacture tools generatively: We not only design tools to solve an immediate problem but also can recombine the parts to create new tools. The wheel, an efficient component of devices for transportation, can be used to extract energy from a flowing river or record information in a compact, easily accessible format. Handedness, then, is most apparent in our use of tools. As an example, right-handers differ only slightly in their ability to use both hands to block balls thrown at them. But when they are asked to catch or throw the balls, the dominant hand has a clear advantage.

In Corballis's scheme, specialization in language became accessible to nonlinguistic functions: As the left-hemisphere GAD allowed language to take on its generative quality, it also imbued the right hand with a functional advantage for skilled actions. Alternatively, the left hemisphere's dominance in language may be a consequence of a specialization in motor control. The asymmetrical use of hands to perform complex actions, including those associated with tool use, may have promoted the development of language. For example, as our ancestors' use of tools became more advanced, a communication system to disseminate that knowledge was needed. From comparative studies of language we believe that most sentence forms convey actions. Not only will an infant issue commands such as "come" or "eat" before using adjectives (e.g., *hungry*), but this sequence is preserved in phylogeny. The earliest forms of communication centered on action commands such as "look" or "throw." If the right hand was being used for many of these actions, there may have been a selective pressure for the left hemisphere to be more proficient in establishing these symbolic representations.

It is also possible that the mechanisms producing hemispheric specialization in language and motor performance are unrelated. There is not a perfect correlation between these two cardinal signs of hemispheric asymmetry. Not only do a small percentage of right-handers exhibit either right-hemisphere language or bilateral language, but also in at least half of the left-handed population the left hemisphere is dominant for language.

These differences may reflect the fact that handedness is affected at least partly by environmental factors. Children may be encouraged to use one hand over the other, perhaps owing to cultural biases or to parental pressure. Or handedness and language dominance may simply reflect different factors. Fred Previc (1991), a researcher with the U.S. Air Force, proposed an intriguing hypothesis along these lines. According to Previc, the left-hemisphere dominance for language is related primarily to a subtle asymmetry in the skull's structure. In most individuals, the orofacial bones on the left side of the face are slightly larger—an enlargement that encroaches on middle-ear function and could limit the sensitivity to certain sound frequencies. Previc maintained that this enlargement has a deleterious effect on the projection of auditory information to the right hemisphere, especially in the frequency region that carries most of the critical information for speech. As such, the left hemisphere is favored for phonemic analysis and develops a specialization for language.

In contrast to this explanation of hemispheric specialization, Previc argued that handedness is determined by the position of the fetus during gestation (Figure 11.41). Most fetuses are oriented with the head downward and the right ear facing the mother's front. This orientation leads to greater in vitro stimulation of the left utricle, part of the vestibular apparatus in the inner ear that is critical for balance. This asymmetrical stimu-

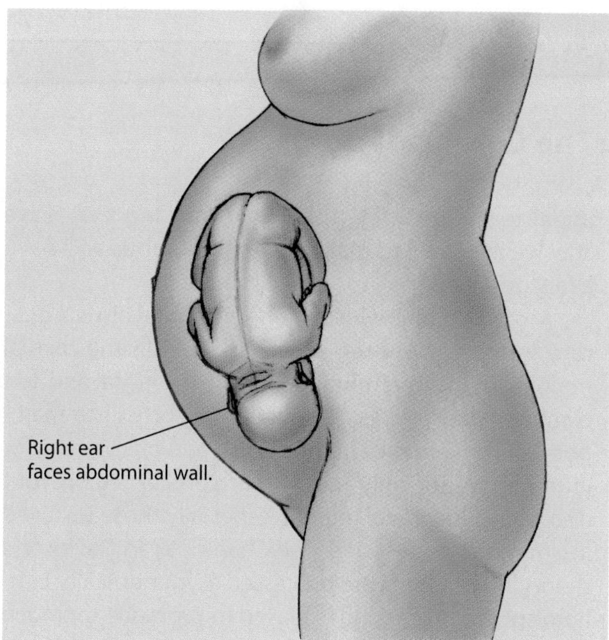

Figure 11.41 According to Fred Previc, functional asymmetries in manual coordination are sometimes attributed to the prenatal environment of the fetus. The position of the fetus in the uterus is thought to influence prenatal vestibular experience. Most fetuses are oriented with the right ear facing outward, resulting in a larger vestibular signal in the right hemisphere. At birth, the left side of the body is more stable, freeing the right hand for exploration.

lation will lead to a more developed vestibular system in the right side of the brain, causing babies to be born with a bias to use the left side of the body for balance and the maintenance of posture. Thus the right side of the body is freed for more exploratory movement, resulting in right-handedness.

According to Previc's theory, then, different factors determine language asymmetries and handedness. At present, the data are too scant for evaluating either of the mechanisms. Previc's own research concerns the demographics of the entire population, not whether language dominance or handedness can be predicted in any one person by orofacial asymmetries or fetal position. Nonetheless, it does raise the interesting possibility that numerous and unrelated factors determine patterns of hemispheric specialization.

Hemispheric Specialization in Nonhumans

Because of the central role of language in hemispheric specialization, laterality research has focused primarily on humans. Asymmetries between the left and right cerebral hemispheres may have arisen only after the evolutionary divergence of the line leading to *Homo sapiens.* But the evolutionary pressures that underlie hemispheric specialization—the need for unified action, rapid communication, reduced costs associated with interhemispheric processing—would also be potentially advantageous to other species. It is now clear that hemispheric specialization is not a unique human feature (Bradshaw & Rogers, 1993).

Anatomical considerations might lead us to expect to find even greater specialization in some nonhuman species, such as birds. In birds, almost all of the optic fibers cross at the optic chiasm, ensuring that all of the visual input from each eye projects to the contralateral hemisphere. The lack of crossed and uncrossed fibers probably reflects the fact that there is little overlap in the visual fields of birds, owing to the lateral placement of the eyes (Figure 11.42). Moreover, birds do not have a corpus callosum, so the communication between the visual systems within each hemisphere is limited and functional asymmetries might result.

Several asymmetries are known in birds. Chickens and pigeons are better at categorizing stimuli viewed by the right eye and left hemisphere than by the left eye and right hemisphere. They are more proficient in discriminating food from nonfood items when stimuli

Figure 11.42 Visual pathways in birds are completely crossed. This organization reflects the fact that there is little overlap in the regions of space seen by each eye, and thus the visual input to the left hemisphere is independent of the visual input to the right hemisphere. This anatomical segregation would be expected to favor the emergence of hemispheric asymmetries.

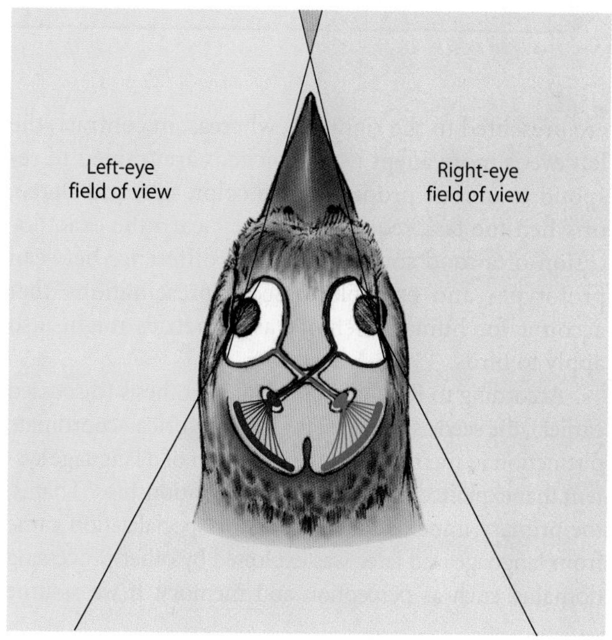

HOW THE BRAIN WORKS

To Approach or Withdraw: The Cerebral Tug-of-War

It is Friday night and you are heading to a party at the apartment of a friend of a friend. You arrive and look around: Loud music and swirling bodies move about the living room, and a throng has gathered in the kitchen around the counter laid out with chips and dips. Unfortunately, your friend is nowhere to be seen and you have yet to recognize a single person among the crowd.

Your reaction will depend on a number of factors: how comfortable you feel mingling with strangers, how lively you are feeling tonight, whether a host approaches and introduces you to a few of the guests. Unless you have a flair for flamboyance, it is unlikely that you will head straight to the dance floor. A more likely response is to head for the kitchen and find yourself something to drink.

Richard Davidson (1995) of the University of Wisconsin proposed that the fundamental tension for any mobile organism is between approach and withdrawal. Is a stimulus a potential food source to be approached and gobbled up, or a potential predator that must be avoided? Even the most primitive organisms display at least a rudimentary distinction between approach and withdrawal behaviors. The evolution of more complex nervous systems has provided mechanisms to modulate the tension between these two behavioral poles: We might overcome our initial reaction to flee the party, knowing that if we stay we are likely to make a few new friends and have a few good laughs.

According to Davidson, this tension involves a delicate interplay between processing within the medial regions of the prefrontal cortex in the right and left cerebral hemispheres. The prefrontal cortex is a major point of convergence in the central nervous system, for information not only from other cortical regions but also from subcortical regions, especially those involved in emotional processing (see Chapter 9). In Davidson's theory, these inputs are processed asymmetrically. Left-hemisphere processing is biased to promote approach behaviors; in contrast, right-hemisphere processing is biased to promote withdrawal behaviors.

This theory has provided an organizing principle to evaluate the changes in behavior that follow neurological damage. For example, damage to the left frontal lobe can result in severe depression, a state in which the primary symptom is withdrawal and inactivity. Although we might expect depression to be a normal response to brain injury, the opposite profile has been reported in patients with right frontal damage. These patients may appear manic. Damage to the right-hemisphere "withdrawal" system biases the patient to be socially engaging, even when such behaviors are no longer appropriate.

are presented to the right eye, whereas, in contrast, the left eye is more adept when chickens are trained to respond to unique properties like color, size, and shape, or when the task requires that they learn the exact location of a food source. Thus, the difference between prototype- and exemplar-based representations that account for human memory asymmetries might also apply to birds.

According to Kosslyn's snowball hypothesis (discussed earlier), the seed asymmetry for the categorical–coordinate distinction in memory was the evolution of a language system that exploited categorical spatial relationships. That is, the primary impetus for hemispheric specialization came from language and later was exploited by other processing domains, such as perception and memory. If we assume that the categorical nature of human language is unique to our species, the same evolutionary story could not be applied to birds.

Almost all birds, though, have a communication system: They vocalize to scare away enemies, mark territory, and lure mates. In many species, the mechanisms of song production depend on structures in the left hemisphere. Fernando Nottebohm of Rockefeller University discovered in the early 1970s (Nottebohm, 1980) that sectioning the canary's hypoglossal nerve in its left hemisphere severely disrupted song production. In contrast, right-hemisphere lesions had little effect. In other bird species a similar effect can be found, although in some cases lesions to either hemisphere can interfere with song production.

More compelling evidence comes from physiological studies that have looked at the brain's response to affective, or emotional, stimuli (Gur et al., 1994). By their very nature, positive stimuli are likely to elicit approach, and negative stimuli will elicit withdrawal or avoidance. Thus, depending on its valence, an affective stimulus is likely to differentially engage the two hemispheres.

Davidson (1995) tested this idea by taking electroencephalographic (EEG) measurements while subjects viewed short video clips, chosen to evoke either positive (e.g., a puppy playing with flowers) or negative (e.g., a leg being amputated) emotional reactions. The EEG activity during these stimuli was compared to that during a baseline condition in which the subjects watched a neutral video segment. As predicted, more neural activity was observed over the left frontal lobe when the subjects watched the positive videos in comparison to the negative videos. In contrast, there was a huge increase in activity over the right frontal lobe while subjects viewed the disturbing video.

Similar results have been found in a variety of related experiments. For example, in one study subjects were required to make rapid responses, either to acquire financial rewards or to avoid financial penalties. Left-hemisphere activation was greater during the reward trials, and right-hemisphere activation was greater during the penalty trials, even when the analysis was restricted to the time period prior to the onset of the stimulus. At this point the subjects had not experienced the reward or punishment; rather they anticipated its consequences.

There are, of course, individual differences in this cerebral tug-of-war between approach and withdrawal. Depression has been linked to an abnormal imbalance favoring neural activity in the right hemisphere. Whether the imbalance preceded or followed the depression remains unclear. More provocative, EEG asymmetries in 3-year-old children are correlated with how well the kids tolerate being separated from their mothers. Children showing higher basal EEG activity in the right hemisphere are more inhibited, staying next to their mother even when surrounded by an array of new toys. Children with higher basal EEG activity in the left hemisphere are quite content to leave their mother to play with the toys.

The study of hemispheric asymmetries in emotion is in its infancy. Prior to the 1990s, physiological studies of emotion generally focused on interactions between subcortical limbic systems and the cortex. In developing his account of cortical differences, Davidson started from a consideration of a marked behavioral dichotomy. What remain to be explored are the computations that might lead to one type of behavior over another, and whether these computations are related to those uncovered in the study of hemispheric specialization in other cognitive domains.

In the interim, however, we might cull from this work one strategy to test the next time we find ourselves alone at a party: Start talking to someone, if just to get the left hemisphere active! Perhaps there is a reason why the left hemisphere appears specialized to promote approach behavior and is dominant in that most social of all behaviors, language.

Nonhuman primates also show differences in hemispheric structure and perhaps function. Old World monkeys and apes have lateral fissures that slope upward in the right hemisphere, similar to the asymmetry found in humans. Whether these anatomical asymmetries are associated with behavioral specializations remains unclear. Unlike humans, nonhuman primates do not show a predominance of right-handedness. Individual animals may show a preference for one hand or the other, but there is no consistent trend for the right hand to be favored over the left hand, either when making manual gestures or when using tools.

Perceptual studies, however, have provided more provocative indications of asymmetrical functions in nonhuman primates. Like humans, rhesus monkeys are superior in making tactile discriminations of shape when using the left hand, but even more impressive is the finding that split-brain monkeys show hemispheric interactions comparable to what split-brain humans demonstrate in visual perception tasks. In a face recognition task, the monkeys have a right-hemisphere advantage; in a line orientation task, the monkeys have a left-hemisphere advantage. In addition, left-hemisphere lesions in the Japanese macaque can impair the animal's ability to comprehend the vocalizations of conspecifics. But unlike the effects on some aphasic patients, this deficit is mild and transient.

In summary, nonhuman species exhibit differences in the function of the two hemispheres. Hemispheric specialization is surely not a unique human characteristic, but how should we interpret these findings? Does the left hemisphere, which specializes in birdsong and human language, reflect a common evolutionary antecedent? If so, this adaptation has a very ancient history because humans and birds have not shared a common ancestor since before the dinosaurs. The fact that hemispheric specialization occurs in many species may instead reflect a general design principle of the brain. Segregation of function within a single hemisphere may simply reflect advantages gained by having cortical areas that are specialized to perform tasks that are important for survival within a specific environmental context. The auditory and visual cortices are each uniquely designed and specialized to solve problems. Hemispheric asymmetries may provide similar benefits.

SUMMARY

Research on laterality has provided extensive insights into the organization of the human brain. Surgical disconnection of the cerebral hemispheres has produced an extraordinary opportunity to study how perceptual and cognitive processes are distributed and coordinated within the cerebral cortex. We have seen how visual perceptual information, for example, remains strictly lateralized to one hemisphere following callosal section. Tactile-patterned information also remains lateralized, but attentional mechanisms are not divided by separation of the two hemispheres. Taken together, cortical disconnection produces two independent sensory information-processing systems that call upon a common attentional resource system in the carrying out of perceptual tasks.

Split-brain studies also have revealed the complex mosaic of mental processes that contribute to human cognition. The two hemispheres do not represent information in an identical manner, as evidenced by the fact that each hemisphere has developed its own set of specialized capacities. In the vast majority of individuals, the left hemisphere is clearly dominant for language and speech and seems to possess a uniquely human capacity to interpret behavior and to construct theories about the relationship between perceived events and feelings. Right-hemisphere superiority, on the other hand, can be seen in tasks such as facial recognition and attentional monitoring. Both hemispheres are likely to be involved in the performance of any complex task, but with each contributing in its specialized manner.

Complementary studies on patients with focal brain lesions and on normal subjects tested with lateralized stimuli have underscored not only the presence, but the importance, of lateralized processes for cognitive and perceptual tasks. Recent work, such as the spatial-frequency hypothesis, has moved laterality research toward a more computational account of hemispheric specialization, seeking to explicate the mechanisms underlying many lateralized perceptual phenomena. These theoretical advances have moved the field away from the popular interpretations of cognitive style and have refocused researchers on understanding the computational differences and specializations of cortical regions in the two hemispheres.

KEY TERMS

amobarbital

categorical spatial relationship

cerebral specialization

coordinate spatial relationship

corpus callosum

dichotic listening task

functional asymmetry

generative assembling device (GAD)

handedness

heterotopic areas

hierarchical structure

homotopic areas

interpreter

planum temporale

spatial-frequency hypothesis

splenium

split-brain research

Sylvian fissure

transcortical

TAKE-HOME MESSAGES

General

- The two cerebral cortices are connected by the largest fiber system in the brain, the corpus callosum. In humans, this bundle of white matter includes more than 200 million axons.
- To relieve his epilepsy, W.J. had split-brain surgery, in which the corpus callosum was severed. Studies on people who have had split-brain surgery help

neuroscientists understand the functional asymmetries of the individual hemispheres.

- During WADA testing, amobarbital is injected into the carotid artery and one hemisphere is temporarily anesthetized. This test is used to identify which hemisphere is responsible for language before brain surgery is performed.
- It is now clear that hemispheric specialization is not a unique human feature, though it is most extensive in humans. The evolutionary pressures that underlie hemispheric specialization—the need for unified action, rapid communication, reduced costs associated with interhemispheric processing—exist across species.

Anatomy of the Corpus Callosum

- The corpus callosum has both homotopic and heterotopic connections. Homotopic fibers connect the corresponding regions of each hemisphere (e.g., V1 on the right to V1 on the left), whereas heterotopic fibers connect different areas (e.g., V1 on the right to V2 on the left).
- In some of the original animal studies on callosotomies, Myers and Sperry demonstrated that visual discrimination learned by one hemisphere did not transfer to the other hemisphere when the hemispheres were disconnected.
- The splenium is the most posterior portion of the corpus callosum. When the posterior half of the callosum is sectioned, transfer of visual, tactile, and auditory sensory information is severely disrupted. The anterior part of the callosum is involved in the higher order transfer of semantic information.

Hemispheric Specialization for Language

- Ninety-six percent of humans, regardless of which hand is dominant, have a left-hemisphere specialization for language.
- The planum temporale encompasses Wernicke's area and is involved in language. The asymmetry of the planum temporale is one of the few examples in which an anatomical index is correlated with a well-defined functional asymmetry.
- Differences have been found in the specifics of cortical microcircuitry between the two hemispheres in both anterior (Broca's) and posterior (Wernicke's) language-associated cortex.
- The left hemisphere is dominant for language, speech, and major problem solving; the right hemisphere appears specialized for visuospatial tasks such as drawing cubes and other three-dimensional patterns. Thus, split-brain patients cannot name or describe visual and tactile stimuli presented to the right hemisphere, because the sensory information is disconnected from the dominant left (speech) hemisphere.
- There may be two lexicons (associations of words with specific meanings), one in each hemisphere. The right hemisphere's lexicon seems organized differently from the left hemisphere's lexicon, and these lexicons are accessed in different ways.
- Corballis believes that the left hemisphere is uniquely equipped with a generative assembling device (GAD), a device that generates complex representations from a small vocabulary of primitive units.
- The right hemisphere has been linked to one aspect of speech perception, prosody, which is the connotative aspects of oral language—the way we vary articulation to convey affect or intonation.

Other Hemispheric Specializations

- Some studies show that the right hemisphere is specialized for visuospatial processing.
- The right hemisphere has special processes devoted to the efficient detection of upright faces. The left hemisphere outperforms the right hemisphere when the faces are familiar, and the right hemisphere outperforms the left when the faces are unfamiliar.
- Although touching any part of the body is noted by either hemisphere, patterned somatosensory information is lateralized. Thus, a split-brain patient who is holding an object in the left hand is unable to find an identical object with the right hand.
- Surprisingly, split-brain patients can use either hemisphere to direct attention to positions in either the left or the right visual field.
- The right hemisphere appears to be specialized for causal perception (the ability to detect that one object is influencing another object in both time and space), and the left hemisphere is more capable with tasks that require causal inference.
- Using Navon's stimuli, investigators showed that patients with left-sided lesions were slow to identify local targets, and patients with right-sided lesions were slow with global targets, demonstrating that the left hemisphere is more adept at representing local information and the right hemisphere is better with global information.
- The spatial-frequency hypothesis might be the computational basis for hemispheric asymmetries in visual perception. The left hemisphere is more adept at representing high-spatial-frequency information, and the right hemisphere is better with low-frequency information.

- Whereas left-hemisphere memories appear to be abstract or categorical, right-hemisphere representations are coordinate, retaining the specific metrics of the stimulus.
- The left hemisphere contains what Michael Gazzaniga has called the *interpreter*, a system that seeks explanations for internal and external events in order to produce appropriate response behaviors.
- In general, many tasks can be performed successfully by either hemisphere, although the two hemispheres may differ in efficiency. In addition, the two hemispheres may work in concert to perform a task, even though their contributions may vary.

THOUGHT QUESTIONS

1. What have we learned from over 40 years of split-brain research? What are some of the outstanding questions that remain to be answered?
2. What are the strengths of testing patients who have suffered brain lesions? Are there any shortcomings to this research approach? If so, what are they? What are some of the ethical considerations?
3. Why are double dissociations diagnostic of cerebral specializations? What pitfalls exist if a conclusion is based on a single dissociation?
4. Why do you think the human brain evolved cognitive systems that are represented asymmetrically between the cerebral hemispheres? What are the advantages of asymmetrical processing? What are some possible disadvantages?
5. What commonalities are shared by the spatial-frequency hypothesis and the categorical–coordinate proposal of Kosslyn?

SUGGESTED READING

BROWN, H., & KOSSLYN, S. (1993). Cerebral lateralization. *Current Opinion in Neurobiology, 3,* 183–186.

CORBALLIS, M. C. (1991). *The lopsided ape: Evolution of the generative mind.* New York: Oxford University Press.

GAZZANIGA, M. S. (2000). Cerebral specialization and interhemispheric communication: Does the corpus callosum enable the human condition? *Brain, 123,* 1293–1326.

GAZZANIGA, M. S. (2005). Forty-five years of split brain research and still going strong. *Nature Reviews Neuroscience, 6,* 653–659.

HELLIGE, J. B. (1993). *Hemispheric asymmetry: What's right and what's left.* Cambridge, MA: Harvard University Press.

HUTSLER, J., & GALUSKE, R. A. (2003). Hemispheric asymmetries in cerebral cortical networks. *Trends in Neuroscience, 26,* 429–435.

IVRY, R. B., & ROBERTSON, L. C. (1998). *The two sides of perception.* Cambridge, MA: MIT Press.

12

Attention and Consciousness

A man in his late 60s is sitting comfortably in his doctor's office. Several weeks before, he suffered a severe stroke which appeared to leave him blind. However, his wife has noted that he can sometimes see things and is hoping that his vision will improve. His doctor, a neurologist, begins to examine the man, and indeed, it is obvious that the man has serious visual problems but is not completely blind, just as the patient's wife has reported. The doctor takes a comb from her pocket and holds it in front of the man (Figure 12.1a). "What do you see?" she asks. "Well, I'm not sure," he replies, "but . . . oh . . . it's a comb, a pocket comb." "Fine," says the doctor.

Next she holds up a spoon whisked from the recesses of her white coat and asks the same question (Figure 12.1b). After a moment the patient replies, "I see a spoon." The doctor says, "Good." The doctor then holds up the spoon and the comb together, asking the man again to tell her what he sees. "I guess . . . I see a spoon," says the man. Then the doctor holds up the comb right behind the spoon in a crossed fashion, so that they overlap in the same location but are still visible, and she asks again what the man sees (Figure 12.1c). He says he sees the comb. When the doctor asks about the spoon, the patient says he does not see it, but then suddenly he says, "Yes, there it is, I see the spoon now." "And what else?" asked the doctor. "Nothing," replies the man. "You don't see anything else, nothing at all?" asks the doctor as she shakes the spoon and the comb vigorously in front of the man's face. The man stares straight ahead, looking intently, and finally says, "Yes, . . . yes, I see them now . . . I see some numbers." "What?" says the puzzled doctor, "Numbers? There are no numbers. What do you see?" The man squints and appears to strain his vision, moving his head ever so slightly, and replies, "Yes, I see numbers." The doctor then notices that the man's gaze seems directed to a point far away and not toward the objects she is holding. Turning to glance over her own shoulder, the doctor spots a large clock on the wall behind her. Turning back toward the man, she says, "Er . . . yes . . . numbers, on the face of that clock on the wall . . . fine. Thank you."

What is interesting about this scene is that the doctor is holding both objects in front of the man at the same time, and even overlapping them in space, in plain view and in good lighting. But the man sees only one item at a time or sees a different item altogether in the direction of his gaze, even when closer items are being presented right in front of his nose. This patient has **Balint's syndrome**, a severe disturbance of visual attention and awareness that results in only one or a small subset of available objects being perceived at any one time, and these being mislocalized in space. The patient can "see" each of the objects presented by the doctor—the comb, the spoon, and even the numbers on the clock. But he fails to see them all together and cannot accurately describe their locations with respect to each other or to himself.

Balint's syndrome informs us about the nature of the normal functioning of attention and awareness in that it is a very severe instance of what we all

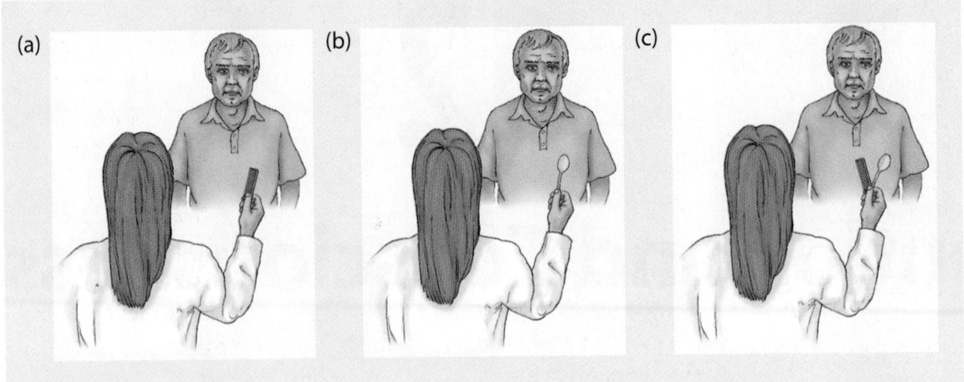

Figure 12.1 Examination of a patient recovering from a stroke affecting the cortex. **(a)** The doctor holds up a pocket comb and asks the patient what he sees. The patient reports seeing the comb. **(b)** The doctor then holds up a spoon, and the patient reports seeing the spoon too. **(c)** But when the doctor holds up both the spoon and the comb at the same time, the patient says he can see only one object at a time. The patient has Balint's syndrome.

experience daily—the fact that we are consciously aware of only a small bit of the vast amount of information available to our sensory systems from moment to moment. How the brain is able to select some information at the expense of other information is the central problem in the study of attention and consciousness, the focus of this chapter. How does this attentional selection occur?

In this chapter we investigate the mechanisms of attention and awareness. First, we will learn that attention involves both top-down (voluntary), goal-directed processes and bottom-up (reflexive), stimulus-driven mechanisms, and that they are in dynamic competition for control of the momentary focus of attention. These effects of attention influence the way information is processed in the brain, and can occur early during sensory processing. Widespread brain networks interact to enable us to attend to relevant events and, importantly, to ignore those that are irrelevant. These attentional networks involve structures in all the lobes of the cortex, as well as many subcortical structures. Damage to different portions of these attentional networks can lead to a variety of attention disorders.

In the last section of the chapter we consider the relationship between attention and consciousness by considering the role of attention in awareness. Recent studies in humans are discussed to help us understand how and why some things gain access to awareness while others are excluded. New models of how attention influences our awareness are considered.

THEORETICAL MODELS OF ATTENTION

Attention, the ability to attend to some things while ignoring others, has proved to be one of the most interesting domains of study in cognitive neuroscience, in part because this cognitive ability supports our momentary awareness and affects how we analyze sensory inputs, encode information in long-term memory, process it semantically, and act on information to survive in a challenging world. In this chapter we will restrict our discussion of attention to its role in perception and awareness. Introspectively, we all have an idea of what is meant by the term *attention*. William James (Figure 12.2), the great psychologist and brother of Henry James, the novelist, wrote at the end of the 19th century,

> Everyone knows what attention is. It is the taking possession by the mind, in clear and vivid form, of one out of what seem several simultaneously possible objects or trains of thought. Focalization, concentration of consciousness are of its essence. It implies withdrawal from some things in order to deal effectively with others, and is a condition which has a real opposite in the confused, dazed, scatterbrain state. (James, 1890)

In this insightful quote, James captured key characteristics of attentional phenomena that are under investigation today. For example, his statement "it is the taking possession by the mind" comments on the voluntary aspects of attention; we can *control* the focus of our attention. And his mention of "one out of what seem

Figure 12.2 William James (1842–1910), the great American psychologist.

several simultaneously possible objects or trains of thought" refers to the inability to attend to many things at once, and hence the *selective* aspects of attention. James reinforces the idea of *limited capacity* in attention by noting that "it implies withdrawal from some things in order to deal effectively with others."

As clear and articulate as James's writings were, very few of the computational mechanisms and virtually none of the neurophysiological implementations of these processes were understood during his lifetime. Even after more than 100 years of investigation, the study of attentional mechanisms continues to accelerate as we seek to understand the neural substrates of attention.

In this chapter we focus on the mechanisms of **selective attention**—those cognitive processes that enable organisms to process relevant inputs, thoughts, or actions while ignoring irrelevant or distracting ones. We do not discuss a different aspect of attention, that associated with nonselective processes such as arousal (for a discussion of the distinctions between selective and nonselective processes, see "How the Brain Works: Behavioral Arousal and Selective Attention," on p. 495). Nor will we discuss the interactions of attention with other cognitive domains, such as memory or linguistic processes. Therefore, we will use the term *attention* as a simple way of referring to the more specific concept of selective attention.

We can divide attention into two broad categories: (a) voluntary and (b) reflexive. **Voluntary attention**, a top-down, goal-directed influence, is our ability to intentionally attend to something. **Reflexive attention**, a bottom-up, stimulus-driven influence, describes the phenomena in which a sensory event captures our attention. These two forms of attention differ in their properties and perhaps their neural mechanisms, as we will see later in this chapter.

Studies of the cognitive neuroscience of attention have three principal goals:

1. To understand how attention enables and influences the detection, perception, and encoding of stimulus events, as well as the generation of actions based on the stimuli
2. To describe the computational processes and mechanisms that enable these effects
3. To uncover how these mechanisms are implemented in the brain's neuronal circuits and neural systems

Understanding these processes will ultimately permit us to comprehend how damage or disease in these systems leads to attentional deficits and the effect that these deficits can have on perception, action, and, indeed, all of cognition.

We begin our discussion with a look at some of the earliest studies of attention. In 1894, Hermann von Helmholtz (Figure 12.3a) performed a fascinating experiment in visual perception. He constructed a screen on which letters were painted at various distances from the center (Figure 12.3b). He hung the screen at one end of his lab and then turned off all the lights to create a completely dark environment. Helmholtz then used an electrical spark to briefly illuminate the screen, essentially just a flash of light, like a camera flash. His goal was to investigate aspects of visual processing when stimuli were briefly perceived. As often happens in science, however, he stumbled on an interesting phenomenon.

Helmholtz noted that the screen was too large to view without moving the eyes. Nonetheless, even when he kept his eyes fixed right at the center of the screen, he could decide in advance where he would pay attention; that is, he made use of something we now refer to as **covert attention**. By *covert* we mean that the location to which he directed his attention could be different from the location at which he was looking. Through these covert shifts of attention, Helmholtz observed that, during the brief period of illumination, he could perceive letters located within the focus of his attention better than letters that fell outside the focus of his attention, even when his eyes remained at the center of the screen.

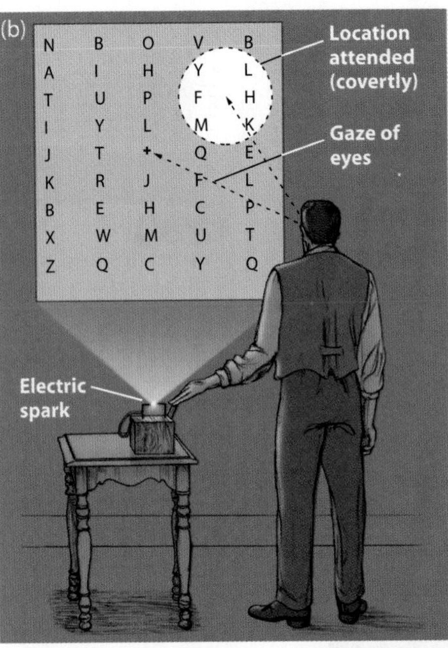

Figure 12.3 **(a)** Hermann von Helmholtz (1821–1894). **(b)** Experimental setup by Helmholtz to study visual attention. Helmholtz observed that, while keeping his eyes fixated in the center of the screen, during a very brief illumination of the screen he could covertly attend to any location on the screen and perceive the letters located within this region but had difficulty perceiving the letters at other locations. He attributed this phenomenon to attention and speculated on the possible mechanisms underlying this ability.

Try this yourself using Figure 12.3: Hold the textbook 12 inches in front of you and stare at the plus sign in the center of Helmholtz's array of letters. Now, without moving your eyes from the plus sign, read out loud the letters closest to the plus sign in a clockwise order. As Helmholtz (1909–1911) wrote in his *Treatise on Physiological Optics*, "These experiments demonstrated, so it seems to me, that by a voluntary kind of intention, even without eye movements, and without changes of accommodation, one can concentrate attention on the sensation from a particular part of our peripheral nervous system and at the same time exclude attention from all other parts."

The pioneering work of James, Helmholtz, and other early psychologists led to an introspective examination of many critical attentional phenomena by the start of the 20th century. These problems, however, were essentially neglected during the first half of the 20th century, largely because attention was considered an inappropriate topic of study during the reign of the behaviorists (see Chapter 1). Not until the 1940s and 1950s did the empirical study of attention begin to flourish. Indeed, the emergence of the study of attention went hand in hand with the emergence of cognitive psychology. The study of attention is, at least in part, the study of the constraints and limitations in how information is processed. As noted in Chapter 4, identifying such constraints is a central feature of cognitive psychology: Understanding the mind means knowing not only its capabilities, but also its limitations. Attention, by definition, indicates that we do not have the capability, nor is it desirable, to process and respond to everything that impinges on our sense organs, especially when we are bombarded by many sights and sounds at once, such as at a party.

The Cocktail Party Effect

British psychologist E. C. Cherry (1953) examined the so-called *cocktail party effect*. How is it that, in the noisy, confusing environment of a cocktail party, people can focus on a single conversation? Is the conversation more salient because of the speaker's and listener's proximity? Although a speaker with a loud voice may certainly try to command our attention, everyday experience indicates that the loudest inputs are not always the best perceived. Indeed, one goal of the listener at the cocktail party is to overcome the louder inputs of the environment (e.g., the music or nearby boisterous conversations) in order to attend to a conversation of interest, even if the person is speaking in a soft, confidential voice.

Selective auditory attention is the mechanism by which you can achieve this goal, even without cupping your ear, requesting the band to play more quietly, or insulting other partygoers by telling them to pipe down. By selectively attending, you can perceive the signal of interest amid the louder noise, and remain charming in a difficult social context. Interestingly, though, if you find the person you are speaking with to be a little boring, you may choose to attend to another conversation while still staring at the person who is talking directly to you (Figure 12.4). In so doing, you are using covert auditory attention to eavesdrop on another conversation, and if you are careful, only you know that you are doing it.

HOW THE BRAIN WORKS

Behavioral Arousal and Selective Attention

Attention has many meanings. It involves consciousness, awareness, and attentiveness, not to mention related deficits. Many scientists concentrated primarily on global states of attention in the late 1950s and early 1960s, prior to the information-processing revolution. The emphasis at that time was distinctions between conscious and unconscious states, such as sleep versus wakefulness. In the late 1940s, Giuseppi Moruzzi and Horace Magoun (1949) at the University of California, Los Angeles, showed that stimulating a cat's brainstem changed its global behavioral state. In some regions of the brainstem, sleep was induced by stimulation; in other regions, wakefulness resulted.

These changes in global state or arousal can be related to specific neurons in the brain and are reflected by changes in the electroencephalogram (EEG), the small voltage fluctuations that accompany neuronal activity in the brains of all animals. The EEG is a clear indicator of the state of global arousal and sleep in normal subjects; one can pinpoint the change from wakefulness to sleep and to different stages of sleep by viewing the EEG alone. Such changes must, however, be distinguished from the changes in brain activity that form the basis for *selective* attention and selective perception.

Attentive behaviors have a hierarchical structure. At the most global level are states of alertness such as sleep and wakefulness. Wakefulness includes more and less attentive and more and less selective states: drowsiness, alertness, and hyperalertness, such as when a life-threatening situation arises. At a finer level of description are levels within each awake, global state of awareness; here we reach levels of description that are appropriate for considering selectivity, as with the *cocktail party effect* described in this chapter.

The cocktail party effect is not just a global change in behavioral arousal or attentive state, but a reflection of a selective attention because the listener's goal is to attend to one source of sound while simultaneously ignoring potentially distracting inputs. This distinction between selective processes and global state changes is essential for its implications in selective attention research, and for the implications that nonselective behavioral changes can have for experimental design. For instance, finding that neurons are more active when an animal is excitedly performing a task, as compared with drowsily watching stimuli, might be an example only of a nonspecific state difference induced by the arousal of the task, and not evidence of neuronal mechanisms of selective processing.

These design considerations plagued the interpretation of many early studies of selective attention, as described in the text. The problems were overcome by controls that cognitive neuroscientists used for studying auditory attention in humans. This victory is largely due to the appreciation of a theoretical framework in the cognitive psychology literature that distinguished between nonspecific global state changes and selective processes—just one example of how hard-fought theories fuel scientific advances.

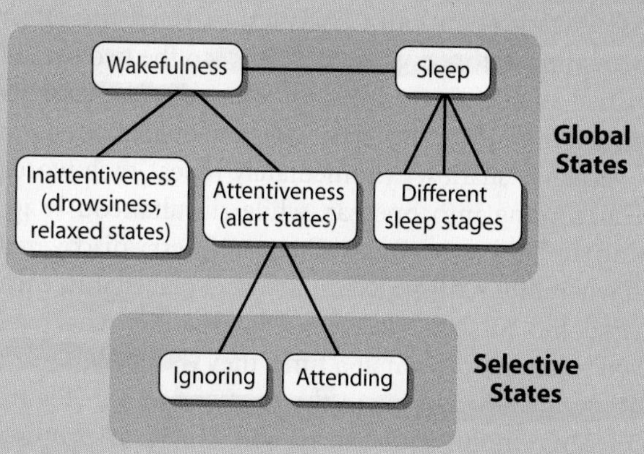

Hierarchical relationships between states of arousal, attentiveness, and selective attention.

Figure 12.4 The cocktail party effect of Cherry (1953), illustrating how, in the noisy, confusing environment of a cocktail party, people are able to focus attention on a single conversation, and, as the woman in the middle right of the cartoon illustrates, to covertly shift attention to listen to a more interesting conversation than the one in which they continue to pretend to be engaged.

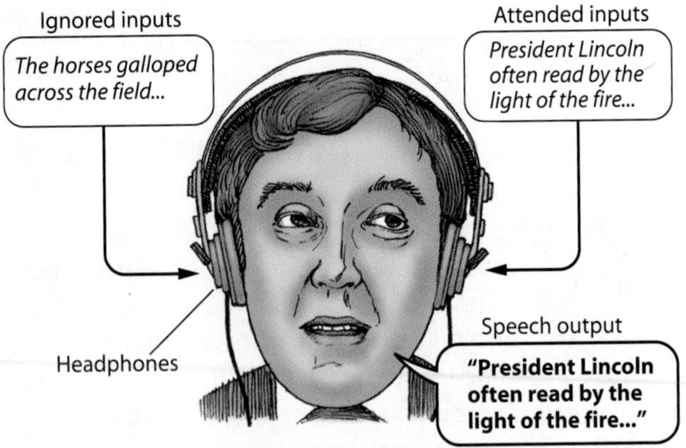

Figure 12.5 Cherry's experimental setup for dichotic listening studies. He presented different auditory information (stories) to each ear of a subject. The subject was asked to "shadow" (immediately repeat) the auditory stimuli from one ear's input (e.g., shadow the left-ear story and ignore the right-ear inputs).

This cocktail party effect clearly demonstrates the kinds of phenomena that interest cognitive psychologists studying attention. Cherry investigated the effect by providing competing speech inputs to the two ears of a normal subject through headphones (**dichotic listening**). In different conditions he asked people to attend to and verbally "shadow" (immediately repeat each word) speech coming into one ear, while simultaneously ignoring similar inputs to the other ear. Cherry discovered that, when different speech inputs were played into each ear and the subjects were asked to shadow what was played into only one ear at a time, they could not report any details of the speech in the unattended ear (Figure 12.5). This finding led Cherry and others to propose that attention to one ear results in better encoding of the inputs to the attended ear, and perhaps loss or degradation of the unattended inputs to the other ear.

It remained unclear, however, *when* the incoming information was modulated to cause the cocktail party effect. Does some sort of gating mechanism allow only some information to be processed? Where might this gate exist in the stream of perceptual processing? Speculation on this topic led to one of the most debated issues in psychology: Are the effects of selective attention *early*—that is, before extensive perceptual analysis? Or do they occur *late*—after the information has been analyzed, but before a later stage of processing, such as that associated with encoding the information as a semantic code or prior to the control of actions. Moreover, the very phenomenon of selection suggested that the amount of incoming information that the human brain can process is limited.

Early and Late Selection

The British psychologist Donald Broadbent (1958), working at Cambridge University, proposed a model of attention to explain data from studies such as that examining the cocktail party phenomenon. He conceptualized the *information-processing system,* a term that encompasses all aspects of the brain's processing of data, including sensory inputs, as having a limited-capacity stage through which only a certain amount of information can pass (Figure 12.6). In this model, the many sensory inputs capable of entering higher levels of the brain for processing had to be screened to let through only the most important, or attended, events. Broadbent described this mechanism as a gate that could be opened for attended information and closed for ignored information. Thus, Broadbent argued for information selection early in the information-processing stream. **Early selection**, then, is the idea that a stimulus need not be completely perceptually analyzed before it can be selected for further processing or rejected as irrelevant.

Some features of Broadbent's model explained the processing limitations revealed in experiments like those of Cherry, but not all data could be understood by a strict gating mechanism. Cherry and his contempo-

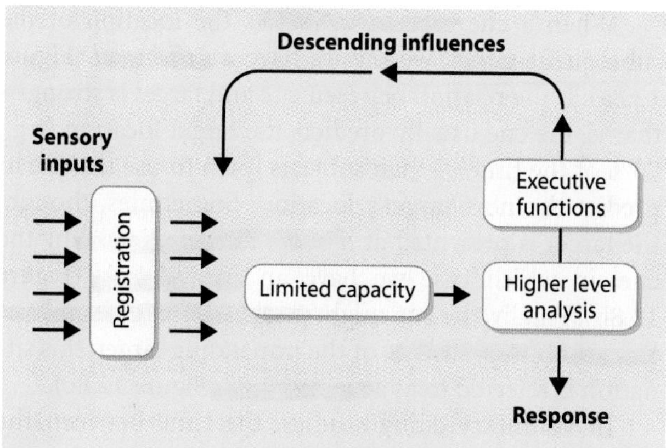

Figure 12.6 Broadbent's model of selective attention. In this model, a gating mechanism determines what limited information is passed on for higher analysis. The gating mechanism shown here takes the form of descending influences on early neural processing, under the control of higher order executive processes.

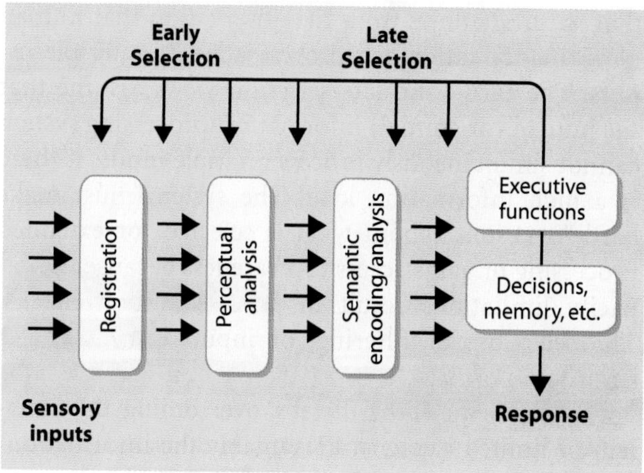

Figure 12.7 Early versus late selection of information processing. This conceptualization is concerned with the extent of processing that an input signal might attain before it can be selected or rejected by internal attentional mechanisms. Early-selection mechanisms of attention would influence the processing of sensory inputs prior to the completion of perceptual analyses. In contrast, late-selection mechanisms of attention would act only after the complete perceptual processing of the sensory inputs, at stages where the information had been recoded as a semantic or categorical representation (e.g., "chair").

raries, such as Neville Moray (1959), noted that some information coming into the unattended ear would capture attention, especially if it contained information of high priority to the subjects. For example, subjects were often able to report when their own name was presented on the unattended channel. This concept of *intrusion of the unattended* inputs led many to believe that all information was extensively analyzed, regardless of whether it was attended or ignored later during processing.

Models of **late selection** hypothesize that attended and ignored inputs are processed equivalently by the perceptual system, reaching a stage of semantic (meaning) encoding and analysis. Thereafter, selection for additional processing and perhaps also representation in awareness can take place. This view implies that attentional processes cannot affect our perceptions of stimuli by changing the way they are processed within the sensory-perceptual processing system. Instead, selection takes place at higher stages of information processing that involve internal decisions about whether the stimuli should gain complete access to awareness, be encoded in memory, or initiate a response. (The term *decisions* in this context refers to nonconscious processes, not conscious decisions on the part of the observer.) Figure 12.7 illustrates the differential stages of early versus late selection.

The strict versions of early-selection models proposed by Broadbent did not permit semantic encoding or analysis of unattended information. Given that high-priority signals could break through from supposedly unattended sources of sensory input (as in the case of subjects hearing their own name in dichotic listening studies), this original view of Broadbent was in need of modification. A simple gating mechanism that assumed that ignored information was lost could not accommodate the fact that sometimes unattended information was not perceived but other times it was. Anne Treisman (1969), now at Princeton University, proposed that perhaps unattended channel information was not completely gated from higher analysis but was merely degraded or attenuated—a point with which Broadbent agreed.

Early-selection versus late-selection models were therefore modified to make room for the possibility that information on the unattended channel could reach higher stages of analysis, but with greatly reduced signal strength. If such information reached the stage at which it could be encoded as a semantic or categorical code (e.g., as "chair," instead of merely the pattern of neural firing triggered in the visual system because of the low-level sensory aspects of the chair), it might lead to an attentional switch to the unattended ear inputs (selection) after the level of semantic encoding, and thereby become available to awareness.

LIMITED-CAPACITY PROCESSES

As noted earlier, one aspect of the debate over early versus late selection is **limited capacity**—a concept that naturally flows from the observation that human performance suffers when overloaded by multiple inputs. The early- and late-selection views assume that the human (or animal) information-processing system cannot simultaneously process multiple inputs if there is a high information load. The system must make hard "decisions" about what is selected for extended processing or gains access to awareness because the capacity limitations result in processing **bottlenecks**. The selection, or filtering, of inputs permits high-priority information to gain access to and pass the bottlenecks efficiently, thereby overcoming the problem of limited capacity. Presumably the information-processing system evolved selection mechanisms to control information flow at these bottlenecks and to establish priorities.

The difference between early- and late-selection theories has sometimes been framed by the following questions: Where does the bottleneck reside, and hence, where must selection take place? Does selection happen at an early perceptual level or at later encoding, decision, or response levels? Let's examine the evidence from studies in which people were asked to perform detection and discrimination tasks under various attentional conditions.

Quantifying Attention in Perception

One way of measuring the effect of attention on information processing is to examine how subjects respond to target stimuli. Various different experimental designs have been used for these explorations. A popular method is to use cues that direct the subject's attention to a particular location or target feature before the task-relevant target stimulus is presented. In these *cuing tasks*, the focus of attention is manipulated by the information in the cue. Cues can direct voluntary attention or be used to attract reflexive attention.

VOLUNTARY ATTENTION

In studies of voluntary spatial attention using cuing tasks, participants are asked to respond as fast as they can following the presentation of a target stimulus. They are instructed that the most likely location for the next target is the one indicated by a prior cue, such as an arrow pointing to that location; this is known as **endogenous cuing** because the orienting of attention to the cue is driven by the subject's goals (perform the task as instructed) rather than merely its physical features (see the next section, "Reflexive Attention," for a contrasting mechanism).

When a cue correctly predicts the location of the subsequent target, we say we have a *valid trial* (Figure 12.8a). If the relation between cue and target is strong—that is, the cue usually predicts the target location (e.g., 80% of the time)—then subjects learn to use the cue to predict the next target's location. Sometimes, though, the target is presented at locations not indicated by the cue, in which case we have an *invalid trial* (Figure 12.8b). Finally, the cue might give no information about the most likely location of the impending target; this situation is referred to as a *neutral trial* (Figure 12.8c).

In voluntary cuing studies, the time between the presentation of the attention-directing cue and the presentation of the subsequent target might be very brief or last up to a second or more. Subjects respond faster to the target stimulus when the cue correctly predicts the target's location, even when they do not move their eyes to the cued spot. That is, if the target appears where subjects expect it, they are faster to respond to it; they are also slower to respond to targets at unexpected locations (Figure 12.9).

Figure 12.8 The spatial cuing paradigm popularized by Michael Posner and colleagues at the University of Oregon. A subject sits in front of a computer screen, fixates on the central cross, and is told never to deviate eye fixation from the cross. An arrow cue indicates the visual hemifield to which the subject should covertly attend. The cue is then followed by a target in either the correctly cued **(a)** or the incorrectly cued **(b)** location. On other trials **(c)**, the cue (e.g., double-headed arrow) tells the subject that it is equally likely that the target will appear in the right or left location.

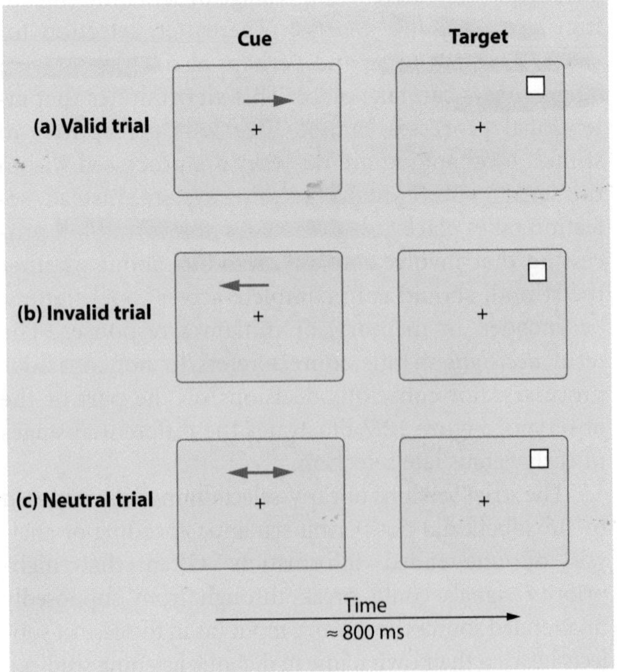

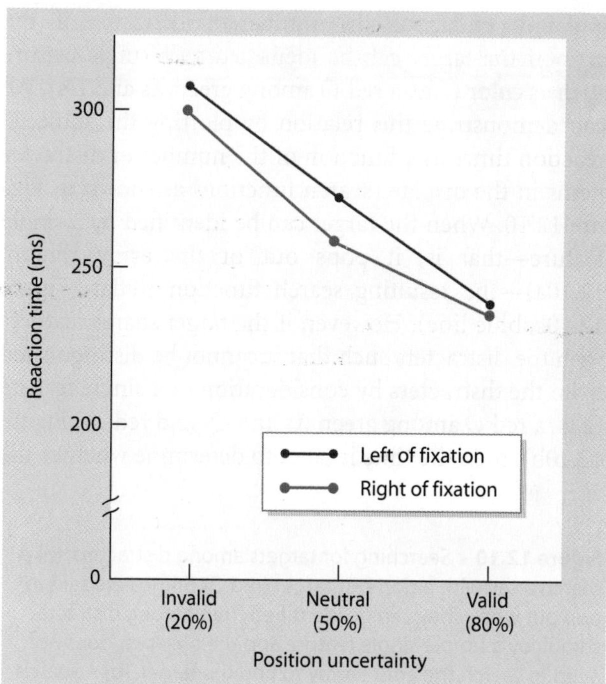

Figure 12.9 Results of the study by Posner and colleagues illustrated in Figure 12.8, as shown by reaction times to unexpected, neutral, and expected-location targets for the right and left visual hemifields. Reaction times for expected locations (valid trials) are significantly faster than those for unexpected locations (invalid trials) or neutral locations.

Differences in reaction time as a function of location expectancy are called *benefits* (speeding of reaction time) and *costs* (slowing of reaction time) with respect to the neutral situation in which the subject does not expect the target at one location more than another. These effects have been attributed to the influence of covert attention on the efficiency of information processing. According to some theories, such effects result when the predictiveness of the cue induces the subjects to internally direct covert attention—a sort of mental "spotlight" of attention—to the cued visual field location. The spotlight is a metaphor to describe how the brain may attend to a spatial location. Because subjects are typically required to keep their eyes on a central fixation spot on the viewing screen, internal or *covert* mechanisms must be at work.

Michael Posner, of the University of Oregon, and his colleagues (1980) suggested that this attentional spotlight may affect reaction times by influencing sensory and perceptual processing; hence, representations of attended-location stimuli are enhanced with respect to unattended-location stimuli. This formulation, a form of an early-selection model, proposes that changes in perceptual processing can happen when the subject is attending a stimulus location. However, these measures of reaction time, or behavioral measures more generally, are not measures of specific stages of neural processing. Rather they provide indirect measures, requiring interpretation in order to be related to hypothesized stages of neural analysis. Later we will see how cognitive neuroscience measures have been combined with the voluntary cuing paradigm described here to test early- and late-selection models more directly.

REFLEXIVE ATTENTION

Introspection and experimental data converge to support the idea that attention can be directed voluntarily to locations or objects in the sensory world—and to internal mental events. In addition, as described earlier, things in the environment sometimes attract our attention without our cooperation, as any student sitting in the back of a classroom has experienced. What happens when the lecturer leaves the door to the hallway open and, in the middle of lecture, someone walks down the hallway passing the open door? Heads turn toward the sounds and sights in the hall and then wag back to the lecturer a moment or two later, and this head wagging may happen before one can prevent it. It is an example of reflexive (automatic) attention leading to overt orienting to the sensory stimulus—*overt* because heads and eyes turn toward the event in the hallway. But even in the absence of overt signs of orienting, covert attention can be attracted to sensory events. Again, a variant of cuing methods allows us to demonstrate this phenomenon experimentally.

One way to demonstrate the effects of reflexive attention is to examine how a task-*irrelevant* flash of light somewhere in the visual field affects the speed of responses to subsequent task-*relevant* target stimuli. This method is referred to as *reflexive cuing* or **exogenous cuing** because attention is controlled by the low-level features of external stimuli and not by internal voluntary control. The typical reflexive cuing design uses cues (light flashes) that do not predict the location of subsequent targets; nonetheless, responses are faster to targets at the reflexively cued location, but only for a short time after the light flash (usually within about 50–200 ms). These types of effects tend to be spatially specific, influencing processing in and around the location of the reflexive cue, and therefore can also be described by the spotlight metaphor introduced earlier; in this case, however, the spotlight is reflexively attracted to a location and short-lived.

When more time passes between the task-irrelevant cuing light flash and the target (more than about 300 ms), the pattern of reaction time effects is reversed:

Subjects now respond more slowly to these stimuli. This slowing of responses is called the *inhibitory aftereffect* or, more commonly, **inhibition of return**; as these names suggest, the recently reflexively attended location becomes inhibited over time such that responses to stimuli occurring there are slowed.

Why would reflexive attentional orienting have such profound variations in its effect over time after a sensory cue? The answer may be rather intuitively simple: If sensory events in the environment caused reflexive orienting that lasted for many seconds or tens of seconds, it would be difficult to function normally in the world. We would be continually distracted by things happening around us. Imagine the potential disaster for someone driving a car if the driver's attention, being attracted reflexively to a sensory events, remained focused on those events for more than an instant. The automatic orienting system has built-in mechanisms to prevent reflexively directed attention from becoming stuck at a location for too long (more than a couple hundred milliseconds); the reflexive capturing of attention subsides and the likelihood that attention will be attracted back to that location is slightly reduced. Does this mean that things that attract our attention reflexively can't be attended for longer than a couple of hundred milliseconds? No. If the event is important, we can rapidly invoke our voluntary mechanisms to sustain attention longer, thereby overriding the inhibition of return. Thus the nervous system has evolved clever, complementary mechanisms to control attention so that we can function in a cluttered, rapidly changing sensory world.

ATTENTION AND VISUAL SEARCH

In everyday perception, we frequently search about for a specific item in a cluttered scene. For example, we look for a friend coming out of the building as classes break at the top of the hour. Or we try to find a suitcase in the baggage claim section of a busy airport. If the suitcase is yellow and covered with purple, flowered stickers, the search is quite easy. But if the suitcase is a medium-sized black bag with rollers, the task can be quite challenging. What role do attentional processes play in this visual search process, and how does visual search relate to the voluntary and reflexive spatial attention mechanisms described in the foregoing?

The mechanisms of visual search were investigated and modeled by Anne Treisman and her colleagues (Treisman & Gelade, 1980). A basic observation from their work is that the time it takes to find a target among distracters is shorter (i.e., targets are located quickly) and independent of the number of distracters in the array if the target can be identified by a single feature such as color (e.g., a red *O* among green *X*s and *O*s). We can demonstrate this relation by plotting the subjects' reaction times as a function of the number of distracter items in the display (search function) as shown in Figure 12.10. When the target can be identified by a single feature—that is, it pops out of the array (Figure 12.10a)—the resulting search function is flat (Figure 12.10c, blue line). However, if the target shares features with the distracters such that it cannot be distinguished from the distracters by consideration of a single feature (e.g., a red *O* among green *X*s and *O*s and red *X*s; Figure 12.10b), then the time it takes to determine whether the

Figure 12.10 Searching for targets among distracters. **(a)** A search array with a pop-out target (red *O*). Stimuli are said to pop out when they can be identified from among distracter stimuli by a simple single feature and the observer does not need to search the entire array to find the target. **(b)** A search array in which the target (red *O*) is defined by a conjunction of features shared with the distracters. **(c)** Idealized plot of reaction times as a function of set size (the number of items in the array) during visual search for pop-out stimuli versus feature conjunction stimuli. In pop-out searches, where an item can be distinguished from distracters by a single feature, the subjects' reaction times do not increase as much as a function of set size as they do in conjunction searches.

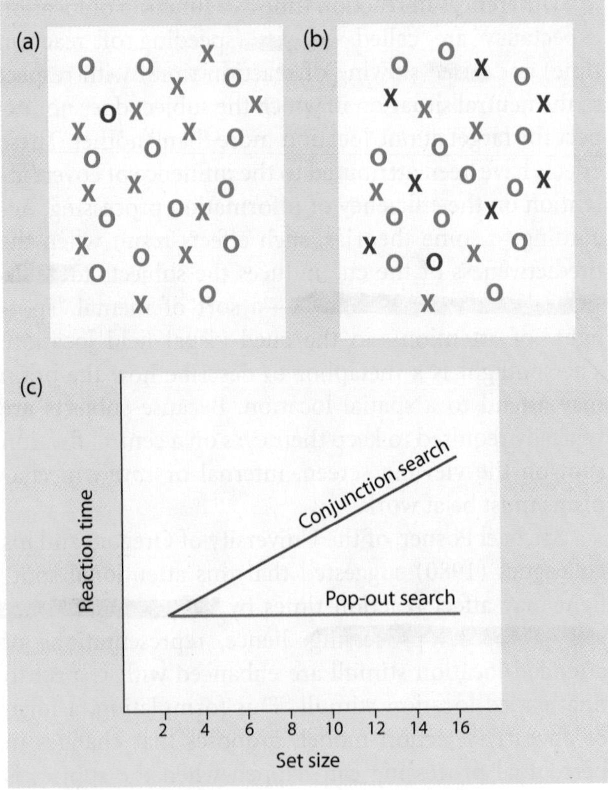

target is present or absent in the array increases with the number of distracters in the array, and the resulting search function is sloped (Figure 12.10c, red line). This is known as *conjunction search* because the target is defined by the conjunction of two or more stimulus features (e.g., the color red and the letter *O*).

It is thought that conjunction targets take longer to find because attention must be deployed in a sequential manner to each item in the array in order to link the information (in this case color and letter shape) in different feature maps so that the target can be analyzed and identified. The idea here is that a sort of spotlight of attention must be moving from one item in the array to another sequentially. How does this concept relate to the metaphorical spotlight of attention for voluntary and reflexive spatial attention?

To investigate whether visual search involves movements of the spatial spotlight of attention, Jeremy Wolfe and his colleagues (2000) at Harvard University examined how voluntary spatial attention modulates visual search. They were able to show that, when deliberate movements of attention were required in a visual search task, people responded more slowly than when deliberate movements of attention were not required and search was permitted to proceed automatically. The striking finding here is that visual search is most rapid when the subject permits the focus of attention to be driven by the visual sensory information in the array, rather than executing a slow, voluntarily controlled search of the items. That is, the brain automatically scans the visual world with a fast, automatic spotlight of attention.

One lingering question is how this automatic spotlight of attention in visual search "determines" where to move to next. In general, most models consider that a low-level map of the visual world provides information about the salience of objects and spatial attention is biased toward the most salient object locations. We will discuss this further when we review evidence about the neural mechanisms of attention later in this chapter.

ATTENTION TO FEATURES AND OBJECTS

So far, much of the theory and experimental evidence that we have presented has focused on spatial attention, the ability to direct attention to some locations at the expense of others in the environment. But, as is evident from the tasks described, especially in the preceding discussion of visual search, the world is full of objects of interest, and these objects are defined by their collections of elementary features. In Chapters 5 and 6 we introduced these relationships, and it is worth touching on these concepts again with selective attention in mind.

As demonstrated earlier, selectively attending to spatial locations, either voluntarily or reflexively, leads to changes in our ability to detect and respond to stimuli in the sensory world; although so far we have limited our discussion of experimental data primarily to visual attention, for completeness we will add that spatial attention also influences auditory and somatosensory information processing. We can also ask whether selectively attending to a stimulus feature (e.g., motion, color, shape) or object properties (e.g., face versus a house) similarly influences information processing. That is, if cued to expect that an upcoming stimulus is moving, are we better able to discriminate the target stimulus if indeed it is moving than if it unexpectedly is not moving?

In a recent example of the effects of feature and spatial attention, Marissa Carrasco and her colleagues at New York University pitted spatial attention against feature attention in a voluntary cuing paradigm using detection accuracy as the dependent measure of attention (Liu et al., 2007). They used arrow cues in one condition to indicate the location to which attention should be directed, and in another condition to indicate the direction of motion of the upcoming target (Figure 12.11a). They found that prior knowledge from the cue produced the typical voluntary cuing effect for spatial attention: Subjects were more accurate (expressed as the signal detection score d') to detect the presence of the target (a change in the velocity of moving dots) at the cued location in comparison to when the cue (a double-headed arrow) did not signal one location over another (Figure 12.11b, red line). In a similar vein, they found that, during the feature attention condition, cuing the direction of motion of the target, independent of whether it appeared in the left or right visual field array, also enhanced accuracy (Figure 12.11b, blue line).

These experiments demonstrated that precuing attention to a visual feature of a stimulus (in this case motion direction) led to improved performance. Interestingly, the effects of attention arose earlier (at shorter lags between the cue and the target) for the spatial attention condition than for the feature attention condition. These sorts of findings for feature attention clearly demonstrate that attention can be directed in advance to nonspatial features of target stimuli, as well as to spatial locations. In the next few sections we will consider the neural bases of selective attention to location, features, and objects.

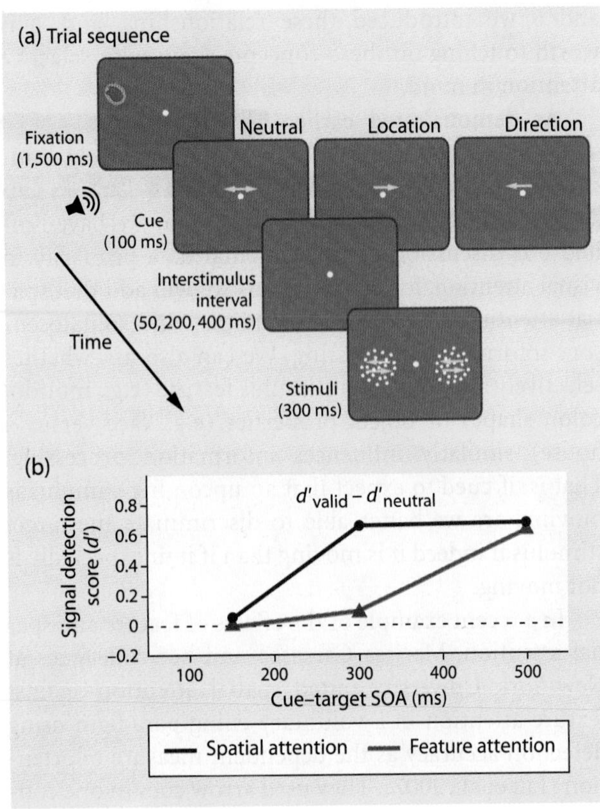

Figure 12.11 Spatial and feature attention. **(a)** Stimuli and trial sequence. Each trial began with a warning tone that was followed by one of three types of cues. In different experimental conditions, the cues indicated either the location of the subsequent target if it was present or the direction of motion of the target if present. The double-headed arrow indicates that the location or direction of motion was equiprobably left or right. **(b)** The difference in accuracy of detection (valid versus neutral cue) of the moving dots is plotted here as a function of cue-to-target stimulus onset asynchrony (SOA) in milliseconds, for both the spatial attention and feature attention conditions.

NEURAL MECHANISMS OF ATTENTION AND SELECTIVE PERCEPTION

In the first part of this chapter we focused on experimental results from cognitive psychology experiments on selective attention, and how these demonstrate that we select some visual high-priority inputs for further analysis while rejecting or attenuating others. Although these studies help identify some fundamental phenomena of attention, they cannot fully describe the neural mechanisms that underlie selective attention, nor do they tell us about the changes that occur in the brain when we attend to one input at the expense of other inputs. For example, where in the human brain does attention influence signal processing? Does an ability to respond more quickly to a target appearing at an attended location imply that the target was more efficiently processed in our visual cortex or instead that motor systems in the frontal lobe were biased to generate faster responses to that target? What brain systems control attention during voluntary and reflexive attention, and are they the same, different, or partly overlapping?

In their search for answers to the question of how attention works, many investigators have turned to physiological methods in humans and animals to determine the neural changes that occur with changes in attention. Physiological recording studies, imaging and stimulation studies, and data from patients with neurological damage or disease provide a wealth of information about the neural mechanisms of attentional processes. In this section we will look at studies that demonstrate how selective attention works in modulating sensory and perceptual processing.

Neurophysiology of Human Selective Attention

More than 50 years ago, interest in the neural mechanisms of attention led neurophysiologists to attempt to measure changes in neural activity with attention. The earliest studies were performed in animals, although, as we will describe shortly, not until somewhat later did neurophysiological work in humans establish that selective attention could influence perceptual processing. But before we begin that story, it is instructive to review a little history, not merely for history's sake, but also to make an important point about how to conduct experimental studies of the neurophysiology of attention.

DESIGN ISSUES IN STUDIES OF SELECTIVE ATTENTION

In the 1950s, the great Mexican neurophysiologist Raúl Hernández-Peón and his colleagues (1956) were investigating the neuroanatomy and neurophysiology of the ascending sensory pathways, and the extent to which incoming information might be influenced by top-down, or descending, neural projections. Since the time of Santiago Ramón y Cajal at the turn of the 19th century (see Chapter 1), it had been known that some neurons in the central nervous system project into the synapse on sensory input neurons in the peripheral nervous system. For example, each neural relay in the ascending auditory pathway sends return axons back down to the preceding processing stage, even out to the cochlea in the form of the olivocochlear bundle (OCB). Indeed, by applying electrical stimulation to the cortex, it can be shown that activity in the cortex can activate the descending OCB pathway all the way to the cochlea. Could the behavioral effects of attention, such as those revealed in dichotic listening studies, be the result of gating that occurred even earlier in auditory processing, such as in the thalamus, brainstem, or even the cochlea?

Hernández-Peón and his colleagues in Mexico, California, and Oregon surmised that, at least in principle, the descending projections of the OCB might exert top-down control over subcortical auditory regions that project to the cortex in the service of early attentional gating of auditory inputs. They attempted to determine whether phenomena like the cocktail party effect might result from such a gating of auditory inputs in the ascending auditory pathways. They recorded the activity in neurons in the subcortical auditory pathway (see Figure 5.1 in Chapter 5) while the cat was either passively listening to the sounds or ignoring the sounds. They induced the animals to ignore the sounds by showing them mice safely contained in a closed bottle and thereby attracting their visual attention to the mice. These researchers reported that the amplitude of activity was greater in the cochlear nucleus when the animals attended to the sounds compared to when they ignored the sounds while visually attending to the mice. They interpreted these neurophysiological findings as evidence that attention could affect the earliest stages of sensory processing—strong evidence for early-selection theories.

Unfortunately, these particular experiments suffered a fatal flaw that is apparent even from the photos included in the original 1956 report in the journal *Science*. The problem was that the sounds delivered to the cat to evoke auditory activity were delivered by speakers near the cat, not via microphones directly into the animal's ear canals. As a result, if the animals differentially oriented their head or ears with respect to the sound-emitting speaker, the amplitude of the sound at the eardrum of the animal would change (Figure 12.12). The result of this change in the relationship between the external ear and the sound source is certainly one mechanism for improving hearing, and does indeed involve attentional orienting in some fashion, but it also presents a significant confounding factor in studies of selective attention where the goal is to investigate covert neural mechanisms.

The principal error of Hernández-Peón and his colleagues related to the control over stimuli. The altered positions of a cat's external ear with respect to the

Figure 12.12 Early study of the neurophysiology of attention. A sound was played to a cat through a loudspeaker under three conditions while recordings from the cochlear nucleus in the brainstem were obtained. **(a)** While the animal sits passively in the cage listening to sounds **(left)**, the evoked response from the cochlear nucleus is robust **(right)**. **(b)** The animal's attention is attracted away from the sounds that it is hearing to visual objects of interest (a mouse in a bottle). **(c)** The animal is once again resting and passively hearing sounds. The arrows indicate the responses of interest and the horizonal lines indicate the onsets and offsets of the sounds from the loudspeaker.

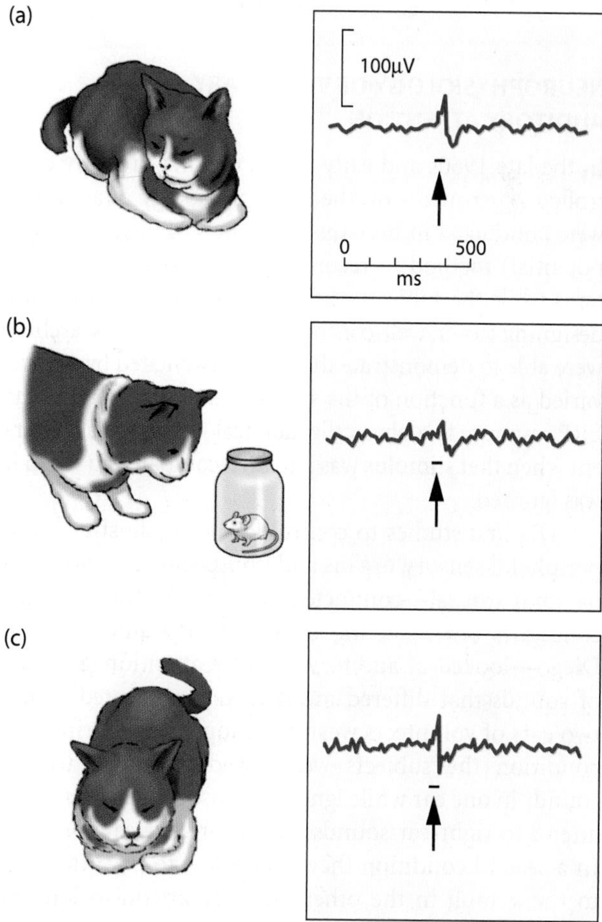

loudspeaker led to signals of varied amplitude reaching the eardrum in the attended versus ignored conditions; hence, differing activity levels were recorded from the auditory structures. We already know that changes in stimulus amplitude at the eardrum will alter the firing rates of neurons. The question was whether such changes in neuronal firing could occur as the result of selective internal neural control over sensory processing.

One lesson that emerges from this work is that experimental controls must prevent any adjustment of the peripheral sensory organs—a lesson that applies to all sensory modalities in attention research. The solution is rigorous monitoring of ear, head, and eye positions, and other experimental controls. For example, when Hernández-Peón's experiment was later repeated by his students, who carefully avoided changes in the sound amplitude at the ear, no differences were found subcortically between the neural response to attended and ignored sound. Hernández-Peón was a pioneer who made many seminal observations about the operation of the nervous system, but like many working at the cutting edge of science, his findings in the field of attention research were not what he believed at the time. Those who followed him were able to capitalize on his advances while also learning from his mistakes.

NEUROPHYSIOLOGY OF VOLUNTARY AUDITORY ATTENTION

In the late 1960s and early 1970s, the first properly controlled experiments on the neurophysiology of attention were conducted in humans using the ERP (event-related potential) method to record activity of the sensory systems while the subjects attended and ignored stimuli. By designing clever, well-controlled experiments, researchers were able to demonstrate that the ERPs elicited by stimuli varied as a function of the subject's attentional state. The ERP response to a physically identical stimulus was different when that stimulus was attended compared to when it was ignored.

The first studies to control for both adjustments of peripheral sensory organs and nonspecific effects of behavioral arousal—conducted by Steven Hillyard and his colleagues (1973) at the University of California, San Diego—looked at auditory selective attention. Streams of sounds that differed in pitch were presented to the two ears of volunteers wearing headphones. During one condition the subjects were asked to attend to the sounds in one ear while ignoring those in the other (e.g., attend to right-ear sounds and ignore left-ear sounds). In a second condition they were asked to pay attention to the stimuli in the other ear (e.g., attend to left-ear sounds and ignore right-ear sounds). In this manner the researchers separately obtained auditory ERPs to stimuli entering one ear when that ear's input was attended and when it was ignored (while attending the other ear).

The significant design feature of the experiment was that, during the two conditions of attention, the subjects were always engaged in a difficult attention task: All that varied was the direction of covert attention—that is, the ear to which the subjects directed their attention. In addition, the researchers controlled the orientation of the subject's head with respect to the sound source by using headphones to deliver the sounds. Thus, they controlled for the confounding factors that had led to failures in previous animal research.

Hillyard and his colleagues discovered that auditory sensory ERPs were enlarged in amplitude when stimuli were attended compared with when they were ignored. This effect in the ERPs appeared as a deflection in the ERP waveform known as the *auditory N1 potential,* so named because it is the first of the large, negative-polarity deflections in the signal-averaged waveform (Figure 12.13). The N1 component is a sensory-evoked wave with a peak latency of less than 90 ms after stimulus onset. Given that this sensory response was labile to manipulation by covert attention, these data provided evidence in support of early-selection models of attention.

In subsequent studies in the 1990s, Marty Woldorff and Steve Hillyard modified the auditory attention experiment so that they could obtain high-fidelity ERP signals from very early in the auditory processing stream, starting as early as the auditory nerve, and ex-

Figure 12.13 Event-related potentials in a dichotic listening task. The solid line represents the average voltage response to an attended input over time; the dashed line, the response to an unattended input. Hillyard and colleagues found that the amplitude of the N1 component was enhanced with attending to a stimulus compared to ignoring a stimulus.

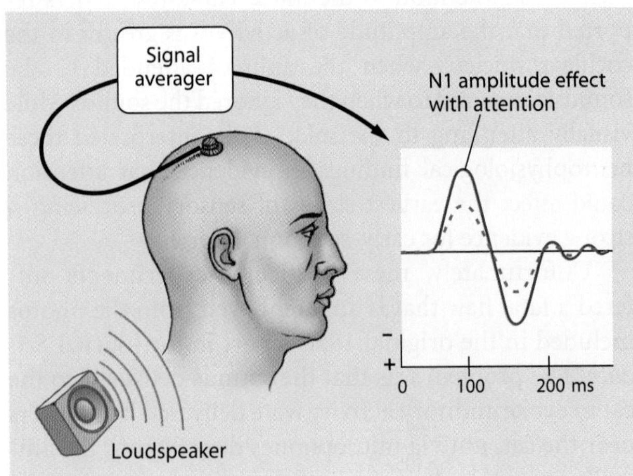

tending through the ascending sensory pathways to the level of the cortex. Woldorff and Hillyard (1991) replicated the prior N1 attention effect: larger N1 responses to tones presented to the attended ear. In addition, they observed that even earlier waveforms—those occurring between 20 and 50 ms after stimulus onset—were also different as a function of selective auditory attention. This finding, the *P20–50 effect*, named for its positive polarity and latency of occurrence (20–50 ms) after stimulus onset, provided extremely compelling evidence in support of early-selection models, because the timing of the P20–50 ERP suggests an early stage of processing, perhaps the primary auditory cortex or even earlier, such as from the medial geniculate nucleus of the thalamus, the auditory thalamic relay. To provide additional neuroanatomical information about this early attention effect, Woldorff and Hillyard and their colleagues (Woldorff et al., 1993) turned to recordings of the magnetoencephalogram (MEG) and signal averaging to obtain event-related fields (ERFs; see Chapter 4) that have a greater ability to localize intracranial activity.

These investigators identified a magnetic correlate of the early electrical P20–50 attention effect: the so-called M20–50 attention effect (*M* for *magnetic*). By estimating the best dipolar model source within the head that would explain the attention-related responses recorded at the surface of the head, and mapping those model dipoles onto structural MRI scans of the subject's brains, the researchers localized the M20–50 effect to the auditory cortex in Heschl's gyri (Figure 12.14). Similar magnetic effects can be observed in the time range of the N1 attention effect (the so-called M1 attention effect), and these effects also appear to be generated within the auditory cortex, but at a later stage of neural processing than the shorter-latency M20–50. Attention, therefore, can affect auditory stimulus processing at initial cortical stages of processing.

These data do not indicate for certain whether the attention effects represent modulations in the primary auditory cortex or in immediately surrounding secondary auditory areas. Even so, attention clearly affects sensory-specific stages of auditory analysis at latencies strongly indicating that auditory sensory analysis has not been completed. At this early stage of processing, the auditory system cannot select information based on higher order aspects of auditory inputs such as speech cues; rather, the ear of entry is the cue for selection. Longer latency changes in an ERP or ERF waveform reflect attentional selection involving the stimuli's higher order properties, such as a speaker's voice or semantic meaning.

If the early stages of cortical auditory processing are influenced by attention, could this influence reflect

Figure 12.14 Mapping attention effects. **(a)** Topographic map of magnetic event-related fields (ERFs) associated with auditory attention in a selective-listening paradigm. The field map was created by subtraction of the field elicited by unattended tones (in the 20- to 50-ms time range after stimulus onset) from the field elicited by the same tones when they were attended. The arrow indicates the location and orientation of a model dipolar neural generator that best explains the surface field. **(b)** The localization of the M20–50 attention effect in the brain. When the three-dimensional location of this model dipolar generator (red asterisk) was mapped onto a structural MRI scan (after coregistration of the data sets), the activity was found to originate in the auditory cortex, in Heschl's gyri in the supratemporal plane.

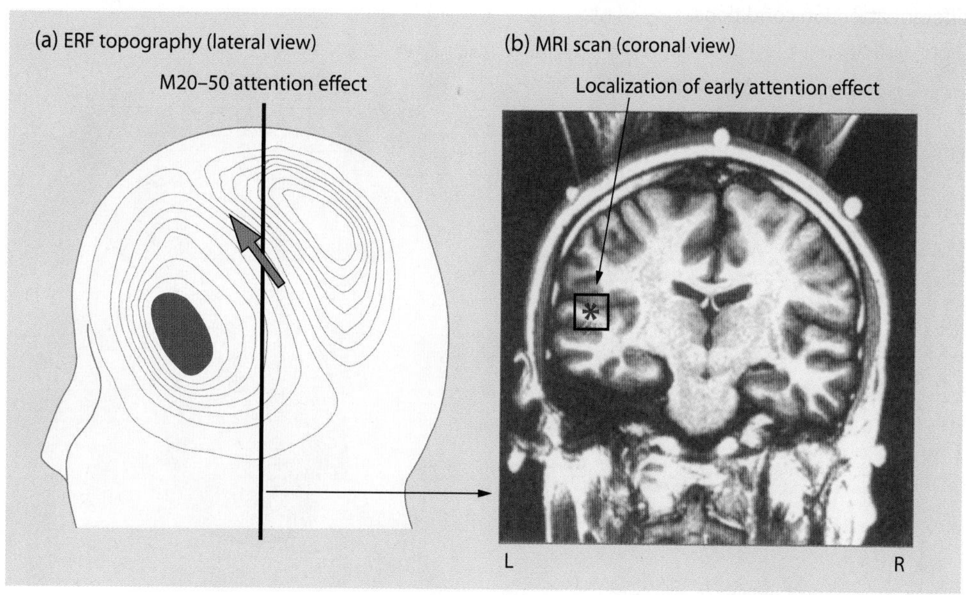

subcortical filtering of sensory inputs? Electrical recordings of human auditory processing from scalp electrodes can pick up sensory activity as early as the brainstem relays, and even the compound action potential of the auditory nerve itself. This activity is called the *auditory brainstem response* (*ABR*) and is manifest as voltage deflections in the auditory ERPs with latencies between 1 and 10 ms after stimulus onset (see Figure 4.29 in Chapter 4). Can these subcortical ERPs be modulated by selective attention? The answer, from many studies, is that voluntary selective attention in the auditory system does not appear to involve modulations of subcortical auditory neurons as measured by the ABR recordings, even when attention must be very highly focused.

Despite a preponderance of negative findings in ERP studies of subcortical attention effects in audition, the issue of brainstem-level gating as a mechanism of auditory selective attention is not yet resolved. Evidence from Marie-Helene Giard and colleagues (2000) in France indicates that, under conditions very similar to those that revealed the P20–50 attention effect, otoacoustic emissions emanating from the ear canal are modulated by auditory selective attention. *Otoacoustic emissions* are minute sounds actually produced by mechanical changes in the cochlea during hearing. These can be recorded with a sensitive microphone placed in the ear canal. Changes in these sounds with attention could reflect attention-related modulations of the mechanical properties of the cochlea, which might represent a form of attentional control.

NEUROPHYSIOLOGY OF VOLUNTARY VISUAL ATTENTION

Neural mechanisms of visual selective attention have been investigated by means of methods similar to those already described for auditory attention. In a typical experiment, participants are given verbal instructions to covertly (without diverting gaze from a central fixation spot) attend to stimuli presented at one location (e.g., right field) and ignore those presented at another

Figure 12.15 Stimulus display used to investigate sustained, spatial selective attention. For periods of seconds to minutes, the subject fixates the eyes on the central crosshairs (+), while stimuli are flashed in random order to the left and right fields. **(a)** During some blocks the subject is instructed to covertly attend left stimuli in order to detect infrequent targets, and to ignore those flashing on the right. **(b)** During other blocks the subject is instructed to attend the right location, ignoring the left. Then the responses to the same physical stimuli, such as the white rectangle being flashed in the figure, are compared when they are attended (the attend-left condition) versus when they are ignored (the attend-right condition). Over the contralateral posterior scalp, beginning about 70 ms after the onset of the stimulus, an increased positive voltage response can be observed for the left stimulus when it is attended **(a)** versus when it is ignored **(b)**. Larger-amplitude positive responses to the stimuli over the occipital scalp are colored more brightly as yellow. The activity is represented in a topographic map where the voltages at a time point or narrow range of times are recorded simultaneously from many electrodes. Then the voltages across the scalp between the electrode sites are estimated by interpolation, and isovoltage contours are drawn as outlines and filled with colors corresponding to different voltage values. The response to the stimulus produces a sort of "mountain peak" of voltage over the contralateral scalp, and the peak is higher, if you will, for attended as opposed to ignored stimuli. The dotted lines from the head to the screen indicate the direction of covert attention for the different attention conditions.

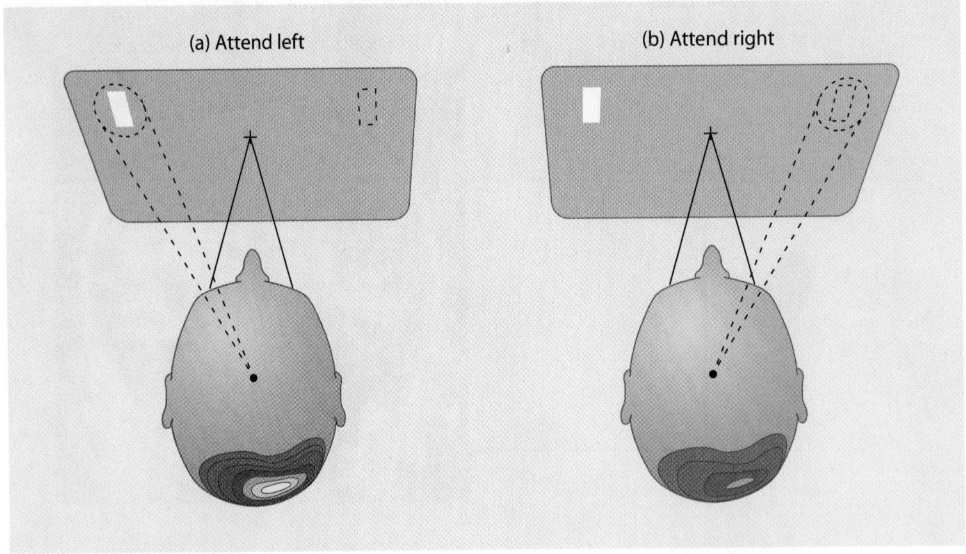

(e.g., left field). Eason and colleagues (1969), and Steve Hillyard and his colleagues (Van Voorhis & Hillyard, 1977), demonstrated that modulations in the visual ERPs begin as early as 70–90 ms after stimulus onset (Figure 12.15). This attention effect is seen in an ERP component known as the occipital *P1*, the first major positive wave. When a visual stimulus appears at a location to which a subject is attending, the P1 is larger in amplitude than when the same stimulus appears at the same location but attention is focused elsewhere (Figure 12.16). Such a pattern is therefore consistent with filtering mechanisms like those observed in studies of auditory selective attention.

These P1 attention effects have been obtained only with manipulations of spatial attention, and they have been shown even when attention is cued on a trial-by-trial basis (Figure 12.17) with cuing methods common in cognitive psychology, as described earlier in this chapter (see Figure 12.8), thereby permitting a close integration of behavioral and neurophysiological attention measures. Interestingly, these early effects of visuospatial selective attention are not reliably found when attentional selection is based on other stimulus features, such as color (e.g., attend to the red circles and ignore the green ones), spatial frequency, orientation, or conjunctions of these features. Similarly, selection of visual inputs based on higher order properties such as what object it is (e.g., attend chairs but ignore tables) does not lead to short-latency modulations of ERP amplitude. Attentional affects for these more complex tasks are observed later in the ERPs (greater than 120-ms latency).

Figure 12.16 Event-related potentials evoked by a left-field stimulus under the two conditions of attention shown in Figure 12.15, and recorded from a single location over the contralateral occipital scalp. These traces are taken from the electrode positioned at the location of the maximal scalp response shown in Figure 12.15. Attended stimuli (solid red trace) elicit greater-amplitude ERPs than do unattended stimuli (dashed blue trace). The shaded area on the ERP shows the difference in amplitude between attended and unattended events in the P1 latency range. The label "topography" indicates that the differences in amplitude of the P1 wave in this time range (from this and adjacent electrodes) were used to generate the topographic maps of Figure 12.15. Time zero ($t = 0$) represents the onset of the stimuli evoking these ERPs. Positive voltage is plotted downward here, and the timescale is from 100 ms before stimulus onset to 400 ms after stimulus onset.

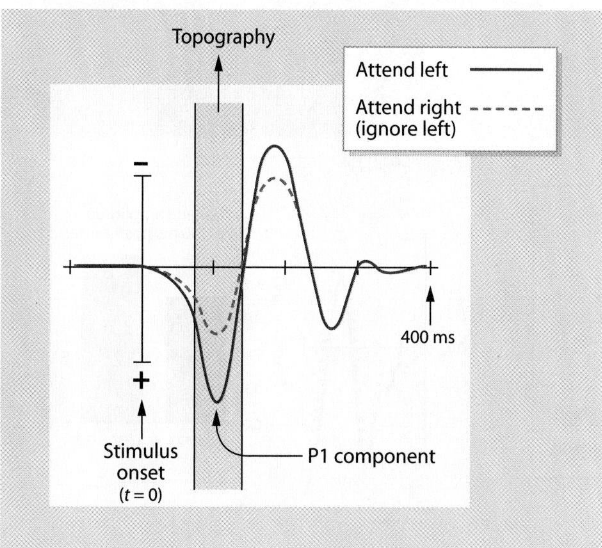

As with the investigation of the neural mechanisms of auditory selective attention, we can ask where within the visual hierarchy the earliest effects of selective visuospatial attention are obtained. The P1 attention effect has an onset latency of about 70 ms from stimulus onset, but what does this value reflect in terms of the functional anatomy of the visual pathways? This point is later than for auditory attention, as reflected in the P20–50 attention effect (onset latency of 20 ms), but the auditory and visual systems have different timing—the visual system is slower—so we cannot directly compare the latency of effects in the two modalities. Indeed, intracranial recordings of activity in primary visual cortex in humans indicates that the first volleys of afferent inputs into striate cortex (V1) take place with a latency longer than 35 ms, and therefore the P1 attention effect reflects cortical activity.

In numerous studies, inverse dipole modeling of the scalp-recorded electrical fields of the P1 attention effect have indicated that the earliest spatial attention effects are generated in extrastriate cortex. Therefore, as for the mechanisms of auditory selective attention, it is clear that robust changes in sensory processing take place early in visual cortex with selective visual attention, but whether incoming signals are influenced at subcortical stages of analysis in humans remains unresolved. In our later discussions of human neuroimaging studies and animal recording studies, we will return to consideration of how early voluntary attention may affect visual processing.

NEUROPHYSIOLOGY OF REFLEXIVE VISUAL ATTENTION

The preceding discussion indicates that voluntarily focusing attention at a location in response to verbal instructions or visual precues will enhance the visual ERPs to stimuli occurring at that location. Do these same changes occur when attention is attracted to locations automatically, via the reflexive mechanisms described

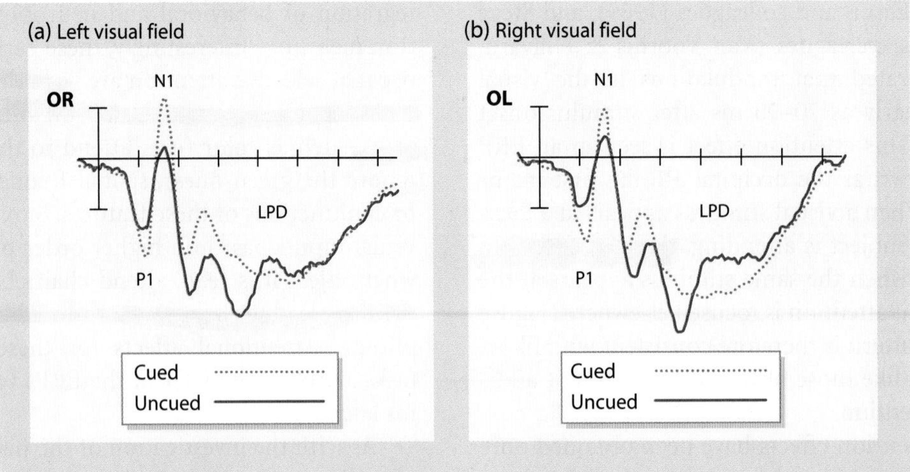

Figure 12.17 ERP waveforms from persons performing a voluntary spatial cuing task like that depicted in Figure 12.8. Shown are modulations of the sensory evoked P1 and N1 ERPs to visual stimuli. The dotted blue traces show the responses to left-field **(a)** and right-field **(b)** targets when cued (valid trials), and the solid red traces show the responses elicited by the same stimuli when uncued (invalid trials). These recordings were made at lateral occipital scalp sites contralateral to the stimulus—that is, at a right occipital site (OR) for left stimuli and at a left occipital site (OL) for right stimuli. LPD = late positive deflection.

Figure 12.18 ERP waveforms from persons performing a reflexive cuing task. **(a)** When attention is attracted to a location by abrupt onset of a visual stimulus, reaction times to subsequent targets are facilitated for short periods of time, as described earlier in this chapter. **(b)** When ERPs are measured to these targets, the same extrastriate cortical response (P1 wave) that is affected by voluntary spatial attention is enhanced by reflexive attention (dotted versus solid lines at left) at short cue-to-target interstimulus intervals (ISIs). The time course of this reflexive attention effect is not the same as that for voluntary cuing, but rather is similar to the pattern observed in reaction times during reflexive cuing. The enhanced response is replaced within a few hundred milliseconds by a relative inhibition of the response **(right)**.

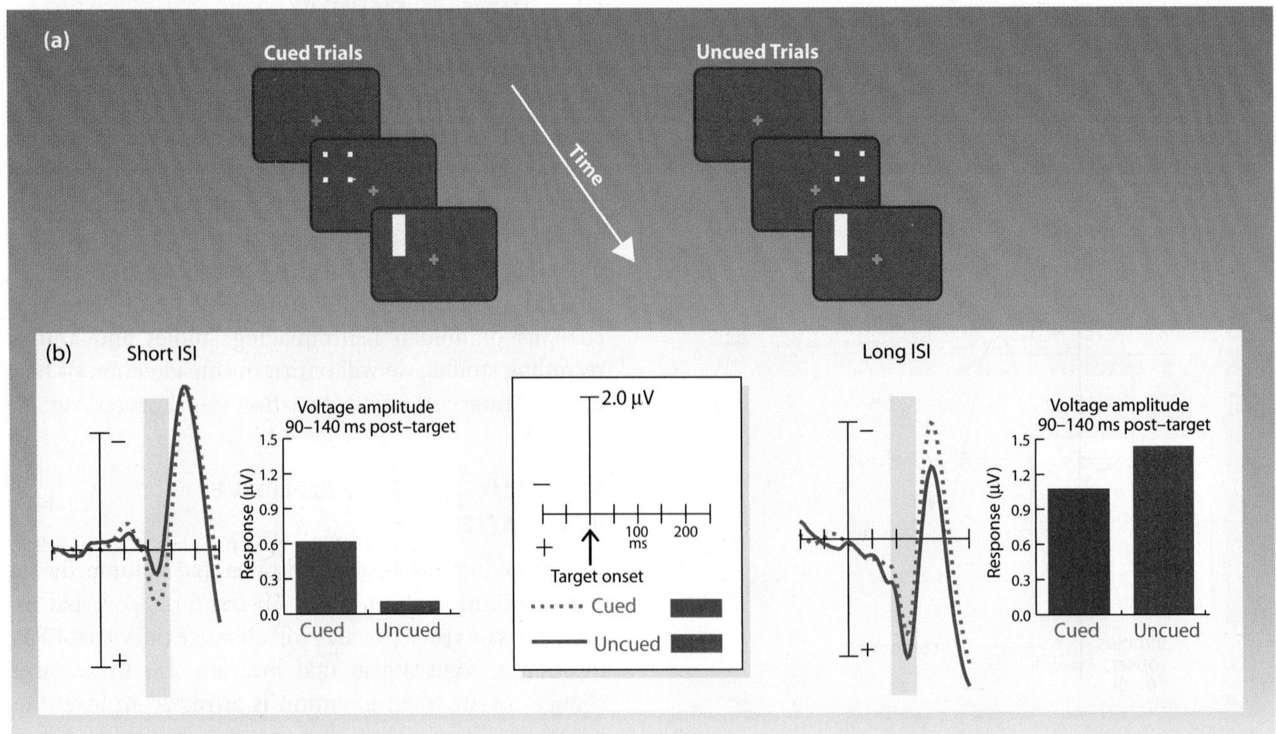

earlier in this chapter? That is, when our attention is reflexively attracted to a location in the visual field by a sensory event, is neural processing in the visual cortex heightened? Here, too, the answer is yes. Remember that reflexive cuing can be observed when a sensory event immediately precedes a target at the same location (Figure 12.18a). Under such conditions, response times are faster at the cued location than at the uncued location, but only when the time between the cuing and target stimuli is short (less than about 250 ms); with longer periods, this effect reverses, producing inhibition of return.

Joseph Hopfinger and colleagues (Hopfinger & Mangun, 1998, 2001) showed that, when ERPs are recorded in response to target stimuli in this type of design, the early occipital P1 wave is enlarged for targets that quickly follow a sensory cue at the same location versus when the sensory cue and target occur at different locations. But as the time after cuing grows longer, this effect reverses and the P1 response diminishes and may even be inhibited, just as in reaction time measures (Figure 12.18b). Therefore, these data indicate that both reflexive (bottom-up) and voluntary (top-down) shifts in spatial attention induce similar physiological modulations in early visual processing. Presumably, the neural networks implementing these attentional modulations of sensory analysis are different, reflecting the differing ways in which attentional control is triggered for the two forms of attention.

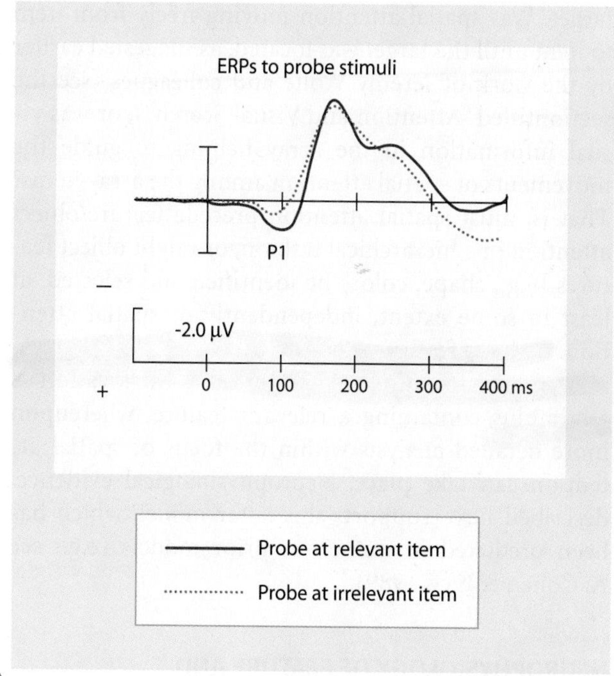

Figure 12.19 ERPs from scalp sites contralateral to a probe stimulus presented 205 ms after a conjunction search array. The probes were flashed to locations where either relevant (solid red line) or irrelevant (dotted blue line) items were located in the conjunction search array. In this way the amplitude of the probe ERP could be taken as an index of the location of spatial attention just after the onset of the conjunction search array at the point where the subjects would have located the relevant item (i.e., the designated target, defined by the conjunction of stimulus features). The irrelevant probe elicited a larger sensory-evoked occipital P1 wave when it occurred at the location of a conjunction target than when it was presented to regions of the array where no target was present, supporting the idea that focal spatial attention is directed to the location of the target in the array.

SPATIAL ATTENTION AND VISUAL SEARCH

The idea that has emerged from studies like the ones reviewed in Figures 12.15 through 12.18 is that, during both voluntary and reflexive attention, a focal "spotlight" of enhanced perceptual processing is focused on a discrete spatial location. Is this hypothetical spotlight similar to the one that searches the array of stimuli during visual search for a target among multiple distracters? In electrophysiological investigations to test this hypothesis, subjects were presented with arrays of targets and distracters in a conjunction search paradigm, like that in Figure 12.10b. At brief time intervals after the search array was presented, a solitary probe stimulus was flashed on the screen to elicit a visual ERP (Figure 12.19). The probe elicited larger early visual responses (P1) at the location of a conjunction target than in regions where nothing other than distracters was present.

This demonstration suggests that similar neural mechanisms for the early selection of visual information are engaged during visual search for targets defined by the conjunction of features among distracters as are engaged during voluntary attention in cuing and sustained attention paradigms. Of course, the difference is that, during visual search, the location of the target is not known until the search concludes, whereas in the cuing paradigms or the sustained attention paradigms, the location to which attention is to be directed is known in advance and is based on either the information in the cue or the verbal instructions given to the subject. Nonetheless, in both cases changes in early visual cortical information processing based on the location of attention can be observed, and these have apparently highly similar neural mechanisms.

One question that remains open is how spatial attention arrived at the location of the conjunction target. Was spatial attention moving freely from item to item until the target was located, as suggested earlier by the work of Jeremy Wolfe and colleagues (see the sectiontitled "Attention and Visual Search"), or was visual information in the array helping to guide the movements of spatial attention among the array items? That is, must spatial attention precede feature/object attention in a hierarchical fashion, or might object features (e.g., shape, color) be identified and selected, at least to some extent, independently of spatial attention. Perhaps feature attention acts as a signal that enables spatial attention to be directed to the location of a stimulus containing a relevant feature, whereupon more detailed analysis within the focus of spatial attention can take place. Neurophysiological evidence, described next, supports this latter model, which has been predicted in numerous prior models (e.g., see A. Cohen & Ivry, 1989).

NEUROPHYSIOLOGY OF FEATURE AND SPATIAL ATTENTION

The foregoing review of the electrophysiological correlates of selective visual attention focused on the physiological signs of early spatial selective attention in humans. However, the field of the human electrophysiology of attention is immense, encompassing hundreds of studies that have investigated spatial and nonspatial attention, identifying several important ERP signs of selective attention. In general, spatial attention produces the shortest-latency ERP signs of attention, but at slightly longer latencies a host of ERPs index nonspatial, feature-based attention (e.g., attending one color while ignoring another), and we will collectively refer to these as *feature selection ERPs*. In addition, a human brain response with the pithy name *N2pc*, which has been identified by Steve Luck and Steve Hillyard (1994), indexes how attention zooms down to focus on objects in visual space when one is searching for a target. Experimental work has established that the N2pc component is a sign of the covert focusing of visual attention, and that it represents a stage of processing that occurs before the completion of object recognition.

Max Hopf and Hans-Jochen Heinze and their colleagues in Germany and Steve Luck at the University of California, Davis (Hopf et al., 2004), investigated the mechanisms of visual search using the feature selection ERP and the N2pc as indices of feature and spatial attention, respectively. They wanted to establish whether features were selected before spatial attention was focused on a target location. They used a visual search task

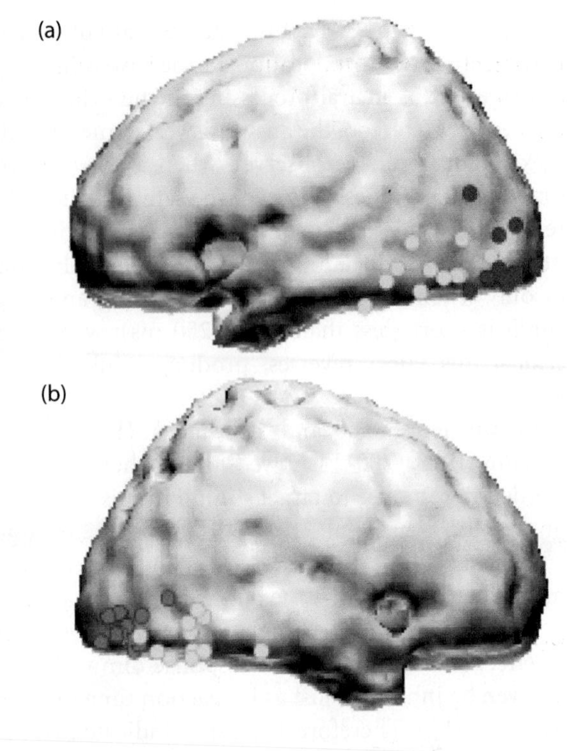

Figure 12.20 Feature and spatial attention mechanisms in visual search. Lateral views of left **(a)** and right **(b)** hemispheres rendered from MRI scans showing the locations of feature (red and blue circles) and spatial (yellow circles) attention effects. Feature selection ERPs occurred earlier (onset of 140 ms) over more posterior regions of occipitotemporal cortex; subsequent spatial attention ERPs (N2pc) were slightly later in time (onset 170 ms) and were localized by means of MEG to slightly more anterior locations in occipitotemporal cortex.

in which the spatial distribution of items containing the task-relevant features was varied independently of the location of the target. Using simultaneous ERP and MEG recordings, they found that, 140 ms after search array onset, a feature selection ERP was generated in ventral occipitotemporal cortex (Figure 12.20). This feature attention effect was then quickly followed (about 30 ms later) by an N2pc response generated in more anterior regions of the occipitotemporal cortex that indicated that the subjects were focusing spatial attention on the target.

These findings clearly demonstrate that feature selective attention precedes visuospatial attention when the location of the target is not known in advance, as is always the case in visual search paradigms. The intriguing aspect of these results is that they suggest that feature selection may guide subsequent shifts of attention to the locations of those features so that higher resolution analyses can identify conjunction targets. Although not done in conjunction with this study, as described earlier, had they also presented an irrelevant probe stimulus at the location of the target and compared that to nontarget locations, there would have been an increased P1 attention effect demonstrating that spatial attention had shifted to the target location (see Figure 12.19).

SUMMARY OF NEUROPHYSIOLOGY OF HUMAN SELECTIVE ATTENTION

Electrophysiological and neuromagnetic recordings provide exceptionally strong evidence in support of the concept of early selection. The general model supported by these data is that incoming sensory signals can be altered within the sensory-specific cortex when stimuli containing the relevant physical features (those to be attended) are encountered. The earliest form of this selection can be defined by location in auditory and visual systems. Projections from attentional control systems appear to affect the excitability of cortical neurons coding the features of the stimuli. These data inform us about the sites (cortical versus subcortical, sensory cortex versus association cortex) where attention effects are manifest during perceptual processing. In the sections to follow we delve more deeply into the mechanisms of attention by presenting evidence from functional brain imaging, animal studies, and finally patient lesion evidence.

Functional Imaging of Brain Attention Systems

Neurophysiological measures in humans have the advantage of providing a strong temporal measure of brain attention systems by recording the neuroelectrical or neuromagnetic responses of populations of neurons in the brain. However, because these measures are taken outside the brain by the use of electrodes or sensors at the scalp (except in cases where neurosurgical recordings can be made in patients), the ability of these methods to localize the brain systems involved in attention mechanisms is limited. Therefore, researchers turn to functional-imaging methods to provide neuroanatomical information about the mechanisms of human attention.

NEUROIMAGING OF SPATIAL ATTENTION

To investigate the mechanisms of visuospatial attention, Hans-Jochen Heinze of the University of Magdeburg, Germany, one of the authors (G.R.M., at the University of California, Davis), and their colleagues (1994; Mangun et al., 1997), combined functional brain imaging using positron emission tomography (PET) with ERP methods. They presented subjects with bilateral stimulus arrays of nonsense symbols (two in each hemifield) flashed at a varying rate averaging about 2 per second (Figure 12.21). In separate conditions, the subjects were required to pay attention to the left half of the array and ignore the right, or vice versa, while keeping their eyes carefully fixated on a central spot and thereby employing covert spatial attention.

In the PET part of the study, the hemodynamic responses (changes in blood flow) in the brain could be

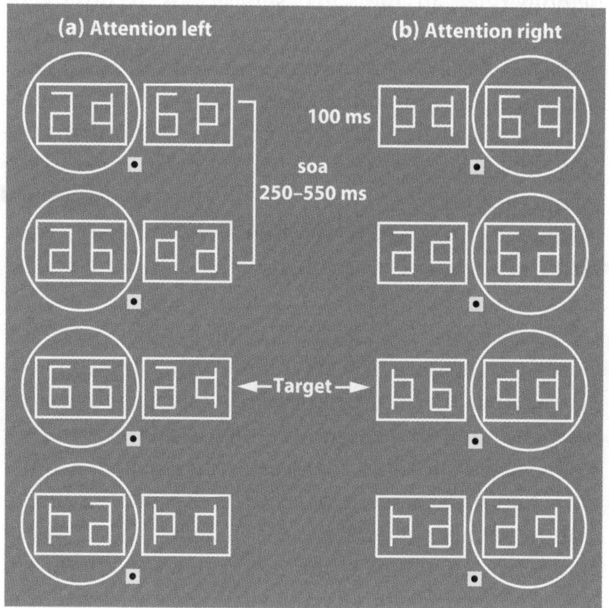

Figure 12.21 Stimuli and task used in a spatial attention study. Two conditions of attention are shown: attention left **(a)** and attention right **(b)**. Subjects viewed rapid sequences of arrays of nonsense symbols (flashed for 100 ms) while maintaining fixation of their eyes on a central fixation spot (yellow box with red dot). The arrays were presented with stimulus onset asynchronies (soa) that varied between 250 and 550 ms. There were always two symbols in the left and two in the right visual hemifield in locations marked by an outline rectangle. The task was to detect and press a button when the symbols in a pair at the attended location matched (labeled "Target"). In the figure (but not in the actual experiment) the focus of covert spatial attention is indicated by a circle.

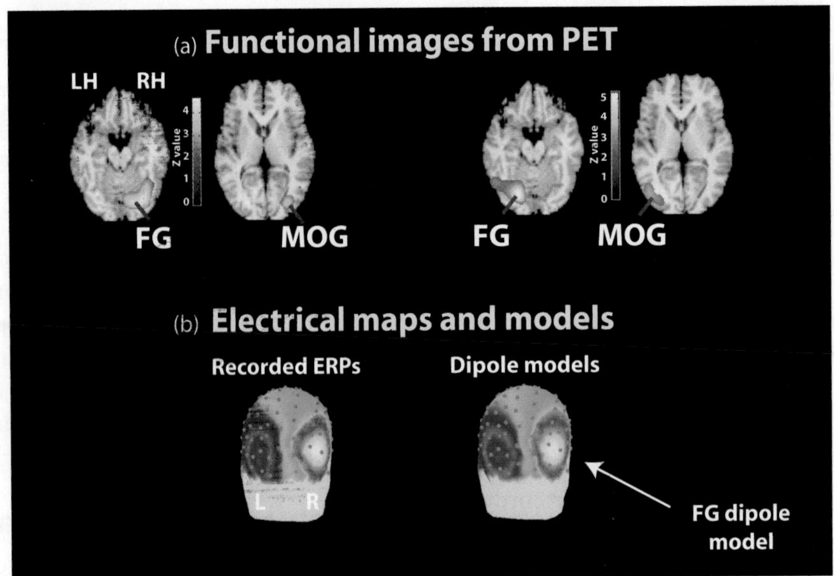

Figure 12.22 PET and ERP data from a study of spatial attention. **(a)** PET scans show activations in contralateral visual cortex with spatial attention in the extrastriate cortex, focused in the posterior fusiform gyrus (FG) and the middle occipital gyrus (MOG). **(b)** Attention effects (attention left minus attention right) as recorded by ERPs and models of the ERPs in simulations. The relationship between the recorded **(left)** and modeled **(right)** data is illustrated for the P1 latency range (100–120 ms latency). The recorded and modeled data are shown as topographic voltage maps on the surface of the head model viewed from the rear (the left side of the brain and head are shown on the left side of the figure). Topographies of the modeled data were very similar to those of the recorded data in the P1 time range for model neural generators placed in the location of the FG activation (compare left and right images).

compared for attend-left versus attend-right conditions (or to passive viewing conditions). The researchers found that spatial attention led to activation in extrastriate cortex in the hemisphere contralateral to the attended side of the bilateral stimulus array, especially in the posterior fusiform gyrus on the ventral cortical surface (Figure 12.22a). Such a finding is in accord with the evidence from prior ERP studies, but was also demonstrated in the same subjects by recording of ERPs during their performance of the same attention task (Figure 12.22b). The scalp-recorded ERPs showed the expected P1 attention effects, and by using simulations to model the intracranial generators of the P1 ERP attention effect (see Chapter 4 for an overview of the method), it was possible to show that the P1 attention effect and the PET attention effect in the posterior fusiform gyrus (extrastriate visual cortex) were apparently related.

These neuroimaging findings on modulations of the visual cortex during attention provide powerful evidence about the stages of processing affected by attention, and they fit well with findings in animals that we will describe shortly. As we learned in Chapter 5, however, the visual system in primate occipital cortex is composed of multiple representations of the visual world. How do these neuroimaging and ERP findings in humans map onto this complexity of visual areas in the brain? Although PET has proved a powerful tool in studies of cognition, for most purposes, as we have already seen, fMRI provides a higher-resolution view of brain activity and is more flexible in permitting event-related imaging.

In an fMRI study of spatial attention, Roger Tootell and Anders Dale at Massachusetts General Hospital (Tootell et al., 1998) addressed questions about the details of the organization of attentional modulations in the visual cortex. In a simple spatial attention task, subjects were required to selectively attend to stimuli located in one visual field quadrant while ignoring those in the other quadrants; different quadrants were attended to in different conditions while the subjects' brains were scanned with fMRI methods. The investigators performed careful retinotopic mapping of the subjects to reveal the borders of the early visual areas from V1 (primary visual cortex) through V4 and beyond (see Chapter 4 for this method). The attentional activations were then mapped onto the flattened computer maps of the visual cortex, permitting the attention effects to be related directly to the multiple visual areas of human visual cortex.

These researchers found that spatial attention was represented by robust modulations of activity in multiple extrastriate visual areas, as well as a smaller modulation of striate cortex (Figure 12.23). This work

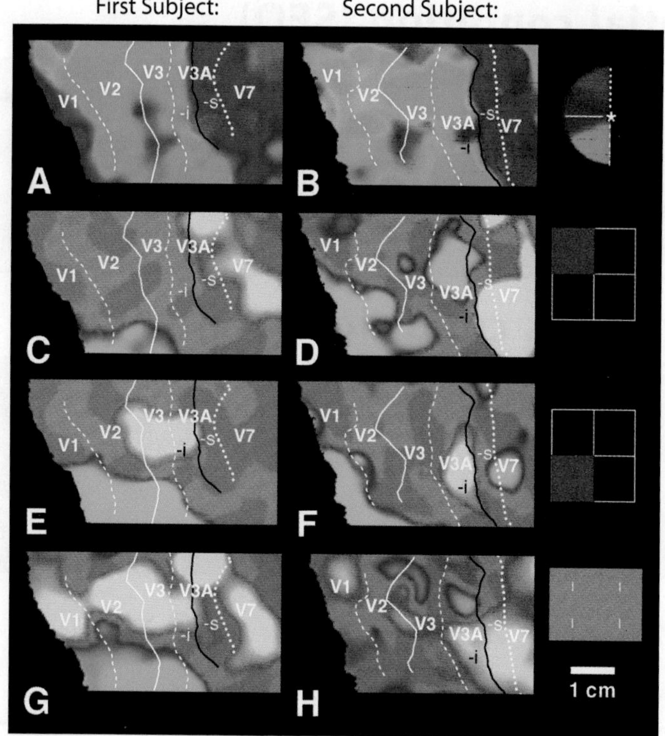

Figure 12.23 Spatial attention effects in multiple visual cortical areas as demonstrated by functional MRI. Activations with spatial attention to left-field stimuli are shown in the flattened right visual cortices of two subjects (one in the left column and the other on the right). The white lines (dotted and solid) indicate the borders of the visual areas as defined by representations of the horizontal and vertical meridians; each area is labeled from V1 (striate cortex) through V7, a retinotopic area adjacent to V3A. The solid black line is the representation of the horizontal meridian in V3A. Panels **A** and **B** show the retinotopic mappings of the left visual field for each subject, corresponding to the polar angles shown at right (which represents the left visual field). Panels **C** and **D** show the attention-related modulations (attended versus unattended) of sensory responses to a target in the upper left quadrant (the quadrant to which attention was directed is shown at right in red). Panels **E** and **F** show the same for stimuli in the lower left quadrant. In **C** through **F**, the yellow to red colors indicate areas where activity was greater when the stimulus was attended to than when ignored; the bluish colors represent the opposite, where the activity was greater when the stimulus was ignored than when attended. The attention effects in **C** through **F** can be compared to the pure sensory responses to the target bars when passively viewed (**G** and **H**.) Note the retinotopic pattern of the attention effects in **C** through **F**: The attention effects to targets in the lower left quadrant produced activity in several lower field representations, which included the appropriate half of V3A (inferior V3A labeled "-i") in both subjects, and V3 and V2 in one subject. In contrast, attention to the upper left quadrant produced activity in the upper field representation of V3A ("-S") and in the adjacent upper field representation of area V7.

provides a high-resolution view of the functional anatomy of multiple areas of extrastriate and striate cortex during sustained spatial attention in human visual cortex.

We now understand that spatial attention influences the processing of visual inputs: Attended stimuli produce greater neural responses than do ignored stimuli, and this difference is observed in multiple visual cortical areas. Two questions about these effects come to mind: First, are such effects limited to visual cortical processing, or might they begin earlier in the subcortical relays? We raised this question earlier in the chapter when we described the work of Hernández-Peón and colleagues in the cat. The second question is this: At the level of neural processing, what does attention do for the brain to permit the attended signal to exert a greater control on perception and awareness? We will address the latter question first, and then come back to the question of subcortical effects of spatial attention.

John Duncan and Robert Desimone proposed a biased competition model for selective attention. In this model, the idea is that different stimuli in a visual scene may fall within the receptive field of a visual neuron, creating a situation in which the two stimuli are *competing* to control the neuron's firing. The biased competition model of attention suggests that attention can help resolve the competition in favor of the attended stimulus.

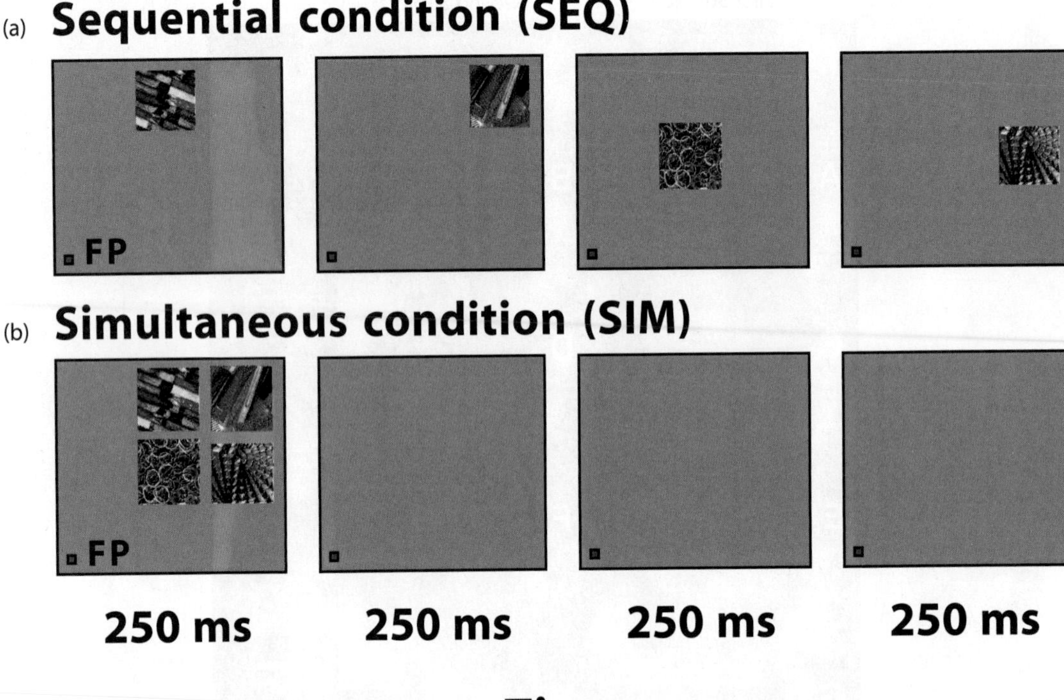

Figure 12.24 Design of the task for attention to competing stimuli to test the biased competition model. Competing stimuli were presented either sequentially **(a)** or simultaneously **(b)**. During the attention condition, covert attention was directed to the stimulus closest to the point of fixation, and the others were merely distracters.

In studies using fMRI, Sabine Kastner, Peter De-Weerd, Robert Desimone, and Leslie Ungerleider (1998) investigated this model for spatial attention (Figure 12.24). They showed that, in the absence of focused spatial attention, nearby stimuli, when presented simultaneously, can interfere with one another (simultaneous condition), reducing the neural response evoked by each stimulus in comparison to when only one stimulus is presented alone (sequential condition). However, when attention is introduced and directed to one stimulus in the array, then simultaneous presentation of the competing stimulus no longer interferes (Figure 12.25). This reduction in interference can be conceptualized as attention attenuating the influence of the distracter (the nearby ignored stimuli), which in this case would produce interference in neuronal activity if attention did not intervene.

Now let's turn to the question of whether effects of attention might be manifest prior to cortical processing, which in vision means in the lateral geniculate nucleus of the thalamus (LGN). Kastner and her colleagues at Princeton have addressed this question using high-resolution fMRI in humans (reviewed in Kastner et al., 2006). They cued subjects to attend to the left or right half of bilateral arrays of flickering checkerboard stimuli (Figure 12.26a on page 516). These stimuli activated the LGN and multiple visual cortical areas (Figure 12.26b), and these activations were greater in amplitude for the attended arrays (e.g., left array) in the contralateral (e.g., right) LGN and visual cortex (Figure 12.26c).

These studies demonstrate that highly focused spatial attention can modulate activity in the visual system in the subcortical relay nuclei in the thalamus, thereby providing strong evidence for early-selection models of attention. One question that remains to be clarified is the extent to which these early modulations form the basis for all spatial attention effects in the visual system by passing these modulations along passively to higher visual areas, or whether instead spatial attention can act at multiple stages of visual processing (i.e., LGN, V1, extrastriate cortical areas) independently or cooperatively. To learn more about this question, see "How the Brain Works: Shocking Studies of Attention," on p. 520.

NEUROIMAGING OF FEATURE SELECTIVE ATTENTION

In one of the first neuroimaging studies of selective attention, Maurizio Corbetta, Steven Petersen, and their

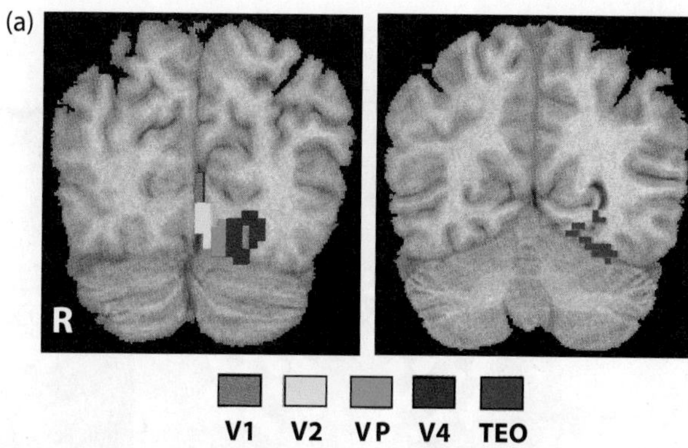

Figure 12.25 Functional-MRI signals in the study investigating the biased competition model of attention. **(a)** Coronal MRI sections in one subject, with the pure sensory responses in multiple visual areas mapped with meridian mapping (similar to that used in Figure 12.23, but without cortical unfolding). **(b)** The percentage of signal changes over time in areas V1 and V4 as a function of whether the stimuli were presented in the sequential (SEQ) or simultaneous (SIM) condition, and as a function of whether they were unattended **(left)** or whether attention was directed to the target stimulus (**right**, shaded blue). In V4 especially, the amplitudes during the SEQ and SIM conditions were more similar when attention was directed to the target stimulus (shaded blue areas at right) than when it was not (unshaded areas). Adapted from Kastner et al., 1998.

colleagues at Washington University (Corbetta et al., 1991) used PET to identify changes that occur in extrastriate cortex when people selectively attend to stimulus features such as color, shape, and motion. While blood flow in the brain was monitored by the use of radioactive water as a tracer, volunteers were shown pairs of visual displays that had arrays of stimulus elements. The first display of each trial was a reference stimulus; the second was a test stimulus. The subjects' task was to view the first array and compare it with the second to detect whether a change had occurred on a specified stimulus dimension (color, shape, or motion in different experimental conditions), or, in divided-attention conditions, to detect a change in any of the three stimulus dimensions. This experimental design permitted the investigators to contrast brain activity under conditions in which the subjects selectively attended a particular stimulus dimension (e.g., color) with the condition in which they divided their attention among all stimulus dimensions (color, shape, and motion).

Selective attention to color, shape, or motion activated distinct, largely nonoverlapping regions of extrastriate cortex (Figure 12.27 on page 517). Extrastriate cortical regions specialized for the perceptual processing of color, form, or motion were modulated during visual attention to the individual stimulus features. These findings provide additional support for the idea that selective attention in modality-specific cortical areas alters the perceptual processing of inputs prior to the completion of feature analysis.

Subsequent studies using fMRI have identified specialized areas of human visual cortex for the processing of features such as stimulus motion or color, in line with evidence from recordings in monkey visual cortex. These specialized feature analysis regions have been shown to be selectively modulated by visual attention as suggested by the work of Corbetta and colleagues. Numerous studies in the past few years have addressed this issue of how attention modulates feature processing in the human brain, and we will review a recent study that combines much of the findings in one study and adds the twist of recording MEG and fMRI to provide temporal as well as spatial resolution.

Ariel Schoenfeld, Hans-Jochen Heinze, Steven Hillyard, and their colleagues at the University of Magdeburg, Germany, and the University of California, San

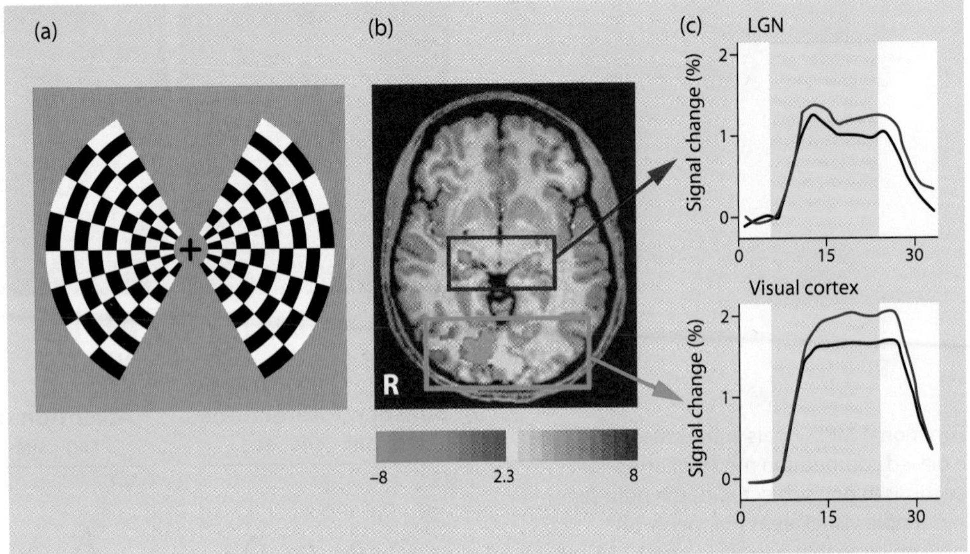

Figure 12.26 Functional-MRI study of spatial attention effects in the LGN. **(a)** Pattern-reversing (7.5-Hz) checkerboard wedge-shaped stimuli presented bilaterally for 18 s (the fixation point is the central plus sign). Prior to stimulus onset, an arrow cue at fixation instructed the subjects which hemifield to attend. The task was to detect randomly occurring luminance changes in the flickering checks along the arc of checks located at 10° eccentricity in the cued hemifield. **(b)** Functional-MRI activations (increased BOLD responses) were observed in the LGN (red box) and in multiple visual cortical areas (green box). **(c)** The activations varied in amplitude (plotted as the percentage of change in the BOLD signal) as a function of whether or not the stimulus in the hemifield contralateral to the brain region measured (i.e., left visual field and right LGN and cortex) was attended (red line) or ignored (black line), which was the condition in which subjects attended the opposite hemifield. The effect was observed both in the LGN **(top)** and in multiple visual cortical areas **(bottom)**.

Diego (Schoenfeld et al., 2007), cued subjects to selectively attend to either changes in color or changes in motion of an upcoming display (Figure 12.28a on page 518). The stimulus sequence randomly presented motion and color changes, permitting the measurement of brain activity in response to changes in either feature as a function of attention to motion or color. Using fMRI to localize brain regions sensitive to selective attention to color or motion, these investigators found, as expected, that attending to the feature of motion resulted to modulations of activity in the visual cortical motion processing area MT/V5 (in the dorsal stream), and that attending to color led to modulations in ventral visual cortex area V4 (in the ventral stream; Figure 12.28b–d). Importantly, though, their related MEG recordings demonstrated that attention-related activity in these areas appeared with a latency of about 100 ms after onset of the motion or color change in the stimulus—much earlier than prior studies had reported.

Such findings exemplify the effects of feature-based selective attention on visual cortical processing, showing that attention acts at relatively early stages of visual cortical processing with relatively short latencies after stimulus onset, in line with early-selection models. Note that, in contrast to the effects of selective spatial attention, the effects of feature attention occur with longer latencies (100 ms versus 70 ms after stimulus onset) and at later stages of the visual hierarchy (extrastriate cortex rather than striate cortex or the subcortical visual relays in the thalamus).

NEUROIMAGING OF ATTENTION TO OBJECTS

We have now described the effects of spatial and feature-based attention in visual cortex. Attention can also act on higher-order stimulus representations—that is, objects. When we search for a friend in a crowd, we don't merely search *where* we think the friend will be, especially if we have no knowledge of this, nor do we merely search for the friend by hair color (unless it is highly salient, like fluorescent pink!). Rather, we look for the conjunction of features that defines the person. For lack of a better word, we can refer to this quality as *object properties*—the collection of elementary stimulus features that, when combined in a particular way, yield an identifiable object or person. Behavioral work has demonstrated evidence for *object-based attention* mechanisms.

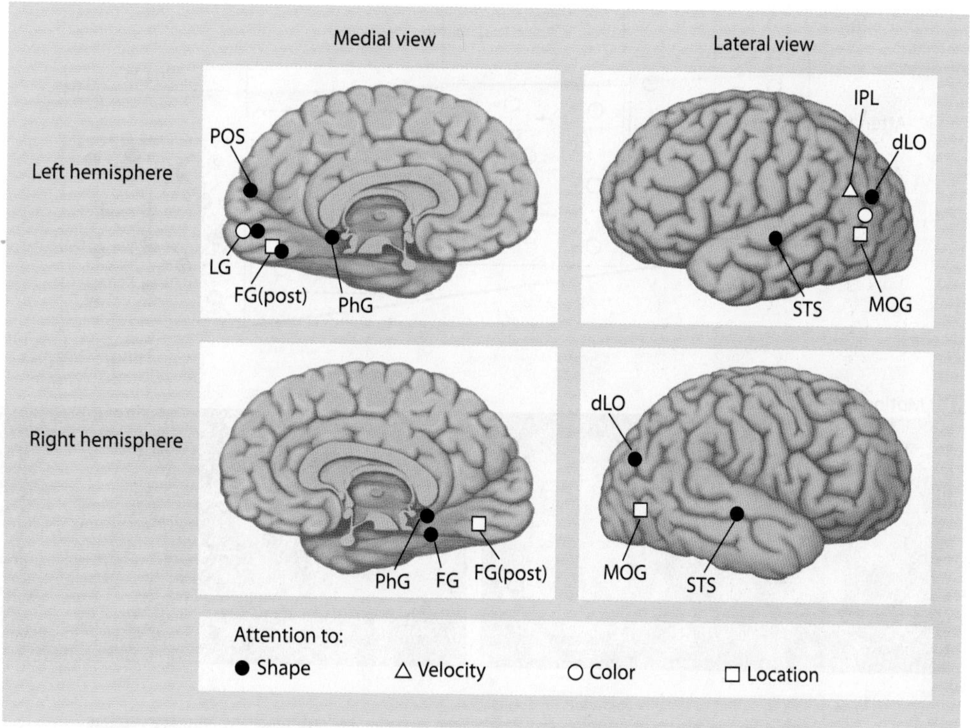

Figure 12.27 Summary of early neuroimaging attention studies using position emission tomography (PET) by Corbetta and colleagues (1991), Heinze and colleagues (1994), and Mangun and colleagues (1997). Regions of extrastriate cortex specialized for the processing of color, shape, or motion (from the work of Corbetta) are selectively modulated during visual attention to these stimulus features (feature selective attention). Selective attention to color activated areas in bilateral extrastriate cortex in the lingual gyrus (LG) and dorsolateral occipital cortex (dLO). Attention to shape led to activations in the lingual gyrus, fusiform gyrus (FG), parahippocampal gyrus (PhG), and superior temporal sulcus (STS). Selective attention to the motion (velocity) of the stimuli especially activated the left inferior parietal lobule (IPL), probably corresponding to motion area MT/V5. The PET study by Heinze and colleagues showed that attention to spatial location (selective spatial attention) produced activations in the posterior fusiform gyrus, and Mangun and colleagues replicated and extended this research to show that the middle occipital gyrus (MOG) was also activated during spatial attention.

In a clever study, John Duncan (1984) contrasted attention to location (spatial attention) with attention to objects (object-based attention). Holding spatial distance constant, he discovered that two perceptual judgments concerning the same object can be made simultaneously without loss of accuracy, whereas the same two judgments about different objects cannot. This processing limitation in attending to two objects implicates an object-based attention system in addition to a space-based system. In line with this view, the behavioral reaction time *costs* (slowing) and *benefits* (speeding) of spatially valid versus invalid cuing are greater *between* two objects compared to those that occur within one object (Egly et al., 1994). This result suggests that the spread of attention is facilitated within the confines of an object or that there is an additional cost to move attention between objects.

This effect of objects on spatial attention is well illustrated both behaviorally and physiologically in an fMRI study by Notger Mueller and Andreas Kleinschmidt (2003) in Germany. They cued subjects on a trial-by-trial basis to expect a target at one location in the visual field (e.g., upper left quadrant), and then presented targets there on most trials (valid trials) or presented them to uncued locations on a minority of trials (invalid trials). So far, this is just the same as the spatial cuing paradigms that we have discussed previously. But following the design of Egly and colleagues (1994), Mueller and Kleinschmidt included objects on the screen such that the uncued target could fall within the same object that was cued (but at another location in the object), or at another location that was not within the bounds of that object.

Their objects were wrenchlike figures, and these figures could be oriented horizontally on the screen or vertically (Figure 12.29a on page 519). For example, when cuing the upper left quadrant location, the upper right quadrant location would be spatially uncued

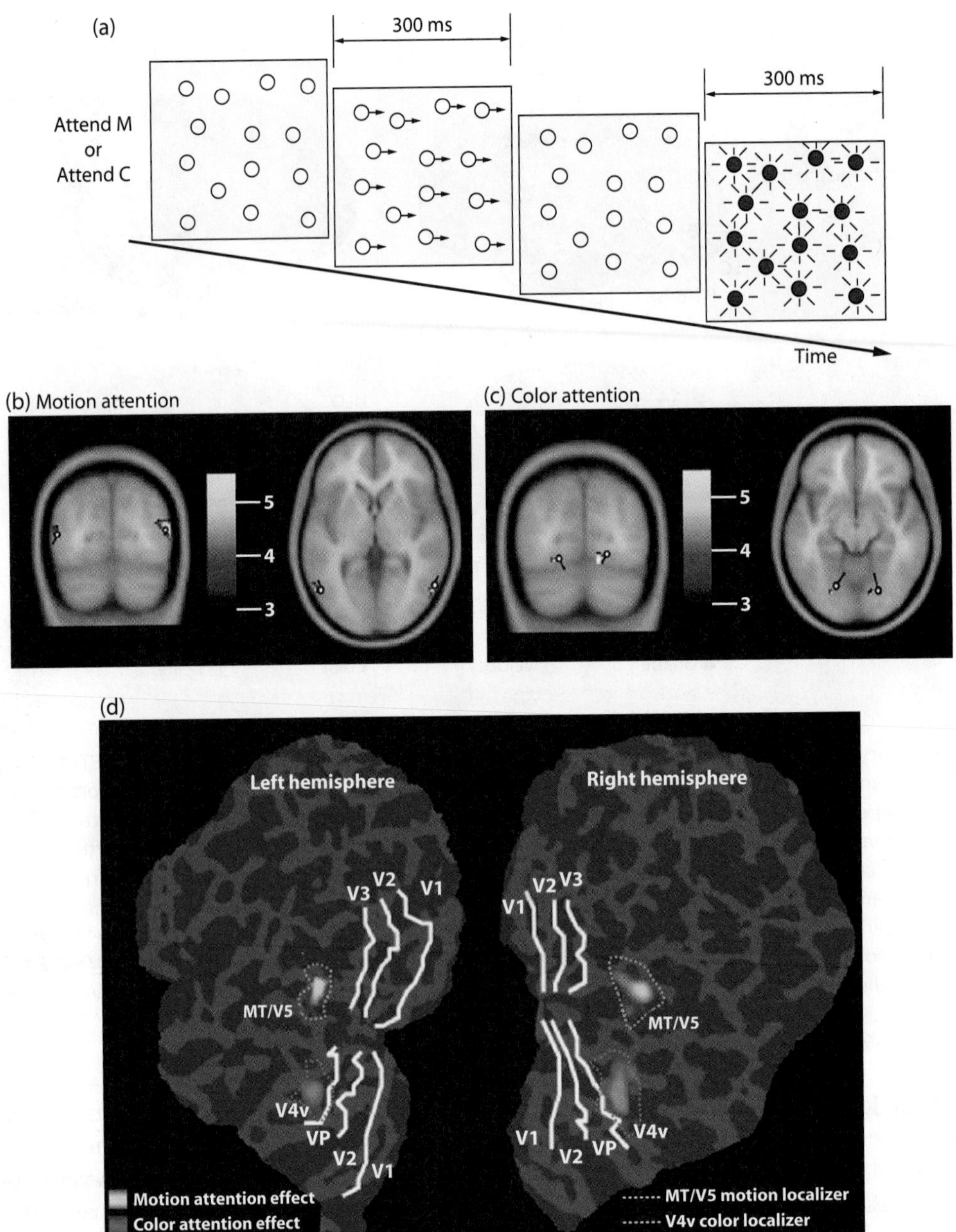

Figure 12.28 Attention modulates activity in feature-specific visual cortex. **(a)** Stimuli and task parameters. Each block of several stimuli began with a letter cue (*M* or *C*) indicating that the subjects should attend to either motion (fast versus slow) or color (red versus orange), respectively, and press a button representing the indicated feature. Dots would appear, and they would either randomly move or change color. In this way, responses to changes in motion (or color) could be contrasted when motion was attended versus when color was attended. **(b)** When motion was attended, activity in lateral occipitotemporal regions (human MT/V5) was modulated. **(c)** When color was attended, ventral area V4 (V4v in the posterior fusiform gyrus) was modulated. This relation was found both for fMRI BOLD responses (shown as the reddish yellow blobs on the MRI), and for MEG measures taken in a separate session (shown as circles with arrows in **(b)** and **(c)**, overlapping regions of significant BOLD signal change). The high temporal resolution afforded by the MEG measures indicated that the latency of the attention effect after the onset of the moving or color arrays was about 100 ms. **(d)** Retinotopic mapping on a single subject verifies the extrastriate region associated with the motion and color attention effects.

(unattended) within the *same* object when the wrenches were oriented horizontally, but would be spatially uncued within a *different* object when the wrenches were vertically oriented. Mueller and Kleinschmidt replicated the behavioral reaction time effects of Egly and colleagues (Figure 12.29b), but they also

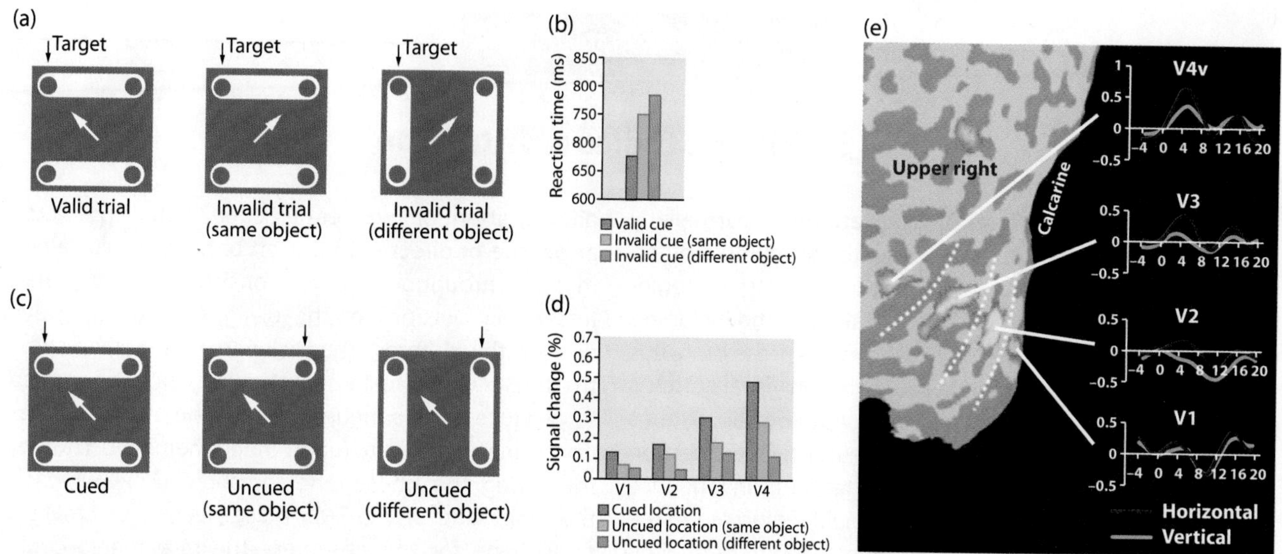

Figure 12.29 Effects of objects on spatial attention. **(a)** Stimulus display used to demonstrate behavioral spatial and object attention effects. Wrenchlike objects were continually presented on the screen and were oriented horizontally **(left and middle)** or vertically **(right)**. On each trial, a centrally located cue (shown here as a white arrow for ease of presentation) indicated the most likely location of subsequent targets that required a fast response whether at the cued location (frequent) or elsewhere (infrequent). **(b)** Reaction times to targets were fastest when the cues validly predicted the target location, were slowest to invalid cue trials when the target appeared on a different object, and were intermediate in speed for invalid trials where the target appeared on the same object. **(c)** Stimulus display for the fMRI experiment where the upper left location was always cued and where the target appeared on most trials. Uncued locations in the upper right quadrant (for example) could be either on the same object as the cued location **(middle)** or on a different object **(right)**. The black arrows above each panel indicate the visual field locations that corresponded to regions of interest in the visual cortex from which hemodynamic responses were extracted. **(d)** Hemodynamic responses (percentage signal change) are shown as bar graphs from regions of interest in visual cortical areas V1 to V4. In each area, the largest response is in the cued location, and smaller responses are obtained from uncued locations (the main effect of spatial attention). Importantly, when the uncued location was on the same object as the cued location, the fMRI activation was larger, demonstrating the effect of object attention. **(e)** Flattened left visual cortex (pole at bottom) from MRI showing retinotopic mapping of V1 to V4, and the hemodynamic responses **(right)** extracted from the activated regions corresponding to the uncued visual field location when that location was in the same (red curve) and different (blue curve) objects as the cued location (which was located in the opposite hemisphere, not shown).

investigated how cuing affects activity in the corresponding brain regions (Figure 12.29c–e). They found that, in visual cortical areas V1 through V4, uncued locations that were located on the same object (the wrench) as the cued location showed increased activity compared to when the uncued location was not on the same object that was cued.

This result demonstrates that the presence of the objects influences the way spatial attention is allocated in space; in essence, attention is drawn along the object, thereby leading to activity for uncued locations on the object. An effect of spatial attention remains because, within the object, the cued location shows greater activity than do uncued locations. Thus, object representations can modulate spatial attention. But can attention to objects operate independently of spatial attention?

Kathleen O'Craven, Paul Downing, and Nancy Kanwisher at the Massachusetts Institute of Technology and Massachusetts General Hospital (1999) provided a fascinating demonstration of the direct action of attention on object representations. They made use of the facts (a) that faces activate a region of the fusiform gyrus, the so-called fusiform face area (FFA; see Chapter 6), that is less active in response to images of other objects, such as houses, and (b) that a region of parahippocampal cortex is more active in response to images of houses than faces (the so-called parahippocampal place area, or PPA).

The researchers then superimposed transparent images of faces and houses so that they occupied the same region of space yet could both be seen at the same point in time (Figure 12.30 on page 522). One of the objects moved back and forth while the other was stationary. The motion of the moving stimulus activated cortical motion area MT/V5. Which stimulus moved and which was stationary varied in different blocks. In these different blocks, subjects were told to attend selectively to

HOW THE BRAIN WORKS

Shocking Studies of Attention

It is clear that effects of visual attention, particularly spatial attention, can be detected at multiple different stages of visual information processing, beginning as early as the LGN of the thalamus, and including early and later stages of visual cortical processing. It is also clear that information processing in visual cortex is influenced by top-down attentional control systems that bias the activity of visual neurons. One question that remains unclear is whether attention can influence visual information processing at multiple loci along the ascending visual pathways, or if instead attentional filtering takes place by influencing a single early stage of processing, such as the subcortical relays, passively transmitting the effects of attention to later stages of visual analysis.

Functional-imaging studies demonstrate that, when subjects prepare for a target in one location in the visual field while ignoring other locations, the background activity in multiple loci in the ascending visual pathways increases, suggesting that attention does act simultaneously at multiple stages. But this evidence is somewhat indirect. In a recent new study, however, Bestmann and colleagues (2007) used transcranial magnetic stimulation (TMS; see Figure 4.26 in Chapter 4) to demonstrate that spatial attention can act directly on sites in the cortex. Using TMS in human volunteers, they were able to demonstrate that visual percepts, called *phosphenes*, elicited by the direct stimulation of visual cortex were influenced by attention.

This clever study was conducted as follows. Attention was covertly (without displacement of gaze) directed toward a particular location (left or right) during a task involving real visual stimuli. In two different conditions, attention was either cued with a predicted arrow cue, or directed to the left or right in a sustained manner throughout a block consisting of many trials (essentially versions of the designs discussed previously in this chapter). The trick here was that, on some trials, instead of a real visual stimulus, TMS was applied to produce a phosphene, either at the attended location or in the opposite (unattended) hemifield. Thus, by measuring the phosphene threshold (PT)—which is the amplitude of the TMS pulse needed to create a phosphene for the observer—the researchers could determine whether perception of the TMS-induced phosphenes was influenced by spatial attention.

Bestmann and colleagues found that PTs were lowered for trials in which the TMS pulse was delivered to the visual cortex that corresponded to the attended (contralateral) visual hemifield: Spatial attention modulated the TMS-induced phosphenes! Because these "signals" in visual cortex did not pass through the thalamic relays to reach visual cortex, this finding provides evidence that attention can act directly within the sensory cortex and does not rely on the modulation of visual inputs in the LGN. That is, the direct activation of visual cortex using transcranial magnetic stimulation in humans provides converging evidence that attentional control is not limited to gating subcortical inputs to cortex. This does not, of course, imply that attention does not influence processing in the LGN (in this chapter we have reviewed evidence from fMRI that this does occur), but rather the TMS study demonstrates that attention can act directly on cortical processing, independently of its actions in subcortical structures.

the face, to the house, or to the motion. The activity in the FFA, the PPA, or MT/V5 provided relatively pure measures of the responses to each of these three stimulus dimensions. The researchers found that, when subjects attended to faces, activity in the FFA increased but activity in the PPA did not, and vice versa when the subjects attended to houses. Interestingly, when they selectively attended to the motion, activity in the MT/MST increased, as did activity in the region (FFA or PPA) that corresponded to the object that was moving (face or house, respectively).

The results from the house/face study demonstrate how attention acts on object representations: Attention facilitates processing of all the features of the attended object. For example, face processing was facilitated when the attended moving stimulus was a face, even though the task did not require identification or attention to the face itself. Importantly, these findings show that, when spatial attention is not involved, object representations can be the level of perceptual analysis affected by top-down attentional control.

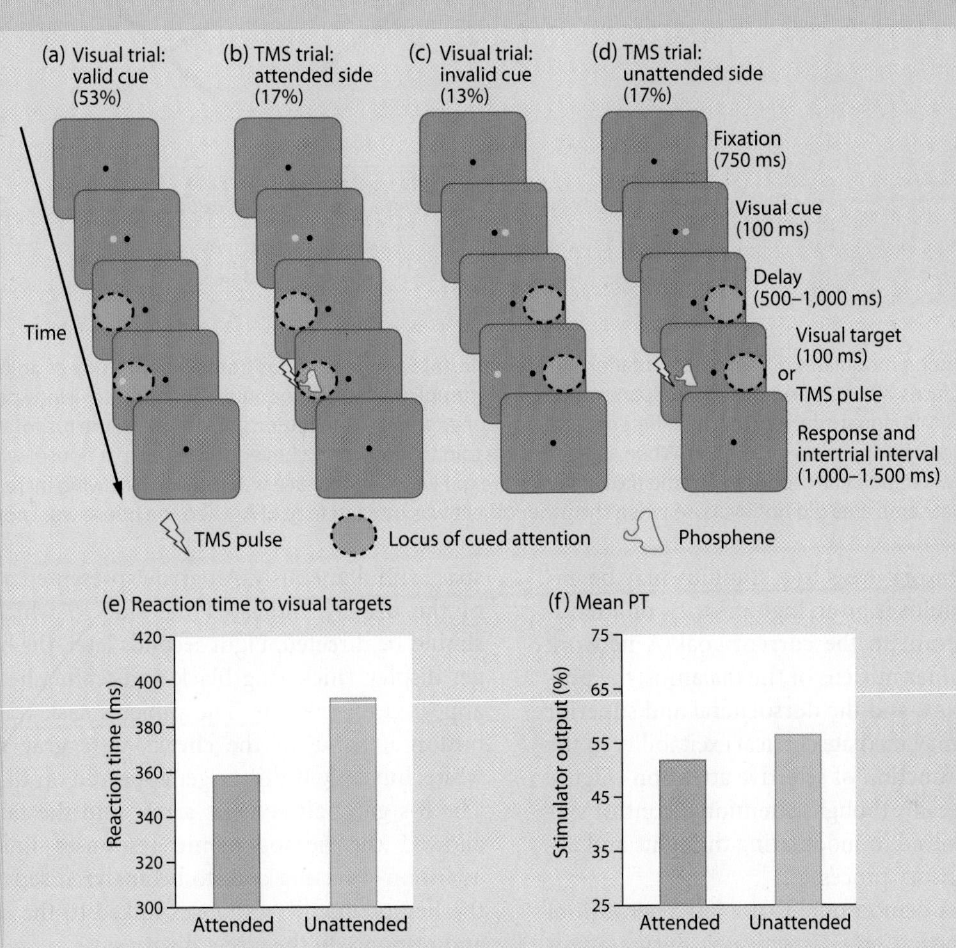

Attentional modulations of phosphenes induced by transcranial magnetic stimulation (TMS) in humans. **(a)–(d)** Stimuli and task sequence in the spatial cuing design. Subjects were shown an arrow cuing them to the left or right visual field. After a delay of 500 to 1,000 ms, they were shown either a target **(a)** or TMS-induced phosphenes **(b)** at the attended location, or a target **(c)** or TMS-induced phosphenes **(d)** at the unattended location. **(e)** Cuing produced the well-known reaction time benefits on target processing: Targets at the attended location were detected faster. **(f)** Similarly, the phosphene threshold (PT) was lower for TMS-induced phosphenes at the attended location.

NEUROIMAGING OF ATTENTIONAL CONTROL NETWORKS

In addition to determining the mechanisms of attention within sensory-specific cortical areas, PET and fMRI studies of selective attention have shed light on the network of cortical and subcortical brain regions that control attention. The idea is simple: Some brain regions are involved in focusing attention in line with momentary behavioral goals, and the result of this neural activity is the modulation of sensory-specific cortex that we described in the preceding sections. Some models have referred to attentional control networks as the *source of attention*, and the sensory (and motor) systems that are affected as the *site of attention.*

This dichotomy is useful because it helps to distinguish the role that attention plays in modulating sensory processing in the sensory systems from neural mechanisms that lead to this effect. Presumably, neuronal projections from executive attentional control systems contact neurons in sensory-specific cortical areas in order to alter their excitability. As a result, the

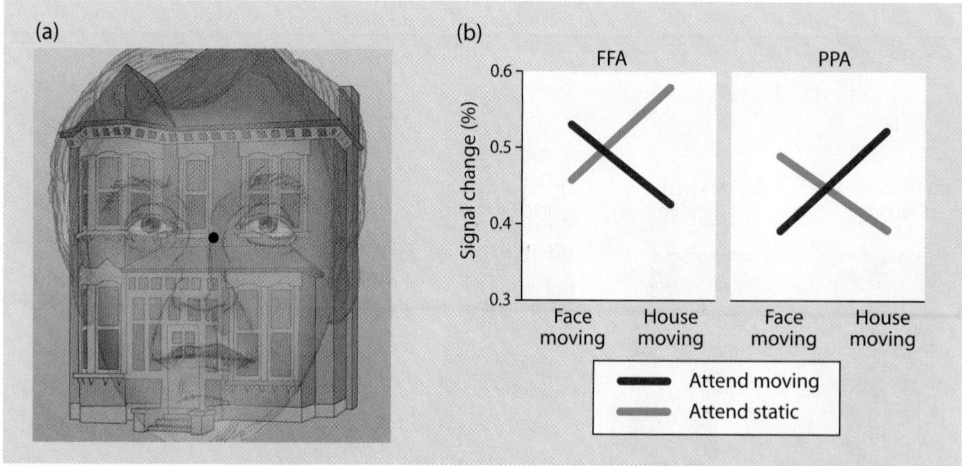

Figure 12.30 Attention modulates object representations in the brain. **(a)** Sample stimulus from an fMRI study of object-based attention. Houses and faces were superimposed transparently to create stimuli that subjects could not attend to using spatial mechanisms. **(b)** Functional-MRI signal intensity for the different conditions of attention from regions of interest in the fusiform face area (FFA) and the parahippocampal place area (PPA). When subjects were told to attend whichever object (face or house) was moving, the activity in the brain region corresponding to the moving object (e.g., FFA when the face was moving) showing increased activity, but the activity in that same area did not increase when the other object was moving (e.g., FFA when the house was moving).

response in the sensory areas to a stimulus may be enhanced, if the stimulus is given high priority, or attenuated, if it is irrelevant to the current goal. A network including the pulvinar nucleus of the thalamus, the posterior parietal cortex, and the dorsolateral and superior prefrontal cortex may mediate cortical excitability in the visual cortex as a function of selective attention (Figure 12.31). More generally, though, attentional control systems could be involved in modulating thoughts and actions, as well as sensory processes.

Imaging studies demonstrate that a large network of cortical and subcortical areas is activated during attentional orienting and selection. How can we measure the activity of the different brain regions during the execution of these tasks, and determine what brain systems and mechanisms are related to which aspects of attentional control and selection? One method that has been exploited for this purpose is event-related fMRI (see Chapter 4). Event-related fMRI has been used to understand attentional control with a specificity not previously available in neuroimaging studies of attention. In related studies, Joseph Hopfinger and colleagues (2000) and Maurizio Corbetta and his coworkers (2000) used event-related fMRI to investigate attentional control mechanisms.

Both teams used a covert spatial cuing paradigm similar to that in Figure 12.8 to investigate the brain's attentional control system. Here we will review the work of the Hopfinger team because this study offers the opportunity to make several points about attentional mechanisms. These investigators modified the paradigm in Figure 12.8 by presenting stimuli on both sides of space simultaneously. An arrow, presented at the center of the display, indicated the side to which attention should be directed. Eight seconds later, the bilateral target display (flickering black-and-white checkerboards) appeared for 500 ms. The subjects' task was to press a button if some of the checks were gray rather than white, but only if this target appeared on the cued side. The 8-s gap between the arrow and the target display allowed the hemodynamic responses linked to the attention-directing cues to be analyzed separately from the hemodynamic responses linked to the detection of and response to the target displays.

Thus, a top-down attentional control network engaged by the appearance of the cue could be identified.

Figure 12.31 Model of executive control systems and the way in which visual cortex processing is affected by the top-down control of a network of brain areas.

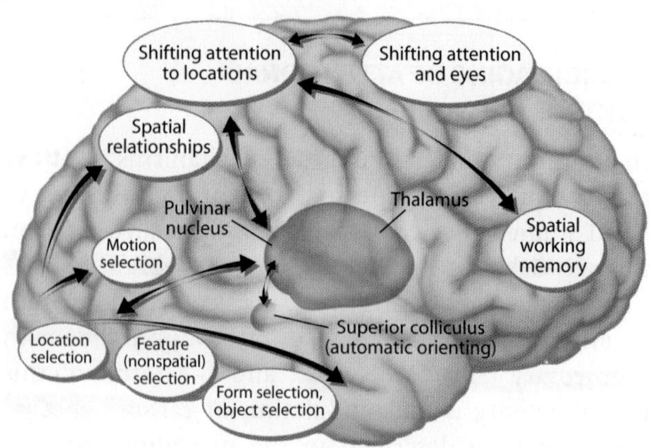

It included the superior frontal cortex, inferior parietal cortex, superior temporal cortex, and portions of the posterior cingulate cortex and insula (Figure 12.32). None of the regions are involved in sensory processing of the visual features of the cue, which were instead reflected by predicted activity in the visual cortex. Rather, this distributed network of frontal, parietal, and temporal brain regions reflects the activity of the brain to control attention, or, in other words, the *sources* of attention signals. This interpretation could be demonstrated because, if the cues were presented but subjects did not have to attend them or act on them (but instead merely passively viewed them), these brain regions were not activated, although the visual cortex was still engaged to process the visual features of the cues.

The effects of attentional selection in visual cortex could be observed by examination of the responses to the target stimuli as a function of the spatial attention. The results are shown in Figure 12.33 in coronal sections through the visual cortex of a single subject in the Hopfinger study. Attention to one visual hemifield activated the visual cortex in the contralateral hemisphere (Figure 12.33a; compare to Figure 12.22), and this activity occurred in multiple extrastriate cortical areas (Figure 12.33b; compare to Figure 12.23). These patterns of modulation of visual cortex are the *sites* of attentional selection, in this case in visual cortex.

Interestingly, this study also demonstrated something about how top-down attention affects visual cortex prior to the presentation of task-relevant targets.

Figure 12.32 Attentional control network activated in response to an attention-directing spatial cue and identified using event-related fMRI in a cuing paradigm. **(a)** Activations time-locked to the cue, indicating attentional control networks. **(b)** Activations time-locked to the targets, indicating target processing and motor responses. The activated areas are shown in different colors to reflect the statistical contrasts that revealed the activations: bluish for brain regions that were more activated to cues than targets, and reddish yellow to indicate regions that were more active to targets than to cues. The activity is collapsed from the data gathered from six normal subjects and is presented on a canonical brain rendered in three dimensions derived from structural MRI scans. The **top row** shows the lateral view of the left hemisphere; the **bottom row** shows its medial surface. The activity was the same for the right hemisphere, which is not shown. The attentional control network included the dorsolateral prefrontal cortex (DLF), inferior parietal lobe (IPL), superior temporal sulcus (STS), medial frontal cortex (MF), and posterior cingulate gyrus (PC). Target processing activated the visual cortex (VC), superior parietal lobe (SPL), anterior cingulate cortex (AC), supplementary motor area (SMA), ventrolateral frontal lobe (VLF), and precentral and postcentral gyri (Pre/Post CS).

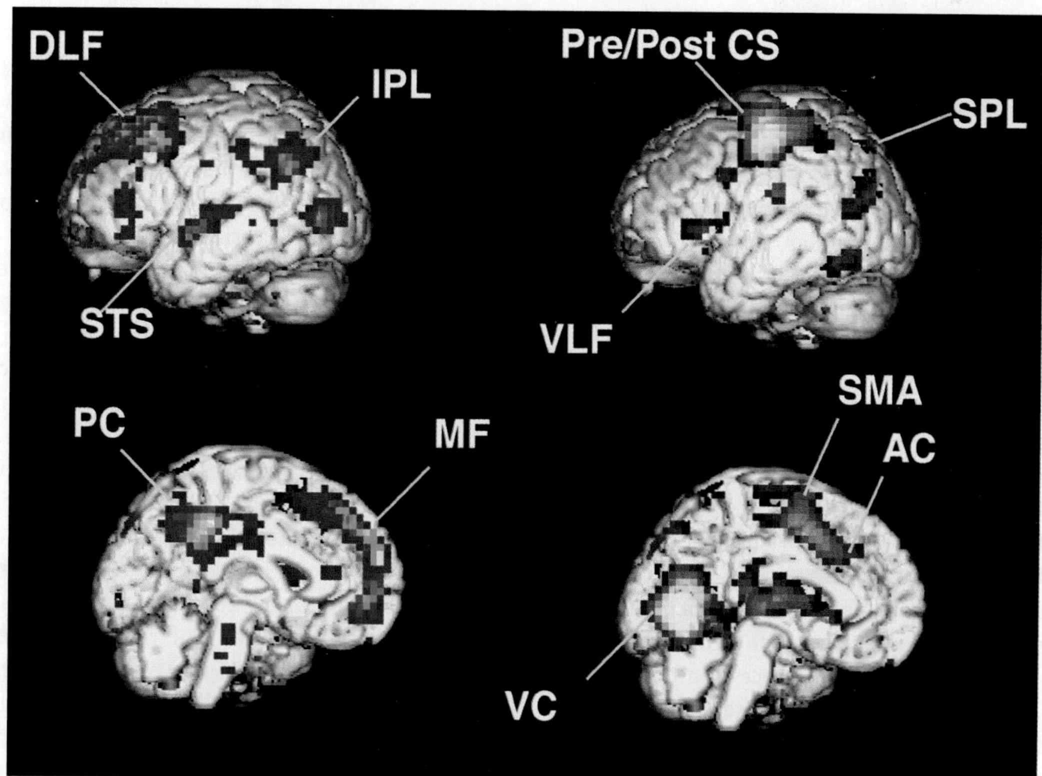

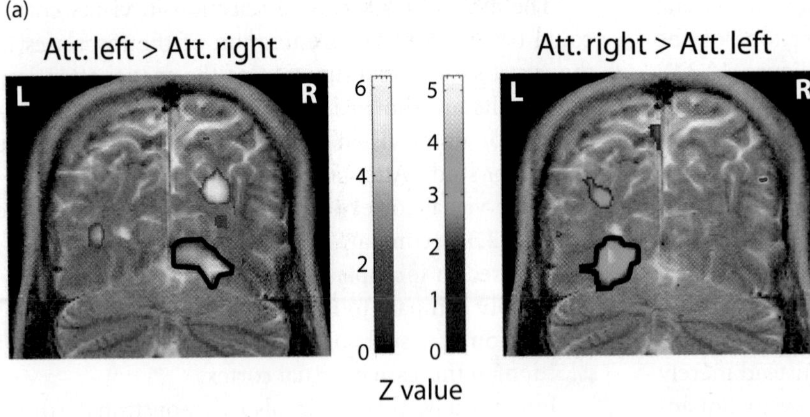

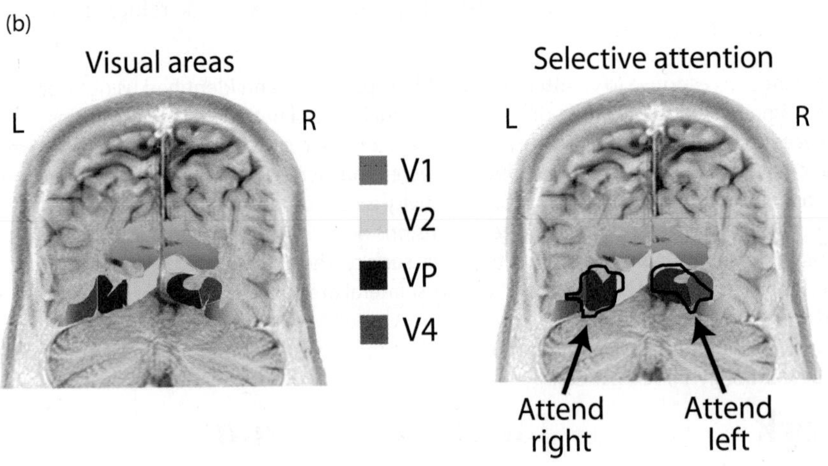

Figure 12.33 Effects of spatial attention in the visual cortex as demonstrated by event-related fMRI. **(a)** Areas of activation in a single subject were overlaid onto a coronal section through the visual cortex (left hemisphere on the left) obtained by structural MRI. The statistical contrasts reveal where attention to the left hemifield produced more activity than attention to the right (reddish to yellow colors, **left**) and the reverse, where attention to the right elicited more activity than did attention to the left (bluish colors, **right**). As demonstrated in prior studies, the effects of spatial attention were activations in the visual cortex contralateral to the attended hemifield. **(b)** Meridian mapping allowed the borders of early visual areas to be defined **(left)** and the effects of attending the left and right fields to be overlaid **(right)**.

After the cue was presented but before the target displays appeared, activations were observed in cortical regions that would later process the incoming target (Figure 12.34). This sort of attentional priming of sensory cortex may form the basis for later selective processing of target inputs, similar to what has been observed in neurophysiological studies in monkeys (Luck & Desimone, 1997) and in fMRI studies by Kastner and Ungerleider (2000).

When a monkey or human is instructed to attend to a particular region of space, activity in the neurons with receptive fields encompassing that region of space increases, even before the appearance of a stimulus. Computationally, such changes are described as an increase in the "gain" of sensory processes (Chawla et al., 1999), or an increase in the sensitivity of the neurons. One way we might achieve such an increase is by increasing the synchronization between neighboring neurons, thereby permitting subsequent stimulus processing to be more efficient if the primed stimulus is presented. One idea, then, is that top-down attentional control may lead to selective changes in sensory processing by changing the background firing rates of neurons, thereby improving their sensitivity.

In addition to the frontoparietal attention network for voluntary spatial attention, other networks have been identified that play a role in attentional processing. In the work of Maurizio Corbetta and colleagues (2002), for example, when a person is selectively attending a region of space, if a relevant stimulus appears somewhere else, a more ventral set of brain areas has been described. In cuing studies that included valid trials (cues predict subsequent target location) and invalid trials (cues do not predict target location), the response to invalid targets (unexpected location) activates a region of the brain at the juncture of the posterior temporal lobe and the inferior parietal lobe. This region has been referred to as the temporoparietal junction (TPJ) (Figure 12.35 on page 526).

Together with regions of the ventrolateral frontal lobe (the inferior and middle frontal gyri), the TPJ has been implicated in the ability to provide an alerting signal that breaks the current attention control set established by the frontoparietal attentional control network.

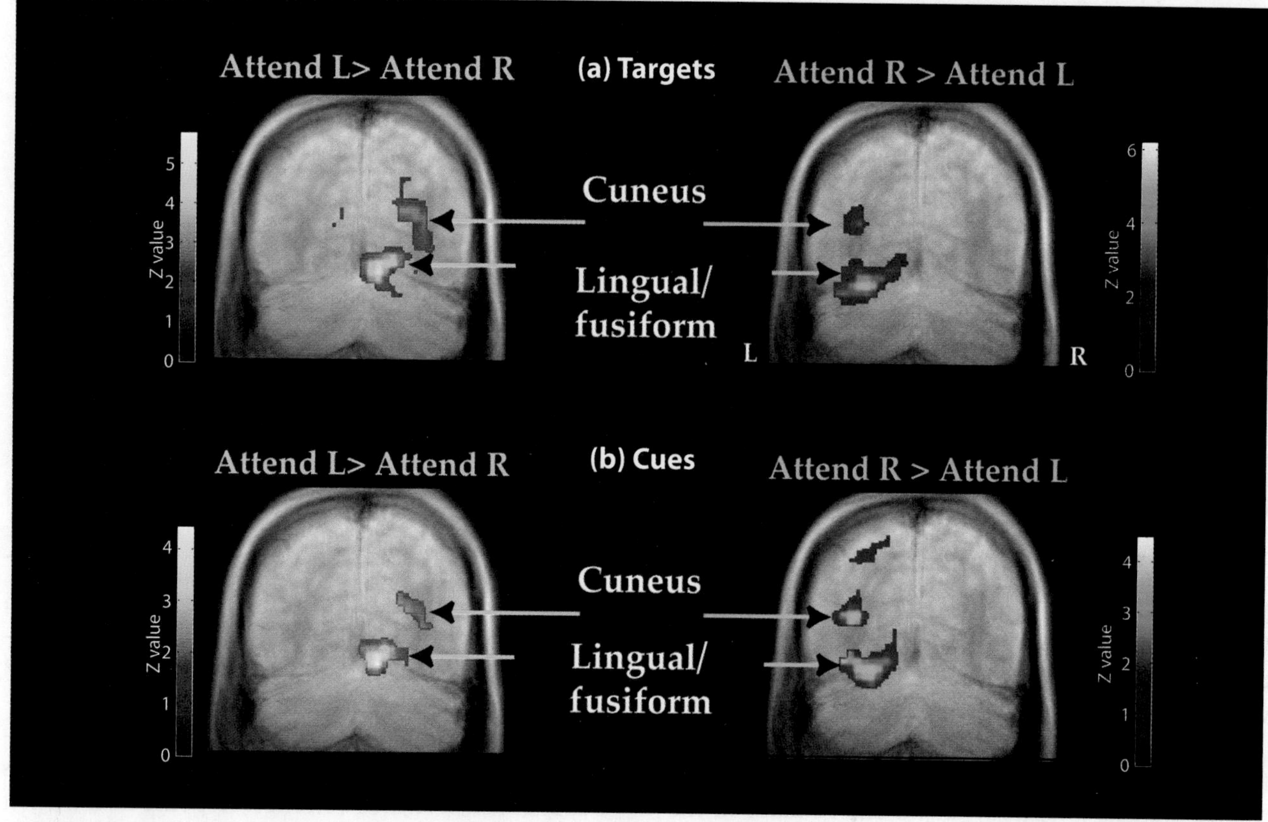

Figure 12.34 Priming of visual cortex by spatial attention. **(a)** The same effects to targets as in Figure 12.33a, but collapsed over a group of six subjects. **(b)** When these same regions of visual cortex are investigated before the targets actually appear but after the cue is presented, a preparatory priming of these areas can be observed as increased activity, and these regions of increased activity precisely overlap with the regions that will later receive the target stimuli shown in **(a)**.

So, in effect, these two systems work together (Figure 12.36a on the next page) to enable attention to be directed to relevant locations and potential targets (frontoparietal system), and to interrupt this attentional state when a novel target appears elsewhere (TPJ and ventrolateral frontal cortex) so that subjects can reorient the focus of attention. As we will discuss further when we consider neurological studies of attention following brain lesions, damage to the more ventral of these systems is most closely associated with the attentional disorder known as *neglect syndrome* (Figure 12.36b).

SUMMARY OF NEUROIMAGING OF BRAIN ATTENTION SYSTEMS

Neuroimaging of brain attention systems has helped us localize the stages of sensory processing influenced by selective attention and provided evidence about the brain networks that control the focus of attention. The results from neuroimaging studies have done much more than replicate work using other methods, such as ERP studies, or the studies in human patients and animals that we will discuss in the next section; they have helped generate new ideas about brain attention systems that are, in many cases, highly complementary but, in other cases, novel, generating new hypotheses to be tested in future research. As is always the case, the more perspectives that can be brought to bear on a problem, the more we learn.

Animal Studies of Attentional Mechanisms

What are the underlying cellular events that support selective attention, and what can we learn from animal studies to confirm, amplify, or perhaps contradict what we have found in humans? Given the event-related-potential studies demonstrating that visual cortical responses are affected by selective attention, and the neuroimaging work showing that activity in the visual cortex is modulated by attention, we can ask how such effects are implemented at the level of single neurons. Indeed, decades of research on the neurophysiology of attention have revealed important insights into the way the mammalian brain selects

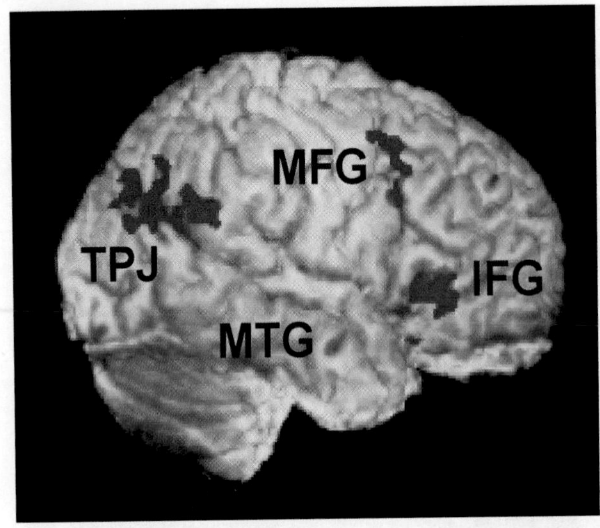

Figure 12.35 Brain regions involved in detection of novelty and attentional reorienting. This MRI reconstruction of the right hemisphere shows regions of temporoparietal junction (TPJ), middle temporal gyrus (MTg), middle frontal gyrus (MFg), and inferior frontal gyrus (IFg) that were activated when subjects received an invalid trial in which a cue incorrectly predicted the target location. The contrast and neural activations are time-locked to the onset of the target stimulus in the unexpected location. These activations are more ventral than those observed to the preceding cue that reflect attentional control. Compare to Figures 12.32 and 12.36.

information on the basis of its behavioral relevance. We will begin with work investigating how visual selective attention affects the firing rates of neurons in the visual cortex of monkeys.

In the 1980s, Jeff Moran and Robert Desimone (1985) of the National Institute of Mental Health trained animals to covertly attend one stimulus in the visual field while ignoring another stimulus. Correct performance with respect to the relevant stimulus led to a reward for the animal. They recorded the responses of single neurons in extrastriate visual area V4 (ventral stream area) when the stimulus that elicited responses from the neuron (e.g., vertical blue bar) was in the receptive field of the neuron and attended, as compared to when (on another trial) the animal attended another stimulus that was located a short distance away and that did not excite the neuron to fire (because the neuron was insensitive to the features of the stimulus—for example, a horizontal white bar). Similar to what ERP studies had demonstrated a decade before with recordings from the human scalp, spatial selective attention affected the firing rates of V4 neurons. When a stimulus was attended, it elicited a stronger response than when it was ignored (Figure 12.37). This was an effect of spatial selective attention because in each case the stimulus display was the same, but merely the location of attention was shifted.

Several studies have now replicated the attention effects observed by Moran and Desimone in V4 and extended this finding to other visual areas, including later stages of the ventral pathway in the inferotemporal region. In addition, work in dorsal-stream visual

Figure 12.36 Cortical regions involved in attentional control. **(a)** MRI activations summarized for attentional control (blue) and novelty and attentional reorienting (orange). FEF = frontal eye field; IPs/SPL = intraparietal sulcus/superior parietal lobule; IPL/STG = inferior parietal lobule/superior temporal gyrus; IFg/MFg = (inferior frontal gyrus/middle frontal gyrus); TPJ = temporoparietal junction; VFC = ventral frontal cortex. **(b)** Approximate regions of human cortex that, when damaged, lead to the neglect syndrome.

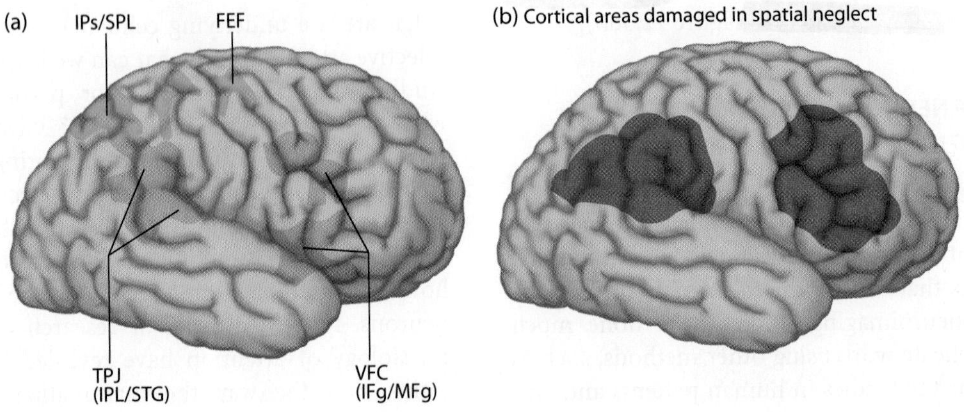

HOW THE BRAIN WORKS

Cell-to-Cell Firing in the Visual System

If attentional selectivity leads to changes in the firing rates of neurons in extrastriate cortical maps, what happens at the neuronal level? We do not really know. Neurons can be modulated by numerous hypothetical mechanisms, but at present it remains unknown which mechanism might produce the effects observed in monkeys. Robert Desimone and his colleagues (1990) at the National Institute of Mental Health described two possible ways that attention might affect neuronal firing rates in a visual area like V4.

One is the input-gating model, in which the receptive fields of hypothesized intermediate neurons correspond to the attended or ignored regions of the visual field. The primary purpose of these neurons is to provide an inhibitory signal to V4 neurons for any regions of the V4 cell's receptive field to which attention is not currently directed. Although in this case it is the V4 neurons that show attention-related modulations of firing, the site of action of the attention effect is on the inputs to V4, not the V4 neurons themselves. The main alternative is a neuron-gating model; the effect here is hypothesized to be on the actual V4 neurons showing enhancement and suppression with attention.

At present, too little is known about cellular interactions that produce attention effects in extrastriate neurons, such as those in V4, to choose between the competing models. Nor can we be certain what the source of the attention-related command may be. In principle, it is possible to obtain the information necessary to precisely specify the neuronal mechanisms underlying selective attention, but it is technically very challenging. There is little doubt, however, that, in the not-too-distant future, these mechanisms will be revealed.

Two models for how attentional gating of extrastriate neurons is represented at the neuronal level. **(a)** In the input-gating model, intermediate neurons provide an inhibitory signal to regions that are outside of the location to be attended. **(b)** In the neuron-gating model, the V4 neurons of interest show both direct enhancement and suppression with attention, with mutual inhibition present between cells coding different stimulus features in the same general region of space.

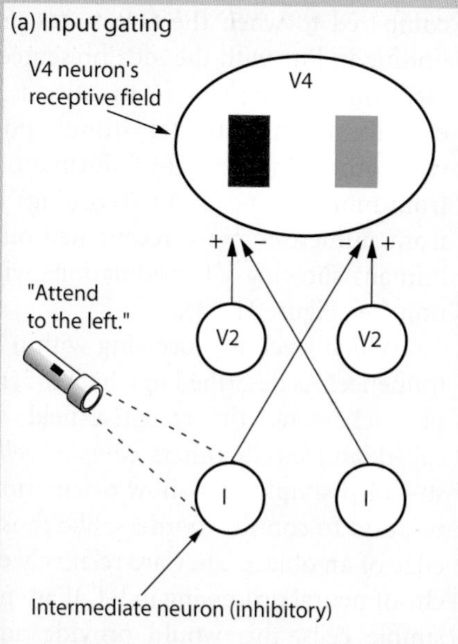

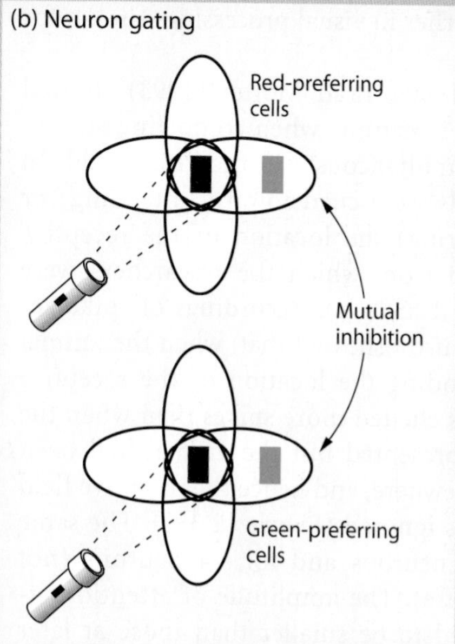

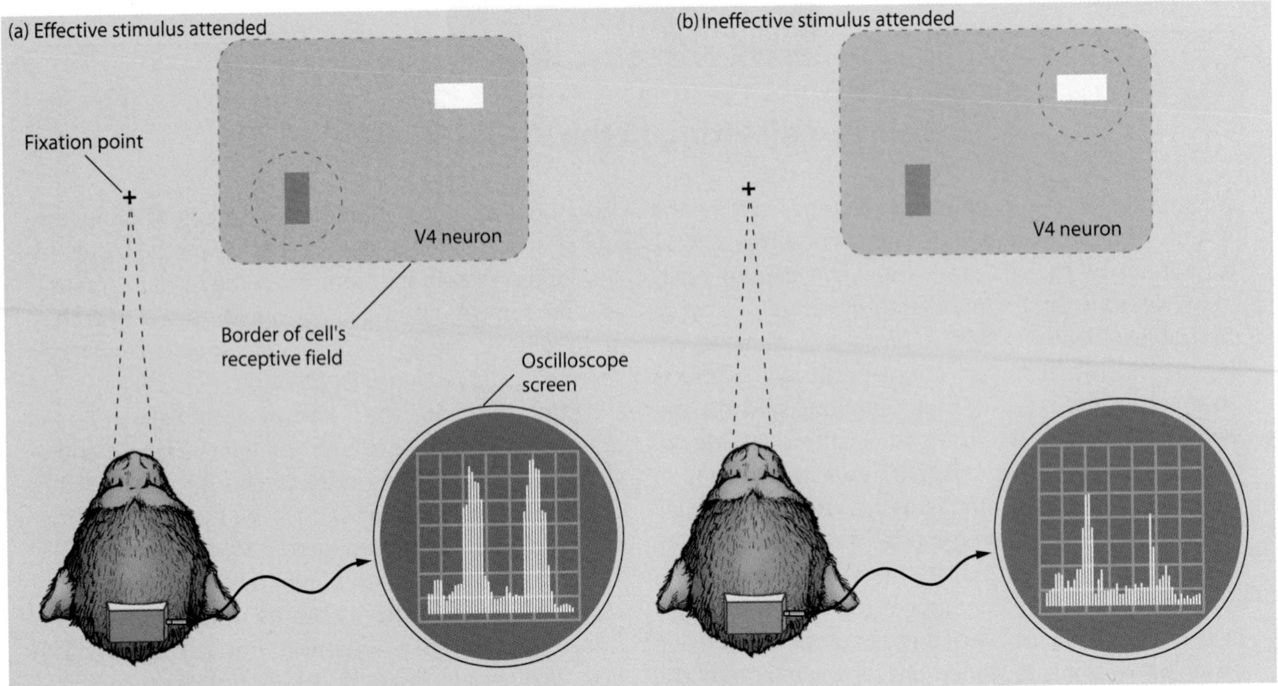

Figure 12.37 Desimone and associates studied the effect of selective attention on the responses of a neuron in area V4 of macaque monkeys. The areas circled by dashed lines indicate the attended locations for each trial. Bars in blue are effective sensory stimuli, and bars without color are ineffective sensory stimuli for this neuron. **(a)** When the animal attended to effective sensory stimuli, the V4 neuron gave a good response. **(b)** When the animal attended to the ineffective sensory stimuli, a poor response was generated. Because both stimuli were presented simultaneously, this effect can be attributed only to the change in the focus of attention from one stimulus to the other; the animal was precued where to attend. The neuronal firing rates are shown to the right of each monkey head. The first burst of activity is to the cue, but the second burst in each image is to the target array, and here the reduction can be observed when the animals attend the ineffective stimulus **(b)**.

areas has demonstrated effects of attention in the motion-processing areas MT and MST of the monkey. But what about earlier in visual processing—in V1, for example?

In the early 1990s, Brad Motter (1993) showed modulations of V1 neurons when competing stimuli were presented simultaneously in the visual field. In this study, animals were cued toward (attending) or away from (ignoring) the location of the receptive field of a neuron from which the researchers were recording (Figure 12.38a–d). Recordings of spike activity from the neuron showed that, when the animal was covertly attending the location of the receptive field, the stimulus elicited more spikes than when the same array was presented but the animal had been cued to attend elsewhere, and hence the receptive field of the neuron was ignored (Figure 12.38e). The same was true for V2 neurons and for V4 neurons (not shown in the figure). The amplitude of attention effects in V1 tended to be smaller than those at later stages of the visual hierarchy.

Interestingly, Motter also found that the amplitude of attention effects in all early visual areas was larger when competing stimuli were present in the visual field, compared to when the target was presented alone—a finding in line with the idea presented earlier about biased competition: That is, attention is most relevant and effective when distracter stimuli potentially interfere with processing relevant information. These findings from monkey single-unit recordings fit well with those from numerous more recent neuroimaging studies in humans showing V1 modulations with selective attention (see Figure 12.23).

Which level of processing within V1 does attention influence? As described in Chapter 5, neurons in V1 display characteristic receptive-field properties—some called *simple cells*, others *complex cells*, and so on. The so-called simple cells show orientation preferences and respond to contrast borders, like those found along the edge of an object. They are relatively early in the hierarchy of neural processing in V1. If attention were to affect simple cells, this would provide additional evidence about how early in processing and by what mechanism spatial attention acted within V1.

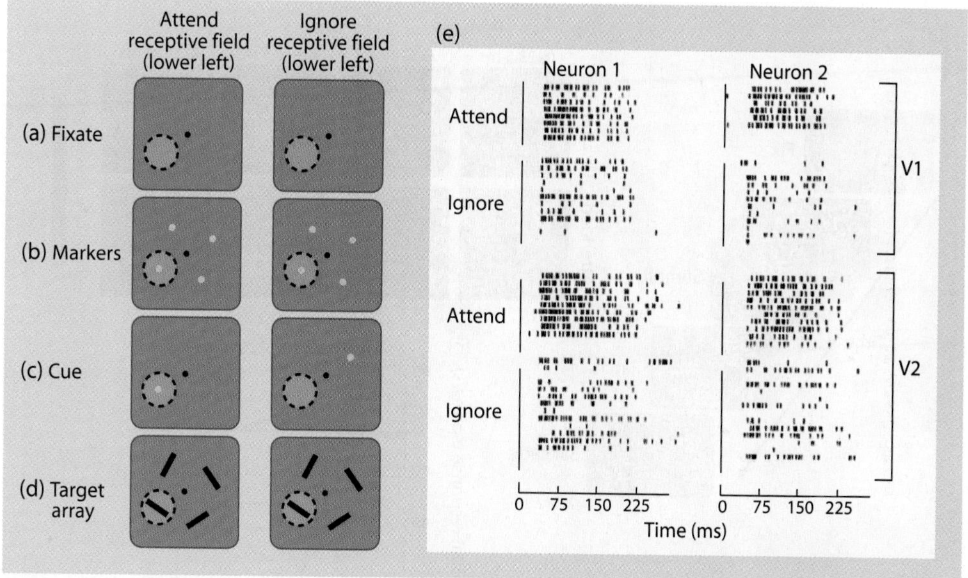

Figure 12.38 Single neuron firing rates in V1 and V2 with spatial attention. The stimuli and task were as follows: **(a)** A fixation point appeared in the middle of the screen. **(b)** Small marker stimuli appeared at all potential target locations. **(c)** The animal was cued to covertly attend to the one location indicated by the marker that remained when the others were extinguished. In the left-hand column the cue indicates that attention should be directed to the lower left location, which was also the location of the receptive field of the neuron (indicated by the dashed circle only). In the right column, the cue directs attention to the upper right location, away from the neuron's receptive field. **(d)** The target array consisting of oriented bars appeared, one bar being in the attended location and the others being at locations that were ignored. **(e)** Raster plots showing the responses (spikes) of two representative neurons from visual areas V1 **(top)** and V2 **(bottom)**. The stimulus array (see part **(d)**) appears at time = 0 ms (upright bars). For each neuron (e.g., Neuron 1) in each visual area (e.g., area V1), the raster shows the firing rates by indicating each spike as a small tick mark. Each row of tick marks indicates an individual trial; for example, for Neuron 1 in V1 eight trials are shown, and for Neuron 2 in V1 six trials are shown. A glance reveals that, for each neuron in both V1 and V2, there are more spikes per unit time (the rasters have more ticks and appear more dense) when the neuron's receptive field was covertly attended than when ignored.

In recent work, Carrie McAdams and Clay Reid (2005) at Harvard Medical School further investigated attention effects in V1 by characterizing the properties of the neurons being recorded, and then assessing whether their activity was influenced by spatial attention. They trained monkeys to fixate a central point and covertly attend a black-and-white flickering noise pattern in order to detect a small, colored pixel that could appear anywhere within the pattern (Figure 12.39a). When the monkeys detected the color, they were to make a rapid eye movement from fixation to the location on the screen that contained that color. The attended location would be positioned either over the receptive field of a recorded V1 neuron or in the opposite visual field, so that the responses of the neuron could be evaluated when that region of space was attended and when it was ignored (in different blocks). The flickering noise pattern could also be used to create a spatiotemporal receptive-field map (Figure 12.39b) that showed regions of the receptive field excited or inhibited by light. In this way the researchers could determine whether the neuron had the properties of simple cells, and they could also see whether attention affected the firing pattern and receptive-field organization. Indeed, they found that spatial attention enhanced the responses of the simple cells but did not affect the spatial or temporal organization of their receptive fields (Figure 12.39c).

Might the existence of these attentional modulations at an early stage of the primary visual cortex reflect earlier gating in the thalamus or even in the retina? Unlike the cochlea, the human retina contains no descending neural projections that could be used to modulate retinal activity by attention. But massive neuronal projections extend from the visual cortex back to the thalamus. These projections synapse on neurons in what is known as the **reticular nucleus** *of the thalamus* or, more specifically for the visual system, on the *perigeniculate nucleus*, the portion of the reticular nucleus that surrounds the lateral geniculate nucleus (Figure 12.40).

These neurons maintain complex interconnections with neurons in the thalamic relays and could, in principle, gate information flow from the thalamus to

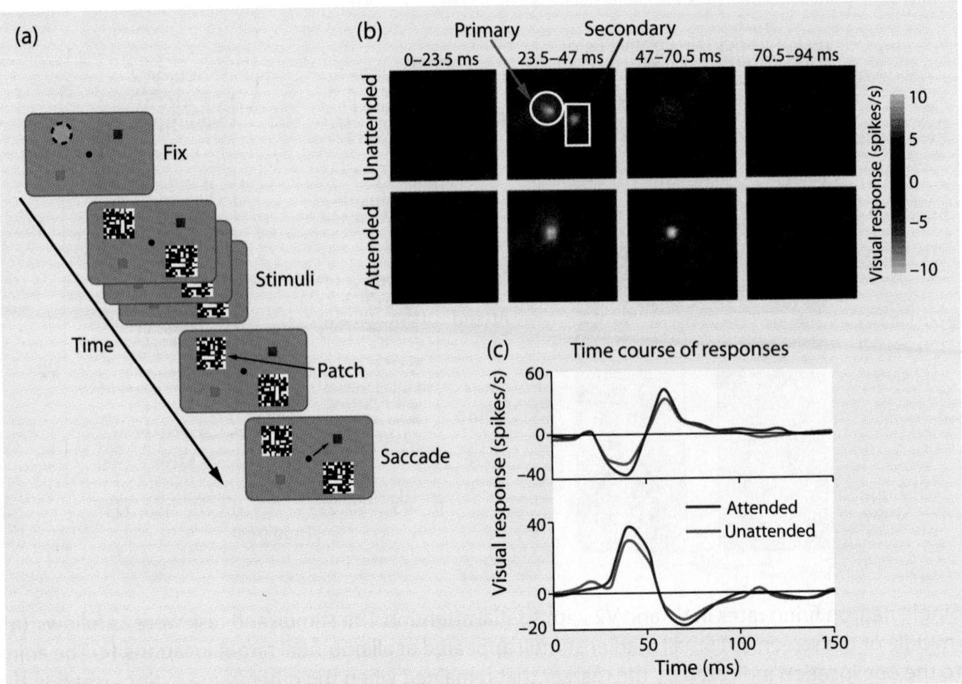

Figure 12.39 Attention effects in V1 simple cells. **(a)** The stimulus sequence began with a fixation point and two color locations that would serve as saccade targets. (The blue circle in the first panel represents the previously mapped receptive-field location and was not shown on the test screen.) Then two flickering black-and-white patches appeared, one over the neuron's receptive field and the other in the opposite visual field. The monkey was instructed which of the two patches to attend prior to the onset of the stimuli. The monkey had been trained to covertly attend the indicated patch to detect a small color pixel that would signal where a subsequent saccade of the eyes was to be made (to the matching color) for a reward. **(b)** The spatiotemporal receptive field of the neuron when unattended (attend opposite visual field patch) and when attended. Each of the eight panels corresponds to the same spatial location (about 3° × 3°) as that of the black-and-white stimulus over the neuron's receptive field. The excitatory (red) and inhibitory (blue) regions of the receptive field are evident, being largest from 23.5 to 70 ms after stimulus onset **(middle two panels)**. Note that the amplitudes of the responses were larger when attended than when unattended. This difference can be seen in these receptive-field maps and is summarized as plots in **(c)**.

the cortex. Indeed, as demonstrated in the cat in the studies of Charles Yingling and James Skinner in 1976, this gating can happen during intermodal (visual–auditory) attention. Such a gating process might also select the visual field location for the current spotlight of attention in perception—an idea proposed by Nobel laureate Francis Crick (1992). The fMRI findings that we reviewed earlier (see Figure 12.26) provide evidence that the lateral geniculate nucleus of the thalamus is influenced by spatial attention. But since no timing information is available from fMRI, it is hard to know whether such effects reflect attentional gating of the afferent volleys heading to V1, or instead are reflections of some more tonic change that supports a different attentional mechanism. Thus, although we can say with confidence that modulations of retinal processing with spatial attention do not occur (given that no neural substrate exists to accomplish this), we must leave open the possibility that the thalamus might be gated during some forms of visual attention. Electrophysiological recordings in the thalamus during selective attention will be necessary to complete the story.

ATTENTIONAL MODULATIONS IN SUBCORTICAL STRUCTURES AND PARIETAL CORTEX

In the early 1970s, Robert Wurtz and his colleagues at the National Eye Institute began to investigate how the superior colliculus, a midbrain nucleus, might play a role in attention. They discovered visually responsive neurons that were affected by how monkeys responded to stimuli. When the animal moved its eyes rapidly from one location to another (a saccadic eye movement) to look at a stimulus, the firing rates increased for cells with receptive fields that included the region of space to be looked at. The eye movement itself did not enhance cell firing; if the same eye movements were made in the dark, no changes in cellular activity were observed (Figure 12.41). Eye movements to other

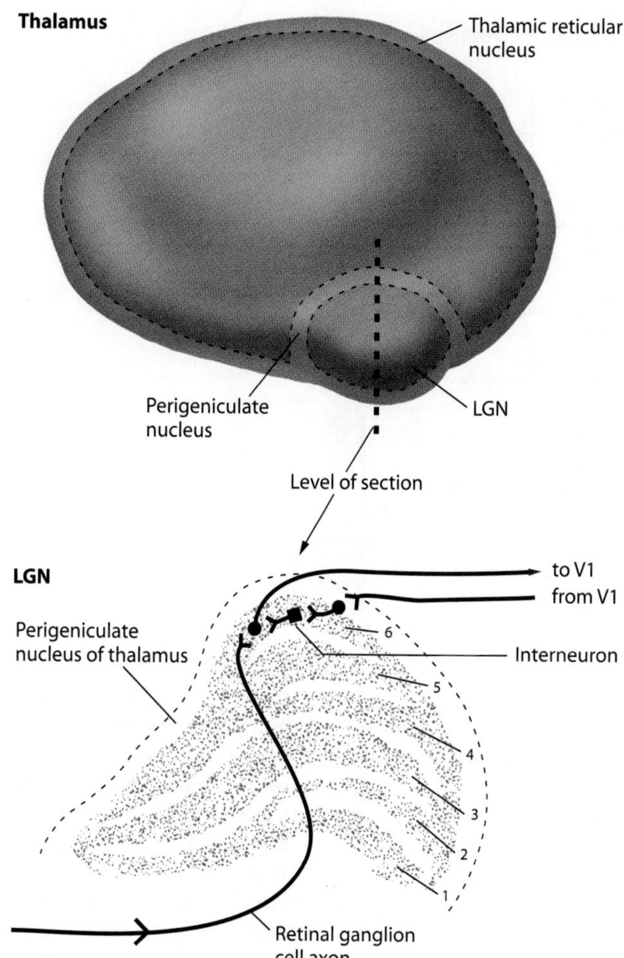

Figure 12.40 The thalamus, perigeniculate nucleus, and projections to and from the thalamus and visual cortex.

locations also did not enhance responses to the stimulus. These cells responded as though they were involved in attentional mechanisms having to do with the stimulus.

In subsequent experiments these investigators found that, when the stimulus was task relevant but was not the target for a saccadic eye movement, the cell did not become more responsive. These neurons, then, were facilitated not just by attending to the stimulus's location, as were cortical neurons in the studies described earlier; they also needed the eyes to move to the target. The conclusion was that cells in the superior colliculus do not participate in voluntary visual selective attention per se, but are part of an eye movement system and may therefore have a role in overt rather than covert aspects of attention. Studies in humans by Ayelet Sapir and Avishai Henik and their colleagues (Sapir et al., 1999) in Israel provide additional information about the role of the colliculus in attention. In a rare patient with a unilateral bleed that damaged only one of the superior colliculi, they demonstrated that inhibition of return (described earlier, see page 500) was reduced for inputs to the lesioned colliculus, indicating that the superior colliculus may have an important role in the inhibitory component of reflexive attention.

Another major subcortical structure that has been implicated in attention is the **pulvinar nucleus** of the thalamus (Figure 12.42). We know that the pulvinar is activated during attentional filtering tasks, and later we will consider human lesions that suggest an orienting role for this nucleus. Here we discuss what has been learned from animal studies about the role of the pulvinar in visual attention.

The pulvinar nucleus has visually responsive neurons that show color, motion, and orientation selectivity. In addition, it has subdivisions containing retinotopic maps of the visual world and interconnections with frontal, parietal, occipital, and temporal cortical areas. Pulvinar neurons show enhanced activity when a stimulus either is the target of a saccadic eye movement or is attended without eye movements to the target. Thus, this structure may be involved in both voluntary and reflexive attention.

Steve Petersen, David Lee Robinson, and their colleagues (Petersen et al., 1987, 1992) examined what happens when a drug is administered that temporarily deactivates pulvinar neurons. In their studies, the drug muscimol, a GABA agonist that inhibits neuronal activity, was injected into the dorsomedial region of the pulvinar in monkeys. Following the injection, the monkey had difficulty orienting attention covertly to targets in the contralateral visual field. In contrast, when a GABA antagonist was administered, the monkey readily directed its attention covertly to contralesional targets. Hence, the pulvinar is central to covert spatial attention (Figure 12.43 on page 534).

The pulvinar may also filter distracting information. Injections of muscimol led to deficits in color or form discrimination when competing distracter stimuli are present in the visual field. A similar result was observed in a PET study conducted by David LaBerge (1990) at the University of California, Irvine, and followed up more recently in an fMRI study by Monte Buchsbaum and colleagues (2006). Pulvinar activation was greatest when the stimulus displays included lots of distracting stimuli that required attentional filtering.

As we will see in the forthcoming discussion of the patient literature, the parietal cortex is a key region for attentional control; this point is also evident in the

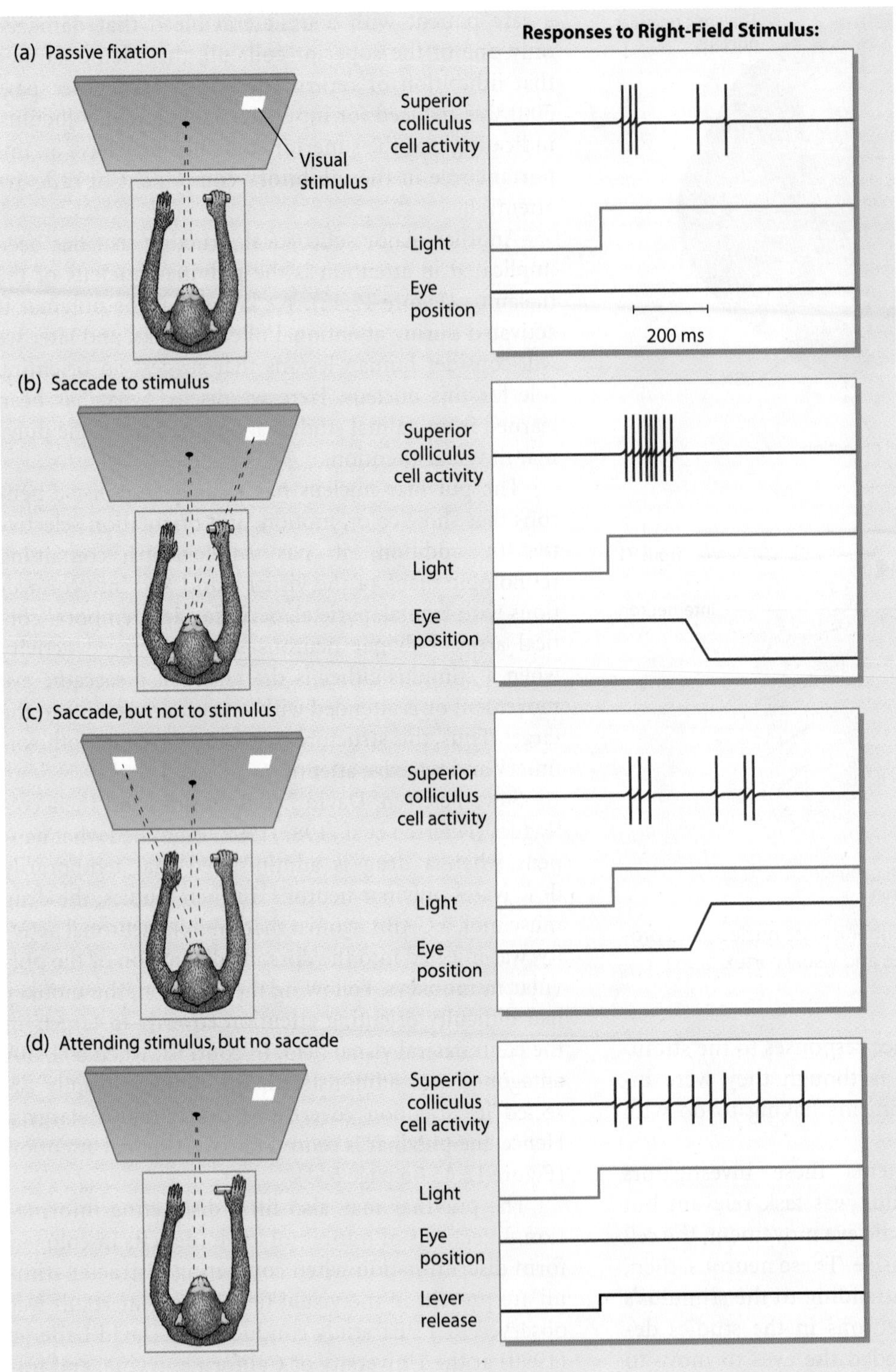

Figure 12.41 Experimental setup and responses of the superior colliculus for four different conditions from Wurtz and colleagues. **(a)** The monkey kept its eyes fixated on the central point and ignored the stimulus that was flashed in the right visual field. A few bursts of activity were found in the superior colliculus. **(b)** The monkey made a rapid saccadic eye movement to the location of a nonfoveal stimulus, and the firing rates of the cells with receptive fields coding that area of space greatly increased. **(c)** The monkey moved its eyes to a location outside the cell's receptive field, and the cells in the superior colliculus did not respond. **(d)** The monkey attended to the location in the field but did not make a saccadic eye movement, and only a few bursts of activity were observed.

many neuroimaging studies of attention (see Figures 12.31 and 12.32). The parietal lobe has extensive connections with subcortical areas like the pulvinar, as well as the frontal cortex and other parts of the visual pathways, and it contains multiple representations of space.

Numerous physiological studies in monkeys have looked at the role of the parietal lobe in attention. Attentional shifts are correlated with significant increases and decreases in the activity of parietal neurons. In the 1970s, Vernon Mountcastle (1976) from Johns Hopkins University discovered that attentive fixation to

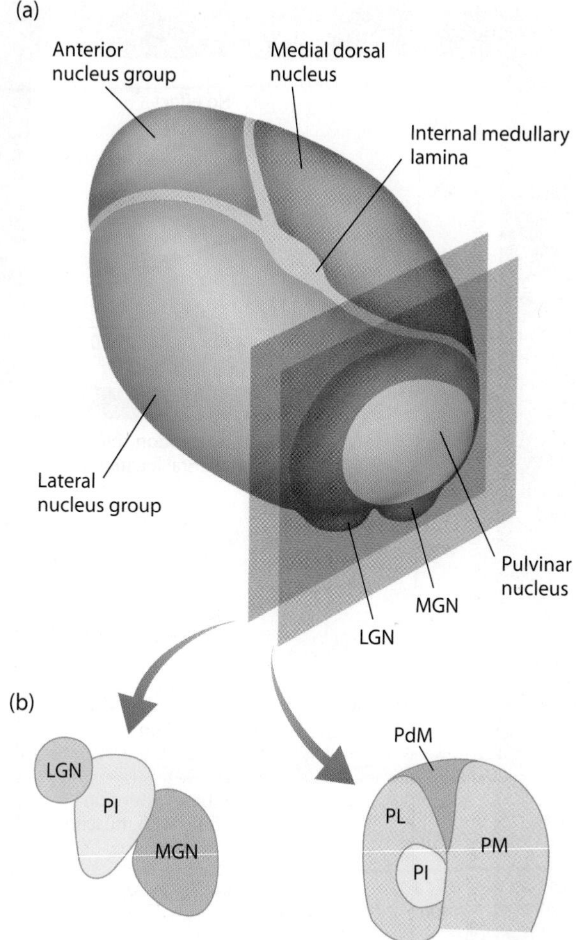

Figure 12.42 Anatomical diagram of the thalamus showing the pulvinar nucleus. **(a)** This diagram of the entire left thalamus shows the divisions of the major groups of nuclei, and the relationships between the visual lateral geniculate (LGN) and auditory medial geniculate (MGN) nuclei, and the pulvinar nucleus. **(b)** These cross sections through the pulvinar at anterior levels show the LGN and MGN, and at more posterior levels, the lateral (PL), dorsomedial (PdM), medial (PM), and inferior (PI) subdivisions.

visual stimuli led to higher firing rates in parietal neurons. What is the role of these attention effects in parietal neurons? Studies by Robert Wurtz and his colleagues (1982) show that the firing rates in neurons of the parietal cortex increase in response to a target stimulus when an animal is using the stimulus as a target for a saccade or covertly discriminating its features. But if a monkey is merely waiting attentively for the next trial in a sequence of trials, the parietal neurons do not usually have enhanced responses to visual stimuli in their receptive fields (Figure 12.44 on page 535). The parietal cortex's response pattern is different from that of the superior colliculus in that parietal neurons become enhanced when stimuli either are the target for saccades or are covertly attended.

What is the role of the parietal cortex in attention? The parietal cortex has many subdivisions, and most studies of attention using single-neuron recording and functional imaging have focused on the intraparietal area, especially the intraparietal sulcus (IPS) and a subregion within the IPS known as the lateral intraparietal (LIP) area in monkeys (Figure 12.45 on page 535). This region is involved in both saccadic eye movements and visuospatial attention.

James Bisley and Micky Goldberg (2006) at the National Eye Institute have been investigating the role of LIP neurons in visuospatial attention. They presented monkeys with a covert attention task that included the occasional introduction of distracter stimuli while the animal was covertly attending a cued location (Figure 12.46a on page 536). They then used a discrimination task that required the animal to detect the properties of a stimulus at the attended location in order to determine whether to execute a planned saccade to the attended location. The scientists compared the neuronal activity for the population of LIP neurons with and without distraction and related this activity to performance.

As shown in Figure 12.46b and c, the best performance (plotted as contrast thresholds for detecting a target feature) was observed when the target feature to be discriminated occurred in the location where neuronal activity was higher. That is, if neuronal activity was highest at the attended location, performance was better for targets presented to that attended location. But if a distracter was presented and neuronal activity in another region of the LIP (corresponding to where the distracter was presented) was temporarily higher than at the location to be attended, then target discrimination was better at that (nominally unattended) location. The distracter could therefore attract attention to that location, but this shift would last only a short period, after which the attended-location activity was once again higher than that at the distracter location, and the advantage for the attended location in performance was regained.

These studies demonstrate that the pattern of activity over the extent of LIP predicts performance and, by inference, the momentary locus of visual attention. Bisley and Goldberg (2006) interpreted this finding as evidence that activity in LIP provides a salience or priority map that is interpreted by the oculomotor system as a saccade goal when a saccade is appropriate, and simultaneously is used by the visual system to determine the locus of attention.

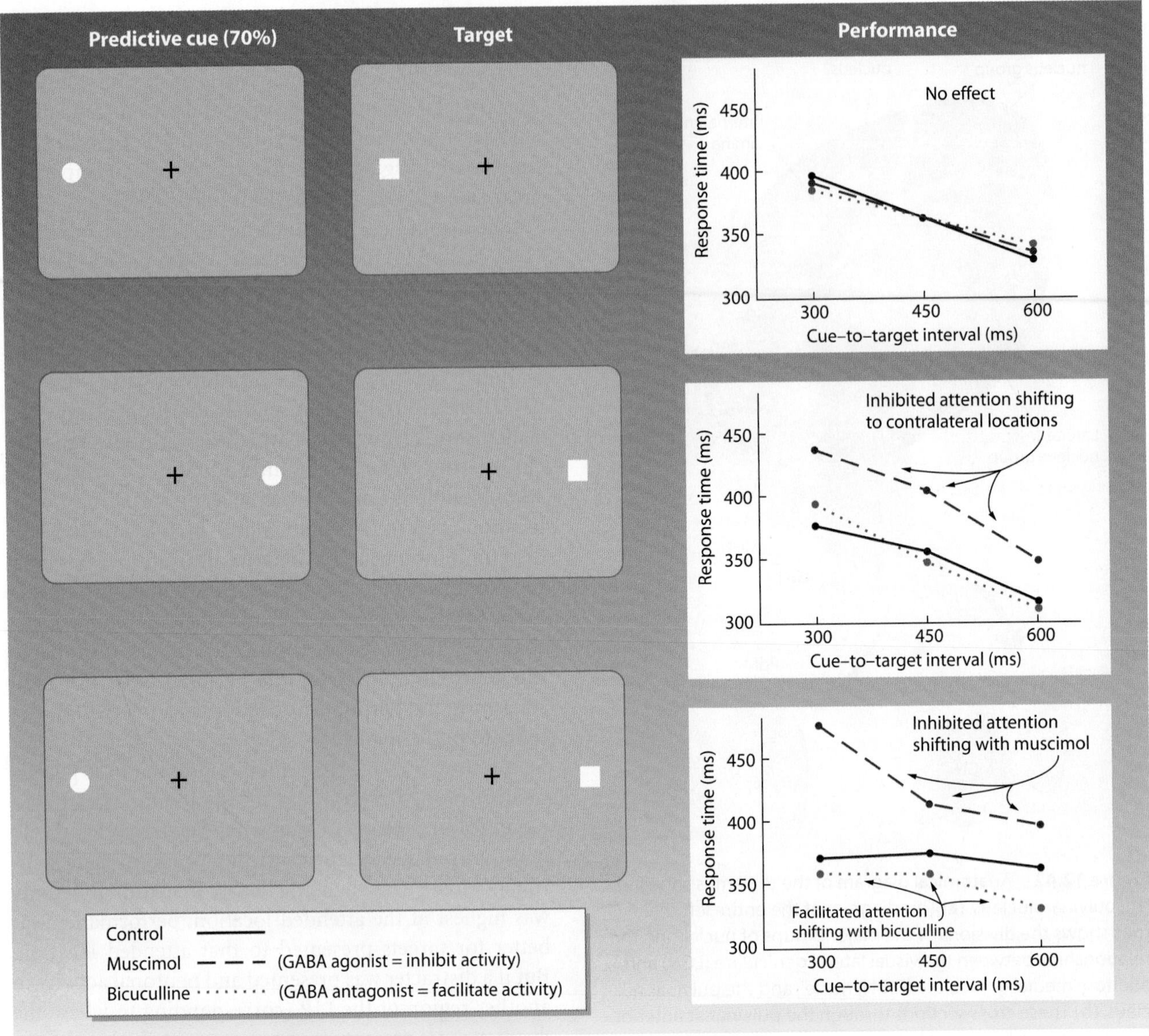

Figure 12.43 Effects on behavior when the pulvinar nucleus is injected with GABA agonists and antagonists. The trial types—predictive peripheral **(left column)** and target **(middle column)**—correspond to the data presented on the **right**. The measure is reaction time to target detection as a function of cue-to-target interval (ms) (see text for description of results).

SUMMARY OF ANIMAL STUDIES OF ATTENTIONAL MECHANISMS

In summary, single-unit recordings and lesion studies in animals have shown that subcortical and cortical brain areas are involved in various aspects of attentional control and selection. Neurons in cortical areas such as the frontal and parietal cortex are also sensitive to attentional processes, and they appear to play a role in coding the locations of behaviorally relevant stimuli and in coordinating shifts of attention, perhaps in conjunction with subcortical networks in the pulvinar and superior colliculus.

Together with evidence from neuroimaging, the take-home message is that the frontal and parietal cortex and subcortical structures are key parts of a system for orienting attention to relevant locations. The consequence of this attentional orienting during perception is seen in the sensory cortex, where analyses of stimulus features and forms are carried out. Convergent evidence for the role of the parietal and subcortical structures in orienting comes from observations of what happens to these abilities in humans with neurological damage. These observations are reviewed in the next section.

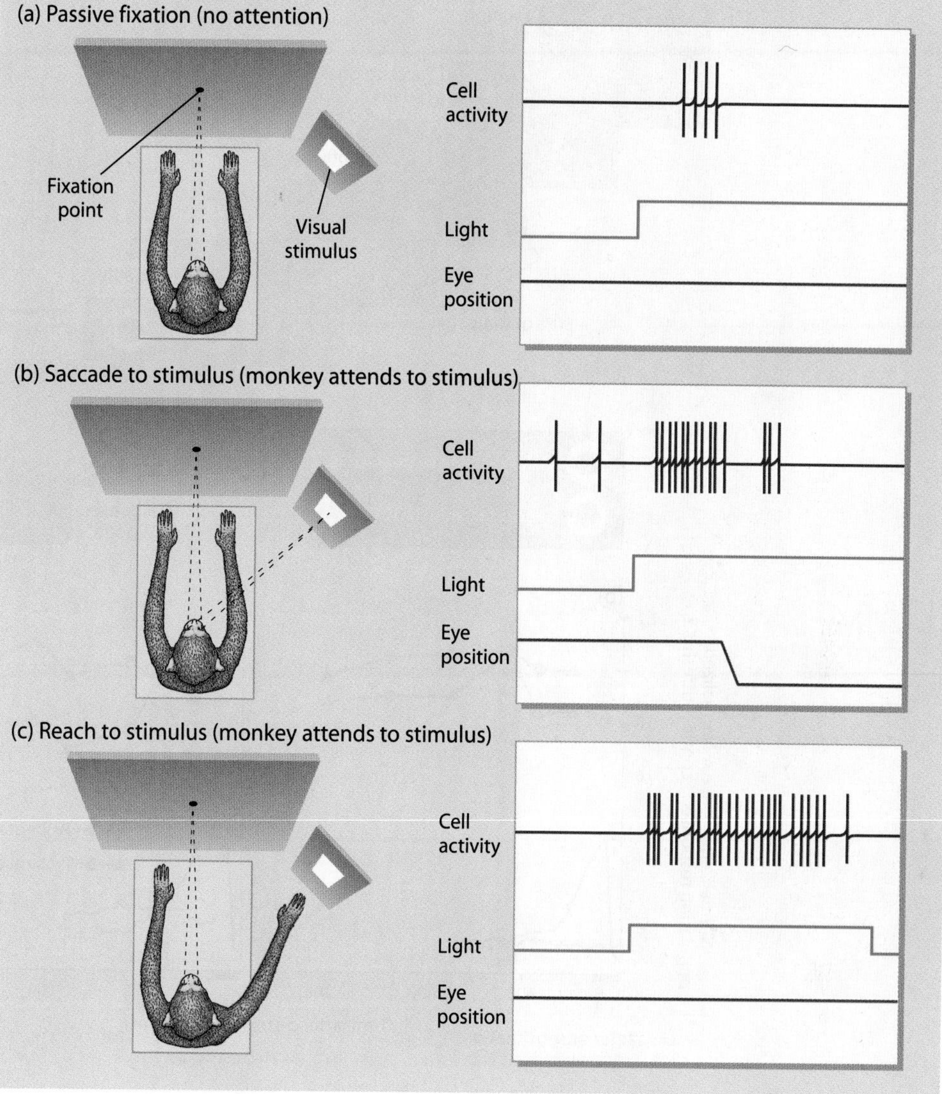

Figure 12.44 Properties of parietal neurons in visual attention. Three conditions are shown. **(a)** The monkey passively fixates while a lateral-field stimulus is presented, generating some action potentials from the neuron **(right)**. **(b)** The monkey has the task of making a saccadic eye movement to the target when it appears, and this saccade increases the rate of neuron firing. **(c)** The neuron increases its firing rate to targets that are presented and covertly attended, when the animal must keep its eyes fixated straight ahead but is required to reach to the target. Thus, the neuron is spatially selective—a sign of covert attention.

Figure 12.45 Left lateral view of macaque monkey brain. The intraparietal sulcus (IPS) in the parietal lobe is shown retracted to reveal the depths of the sulcus, which contains several distinct areas. One of these distinct areas, the lateral intraparietal area (LIP), is also identified in the figure. Neurons in the LIP receive inputs from and project to neurons in the frontal eye field and the superior colliculus, and they have been related to many functions, but principally to saccadic eye movements and visuospatial attention. In humans, functional-imaging data suggest that the functional equivalent of the monkey LIP is located also in the IPS, but along its medial aspect.

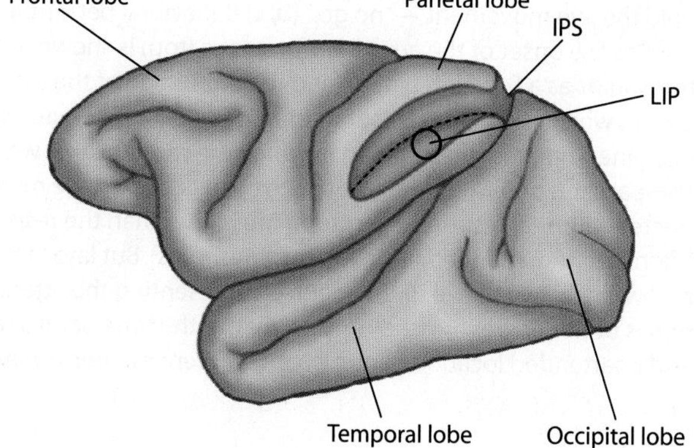

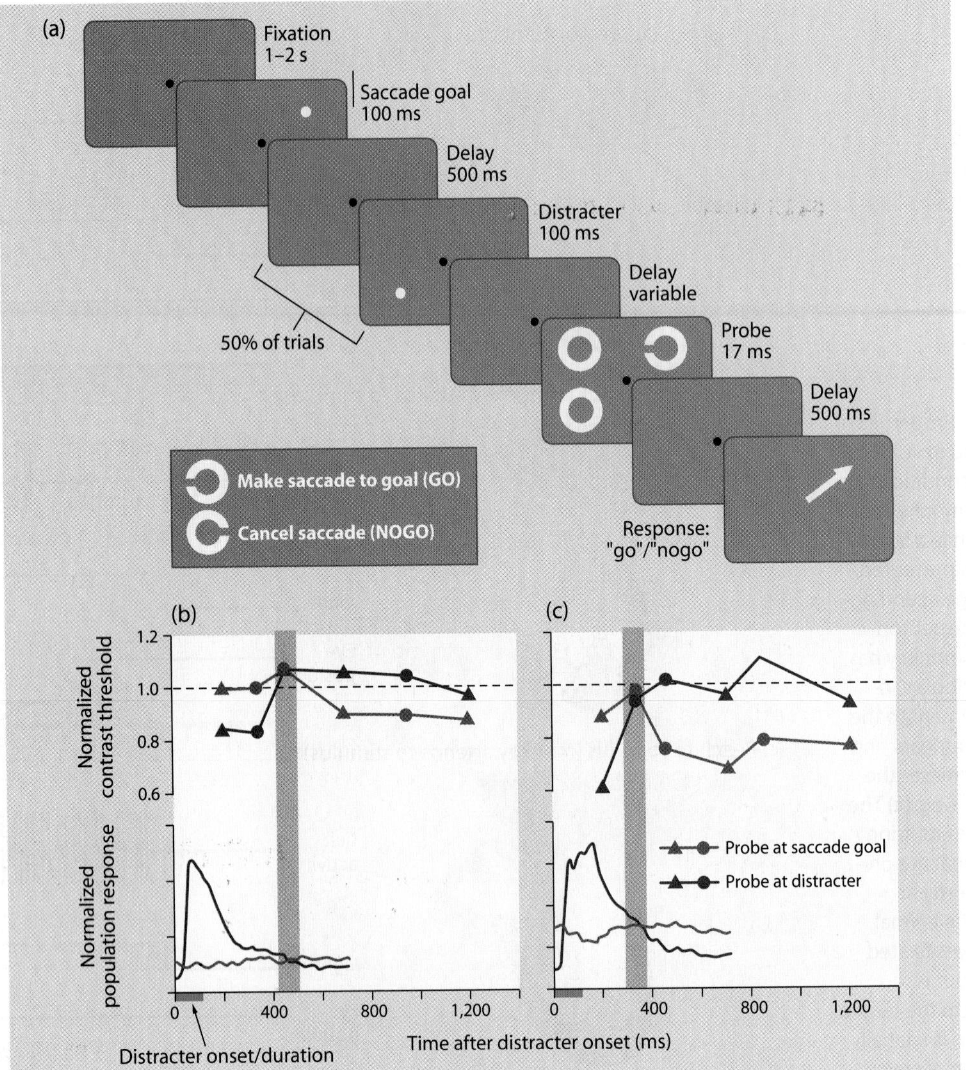

Figure 12.46 Behavior and neuronal attention effects in monkey parietal cortex during visuospatial attention. **(a)** Stimulus sequence. Each trial started with a fixation spot to which the animals directed their eyes until the end of the trial. Then a dot appeared that could be in the recorded neuron's receptive field or not, but that always instructed the animal where to make a saccade later if a subsequent probe at the same location contained the correct feature. On some trials a distracter could appear at another location that might be within or outside the neuron's receptive field. Then the probe array appeared, and the animal's task was to covertly attend the item in the saccade location (attended location) and discriminate whether the shape had a gap on the left or right. If the gap was on the left, the animal was to move its eyes to the goal (the attended location)—"go." If not, then the animal was to withhold the eye movement —"no go." **(b, c)** Behavioral performance and neuronal responses from two monkeys in the period 700 ms prior to the onset of the arrays. Performance (top) is shown as threshold, so the plots show lower (downward) and higher (upward) thresholds as a function of time and the amplitude of the associated responses in populations of LIP neurons. Red lines indicate the case in which the distracter stimulus appeared in the neuron's receptive field and the animal was therefore attending elsewhere; blue lines indicate the situation in which the saccade goal was in the neuron's receptive field. To appreciate the interesting finding, compare the behavioral trace (use the color codes) to the neuronal responses over time prior to the onset of the probes. If the distracter neuronal responses (bottom) are higher than the responses for the neuron at the attended location, then performance is poorer for the attended item (higher thresholds). But late in the sequence, when the response amplitude for the distracter decays to below the activity level for the neuron representing the attended location (blue), performance on the target at the attended location is better (lower threshold). Note that, at the time point shaded gray, there is no difference in the neuronal activity for attended and unattended locations, and also no difference in performance.

NEUROLOGY AND NEUROPSYCHOLOGY OF ATTENTION

One fascinating syndrome associated with brain damage is **unilateral spatial neglect**, or simply *neglect*. Following damage to one hemisphere, typically associated with right parietal and frontal cortical areas, this disorder is common. The syndrome of neglect is unfortunate for those afflicted, yet fascinating to contemplate. In this disorder, patients behave as though parts of objects and the world around them do not exist, and they are unaware of this deficit. That is, they neglect the information.

A graphic example comes from paintings by the late German artist Anton Raederscheidt. Raederscheidt suffered a stroke in the right hemisphere that left him with neglect; the pictures in Figure 12.47 are self-portraits that he painted at different times after the stroke occurred and during his partial recovery. The paintings show his failure to represent portions of contralateral space, including, remarkably, portions of his own face! In the first painting (Figure 12.47a), done shortly after his stroke, notice that almost the entire left half of the canvas is untouched. And interestingly, the image he paints of himself, in addition to be poorly formed, is also missing the left half. One can make out one eye, part of a nose, one ear, but toward the left the painting fades away. With each of the next three paintings (Figure 12.47b–d), made over the following several weeks and months, notice that Raederscheidt's use of the canvas improves, and so does his representation of his face, until in Figure 12.47d he uses the whole canvas and has a bilaterally symmetrical face. Fascinating!

Figure 12.47 Self-portraits by the late German artist Anton Raederscheidt, painted at different times following a severe stroke, which left him with neglect to contralesional space.

(a)

(b)

(c)

(d)

In some cases, as suggested by Raederscheidt's self-portraits, patients with unilateral brain damage showing neglect not only ignore the presence of persons or objects in the contralesional hemispace, but they might also fail to groom (e.g., shave or comb hair) on the contralesional side of the body, or even, remarkably, not recognize their own limbs on the contralesional side of the body as their own. Typically, patients show only a subset of these extreme signs of neglect, and indeed, neglect can manifest itself in different ways, but the common thread is that neglect involves deficits in attending to and acting in the direction contralesional to the unilateral brain damage.

Extinction

A prominent feature of neglect is **extinction**, the failure to perceive or act on stimuli contralateral to the lesion (contralesional stimuli) when presented simultaneously with stimuli ipsilateral to the lesion (ipsilesional stimuli). Signs of extinction can often be observed with careful testing even after the most obvious signs of neglect have remitted as the patient recovers. Figure 12.48 shows a neurologist testing a patient with right parietal damage. In this example the neurologist is both verifying that the patient has no primary vision problems and performing a test for extinction. When confronted with simultaneous stimuli in the left and right visual fields, the patient responds to only the one in his unaffected (right) visual field, extinguishing (failing to perceive) the stimulus in the contralesional (left) visual field. Because the patient can detect the stimuli when they are presented unilaterally, we know that his visual system is intact and therefore visual field defects cannot explain the extinction.

Neglect of contralesional space is also diagnosed by other neuropsychological tests, such as line cancellation.

THE COGNITIVE NEUROSCIENTIST'S TOOLKIT

Two Brains Are Better Than One

The human visual system is remarkably adept at searching for target items in complex scenes. But when a target differs from other items by a conjunction of simple features like brightness and shape, search time grows linearly with the number of distracters. What is happening, then, is a serial process in which a unitary focus of attention searches the representation of the visual scene in the normal brain. But how would such a unitary process function after the cerebral hemispheres in split-brain patients were disconnected by surgical sectioning of the corpus callosum?

Because split-brain patients have had the corpus callosum cut to treat epilepsy, there is little or no perceptual or cognitive interaction between the hemispheres. Thus, specializations of the two halves of the brain can be investigated separately. From studies of visual search in these patients, we know that they, unlike subjects with an intact corpus callosum, can search at twice the rate when items are split between hemifields rather than concentrated within a single field. It is clear that each disconnected hemisphere possesses its own attentional scanning mechanism. So the old adage that "two brains are better than one" has real meaning for this cognitive mechanism in split-brain patients.

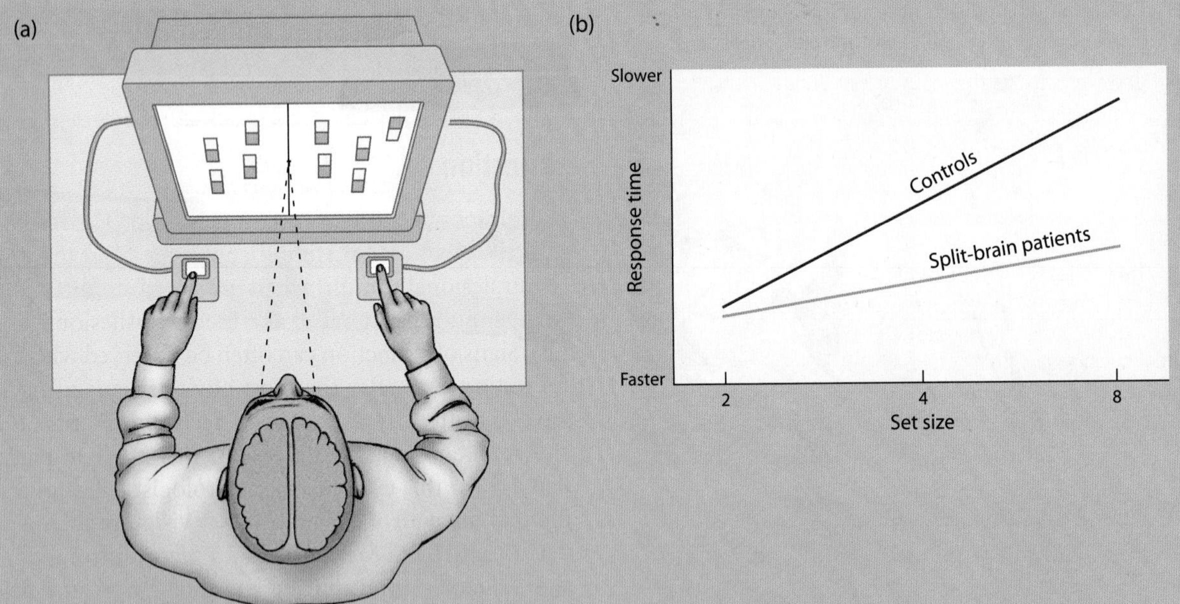

(a) A split-brain patient seated in front of a computer monitor and performing a visual search task for conjunction targets. **(b)** Graphs of the patient's reaction times in comparison to healthy control subjects for bilateral stimulus arrays of various set sizes. Control subjects take longer to perform the task (red line) than does the split-brain patient (green line) as set size increases. The split-brain patient has a search rate that is twice as fast, indicating that he is searching the array for the target separately with each hemisphere.

Patients suffering from neglect are given a sheet of paper containing many horizontal lines and are asked under free-viewing conditions to bisect the lines precisely in the middle by drawing a vertical line. Patients with lesions of the right hemisphere tend to bisect the lines to the right of the midline. They may also miss lines altogether in the direction opposite the lesioned hemisphere (Figure 12.49). In this example, the pattern of line cancellation provides evidence for neglect at the level of both object representations (each line) and visual space (the visual scene represented by the test paper); we will return to this point later.

Interestingly, neglect is much more common as a result of damage to the right hemisphere than of damage to the left hemisphere in patients who are left dominant for language (most of the population). This asymmetry has not been observed in nonhuman primates with unilateral brain damage resulting in contralesional attention deficits. Why might neglect be more likely after right-hemisphere lesions in humans? Two prominent models have been put forth to explain this preponderance of neglect following damage to the right hemisphere.

In the *representational model*, the right hemisphere is considered to have attentional representations of right and left hemispace, while the left hemisphere contains only representations of the right hemispace. Therefore, damage to the left hemisphere does not lead to significant contralesional neglect, because the intact right hemisphere is capable of representing space and allocating spatial attention toward left and right hemispace.

The *attentional bias model* proposes that the left and right hemispheres have natural biases toward attention contralaterally, but that this bias is asymmetrical, with the left hemisphere being more strongly biased toward right hemispace than the right hemisphere is to the left. Under normal circumstances, this asymmetry is not obvious, because inhibitory circuitry maintains a balance in rightward and leftward attention (Figure 12.50a). With a right-hemisphere lesion, however, this model proposes that a bias of attention develops as follows: First, the strong contralateral attentional bias of the left hemisphere is unopposed by the action of the right hemisphere. Second, the inhibitory inputs from the right hemisphere onto the left are removed, and the bias of the left hemisphere to direct attention to the right increases (Figure 12.50b). In the converse situation, a left-hemisphere lesion resulting in neglect of the right field is correspondingly less severe. These models have helped guide investigations of the neural correlates of unilateral hemispatial neglect, as we will review later.

COMPONENTS OF SPATIAL ATTENTION

To understand the clinical syndrome of neglect and relate it to attention in normal volunteers, researchers have tried to determine which components of normal attentional control and selection are lost or damaged after unilateral brain damage. Michael Posner, Robert Rafal, and their colleagues (Posner et al., 1984) studied neglect patients with mild to moderate symptoms who

Figure 12.48 Test of neglect and extinction. To a patient with a right-hemisphere lesion from a stroke, a neurologist presented a visual stimulus first in the left hemifield **(a)** and then in the right hemifield **(b)**. The patient correctly detected and responded (by pointing) to the stimuli if presented one at a time, demonstrating an ability to see both stimuli and therefore no major visual field defects. When the stimuli were presented simultaneously in the left and right visual fields **(c)**, however, the patient reported seeing only the one in the right visual field. This effect is called *extinction* because the simultaneous presence of the stimulus in the right field leads to the stimulus on the left being extinguished from awareness.

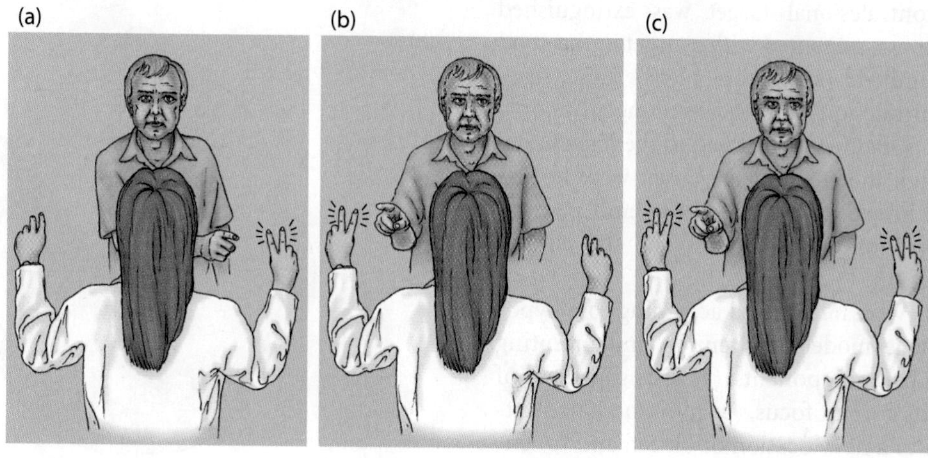

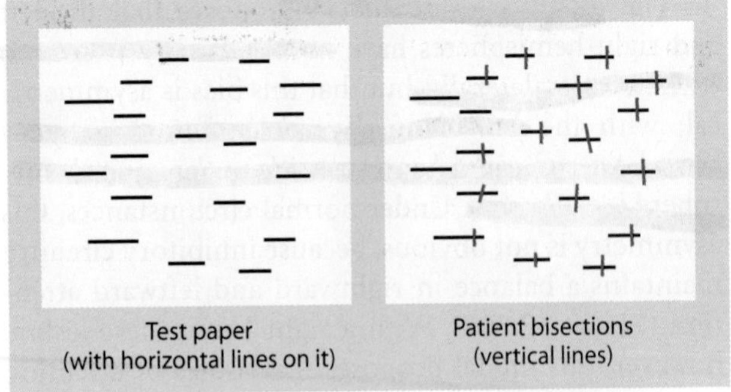

Figure 12.49 Patients suffering from neglect are given a sheet of paper containing many horizontal lines and asked under free-viewing conditions to bisect the lines precisely in the middle with a vertical line. They tend to bisect the lines to the right (for a right-hemisphere lesion) of the midline of each page and/or each line, owing to neglect for contralesional space.

had unilateral lesions involving the parietal, temporoparietal, and frontal cortex. They tested the patients using a trial-by-trial cuing design like the one shown in Figure 12.8, in which they had to press a button as fast as possible in response to target stimuli.

In the cuing paradigm, when they were cued to attend to locations in the contralesional hemifield, patients responded relatively quickly to target stimuli there. But if they were cued to expect the target stimulus in the ipsilesional field—for example, the right visual field for a patient with a right-sided lesion—they were unusually slow to respond to the target when it unexpectedly appeared in the contralesional field. The reaction times to uncued contralesional targets were much longer even than the reaction times to uncued trials presented to the ipsilesional field (Figure 12.51).

This reaction time pattern has been described as an "extinction-like reaction time pattern," to indicate its similarity to the clinical finding of extinction in bedside neurological testing of these patients. Recall that, in extinction, the contralesional target was extinguished when the subject was presented with a target in the good (ipsilesional) hemifield (see Figure 12.48). Here, reaction times to contralesional targets were longer but only when the patients had first been cued to the ipsilesional field. Even though the cue and the target were not simultaneous, the investigators noted the resemblance between the pattern of reaction times and the clinical finding of extinction.

These results were interpreted according to a hypothetical three-stage model of attention and orienting having the following components: (a) disengagement of attention from its current focus, (b) movement or shifting of attention to a new location or object, and (c) engagement of attention on the new location or object to facilitate perceptual processing of the stimuli (Figure 12.52). The patients' exceptionally long reaction times when the cue was in the ipsilesional field and the target was in the contralateral field could be interpreted as a deficit in the disengage operation. That is, when the patients were cued to engage attention to the location in the ipsilesional field, the appearance of the target in the uncued contralesional field required them to first disengage attention from the ipsilesional field and then shift and engage it contralesionally. Disengagement problems are thought to lead to the deficits in reaction times in this study because the patients could shift attention to

Figure 12.50 Model of hemispheric biases in spatial attention. **(a)** Under normal circumstances, the asymmetry in the contralateral attentional biases of the left and right hemispheres (red arrows) is well balanced by the opposing action of each hemisphere and the crossed inhibitory inputs from each hemisphere's attentional system onto the other. **(b)** If the right hemisphere is lesioned, however, then not only is the attentional action of the right hemisphere removed or diminished, but the crossed inhibition of the right onto the left is removed. The result is a rightward attentional bias (larger red arrow).

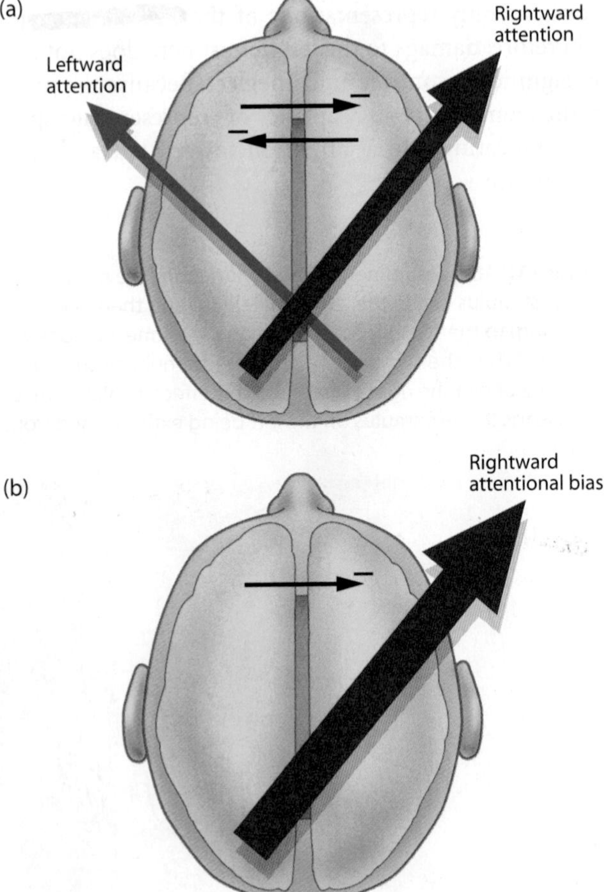

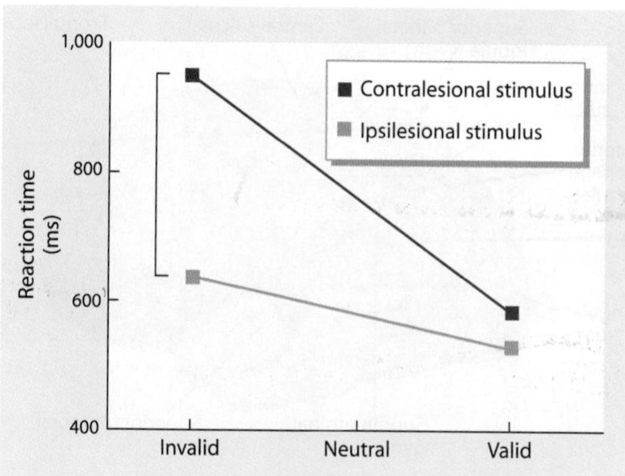

Figure 12.51 Extinction-like reaction time pattern in patients with unilateral lesions of the parietal cortex. Reaction times to precued (valid) targets contralateral to the lesion were almost "normal"; that is, although reactions were slower than those of healthy control subjects, they were not much slower than the patients' reactions to targets that occurred in the ipsilesional hemifield when that field was cued. But when patients were cued to expect the target stimulus in the field ipsilateral to the lesion (e.g., right visual field for a right parietal lesion), they were unusually slow to respond to the target when it occurred in the opposite field (invalid trials).

contralesional space and engage targets if cued there, but they showed particular impairment when their attention was first attracted somewhere else in the visual field and then had to be moved toward the contralesional hemispace.

CORTICAL MECHANISMS OF NEGLECT

The finding of a variety of spatial attention deficits following unilateral cortical damage clearly points to disruption of brain attention mechanisms. What is known about the precise cortical areas and networks involved in neglect? We have already pointed to the fact that right-hemisphere lesions produce more profound neglect than do left-hemisphere lesions, and the long history of neurology has implicated posterior parietal and frontal cortex in neglect. However, it is possible to be more precise in localizing the damage that leads to this disorder. Using high-resolution imaging methods, we should be able to elucidate the neural correlates of neglect. Indeed, we have already told you some of this unfolding story.

Recall the fMRI studies of Corbetta and colleagues that identified a region of right temporoparietal cortex that was activated when subjects received an invalid cue and then had to reorient their attention (see Figures 12.35 and 12.36 and the associated text). Those results were interpreted to mean that a ventral parietal, posterior temporal, and inferior frontal network was involved in disengaging attention in order to reorient it elsewhere. Together with the evidence from the reaction time studies in patients already described, these findings strongly suggest that lesions to this network result in the major symptoms of neglect. Is there more direct evidence from patients?

The specific brain damage that causes unilateral spatial neglect is still a matter of debate. Some studies have provided evidence that lesions of the right inferior parietal lobe centered on the angular gyrus are most likely to cause neglect, but other studies have provided compelling evidence that lesions of the right superior temporal cortex are the most likely culprit. Kenneth Heilman and his colleagues (1983) in the United States conducted one of the first modern imaging analyses of the brain correlates of neglect. Using the CT scans of 10 neglect patients, they found that the right inferior parietal lobule and the temporoparietal junction were the sites of maximum overlap of the lesion across the

Figure 12.52 The model of attention hypothesized by Posner and colleagues (1984). A sensory event generates a signal that produces localization of the event spatially. Thereupon an interrupt signal is generated and attention disengages from the current focus, moves to the location of the event, and engages the stimulus. Attentional engagement may be followed by a spatially mediated inhibition if this is purely reflexive orienting to the sensory event—the phenomenon of inhibition of return.

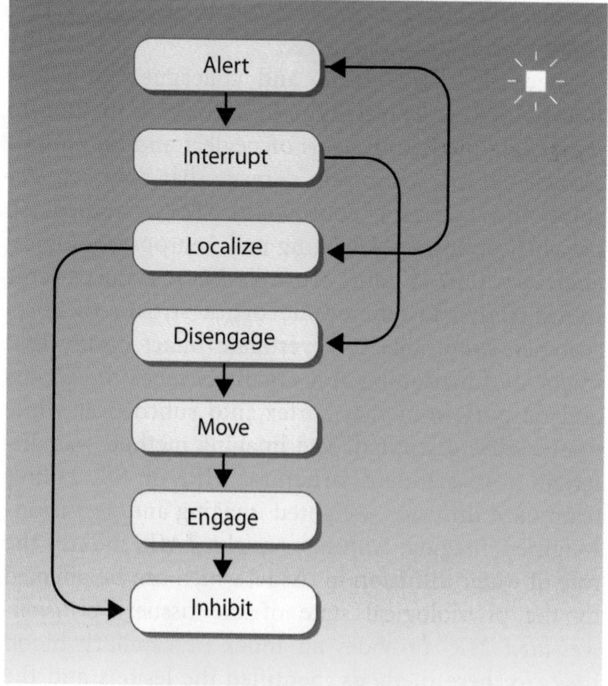

patient group. Similarly, Giuseppe Vallar and Daniela Perani (1986) in Italy also examined imaging data from right-hemispheric neglect patients and found involvement of the inferior parietal lobule and temporoparietal junction (Figure 12.53).

However, more recent work in larger patient populations has implicated regions in the posterior superior temporal gyrus that are most related to neglect. Hans-Otto Karnath and his colleagues (2001, 2004) investigated large groups of neglect patients in order to learn which brain regions result in neglect. In this work they studied patients with lesions confined to the right hemisphere that could be clearly visualized using MRI or CT scans. The lesions were identified and transposed onto standardized brain templates so that they could be compared across the patient sample. Like the other studies mentioned here, this method looks for the lesioned brain areas that are damaged in neglect patients studied but not in control patients who have brain lesions but no neglect. These scientists found that the brain regions most commonly associated with spatial neglect were the superior temporal gyrus, insula, and basal ganglia (Figure 12.54).

The variations in the findings from different studies in patients regarding the site of brain lesion that produces neglect may result from differences in the methods used to analyze the data. Or they might result from differences in how the patients were selected (e.g., those with and those without neglect defined by particular neuropsychological tests, or those with versus without visual field defects). However, they may also be related to other organizational principles in the inferior parietal and posterior temporal cortex.

Recently, Argye Hillis and colleagues (2005) at Johns Hopkins University used a different method to investigate the neural bases of neglect and find a pattern of deficits with brain damage that may help resolve the apparent controversy. They studied 50 patients, performing imaging and neuropsychological analysis within 48 hours of stroke. Because the patients in this study had suffered subcortical strokes, these researchers were able to investigate intact cortex that might be functioning abnormally because the inputs and outputs from that cortex into subcortical white matter were disrupted. The imaging method was different from standard structural MRI or CT. Hillis's team used diffusion-weighted imaging and perfusion-weighted imaging. *Diffusion-weighted MRI* indexes the rate of water diffusion in tissue, which can be affected by the physiological state of the tissue. *Perfusion-weighted MRI* provides an index of capillary blood flow. So these methods identified the lesions and the

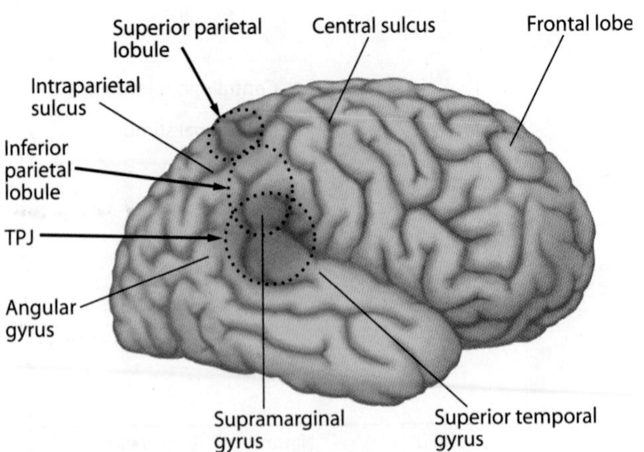

Figure 12.53 Lateral view of the right hemisphere, showing the major anatomical regions implicated in neglect, including the temporoparietal junction (TPJ), angular gyrus, supramarginal gyrus, and superior temporal gyrus. The parietal lobe is colored bluish, frontal lobe pink, temporal lobe orange, and occipital lobe green.

effect of those lesions on the functioning of intact cortex.

First, Hillis and colleagues demonstrated that patients who showed no cortical hypoperfusion (reduced blood flow) did not demonstrate neglect. Those with cortical hypoperfusion who showed neglect could be divided into two groups based on the type of neglect they showed: Importantly, this categorization also implicated different brain regions in each form of neglect. Some patients showed neglect for the left sides of objects but not the left sides of personal space (object-based neglect); the other group showed the inverse pattern—no object-based neglect but instead clear signs of spatial neglect for extrapersonal space.

The interesting finding was that patients with object-based neglect showed cortical hypoperfusion centered on the right superior temporal gyrus, but those with neglect for extrapersonal space showed hypoperfusion in the right angular gyrus, in the region considered the inferior parietal lobule and temporoparietal junction (Figure 12.55). This interesting finding helps us understand the controversy in the literature regarding the brain regions associated with neglect by suggesting that different forms of neglect may correlate with different brain lesions. We will return to the issue of the coordinates of neglect in the next section, but let's first consider how these data from patient lesion analyses can be integrated with functional imaging in healthy subjects and with lesion studies in animals.

The fMRI studies described earlier have implicated the posterior parietal lobe (intraparietal sulcus) in attentional control and the temporoparietal junction, in-

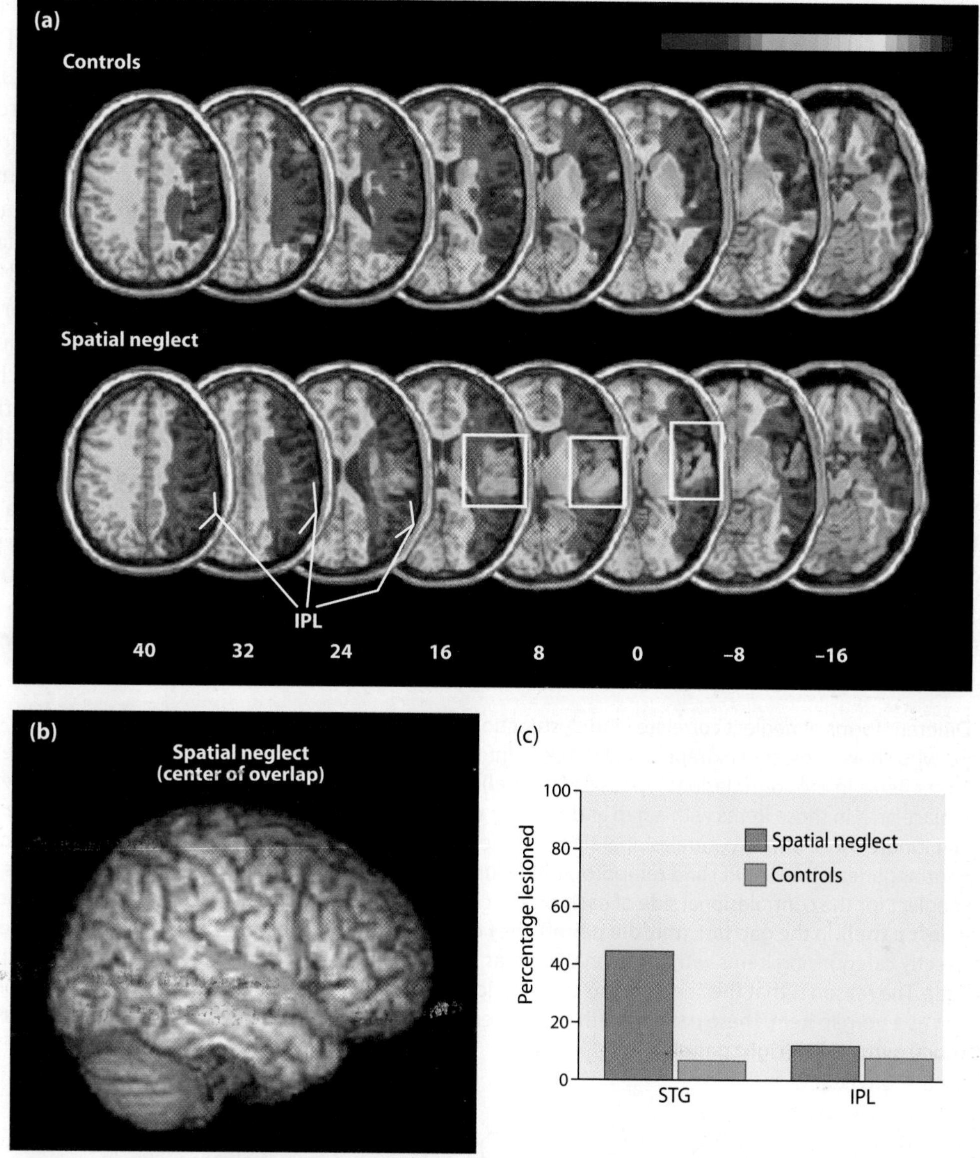

Figure 12.54 Brain damage associated with unilateral spatial neglect. **(a)** Regions of maximum lesion overlap in patients with right-hemisphere damage without **(top row)** and with **(bottom row)** spatial neglect are evident on horizontal slices from a standard brain atlas. Purple indicates less overlap, and blue to green indicates more overlap in the lesions across the population. The numbers at the bottom refer to the slice location in standard coordinates from more superior **(left)** to more inferior **(right)**. IPL = inferior parietal lobule. **(b)** Lateral three-dimensional reconstruction of the right hemisphere showing the regions in the right superior temporal lobe (green) that most overlapped in the neglect patient group. **(c)** Quantitative comparison of brain regions lesioned in the neglect and control group in the superior temporal gyrus (STG) and IPL. The region showing the most overlap in the neglect patient group was in the STG.

cluding the superior temporal sulcus, in reorienting attention (see Figure 12.36); and in some studies the superior temporal cortex has been observed to be activated when healthy subjects focus spatial attention voluntarily (see Figure 12.32). All these regions have now also been implicated in neglect in studies of neurological patients, as described in the foregoing. The combination of fMRI in healthy subjects and structural and perfusion imaging in patients is progressively converging on a network of brain areas supporting attentional function. Similarly, a long history of monkey lesion studies had failed to develop animal models of neglect when the posterior parietal cortex was lesioned. However, neglectlike symptoms could be produced when the superior temporal and temporoparietal junction regions were lesioned—a finding that now makes sense in light of the new patient lesion analyses (see Figure 12.54).

COORDINATE SYSTEMS OF ATTENTION AND NEGLECT

As we indicated in our review of the studies of Hillis and colleagues (see Figure 12.55), patients with unilateral brain damage resulting in extinction and neglect sometimes have disturbed attention in object-based coordinates (left and right sides of individual objects) and not only extrapersonal space (left versus right hemispace). In tests of line bisections, for example, patients may neglect the left half of the page (neglect in extrapersonal space) or the left half of each object (each line) on the page (object-based neglect), or they may exhibit both patterns. Such effects are still spatially defined because the side of each object (the line or the page) contralateral to the lesion is neglected. But these neuropsychological findings show that object-based coordinates for neglect can exist even when the objects themselves are not in the neglected hemispace (i.e., an object in the ipsilesional hemispace).

So far, we have considered neglect for items actually present in the visual world, like stimuli presented to the patients on a page during neuropsychological testing. Does neglect affect only external personal hemispace and objects? This major question about neglect was illustrated in a clever study by Eduordo Bisiach and Claudio Luzzatti (1978) in Italy. They studied patients with neglect who had lived in the same town for most of their lives and were familiar with the city's major landmarks, especially the central piazza, which has a church, restaurants, shops, and buildings known to all the townspeople. They asked patients who showed neglect following stroke, but who had recovered from the acute symptoms, to imagine themselves in the piazza standing in a certain location, such as on the church steps, and to describe the piazza and the buildings surrounding it.

Amazingly, in their description from memory, the patients neglected things on the side of the piazza con-

Figure 12.55 Different forms of neglect correlate with dysfunction in different brain regions. **(a)** Patients with right-hemisphere subcortical lesions who show neglect of extrapersonal space faithfully copy the entire object in the ipsilesional space (the tree) but neglect to copy other items in the contralesional space **(left panel)**. Similarly, in the gap detection task **(middle panel)**, in which they are asked to place an *X* in those items with a gap and to circle those without a gap, they correctly categorize the items in the ipsilesional space but ignore those on the contralesional side of the page. These patients show hypoperfusion (reduced blood flow) centered in the inferior parietal lobule (IPL) and temporoparietal junction (TPJ) **(right panel)**. **(b)** In contrast, patients who show object-centered neglect for the contralesional side of each object copy all items in the sample picture but neglect the contralesional side of each item **(left panel)**. In the gap task **(middle panel)**, they categorize items across the sheet of paper but show a characteristic error in incorrectly categorizing items with a gap on the left as having no gap and circling them just as they do the items that actually have no gap. The reason is that they neglect the contralesional side of each object, do not detect the gap if on the left, and categorize the item as a no-gap item. These patients with object-centered neglect showed the focus of their hypoperfusion to be in the superior temporal gyrus (STG) **(right panel)**.

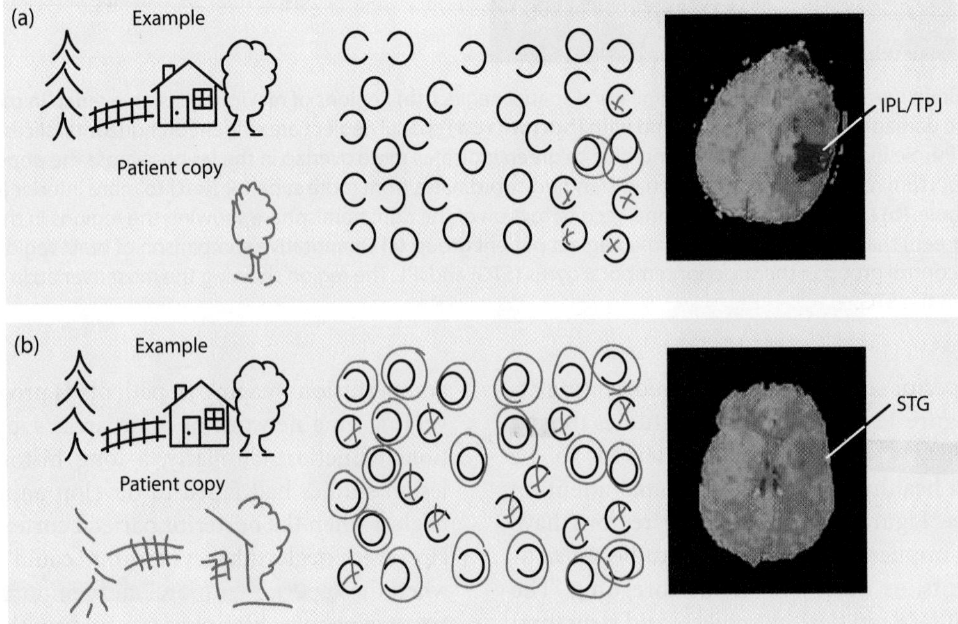

tralateral to their lesion as defined from their perspective looking out from the church steps, just as if they had actually been standing there surveying the scene. The clincher, however, is that, when the researchers asked the patients to now imagine themselves standing at the other end of the piazza, facing the other way, *toward* the church, they reported items from visual memory that they had previously neglected, and they now neglected the side of the piazza that they had previously reported!

Thus, in this striking demonstration, neglect was found not merely for items in the external sensory world, but also for items in visual memory during remembrance of a known scene (Figure 12.56). The key point is that the piazza was well known to the patients prior to the damage; thus, their neglect of buildings and objects on the side contralateral to the lesion could not be attributed to not having memories of previously neglected scenes, but rather indicated that attention to parts of the recalled images was biased by parietal damage.

SUBCORTICAL SYSTEMS AND NEGLECT

As would be expected from the imaging studies in humans and physiological studies in monkeys described earlier, attentional deficits are not limited to patients with cortical lesions. Patients with lesions of the pulvinar may also show deficits in attentional orienting. Cuing methods can be used to show that these patients have a problem with engaging attention at a cued location. This deficit in engaging attention is revealed as reaction times that are increased for both validly cued and invalidly cued targets that appear in the contralesional space. Note that this pattern differs from the pattern resulting from lesions of the inferior parietal and temporoparietal junction patients studied by Posner and colleagues, whose main deficit was greatly increased reaction times to invalid targets in the contralesional space (see Figure 12.51).

A different pattern of results was obtained in studies of patients with lesions of the midbrain, including the superior colliculus, associated with a neurological disease called progressive supranuclear palsy (PSP). These patients were slow to respond to cued targets in the direction of their orienting deficit, thus displaying a deficit in the hypothetical move operation. These patterns of reaction time deficits in the different patients can be interpreted within the predictions of the three-stage model of attention (see Figure 12.52), and therefore relate specific brain regions with specific components of the model: the inferior parietal cortex and temporoparietal junction with attentional disengagement, the midbrain with the hypothetical move operation, and the pulvinar of the thalamus with attentional engagement (Table 12.1).

The Fate of Neglected Information

We have learned that patients with unilateral brain damage can suffer from neglect, a deficit that results in an apparent loss in awareness of information presented in the visual world, as well as derived from visual memory. What happens to this neglected information? Does it fail to engage neural systems beyond the earliest visual areas? Or does the information undergo extensive processing yet remain outside of awareness?

Figure 12.56 Visual recollections of two ends of an Italian piazza by a neglect patient. The neglected side in visual memory (shaded gray) was contralateral to the side with cortical damage. The actual study was performed using the famous Piazza del Duomo in Milan.

Table 12.1 Reaction Times in Spatial Cuing Paradigm in Neglect

Lesion Site	Valid Target		Invalid Target		Deficient Attentional Operation
	Contralesional	Ipsilesional	Contralesional	Ipsilesional	
Right IPL/TPJ	Normal	Normal	Slowed	Normal	Disengage
Superior colliculus	Slowed	Normal	Normal	Normal	Move
Pulvinar of thalamus	Slowed	Normal	Slowed	Normal	Engage

Let's begin by considering a clinical observation. As we have described, neglect patients often display extinction for simultaneous bilateral stimulus presentations. Interestingly, in some cases extinction may be influenced by the object categories of the two stimuli shown to the patient. In testing visual extinction, for example, a neurologist might simultaneously present to a neglect patient two items—one in each visual field—that are the same (e.g., two forks) or different (e.g., a fork and a key). Results of such studies suggest that extinction is less severe when the two items are different than when they are the same (Figure 12.57). This finding tells us that neglect patients process information in the neglected field at least to the extent that they can detect that it is different from information in the intact field.

Many experimental studies have now shown that, despite an inability to orient to contralesional stimuli, this neglected information is highly processed. In one early example, neglect patients were shown to be highly accurate in making same–different judgments between items in the intact versus the neglected field, even when they could not identify items on the neglected side of visual hemispace (Volpe et al., 1979). Subsequent studies have replicated and extended this effect, showing that information in the neglected field is processed to a high level even when the patient is not required to make an explicit report on that information. These provocative findings suggest that information on the neglected side can be processed to the level of perceptual representation, even though it may not be accessible to the patient's awareness.

Given that information in the neglected hemispace can be processed to at least a perceptual level, it would not be surprising if that information could somehow influence the patient's performance. Indeed, this is the case. For example, in visual search tasks the presence of distracter stimuli in the more peripheral regions of the neglected, contralesional hemifield actually *helps* improve the detection of targets closer to the vertical midline but still in the neglected field (Figure 12.58).

Figure 12.57 Extinction test in a patient with neglect. When two identical items are held up in two hemifields **(a)**, the patient exhibits extinction of the item on the neglected side. When two different items are held up **(b)**, the patient exhibits less extinction.

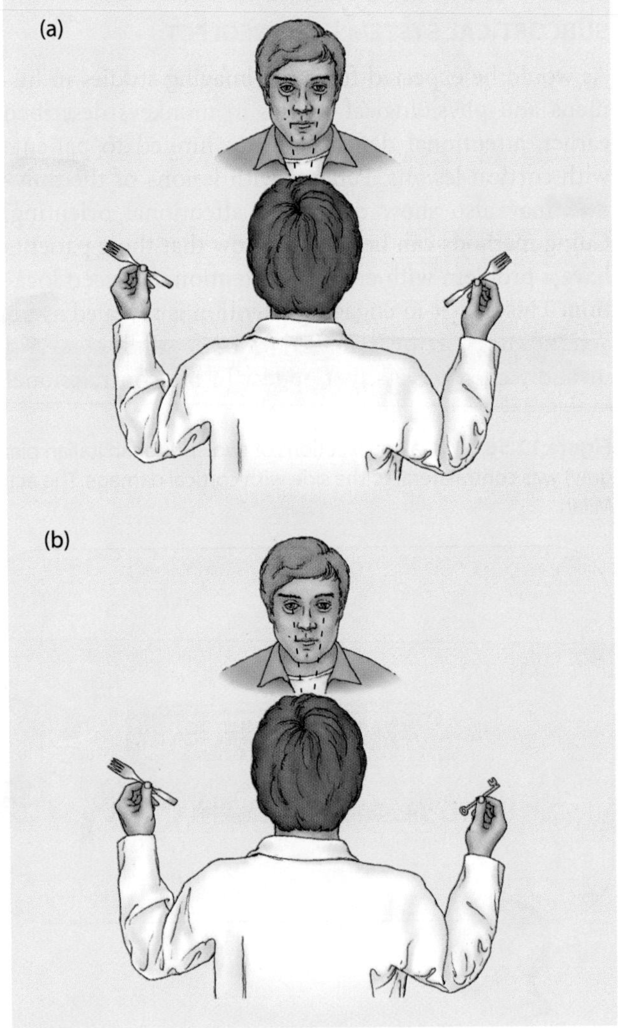

This effect was observed as a reduction in deficits induced by the presence of distracters ipsilateral to the lesion. The logic is that normally the patients are biased toward the right (for right-hemisphere lesions) and therefore neglect the left. But if distracter stimuli are presented bilaterally, the stimuli contralateral to the lesion partially attract attention to that field or, rather, reduce the asymmetrical contralateral–ipsilateral attentional bias caused by the unilateral brain damage. Targets near the visual field's midline are now more likely to be quickly detected, even when located in the neglected field (or more generally, the neglected direction). One interpretation for this finding is that, even though the targets are in the neglected field, the center of mass of the stimulus array has shifted to the direction contralateral to the lesion and thus helped the patients direct attention leftward.

In another related study, colored letters were presented to both fields. The letters were either different but of the same color, the same but of a different color, or different with different colors. The patients were required to say where the stimulus occurred, and what letter or color it was. If the color was the same when the relevant dimension was to be reported, then extinction was observed (i.e., patients failed to report the item on the neglected side). But when the letters were the same on the left and the right but the colors were different, there was no extinction. Hence, both the neglected and intact fields show normal extraction of visual feature information even if that information does not always reach awareness in the neglected regions of space. Yet we can still calculate a difference signal between contralesional and ipsilesional visual fields using the visual feature information that is unconsciously represented. As a result, patients both exhibit greater extinction for similar items in the two fields and can make same–different judgments about items in the intact versus neglected field even without knowing what exactly was in the neglected field.

The idea that information in the neglected field is processed to a high level has been extended to include the meanings of items—that is, to the level of semantic, not merely perceptual, representations. Words presented in the neglected field are processed to a semantic level even when patients are unaware of the stimuli because of their neglect. Hence, for instance, the word *doctor* in the neglected field primes associated words like *nurse* subsequently presented in the good field such that patients are faster to decide whether *nurse* is a real word versus a nonword in a lexical decision task (Ladavas et al., 1993). These types of

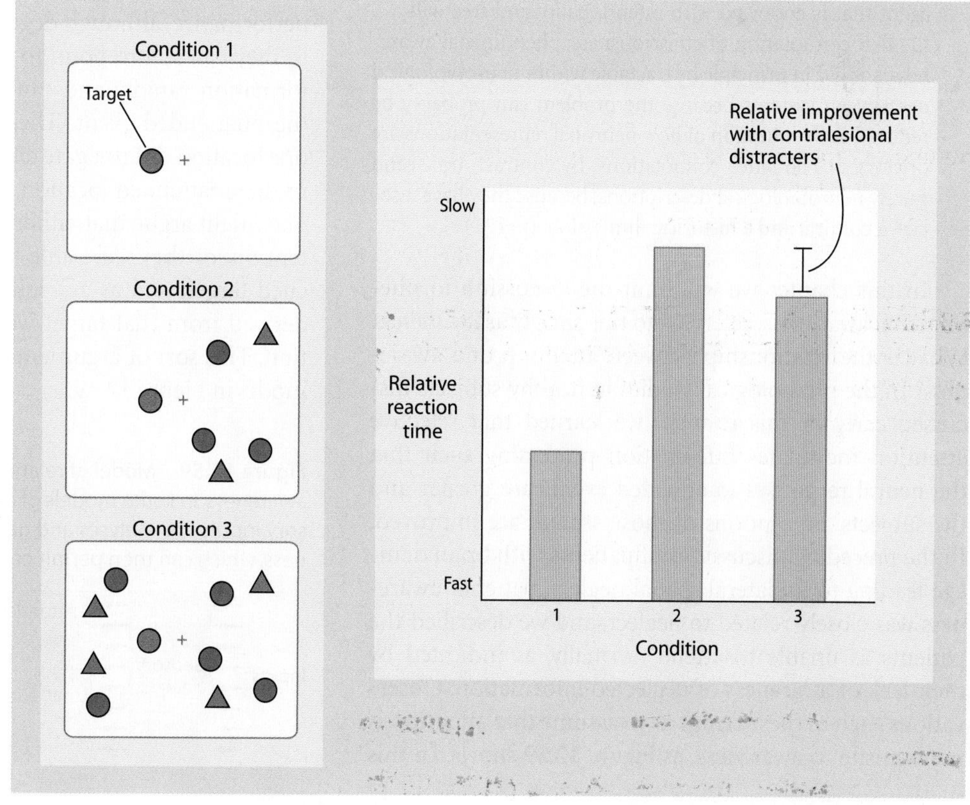

Figure 12.58 The bias toward the field ipsilateral to the lesion in unilateral neglect patients can be reduced by the presentation of target or distracter items in the neglected hemifield. This reduction in bias is indicated by the improvement in the detection of the target near the midline (i.e., in the direction of the neglected field) in the good hemifield. The logic for this effect is described in the text.

findings represent one form of evidence for **unconscious processing** resulting from damage to the brain—*unconscious* because the patients are unaware (not conscious) of it, and *processing* because these studies show that the information can influence behavior.

MODELS OF ATTENTION AND AWARENESS

So far, we have concentrated on the mechanisms of selective attention, and the role of attention has seemingly been closely associated with awareness. We have used the term *awareness* at various points in this chapter but have not defined it. As a first stab we can define awareness as our immediate experience of sensations and feelings. This is sometimes referred to as *phenomenal awareness* (being aware of the phenomena of sensations and feelings) which can be distinguished, in some models, from *access awareness*, a state in which it is possible to report and act on those things of which we are aware.

How does the concept of consciousness relate to awareness? Roughly, the terms are synonyms, but *consciousness*, like *awareness*, can refer to different states. German neuroscientist Wolf Singer (2000) described awareness and consciousness as follows:

> The term "consciousness" has a number of different connotations ranging from awareness of one's perceptions and sensations to self-awareness, the perception of oneself as an agent that is endowed with intentionality and free will . . . the first connotation of consciousness, phenomenal awareness, should in principle be tractable within neurobiological description systems because the problem can probably be reduced to the question of how neuronal representations are organized. The latter connotations, by contrast, transcend purely neurobiological descriptions, because they have a social, a cultural and a historical dimension. (p. 121)

In this chapter we will limit the discussion to phenomenal awareness, referring to this simply as *awareness*. What is the relationship between attention and awareness? In the physiological studies in healthy subjects discussed early in this chapter, we learned that selective attention modulates information processing such that the neural responses to attended events are greater and the subjects' perceptions of those stimuli are improved. In the preceding discussions of patients with brain damage leading to unilateral spatial neglect, patients' awareness was closely related to neglect, and we described the patients as unable to attend normally, as indicated by their lack of awareness of neglected information. Observations such as these tempt us to assume that attention is prerequisite to awareness, as Figure 12.59 shows. In this model, sensory information is processed according to its featural information, and then attention gates some information into awareness, which may then enable conscious report of the information. Most theorists, however, would not endorse such a model, as we will discuss next.

Unattended Information and Awareness

Let's consider the attention studies in healthy subjects that we described in the first part of the chapter. One of the points we made was that subjects were better at responding to and discriminating attended information in comparison to nominally unattended information. Were the subjects unaware of the information that was to be ignored? Consider the spatial cuing paradigms (see Figure 12.8); in these paradigms, the subject expects a target at the cued location and therefore covertly attends to that location, but when the target appears elsewhere the subject must still respond to it. As Figure 12.9 shows, their performance, although degraded, is still quite good. That is, they can still respond to the uncued (unattended) information rapidly and can discriminate the features of the unattended event. Therefore, in this case attending one location did not gate all information from awareness in the unattended location. But in this sort of paradigm one might argue that either the subjects divided their attention, or they were able to reorient rapidly to the uncued target; and as a result, whatever information they derived from that target was in fact mediated by attention. This sort of argument could still be in line with the model in Figure 12.59.

Figure 12.59 Model of relationship between attention and awareness. In some models of attention and awareness, sensory inputs are analyses and gated by attention into awareness, which can then permit conscious report.

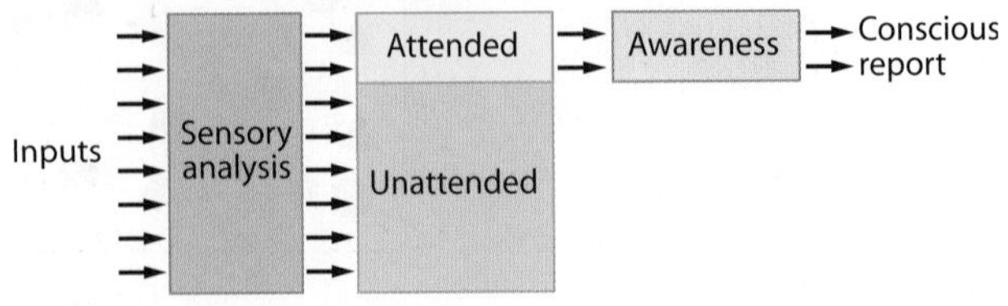

Physiological studies can help us gain more insight into this issue because we can ask subjects to totally ignore stimuli at the unattended location, because the unattended stimuli can be completely irrelevant to the task. In this type of work, the physiological measures (ERPs and fMRI) provide an index of attentional processing. We can show that the unattended information still evokes neural responses, albeit of reduced amplitude (see Figure 12.16). We would interpret this sort of information as evidence that the brain responded to the unattended stimuli, but in most such studies we do not know that those stimuli were represented in awareness, or that they produced any influence on information processing.

Using so-called **flanker paradigms**, it is possible to show that completely ignored information can influence the processing of attended information by producing interference. For example, one can measure the reaction time to discriminate target letters at fixation in the presence of distracting letters located next to the target location. The target letters require one response (right-hand button press) when, for example, they are the letter *A*, but another response (left hand) when the letter is *E*. The reaction time to make these responses can be compared when the nearby distracter letters are the same (congruent) as the targets on that trial, or signal a response opposite the response signaled by the target letter (incongruent), or are neutral (e.g., a series of *X*s). In this type of study in the 1970s, Charles Eriksen and his colleagues at the University of Illinois at Urbana-Champaign (Eriksen & Eriksen, 1971) showed that reaction times to the target letters were slowed when the distracters were incongruent, as compared to congruent or neutral. This finding makes it clear that the unattended information can influence the processing of attended information. But in such studies, the extent to which the subjects were aware of the unattended information is also not typically assessed.

In a similar vein, we can consider the evidence from work in patients described in the preceding section. There we relayed that neglected (unattended) information (e.g., in the contralesional hemispace) was not available to awareness in the patients. In the most severe cases, portions of the patients' own bodies might even be neglected (see Figure 12.47). Still, we also learned that neglected information was processed to a fairly high level, including semantic levels of encoding. This finding again indicates that attention and awareness are linked. But does this tell us that attention gates information into awareness?

Unconscious Processing and Attention

One distinction that we might want to add to the model shown in Figure 12.59 is that of conscious and unconscious processing. Indeed, most of the processing that goes on in the brain can be considered unconscious. For example, we are not aware of the analyses that take place in the retina, lateral geniculate, and perhaps V1 of the visual pathways. Or, to put it another way, we are not aware of the extraction of luminance, spatial frequency, or contrast information in the visual scene. Nor are we directly aware of a host of visual processes that may ultimately lead to our visual percepts and visual awareness. This is no mystery, although it is interesting.

Models of attention typically include a fast, parallel, preattentive stage of sensory analysis that is followed by a limited-capacity attentional stage, the output of which may result in awareness. We can modify our model of attention and awareness, then, to take this into consideration (Figure 12.60). Such a model parses processing rather early into conscious processing (that which is accessible to awareness) and unconscious processing (that which is not accessible to awareness), with attention operating later to influence how conscious information can be perceived, encoded, reported, and acted upon.

One way to investigate the role of attention in awareness is to make use of paradigms in which attended stimuli might or might not be perceived. For example, René Marois, Do-Joon Yi, and Marvin Chun (2004) investigated the neural correlates of unconscious stages of processing from later attention-dependent stages of analysis and related these to the awareness of visual inputs. They used the attentional blink paradigm. The *attentional blink paradigm* uses the rapid serial visual presentation (RSVP—approximately 10 items per second) of target and distracter stimuli under single- or dual-task conditions.

In the single-task condition, the subjects are asked to detect a single target in the RSVP display. In the dual-task condition, they are assigned the detection of two targets in the display. The time between the first target (T1) and the second target (T2)—the "lag"—can be varied from a few hundred milliseconds to over 1 s or more. Under dual-task conditions, performance in detecting the T2 stimulus is reduced when T1 must also be detected, but only when the lag between T1 and T2 is short (e.g., 500 ms). This pattern of effects is known as the attentional blink, the *blink* being the loss in the ability to detect the T2 stimulus during a short window after the attended T1 (by comparison, in the single-task case the T1 is not attended but T2 must be detected).

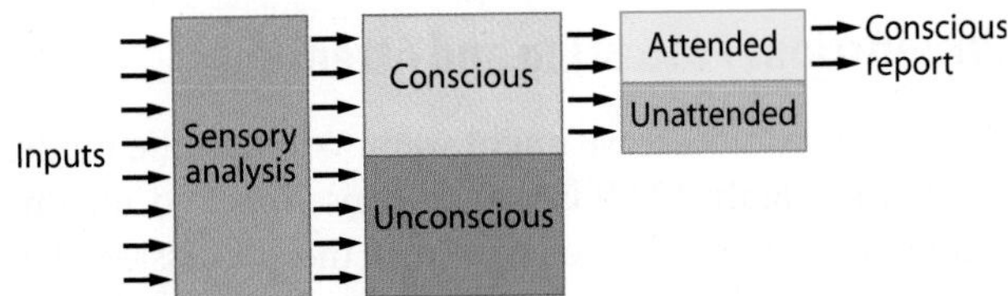

Figure 12.60 Model of the relationship between attention and awareness that incorporates conscious and unconscious processing. In this model, attention does not control access to awareness; rather, access to awareness is determined at a preattentive stage, with attention acting subsequently to bias the processing of information available to awareness.

Marois and colleagues used faces as the T1 stimulus and scenes as the T2 stimulus in their design (Figure 12.61), and they conducted fMRI scanning to reveal the brain regions and activities related to the attentional blink and awareness of the targets. They found that, under dual-task conditions, when the T2 targets (scenes) were detected, the parahippocampal place area (PPA) was activated. Interestingly, the PPA was also activated to T2 scenes that were not perceived (not correctly detected—misses in the task). In contrast, in the lateral frontal cortex and anterior cingulate gyrus, the responses were more selective: Responses in frontal cortex were larger for T2 targets that the subjects consciously perceived, and similarly reduced to the targets that were not perceived or not presented (Figure 12.62). These findings distinguish between regions of the brain that are driven primarily by the physical features of the stimulus (PPA) and brain regions whose activity reflects visual awareness (frontal cortex).

Subliminal, Preconscious, and Conscious Processing

The work of Marois and colleagues described in the preceding section points out the interactions of bottom-up stimulus influences and top-down attentional constraints in awareness. In a recent model, Stanislas Dehaene and his colleagues (2006) in France laid out how stimulus salience (defined by a combination of stimulus strength and information availability) and top-down voluntary attentional control interact to produce different degrees of brain activation, and subsequently to produce states of awareness. These different brain states can be describe in a tripartite model (Figure 12.63) that includes

1. **Subliminal processing**—that is, brain activity evoked by a stimulus below the threshold for awareness. When processing is subliminal, the information is inaccessible to awareness.
2. **Preconscious processing**, the brain state in which stimulus-driven activity is strong enough to generate

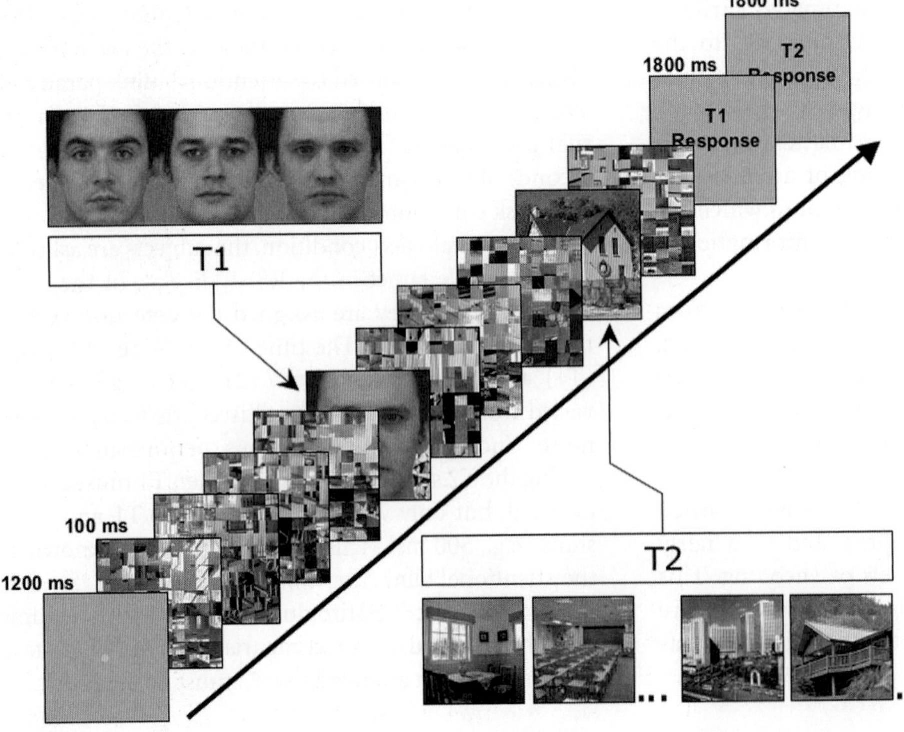

Figure 12.61 Attentional blink paradigm used in dual-task and single-task conditions. In the dual-task condition, subjects searched for a face target (T1) and a scene target (T2) presented in a rapid-serial-visual-presentation (RSVP) stream of scrambled distracter scenes. The stimulus onset asynchrony between T1 and T2 varied. The single-task experiment was identical to that shown here, but the subjects attempted to detect only the target scene. Insets show the three face targets and examples of both indoor and outdoor scene targets.

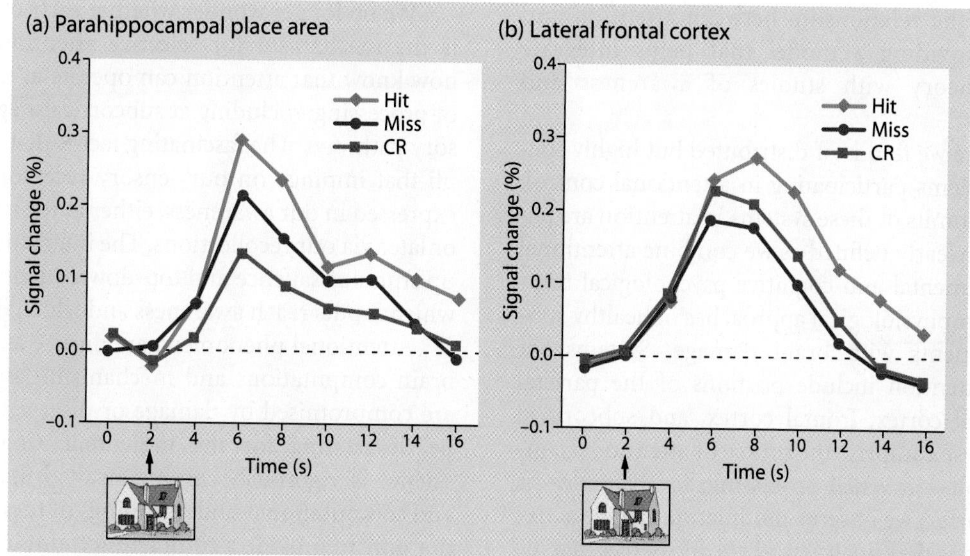

Figure 12.62 Hemodynamic responses from parahippocampal place area and lateral frontal cortex in the attentional blink paradigm. **(a)** Responses in the PPA were robust for correctly detected T2 targets (scenes) whether the scene was correctly detected (hit) or not (miss). Responses in the PPA when the subjects correctly indicated that there was no scene target (correct rejections, labeled "CR") were reduced. **(b)** In contrast, in the lateral frontal cortex the fMRI responses were different for correctly detected T2 targets (hits) and those that were missed and trials where no scene target was presented.

significant sensory processing, but in the absence of top-down attention to amplify the signal, it does not reach the threshold for awareness.

3. **Conscious processing** (awareness), which occurs when stimulus salience is sufficiently strong *and* the signals are amplified by top-down attention such that they exceed the threshold for awareness.

Such a model fits well with classical models of attention and is able to describe various findings in studies of attention and awareness. To relate this model to those described earlier, note that attention is not itself sufficient to gate information into awareness (see Figure 12.59), nor is all unconscious information equivalent in whether it gains access to awareness, even with attention (see Figure 12.60). Rather, the Dehaene model points out that both stimulus factors and attentional factors must come together under the right circumstances to achieve awareness of stimulus inputs.

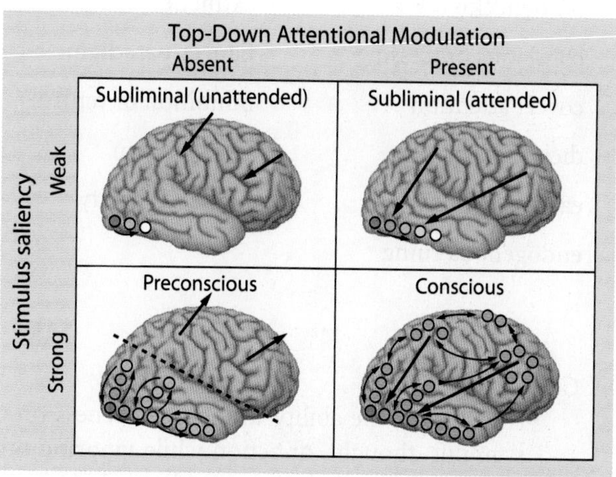

Figure 12.63 Tripartite model of attention and awareness. The dual influences of bottom-up stimulus salience and top-down attentional modulation determine whether a stimulus reaches awareness **(lower right)**.

SUMMARY

If William James and Hermann von Helmholtz were alive today, they would marvel at how much behavioral and physiological data we can provide to answer their questions about attention and awareness. Although in this chapter we did not address the whole of attention, we did look at key aspects of attentional mechanisms and examine the top-down executive systems and bottom-up stimulus-driven mechanisms that engender orienting and selection within the sensory pathways. Finally, we discussed the relationship between attention and awareness, providing a model that helps integrate attentional theory with studies of awareness and consciousness.

The picture we find is of distributed but highly specific brain systems participating in attentional control. The roles and limits of these systems in attention are becoming more clearly defined as we combine attentional theory, experimental and cognitive psychological findings, and neurophysiological approaches in healthy subjects and patients with brain damage. Systems for controlling attention include portions of the parietal lobe, temporal cortex, frontal cortex, and subcortical structures; these comprise the source of attentional control. The result—in visual processing, for example—is that, in the cortex, we observe modulations in the activity of neurons as they analyze and encode perceptual information as a function of their relevance; these areas of modulation are the sites of attentional selection.

We no longer wonder whether early or late selection is the mechanism for selective attention, because we now know that attention can operate at multiple stages of processing, including at subcortical stages of the sensory pathways. The fascinating fact is that physical stimuli that impinge on our sensory receptors may not be expressed in our awareness, either at the time they occur or later via our recollections. The interaction of bottom-up stimulus salience and top-down attention determine which inputs reach awareness and which do not.

Attentional phenomena are diverse and entail many brain computations and mechanisms, and when these are compromised by damage or disease the results can be devastating for the individual. Cognitive neuroscience is vigorously carving away at the physiological and computational underpinnings of these phenomena, not only to provide a complete account of the functioning of the healthy brain but also to shed light on how to ameliorate attentional deficits in all their forms.

KEY TERMS

Balint's syndrome
bottleneck
conscious processing
covert attention
dichotic listening
early selection
endogenous cuing
exogenous cuing
extinction
flanker paradigm
inhibition of return
late selection
limited capacity
neglect
preconscious processing
pulvinar nucleus
reflexive attention
reticular nucleus
selective attention
subliminal processing
superior colliculus
thalamic reticular nucleus
unconscious processing
unilateral spatial neglect
voluntary attention

TAKE-HOME MESSAGES

General

- Attention is the ability to focus awareness on one stimulus, thought, or action while ignoring other, irrelevant stimuli, thoughts, and actions.
- Helmholtz's studies revealed covert attention—the idea that we can attend to something without actually looking at it.
- Cherry examined the cocktail party effect, the ability to attend to a single conversation even in a noisy room full of different conversations.
- In the experimental technique of dichotic listening, the subject wears headphones and sound is presented to only one ear at a time.

Early Versus Late Attentional Processing

- According to early-selection models, a stimulus need not be completely perceptually analyzed before it can be selected for further processing or rejected as irrelevant. Broadbent proposed such a model of attention. Late-selection models hypothesize that attended and ignored inputs are processed equivalently by the perceptual system, reaching a stage of semantic (meaning) encoding and analysis.
- Our attentional system has a limited capacity; that is, it can hold only a certain amount of information online at any given time. The selection, or filtering, of information due to a limited capacity is referred to as a *processing bottleneck*.
- The difference between early- and late-selection theories has sometimes been framed by the following questions: Where does the bottleneck reside, and hence, where must selection take place? Is it at an early perceptual level or at later encoding, decision, or response levels?

Voluntary Versus Reflexive Attention

- Attention involves both top-down (voluntary), goal-directed processes and bottom-up (reflexive), stimulus-driven mechanisms.
- In experiments of voluntary attention, endogenous cuing (cuing driven by the subject's goals) is often used. Studies of reflexive attention often use exogenous cuing, where the cuing (like a flash of light) is task irrelevant.
- Voluntary attention is often thought of as a "spotlight" of attention that can move around as the person consciously desires.
- One of the hallmarks of reflexive attention is the inhibition of return—the phenomenon in which the recently reflexively attended location becomes inhibited over time such that responses to stimuli occurring there are slowed.

Visual Search

- Anne Treisman led the main investigations into the mechanisms by which we search visual space for items of interest.
- In a conjunction visual search task the target is defined by two or more stimulus features (e.g., color and shape).

Electrophysiology of Attention

- Hillyard and his colleagues discovered that auditory sensory ERPs were enlarged in amplitude when stimuli were attended compared with when they were ignored.
- Woldorff and Hillyard observed that ERPs between 20 and 50 ms after stimulus onset were different as a function of selective auditory attention. This finding, the P20–50 effect, named for its positive polarity and latency of occurrence, 20–50 ms, after stimulus onset), provided extremely compelling evidence in support of early-selection models. The brain region most likely involved in this effect is the auditory cortex in Heschl's gyrus.
- Attentional modulation in the visual ERPs begins as early as 70 to 90 ms after stimulus onset. This attention effect is seen in an ERP component known as the occipital P1, the first major positive wave.
- Experimental work has established that the N2pc component is a sign of the covert focusing of visual attention, and that it represents a stage of processing that occurs before the completion of object recognition.

Neuroimaging of Attention

- Spatial attention influences the processing of visual inputs: Attended stimuli produce greater neural responses than do ignored stimuli, and this happens in multiple visual cortical areas.
- Extrastriate cortical regions specialized for the perceptual processing of color, form, or motion can be modulated during visual attention to the individual stimulus features.
- Highly focused spatial attention can modulate activity in the visual system in the subcortical relay nuclei in the thalamus, thereby providing strong evidence for early-selection models of attention.
- A network including the pulvinar nucleus of the thalamus, the posterior parietal cortex, and the dorsolateral and superior prefrontal cortex mediate cortical excitability in the visual cortex as a function of selective attention.
- In addition to the frontoparietal attention network for voluntary spatial attention, other networks have been identified that play a role in attentional processing. For example, when a person is selectively attending a region of space, if a relevant stimulus appears somewhere else a more ventral set of brain areas has been described that include the temporoparietal junction and lateral inferior frontal cortex.

Animal Studies of Attentional Mechanisms

- Single-unit recordings and lesion studies in animals have shown that subcortical and cortical brain areas are involved in various aspects of attentional control and selection.
- Neurons in cortical areas such as the frontal and parietal cortex are sensitive to attentional processes, and they appear to play a role in coding the locations of behaviorally relevant stimuli and in coordinating shifts of attention, in conjunction with subcortical networks in the pulvinar and superior colliculus.

Neurology of Attention

- Balint's syndrome is a severe disturbance of spatial orientation, attention, and awareness marked by a narrowing of visual attention to the point where only one object reaches awareness at a time and the patient cannot localize the object in space.
- Balint's is an extreme example of what we all experience: a focusing of our attention such that we are consciously aware of only a small portion of the vast amount of information that enters our sensory organs at any given time.
- Unilateral spatial neglect typically results from damage to the right parietal, temporal or frontal cortices and subcortical structures, and leads to a neglect of the left-hand side of objects and the spatial world.

- A prominent feature of neglect is extinction, the failure to perceive or act on stimuli contralateral to the lesion (contralesional stimuli) when presented simultaneously with a stimulus ipsilateral to the lesion (ipsilesional stimulus).
- Neglect affects not only external personal hemispace and objects, but also internal memory for space.
- Neglect patients process information in the neglected field at least to the extent that they can detect that it is different from information in the intact field.
- Patients with lesions of the pulvinar may also show deficits in attentional orienting. Using cuing methods, these patients can be shown to have a problem engaging attention at a cued location.
- A different pattern of results was obtained in studies involving patients with lesions of the midbrain, including the superior colliculus, due to the neurological disease progressive supranuclear palsy. These patients were slow to respond to cued targets in the direction of their orienting deficit, thus displaying a deficit in the hypothetical move operation.

Awareness and Consciousness

- Most of the processing that goes on in the brain is considered to be unconscious.
- Phenomenal awareness is the awareness of the phenomenon of sensations and feelings. Access awareness is a state in which it is possible to report and act on those things of which we are aware.
- Using flanker paradigms, we can show that completely ignored information can influence the processing of attended information by producing interference.
- Subliminal processing is defined as brain activity evoked by a stimulus that is below the threshold for awareness. When processing is subliminal, the information is inaccessible to awareness.
- Preconscious processing is the brain state in which stimulus-driven activity is strong enough to generate significant sensory processing, but in the absence of top-down attention to amplify the signal it does not reach the threshold for awareness.
- Conscious processing (awareness) occurs when stimulus salience is sufficiently strong and the signals are amplified by top-down attention such that they exceed the threshold for awareness.

THOUGHT QUESTIONS

1. Do we perceive everything that strikes the retina? If not, does something interfere with vision? What might be the fate of stimuli that we do not perceive but that nonetheless stimulate our sensory receptors?
2. Are the same brain mechanisms involved when we focus our intention voluntarily as when our attention is captured by a sensory event, such as a flash of light?
3. Does attention act on inputs from locations or object representations or both? If both, how are the two levels of representation related during selective attention?
4. Is neglect following brain damage a deficit in perception, attention, or awareness?
5. Compare and contrast the way attention is reflected in the activity of single neurons in visual cortex versus parietal cortex. Can these differences be mapped onto the distinction between attentional control and attentional selection?

SUGGESTED READING

Corbetta, M., & Shulman, G. L. (2002). Control of goal-directed and stimulus-driven attention in the brain. *Nature Reviews Neuroscience, 3,* 201–215.

Hillis, A. E. (2006). Neurobiology of unilateral spatial neglect. *Neuroscientist, 12,* 153–163.

Luck, S. J., Woodman, G. F., & Vogel, E. K. (2000). Event-related potential studies of attention. *Trends in Cognitive Sciences, 4,* 432–440.

Moore, T. (2006). The neurobiology of visual attention: Finding sources. *Current Opinion in Neurobiology, 16,* 1–7.

Rees, G., Kreiman, G., & Koch, C. (2002). Neural correlates of consciousness in humans. *Nature Reviews Neuroscience, 3,* 261–270.

Wolfe, J. M., & Horowitz, T. S. (2004). What attributes guide the deployment of visual attention and how do they do it? *Nature Reviews Neuroscience, 5,* 495–501.

13

Cognitive Control

The attending physician at a neurology clinic had heard many bizarre reports over the 20 years of his practice. Most of the people he had seen in his outpatient clinic had symptoms of backaches or headaches. And he had seen his share of stroke and head trauma patients, people who had suffered an acute neurological disorder that had immediately wrought dramatic changes in mental function. But this morning an unusual new patient, W.R., had come to his office accompanied by his brother. The patient recounted his life history and hit upon what he saw as his novel ailment. It was one that was unlikely to be prominent among the medical textbooks that lined the neurologist's shelves. The patient's chief complaint was that "he had lost his ego" (Knight & Grabowecky, 1995).

The neurologist observed the well-dressed man describe the previous 10 years of his life. In many ways it was typical of a young professional. Early on, W.R. had decided to become a lawyer. He described a college tenure that was focused on this goal, with intense study in a prelaw program, and a time of social indulgences—hours on the tennis court, parties, and numerous girlfriends. W.R. had been admitted to the law school of his choice and had completed the program with a solid, if not stellar, academic record. But when he earned his degree, his life suddenly seemed to change course. He no longer found himself driven to secure a job with a top law firm. Indeed, 4 years had passed and he had still not taken the bar exam or even looked for a job in the legal profession. Rather, he had been hired as an instructor at a tennis club.

The family had been extremely disturbed to see the changes in W.R.'s fortunes. After law school, they thought he was experiencing an early midlife crisis that was not atypical of the times. Many of W.R.'s peers were having second thoughts about entering the mainstream of American life, and the family only hoped that either he would find satisfaction in his passion for tennis or he would eventually resume his pursuit of a career in law. But as time passed, it became more and more difficult to tolerate the changes. W.R. seemed to drift along. He was unable to support himself, hitting his brother up with increasing frequency for "temporary" loans.

It was clear to the neurologist that W.R. was a highly intelligent man. Not only could W.R. clearly recount the many details of his life history, but also he was cognizant that something was amiss. He realized that he had become a burden to his family, even expressing repeatedly that he wished he could pull things together. But he simply could not get his life organized to take the necessary steps to find a job or get a place to live. W.R. had even given up playing tennis. His opponents would quickly become frustrated because, shortly after commencing a match, W.R. would project an aura of nonchalance, forgetting to keep track of the score or even whose turn it was for service.

His brother noted another radical change in W.R.'s interests. He pointed out that his brother had not been on a date for a number of years and seemed to have lost all interest in romantic pursuits. W.R. sheepishly agreed. He recalled that he had been sexually active throughout his college years and had even lived with a woman for a number of years. But now that his brother mentioned it, why yes, it was true, he had not dated anyone in years and had not even given it a second thought. It was another sign of the lost ego. W.R. had little regard for his own future, for his successes, even for his own happiness. Though aware that his life had drifted off course, he just was not able to make the plans to effect any changes.

If this had been the whole story, the neurologist might have thought that a lost ego was not something he was equipped to treat. A psychiatrist might be a better option. But W.R. had suffered a seizure during his last year in law school, after staying up all night and drinking large amounts of coffee so that he could study for a midterm exam. An extensive neurological examination at that time, including positron emission tomography (PET) and computed tomography (CT), had failed to identify the cause of the seizure. But given the claims of a lost ego and the patient's obvious distractibility, the neurologist was suspicious.

A CT scan that day confirmed his worst fears. W.R. had an astrocytoma. Not only was the tumor extremely large, but also it had followed an unusual course, traversing along the fibers of the corpus callosum so that it now extensively invaded the lateral prefrontal cortex in the left hemisphere and a considerable portion of the right frontal lobe. This tumor had very likely caused the initial seizure, even though it was not detected at the time. Over the previous 4 years, it had spread slowly.

The next day the neurologist informed the two brothers of the diagnosis. Containment of the tumor was all but impossible. They could try radiation, but the prognosis was poor: W.R. was unlikely to live more than a year. His brother was devastated. Not only did he face the loss of W.R., but also he felt guilty over the frustration he had felt and expressed in the previous 10 years. More perplexing, though, was W.R.'s response: Though his brother shed tears upon hearing the news, W.R. remained relatively passive and detached. He understood that the tumor was the culprit behind the dramatic life changes he had experienced. But there was no rage, minimal anguish, and indeed, a seeming absence of great concern. He understood the seriousness of his condition, but the news, as with so many of his recent life events, failed to evoke a clear response, a resolve to take some action. W.R.'s self-diagnosis seemed to be right on target: He had lost his ego and, with it, the ability to take command of his own life.

The study of the ego is something that would make most neuroscientists squeamish. Compared to color perception or procedural learning, it is difficult to define this concept, let alone figure out how to investigate its neural basis. Animal models seem unlikely. And yet, from W.R.'s actions, or rather nonactions, we can distill a sense of an essential aspect of having an ego. W.R. had lost the ability to engage in goal-oriented behavior. He could handle the daily chores required to groom and feed himself, although even here he had needed the financial assistance of his family. But these actions were performed without the context of an overriding goal. He was not getting up in the morning, brushing his teeth, and eating breakfast so that he would be full of energy, ready to tussle in the legal system. He had few plans beyond satisfying his immediate needs, and even these seemed minimal. He could step back and see that things were not going as well for him as others hoped, but on a day-to-day basis, the signals that he was not making progress just seemed to pass him by.

In this chapter, our focus turns to the more complex aspects of cognition. We will consider the processes that are essential for goal-oriented behavior, the behaviors that allow us to interact in the world in a purposive manner. As we will see, there are many challenges to the successful completion of **goal-oriented behavior**. We must formulate a plan of action, one that draws on our past experiences yet is tailored to the current environment. Such actions must be flexible and adaptive. The best route from the dorm room to the eatery might be blocked by a construction project, but a highly evolved system like a hungry college student will still succeed in getting to dinner. To switch from one plan to another requires a means for monitoring the success of our ongoing actions. These operations are commonly referred to as **cognitive control**, based on the idea that their operation controls and regulates information processing across the brain. The study of cognitive control brings us to the part of the cerebral cortex that has received little attention in the preceding chapters—the prefrontal cortex.

SUBDIVISIONS OF THE FRONTAL LOBES

The frontal lobes comprise about a third of the cerebral cortex in humans (Figure 13.1). The posterior border with the parietal lobe is marked by the central sulcus, the only sulcus that extends the entire length of the brain's lateral surface and down along the medial surface. The frontal

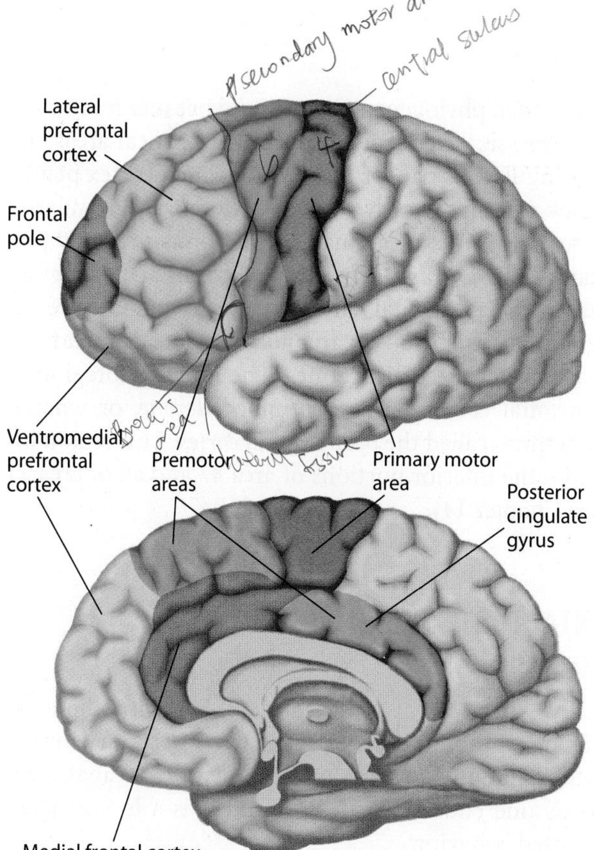

Figure 13.1 Areas of the frontal lobe. The prefrontal cortex includes all of the areas in front of the primary and secondary motor areas. The four subdivisions of prefrontal cortex are the lateral prefrontal cortex, ventromedial prefrontal cortex, frontal pole, and medial frontal cortex.

and temporal lobes are separated by the lateral fissure. Though the frontal cortex is present in all mammalian species, it has undergone tremendous expansion in human evolution, especially in the most anterior aspects. Since the development of functional capabilities parallels phylogenetic trends, the frontal lobe's expansion is related to the emergence of capabilities associated with cognition.

The most posterior part of the frontal lobe is the primary motor cortex (area 4), encompassing the gyrus in front of the central sulcus and extending into the central sulcus itself. Anterior and ventral to area 4 are the secondary motor areas, including the lateral premotor cortex and supplementary motor area (area 6), the frontal eye field (area 8), Broca's area (area 44), and the posterior portion of the cingulate cortex. The remainder of the frontal lobe is termed the *prefrontal cortex.* The prefrontal cortex includes half of the entire frontal lobe in humans. The ratio is considerably smaller for nonprimate species (Figure 13.2). Interestingly, when compared to other primate species, the expansion of prefrontal cortex in the human brain is more pronounced in the white matter (the axonal tracts) than in the gray matter (the cell bodies; Schoenemann et al., 2005).

Prefrontal cortex constitutes a massive network that links the brain's motor, perceptual, and limbic regions (Goldman-Rakic, 1995; Passingham, 1993). Extensive projections connect the prefrontal cortex to almost all regions of the parietal and temporal cortices, and even prestriate regions of the occipital cortex. Subcortical structures, including the basal ganglia, cerebellum, and various brainstem nuclei, project indirectly to the prefrontal cortex via thalamic connections. Indeed, almost all cortical and subcortical areas influence the prefrontal cortex either through direct projections or indirectly via a few synapses. The prefrontal cortex also sends reciprocal connections to most areas that project to it, and to premotor and motor areas. The prefrontal cortex has many projections to the contralateral hemisphere—not only projections to homologous prefrontal areas via the corpus callosum but also bilateral projections to premotor and subcortical regions. From these neuroanatomical considerations we can assume that the prefrontal cortex is in an excellent position to

Figure 13.2 The extent of prefrontal cortex in six species, as indicated by the shading. Note how small this region is in the cat, dog, and squirrel monkey. It is greatly enlarged in humans. (The brains are not drawn to scale.)

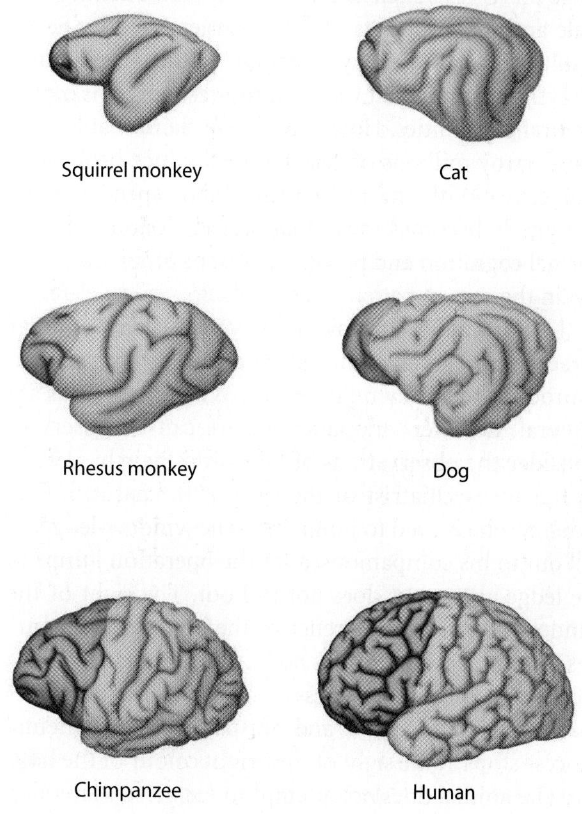

coordinate processing across wide regions of the central nervous system (CNS).

In this chapter we focus on three regions of prefrontal cortex. The first region, the **lateral prefrontal cortex**, includes areas 45 and 46, the lateral aspects of area 9, and the superior portions of area 47. The second region, the **frontal pole**, includes area 10 and the medial aspect of area 9. The third region, the **medial frontal cortex**, includes the cingulate cortex (areas 24, 25, 32) and the inferior aspects of the medial wall of areas 6 and 8—a region that is referred to as *presupplementary motor area.*

Note that the cingulate is not always included in considerations of prefrontal function, perhaps because of its older, phylogenetic history and because it lacks the granular, six-layer structure of other cortical areas. Yet the cingulate as part of the medial frontal cortex plays a major role in cognitive control. Moreover, granularity appears to be a questionable criterion, since only primates have a granular prefrontal cortex. For all other mammals, prefrontal and cingulate regions have an agranular structure—an architecture quite distinct from more posterior cortical zones. The fourth subregion of prefrontal cortex is the *ventromedial zone,* or what is sometimes called the *orbitofrontal cortex.* This region includes the inferior portions of area 47 and all of area 11 (see Chapter 14).

THE LATERAL PREFRONTAL CORTEX AND WORKING MEMORY

Patients with frontal lobe lesions present a paradox. From their everyday behavior, it is frequently difficult to detect a neurological disorder. They do not display obvious disorders in any of their perceptual abilities, and their speech is fluent and coherent. On conventional neuropsychological tests of intelligence, the patients may perform normally. For example, when matched for education and age, patients with frontal lobe lesions generally score within the normal range on IQ tests such as the Wechsler Adult Intelligence Scale and most subtests of the Wechsler Memory Scale. Results such as these may contribute to the perpetuation of myths claiming that we fail to use vast portions of our cerebral capabilities. How else can we claim that lesions that destroy millions of cells fail to produce behavioral problems? With more sensitive and specific tests, though, it becomes clear that frontal lesions disrupt normal cognition and produce a host of problems, as we saw in the case of patient W.R.

Lesion studies in animals have revealed a similar paradox. Unilateral lesions of prefrontal cortex also tend to produce relatively mild deficits. When the lesions are bilateral, however, dramatic changes can be observed. Consider the observations of Leonardo Bianchi (1922), an Italian psychiatrist of the early 20th century: "The monkey which used to jump on to the window-ledge, to call out to his companions, after the operation jumps to the ledge again, but does not call out. The sight of the window determines the reflex of the jump, but the purpose is now lacking, for it is no longer represented in the focal point of consciousness . . . Another monkey sees the handle of the door and grasps it, but the mental process stops at the sight of the bright colour of the handle. The animal does not attempt to turn it so as to open the door . . . Evidently there are lacking all those other images that are necessary for the determination of a series of movements coordinated towards one end." As with W.R., there is a loss of goal-oriented behavior.

The behavior of these monkeys underscores an important aspect of goal-oriented behavior. Following the lesions, the behavior is **stimulus driven.** The animal sees the ledge and jumps up; another grasps the door but fails to open it. What is lacking is the knowledge of how these actions have served the animal in the past. The animal acts as if it does not remember the purpose for these actions. The sight of the door is no longer a sufficient cue to remind the animal of the food and other animals that can be found in the other room. Is this deficit a motivational problem? Perhaps. The animals continue to be active, but their actions lack purpose. Alternatively, the problem could be a type of memory deficit. The animals may fail to remember the rewards that can be found in the other room.

Distinguishing Between Stored Knowledge and Activated Information

We need to distinguish between memory functions associated with the long-term storage of information and those associated with the activation of that information when it is relevant for online processing. The initial impetus for this work grew out of cognitive psychology when researchers emphasized a distinction between long-term and short-term memory. Here, too, we face a paradox. There are many dramatic demonstrations of the unbounded capacity of humans and animals to remember even the most minute details of past experiences. We can recall our first-grade classroom or recognize the face of a person only briefly encountered at a party. In contrast, sometimes when we are introduced to a person or given a new phone number, within seconds this information slips away—in one ear and out the other. (As mentioned in Chapter 8, studies of implicit learning convincingly demonstrate that the information often is not lost but is buried in the cortical abyss.) Studies of short-term memory have shown that our ability to keep information active is severely limited: We can keep track of only a few pieces of information at a time.

Short-term memory and long-term memory depend on dissociable systems. Cognitive studies have indicated that the way we represent information may shift over time. For example, when people are asked to immediately recall a visually presented list of words, memory failures are much more frequent when the list contains phonologically similar words (e.g., *man, mat, cap*) than when the list contains semantically similar words. But if the recall is delayed, the pattern of errors reverses. Now, performance is poorer for lists whose words are similar in meaning. Hence, we translate verbal information into an acoustic code immediately after its presentation, but long-term storage may be in a network that represents semantic properties.

Early work on memory dichotomies emphasized that the critical function of short-term memory was to assist in the translation of newly acquired information into a format for longer-term storage. More recent work has reconceptualized the functional role of a different form of short-term memory—what is called **working memory**. Working memory refers to transient representations of task-relevant information. These representations may be from the distant past: When returning to a high school reunion, we can anticipate what the cafeteria will look like or where our old homeroom was as we enter the front door. This knowledge had been buried deep within the recesses of our long-term memory. But as we approach the school, it is reactivated into working memory, with the representations now available to guide our actions. Representations in working memory also might be closely related to something that is currently in the environment or has been experienced recently. If we are introduced to the spouse of an old classmate, our ability to recall her name 20 minutes later will depend on bringing that information back into working memory.

The emphasis here is on how past knowledge influences and constrains current behavior. We do not process information simply so that we can put it to use later—a view that would be oriented only toward future behavior. Rather, representations are activated to shape behavior in the present. Reflecting this idea, the concept of a working memory system has surfaced as an apt characterization of processes that represent the current contents of cognition. Patricia Goldman-Rakic has called working memory the "blackboard of the mind."

Working memory is critical for animals whose behavior is not stimulus driven. What is immediately in front of us surely will influence our behavior, but we are not automatons. We can hold off eating until all the guests are sitting around the table. We can resist jumping onto the city bus that pulls over to the curb as we walk down the street. This capacity reflects the fact that, in addition to reacting to stimuli that currently dominate our perceptual pathways, we can represent information that is not immediately evident. We can mind our dinner manners or choose to respond to some stimuli while ignoring other stimuli. This process requires integrating current perceptual information with stored knowledge.

Prefrontal Cortex Is Necessary for Working Memory but Not Associative Memory

The lateral prefrontal cortex is the primary repository for the interaction between current perceptual information and stored knowledge, and thus constitutes a major component of the working memory system. A classic demonstration comes from delayed-response tasks. In the simplest version, sketched in Figure 13.3, a monkey is situated within reach of two food wells. At the start of a trial, the monkey observes the experimenter placing a food morsel in one of the two wells. Then the two wells are covered, and a curtain is lowered to prevent the monkey from reaching toward either well. After a delay period, the curtain is raised and the monkey is allowed to choose one of the two wells and recover the food. Although this appears to be a simple task, it demands one critical cognitive capability: The animal must continue to represent the location of the unseen food during the delay period. Monkeys with lesions of the lateral prefrontal cortex do poorly on the task.

This inability does not imply a general deficit in forming associations. In an experiment to test associative memory, the food wells are covered with distinctive visual cues: One cue is associated with the food location and the other with the position of the empty well. In this condition, the food morsel's location may be shifted during the delay period, but the visual cue also will be relocated so that it continues to cover the food. Prefrontal lesions do not disrupt performance in this task.

These two tasks clarify the concept of working memory (Goldman-Rakic, 1992). In the **delayed-response task** (see Figure 13.3a), no explicit cue remains constant from one trial to the next. In half of the trials, the food is

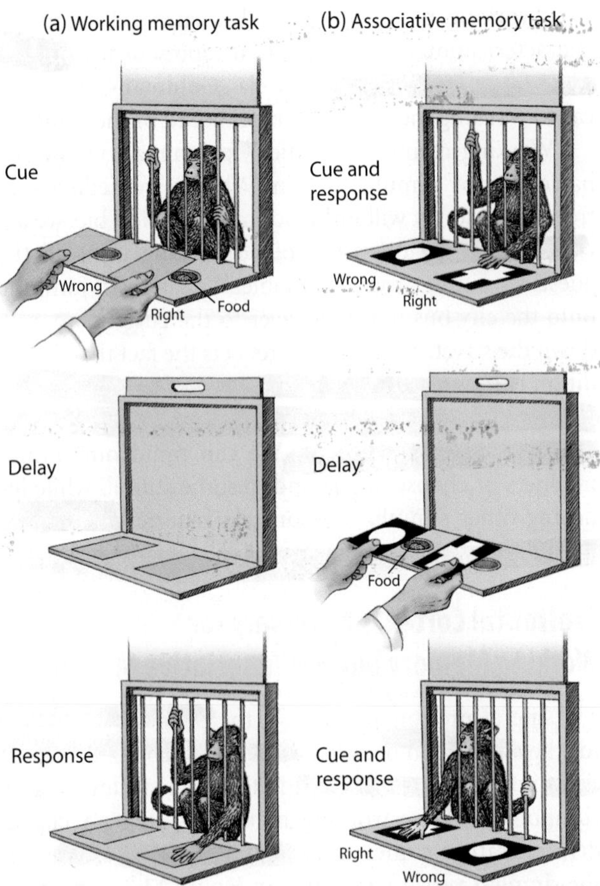

Figure 13.3 Monkeys with prefrontal lesions demonstrate selective impairment on the delayed-response task. **(a)** In the working memory task, the monkey observes one well being baited with food. After a delay period, the animal retrieves the food. The location of the food is determined randomly. **(b)** In the associative memory task, the food reward is always associated with one of the two visual cues. The location of the cues (and food) is determined randomly. Working memory is required in the first task because, at the time the animal responds, no external cues indicate the location of the food. Long-term memory is required in the second task because the animal must remember which visual cue is associated with the reward.

placed in the left well; in the other half, the right well is baited. Thus, there is no bias for either side to become associated with the reward over the long term. Rather, the associations fluctuate from trial to trial and the animal must remember the currently baited location during the delay period. In contrast, in the associative learning condition (see Figure 13.3b), it is necessary only that the visual cue reactivate a long-term association of which cue is associated with the reward. The reappearance of the two visual cues can trigger recall and guide the animal's performance.

Prefrontal lesions do not disrupt recognition memory. In another experiment, monkeys are shown three objects and allowed to select one. A curtain is lowered, and the experimenter quickly rearranges the display. In the working memory condition, two objects are presented, one of which was just selected. The monkey is rewarded for choosing the other object. In the recognition memory condition, the previously selected object is again presented, but now it is paired with a novel object. The animal is rewarded for choosing the novel object. In both conditions, then, the animal is rewarded for picking a previously unselected object.

Despite this similarity, animals with lesions that encompassed areas 46 and 9 of the dorsolateral prefrontal cortex had selectively impaired working memories. As a group, their performance was barely above the level of chance. In the recognition memory task, this group performed as well as control subjects. Here, it was sufficient to recognize that one object was novel—or that the other was familiar. In the working memory condition, both objects were familiar and the animal had to keep track of which had been previously selected. An important control in this study was the inclusion of animals who received frontal lesions in the vicinity of areas 6 and 8. These animals performed as well as the control animals on both versions of the task.

Humans also display frontal involvement in working memory. Adele Diamond of the University of Pennsylvania (1990) pointed out that a common marker of conceptual intelligence, Piaget's Object Permanence Test, is logically similar to the delayed-response task. In this task, a child observes the experimenter hiding a reward in one of two locations. After a delay of a few seconds, the child is encouraged to find the reward. Children younger than 1 year are unable to accomplish this task. At this age, the frontal lobes are still maturing. Diamond maintained that the ability to succeed in tasks such as the Object Permanence Test parallels the development of the frontal lobes. Prior to this development, the child acts as though the object is "out of sight, out of mind." As the frontal lobes mature, the child can be guided by representations of objects and no longer depends on their presence.

Tasks similar to the ones used with animals do not sufficiently elicit deficits in adult human subjects. To challenge adults, a variant of the delayed-response task, the delayed-alternation task, is used. Here, a correct response requires the subject to choose the location opposite that of the previously reinforced one. Patients with frontal lesions have difficulty with this task, especially if the lesions are bilateral.

Physiological Correlates of Working Memory

How is information activated and maintained in working memory? In Chapter 8 we described the critical role of the hippocampus in forming long-term memories. The idea was that the hippocampus operates as a consolidation device, strengthening connections between conceptual and perceptual processing centers so that further experiences with similar stimuli produce more efficient activation and thus facilitate recognition. In the working memory tasks just described, it is not enough for a stimulus to be recognized; subjects need to retain a record of its relevance, regardless of whether it pertained to the task at hand.

Two conditions are sufficient for a working memory system: First, it should have a mechanism to access stored information; second, there should be a way to keep the information active. The prefrontal cortex can perform both operations. Clues to the neural basis for working memory have been provided by single-cell recordings in the lateral prefrontal cortex. Recall that, in the delayed-response task, the animal first is shown a cue, the placing of a food morsel in one of two food wells. This cue is followed by a delay during which the animal is prevented from viewing the food wells. The occluding blind is then removed, and the animal tries to retrieve the morsel. Cells in the prefrontal cortex such as the ones recorded in Figure 13.4 become active during this task and show sustained activity throughout the delay period (Fuster, 1989). Indeed, for some cells activation does not commence until after the delay begins and can be maintained up to 1 minute. These cells, then, provide a neural correlate for keeping active a representation after the triggering stimulus is no longer visible. The cells provide a continuous record of the response required for the animal to obtain the reward.

Earl Miller and his colleagues at the Massachusetts Institute of Technology have conducted a series of experiments to determine the specificity of prefrontal neurons (Rao et al., 1997). Do prefrontal neurons simply provide a generic signal that supports representations in other cortical areas, or do the neurons code specific stimulus features? To look at this question, monkeys were trained on a working memory task that required successive coding of two stimulus attributes: identity and location. The sequence of events in each trial is depicted in Figure 13.5a. A sample stimulus is presented, and the animal must remember the identity of this object for a 1-s delay period in which the screen is blank. Then two objects are shown, one of which matches the sample. The position of the matching stimulus indicates the target location for a forthcoming response. However, this response must be withheld until the end of a second delay. Within the lateral prefrontal cortex, cells characterized as "what," "where," and "what–where" were observed. For example, "what" cells responded to specific objects, and this response was sustained over the delay period (Figure 13.5b). "Where" cells showed selectivity to certain locations (Figure 13.5c). In addition, about half of the cells were "what–where" cells, responding to specific combinations of "what" and "where" information. A cell of this type exhibited an increase in firing rate during the first delay period when the target was the preferred stimulus. Moreover, the same cell continued to fire during the

Figure 13.4 Prefrontal neurons can show sustained activity during delayed-response tasks. Each line here represents a single trial. The cue indicated the location for a forthcoming response. The monkey was trained to withhold the response until a "Go" signal (arrows) appeared. Each vertical tick represents an action potential. This cell did not respond during the cue interval. Rather, its activity increased when the cue was turned off, and persisted until the response.

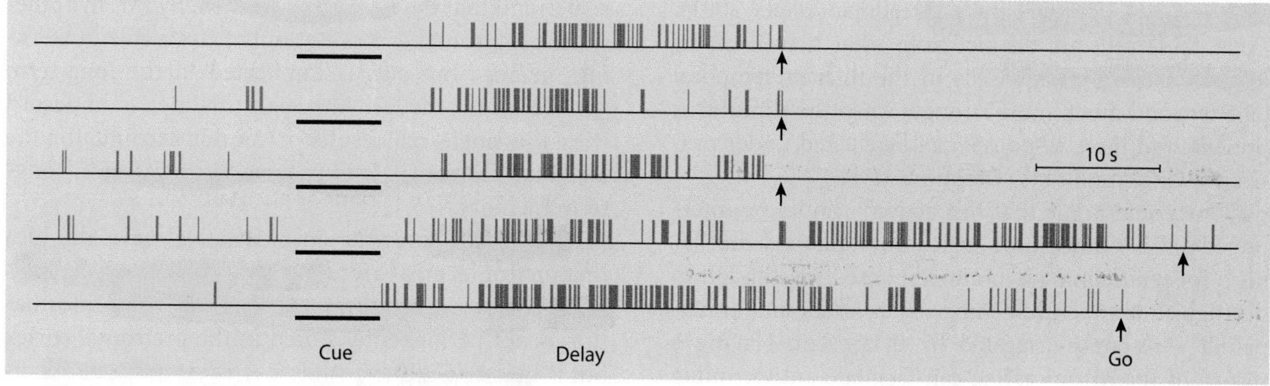

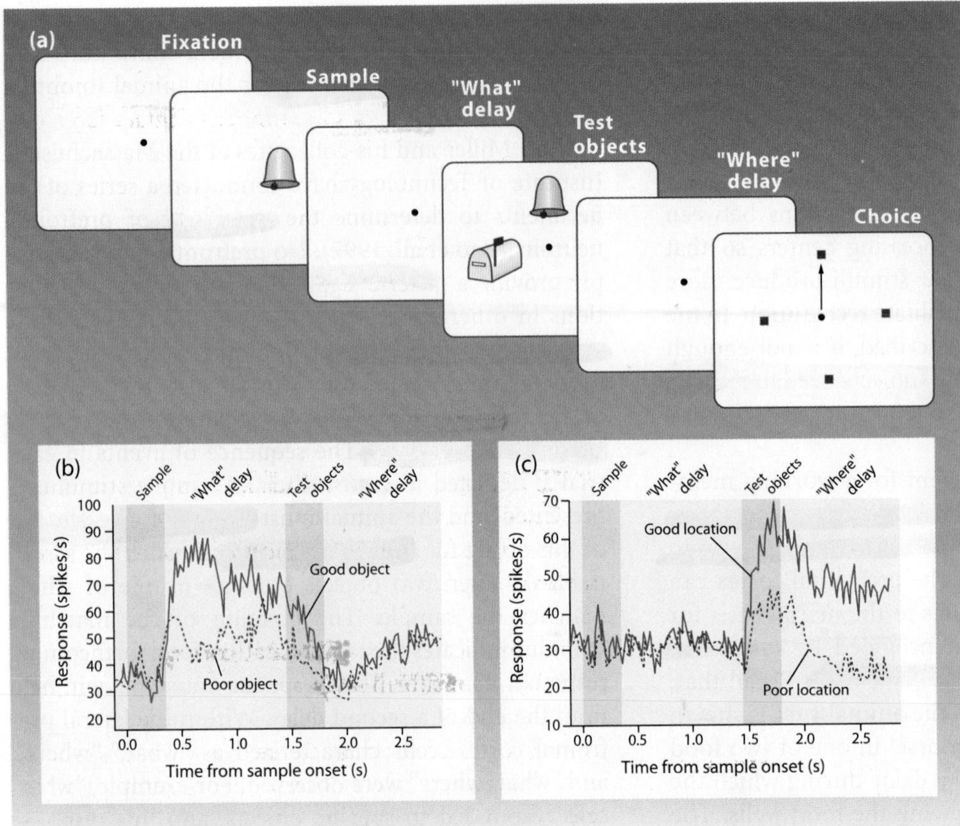

Figure 13.5 Coding of "what" and "where" information in single neurons of the prefrontal cortex in the macaque. **(a)** Sequence of events in a single trial. See text for details. **(b)** Firing profile of a neuron that shows a preference for one object over another during the "what" delay. The neural activity is low once the response location is cued. **(c)** Firing profile of a neuron that shows a preference for one location. This neuron was not activated during the "what" delay.

second delay period if the response was directed to a specific location.

These results indicate that cells in the prefrontal cortex exhibit selectivity in terms of stimulus attributes. Such selectivity is task specific. In these studies, the cell activity is dependent on the monkey's using that information to obtain a response. If the animal is required simply to passively view the stimuli, the response of these cells is minimal right after the stimulus is presented and entirely absent during the delay period. Moreover, the response of these cells is malleable. If the task conditions change, the same cells become responsive to a new set of stimuli (Freedman et al., 2001). Thus, these cells are distinct from what is seen in the ventral visual pathway. Cells in the inferior temporal lobe respond much more strongly when the stimulus is present, and these responses can be elicited under passive viewing conditions (Desimone, 1996).

One could argue that this activity should be interpreted not as a mnemonic device, but rather as a mechanism for maintaining a motor response. It is difficult to distinguish between remembering an event and anticipating a response triggered by that event. Having a record of recent processing can facilitate an upcoming action. Yet these cells are more closely linked to memory than to motor processes, because their activity is modified by past experience. Fewer sustained responses are observed in an untrained animal, even though the animal will respond on every trial. As the animal becomes skilled in using the cue to guide performance, the activity during the delay period becomes more pronounced. Sustained activity cannot be attributed to arousal. Some cells are activated after one cue; others fire more after the other cue appears.

Cellular responses like these could indicate that long-term representations are stored in the prefrontal cortex and that the cues activate them. By this hypothesis, the prefrontal cortex not only plays a role in working memory but also is implicated in the long-term storage of knowledge. Although this idea is in accord with the single-cell results, it cannot account for the fact that prefrontal lesions have little effect on long-term memory.

Figure 13.6 presents an alternative view: the idea that prefrontal areas are a temporary repository for representations accessed from other neural sites. Information is not permanently stored in the prefrontal cortex but is maintained there while it is relevant for perform-

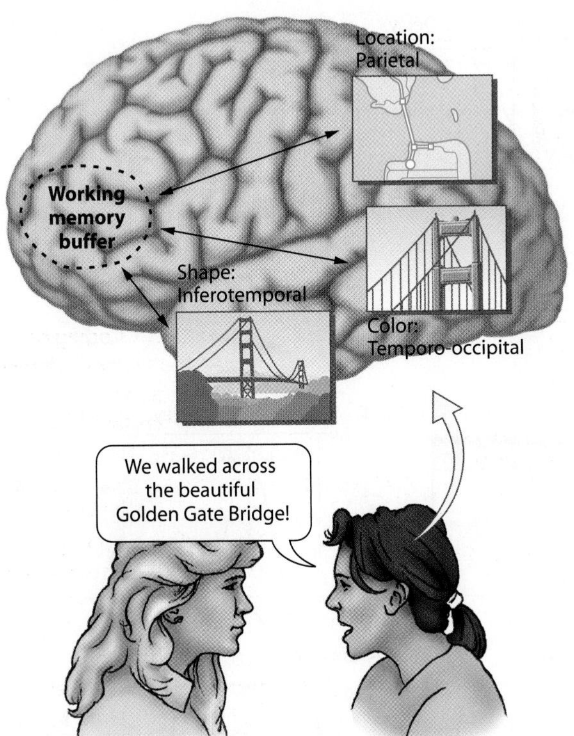

Figure 13.6 Lateral prefrontal cortex may provide a transient buffer for sustaining information stored in other cortical regions. In this example, the woman on the right is telling a friend about her walk across the Golden Gate Bridge during a visit to San Francisco. Long-term knowledge is reactivated and temporarily maintained through the reciprocal connections between the prefrontal cortex and the more posterior regions of the cortex. Note that the long-term memories of the Golden Gate Bridge are stored in dimension-specific cortical regions.

ing a task. This hypothesis jibes nicely with the fact that the prefrontal cortex is connected intimately with post-sensory regions of the temporal and parietal cortices. When a stimulus is perceived, a temporary representation is instantiated in the prefrontal cortex via these connections to posterior brain regions. The sustained activation of prefrontal cells probably requires continuous reverberation across this network.

This hypothesis has been examined in many functional-imaging studies over the past 15 years; indeed, working memory has been one of the favorite topics in the fMRI literature, in part because the tasks tend to extend over many seconds and thus are amenable to the relatively sluggish BOLD response and because humans can readily learn to perform delayed-response tasks—something that can be quite challenging to teach a monkey. In one representative study, a variant of a delayed-response task was employed (Figure 13.7a). On each trial, four stimuli were presented successively for 1 s each during an encoding interval. The stimuli were either intact faces or scrambled faces. The participants were instructed to remember only the faces. Thus, by varying the number of intact faces presented during the encoding interval, the processing demands on working memory were manipulated. After an 8-s delay, a face stimulus, the probe, was presented and the participant had to decide if the probe matched one of the faces presented during the encoding period. The BOLD response in the lateral prefrontal cortex, bilaterally, began to rise with the onset of the encoding period and was maintained across the delay period even though the screen was now blank (Figure 13.7b). This prefrontal response was sensitive to the demands on working memory, with the sustained response during the delay period greater when the person had to remember three or four intact faces compared to just one or two intact faces.

By using faces, the experimenters could also compare activation in the prefrontal cortex with that observed in the fusiform face area, the inferotemporal lobe region that was discussed in Chapter 6. The BOLD responses for these two regions are shown in Figure 13.7c, with the data combined over the different memory loads. When the stimuli are presented, either during the encoding phase or to the probe, the BOLD response is much stronger in the FFA than in the prefrontal cortex. As noted already, the prefrontal response remains high across the delay period. Although there is a substantial drop in the FFA response, the drop is not to baseline, suggesting that this area continues to be active during the delay period. In fact, the BOLD response in other perceptual areas of the inferotemporal cortex actually goes below baseline—the so-called rebound effect. Thus, although the sustained response is small in the FFA, it is considerably higher than what would be observed with nonfacial stimuli.

The timing of the peak activation in the prefrontal cortex and the FFA is also intriguing. During encoding, the peak response is slightly earlier in the FFA compared to the prefrontal cortex. In contrast, during memory retrieval the peak response is slightly earlier in the prefrontal cortex. Although this study does not allow us to make causal inferences, the results are consistent with the general tenets of the model sketched in Figure 13.6. In this experiment, lateral prefrontal cortex serves as a working memory buffer for faces and, through its links to inferotemporal cortex, helps maintain representations of the stimuli studied during the delay period that can be compared to the probe stimulus.

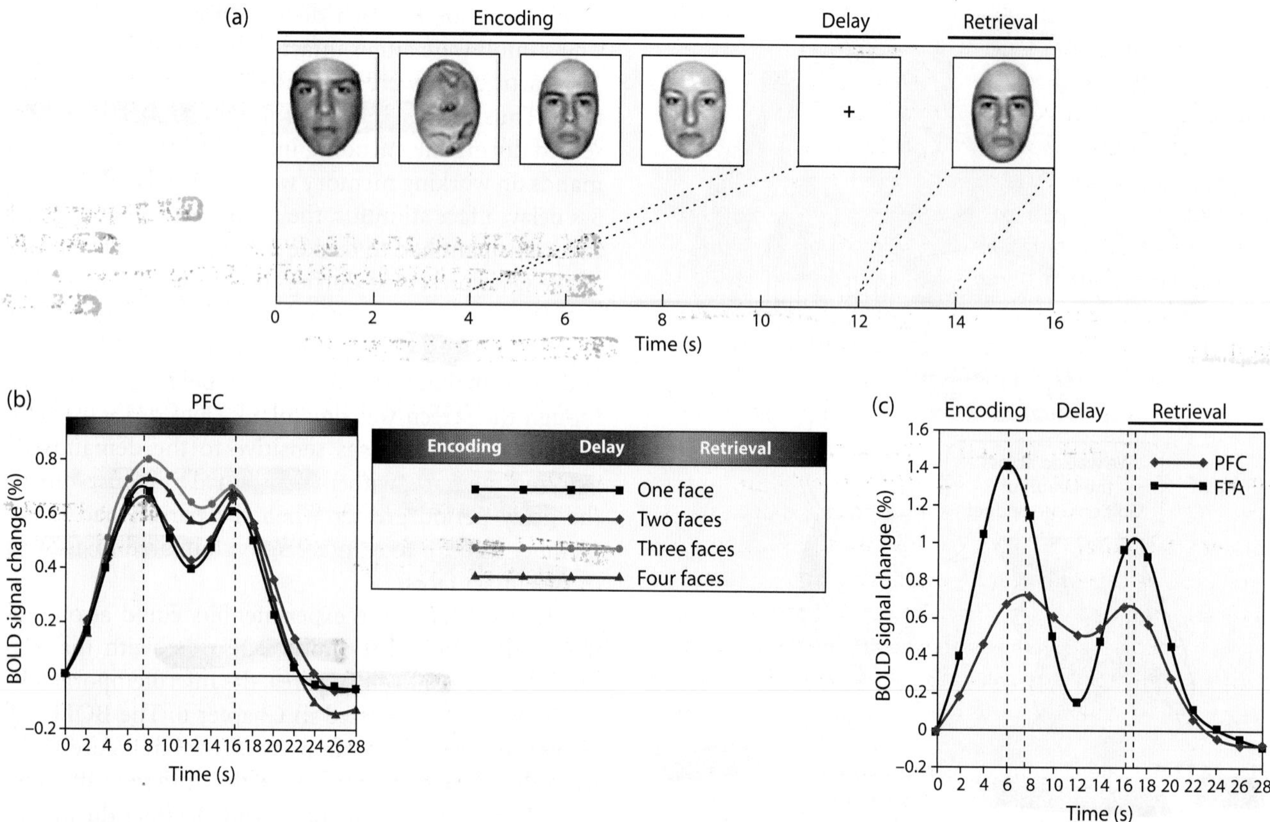

Figure 13.7 Functional-MRI study of working memory. **(a)** In a delayed-response task, a set of intact faces or scrambled faces is presented during an encoding period. After a delay period, a probe stimulus is presented and the subject indicates if that face was part of the memory set. **(b)** The BOLD response in lateral prefrontal cortex (PFC) rises during the encoding phase and remains high during the delay period. The magnitude of this effect is related to the number of faces that must be maintained in working memory. **(c)** The BOLD response in the lateral prefrontal cortex and the fusiform face area (FFA) rises during the encoding and retrieval periods. The black dotted and red dotted lines indicate the peak of activation in the FFA and PFC. During encoding, the peak is earlier in the FFA; during retrieval, the peak is earlier in the PFC.

THE PREFRONTAL CORTEX AND OTHER MEMORY DOMAINS

Up to now, studies of working memory have focused on variants of the delayed-response task. Other tasks, however, have been used to study the contribution of the prefrontal cortex to memory. In this section, we will review this literature. We will then consider whether these problems reflect a common processing deficit or suggest a heterogeneity of function within the prefrontal cortex.

The Frontal Lobes and the Temporal Organization of Memory

Memory fades with time. It is impossible to remember all the details of our lives. We have a few memories of our childhood, perhaps a special birthday party, or a cross-country trip, or our first-grade classroom. But the details of most experiences become difficult to reconstruct as time passes. This information is not necessarily lost; it is absorbed into new experiences. We remember how to play Monopoly or how to bake a favorite cake, not by recalling our initial attempts but by repeating the activities. Practice makes perfect. By measuring and sifting flour, salt, and baking powder; by blending egg yolks and sugar; and by folding this mixture into the dry ingredients, we remember how to prepare the cake. These actions must be executed in the proper order for the cake to come out as planned. Something does not taste right if the sugar is added to the flour mix without first having been stirred with the eggs.

Even when it is unnecessary to remember a sequence of actions, our memories include temporal tags. Think about what you did yesterday. Perhaps the events have not yet faded from your memory. Most likely, you can recall waking up and what you ate for breakfast, which classes you attended, where you ate lunch, and how you spent the evening, perhaps poring over books in preparation for an exam or relaxing with friends. Although no one required that the events be recalled in order, you probably used temporal cues to organize the information. Time continually moves forward, and our reconstruction of the past obeys this principle.

People with frontal lobe lesions may be impaired in their ability to organize and segregate events in memory—an ability referred to as **recency memory** (B. Milner, 1995). A recency discrimination task has been used to study temporal memory. In this task the subjects are presented with study cards, each having two stimuli, such as a pair of pictures. The subjects are instructed to study the pictures. Every so often, a test card is presented with two question marks in addition to the two pictures (Figure 13.8). The subject must decide which of the two pictures was seen most recently. For example, one of the pictures might have been on a study card presented 4 trials previously, and the other, on a study card shown 32 trials ago. For a control task, the procedure is modified: The test card contains two pictures and the question marks, but only one of the two pictures was presented previously. Following the same instructions, the subject should choose that picture since, by definition, it is the one seen most recently. Note, though, that the task is really one of recognition memory. There is no need to evaluate the temporal position of the two choices.

Frontal lobe lesions were associated with a selective deficit in recency judgments. Patients performed as well as control subjects did on the recognition memory task, with both groups scoring above 90% correct. The recency task proved considerably more difficult, and most important, this effect was even more marked in patients with frontal lobe lesions, which provided a single dissociation. Temporal lobe lesions did not affect performance on either task.

All the patients had undergone a unilateral brain operation for the treatment of severe, focal epilepsy. With this procedure, the extent of the surgically induced lesion can be limited and is precisely known. Hence, one can distinguish between patients in whom the lesion encompassed dorsolateral prefrontal regions (area 46)

Figure 13.8 Recency memory is impaired in patients with prefrontal lesions. **(a)** Subjects were presented with a series of cards, each one showing a pair of objects. On test cards the objects were flanked by question marks, and the subject had to indicate which object was seen most recently. In the recency test, both objects on the test cards had been seen previously. In the item recognition test, only one object had appeared previously. **(b)** The results reveal a single dissociation. Patients who had had a frontal lobectomy performed more poorly on the recency task compared to both control subjects and patients who had had a temporal lobectomy. The frontal group was not impaired on the item recognition task.

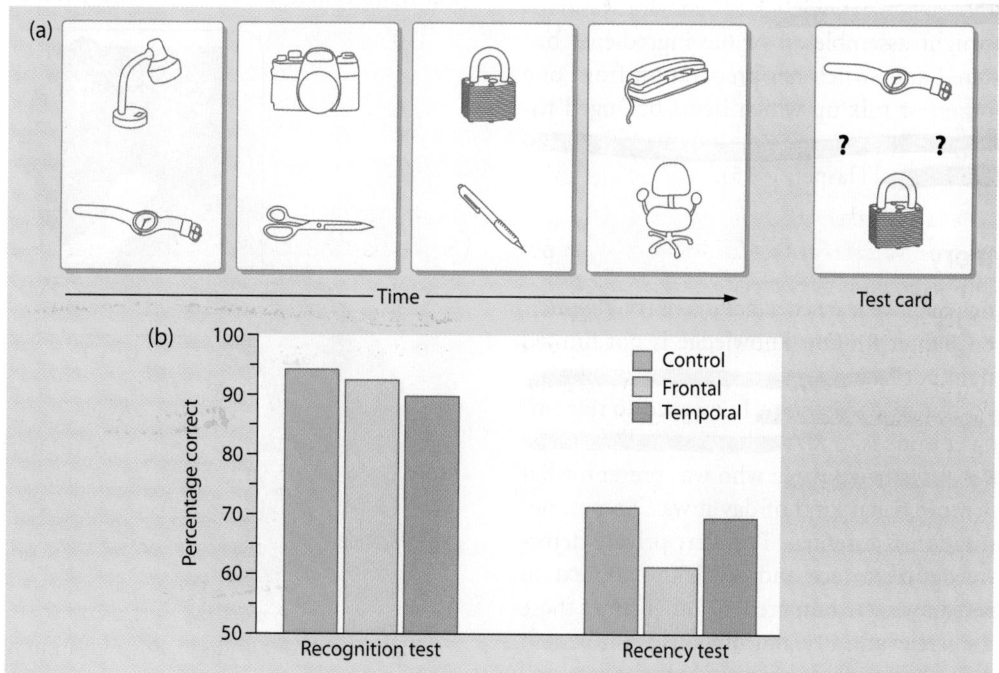

from those in whom this area was spared. This analysis revealed that deficits in the recency task were restricted to patients in the dorsolateral group. Thus, the same area implicated in working memory tasks, such as delayed response, is associated with the memory for temporal order. Moreover, a laterality effect was a function of the type of stimulus. With word stimuli, the deficit was most evident in patients with left-hemisphere lesions, whereas right-hemisphere lobectomies were associated with impaired performance when drawings of common objects or abstract paintings were substituted for words.

A variant of the recency discrimination task is the self-ordered pointing task. Here, a series of 6 to 12 cards is presented, each with the same set of 6 to 12 objects. The positions of the objects are shuffled about from card to card. The subject must point to a new object on each card. Thus, successful performance requires that the subject keep track of which items had been responded to on previous cards. As in the recency discrimination tasks, patients with frontal lesions make more errors than do control subjects, and the deficit becomes more pronounced as the number of items per card increases.

The breakdown in the temporal structure of memory may account for more bizarre aspects of frontal lobe syndrome. For example, in a classic report of frontal lobe dysfunction, Wilder Penfield described a patient who was troubled by her inability to prepare her family's evening meal. This patient could remember the ingredients for dishes, but she could not organize her actions into a proper temporal sequence. Her behavior was haphazard. She might assemble all of the ingredients but become flustered and switch her preparation from one dish to the other, or mix up which items belonged together. No longer could she generate a temporal plan to achieve a coherent goal (Jasper, 1995).

Source Memory

Remembering when we learned a fact is a part of *episodic memory* (see Chapter 8). Our knowledge is not limited solely to content but includes the context in which learning took place, or **source memory.** In essence, to remember a learning episode is to remember details about time and place, and the episode itself: who was present, what those present wore, what kind of day it was. Sometimes source information is essential. The alert private detective has to recognize a face and recall the context in which that person was encountered. At other times these details may be irrelevant. It is not obvious what benefit there is in remembering that the professor who lectured on Freud and his theory of dream interpretation was wearing a bright-green suit. Are these details simply information cluttering up our cranial warehouse? Or can they facilitate memory? These obscure details are actually useful retrieval cues (Figure 13.9).

Source memory depends on the integrity of the frontal lobes. To show this, Larry Squire and his colleagues (Janowsky et al., 1989) at the Veterans Administration Medical Center in San Diego had control subjects and frontal lobe patients learn facts such as "The name of the dog on the Cracker Jack box is Bingo," or "The body of water between Russia and Iran is the Caspian Sea." After a 6- to 8-day retention interval, the subjects were tested on these statements plus new ones with equally obscure facts or easy questions. Whenever subjects correctly answered a question, they were asked to recollect how they had learned the information. Subjects could answer that they had learned it during the previous testing session, or they could attribute it to something they had learned in school or read in the paper. There was a dissociation between recall and source memory tasks: Patients performed as well as control subjects on the recall task but made more errors on the source task.

Healthy subjects also provided novel evidence linking the frontal lobes to source memory (Glisky et al., 1995). Although the subjects never had a neurological

Figure 13.9 Source memory is knowledge concerning the source of information or the context in which the information was learned. This student is recalling the specific episode in which she learned about Freud's theory of the unconscious.

disorder, they were given neuropsychological tests. According to their performance on tests designed to assess frontal lobe function, they were divided into groups based on "high" and "low" frontal function (the "low" group still performed higher than patients who had incurred a neurological insult in the frontal lobes). A similar division was based on their performance on tests designed to assess temporal lobe function. The two tests had minimal correlation. Subjects who scored well on the frontal test did not necessarily score well on the temporal lobe test.

In the primary experiment, subjects were tested on item and source memory. During the study phase, the participants heard a series of sentences expressing common events (e.g., "The boy went to the store to buy some apples and oranges"). Half of the sentences were read by a woman and the other half by a man. The investigators tested item memory by pairing a study sentence with a novel sentence and asking subjects to choose the sentence that they had heard in the study phase; and they tested source memory by having the subjects hear the same sentence read by both speakers and then judge which voice matched the original presentation.

The results, presented in Figure 13.10, reveal a double dissociation. High temporal lobe function was associated with good performance on the item memory test, but the two frontal lobe function groups did not differ significantly. In contrast, only the frontal lobe function groups differed on the source memory task. Participants rated as having low frontal function performed barely above chance, whereas those whose function was rated high did considerably better. Thus, healthy people dissociate item and source memory, and the two tasks correlate with differences in temporal and frontal lobe function.

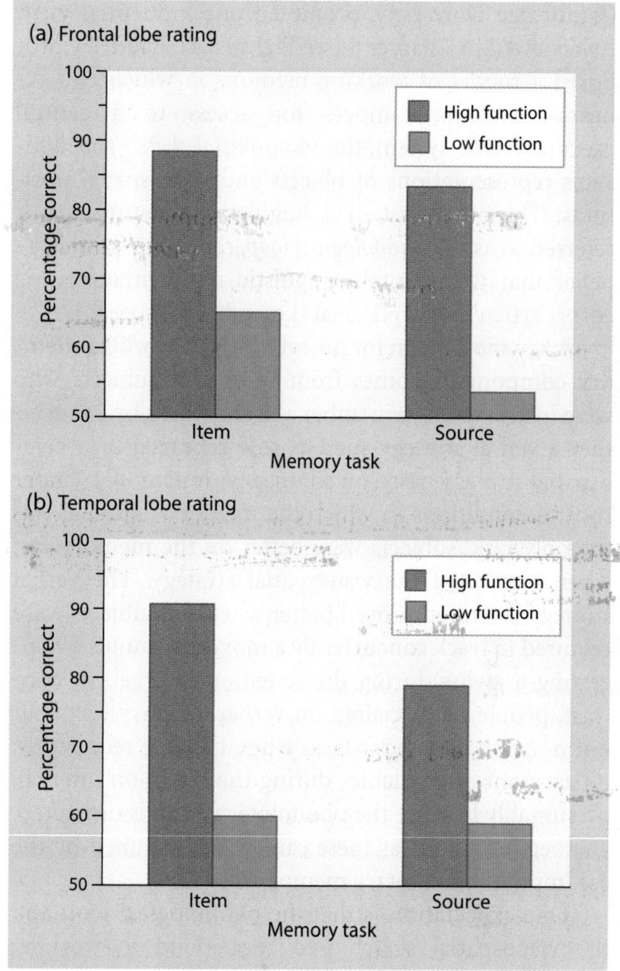

Figure 13.10 Double dissociation on tests of item and source memory in healthy elderly adults who were rated as "high" or "low" on tests of frontal and temporal lobe function. **(a)** Low frontal lobe function was associated with poor performance on the source memory test. **(b)** Low temporal lobe function was associated with relatively poor performance on the item memory test.

COMPONENT ANALYSIS OF THE PREFRONTAL CORTEX

Working memory is conceptualized as a temporary network to sustain the current contents of processing. As reviewed earlier, the evidence overwhelmingly demonstrates that the lateral prefrontal cortex is a key component of working memory. But, as Figure 13.1 shows, the lateral prefrontal cortex encompasses a large area. A question of intense debate has been how best to characterize the different contributions of the prefrontal cortex.

Content-Based Accounts of Functional Specialization Within the Prefrontal Cortex

One approach focuses on the content of the represented information. **Content-based hypotheses** have been motivated by psychological models of working memory. Alan Baddeley (1995) of the Applied Psychology Unit (now called the Cognition and Brain Sciences Unit) at

Cambridge University, promoted one influential view. As reviewed in Chapter 8 (see Figure 8.4), Baddeley proposed a model of working memory in which two rehearsal systems compete for access to a central executive. One system, the *visuospatial sketch pad*, activates representations of objects and their spatial positions. The other system is linguistic in nature and is referred to as the *phonological loop*, reflecting Baddeley's belief that we maintain linguistic representations via covert articulatory rehearsal (i.e., subvocal speech).

A key motivation for postulating two working memory components comes from studies of subjects who were instructed to remember a list of words by using either a verbal strategy such as rote rehearsal or a visuospatial strategy based on an imagery mnemonic. Under control conditions in which the memory rehearsal was the only task, subjects were better on the memory test when they used the visuospatial strategy. The verbal strategy, however, proved better when the subjects were required to track concurrently a moving stimulus by operating a stylus during the retention interval. In contrast, people are impaired on verbal memory tasks but not nonverbal memory tasks when they are required to repeat nonsense syllables during the retention interval, presumably because the phonological loop is disrupted. Dissociations such as these cannot be explained by the assumption of a unitary memory system.

One expectation is that the phonological loop and the visuospatial sketch pad correspond to working memory functions of the left and right hemispheres, respectively—an idea consistent with the general picture of hemispheric specialization (see Chapter 11). A metareview of 60 PET and fMRI studies revealed that activation in the lateral prefrontal cortex is found in working memory tasks with verbal stimuli (Wager & Smith, 2003). This lateralization is especially pronounced in areas 44 and 45, regions including and anterior to Broca's area. For example, these left prefrontal regions are recruited when working memory is explicitly taxed during delayed-response tasks with word lists, as well as in studies in which people have to generate semantic associates—a situation in which working memory is required online and subjects are asked to retain a short list of words for subsequent recall or to sort through the various possibilities. As discussed previously, working memory entails interactions between prefrontal and posterior cortex (Figure 13.11). The rehearsal processes that keep information active in verbal working memory, the phonological loop, involves interactions between these prefrontal regions and left-hemisphere regions of secondary auditory cortex and inferior parietal lobe that support phonological representations. These posterior activations are also observed primarily in the left hemisphere.

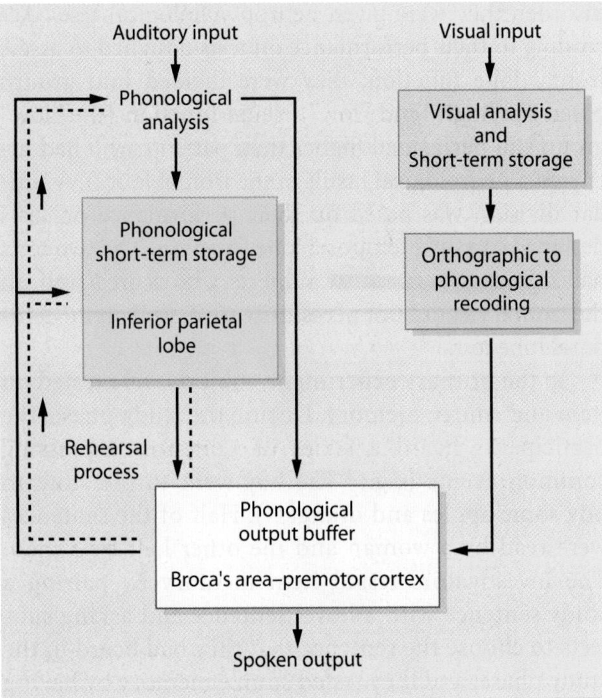

Figure 13.11 Components of the phonological loop. The loop can be engaged by speech (auditory input) or reading (visual input). For speech, the auditory input leads to the activation of phonological representations that are internally rehearsed for maintenance. For reading, the letters must be mapped onto their phonological representations before entering the phonological loop.

The picture is not as clear for spatial working memory. Activation in area 46 is generally bilateral, and even when it is asymmetrical the effect is as likely to be more pronounced in the left hemisphere as in the right hemisphere. In fact, in more anterior regions of the prefrontal cortex, spatial working memory tasks also tend to engage the left hemisphere more than the right hemisphere. The bias for left-hemisphere activity during spatial working memory may reflect, at least in some studies, a verbal recoding of the nonverbal stimuli. For example, when asked to remember the locations of a set of stimuli, we might think "upper left" and "lower right."

A different content-based hypothesis builds on the idea of two cortical visual systems. As described in Chapter 6, the dorsal visual pathway is prominent in the analysis of spatial information; the ventral pathway is essential in the analysis of object information. It has been hypothesized that this dorsal–ventral distinction may extend into the prefrontal cortex (F. A.

Wilson et al., 1993). This distinction does appear to have some validity, although, as we shall see below, the effect may be limited to only certain regions within the prefrontal cortex.

Consider the experiment outlined in Figure 13.12a, which was conducted by Richard Passingham and his colleagues at Oxford University. An instruction cue was presented at the beginning of the trial, indicating whether the trial would involve a verbal or spatial delayed-response task, as well as whether the participant would be required to respond according to the actual presentation order of the stimuli or in a reversed order. Following the instruction cue, and continuing through the stimulation and delay periods, the superior frontal sulcus was activated in both hemispheres for the spatial working memory task (Figure 13.12b and c). In contrast, ventral prefrontal regions, limited to the left hemisphere, were activated during the verbal working memory task.

Process-Based Accounts of Functional Specialization Within the Prefrontal Cortex

A second approach for partitioning prefrontal cortex centers is process based: Are different regions recruited as a function of the type of processing required for a particular task? Consider the two ways in which memory was probed in Figure 13.12a: When the judgment requires that the items be remembered in the forward direction, the subjects must internally maintain a

Figure 13.12 Subregions of the prefrontal cortex are sensitive to either contents or processing requirements of working memory. **(a)** An instruction cue indicates the task required for the forthcoming trial. Following a delay period, a series of pictures containing letters and squares at various locations is presented. The participant must remember the order of the instruction-relevant stimuli to respond after the memory probe is presented. **(b)** When subjects are required to remember the location of the squares, activation is greater in the parietal and dorsal prefrontal regions. In contrast, remembering the letters leads to greater activation in the temporal lobe and inferior frontal cortex of the left hemisphere. **(c)** Time course of the BOLD signal in four brain regions. Content specificity is observed in the superior parietal sulcus (SPS) and inferior frontal gyrus (IFG). Anterior prefrontal cortex (APF) is activated in a consistent fashion for all four tasks. Dorsolateral prefrontal cortex (DLPF) is more active when the stimuli must be remembered in reverse order, independent of whether the set is composed of locations or letters.

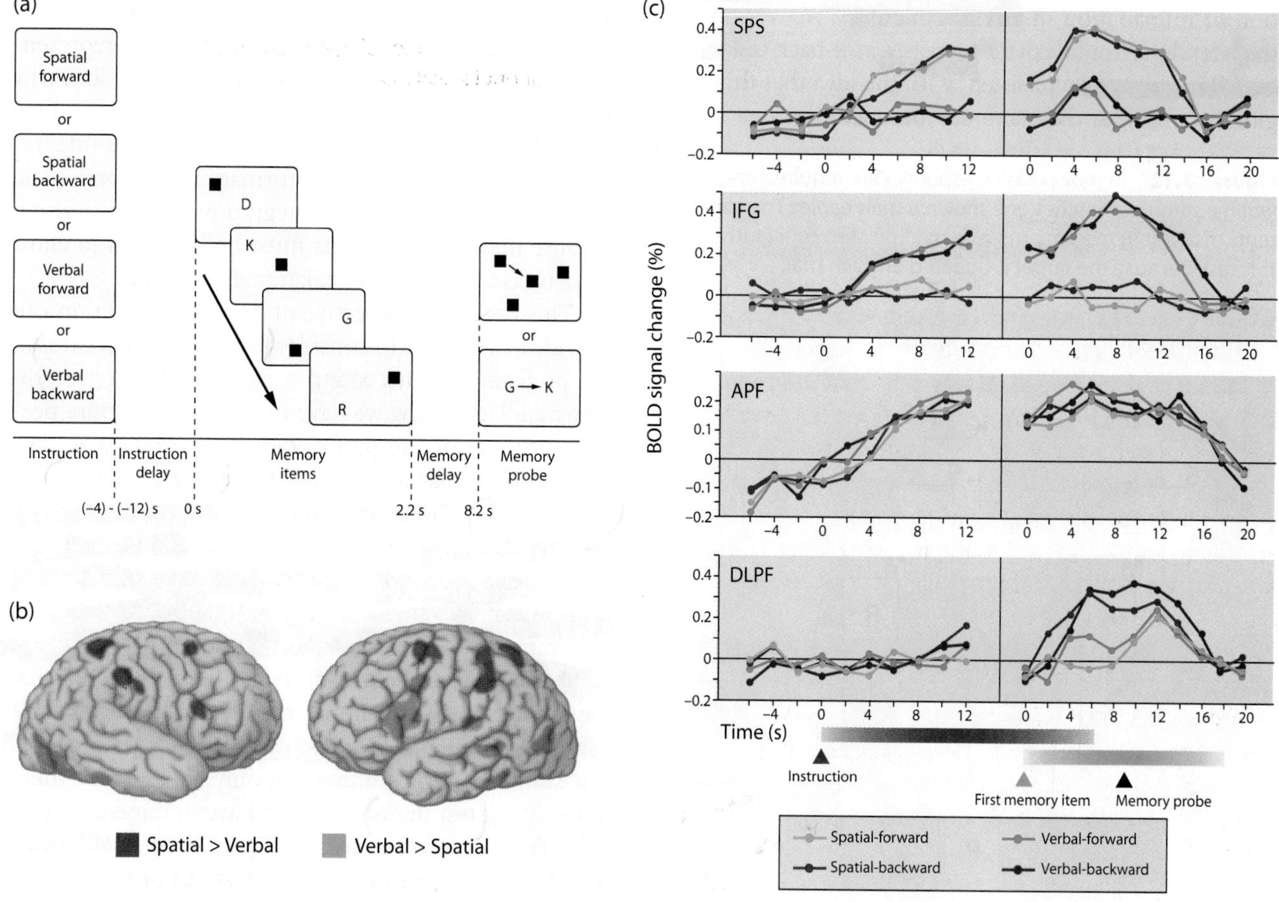

representation of the stimuli, using a natural scheme in which the items can be rehearsed in the order presented. The backward conditions, however, are more challenging. Here the items must be shuffled in memory to recode the presentation order. Thus, the information must be not only remembered, but also manipulated. As Figure 13.12c shows, the backward condition selectively recruited lateral prefrontal cortex, and the effect was similar for the verbal and spatial conditions.

A similar pattern is observed in many imaging studies, suggesting that the lateral prefrontal cortex is critical when the contents of working memory must be manipulated. One favorite testing variant is the "*n*-back" task (Figure 13.13). Here the display consists of a continuous stream of stimuli. Responses are required only when the current stimulus matches a stimulus that was presented *n* items previously. In the simplest version, *n* equals 1, responses are made when the same stimulus is presented on two successive trials. In more complicated versions, *n* can equal 2 or more. With *n*-back tasks, it is not sufficient to simply maintain a representation of recently presented items; the working memory buffer must be updated continually to keep track of what the current stimulus must be compared to. Tasks such as *n*-back tasks require both the maintenance and the manipulation of information in working memory. Activation in the lateral prefrontal cortex increases as *n*-back task difficulty is increased, consistent with the idea that this region is critical for the manipulation operation.

Figure 13.13 In *n*-back tasks, responses are required only when a stimulus matches one shown *n* trials earlier. The contents of working memory must be manipulated constantly in this task because the target is updated on each trial.

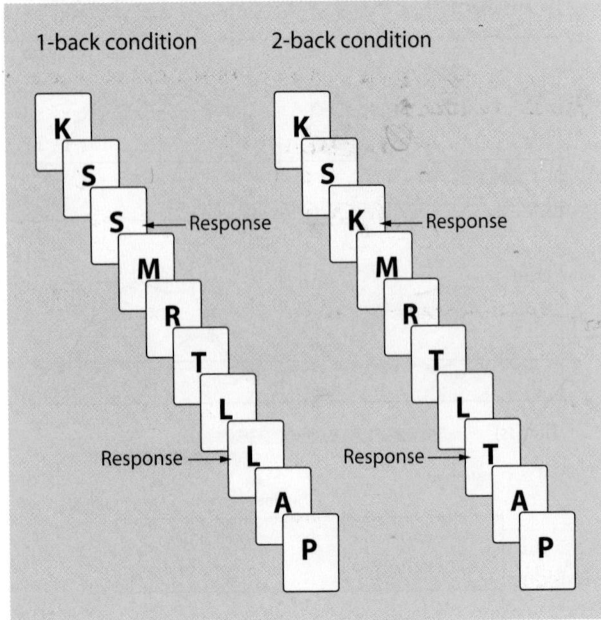

The *n*-back tasks capture an essential aspect of prefrontal function, putting the emphasis on the active part of working memory. Think about what happens when you reach for your wallet to pay a bill after dinner at a restaurant. Not only must you remember the price of the dinner, but also you have to calculate the tip. Working memory is not only about keeping task-relevant information active; it is also about manipulating that information to accomplish behavioral goals (Petrides, 2000). The recency and self-oriented pointing tasks also reflect the updating aspect of working memory. Both require that the subjects remember whether something is familiar and the context in which the stimulus was previously encountered.

The link between source memory and working memory is not as obvious. On the one hand, source memory is a form of contextual memory. By definition, it requires remembering the context in which something was experienced. But source memory is a form of a long-term memory, and in general, patients with prefrontal lesions do not show impairment on long-term memory tasks. However, the deficit on source memory tasks is primarily in terms of learning source information. It is not clear that the patients would have similar problems if they were asked about the source of information that they had learned prior to the onset of their neurological condition. Nonetheless, if we think of working memory as a repository of transient representations and the manipulation of this information, why should source memory be especially disrupted? One possibility is that source memory requires the integration of distinct sources of information. The prefrontal cortex is important in this integration process, perhaps because the representations must be sustained to allow these links to occur (Prabhakaran et al., 2000).

This broader perspective of prefrontal function can provide a novel way to consider functional differences in the prefrontal cortex along the anterior–posterior dimension. Up to now we have focused on the more posterior aspects of the prefrontal cortex: areas 9, 44, 45, and 46. But what about the most anterior region, the frontal pole? The study comparing verbal and spatial working memory provides one hint. The frontal pole was the one region that was recruited upon the presentation of the instruction cue in all four conditions and maintained a high level of activity across the extent of the trial (see Figure 13.12c). It has been proposed that the frontal pole is essential for integrating the specific contents of mental activity into a general framework. The subjects in the scanner not only have to remember to study the test items; they also have to remember that they have volunteered to participate in an fMRI study and that there are some general instructions to keep in mind. For example, they should stay awake, minimize all

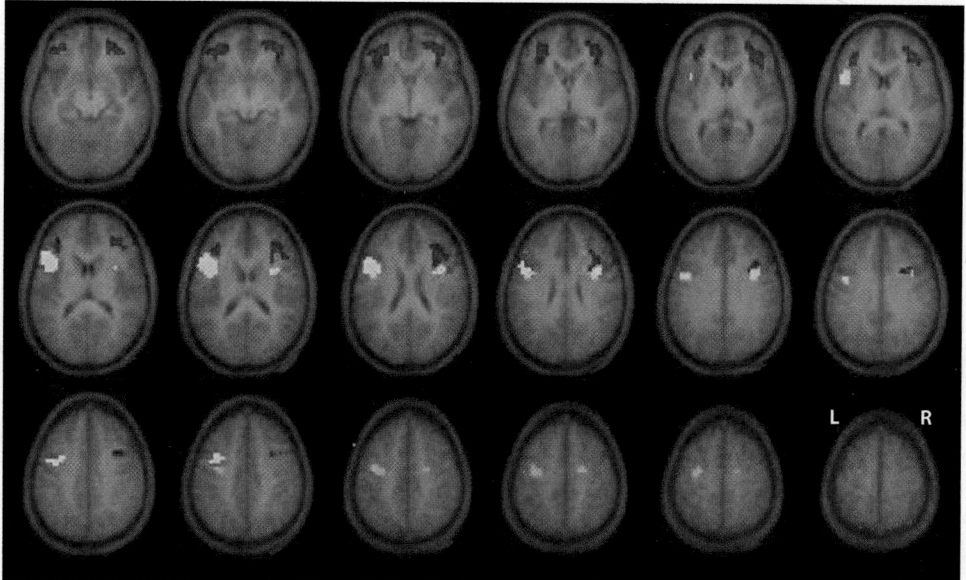

Figure 13.14 Hierarchical organization of the prefrontal cortex. Prefrontal activation in an fMRI study increased along a posterior–anterior gradient as the experimental task became more complex. Activation in the regions shown in green was related to the number of stimulus–response mappings that had to be maintained. Activation in regions shown in yellow was related to the contextual demands of the task. For example, a response to a letter might be made if the color of the letter was green, but not if it was white. Activation in regions shown in red was related to variation in the instructions from one scanning run to the next. For example, the rules in one run might be reversed in the next run.

movements, and respond as fast as possible. In a sense, the working memory operations required here take place within a particular context.

Studies that focus on frontal pole function are much more rare than those that look at the lateral prefrontal cortex. The dearth of work here is, in part, methodological. The most anterior region of the prefrontal cortex tends to be susceptible to imaging artifacts, rendering the signal:noise ratio weaker. Moreover, a general feature of brain evolution is that individual differences are more pronounced in recently evolved structures. Because the anterior pole is one of the most recent extensions of primate cortex, variability is likely to be substantial, making it difficult to observe consistent effects when the analytical methods require alignment of the brains of different individuals onto a common brain template.

Nonetheless, some recent work has focused on the anterior–posterior gradient. The results of this work suggest that activation patterns follow a crude hierarchy: For the simplest of working memory tasks, the activation may be limited to more posterior prefrontal regions or even secondary motor areas. For example, if the task requires the subject to press one key upon seeing a flower and another upon seeing an automobile, then these relatively simple stimulus–response rules can be sustained by the ventral prefrontal cortex and lateral premotor cortex. However, if the stimulus–response rule is defined not by the objects themselves, but by a color surrounding the object, then the frontal pole is also recruited (Bunge, 2004).

When such contingencies are made even more challenging by a changing of the rules from one block of trials to the next, activation extends even farther in the anterior direction (Figure 13.14). These complex experiments demonstrate, in a sense, the intertwined nature of working memory, recency memory, and source memory, at least within the time frame of an experimental session. The participants must integrate multiple pieces of information in order to comply with the task instructions.

GOAL-ORIENTED BEHAVIOR

Our actions are not aimless, nor are they entirely dictated by events and stimuli immediately at hand. We choose to act because we want to accomplish goals, to gratify personal needs. Goal-driven behavior can be as mundane as turning on a computer to play a game, or as complex as attending lectures, reviewing notes, and reading to learn. Goals dwell within a hierarchy. We can describe the immediate goal of an action—to learn—but also recognize that this is really a subgoal for a larger plan. Learning subjects is necessary for admission to graduate or professional school, and these institutions can be a ticket to fame, fortune, and personal satisfaction.

The ability to form a coherent plan of action is compromised after damage to the prefrontal lobe. Patients like W.R., the wayward lawyer, are plagued by this problem. They are unable to resurrect a normal life even after the acute symptoms of their illness have passed. It is difficult to attribute the problem to a lack of knowledge. These patients are aware of their deteriorating social situation and have the intellectual capabilities to generate ideas that may alleviate their condition. But their efforts to overcome inertia are haphazard at best. They are unable to sustain a plan of action and meet their goals.

Tim Shallice at the National Hospital for Neurology and Neurosurgery in London (Shallice & Burgess, 1991) documented this problem in three patients who suffered frontal lesions from head traumas. On many neuropsychological assessment procedures, the patients demonstrated intact, perhaps even superior, cognitive abilities. Not only did they all score at least one standard deviation above average on an IQ test, but also they had few problems on standard tests of frontal lobe function, including the Wisconsin Card Sorting Task, which we will describe shortly.

To examine their ability to engage in goal-oriented behavior, the experimenters designed tasks that mimicked the errands a person might have to run on a Saturday morning. Patients were asked to go to a shopping center and purchase items (e.g., a loaf of bread, a packet of throat lozenges), to keep an appointment at a certain time, and to collect four pieces of information, such as the price of a pound of tomatoes or the exchange rate of the rupee. The task was not designed to tap memory. The patients were given a list of the errands and instructions to follow, such as to spend as little money as possible.

Despite their superior intellectual abilities, all three patients had difficulty executing this assignment. One patient failed to purchase soap because the store she visited did not carry her favorite brand; another wandered outside the designated shopping center in pursuit of an item that could be found within the designated region. All became embroiled in social complications. One succeeded in obtaining the newspaper but was pursued by the merchant for failing to pay! In a related experiment, patients were asked to work on three tasks for 15 minutes. Whereas control subjects successfully juggled their schedule to ensure that they made enough progress on each task, the patients got bogged down on one or two tasks.

Planning and Selecting an Action

In preparing for an exam, a good student develops an action plan such as the one in Figure 13.15. This plan can be represented as a hierarchy of subgoals, each requiring actions to achieve the goal. At the top is the goal of doing well on the exam. To do so, subgoals are designed: Reading must be completed, lecture notes reviewed, and material integrated to identify themes and facts. Perhaps the student will generate essay questions and practice writing answers. A timeline might include when the subgoals will be completed and how to devote the day before the exam to study.

Three components are essential for successfully executing an action plan (Duncan, 1995). First, one must identify the goal and develop subgoals. Perhaps the student has noticed that the professor often includes readings on exams, so a subgoal might be to maximize the effort devoted to reading. Second, in choosing among goals, consequences must be anticipated. Will the information be remembered better if the student sets aside 1 hour a day for study during the week preceding the exam, or is it better to cram intensively the night before? Third, the student must determine what is required to achieve the subgoals. A place must be identified for study. The coffee supply must be adequately stocked. A pen must be

Figure 13.15 Action hierarchy. Successfully achieving a complex goal such as doing well on an exam requires planning and organization at multiple levels of behavior.

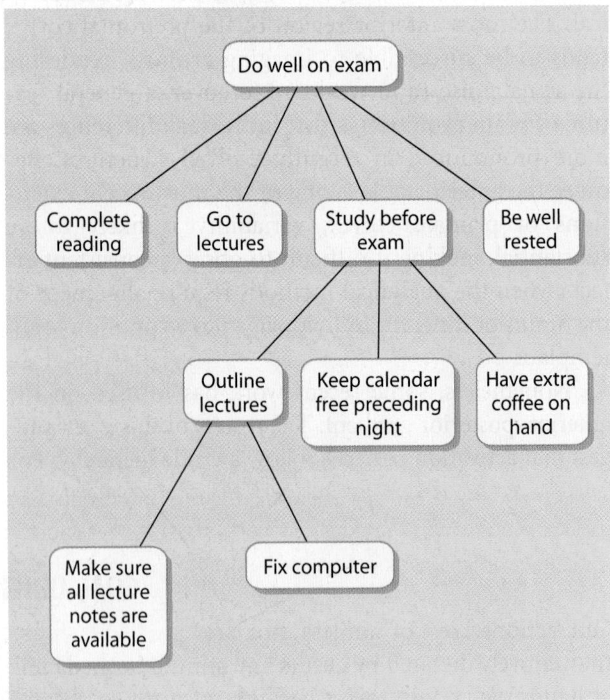

available for marking critical passages. It is easy to see that these components are not entirely separate. Purchasing coffee, for example, can be an action and a goal.

When an action plan is viewed as a hierarchical representation, it is easy to see that failure to achieve a goal can happen in many ways. In the example illustrated in Figure 13.15, if reading is not completed, the student may lack knowledge essential for an exam. If a friend arrives unannounced to celebrate his birthday the weekend before the exam, critical study time can be lost. If coffee is not handy, the student may lack the stamina to stay awake for the final all-nighter. The failures of goal-oriented behavior in patients with prefrontal lesions can be traced to many potential sources. Problems can arise because of deficits in filtering irrelevant information, in keeping one's eyes on the prize. Or the challenge may come in selecting the best way to achieve a particular goal. Developing an action plan means a simultaneous consideration of possible subgoals. We must evaluate these different plans of attack to establish sensible goals.

A clever demonstration of the importance of the frontal lobes in this evaluation process comes from a study carried out in Jordan Grafman's laboratory at the National Institutes of Health (Goel et al., 1997). The researchers sought to capture the real-world problems that patients with penetrating head injuries face. To this end, they asked the patients to help an upwardly mobile couple plan their family budget. The patients were told of the family's long-term financial goals: to purchase a home within 2 years, send the kids to college in 15 years, and retire in 35 years. But like many young couples, this family was having trouble living within its means. The family was actually falling further into debt rather than building a nest egg. When shown the list of family expenditures, control participants focused on a few categories. The expenses for clothing, $175 a month, seemed like a lot for a family of four with two young children. Perhaps substantial savings could be found by dressing the younger child in hand-me-downs from the oldest.

The responses of the frontal patients were revealing. They understood the overriding need to identify places where savings could be achieved. They could appreciate the need to budget. But their solutions did not always seem reasonable. One patient focused on the family's rent. Noting that the $10,800 yearly expense for rent was by far the biggest expense in the family budget, he proposed that it be eliminated. When the experimenter pointed out that the family would need a place to live, the patient was quick with an answer: "Yes. Course I know a place that sells tents cheap. You can buy one of those." We see in this naturalistic domain another manifestation of the selection problems reviewed earlier.

Cognitive Control of Goal-Oriented Behavior

By focusing on the housing costs, the patient is demonstrating a certain inflexibility in his decision making. The large price tag assigned to rent was a particularly salient piece of information, and the patient's budgeting efforts were captured by the potential savings to be found here. From a strictly monetary perspective, this decision makes sense. But at a practical level, we realize the inappropriateness of this choice. Making wise decisions with complex matters such as one's long-term financial goals requires keeping an eye on the overall picture. We must not lose track of the forest for the trees. It is essential that we monitor and evaluate the different subgoals. To do so requires an ability to shift our focus from one subgoal to another, an essential feature of cognitive control.

We are all familiar with the importance of task control. It is common to hear someone describe a particularly active friend as someone who is good at "multitasking." Globally, this description might apply to someone who can keep up with all of her studies, manage a part-time job, and still find time to exercise 2 hours each afternoon. Locally, this phrase is used to describe someone who, while checking e-mail and transferring files on the computer, is also able to scan her phone messages. Cognitive control provides the interface through which goals influence behavior. Complex actions require that we maintain our current goal, focusing on the information that is relevant to achieving that goal, ignore irrelevant information, and be able to shift from one subgoal to another in a coordinated manner.

These multiple components of cognitive control are highlighted in one of the most widely accepted tests of frontal disorders, the **Wisconsin Card Sorting Task**. This task involves cards containing objects that vary along three dimensions: shape, color, and numerosity (Figure 13.16). The cards are presented one at a time, and the subject is instructed to sort the cards according to an experimenter-defined sorting rule.

The task has two catches. First, the subject is not informed of the sorting rule but must discover it through trial and error; the experimenter simply says "Correct" or "Incorrect" after each card is played. Thus, recognition of the stimulus by itself is insufficient to guide subjects to the correct response but must be integrated with how that information was relevant on previous trials. The subject's working memory must retain knowledge about the relevance of certain features in their previous responses.

Second, and especially devilish, once the subject has learned to sort by one dimension, the experimenter

Figure 13.16 Patients with damage in the lateral prefrontal cortex have difficulty on the Wisconsin Card Sorting Task. On each trial, the subjects place the top card of the deck under one of the four target cards. The experimenter indicates whether the response is correct or incorrect, allowing the subject to learn the sorting rule by trial and error. The sorting rule changes whenever the subject makes 10 consecutive correct responses.

changes the rule without informing the subject. So the subject not only must seek the appropriate sorting rule but also must be flexible enough to discard a previously reinforced hypothesis and begin the discovery anew. In doing so, the subject must recognize that previously relevant information has now become irrelevant.

Patients with frontal lobe lesions have difficulty with this task. Not only is it a challenge to keep track of previous responses in order to evaluate a current hypothesis, but the patients tend to **perseverate**, applying the initial rule over and over again after the switch, despite the experimenter's continued admonishment that the responses are incorrect. In the following sections, we explore in detail these different aspects of cognitive control.

Retrieval and Selection of Task-Relevant Information

Goal-oriented behavior requires the selection of task-relevant information. Indeed, this selection process is a cardinal feature of tasks associated with the lateral prefrontal cortex. Within this framework, the emphasis on prefrontal function shifts from a role in memory to a role in the allocation of attentional resources.

Suppose that you are telling a friend about your recent trip to San Francisco (Figure 13.17). One highlight was your walk across the Golden Gate Bridge. In describing the beauty of this structure, how its two towers span the mouth of the bay linking the city with the Marin Headlands, you will have activated a lot of semantic information from long-term memory; information about the location, shape, and color of the bridge; and episodic information related to your visit to the bridge. In the working memory model, a transient file is established to hold this information. Suppose your friend asks you about a particular feature, such as the color of the bridge. This query requires that one piece of information be made more salient than others. To answer the question, you must be able to select this information from the contents of working memory.

Art Shimamura (2000) of the University of California, Berkeley, has argued that the prefrontal cortex can be conceptualized as a **dynamic filtering** mechanism. The frontal cortex is a repository of representations and

Figure 13.17 The prefrontal cortex operates as a filtering device in the retrieval of task-relevant information from long-term memory. When the subject is asked about the color of the Golden Gate Bridge, information regarding the long-term memory of the color of the bridge is amplified, while information about the location and shape of the bridge is inhibited.

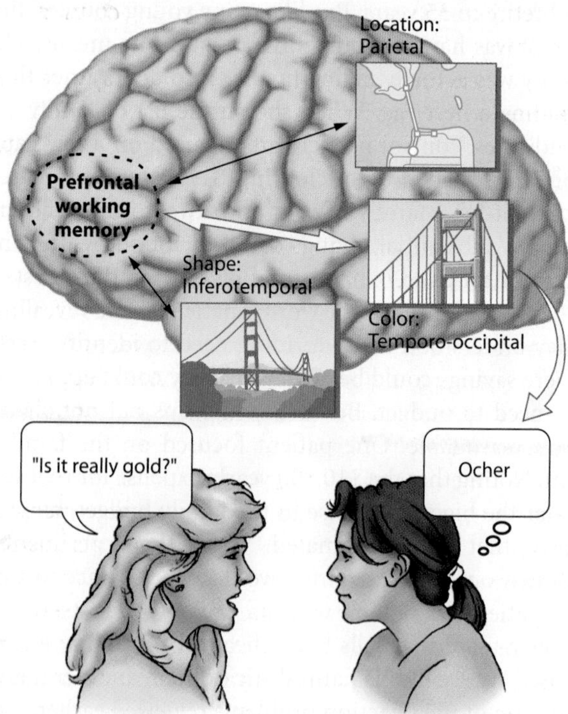

selects information most relevant for meeting the task's demands. Working memory is more than the passive sustaining of representations; it requires an attentional component in which the subject's goals modify the salience of sources of information. In a spatial delayed-response task, the critical information is the object's location. In an object version of this task, the critical information is the shape of the stimulus.

Can a deficit in dynamic filtering account for the range of deficits exhibited by patients with lesions of the lateral prefrontal cortex? Could it provide an alternative account for the difficulty these patients have on source memory tasks? Perhaps, if we consider that memory for context is generally secondary to memory for content. We rarely need to recall where we learned something; it is usually sufficient to remember the information itself. We can successfully bake a cake by remembering how to combine the ingredients without recalling that we first learned to make this recipe from *The Joy of Cooking.* (But when we forget a step, it is useful to know where the information can be obtained.)

With the asymmetry between memory for content and memory for context, it is reasonable to suppose that source memory requires disproportionate attention. Content representations can be expected to be more salient and thus less sensitive to a loss of attention. Greater resources are required when we must ignore content and attempt to retrieve context. When we read a sentence, we derive its meaning while paying little attention to superficial aspects such as the font in which it is printed or where it is in the text. We can recall this surface information, but only when we make an effort to encode it.

The hypothesis that the frontal lobes play a critical role in selecting task-relevant information can account for frontal lobe patients' problems with the Wisconsin Card Sorting Task (see Figure 13.16). They learn by trial and error; they hypothesize which information is relevant and which is not. Subjects, then, must learn to attend to the correct dimension while filtering the other two dimensions. Frontal lobe patients have difficulty doing this. Their susceptibility to perseverative errors can be viewed as a failure in selection. After learning to attend to one dimension, a person with frontal lobe damage continues to focus on it.

The filtering hypothesis also offers a way to appreciate the role of the frontal lobe in tasks where memory demands are minimal. Frontal lobe patients display heightened interference on the Stroop task, in which subjects are shown a list of colored words and the words spell color names such as *red*, *green*, or *blue*. In the congruent condition, the colors of the words correspond to their names; in the incongruent condition, the word names and colors do not correspond (see Figure 4.5). With years of reading experience, we have a strong urge to read words even when the task requires us to ignore them in favor of color; thus, everyone is slower in responding to incongruent stimuli in comparison with congruent stimuli. This difference is even greater in patients with frontal lobe lesions.

Support for the dynamic filtering hypothesis comes from an elegant series of experiments conducted by Sharon Thompson-Schill, Mark D'Esposito, and their colleagues (Thompson-Schill et al., 1997, 1998). The studies involved the semantic generation task. On each trial, a noun is presented and the subjects generate a word that is semantically associated. Early PET studies on language had found that, in comparison to a task in which subjects simply read the nouns, the generation task produced increased activation in the inferior frontal gyrus of the left hemisphere. Building on ideas regarding working memory, Thompson-Schill hypothesized that this prefrontal activation reflected the prefrontal filtering of transient representations of semantic associates to the target item—information that is stored in posterior regions of the cortex.

To test this hypothesis, researchers compared brain activation during two types of verb generation tasks, varying the demands on a filtering process (Figure 13.18). In the low-filtering condition, each noun was associated with a single verb. For example, when asked to name the action that goes with *scissors*, almost everyone will respond "cut," and thus there is no need to filter out competing, alternative responses. In the high-filtering condition, each noun had numerous associates. For example, for the word *rope*, multiple answers are reasonable: "tie," "lasso," "twirl." Here, a filtering process is required to ensure that one answer is selected. Note that, in both conditions, the demands on semantic memory are similar. The subject must comprehend the target noun and retrieve semantic information associated with that noun. However, if this region is involved in the active retrieval of goal-related information, then activation should be greater in the high-filtering condition. The results supported this prediction.

Converging evidence was obtained in a neuropsychological study (Thompson-Schill et al., 1998). Patients with lesions that spanned the inferior frontal cortex in the left hemisphere failed on about 15% of the trials in the high-filtering condition. Interestingly, these errors did not result from the generation of an erroneous verb. Rather, the patients either failed to come up with a single verb within 30 s or simply read the nouns. Such errors did not occur in the low-filtering condition; in fact, the patients made essentially no errors in this condition.

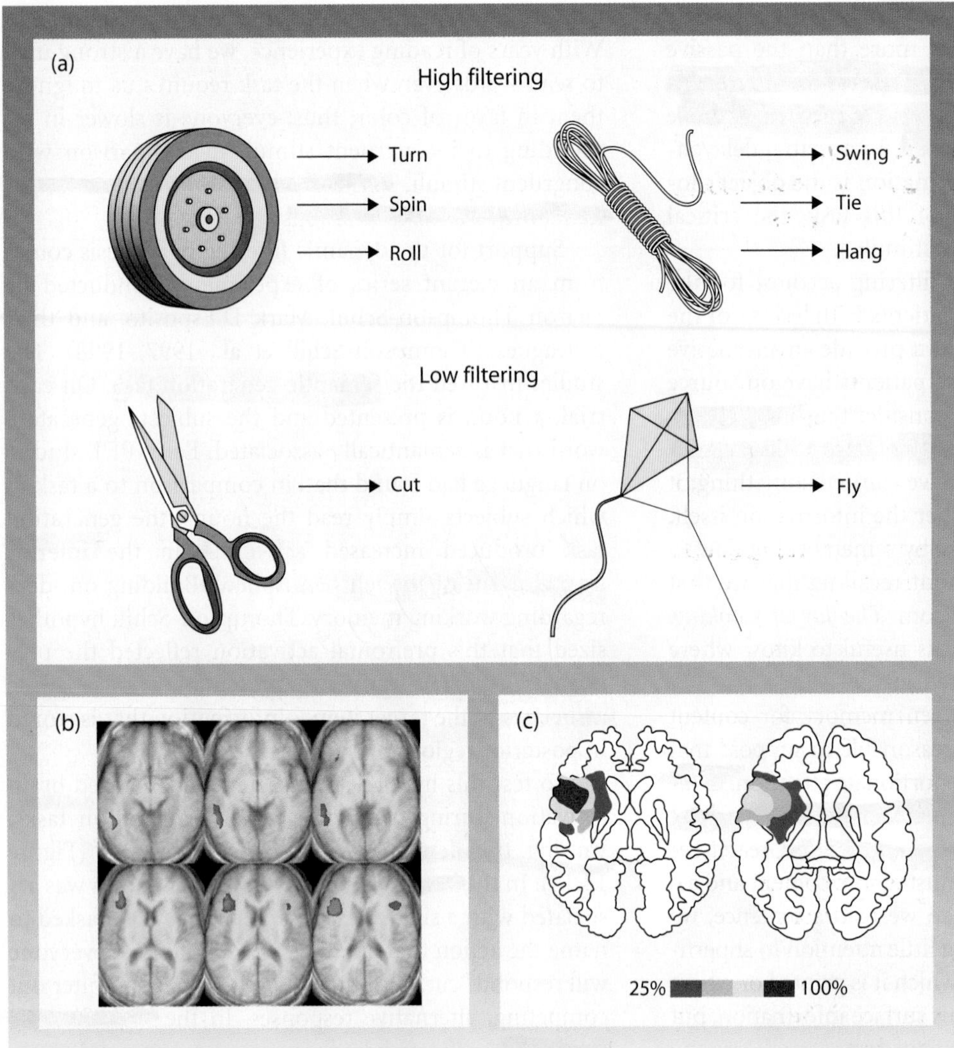

Figure 13.18 Involvement of inferior frontal cortex in memory retrieval and response selection. **(a)** The verb generation task can be performed with nouns that are associated with many actions (high filtering) or few actions (low filtering). **(b)** In these scans, areas showing higher activity in the high-filtering condition are shown in yellow. **(c)** Lesion overlap in patients who had difficulty in the high-filtering condition. Colors indicate the percentage of patients with damage in the highlighted regions.

The inability of the patients to come up with a verb points to a problem, not only with filtering, but also with semantic retrieval. These same patients would have no trouble judging that the words *rope* and *twirl* go together; thus, their semantic knowledge is intact. But when they have to select one response from among a set of viable candidates, either they are unable to filter out irrelevant or suboptimal responses, or they get stuck and fail to succeed in semantic retrieval.

Note that the generation task also increased activation in the left temporal lobe in comparison to a baseline repeat task. This area is a reasonable candidate for the long-term storage of semantic information. Indeed, the results of a follow-up study support this hypothesis (Thompson-Schill et al., 1999). Subjects were trained to make two types of generation responses, one based on naming an action associated with the noun and another based on naming the color associated with the noun. The initial scanning run revealed a replication of the prefrontal and temporal cortical engagement during the generation tasks, demonstrating that the same inferior frontal region was recruited for both types of semantic associations.

Of interest here is what happened in subsequent scanning runs. The list of nouns was repeated. In one condition, the subjects performed the same generation task as for the first run; in the other, they were required to perform the alternative generation task. This manipulation led to an interesting dissociation between the BOLD response in the prefrontal and temporal cortices. Prefrontal activation increased in scanning runs in which the generation requirements changed. Selection and filtering would likely be high under such conditions. A different pattern was seen in the temporal lobe. Here the activation decreased on the second run for both the same and the different generation conditions. Such decreases with repetition have been seen in many imaging studies of priming (see Chapter 8). The fact that the decrease was observed even when the generation requirements changed is consistent with the idea that semantic attributes, whether relevant or irrelevant to the task at hand, are automatically activated upon presentation of the nouns. The prefrontal cortex applies a dynamic filter to help retrieve and select information that is relevant to the current task requirements.

Task Switching

The loss of dynamic filtering captures an essential feature of prefrontal damage. Basic cognitive capabilities are generally spared. The patients' intelligence shows little evidence of change, and they can perform normally on many tests of psychological function. But they are in a particularly vulnerable condition. In an environment in which multiple sources of information compete for attention, the patients have difficulty maintaining their focus.

Task-switching experiments have been designed to examine this aspect of cognitive control. We already introduced one such example, the Wisconsin Card Sorting Task (see Figure 13.16). This task tests how flexible a person can be in sorting multidimensional stimuli. As with many other neuropsychological tests, however, the Wisconsin Card Sorting Task is limited in terms of how well it can isolate particular mental operations. It was developed as a diagnostic tool: Poor performance on the test correlates with frontal lobe damage. Thus, it is an important tool for clinical neuropsychologists who wish to assess frontal function in patients with head trauma or degenerative disorders, but the source of the patients' failure remains unclear. It may reflect the strategic requirements involved in trial-and-error learning, a tendency to focus on one stimulus dimension at the expense of others, or an inability to ignore a dimension that was reinforced previously.

To get around this limitation, simplified *task-switching* experiments are used. In Chapter 7 (see Figure 7.46) we described a task-switching study with Parkinson's disease patients, showing that they had a deficit in their ability to change mental set that is similar to their problems in changing motor set. Another example of a task-switching experiment is shown in Figure 13.19. On each trial, a letter–digit pair is presented. The task goal is switched every two trials, alternating between trials in which the subject is required to name the digit and trials in which the subject is required to name the letter. Thus, in the first trial for each pair the task goal switches (e.g., changes from naming the letter to naming the digit), and in the second the task goal remains the same. The time required to change from one goal to the other, the

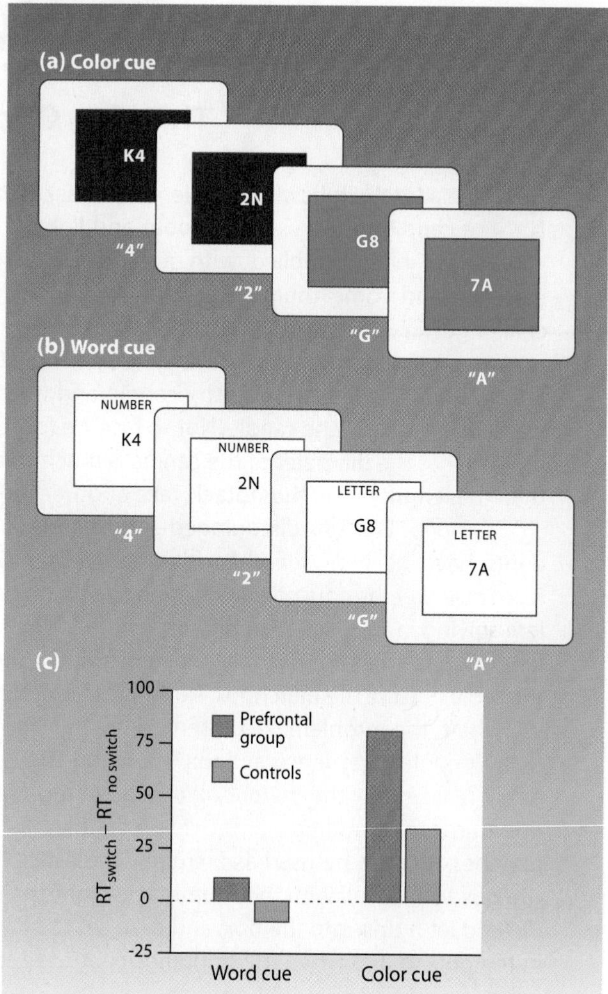

Figure 13.19 Task-switching experiment, with the task cued by either a color **(a)** or a word **(b)**. **(c)** Switching cost, the time required to switch from one task to the other (e.g., from naming the digit to naming the letter), is measured as the difference in reaction time (RT) on switch trials and no-switch trials. Patients with prefrontal lesions showed impairment only on the color cue condition.

switching cost, is measured by the difference in reaction time on these two types of trials.

A second important variable in this experiment is the manner in which the task goal is specified. Given that the trials alternate in a consistent manner, it is possible for subjects to keep track of their place, but doing so would increase the processing requirements for the subjects. To avoid complicating the processing, the task goal is cued by an external cue. In one condition, this cue is indicated by the background color (Figure 13.19a). In the other condition, a visual word cue is used (Figure 13.19b).

As Figure 13.19c shows, the cuing variable turned out to be critical. When a visual word cue was used to

HOW THE BRAIN WORKS

Thinking Outside the (Match)Box

Consider the following problem: Your task is to fix a candle to the wall of a room and light it. You have been supplied with a candle, a box of matches, and some thumbtacks. Are you up for the challenge? Go.

You probably solved this rather quickly. Simply take a thumbtack, stick it through the candle and into the wall, and then light the candle. Not so fast. We forgot to tell you that the diameter of the candle is much thicker than the length of the thumbtack. Take another shot.

Stumped? Don't be discouraged—thousands of students have been mystified by this brainteaser since Rainer Dunker introduced it in his monograph on problem solving in 1945 (cited in Wickelgren, 1974). Here's a hint: Suppose that there is only one match, and it sits on the table outside the matchbox. Now give it another go.

When the problem is presented in this format, many people experience an "aha" moment. They suddenly realize that the matchbox can serve more than one purpose. In addition to providing a striker for the matches, it could be used as a crude candlestick. Tack the box to the wall with the thumbtacks, light the candle and let it drip into the box, and then set the candle in the goo so that when the drippings cool, the candle will be secure in an upright position.

These problems are challenging because, in developing an action plan, we tend to think narrowly about the possible uses of an object—a phenomenon that psychologists refer to as *functional fixedness*. Functional fixedness might be seen as an undesired consequence of having evolved the kind of rapid-response selection ability associated with the prefrontal cortex. As we have seen in the work on semantic generation, the lateral prefrontal cortex facilitates the selection of viable responses from a set of automatically activated long-term representations. With the matchbox, we immediately think of its common use—to light matches—and then mull over how those thumbtacks can be applied to the candle. By emptying the box of matches, we might realize new possibilities; but even here, many people continue to be unable to see novel uses because of the strong association between the stimulus and an action. Chris Frith (2000) has referred to the selection process of lateral prefrontal cortex as "sculpting the response space."

Ready for your next brainteaser? Here is a false arithmetic statement in Roman numerals:

Problem 1: VI = VII + I

Provide a correct solution by moving only one stick. Not too hard. Moving one of the *I*s from the VII to the VI renders the correct statement VII = VI + I.

Now try a problem that, with the one-move rule, is much more difficult:

Problem 2: VI = VI + VI

Stuck again? Moving a matchstick from one of the VI's on the right side of the equation to the left won't do it. Nor will turning a VI into a IV. The answer here requires an unusual transformation of one of the operators and a kind of arithmetic statement that we rarely encounter: VI = VI = VI.

specify the task goal, the patients with lateral prefrontal lesions performed similarly to matched control subjects. When a color cue was used, however, the patients were slow on the switch trials. This dissociation reinforces the idea that the prefrontal cortex is important for coordinating goal-oriented behavior. Moreover, this form of control is needed especially when the goal must be retrieved from memory. With the color cue, the patients must remember the associations between the colors and the tasks (e.g., blue with digit naming). The word cues do not require this referencing back to memory.

One result of this experiment is noteworthy. Parkinson's disease patients who were tested on the same task had no difficulty in either the color cue or the word cue condition. This finding would seem to be at odds with that shown in Figure 7.46. One difference between the two studies is the use of a fixed sequence in which the two tasks alternated every other trial. Perhaps the Parkinson's disease patients were able to anticipate the switch from one goal to the next. Frontal patients failed to exhibit the kind of insight needed to come up with such strategies.

On the basis of the selection hypothesis, Carlo Reverberi and his colleagues at the University of Milan made an unusual prediction. They proposed that patients with lateral prefrontal cortex would actually do *better* on Problem 2 than would healthy control subjects. This prediction was based on the idea that an impaired selection process would make it easier for the patients to represent atypical actions. Indeed, this is exactly what they found. The superior performance of the patients was especially striking, given that these individuals were worse than the controls when presented with equations such as that of Problem 1 or equations in which standard operator transformations were required (e.g., V = III − II in which the equal and minus signs are swapped by the movement of one matchstick). Here the patients' impairment became greater as the number of possible moves increased, consistent with the idea that the lateral prefrontal cortex is especially critical when the response space must be narrowed. But for equations like Problem 2, the "sculpting" process of prefrontal cortex led the controls to focus on the numbers or simple changes in the operators (e.g., turn the plus sign into a minus).

These results are especially compelling when we consider that neuropsychological studies rarely involve tasks in which a patient group performs better than a control group. By thinking deeply about the implications of a theory regarding prefrontal function, the researchers were able to recognize that processes that confer a functional advantage in most situations—rapidly selecting task-relevant responses—may not be optimal in certain situations. Like the patients with lateral prefrontal cortex, they were thinking outside the box.

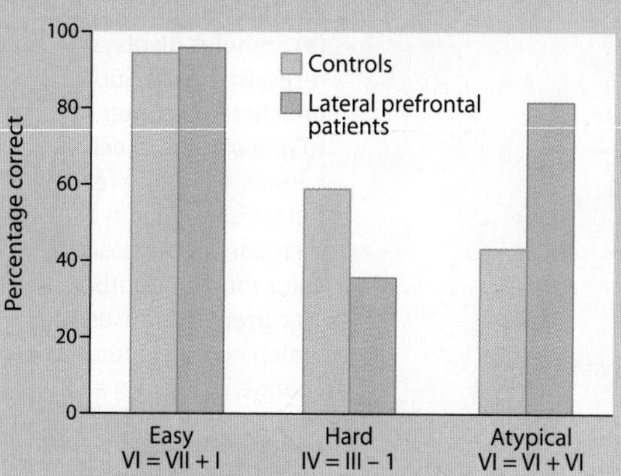

Patients with lateral prefrontal lesions do better than healthy control subjects on a problem-solving task that requires unusual solutions. For the easy and hard conditions, the solution requires moving a matchstick from one side of the equation to the other to transform a numeral or the operators. For the atypical condition, the solution requires rotating a matchstick to create a three-part equality.

Seiki Konishi of the University of Tokyo School of Medicine and colleagues (1998) used fMRI and a computerized version of the Wisconsin Card Sorting Task to specify regions within the prefrontal cortex that are involved in task switching. Recognizing the complexity of the mental operations involved in this task, they focused their analysis on neural responses following a feedback message indicating that a dimensional shift was required (Figure 13.20). The most prominent foci were in the inferior frontal sulci in both hemispheres. The magnitude of the hemodynamic response during task switching was a function of the number of possible dimensions. Larger responses were observed when there were three potential new dimensions rather than just one or two new dimensions. Although the function of this area may be important for inhibiting the dimension that is no longer relevant, it also appears to be related to the demands of selecting between new courses of action. Selection is required to determine the appropriate goal, and once an action has been selected, the subject must bring into working memory the new categorization rule that will guide the processing of forthcoming stimulus information.

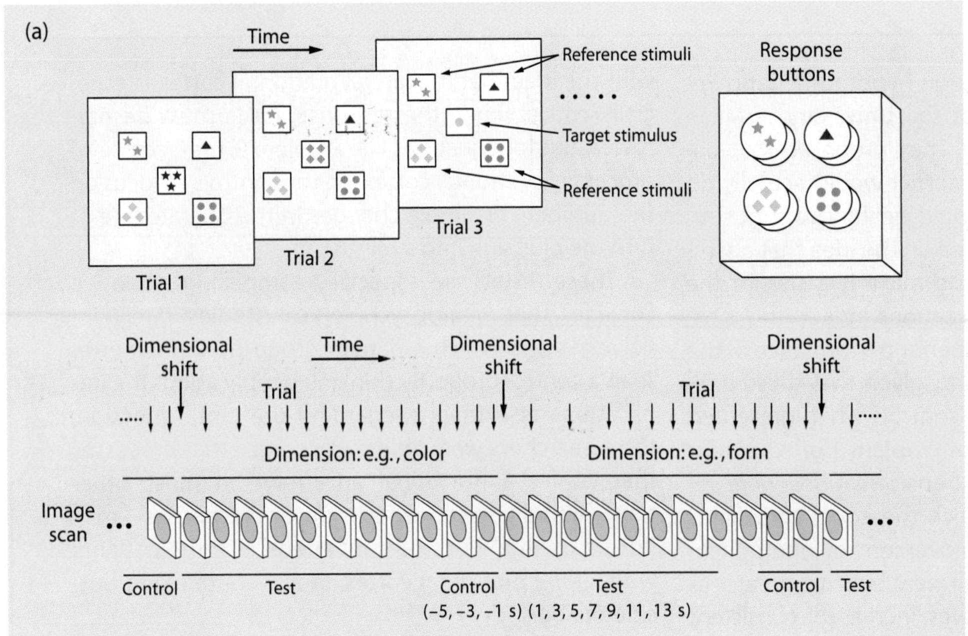

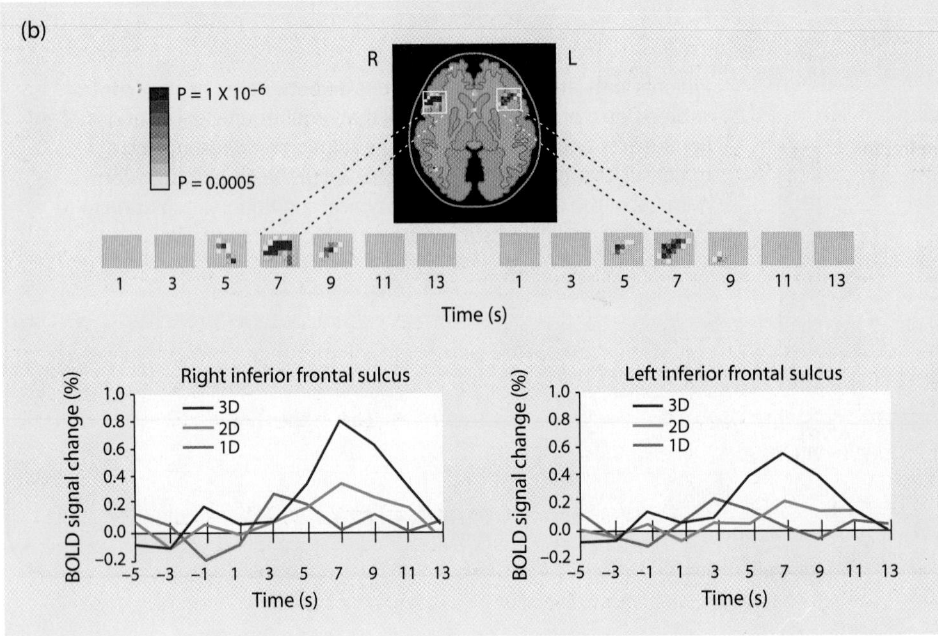

Figure 13.20 Modified Wisconsin Card Sorting Task for event-related fMRI. **(a)** Stimulus displays and response board. Subjects matched the center object to one of four objects in the corners, using the response buttons. The match could be made on the basis of color, form, or number. After 10 correct responses, the matching rule would change, indicating a dimensional shift. **(b)** Increased activation was observed bilaterally in the inferior frontal cortex following the signal to shift dimensions. Note that the hemodynamic response peaks about 7 s after the shift.

TOP-DOWN COGNITIVE CONTROL

Dynamic filtering is a form of *top-down control* (see Chapter 12). In the Golden Gate Bridge and semantic associate examples, this top-down control was seen as facilitating the retrieval of some information from long-term memory. In the Stroop task, top-down control facilitates online processing in a similar manner. The task goal requires that we attend to one visual dimension (the color of the ink) while ignoring another visual dimension (the word). A focus of considerable research has been to understand the neural mechanisms through which top-down control is achieved. This problem is especially challenging because it requires understanding interactions between brain regions that are considerably far apart. Neurophysiological studies in primates are difficult because it would be extremely challenging to identify neurons in frontal and parietal cortices that were functionally or causally linked.

For these reasons, much of the work on top-down control has involved human studies and has required rather clever experimental strategies. Jon Driver and his colleagues at University College London provide one remarkable example in which they concurrently used transcranial magnetic stimulation and functional MRI (Ruff et al., 2006). Using a TMS machine in the scanner environment requires considerable technical innovation. The stimulator must be secured so that it does not move when exposed to the scanner's magnet field. It must also be strong enough to withstand the powerful magnetic field exerted by the scanner. Finally, the magnetic and electrical fields produced by the TMS device can distort the fMRI measurements of brain activity. To overcome these problems, a special magnet was built and combined with an fMRI protocol in which the TMS pulses were timed to occur between pulse sequences generated by the MRI scanner.

In this way the researchers were able to ask how TMS over a particular region of the frontal lobe, the frontal eye fields (FEFs), influenced the BOLD response in posterior cortex. As described in Chapter 12, the FEFs are known to play a role in spatial attention, working in tandem with the superior colliculus to control eye movements. Attention requires a balance between maintaining the current focus and shifting to novel salient stimuli, and the FEF appears to be critical for overcoming the tendency to look at novel stimuli. Thus, the researchers were interested in how TMS over the FEF would influence retinotopic maps in early visual areas. They repeated the well-tested fMRI method of mapping visual areas (see Chapter 5) but interspersed the visual stimulus with short bursts of TMS pulses under the assumption that these pulses would cause transient disruption of the FEF (Figure 13.21).

Compared to a condition in which the TMS was directed to a control site, the BOLD response was attenuated in those portions of the visual areas that represented central vision. More surprising, activation was increased in the regions that represented peripheral vision. These results suggest that, without the top-down influence from the FEF, perceptual signals arising in the fovea are attenuated and those from the periphery become more salient. This prediction was confirmed in a follow-up behavioral study. Subjects judged flashes of light in the periphery as brighter following FEF TMS compared to TMS over a control site.

Inhibitory and Facilitatory Mechanisms for Top-Down Control

Top-down control could influence the contents of information processing in at least two distinct ways. One is to accentuate the attended information. For example, when we attend to a location, our sensitivity to detect a stimulus at that location is enhanced. Or we can selectively attend by excluding information from other locations. Similarly, when multiple sources of information come from the same location, we might selectively enhance the task-relevant information or inhibit the irrelevant information. In behavioral tasks it is often difficult to distinguish between facilitatory and inhibitory modes of control. Moreover, as seen in times of budgetary crises, the hypotheses are not mutually

Figure 13.21 Combined use of TMS and fMRI to study top-down prefrontal control of visual cortex. **(a)** TMS was targeted to disrupt activity in the frontal eye fields (red) or a control site (blue). **(b, c)** A series of five TMS pulses was applied during a 570-ms interval that separated phases during which fMRI data were collected while subjects viewed either visual stimuli **(b)** or a blank screen **(c)**. By comparing these conditions, the experimenters could assess whether the retinotopic maps in visual cortex were altered when top-down signals from the frontal cortex were disrupted.

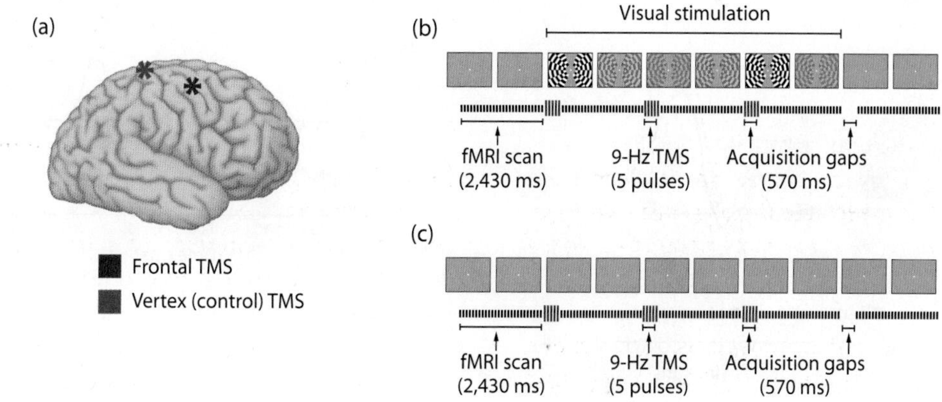

exclusive. If we have fixed resources, allocating resources to one thing places a limit on what is available for others; thus, the form of top-down control may vary as a function of task demands.

Evidence for a loss of **inhibitory control** comes from electrophysiological studies involving patients with frontal lobe dysfunction. Robert Knight of the University of California, Berkeley, recorded the evoked potentials in groups of patients with localized neurological disorders (Knight & Grabowecky, 1995). In the simplest experiment, subjects were presented with tones, and no response was required. As might be expected, the evoked responses were attenuated in patients with lesions in the temporoparietal cortex in comparison to control subjects. This difference was apparent about 30 ms after stimulus onset, the time when stimuli would be expected to reach the primary auditory cortex. The attenuation presumably reflects tissue loss in the region that generates the evoked signal. A more curious aspect is shown in Figure 13.22: Patients with frontal lobe lesions have enhanced evoked responses. This enhancement was not seen in the evoked responses at subcortical levels; the effect did not reflect a generalized increase in sensory responsiveness but was limited to the cortex.

The failure to inhibit irrelevant information was more apparent when the subjects were instructed to attend to auditory signals in one ear and ignore similar sounds in the opposite ear, with the attended ear varied between blocks (see Figure 13.22b). In this way, one can assess the evoked response to identical stimuli under

Figure 13.22 Evoked potentials reveal filtering deficits in patients with lesions in the lateral prefrontal cortex. **(a)** Evoked responses to auditory clicks in three groups of neurological patients. The subjects were not required to respond to the clicks. The first positive peak occurs at about 8 ms and reflects neural activity in the inferior colliculus (IC). The second positive peak occurs at about 30 ms (the P30), reflecting neural responses in the primary auditory cortex. Both responses are normal in patients with parietal damage **(top)**. The second peak is reduced in patients with temporoparietal damage **(middle)**, reflecting the loss of neurons in the primary auditory cortex. The auditory cortex response is amplified in patients with frontal damage **(bottom)**, suggesting a loss of inhibition from frontal lobe to temporal lobe. Note that the evoked response for control subjects is repeated in each panel. **(b)** Difference waves for attended and unattended auditory signals. Subjects were instructed to monitor tones in either the left or the right ear. The evoked response to the unattended tones is subtracted from the evoked response to the attended tones. In healthy individuals, the effects of attention are seen at approximately 100 ms, marked by a larger negativity (N100). Patients with right prefrontal lesions show no attention effect for contralesional tones presented in the left ear but show a normal effect for ipsilesional tones. Patients with left prefrontal lesions show reduced attention effects for both contralateral and ipsilateral tones.

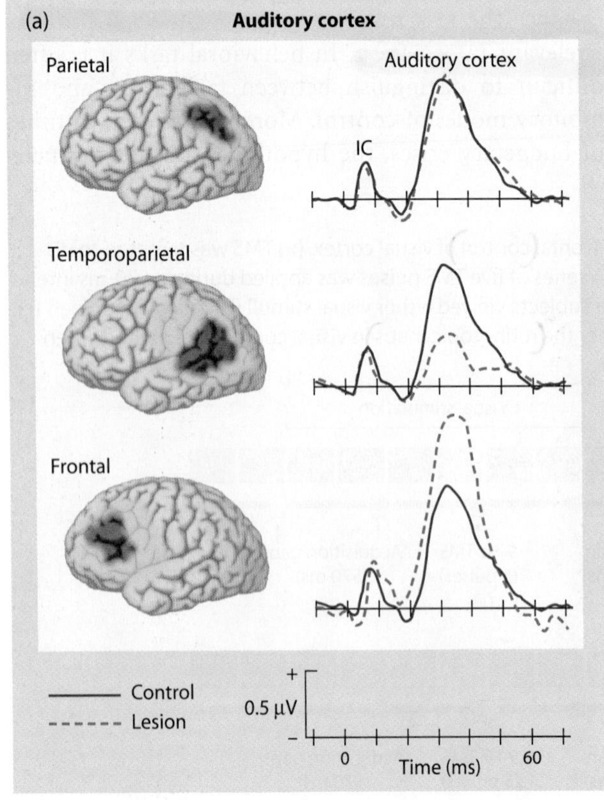

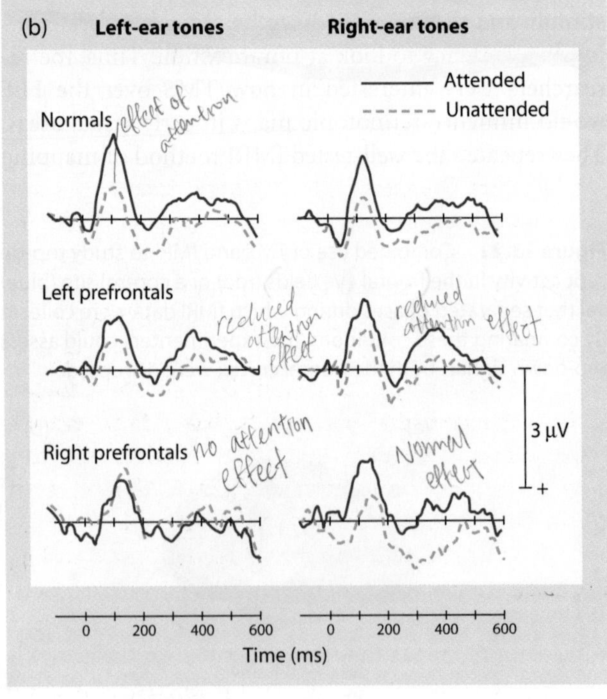

different attentional sets (e.g., response to left-ear sounds when they are attended or ignored). With healthy subjects, these responses diverge at about 100 ms; the evoked response to the attended signal becomes greater. This difference is absent in patients with prefrontal lesions, especially for stimuli presented to the ear contralateral to the lesion. What happens is that the unattended stimulus receives a heightened response, which accords with the notion that the frontal lobes modulate the salience of perceptual signals by inhibiting unattended information. We are bombarded with stimuli: Our ability to respond appropriately requires that we select information relevant to the task.

In the study just described, we can see inhibition operating to minimize the impact of irrelevant perceptual information. This same mechanism can be applied to memory tasks for which information must be internally maintained. Again, consider the monkey attempting to perform a delayed-response task (see Figure 13.3). The monkey views the target being placed in one of the food wells, and then the blind is closed during the delay period. The monkey's mind does not just shut down; it sees and hears the blind being drawn, looks about the room during the delay interval, and perhaps contemplates its hunger. All such intervening events can distract the animal and cause it to lose track of which location is baited. To succeed, it must ignore the distractions and sustain the representation of its forthcoming response. We have all experienced failures in similar situations. A friend gives us her telephone number, but we forget it. The problem is not a failure to encode the number. Something else captures our attention, and we fail to block out the distraction. This point is underscored by the fact that primates with prefrontal lesions perform better on delayed-response tasks when the room is darkened during the delay (Malmo, 1942) or when they are given drugs that decrease distractibility.

Failure of inhibition also can account for the dissociation between recognition and recency memory. Subjects must remember all stimuli because they do not know which will be tested in probe trials. As we encode each stimulus, we pay attention to it, with one cost being the inhibition of previous stimuli. The degree of activation of a representation is inversely related to how long ago the stimulus was presented. As shown in Figure 13.23, recency judgments can be made by comparison of the magnitude of the two target items. Whichever item has the strongest residual activation is judged most recent. For healthy subjects, inhibition could quickly lower the activation of distinct items. But for frontal lobe patients, the loss of inhibition would result in lingering activations and render such judgments difficult. Paradoxically, though, these patients would not have a problem with recognition, because their memory is so high.

The preceding discussion emphasized how top-down control might be achieved by the inhibition of task-irrelevant information. However, top-down control may also involve the amplification of task-relevant information. This issue has been studied in a series of experiments by Mark D'Esposito and his colleagues at the University of California, Berkeley. As we saw in Chapter 6, regions in the inferior temporal lobe are preferentially activated by face and place stimuli—the so-called FFA (fusiform face area) and PPA (parahippocampal place area), respectively. Exploiting this fact, this group of researchers asked whether activation in these regions is modulated when people are instructed to remember either faces or places for a subsequent memory test (Figure 13.24a). At the start of each trial, an instruction cue indicated the current task. Then a set of four pictures was presented: two faces and two scenes.

Figure 13.23 When a subject is presented with a series of items, activation for each item decays. A loss of inhibitory mechanisms following frontal lobe damage will lead to a slower decay process. Judgments on a recency memory task may be based on a comparison of the residual activation of the series of stimuli. In healthy people, the rapid decay of activation allows the temporal tag for each item to be distinct. In frontal lobe patients, the sustained activation leads to errors due to the similar activation states associated with successive items.

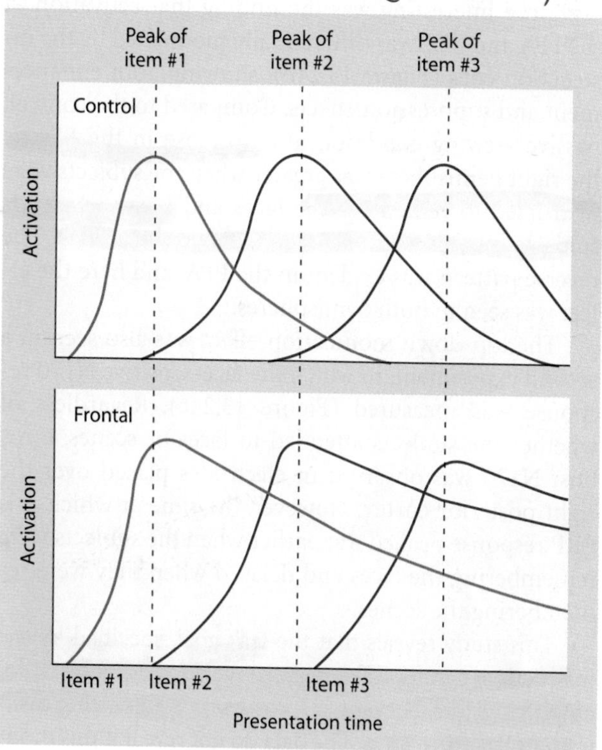

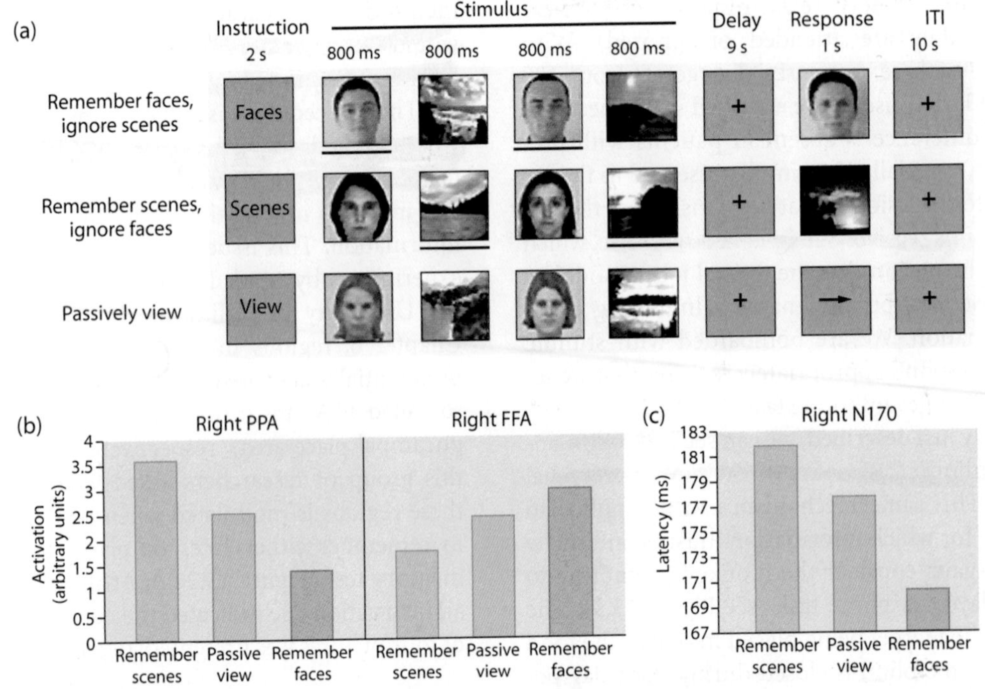

Figure 13.24 Modulation in posterior cortex as a function of task goals. **(a)** In a delayed-response task, subjects had to remember either faces or scenes. **(b)** Compared to a passive viewing control condition, activation in the parahippocampal place area (PPA) was greater when subjects attended to scenes and reduced when subjects attended to faces. The reverse effect was observed in the fusiform face area (FFA). **(c)** The latency of the N170, a face-selective ERP, was also modulated by the task goal. When subjects were attending to faces, this response peaked earlier; when they were attending to scenes, the peak response was delayed.

As expected, a subsequent memory test verified that the subjects selectively attended to the relevant dimension.

More interesting was the finding that activation in the FFA and PPA was differentially modulated by the instruction cues (Figure 13.24b), showing both enhancement and suppression effects. Compared to the control, passive viewing condition, the response in the FFA of the right hemisphere was greater when the subjects were instructed to remember the faces and lower when the subjects were instructed to remember the scenes. The reverse pattern was evident in the PPA, and here the effect was seen in both hemispheres.

The top-down modulation effect was also seen in a second experiment, in which the face-sensitive N170 response was measured (Figure 13.24c). Regardless of whether the subjects attended to faces or scenes, a robust N170 was observed in electrodes placed over the right posterior cortex. However, the time at which this ERP response peaked was earlier when the subjects were remembering the faces and delayed when they were remembering the scenes.

This study reveals that the task goal, specified by the instruction, can modulate perceptual processing by either amplifying task-relevant information or inhibiting task-irrelevant information. The data do not reveal if this modulation is the result of prefrontal activation. However, various lines of evidence indicate that representation of the task goal is maintained in prefrontal cortex, suggesting a causal role. A direct test would require analyzing whether activation in the prefrontal cortex is correlated with the changes observed in the FFA or PPA, or asking if damage to the prefrontal cortex, either in neurological patients or with TMS, interfered with subjects' ability to use the instruction cue. These predictions have not yet been tested.

An interesting extension of this work provides a first stab at answering this question. Here the same experiment was repeated, but this time the participants were older, neurologically healthy individuals (Gazzaley, Cooney, Rissman, et al., 2005). Unlike college-age subjects, the older subjects showed only an enhancement effect; they did not show the suppression effect in either FFA or PPA compared to the passive viewing condition. These findings are intriguing for two reasons. First, they suggest that enhancement (i.e., amplification) and suppression (i.e., inhibition) involve different neural mechanisms, with the latter more sensitive to the effects of aging. Second, given that aging is thought to disproportionately affect prefrontal function, perhaps inhibitory top-down control is more dependent on prefrontal cortex than are the attentional mechanisms that underlie the amplification of task-relevant information.

An alternative way to look at the role of prefrontal cortex in top-down control is to consider what happens when attentional resources are challenged by the requirement that two tasks be performed simultaneously. Consider the experiment outlined in Figure 13.25. Subjects were required to switch back and forth between two tasks: one designed to involve working memory, and a second that looked at selective attention. For the former, the subject had to remember a string of digits in order to judge if a probe digit was part of the memory set. In one condition, the demands on working memory were high because the digit set varied from trial to trial. In another condition, the demands on working memory were low because the same set was used on each trial. In the selective-attention task, subjects judged if a name was associated with a politician or a pop star. The names were presented over a face; thus, the task required selective attention because the subjects had to ignore the faces. As predicted, the manipulation of working memory led to an increase in activation in prefrontal cortex. Moreover, the response in the FFA to the irrelevant faces was greater when working memory was taxed by varying of the digit set from trial to trial. These results indicate that when prefrontal cortex is occupied by one task, the ability to ignore irrelevant information, the faces, is reduced.

In most situations, our goals specify the information that we want to highlight. When scanning a crowd at the airport for our parents, we may activate perceptual units that correspond to their salient features. Or when driving to our favorite restaurant, we may look for familiar landmarks. However, we also appear to be capable of actively preventing some information from entering working memory. This form of suppression is different from that required when we want to avoid being distracted by irrelevant information. Rather, top-down control in this context might be useful for preventing undesirable information from gaining access to long-term memory. This kind of control is, in a sense, reminiscent of the idea that Sigmund Freud had when he developed his theory of the unconscious mind, suggesting that we repress unwanted thoughts and desires.

Michael Anderson at the University of Oregon offers a 21st-century perspective on the question of active repression using a clever experimental design. Subjects initially learn a set of word–pair associations such as *steam–train*. Later they are given the first word as a cue and told *not* to think of the associated word. This is, of course, a hard thing to do. If you are told to try *not* to think about pink elephants, probably the first thing that pops into your mind is an image of Dumbo's nightmare with pink elephants flying across the sky. Nonetheless, in subsequent memory tests, people are poorer at remembering the word pairs that they were instructed to keep out of mind.

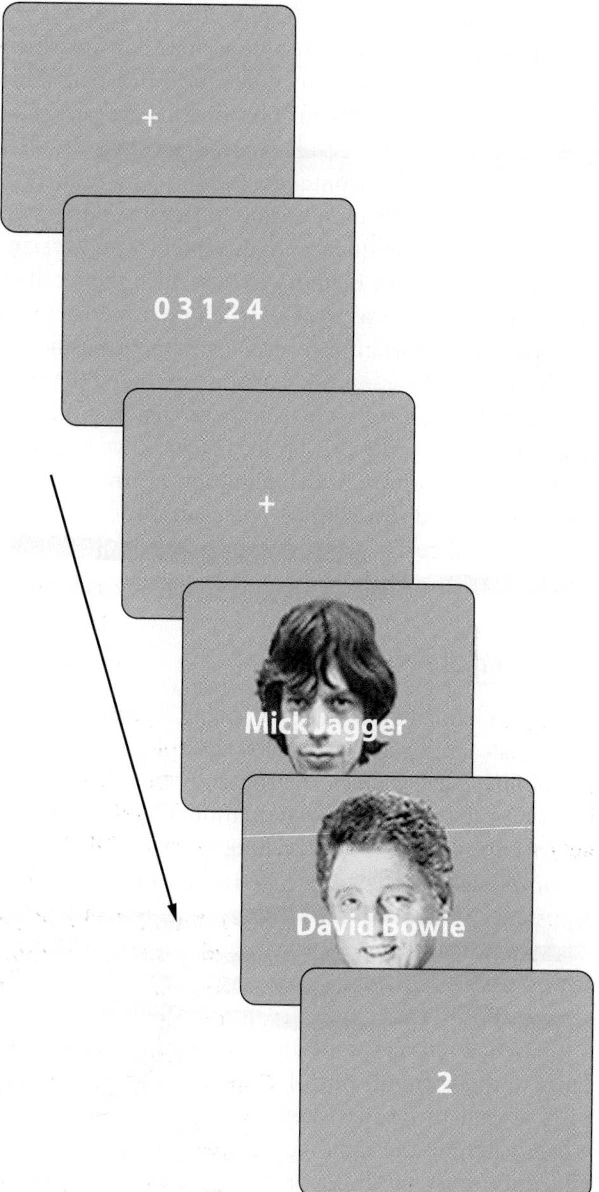

Figure 13.25 Method to study the role of attention in top-down control. The primary task required subjects to judge if the name belonged to a politician or a pop star. The background face could either be congruent or incongruent with the name (and category), creating a form of Stroop effect. The experimenters challenged the subjects' ability to ignore the faces by having them simultaneously remember a list of digits.

Anderson has shown that this active repression involves another form of top-down control. Activation in the prefrontal cortex was greater when subjects were presented with the single word cues and instructed not to think about its associate (e.g., if cued with *steam*, do not think of *train*) compared to a condition in which they were instructed to remember the word pair. This finding is consistent with our phenomenal experience—it requires effort not to think about something. Paralleling this enhanced prefrontal activation was a reduction in hippocampal activation during retrieval suppression. The behavioral consequences of this interaction were evident in a subsequent memory test in which the recall of the associated item was weakest when prefrontal activity was greatest. Importantly, control experiments, using indirect methods to assess performance, excluded the possibility that subjects were simply pretending not to remember the word pairs. From this work we can conclude that, in addition to the inhibition of irrelevant information, top-down control processes associated with the prefrontal cortex can either amplify or inhibit relevant information, depending on the behavioral goals.

Inhibition of Action

Inhibitory control can take on many forms. We have seen that failures of inhibition lead to greater distractibility, a hallmark of prefrontal dysfunction. As described in the preceding section, inhibition may also be deployed to control access to long-term memory. Inhibition is useful for cognitive control also in a third circumstance: when we are about to take an action and something causes us to change our mind; we suddenly realize that a selected response is not appropriate and seek to abort the action before it is fully realized.

Baseball players constantly recognize the importance of this form of control. A hitter has only a fraction of a second to decide whether or not to swing a bat when watching the rapid approach of the pitched ball. Not only must the hitter track an object moving at a speed that pushes the limits of the human visual system, but a skilled pitcher is devious, putting exotic spins on the ball. The hitter may decide to swing the bat, only to recognize suddenly that the ball is about to take a dive or curve outside of reach. Sometimes the hitter can quickly halt the action—what is commonly referred to as a *check-swing*. This form of inhibition—the cancellation of a planned action—is actually quite common even for those of us who never play baseball. At a party, we often find ourselves ready to jump in with a pithy idea, only to find that the loudmouth bore has once again commandeered the conversation. Politely, we hold back, waiting for another opportunity.

Inhibition of this form can be seen as the opposite of action selection. But are the neural mechanisms the same? That is, to inhibit an action, do we *deselect* that action by generating some sort of negative image of the brain activation? Even if this were possible, it might not be sufficient to inhibit the unwanted action. The commands to produce the planned action have already been sent to the motor system, and simply to deactivate the plan would not result in termination of an initiated movement.

This form of inhibitory control has been studied with the *stop-signal task*. In the standard form of this experiment, subjects are tested in a reaction time task in which they have to choose between two alternatives. For example, if an arrow points to the left, press one button; if to the right, another button. The twist here, though, is that, on a certain percentage of the trials, a signal indicates that the response should be aborted. This stop signal might be a change in color or the presentation of a sound. The time between the onset of the initial stimulus and the stop signal can be adjusted, creating a situation in which the subject sometimes succeeds in aborting the planned response and sometimes fails to abort the response. Three conditions result (a) trials without a stop signal (go trials), (b) trials in which the person is able to stop (successful stop trials), and (c) trials in which the person fails to stop (failed stop trials; Figure 13.26).

Adam Aron at the University of California, San Diego, has employed a multimethod approach to establish the neural network that underlies this form of cognitive control. Patients with lesions of the frontal lobe are slow to abort a planned response. This impairment appears to be specific to lesions of the inferior frontal gyrus on the right side, since the deficit is not present in patients with left frontal lesions or in patients with damage restricted to more dorsal parts of the right prefrontal cortex. The association of the right prefrontal cortex with this form of inhibitory control is also supported by fMRI data obtained in young adults. Here the BOLD response can be plotted for each of the three trial types (Figure 13.26b). Both successful stop trials and failed stop trials produce a strong response in the right inferior frontal gyrus. In contrast, this area is silent on go trials. The fact that the BOLD signal is very similar for both types of stop trials suggests that an inhibitory process is recruited in both situations, even though the control signal to abort the response is effective on only some trials.

Why might this be? The BOLD response in motor cortex is revealing. Here we see strong activation on both go trials and failed stop trials. However, the activation in motor cortex on the failed stop trials is already high when the initial stimulus is presented (time = 0). Remember that the participants are under a lot of pressure in these experiments to go as fast as possible. It is likely that this prestimulus activation reflects a high state of anticipation. Even though the right prefrontal cortex generates a stop command, the initial level of ac-

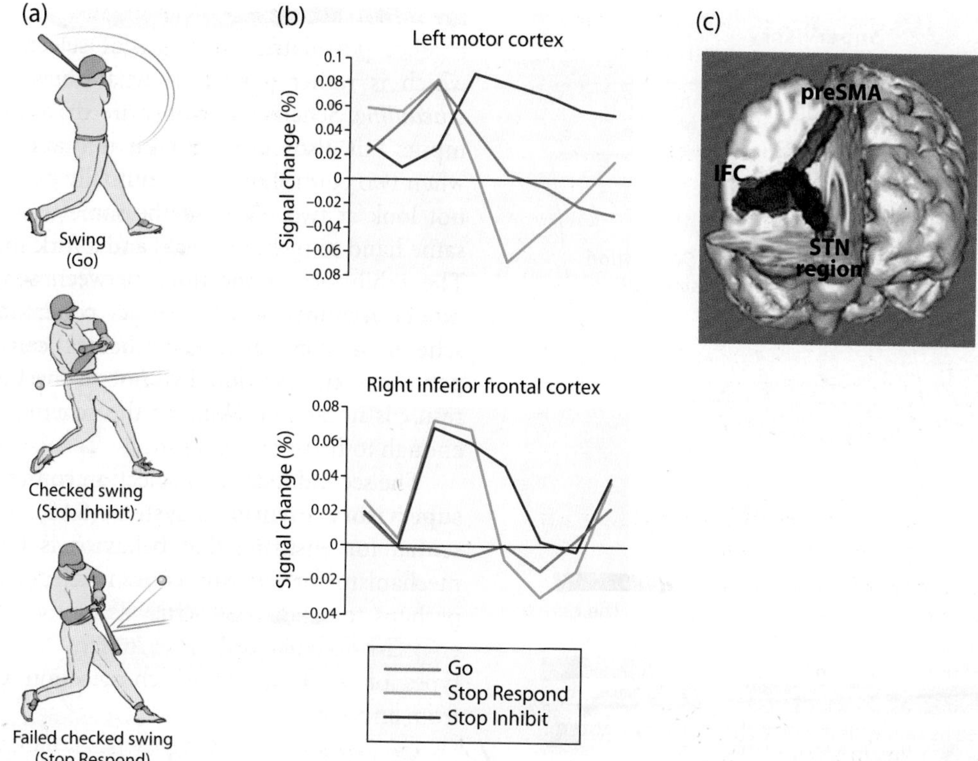

Figure 13.26 Role of the right inferior prefrontal gyrus in inhibitory control. **(a)** Successful actions sometimes require the ability to abort a planned response. **(b)** BOLD response in motor cortex (M1) and right inferior frontal cortex (IFC) on trials in which a required response is performed (Go), a planned response is successfully aborted (Stop Inhibit), or a planned response that should be aborted is erroneously executed (Stop Respond). The IFC responds on all stop trials, regardless of whether the person is able to abort the response. In M1, activation is high at the start of the trial on failed stop trials, likely reflecting a high state of anticipation in the motor system. **(c)** Diffusion tensor imaging reveals an anatomical network linking IFC with presupplementary motor area (preSMA) and the subthalamic nucleus (STN) of the basal ganglia.

tivation in motor cortex has led to a fast response, and the person is unable to abort the movement. For an antsy baseball player, it's strike three.

The right inferior frontal gyrus pattern was also present in the subthalamic nucleus (STN) of the basal ganglia. As we saw in Chapter 7, the basal ganglia are implicated in response initiation. Within this subcortical system, the STN provides a strong excitatory signal to the globus pallidus, helping maintain inhibition of the cortex. The stop-signal work suggests how this inhibition might be recruited within the context of cognitive control. Activation of the right prefrontal cortex generates the command to abort a response, and this command is implemented through the recruitment of the STN. This hypothesis led Aron and his colleagues to predict the existence of an anatomical connection between the right prefrontal cortex and the STN. Using diffusion tensor imaging (DTI), they confirmed this prediction (Figure 13.26c). The reason that this works so elegantly is that behavioral and fMRI results led the researchers to uncover an anatomical pathway that had never been described in the literature. This anatomical pathway includes the presupplementary motor area, a part of the medial frontal cortex. As we will see shortly, this region is activated in functional-imaging studies when there is response conflict—something that is obviously present in the stop-signal task.

ENSURING THAT GOAL-ORIENTED BEHAVIORS SUCCEED

Tim Shallice, together with Donald Norman of the University of California, San Diego (D. A. Norman & Shallice, 1986), developed the model in Figure 13.27 to account for goal-oriented behavior. Like concepts developed in Chapter 7, this model conceptualizes the selection of an action as a competitive process. At the heart of the model is the notion of *schema control units*, or *representations*

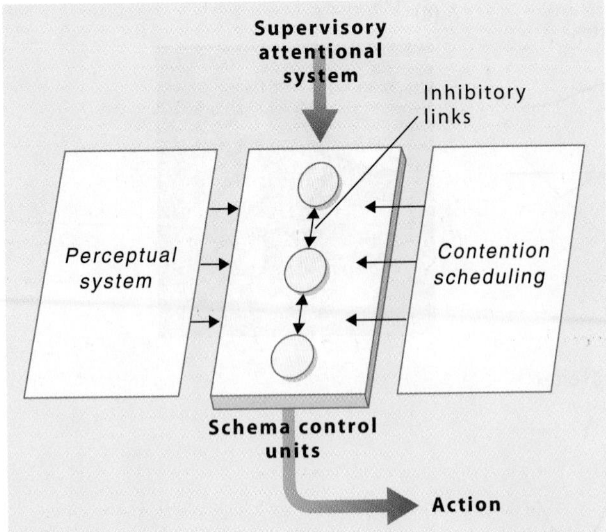

Figure 13.27 Norman and Shallice's model of response selection. Actions are linked to schema control units. The perceptual system produces input to these control units. However, selection of these units can be biased by the contention scheduling units and the supervisory attentional system (SAS). The SAS provides flexibility in the response selection system.

of responses (a term used in a generic sense here). These schemas can correspond to explicit movements or to the activation of long-term representations that lead to purposeful behaviors. For example, when we see a word printed on paper, an action schema could be the articulatory gestures required to pronounce the word. Or, in reading the word, its semantic meaning and associated representations may be activated.

Schema control units receive input from many sources. Norman and Shallice emphasized perceptual inputs and their link to these control units. The strength of the connections, however, reflects the effects of learning. If we have had experience in restaurant dining, walking into a restaurant will activate behaviors associated with waiting for the hostess or looking at the menu. Moreover, walking into the restaurant can elicit varied affective responses—which is how somatic markers influence schema control units. A restaurant setting is often associated with pleasant memories of fine meals and good company. For some, though, it may reawaken painful thoughts of washing dishes or waiting for grown-ups to end dull conversations.

External inputs can be sufficient to trigger schema control units. For example, it is hard not to move your eyes when tracking a moving object. But in most situations our actions are not dictated solely by the input; many schema control units can be activated simultaneously, and a control process is needed to ensure that the appropriate control units are selected. Norman and Shallice postulated two types of selection. One type, which is rather passive, is what they call *contention scheduling*. Schemas not only are driven by perceptual inputs but also compete with one another, especially when two control units are mutually exclusive. We cannot look at two places at the same time or move the same hand to pick up a glass and a fork simultaneously. The inhibitory connections between schemas in this model account for why we act coherently. Only one schema (or nonoverlapping schemas) can win the competition. If competition does not resolve the conflict, the result is no action. None of the schemas are activated enough to trigger a response.

The second means for selection comes by way of the **supervisory attentional system (SAS)**. The SAS is essential for ensuring that behavior is flexible. It is a mechanism for favoring certain schema control units, perhaps to reflect the demands of the situation or to emphasize some goals over others. We can postulate types of situations in which selection would benefit from an SAS:

1. Planning or decision making is required
2. Links between the input and schema control units are novel or not well learned
3. The required response competes with a strong, habitual response
4. Error correction or troubleshooting is required
5. The situation is difficult or dangerous

The SAS is a psychological model of cognitive control. It specifies some of the key situations in which control operations would be useful. Although the SAS in this model is sketched as a single entity, it is unlikely that only one neural structure would be involved in all of these operations. It would be more plausible to expect the functions embodied in the SAS to be part of a distributed network, a set of neural regions that, as a group, come into play in the situations that we have described.

Much of the discussion in this chapter has emphasized the first type of situation. We have seen various ways in which prefrontal cortex is important for goal-oriented behavior: It provides a way to represent the goals that guide our actions and thus select, maintain, and manipulate the information that is essential for accomplishing these goals. Complex behaviors require an ability to switch from one subgoal to another or, in multitask situations, to switch between subtasks. Again, the evidence suggests a key role for prefrontal cortex in this function.

The last four situations listed share one aspect of cognitive control that has not been discussed in detail to this point. For a person engaged in goal-oriented behavior, especially a behavior that includes subgoals, it is important that there be a way to monitor progress. If this is a well-learned process, there should be a means for signaling deviations from the expected course of events. The cook must recognize that the stove thermostat is off when his favorite soufflé has failed to puff up. If the behavior is novel, or being performed in an unusual context, then different actions must be evaluated to determine if progress is being made toward achieving the goal. The cook may experiment with a few new spices in the soufflé for a special dinner. But if the combination turns out all wrong, he will want to whip together a last-minute concoction.

The Medial Frontal Cortex as a Monitoring System

One might expect the task of a **monitoring** system to be like that of a supervisor, whether in a busy high-class restaurant or on the floor of an assembly line. This supervisor keeps an eye on the overall flow of activity, ready to step in whenever a problem arises. The soufflé cook can attend to the chores that will ensure that his specialty turns out just right. But his actions must be combined with all the other activities that must be coordinated to produce the perfect meal. If the salad course is delayed because the prep chef has taken an extended break, the entire production can collapse: Even the perfect soufflé will collapse if it has to sit in the warmer for a long time. By monitoring the various components of the operation, the supervisor can make online adjustments, by either stepping in to take over the role of the prep chef or instructing the soufflé cook to slow down.

The last 20 years have witnessed burgeoning interest in the medial frontal cortex, especially the **anterior cingulate cortex**, as a critical component of a monitoring system. The anterior cingulate cortex provides an especially interesting story within the history of cognitive neuroscience. Buried in the depths of the frontal lobes and characterized by a primitive cytoarchitecture, this structure was assumed to be a component of the limbic system, helping to modulate autonomic responses during painful or threatening situations. Whereas functional roles for most cortical regions have been inspired by behavioral problems associated with neurological disorders, interest in the anterior cingulate has been inspired by serendipitous activations found in this region during neuroimaging studies. For example, cingulate activation increases during semantic generation tasks, similar to what is found in the inferior prefrontal cortex. This activation was especially surprising in these initial studies, given that the lesions of this region were not associated with language disorders.

Subsequent imaging studies led to the recognition that the cingulate activation was not specific to language tasks. Indeed, perhaps the most consistent finding in the entire neuroimaging literature is that the medial frontal cortex is engaged whenever a task becomes more difficult. Figure 13.28 shows the results of a meta-analysis highlighting the center of activation in 38 fMRI studies that included conditions in which monitoring demands were high. The activations are clustered in the anterior cingulate regions (areas 24 and 32) but also extend into areas 8 and 6; thus we refer to this region as *medial frontal cortex.*

Making sense of the functional role of the medial frontal cortex has proved to be an area of lively debate. One hypothesis centered on the idea that the medial frontal cortex should be conceptualized as part of an attentional hierarchy. In this view, the medial frontal cortex occupies an upper rung on the hierarchy, playing a critical role in coordinating activity across attentional systems (Figure 13.29).

Consider a PET study of visual attention in which subjects must selectively attend to a visual feature (color, motion, shape) or monitor changes in all three features simultaneously—a condition in which attentional resources must be divided (Corbetta et al., 1991). Compared to control conditions in which stimuli are viewed passively, the selective-attention conditions were associated with enhanced activity in feature-specific regions of visual association areas. For example, attending to motion was correlated with greater blood flow in the lateral prestriate cortex, whereas attending to color stimulated blood flow in more medial

Figure 13.28 Meta-analysis showing activation foci in the medial frontal cortex during a range of tasks in which demands on performance monitoring were high. The data are assembled from 38 fMRI studies and result from contrasts looking at four different types of monitoring functions.

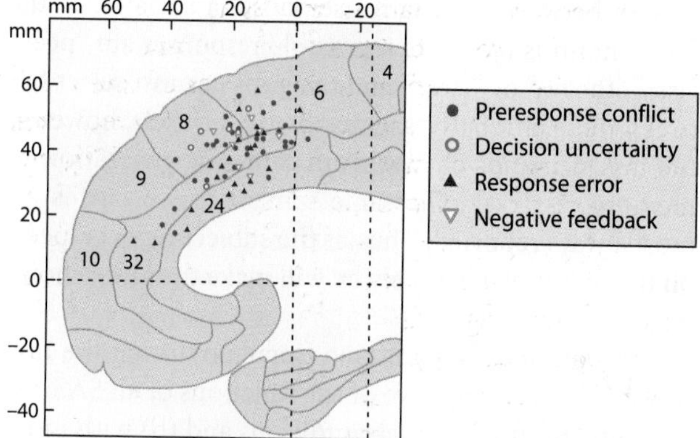

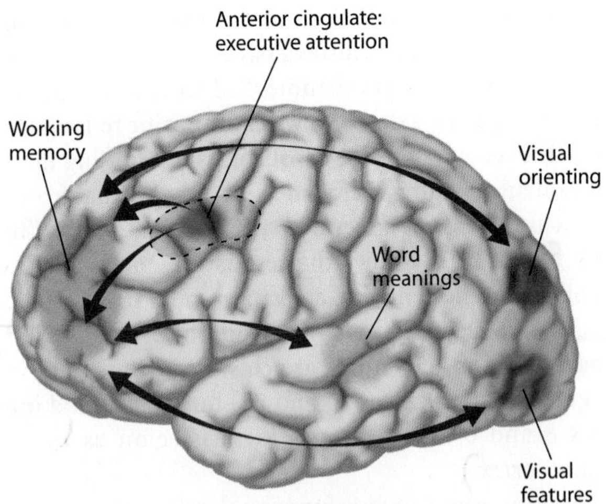

Figure 13.29 The anterior cingulate has been hypothesized to operate as an executive attention system. This system ensures that processing in other brain regions is most efficient, given the current task demands. Interactions with the prefrontal cortex may select working memory buffers; interactions with the posterior cortex can amplify activity in one perceptual module over others. The interactions with the posterior cortex may be direct, or they may be mediated by connections with the prefrontal cortex.

regions. In contrast, during the divided-attention task the most prominent activation was in the anterior cingulate cortex. These findings suggest that selective attention causes local changes in regions specialized to process certain features. The divided-attention condition, in contrast, requires a higher level attentional system—one that simultaneously monitors information across these specialized modules.

An association between the medial frontal cortex and attention is further shown by how activation in this region changes as attentional demands decrease. If the verb generation task is repeated over successive blocks, the primary activation shifts from the cingulate and prefrontal regions to the insular cortex of the temporal lobe (Raichle et al., 1994). This shift reflects the fact that the task has changed. In the initial trial, the subjects have to choose between alternative semantic associates. If the target noun is *apple*, then possible responses are "peel," "eat," "throw," or "type," and the subject must select between these alternatives. On subsequent trials, however, the task demands change from semantic generation to memory retrieval. The same semantic associate is almost always reported. Thus, if the subject reports "peel" on the first trial, invariably he will make the same choice on subsequent trials.

Activation of the anterior cingulate during the first trial can be related to two of the functions of an SAS: responding (a) under novel conditions and (b) with more difficult tasks. The generation condition is more difficult than the repeat condition because the response is not constrained. But over subsequent trials, the generation condition becomes easier (as evidenced by markedly reduced response times), and the items are no longer novel. Thus, the higher blood flow in the cingulate disappears, reflecting a reduced need for the SAS. That this shift indicates the loss of novelty rather than a general decrease in the medial frontal cortex with practice is shown by the fact that, when a new list of nouns is used, the cingulate activation returns.

One concern with the hierarchy model is that it is descriptive rather than mechanistic. The model captures the fact that the medial frontal cortex is recruited when attentional demands are high, but it does not specify how this recruitment occurs, nor does it specify the kinds of representations supported by the medial frontal cortex. We might suppose that the representation is akin to our kitchen supervisor, one that includes the current goal, as well as all the suboperations that are required to achieve that goal. But this type of representation is quite complex. Moreover, even if all of this information were represented in the medial frontal cortex, we would still lack an explanation of how it uses this information to implement cognitive control. In a sense, the hierarchical attention model is reminiscent of the homunculus problem: To explain control we postulate a controller without providing an explanation of how the homunculus works.

This concern has led researchers to consider other models of how medial frontal cortex might be involved in monitoring behavior. The starting point for one such model comes from evidence implicating this region in the detection of errors. Evoked-potential studies have shown that the medial frontal cortex provides an electrophysiological signal correlated with the occurrence of errors. As Figure 13.30 illustrates, when people make an incorrect response, a large evoked response sweeps over the prefrontal cortex just after the movement is initiated. This signal, referred to as the **error-related negativity**, or **ERN**, response, has been localized to the anterior cingulate (Dehaene et al., 1994). The ERN response, interestingly enough, is absent when the subject is unaware that the response is erroneous, and its magnitude is correlated with the intensity of the incorrect response (Gehring et al., 1993). One might suppose that a monitoring system detects when an error has occurred and that this information is used to increase cognitive control.

This hypothesis provides a different perspective on the co-occurrence of activation in medial and lateral prefrontal cortex—one that captures many of the functional benefits of an attentional system. Typically we make errors when we are not paying sufficient attention to the task at hand. Consider a subject being asked to perform the Stroop task for 30 minutes (see Figure 4.5). At some point she might start thinking about her evening plans to attend the premiere of a new summer blockbuster. This new goal begins to occupy working memory, displacing the experimentally defined (boring) goal to name the colors. Oops—she suddenly finds herself reading the word rather than naming the color. This error, and the subsequent generation of the ERN response could be used to reactivate the experimental goal in working memory. In a sense, the interaction of medial and lateral prefrontal cortex can accomplish much

Figure 13.30 Subjects were tested on a two-choice letter discrimination task in which they made accelerated responses with either the right or the left hand. Errors were made when speed was emphasized and when targets were flanked by irrelevant distracters. Evoked potentials for incorrect responses deviated from those obtained on trials with correct responses just after the onset of peripheral motor activity. This error detection signal is maximal over a central electrode positioned above the prefrontal cortex and it has been hypothesized to originate in the anterior cingulate. The zero position on the *x*-axis indicates the onset of electromyographic (EMG) activity. Actual movement would be observed about 50 to 100 ms later.

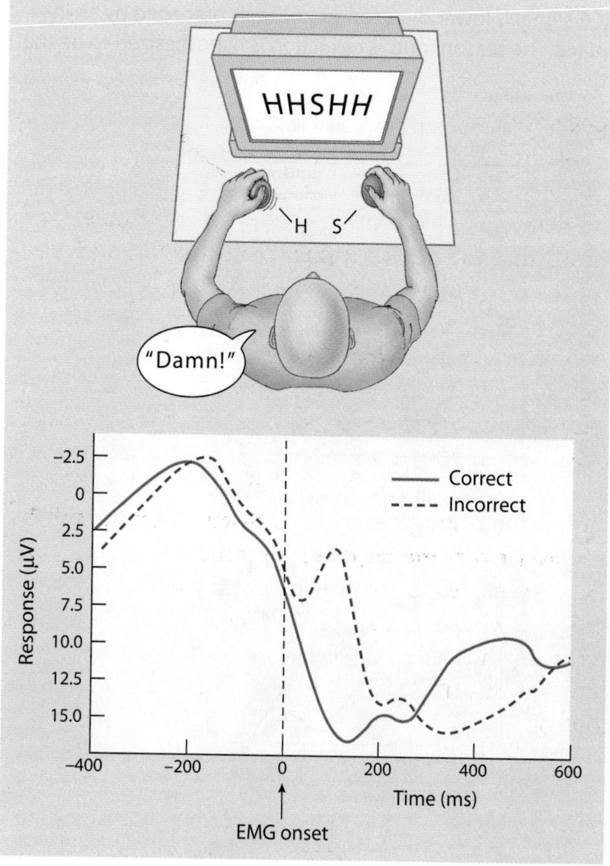

of what was expected of the SAS: We can succeed on a difficult task (Stroop) in which input–output links are relatively novel (name the ink color of a printed word) and there is a need to overcome a habitual response (to read the word). An error detection function would be essential for modulating the degree of cognitive control.

The ERN is an especially salient signal of a monitoring system. But the engagement of medial frontal cortex is not limited to conditions in which people make errors. Cingulate activation is prominent in many tasks in which errors rarely occur. The Stroop task is one such example. The difficulty that people have when the words and colors are incongruent is typically manifest in the reaction time data and only minimally, if at all, in measures of accuracy. Nonetheless, activation of the anterior cingulate is much higher on incongruent trials compared to when the words and colors are congruent (Bush et al., 2000). Similarly, medial frontal activation is higher when people are asked to generate the verbs associated with nouns compared to when they just repeat the nouns, even though errors rarely occur.

Jonathan Cohen and his colleagues (2000) at Princeton University have hypothesized that a key function of the medial frontal cortex is to evaluate **response conflict**. This hypothesis is intended to provide an umbrella account of the monitoring role of this region, subsuming earlier models that focused on attentional hierarchies or error detection. Difficult and novel situations should engender high response conflict. In the verb generation task, there is a conflict between acceptable alternative responses. Errors, by definition, are situations in which conflict exists. Similarly, tasks such as the Stroop task entail conflict in that the required response is in conflict with a more habitual response. In Cohen's view, conflict monitoring is a computationally appealing way to allocate attentional resources. When the monitoring system detects that conflict is high, there is a need to increase attentional vigilance. Increases in anterior cingulate activity can be used to modulate activity in other cortical areas.

Event-related fMRI has been used to pit the error detection and conflict-monitoring hypotheses against one another. One such study used the flanker task, similar to that shown in Figure 13.30, except that the letters were replaced by a row of five arrows (Botvinick et al., 1999). Subjects responded to the direction of the central arrow, pressing a button on the right side if this arrow pointed to the right and pressing a button on the left side if this arrow pointed to the left. On compatible trials, the flanking arrows pointed in the same direction; on incompatible trials, the flanking arrows pointed in opposite directions. Neural activity in the medial frontal cortex was higher on the incompatible trials compared to the compatible trials. Importantly, this increase was observed even when subjects responded correctly. These results strongly suggest that it is the monitoring demands, and not the occurrence of an error, that engage the medial frontal cortex.

Subsequent work has sought to clarify how a conflict-monitoring process might be part of a network for cognitive control. Consider the variant of the Stroop task depicted in Figure 13.31a, a very boring variant in which each trial lasted 25 s! A cue appeared at the beginning of each trial indicating whether the subject was to read the word or name the color. After a lengthy delay, the cue was replaced by a Stroop stimulus. Thus, the design manipulated two factors: (a) goal difficulty, given the assumption that it is easier to read words than to name their ink color; and (b) color–word congruency. By using long delays after the cue and response, the experimenters could separately examine neural responses related to goal selection and neural responses related to response conflict. The results showed distinct neural correlates of these two factors (Figure 13.31b).

The degree of difficulty for goal selection is evident in the activation of the lateral prefrontal cortex. When the task was made more difficult, the BOLD response in this region increased even before the actual stimulus was presented. In contrast, activation in the anterior cingulate was sensitive to the degree of response conflict, being greater when the word and stimulus color were different. The picture here is similar to that observed in the ERN literature. The lateral prefrontal cortex represents the task goal, and the medial frontal cortex monitors whether that goal is being achieved. One difference with the error detection model, though, is that the medial monitoring process is recruited not just when errors occur; it is engaged whenever there is conflict—which we would expect to be quite high in novel contexts or with particularly demanding tasks.

Figure 13.31 Interactions between the medial and lateral frontal cortex to facilitate goal-oriented behavior. **(a)** Subjects performed a series of Stroop trials, responding to either the word or the color as indicated by a cue. C = congruent; I = incongruent. **(b)** Functional MRI showing double dissociation between the lateral prefrontal cortex (PFC) and the anterior cingulate cortex (ACC). PFC activation in the instruction phase differs between conditions in which the cue indicates that the task will be easy (word) or hard (color). ACC activation varies in the stimulus phase as a function of response conflict (incongruent [greater than] congruent). **(c)** Correlation between ACC and PFC activation across successive trials. The PFC representation of the task goal is enhanced following the detection of a conflict by the ACC monitoring system. **(d)** The ACC signal is lower on incongruent trials preceded by an incongruent trial (iI) compared to when the preceding trial was congruent (cI). The reason for this reduction is hypothesized to be that the goal representation in PFC is stronger and thus there is less conflict.

(a)

Series of trials

Cue	Stimulus	Previous trial	Current trial
Word	GREEN		C
Color	BLUE	I	C
Color	RED	C	I
Word	BLUE	I	I
Word	RED	I	C
Color	GREEN	C	C
Color	RED	C	I

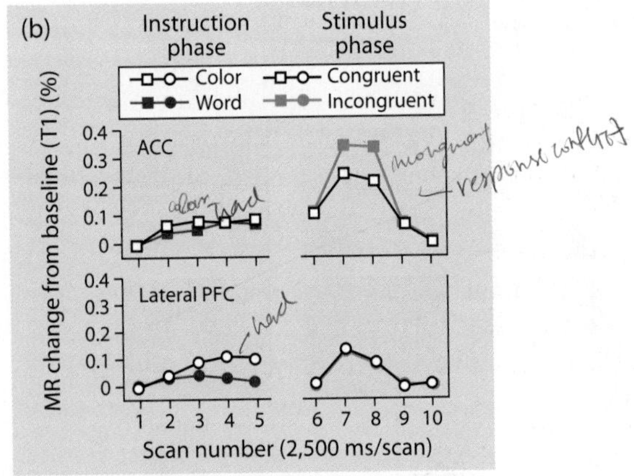

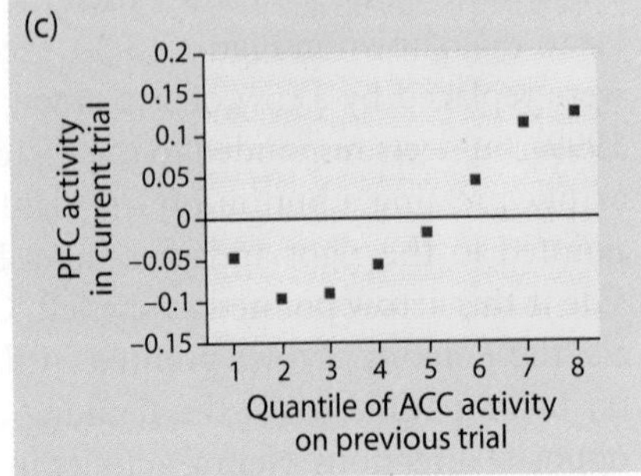

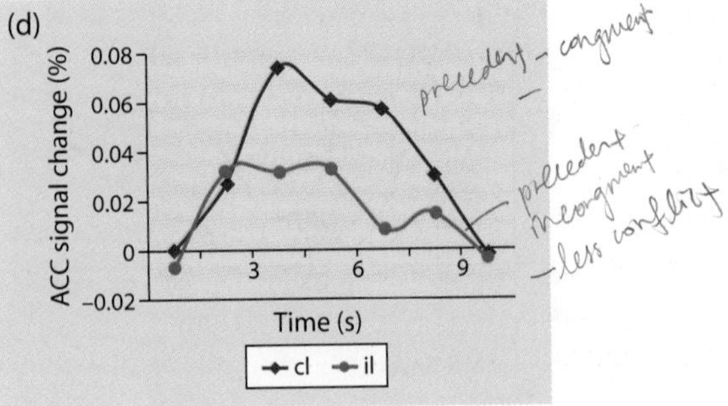

Note that the preceding study shows only the distinct contributions of the lateral and medial frontal regions. A subsequent event-related fMRI study provided direct evidence that these two regions work in tandem to provide cognitive control. Activation in the lateral prefrontal cortex was highly correlated with activation in the medial frontal cortex on the *preceding* trial (Figure 13.31c). Thus, a signal of high response conflict on an incongruent Stroop trial led to a stronger response in the lateral prefrontal cortex. As with the error model, the medial monitoring function can be used to modulate the activation of the goal in working memory. Difficult trials help remind the person to stay on task. We can hypothesize that the medial frontal activity modulates filtering operations of the prefrontal cortex, ensuring that the irrelevant word names are ignored. Interestingly, activation in the medial frontal cortex on incongruent trials was lower when the previous trial was also incongruent (Figure 13.31d). Assuming that an incongruent trial leads to a stronger activation of the task goal in working memory and, as a result, there is better filtering of irrelevant information on the next trial, the degree of conflict generated on that trial will be attenuated.

Advances in understanding how the medial frontal cortex contributes to cognitive control provide a model case study for the maturation of cognitive neuroscience. We began with a mystery—why is this region active in so many neuroimaging studies of cognitive function? The hierarchical attention model offered a description of medial frontal function, placing it within the context of a cognitive model, the supervisory attentional system (SAS), that captured many essential features of goal-oriented behavior. The error detection hypothesis offered an initial mechanistic account of how control might be recruited when our actions fail to meet these goals. This hypothesis was limited in that it did not offer an account of many of the conditions that led to recruitment of the medial frontal cortex.

This shortcoming led to the conflict-monitoring hypothesis, in which the core mechanism modulated cognitive control by continuously evaluating the level of uncertainty. This hypothesis bears many similarities to the error detection model but suggests a more generic use of monitoring—one that is not limited to conditions in which errors occur. As such, the conflict-monitoring hypothesis is parsimonious, accounting for a large range of observations within a framework that retains the appealing features of the attentional network and error detection hypotheses. More generally, the error detection and conflict-monitoring hypotheses suggest a way in which rather sophisticated control can be achieved. One can easily envision a rather simple neural mechanism that assesses the degree to which multiple responses are concurrently active. Thus, without resorting to homunculus-like notions these models provide examples of how rather sophisticated control can be achieved.

We can, of course, expect that future work will reveal shortcomings with the conflict-monitoring hypothesis. Indeed, the literature already suggests some problems that need to be addressed. A recent imaging study has shown that activation in the anterior cingulate is more closely linked with the subject's anticipation of possible errors than with the degree of conflict (J. W. Brown & Braver, 2005). More perplexing are the results of studies involving patients with lesions of the medial frontal cortex. These patients show little evidence of impairment on various tasks that would appear to require cognitive control. For example, they are as sensitive to the effects of an error on the Stroop task as are control subjects (Fellows & Farah, 2005). In fact, the patient data fail to confirm a number of behavioral predictions derived from models of how medial frontal function contributes to cognitive control.

Although their cognitive performance appears to be relatively normal, these patients do exhibit one marked impairment: They fail to show normal changes in arousal, when challenged either physically through exercise or mentally with math problems (Critchley et al., 2003). This finding suggests that medial frontal cortex may provide an interface between cognition and arousal, modulating autonomic activity in response to the current context. This modulation would also constitute a form of control, but in a rather indirect manner—one that is linked to regulatory mechanisms in the brainstem rather than through direct interactions with the cognitive representations of prefrontal cortex.

This chapter has focused on higher level aspects of cognition—those that allow us to perform complex behaviors that satisfy both immediate and long-term goals. Although it is laudable, and indeed essential, that we tackle such problems, these complex processes still depend on the operation of the same basic physiological processes that underlie even elementary perceptual problems, such as detecting the presence of an edge. Without resorting to homunculus-like notions, the error detection and conflict-monitoring hypotheses suggest a way in which rather sophisticated control can be achieved. One can easily envision a rather simple neural mechanism that assesses the degree to which multiple responses are concurrently active. Whether these ideas prove to have lasting value, they do offer a very encouraging example of how even the most advanced of our cognitive competencies can be subject to rigorous experimental investigation, given the many tools of cognitive neuroscience.

HOW THE BRAIN WORKS

Understanding Substance Abuse: Insights from the Study of Cognitive Control

Ticket to ride, white line highway . . .
Pay your toll, sell your soul
Pound for pound costs more than gold
The longer you stay, the more you pay

—"White Lines (Don't Do It)," by Melle Mel and Grandmaster Flash (Sugar Hill Records, 1983)

A hallmark of drug addiction is the sense of a loss of control. The alcoholic will throw away a week's paycheck buying rounds at the bar, momentarily ignoring that the rent is due next week and her credit card bill has gone unpaid for months. The addict feels like a slave to his drug of choice, forsaking all responsibilities when in need of his next fix. Given the physical, mental, and financial costs, both for the afflicted individual and for society in general, the study of drug abuse has been a top priority in the neuroscience community.

This research can be especially challenging because it is usually not possible to randomly assign participants to different experimental groups. We cannot designate certain individuals to become drug addicts, others to be abstinent. Rather, the assignments are based on individual histories, so it is often difficult to control for various secondary factors associated with drug addiction. Nonetheless, studies on addiction have begun to offer new insights into some of the short- and long-term changes that occur in cognitive control with substance abuse.

One approach is to look at how mind-altering substances affect healthy individuals. In one such study (Ridderinkhof et al., 2002), young adults were tested on the flanker task (see Figure 13.30) after consuming alcohol that raised their blood alcohol content to 0.40% (low) or 0.97% (high). Compared to a control condition in which the participants consumed a placebo drink, the ERP response following errors was reduced in both the low- and high-dose conditions. In addition, alcohol affected how the participants adjusted their behavior across trials. In the placebo condition, the participants showed a reduced conflict effect (incongruent reaction time minus congruent reaction time) after making an error—an indicator of increased cognitive control. This effect was also attenuated when the task was performed after the consumption of alcohol. Thus, alcohol appears to reduce our ability to react appropriately to the immediate consequences of erroneous behavior and impairs our ability to make adjustments in response to our mistakes. The effects of the low dose are of special interest, given that this level of alcohol is within the legal limits for driving in most countries.

A related line of research has focused on changes in cognitive control networks associated with chronic drug abuse. Hugh Garavan at Trinity College in Dublin, Ireland, has conducted a series of studies to look at this question in cocaine users. One of their tasks involves a simple test of inhibitory control. Participants view a stream of stimuli that alternate between two letters and quickly press a button (go trial) with the presentation of each letter (see the figure). In rare instances, the same letter is repeated on successive trials. For these trials, they are instructed to withhold their response (no-go trials).

Chronic cocaine users, none of whom had used cocaine for 18 hours prior to testing, were more likely to respond on no-go trials than were matched controls, and they showed lower activation in the medial frontal cortex when they produced these erroneous responses, indicating that they had difficulty monitoring their performance. Moreover, even when they succeeded in inhibiting the response, the medial frontal cortex response was lower in the cocaine users. Interestingly, they showed a stronger response in other brain areas, such as the cerebellum, that may reflect a compensatory process. Thus, even when the addicts were not under the influence of cocaine, changes in their cognitive control network persisted.

In subsequent work, Garavan and his colleagues have found that this impairment in inhibitory control is especially pronounced when working memory demands are high. This interaction of working memory and cognitive control may help us understand, at least in part, why addiction can be so hard to break. When addicts experience the craving for their drug of choice, working memory is taxed: Not only must these individuals attend to whatever they are currently doing, but the goal of obtaining the drug is highly activated and has been shown to produce strong responses to environmental cues associated with that drug. Under such conditions, the ability to monitor and inhibit behavior is compromised, increasing the likelihood of relapse.

This vicious cycle can interfere with recovery, even in individuals who are highly motivated to escape their drug addiction. By appreciating how motivation must be coupled with the appropriate mechanisms of cognitive control, researchers can consider therapeutic options that might facilitate the process. For example, prescription drugs that restore medial frontal activity to normal levels might prove useful in treating addiction.

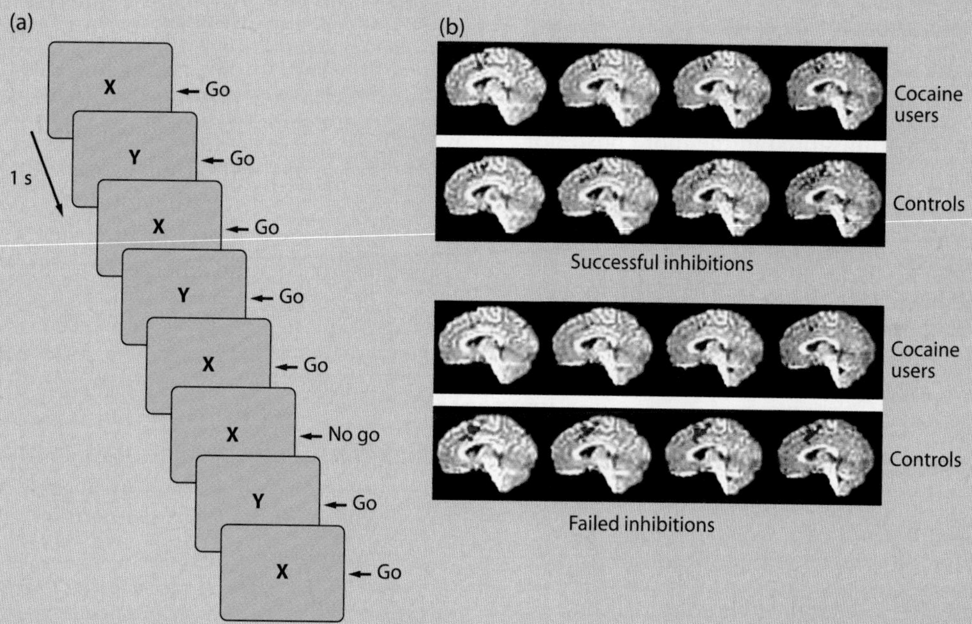

Reduced inhibitory control in chronic cocaine users. **(a)** Subjects view a stream of letters and press a key whenever the letters alternate between X and Y (go trials). In a small percentage of the trials, the same letter appears in successive displays, and here the subjects must withhold their responses (no go). **(b)** Activation in the medial frontal cortex is lower in the cocaine users on all no-go trials—whether inhibition of the response succeeds or fails.

SUMMARY

The prefrontal cortex plays a crucial role in goal-oriented behavior. Working memory is essential for representing information that is not immediately present in the environment. It allows for the interaction of current goals with perceptual information and knowledge accumulated from past experience. Not only must we be able to represent our goals, but also these representations must persist for an extended period of time. Working memory must be dynamic. It requires the retrieval and amplification of representations that are useful for the task at hand, as well as the ability to ignore potential distractions. Yet we must also be flexible. If our goals change, or if the context demands an alternative course of action, we must be able to switch from one plan to another. These operations require a system that can monitor ongoing behavior, signaling when we fail or when there are potential sources of conflict.

Two functional systems have been emphasized in this chapter: (a) The lateral prefrontal cortex and frontal pole support goal-oriented behavior, providing a working memory system that recruits and selects task-relevant information stored in the more posterior regions of the cortex. (b) The medial frontal cortex is hypothesized to work in tandem with the prefrontal cortex, monitoring ongoing activity so as to be able to modulate the degree of cognitive control. As we emphasized in this chapter and in Chapter 7, the control of action has a hierarchical nature. Just as control in the motor system is delegated across many functional systems, an analogous organization characterizes prefrontal function. With control distributed in this manner, the need for an all-powerful controller, a homunculus, is minimized. The prefrontal cortex can be a reservoir of the current contents of processing by linking up to stored representations in the more posterior regions of the cortex—representations that help to select actions.

However, these representations, the content of ongoing processing, are embedded in a context that reflects the history and current goals of the actor. Up to now we have focused on relatively impersonal goals: naming words, attending to colors, remembering locations. But most of our actions are socially oriented. They reflect our personal desires, both as individuals and as members of social groups. To gain a more complete appreciation of goal-oriented behavior, we must turn to the study of the social brain, asking how our behavior is influenced by our interactions with others. In Chapter 14 we will address this topic, turning the spotlight to the third division of the prefrontal cortex: the ventromedial cortex. By recognizing the intimate connections between the regions of prefrontal cortex, we can start to appreciate how a mind emerges from the architecture of the human brain.

KEY TERMS

anterior cingulate cortex
cognitive control
content-based hypotheses
delayed-response task
dynamic filtering
error-related negativity (ERN)
frontal pole
goal-oriented behavior
inhibitory control
lateral prefrontal cortex
medial frontal cortex
monitoring
perseverate
recency memory
response conflict
source memory
stimulus driven
supervisory attentional system (SAS)
Wisconsin Card Sorting Task
working memory

TAKE-HOME MESSAGES

General

- As a result of a large tumor that traversed the corpus callosum, invading the left lateral prefrontal cortex and a large portion of the right frontal lobe, W.R. "lost his ego" and the cognitive capability to organize his own life. W.R.'s actions became reactive, or stimulus driven, as opposed to proactive, or goal-oriented.
- *Cognitive control* refers to mental abilities that involve planning, controlling, and regulating the flow of information processing.
- The prefrontal cortex constitutes a massive network that links the brain's motor, perceptual, and limbic systems. There are four major components of the prefrontal cortex: lateral prefrontal cortex, frontal pole, medial frontal cortex, and ventrome-

dial prefrontal cortex. All are associated with cognitive control.

Memory Functions of the Prefrontal Cortex

- Working memory consists of transient representations of task-relevant information. It is a type of short-term memory, critical for goal-oriented behavior.
- The prefrontal cortex (especially the lateral prefrontal cortex) is a key component in a working memory network. Although patients with prefrontal lesions show little impairment on many types of memory tests, especially those involving long-term memory, they have difficulty on tasks involving working memory. Delayed-response tasks are one of the best-studied types of working memory tasks.
- Physiological studies in primates show that cells in the prefrontal cortex remain active during the delay in delayed-response tasks. Thus, these cells can maintain the representation of a stimulus even when that stimulus is no longer present. Some of these cells exhibit selectivity in terms of stimulus attributes (e.g., "what" and "where" information).
- In humans, functional-imaging studies have shown sustained activity in the prefrontal cortex during working memory tasks. These studies also demonstrate that working memory requires the interaction of the prefrontal cortex with other brain regions.
- Recency memory is the ability to organize and segregate events in memory. Source memory consists of information concerning the context in which something was learned. It might be the place in which learning occurred or a person associated with the experience. Recency and source memory are impaired in frontal lobe patients.

Component Analysis of the Prefrontal Cortex

- Alan Baddeley proposed a content-based model of working memory that includes two working memory systems. A visuospatial sketch pad maintains representations of visual information such as what was recently seen and where it was located. A phonological loop maintains linguistic representations through covert articulatory rehearsal. These systems are under the control of a shared central executive.
- The phonological loop engages a network of left-hemisphere regions. Tasks involving the visuospatial sketch pad produce more bilateral brain activity.
- Another content-based hypothesis is that the dorsal and ventral visual streams in the posterior cortex are also maintained in the prefrontal cortex. By this view, dorsolateral prefrontal cortex is part of a working memory system for spatial information, whereas more ventral aspects of the lateral prefrontal cortex are essential for object working memory.
- Process-based accounts offer an alternative approach to understanding functional specialization within the prefrontal cortex. The emphasis here is on identifying how different subregions are specialized to perform certain types of mental operations or transformations. The evidence suggests that dorsolateral prefrontal cortex is essential for manipulating information in working memory.
- Processing within the prefrontal cortex is hierarchical, with more anterior regions associated with the representation of more complex, higher order information.

Goal-Oriented Behaviors

- Goal-oriented behaviors allow us to interact in the world in a purposeful manner.
- The ability to make goal-directed decisions is impaired in patients with frontal cortex lesions, even if their general intellectual capabilities remain unaffected.
- There are three components to successfully executing an action plan: (a) identifying the goal and developing subgoals, (b) anticipating consequences when choosing among goals, and (c) determining what is required to achieve the goals.
- An important part of cognitive control is the ability to shift focus from one subgoal to another. People who cannot shift focus are said to "perseverate."
- Goal-oriented behavior requires the retrieval and selection of task-relevant information. The prefrontal cortex can be conceptualized as a dynamic filtering mechanism through which information is brought in and maintained in working memory.
- Dynamic filtering can influence the contents of information processing by accentuating the attended information or by excluding irrelevant information.
- Task switching requires that the information retrieved and maintained by a filtering mechanism be adjusted as task demands change.
- In top-down control, information processing is influenced by goals and the allocation of attentional resources. Dynamic-filtering is a type of top-down control. Top-down control involves accentuating task-relevant information and excluding irrelevant information. This dynamic process is revealed in brain-imaging studies showing that, as task goals are modified, activation in perceptual areas is either increased or decreased compared to baseline conditions.

- The inhibition of action constitutes another form of cognitive control. In the stop-signal task, subjects attempt to abort a planned response. This form of control involves the right inferior frontal gyrus.
- Patients with prefrontal cortex damage lose inhibitory control. For example, they cannot inhibit task-irrelevant information.

Ensuring That Goal-Oriented Behavior Succeeds

- The supervisory attentional system (SAS) is a psychological model to account for how goal-oriented behavior succeeds. It is proposed to describe cognitive control required for planning an action, performing in novel situations that do not involve well-learned responses and when errors are likely to occur.
- The medial frontal cortex is thought to be a critical part of a monitoring system, identifying situations in which cognitive control is required.
- The error-related negativity (ERN) response is an ERP component that occurs when an error is produced. This response is generated by the medial frontal cortex.
- The medial frontal cortex is engaged when response conflict is high. Through its interactions with lateral regions of the prefrontal cortex, a monitoring system can regulate the level of cognitive control.

THOUGHT QUESTIONS

1. What memory functions are associated with the prefrontal cortex? How do these mnemonic functions differ from other types of memory?
2. Compared to the visual cortex, it has been difficult to identify subregions of the prefrontal cortex. What are some of the current hypotheses concerning functional specialization within the prefrontal cortex? Does the lack of specificity reflect the current lack of knowledge or a difference between anterior and posterior cortex? Explain your answer.
3. One of the cardinal features of human cognition is that we exhibit great flexibility in our behavior. Flexibility implies choice, and choice entails competition between alternatives. Describe some of the neural systems involved in response selection.
4. Review and contrast some of the ways in which the prefrontal cortex and the anterior cingulate are involved in monitoring and controlling processing.
5. The notion of a supervisory attentional system does not sit well with some researchers, because it seems like a homuncular concept. Is such a system a necessary part of a network for cognitive control? Explain your answer.

SUGGESTED READING

BADDELEY, A. (1995). Working memory. In M. S. Gazzaniga (Ed.), *The cognitive neurosciences* (pp. 755–764). Cambridge, MA: MIT Press.

BUNGE, S. A. (2004). How we use rules to select actions: A review of evidence from cognitive neuroscience. *Cognitive and Affective Behavioral Neuroscience, 4,* 564–579.

FUSTER, J. M. (1989). *The prefrontal cortex: Anatomy, physiology, and neuropsychology of the frontal lobe* (2nd ed.). New York: Raven.

MILLER, E. K., & COHEN, J. D. (2001). An integrative theory of prefrontal cortex function. *Annual Review of Neuroscience, 24,* 167–202.

MONSELL, S., & DRIVER, J. (2000). *Control of cognitive processes. Attention and performance XVIII.* Cambridge, MA: MIT Press.

RIDDERINKHOF, K. R., ULLSPERGER, M., CRONE, E. A., & NIEUWENHUIS, S. (2004). The role of the medial frontal cortex in cognitive control. *Science, 306,* 443–447.

14

Social Cognition

Patient M.R. has extensive damage to his **orbitofrontal cortex**, the portion of the frontal lobes that rests behind the eye orbits. His damage is the unfortunate consequence of his crashing a motorcycle into an inanimate object, coupled with his evolutionary history. The human skull is helpfully designed with sockets for the eyes. Jagged ridges around the sockets provide protective support for the eye orbits, but in the aftermath of the sort of high-speed collision that is associated with modern-day vehicles, they can become essentially like a set of knives slicing away brain tissue (see Figure 4.19). M.R.'s injury is commonly known as a *coup-contra-coup* injury and occurs when impact causes the brain to first bounce against the back of the skull and then rebound. Coup-contra-coup injuries are especially pronounced in the orbitofrontal cortex because of the jagged ridges around the eye sockets.

Despite his extensive brain damage, M.R. has a surprising ability to perform standard neuropsychological tests of memory, motor, and language skills. M.R. does well on all of these tests. At the start of a casual conversation with him, however, you would notice that something was amiss. Patients who have orbitofrontal damage like M.R.'s tend to exhibit inappropriate social behavior (Beer et al., 2003). They might choose to discuss personal topics with a complete stranger or talk endlessly about topics that clearly bore their conversation partner; for example, M.R. would readily provide a detailed account of the precise cuts he recently used to trim a bonsai tree. Orbitofrontal patients might greet a stranger with a hug, sit a little too close for comfort, or stare just a little too long.

Cases of orbitofrontal damage are certainly not new in the history of neuroscience. In fact, the most famous case, one familiar to most neuroscience students, was recorded in 1848. On a summer day in June that year, Phineas Gage, the foreman of a railroad construction crew, made a mistake that would change his life irrevocably. One of Gage's responsibilities was to create controlled explosions to blast through rock so that railroad tracks could be laid over a smooth surface. For each explosion, Gage would make a small hole in the rock and fill it with explosive powder and a fuse. He would then cover the explosive powder with sand and pat it down with a tamping iron. On this day, however, he failed to notice that some of the explosive powder was uncovered. The iron set off a spark that ignited the exposed powder. The explosion made the tamping iron a lethal projectile that shot out and passed through Gage's skull, entering just below the chin and exiting at the top of his head, and creating a large hole in his orbitofrontal cortex (Figure 14.1).

Amazingly, Gage remained conscious and seemed quite alert, even greeting the town physician, Dr. Harlow, who was asked to treat him. But although his physical wounds healed after a few months, Gage would never be the same. Harlow described the postinjury Gage as "irreverent, indulging in the grossest profanity (which was not previously his custom), manifesting

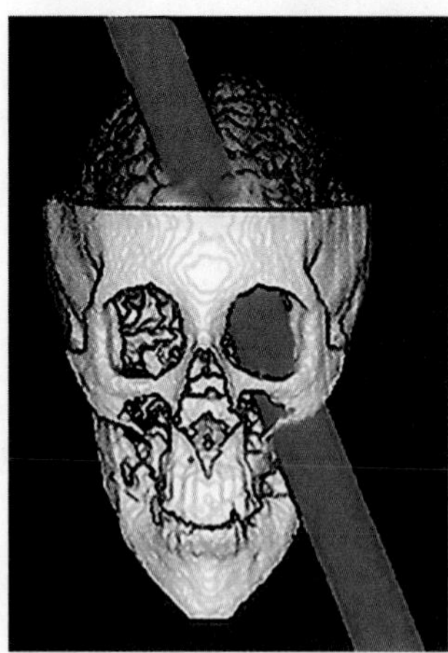

Figure 14.1 This computer reconstruction shows how the tamping iron passed through Phineas Gage's brain. The iron entered just below the left eye and exited from the top. It destroyed much of the medial region of the prefrontal cortex.

little deference to his fellows, impatient of restraint or advice when it conflicts with his desires." Another physician noted that Gage's "society was intolerable to decent people" (MacMillan, 1986).

Although Gage had been a respected citizen, exemplary worker, and well-liked man, he became a different man after his injury. His employers with the railroad soon fired him. Many fantastic stories have been told about Gage's life after he healed from his injury. Some of these stories suggest that Gage was never able to hold a steady job and even traveled with Barnum's freak show for a time. Malcolm MacMillan at Deakin University in Australia (2000) has spent years investigating Gage's life and has uncovered documentation reporting that Gage spent most of his postinjury life employed as a stagecoach driver both in the United States and in Chile. Gage eventually moved to San Francisco to live with his mother, and it was there that he died. Although his preinjury life had been filled with promise, he never again held a job as prestigious as railroad foreman.

Only very recently have scientists begun to tackle the problem of why some kinds of brain damage impair social behavior while sparing other complex cognitive abilities. As recently as 2002, media headlines boasted, "Man speared in head survives because spear passed through a place in the brain that is non-functional." Much like Phineas Gage, this man had had his orbitofrontal cortex pierced. Although damage to this region does not impair performance on many cognitive tests, the dysfunctional social behavior of patient M.R. and Phineas Gage make it clear that the orbitofrontal cortex is anything but nonfunctional.

Social cognitive neuroscience is a new field that aims to tackle the problem of understanding how brain function supports the cognitive processes underlying social behavior. Much of the research in this field builds on scientific findings that you have learned about throughout this textbook. Social interactions are an essential aspect of human behavior, involving romantic partners, friends, family, coworkers, and, quite frequently, strangers. Through these interactions, we form a sense of self and also develop impressions of other people.

In this chapter we focus on some of the most fundamental questions that psychologists study: How do we get to know ourselves? How do we get to know others? What can the brain tell us about possible similarities in the processes through which we come to know ourselves and other people? Understanding ourselves and other people is only part of successfully navigating our social worlds. We also need to learn social rules and use them to guide our behavior. How do we make decisions that are guided by social knowledge? What can the brain tell us about the psychological functions that might be involved in this process? The answers to these questions will give us insight into our everyday experiences. This chapter discusses social cognitive neuroscience research concerning the neural representation of self, other people, and social knowledge and procedures. Note that social responses, including facial expression, social group evaluation, and racial stereotyping—which are also considered to be social cognitive neuroscience topics—were covered earlier, in Chapter 9, which focused on emotion.

SELF-PERCEPTION AND SELF-KNOWLEDGE

Socrates emphasized the importance of "knowing thyself." How exactly do we do that? We develop our self-knowledge (e.g., information about our characteristics, desires, and thoughts) through self-perception processes designed to gather information about the self. Self-perception is a unique social cognitive process because the self is simultaneously the perceiver and the perceived. In other words, when we think about ourselves, the self is doing the thinking and it is also the subject of our thoughts. In addition, our sense of self relies partially on perceiving a distinction between our self-knowledge and the characteristics, desires, and thoughts of other individuals. For example, even if you are one of those unusual individuals who favor marzipan candy, you can readily acknowledge that most people prefer other kinds of candy. Your individual preference helps define a little bit of what makes you an individual who is unique from other people.

In this section we focus on how people represent and gather information about themselves. Do unique neural and psychological mechanisms support the processing of information about the self in comparison to that about other people? What can the brain tell us about the nature of self-perception? Do we always want to know ourselves, or just the good things about ourselves? If we want to focus on the positive, how does the brain help us do that?

Self-Referential Processing

Why do we remember some information better than other information? According to Fergus Craik and Robert Lockhart's levels-of-processing model of memory (1972), the depth of processing profoundly affects the storage of information. Craik and Lockhart found that information processed in a more meaningful manner is remembered better than information processed in a more superficial manner. For example, if you were presented with a list of words and had to consider their meaning, you would be much more likely to remember the words than if you considered their font. In the late 1970s, two groups of scientists extended these ideas, simultaneously discovering that information that becomes related to the self is processed at the deepest possible level (Markus, 1977; Rogers et al., 1977). People remember significantly more information that they process in relation to themselves than information that they process in other ways. For example, people are more likely to remember the adjective *happy* if they have to judge how well it describes themselves than if they have to judge how well it describes the president of the United States (Figure 14.2). This is true even if they do not know that they will be asked to remember the adjectives when judging their descriptiveness. The enhanced memory for information processed in relation to the self is known as the **self-referent effect.**

Why is memory so much better for information processed in relation to the self? Two hypotheses have been considered. One hypothesis is that the self represents an extreme endpoint of the depth-of-processing effect, by which memory is significantly improved as information is processed more deeply. The reason we may process information in relation to ourselves more deeply might be that anything related to the self is naturally more engaging and we pay more attention. Or the greater depth of processing might result because participants have to consider the personality adjective in relation to the wealth of stored information about the self. In contrast, their judgment of the number of syllables in the personality adjective is considered only in relation to a single dimension that they may have stored about that word. Another hypothesis is that the self is actually a special cognitive structure with unique mnemonic or organizational elements that promote processing in a way that is distinct from all other cognitive structures.

Although numerous behavioral studies have been conducted to examine these hypotheses, substantial knowledge has been gained with our newfound understanding of the neural systems underlying the self-referent effect. If the self is a special cognitive structure characterized by unique information processing, then distinct neural regions should be activated in relation to the self-referent effect. One of the first fMRI studies

Figure 14.2 A typical self-referential processing experiment. **(a)** Participants answer a series of questions about their own personality traits as well as the personality traits of someone else. **(b)** Then they are asked which of the trait words they can remember.

to test this hypothesis was conducted by William Kelley and his colleagues at Dartmouth College. Participants judged personality adjectives in one of three experimental conditions: in relation to the self ("Does this trait describe you?"), in relation to another person ("Does this trait describe George Bush?"—the president at the time the study was conducted), or in relation to its printed format ("Is this word presented in uppercase letters?"). As found in numerous other studies of the self-referent effect, participants were most likely to remember words from the self condition and least likely to remember words from the printed-format condition.

Was there unique brain activity, then, when participants were making judgments in the self condition? The study did find unique activity in the self condition, but the results do not explain the social deficits associated with orbitofrontal cortex damage described at the beginning of this chapter. Instead, the medial prefrontal cortex (MPFC) was differentially activated in the self condition compared to the other two conditions (Figure 14.3). Later studies found that the level of activity in the MPFC predicted which items would be remembered on the surprise memory test (Macrae et al., 2004). The relation of MPFC and self-reference also extends to instances in which participants have to view themselves through the eyes of another person. A similar region of MPFC is activated when people are asked to judge whether another individual would use particular adjectives to describe them (Ochsner et al., 2005).

Although much of this research has been conducted with functional MRI, studies using ERP provide convergent results. Self-referential processing produces positive-going shifts in ERPs that emerge from a midline location consistent with the location of medial prefrontal cortex (Magno & Allan, 2007). Together, these studies suggest that self-referential processing is more strongly associated with medial prefrontal cortex function when compared to the processing of information about other people not personally known, such as the president of the United States.

The self-referent effect is just one example of the unique effect that the self has on cognition. What about other processes that are unique to self-perception? How can neuroscience research help us understand these processes? A series of behavioral studies has suggested that people use different sources of information when deciding whether they possess a trait compared to deciding whether another person possesses that trait. In other words, people not only have uniquely strong memory for traits that they judge in relation to themselves, but the process of deciding whether the trait is self-descriptive is conducted in a unique manner as well. Specifically, when we decide whether an adjective is self-descriptive, we rely on self-perceptions that are summaries of our personality traits rather than considering various episodes in our lives. In contrast, when making judgments of other individuals, we often focus on specific instances in which the person might have exhibited behaviors associated with the adjective.

Stanley Klein and his colleagues at the University of California, Santa Barbara (1992), have conducted a series of studies showing that self-description judgments do not rely on recall of specific autobiographical episodes. Their experimental paradigm examines the effect of self-description judgments on the accessibility of autobiographical memories. Participants either rated personality adjectives for self-descriptiveness or, in a comparison condition, generated a definition for the adjectives. After the first task, participants were asked to recall a particular instance from their lives in which

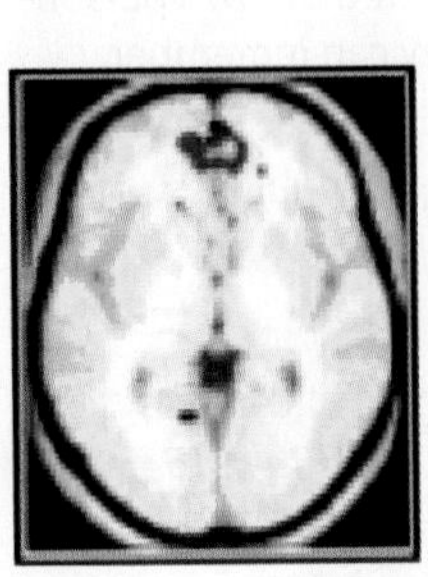

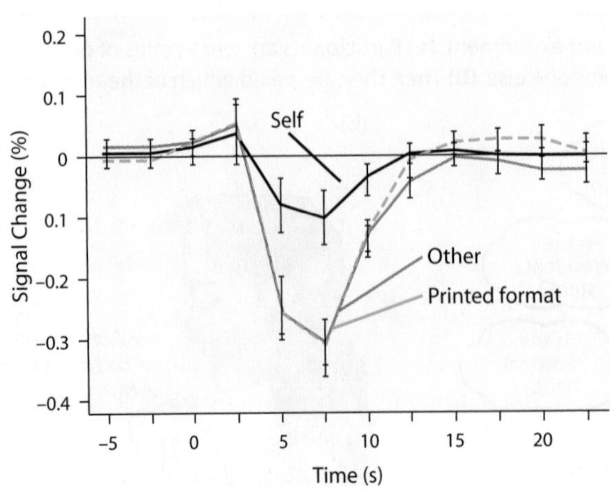

Figure 14.3 Medial prefrontal cortex (MPFC) activity is associated with self-referential processing when compared to processing words in relation to another person ("Other") or the printed format of the words.

they had exhibited the personality characteristic. If self-descriptions rely on searches through episodic memory, participants should have been faster to recall a time in which they exhibited the personality characteristic after making a self-description judgment compared to when they simply generated a definition. However, no differences were found between the self-judgment and definition conditions, suggesting that our judgments about self-characteristics are not linked to recall of specific past behaviors.

If this conclusion is correct, then we should be able to maintain a sense of self even if we are robbed of autobiographical memories across our lives. Is this possible? The ability to maintain a sense of self in the absence of specific autobiographical memories is demonstrated in case studies of patients with dense amnesia (Klein et al., 2002; Tulving, 1993). Consider two patients who developed retrograde and anterograde amnesia (see Chapter 8). Patient R.B.'s memory problems developed after a heart attack as a result of the transient loss of oxygen to the brain—a condition known as *hypoxia*. Patient K.C. was in a motorcycle accident and sustained brain damage that result in amnesia. Neither R.B. nor K.C. is able to recall personal events from the past, but they are both able to accurately describe their own personality. For example, R.B.'s and K.C.'s personality judgments are consistent with judgments provided by their family members.

Together, this research suggests that the unique mechanisms of self-referential processing rely on neural systems distinct from the neural systems used to process information about other people who are not well-known to us. Our memory for information processed in relation to ourselves is significantly stronger than for information processed in other ways. The deep processing associated with self relies on medial prefrontal cortex function. A more complete understanding of the psychological role of the medial prefrontal cortex function in self-judgment requires more research. For example, patients with selective damage to the MPFC region found in the fMRI studies of self-reference are rare, so we do not yet know how (or whether) damage to this region impairs the ability to make accurate personality judgments. The MPFC region may be important for storing knowledge about the self or for retrieving this knowledge. Finally, people may be able draw on unique information sources when making self-descriptive judgments because unique neural systems play a role in the different kinds of information sources used to make these judgments. Judgments about the self rely on summaries of our personality traits, and judgments about other people rely on memories of specific life events. Patients with amnesia, although unable to remember specific events in their lives, can make self-descriptive judgments, and this ability suggests that the summaries of personality traits are supported by neural systems distinct from the neural systems that support memories of specific life events.

Self-Reference as a Baseline Mode of Brain Function

What can the brain tell us about the prevalence of self-referential processing? Some research suggests that the medial prefrontal cortex, the region associated with self-referential processing, has unique physiological properties that may permit self-referential processing to occur even when we are not actively trying to think about ourselves.

Usually, fMRI studies report increased brain activation in relation to a particular cognitive process. However, many of the fMRI studies of the self-referent effect show a different pattern. Although there are significant differences in MPFC activity in relation to self-referential judgments compared to other kinds of judgments, the data show that the MPFC *deactivates less* when people make self-referential judgments (Figure 14.4). What does this finding mean? Marcus Raichle and Debra Gusnard at Washington University in St. Louis argue that the answer lies in understanding the physiological properties of the MPFC when the brain is at rest, as well as how this region's activity relates to specific cognitive tasks.

What does it mean to say the brain is at rest? Even when you are resting quietly and not trying to think about something in particular, your brain continually circulates blood and uses oxygen. These circulatory and metabolic changes are costly because they take blood and oxygen away from other organs. And the costs may be even higher in particular brain regions. For example, some evidence suggests that a network of brain regions including the MPFC has higher metabolic rates at rest. Why would the brain consume so much of the body's energy when it is not engaged in a specific cognitive task? Raichle, Gusnard, and their colleagues argue that these effects reflect the fact that when individuals are at "rest," their brains continue to engage in a number of psychological processes. The psychological processes represent a default mode of brain function (Gusnard & Raichle, 2001). For example, they suggest that the higher metabolism in the medial prefrontal cortex reflects self-referential processing, such as thinking about what we might be getting ready to do, or evaluating our current condition. The default mode of brain function ensures

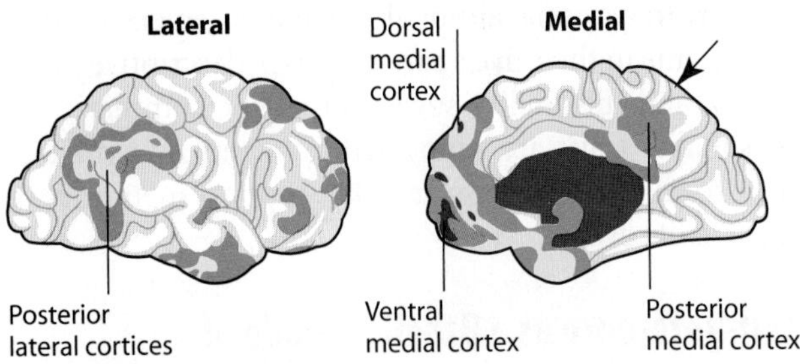

Figure 14.4 Regions of the brain associated with high levels of metabolism when the brain is at rest and with deactivation when the brain is focusing on specific task instructions. Regions in the ventral and dorsal medial prefrontal cortex, as well as the posterior lateral cortices, tend to have a high level of metabolism when people are not engaged in a particular task. When people are instructed to focus on a particular task, many of these regions then deactivate from their resting level of activity.

that we always have some idea of what is going on around us.

If the brain is already making a set of default psychological computations, then what are the implications for brain activation when we deviate from the "default state" and actively try to think about something else? Because supplies of blood and oxygen in the brain are limited, these resources are directed away from baseline regions, resulting in their deactivation.

From this perspective, the MPFC is theorized to perform self-referential functions when people are at rest. When people are left to daydream, we generally think about ourselves. Given this assumption, a self-referential task would not elicit a significant change in activation in the MPFC, because it chronically engages in self-referential thinking, even during the "rest" or baseline condition. In the self-reference studies, the president and printed-format conditions direct cognitive resources away from self-referential thinking, and therefore the MPFC shows a strong deactivation relative to baseline.

The perspective of a default mode of brain activation suggests that any understanding of brain function must consider activation that occurs when people try to think about something, as well as the implications of baseline physiology and function when people are at "rest." However, some researchers, such as Alexa Morcom and Paul Fletcher at the University of Cambridge, have questioned why rest is assigned special status as the "baseline" of brain function. They point out that rest is a fairly infrequent state in our daily lives. In addition, the psychological meaning assigned to various regions in the default network is based on studies that found activation above baseline.

Although Kelley and colleagues found that the MPFC does not deactivate as much for self-reference, other studies have found that activity in the MPFC is significantly above baseline in relation to self-reference. It is unclear why the MPFC would activate above baseline for a self-referential task if it chronically performs this psychological function at baseline. More research is needed before we can strongly conclude that there is a default mode of brain function, but this line of research is intriguing because it suggests that self-referential processing occurs as a "baseline" function of the brain.

Self-Perception as a Motivated Process

The studies described in the preceding discussion examine a number of ways we process information about the self, but they do not address the question of how accurately we process this information. Judgments about the self are somewhat unique because this process is often inaccurate; people are motivated to see themselves in a positive manner. A wide range of behavioral studies have shown that people often have unrealistically positive self-perceptions (Taylor & Brown, 1988). More than 50% of people believe they are above average in intelligence, physical attractiveness, and a host of other positive characteristics—as humorist Garrison Keillor's description of his fictitious hometown, Lake Wobegon, attests: "where all the women are strong, all the men are good-looking, and all the children are above average." This rose-colored view extends to our expectations in life. People believe they are more likely than others to experience positive future events, such as winning the lottery, and less likely than others to experience negative future events, such as getting a divorce.

How does the brain allow us to maintain these positive illusions about ourselves? Chapter 5 described how visual illusions arise from higher order visual areas. Although research on self-perceptual biases is still unfolding, the results of recent studies suggest that distinct higher order prefrontal regions allow people to selectively focus on positive aspects of themselves and at the same time prevent them from deviating too far from reality.

Two studies suggest that the most ventral portion of the anterior cingulate cortex is responsible for focusing attention on positive information about the self compared to negative information. An fMRI study conducted at Dartmouth College by Joseph Moran and his colleagues (2006) asked participants to make a series of self-descriptiveness judgments just like those in the self-reference studies. As expected from research on positive biases in self-perception, the participants tended to claim more positive adjectives and fewer negative adjectives as self-descriptive. Differences in activity in the ventral anterior cingulate cortex were associated with making judgments of positive compared to negative adjectives, and this was particularly true for adjectives considered to be self-descriptive (Figure 14.5). Another fMRI study found that a similar region of anterior cingulate cortex was activated differentially when participants imagined experiencing a positive event in the future compared to a negative event (Sharot et al., 2007). These studies suggest that the anterior cingulate cortex is important for distinguishing positive self-relevant information from negative self-relevant information. Marking information as positive versus negative may permit people to focus more on the positive information.

Although self-perceptions are sometimes biased in a positive direction, on average self-perceptions are not delusional or completely detached from reality. Accurate self-perception is essential for appropriate social behavior. For example, people must have some insight into their behavior to make sure they are following social norms and avoid social mistakes. Research conducted by the author (J.S.B.) suggests that the orbitofrontal cortex is one brain region that may help people have relatively accurate insight into their behavior. Patients with damage to the orbitofrontal cortex (like M.R. at the beginning of this chapter) tend to have unrealistically positive self-views. Patients with damage to either the orbitofrontal cortex or the lateral prefrontal cortex, as well as healthy control participants, were videotaped while they engaged in a structured social interaction with a stranger (Beer et al., 2006). In this interaction, the stranger made conversation with the participants by asking them a series of questions. In comparison to patients with lateral prefrontal cortex damage and healthy control participants, patients with orbitofrontal damage tended to bring up impolite conversation topics. Patients with orbitofrontal damage were unaware of their social mistakes; instead, they believed they had performed very well on the social interaction task. These patients became embarrassed by their social mistakes only after gaining insight into their behavior by watching their videotaped performance (Figure 14.6). This study suggests that the

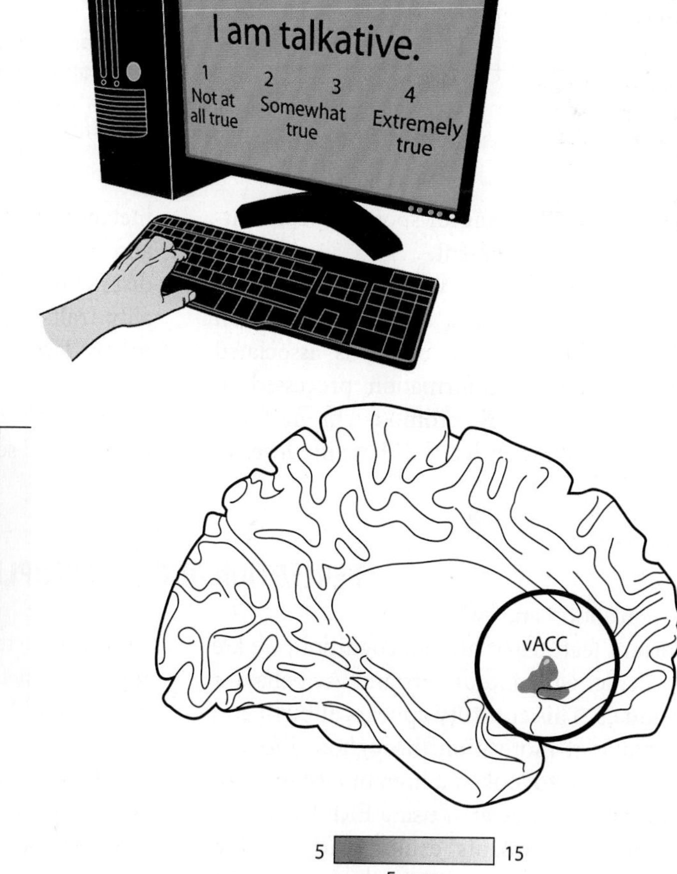

Figure 14.5 Neural activity in relation to judging positive information about the self. **(a)** Participants rated the self-descriptiveness of a variety of personality traits. **(b)** Less deactivation in the anterior cingulate was associated with rating positive personality traits in comparison to negative personality traits.

(a)

(b)

(c)

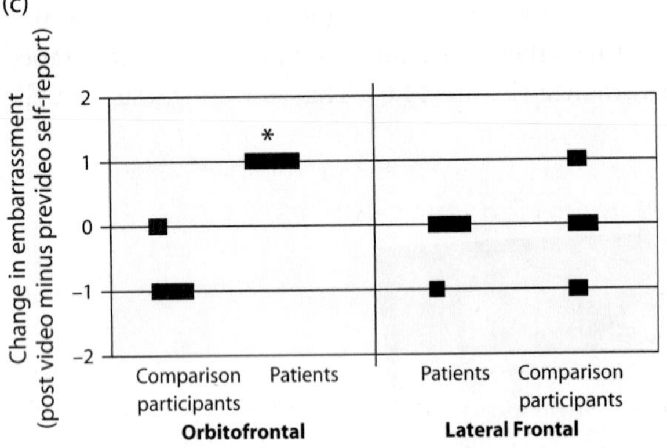

Figure 14.6 Study of self-insight in patients with orbitofrontal damage. **(a)** Participants first performed a social skills task that required them to make conversation with an experimenter they did not know well. **(b)** After performing the task and reporting on their perceptions of their own social appropriateness and emotions, participants watched a videotape of their task performance to see whether it gave them a different impression of their social appropriateness. **(c)** In contrast to the other brain-damaged participants and the healthy control participants, patients with orbitofrontal damage became embarrassed after viewing their social mistakes on videotape.

orbitofrontal cortex is important for spontaneous, accurate self-perceptions in the moment.

In summary, several regions within the prefrontal cortex support the unique effects that the self has on cognition. The medial prefrontal cortex is associated with superior memory for information processed in relation to the self and may promote chronic self-referential processing through its high baseline level of metabolism. It is possible to maintain a sense of self in the absence of specific autobiographical memories because a distinct neural system supports the summaries of personality traits typically used to make self-descriptive judgments. Finally, the anterior cingulate cortex is important for selectively attending to positive information about the self, but orbitofrontal cortex function ensures that positively biased self-views do not deviate too far from reality.

PERCEPTION OF OTHER PEOPLE

Although self-perception and awareness are important features of human cognition, we are also eager to interact with and understand the behavior of other individuals. This curiosity appears at birth and is a primary source of motivation throughout life. For example, infants prefer to look at a human face in comparison to other objects. Research using ERP has found that even 4-month-old infants exhibit early evoked gamma activity at occipital channels and a late gamma burst over right prefrontal cortex channels in response to direct eye contact. These findings suggest that infants are quick to process information about faces and use neural structures similar to those found in adults (Grossmann et al., 2007). In adulthood, much of conversation is spent on gossip about other people. Social psychologists recognize that understanding other people is a unique challenge when it comes to perceiving our social world. Consider a situation in which you are walking by the window of a candy store with a friend. At the sight of the elaborate marzipans in the window, your love of this candy sends an electric thrill down your spine. The two of you are already running late, but you wonder if she would be willing to take a minute to go into the store. Will she be offended if you voice your request? How would you figure that out?

Our self-perceptions have privileged access to our rich autobiographical memories, mental states that may not be expressed, and internal physiological signals. In contrast, our perceptions of other people are made without direct access to their mental and physiological states; instead, we have direct access to only the verbal and nonverbal cues they exhibit. Although we do not have direct access to the mental states of others, we often try to understand them by reasoning about what they might be thinking.

Understanding the Mental States of Others

The ability to infer the current mental state of others—their beliefs and desires—is critical for successful performance across a wide range of social actions, such as cooperating, empathizing, and accurately anticipating behavior. David Premack and Guy Woodruff of the University of Pennsylvania (1978) coined the term **theory of mind** to describe our ability to make inferences about the mental states of other people. Premack and Woodruff developed the idea when considering what might account for differences in cognition across species. They suggested that chimpanzees might be capable of inferring information about the mental states of other chimpanzees. Although considerable debate continues on the competence of social cognition in nonhuman species (Herrmann et al., 2007), the work of Premack and Woodruff sparked a deep interest in theory-of-mind research in humans. Theory of mind, also known as *mentalizing*, has received a considerable amount of attention in the developmental psychology literature and, more recently, in cognitive neuroscience studies.

Understanding the mental states of other people is important because those states do not always match their visible cues. In the case of the candy store scenario, for example, your friend may agree to go into the store but may still feel annoyed at your lack of consideration, given how late you are for your appointment. It is important to recognize that even though her words communicate a shared preference to go in the store, her true preference is the exact opposite. This knowledge can then help you decide whether the marzipan is important enough to make it worthwhile to momentarily upset your friend. Our daily lives are filled with instances in which people hide their true thoughts and feelings. In more extreme cases, our ability to recognize the mismatch between outward behavior and intentions will be useful for recognizing people who should not be trusted.

Much of the behavioral work on theory of mind has examined how this ability develops over the life span. At about age 3 or 4, children recognize that their physical vantage point gives them an individual perspective on the world that is different from the vantage point of other people. By 5 or 6 years of age, children appreciate that their mental states are distinct from the mental states of other people. Specifically, they are aware that two people can have different beliefs about the state of the world. At about 6 or 7 years of age, children can appreciate when the literal meanings of words communicate only part of the speaker's intention, or that the actual intention may be quite different from the literal meaning of what is said. For example, they can understand irony and differentiate between a joke and a lie. At about 9 to 11 years of age, children are able to simultaneously represent more than one person's mental state, and to discern when one person hurts another person's feelings.

The Neural Correlates of Theory of Mind

Social cognitive neuroscientists are interested in how the brain supports our ability to make inferences about other people's minds, read their nonverbal cues, and understand the relation between the two. What kinds of brain regions are associated with this ability, and what can this network of brain regions tell us about how we perform this important psychological function?

A series of studies indicates that the medial prefrontal cortex plays an important role in making inferences about other people's minds. Jason Mitchell and his colleagues at Harvard University found that the MPFC plays a strong role when people form impressions of the personality of another individual compared to when they are required to process other information about another individual. Participants were presented with pictures of people paired with statements about their personality, such as, "At the party, he was the first to start dancing on the table." A cue indicated how the participants should think about the faces and statements. In the impression formation task, the cue indicated that participants should make an inference about the personality of the person in the picture. In the sequencing task, the cue indicated that participants should remember the order in which specific statements were presented in relation to a particular face. Both conditions required participants to think about other people, but only the impression formation task required them to think about the internal states of those people. The impression formation task engaged the MPFC much more than the sequencing task did (Figure 14.7).

The results of this study suggest that MPFC activation plays a strong role in forming impressions about the internal states of other people rather than in thinking about other types of information pertaining to another person. Subsequent studies have shown that the relation between the MPFC and impression formation is specific to animate beings such as dogs (Mitchell et al., 2005); it is not present when individuals form impressions of inanimate objects. Together, this work indicates that the MPFC is important for reasoning about the intangible mental states of other beings.

Another brain region that has been associated with making inferences about other people's mental states is the temporoparietal junction in the right hemisphere (rTPJ). Rebecca Saxe at the Massachusetts Institute of Technology conducted a series of studies to examine the specificity of this region, building on the logic developed in fMRI studies of face perception. Recall from Chapter 6 that investigators explore the response characteristics of the fusiform face area (FFA) by identifying this region on an individual basis through the use of a localizer task. For example, participants might view faces or places, and the difference between the two conditions is used to specify the FFA on an individual basis. Once identified, further manipulations can be done to ask how activity in the FFA varies as a function of other experimental manipulations (see Chapter 13).

Saxe developed a similar method to identify the rTPJ region that is engaged during theory-of-mind judgments. The localizer task is based on the *Sally–Anne False-Belief Task* (Figure 14.8), a task that has been used in many developmental studies of theory of mind. In one version of this task, participants view a series of cartoons that depict scenarios involving the characters Sally and Anne. The pictures begin with Sally placing a marble in a basket and then leaving the room. Anne enters the empty room and moves the marble into a drawer. Sally then comes back into the room. The key question here is, where will Sally look for the marble? To answer the question correctly, participants have to ignore their own knowledge about the location of the marble and answer from the perspective of Sally. Sally is unaware of the devious behavior of Anne, so she expects the marble to be in the basket where she left it. Participants who are unable to recognize that Sally does not share their knowledge predict that she will look in the drawer. To solve the Sally–Anne task, participants must understand that Sally and Anne can have different beliefs about the world; that is, they must understand that people have different perspectives.

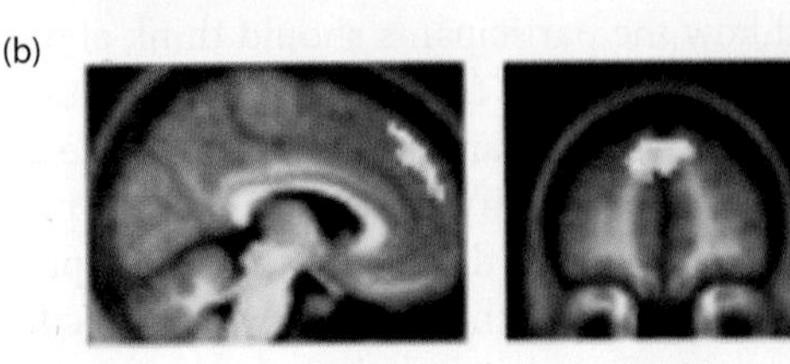

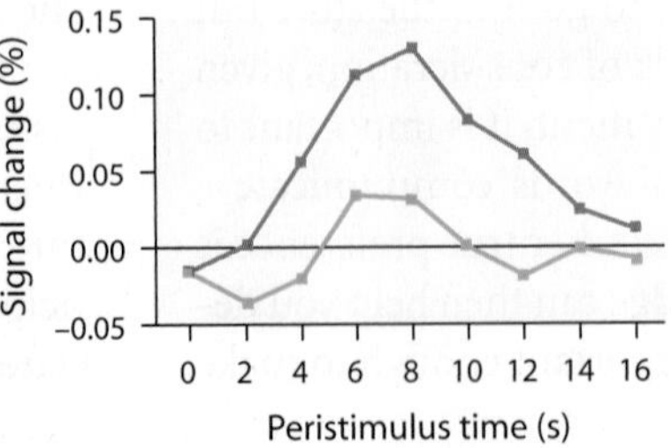

Figure 14.7 A study of personality inference. **(a)** Participants were presented with a series of pictures that paired faces with statements about personality. They were instructed either to make an inference about the person's personality or to pay attention to the order in which the statements were presented. **(b)** Medial prefrontal cortex activity was associated with forming impressions of personality in comparison to remembering sequence order.

Figure 14.8 The Sally–Anne False-Belief Task for investigating theory of mind. This task is used with children to determine whether they can interpret what Sally is thinking about the location of the marble. Because Sally does not see Anne move the marble from the basket to the drawer, Sally should look for the marble in the basket.

Saxe's localizer task presents a series of false-belief stories like the Sally–Anne task, as well as control scenarios involving falsehoods that have nothing to do with the mental states of other people. For example, participants view photographs of outdated maps. When these conditions are compared, a region of the rTPJ is consistently more active in the theory-of-mind condition. The exact location within the rTPJ is defined on an individual basis. Activity in this region is then examined for differential activity in relation to a series of other tasks that measure person perception (Figure 14.9).

Activity in the rTPJ is associated with reasoning about other people's mental states. Note that this area does not respond to *any* condition involving socially relevant information about other people. In one study, participants were presented with three kinds of information about a person: social background, mental states, and a life event. For example, participants might learn about "Lisa." Lisa lives in New York City with her parents (social background) but wants to move to her own apartment (mental state), and she finds out that the apartment she wants is available (life event). The study found that the rTPJ was significantly activated when participants where presented with the information about mental state compared to information about social background or life event (Saxe & Wexler, 2005).

As you know from Chapter 1, neuroscientists favor a network approach to the relation between brain regions and psychological function rather than a strict localization approach. It is unlikely that a psychological process as complicated as thinking about another person's mental states would be supported by a single brain region. Although the rTPJ is theorized to be specialized for reasoning about the mental states of other people, a large number of studies have also identified the MPFC in this process. How should we think about the roles of the rTPJ and MPFC in reasoning about mental states?

Currently, two different hypotheses have been suggested. One hypothesis is that the rTPJ is specialized for reasoning about the mental states of other people and the MPFC more broadly supports reasoning about other people including *but not limited to* their mental states. A second hypothesis is that the MPFC supports reasoning about social tasks but the rTPJ is important for redirecting attention in both social *and nonsocial* tasks. Let's look at the evidence for the first hypothesis. Participants' brain activity was examined in relation to processing information about a person's physical appearance ("Joe was a heavy-set man"), internal physiology ("Sheila's stomach was starving because she skipped breakfast"), or mental states ("Nicky knew that his sister's flight was delayed by ten hours"). The study found that the MPFC activated in relation to information about physical appearance and internally physiology. In contrast, the rTPJ was selectively activated for the information about mental states (see Figure 14.9; Saxe & Powell, 2006).

What about evidence for the second hypothesis? Chapter 12 described the attentional cuing procedure popularized by Michael Posner and his colleagues. In that procedure, participants are presented with cues that provide either valid or invalid information about where to direct their attention to successfully identify a target object (see Figure 12.8). Many of the studies that have found activation of the rTPJ in relation to mental states use **false-belief tasks** that require participants to direct their attention away from invalid information to answer questions about a person's mental states. Consider again

(a)

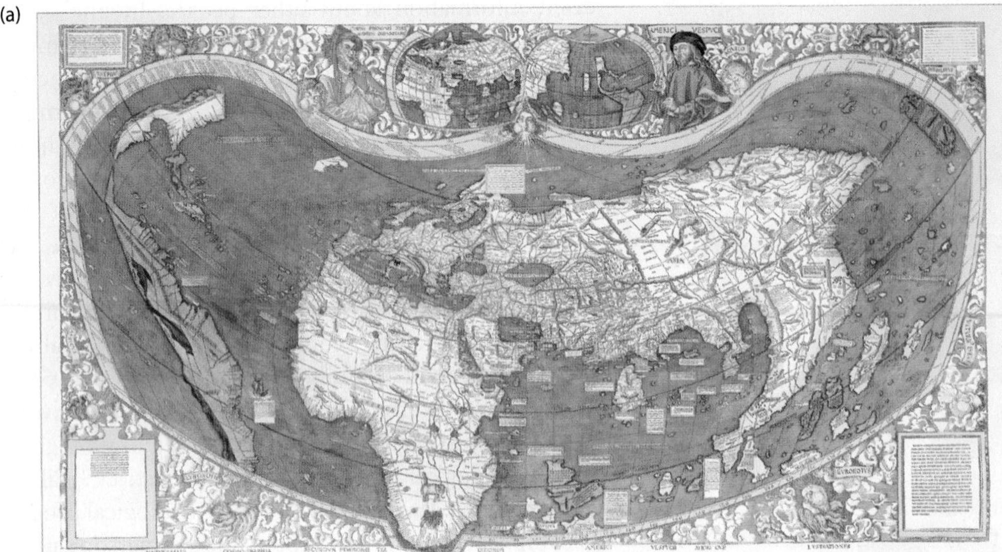

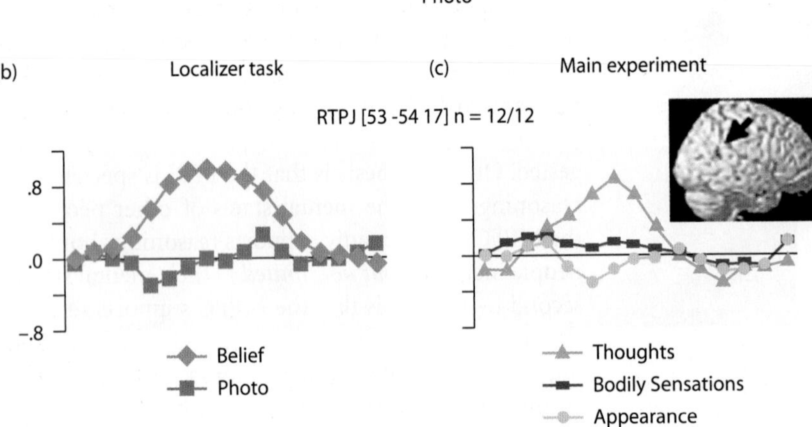

Figure 14.9 The localizer procedure for theory of mind and the right temporoparietal junction. Participants complete false-belief tasks that involve false beliefs about either people (as illustrated, for example, in Figure 14.8) or photos, as in this case of an outdated 1507 world map **(a)**. **(b)** Researchers identify a specific region in the brain that activates more strongly to the false beliefs of people when compared to false photographs. **(c)** They then examine this region of the brain for differential activity in relation to forming impressions about different aspects of people, such as their thoughts, body sensations, or physical appearance.

the structure of a typical false-belief task (see Figure 14.8). Participants are told a story in which Sally puts her marble away in the basket. Then she goes outside. Anne comes in the room and moves the marble to the drawer. Sally returns, and participants must decide where she will look for the marble. We know that participants' most current representation of the marble is in the drawer. Therefore, they have to redirect their attention to other information to correctly answer that she will think the marble is in the basket. Although this task is specifically about mental states rather than someone's physical appearance or other socially relevant information, it is also unique in its requirement that participants redirect their attention.

A recent study found that the *same* region of rTPJ is significantly activated in relation to the false-belief localizer task used by Saxe and her colleagues *and* in relation to redirecting attention away from nonsocial cues that signaled invalid information in the attentional cuing procedure (Mitchell, 2008). This finding suggests that the same region of rTPJ supports the control of attention for social and nonsocial stimuli. Although currently there is no definitive answer about the differential roles of the rTPJ and MPFC in person perception, research continues to be conducted on this question and promises to deepen our understanding of how we accomplish the difficult task of understanding the minds of other people.

Integrating Nonverbal Cues and Mental States

The studies described in the preceding discussion provide information about someone's mental states and then examine the brain systems that are recruited for reasoning about mental states in comparison to reasoning about other kinds of information. In the real world, however, we are not given a paragraph about what someone is thinking, nor can we count on people telling us exactly what they are thinking. In fact, paying attention to nonverbal cues rather than verbal cues may be your best strategy when people try to hide their mental state from you! We know this to be a good strategy because patients with language comprehension deficits are actually better at detecting when someone is lying than are patients without language deficits or control participants (Etcoff et al., 2000).

Nonverbal cues play a powerful role in person perception. You have already learned about the neuroscience of facial perception, which involves regions such as the fusiform face area (Chapter 6) and the role of the amygdala in using the face to make social judgments (Chapter 9). What about other kinds of nonverbal information? What behavioral cues signal this information, and what neural systems are sensitive to these cues? Research has shown that attention to the direction of eye gaze provides an important source of information concerning another individual's attentional state.

Within their first year of life, children develop **joint attention**, the ability to monitor another person's attention. One of the most typical ways that children monitor where other people are directing their attention is by noting the direction of their eye gaze. Eye gaze may also be helpful for understanding when people's words may not match their mental states. For example, when your friend agrees to go in the candy store with you, does she make eye contact while agreeing? Or does she avoid your gaze so that you cannot see her annoyance? What neural systems support the ability to attend to another person's eye gaze and use this information to reason about their mental state?

One of the earliest lines of research examining this question comes from single-cell recording studies in monkeys. David Perrett of the University of St. Andrews in Scotland discovered that cells in the superior temporal sulcus (STS) are helpful for identifying head position and gaze direction. The STS lies below the superior temporal gyrus and above the middle temporal gyrus. Amazingly, some cells responded to head position while others responded to gaze direction. Although head position and direction of eye gaze are often consistent, the ability to distinguish head position from eye gaze opens the door for using these cues to make inferences about mental states. Individuals who turn their head in the same direction as their gaze may be thinking something very different from individuals who keep their head facing forward but direct their gaze in a different direction.

Converging evidence showing that the STS is important for interpreting eye gaze in relation to mental states comes from human neuroimaging studies. Kevin Pelphrey and his colleagues at Duke University examined whether activity in the STS depends on the mental states indicated by shifts of eye gaze in another person. Participants watched as an animated woman directed her attention either toward or away from a checkerboard that flickered in either her left or right visual field (Figure 14.10 on p. 615). If the STS is involved in tracking shifts in eye gaze, then it will be activated in relation to any shift in eye gaze. However, if the STS is involved in integrating shifts in eye gaze with mental states, then activation of the STS should be related to where the character directs her attention, because eye gaze shifted toward the checkerboard and eye gaze shifted away from the checkerboard indicate two different mind states.

Consistent with the latter prediction, activity in a posterior region of the STS was related to shifts in eye gaze when they were directed away from the checkerboards (Pelphrey et al., 2003). In a related study, a similar region in the STS was activated when a virtual-reality character made eye contact with the participant compared to when the character looked away from the participant (Pelphrey et al., 2004). Thus, the STS appears not only to signal the focus of attention of another individual, but also to provide very important social signals—when that individual may be trying to direct our attention away from a novel object and when we have become the focus of another person's attention.

Autism: Deficits in Understanding the Minds and Nonverbal Cues of Other People?

Although different brain regions support our ability to make sense of other people's minds and visible cues, the study of autism suggests that they function as a network. For other disorders that affect a wide range of brain regions involved in social cognition, see "Milestones in Cognitive Neuroscience: Psychiatric Disorders and the Frontal Lobes," on the following page. **Autism** is a pervasive developmental disorder associated with impaired social interaction. People with autism tend to reason in a very concrete manner, so it is difficult for them to appreciate the mental and emotional states of other people. In Mark Haddon's book *The Curious Incident of the Dog in the Night-time*, a character with an autism spectrum disorder states, "I find people confusing ... The first main reason is that people do a lot of talking without using any words ... the second main reason is that people often talk using metaphors." We all recognize that many social situations are inherently confusing. Imagine how much more confusing this would be if you could not understand that teasing words were meant as a joke rather than criticism (Heerey et al., 2005)—or if you thought that someone had literally "laughed his socks off."

Individuals with autism tend to show little interest in other individuals or social interactions, preferring to focus on their internal thoughts or inanimate external stimuli. Individuals with autism may prefer routine activities and

MILESTONES IN COGNITIVE NEUROSCIENCE

Psychiatric Disorders and the Frontal Lobes

Psychiatric disorders such as schizophrenia and depression represent a widespread breakdown in mental function. Problems faced by patients suffering from these disorders affect almost all aspects of their behavior. Most likely their problems are not linked to a simple physiological mechanism. Rather the disorders are thought to arise from a delicate interplay of physiological mechanisms that reflect endogenous dispositions and a person's idiosyncratic experiences.

One of the most promising aspects of cognitive neuroscience is that it may offer new insights concerning the functional deficits associated with severe psychiatric disorders. Simple neuropsychological descriptions do not adequately account for these disorders. Schizophrenia cannot be thought of as a temporal lobe or frontal lobe problem; it arises as a disturbance in cognitive systems that span cortical and subcortical systems. For example, some imaging studies (Figure 1) have shown that schizophrenics have an underactive frontal cortex, especially in lateral regions. Losing their working memory and inhibitory capabilities renders them more reliant on activity in the posterior cortex. They may be easier to distract, and hence fail to inhibit irrelevant representations such as the ones related to persistent hallucinations.

Depressed patients, on the other hand, tend to exhibit a profile of overactivity in prefrontal regions associated with working memory and in areas linked to the generation of affective memories. With these people, representations persist for a long time and are imbued with heightened affect. A situation that a normal person might find neutral, or at most mildly aggravating, becomes amplified and often highly unpleasant. The depressed patient cannot let a situation go; the representation of a thought or obsession persists, sustained by input from inappropriate somatic markers.

With a cognitive neuroscience perspective, we can make sense of the outcome of one of the great debacles of neurosurgery: frontal lobotomies for treating psychiatric disorders (Valenstein, 1986). Prior to the implementation of drug therapies in the 1950s and 1960s, mental institutions were overflowing with desperate patients and doctors, eager to try any procedure that promised relief. In the 1930s, Egas Moniz, a renowned Portuguese neurologist who had developed cerebral angiography in 1927, introduced a psychosurgical procedure for treating patients with severe schizophrenia and obsessive-compulsive disorder.

Moniz's inspiration came from an international scientific conference at which two American researchers had reported the effects of frontal lobectomy in chimpanzees. One animal appeared to have undergone a personality change. Before the operation, the chimp had been uncooperative and would throw temper tantrums. After removal of most of her frontal lobes, the animal was cheerful and participated in experimental tests without hesitation. Moniz reasoned that the procedure might bring relief to severely agitated patients—a well-intended thought, given the paucity of alternatives.

Removing large amounts of tissue from the frontal lobes seemed excessive. Instead, Moniz decided to isolate the prefrontal cortex from the rest of the brain by severing the white matter's connecting fibers. In his early efforts he applied toxic levels of alcohol through holes in the skull's lateral surface. Later he switched to a procedure in which a leukotome (a plunger with an extractable blade) could be lowered into the brain to sever fibers in targeted regions.

Walter Freeman at Georgetown University refined this procedure. He developed a simple technique that did not require a surgeon. The patient was first given an anesthetic consisting of a severe electrical shock. While the patient was unconscious for 15 minutes, the surgeon performed the lobotomy by jabbing an ice pick through the bone above each eye and wiggling it back and forth. Freeman assembled a portable kit containing his electroshock apparatus, ice picks, and a small hammer, and set off on a barnstorming trip to promote the benefits of this miracle cure (Figure 2). The public and scientific community were welcoming. Thousands of procedures were performed over the next few decades, and Moniz received the Nobel Prize in Physiology or Medicine in 1949.

With the advantage of hindsight, we now recognize the abject failings of the lobotomy craze. The few

(a)

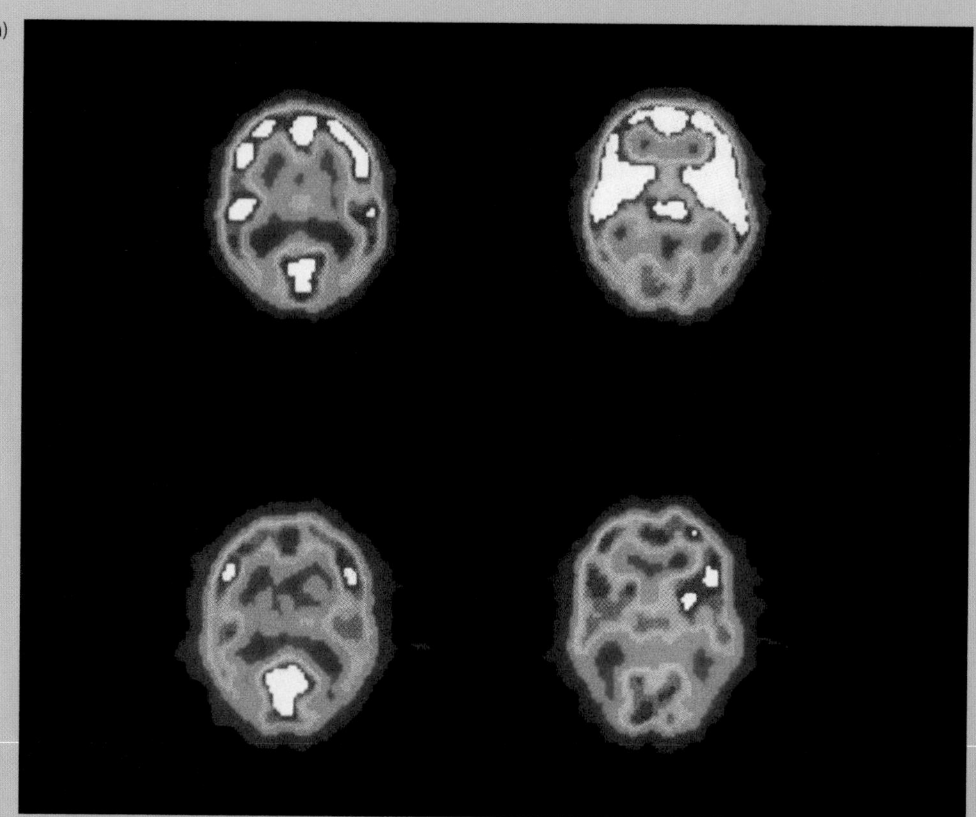

(b)

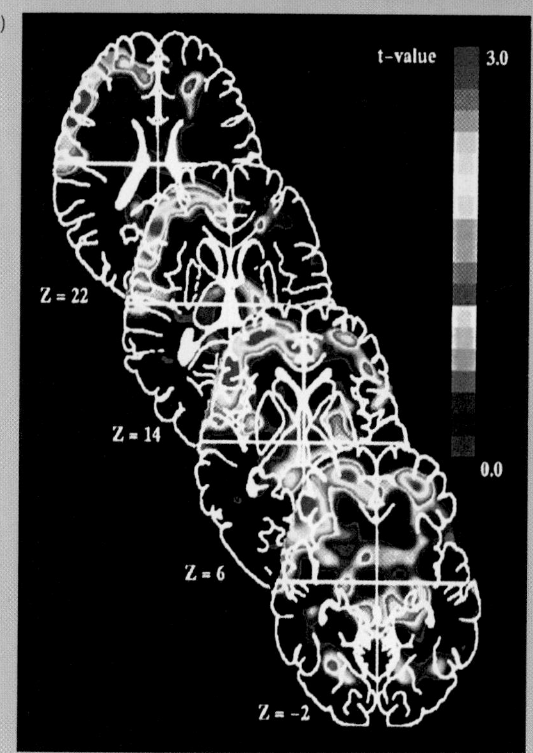

Figure 1 Positron emission tomography (PET) reveals abnormal patterns of blood flow in patients with psychiatric disorders. **(a)** Schizophrenic patients show hypometabolism in the prefrontal cortex. This abnormality is especially marked during tasks that produce increased blood flow in this area in healthy subjects. In this study, subjects were involved in a continuous auditory discrimination task. Compared to the control subjects **(top)**, uptake of the tracer is much lower in schizophrenic patients **(bottom)**. **(b)** Blood flow at rest was measured in control subjects and patients with depression. Colored areas indicate regions of increased blood flow in the depressed patients. These areas are centered in the lateral prefrontal cortex in the left hemisphere.

Continued on the following page

Continued from the previous page

outcome studies that were done revealed that the discharge rate from mental institutions was no greater for lobotomy patients than it was for control subjects. Scant concern was given to the patients selected; the procedure had minimal effect on schizophrenics but drastically altered patients with affective disorders like depression or severe neurosis, who felt much less anxious, impulsive, and depressed. But these feelings brought new problems that rendered these patients incapable of functioning outside the institutional setting. They were now withdrawn and underactive, lacking in affect or responsiveness. The benefits, if any, were experienced by attendants, who rejoiced that the patients were docile and easy to manage. As with Phineas Gage, the patients' personalities had been transformed.

These differential outcomes make sense in light of metabolic studies. Lobotomies targeted the prefrontal cortex, a region already underactive in schizophrenia. As such, we might expect little effect on schizophrenics, or maybe new problems for those with an excessive dominance of posterior brain function. For affective disorders, though, lobotomies isolated an overactive region. Moreover, the primary foci were medial regions, so the procedure may have eliminated behaviors associated with exaggerated emotionality but turned patients into affectless zombies.

(a)

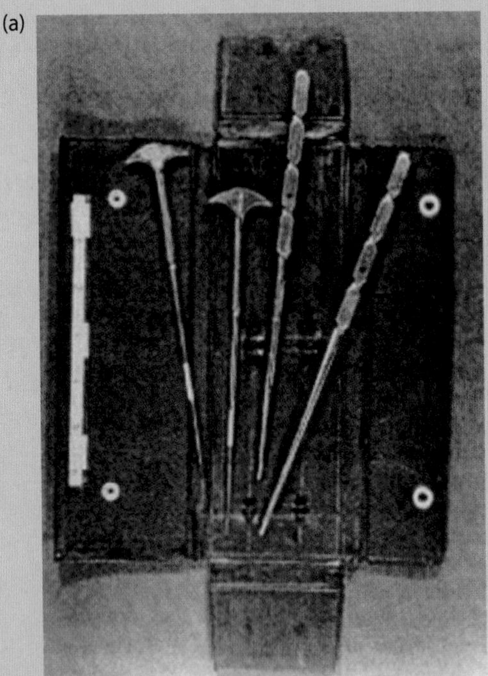

(b)

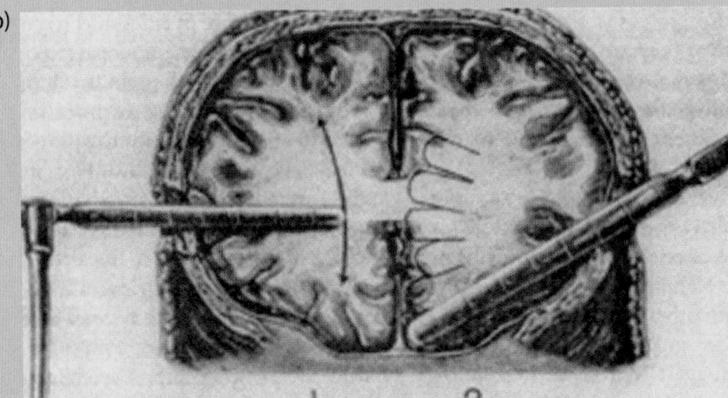

Figure 2 **(a)** The portable toolkit for performing prefrontal lobotomies. The kit included various tools for penetrating the skull and cutting through brain tissue. **(b)** Freeman's sketch of two lobotomy procedures. In one, the blade is rotated back and forth, forming a radial cut. In the other, the blade is inserted at various angles.

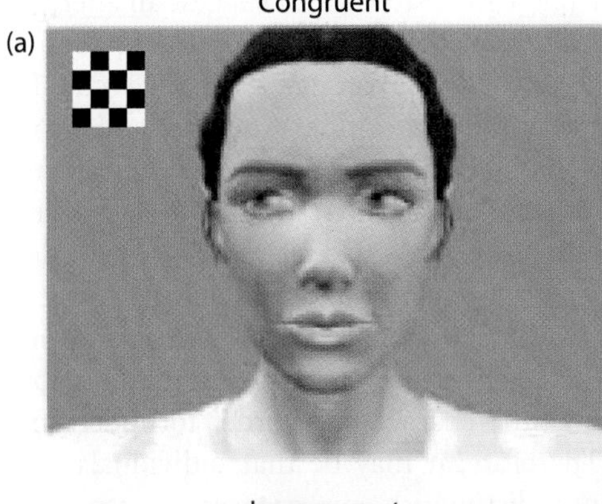

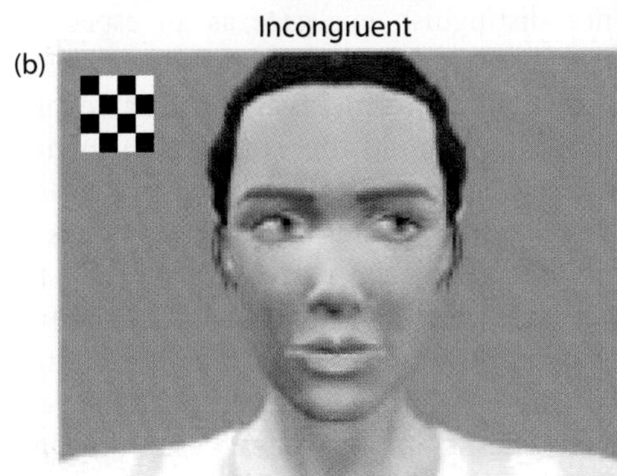

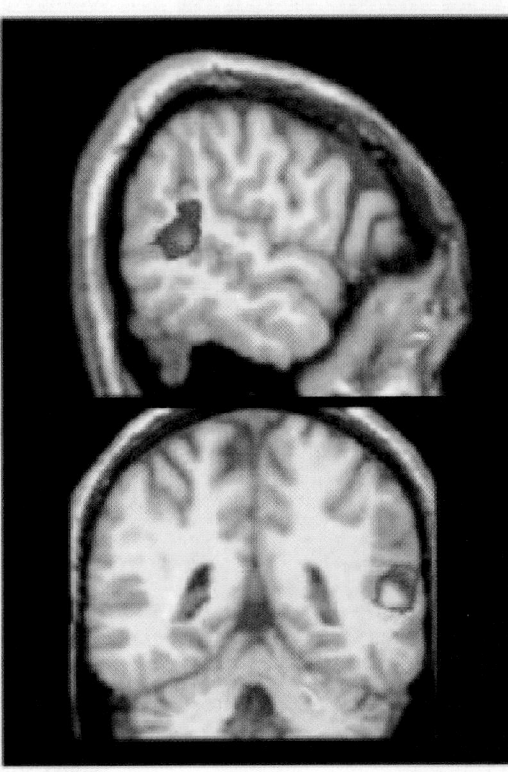

Figure 14.10 Participants viewed a virtual-reality character who moved her eye gaze either **(a)** in a congruent manner toward a flashing checkerboard or **(b)** in an incongruent manner away from a flashing checkerboard. The superior temporal sulcus tracked the intention behind eye gaze shifts rather than all shifts in eye gaze.

may become upset if these routines are interrupted. For example, the author (J.S.B.) observed a therapy session with a young girl who had autism in which she became extremely distressed when a new volunteer set the table for lunch in a different order than was the typical routine. Instead of seeking out social interaction, individuals with autism may prefer to engage in repetitive behavior by themselves, such as flicking a string back and forth repeatedly. Rather than seeking out a hug, these individuals may comfort themselves by rocking their bodies back and forth or twisting their hands and fingers.

Simon Baron-Cohen of Cambridge University (Baron-Cohen et al., 1985) has proposed that individuals with autism direct their attention away from other people because of theory-of-mind deficiencies. Chapter 6 described people with prosopagnosia, patients who become "face-blind" because they are unable to identify people on the basis of facial information. Drawing on this notion, Baron-Cohen coined the term *mindblindness* to reflect the inability of children with autism to properly represent the mental states of others (Baron-Cohen, 1995). False-belief tasks are particularly challenging for children with autism. Even when they are well past the age at which most children are able to solve these problems, autistic individuals perform these tasks as if the characters have access to all of the information in the story. For example, although they understand that Sally initially put the marble in the basket, they also act as if Sally were aware that Anne moved the marble to the drawer; that is, they report that Sally will look for the marble in the drawer.

As mentioned earlier, false-belief tasks often provide participants with information about other people's mental states, but in real life we are often left to infer these states from nonverbal cues such as facial expression and eye gaze. The mindblindness associated with autism extends to impaired use of nonverbal cues to reason about another person's internal states. A large body of research shows that people with autism are impaired on a variety of tasks requiring the use of facial perception for social judgments (e.g., Baron-Cohen, 1995; Klin et al., 1999; Weeks & Hobson, 1987).

People with autism have difficulty identifying emotion and mental states from facial expressions and do not use this information in the same way that healthy control participants do. When asked to sort a set of facial pictures, most children organize them according to the emotional expressions on the faces. In other words, they put pictures of people expressing happiness in one pile, pictures of people expressing sadness in another pile, and so on. In contrast, children with autism are more likely to sort these pictures on the basis of physical features such as clothing. Recall from Chapter 9 that Ralph Adolphs and his colleagues investigated the facial

(a)

(b)

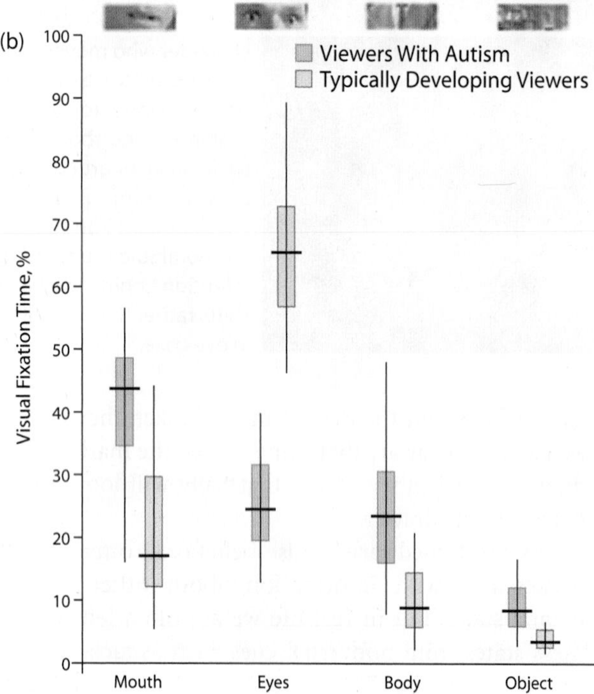

Figure 14.11 Study of eye gaze in healthy and autistic participants. **(a)** The eye gaze of healthy participants is compared to that of participants with autism while they are watching characters in a film. **(b)** Healthy participants tend to focus on the eyes of characters in a film. In comparison, participants with autism do not show selective attention to the eyes in comparison to more noninformative aspects of the face.

perception abilities of patients with amygdala lesions by using computer software that presented small pieces of facial expressions at a time. They also conducted a study in which people with autism performed these procedures, and found that they do not attend to eye gaze as much as healthy controls do (Spezio et al., 2007).

Why don't people with autism pay attention to eye gaze? Some researchers have suggested that people with autism may avoid the eye gaze of others because they find eye contact unpleasant. However, Ami Klin and his colleagues at Yale University (2002) suggest an alternate hypothesis. Individuals with autism may fail to recognize the importance of eye gaze as a cue for understanding their social worlds. When nonautistic individuals watched the movie *Who's Afraid of Virginia Woolf?* (Figure 14.11), they spent much of their viewing time paying attention to the faces and eyes of the characters in order to understand their intentions and feelings. In contrast, individuals with autism did not allocate much of their attention to the facial expressions and eye gaze of the characters in order to understand the movie. Therefore, it may be that individuals with autism do not distinguish eye gaze as an especially meaningful cue for perceiving other people.

If theory-of-mind impairments are a central feature of autism, then autism should affect many of the neural regions involved in person perception. Is this the case? The neural correlates of autism have been the focus of intense investigation over the past 25 years, with researchers employing a host of methodologies. Anatomical studies suggest that a host of brain abnormalities are associated with autism beginning at birth. For example, Eric Courchesne and his colleagues at the University of San Diego have discovered that infants with autism tend to have small head circumference at birth, which is followed by an abrupt inflation of head circumference in the first year of life. Brain abnormalities persist over the course of development, and studies suggest that autism is associated with reduced volume in a range of brain areas, including the frontal lobes, STS, amygdala, cerebellum, and hippocampus. In addition to reduced structural volume, autism has been associated with abnormal function in a number of regions associated with person perception, including the MPFC, amygdala, FFA, and STS.

How is the "mindblindness" and specifically the lack of interest in eye gaze associated with autism reflected in abnormal brain function? Unsurprisingly, people with autism exhibit significantly less activation in the MPFC and STS when performing theory-of-mind tasks (see Frith, 2003, for a review). In other tasks, individuals with autism do not show reduced STS activation but instead activate this region for a broader range of conditions. When performing the eye gaze and checkerboard task developed by Kevin Pelphrey and his colleagues at Duke (see Figure 14.10), participants with autism show increased STS activation to *any* shift in eye gaze rather than specifically in response to eye gaze away from the checkerboard. To the extent that participants with autism attend to eye gaze, they engage the FFA when viewing faces (Dalton et al., 2005). The failure to pay attention to eye gaze is accounted for at least partially by the smaller amygdala size that is characteristic of autism. In fact, amygdala size correlates with attention to the eyes of other people. The smaller the amygdala, the less likely an individual with autism is to attend to the eyes of another person (Nacewicz et al., 2006).

Together, these studies suggest that individuals with autism do not activate the neural regions associated with person perception in the same manner that individuals without autism do. Sometimes autism is associated with reduced function or volume, and sometimes it is associated with more inclusive activation that is not sensitive to subtle social cues such as eye gaze specifically oriented toward an object of interest.

In addition to being associated with abnormal brain function and volume, autism may affect the default brain network. As mentioned earlier in the chapter, the MPFC is part of a brain network that has a higher level of metabolism at rest—activity that may reflect self-referential processing. The relation between autism and abnormalities in MPFC function may also extend to this region's baseline mode. When healthy participants engage in thinking that takes their attention away from this self-referential processing, they experience deactivation in the MPFC. Participants with autism do not significantly deactivate their MPFC when performing non-self-referential tasks (Kennedy et al., 2006). This failure to deactivate may result from an unusual focus on internal states rather than the external world (which would include the minds of other people). In other words, unlike healthy control participants, people with autism may continuously maintain a high level of self-referential focus.

The study of autism provides a fascinating window into the important role of theory-of-mind abilities in navigating our social worlds. Individuals with autism prefer routine and repetitive behavior that does not often involve other people. Autism is associated with difficulty in appreciating the minds and nonverbal cues of other people and may reflect an intense self-referential focus. The difficulty in understanding other people and intense self-referential focus may be reflected in the abnormal brain development and function associated with autism. These brain abnormalities are far-reaching: this disorder affects all of the major neural regions important for person perception and self-referential processing.

CONVERGENCE IN THE PERCEPTION OF SELF AND OTHERS

You may have noticed in the preceding discussion that MPFC activation is associated with the perception of both self and other people. Why would a common brain region be involved in both processes? One possibility is that a common brain region is recruited for both kinds of tasks because a common psychological function can be used to perform both kinds of tasks. For example, people may draw on their self-representations to make inferences about another person. **Simulation theory** suggests that theory of mind is based on an ability to put ourselves in the shoes of another person, using our own minds to simulate what might be going on in the minds of someone else (Harris, 1992; Figure 14.12). How is the process of simulation reflected in brain activity?

Medial Prefrontal Cortex: Similar and Close Others

The theory of simulation suggests an intrinsic relation between the perception of self and the perception of others. Therefore, the reason for the MPFC's involvement in both types of perception may be that the perception of self is sometimes used to accomplish the perception of others. For example, in one fMRI study, scientists found that a similar region of the MPFC was significantly activated for self-perception and perception of a similar other, but not for perception of a dissimilar other (Mitchell et al., 2006). Participants read descriptions of two people; one person shared similar political views with the participants, and the other held the opposite political views. Subsequently, the participants' brain activity was measured while they answered questions about their preferences, as well as when they speculated about the preferences of the person with similar views and the one with dissimilar views. A ventral subregion of the MPFC was found to increase its activity for self-perceptions and perceptions of the similar person, whereas a more dorsal region of the MPFC was significantly activated for perceptions of the dissimilar person. This pattern of different regions of the MPFC being involved for speculations about similar and dissimilar persons has been interpreted as evidence that the participants may have reasoned that their own preferences would predict the preference of someone like them but would not be informative for speculating about the preferences of someone dissimilar.

Another reason why the MPFC may support self-perception and the perception of others is that we may

Figure 14.12 Simulation theory. People make inferences about the actions of others using their own expectations based on past experiences from their own lives.

store highly elaborate and emotional information about ourselves *and* the special people in our lives. The study conducted by Kevin Ochsner and the author (J.S.B.) mentioned earlier in this chapter provides some support for this view. A similar region of the MPFC was activated for self-perception and the perception of a current romantic partner (Ochsner et al., 2005). This effect was not driven by perceived similarities between the self and the romantic partner. Instead, this activation likely represents commonalities in the complexity or emotional nature of information stored about ourselves and romantic partners. Together, these studies suggest that the MPFC is important for thinking about the self and other people when a common psychological process underlies the thought processes. Sometimes we may use ourselves as a way of understanding someone whom we do not know well but who appears to be similar to us. At other times, these processes may be linked because we create incredibly rich stores of information about ourselves as well as our close others.

Empathy

The strong relation between self-perception and the perception of others is epitomized in the process of empathy. **Empathy** is the process of purposely putting oneself in another person's shoes in order to understand that person's thoughts and feelings. Although we recognize the distinction between ourselves and the other person, we momentarily try to create the other person's internal state within ourselves to better understand that perspective. What brain mechanism permits us to share the experience of another person?

Recall from Chapter 7 that mirror neurons are activated both for executing an action and for perceiving the same type of action when executed by someone else. Mirror neurons may also be a critical physiological mechanism that supports our ability to empathize with others by permitting us to simulate their internal states within our own bodies. A large body of research suggests that the brain regions supporting our emotional states are also activated when we perceive these emotional states in other people. Chapter 7 described mirror neurons in the premotor and parietal cortex that link action and perception for object use. Mirror neurons associated with empathy are located in regions more typically associated with emotional states.

For example, a series of experiments using a wide range of methodologies has found that the experience of disgust and the perception of facial expressions of disgust activate similar regions within the insula. For example, one fMRI study found that when people become disgusted by images of insects, poor hygiene, or rotten food, the intensity of their disgust is correlated with the magnitude of their insula activity. Similarly, an fMRI study showed that the magnitude of insula activation is associated with the intensity of another person's facial expression of disgust (Figure 14.13).

The fMRI studies are consistent with a study using depth electrodes that was conducted by Pierre Krolak-Salmon and his colleagues at University College London (2003). Patients with epilepsy who were undergoing neurosurgery had depth electrodes placed in the insula. The researchers found that neurons in the anterior insula fired when these patients viewed disgusting facial expressions. Finally, a single-patient case study of insula damage provides additional support for mirror neurons in the insula: after sustaining a lesion to the insula, this patient lost the ability to recognize disgust (Adolphs et al., 2003). Together, these studies suggest that the insula is important for experiencing disgust, as well as for perceiving it in others.

What about internal states other than disgust? A study conducted by Tania Singer and her colleagues at

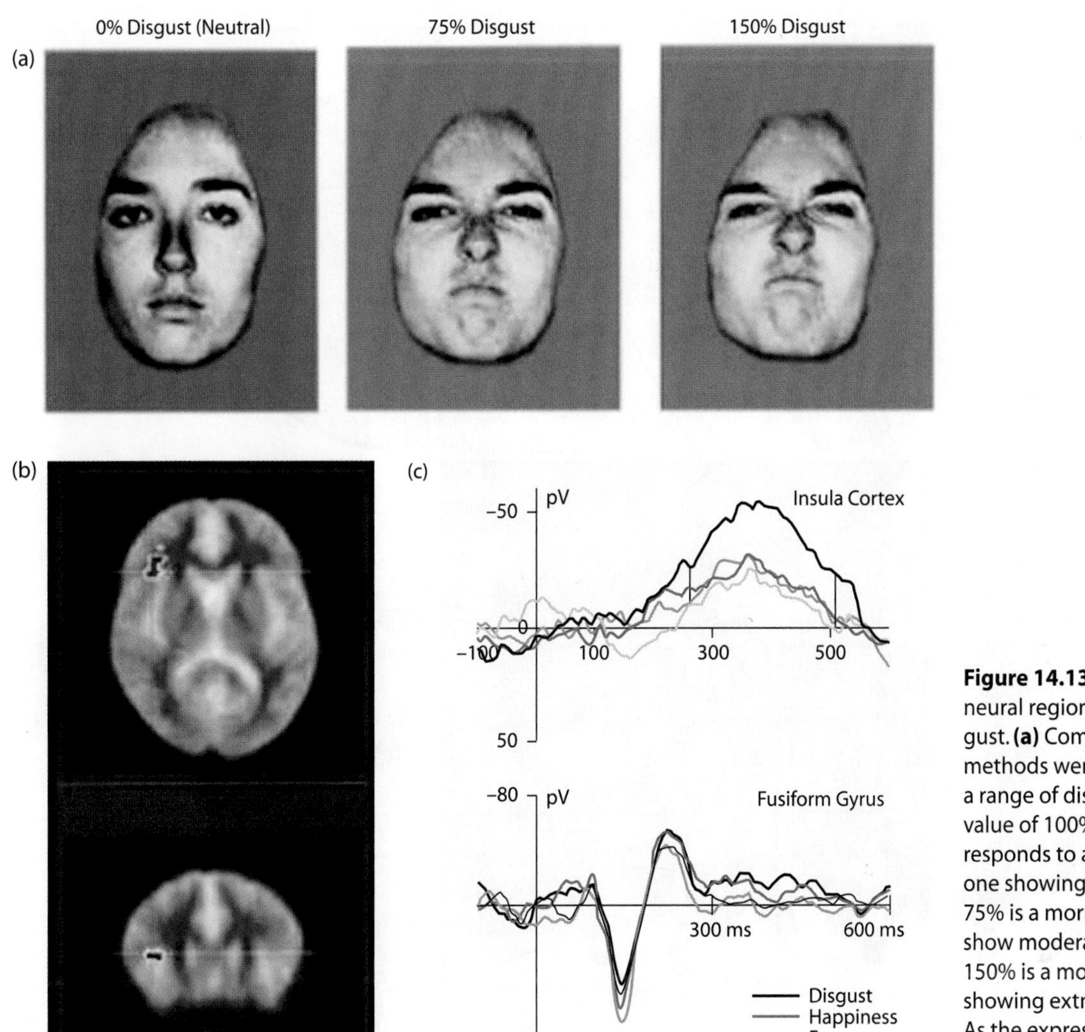

Figure 14.13 Exploring the neural regions responsive to disgust. **(a)** Computer morphing methods were used to generate a range of disgusted faces. A value of 100% (not shown) corresponds to a photo of someone showing actual disgust, 75% is a morphed version to show moderate disgust, and 150% is a morphed version showing extreme disgust. **(b,c)** As the expressions of disgust became more intense, the BOLD response in the insula increased.

University College London found that both experiencing physical pain in oneself and perceiving physical pain in others activate the insula and anterior cingulate (Singer et al., 2004). In the study, participants' brain activity was examined when they received painful stimulation through an electrode on their hand or saw the painful stimulation delivered through an electrode to a romantic partner's hand (Figure 14.14). Although the experience of pain activated a larger network of brain structures, both the experience of pain and the perception of a loved one's pain activated the insula and anterior cingulate. Furthermore, participants who scored high on a questionnaire measure of empathy showed the most insula and anterior cingulate activation when perceiving pain in their romantic partners. This result suggests that the mirror neurons that are activated in relation to the experience and perception of pain are particularly active for people who generally tend to be empathic.

An inventive experiment conducted by Jean Decety and his colleagues in Taiwan provides converging evidence that individual differences in empathy modulate the activation of the mirror neurons related to physical pain (Cheng et al., 2007). In this study, the brain activity of two groups of participants was examined while they watched video clips depicting body parts receiving nonpainful stimulation (touch with cotton swab) or painful stimulation (acupuncture needles). One group of participants had no experience with acupuncture practices; the other group were physicians who had at least 2 years of experience with acupuncture. It was hypothesized that regions typically associated with

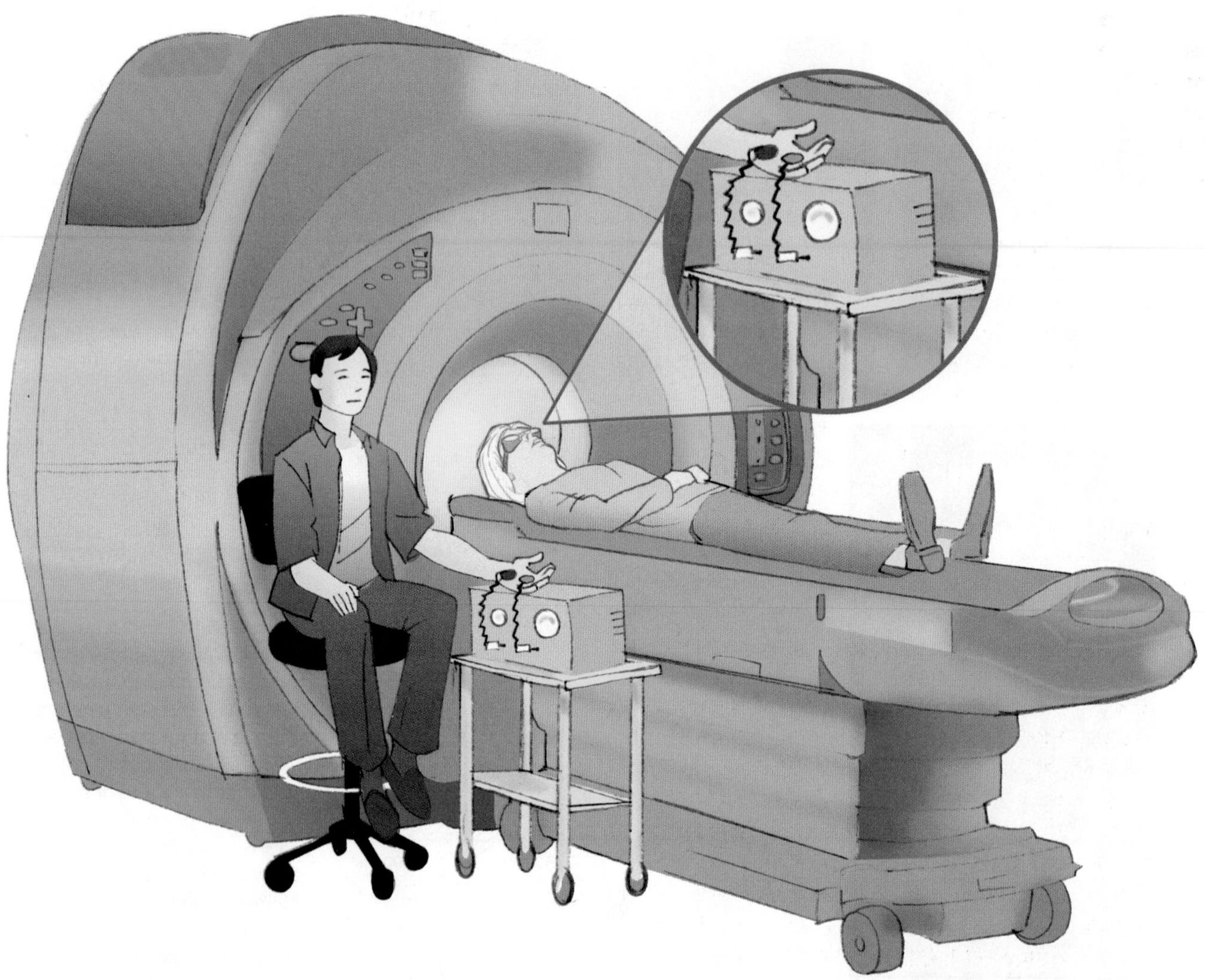

Figure 14.14 Study of empathy for pain. Each participant watched as a partner's hand received a shock through a set of electrodes. Brain activity was very similar for one's own pain and the pain of the partner, and the degree of brain activation was correlated with empathy.

perceptions of physical pain would not be activated in physicians, because their jobs require that they detach themselves from the painful aspect of administering acupuncture and focus on the long-term benefit to the patient. Consistent with previous research, the study found that regions associated with the experience of pain—including the insula, anterior cingulate, and somatosensory cortex—were activated in nonexperts. In the physicians, by contrast, these regions were not significantly activated; but regions associated with mentalizing about others, such as the MPFC and rTPJ, were activated.

Although the somatosensory cortex has not been found to be activated in relation to the perception of pain in other studies, an extensive study of lesion patients found that patients with damage to the somatosensory cortex were significantly impaired in their ability to identify another person's emotional state when compared to patients who had damage to other brain regions (Adolphs et al., 2000). Together, these studies suggest that the principle of mirror neurons likely plays a role in our ability to empathize. The regions associated with emotional states such as disgust or pain are also activated when we are perceiving these states in other people. Furthermore, their activation depends on whether a particular individual is empathizing with the person experiencing the emotion.

SOCIAL KNOWLEDGE

In 1985, Simon Yates and Joe Simpson were the first mountaineers ever to reach the summit of Siula Grande in the Peruvian Andes. Their climb would be remembered as much for this accomplishment as it was for the moral dilemma faced by the climbers during their descent. Early in the descent, Joe fell and broke his leg. How could he climb down the mountain now? The two men developed a system in which Simon would brace himself with his climbing axes and then lower Joe down using a 300-meter rope. Once Joe had been lowered as far as the rope would permit, often out of Simon's view, he would brace himself in the mountain with his climbing axes and tug on the rope. Simon would then climb down to meet Joe and repeat the process. Their slow progress became even slower and more treacherous when a storm hit, causing temperatures to drop even further on the icy mountain. Simon lowered Joe down as usual and waited for the tug indicating he should begin climbing down. But no tug came. Simon did not know it, but he had lowered Joe over an overhang of ice and there was no way for Joe to brace himself in the mountain. Joe tried to yell to Simon, but he could not be heard over the storm. Simon grew colder and felt himself begin to slip off the mountain from Joe's weight on the other end of the rope. He grew concerned that he would freeze to death or they would both be pulled off the mountain if he did not begin climbing again soon.

Simon measured his concern against his knowledge that the biggest taboo in the mountaineering community is to cut the rope attaching you to your partner. In the 2003 documentary *Touching the Void*, Simon discusses how he made the decision to save his own life by cutting the rope. Simon managed to make it down off the mountain and, incredibly, so did Joe. Ironically, Simon's decision to violate the moral code of mountaineering may have been the only reason they both survived. It is likely that both men would have frozen on the mountain if they had remained where they were. Joe forgave Simon, but the two men do not remain in contact, and Simon was ostracized by much of the mountaineering community.

Simon broke the moral code of the mountaineering community in order to save his own life. Do you think he was justified in endangering someone else's life to save his own? Simon and Joe's story is certainly an extreme case, but it illustrates the reality that social behavior is shaped by multiple influences. To successfully negotiate our social worlds, we must not only understand the rules for appropriate behavior, but make choices consistent with those rules. In this section we will consider questions about social knowledge and its use in decision making. How do we know which aspects of knowledge to apply to a particular situation? If our own interests conflict with societal norms, deciding how to proceed can be difficult. What can the brain systems used to make these sorts of decisions tell us about this psychological process?

Representations of Social Knowledge

One of the most complicated aspects of social behavior is that there are few straightforward rules. The very same behavior that is appropriate in one context may be wildly inappropriate in another. For example, hugging a close friend is an act of affection, but hugging a stranger may be considered intrusive. And what about someone who you are getting to know better but do not yet consider a close friend? When is it appropriate to greet that person with a hug? Social cognitive neuroscience has only begun to research the neural systems that help us make these decisions, and there is much left to be learned. At present, most research findings suggest that the frontal lobes are important for taking into account the particular situation in order to apply the appropriate rules.

Patients with prefrontal cortex damage do not take context into account. Instead, they execute prototypical responses to objects in their environment, even if these responses are inappropriate for the context. A classic demonstration of this tendency is evident from the medical practice of Francois Lhermitte of the Hôpital de la Salpêtrière in Paris (Lhermitte, 1983; Lhermitte et al., 1986). Lhermitte invited a patient with frontal lobe damage to meet him in his office. At the entrance to the room, Lhermitte placed a hammer, a nail, and a picture. Upon entering the room and seeing these objects, the patient spontaneously used the hammer and nail to hang the picture on the wall.

In a more extreme example, Lhermitte put a hypodermic needle on his desk, dropped his trousers, and turned his back to his patient. Whereas most people would consider filing ethical charges in this situation, the frontal lobe patient was unfazed. He simply picked up the needle and gave his doctor a healthy jab in the buttocks! Lhermitte coined the term **utilization behavior** to characterize this extreme dependency on prototypical responses for guiding behavior. The patients with frontal lobe damage retained knowledge about prototypical uses of objects such as a hammer or needle, but could not arrive at appropriate decisions about whether to use those items in the particular circumstance of the visit to the doctor's office.

Consistent with the perspective that patients with frontal lobe damage are overly reliant on environmental cues, Lhermitte also found that some of his patients exhibited **imitative behaviors**. Lhermitte would sit opposite his patient and engage in behaviors that were inappropriate for an office visit. Sometimes he would fold paper, comb his hair, or tap his leg. At other times he would engage in wildly inappropriate behaviors, such as thumbing his nose, chewing paper, or kneeling in prayer. A subset of patients with frontal lesions would imitate these actions—both the appropriate ones and the inappropriate ones. It is tempting to argue that these patients may have imitated the behaviors because they believed that those behaviors must be appropriate if they were performed by a doctor. However, healthy participants and patients with lesions outside the prefrontal cortex did not imitate the doctor.

As we learned earlier in the book, brain lesions do not typically naturally occur in perfectly prescribed brain regions. Lhermitte worked with patients who had large lateral prefrontal lesions that sometimes extended into the orbitofrontal cortex and basal ganglia. We now know that subregions in the frontal lobes are responsible for diverse psychological functions. Therefore, more recent research has examined the social knowledge of patients with lesions to specific subregions of the frontal cortex. Although Lhermitte found that his patients with lateral prefrontal lesions could not stop themselves from using objects in a prototypical manner, more recent research suggests that patients with orbitofrontal cortex damage have the most difficulty when they need to draw on their social knowledge to make sense of social interactions.

In one fascinating line of work, Valerie Stone and her colleagues developed a social faux pas task that measures one's ability to reason about the world. The task presents participants with a series of scenarios in which one of the characters commits a social faux pas by accidentally saying something impolite. One scenario tells the story of Jeannette and Anne. Anne receives a vase as a wedding gift from Jeannette. A year later, Anne has forgotten that the vase was from Jeannette. Jeannette accidentally breaks the vase while at Anne's house. Anne tells Jeannette not to worry because it was a wedding gift that she never liked anyway. The researchers then measure social reasoning by asking participants to identify whether someone in this scenario made a social mistake and if so, why. Stone and her colleagues gave this test to patients with orbitofrontal damage, patients with lateral prefrontal cortex damage, and healthy control participants (Stone et al., 1998).

In comparison to all other participants, patients with orbitofrontal damage performed poorly on the test because of their inability to apply their social knowledge to the scenarios (Table 14.1). Patients with orbitofrontal damage understood that a character like Jeannette would feel badly, but they did not understand that Anne's comment about not liking the vase was actually intended to reassure Jeannette. Instead, they often believed that Anne had intended to hurt Jeannette's feelings. These results suggest that orbitofrontal damage impairs the ability to use social knowledge to reason about social interactions. The patients with orbitofrontal damage were not able to take the context into account when reasoning about the social mistakes.

A series of studies conducted by the author (J.S.B.) provides some important clues that orbitofrontal cortex supports appropriate social behavior (Beer et al., 2003, 2006). In a study reported earlier in the chapter, patients with orbitofrontal damage, patients with lateral prefrontal damage, and healthy controls took part in a structured conversation with a stranger. Compared to the other participants, patients with orbitofrontal

Table 14.1 Types of Errors

Group Tested	Detected Faux Pas
DFC patients	
L.S.	10
R.T.	10
O.A.	10
W.E.	10
Mean	10
OFC patients	
D.H.	9
M.R.	6
R.V.	7
R.M.	8
R.B.	10
Mean	8
Anterior temporal control	
B.G.	10
Normal controls	
Mean	10

Source. From Stone et al., 1998.

damage were likely to introduce impolite conversation topics. However, all of the participants reported that it was inappropriate to discuss emotional and personal information with strangers before they began the social interaction task. The patients were unaware that their actual social behavior violated these social rules for conversations with a stranger.

This lack of awareness may be particularly problematic because it makes it difficult for patients with orbitofrontal damage to experience embarrassment that might motivate them to behave differently in the future. In another study, patients with orbitofrontal damage and healthy control participants took part in a teasing task that required them to make up nicknames for an experimenter they did not know well. Healthy control participants were careful to come up with flattering nicknames and to apologize for having to tease someone they did not know well. In contrast, patients with orbitofrontal damage offered unflattering nicknames and were likely to announce them in a singsong voice more often used for teasing someone you know well. The orbitofrontal patients were not embarrassed by their inappropriate teasing, but instead they reported feeling especially proud of their social behavior.

Without awareness of their social mistakes, patients with orbitofrontal damage never generate the emotional feedback they need to change their future behavior. When we do something that makes us feel embarrassed, we are strongly motivated to avoid feeling that way again. But when we do something that makes us feel proud, we are likely to repeat the action in order to continue the good feeling. These findings suggest that even though patients with orbitofrontal damage report an understanding of social rules, they do not apply this knowledge to their own social interactions (Figure 14.15). They are also unlikely to spontaneously recognize that their behavior is inappropriate, because they lack self-insight and do not generate the social emotions needed to correct their social mistakes in future social interactions.

Although patients with orbitofrontal damage who behave inappropriately do retain intact social knowledge about what is proper, they appear to have trouble learning new social knowledge. This view is supported by case studies of orbitofrontal damage sustained in childhood. These patients also have inappropriate social behavior but, in contrast to patients who receive this damage in adulthood, orbitofrontal patients who sustained their damage in childhood do not understand social rules (Anderson et al., 1999). This finding suggests that the orbitofrontal cortex is important for learning social knowledge and applying it to specific social interactions.

Using Social Knowledge to Make Decisions

The research described in the preceding discussion suggests that the orbitofrontal cortex is important for identifying what kinds of social knowledge are relevant for a particular situation. Even if we know the rules for a given social situation, we still have to decide what to do to ensure that we abide by the rules. Consider the following scenario. When you go to a friend's house for a party, you know that there are certain rules for being a polite guest. These rules may help you avoid inappropriate behavior, but they do not always point to one specific behavioral choice. For example, there may be a number of things you can do and still be polite. Do you greet first your friends or someone new? Do you get something to eat now or wait until later? How do we make decisions about our social behavior? What are the brain mechanisms that support decision making using social knowledge?

One of the earliest theories of how the brain supports the application of social knowledge to decision making was proposed by Antonio Damasio. In the early 1990s, Damasio and his colleagues at the University of Iowa made a surprising discovery when working with E.V.R., a patient with orbitofrontal cortex damage. When faced with social reasoning tasks, E.V.R. could generate solutions to problems but he could not prioritize his various solutions on the basis of their ability to solve the problem (Saver & Damasio, 1991). E.V.R. could describe a number of ways to address social dilemmas (e.g., a disagreement between two roommates about which television program to watch), but he could not distinguish which solutions were most likely to be effective in resolving the dilemma. One of the reasons this was such a surprising discovery was that, at that time, the orbitofrontal cortex was considered to handle emotional functions. Because emotion was considered a disruptive force in decision making, it was surprising that impairing a region involved in emotion would result in impaired decision making. Damasio wondered whether damage to the orbitofrontal cortex impaired decision making because emotion was actually needed to optimize decision making.

On the basis of the case study of E.V.R. and subsequent research, Damasio developed the somatic marker hypothesis to explain the process through which emotion is necessary for successful decision making and the involvement of the orbitofrontal cortex (Figure 14.16). The somatic marker hypothesis states that emotional

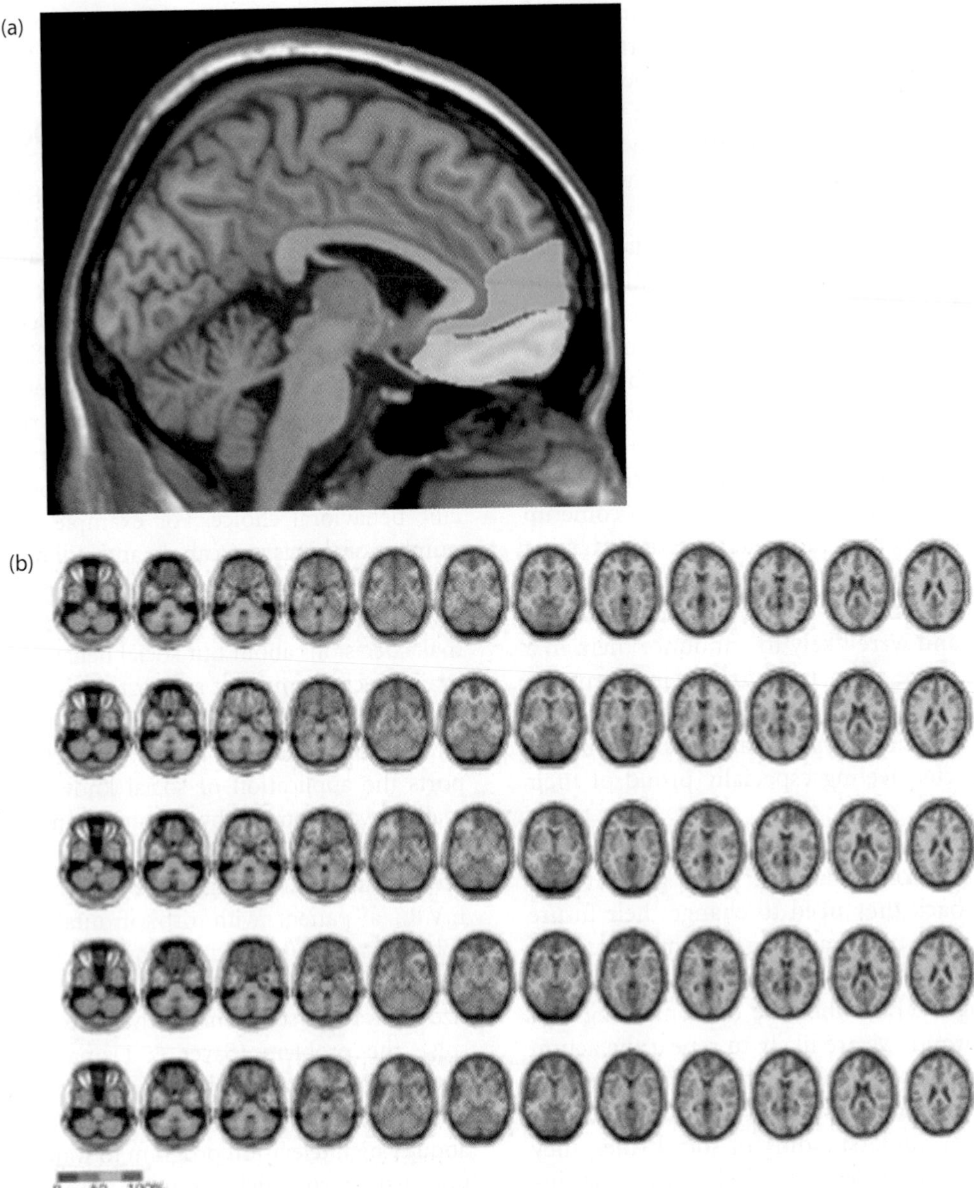

Figure 14.15 Patients with orbitofrontal damage may lack insight into their behavior at a particular moment while maintaining accurate summaries of their traits. **(a)** The orbitofrontal cortex (yellow) lies just beneath the medial prefrontal cortex region (green) associated with the summaries of personality traits. **(b)** Typical orbitofrontal damage. Damage is indicated in red. Each row represents ascending brain slices of a single patient. The bottom row indicates the extent of overlap in lesion location across the whole group.

information in the form of physiological arousal is needed to guide decision making. When presented with a situation in which we need to make a decision, we may react emotionally to the situation around us. This emotional reaction is manifest in our bodies as **somatic markers**—changes in physiological arousal. Orbitofrontal structures are theorized to support learning of associations between complex situations and the somatic changes (i.e., emotional state) usually associated with a particular situation. The orbitofrontal cortex works with other brain regions to consider previous situations that elicited similar patterns of somatic change. Once previous situations that elicited similar somatic markers are identified, then the orbitofrontal cortex can use these past experiences to rapidly evaluate possible behavioral responses and their likelihood for reward. Decision making can then selectively focus on option–outcome pairings that are potentially rewarding.

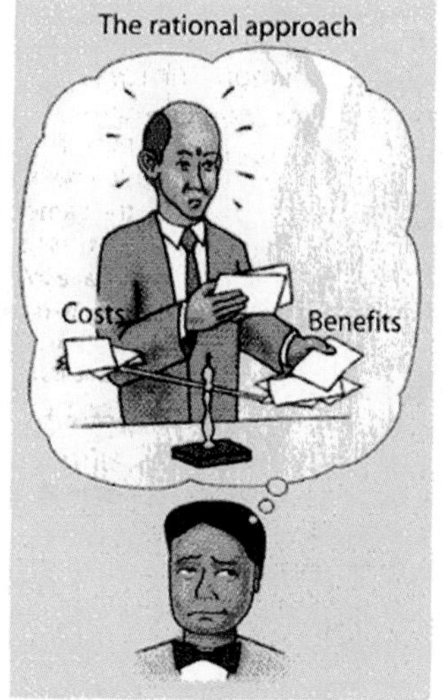

Figure 14.16 Somatic markers facilitate decision making by influencing candidate responses based on their affective value. The rational economist might assess the benefits and costs of each option, and then choose the one with the highest value. Limitations in information processing, coupled with the need for expedience, favor a faster system that can quickly eliminate actions associated with unpleasant consequences, while boosting those that experience has shown to be rewarding.

The somatic marker hypothesis is supported by studies in patients with brain lesions who performed a task called the Iowa Gambling Task (Figure 14.17; Bechara et al., 1997). In the Iowa Gambling Task, skin conductance response (SCR) is measured while participants continually draw cards from their choice of four decks. The cards indicate monetary amounts resulting in either gain or loss. Unbeknownst to the participants, two decks are associated with net winnings; they have low payoffs but even lower losses. The other two decks are associated with net losses; they have high payoffs but even larger losses. Participants must figure out that they need to favor the decks associated with net winnings in order to earn the most money.

Healthy adults and patients with damage outside the orbitofrontal cortex (either within the frontal lobes or outside the frontal lobes) learn the task and gamble in a manner that maximizes winnings. In contrast, patients with orbitofrontal damage learn the task but fail to favor the decks that result in net winnings. The studies claim that this failure arises because the patients do not generate the somatic markers needed to successfully complete the task. Healthy adults show an increased skin conductance response (SCR) in anticipation of making a risky gamble. In contrast, patients with orbitofrontal damage show no anticipatory change in SCR.

More recently, researchers have begun to search for alternative explanations of the role of the orbitofrontal cortex and emotion in successful decision making (Dunn et al., 2006). Empirical evidence challenges the claim that the main function of the orbitofrontal cortex is to interpret physiological arousal so that emotional experience can then enhance cognition. People are not very good at correctly attributing the source of their physiological arousal (Schachter & Singer, 1962). Studies have also shown that patients with spinal cord injuries, bereft of physiological feedback, report subjective experiences of emotion like those of normal study participants (Bermond et al., 1991; Chwalisz et al., 1988) and can perform the Iowa Gambling Task without impairment (North & O'Carroll, 2001). Therefore, it is unlikely that patterns of physiological arousal (or mentally represented patterns of arousal) are all that useful for ensuring successful decisions.

Finally, a recent study found that the Iowa Gambling Task may be challenging for patients with orbitofrontal damage because it requires them to change their initial perceptions of the potential for rewards in the risky decks (Fellows & Farah, 2005). The decks with the net losses are very appealing in the beginning of the task because the rewards are so large. Because cards are continually drawn from those decks, however, the monumental losses begin to appear. If the task is modified so that the card order in the decks makes it clear earlier in the task that there are large wins but even larger losses, then patients with orbitofrontal damage perform this task as well as healthy control participants. This finding is consistent with research in monkeys that found that orbitofrontal damage makes it difficult to reverse an association once it has been learned (Jones & Mishkin, 1972).

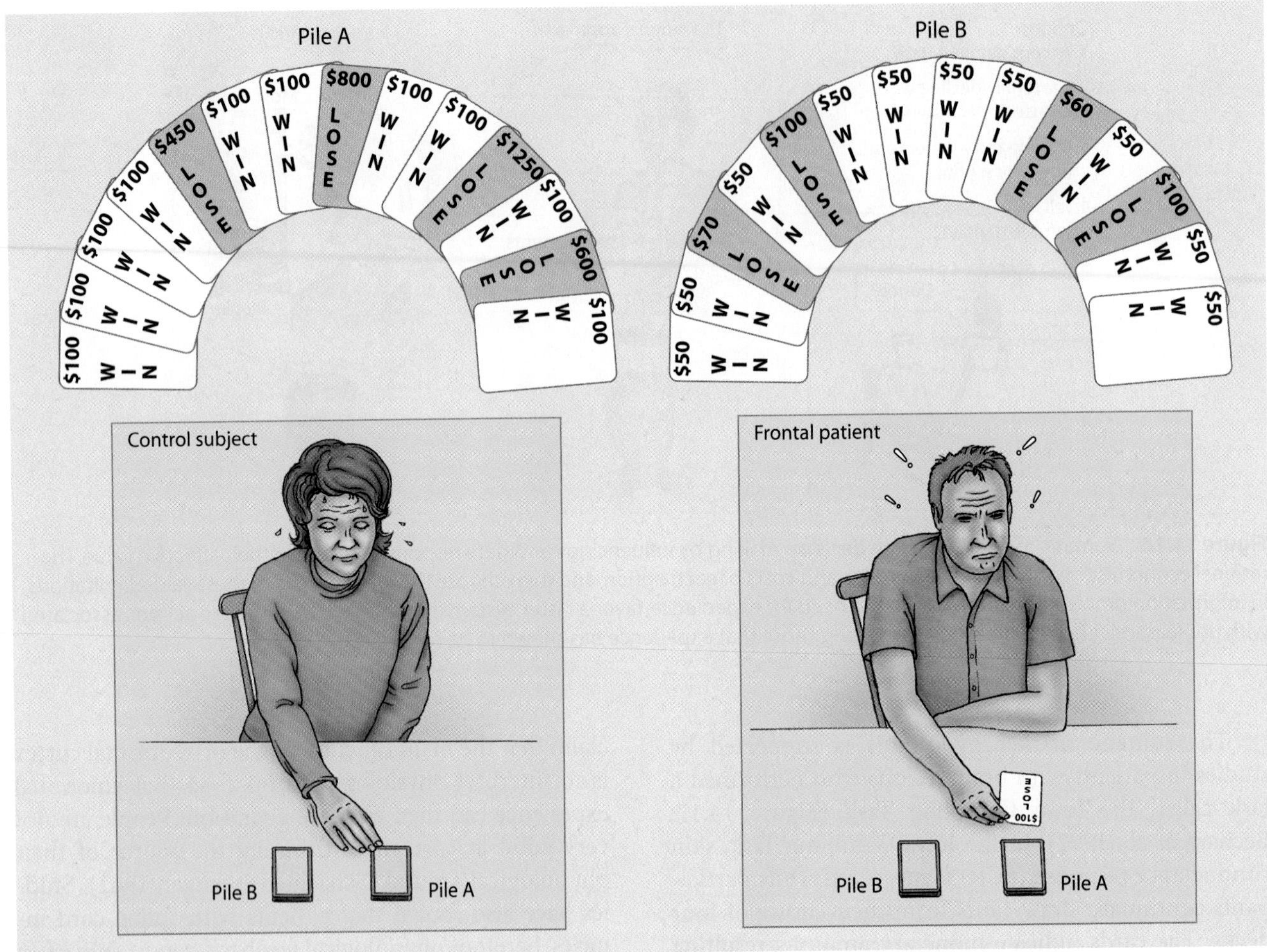

Figure 14.17 Emotional responses in reaction to stimuli are useful in guiding our decision processes. Subjects in this experiment were required to choose cards from one pile or the other, with each card specifying an amount won or lost. Through trial and error, the subjects learned that Pile A was riskier than Pile B. Control subjects not only tended to avoid the high-risk pile but also showed a large skin conductance response (SCR) when considering choosing a card from this pile **(a)**. The patients with prefrontal lesions failed to show anticipatory SCRs. Interestingly, they did show a large SCR **(b)** upon turning over a card and discovering they had lost $1,000 (of play money).

As suggested in the previous section, the orbitofrontal cortex plays a strong role in applying social knowledge to our decisions in social settings. It is likely that this region helps us choose the correct behaviors not by accessing somatic markers but by recognizing which rules are applicable in a particular situation. As the case of patient M.R. from the beginning of the chapter illustrates, the orbitofrontal cortex is helpful for recognizing when a hug is appropriate and when it is not.

Neuroeconomics

A recent perspective on the problem of how we make decisions using social knowledge comes from a new field called **neuroeconomics.** Neuroeconomics integrates psychology, neuroscience, and economics to yield an understanding of how people make decisions (Sanfey et al., 2006). Economic models of decision making assume that people should make rational decisions—that is, decisions that maximize their rewards and minimize their losses. Specifically, rational decision making focuses on the choice that will reap the largest monetary outcomes. However, these models have begun to incorporate the role of emotion and recognize that people do not always make decisions on the basis of financial outcomes. People sometimes follow their emotions and make decisions that do not reap the largest monetary outcomes. The emotional reactions often arise in relation to concerns that are not financial. Therefore, emotions may sometimes help make optimal decisions by taking into account a wider range of consequences. Neuroeconomists are interested in understanding how neural regions that

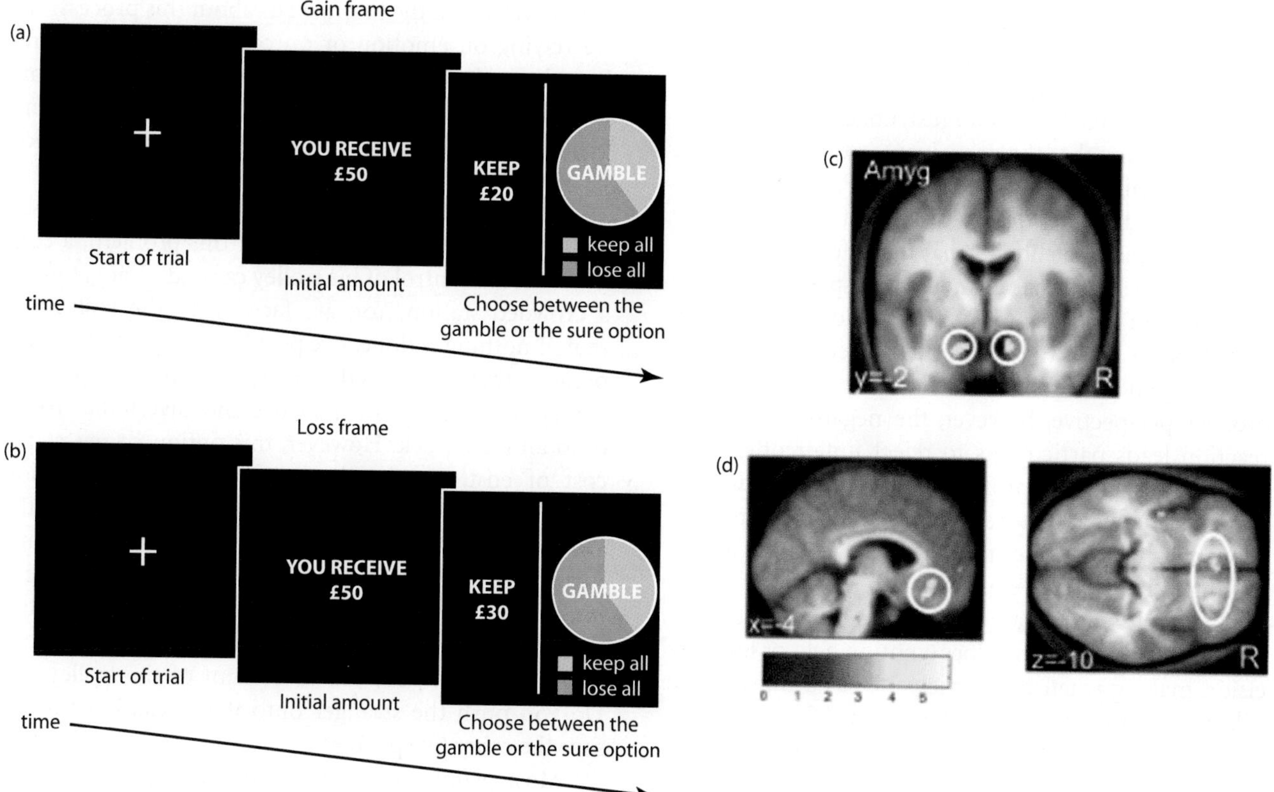

Figure 14.18 A gambling task in which participants can choose to gamble in the context of a guaranteed gain **(a)** or a guaranteed loss **(b)**. In both guaranteed cases, the outcome is the same; it is merely couched in different terms. **(c)** Participants who react to the condition of gain or loss rather than actual money amounts activate their amygdala when placing a bet. **(d)** Participants who bet on the basis of money amounts and are not swayed by a guaranteed gain versus loss activate their medial and lateral orbitofrontal cortex.

are associated with emotion and cognition are engaged by decisions that are more or less rational.

Suppose you are given $50 and a chance to gamble it. If you were presented with a guarantee of keeping $20 or a chance to gamble it all, what would you choose? What if you had a guarantee of losing $30 or a chance to gamble it all? What would you choose then? Most people prefer to gamble when faced with a guaranteed loss, even when the monetary consequences of the guaranteed options are the same, as they are in the two bets outlined here (Figure 14.18). A guaranteed loss elicits a negative emotional response and makes people focus on any option that will help them avoid the guaranteed loss. However, acting on emotion is detrimental because, as mentioned already, participants are not making decisions on the basis of actual monetary consequences. Benedetto De Martino and his colleagues at University College London (De Martino et al., 2006) conducted an fMRI study to understand the neural systems that underlie emotion-driven and rational decision making in this task. They found that participants who were misled by the loss frame tended to show activation in the amygdala. Orbitofrontal cortex activation was correlated with rational decision making. Specifically, participants who made decisions on the basis of monetary principles had significantly more orbitofrontal cortex activation than did participants who based their decisions on emotion.

In the preceding example, emotion shaped decision making in a detrimental manner. But what about when we make financial decisions in the context of an interaction with another person? Some research suggests that emotions may lead to decision making that is irrational because money will be lost but beneficial for defending social reputation. One study examined decision making using the ultimatum game (Sanfey et al., 2003). In the ultimatum game, each participant must split a sum of money with another player. The other player offers a portion of the sum to the participant and the participant must decide to accept or reject the offer. The offers may be fair (e.g., very close to 50% for each person) or unfair (e.g., 80% for the player and 20% for the participant).

In this study, the consideration of unfair offers was associated with dorsolateral prefrontal cortex and insula activity. Insula activity has often been associated with negative emotions such as disgust, anger, pain, and distress, suggesting that the participants experienced these emotions while considering the offer. Furthermore, increased insula activity during consideration of an unfair offer predicted a likelihood that the offer would be rejected. From a rational economic perspective, participants should not let their negative emotional reaction lead them to reject the unfair offer. Even if it is unfair, they can gain some money instead of no money. From a broader perspective, however, the negative emotional reaction leads participants to reject unfair offers that might otherwise compromise their social standing. If you continually accept less than your share, word may get around and people may begin to view you as deserving of less than an equal share.

In the ultimatum game, players can only react to the other person's offer. How does emotion help or hurt decision making when the participant has a more active role and has to speculate on the actions of another person? An fMRI study used the prisoner's dilemma game to test this question (Rilling et al., 2002). In the prisoner's dilemma game, participants again make decisions about how to divide a sum of money. Participants' winnings are determined by various combinations of their own decision to cooperate or betray their partners and their partners' decisions to cooperate or betray them (e.g., combinations of whether each makes fair or unfair offers). The choice to cooperate is a double-edged sword; participants win the most if both players choose to cooperate but lose the most if one player decides to cooperate and the other player decides to betray.

In this study, cooperation was related to areas associated with reward states, such as the nucleus accumbens, orbitofrontal cortex, anterior cingulate, and caudate nucleus. The authors suggest that this activation reflects a positive emotion experience that reinforces prosocial decision making. The positive emotional reaction is adaptive because even though money might be lost in specific rounds of the game, social cooperation is considered the "right" thing to do and therefore ensures that the individual will not be rejected by others.

Moral Decisions

Neuroeconomics focuses on financial decisions, but the relative contributions of emotion and cognition have also been theorized to support other kinds of social decision making. How do we resolve moral dilemmas like the one that Simon Yates faced on the Siula Grande climb? What can the brain tell us about this process? Are we relying on emotion or on cognitive computations? For discussion of the implications of the relations among brain function, moral judgment, and criminal behavior, see "The Cognitive Neuroscientist's Toolkit: Neuroethics."

Simon's dilemma is a real-life example of the classic trolley dilemma in philosophy. In this problem, a conductor loses control of his trolley car and it races toward a crowded station. You are faced with the realization that, if nothing is done, five people are likely to be killed because they are directly in the path of the speeding trolley. You can throw a switch and divert the trolley onto another track. However, this option comes at the cost of ensuring the death of a single construction worker who is on the alternate track. Do you throw the switch or not? Now consider the footbridge dilemma. Again, you witness an out-of-control trolley car speeding toward five people. This time, the only way to stop the trolley car is to push a person off a footbridge above the tracks to impede the movement of the trolley car. Do you push the stranger onto the tracks in order to save the other five people?

Most people agree that is acceptable to throw the switch in the trolley dilemma but find it immoral to push the stranger in the footbridge dilemma. In both cases, one person's life is sacrificed to save five others, so why do we make such different choices in each dilemma (Figure 14.19)? Simon's dilemma on Siula Grande draws on aspects of both the trolley car and the footbridge dilemmas. We know already that Simon could not simply walk away from Joe, while he was alive. Thus, he was willing for a time at least to sacrifice his life or put it at great risk to try to save Joe's. When his life was again threatened, he made the opposite decision to save his own life and cut the rope, believing that, in so doing, he would be sending Joe to his demise. What do you think Simon would have done if he had had to cut the rope while looking right at Joe? What would you have done if you were in Simon's position on Siula Grande?

Joshua Greene and his colleagues at Princeton University (2004) argue that we make different choices in the trolley and footbridge dilemmas because the level of personal involvement in causing the single death differentially engages emotional decision making. If you throw a switch, you still maintain some distance from the death of the construction worker. When you actually push the stranger, you perceive yourself as causing the death in a more proximal manner. Greene and his colleagues conducted a series of fMRI studies that contrasted moral dilemmas involving high levels of personal engagement with dilemmas involving low levels of

THE COGNITIVE NEUROSCIENTIST'S TOOLKIT

Neuroethics: An Emerging Field

On July 10, 2003, William Safire of the *New York Times* coined the term *neuroethics* to refer to "the field of philosophy that discusses the rights and wrongs of the treatment of, or enhancement of, the human brain." In the past few years, the term has come to encompass how society will "deal with social issues of disease, normality, morality, lifestyle and the philosophy of living" as informed by our understanding of the underlying brain mechanisms (Gazzaniga, 2005).

Antisocial personality disorder (APD) is a mental illness characterized by the utter disregard for social rules and the rights of others and is almost always accompanied by violence, aggression, deceitfulness, impulsivity, and lack of remorse. Genetic research on twins who were reared apart reveals that there are genetic influences on APD and aggressive behavior (Rowe, 2001). But genetic influences are not always sufficient to produce the behaviors associated with APD. Such behaviors are most often expressed when environmental influences are also present.

Evidence for this observation comes from research on adopted children. In a study of Swedish male adoptees, researchers determined that, when both genetic factors for violence and environmental factors encouraging violence were present, 40% of adoptees had engaged in criminal behavior. When genetic factors were present in the absence of environmental factors encouraging violence, only 12% of adoptees had committed illegal acts. The percentages dropped to 7% of adoptees when genetic factors were absent and only environmental factors remained, and to just 3% when neither environmental nor genetic factors were present.

Adriane Raine of the University of Southern California (2002) proposed a biosocial model for the development of violent behavior based on this evidence (Figure 1). The model outlines how genetic and environmental dispositions for violence, as well as genetic and environmental protective factors against violence, can influence the likelihood of violent behavior. In effect, this is a demonstration of the subtle interplay between nature and nurture. Raine and his colleagues employed a variety of imaging techniques to assess this model. Using positron emission tomography (PET), they found that individuals with violent and antisocial histories had reduced glucose metabolism in the orbitofrontal cortex. In terms of structural abnormalities, people with APD have reduced volume of prefrontal gray matter (Figure 2). These findings suggest that a dysfunctional orbitofrontal cortex—resulting from environmental factors, genetic factors, and the interaction of environmental and genetic factors—is associated with abnormal social behavior and violence.

The advances of neuroscience raise important ethical questions. APD is present in overwhelming proportions in the prison community (65%–80%). If there is a

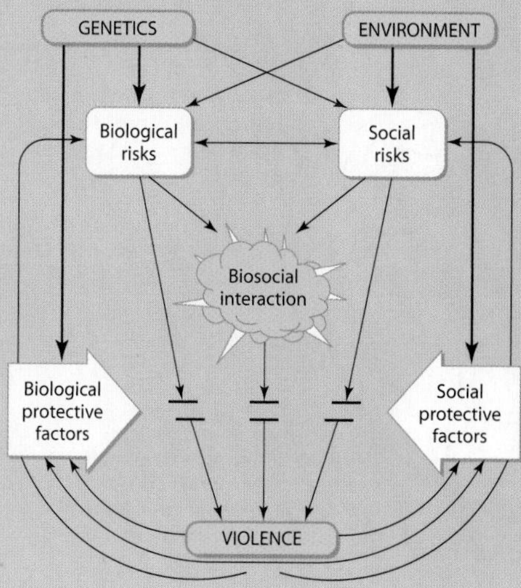

Figure 1 According to Adriane Raine's biosocial model of violence, both genetic and environmental factors are necessary for the behavioral result of violence.

Continued on the following page

Continued from previous page

neural correlate for such behavior, then is the person at fault for committing the crime? Could that person have done otherwise? Or did the person's brain make him commit the crime, thus absolving him of responsibility for the crime?

One of the authors of this book (M.S.G.) argues in his book *The Ethical Brain* that the questions the law asks are not the same as those that neuroscience answers. We do not know that a specific amount of loss of prefrontal gray matter will cause antisocial behavior, nor do we know exactly how much neuronal loss or dysfunction correlates with the inability to choose to do the right thing. It is the fervent hope of those studying these issues in cognitive neuroscience that these correlations will be further understood in the future.

This is just one example of the intersection of neuroscience and ethics. Many others are beginning to emerge (Figure 3), and it will be important to engage in a societal discussion of these issues in the years to come.

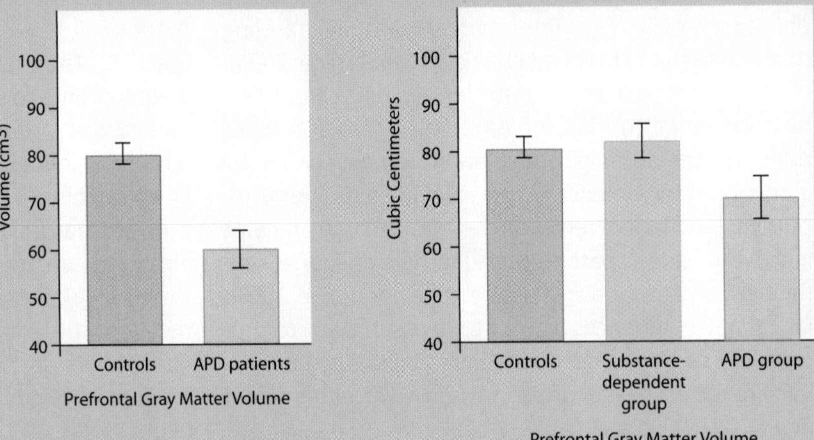

Figure 2 In patients with antisocial personality disorder, the volume of cortex (gray matter) in the prefrontal region of the brain is significantly reduced from normal.

Figure 3 Issues facing neuroethics. Current topics of neuroethical debate include free will, the neural basis of criminal behavior, neuroenhancement, the reliability of memory, the possibility of a neural correlate of the soul, when consciousness begins, and when consciousness ends.

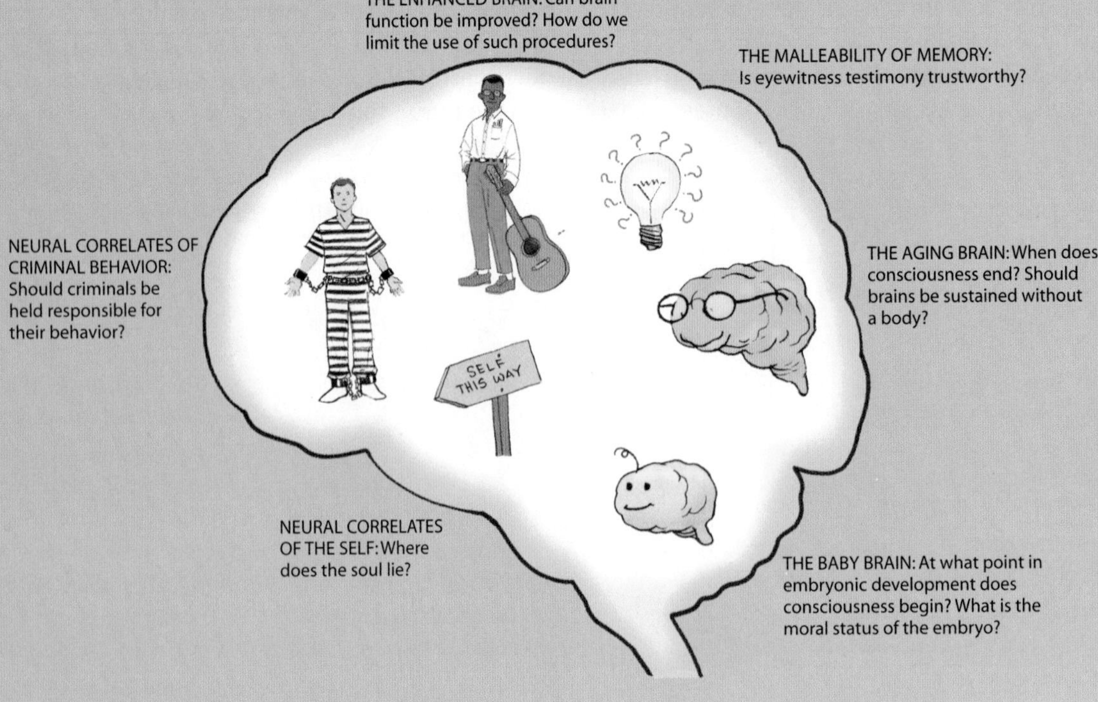

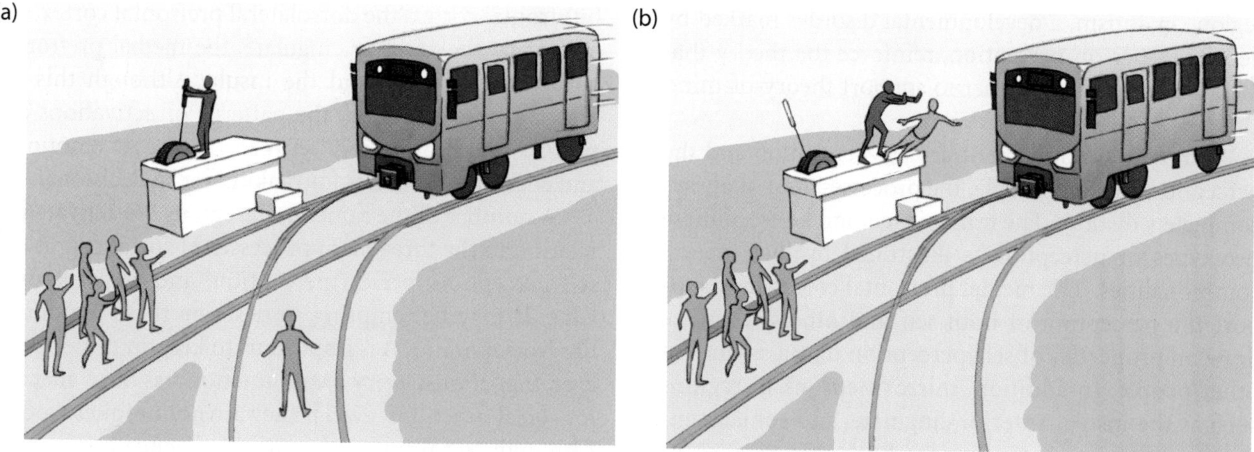

Figure 14.19 The trolley problem. Would you be willing to sacrifice one life in order to save five lives? Would your decision be different if you had to **(a)** pull a switch to direct a trolley toward one person or **(b)** physically push a person in front of a trolley car? Research suggests that the strong emotional response to actually pushing someone would make you decide differently in these two scenarios.

personal engagement (Greene et al., 2001, 2004). As predicted, personal dilemmas and impersonal dilemmas were associated with distinct patterns of activation. Across the studies, impersonal decisions were associated with greater activation in the right lateral prefrontal cortex and bilateral parietal lobe, areas associated with working memory (Chapter 13). In contrast, when participants chose options that required more personal effort, regions such as the medial frontal cortex, the posterior cingulate gyrus, and the amygdala were significantly activated. These regions have been associated with emotional and social cognitive processes. Together, these studies suggest that the differences in our moral decisions arise in relation to the extent that we permit emotions to influence our decisions about what is morally acceptable.

SUMMARY

Given that over 100 years separate the cases of Phineas Gage and patient M.R., it is surprising that we have learned so little about the relation between brain function and social cognition in that time. But with the development of exciting new research tools and new theories, the fields of social cognitive neuroscience and neuroeconomics have begun to develop and have already yielded exciting insights into how the brain supports our ability to know ourselves, to know other people, and to make decisions about our social worlds. We still have a long way to go, but we have begun down an exciting pathway.

We know from behavioral research that self-perception is unique in many regards, and we have gained further insight by understanding the unique features of self-perception at the neural level. We store incredibly elaborate information about ourselves, and the medial prefrontal cortex supports the particularly deep manner in which we encode information about ourselves. The increased baseline metabolism in this region may indicate that we chronically engage in self-referential thought, and many other processes represent momentary diversions of our cognitive resources from self-referential thought. Although the orbitofrontal cortex helps us consider contextual information so that we remain relatively accurate in our self-perceptions, the anterior cingulate may help us view ourselves through rose-colored glasses by marking positive information about the self.

When we try to understand other people, we are faced with the difficult task of trying to reason about their mental states, which are not directly accessible to us. This process heavily relies on our ability to use nonverbal cues such as facial expression and eye gaze to gather information about possible mental states. Then we have to represent this abstract information and use it to form an impression of what the person might be thinking. A number of structures, such as the medial prefrontal cortex, right temporoparietal junction, superior temporal sulcus, fusiform face area, and amygdala, support our ability to make inferences about other people's minds. The widespread impairment of these regions in autism, a developmental disorder marked by deficits in person perception, reinforce the theory that these regions work together to support theory-of-mind abilities.

Although we often contrast self-perception and the perception of other people, the processes are not always completely distinct. The intrinsic relation between these two types of perception is illustrated by their neural commonalities. The medial prefrontal cortex may support the perception of both self and others when we draw on properties of self-perception to make sense of other people. In addition, mirror neurons in regions such as the insula, anterior cingulate, and somatosensory cortex appear to support both our own emotional experiences and the extent to which we empathize with the same emotional states in other people.

In addition to understanding ourselves and other people, we need to understand the rules for social interactions and how to make decisions to satisfy the multitude of rules that govern a particular social interaction. The process of making social decisions engages a large network of neural structures, including the orbitofrontal cortex, the dorsolateral prefrontal cortex, the amygdala, the anterior cingulate, the medial prefrontal cortex, the caudate, and the insula. Although this research is just emerging, the patterns of activations appear to reflect a tension between the use of emotional and cognitive processes for making social decisions.

A number of the same brain regions are activated in relation to the three main processes of social cognition: self-perception, person perception, and social knowledge. It may be tempting to describe these regions as the "social brain." It is important to keep in mind, however, that almost every brain function has been adapted for social functions, even if they are not uniquely social. Although social interaction may influence how we select motor movements or where we direct our attention, motor movement and vision are also useful for finding food and other nonsocial functions. However, disorders like autism suggest that abnormal function in certain brain regions most powerfully affects social function. The interdisciplinary perspectives of social cognitive neuroscience and neuroeconomics promise to give us a deeper understanding of the processes that are most fundamental to social behavior.

KEY TERMS

autism
empathy
false-belief task
imitative behavior
joint attention
neuroeconomics
orbitofrontal cortex
self-referent effect
simulation theory
social cognitive neuroscience
somatic marker
theory of mind
utilization behavior

TAKE-HOME MESSAGES

General

- The damage that Phineas Gage suffered to the orbitofrontal region of his frontal lobe resulted in a change of his behavior and personality such that, as one person commented, "Gage was no longer Gage."
- Social cognitive neuroscience research explores the neural mechanisms involved in human social interaction.

Self-Perception and Self-Knowledge

- Social interactions require a sense of the self as distinct from other individuals.
- Knowledge of the self is strongly supported by the medial prefrontal cortex. This region is involved in the perception of others when we use ourselves to understand others or we represent information about the other person in a manner that is as complex as the way we store information about ourselves.
- The evidence suggests that our self-knowledge does not depend on reflecting on past experiences to understand personality features, but rather is based on information abstracted from these experiences.
- We often view ourselves through rose-colored glasses. Regions within the frontal cortex may work together to permit a focus on positive aspects of the self without deviating too far from reality.

Perception of Other People

- Part of distinguishing between the self and others involves the development of theory of mind, the ability to infer that the mental states of others are different from our own. Theory of mind is essential for social development and interactions. For example, it underlies the capacity to cooperate, empathize, and accurately anticipate the behavior of others.

- Mirror neurons provide a neural mechanism for engaging in mental simulation. Just as researchers in motor control emphasize the role of mirror neurons in understanding the actions of other individuals, social cognitive neuroscientists have argued that mirror neurons could be essential for understanding the intentions and emotions of other individuals.
- Understanding the consistency or discrepancy between the nonverbal cues and mental states of others helps us to judge their actions and determine subtle characteristics such as trustworthiness. It is also essential for the development of complex social responses such as empathy.
- Autism is a developmental disorder marked by abnormal social behavior. People with autism do not engage in normal social interactions, frequently focused on self-stimulation with attenuated interest in the actions of other individuals.
- One hypothesis is that people with autism fail to properly develop theory-of-mind skills; that is, their understanding and/or appreciation of the mental states of others is abnormal.

Social Knowledge

- Patients with orbitofrontal damage demonstrate many socially inappropriate behaviors. Although they understand social rules, they fail to recognize when they have broken these rules "in the moment."
- An early model of the role of the orbitofrontal cortex in social decision making focused on somatic markers. Somatic markers are physiological changes in the body that are associated with past experiences. The orbitofrontal cortex was theorized to be important for using these somatic markers to identify behavioral choices that maximize reward and minimize punishment.
- Current models of the role of the orbitofrontal cortex in social decision making propose that this region helps individuals identify which social rules are appropriate for a given situation so that they may flexibly change their behavior.
- The field of neuroeconomics integrates psychology, neuroscience, and economics to yield an understanding of how people make decisions.
- Decision making—whether about social behavior, money, or morality—may rely on a combination of emotional and cognitive systems.

THOUGHT QUESTIONS

1. Why do we have regions in our brain dedicated to processing information about the self? Why is it important to distinguish the self?
2. What kinds of social and emotional behaviors might be accounted for by the concept of mirror neurons? Would these behaviors be possible without some sort of mirrorlike system?
3. What might have been the evolutionary advantage for the development of empathy and theory of mind?
4. How might emotion help social decision making? How might emotion impair social decision making?

SUGGESTED READING

Adolphs, R. (2003). Cognitive neuroscience of human social behaviour. *Nature Reviews Neuroscience, 3,* 165–178.

Baron-Cohen, S., & Belmonte, M. K. (2005). Autism: A window onto the development of the social and the analytic brain. *Annual Review of Neuroscience, 28,* 109–126.

Gazzaniga, M. S. (2005). *The ethical brain.* New York: Dana Press.

Lieberman, M. D. (2007). Social cognitive neuroscience: A review of core processes. *Annual Review of Psychology, 58,* 259–289.

Macmillan, M. (2002). *An odd kind of fame: Stories of Phineas Gage* (reprint ed.). Cambridge, MA: MIT Press.

15

Evolutionary Perspectives

When the practice was first documented, evolutionary biologists were flummoxed: Why were langur monkeys killing their young? Surely such a practice must be maladaptive! As it turns out, infanticide, the killing of one's own young, is quite common: It can be observed in monkeys, lions, woodpeckers, and even humans, to name just a few species. How can this be?

A central tenet of Darwin's great theory of evolution is that behaviors that encourage survival and reproduction are adaptive and thus have a high probability of being passed on to future generations. In contrast, behaviors that discourage survival are maladaptive and should not be passed on to future generations. This is **natural selection** at its finest. How could the behavior of infanticide have survived natural selection in so many species? How could it possibly be adaptive?

For many years, scientists believed that infanticide occurred by the hands of the infant's genetic mother or father—a fact that seemed to be directly at odds with Darwinian laws. Recently, however, scientists have discovered that, in many cases of infanticide—at least in the langur monkey—the killer is not the genetic father of the infant, but rather a dominant monkey seeking to impregnate the mother of another male's infant. To ensure that the dominant male's genes are passed on (and not someone else's genes) and to decrease the time necessary for the mother to become ready to reproduce again, the dominant male kills the mother's current infants.

Sometimes, apparently, even the genetic mother of an infant commits infanticide—particularly if sources of food are scarce or if one infant is weak or deformed—in order to encourage the survival of the strongest siblings. This practice, though emotionally disturbing, is a stark example of evolutionary biology at work. Behaviors that currently exist in any given species are the result of a long line of natural selection within that species that favored traits and behaviors adaptive for the survival of its strongest, healthiest members.

This fascinating example raises several questions: How did we get here? How has evolution shaped our brain and behavior? What can we learn from existing animals about our origins? What does evolutionary theory have to say about the nature of human cognition? Neuroscience and cognitive science are beginning to incorporate the facts and theories of comparative anatomists and evolutionary biologists to address these questions.

We start this chapter by reviewing the history of this approach. We then discuss the basic terminology and concepts used by comparative neuroanatomists to illuminate how examining the brains of existing animals can teach us about our evolutionary roots. This enterprise is tricky because the structure of animal bodies and brains can vary dramatically, and trying to deduce similar features of brain organization and unique features is difficult. Therefore, we must learn the strategy that comparative neuroscientists use to avoid the pitfalls of applying conclusions about the brain of one species to that of another.

In the second half of the chapter we show how evolutionary theory is important for understanding learning and cognition. The mind is a collection of old adaptations designed to solve problems that our prehistoric ancestors faced, and newly developed features that take shape via activity-dependent mechanisms. Appreciation of the roots of our mental behavior is essential to the exploration of current cognitive capabilities and limitations.

EVOLUTION OF THE BRAIN

The brain is a compromise, and therefore the functions it generates are absolutely imperfect, although relatively optimal. This statement may be bothersome to some, because it implies that humans must be imperfect. This notion, and our long history of struggles to prove just the opposite, has had a dramatic impact on our current thinking about the mind, the brain, and the complex behaviors that they generate. In addition, the notion goes against a history of dogma regarding two major tenets of human design that shaped the direction of science in earlier times and often form the basis of modern theory.

The first is that humans are the pinnacle of life or the center of the cosmos; the second is that the mind or soul is somehow distinct from the body. The former idea affects how we view humans and the human brain compared to the brains of other animals. We tend to view evolution as linear, with humans at the top and other animals as degraded forms of ourselves, and therefore we view brain evolution as additive rather than in the nonlinear fashion in which it should be regarded. For example, complex brains like those of humans are not simply monkey brains or chimpanzee brains with a few new parts added, such as Broca's area and the prefrontal cortex. Rather, the human brain is a unique amalgamation of evolutionarily old areas and new areas that have been modified in predictable ways through the expansion or reduction of existing parts, the formation of new connections, and the adaptation to new environmental demands. The latter notion—that there is a unique aspect of the human condition that is different from the condition of other animals—affects how we compare animal brains to human brains and what conclusions we reach regarding cortical evolution in mammals.

Before we can talk about the basic principles of evolution and their impact on our thinking about the brain and cognition, it is necessary to discuss the history of evolutionary thought. History shapes our current understanding of the brain and our beliefs about how things work. Indeed, as already noted, two very old ideas are embedded in our culture and form the basis of our thinking on issues regarding cognition and the evolution of the nervous system.

Historical Underpinnings of Contemporary Evolutionary Neurobiology

Probably the most significant event in the biological sciences during the 19th century was the discovery by Charles Darwin (1859) and Alfred Russel Wallace that *natural selection* is the vehicle of evolutionary change. The basic observations were that individuals within a population vary and that changes in individuals arise via natural selection of these variants. The **trait**, or *characteristic*, that is selected has no absolute value; rather its *value is measured by how well it contributes to the individual's fitness within a particular environment.* The details of this theory deserve a more in-depth discussion and are dealt with later. Here, we wish only to underscore the historical importance of this discovery and its impact on modern evolutionary biology.

A number of 20th-century scientists have contributed to our understanding of the brain and its evolution. Investigators in the early 1900s, such as Korbinian Brodmann (1909/1960), utilized the technique of Franz Nissl to distinguish the architecture of the cerebral cortex in humans from that in other mammals. Most of us know Brodmann for his cytoarchitectonic descriptions of the human brain (see Chapter 3), but perhaps his most important contribution was his cross-species comparisons of the cytoarchitecture of the cerebral cortex (Figure 15.1). He observed that some cytoarchitectonic areas of the brain, such as area 17, could be found in all of the species he examined, and the ubiquity of these fields suggested that they must have been inherited from a common ancestor. Brodmann proposed that these cytoarchitectonic areas had different functions, although there was no direct evidence for this hypothesis. We now know that area 17 corresponds to the primary visual area (V1) in all mammals. Contemporaries of Brodmann, such as Joseph Shaw Bolton, George Elliot Smith, and Constantin von Economo, devoted much time to parceling the human cerebral cortex into separate divisions on the basis of cytoarchitecture. These early investigators established a common view of the functional organization of the human brain that still persists today.

This view, outlined by Michael Merzenich of the University of California, San Francisco, and Jon Kaas of Vanderbilt University (1980), is that sensory input is relayed from subcortical structures to primary receiving areas of the neocortex (such as V1). These primary areas send this sensory information to secondary cortex, where more complex perceptual functions are performed. This information is finally relayed to multimodal association areas for higher-order processing (see Chapter 6). With the caveat that humans possess more association cortex than do any other mammals, this traditional view of serially and hierarchically ordered cortical regions still dominates neuroscience. Note, however,

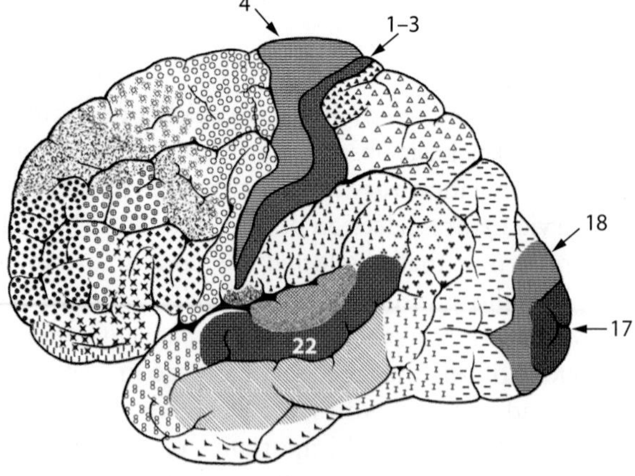

(a) *Homo sapiens* (human)

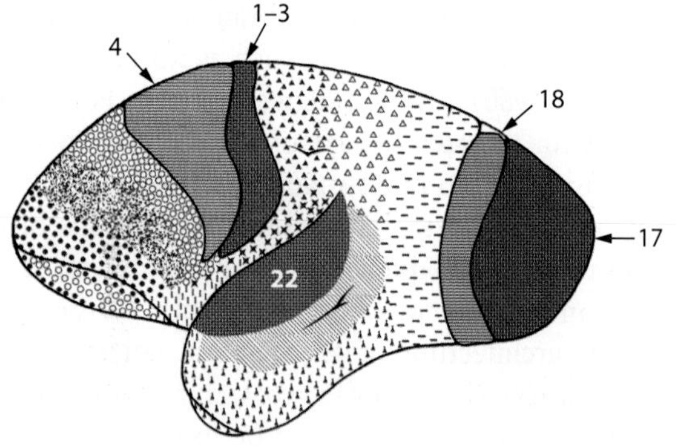

(b) *Callithrix jacchus* (common marmoset)

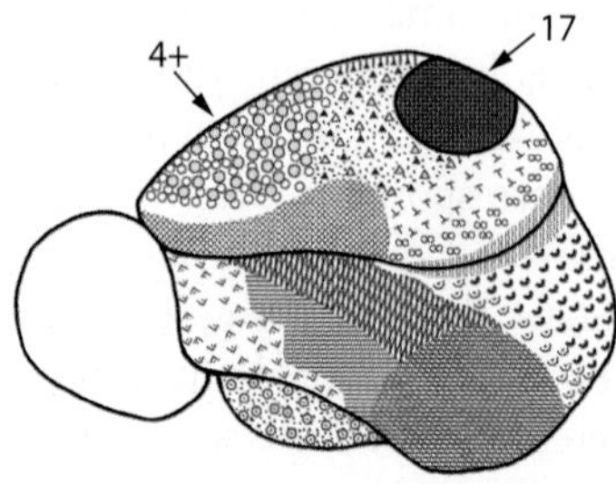

(c) *Erinaceus europaeus* (European hedgehog)

Figure 15.1 Cytoarchitectonic divisions of the human **(a)**, marmoset **(b)**, and hedgehog **(c)** neocortex as described by Brodmann (1909/1960). The different patterns of black-and-white stipple denote separate regions of the neocortex that have different architectonic appearances. Some cortical areas, such as areas 17 and 4, were present in all animals investigated, suggesting that these regions are homologous. Other regions, such as area 22, were present only in primates.

that more recently Kaas (1999) has suggested a dramatic revision of this historical view. Most of the neocortex is either sensory or motor, rather than associative in nature, and connections between regions may be the primary basis of more complex cognitive functions.

Major events occurring in other disciplines in the middle of the 20th century were to have a tremendous impact on neuroscience in general and on evolutionary neurobiology in particular. James Watson, Francis Crick, and Maurice Wilkins discovered the molecular structure of DNA, the "double helix," and its significance for information transfer in living organisms. Their discovery that life could be reduced to this very basic unit of organization, which continually replicates itself, rocked the world.

On the heels of this discovery, a quiet revolution was brewing. From the 1950s through the 1970s, Konrad Lorenz of the Institute of Zoology in Munich, Germany; Nikolaas Tinbergen of the Institute of Ethology in Vienna, Austria; and Karl von Frisch at Oxford University in England—all of whom shared the Nobel Prize in Physiology or Medicine in 1973—led the fields of **ethology** (the study of animal behavior) and its counterpart, **neuroethology** (the study of the neurobiology of animal behavior). Lorenz and Tinbergen contributed to the fields in two fundamental ways: They focused attention on the innate aspects of behavior, and they provided empirical data from animal studies that allowed behavior to be understood from a more biological perspective.

Probably the most famous study of Tinbergen and Lorenz (see Lorenz & Tinbergen, 1957) was on the egg-rolling response in greylag geese. When the brooding goose notices that an egg has rolled outside the nest, a very stereotypical behavior ensues. First the goose fixates on the misplaced egg; then she rises and extends her neck to touch the egg. She then places her bill over the egg and carefully rolls it back into the nest. Tinbergen and Lorenz at first believed that the goose was thoughtfully performing a behavior to return a lost egg to the nest. However, when these scientists removed the egg after the goose had initiated the behavior, the goose continued with the behavior despite the absence of the egg. Thus, this behavior has an initial stimulus (the sight of the egg out of the nest) that triggers it and then an innate, highly stereotypical pattern that they termed a *fixed action pattern.* A fixed action pattern, once initiated, continues through to completion, independent of feedback.

Ethologists and neuroethologists stressed the importance of invoking evolutionary theory to understand animal behavior. But although evolutionary theory was used to understand animal behavior, it was still excluded from explanations of human behavior. Indeed, at this point sociology and psychology were largely devoid of any theory incorporating evolutionary principles (Hodos & Campbell, 1969).

In the early 1970s, E. O. Wilson sought to "reformulate the foundations of the social sciences" by giving them a biological basis. He invoked evolutionary theory to explain social phenomena, and in 1975 he promoted the new field of **sociobiology**, which he defined as the systematic study of the biological basis of all social behavior. Sociobiology allowed for a logical explanation of animal behavior that, at first glance, seemed counter to natural selection. For example, highly social insects, such as ants, have cooperative care for their young and a reproductive division of labor in which multiple sterile individuals work on behalf of reproductive nestmates. The inability of some individuals to reproduce may seem at odds with what is known about evolution and natural selection. However, others described the reproductive benefits of colonial life by examining how individuals within the colony are related. According to this viewpoint, even individuals that do not reproduce are working to propagate their genes into future generations by maximizing the reproductive fitness of their close relatives.

Wilson (1975) observed that "in evolutionary time the individual organism counts for almost nothing. In a Darwinist sense the organism does not live for itself. Its primary function is not even to reproduce other organisms; it reproduces genes, and it serves as their temporary carrier." This idea represented a large shift in paradigm from traditional psychology, sociology, and ethology and constituted a virtual revolution in perspective. The contributions of Maynard Smith, William Hamilton, Robert Trivers, and David Barrash, along with many other scientists, helped shape the field of sociobiology during its infancy in the late 1970s and 1980s. In 1976, the highly popular book *The Selfish Gene*, by Richard Dawkins, drew attention to the field and placed the gene, rather than the individual, at the center of importance. Dawkins's contention is that life is simply about the replication of genes and the propagation of "good" genes into the future.

Since its introduction, sociobiology has undergone a rebirth and has been strongly embraced by psychology and sociology, resulting in the field of **evolutionary psychology**. Proponents of this new viewpoint, such as Steven Pinker, Leda Cosmides, and John Tooby, use the framework of evolutionary theory to explain cognitive behavior. Evolutionary psychologists have painted a picture different from that portrayed by sociobiologists. They do not believe that all behaviors are driven by genetic mechanisms. Rather, they believe that the brain has built into it a flexible set of adaptations. These adaptations are a set of rules that govern behavior and that can be applied differently depending on the environmental context, resulting in an infinite number of behaviors. This view is quite different from that of traditional sociobiologists and traditional cognitive psychologists, because it allows for a more objective, biologically compatible view of human behavior compared to traditional psychology-based interpretations.

Understanding the neural organization of the brain depends on understanding the functional organization of its cognitive devices. The brain originally came into existence and accumulated its particular set of design features only because these features functionally contributed to the organism's propagation. This contribution—that is, the evolutionary function of the brain—is obviously the adaptive regulation of behavior and physiology on the basis of information derived from the body and from the environment. The brain performs no significant mechanical, metabolic, or chemical service for the organism; its function is purely informational, computational, and regulatory in nature. Because the function of the brain is informational, its precise functional organization can be described accurately only in a language capable of expressing its informational functions—that is, in cognitive terms rather than in cellular, anatomical, or chemical terms. Cognitive investigations are not an optional activity. Mapping the computational adaptations of the brain is an indispensable step in the neuroscience research enterprise.

We will return to these ideas after considering how current neurobiologists approach studying the brain from a comparative perspective.

Modern Evolutionary Neurobiology: Assumptions and Aims

Modern evolutionary neurobiology, or **comparative neuroscience** (Bullock, 1984a)—while not incompatible with sociobiology, evolutionary psychology, or neuroethology—differs from these disciplines in that it is more brain and systems oriented. Furthermore, although it has an appreciation of the fundamental role of genes in evolution, it also has an appreciation of the complex interaction between genes and the environment in the construction of a nervous system. Comparative neuroscience probably began with Brodmann (1909/1960) and his demonstration that mammals have neocortical areas in common, despite very distant phylogenetic relationships.

Around the middle of the 20th century, Clinton Woolsey of the University of Wisconsin (1952, 1958) and colleagues used electrophysiological recording techniques to divide the neocortex into functional subregions in a variety of mammals (Figure 15.2). Woolsey's work empirically demonstrated what Brodmann had only proposed: that the separate architectonic areas of the neocortex correspond to different functions.

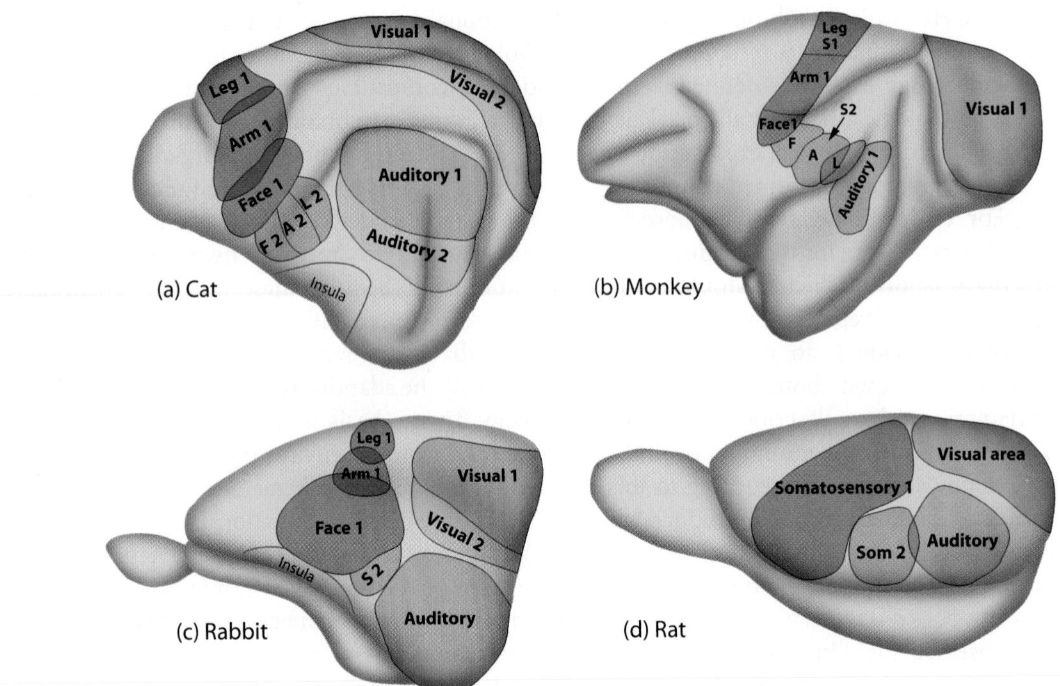

Figure 15.2 Functional subdivisions of the neocortex as described by Woolsey (1952, 1958) and colleagues in the middle of the 20th century. Evoked potentials in response to mechanical stimulation of the sensory surface were used to determine the number and topographic organization of different sensory neocortical areas in a variety of mammals. Some areas, such as the primary visual area (V1), somatosensory area (S1), and auditory area (A1), were in all the mammals they investigated, suggesting descent from a common ancestor. Additional sensory areas, such as S2 and V2, also were present in most of the mammals investigated.

Charles Judson Herrick, a contemporary of Woolsey, also advanced the field of comparative neuroanatomy. As a result of his numerous cross-species comparisons of neural structures, Herrick reached profound conclusions regarding how complexity is achieved in the nervous system. After examining the connections of the brain in a variety of species, he hypothesized that a slight increase in the connectivity of homologous structures could exponentially increase the processing capacity of the brain. Herrick (1963) proposed that "during a few minutes of intense cortical activity the number of interneuronic connections actually made may well be as great as the total number of atoms in the solar system. Certainly not all anatomically present connections of nervous elements are ever used, but the *potentialities* of diversity of cortical associational combinations are practically unlimited and the personal experience of the individual is probably an important factor in determining which of these possibilities will be actually realized."

From the 1960s through the 1980s, Irving Diamond focused his research on the evolution of the mammalian brain and used the comparative approach to understand the brain and the evolution of thalamocortical relationships. He was a pioneer in the use of modern neuroanatomical techniques, and he trained a number of contemporary comparative neuroscientists.

Kaas, one of Diamond's graduate students, has advanced our understanding of the evolution of the mammalian brain. As mentioned previously, he has challenged the traditional view that primate neocortex, particularly human neocortex, is composed predominantly of association areas. By default, association cortex is defined as cortex that is not sensory and presumably is involved in high-level perceptual and cognitive processing. Kaas's work in primates over the past several decades has demonstrated that almost all of the neocortex is sensory and motor in nature, and that complex brains evolve not by simple expansion of the association cortex, but by an increase in the number of sensory and motor areas and the connections between them. As Kaas (1997) himself put it, "The validity of a comparative approach depends on the basic premise that theories of brain organization applied to any given species, say humans, should be compatible with evidence and theories of brain organization for other species, with the evidence and theories for closely related species being most relevant."

Scientists who compare animal brains to deduce how they are constructed by evolutionary processes use a variety of names to identify themselves, including *comparative neuroanatomists, physiological psychologists, evolutionary neurobiologists,* and *comparative neuroscientists.* However, all modern comparative studies are based on a few underlying assumptions. The first assumption is that all behavior in all animals is generated by the nervous system. This definition of behavior is not limited to sensory, perceptual, and motor behaviors. It also includes cognitive behaviors that are difficult to define and measure, such as consciousness. The second assumption is that brains evolve, and therefore behaviors evolve. Thus, behavior cannot be completely understood without an evolutionary perspective. The final assumption is that we can gain significant insight into the evolution of the brain and behavior by examining the products of the process—namely, existing animals.

Theodore Bullock of the University of California, San Diego (1984a), has led the field of comparative neurobiology for nearly half a century. Bullock describes three aims of comparative neuroscience:

1. *Roots.* The evolutionary history of the brain and behavior. How did the brain come to have its current organization?
2. *Rules.* The mechanisms that give rise to changes in the nervous system. Under what constraints did evolving nervous systems develop?
3. *Relevance.* The general principles of organization and functions that can be extrapolated from a particular animal studied to all animals, including humans.

The choice of animal that researchers use for their experiments depends on their goals. For instance, if they are interested in how sodium channels work in neurons, the squid is an excellent choice because it contains axons that are large and easily accessible. Because sodium channels evolved early, are shared across a wide variety of species, and make a basic contribution to the action potential that has not changed over time, findings in the squid are likely to be relevant to human neurons.

If, on the other hand, researchers are interested in when the visual area MT (see Chapter 5), an area linked to motion perception in primates, first appeared (i.e., the *roots* of MT), then their choice of animals should include representatives of early primate lineages such as lemurs, galagos, and lorises, as well as other archontans, such as tree shrews (Figure 15.3). Tree shrews (squirrel-like mammals) belong to a family of mammals termed Tupaiidae, whose ancestors are believed to have formed an early branch of the primate lineage. Lemurs form a unique family of primates and exist only on the island of Madagascar, off the southeastern coast of Africa, and galagos and lorises are members of another primate family (Lorisidae) and are found in Africa and Southeast Asia. The ancestor of these primates diverged early in primate evolution, and extant species are believed to share many features of our primate ancestors.

Kaas has addressed the question of when area MT arose in primate evolution by examining a variety of primates from different orders, including Lorisiformes, New World monkeys, and Old World monkeys. Interestingly, all of these primates have an area MT. Although lemurs have not been studied, Kaas's examination of tree shrews demonstrated a V1 projection zone sharing some features of MT (however, a distinct MT, like that found in numerous other primates, does not appear to be present). This pattern of results suggests that MT may have had some primitive underpinning early in primate evolution but probably arose after the Tupaiidae radiation and sometime before the emergence of Lorisiformes.

If researchers are interested in the rules of change for specialized peripheral structures and the behaviors associated with these structures, they might use a variety of highly specialized mammals such as the duck-billed platypus (Krubitzer et al., 1995; Krubitzer, 1998) or the star-nosed mole (Catania et al., 1993; Catania & Kaas, 1995) to determine how the somatosensory and motor cortex is modified in relation to specialization. For instance, the duck-billed platypus has a specialized bill (Figure 15.4a), and approximately 80% of its nervous system is devoted to processing inputs from the bill. Likewise, the star-nosed mole has an extraordinary specialization of the nose (Figure 15.4b), and like the platypus, a large portion of its nervous system is devoted to processing inputs from the nose. This neural magnification of specialized body parts arose independently in these mammals and is a feature of modifications shared by a number of mammals. Because the neural specialization looks remarkably similar, it seems likely that its nervous system implements certain rules when generating representations of specialized body parts. Thus, studying the neural organization and connections in these mammals may provide some insight into these rules.

Now that we have an overview of the theoretical basis of an evolutionary perspective, we need to delve more deeply into evolution via natural selection, the terms associated with the field of evolutionary neurobiology, and the use of the comparative approach to formulate hypotheses and make valid inferences regarding the human condition.

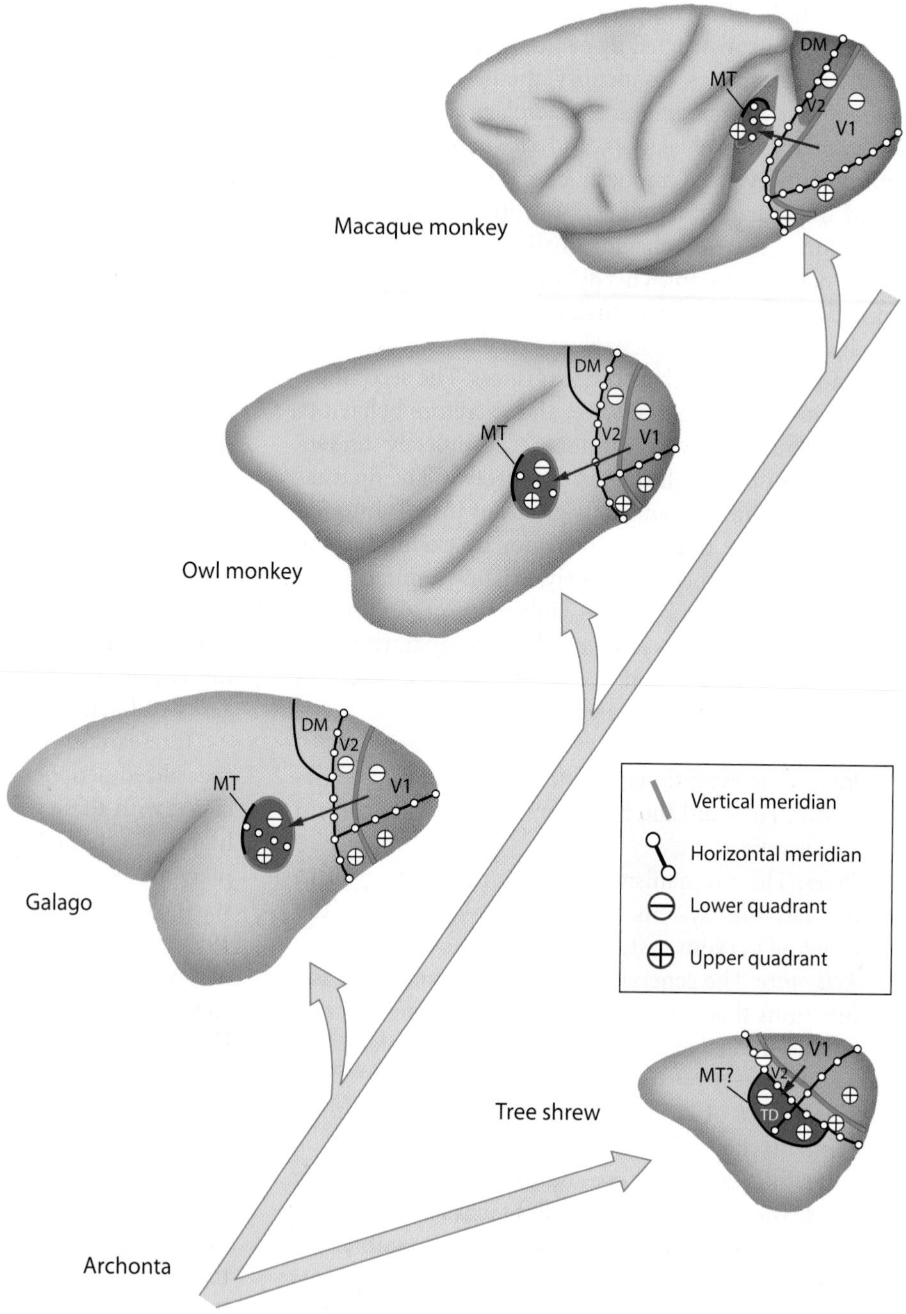

Figure 15.3 A comparative analysis can be used to determine when area MT (blue) evolved in primates. The visuotopic organization and relative location of MT are similar in prosimians (galagos), New World monkeys (owl monkeys), and Old World monkeys (macaque monkeys). The architectonic appearance of area MT and the presence of direct connections from the primary visual area add further support to the hypothesis that area MT is homologous in all of these primates. An out-group analysis of a more distantly related group (tree shrews) indicates that some features of an MT-like area are present in the area labeled "TD." However, further evidence needs to be gathered to determine if TD is homologous to MT in primates. Without this evidence, it appears that area MT evolved sometime before the emergence of prosimians, but after the radiation of early archontans such as tree shrews. Shaded gray areas indicate cortex that resides in fissures.

FIRST PRINCIPLES

Charles Darwin's (1859) theory of evolution via natural selection is a powerful and pervasive force in modern biology. Although a number of popular concepts spring to mind when we think of evolution—including our own evolution from lower animals and survival of the fittest—the principles of evolutionary theory are often misapplied and misunderstood. If we are to thoroughly understand its importance and how we can apply the evolutionary perspective to our theories of cognition, we must learn a few basic principles of the evolutionary theory (Williams, 1966).

The concept of evolution was appreciated well before Darwin's time. Early scientists noted that animals had a number of features in common and therefore all animals must be related; in other words, there must be a common ancestor. Early scientists further reasoned

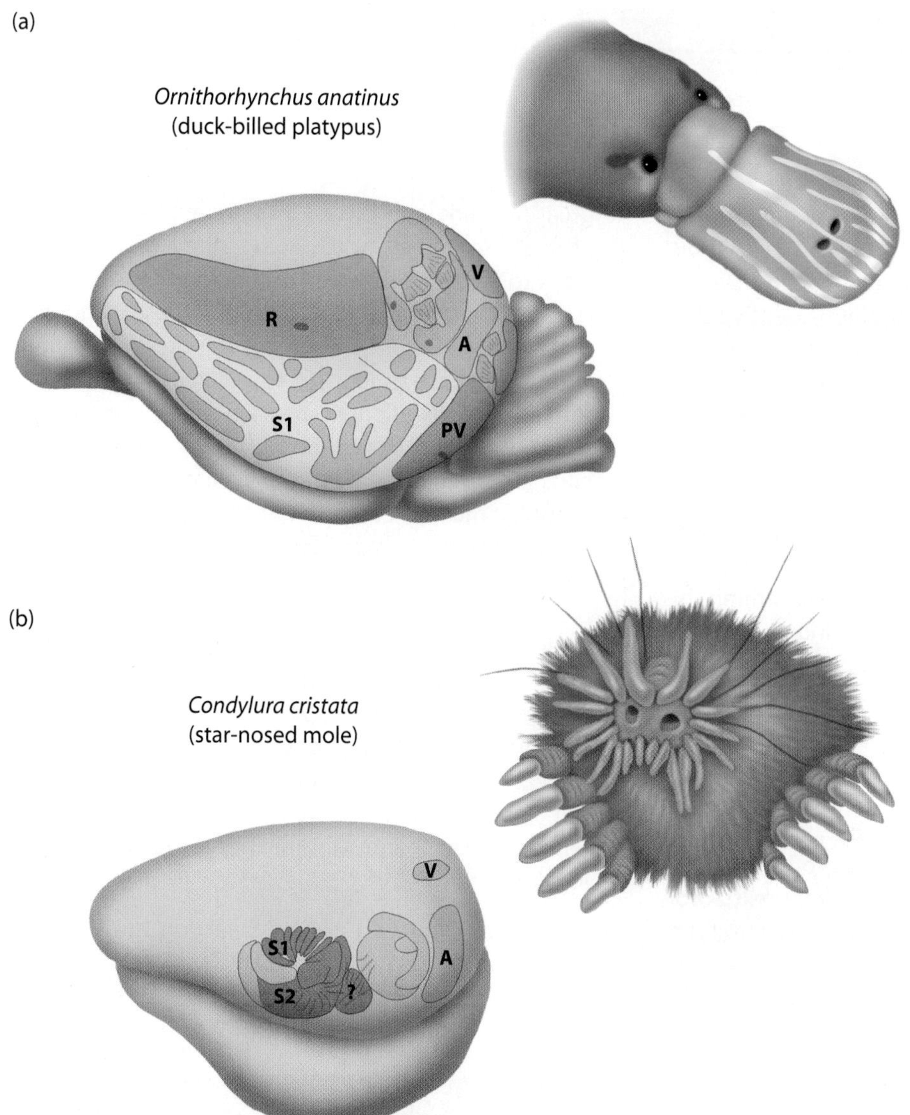

Figure 15.4 Some mammals are highly derived (have extreme specializations of a particular body part, behavior, or piece of neural tissue). **(a)** The bill of the platypus contains both mechanosensory (gray) and electrosensory (white) receptors arranged in stripes. In the primary somatosensory area (S1), neurons are aggregated in groups of mechanosensory (gray) and electrosensory (white) inputs. The magnification of the bill representation in the neocortex is extreme, assuming about 75% of the entire neocortex. **(b)** Specializations of the face have evolved independently in a number of lineages. The nose of the star-nosed mole, for example, has evolved a number of movable appendages used for exploration, prey capture, and feeding. An independent magnification of the representation of this highly derived nose is found in the primary (S1) and secondary (S2) somatosensory areas in the neocortex. These examples illustrate that the types of modifications to the neocortex are highly constrained.

that if God had indeed created all animals simultaneously, and if all animals are complete, why do some animals have features or parts that they apparently do not use? Although speculation regarding evolution was rife, however, the vehicle by which it proceeded was not appreciated.

In the mid 1800s, both Charles Darwin and Alfred Russell Wallace discovered the force that drives evolutionary change in animals. Three observations led to Darwin's theory of evolution by natural selection: first, individuals within a population of animals vary and are not all absolutely identical; second, some of this variation is inherited or **heritable**; and third, not all individuals within a population are equally successful at reproducing. How variability between individuals was generated was not appreciated until much later, when Gregor Johann Mendel's (1822–1884) principles of heredity were rediscovered in the early 20th century.

Evolution proceeds by differential reproductive success. Within any group, some individuals are better than others at reproducing in a particular environment. The reproductive success of these individuals results in the natural selection of certain traits or characteristics over others. These selected traits or characteristics may endow a particular benefit on the individual organisms that possess them. Note that no absolute value is given to any trait that is selected (e.g., big brains with many parts are not absolutely better); rather, a trait can be beneficial only within the context of a specific environment. In this case, environment includes not only the organism's habitat but also its conspecifics, predators, group size, and the other biological characteristics of the

MILESTONES IN COGNITIVE NEUROSCIENCE

Darwin's Big Idea

Charles Darwin was a genius by any measure. He provided humankind with the key idea about our origins: the idea of natural selection. Darwin was the first one who brought together extensive data that the idea of natural selection had sustaining value for understanding human origins. He summarized his idea in two long sentences, as recently recounted by Daniel Dennett in his fascinating book, *Darwin's Dangerous Idea* (1995). Here is that idea:

> If during the long course of ages and under varying conditions of life, organic beings vary at all in the several parts of their organization, and I think this cannot be disputed; if thereby, owing to the high geometric powers of increase of each species, at some age, season, or year, a severe struggle for life, and this certainly cannot be disputed; then considering the infinite complexity of the relations of all organic beings to each other and to their conditions of existence, causing an infinite diversity in structure, constitution, and habits, to be advantageous to them, I think it would be a most extraordinary fact if no variation ever had occurred useful to each being's own welfare, in the same way as so many variations have occurred useful to man. But if variations useful to any organic being do occur, assuredly individuals thus characterized will have the best chance of being preserved in the struggle for life; and from the strong principle of inheritance they will tend to produce offspring similarly characterized. This principle of preservation, I have called, for the sake of brevity, Natural Selection.

Now, although Darwin could have used an editor, he did condense the most powerful idea in biology into two sentences. And yet, as Dennett pointed out in his book, his brilliant idea was not born from whole cloth. In his *Dialogues*, the great philosopher David Hume had three characters carry out a fictional debate about whether the world exists as a result of a design; that is, any complex entity must have a designer and in this case it is God. Cleanthes, the Greek philosopher, had previously defended the argument for design:

> Look round the world: Contemplate the whole and every part of it: You will find it to be nothing but one great machine, subdivided into an infinite number of lesser machines, which again admit of subdivisions to a degree beyond what human senses and faculties can trace and explain. All these various machines, and even their most minute parts, are adjusted to each other with an accuracy which ravished into admiration all men who have ever contemplated them. The curious adapting of means to ends, throughout all nature, resembles, exactly, though it much exceeds, the productions of human contrivance, of human design, thought, wisdom, and intelligence. Since therefore the effects resemble each other, we are led to infer, by all the rules of analogy, that the causes also resemble, and that the Author of Nature is somewhat similar to the mind of man, though possessed of much larger faculties, proportioned to the grandeur of the work which he has executed. By this argument a posteriori, and by this argument alone, do we prove at once the existence of a Deity and his similarity to human mind and intelligence.

Replace "a Deity" with "Natural Selection" and a tangible mechanism has been articulated, which was Darwin's genius. Yet the idea was in the air 80 years before he wrote about it.

Charles Darwin (1809–1882).

individual. In short, a trait's environment includes a wide array of factors at many levels of analysis.

Natural selection acts on the variations of the **phenotype** within the population. The phenotype is an observable trait, or set of characteristics, of an organism. A phenotype can refer to a morphological structure, like the hand, foot, leg, heart, or kidney, as well as a neural structure, such as the lateral geniculate nucleus, the superior colliculus, the neocortex, or a cortical field within the neocortex. We can also describe neural properties as having a particular phenotype, such as the on/off responses of ganglion cells in the retina. Even the behaviors that an organism produces constitute an important part of its phenotype—for example, the food-caching behaviors exhibited by squirrels. In contrast, the **genotype** is the genetic composition of an organism. Phenotypes are produced by an organism's genotype in combination with environmental and activity-dependent mechanisms (see Chapter 3).

Evolutionary success can be measured in terms of a gene, trait, or behavior that is represented in future generations. The prevalence of these characteristics is a measure of their **fitness**. An **adaptation** is a characteristic of a living thing that contributes to its fitness. Thus, an adaptation is either a process by which a species adjusts to environmental change, or a feature of an organism that is suited to the environment. For example, the hand in primates is an adaptation of the distal forelimb, used for tactile exploration and active reaching. This same structure has been adapted in bats for flying, in dolphins for swimming, and in moles for digging. The acquisition of adaptations through natural selection is the heart of the evolutionary process. This process of evolution by adaptation and natural selection applies to morphological structures, behaviors, and the underlying nervous system that generates them.

A related term is *exaptation*, first coined by Stephen Jay Gould of Harvard University. **Exaptation** refers to a structure that serves a particular function but then is co-opted for another, very different function. For instance, the lateral line in aquatic anamniotes (e.g., jawless vertebrates, cartilaginous fishes, amphibians) contains hair cell–like receptors used for electroreception (the ability to detect changes in electrical current) or mechanoreception (the ability to detect mechanical displacement of a structure—e.g., a hair follicle, skin, and the cilia of hair cells). In mammals, the inner ear is an exaptation of the lateral line. The hair cells in the inner ear of mammals are involved in transducing air pressure changes (sound) into neural activity via hydraulic and mechanosensory mechanisms.

Although natural selection acts on the phenotype of an organism, the only heritable part of the natural selection equation is the gene. **Genes** are composed of a complex organic molecule termed *deoxyribonucleic acid*, or *DNA*, and have alternative forms called **alleles**. For instance, if two alleles of a gene responsible for height exist in the population (*A* for tall and *a* for short), three allelic combinations (*AA*, *aa*, and *Aa*) are possible. The term *homozygous* describes the occurrence of identical alleles at one or more genetic loci (e.g., *AA* or *aa*); *heterozygous* describes the occurrence of different alleles at one or more genetic loci (e.g., *Aa*). From an evolutionary perspective, within the genes of an organism different alleles compete with each other over time.

At this point it is useful to introduce two terms regarding genes and the characteristics or functions that they generate: *genetic specificity* and *genetic pleiotropy*. According to the concept of **genetic specificity**, a particular gene is responsible for a single function or behavior, as is, for example, the gene that encodes the egg-laying peptide prohormone in mollusks (Geraerts et al., 1994). Thus, a very specific behavior, egg-laying, appears to be encoded by a single gene. The general idea in sociobiology—that complex behaviors such as altruism, aggression, and even some aspects of cognition are controlled by a gene or a set of genes directly responsible for that behavior, at least in part—subscribes to genetic specificity. Though this notion is attractive and has gained much notoriety because of its simplicity, most consider genetic specificity to be the exception to the rule, rather than a common occurrence. The second concept is **genetic pleiotropy**, according to which one gene has many functions. From a developmental perspective, one gene can participate in the generation of a number of different events and can be expressed differentially at various times for different purposes.

For example, one might ask why diseases like Alzheimer's or even schizophrenia survive in the population. Alzheimer's disease appears late in life, and accumulating evidence indicates that this disease has a strong genetic underpinning (Gatz et al., 2006). Why would such genes be selected and persist if they are so detrimental to the individual organism? One likely answer to this question is that their selection is due to genetic pleiotropy. The genes responsible for unleashing the neuropathological state of this disease may be selected because they play a positive role early in life. The fact that the same gene has detrimental effects later in life is irrelevant in evolutionary terms because its negative effects occur well after the age when an organism can reproduce. Even the genes for schizophrenia, which have a wide distribution throughout the species, may have both a positive role and a negative effect in the environment in which they are currently expressed (Burns, 2006).

Because of genetic pleiotropy, structures, components of structures, functions, and behaviors are carried along in evolution as a package of positive, negative, and neutral events. The assignment of a trait as negative or positive depends on the environment in which it is expressed. This is why the brain is a compromise. It is a well-adapted structure, yet it consists of a combination of positive, negative, and neutral characteristics, with a net effect that is determined by the particular environment in which it finds itself. Should the environment change, the value or fitness of the package can change dramatically and lead to eventual genetic changes, speciation, or extinction.

The problem for neuroscientists is to decipher whether a structure, receptor type, connection, neural property, or behavior under investigation is functionally significant to the organism in the environment to which it is adapted or whether it is an epiphenomenon of evolution. The term *epiphenomenon* refers to a trait that is not directly caused by natural selection, but is instead a by-product of the selection of a different trait. For example, ocular dominance columns are the result of correlated activity within each eye and discorrelated activity between the two eyes during development (see Chapter 5). Thus, although ocular dominance columns are an important trait in animals with stereopsis and binocular vision, they are an epiphenomenon of correlated activity during development. Indeed, this system in cats and monkeys has been used extensively as a model to study the role of correlated activity in the wiring of the nervous system.

Another example of an epiphenomenon may be consciousness. Has the actual behavior that we term *consciousness* been selected for in evolution, or is it an epiphenomenon of the neural circuitry of a brain that evolved to solve complex sensory and motor problems? Although consciousness certainly may have arisen as a by-product of complexly organized brains, that does not mean that consciousness could not have ultimately been exposed to selection pressures. Traits that may start out as epiphenomena can become highly adaptive in certain environments.

From an evolutionary perspective, complex behaviors are very difficult to study. The genetic contribution to a complex phenomenon like consciousness is rarely straightforward. Instead, complex traits probably contain within their history the processes of adaptation and exaptation, and they may also have co-opted components that initially started out as epiphenomena. As François Jacob (1977) notes, "Natural selection does not work as an engineer works. It works like a tinkerer—a tinkerer who does not know exactly what he is going to produce but uses whatever he finds around him whether it be pieces of string, fragments of wood, or old cardboard; in short it works like a tinkerer who uses everything at his disposal to produce some kind of workable object . . . The tinkerer gives his material unexpected functions to produce a new object . . . Tinkerers who tackle the same problem are likely to end up with different solutions."

As noted earlier, because of genetic pleiotropy, what we observe, while appearing functionally optimal, may not be the best or only method of accomplishing a particular task. For example, the method of information transmission that has evolved in animal nervous systems, the action potential, is only one of a number of possible ways in which cells can communicate. Indeed, synaptic transmission, with its highly intricate molecular mechanisms, is a superb example of evolutionary tinkering (see Chapter 2).

Our nervous system is a snapshot in evolutionary time of a very fluid process, and it is composed of various adaptations for previous environments, exaptations, and epiphenomenal characteristics that may or may not be functionally important and ultimately selected.

Evolutionary Mechanisms

How is phenotypic variability achieved within a population? We know that genes are ultimately responsible for evolutionary changes in the phenotype and that phenotypic variability is achieved by genetic mechanisms. The first of these mechanisms is mutation. **Mutation** is a sudden change in the genetic structure of an organism that affects the development of the organism. Mutations can have a positive, negative, or neutral effect on the organism. Recent work on mutant and transgenic mice demonstrates well the mixed effects that a mutation can have on the phenotype. For instance, molecular neurobiologists have begun to use mutant mice to genetically alter a molecule, brain area, or connection pathway, in an effort to understand the contributions that specific genes make to the generation and maintenance of the phenotype.

Unfortunately, there are several problems with this marvelous new tool. The first is that a large percentage of mutants die very early in development. The second, related problem is that the "genetic lesion" of the characteristic under study is never really specific. Thus, the mutants, if they are viable, have a plethora of other phenotypic changes associated with the lesion. Both problems are due to genetic pleiotropy. In the first instance—nonviable offspring—the mice generally do not die from the targeted characteristic that was genetically lesioned, but from other effects, such as kidney failure, respiratory abnormalities, or cardiac dysfunction. The point is that the single gene controls not only the characteristic in question but also a number of other functions. This is why viable, or good, mutations are relatively rare and genetic change across species is small. Indeed, modern DNA-sequencing techniques indicate that humans are very closely related to chimpanzees, and our genetic relationship to something as simply organized as a sea anemone is also remarkably similar, considering the large phenotypic differences in the two species.

Despite the very close genetic relationship that we share with other primates, and even other animals, there is a remarkable degree of phenotypic variability in both external morphology and organization of the brain and behaviors. This variability indicates that (a) a slight change to the genotype can produce very large changes in the phenotype, (b) phenotypic change via genetic change is rarely successful, and (c) other factors that are not directly dictated by an organism's genes must provide a large contribution to phenotypic variability.

In addition to genetic mutation, genetic recombination can also increase phenotypic variability. The term **recombination** refers to a change in the array of alleles of existing genes. Here, the manner in which existing alleles are combined, rather than the frequency of an allele within a population, is changed. Factors that affect the frequency of any given allele within a population include genetic flow and genetic isolation. *Genetic flow* refers to the migration of individuals within the same species into particular populations and their interbreeding with that population's members. *Genetic isolation* is usually the result of the geographic separation of one group from another. A population of individuals of the same species can become separated because of shifts in landmasses or bodies of water, and ultimately unable to mate with others outside of this geographically isolated population. Genetic isolation may be an important factor in speciation in cases where the isolated subgroup diverges significantly from the remaining population.

THE COMPARATIVE APPROACH

Often, because of technical and pragmatic constraints, we must rely on studies of other animals to provide insights into a number of aspects of organization and function in the human brain. In addition, the comparative approach is critical for gaining insight into the evolution of the human brain (as discussed earlier in the chapter), so it is important to understand the theory and defining principles behind the comparative approach.

One of the most misunderstood and misused concepts in this approach is *homology*. Simply put, **homology** is the retention of a structure, behavior, or gene from a common ancestor. That is, a particular structure in one species is homologous to a structure in another species. The hand of a monkey and the hand of a human are homologous. The wing of a bat and the hand of a human are also homologous, because both structures have the same evolutionary descent. *Homology* is also used to refer to structures in the brain. For instance, area MT in the macaque monkey is homologous to area MT in the owl monkey and galago (see Figure 15.3).

Keep in mind that homologous structures do not necessarily have the same function. For example, V1 in humans is homologous to V1 in monkeys, and it probably functions in a very similar fashion. V1 in humans and other primates and V1 in the duck-billed platypus are also homologous. However, the internal organization and connections of V1 in these species vary dramatically. In some cases homologous structures may not look the same. For example, although the wing of a bat and the hand of a monkey are homologous, the wing of a bat is considered to be a derived feature that has been co-opted for different functions (an exaptation). Thus, the two appendages look quite different and serve very different functions. A *derived trait* is one that is specialized and limited to a particular group or species. Examples of derived features include the bill of a duck-billed platypus, the flipper of a dolphin, and the nose of the star-nosed mole. We can also examine derived features of the nervous system. For example, the primary somatosensory cortex of murine rodents (mice and rats) contains a highly derived feature called *barrel fields*, which are related to whiskers. A **plesiomorphic** trait is one that is a general feature of a particular group or lineage. For instance, area MT is a plesiomorphic trait of primates.

Homoplasy refers to structures that look the same but do not necessarily have a common ancestry. For instance, the wing of a bat and the wing of a fly are homoplastic and have similar functions but are not

(a) Brush-tailed possum

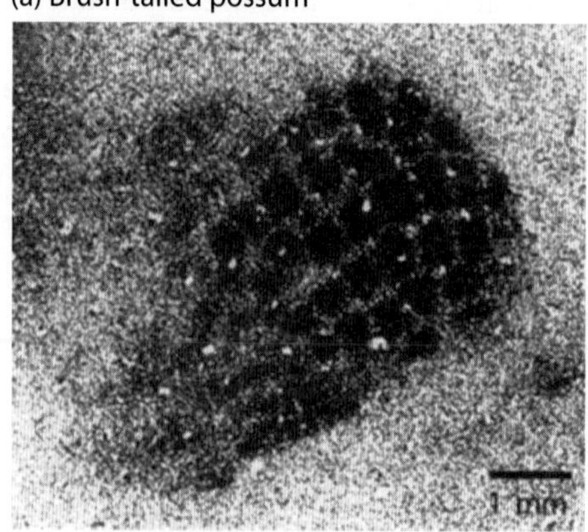

(b) Mouse

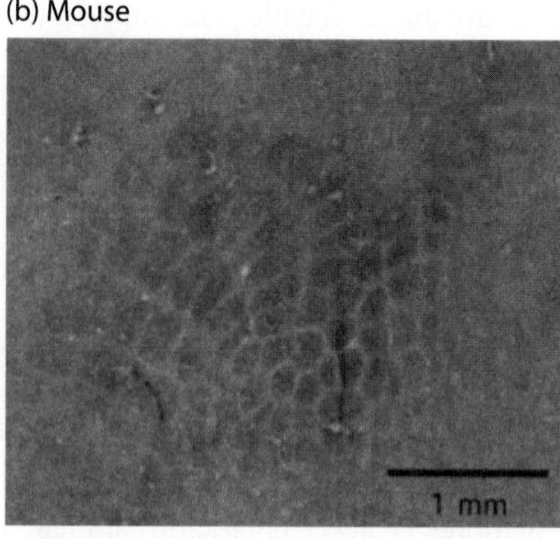

Figure 15.5 The barrel cortex in the primary somatosensory area (S1) in the brush-tailed possum **(a)** and the mouse **(b)**, as demonstrated with Nissl stains and cytochrome oxidase stains, respectively. The barrel cortex represents the mystacial vibrissae in these mammals. Despite more than 100 million years of independent evolution, the neural organization of this peripheral specialization looks remarkably similar.

homologous. This also holds true for features of the brain as well. A barrel field has been identified in the primary somatosensory area of murine rodents (T. A. Woolsey et al., 1975) and in some marsupials, such as opossums (Weller, 1993). The barrel fields in each group are considered to be homoplastic but not homologous (Figure 15.5). The remarkable similarity in appearance of the barrel fields in these very distantly related mammals (approximately 125 million years of independent evolution) indicates that the rules governing neocortex development and evolution are very highly constrained.

Likewise, visual motion areas have been identified in other mammals as homoplastic and similar in function to area MT of the primate; an example is the posteromedial lateral suprasylvian area (PMLS) in cats (Figure 15.6). The implication that similar structures with similar functions can arise independently in different lineages (**convergent evolution**) is a sign of the limited and constrained rules by which the brain evolves.

An **out-group comparison** can determine whether features of the brain are homologous or homoplastic, or merely share similar functions. An out-group comparison defines phylogenetic relationships among animals (Figure 15.7). Close sister groups of a species are examined to determine if they possess the structure in question. The probability that close sister groups will have the characteristic in question is higher than for a distantly related species. For instance, the middle temporal visual area (area MT) was first identified in owl monkeys. The question that arose after its discovery was this: Is this a derived feature of owl monkey brains, or is this a general feature of primate brains, including humans?

Decades of research on a number of sister groups (such as New World monkeys, Old World monkeys, and prosimians) indicate that MT is indeed a general feature of most, if not all, of the primate brains studied. Functional-imaging studies suggest that MT is also likely to be a feature of human brains (see Chapter 5).

Because the connections of MT appear similar across primates, and neurons in area MT have similar response properties, area MT may have a similar function in all primates, even though this remains to be directly demonstrated.

Figure 15.6 A motion area has been identified in both cats (a) and primates (b). The area in cats is termed the *posteromedial lateral suprasylvian area (PMLS)*; the area in primates is termed *middle temporal visual area (MT)*. Although neurons in both of these regions respond to moving stimuli, and these areas receive direct inputs from the primary visual area (V1), it is unlikely that they are homologous, because of the very distant phylogenetic relationship between cats and primates and the lack of such an area in a number of intervening groups. These areas are homoplastic, and likely emerged owing to similar selective pressures for detecting moving objects in the environment.

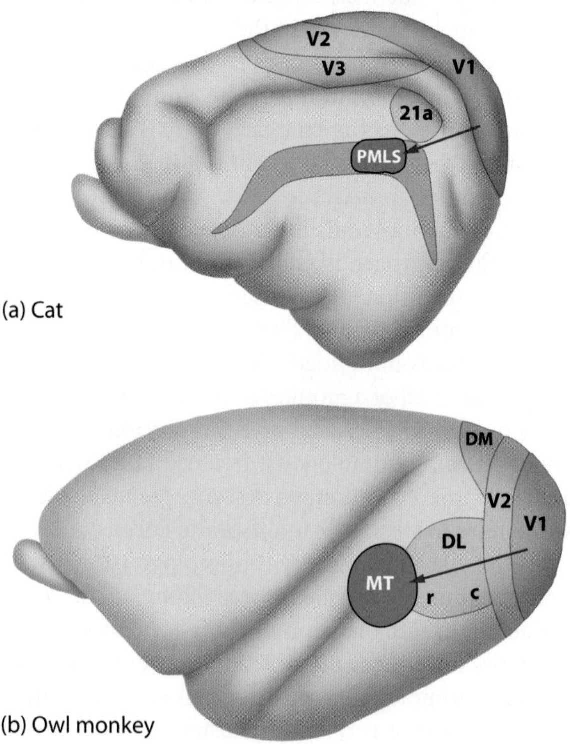

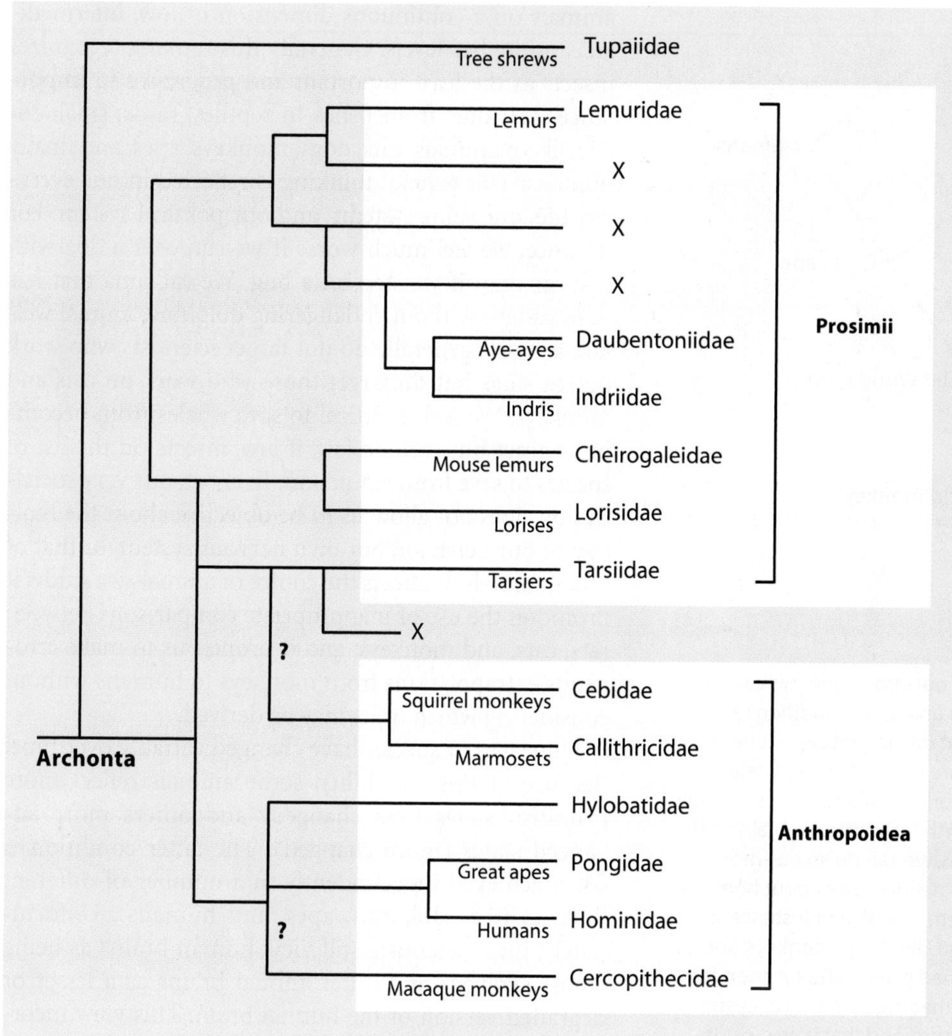

Figure 15.7 The phylogenetic relationships between extant primates. Archonta is the grand order to which the order of primates belongs. Primates are divided into two suborders: Prosimii and Anthropoidea. Each suborder is divided into several families (e.g., Lorisidae and Tarsiidae for Prosimii, and Hominidae and Cercopithecidae for Anthropoidea). The common names of some representatives, or groups, are found just to the left of the family names. Although no dates are given, and some of the details of the relationships are still in dispute, this diagram gives a general overview of relationships and is used in comparative analysis. The family Tupaiidae diverged early in the archontan line and its members are not considered primates, but the neocortex in this family does possess some primate-like features.

When researchers use the comparative approach, the **principle of parsimony** is applied to arrive at the most accurate inference regarding the unknown condition. In this case, after researchers have done an out-group comparison, the best hypothesis is the one that requires the fewest number of *transformations* to explain a phenomenon. For example, consider a hypothetical brain trait or cognitive behavior, which we'll call Trait A (Figure 15.8). We are interested in whether Trait A exists in humans, but we cannot directly test for it in humans. An out-group analysis of three great apes indicates that Trait A is present in two of these animals but not the other. A further analysis of Old World monkeys indicates that Trait A is present in four of the five species examined. Finally, an examination of six species of New World monkeys indicates that Trait A is present in all of them.

The most parsimonious explanation is that Trait A is a plesiomorphic feature (general characteristic) of primates that was lost in two of the species examined. Therefore, it is highly probable that humans also have Trait A. A less parsimonious explanation, because the number of transformations is considerably greater, would be that Trait A has arisen independently in six New World monkeys, four Old World monkeys, and two great apes. According to this explanation, Trait A is not likely to be present in humans.

Let's apply the principle of parsimony to the example of area MT. We have concluded that MT is a general feature of all primates; it looks the same and is likely to have a similar function. Is the motion area identified in cats (PMLS) homologous to MT in primates? This question has been vigorously contested. An out-group comparison, which includes representatives of all the major mammalian radiations, indicates that MT is not present in rodents, ungulates, or other carnivores. The most parsimonious explanation is that a motion area evolved independently in primates and cats. MT and PMLS are homoplastic and may have similar functions, but they

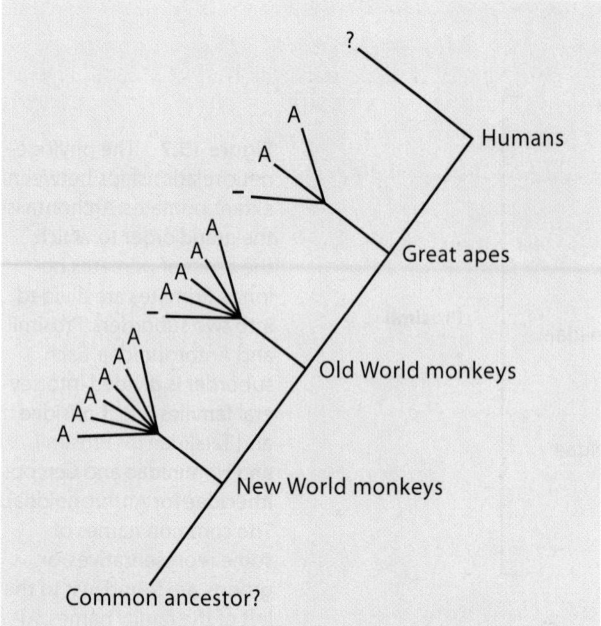

Figure 15.8 Example of how an out-group analysis can be used to make inferences about an unknown condition (e.g., the common ancestor, or an extant group that cannot be studied, such as humans). Great apes are relatively closely related to humans; Old World and New World monkeys are less closely related. If we are interested in whether a particular brain characteristic (Trait A) exists in humans, we can do an out-group comparison to make a fairly accurate inference about humans, even though we cannot study them directly. For instance, if two of three great apes, four of five Old World monkeys, and six of six New World monkeys examined possess Trait A, then the most parsimonious conclusion is that the common ancestor of these primates possessed this feature, and that it was lost in one group of Old World monkeys and one group of great apes.

do not appear to be homologous. Does this mean that it is not worthwhile to study the motion area in cats? Absolutely not. It is not a simple coincidence that two areas that have a number of similar features of organization arose independently in two distinct lineages. The implication here is that, although the roots of the motion area are different, the rules of how the brain constructs a motion area in evolution must be highly constrained. Homoplasy allows us to examine the rules of how brains can change over time and the limitations inherent in constructing nervous systems.

The Scale of Nature Revisited

Despite the many advances that we have made in understanding the brain, we still find it hard to move away from a human-centered, or *anthropocentric*, view of life, the brain, and the behavior it generates. We tend to rank animals on a continuous dimension of low, intermediate, and higher levels. Generally this ranking recognizes insects as the least important and progresses in importance, or value, from fishes to reptiles, birds, small rodentlike mammals, cats, dogs, monkeys, apes, and finally humans. This general thinking is reflected in our everyday life, our value systems, and our political system. For instance, we feel much worse if we run over a dog with our car than if we step on a bug. We eat tuna that has been caught without endangering dolphins. Animal welfare activists generally do not target scientists who work on sea slugs but do target those who work on cats and monkeys. We feel it critical to save whales from becoming extinct but include few, if any, insects on the list of species to save from extinction. In short, our very socialization does not allow us to be objective about the biology of our behavior, our own nervous system, or that of other animals. It affects the choice of animals we study; it promotes the use of inappropriate comparisons between rats, cats, and monkeys; and it propels us to make erroneous extrapolations from monkeys to humans without considering which traits may be derived.

Lineages of species have changed variably over time. Because of this variability, some animals reflect more primitive states (less changed) and others more advanced states (more changed). The latter condition is often achieved independently in a number of different lineages (e.g., dolphins, apes, and humans). Unfortunately, most scientists still view human brains as being "most evolved" and other animal brains as a lesser or degraded version of the human brain. This view incorrectly suggests that evolution is linear or simply additive and promotes the idea that "higher order" brain areas subserving behaviors such as language, cognition, and even consciousness should be distinguishable as a part that was added on to "lower animal" brains.

Two brain areas that are considered higher order areas in humans can best be understood from an evolutionary perspective: the prefrontal cortex and Broca's area. The prefrontal cortex is commonly considered the hallmark of the human brain. A comparative, or evolutionary, perspective suggests that the prefrontal cortex actually arose from a very primitive brain system, the olfactory system, and has been modified in the primate lineage with the expansion of sensory cortex, to which it is connected via multisynaptic pathways. All mammals have (homologous) orbitofrontal pathways similar to those described in nonhuman primates and presumably humans as well. For instance, orbitofrontal cortex receives indirect inputs from higher order sensory cortex in many primates (Kupfermann, 1991). In humans, orbitofrontal cortex may have expanded to become prefrontal cortex (which consists of several divisions), and this expansion was likely tied to the expansion of sensory neocortex. Although the functions of the orbitofrontal cortex mediated by homologous neural pathways may overlap somewhat among mammals, in the human brain this region of cortex has been co-opted for more varied functions.

Interestingly, other mammals, such as echidnas, have independently "added on" a large prefrontal cortex (Figure 15.9). In this species, however, we do not automatically liken this expansion to increased intelligence or a "more evolved" state. Echidnas are monotremes, mammals whose ancestor diverged very early in mammalian evolution (some 200 million years ago). These egg-laying mammals are thought to represent a primitive mammalian form, and they possess a fairly limited behavioral repertoire compared to that of humans and other primates. Although there is clearly a tie between evolution of the prefrontal cortex and complex human abilities, the presence of the prefrontal cortex is not the defining characteristic of advanced neocortical evolution.

Figure 15.9 The location and extent of prefrontal cortex (gray) in three different species. The brains have been scaled to approximately the same size. The proportion of the entire neocortex that the prefrontal cortex assumes in humans **(a)** is larger than in other primates, such as macaque monkeys **(b)**. In other species, such as the spiny anteater or the echidna **(c)**, an expanded prefrontal cortex (relatively larger than that in humans) has evolved independently. The pressure that drove this expansion is likely to be quite different in humans and echidnas, and therefore the prefrontal cortex in each group is not analogous.

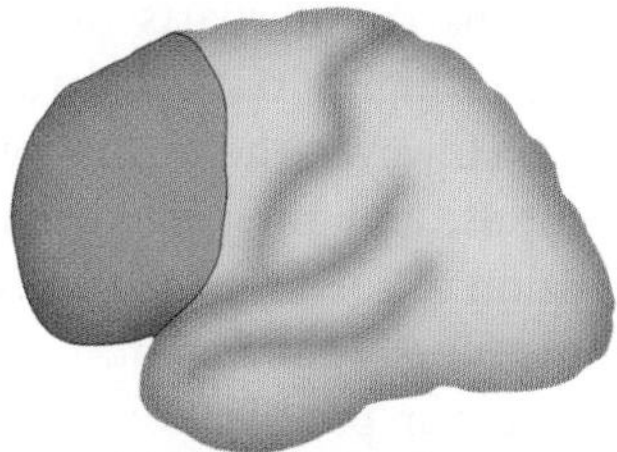

(a) *Homo sapiens* (human)

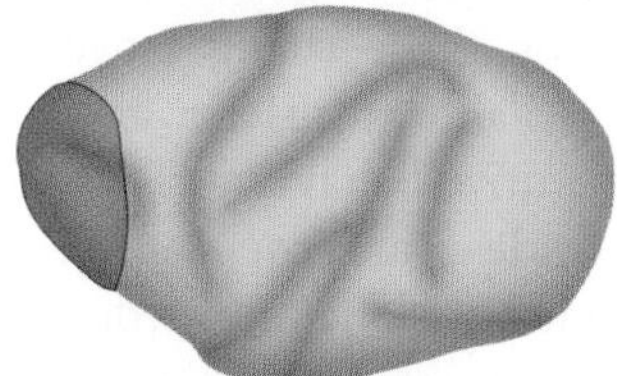

(b) *Macaca mulatta* (rhesus monkey)

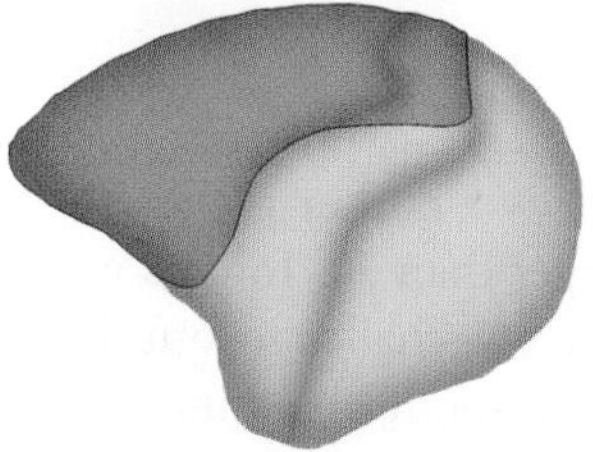

(c) *Tachyglossus aculeatus* (echidna)

Broca's area is intimately involved with language capabilities in the human brain. An evolutionary perspective suggests that, although language capabilities in the human brain are qualitatively unique, other species may have cortical regions quite similar to Broca's area. We know from a number of experiments on sensory and motor cortex in a variety of mammals that morphological and behavioral specializations are associated with cortical specialization. Such specializations usually take the form of enlargement or modularization of the cortical area representing the specialized portion of the sensory epithelium or muscle group (Figure 15.10).

For instance, the duck-billed platypus has evolved a bill with a unique distribution of mechanosensory (touch) receptors interfaced with a novel type of sensory receptor called an *electroreceptor*. Specialized motor programs have evolved in the platypus in which oscillatory movements of the bill are used to help localize and identify prey. The representation of the bill along the entire neuroaxis has been modified, particularly in the neocortex. This modification takes the form of an enlargement in the amount of neural space devoted to the specialized structure and its receptors, as well as specialized motor programs that generate foraging behaviors associated with the bill.

Other examples of neural specializations that reflect morphological specializations abound. For instance, the hairless hands of most primates and the raccoon show a similar magnification of representation along the entire neuroaxis, as does the nose of the star-nosed mole. All of these neural specializations have arisen independently, although all reside in the primary somatosensory area and appear to follow the same rules of specialization. Thus, although all mammals have a primary somatosensory area (S1), only the platypus cortex has a bill representation that has been modified to such a large extent. In the star-nosed mole, the nose representation has been modified in a similar fashion, and in the raccoon and some primates the hand representation has been similarly modified.

In humans, if we view the changes in the density and distribution of receptors for the tongue, lips, and teeth, as well as the physical changes to the structure of the larynx and the motor programs associated with it, in the same way that we view other mammalian specializations, then we might think of Broca's area very differently. We might not view this region of the brain as uniquely human, but as a region that many mammals, and certainly all primates, share. In humans, this region has become highly derived. This derived state is a magnification of the cortical representation of the face and oral structures in the premotor

(a) New World monkey hand

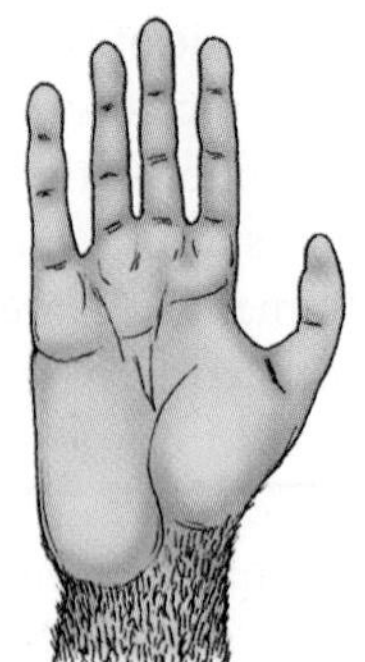

(b) Owl monkey cuneate nucleus (brainstem)

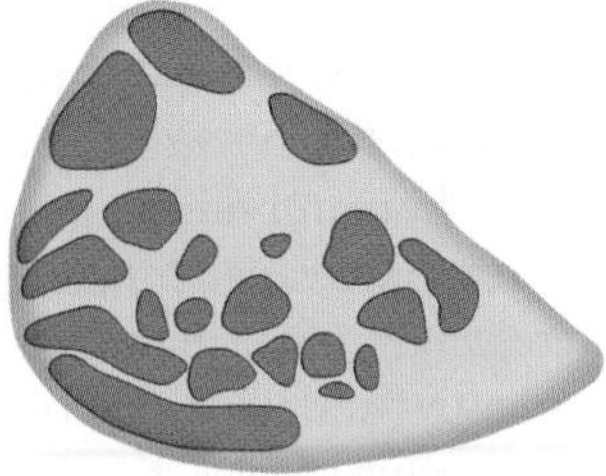

(c) Squirrel monkey ventral posterior nucleus (thalamus)

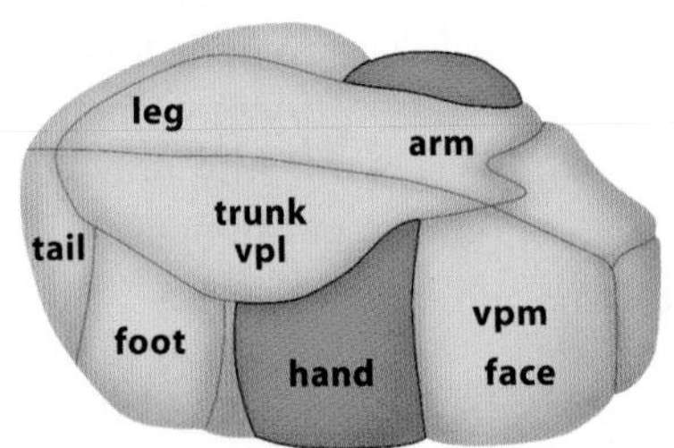

(d) Owl monkey somatosensory cortex

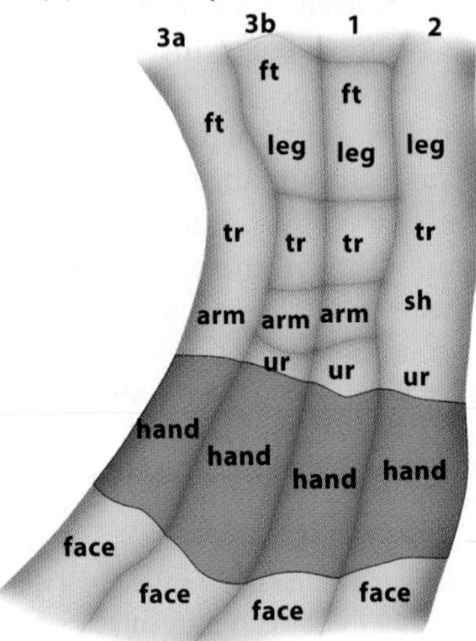

Figure 15.10 The organization of the hand representation in New World primates at all levels of the nervous system. **(a)** The glabrous hand is a specialized structure in primates adapted for tactile exploration, recognition, and goal-directed grasping and reaching. A greatly magnified representation of this structure appears in the cuneate nucleus of the brainstem **(b)**, the ventral posterior nucleus of the thalamus **(c)**, and the anterior parietal somatosensory areas of the neocortex **(d)**. The red indicates the amount of each of these nuclei and fields associated with the specialized representation.

cortex (PMC), as well as M1 and S1, as a consequence of, or in conjunction with, changes in the periphery.

As in other species with sensory and motor specializations, changes in the connections and the motor programs direct the use of these structures (e.g., the mole's nose is used for exploration, the platypus's bill is used for oscillation, and the primate's hand is used for reaching and grasping). In the case of Broca's area, interconnections with specialized auditory regions of the brain (such as Wernicke's area) have formed. Thus, although all mammals have an M1, and certainly all primates have a PMC, only in humans have the motor and sensory representations of oral and facial structures been modified in such an elaborate manner.

A comparative analysis suggests that the most parsimonious and biologically compatible explanation is that the modification to the human brain known as Broca's area has homologous counterparts in other primates and certainly follows highly restricted rules of cortical field modification. However, the formation of new patterns of connections, and the clear behavioral differences that this region of cortex generates, indicate that it is not entirely functionally equivalent.

If we overcome our predilection for thinking of a "scale of nature" with humans at the top, but instead invoke the history of change (roots) and mechanisms (rules) generating those changes over time in other mammals, we can allow for richer and more varied hypotheses of cognitive behaviors. These hypotheses are more objective, less anthropocentric, and certainly more compatible with our knowledge of evolutionary neurobiology.

ADAPTATION AND THE BRAIN

Evolutionists interested in human behavior believe that the modern human brain was adapted to deal with the world as it was in Pleistocene hunter-gatherer societies of 100,000 years ago. This period was chosen for its slowness of new adaptations. In hunter-gatherer times, groups were rarely larger than 50. Today's vast cities and social structures severely challenge our brains to cope. So when we think about the functions of the modern brain and what it does and does not do well, we should take into account what the early hunter-gatherers had to solve.

This proposal takes a novel tack in the study of decision-making. Wendy Wang of the University of South Dakota (X. T. Wang, 1996) argues that mechanisms for decision making evolved in a particular social context. Specifically, he focuses on the idea that, for most of our evolutionary history, humans lived in small groups. Wang's experiments to date have centered on the framing effect. In a framing experiment, people are presented with two choices regarding a particular risky situation, such as which of two treatments should be administered to combat a potentially fatal medical condition. In the classic framing-effect demonstration (Tversky & Kahneman, 1988), the treatments are posed in either a positive or a negative light (e.g., treatments to save lives or treatments to minimize death). Risk-taking behavior differs in these two situations. When the treatment is framed in a positive manner, people tend to choose sure bets—treatments that are guaranteed to work. When it is framed in a negative manner, people tend to choose more probabilistic options. The framing effect is one demonstration of human irrationality, since a strict cost–benefit analysis is not sufficient to account for human decision making.

This example clearly illustrates that, in a number of respects, our behaviors are adapted to a simpler life, the life of the Stone Age human. Back then we had to be ready to defend ourselves, detect cheaters, hunt, forage, recognize kin, and read others' facial expressions and intentions.

According to evolutionary thinking, each of these special capacities grows from separate and individual adaptations. The cognitive systems that evolved for these individual adaptations are not necessarily a unified system. Still, they must work together to solve individual problems. This fundamental point is at the heart of the evolutionary perspective, and it concurs with a vast amount of neuropsychological research. Localized brain lesions can lead to a loss of a particular capacity—say, facial recognition—but they can also have numerous mild effects on specific functions.

The adaptations built into the neural circuitry of our brains are the structural devices that we should try to understand when trying to figure out how the brain works. As pointed out earlier, it is important to focus on the adaptation itself, and not on the ancillary events associated with the adaptation. Bones are an adaptation that provide a rigid structure for an organism, but their whiteness is a by-product, or epiphenomenon, of the calcium that gives them their rigidity. If we want to study bones and how they came to be, it would be a mistake to delve into the fact that they are white. Instead we must distinguish between *proximate* factors (i.e., whiteness as a by-product of the presence of calcium) and *ultimate* factors (i.e., the usefulness of a rigid structure) when we consider why something evolved. Proximate factors are those at hand and are a part of the structure, but their presence may not be why the structure evolved.

Evolutionary biologists must also distinguish between the function and current use of an adaptation. The *function* of an adaptation is the original purpose for which it evolved over time, and the *current use* is a new purpose for which a previous adaptation is exploited. Both functions and current uses may be adaptive in the sense that they lead to greater reproductive success of the organism. A simple example of the distinction between function and use is the wing of a crane. The crane will sometimes hold its wing up to shade the surface of the water so that it can more easily see the fish that it is attempting to catch. This behavioral use of the wing is certainly adaptive, but this is the current use of the wing. The purpose for which the wing evolved and adapted was flying. Flying is the wing's ultimate function; assisting in fishing behavior is one of its current uses. Current use may not inform us of the original adaptive significance of a structure in the context of past evolutionary pressures, but it may be important for the continued maintenance of such structures.

Adaptations at Multiple Brain Levels

It is easy to see how perceptual adaptations may have developed in primates; they likely occurred within primary sensory systems like our visual and auditory systems. But we also have adaptations for more complex behaviors, such as our capacity to have a theory of mind about someone else. We look at other humans and quickly theorize about their intentions toward us and how we should respond. At these varying levels evolutionary processes operate—and deserve comment.

At the simpler level of understanding vision, today's researcher may have insights that are consonant with the realities of the Pleistocene landscape. After all, the physical world of light and object has not changed all that much. Our visual system is built to take a two-dimensional retinal image and turn it into a real-world representation of the visual scene. David Marr of the Massachusetts Institute of Technology first articulated the true problems associated with understanding how vision must work. As Marr (1982) put it, "Trying to understand perception by studying only neurons is like trying to understand bird flight by studying only feathers: It just cannot be done."

In general terms, Marr suggested three levels of description for any information-processing device, whether a cash register or a brain. He based his ideas on the following logic: that information-processing devices are designed to solve problems, that they solve problems by virtue of their structure, and that a device's structure can be explained when one knows what problem it was designed to solve.

Using this approach, Marr proposed that the evolutionary function of vision is scene analysis: The brain must reconstruct a model of real-world conditions from a two-dimensional visual array—the information on the retina. But constructing a model of the real world from such limited input is not an easy undertaking. Scene analysis is far more complicated than had been imagined. First, a simple object sitting on the horizon in the morning light looks completely different when the sun reaches high noon and then falls over the opposite horizon. An intricately specialized system must have been built into the primary visual system to allow for this natural progression and enable us to see the object as constant. Second, investigators discovered that our visual system apprehends far more information about a scene than can any artifact. The system has many adaptations built in for this capability, all specific to vision. Finally—and this is the tricky part—our evolved visual system must have a cognitive, built-in component that has deduced that objects in the world have regularities that allow for the proper computations. This built-in component is what developmentalists mean by biologically prepared implicit knowledge in infants and children.

As we move up the scale to more complex adaptations, such as those associated with problem solving and social exchange, the insights we might gain by looking around us in our present world are probably not as helpful. Most studies do not take into account the sorts of ways that Stone Age humans dealt with social problems. In many of today's attempts to understand human rational processes, subjects are presented with artificial thought problems developed in the laboratory, yet our brains are adapted only for real-world problems. For instance, many logic tests on issues of social exchange stump college sophomores because they are posed in the abstract. Does their failure mean that sophomores are illogical? The answer is a resounding no, because when the same logic problem is based on a real-life story about obtaining beer or food, their logic systems work just fine.

Leda Cosmides at the University of California, Santa Barbara (1984), worked out a telling example of this fact. She built on a test first developed by Peter Wason of University College London, who showed how poorly educated people can perform a simple logical task. Try it yourself: Each card below has a number on one side and a letter on the other. Examine the following four cards:

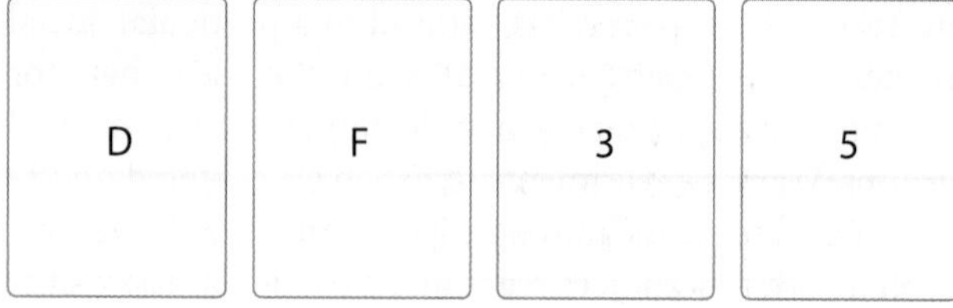

The task is simple. You are to determine if the following rule has any exceptions: If a card has a D on one side, it has a 3 on the other side. Which cards do you need to turn over to discover if this is true? Do you feel your mind rattling? Now consider the following problem: You are a bouncer at a bar, and your job is to make sure no one under 21 drinks beer at the bar. The following cards have information about age on one side and what the patron is drinking on the other. Again, which cards do you need to turn over?

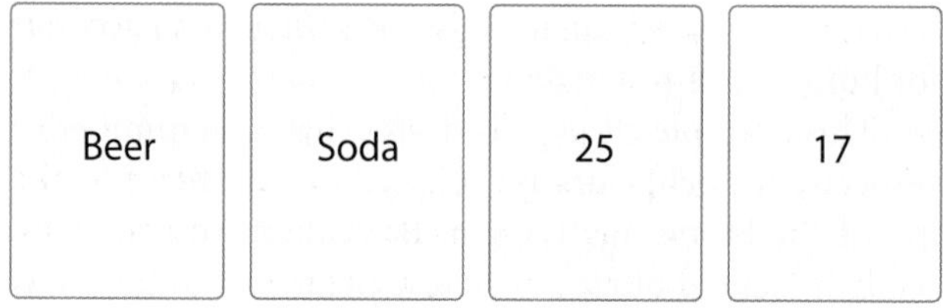

In this case, obviously the first and last cards must be turned over, just as in the previous more abstract example. Why is it easy to solve the second task and so difficult to solve the first, when both problems have exactly the same structure and the same solution? Cosmides and Tooby (1992) maintained that we have a built-in cheater detector system that has been a necessary part of our brains ever since we, as a species, began to exist in social groups. When survival becomes contingent on what a group does, as opposed to what an individual does, there must be a way to ensure that individual members are not violating the rules of the group. In other words, we have the beginnings of a social contract.

This social exchange can be expressed by the conditional statement that, if you take the benefit, then you must pay the cost. For example, if you play on the hotel's golf course, then you must be a guest at the hotel. A cheater is someone who takes a benefit without paying the cost. People are quite good at detecting potential violations of these kinds of conditional rules (i.e., catching potential cheaters), whereas they cannot detect potential violations of purely descriptive rules. Descriptive rules

HOW THE BRAIN WORKS

Lessons from a Frog

Wonderful examples illustrate how evolutionary theory has led to great insights into brain function. Perhaps the most famous example is the work of Jerome Lettvin, one of the fathers of modern neuroscience and an extremely lively intellect. In 1959 he and his colleagues wrote a well-known paper titled "What the Frog's Eye Tells the Frog's Brain." Lettvin broke with his predecessors and asked questions about the visual system based on his understanding of how a frog views the world.

Prior to Lettvin's work, the eye was regarded as an organ that translated an image into electrical impulses, and the brain was then believed to sort out and interpret this retinal information. The great American physiologist Haldan Keffer Hartline gave support to this idea in 1938 by studying the retina with simple points of light and dark. Using these abstract stimuli, Hartline and his colleagues concluded that the frog's retina passed on to the brain information about the tone of various objects. They concluded that the retina's ganglion cells had but one function, and that was it.

Lettvin changed this interpretation. While recording from the frog's ganglion cells and stimulating the frog's visual system with bugs, twigs, and other ecologically relevant material, he and his colleagues discovered several types of ganglion cells—five, to be exact. In simple terms, Lettvin showed how much information is weeded out by biological systems like the retina. Evolution has seen to it that the frog's brain does not detect things about the visual environment that it does not need in order to function and survive. Hence, the male frog's brain does not spend energy on noticing the actor Melanie Griffith but does detect the movement of female frogs.

Continued on the following page

Table 15.1 Types of Detectors in the Frog's Retina

Detector Type	Stimulus Evoking the Greatest Response
Sustained-edge detector (SED)	Small, moving edge entering and remaining in the SED's receptive field. Immobile or long edges do not evoke a response.
Convex-edge detector (CED)	Small, dark object with a convex outline, such as a beetle or other bug.
Moving-edge detector (MED)	Edge moving in and out of the MED's receptive field.
Dimming detector (DD)	Decrease in light intensity, such as a shadow cast suddenly over the frog.
Light-intensity detector (LID)	Dim light. Responses are inversely proportional to light intensity.

take the form that, if a man wears a tuxedo, then he must wear a bow tie. In studies of undergraduates in the United States and Germany, 75% to 90% of people reason correctly about social exchanges, compared to only 4% to 25% when the focus is abstract or descriptive rules. Detecting potential cheaters is an important evolutionary problem: Those who cannot detect cheating lose out on precious resources and therefore are at a significant disadvantage in social groups. Conversely, there is little evolutionary benefit to detecting descriptive rules.

This type of work has built on the insights of Robert Trivers of Rutgers University (1971). Trivers showed that the elements of social exchange are based on the evolution of reciprocal altruism. Reciprocity amounts to roughly equal amounts of give and take in social relationships. The associated cognitive, psychological, and emotional systems allow us to develop and maintain friendships with nonkin. Children implicitly recognize the reciprocal nature of friendships and socially reject those who do not reciprocate.

Trivers argued that many emotional reactions regulate social exchange. If we give more than we take in a social relationship, we get angry; if we take more than we give, we feel guilty. Guilt motivates us to return the favor; anger motivates us to break off relationships with people who cheat or who do not reciprocate.

Sexual Selection and Evolutionary Pressures on Behavior

Sex has realities that are at once clear and puzzling. Darwin knew that natural selection was at work, but he was

Continued from previous page

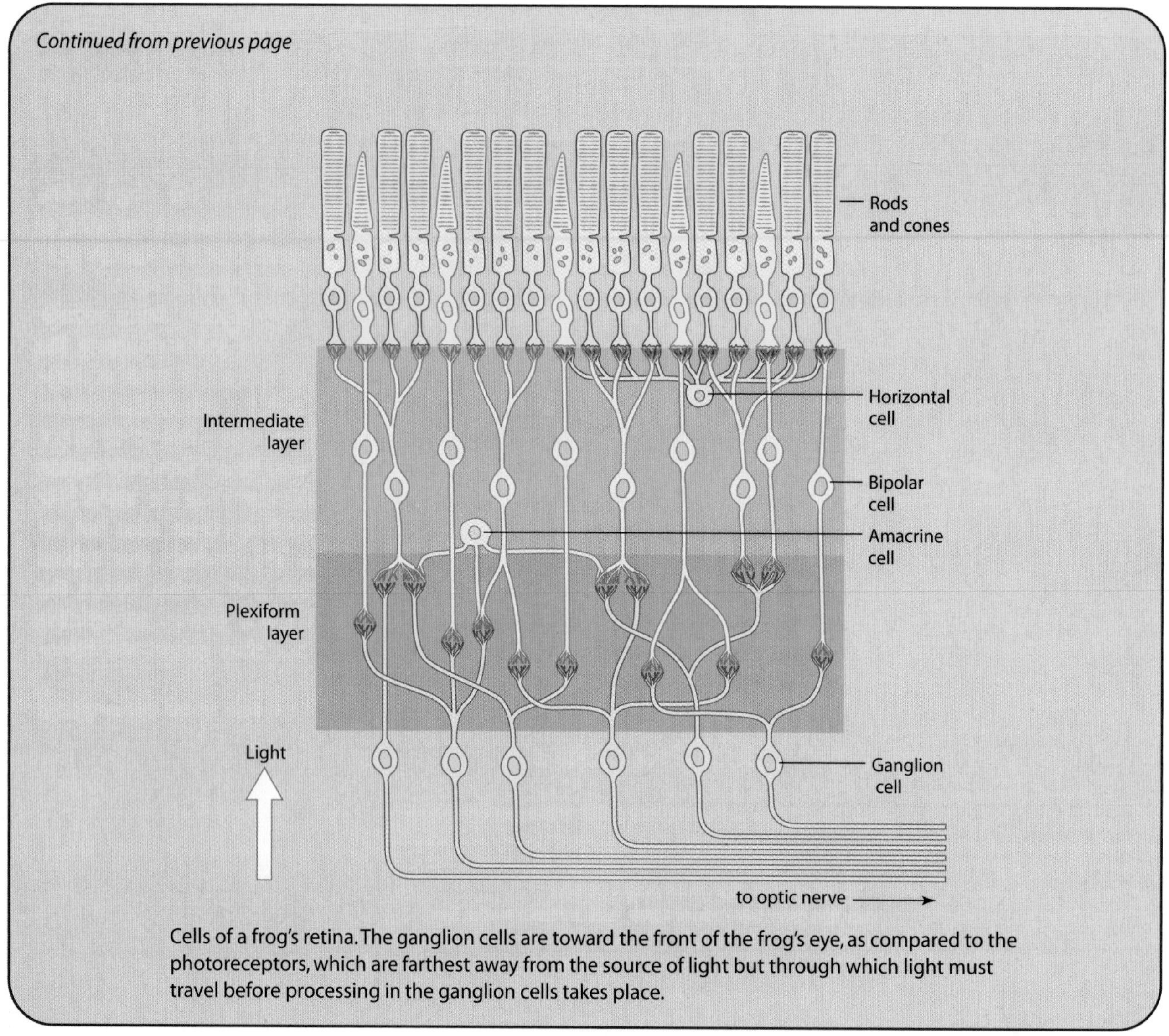

Cells of a frog's retina. The ganglion cells are toward the front of the frog's eye, as compared to the photoreceptors, which are farthest away from the source of light but through which light must travel before processing in the ganglion cells takes place.

bothered by why males and females differ so much, given their mutual goal of trying to survive in the same niche. It is easy to understand why genitalia are different, but it is not easy to understand why such big differences exist in behavior and body structure.

Some dispute whether sexual selection should be distinguished from natural selection, but leading researchers, such as Steven Gaulin at the University of Pittsburgh (1995), argue that it should be. Gaulin maintains that a distinction between sexual selection and natural selection explains how characteristics that appear to have no role in survival, such as the colored feathers of a peacock, have evolved and survived. Although not necessary for functions such as food gathering, these characteristics are important in enhancing sexual contact.

Similarly, the very large antlers of the male deer enhance sexual contact and illustrate how selection might cause the sexes within a species to diverge. Once a female deer has mated and conceived her maximum litter, she has no need for additional sexual contact. The male, though, can maximize his reproductive success by continuing to impregnate as many females as he can. Thus, any somatic event—for example, the development of large antlers—that would enhance a male's reproductive fitness would be selected for, whereas a similar change for the female would not. The female would not gain, because her reproductive limit has been met (Figure 15.11).

This pattern for mammals has exceptions, and the exceptions strengthen the idea that sexual selection is distinct from natural selection. First, male mammals have small and many sex cells (sperm), whereas females

Figure 15.11 The typical morphology of **(a)** a female doe that invests her energy in raising her offspring and **(b)** a polygamous male elk that invests a lot of energy in growing a massive set of antlers, which aid his ability to attract mates and fight off competitors.

have large sex cells (eggs). In other animals, the quickly reproducing sex is the female, and the male stays home with the young. In some shorebirds, the male stays in the nest to incubate the egg, and the female, right after laying the egg, leaves the nest to seek other males so that she can lay yet more eggs for them to incubate. In this turnabout of roles, the fast-sexed females are larger, more brightly colored, and aggressive. It is clear, then, that the flamboyant characteristics of most males and of the less common fast-sexed females enhance their capacity for a higher reproductive rate. But this does not mean that there are no monogamous species: Over 90% of foxes and birds are deeply committed to each other because both must participate in child rearing if their species is to survive.

Another significant difference between mammals and birds is that mammals have an internal gestation period. Female mammals make a larger commitment to offspring than do males, underscoring the known difference in how much the male and female invest in their offspring as compared to how much time they spend on mating. For birds and many fish species, external gestation creates the potential for females to force parental care onto males—a more difficult trick with mammals.

The Effect of Sex on Spatial Abilities

In addition to diverging physical characteristics, there are differences in the cognitive abilities of males and females. For example, spatial abilities, on average, vary according to sex—and they likely do so because of selective pressures. Spatial skills differ not only in humans but also in a variety of other animals, suggesting that male and female brains manage spatial representations differently.

Natural selection ensures that males and females have basic navigational skills. Both meet the same challenges for reward and risk in food gathering and other life-perpetuating activities. Sexual selection might start to mold differences when males of a species are polygamous, because the males might need better spatial skills to find available females for sex and then return home (Figure 15.12). In trying to test the hypothesis that polygamous males have greater spatial skills than females, we run into a problem: Over 95% of mammalian species are polygamous. In fact, verifiable sex differences in spatial skills have been discovered in rats, mice, and humans. The best way to test this hypothesis would be to use a species with both monogamous and polygamous strains, and to evaluate each group's spatial skills.

Figure 15.12 Typical home range patterns for polygamous versus monogamous mammals. **(a)** For many polygamous species, male home ranges overlap with numerous, smaller female ranges. **(b)** Females and males in monogamous species in which parenting by both sexes is necessary for the raising of young tend to have smaller, isomorphic home ranges.

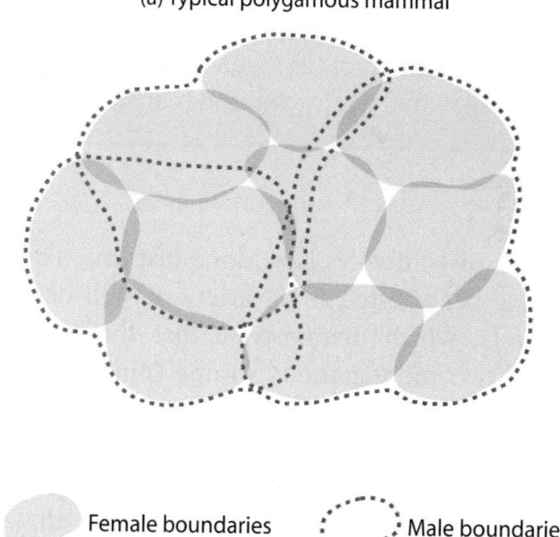

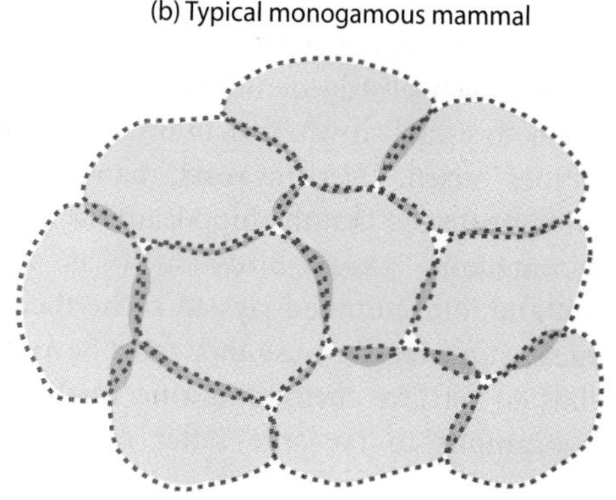

HOW THE BRAIN WORKS

Sexual Selection and Mathematics

The perennial topic of sex-related differences in mathematical abilities has been exhaustively studied by David Geary at Columbia University (1995). He observed that there are no sex-related differences in primary mathematical skills, even in nonhuman primates. This is true for all cultures. Yet there are sex-related differences in secondary mathematical skills—the kinds of math taught in schools in the industrialized world: Males consistently outperform females in word and geometry problems. Geary suggested that this capacity builds on the sort of male superiority in spatial skills that is seen in many species, such as the ones described in this chapter. In short, it is a secondary benefit to males, arising out of the sexual selection process that we have described.

Geary went on to show that sex hormones, which are the proximate mechanisms associated with sexual selection, appear to influence mathematical ability indirectly. He argued that sexual selection resulted in greater elaboration of the neurocognitive systems that support navigation in three-dimensional space in males than in females. These navigational systems have evolved in the three-dimensional physical world, so some information about the structure of the physical world is built into these systems. Features of Euclidean geometry appear to be a mathematical representation of the organization of the physical world; thus, an implicit understanding of aspects of geometry is built into the spatial system. In geometry, males do better than females because evolution has provided males with more built-in knowledge of geometry. These same spatial skills can be used to solve other types of math problems, such as word problems, because solving word problems is much easier if important information in the problems is diagrammed or spatially represented.

The same study also observed that many sex differences are found in social styles and interests, which play into the superior acquired math skills of males. Because of these differences, males are more likely to engage in mathematical problems, further enhancing their ability.

Studies of wild voles have done just this. These rodents have been tested in a variety of well-developed spatial tests, which demonstrate that the geographic ranges of two monogamous strains (pine and prairie voles) do not differ (Figure 15.13). In contrast, polygamous male and female meadow voles demonstrate huge differences in range size. Gaulin and his colleagues confirmed these spatial differences by testing the same species in laboratory spatial tasks. They found that polygamous males with larger range sizes had better spatial skills (Figure 15.14).

Once the differences in spatial abilities between the two sexes had been clearly demonstrated, researchers became eager to establish whether brain structures for spatial abilities varied. Over the years, many investigators have demonstrated that the hippocampus is crucial to spatial memory tasks. Birds such as titmice, nuthatches, and loudmouthed jays all cache their food over a large spatial area. Because they must have superb spatial skills to retrieve their food, one might expect their hippocampus to be large (after correcting for whole-brain volume) when compared to birds that do not store food in this manner. This is exactly what researchers found in a number of species, including the vole (Figure 15.15).

Lucy Jacobs and her colleagues at the University of California, Berkeley (1990), asked similar questions about the kangaroo rat. In two species of these animals, she found that the hippocampus is larger in males, which range more widely than females, than in their female counterparts. Just as fascinating is the cowbird, a species whose females sneak their eggs into the nests of other species. The cowbird's timing has to be just right, and she has to search a wide area to find the unsuspecting host nest. As you might predict, a female cowbird's hippocampus is much larger than a male cowbird's hippocampus. Males do none of these wide-ranging activities; they are the avian equivalent of couch potatoes.

Hormones play a fascinating role in the development of spatial abilities (Dawson et al., 1973). Investigators showed that sex-typical patterns of maze

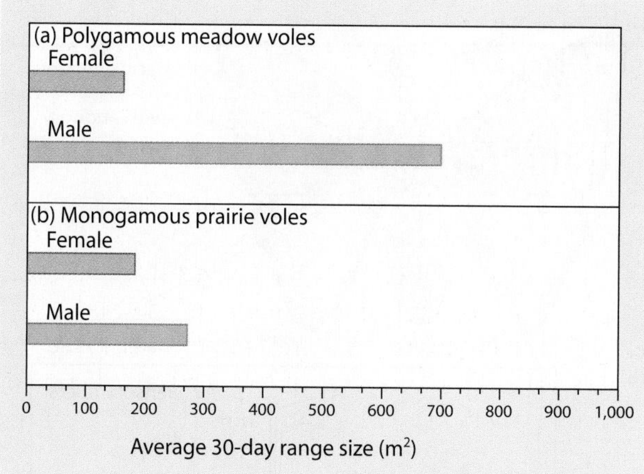

Figure 15.13 Average range area of polygamous meadow voles **(a)** and monogamous prairie voles **(b)** over 30 days.

Figure 15.14 Gender-specific performance in symmetrical mazes by monogamous prairie voles **(a)** and polygamous meadow voles **(b)**.

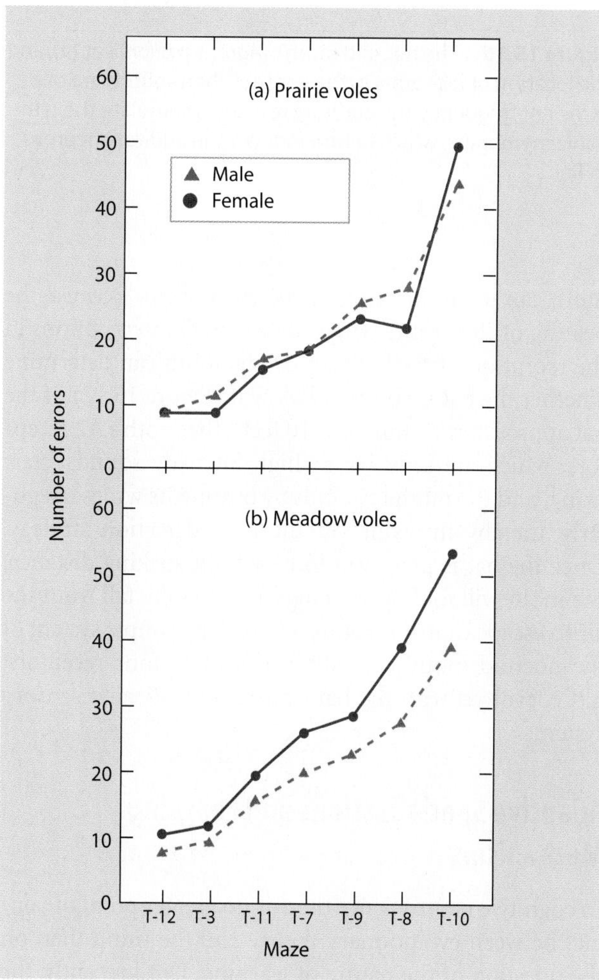

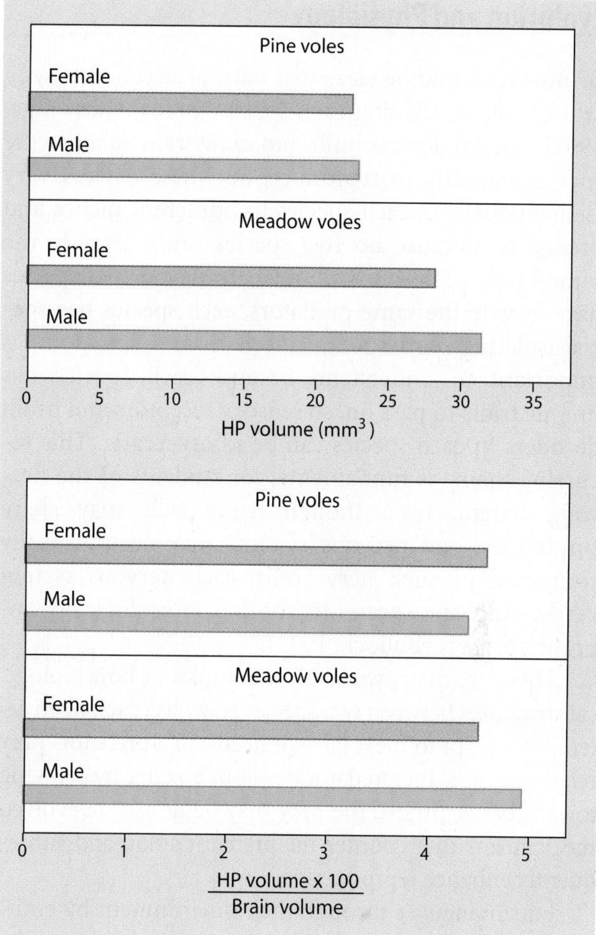

Figure 15.15 Comparison of hippocampal volume for monogamous pine voles and polygamous meadow voles.

performance can be reversed by the early administration of appropriate hormones. How can hormones affect the genetic blueprint for sex differences such as spatial skills?

The expression of sexual differences involves developmental events occurring during the fetal stage. The true genetic differences between males and females are slight, and they are expressed by factors such as the local hormone environment. For example, in humans who have Turner's syndrome, a neuroendocrine genetic disorder, the gonads remain undifferentiated. As a result, a phenotypic female deprived of androgen and estrogen during development has spatial abilities significantly below her verbal skills. The same is true for males with low androgen levels during development, such as in Klinefelter's syndrome, another genetically based neuroendocrine disorder. They, too, exhibit depressed spatial skills.

Evolution and Physiology

By now it should be clear that natural selection plays a crucial role in shaping each species' brain (Gazzaniga, 1992). Special devices built into each brain enhance the species' capacity to reproduce, but these devices vary tremendously, as each species has different niches and predators. Because no two species utilize exactly the same kinds of resources, and because no two species have exactly the same predators, each species has special isolating reproduction mechanisms. This point is important to understand because each species has unique traits to pass on, so sensory receptors and brain decoders in each species can be idiosyncratic. This recurring theme is fundamental for students of the nervous system. Even though nerve cells may share similarities, and nervous systems may be universally composed of such nerve cells, each nervous system varies from one species to another in ecologically appropriate ways (Bullock, 1993).

There are many wonderful examples of how biological structures between two species coevolve, each in an attempt to adapt to meet its own needs. In a predator–prey relationship, as the predator develops an edge by evolving toward better fitness, the prey may demonstrate evolved mechanisms that counter the predator's skill and subsequently enhance reproduction.

Bats maneuver through their environment by emitting high-frequency sound waves and detecting the weak echoes of those sounds off surfaces. The bat's nervous system has evolved sophisticated adaptations that enable the bat to be sensitive to these weak echoes. As the bat approaches an object, such as a moth, it emits more sound waves to gain exact information on the object's direction and distance. Because of their mode of transportation, flying insects give the bat more clues. As an insect moves its wings for flight, rhythmic reflections of the bat's sound waves strike the upper and lower surfaces of the insect's wings and return to the bat. The bat uses these echoes to distinguish between moths and tree leaves. With such an accurate detection system, it is hard to believe bats' prey stand a chance of survival.

Prey such as the noctuid moth, however, have evolved adaptations to avoid becoming the next meal. The noctuid moth has two ears, each with only two receptors, the A1 and A2 receptors, with which to perceive an approaching bat (Figure 15.16). The A1 receptor responds to low-intensity sounds such as those from a bat 3 to 30 m (10 to 100 feet) away. The moth's ears work as ours do to locate a sound source; the moth relies on its knowledge that the receptor closer to the sound will be activated slightly before the receptor that is farther from it. In this way, the moth can tell if the bat is to its left or right. Because the beating of the moth's wings makes small interruptions in the reception of the bat's signal, the moth can determine whether the bat is above or below it (Figure 15.17). If the bat approaches within 3 m (10 feet), the moth's A2 receptors, which are sensitive to high-intensity sounds, start firing, and the moth responds by beating its wings irregularly, thereby throwing off the bat's detection strategy. Once the bat is perceived to be within striking distance, the moth will fold up its wings and literally fall from the air to escape capture (Figure 15.18). The simple system of the noctuid moth, consisting of a mere four receptors, has coevolved with the bat's more sophisticated sensory system.

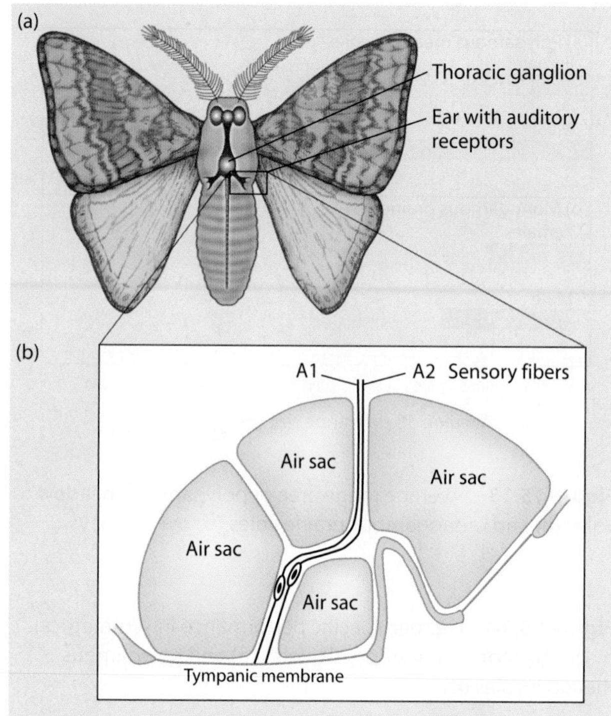

Figure 15.16 The noctuid moth's (*Agrotis ypsilon*) ear **(a)**, and the location of receptors in the ear **(b)**. When sounds are of a sufficient frequency, the auditory receptors stimulate the tympanic membrane, which in turn induces the auditory neurons to fire.

Adaptive Specializations and Learning Mechanisms

In cognitive neuroscience there is no greater point of contact between evolutionary theory and the mind than on the question of the nature of learning. Until recently, the leading theory of learning posited that the brains of

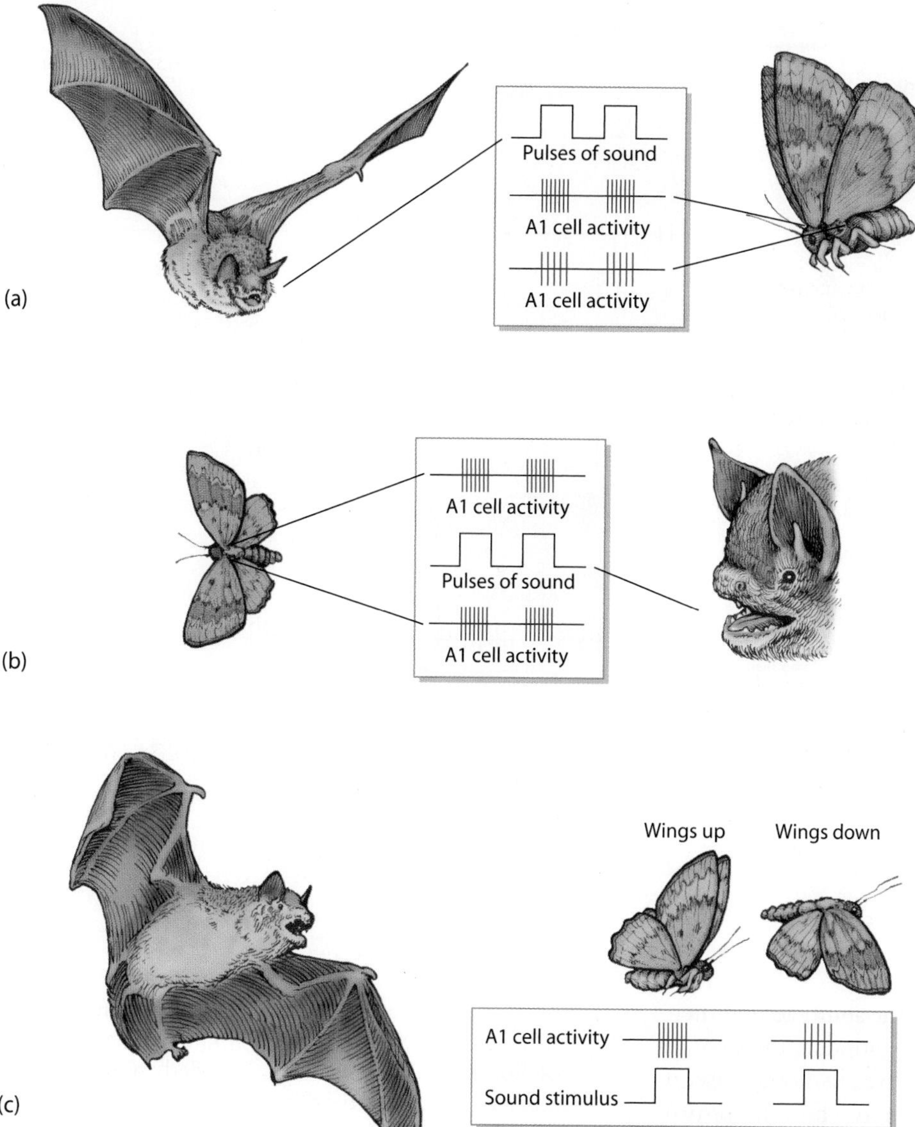

Figure 15.17 Noctuid moths can detect the presence of a bat. **(a)** Differential firing of the bilaterally located A1 receptors indicates from which direction, left or right, a bat is approaching. The receptor that fires with a higher frequency is closer to the source of the sound and thus indicates the direction from which the bat approaches. **(b)** Symmetrical firing of the A1 receptors on either side of the moth indicates that the bat is directly behind the moth. **(c)** The interruption of the bat's sounds due to the location of the moth's beating wings indicates whether the bat is approaching from above or below.

animals and humans have a learning system with a general-purpose capacity to acquire information during any and all kinds of tasks. Indeed, the idea of simple associationism was prevalent and, in early American experimental hands, became known as *stimulus–response*, or *SR*, *psychology*. With the right reinforcement contingencies and the right brain state, learning could proceed with ease.

This dominant view has changed in the past few years. Leading the charge has been Randy Gallistel (1995), at the University of California, Los Angeles. He argues for the idea that there are many learning mechanisms, each computationally specialized for solving problems. He takes the strong view that the association formation mechanisms so ubiquitously touted by psychologists are not even responsible for classical and instrumental conditioning. To support his ideas, Gallistel recounts how migratory thrushes must learn the center of rotation of the night sky when they are mere nestlings. This knowledge, gained as a young bird, is called upon only in adulthood when the bird uses knowledge of the night sky's celestial pole to maintain a southerly route during its first migratory flight (Figure 15.19). A simple associationism could never explain this behavioral capacity, because the knowledge gained as a young nestling is not used at that stage of its life. There are no contingencies; the knowledge is called on only at a later time.

We have no shortage of examples of what is called *nonassociative learning*. The field of *ethology*—the study of animal behavior in the real world as opposed to the world of the laboratory rat maze—has many rich examples. An often-cited example has to do with the capacity

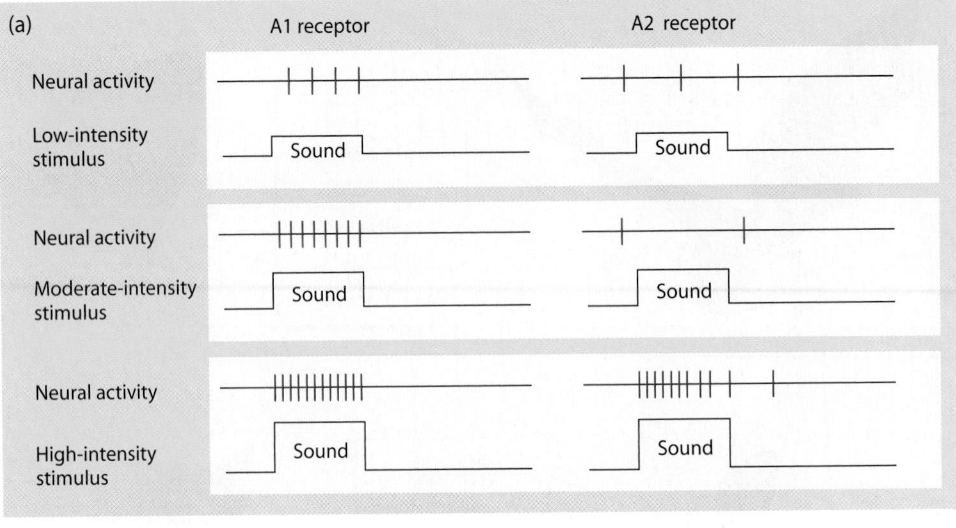

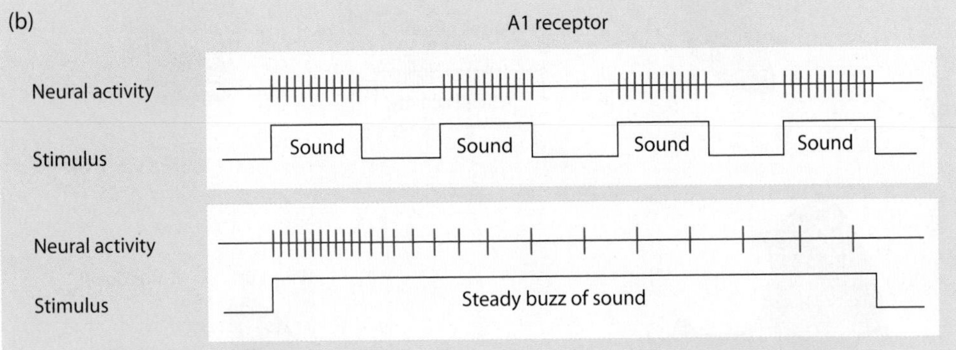

Figure 15.18 The simplistic A1 and A2 receptors work together to process information about sounds of different intensities and frequencies. **(a)** When the bat is farther away, sounds of lower intensity affect the A1 receptor but not the A2 receptor. As the intensity increases, the A2 receptor starts firing to give the moth more detailed information about the location of the sound source. **(b)** The A1 receptor reacts strongly to high-frequency sounds that are detected in pulses. If the stimulus is a steady sound of the same frequency and intensity, the A1 receptor will cease firing after a short while. This cessation prevents the moth from being overly sensitive to persistent, irrelevant sounds in its environment, and reserves the functioning of these receptors for ecologically important situations, such as detecting a hunting bat.

of insects to learn *dead reckoning*, the ability to find their way home after foraging, without retracing their entire circuitous route. When the ant leaves its home base, it computes and stores information on how to return home (Figure 15.20).

These sorts of examples have led several ethologists to the view that an animal has a constellation of specialized learning mechanisms. The learning capacity exhibited in one situation works only in that situation and no other. Peter Marler (1991) at the University of California, Davis, and others called these cases examples of *problem-specific learning mechanisms.* In cognitive neuroscience, when we are trying to understand how the brain enables learning, we must realize that there may be several mechanisms, not just one. For example, in Chapter 7 we saw that the cerebellum is essential for representing the temporal relationship between a tone and a forthcoming air puff in order to respond at the right time.

Gallistel (1995) argued that, although there are many different learning mechanisms, there may still be some commonalities. The basic computational operations may be quite similar. As he puts it,

> In computer terms, they may all use the same basic instruction set. (Of course, they may not. At a time when we cannot specify the instruction set underlying any computation of any substantial complexity, we are in no position to say whether different complex computations use the same elementary computational operations.)
>
> The other thing that all learning mechanisms must do is store and retrieve the values of variables. The bird has to store values that represent the center of rotation of the night sky and retrieve them when it determines what orientation to adopt with respect to whatever constellation of circumpolar stars it can see at the moment. The foraging bee must store the distance and direction of the food source and retrieve that information when it gives the dance that transmits the values to other foragers. The dead-reckoning mechanism must store the values that represent the animal's current position and then add to them whenever the animal moves, because dead reckoning amounts to keeping a running sum of displacements.

These various examples from the animal world show us that, from an evolutionary perspective, humans

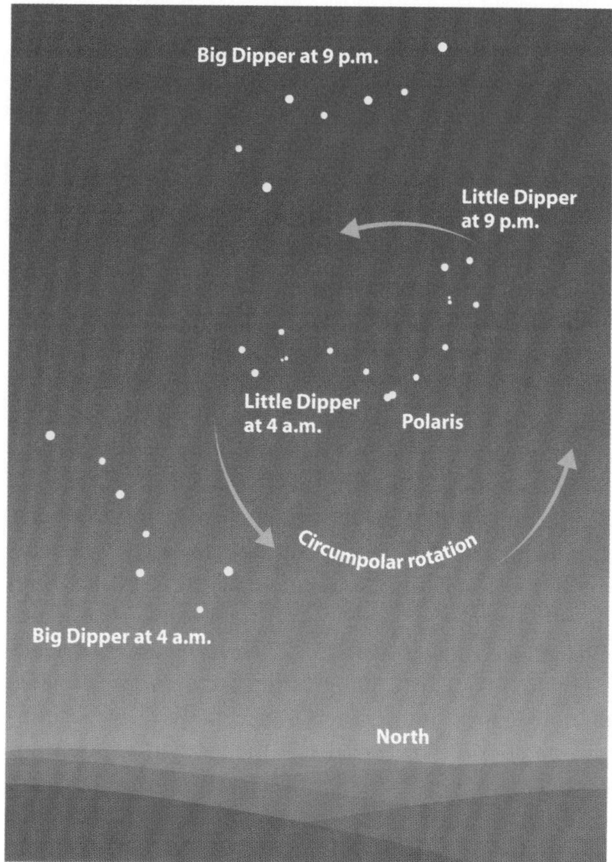

Figure 15.19 Two of the most prominent circumpolar constellations are the Big Dipper and the Little Dipper. Here, the Big and Little Dippers are seen as they would appear at 9:00 p.m. and 4:00 a.m. from temperate latitudes in the Northern Hemisphere in the spring. Migratory birds learn the directions north and south by observing the rotation of the circumpolar stars around the celestial pole (near Polaris now).

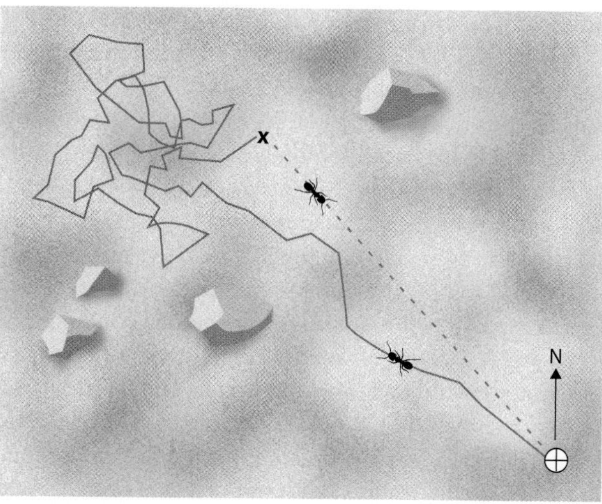

Figure 15.20 A foraging ant's path. The solid line represents the outward, searching journey until food was found at the location marked "x". Even after making numerous turns in all directions, however, the ant is able to take a direct route (dead reckoning) home, as designated by the dashed line.

must possess special devices for learning. William James stated that the human has more instincts than animals, not fewer. In this setting, Noam Chomsky and Steven Pinker argued for the view that there is a special learning module for human language. It has specific features and capacities and most likely a definite neural organization. In short, the work on animals, where specialized systems are easily identified, raises provocative notions about the human brain's organization and cognitive powers and the evolution of human-specific cognitive traits.

EVOLUTIONARY INSIGHTS INTO HUMAN BRAIN ORGANIZATION

A major assumption in neuroscience is being challenged: the idea that a larger brain with more cells is responsible for the greater computational capacity of the human being. This traditional view is exemplified by the following passage:

> Simple changes in the genetic control of growth can have far-reaching effects on form. The human brain differs from the chimpanzee brain in its extreme development of cortical structures, in particular the cerebellar cortex and the association areas of the neocortex. The proportions of these areas are predictable from rules governing the construction of primate brains of differing size. Furthermore, there appears to be a uniformity in the number and type of cells used in building neocortical areas; the human brain follows the general pattern for mammals. Even with two speech areas we believe we can detect regions in the monkey brain that are alike in cellular organization. The evolution of the human brain is characterized more by expansion of areas than by radical reconstructions (Passingham, 1982).

The uniqueness of the human brain, it is commonly believed, can be traced to its large size. It has more neurons and more cortical columns than does the brain of any other animal, and in that truth lies (somewhere) the secret to human experience. This point is entirely consistent with many other observations of humans and animals. The disproportionately large representation of some sensory and motor regions of the cortex in animals and humans is well established. The recognized correlation between the large inferior colliculus for echolocating bats and dolphins, and the enlarged optic lobes for species of fish that use vision for navigation are well known. In short, the idea that a larger brain structure reflects an increase in function is prevalent.

Even Charles Darwin promoted the idea that big brains explain the uniqueness of the human condition. In *The Descent of Man and Selection in Relation to Sex* (1871), he wrote that there is no fundamental difference in the mental faculties of humans and the higher mammals. He went on to add that the difference in mind between humans and the higher animals, great as it is, is certainly one of degree and not of kind. He did not want to be part of any thinking that there may be critical qualitative differences between the subhuman primate and humans.

Darwin left the actual anatomy to his colleague Thomas Henry Huxley. At that time, Richard Owen, another anatomist, maintained that the human brain contained a special structure: the hippocampus minor. Yet Huxley proved that this structure was also found in other primates, thereby undercutting the idea that human and primate brains were qualitatively different. Thus Darwin, the genius who had articulated natural selection and diversity, argued for a straight-line evolution between primates and humans. Organisms, the product of selection pressures, displayed rich diversity in the evolution of species. But when it came to brain and mind, Darwin thought the human brain was merely a large primate brain, a nervous system with a monotonic relation to its closest ancestor.

Nonetheless, a lot of evidence shows that the human brain's unique capacities do not rely on an increase in cell number so much as on the appearance of specialized circuits (Hutsler & Galuske, 2003). That the human brain has more cells does not explain greater capacities. Evolutionary perspectives would find the human brain adapted to its own biological niche, and one would predict differences in brain organization from other animals. After millions of years of natural selection, we have accumulated circuits that enable us to carry out specific aspects of human cognition. In short, just as comparative neurobiologists have demonstrated the presence of specialized circuitry in lower animals that reflect adaptations to niches, similar demonstrations have been made in humans.

Let's look at more evidence for specialized circuits. Consider the human brain's two halves: left and right. We know that the left cortex is specialized for language and speech, and the right has specializations of its own (see Chapter 11). Each half is the same size and has roughly the same number of nerve cells. The cortices are connected by the corpus callosum. The total, linked cortical mass contributes to our unique human intelligence. What would happen to intelligence if the halves were disconnected, leaving the left operating independently of the right, and vice versa? Would split-brain patients lose half of their cognitive capacity because the left, talking hemisphere would now operate with only half of the total brain cortex?

A cardinal feature of split-brain research is that, after cerebral hemispheres are disconnected, the patient's verbal IQ remains intact, and the problem-solving capacity of the left hemisphere, such as hypothesis formation, remains unchanged. Although there can be deficits in recall capacity and in other performance measures, the total capacity for problem solving remains unaffected. Isolating essentially half of the cortex from the dominant left hemisphere, then, causes no major change in cognitive functions. Following surgery, the integrated 1,200- to 1,300-g brain becomes two isolated 600- to 650-g brains, each about the size of a chimpanzee's brain. The capacity of the left half remains unchanged from its preoperative level—strong evidence that cortical cell numbers do not fully account for human intelligence.

Many lines of anatomical and physiological research suggest that cortical areas within a species contain variable proportions of morphologically and neurochemically defined cell types. For example, primary and secondary visual, somatosensory, and auditory cortices express varying distributions of specific nerve fibers, and the density of certain nerve cells, called *chandelier cells*, differs between prefrontal and visual cortical regions (Lewis & Lund, 1990).

Cortical connectivity and physiology vary among species, possibly reflecting each organism's niche. For example, the physiological properties of dendritic spines in humans might differ from those in other animals. Gordon Shepherd and his colleagues at Yale University (1989) studied presumed normal cortical tissue that had been removed from epileptic patients. Comparing the membrane and synaptic properties of human and rodent dentate granule cells, they noticed important variations. First, humans had less spike-frequency adaptation in comparison to rodents; second, only feedback was inhibited in human tissue, whereas rodent tissue showed both feed-forward and feedback inhibition—consistent with Shepherd's neuronal modeling. This work suggests that the simple addition of a few calcium channels to the dendritic spines allows them to handle vastly complex computations, leading to more information-processing capability. These suggestive study results are exciting and may point to new ways of thinking about variations in neuronal physiology among species (Williamson et al., 1993).

Nonhuman primate and human visual systems also have different organizational properties. When comparing, for example, the anterior commissure between humans and other primates, it is easy to see how the species differ in neural organization. The anterior commissure is one of the neural connections between the two halves of the brain. It is the smaller of the two cortical connections, second in size to the huge corpus callosum. When this structure is left intact but the corpus callosum is sectioned, visual information easily transfers in monkeys but not in humans. Thus, primate species vary in how they transfer visual information between hemispheres.

Examples of system-level variations between primates and other lower animals are abundant, but less attention is paid to the variations between nonhuman primates and humans. Yet some observations, like the one above, indicate major anatomical differences between two closely related species, even though the monkey's visual system and the human's visual system have virtually identical sensory capacities. Psychophysical measurements of acuity, color, and other parameters reveal identical sensitivities. Additionally, even though the gray matter volume of the primary visual cortex (V1) in humans is three times larger than in the rhesus monkey and five times larger than in owl monkeys, this cortical area has the same number of cells in rhesus monkeys and humans.

In grasping the differences between monkey and human behavior, one has to consider the variations in the neuronal organization of each visual system. Can these differences be understood in relation to the connectivity of major processing areas or to the level of synaptic function? We do not know.

Arguing about similarities between species has been the target of much criticism. Take the problem of intelligence. It is naive anthropomorphism to apply the concept of human intelligence to the behavior of animals. It is simply a fact that each species has developed behavioral capabilities that are advantageous to its own survival, and that each member of that species possesses these capacities. There have been many attempts to raise the intelligence of a rat by selective breeding. All have failed. A rat that might be better at running a maze turns out to be lousy at discrimination learning. Our human brains are larger because they have more devices for solving problems, and the devices are shared by all members of the species. It is not likely that the variations seen in our own species' capacity to solve problems will vary with brain size; recent direct measures have shown that there is no correlation.

Even though brain size cannot explain the unique capacities of the human, Noam Chomsky of the Massachusetts Institute of Technology (1957) favored the view that, although language is deeply biological in nature, it is not a product of natural selection. Chomsky left open the possibility that language is the result, the concomitant, of massive interactions of millions of neurons. So, in the heart of the great Chomsky, the one who argued deeply for the biological basis of language, the idea that bigger is better lingers.

Steven Pinker (1997a) challenged this bit of backsliding by Chomsky. Cranking up his unusually insightful and lively style, Pinker chided his colleague, "If Chomsky maintains that grammar shows signs of complex design, but is skeptical that natural selection manufactured it, what alternative does he have in mind? What he repeatedly mentions is physical law. Just as the flying fish is compelled to return to the water and calcium-filled bones are compelled to be white, human brains might, for all we know, be compelled to contain circuits for Universal Grammar."

Chomsky wrote (Pinker, 1994),

> These skills [e.g., learning a grammar] may well have arisen as a concomitant of structural properties of the brain that developed for other reasons. Suppose that there was selection for bigger brains, more cortical surface, hemispheric specialization for analytic processing, or many other structural properties that can be imagined. The brain that evolved might well have all sorts of special properties that are not individually selected; there would be no miracle in this—only the normal workings of evolution. We have no idea, at present, how physical laws apply when 10^{10} neurons are placed in an object the size of a basketball, under the special conditions that arose during human evolution.

Pinker (1994) cleverly responds,

> We may have no idea—just as we do not know how physical laws apply under the special conditions of hurricanes sweeping through junkyards—but it seems unlikely that an undiscovered corollary of the laws of physics causes human-size and -shaped brains to develop the circuitry for Universal Grammar.

Neuroscientists have had a hard time accepting the view that big brains may be a by-product of other processes for establishing the uniqueness of each species' nervous system. Yet biologists have known for years how specialized circuits define differences between fish and reptile, reptile and mammal, snail and octopus. It is only logical that this information would help define the neural processes supporting unique human capacities, especially language, and that big brains (corrected for body size) might get bigger because they collect more specialized circuits.

SUMMARY

Complex capacities like language and social behavior are not constructs that arise out of our brain simply because it is bigger than a chimpanzee's brain. Instead, these capacities reflect specialized devices that natural selection has built into our brains. Individuals within a species vary, and if this variation produces a slightly unique state of affairs that helps our brains make better decisions about enhancing reproductive success, the new capacities will survive. Variations that further enhance the capacity in question will also survive. The brain was not built in a day. It started as something that worked a little bit, which was better than something that did not work at all. As it evolved, it became the finely tuned device it is now, with language and other mental abilities. The positive-feedback mechanism of natural selection, not experience, builds complexity into organisms.

The structure of animal bodies and brains can vary dramatically, and trying to deduce similar features of brain organization and unique features is difficult. Therefore, the strategy that comparative neuroscientists use is crucial. Bullock described three aims of comparative neuroscience: roots, rules, and relevance. By *roots*, he means the evolutionary history of the brain and behavior. How did the brain come to have its current organization? What led us to our current state? The *rules* of change are the mechanisms that result in modifications to the nervous system, as well as the constraints under which evolving nervous systems develop. Finally, the *relevance* of our observations refers to how the principles of organization and function found in one species can be extrapolated to other species, including humans.

Finally, a multitude of commonalities connect all species and lend strength to much of biological research. At the same time, species exhibit crucial differences, such as those reviewed here, and human brain research has uncovered unique aspects of human behavior (e.g., language) that may be supported by specialized and specifically evolved neural circuitry.

KEY TERMS

adaptation
alleles
comparative neuroscience
convergent evolution
ethology
evolutionary psychology
exaptation
fitness
genes
genetic pleiotropy
genetic specificity
genotype
heritable
homology
homoplasy
mutation
natural selection
neuroethology
out-group comparison
phenotype
plesiomorphic
principle of parsimony
recombination
sociobiology
trait

TAKE-HOME MESSAGES

General

- Darwin's great theory of evolution (natural selection) is that behaviors that encourage survival and reproduction are adaptive, and thus have a high probability of being passed on to future generations. In contrast, behaviors that discourage survival are maladaptive and should not be passed on to future generations.
- Infanticide, the intentional killing of an infant of one's own species, occurs in monkeys, lions, woodpeckers, and humans, among others.
- Although at first infanticide appears at odds with evolutionary theory, it can be seen as evolutionarily beneficial when one realizes that it is often a nonparental male who kills the young to gain access to the mother to increase his chances of

reproducing. If resources are scarce, the mother may also kill her young (especially the weak), to increase the chances of survival of the healthiest offspring.

Evolutionary Psychology

- Evolutionary psychologists use an evolutionary framework to help understand cognitive behavior.
- The brain is a result of evolutionary compromise and is therefore imperfect, though nearly ideal.
- Traits or characteristics have no absolute value. Instead, their value is measured by how well they contribute to the individual fitness within a particular environment.
- The discovery of DNA and its importance in transferring information from one organism to another was central to the field of evolutionary biology.
- A phenotype is an observable trait or set of characteristics of an organism; a genotype is the genetic composition of an organism.
- Adaptation is a characteristic of an organism that contributes to its fitness; exaptation is the process whereby a structure that serves a particular function is co-opted for another, very different function.
- Ethology is the study of animal behavior; neuroethology is the study of the neurobiology of animal behavior.
- Sociobiology, the study of the biological basis of social behavior, allows for a new view of natural selection that looks at the propagation of the genes of a colony, rather than just the individual.

Comparative Neuroscience

- Brodmann compared cytoarchitecture across species and found that some areas, such as BA17, are common among many species.
- Comparative anatomists compare the brains of various animals to deduce how brains are constructed by evolutionary processes.
- The three aims of comparative neuroscience are (a) roots (the evolutionary history of brain and behavior), (b) rules (the mechanisms that give rise to changes in the nervous system), and (c) relevance (the general principles of organization and functions that can be extrapolated from a particular animal studied to all animals).
- Genetic isolation (e.g., the separation of genetically similar groups by shifts in landmasses or water) can lead to speciation in which the isolated groups cannot interbreed and subsequently begin to diverge significantly in genotype or phenotype.
- Homologous features or traits have been retained from a common ancestor but do not necessarily have the same function across species. Homoplastic structures look the same but do not necessarily have a common ancestry.
- A plesiomorphic trait is a general feature of a group or lineage.
- Genetic specificity is the idea that one gene can be responsible for one trait; genetic pleiotropy is the idea that one gene can have many separate functions.
- Genetic recombination is the process by which the array of alleles in existing genes are changed.
- We tend to have an anthropocentric (human-centered) view of life, with humans at the top and insects at the bottom of the "phylogenetic scale." This view incorrectly suggests that evolution is linear or simply additive.
- Evolutionary scientists believe that the modern human brain was adapted to deal with the world of the Pleistocene hunter-gatherer of 100,000 years ago.
- The current use of a structure may not indicate its adaptive significance, but it can be important for its continued maintenance.
- Humans are good at detecting potential violations of conditional rules, especially when they are described in a social context, because it is evolutionarily advantageous to have this capability. We are not as effective, however, at detecting descriptive rule violations, which have little evolutionary advantage.
- Some people believe that sexual selection should be distinguished from natural selection because some traits (e.g., the colored feathers of a male peacock) have been selected for not by virtue of their importance to survival, but only because they increase the likelihood of sexual contact.
- From an evolutionary perspective, animals must possess special devices for learning. Some (e.g., Steven Pinker and Noam Chomsky) believe that humans have a special learning module for language.
- The difference between the human brain and that of other animals is not just its increased size. Rather, the human brain's unique capacities appear to rely not on cell number so much as on specialized circuits.

THOUGHT QUESTIONS

1. A hypothetical cortical area—let's call it *DF*—has been newly discovered in macaque monkeys. The investigators who first described it hypothesize that it is involved in tactile object discrimination and propose that it might be present in humans as well. How can they test this hypothesis without performing experiments using functional MRI or PET?
2. What are the three major aims of comparative neuroscience? Briefly explain each.
3. Why is the study of convergent evolution of brain structures or fields important?
4. An area MT has been described in humans. This region does not reside at the tip of the superior temporal sulcus as it does in all other primates that have been investigated. Furthermore, the cortical architecture (how it looks in neural tissue that has been histologically processed) is quite different from that in other primates. Although it becomes active in response to moving stimuli, so do a number of other areas of human neocortex. Is this field homologous to the area MT described in other primates? Why or why not?
5. Should a genetic explanation be sought for every behavior? Explain your answer.

SUGGESTED READING

BULLOCK, T. H. (1984). Comparative neuroscience holds promise for a quiet revolution. *Science, 225,* 473–478.

JACOB, F. (1977). Evolution and tinkering. *Science, 196,* 1161–1166.

MERZENICH, M. M., & KAAS, J. H. (1980). *Principles of organization of sensory-perceptual systems of mammals.* New York: Academic Press.

PINKER, S. (1997). *How the mind works.* New York: Norton.

WILSON, E. O. (1975). *Sociobiology: The new synthesis.* Cambridge, MA: Belknap Press of Harvard University Press.

GLOSSARY

A1 See *primary auditory cortex.*

ABR See *auditory brainstem response.*

access awareness Our ability to report and act on information in our minds. Compare *phenomenal awareness.*

achromatopsia A selective disorder of color perception resulting from a lesion or lesions of the central nervous system, typically in the ventral pathway of the visual cortex. In achromatopsia, the deficit in color perception is disproportionately greater than that associated with form perception. Colors, if perceived at all, tend to be muted.

acquired alexia See *alexia.*

acquisition The registration of inputs in sensory buffers and sensory analysis stages.

action potential The active or regenerative electrical signal that is required for synaptic communication. Action potentials are propagated along the axon and result in the release of neurotransmitter.

adaptation A characteristic of a living thing that contributes to its fitness. Compare *exaptation.*

affective Having an emotional value, either positive or negative; not neutral.

aggregate field theory The belief that the whole brain participates in behavior.

aggression A socially inappropriate expression of emotion, marked by an intent to dominate or control another's actions through the infliction of physical harm or verbal assault.

agnosia A neurological syndrome in which disturbances of perceptual recognition cannot be attributed to impairments in basic sensory processes. Agnosia can be restricted to a single modality, such as vision or audition.

agrammatic aphasia Difficulty producing and/or understanding the structure of sentences. Agrammatic aphasia is seen in brain-damaged patients who may speak using only content words, leaving out function words such as *the* and *a.*

akinetopsia A selective disorder of motion perception resulting from a lesion or lesions of the central nervous system. Patients with akinetopsia fail to perceive stimulus movement, created by either a moving object or their own motion, in a smooth manner. In severe cases, the patient may only infer motion by noting that the position of objects in the environment has changed over time, as if the patient were constructing dynamics through a series of successive static snapshots.

alexia A neurological syndrome in which the ability to read is disrupted. Alexia is frequently referred to as *acquired alexia* to indicate that it results from a neurological disturbance such as a stroke, usually including the occipitoparietal region of the left hemisphere. In contrast, refers to problems in reading that are apparent during childhood development. The phrases and *developmental dyslexia* are commonly used to indicate that reading is abnormal, either from a neurological disturbance of as part of development.

alleles Alternate forms of genes.

alpha motor neurons The neurons that terminate on muscle fibers, causing contractions that produce movements. Alpha motor neurons originate in the spinal cord and exit through the ventral root of the cord.

amnesia The loss of memory.

amobarbital A barbiturate used to produce rapid and brief anesthesia.

amygdala Groups of neurons anterior to the hippocampus in the medial temporal lobe that are involved in emotional processing.

analytic processing Perceptual analysis that emphasizes the component parts of an object. Reading is thought to be a prime example of analytic processing in that the recognition of words requires the analysis of at least some of the component letters. Compare *holistic processing.*

angiography An imaging method used to evaluate the circulatory system in the brain.

anterior cingulate cortex Anterior portion of the cingulate cortex, located below the frontal lobe along the medial surface. This region is characterized by a primitive cytoarchitecture (three-layered cortex) and is part of the interface between the frontal lobe and the limbic system. The anterior cingulate cortex is implicated in various executive functions, such as response monitoring, error detection, and attention.

anterograde amnesia The loss of the ability to form new memories. Compare *retrograde amnesia.*

aphasia A language deficit following brain damage or disease.

apperceptive agnosia A form of agnosia associated with deficits in the operation of higher-level perceptual analyses. A patient with apperceptive agnosia may recognize an object when seen from a typical viewpoint. However, if the orientation is unusual, or the object is occluded by shadows, recognition deteriorates. Compare *associative agnosia.*

apraxia A neurological syndrome characterized by loss of skilled or purposeful movement that cannot be attributed to weakness or an inability to innervate the muscles. Apraxia results from lesions of the cerebral cortex, usually in the left hemisphere.

apraxia of speech Difficulty pronouncing words.

arcuate fasciculus A white matter tract that connects the posterior temporal region with frontal brain regions and is believed to transmit language-related information between the posterior and anterior brain regions.

area MT A region in the visual cortex containing cells that are highly responsive to motion. Area MT is part of the dorsal pathway, thought to play a role not only in motion perception but also in representing spatial information.

area V4 A region in the visual cortex containing cells that are thought to process color information.

association cortex The volume of the neocortex that is not strictly sensory or motor, but receives inputs from multiple sensorimotor modalities.

associationism The theory that the aggregate of a person's experience determines the course of mental development.

associative agnosia A form of agnosia in which the patient has difficulty linking perceptual representations with long-term knowledge of the percepts. For example, the patient may be able to identify that two pictures are of the same object, yet fail to demonstrate an understanding of what the object is used for or where it is likely to be found. Compare *apperceptive agnosia.*

ataxia A movement disorder associated with lesions or atrophy of the cerebellum. Ataxic movements are clumsy and erratic, even though muscle strength is normal.

auditory brainstem response (ABR) Electrical responses from ascending auditory pathways in the brainstem recorded from electrodes on the human scalp using signal averaging to extract the small signals from the ongoing background EEG.

autism A neurological disorder characterized by deficits in social cognition and social communication often associated with an increase in repetitive behavior or obsessive interests.

autonomic motor system See *autonomic nervous system.*

autonomic nervous system Also *autonomic motor system* or *visceral motor system.* The body system that regulates heart rate, breathing, and glandular secretions and may become activated during emotional arousal, initiating a "fight or flight" behavioral response to a stimulus. It has two subdivisions, the sympathetic and parasympathetic branches.

awareness Our immediate experience of sensations, thoughts and feelings.

axon The process extending away from a neuron down which action potentials travel. The terminals of axons contact other neurons at synapses.

Balint's syndrome A disorder following bilateral occipitoparietal stroke, characterized by difficulty in perceiving visual objects. Patients with the disorder can correctly identify objects but have difficulty relating objects to one another. They tend to focus attention on one object to the exclusion of others when the objects are presented simultaneously.

basal ganglia A collection of five subcortical nuclei: the caudate, putamen, globus pallidus, subthalamic nucleus, and substantia nigra. The basal ganglia are involved in motor control and learning. Reciprocal neuronal loops project from cortical areas to the basal ganglia and back to the cortex. Two prominent basal ganglia disorders are Parkinson's disease and Huntington's disease.

BBB See *blood–brain barrier.*

behaviorism The theory that environment and learning are the primary factors in mental development, and that people should be studied by outside observation.

benefit An improvement in performance or physiological response as a function of selective attention.

biased competition model A theoretical model positing that attention acts at each stage of information processing in order to enable the relevant stimulus to influence the responses of neurons at that stage of processing.

blindsight Residual visual abilities within a field defect in the absence of awareness. Blindsight can be observed when there is damage in the primary visual cortex. The residual function is usually observed with indirect measures such as by prodding the patient to look at or point to the location of a stimulus, even if the patient denies having seen the stimulus.

blood–brain barrier (BBB) A physical barrier formed by the end feet of astrocytes between the blood vessels in the brain and the tissues of the brain. The BBB limits which materials in the blood can gain access to neurons in the nervous system.

blood oxygenation level–dependent (BOLD) Characterized by a dependence on the level of oxygen in the blood. Hemoglobin carries oxygen in the bloodstream, and when the oxygen is absorbed, the hemoglobin becomes deoxygenated. Deoxygenated hemoglobin is more sensitive, or paramagnetic than oxygenated hemoglobin. The magnetic detectors in a magnetic resonance imaging machine measure changes in the ratio of oxygenated to deoxygenated blood, or what is called the *BOLD signal.* When neural regions are active, this ratio increases as the blood supply to the active tissue increases.

BMI See *brain–machine interface.*

BOLD See *blood oxygenation level–dependent.*

bottleneck A stage of processing where not all of the inputs can gain access or pass through.

bradykinesia Slowness in the initiation and execution of movements. Bradykinesia is a prominent symptom in Parkinson's disease.

brain lesion Structural damage to the white or gray matter of the brain. Lesions result from many causes, including tumor, stroke, and degenerative disorders such as Alzheimer's disease.

brain–machine interface (BMI) A device that uses the interpretation of neuronal signals to perform desired operations with a mechanical device outside the body. For instance, signals recorded from neurons or EEG can be used to move a prosthetic arm.

brainstem The region of the nervous system that contains groups of motor and sensory nuclei, nuclei of widespread modulatory neurotransmitter systems, and white matter tracts of ascending sensory information and descending motor signals.

Broca's aphasia The oldest and perhaps best-studied form of aphasia, characterized by speech difficulties in the absence of severe comprehension problems. However, Broca's aphasics may also suffer from problems in fully comprehending grammatically complex sentences. Compare *Wernicke's aphasia.*

CAT See *computed tomography.*

categorical spatial relationship One manner of representing the spatial information of objects. Categorical spatial relationships capture basic relational information such as the relative position of two objects from a particular viewpoint. Compare *coordinate spatial relationship.*

category-specific deficit Recognition impairment that is restricted to a certain class of objects. Some rare individuals demonstrate an impairment in their ability to recognize living things, yet exhibit near-normal performance in recognizing nonliving things. Such deficits are useful in the development of models about how perceptual and semantic knowledge is organized in the brain.

cellular architecture See *cytoarchitectonics.*

central nervous system (CNS) The brain and spinal cord. Compare *peripheral nervous system.*

cerebellum Also known as "little cerebrum." A large, highly convoluted (infolded) structure located dorsal to the brainstem at the level of the pons. The cerebellum maintains (directly or indirectly) interconnectivity with widespread cortical, subcortical, brainstem, and spinal cord structures, and plays a role in various aspects of coordination ranging from locomotion to skilled, volitional movement.

cerebral cortex The layered sheet of neurons that overlies the forebrain. The cerebral cortex consists of neuronal subdivisions (areas) interconnected with other cortical areas, subcortical structures, and the cerebellum and spinal cortex.

cerebral specialization The adaptation of the activity in a particular brain region to subserve a given cognitive function or behavior.

characteristic See *trait.*

chemical senses The two senses that depend on environmental molecules for stimulation: taste and smell.

CNS See *central nervous system.*

cochlear nucleus A midbrain nucleus that is one of the primary receiving regions of the output from the cochlea of the inner ear. Axons from the cochlear nucleus project to the inferior colliculus, and from there to the medial geniculate nucleus of the thalamus and the auditory cortex.

cognitive control Processes that facilitate information processing. Control operations are thought to help coordinate activity across different neural regions; for example, the representation of a current goal in the prefrontal cortex can help control the retrieval of information in long-term memory. See also *executive functions.*

cognitive neuroscience The study of how the brain enables the mind.

cognitive psychology The branch of psychology that studies how the mind internally represents the external world and performs the mental computations required for all aspects of thinking. Cognitive psychologists study the vast set of mental operations associated with such things as perception, attention, memory, language, and problem solving.

commissure White matter tracts that cross from the left to the right side, or vice versa, of the central nervous system.

comparative neuroscience The investigation of the organization and mechanisms of the nervous systems of different species in order to understand the functions of specialized brain systems.

computed tomography (CT or CAT) An noninvasive neuroimaging method that provides images of internal structures such as the brain. CT is an advanced version of the conventional X-ray. Whereas conventional X-rays compress three-dimensional objects into two dimensions, CT allows for the reconstruction of three-dimensional space from the compressed two-dimensional images through computer algorithms.

conduction aphasia A form of aphasia that is considered a disconnection syndrome. Conduction aphasia may occur when the arcuate fasciculus, the pathway from Wernicke's area to Broca's area, is damaged, thereby disconnecting the posterior and anterior language areas.

conscious processing Information processing that involves attention and awareness. Compare *preconscious processing* and *subliminal processing.*

consciousness The human ability to be aware of some of the contents of mental activity and potentially describe these mental states to other individuals.

consolidation The process by which memory representations become stronger over time. Consolidation is believed to include changes in the brain system participating in the storage of information.

content-based hypothesis The proposal that memory systems are defined in terms of their content. An influential content-based hypothesis of working memory proposes that there are two distinct systems: one that keeps active selected verbal representations, and a second that keeps active selected visuospatial representations.

convergent evolution The process by which similar structures with similar functions arise independently in different species.

coordinate spatial relationship One manner of representing the spatial information of objects. Coordinate spatial relationships specify the exact positions of the objects and the distances between them. Compare *categorical spatial relationship.*

corpus callosum A fiber system composed of axons that connect the cortex of the two cerebral hemispheres.

corpuscle A globular mass of cells that are part of the somatosensory system.

cortical visual areas Regions of visual cortex that are identified on the basis of their distinct retinotopic maps. The areas are specialized to represent certain types of stimulus information, and through their integrated activity they provide the neural basis for visually based behavior.

corticogenesis The creation of the cortex during development: how neurons are born, are specified to be a certain neuronal type or class, and are placed in the correct anatomical position accordingly.

corticospinal tract Also *pyramidal tract.* A bundle of axons that originate in the cortex and terminate monosynaptically on alpha motor neurons and spinal interneurons in the spinal cord. Many of these fibers originate in the primary motor cortex, although some come from secondary motor areas. The corticospinal tract is important for the control of voluntary movements.

covert attention The ability to direct attention without overt alterations or changes in sensory receptors—for example, attending to a conversation without turning the eyes and head toward the speakers.

critical period Also *sensitive period.* A specific time range during development in which experience can maximally influence the organization and function of the nervous system. Critical periods for behavioral development likely correspond to specific stages of neural development, such as the formation of synaptic connections or the presence and activity of molecular cues for specifying neuronal connectivity.

CT See *computed tomography.*

cytoarchitectonic map A diagram showing regions of the cerebral cortex that contain neurons and neuronal organization of similar type.

There are as many as 50 different cytoarchitectonic areas, defined by histological analysis of the cortex.

cytoarchitectonics Also *cellular architecture.* The way in which cells differ between brain regions.

DBS See *deep-brain stimulation.*

decision making The process of making a choice between different behavioral options. The evaluation process likely involves some assessment of the potential rewards and costs for the different options.

declarative memory Knowledge to which we have conscious access, including personal and world knowledge (events and facts). The term *declarative* signals the idea that declarations can be made about this knowledge, and that for the most part, we are aware that we possess the information. Compare *nondeclarative memory.*

deep-brain stimulation (DBS) The electrical stimulation of brain structures via an implanted electrode. Stimulation of the subthalamic nucleus, one of the nuclei of the basal ganglia, is used as a treatment for Parkinson's disease.

delayed-response task A task in which the correct response must be produced after a delay period of several seconds. Such tasks require the operation of working memory because the animal or person must maintain a record of the stimulus information during the delay period.

dendrites Large treelike processes of neurons that receive inputs from other neurons at locations called synapses.

depolarization A change in the membrane potential in which the electrical current inside the cell becomes less negative. With respect to the resting potential, a depolarized membrane potential is closer to the firing threshold. Compare *hyperpolarization.*

developmental alexia See *alexia.*

dichotic listening An experimental technique in which subjects listen to a different message in each ear at the same time.

dichotic listening task An auditory task in which two competing messages are presented simultaneously, one to each ear, while the subject tries to report both messages. The ipsilateral projections from each ear are presumably suppressed when a message comes over the contralateral pathway from the other ear.

diffusion tensor imaging (DTI) A neuroimaging technique employed using an MRI scanner that allows white matter pathways in the brain to be imaged.

distributed representation The idea that information may be stored in large populations of neurons located in relatively widespread regions of the brain. This idea is in contrast to the idea that the representations of some items in memory are stored in a discrete, highly localized set of neurons.

dorsal pathway Also *occipitoparietal pathway.* One of the two main processing streams for visual information in the cerebral cortex. The dorsal pathway extends from the occipital lobe into the superior temporal and parietal lobes. Functional hypotheses have centered on the idea that this pathway is important for the representation of spatial information and for guiding visually directed actions. Compare *ventral pathway.*

double dissociation A method used to develop functional models of mental and/or neural processes. Evidence of a double dissociation requires a minimum of two groups and two tasks. In neuropsychological research, a double dissociation is present when one group is impaired on one task and the other group is impaired on the other task. In imaging research, a double dissociation is present when one experimental manipulation produces changes in activation in one neural region and a different manipulation produces changes in activation in a different neural region. Double dissociations provide a strong argument that the observed differences in performance reflect functional differences between the groups, rather than unequal sensitivity of the two tasks. Compare *single dissociation.*

DTI See *diffusion tensor imaging.*

dualism A major philosophical approach to describing consciousness, which holds that the mind and brain are two separate phenomena. Variations include popular dualism, property dualism, epiphenomenalism, and interactionist property dualism.

dura mater Dense layers of collagenous fibers that surround the brain and spinal cord.

dynamic filtering The hypothesis that a key component of working memory involves the selection of information that is most relevant, given current task demands. This selection is thought to be accomplished through the filtering, or exclusion of, potentially interfering and irrelevant information.

dyslexia See *alexia.*

early selection The theoretical model positing that attention can select (partially or completely) incoming information prior to complete perceptual analysis and its encoding as categorical or semantic information. Compare *late selection.*

ectoderm The cell line in the blastula of a developing embryo from which neural ectoderm will form, leading to the development of the nervous system.

EEG See *electroencephalography.*

effector Any part of the body that can move, such as an arm, finger, or leg.

electrical gradient A force that develops when a charge distribution across the neuronal membrane develops such that the charge inside is more positive or negative than the one outside. Electrical gradients result from asymmetrical distributions of ions across the membrane.

electroencephalography (EEG) A technique to measure the electrical activity of the brain. In EEG, surface recordings are made with electrodes placed on the scalp. The EEG signal includes endogenous changes in electrical activity (e.g., due to changes in arousal), as well as those triggered by specific events (e.g., stimuli or movements).

electrotonic conduction Passive current flow through neurons that accompanies activated electrical currents.

emotion An affective (positive or negative) mental response to a stimulus that also may be expressed physically (e.g., by change in heart rate, facial expression, and speech).

empathy The ability to experience and understand what others feel while still knowing the difference between oneself and others. Empathy is often described as the ability to "put oneself in another person's shoes."

empiricism The idea that all knowledge comes from sensory experience.

encoding The processing of incoming information to be stored. Encoding consists of two stages: acquisition and consolidation. Compare *retrieval.*

endogenous cuing The control of attention by internal stimuli under voluntary control. Compare *exogenous cuing.*

endpoint control A hypothesis concerning how movements are planned in terms of the desired final location. Endpoint control models emphasize that the motor representation is based on the final position required of the limbs to achieve the movement goal.

episodic memory Stored information about events in one's life, including information about when they happened and what happened. Episodic memory is a form of declarative memory.

equilibrium potential The membrane potential at which a given ion (e.g., K^+) has no net flux across the membrane; that is, as many of the ion move outward as inward across the membrane.

ERN See *error-related negativity.*

ERP See *event-related potential.*

error-related negativity (ERN) An electrical signal that is derived from the EEG record following an erroneous response. The ERN is seen as a prominent negative deflection in the ERP, and it is hypothesized to originate in the anterior cingulate.

ethology The study of animal behavior. Compare *neuroethology.*

event-related potential (ERP) A change in electrical activity that is time-locked to specific events such as the presentation of a stimulus or the onset of a response. When the events are repeated many times, averaging the EEG signals reveals the relatively small changes in neural activity triggered by these events. In this manner, the background fluctuations in the EEG signal are removed, revealing the event-related signal with great temporal resolution.

evolutionary psychology The field of study that uses an evolutionary framework to explain cognitive behavior.

exaptation The process whereby a structure that serves a particular function is co-opted for another, very different function. Compare *adaptation.*

executive functions The set of higher-level cognitive operations that are essential for the production of goal-oriented behavior. Executive functions involve the maintenance and manipulation of information that is essential for dealing with situations in which the appropriate response is not dictated by the current stimulus information. Executive functions include processes such as working memory, attention, goal representation and planning, response monitoring, and error detection. See also *cognitive control.*

exogenous cuing Also *reflexive cuing.* The control of attention by external stimuli and not by internal voluntary control. Compare *endogenous cuing.*

extinction The failure to perceive or respond to a stimulus contralateral to a lesion (contralesional) when presented with a simultaneous stimulus ipsilateral to the lesion (ipsilesional).

extrapyramidal tracts A collection of motor tracts that originate in various subcortical structures, including the vestibular nucleus and the red nucleus. These tracts are especially important for maintaining posture and balance.

extrastriate visual areas Visual areas that lie outside the striate cortex (Brodmann area 17, the primary visual cortex) and are considered secondary visual areas because they receive input either directly or indirectly from the primary visual cortex.

facial expression The nonverbal communication of emotion by manipulation of particular groups of facial muscles. Research findings suggest six basic human facial expressions represent the emotional states anger, fear, disgust, happiness, sadness, and surprise.

false-belief task A task that measures the ability to simultaneously represent the individual, and sometimes different, mental states of at least two different people.

familiarity A memory that does not contain episodic awareness of the prior event but is recognized by the feeling that the item was seen before—that is, by its feeling familiar.

fear conditioning Learning in which a neutral stimulus acquires aversive properties by virtue of being paired with an aversive event.

FFA See *fusiform face area.*

fissure See *sulcus.*

fitness The measure of evolutionary success in terms of a gene, trait, or behavior that is represented in future generations.

flanker paradigm A behavioral task that measures the effects of spatial selective attention to a stimulus by assessing the degree of interference, measured in slowed reaction time, produced by distracters flanking the target stimulus to be discriminated. Typically, the distracters require no response, since they are at a location that is to be ignored, but they contain features that would require a response different from that required to the target.

fMRI See *functional magnetic resonance imaging.*

frontal lobe The mass of cortex anterior to the central sulcus and dorsal to the Sylvian fissure. The frontal lobe contains two principal regions—the motor cortex and the prefrontal cortex—each of which can be further subdivided into specific areas both architectonically and functionally.

frontal pole The most anterior part of the prefrontal cortex, including area 10 and parts of area 9. This region is hypothesized to play a critical role in the hierarchical representation of action goals.

functional asymmetries Differences in the functions that each hemisphere subserves.

functional magnetic resonance imaging (fMRI) A neuroimaging method that utilizes MRI to track blood flow changes in the brain that are thought to be correlated with local changes in neuronal activity.

fusiform face area (FFA) An area of the brain, located in the ventral surface of the temporal lobe in the fusiform gyrus, that responds to selective stimuli, such as faces.

fusiform gyrus A gyrus located along the ventral surface of the temporal lobe. This area has been shown in neuroimaging studies to be consistently activated when people view face stimuli. Neurological lesions that include the fusiform gyrus are associated with prosopagnosia, although the damage also extends to other regions of the cortex.

GAD See *generative assembling device.*

gate Conceptualization of the attentional mechanism that prevents ignored stimuli from gaining access to further processing.

gene A hereditary unit composed of the complex organic molecule deoxyribonucleic acid (DNA). Compare *alleles.*

generative assembling device (GAD) A device that generates complex representations from a small vocabulary of primitive units.

genetic pleiotropy The idea that a single gene has many functions. Compare *genetic specificity.*

genetic specificity The idea that one gene is responsible for a single function or behavior. Compare *genetic pleiotropy.*

genotype The genetic composition of an organism. Compare *phenotype.*

glial cell Also *neuroglial cell.* One of two cell types (along with the *neuron*) in the nervous system. Glial cells are more numerous than neurons, by perhaps a factor of 10, and may account for more than half of the brain's volume. They typically do not conduct signals themselves; but without them, the functionality of neurons would be severely diminished. Tissue made of glial cells is termed *glia.*

glomeruli (s. glomerulus) The neurons of the olfactory bulb.

gnostic unit A neuron or small set of neurons tuned for a specific percept (e.g., an apple). The concept of the gnostic unit is based on the idea that hierarchical models of perception imply that, at higher levels in the system, neurons become much more selective in terms of what they respond to.

goal-oriented behavior Behavior that allows us to interact in the world in a purposeful manner. Goals reflect the intersection of our internal desires and drives, coupled with the current environmental context.

gray matter Regions of the nervous system that contain primarily neuronal cell bodies. Gray matter includes the cerebral cortex, the basal ganglia, and the nuclei of the thalamus. Gray matter is so called because, in preservative solution, these structures look gray in comparison to the *white matter* where myelinated axons are found (which look more white).

gyrus (pl. gyri) A protruding rounded surface of the cerebral cortex that one can see upon gross anatomical viewing of the intact brain. Compare *sulcus.*

handedness The tendency to perform the majority of one's manual actions with either the right or left hand.

Hebbian learning The theory that, if a weak and a strong input act on a cell at the same time, the weak synapse becomes stronger. The theory is named for Donald Hebb, who postulated this mechanism as a means for the connectional strength between neurons to change in order to store information.

hemianopia A condition resulting from destruction of the primary visual cortex in one hemisphere. The patient is unaware of any visual stimulation presented in the side of space contralateral to the lesion.

hemiplegia A neurological condition characterized by the loss of voluntary movements on one side of the body. Hemiplegia typically results from damage to the corticospinal tract, either from lesions to the motor cortex or from white matter lesions that destroy the descending fibers.

heritable Capable of being inherited or passed on to successive generations.

heterotopic areas Noncorresponding areas of the brain. Usually such areas are referred to as *heterotopic* because of their connections with one another. For instance, a connection between M1 on the left side and V2 on the right side would be a connection joining heterotopic areas of the brain. Compare *homotopic areas.*

hierarchical structure A configuration that may be described at multiple levels, from global features to local features; the finer components are embedded within the higher level components.

hippocampus (pl. hippocampi) The "seahorse" of the brain. A layered structure in the medial temporal lobe that receives inputs from wide regions of the cortex via inputs from the surrounding regions of the temporal lobe, and sends projections out to subcortical targets. The hippocampus is involved in learning and memory, particularly memory for spatial locations in mammals and episodic memory in humans.

holistic processing Perceptual analysis that emphasizes the overall shape of an object. Face perception has been hypothesized to be the best example of holistic processing, in that the recognition of an individual appears to reflect the composition of the person's facial features rather than being based on the recognition of the individual features themselves. Compare *analytic processing.*

homology The retention of a structure, behavior, or gene from a common ancestor. Compare *homoplasy.*

homoplasy The existence of structures in different species that look the same, but not necessarily because of common ancestry. Compare *homology.*

homotopic areas Areas in corresponding locations in the two hemispheres. A connection between M1 on the right side and M1 on the left side would be joining homotopic areas. Compare *heterotopic areas.*

homunculus See *primary somatosensory cortex.*

Huntington's disease A genetic degenerative disorder in which the primary pathology, at least in the early stages of the disease, is observed in the striatum (caudate and putamen) of the basal ganglia. Prominent symptoms include clumsiness and involuntary movements of the head and trunk. Cognitive impairments are also seen and become pronounced over time. Compare *Parkinson's disease.*

hyperpolarization A change in the membrane potential in which the electrical current inside of the cell becomes more negative. With respect to the resting potential, a hyperpolarized membrane potential is farther from the firing threshold. Compare *depolarization.*

hypothalamus A small collection of nuclei that form the floor of the third ventricle. The hypothalamus is important for the autonomic nervous system and the endocrine system, and it controls functions necessary for the maintenance of homeostasis.

ideational apraxia A severe form of apraxia in which the patient's knowledge about the intent of an action is impaired. For example, the patient may no longer comprehend the appropriate use for a tool, even though still capable of producing the required movement. Compare *ideomotor apraxia.*

ideomotor apraxia A form of apraxia in which the patient has difficulty executing the desired action properly. Patients with ideomotor apraxia appear to have a general idea about how the action should be performed and how tools are used, but they are unable to coordinate the movements to produce the action in a coherent manner. Compare *ideational apraxia.*

imitative behavior The spontaneous and uncontrolled mimicking of another person's behavior that is sometimes exhibited by patients with frontal lobe damage.

inferior colliculus A part of the midbrain that is involved in auditory processing. Compare *superior colliculus.*

information processing A conceptualization of sensory, perceptual, conceptual, and response processes in the brain that focuses on the flow of information from input through storage and analysis to output.

inhibition of return A hypothesized process underlying the slowing of motor responses observed over time when attention is reflexively attracted to a location by a sensory event (i.e., reflexive cue). As the name implies, inhibition of return is conceptualized as inhibition of recently attended locations such that attention is inhibited in returning to that location (or object).

inhibitory control The hypothesis that one aspect of executive functions is the regulation of actions by active inhibition of the tendency to produce habitual responses or environmentally dictated actions. A loss of inhibitory control is assumed to underlie the tendency of some patients with prefrontal lesions to produce socially inappropriate behavior.

innate An ability or behavior that an organism is born capable of exhibiting, and that therefore is under genetic control, being prespecified by the genetic code (as opposed to learned).

insula A part of cortex known to process gustatory information.

integrative agnosia A form of agnosia associated with deficits in the recognition of objects due to the failure to group and integrate the component parts into a coherent whole. Patients with this deficit can faithfully reproduce drawings of objects; however, their percept is of isolated, unconnected parts or contours.

interaural time The difference in time between when a sound reaches each of the two ears. This information is represented at various stages in the auditory pathway and provides an important cue for sound localization.

interpreter A left-brain system that seeks explanations for internal and external events in order to produce appropriate response behaviors.

ion channel A passageway in the cell membrane, formed by a transmembrane protein that creates a pore, through which ions (charged atoms in solution) of sodium, potassium, and chloride (Na^+, K^+, and Cl^-) might pass into or out of the cell.

joint attention The ability to monitor someone else's attention by observing that person's gaze or actions and directing one's own attention similarly.

knockout procedure A technique for creating a genetically altered version of a species. In the knockout species, specific genes are altered or eliminated. Knockout procedures can be used to study behavioral changes occurring animals that have developed without the targeted gene, or to observe how genes code the development of the nervous system.

late selection The theoretical model positing that all inputs are equally processed perceptually but attention acts to differentially filter these inputs at later stages of information processing. Compare *early selection*.

lateral fissure See *Sylvian fissure*.

lateral geniculate nucleus (LGN) The thalamic nucleus that is the main target of axons of the optic tract. Output from the LGN is directed primarily to the primary visual cortex (Brodmann area 17). Compare *medial geniculate nucleus*.

lateral prefrontal cortex The region of the cerebral cortex that lies anterior to Brodmann area 6, along the lateral surface. This region has been implicated in various executive functions, such as working memory and response selection.

laterality effect Asymmetries in performance thought to result from differences in how the two cerebral hemispheres influence cognitive function or behavior. For example, people are usually better on visual word recognition when the stimuli are presented in the right visual field (with initial projection to the left hemisphere).

learning The process of acquiring new information.

lexical access The process by which perceptual inputs activate word information in the mental lexicon, including semantic and syntactic information about the word.

lexical selection The process of selecting from a collection of representations the activated word that best matches the sensory input.

LGN See *lateral geniculate nucleus*.

limbic system Several structures that form a border (*limbus* in Latin) around the brainstem, named the *grand lobe limbique* ("limbic lobe") by Paul Broca. The limbic system is the emotional network that includes the amygdala, orbitofrontal cortex, and portions of the basal ganglia.

limited capacity The concept that the stages of information processing have a finite processing capability, leading to the need for the system to select high-priority information for access to these stages of analysis.

localizationist view The belief that individual behaviors and perceptions are controlled by distinct regions of the brain.

long-term memory The retention of information over the long term, from hours to days and years. Compare *sensory memory* and *short-term memory*.

M system See *magnocellular system*.

M1 See *primary motor cortex*.

magnetic resonance imaging (MRI) A neuroimaging technique that exploits the magnetic properties of organic tissue. Certain atoms are especially sensitized to magnetic forces because of the number of protons and neutrons in their nuclei. The orientation of these atoms can be altered by the presence of a strong magnetic field. When the magnetic field is removed, the atoms will gradually return to a randomly distributed orientation and, in the process of this transition, will generate a small magnetic field that can be measured by sensitive detectors. Structural MRI studies usually measure variations in the density of hydrogen. Functional MRI measures changes over time in the distribution of the targeted atom.

magnetoencephalography (MEG) A measure of the magnetic signals generated by the brain. The electrical activity of neurons also produces small magnetic fields, which can be measured by sensitive magnetic detectors placed along the scalp, similar to the way EEG measures the surface electrical activity. MEG can be used in an event-related manner similar to ERP studies, with similar temporal resolution. The spatial resolution, in theory, can be superior with MEG because magnetic signals are minimally distorted by organic tissue such as the brain or skull.

magnocellular (M) system A system of visually responsive cells characterized by relatively large axons. The magnocellular cells of the optic tract terminate in the bottom two layers of the lateral geniculate nucleus, and from there project to the cerebral cortex, contributing primarily to the dorsal pathway. Compare *parvocellular system*.

masking stimulus A stimulus that immediately follows a briefly presented stimulus, to prevent further conscious processing of the original stimulus.

materialism A major philosophical approach to describing consciousness, based on the theory that the mind and brain are both physical mediums. Variations include: philosophical behaviorism, reductive materialism, and functionalism.

medial frontal cortex The medial region of the frontal cortex that includes parts of areas 24, 32, and inferior aspects of 6 and 8. The medial frontal cortex is associated with cognitive control—in particular, monitoring functions for error detection and resolving conflict.

medial geniculate nucleus (MGN) A collection of cell bodies in the medial portion of the thalamus involved in processing auditory information. Output from the MGN is directed primarily to the primary auditory cortex. Compare *lateral geniculate nucleus*.

medulla Also *myelencephalon*. The brainstem's most caudal portion. The medulla is continuous with the spinal cord and contains the prominent, dorsally positioned nuclear groups known as the *gracile* and *cuneate nuclei*, which relay somatosensory information from the spinal cord to the brain, and the ventral pyramidal tracts, containing descending projection axons from the brain to the spinal cord. Various sensory and motor nuclei are found in the medulla.

MEG See *magnetoencephalography*.

memory The persistence of learning in a state that can be revealed later.

mental lexicon A mental store of information about words, including semantic information (meanings of the words), syntactic information (rules for using the words), and the details of word forms (spellings and sound patterns).

mentalizing See *theory of mind*.

MGN See *medial geniculate nucleus*.

microstimulation Injection of electrical current in the vicinity of a group of neurons of interest, in order to induce neural activity. Microstimulation allows the experimenter to manipulate normal neural activity and observe the consequences on behavior.

midbrain The part of the brain consisting of the *tectum* (meaning "roof," and representing the dorsal portion of the mesencephalon), *tegmentum* (the main portion of the midbrain), and ventral regions occupied by large fiber tracts (*crus cerebri*) from the forebrain to the spinal cord (corticospinal tract), cerebellum, and brainstem (corticobulbar tract). The midbrain contains neurons that participate in visuomotor functions (e.g., superior colliculus, oculomotor nucleus, trochlear nucleus), visual reflexes (e.g., pretectal region), auditory relays (inferior colliculus), and the mesencephalic tegmental nuclei involved in motor coordination (red nucleus). It is bordered anteriorly by the diencephalon, and caudally by the pons.

mirror system A distributed network of neurons that respond not only to one's own action but also to *perceived* actions. For instance, a mirror neuron responds when you pick up a pencil and when you watch someone else pick up a pencil.

monitoring The executive function associated with evaluating whether current representations and/or actions are conducive to the achievement of current goals. Errors can be avoided or corrected by a monitoring system. One of the hypothesized operations of a supervisory attentional system.

MRI See *magnetic resonance imaging*.

multisensory integration The integration of information from more than one sensory modality. Watching someone speak requires the integration of auditory and visual information.

multiunit recording A physiological procedure in which an array of electrodes is inserted in the brain such that the activity of many cells can be recorded simultaneously.

mutation A sudden change in the genetic structure of an organism that affects the development of the organism.

myelencephalon See *medulla.*

myelin A fatty substance that surrounds the axons of many neurons and increases the effective membrane resistance, helping to speed the conduction of action potentials.

N170 response Also simply "the N170." A negative evoked response in the EEG signal that occurs approximately 170 ms after the onset of a stimulus.

N400 response Also simply "the N400." A negative-polarity event-related potential that is elicited by words, and that is larger in amplitude for words that do not fit well into the sentence context. Compare *P600 response.*

natural selection Darwin's mechanism for evolution, which states that individuals with characteristics that best suit an environment are more likely to survive and reproduce.

neglect See *unilateral spatial neglect.*

neocortex The portion of the cortex that typically contains six main cortical layers (with sublayers) and has a high degree of specialization of neuronal organization. The neocortex is composed of areas like the primary sensory and motor cortex and association cortex, and as its name suggests, is the most modern (evolved) type of cortex.

neural plate The dorsal surface of a developing embryo early in embryogenesis, formed by ectoderm cells. The developing nervous system arises from the neural plate.

neuroeconomics An emerging field of brain science that combines economics and cognitive neuroscience with the goal of understanding the neural mechanisms involved in decision making.

neuroethology The study of the neurobiology of animal behavior. Compare *ethology.*

neuroglial cell See *glial cell.*

neurology The branch of medicine that focuses on the function and dysfunction of the nervous system. Clinical neurologists treat patients with a wide range of problems, such as headache, trauma, stroke, and changes in mental ability. They may also study patients as a way of understanding the operation of the nervous system in normal function.

neuron One of two cell types (along with the *glial cell*) in the nervous system. Neurons are responsible for processing neural information.

neuron doctrine The belief that brain functions are carried out through the synchronized activity of independent neurons.

neuronal determination and differentiation The specification of neuronal cell type during development. Cells produced from nondifferentiated precursor cells must take on the phenotype appropriate for their ultimate role in the nervous system.

neuronal migration The movement of new neurons to their final and appropriate location in the developing brain. Neuronal migration involves molecular cues and the assistance of special glial cells (in the cortex) that provide a superstructure (radial glial cells) for neurons to climb along en route to their position in the brain (e.g., specific layers of cortex).

neuronal proliferation Cell division in the developing embryo and fetus occurring over time, which populates the nervous system with the complete complement of neurons needed for the organism.

neurophysiology The study of the physiological processes of the nervous system. Neural activity is characterized by physiological changes that can be described both electrically and chemically. The changes can be observed at many different levels, ranging from the gross changes recorded with EEG, to the firing of individual neurons, to the molecular changes that occur at the synapse.

neurotransmitter A chemical substance that transmits the signal between neurons at chemical synapses.

nociceptors The somatosensory receptors that convey pain information.

node of Ranvier A location at which myelin is interrupted between successive patches of axon, and where an action potential can be generated.

nondeclarative memory Knowledge to which we typically have no conscious access, such as motor and cognitive skills (procedural knowledge). For example, the ability to ride a bicycle is a nondeclarative form of knowledge. Although we can describe the action itself, the actual information one needs to ride a bicycle is not easy to describe. Compare *declarative memory.*

nucleus (pl. nuclei) 1. In neuroanatomy, a collection of cell bodies in the central nervous system—for example, the lateral geniculate nucleus. 2. In biology, a cellular organelle where DNA is stored.

nucleus reticularis thalami See *reticular nucleus.*

object-based attention Selective attention that is based on object representations. Compare *spatial attention.*

object constancy The ability to recognize invariant properties of an object across a wide range of contexts. For example, although the size of the retinal image changes dramatically when a car recedes in the distance, our percept is that the car remains the same size. Similarly, we are able to recognize that an object is the same when seen from different perspectives.

OCB See *olivocochlear bundle.*

occipital lobe A cortical lobe located at the posterior of the cerebral cortex that contains primarily neurons involved in visual information processing.

occipitoparietal pathway See *dorsal pathway.*

occipitotemporal pathway Also *ventral pathway.*

odorant A molecule conducted through the air that leads to activation of the olfactory receptors and may be perceived as having a smell when processed through the olfactory system. Compare *tastant.*

olivocochlear bundle (OCB) A neural projection from the neurons in the brainstem that project to the hair cells of the cochlea.

operculum A part of the cortex known to process gustatory information.

optic ataxia A neurological syndrome in which the patient has great difficulty using visual information to guide her actions, even though she is unimpaired in her ability to recognize objects. Optic ataxia is associated with lesions of the parietal lobe.

orbitofrontal cortex A region of the frontal lobe, located above the orbits of the eyes, that is implicated in a range of functions, including perceptual processes associated with olfaction and taste, as well as those associated with monitoring whether one's behavior is appropriate.

out-group comparison A comparison that defines phylogenetic relationships among animals. In such comparisons, close sister groups of a species are examined to determine whether they possess the structure in question to ascertain whether the structure is ancestral or has evolved in one group.

P system See *parvocellular system.*

P600 response Also *syntactic positive shift.* A positive-polarity event-related potential elicited when words violate syntactic rules in sentences. Compare *N400 response.*

parietal lobe A cortical lobe located posterior to the central sulcus, anterior to the occipital lobe, and superior to the posterior temporal cortex. This cortical region contains a variety of neurons, including the somatosensory cortex, gustatory cortex, and parietal association cortex, which includes regions involved in visuomotor orienting, attention, and representation of space.

Parkinson's disease A degenerative disorder of the basal ganglia in which the pathology results from the loss of dopaminergic cells in the substantia nigra. Primary symptoms include difficulty in initiating movement, slowness of movement, poorly articulated speech, and, in some cases, resting tremor. Compare *Huntington's disease.*

parsing The immediate assignment of syntactic structure to incoming words.

parvocellular (P) system A system of visually responsive cells characterized by relatively small axons. The parvocellular cells of the optic tract terminate in the top four layers of the lateral geniculate nucleus, and from there project to the cerebral cortex, contributing primarily to the ventral pathway. Compare *magnocellular system.*

perceptual representation system (PRS) A form of nondeclarative memory, acting within the perceptual system, in which the structure and form of objects and words can be primed by prior experience and can be revealed later through implicit memory tests.

peripheral nervous system (PNS) A courier network that delivers sensory information to the CNS and then conducts the motor commands of the CNS to control muscles of the body; anything outside the brain and spinal cord. Compare *central nervous system.*

permeability The extent to which ions can cross a neuronal membrane.

perseveration The tendency to produce a particular response on successive trials, even when the context has changed such that the response is no longer appropriate. Commonly observed in patients with prefrontal damage, perseveration is thought to reflect a loss of inhibitory control.

PET See *positron emission tomography.*

phenomenal awareness Our experience of sensations and thoughts. Compare *access awareness.*

phenotype An observable trait or set of characteristics of an organism. Compare *genotype.*

photoreceptor A specialized cell in the retina that transduces light energy into changes in membrane potential. The photoreceptors are the interface for the visual system between the external world and the nervous system.

phrenology The study of the physical shape of the human head, based on the belief that variations in the skull's surface can reveal specific intellectual and personality traits. Today phrenology is understood to lack validity.

planum temporale The surface area of the temporal lobe that includes Wernicke's area. The planum temporale has long been believed to be larger in the left hemisphere because of the lateralization of language function, although this theory is currently controversial.

plastic Referring to the capacity to adapt or change (i.e., plasticity). For example, neurons in the visual cortex are considered plastic because, following visual deprivation, they can remap to process information other sensory information, like touch or audition.

plesiomorphic Describing a trait that is a general feature of a particular group or lineage.

PNS See *peripheral nervous system.*

pons A region in the brain that includes the pontine tegmental regions on the floor of the fourth ventricle, and the pons itself, a vast system of fiber tracts interspersed with pontine nuclei. The fibers are continuations of the cortical projections to the spinal cord, brainstem, and cerebellar regions. The pons also includes the primary sensory nuclear groups for auditory and vestibular inputs, and somatosensory inputs from, and motor nuclei projecting to, the face and mouth. Neurons of the reticular formation can also be found in the anterior regions of the pons.

pop-out A phenomenon in which target objects in a cluttered scene can be detected rapidly when they are defined by a unique feature (e.g., color) that distinguishes them from distracters in the scene. The result is a flat search function, which plots reaction time to target detection as a function of the number of distracter stimuli. Pop-out implies that preattentive mechanisms can achieve target detection.

population vector A statistical procedure to represent the activity across a group of neurons. Population vectors reflect the aggregate activity across the cells, providing a better correlation with behavior than that obtained from the analysis of individual neurons. For example, the population vector calculated from neurons in the motor cortex can predict the direction of a limb movement.

positron emission tomography (PET) A neuroimaging method that measures metabolic activity in the brain by monitoring the distribution of a radioactive tracer. The PET scanner measures the photons that are produced during the decay of a tracer. A popular tracer is O^{15} because its decay time is rapid and the distribution of oxygen increases to neural regions that are active.

postsynaptic Referring to the neuron located after the synapse with respect to information flow. Compare *presynaptic.*

preconscious processing Information processing that is automatic (i.e., we are not aware of it) but that leads to awareness. Compare *conscious processing* and *subliminal processing.*

precursor cells Undifferentiated cells from which all neurons are produced by cell division. Precursor cells are located in the ventricular zone.

prefrontal cortex A region of cortex that takes part in the higher aspects of motor control and the planning and execution of behavior, perhaps especially tasks that require the integration of information over time and thus mandate the involvement of working memory mechanisms. The prefrontal cortex has three or more main areas that are commonly referred to in descriptions of the gross anatomy of the frontal lobe: the dorsolateral prefrontal cortex, the anterior cingulate and medial frontal regions, and the orbitofrontal cortex.

premotor cortex A secondary motor area that includes the lateral aspect of Brodmann area 6, just anterior to the primary motor cortex. Although some neurons in the premotor cortex project to the corticospinal tract, many terminate on neurons in the primary motor cortex and help shape the forthcoming movement.

presynaptic Referring to the neuron located before the synapse with respect to information flow. Compare *postsynaptic.*

primary auditory cortex (A1) The initial cortical processing area of the auditory system.

primary gustatory cortex The initial cortical processing area for gustation, located in the insula and operculum.

primary motor cortex (M1) A region of the cerebral cortex that lies along the anterior bank of the central sulcus and precentral gyrus, forming Brodmann area 4. Some axons originating in the primary motor cortex form the majority of the corticospinal tract; others project to cortical and subcortical regions involved in motor control. The primary motor cortex contains a prominent somatotopic representation of the body.

primary olfactory cortex The initial cortical processing area for olfaction, located at the ventral junction of the frontal and temporal cortices, near the limbic cortex.

primary somatosensory cortex (S1) The initial cortical processing area for somatosensation, including Brodmann areas 1, 2, and 3. This area of the brain contains a somatotopic representation of the body called the sensory *homunculus.*

primary visual cortex (V1) The initial cortical processing area for vision, located in the most posterior portion of the occipital lobe, known as Brodmann area 17.

principle of parsimony The idea that the best hypothesis is one that requires the fewest number of transformations to explain a phenomenon; the simplest of competing theories is preferred.

procedural memory A form of nondeclarative memory that involves the learning of a variety of motor skills (e.g., knowledge of how to ride a bike) and cognitive skills (e.g., knowledge of how to read).

propagation The movement of electrical signals down the axon during neuronal signaling.

proprioception The awareness of the position of one's own body parts, such as limbs. This awareness arises from the information provided by specialized nerve cells at the linkage of the muscles and tendons.
prosopagnosia A neurological syndrome characterized by a deficit in the ability to recognize faces. Some patients will show a selective deficit in face perception, a type of category-specific deficit. In others, the prosopagnosia is one part of a more general agnosia. Prosopagnosia is frequently associated with bilateral lesions in the ventral pathway, although it can also occur with unilateral lesions of the right hemisphere.
PRS See *perceptual representation system.*
pulvinar nucleus A large group of nuclei in the thalamus, located at the posterior end.
pyramidal tract See *corticospinal tract.*
radial glial cell A special type of glial cell that is anchored on one end at the ventricular zone and at the other end at the cortical surface. Migrating neurons "crawl" along radial glial cells, which act as scaffolding during corticogenesis.
rationalism The idea that, through right thinking and rejection of unsupportable or superstitious beliefs, true beliefs can be determined.
rCBF See *regional cerebral blood flow.*
recency memory Memory for the temporal order of previous events. Recency memory is a form of episodic memory in that it involves remembering when a specific event took place. Patients with prefrontal lesions do poorly on tests of recency memory, even though their long-term memory is relatively intact.
receptive field The area of external space within a stimulus that must be presented in order to activate a cell. For example, cells in the visual cortex respond to stimuli that appear within a restricted region of space. In addition to spatial position, the cells may be selective to other stimulus features, such as color or shape. Cells in the auditory cortex also have receptive fields. The cell's firing rate increases when the sound comes from the region of space that defines its receptive field.
receptor 1. A sensory cell such, as a photoreceptor in the eye, that transduces physical signals in the environment (e.g., light energy) to neuron signals. 2. A transmembrane protein on the postsynaptic side of a synapse that binds neurotransmitters, leading to changes in the membrane potential of the postsynaptic neuron.
receptor potential An electrical potential generated by an active process (the opening of an ion channel) in a sensory receptor, such as a photoreceptor in the eye.
recombination A change in the array of alleles of existing genes.
reflexive attention The automatic orienting of attention induced by bottom-up, or stimulus-driven, effects, such as when a flash of light in the periphery captures one's attention. Compare *voluntary attention.*
reflexive cuing See *exogenous cuing.*
refractory period The short period of time following an action potential during which the neuron may not be able to generate action potentials or may be able to do so only with larger-than-normal depolarizing currents.
regional cerebral blood flow (rCBF) The distribution of the brain's blood supply, which can be measured with various imaging techniques. In PET scanning, rCBF is used as a measure of metabolic changes following increased neural activity in restricted regions of the brain.
repetition suppression effect The phenomenon seen during functional MRI in which the BOLD response to a stimulus decreases with each subsequent stimulus repetition.
response conflict A situation in which more than one response is activated, usually because of some ambiguity in the stimulus information. It has been hypothesized that the anterior cingulate monitors the level of response conflict and modulates processing in active systems when conflict is high.
resting membrane potential The difference in voltage across the neuronal membrane at rest, when the neuron is not signaling.
reticular nucleus Also *nucleus reticularis thalami.* A thin sheet of neurons surrounding the thalamus and containing local interneurons, which receive input from the cortex and make projections onto thalamic relay neurons.
retina A layer of neurons along the back surface of the eye. The retina contains a variety of cells, including photoreceptors (the cells that respond to light) and ganglion cells (the cells whose axons form the optic nerve).
retinotopic Referring to a topographic map of visual space across a restricted region of the brain. Activation across the retina is determined by the reflectance of light from the environment. A retinotopic map in the brain is a representation in which some sort of orderly spatial relationship is maintained. Multiple retinotopic maps have been identified in the cortex and subcortex.
retrieval The utilization of stored information to create a conscious representation or to execute a learned behavior like a motor act. Compare *encoding.*
retrograde amnesia The loss of memory for events that happened in the past. Compare *anterograde amnesia.*
S1 See *primary somatosensory cortex.*
S2 See *secondary somatosensory cortex.*
saltatory conduction The mode of conduction in myelinated neurons, in which action potentials are generated down the axon only at nodes of Ranvier. Measurement of the propagation of the action potential gives it the appearance of jumping from node to node—hence the term *saltatory*, which comes from the Latin *saltare*, meaning "to jump."
SAS See *supervisory attentional system.*
scotoma A region in external space in which a person or animal fails to perceive a stimulus following neural damage. Scotomas occur following lesions of primary visual cortex or partial lesions of ascending visual pathways. The size and location of scotomas vary depending on the extent and location of the lesions.
second messenger A substance that transmits information from the postsynaptic receptor to ion channels or to other intracellular entities in the postsynaptic neuron (e.g., the nucleus).
secondary somatosensory cortex (S2) The area of the brain that receives inputs from primary somatosensory cortex and processes higher level somatosensory information.
selective attention The ability to focus one's concentration on a subset of sensory inputs, trains of thought, or actions, while simultaneously ignoring others. Selective attention can be distinguished from nonselective attention, which includes simple behavioral arousal (i.e., being generally more versus less attentive).
self-referent effect An effect rooted in the theoretical perspective that the recall of information is related to how deeply the information was initially processed. Specifically, the self-reference effect is the superior memory for information that is encoded in relation to oneself.
semantic paraphasia The production of a word related in meaning to the intended word (e.g., *horse* for *cow*) instead of the intended word itself. Wernicke's aphasia patients often produce semantic paraphasias.
sensitive period See *critical period.*
sensory memory The short-lived retention of sensory information, measurable in milliseconds to seconds, as when we recover what was said to us a moment before when we were not paying close attention to the speaker. Sensory memory for audition is called *echoic memory*; sensory memory for vision is called *iconic memory*. Compare *short-term memory* and *long-term memory.*
short-term memory The retention of information over seconds to minutes. See also *working memory.* Compare *long-term memory* and *sensory memory.*

simulation A method used in computer modeling to mimic a certain behavior or process. Simulations require a program that explicitly specifies the manner in which information is represented and processed. The resulting model can be tested to see if its output matches the simulated behavior or process. The program can then be used to generate new predictions.

simulation theory A theoretical account of how we understand other people's minds. From this perspective, we try to make inferences about other people's minds by considering what we might do if we were in their position.

single-cell recording A neurophysiological method used to monitor the activity of individual neurons. The procedure requires positioning a small recording electrode either inside a cell or, more typically, near the outer membrane of a neuron. The electrode measures changes in the membrane potential and can be used to determine the conditions that cause the cell to respond.

single dissociation A method used to develop functional models of mental and/or neural processes. Evidence of a single dissociation requires a minimum of two groups and two tasks. A single dissociation is present when the groups differ in their performance on one task but not the other. Single dissociations provide weak evidence of functional specialization since it is possible that the two tasks differ in terms of their sensitivity to detect group differences. Compare *double dissociation.*

SMA See *supplementary motor area.*

social cognitive neuroscience An emerging field of brain science that combines social-personality psychology and cognitive neuroscience with the goal of understanding the neural mechanisms involved in social interaction in humans.

sociobiology The systematic study of the biological basis of all social behavior.

soma (pl. somata) The cell body of a neuron.

somatic marker A physiological-emotional mechanism that was once theorized to help us sort through possible options and make a decision. Somatic markers were thought to provide a common metric for evaluating options with respect to their potential benefit.

somatotopy A point-for-point representation of the body surface in the nervous system. In the somatosensory cortex, regions of the body near one another (e.g., the index and middle fingers) are represented by neurons located near one another. Regions that are farther apart on the body surface (e.g., the nose and the big toe) are coded by neurons located farther apart in the somatosensory cortex.

source memory Memory for the context in which something was learned; a form of episodic memory. Patients with lateral prefrontal lesions may do well at remembering a list of facts, but they have difficulty identifying the place and time at which the facts were learned.

spatial attention Selective attention that is based on location in the sensory world. For example, visuospatial attention is attention to one location while simultaneously ignoring another location. Compare *object-based attention.*

spatial-frequency hypothesis The hypothesis that the two hemispheres differ in how they process complex information, with the left hemisphere biased toward processing high-frequency information and the right hemisphere biased toward processing low-frequency information.

spike-triggering zone The location, at the juncture of the soma and the axon of a neuron, where currents from synaptic inputs on the soma and distant dendrites are summed and where voltage-gated Na^+ channels are located that can be triggered to generate action potentials that can propagate down the axon.

spine A little knob attached by a small neck to the surface of a dendrite. Synapses are located on spines.

splenium The posterior area of the corpus callosum that interconnects the occipital lobe.

split-brain research The study of patients who have had the corpus callosum severed, typically as a radical treatment for intractable epilepsy.

SPS See *syntactic positive shift.*

stimulus-driven Describing behavior that is dictated by the environmental context and fails to incorporate an animal's or person's goals. For example, a person with a lesion of prefrontal cortex might drink from a glass placed in front of him even if he isn't thirsty.

storage The result of the acquisition and consolidation of information, which create and maintain, respectively, a permanent record.

subliminal processing Information processing that is triggered by bottom-up inputs and does not reach the level of awareness. Compare *conscious processing* and *preconscious processing.*

substantia nigra One of the nuclei that form the basal ganglia. The substantia nigra is composed of two parts: The axons of the substantia nigra *pars compacta* provide the primary source of the neurotransmitter dopamine and terminate in the striatum (caudate and putamen). The substantia nigra *pars reticularis* is one of the output nuclei from the basal ganglia.

subthreshold Referring to stimuli and events that are available only to unconscious processing. Subthreshold stimuli and events are perceived, maintained, and manipulated below the level of conscious awareness.

sulcus (pl. sulci) Also *fissure.* An invaginated region that appears as a line or crease of the surface of the cerebral cortex. Compare *gyrus.*

superior colliculus A subcortical visual structure located in the midbrain. The superior colliculus receives input from the retinal system and is interconnected with the subcortical and cortical systems. It plays a key role in visuomotor processes and may be involved in the inhibitory component of reflexive attentional orienting. Compare *inferior colliculus.*

supervisory attentional system (SAS) The psychological model used to explain how response selection is achieved in a flexible manner. Without the SAS, behavior is dictated by context, with the selected action being the one that has been produced most often in the current context. The SAS allows for flexible behavior by biasing certain actions based on current goals or helping to determine actions in unfamiliar situations.

supplementary motor area (SMA) A secondary motor area that includes the medial aspect of Brodmann area 6, just anterior to the primary motor cortex. The SMA plays an important role in the production of sequential movements, especially those that have been well learned.

Sylvian fissure Also *lateral fissure.* A large fissure (sulcus) on the lateral surface of the cerebral cortex first described by the anatomist Franciscus Sylvius. The Sylvian fissure separates the frontal cortex from the temporal lobe below.

synapse The specialized site on the neural membrane where a neuron comes in close position to another neuron to transmit information. Synapses include both presynaptic (e.g., synaptic vesicles with neurotransmitter) and postsynaptic (e.g., receptors) specializations in the neurons that are involved in chemical transmission. Electrical synapses involve special structures called gap junctions that make direct cytoplasmic connections between neurons.

synapse elimination The elimination of some synaptic contacts between neurons during development, including postnatally.

synaptic potential The voltage difference across the membrane at the synapse during synaptic transmission.

synaptogenesis The formation of synaptic connections between neurons in the developing nervous system.

syncytium (pl. syncytia) A continuous mass of tissue that shares a common cytoplasm.

synesthesia A mixing of the senses whereby stimulation of one sense (e.g., touch) automatically causes an illusory perceptual experience in the same or another sense (e.g., vision).
syntactic positive shift (SPS) See *P600 response.*
task switching An experimental method used to study the processes involved in changing from one goal to another—an important feature of flexible behavior. In these studies, participants alternate between two or more tasks, allowing the experimenter to observe the processes involved in retrieving a new goal, discarding an old goal, and establishing a new set of stimulus-response conditions.
tastant A food molecule that stimulates a receptor in a taste cell to initiate the sensory transduction of gustation. Compare *odorant.*
temporal lobe Lateral ventral portions of the cerebral cortex bounded superiorly by the Sylvian fissure and posteriorly by the anterior edge of the occipital lobe and ventral portion of the parietal lobe. The ventromedial portions contain the hippocampal complex and amygdala. The lateral neocortical regions are involved in higher order vision (object analysis), the representation of conceptual information about the visual world, and linguistic representations. The superior portions within the depths of the Sylvian fissure contain auditory cortex.
thalamus A group of nuclei, primarily major sensory relay nuclei for somatosensory, gustatory, auditory, visual, and vestibular inputs to the cerebral cortex. The thalamus also contains nuclei involved in basal ganglia–cortical loops, and other specialized nuclear groups. It is a part of the diencephalon, a subcortical region, located in the center of the mass of the forebrain. Each hemisphere contains one thalamus, and they are connected at the midline in most humans by the massa intermedia.
theory of mind Also *mentalizing.* The ability to self-reflect and think about the mental states of others, which allows predictions of what others can understand, and how they will interact and behave in a given situation. This trait is considered unique to the human species.
threshold The membrane potential value to which the membrane must be depolarized for an action potential to be initiated.
TMS See *transcranial magnetic stimulation.*
topography The systematic relationship between a particular property of the external world and the neural representation of that property. Examples of topographic representations include retinotopic maps in the visual cortex, tonotopic maps in the auditory cortex, and somatosensory maps in the motor and sensory cortices.
tract A bundle of axons in the central nervous system.
trait Also *characteristic.* A distinguishing quality or attribute.
transcortical Pertaining to communication between the left and right hemispheres, either via the corpus callosum or via subcortical connections.
transcranial magnetic stimulation (TMS) A noninvasive method used to stimulate the cerebral cortex or motor neurons. A strong electrical current is rapidly generated in a coil placed over the targeted region. This current generates a magnetic field that causes the neurons in the underlying region to discharge. TMS is used in clinical settings to evaluate motor function by direct stimulation of the motor cortex. Experimentally, the procedure is used to transiently disrupt neural processing, thus creating brief, reversible lesions.
unconscious processing Brain-mediated processing of the features of a given stimulus that presumably precede and give rise to conscious awareness of that stimulus.
unilateral spatial neglect Also simply *neglect.* A behavioral pattern exhibited by neurological patients with lesions to the forebrain, in which they fail at or are slowed in acknowledging that objects or events exist in the hemispace opposite their lesion. Neglect is most closely associated with damage to the right parietal cortex.
universal grammar A linguistic theory stating that the principles of grammar are shared by all languages because these principles arise from the organization of the human brain, which is identical in all races and ethnic groups around the world.
utilization behavior An extreme dependency on the prototypical use of an object without regard for its use in a particular context.
V1 See *primary visual cortex.*
ventral pathway Also *occipitotemporal pathway.* One of the two main processing streams for visual information in the cerebral cortex. The ventral pathway extends from the occipital lobe into the inferior and middle temporal lobe. Functional hypotheses have centered on the idea that this pathway is important for the recognition of objects, including faces. Compare *dorsal pathway.*
vesicle A small intracellular organelle, located in the presynaptic terminals at synapses, that contains neurotransmitter.
view-dependent frame of reference A theory based on the idea that perception involves recognizing an object from a certain viewpoint. View-dependent theories assume that visual memory is based on previous experiences with objects in specific orientations and that the recognition of an object in a novel orientation involves an approximation process to the stored representations of specific perspectives. Compare *view-invariant frame of reference.*
view-invariant frame of reference A theory based on the idea that perception involves recognizing certain properties of an object that remain invariant, or constant across different perspectives. In this view, these properties form the basis of visual memory, and recognition entails matching the perceived properties to this knowledge base. Compare *view-dependent frame of reference.*
visceral motor system See *autonomic nervous system.*
visual agnosia A failure of perception that is limited to the visual modality. In visual agnosia, the patient is relatively good at perceiving properties such as color, shape, or motion yet cannot recognize objects or identify their uses.
visual search The process of searching a cluttered visual scene for a relevant item using covert attention.
visual search task An experiment designed by Anne Treisman to study the level of attentional processing necessary for various types of visual discrimination.
voluntary attention The volitional, or intentional, focusing of attention on a source of input, train of thought, or action. Compare *reflexive attention.*
voxel The smallest unit of three-dimensional data that can be represented in an MRI.
Wernicke's aphasia A language deficit usually caused by brain lesions in the posterior parts of the left hemisphere, resulting in comprehension deficits. Compare *Broca's aphasia.*
white matter Regions of the nervous system composed of millions of individual axons, each surrounded by myelin. The myelin is what gives the fibers their whitish color—hence the name *white matter.* Compare *gray matter.*
Wisconsin Card Sorting Task A neuropsychological test that assesses various aspects of executive control. Although the test has traditionally been viewed as an excellent diagnostic of prefrontal function, impaired performance is frequently observed in other patient groups, probably reflecting the complexity of this multidimensional sorting task, in which rules are learned through trial and error.
working memory Transient representations of task-relevant information. These representations may be related to information that has just been activated from long-term memory or something recently experienced. Representations in working memory guide behavior in the present, constituting what has been called, "the blackboard of the mind." See also *short-term memory.*

REFERENCES

ADOLPHS, R., GOSSELIN, F., BUCHANAN, T. W., TRANEL, D., SCHYNS, P., & DAMASIO, A. R. (2005). A mechanism for impaired fear recognition after amygdala damage. *Nature, 433*, 68–72.

ADOLPHS, R., & TRANEL, D. (1999). Intact recognition of emotional prosody following amygdala damage. *Neuropsychologia, 37*, 1285–1292.

ADOLPHS, R., & TRANEL, D. (2004). Impaired judgments of sadness but not happiness following bilateral amygdala damage. *Journal of Cognitive Neuroscience, 16*, 453–462.

ADOLPHS, R., TRANEL, D., & DAMASIO, A. R. (2003). Dissociable neural systems for recognizing emotions. *Brain and Cognition, 52*, 61–69.

ADOLPHS, R. A., TRANEL, D., DAMASIO, H., & DAMASIO, A. R. (1994). Impaired recognition of emotion in facial expressions following bilateral amygdala damage to the human amygdala. *Nature, 372*, 669–672.

ADOLPHS, R., TRANEL, D., DAMASIO, H., & DAMASIO, A. R. (1995). Fear and the human amygdala. *Journal of Neuroscience, 75*, 5879–5891.

ADOLPHS, R., TRANEL, D., & DENBURG, N. (2000). Impaired emotional declarative memory following unilateral amygdala damage. *Learning & Memory, 7*, 180–186.

ADOLPHS, R., TRANEL, D., HAMANN, S., YOUNG, A. W., CALDER, A. J., PHELPS, E. A., ET AL. (1999). Recognition of facial emotion in nine individuals with bilateral amygdala damage. *Neuropsychologia, 37*, 1111–1117.

AGUIRRE, G. K., & D'ESPOSITO M. E. (1999). Topographical disorientation: A synthesis and taxonomy. *Brain, 122*, 1613–1628.

AKELAITIS, A. J. (1941). Studies on the corpus callosum: Higher visual functions in each homonymous visual field following complete section of corpus callosum. *Archives of Neurology and Psychiatry, 45*, 788.

ALLEN, M. (1983). Models of hemisphere specialization. *Psychological Bulletin, 93*, 73–104.

ANDERSEN, R. A., & BUNEO, C. A. (2002). Intentional maps in posterior parietal cortex. *Annual Review of Neuroscience, 25*, 189–220. [Epub, March 27]

ANDERSON, A. K., & PHELPS, E. A. (1998). Intact recognition of vocal expressions of fear following bilateral lesions of the human amygdala. *Neuroreport, 9*, 3607–3613.

ANDERSON, A. K., & PHELPS, E. A. (2000). Expression without recognition: Contributions of the human amygdala to emotional communication. *Psychological Science, 11*, 106–111.

ANDERSON, A. K., & PHELPS, E. A. (2001). Lesions of the human amygdala impair enhanced perception of emotionally salient events. *Nature, 411*, 305–309.

ANDERSON, S. W., BECHARA, A., DAMASIO, H., TRANEL, D., & DAMASIO, A. R. (1999). Impairment of social and moral behavior related to early damage in human prefrontal cortex. *Nature Neuroscience, 2*, 1032–1037.

ANGRILLI, A., MARUI, A., PALOMBA, D., FLOR, H., BIRBAUMER, N., SARTORI, G., ET AL. (1996). Startle reflex and emotion modulation impairment after a right amygdala lesion. *Brain, 119*, 1991–2000.

ARON, A. R., BEHRENS, T. E., SMITH, S., FRANK, M. J., & POLDRACK, R. A. (2007). Triangulating a cognitive control network using diffusion-weighted magnetic resonance imaging (MRI) and functional MRI. *Journal of Neuroscience, 27*, 3743–3752.

ARON, A. R., & POLDRACK, R. A. (2006). Cortical and subcortical contributions to Stop signal response inhibition: Role of the subthalamic nucleus. *Journal of Neuroscience, 26*, 2424–2433.

ARVANITAKI, A. (1939). Recherches sur la résponse oscillatoire locale de l'axone géant isolé de 'Sepia.' *Archives Internationales de Physiologie, 49*, 209–256.

ATKINSON, R. C., & SHIFFRIN, R. M. (1968). Human memory: A proposed system and its control processes. In K. W. Spence & J. T. Spence (Eds.), *The psychology of learning and motivation* (Vol. 2, pp. 89–195). New York: Academic Press.

ATKINSON, R. C., & SHIFFRIN, R. M. (1971). The control of short-term memory. *Scientific American, 225*(2), 82–90.

BADDELEY, A. (1995). Working memory. In M. S. Gazzaniga (Ed.), *The cognitive neurosciences* (pp. 755–764). Cambridge, MA: MIT Press.

BADDELEY, A. (2003). Working memory: Looking back and looking forward. *Nature Reviews Neuroscience, 4*, 829–839.

BADDELEY, A., & HITCH, G. (1974). Working memory. In G. H. Bower (Ed.), *The psychology of learning and motivation* (Vol. 8, pp. 47–89). New York: Academic Press.

BAIRD, A. A., COLVIN, M. K., VANHORN, J. D., INATI, S., & GAZZANIGA, M. S. (2005). Functional connectivity: Integrating behavioral, diffusion tensor imaging, and functional magnetic resonance imaging data sets. *Journal of Cognitive Neuroscience, 17*, 687–693.

BANNERMAN, D. M., GOOD, M. A., BUTCHER, S. P., RAMSAY, M., & MORRIS, R. G. M. (1995). Distinct components of spatial learning revealed by prior training and NMDA receptor blockade. *Nature, 378,* 182–186.

BANSAFI, M., ZELANO, C., JOHNSON, B., MAINLAND, J., KHAN, R., & SOBEL, N. (2004). Olfaction: From sniff to percept. In M. S. Gazzaniga (Ed.), *The cognitive neurosciences III* (pp. 259–280). Cambridge, MA: MIT Press

BARBUR, J. L., WATSON, J. D. G., FRACKOWIAK, R. S. J., & ZEKI, S. (1993). Conscious visual perception without V1. *Brain, 116,* 1293–1302.

BARON-COHEN, S. (1995). *Mindblindness: An essay on autism and theory of mind.* Cambridge, MA: MIT Press.

BARON-COHEN, S., BURT, L., SMITH-LAITTAN, F., HARRISON, J., & BOLTON, P. (1996). Synaesthesia: Prevalence and familiality. *Perception, 25,* 1073–1079.

BARON-COHEN, S., LESLIE, A. M., & FRITH, U. (1985). Does the autistic child have a "theory of mind"? *Cognition, 21,* 37–46.

BARON-COHEN, S., LESLIE, A. M., & FRITH, U. (1986). Mechanical, behavioural and intentional understanding of picture stories in autistic children. *British Journal of Developmental Psychology, 4,* 113–125.

BARRETT, A. M., CRUCIAN, G. P., RAYMER, A. M., & HEILMAN, K. M. (1999). Spared comprehension of emotional prosody in a patient with global aphasia. *Neuropsychiatry, Neuropsychology, and Behavioral Neurology, 12,* 117–120.

BARTHOLOMEUS, B. (1974). Effects of task requirements on ear superiority for sung speech. *Cortex, 10,* 215–223.

BATISTA, A. P., BUNEO, C. A., SNYDER, L. H., & ANDERSON, R. A. (1999). Reach plans in eye-centered coordinates. *Science, 285,* 257–260.

BAXTER, M. G., PARKER, A., LINDNER, C. C., IZQUIERDO, A. D., & MURRAY, E. A. (2000). Control of response selection by reinforcer value requires interaction of amygdala and orbital prefrontal cortex. *Journal of Neuroscience, 20,* 4311–4319.

BAYLIS, G. C., ROLLS, E. T., & LEONARD, C. M. (1985). Selectivity between faces in the responses of a population of neurons in the cortex in the superior temporal sulcus of the monkey. *Brain Research, 342,* 91–102.

BEAR, M. F., CONNORS, B. W., & PARADISO, M. A. (1996). *Neuroscience: Exploring the brain.* Baltimore: Williams & Wilkins.

BECHARA, A., DAMASIO, H., TRANEL, D., & DAMASIO, A. R. (1997). Deciding advantageously before knowing the advantageous strategy. *Science, 275,* 1293–1295.

BECHARA, A., TRANEL, D., DAMASIO, H., ADOLPHS, R., ROCKLAND, C., & DAMASIO, A. R. (1995). Double dissociation of conditioning and declarative knowledge relative to the amygdala and hippocampus in human. *Science, 269,* 1115–1118.

BECKERS, G., & ZEKI, S. (1995). The consequences of inactivating areas V1 and V5 on visual motion perception. *Brain, 118,* 49–60.

BEER, J. S. (2007). The default self: Feeling good or being right? *Trends in Cognitive Sciences, 11,* 187–189.

BEER, J. S., HEEREY, E. H., KELTNER, D., SCABINI, D., & KNIGHT, R. T. (2003). The regulatory function of self-conscious emotion: Insights from patients with orbitofrontal damage. *Journal of Personality and Social Psychology, 85,* 594–604.

BEER, J. S., JOHN, O. P., SCABINI, D., & KNIGHT, R. T. (2006). Orbitofrontal cortex and social behavior: Integrating self-monitoring and emotion-cognition interactions. *Journal of Cognitive Neuroscience, 18,* 871–880.

BEHRENS, T. E., WOOLRICH, M. W., JENKINSON, M., JOHANSEN-BERQ, H., NUNES, R. G., CLARE, S., ET AL. (2003). Characterization and propagation of uncertainty in diffusion-weighted MR imaging. *Magnetic Resonance in Medicine, 50,* 1077–1088.

BEHRMANN, M., MOSCOVITCH, M., & WINOCUR, G. (1994). Intact visual imagery and impaired visual perception in a patient with visual agnosia. *Journal of Experimental Psychology. Human Perception and Performance, 20,* 1068–1087.

BENTIN, S., DEOUELL, L. Y., & SOROKER, N. (1999). Selective visual streaming in face recognition: Evidence from developmental prosopagnosia. *Neuroreport, 10,* 823–827.

BERMAN, R. A., HEISER, L. M., SAUNDERS, R. C., & COLBY, C. L. (2005). Dynamic circuitry for updating spatial representations. I. Behavioral evidence for interhemispheric transfer in the split-brain macaque. *Journal of Neurophysiology, 94,* 3228–3248.

BERMOND, B., NIEUWENHUYSEDR, B., FASOTTI, L., & SCHUERMAN, J. (1991). Spinal cord lesions, peripheral feedback and intensities of emotional feelings. *Cognition and Emotion, 5,* 201–220.

BERNARD, C. (1865). *An introduction to the study of experimental medicine,* 1865. First English translation by Henry Copley Greene, published by Macmillan & Co., Ltd., 1927; reprinted in 1949. The Dover Edition of 1957 is a reprint of the original translation with a new Foreword by I. Bernard Cohen of Harvard University.

BERNS, G. S., & SEJNOWSKI, T. (1996). How the basal ganglia makes decisions. In A. Damasio, H. Damasio, & Y. Christen (Eds.), *The neurobiology of decision making* (pp. 101–113). Cambridge, MA: MIT Press.

BERTOLINO, A., CAFORIO, G., BLASI, G., DE CANDIA, M., LATORRE, V., PETRUZZELLA, V., ET AL. (2004). Interaction of COMT (Val(108/158)Met) genotype and olanzapine treatment on prefrontal cortical function in patients with schizophrenia. *American Journal of Psychiatry, 161,* 1798–1805.

BESTMANN, S., RUFF, C., BLAKEMORE, C., DRIVER, J., & THILO, K. (2007). Spatial attention changes excitability of human visual cortex to direct stimulation. *Current Biology, 17,* 134–139.

BIANCHI, L. (1922). *The mechanism of the brain* (J. H. MacDonald, Trans.). Edinburgh, Scotland: E. & S. Livingstone.

BINDER, J., & PRICE, C. J. (2001). Functional neuroimaging of language processes. In R. Cabeza & A. Kingstone (Eds.), *Handbook of functional neuroimaging of cognition* (pp. 187–251). Cambridge, MA: MIT Press.

Binder, J. R., Frost, J. A., Hammeke, T. A., Bellgowan, P. S. F., Rao, S. M., & Cox, J. A. (1999). Conceptual processing during the conscious resting state: A functional MRI study. *Journal of Cognitive Neuroscience, 11,* 80–93.

Binder, J. R., Frost, J. A., Hammeke, T. A., Bellgowan, P. S. F., Springer, J. A., Kaufman, J. N., ET AL. (2000). Human temporal lobe activation by speech and non-speech sounds. *Cerebral Cortex, 10,* 512–528.

BISIACH, E., & LUZZATTI, C. (1978). Unilateral neglect of representational space. *Cortex, 14,* 129–133.

BISLEY, J. W., & GOLDBERG, M. E. (2006). Neural correlates of attention and distractibility in the lateral intraparietal area. *Journal of Neurophysiology, 95,* 1696–1717.

BIZZI, E., ACCORNERO, N., CHAPPLE, W., & HOGAN, N. (1984). Posture control and trajectory formation during arm movement. *Journal of Neuroscience, 4,* 2738–2744.

BLAIR, R. J. R., MORRIS, J. S., FRITH, C. D., PERRETT, D. I., & DOLAN, R. J. (1999). Dissociable neural responses to facial expressions of sadness and anger. *Brain, 122,* 883–893.

BLEULER, E. (1911). *Dementia praecox: Oder die Gruppe der Schizofrenien* (Handbuch der Psychiatrie. Spezieller Teil, Abt. 4, Hälfte 1). Leipzig, Germany: Deuticke.

BLISS, T. V. P., & LØMO, T. (1973). Long-lasting potentiation of synaptic transmission in the dentate area of the anaesthetized rabbit following stimulation of the perforant pathway. *Journal of Physiology, 232,* 331–356.

BLOCK, J. R., & YUKER, H. E. (1992). *Can you believe your eyes?: Over 250 illusions and other visual oddities.* Mattituck, NY: Amereon.

BLONDERS, L. X., BOWERS, D., & HEILMAN, K. M. (1991). The role of the right hemisphere in emotional communication. *Brain, 114,* 1115–1127.

BOOKHEIMER, S. (2002). Functional MRI of language: New approaches to understanding the cortical organization of semantic processing. *Annual Review of Neuroscience, 25,* 151–188.

BOTVINICK, M., NYSTROM, L. E., FISSELL, K., CARTER, C. S., & COHEN, J. D. (1999). Conflict monitoring versus selection-for-action in anterior cingulate cortex. *Nature, 402,* 179–181.

BOWER, J. M. (1997). Control of sensory data acquisition. *International Review of Neurobiology, 41,* 489–513.

BRADSHAW, J. L., & ROGERS, L. J. (1993). *The evolution of lateral asymmetries, language, tool use, and intellect.* San Diego, CA: Academic Press.

BRADSHAW, J. L., & NETTLETON, N. C. (1981). The nature of hemispheric specialization in man. *Behavioral and Brain Sciences, 4,* 51–91.

BRAITENBERG, V. (1984). *Vehicles: Experiments in synthetic psychology.* Cambridge, MA: MIT Press.

BRANSFORD, J. D., & JOHNSON, M. K. (1972). Contextual prerequisites for understanding: Some investigations of comprehension and recall. *Journal of Verbal Learning and Verbal Behavior, 11,* 717–726.

BREITER, H. C., ETCOFF, H. L., WHALAN, P. J., KENNEDY, W. A., RAUCH, S. L., BUCKNER, R. L., ET AL. (1996). Response and habituation of the human amygdala during visual processing of facial expression. *Neuron, 17,* 875–887.

BREMNER, J. D., RANDALL, P., VERMETTEN, E., STAIB, L., BRONEN, R. A., MAZURE, C., ET AL. (1997). Magnetic resonance imaging-based measurement of hippocampal volume in posttraumatic stress disorder to childhood physical and sexual abuse: A preliminary report. *Biological Psychiatry, 41,* 23–32.

BROADBENT, D. A. (1958). *Perception and communication.* New York: Pergamon.

BRODAL, A. (1982). *Neurological anatomy.* New York: Oxford University Press.

BRODMANN, K. (1960). On the comparative localization of the cortex (translated from the French and German). In G. von Bonin, *Some papers on the cerebral cortex* (pp. 201–230). Springfield, IL: Thomas, 1960. (Original work published 1909)

BROTCHIE, P., IANSEK, R., & HORNE, M. K. (1991). Motor function of the monkey globus pallidus. *Brain, 114,* 1685–1702.

BROWN, J. W., & BRAVER, T. S. (2005). Learned predictions of error likelihood in the anterior cingulate cortex. *Science, 307,* 1118–1121.

BROWN, T. (1911). The intrinsic factors in the act of progression in the mammal. *Proceedings of the Royal Society of London, Series B, 84,* 308–319.

BRYDEN, M. P. (1982). *Laterality: Functional asymmetry in the intact human brain.* New York: Academic Press.

BUCHANAN, T. W., TRANEL, D., & ADOLPHS, R. (2006). Memories for emotional autobiographical events following unilateral damage to medial temporal lobe. *Brain, 129,* 115–127.

BUCHSBAUM, M. S., BUCHSBAUM, B. R., CHOKRON, S., TANG, C., WEI, T. C., & BYNE, W. (2006). Thalamocortical circuits: fMRI assessment of the pulvinar and medial dorsal nucleus in normal volunteers. *Neuroscience Letters, 404,* 282–287.

BUCKNER, R. L., KELLEY, W. M., & PETERSEN, S. E. (1999). Frontal cortex contributes to human memory formation. *Nature Reviews Neuroscience, 2,* 311–314.

BUDGE, J. (1862). *Lehrbuch der speciellen Physiologie des Menschen.* Leipzig, Germany: Voigt & Günther.

BULLOCK, T. H. (1984a). Comparative neuroscience holds promise for a quiet revolution. *Science, 225,* 473–478.

BULLOCK, T. H. (1993). How are more complex brains different? One view and an agenda for comparative neurobiology. *Brain, Behavior and Evolution, 41,* 88–96.

BUNGE, S. A. (2004). How we use rules to select actions: A review of evidence from cognitive neuroscience. *Cognitive, Affective & Behavioral Neuroscience, 4,* 564–579.

BURNS, J. K. (2006). Psychosis: A costly by-product of social brain evolution in *Homo sapiens. Progress in Neuropsychopharmacological and Biological Psychiatry, 30,* 797–814.

BUSH, G., LUU, P., & POSNER, M. I. (2000). Cognitive and emotional influences in anterior cingulate cortex. *Trends in Cognitive Sciences, 4,* 215–222.

CABEZA, R., RAO, S. M., WAGNER, A. D., MAYER, A. R., & SCHACTER, D. L. (2001). Can medial temporal lobe regions distinguish true from false? An event-related fMRI study of veridical and illusory recognition memory. *Proceedings of the National Academy of Sciences, USA, 98,* 4805–4810.

CAHILL, L., BABINSKY, R., MARKOWITSCH, H. J., & MCGAUGH, J. L. (1995). The amygdala and emotional memory. *Science, 377,* 295–296.

CAHILL, L, HAIER, R. J., FALLON, J., ALKIRE, M. T., TANG, C., KEATOR, D., ET AL. (1996). Amygdala activity at encoding correlated with long-term, free recall of emotional information. *Proceedings of the National Academy of Sciences, USA, 93,* 8016–8021.

CALDER, A. J., KEANE, J., MANES, F., ANTOUN, N., & YOUNG, A. W. (2000). Impaired recognition and experience of disgust following brain injury. *Nature Neuroscience, 3,* 1077–1078.

CALVERT, G. A., BULLMORE, E. T., BRAMMER, M. J., CAMPBELL, R., WILLIAMS, S. C., MCGUIRE, P. K., ET AL. (1997). Activation of auditory cortex during silent lipreading. *Science, 276,* 593–596.

CALVO-MERINO, B., GLASER, D. E., GRÈZES, J., PASSINGHAM, R. E., & HAGGARD, P. (2005). Action observation and acquired motor skills: An fMRI study with expert dancers. *Cerebral Cortex, 15,* 1243–1249.

CAPLAN, D. (1994). Language and the brain. In M. A. Gernsbacher (Ed.), *Handbook of psycholinguistics* (pp. 1023–1053). San Diego, CA: Academic Press.

CAPLAN, D., ALPERT, N., WATERS, G., & OLIVIERI, A. (2000). Activation of Broca's area by syntactic processing under conditions of concurrent articulation. *Human Brain Mapping, 9,* 65–71.

CARAMAZZA, A. (1992). Is cognitive neuropsychology possible? *Journal of Cognitive Neuroscience, 4,* 80–95.

CARAMAZZA, A. (1996). The brain's dictionary. *Nature, 380,* 485–486.

CARAMAZZA, A., & SHELTON, J. (1998). Domain-specific knowledge systems in the brain: The animate-inanimate distinction. *Journal of Cognitive Neuroscience, 10,* 1–34.

CARMEL, D., & BENTIN, S. (2002). Domain specificity versus expertise: Factors influencing distinct processing of faces. *Cognition, 83,* 1–29.

CARMENA, J. M., LEBEDEV, M. A., CRIST, R. E., O'DOHERTY J. E., SANTUCCI, D. M., DIMITROV, D. F., ET AL. (2003). Learning to control a brain-machine interface for reaching and grasping by primates. *PLoS Biology, 1*(2), E42. [Epub, October 13]

CARPENTER, M. (1976). *Human neuroanatomy* (7th ed.). Baltimore: Williams & Wilkins.

CASPI, A., MCCLAY, J., MOFFITT, T. E., MILL, J., MARTIN, J., CRAIG, I. W., ET AL. (2002). Role of genotype in the cycle of violence in maltreated children. *Science, 297,* 851–854.

CASTAIGNE, P., LHERMITTE, F., SIGNORET, J. L., & ABELANET, R. (1980). Description et étude scannographique du cerveau de Leborgne: La découverte de Broca. *Revue Neurologique, 136,* 563–583.

CASTRIOTA-SCANDERBEG, A., HAGBERG, G. E., CERASA, A., COMMITTERI, G., GALATI, G., PATRIA, F., ET AL. (2005). The appreciation of wine by sommeliers: A functional magnetic resonance study of sensory integration. *Neuroimage, 25,* 570–578.

CATANIA, K. C., & KAAS, J. H. (1995). Organization of the somatosensory cortex of the star-nosed mole. *Journal of Comparative Neurology, 351,* 549–567.

CATANIA, K. C., NORTHCUTT, R. G., KAAS, J. H., & BECK, P. D. (1993). Nose stars and brain stripes. *Nature, 364,* 493.

CHAO, L. L., & MARTIN, A. (2000). Representation of manipulable man-made objects in the dorsal stream. *Neuroimage, 12,* 478–484.

CHAPIN, J. K., MOXON, K. A., MARKOWITZ, R. S., & NICOLELIS, M. A. (1999). Real-time control of a robot arm using simultaneously recorded neurons in the motor cortex. *Nature Neuroscience, 2,* 664–670.

CHAWLA, D., LUMER, E. D., & FRISTON, K. J. (1999). The relationship between synchronization among neuronal populations and their mean activity levels. *Neural Computation, 11,* 1389–1411.

CHENG, Y., LIN, C. P., LIU, H. L., HSU, Y. Y., LIM, K. E., HUNG, D., ET AL. (2007). Expertise modulates the perception of pain in others. *Current Biology, 17,* 1708–1713.

CHERRY, E. C. (1953). Some experiments on the recognition of speech, with one and two ears. *Journal of the Acoustical Society of America, 25,* 975–979.

CHIARELLO, C. (1991). Interpretation of word meanings by the cerebral hemispheres: One is not enough. In P. J. Schwanenflugel (Ed.), *The psychology of word meanings* (pp. 251–278). Hillsdale, NJ: Erlbaum.

CHOMSKY, N. (1956). Three models for the description of language. *IEEE Transactions on Information Theory, 2*(3), 113–124.

CHOMSKY, N. (1957). *Syntactic structures.* The Hague, Netherlands: Mouton.

CHOMSKY, N. (2006). *Language and mind* (3rd ed.). Cambridge, England: Cambridge University Press.

CHRISTIANSON, S. A. (1992). *The handbook of emotion and memory: Research and theory.* Hillsdale, NJ: Erlbaum.

CHUGANI, H. T. (1998). A critical period of brain development: Studies of cerebral glucose utilization with PET. *Preventive Medicine, 27,* 184–188.

CHURCHILL, W. (1930). *My early life: A roving commission.* New York: Scribner.

CHWALISZ, K., DIENER, E., & GALLAGHER, D. (1988). Autonomic arousal feedback and emotional experience: Evidence from the spinal cord injured. *Journal of Personality and Social Psychology, 54,* 820–828.

CLASSEN, J., LIEPERT, J., WISE, S. P., HALLETT, M., & COHEN, L. G. (1998). Rapid plasticity of human cortical movement representation induced by practice. *Journal of Neurophysiology, 79,* 1117–1123.

COHEN, A., & IVRY, R. (1989). Illusory conjunctions inside and outside the focus of attention. *Journal of Experimental Psychology. Human Perception and Performance, 15,* 650–663.

COHEN, J. D., BOTVINICK, M., & CARTER, C. S. (2000). Anterior cingulate and prefrontal cortex: Who's in control? *Nature Neuroscience, 3,* 421–423.

COHEN, L., LEHERICY, S., CHOCHON, F., LEMER, C., RIVAUD, S., & DEHAENE, S. (2002). Language-specific tuning of visual cortex? Functional properties of the Visual Word Form Area. *Brain, 125*(Pt.5), 1054–1069.

COHEN, N. J., & EICHENBAUM, H. (1993). *Memory, amnesia and the hippocampal system.* Cambridge, MA: MIT Press.

COLLINS, A. M., & LOFTUS, E. F. (1975). A spreading-activation theory of semantic processing. *Psychological Review, 82,* 407–428.

COLTHEART, M., CURTIS, B., ATKINS, P., & HALLER, M. (1993). Models of reading aloud: Dual route and parallel-distributed-processing approaches. *Psychological Review, 100,* 589–608.

CORBALLIS, M. C. (1991). *The lopsided ape: Evolution of the generative mind.* New York: Oxford University Press.

CORBETTA, M., KINCADE, J. M., OLLINGER, J. M., MCAVOY, M. P., & SHULMAN, G. L. (2000). Voluntary orienting is dissociated from target detection in human posterior parietal cortex. *Nature Neuroscience, 3,* 292–297.

CORBETTA, M., MIEZIN, F. M., DOBMEYER, S., SHULMAN, G. L., & PETERSEN, S. E. (1991). Selective and divided attention during visual discriminations of shape, color and speed: Functional anatomy by positron emission tomography. *Journal of Neuroscience, 11,* 2383–2402.

CORBETTA, M., & SHULMAN, G. (2002). Control of goal-directed and stimulus-driven attention in the brain. *Nature Reviews Neuroscience, 3,* 201–215.

COREN, S., WARD, L. M., & ENNS, J. T. (1994). *Sensation and perception* (4th ed.). Ft. Worth, TX: Harcourt Brace.

CORKIN, S. (2002). What's new with the amnesic patient H.M.? *Nature Reviews Neuroscience, 3,* 153–160.

CORKIN, S., AMARAL, D., GONZALEZ, R., JOHNSON, K., & HYMAN, B. T. (1997). H.M.'s medial temporal lobe lesion: Findings from magnetic resonance imaging. *Journal of Neuroscience, 17,* 3964–3979.

CORTHOUT, E., UTTL, B., ZIEMANN, U., COWEY, A., & HALLETT, M. (1999). Two periods of processing in the (circum)striate visual cortex as revealed by transcranial magnetic stimulation. *Neuropsychologia, 37,* 137–145.

COSMIDES, L. (1984). The logic of social exchange: Has natural selection shaped how humans reason? Studies with the Wason selection task. *Cognition, 31,* 187–276.

COSMIDES, L., & TOOBY, J. (1992). Cognitive adaptations for social exchange. In J. H. Barkow, L. Cosmides, & J. Tooby (Eds.), *The adapted mind* (pp. 163–228). New York: Oxford University Press.

CRAIK, F. I. M., & LOCKHART, R. S. (1972). Levels of processing: A framework for memory research. *Journal of Verbal Learning and Verbal Behavior, 11,* 671–684.

CRICK, F. (1992). Function of the thalamic reticular complex: The searchlight hypothesis. In S. M. Kosslyn & R. A. Andersen (Eds.), *Frontiers in cognitive neuroscience* (pp. 366–372). Cambridge, MA: MIT Press.

CRITCHLEY, H. D., MATHIAS, C. J., JOSEPHS, O., O'DOHERTY, J., ZANINI, S., DEWAR, B. K., ET AL. (2003). Human cingulate cortex and autonomic control: Converging neuroimaging and clinical evidence. *Brain, 126,* 2139–2152.

CULHAM, J. C., DANCKERT, S. L., DESOUZA, J. F., GATI, J. S., MENON, R. S., & GOODALE, M. A. (2003). Visually guided grasping produces fMRI activation in dorsal but not ventral stream brain areas. *Experimental Brain Research, 153,* 180–189.

CUNNINGHAM, W. A., JOHNSON, M. K., RAYE, C. L., GATENBY, J. C., GORE, J. C., & BANAJI, M. R. (2004). Separable neural components in the processing of black and white faces. *Psychological Science, 15,* 806–813.

DALTON, K. M., NACEWICZ, B. M., JOHNSTONE, T., SCHAEFER, H. S., GERNSBACHER, M. A., GOLDSMITH, H. H., ET AL. (2005). Gaze fixation and the neural circuitry of face processing in autism. *Nature Neuroscience, 8,* 519–526.

DAMASIO, A. R. (1990). Category-related recognition defects as a clue to the neural substrates of knowledge. *Trends in Neurosciences, 13,* 95–98.

DAMASIO, A. R. (1994). *Descartes' error: Emotion, reason, and the human brain.* New York: Putnam.

DAMASIO, H., GRABOWSKI, T., FRANK, R., GALABURDA, A. M., & DAMASIO, A. R. (1994). The return of Phineas Gage: Clues about the brain from the skull of a famous patient. *Science, 264,* 1102–1105.

DAMASIO, H., GRABOWSKI, T. J., TRANEL, D., HICHWA, R. D., & DAMASIO, A. R. (1996). A neural basis for lexical retrieval. *Nature, 380,* 499–505.

DAMASIO, H., TRANEL, D., GRABOWSKI, T., ADOLPHS, R., & DAMASIO, A. (2004). Neural systems behind word and concept retrieval. *Cognition, 92,* 179–229.

DARWIN, C. (1859). *On the origin of species.* London: Murray. (Reprint, Cambridge, MA: Harvard University Press)

DARWIN, C. (1871). *The descent of man and selection in relation to sex.* London: Murray.

DASILVA, A. F., TUCH, D. S., WIEGELL, M. R., & HADJIKHANI, N. (2003). A primer on diffusion tensor imaging of anatomical substructures. *Neurosurgical Focus, 15,* E4.

DAVIDSON, R. J. (1995). Cerebral asymmetry, emotion, and affective style. In R. J. Davidson & K. Hugdahl (Eds.), *Brain asymmetry* (pp. 361–387). Cambridge, MA: MIT Press.

DAVIDSON, R. J., EKMAN, P., SARON, C., SENULIS, J., & FRIESEN, W. V. (1990). Approach-withdrawal and cerebral asymmetry: Emotional expression and brain physiology. *Journal of Personality and Social Psychology, 58,* 330–341.

DAVIDSON, R. J., JACKSON, D. C., & KALIN, N. H. (2000). Emotion, plasticity, context, and regulation: Perspectives from affective neuroscience. *Psychological Bulletin, 126,* 890–909.

DAVIS, M. (1992). The role of the amygdala in conditioned fear. In J. P. Aggleton (Ed.), *The amygdala: Neurobiological aspects of emotion, memory and mental dysfunction* (pp. 255–306). New York: Wiley-Liss.

DAWKINS, R. (1976). *The selfish gene.* New York: Oxford University Press.

DAWSON, J. L. M., CHEUNG, Y. M., & LAU, R. T. S. (1973). Effects of neonatal sex hormones on sex-based cognitive abilities in the white rat. *Psychologia, 16,* 17–24.

DEARMOND, S., FUSCO, M., & DEWEY, M. (1976). *A photographic atlas: Structure of the human brain* (2nd ed.). New York: Oxford University Press.

DE BIE, R. M., DE HAAN, R. J., SCHUURMAN, P. R., ESSELINK, R. A., BOSCH, D. A., & SPEELMAN, J. D. (2002) Morbidity and mortality following pallidotomy in Parkinson's disease: A systematic review. *Neurology, 58,* 1008–1012.

DECETY, J., & GREZES, J. (1999). Neural mechanisms subserving the perception of human actions. *Trends in Cognitive Sciences, 3,* 172–178.

DEEP-BRAIN STIMULATION FOR PARKINSON'S DISEASE STUDY GROUP. (2001). Deep-brain stimulation of the subthalamic nucleus or the pars interna of the globus pallidus in Parkinson's disease. *New England Journal of Medicine, 345,* 956–963.

DE FOCKERT, J. W., REES, G., FRITH, C. D., & LAVIE, N. (2001). The role of working memory in visual selective attention. *Science, 291,* 1803–1806.

DEHAENE, S., CHANGEUX, J. P., NACCACHE, L., SACKUR, J., & SERGENT, C. (2006). Conscious, preconscious, and subliminal processing: A testable taxonomy. *Trends in Cognitive Sciences, 10,* 204–211.

DEHAENE, S., POSNER, M. I., & TUCKER, D. M. (1994). Localization of a neural system for error detection and compensation. *Psychological Science, 5,* 303–305.

DEIBERT, E., KRAUT, M., KREMEN, S., & HART, J., JR. (1999). Neural pathways in tactile object recognition. *Neurology, 52,* 1413–1417.

DELBRÜCK, M. (1986). *Mind from matter? An essay on evolutionary epistemology.* London: Blackwell.

DELIS, D., ROBERTSON, L., & EFRON, R. (1986). Hemispheric specialization of memory for visual hierarchical stimuli. *Neuropsychologia, 24,* 205–214.

DELL, G. S. (1986). A spreading activation theory of retrieval in sentence production. *Psychological Review, 93,* 283–321.

DELONG, M. R. (1990). Primate models of movement disorders of basal ganglia origin. *Trends in Neurosciences, 13,* 281–285.

DE MARTINO, B., KUMARAN, D., SEYMOUR, & DOLAN, R. J. (2006). Frames, biases, and rational decision-making in the human brain. *Science, 313,* 684–687.

DÉMONET, J. F., CHOLLET, F., RAMSAY, S., CERDEBAT, D., NESPOULES, J. D., WISE, R., ET AL. (1992). The anatomy of phonological and semantic processing in normal subjects. *Brain, 115,* 1753–1768.

DÉMONET, J. F., PRICE, C. J., WISE, R., & FRACKOWIAK, R. S. J. (1994). Differential activation of right and left posterior sylvian regions by semantic and phonological tasks: A positron emission tomography study. *Neuroscience Letters, 182,* 25–28.

DENNETT, D. (1995). *Darwin's dangerous idea.* New York: Simon and Schuster.

DE RENZI, E., PERANI, D., CARLESIMO, G. A., SILVERI, M. C., & FAZIO, F. (1994). Prosopagnosia can be associated with damage confined to the right hemisphere—An MRI and PET study and a review of the literature. *Neuropsychologia, 32,* 893–902.

DESIMONE, R. (1991). Face-selective cells in the temporal cortex of monkeys. *Journal of Cognitive Neuroscience, 3,* 1–8.

DESIMONE, R. (1996). Neural mechanisms for visual memory and their role in attention. *Proceedings of the National Academy of Sciences, USA, 93,* 13494–13499.

DESIMONE, R., ALBRIGHT, T. D., GROSS, C. G., & BRUCE, C. (1984). Stimulus-selective properties of inferior temporal neurons in the macaque. *Journal of Neuroscience, 4,* 2051–2062.

DESIMONE, R., WESSINGER, M., THOMAS, L., & SCHNEIDER, W. (1990). Attentional control of visual perception: Cortical and subcortical mechanisms. *Cold Spring Harbor Symposia on Quantitative Biology, 55,* 963–971.

DESMURGET, M., EPSTEIN, C. M., TURNER, R. S., PRABLANC, C., ALEXANDER, G. E., & GRAFTON, S. T. (1999). Role of the posterior parietal cortex in updating reaching movements to a visual target. *Nature Neuroscience, 2,* 563–567.

DEVINSKY, O., MORRELL, M. J., & VOGT, B. A. (1995). Contributions of anterior cingulate cortex to behavior. *Brain, 118,* 279–306.

DIAMOND, A. (1990). The development and neural bases of memory functions as indexed by the A(not)B and delayed response tasks in human infants and infant monkeys. In A. Diamond (Ed.), *The development and neural bases of higher cognitive functions* (pp. 267–317). New York: New York Academy of Sciences.

DOLCOS, F., LABAR, K. S., & CABEZA, R. (2004). Interaction between the amygdala and the medial temporal lobe memory system predicts better memory for emotional events. *Neuron, 42,* 855–863.

DOYLE, D., CABRAL, J., PFUETZNER, R., KUO, A., GULBIS, J., COHEN, S., ET AL. (1998). The structure of the potassium channel: Molecular basis of K^+ conduction and selectivity. *Science, 280,* 69–77.

DRACHMAN, D. A., & ARBIT, J. (1966). Memory and the hippocampal complex. II. Is memory a multiple process? *Archives of Neurology, 15,* 52–61.

DREVETS, W. C. (1998). Functional neuroimaging studies of depression: The anatomy of melancholia. *Annual Review of Medicine, 49,* 341–361.

DRONKERS, N. F. (1996). A new brain region for coordinating speech articulation. *Nature, 384,* 159–161.

DRONKERS, N. F., WILKINS, D. P., VAN VALIN, R. D., REDFERN, B. B., & JAEGER, J. J. (1994). A reconsideration of the brain areas involved in the disruption of morphosyntactic comprehension. *Brain and Language, 47,* 461–462.

DRUZGAL, T. J., & D'ESPOSITO, M. (2003). Dissecting contributions of prefrontal cortex and fusiform face area to face working memory. *Journal of Cognitive Neuroscience, 15,* 771–784.

DUM, R. P., & STRICK, P. L. (2002). Motor areas in the frontal lobe of the primate. *Physiology & Behavior, 77,* 677–682.

DUNCAN, J. (1984). Selective attention and the organization of visual information. *Journal of Experimental Psychology. General, 113,* 501–517.

DUNCAN, J. (1995). Attention, intelligence, and the frontal lobes. In M. S. Gazzaniga (Ed.), *The cognitive neurosciences* (pp. 721–733). Cambridge, MA: MIT Press.

DUNN, B. B., DALGLEISH, T., & LAWRENCE, A. D. (2006). The somatic marker hypothesis: A critical evaluation. *Neuroscience and Biobehavioral Reviews, 30,* 239–271.

DUONG, T. Q., KIM, D. S., UGURBIL, K., & KIM, S. G. (2000). Spatiotemporal dynamics of the BOLD fMRI signals: Toward mapping submillimeter cortical columns using the early negative response. *Magnetic Resonance in Medicine, 44,* 231–242.

EASON, R., HARTER, M., & WHITE, C. (1969). Effects of attention and arousal on visually evoked cortical potentials and reaction time in man. *Physiology & Behavior, 4,* 283–289.

EFRON, R. (1990). *The decline and fall of hemispheric specialization.* Hillsdale, NJ: Erlbaum.

EGLY, R., DRIVER, J., & RAFAL, R. D. (1994). Shifting visual attention between objects and locations—Evidence from normal and parietal lesion subjects. *Journal of Experimental Psychology. General, 123,* 161–177.

EICHENBAUM, H. (2000). A cortical-hippocampal system for declarative memory. *Nature Reviews. Neuroscience, 1,* 41–50.

EISENBERG, J. F. (1981). *The mammalian radiations: An analysis of trends in evolution, adaptation and behavior.* Chicago: University of Chicago Press.

EKMAN, P. (1973). Cross-cultural studies in facial expression. In P. Ekman (Ed.), *Darwin and facial expressions: A century of research in review.* New York: Academic Press.

EKMAN, P., & FRIESEN, W. V. (1971). Constants across cultures in the face and emotion. *Journal of Personality and Social Psychology, 17,* 124–129.

ELBERT, T., PANTEV, C., WIENBRUCH, C., ROCKSTROH, B., & TAUB, E. (1995). Increased cortical representation of the fingers of the left hand in string players. *Science, 270,* 305–307.

ELDRIDGE, L. L., KNOWLTON, B. J., FURMANSKI, C. S., BOOKHEIMER, S. Y., & ENGEL, S. A. (2000). Remembering episodes: A selective role for the hippocampus during retrieval. *Nature Neuroscience, 3,* 1149–1152.

ENGEL, A. K., KREITER, A. K., KONIG, P., & SINGER, W. (1991). Synchronization of oscillatory neuronal responses between striate and extrastriate visual cortical areas of the cat. *Proceedings of the National Academy of Sciences, USA, 88,* 6048–6052.

EPSTEIN, R., & KANWISHER, N. (1998). A cortical representation of the local visual environment. *Nature, 392,* 598–601.

ERIKSEN, C. W., & ERIKSEN, B. (1971). Visual perceptual processing rates and backward and forward masking. *Journal of Experimental Psychology, 89,* 306–313.

ERIKSSON, P. S., PERFILIEVA, E., BJÖRK-ERIKSSON, T., ALBORN, A., NORDBORG, C., PETERSON, D., ET AL. (1998). Neurogenesis in the adult human hippocampus. *Nature Medicine, 4,* 1313–1317.

ESTERMAN, M., VERSTYNEN, T., IVRY, R. B., & ROBERTSON, L. C. (2006). Coming unbound: Disrupting automatic integration of synesthetic color and graphemes by transcranial magnetic stimulation of the right parietal lobe. *Journal of Cognitive Neuroscience, 18,* 1570–1576.

ETCOFF, N. L., EKMAN, P., MAGEE, J. J., & FRANK, M. G. (2000). Lie detection and language comprehension. *Nature, 405,* 139.

FARAH, M. J. (1988). Is visual imagery really visual? Overlooked evidence from neuropsychology. *Psychological Review, 95,* 307–317.

FARAH, M. J. (1990). *Visual agnosia: Disorders of object recognition and what they tell us about normal vision.* Cambridge, MA: MIT Press.

FARAH, M. J. (1994). Specialization within visual object recognition: Clues from prosopagnosia and alexia. In M. J. Farah & G. Ratcliff (Eds.), *The neuropsychology of high-level vision: Collected tutorial essays* (pp. 133–146). Hillsdale, NJ: Erlbaum.

FARAH, M. (2004). *Visual agnosia* (2nd ed.). Cambridge, MA: MIT Press.

FARAH, M. J., & MCCLELLAND, J. L. (1991). A computational model of semantic memory impairment: Modality specificity and emergent category specificity. *Journal of Experimental Psychology. General, 120,* 339–357.

FELLOWS, L. K., & FARAH, M. J. (2005). Is anterior cingulate cortex necessary for cognitive control? *Brain, 128,* 788–796.

FENDRICH, R., WESSINGER, C. M., & GAZZANIGA, M. S. (1992). Residual vision in a scotoma: Implications for blindsight. *Science, 258,* 1489–1491.

FERRY, B., & MCGAUGH, J. L. (2000). Role of amygdala norepinephrine in mediating stress hormone regulation of memory storage. *Acta Pharmacologica Sinica, 21,* 481–493.

FINGER, S. (1994). *Origins of neuroscience.* New York: Oxford University Press.

FLORENCE, S. L., & KAAS, J. H. (1995). Large-scale reorganization at multiple levels of the somatosensory pathway follows therapeutic amputation of the hand in monkeys. *Journal of Neuroscience, 15,* 8083–8095.

FLOURENS, M.-J. P. (1824). *Recherches expérimentales sur les proprieties et les functiones du systeme nerveux dans le animaux vertébrés.* Paris: Ballière.

FODOR, J. A. (1983). *The modularity of mind.* Cambridge, MA: MIT Press.

FOSTER, D., & WILSON, M. (2006). Reverse replay of behavioral sequences in hippocampal place cells during the awake state. *Nature, 440,* 680–683.

FOX, P. T., MIEZIN, F. M., ALLMAN, J. M., VAN ESSEN, D. C., & RAICHLE, M. E. (1987). Retinotopic organization of human visual cortex mapped with positron-emission tomography. *Journal of Neuroscience, 7,* 913–922.

FRANZ, E., ELIASSEN, J., IVRY, R., & GAZZANIGA, M. (1996). Dissociation of spatial and temporal coupling in the bimanual movements of callosotomy patients. *Psychological Science, 7,* 306–310.

FRAZIER, L. (1987). Structure in auditory word recognition. *Cognition, 25,* 157–187.

FREEDMAN, D. J., RIESENHUBER, M., POGGIO, T., & MILLER, E. K. (2001). Categorical representations of visual stimuli in the primate prefontal cortex. *Science, 291,* 312–316.

FREEMAN, W., & WATTS, J. W. (1950). *Psychosurgery: In the treatment of mental disorders and intractable pain* (2nd ed.). Springfield, IL: Charles C. Thomas.

FREUD, S. (1882) *Über den Bau der Nervenfasern und Nervenzellen beim Flusskrebs* (Sitzungsberichte der Kaiserliche Akademie der Wissenschaften, Mathematisch-Naturwissenschaftliche Classe, v. 85). [Vienna: K. K. Hof- und Staatsdruckerei].

FREY, S. H., FUNNELL, M. G., GERRY, V. E., & GAZZANIGA, M. S. (2005). A dissociation between the representation of tool-use skills and hand dominance: Insights from left- and right-handed callosotomy patients. *Journal of Cognitive Neuroscience, 17,* 262–272.

FRICKER-GATES, R. A., SHIN, J. J., TAI, C. C., CATAPANO, L. A., & MACKLIS, J. D. (2002). Late-stage immature neocortical neurons reconstruct interhemispheric connections and form synaptic contacts with increased efficiency in adult mouse cortex undergoing targeted neurodegeneration. *Journal of Neuroscience, 22,* 4045–4056.

FRIEDERICI, A., PFEIFER, E., & HAHNE, A. (1993). Event-related brain potentials during natural speech processing: Effects of semantic, morphological and syntactic violations. *Cognitive Brain Research, 1,* 183–192.

FRITH, C. D. (2000). The role of the dorsolateral prefrontal cortex in the selection of action as revealed by functional imaging. In S. Monsell & J. Driver (Eds.), *Attention and performance: Vol. 18. Control of cognitive processes* (pp. 549–565). Cambridge, MA: MIT Press.

FRITH, C. (2003). What do imaging studies tell us about the neural basis of autism? *Novartis Foundation Symposium, 251,* 149–166.

FRITSCH, G., & HITZIG, E. (1870). Ueber die elektrische Erregbarkeit des Grosshirns (On the electrical excitability of the cerebrum). *Archiv fur Anatomie, Physiologie und wissenschaftliche Medizin, 37,* 300–332.

FUNAYAMA, E. S., GRILLON, C. G., DAVIS, M., & PHELPS, E. A. (2001). A double dissociation in the affective modulation of startle in humans: Effects of unilateral temporal lobectomy. *Journal of Cognitive Neuroscience, 13,* 721–729.

FUSTER, J. M. (1989). *The prefrontal cortex: Anatomy, physiology, and neuropsychology of the frontal lobe* (2nd ed.). New York: Raven.

GAFFAN, D., & HARRISON, S. (1987). Amygdalectomy and disconnection in visual learning for auditory secondary reinforcement by monkeys. *Journal of Neuroscience, 7,* 2285–2292.

GALL, F. J., & SPURZHEIM, J. (1810–1819). *Anatomie et physiologie du système nerveux en général, et du cerveau en particulier.* Paris: Schoell.

GALLAGHER, M., & HOLLAND, P. C. (1992). Understanding the function of the central nucleus: Is simple conditioning enough? In J. P. Aggleton (Ed.), *The amygdala: Neurobiological aspects of emotion, memory, and mental dysfunction* (pp. 307–321). New York: Wiley-Liss.

GALLANT, J. L., SHOUP, R. E., & MAZER, J. A. (2000). A human extrastriate area functionally homologous to macaque V4. *Neuron, 27,* 227–235.

GALLISTEL, C. R. (1995). The replacement of general-purpose theories with adaptive specializations. In M. S. Gazzaniga (Ed.), *The cognitive neurosciences* (pp. 1255–1267). Cambridge, MA: MIT Press.

GALUSKE, R. A., SCHLOTE, W., BRATZKE, H., & SINGER, W. (2000). Interhemispheric asymmetries of the modular structure in human temporal cortex. *Science, 289,* 1946–1949.

GASH, D. M., ZHANG, Z., OVADIA, A., CASS, W. A., YI, A., SIMMERMAN, L., ET AL. (1996). Functional recovery in parkinsonian monkeys treated with GDNF. *Nature, 380,* 252–255.

GATZ, M., REYNOLDS, C. A., FRATIGLIONI, L., JOHANSSON, B., MORTIMER, J. A., BERG, S., ET AL. (2006). Role of genes and environments for explaining Alzheimer disease. *Archives of General Psychiatry, 63,* 168–174.

GAULIN, S. J. C. (1995). Does evolutionary theory predict sex differences in the brain? In M. S. Gazzaniga (Ed.), *The cognitive neurosciences* (pp. 1211–1225). Cambridge, MA: MIT Press.

GAULIN, S. J. C., & FITZGERALD, R. W. (1989). Sexual selection for spatial-learning ability. *Animal Behaviour, 37,* 322–331.

GAUTHIER, I. L., BEHRMANN, M., & TARR, M. J. (1999). Can face recognition really be dissociated from object recognition? *Journal of Cognitive Neuroscience, 11,* 349–370.

GAUTHIER, I., SKUDLARSKI, P., GORE, J. C., & ANDERSON, A. W. (2000). Expertise for cars and birds recruits brain areas involved in face recognition. *Nature Neuroscience, 3,* 191–197.

GAUTHIER, I., TARR, M. J., ANDERSON, A. W., SKUDLARSKI, P., & GORE, J. C. (1999). Activation of the middle fusiform 'face area' increases with expertise in recognizing novel objects. *Nature Neuroscience, 2,* 568–573.

GAZZALEY, A., COONEY, J. W., MCEVOY, K., KNIGHT, R. T., & D'ESPOSITO, M. (2005). Top-down enhancement and suppression of the magnitude and speed of neural activity. *Journal of Cognitive Neuroscience, 17,* 507–517.

GAZZALEY, A., COONEY, J. W., RISSMAN, J., & D'ESPOSITO, M. (2005). Top-down suppression deficit underlies working memory impairment in normal aging. *Nature Neuroscience, 8,* 1298–1300.

GAZZANIGA, M. S. (1992). *Nature's mind: The biological roots of thinking, emotions, sexuality, language, and intelligence.* New York: Basic Books.

GAZZANIGA, M. S. (1995c). Principles of human brain organization derived from split-brain studies. *Neuron, 14,* 217–228.

GAZZANIGA, M. S. (2000). Cerebral specialization and interhemispheric communication: Does the corpus callosum enable the human condition? *Brain, 123,* 1293–1326.

GAZZANIGA, M. S. (2005). Forty-five years of split brain research and still going strong. *Nature Reviews Neuroscience, 6,* 653–659.

GAZZANIGA, M. S., & LEDOUX, J. E. (1978). *The integrated mind.* New York: Plenum.

GAZZANIGA, M. S., & SMYLIE, C. S. (1983). Facial recognition and brain asymmetries: Clues to underlying mechanisms. *Annals of Neurology, 13,* 536–540.

GAZZANIGA, M. S., & SMYLIE, C. S. (1990). Hemispheric mechanisms controlling voluntary and spontaneous facial expressions. *Journal of Cognitive Neuroscience, 2,* 239–245.

GAZZANIGA, M. S., & SPERRY, R. W. (1967). Language after section of the cerebral commissures. *Brain, 90,* 131–148.

GEARY, D. C. (1995). Reflections of evolution and culture in children's cognition. Implications for mathematical development and instruction. *American Psychologist, 50,* 24–37.

GEHRING, W. J., GOSS, B., COLES, M. G. H., MEYER, D. E., & DONCHIN, E. (1993). A neural system for error detection and compensation. *Psychological Science, 4,* 385–390.

GEORGOPOULOS, A. P. (1990). Neurophysiology of reaching. In M. Jeannerod (Ed.), *Attention and performance XIII: Motor representation and control* (pp. 227–263). Hillsdale, NJ: Erlbaum.

GEORGOPOULOS, A. P. (1995). Motor cortex and cognitive processing. In M. S. Gazzaniga (Ed.), *The cognitive neurosciences* (pp. 507–517). Cambridge, MA: MIT Press.

GERAERTS, W. P. M., SMIT, A. B., & LI, K. W. (1994). Constraints and innovations in the molecular evolution of neuronal signaling: Implications for behavior. In R. J. Greenspan & C. P. Kyriacou (Eds.), *Flexibility and constraint in behavioral systems* (pp. 207–235). New York: Wiley.

GERLACH, C., LAW, I., & PAULSON, O. B. (2002). When action turns into words. Activation of motor-based knowledge during categorization of manipulable objects. *Journal of Cognitive Neuroscience, 14,* 1230–1239.

GERLOFF, C., CORWELL, B., CHEN, R., HALLETT, M., & COHEN, L. G. (1997). Stimulation over the human supplementary motor area interferes with the organization of future elements in complex motor sequences. *Brain, 120,* 1587–1602.

GESCHWIND, N. (1967). The varieties of naming errors. *Cortex, 3,* 97–112.

GESCHWIND, N., & GALABURDA, A. M. (1987). *Cerebral lateralization: Biological mechanisms, associations, and pathology.* Cambridge, MA: MIT Press.

GESCHWIND, N., & LEVITSKY, W. (1968). Human brain: Left-right asymmetries in temporal speech region. *Science, 161,* 186–187.

GIARD, M.-H., FORT, A., MOUCHETANT-ROSTAING, Y., & PERNIER, J. (2000). Neurophysiological mechanisms of auditory selective attention in humans. *Frontiers in Bioscience, 5,* D84–D94.

GIBSON, J., BEIERLEIN, M., & CONNORS, B. (1999). Two networks of electrically coupled inhibitory neurons in neocortex. *Nature, 402,* 75–79.

GIEDD, J. N., BLUMENTHAL, J., JEFFRIES, N. O., CASTELLANOS, F. X., LIU, H., ZIJDENBOS, A., ET AL. (1999). Brain development during childhood and adolescense: A longitudinal MRI study. *Nature Neuroscience, 2,* 861–863.

GILBERTSON, M. W., SHENTON, M. E., CISZEWSKI, A., KASAI, K., LASKO, N. B., ORR, S. P., ET AL. (2002). Smaller hippocampal volume predicts pathologic vulnerability to psychological trauma. *Nature Neuroscience, 5,* 1242–1247.

GLISKY, E. L., POLSTER, M. R., & ROUTHUIEAUX, B. C. (1995). Double dissociation between item and source memory. *Neuropsychology, 9,* 229–235.

GOEL, V., GRAFMAN, J., TAJIK, J., GANA, S., & DANTO, D. (1997). A study of the performance of patients with frontal lobe lesions in a financial planning task. *Brain, 120,* 1805–1822.

GOLDBERG, G. (1985). Supplementary motor area structure and function: Review and hypothesis. *Behavioral and Brain Sciences, 8,* 567–616.

GOLDMAN-RAKIC, P. S. (1992). Working memory and the mind. *Scientific American, 267*(3), 111–117.

GOLDMAN-RAKIC, P. S. (1995). Architecture of the prefrontal cortex and the central executive. In J. Grafman, K. J. Holyoak, & F. Boller (Eds.), *Structure and functions of the human prefrontal cortex* (pp. 71–83). New York: New York Academy of Sciences.

GOLDSBY, R. A. (1976). *Basic biology.* New York: Harper and Row.

GOLGI, C. (1894). *Untersuchungen über den feineren Bau des centralen und peripherischen Nervensystems.* Jena, Germany: Fischer.

GOODALE, M. A., & MILNER, A. D. (1992). Separate visual pathways for perception and action. *Trends in Neurosciences, 15,* 22–25.

GOODALE, M. A., & MILNER, A. D. (2004). *Sight unseen: An exploration of conscious and unconscious vision.* Oxford: Oxford University Press.

GOODMAN, G., QUAS, J., BATTERMAN-FAUNEE, J., RIDDLESBERGER, M., & KUHN, J. (1994). Predictors of accurate and inaccurate memories of traumatic events experienced in childhood. *Consciousness and Cognition, 3,* 269–294.

GRABOWECKY, M., ROBERTSON, L. C., & TREISMAN, A. (1993). Preattentive processes guide visual search. *Journal of Cognitive Neuroscience, 5,* 288–302.

GRAFTON, S. T., FADIGA, L., ARBIB, M. A., & RIZZOLATTI, G. (1997). Premotor cortex activation during observation and naming of familiar tools. *Neuroimage, 6,* 231–236.

GRAFTON, S. T., HAZELTINE, E., & IVRY, R. (1995). Functional mapping of sequence learning in normal humans. *Journal of Cognitive Neuroscience, 7,* 497–510.

GRAHAM, J., CARLSON, G. R., & GERARD, R. W. (1942). Membrane and injury potentials of single muscle fibers. *Federation Proceedings, 1,* 31.

GRATTON, G., & FABIANI, M. (1998). Dynamic brain imaging: Event-related optical signal (EROS) measures of the time course and localization of cognitive-related activity. *Psychonomic Bulletin & Review, 5,* 535–563.

GRAY, C. M., KONIG, P., ENGEL, A. K., & SINGER, W. (1989). Oscillatory responses in cat visual cortex exhibit inter-columnar synchronization which reflects global stimulus properties. *Nature, 338,* 334–337.

GRAZIANO, M. S. A., & GROSS, C. G. (1994). Mapping space with neurons. *Current Directions in Psychological Science, 3,* 164–167.

GREENBERG, J. O. (1995). *Neuroimaging: A companion to Adams and Victor's Principles of neurology.* New York: McGraw-Hill.

GREENE, J. D., NYSTROM, L. E., ENGELL, A. D., DARLEY, J. M., & COHEN, J. D. (2004). The neural bases of cognitive conflict and control in moral judgement. *Neuron, 44,* 389–400.

GREENE, J. D., SOMMERVILLE, R. B., NYSTROM, L. E., DARLEY, J. M., & COHEN, J. D. (2001). An fMRI investigation of emotional engagement in moral judgment. *Science, 293,* 2105–2108.

GREENWALD, A. G., MCGHEE, J. L., & SCHWARTZ, J. L. (1998). Measuring individual differences in social cognition: The Implicit Association Test. *Journal of Personality and Social Psychology, 74,* 1474–1480.

GREFKES, C., & FINK, G. R. (2005). The functional organization of the intraparietal sulcus in humans and monkeys. *Journal of Anatomy, 207,* 3–17.

GRILL-SPECTOR, K., KNOUF, N., & KANWISHER, N. (2004). The fusiform face area subserves face perception, not generic within-category identification. *Nature Neuroscience, 7,* 555–562.

GRILL-SPECTOR, K., KOURTZI, Z., & KANWISHER, N. (2001). The lateral occipital complex and its role in object recognition. *Vision Research, 41,* 1409–1422.

GROSSENBACHER, P. G., & LOVELACE, C. T. (2001). Mechanisms of synesthesia: Cognitive and physiological constraints. *Trends in Cognitive Sciences, 5,* 36–41.

GROSSMANN, T., JOHNSON, M. H., FARRONI, T., & CSIBRA, G. (2007). Social perception in the infant brain: Gamma oscillatory activity in response to eye gaze. *Social, Cognitive, and Affective Neuroscience, 2,* 284–291.

GRZIMEK'S ENCYCLOPEDIA OF MAMMALS, VOL. 3. (1990). New York: McGraw-Hill.

GUR, R. C., SKOLNICK, B. E., & GUR, R. E. (1994). Effects of emotional discrimination tasks on cerebral blood flow: Regional activation and its relation to performance. *Brain and Cognition, 25,* 271–286.

GUSNARD, D. A., & RAICHLE, M. E. (2001). Searching for a baseline: Functional imaging and the resting human brain. *Nature Reviews Neuroscience, 2,* 685–694.

HABIB, M., & SIRIGU, A. (1987). Pure topographical disorientation: A definition and anatomical basis. *Cortex, 23,* 73–85.

HADAMARD, J. (1945). *An essay on the psychology of invention in the mathematical field.* Princeton, NJ: Princeton University Press.

HADJIKHANI, N., LIU, A. K., DALE, A. M., CAVANAGH, P., & TOOTELL, R. B. (1998). Retinotopy and color sensitivity in human visual cortical area V8. *Nature Neuroscience, 1,* 235–241.

HAERER, A. F. (1992). *DeJong's The Neurologic Examination* (5th ed.; rev. ed. of *The Neurologic Examination*, R. N. DeJong, 4th ed., 1979). Philadelphia: Lippincott.

HAEUSSER, M. (2000). The Hodgkin-Huxley theory of the action potential. *Nature Reviews. Neuroscience, 3*, 1165.

HAGOORT, P. (2005). On Broca, brain, and binding: A new framework. *Trends in Cognitive Neurosciences, 9*, 416–423.

HAGOORT, P., BROWN, C., & GROOTHUSEN, J. (1993). The syntactic positive shift (SPS) as an ERP measure of syntactic processing. *Language and Cognitive Processes, 8*, 439–483.

HAGOORT, P., BROWN, C., & SWAAB, T. (1996). Lexical semantic event-related potential effects in patients with left hemisphere lesions and aphasia, and patients with right hemisphere lesions without aphasia. *Brain, 119*, 627–649.

HAGOORT, P., HALD, L., BASTIAANSEN, M., & PETERSSON, K. (2004). Integration of word meaning and world knowledge in language comprehension. *Science, 403*, 438–441.

HAMANI, C., NEIMAT, J., & LOZANO, A. M. (2006). Deep brain stimulation for the treatment of Parkinson's disease. *Journal of Neural Transmission, 70*(Suppl.), 393–399.

HAMANN, S. B., ELY, T. D., GRAFTON, S. T., & KILTS, C. D. (1999). Amygdala activity related to enhanced memory for pleasant and aversive stimuli. *Nature Neuroscience, 2*, 289–293.

HAMANN, S. B., & SQUIRE, L. R. (1995). On the acquisition of new declarative knowledge in amnesia. *Behavioral Neuroscience, 109*, 1027–1044.

HAMPTON, A. N., ADOLPHS, R., TYSZKA, J. M., & O'DOHERTY, J. P. (2007). Contributions of the amygdala to reward expectancy and choice signals in human prefrontal cortex. *Neuron, 55*, 545–555.

HAREL, N. Y., & STRITTMATTER, S. M. (2006). Can regenerating axons recapitulate developmental guidance during recovery from spinal cord injury? *Nature Reviews Neuroscience, 7*, 603–616.

HARKNESS, R. D., & MAROUDAS, N. G. (1985). Central place foraging by an ant (*Cataglyphis bicolor* Fab.): A model of searching. *Animal Behaviour, 33*, 916–928.

HARRIS, P. L. (1992). From simulation to folk psychology: The case for development. *Mind and Language, 7*, 120–144.

HART, J., BERNDT, R. S., & CARAMAZZA, A. (1985). Category-specific naming deficit following cerebral infarction. *Nature, 316*, 439–440.

HARTLINE, H. K. (1938). The response of single optic nerve fibers of the vertebrate eye to illumination of the retina. *American Journal of Physiology, 121*, 400–415.

HAXBY J. V., HORWITZ B., UNGERLEIDER, L. G., MAISOG, J. M., PIETRINI, P., & GRADY, C. L. (1994). The functional organization of human extrastriate cortex: A PET-rCBF study of selective attention to faces and locations. *Journal of Neuroscience, 14*, 6336–6353.

HAYES, A., DAVIDSON, M., KEELE, S. W., & RAFAL, R. (1998). Toward a functional analysis of the basal ganglia. *Journal of Cognitive Neuroscience, 10*, 178–198.

HAZELTINE, E., GRAFTON, S. T., & IVRY, R. (1997). Attention and stimulus characteristics determine the locus of motor-sequence encoding. A PET study. *Brain, 120*, 123–40.

HEBB, D. (1949). *The organization of behavior: A neuropsychological theory.* New York: Wiley.

HEEREY, E. A., CAPPS, L. M., KELTNER, D., & KRING, A. M. (2005). Understanding teasing: Lessons from children with autism. *Journal of Abnormal Child Psychology, 33*, 55–68.

HEILMAN, K. M., BOWERS, D., & WATSON, R. T. (1983). Performance on hemispatial pointing task by patients with neglect syndrome. *Neurology, 33*, 661–664.

HEILMAN, K. M., ROTHI, L. J., & VALENSTEIN, E. (1982). Two forms of ideomotor apraxia. *Neurology, 32*, 342–346.

HEILMAN, K. M., SCHOLES, R., & WATSON, R. T. (1975). Auditory affective agnosia: Disturbed comprehension of affective speech. *Journal of Neurology, Neurosurgery, and Psychiatry, 38*, 69–72.

HEINZE, H. J., MANGUN, G. R., BURCHERT, W., HINRICHS, H., SCHOLZ, M., MÜNTE, T. F., ET AL. (1994). Combined spatial and temporal imaging of brain activity during visual selective attention in humans. *Nature, 372*, 543–546.

HELMHOLTZ, H. VON. (1909–1911). *Handbuch der Physiologischen Optik* [Treatise on Physiological Optics]. Leipzig, Germany: L. Vos. (Translated in R. M. Warren and R. P. Warren, *Helmholtz on Perception: Its Physiology and Development.* New York: Wiley, 1968.)

HERNÁNDEZ-PEÓN, R., SCHERRER, H., & JOUVET, M. (1956). Modification of electrical activity in cochlear nucleus during attention in unanesthetized cats. *Science, 123*, 331–332.

HERRMANN, E., CALL, J., HERNÀNDEZ-LLOREDA, M. V., HARE, B., & TOMASELLO, M. (2007). Humans have evolved specialized skills of social cognition: The cultural intelligence hypothesis. *Science, 317*, 1360–1366.

HERRICK, C. J. (1963). *Brains of rats and men.* New York: Hafner.

HERZ, R. S., ELIASSEN, J., BELAND, S., & SOUZA, T. (2004). Neuroimaging evidence for the emotional potency of odor-evoked memory. *Neuropsychologia, 42*, 371–378.

HEYWOOD, C. A., WILSON, B., & COWEY, A. (1987). A case study of cortical colour "blindness" with relatively intact achromatic discrimination. *Journal of Neurology, Neurosurgery, and Psychiatry, 50*, 22–29.

HIKOSAKA, K., IWAI, E., SAITO, H., & TANAKA, K. (1988). Polysensory properties of neurons in the anterior bank of the caudal superior temporal sulcus of the macaque monkey. *Journal of Neurophysiology, 60*, 1615–1637.

HILLIS, A. E. (2006). Neuroboiology of unilateral spatial neglect. *Neuroscientist, 12*, 153–163.

HILLIS, A. E., NEWHART, M., HEIDLER, J., BARKER, P. B., HERSKOVITS, E. H., & DEGAONKAR, M. (2005). Anatomy of spatial attention: Insights from perfusion imaging and hemispatial neglect in acute stroke. *Journal of Neuroscience, 25*, 3161–3167.

HILLIS, A. E., WORK, M., BARKER, P. B., JACOBS, M. A., BREESE, E. L., & MAURER, K. (2004). Re-examining the brain regions crucial for orchestrating speech articulation. *Brain, 127*, 1461–1462.

HILLYARD, S. A., HINK, R. F., SCHWENT, V. L., & PICTON, T. W. (1973). Electrical signs of selective attention in the human brain. *Science, 182*, 177–180.

HILTS, P. J. (1995). *Memory's ghost: The strange tale of Mr. M. and the nature of memory.* New York: Simon and Schuster.

HOCHBERG, L. R., SERRUYA, M. D., FRIEHS, G. M., MUKAND, J. A., SALEH, M., CAPLAN, A. H., ET AL. (2006). Neuronal ensemble control of prosthetic devices by a human with tetraplegia. *Nature, 442*, 164–171.

HODGKIN, A. L., & HUXLEY, A. F. (1939). Action potentials recorded from inside a nerve fibre. *Nature, 144*, 710–711.

HODOS, W., & CAMPBELL, C. B. G. (1969). Scala naturae: Why there is no theory in comparative psychology. *Psychological Review, 76*, 337–350.

HOLBOURN, A. H. S. (1943). Mechanics of head injury. *Lancet, 2*, 438–441.

HOLMES, G. (1919). Disturbances of visual orientation. *British Journal of Ophthalmology, 2*, 449–468.

HOLMES, N. P., & SPENCE, C. (2005). Multisensory integration: Space, time and superadditivity. *Current Biology, 15*, R762–R764.

HOLTZMAN, J. D., & GAZZANIGA, M. S. (1982). Dual task interactions due exclusively to limits in processing resources. *Science, 218,* 1325–1327.

HOPF, J. M., BOELMANS, K., SCHOENFELD, M. A., LUCK, S. J., & HEINZE, H. J. (2004). Attention to features precedes attention to locations in visual search: Evidence from electromagnetic brain responses in humans. *Journal of Neuroscience, 24,* 1822–1832.

HOPFINGER, J. B., & MANGUN, G. R. (1998). Reflexive attention modulates visual processing in human extrastriate cortex. *Psychological Science, 9,* 441–447.

HOPFINGER, J. B., & MANGUN, G. R. (2001). Tracking the influence of reflexive attention on sensory and cognitive processing. *Cognitive, Affective & Behavioral Neuroscience, 1,* 56–65.

HOPFINGER, J. B., BUONOCORE, M. H., & MANGUN, G. R. (2000). The neural mechanisms of top-down attentional control. *Nature Neuroscience, 3,* 284–291.

HORE, J., WILD, B., & DIENER, H. (1991). Cerebellar dysmetria at the elbow, wrist, and fingers. *Journal of Neurophysiology, 65,* 563–571.

HUANG, Y.-Y., BATTISTUZZI, C., OQUENDO, M. A., HARKAVY-FRIEDMAN, J., GREENHILL, L., ZALSMAN, G., ET AL. (2004). Human 5-HT1A receptor C(–1019)G polymorphism and psychopathology. *International Journal of Neuropsychopharmacology, 7,* 441–451.

HUBEL, D. H., & WIESEL, T. N. (1968). Receptive fields and functional architecture of monkey striate cortex. *Journal of Physiology, 195,* 215–243.

HUBEL, D. H., & WIESEL, T. N. (1977). Ferrier lecture. Functional architecture of macaque monkey visual cortex. *Proceedings of the Royal Society of London. Series B, 198,* 1–59.

HUMPHREYS, G. W., & RIDDOCH, M. J. (1987). The fractionation of visual agnosia. In G. W. Humphreys & M. J. Riddoch (Eds.), *Visual object processing: A cognitive neuropsychological approach.* Hove, England: Erlbaum.

HUMPHREYS, G. W., RIDDOCH, M. J., DONNELLY, N., FREEMAN, T., BOUCART, M., & MULLER, H. M. (1994). Intermediate visual processing and visual agnosia. In M. J. Farah and G. Ratcliff (Eds.), *The neuropsychology of high-level vision: Collected tutorial essays* (pp. 63–102). Hillsdale, NJ: Erlbaum.

HUTCHISON, W. D., DOSTROVSKY, J. O., WALTERS, J. R., COURTEMANCHE, R., BORAUD, T., GOLDBERG, J., ET AL. (2004). Neuronal oscillations in the basal ganglia and movement disorders: Evidence from whole animal and human recordings. *Journal of Neuroscience, 24,* 9240–9243.

HUTSLER, J., & GALUSKE, R. A. (2003). Hemispheric asymmetries in cerebral cortical networks. *Trends in Neuroscience, 26,* 429–435.

HUTTENLOCHER, P. R., & DABHOLKAR, A. S. (1997). Regional differences in synaptogenesis in human cerebral cortex. *Journal of Comparative Neurology, 387,* 167–178.

HYDE, I. H. (1921). A micro-electrode and unicellular stimulation. *Biological Bulletin, 40,* 130–133.

IGAZ, L. M., BEKINSCHTEIN, P., VIANNA, M. M., IZQUIERDO, I., & MEDINA, J. H. (2004). Gene expression during memory formation. *Neurotoxicity Research, 6,* 189–204.

IMAMIZU, H., MIYAUCHI, S., TAMADA, T., SASAKI, Y., TAKINO, R., PUTZ, B., ET AL. (2000). Human cerebellar activity reflecting an acquired internal model of a new tool. *Nature, 403,* 192–195.

ITO, M., TAMURA, H., FUJITA, I., & TANAKA, K. (1995). Size and position invariance of neuronal responses in monkey inferotemporal cortex. *Journal of Neurophysiology, 73,* 218–226.

IVRY, R. B., & LEBBY, P. C. (1993). Hemispheric differences in auditory perception are similar to those found in visual perception. *Psychological Science, 4,* 41–45.

IVRY, R. B., & ROBERTSON, L. C. (1998). *The two sides of perception.* Cambridge, MA: MIT Press.

IVRY, R. B., SPENCER, R. M., ZELAZNIK, H. N., & DIEDRICHSEN, J. (2002). The cerebellum and event timing. In S. M. Highstein and W. T. Thach (Eds.), *The cerebellum: Recent developments in cerebellar research* [Annals of the New York Academy of Sciences, vol. 978] (pp. 302–317). New York: New York Academy of Sciences.

JACK, C. R., JR., DICKSON, D. W., PARISI, J. E., XU, Y. C., CHA, R. H., O'BRIEN, P. C., ET AL. (2002). Antemortem MRI findings correlate with hippocampal neuropathology in typical aging and dementia. *Neurology, 58,* 750–757.

JACOB, F. (1977). Evolution and tinkering. *Science, 196,* 1161–1166.

JACOBS, L. F., GAULIN, S. J. C., SHERRY, D. F., & HOFFMAN, G. E. (1990). Evolution of spatial cognition: Sex-specific patterns of spatial behavior predict hippocampal size. *Proceedings of the National Academy of Sciences, USA, 87,* 6349–6352.

JAMES, T. W., CULHAM, J., HUMPHREY, G. K., MILNER, A. D., & GOODALE, M. A. (2003). Ventral occipital lesions impair object recognition but not object-directed grasping: An fMRI study. *Brain, 126*(Pt.11), 2463–2475.

JAMES, W. (1890). *Principles of psychology.* New York: Holt.

JANOWSKY, J. S., SHIMAMURA, A. P., & SQUIRE, L. R. (1989). Source memory impairment in patients with frontal lobe lesions. *Neuropsychologia, 27,* 1043–1056.

JASPER, H. H. (1995). A historical perspective: The rise and fall of prefrontal lobotomy. *Advances in Neurology, 66,* 97–114.

JENKINS, I. H., BROOKS, D. J., NIXON, P. D., FRACKOWIAK, R. S. J., & PASSINGHAM, R. E. (1994). Motor sequence learning: A study with positron emission tomography. *Journal of Neuroscience, 14,* 3775–3790.

JOBST, K. A., SMITH, A. D., SZATMARI, M., ESIRI, M. M., JASKOWSKI, A., HINDLEY, N., ET AL. (1994). Rapidly progressing atrophy of medial temporal lobe in Alzheimer's disease. *Lancet, 343,* 829–830.

JOHNSON-FREY, S. H., NEWMAN-NORLUND, R., & GRAFTON, S. T. (2004). A distributed left hemisphere network active during planning of everyday tool use skills. *Cerebral Cortex, 15,* 681–695.

JOHNSRUDE, I. S., OWEN, A. M., WHITE, N. M., ZHAO, W. V., & BOHBOT, V. (2000). Impaired preference conditioning after anterior temporal lobe resection in humans. *Journal of Neuroscience, 20,* 2649–2656.

JONES, B., & MISHKIN, M. (1972). Limbic lesions and the problem of stimulus-reinforcement associations. *Experimental Neurology, 36,* 362–377.

JUST, M., CARPENTER, P., KELLER, T., EDDY, W., & THULBORN, K. (1996). Brain activation modulated by sentence comprehension. *Science, 274,* 114–116.

KAAS, J. H. (1995). The reorganization of sensory and motor maps in adult mammals. In M. S. Gazzaniga (Ed.), *The cognitive neurosciences* (pp. 51–71). Cambridge, MA: MIT Press.

KAAS, J. H. (1997). What comparative studies of neocortex tell us about the human brain. *Revista Brasileira de Biologia, 56,* 315–322.

KAAS, J. H. (1999). The transformation of association cortex into sensory cortex. *Brain Research Bulletin, 50,* 425.

KAAS, J. H., NELSON, R. J., SUR, M., DYKES, R. W., & MERZENICH, M. M. (1984). The somatotopic organization of the ventroposterior thalamus of the squirrel monkey, *Saimiri sciureus. Journal of Comparative Neurology, 226,* 111–140.

KAKEI, S., HOFFMAN, D. S., & STRICK, P. L. (1999). Muscle and movement representations in the primary motor cortex. *Science, 285,* 2136–2139.

KAKEI, S., HOFFMAN, D. S., & STRICK P. L. (2001). Direction of action is represented in the ventral premotor cortex. *Nature Neuroscience, 4,* 1020–1025.

KALI, S., & DAYAN, P. (2004). Off-line replay maintains declarative memories in a model of hippocampal-neocortical interactions. *Nature Neuroscience, 7,* 286–294.

KANDEL, E. R., SCHWARTZ, J. H., & JESSELL, T. M. (EDS.). (1991). *Principles of neural science* (3rd ed.). New York: Elsevier.

KANWISHER, N. (2000). Domain specificity in face perception. *Nature Neuroscience, 3,* 759–763.

KANWISHER, N., MCDERMOTT, J., & CHUN, M. M. (1997). The fusiform face area: A module in human extrastriate cortex specialized for face perception. *Journal of Neuroscience, 17,* 4302–4311.

KANWISHER, N., WOODS, R., IACOBONI, M., & MAZZIOTTA, J. C. (1997). A locus in human extrastriate cortex for visual shape analysis. *Journal of Cognitive Neuroscience, 9,* 133–142.

KAPP, B. S., PASCOE, J. P., & BIXLER, M. A. (1984). The amygdala: A neuroanatomical systems approach to its contributions to aversive conditioning. In N. Butters and L. R. Squire (Eds.), *Neuropsychology of memory* (pp. 473–488). New York: Guilford.

KARNATH, H., FERBER, S. & HIMMELBACH, M. (2001). Spatial awareness is a function of the temporal lobe not the posterior parietal lobe. *Nature, 411,* 950–953.

KARNATH, H., FRUHMANN BERGER, M., KÜKER, W., & RORDEN, C. (2004). The anatomy of spatial neglect based on voxelwise statistical analysis: A study of 140 patients. *Cerebral Cortex, 14,* 1165–1172.

KARNI, A., MEYER, G., JEZZARD, P., ADAMS, M. M., TURNER, R., & UNGERLEIDER, L. G. (1995). Functional MRI evidence for adult motor cortex plasticity during motor skill learning. *Nature, 377,* 155–158.

KARNI, A., MEYER, G., REY-HIPOLITO, C., JEZZARD, P., ADAMS, M., TURNER, R., ET AL. (1998). The acquisition of skilled motor performance: Fast and slow experience-driven changes in primary motor cortex. *Proceedings of the National Academy of Sciences, USA, 95,* 861–868.

KASTNER, S., DEWEERD, P., DESIMONE, R., & UNGERLEIDER, L. C. (1998). Mechanisms of directed attention in the human extrastriate cortex as revealed by functional MRI. *Science, 282,* 108–111.

KASTNER, S., SCHNEIDER, K., & WUNDERLICH, K. (2006). Beyond a relay nucleus: Neuroimaging views on the human LGN. *Progress in Brain Research, 155,* 125–143.

KASTNER, S., & UNGERLEIDER, L. (2000). Mechanisms of visual attention in the human cortex. *Annual Review of Neuroscience, 23,* 315–341.

KAUFFMAN, T., THEORET, H., & PASCUAL-LEONE, A. (2002). Braille character discrimination in blindfolded human subjects. *Neuroreport, 13,* 571–574.

KAUFMAN, J. N., ROSS, T. J., STEIN, E. A., & GARAVAN, H. (2003). Cingulate hypoactivity in cocaine users during a GO-NOGO task as revealed by event-related functional magnetic resonance imaging. *Journal of Neuroscience, 23,* 7839–7843.

KEELE, S. (1986). Motor control. In K. R. Boff, L. Kaufman, & J. P. Thomas (Eds.), *Handbook of perception and human performance* (Vol. 2, pp. 1–60). New York: Wiley.

KEELE, S. W., IVRY, R., MAYR, U., HAZELTINE, E., & HEUER, H. (2003). The cognitive and neural architecture of sequence representation. *Psychological Review, 110,* 316–339.

KEENAN, J. P., NELSON, A., O'CONNOR, M., & PASCUAL-LEONE, A. (2001). Self-recognition and the right hemisphere. *Nature, 409,* 305.

KELLENBACH, M. L., BRETT, M., & PATTERSON, K. (2003). Actions speak louder than functions: The importance of manipulability and action in tool representation. *Journal of Cognitive Neuroscience, 15,* 30–46.

KELLEY, W. M., MACRAE, C. N., WYLAND, C. L., CAGLAR, S., INATI, S., & HEATHERTON, T. F. (2002). Finding the self? An event-related fMRI study. *Journal of Cognitive Neuroscience, 14,* 785–794.

KENNEDY, D. P., REDCAY, E., & COURCHESNE, E. (2006). Failing to deactivate: Resting functional abnormalities in autism. *Proceedings of the National Academy of Sciences, 103,* 8275–8280.

KERETSZ, A., & HOOPER, P. (1982). Praxis and language: The extent and variety of apraxia in aphasia. *Neuropsychologia, 20,* 275–286.

KERNS, J. G., COHEN, J. D., MACDONALD, A. W., CHO, R. Y., STENGER, V. A., & CARTER, C. S. (2004). Anterior cingulate conflict monitoring and adjustments in control. *Science, 303,* 1023–1026.

KILLGORE, W. D. S., & YURGELUN-TODD, D. A. (2004). Activation of the amygdala and anterior cingulate during nonconscious processing of sad versus happy faces. *Neuroimage, 21,* 1215–1223.

KIMURA, D. (1973). The asymmetry of the human brain. *Scientific American, 228*(3), 70–78.

KINGSTONE, A., ENNS, J., MANGUN, G. R., & GAZZANIGA, M. S. (1995). Guided visual search is a left hemisphere process in split-brain patients. *Psychological Science, 6,* 118–121.

KINGSTONE, A., FRIESEN, C. K., & GAZZANIGA, M. S. (2000). Reflexive joint attention depends on lateralized cortical connections. *Psychological Science, 11,* 159–166.

KINGSTONE, A., & GAZZANIGA, M. S. (1995). Subcortical transfer of higher order information: More illusory than real? *Neuropsychology, 9,* 321–328.

KINSBOURNE, M. (1982). Hemispheric specialization and the growth of human understanding. *American Psychologist, 37,* 411–420.

KIRCHER, T. T., SENIOR, C., PHILLIPS, M. L., RABE-HESKETH, S., BENSON, P. J., BULLMORE, E. T., ET AL. (2001). Recognizing one's own face. *Cognition, 78,* B1–B15.

KIRSCHBAUM, C., WOLF, O. T., MAY, M., WIPPICH, W., & HELLHAMMER, D. H. (1996). Stress- and treatment-induced elevations of cortisol levels associated with impaired declarative memory in healthy adults. *Life Sciences, 58,* 1475–1483.

KITTERLE, F., CHRISTMAN, S., & HELLIGE, J. (1990). Hemispheric differences are found in identification, but not detection of low versus high spatial frequencies. *Perception & Psychophysics, 48,* 297–306.

KLATT, D. H. (1989). Review of selected models of speech perception. In W. Marslen-Wilson (Ed.), *Lexical representation and process* (pp. 169–226). Cambridge, MA: MIT Press.

KLEIM, J. A., CHAN, S., PRINGLE, E., SCHALLERT, K., PROCACCIO, V., JIMENEZ, R., ET AL. (2006). BDNF val66met polymorphism is associated with modified experience-dependent plasticity in human motor cortex. *Nature Neuroscience, 9,* 735–737.

KLEIN, S. B., LOFTUS, J., & PLOG, A. E. (1992). Trait judgments about the self: Evidence from the encoding specificity paradigm. *Personality and Social Psychology Bulletin, 18,* 730–735.

KLEIN, S. B., ROZENDAL, K., & COSMIDES, L. (2002). A social cognitive neuroscience analysis of the self. *Social Cognition, 20,* 105–135.

KLEINSMITH, L. J., & KAPLAN, S. (1963). Paired-associate learning as a function of arousal and interpolated interval. *Journal of Experimental Psychology, 65,* 190–193.

KLIN, A., JONES, W., SCHULTZ, R., VOLKMAR, F., & COHEN, D. (2002a). Defining and quantifying the social phenotype in autism. *American Journal of Psychiatry, 159,* 895–908.

KLIN, A., JONES, W., SCHULTZ, R., VOLKMAR, F., & COHEN, D. (2002b). Visual fixation patterns during viewing of naturalistic social situations as predictors of social competence in individuals with autism. *Archives of General Psychiatry, 59,* 809–816.

KLIN, A., SPARROW, S. S., DE BILDT, A., CICCHETTI, D. V., COHEN, D. J., & VOLKMAR F. R. (1999). A normed study of face recognition in autism and related disorders. *Journal of Autism and Developmental Disorders, 29,* 499–508.

KLINGBERG, T., HEDEHUS, M., TEMPLE, E., SALZ, T., GABRIELI, J. D., MOSELEY, M. E., ET AL. (2000). Microstructure of temporoparietal white matter as a basis for reading ability: Evidence from diffusion tensor magnetic resonance imaging. *Neuron, 25,* 493–500.

KLÜVER, H., & BUCY, P. C. (1939). Preliminary analysis of functions of the temporal lobes in monkeys. *Archives of Neurology, 42,* 979–1000.

KNIGHT, R. T., & GRABOWECKY, M. (1995). Escape from linear time: Prefrontal cortex and conscious experience. In M. S. Gazzaniga (Ed.), *The cognitive neurosciences* (pp. 1357–1371). Cambridge, MA: MIT Press.

KOECHLIN, E., ODY, C., & KONNEIHER, F. (2003). The architecture of cognitive control in the human prefrontal cortex. *Science, 302,* 1181–1185.

KOHLER, E., KEYSERS, C., UMILTA, A., FOGASSI, L., GALLESE, V., & RIZOLATT, G. (2002). Hearing sounds, understanding actions: Action representation in mirror neurons. *Science, 297,* 846–848.

KOHLER, S., KAPUR, S., MOSCOVITCH, M., WINOCUR, G., & HOULE, S. (1995). Dissociation of pathways for object and spatial vision: A PET study in humans. *Neuroreport, 6,* 1865–1868.

KOLB, B., & WHISHAW, I. Q. (1996). *Fundamentals of human neuropsychology* (4th ed.). New York: Freeman.

KONISHI, M. (1993). Listening with two ears. *Scientific American, 268*(4), 66–73.

KONISHI, S., NAKAJIMA, K., UCHIDA, I., KAMEYAMA, M., NAKAHARA, K., SEKIHARA, K., ET AL. (1998). Transient activation of inferior prefrontal cortex during cognitive set shifting. *Nature Neuroscience, 1,* 80–84.

KORDOWER, J. H., FREEMAN, T. B., SNOW, B. J., VINGERHOETS, F. J., MUFSON, E. J., SANBERG, P. R., ET AL. (1995). Neuropathological evidence of graft survival and striatal reinnervation after the transplantation of fetal mesencephalic tissue in a patient with Parkinson's disease. *New England Journal of Medicine, 332,* 1118–1124.

KOSSLYN, S. M. (1987). Seeing and imagining in the cerebral hemispheres: A computational approach. *Psychological Review, 94,* 148–175.

KOSSLYN, S. M. (1988). Aspects of cognitive neuroscience of mental imagery. *Science, 240,* 1621–1626.

KOSSLYN, S. M., ALPERT, N. M., THOMPSON, W. L., MALJKOVIK, V., WEISE, S. B., CHABRIS, C. F., ET AL. (1993). Visual mental imagery activates topographically organized visual cortex: PET investigations. *Journal of Cognitive Neuroscience, 5,* 263–287.

KOSSLYN, S. M., KOENIG, O., BARRET, A., CAVE, C. B., TANG, J., & GABRIELI, J. D. E. (1989). Evidence for two types of spatial representations: Hemispheric specialization for categorical and coordinate relations. *Journal of Experimental Psychology. Human Perception and Performance, 15,* 723–735.

KOTTER, R., & MEYER, N. (1992). The limbic system: A review of its empirical foundation. *Behavioural Brain Research, 52,* 105–127.

KRACK, P., POLLAK, P., LIMOUSIN, P., HOFFMANN, D., XIE, J., BENAZZOUZ, A., ET AL. (1998). Subthalamic nucleus or internal pallidal stimulation in young onset Parkinson's disease. *Brain, 121,* 451–457.

KROLAK-SALMON, P., HÉNAFF, M. A., ISNARD, J., TALLON-BAUDRY, C., GUÉNOT, M., VIGHETTO, A., ET AL. (2003). An attention modulated response to disgust in human ventral anterior insula. *Annals of Neurology, 53,* 446–453.

KRUBITZER, L. (1998). What can monotremes tell us about brain evolution? *Philosophical Transactions of the Royal Society of London. Series B, Biological Sciences, 353,* 1127–1146.

KRUBITZER, L. A. (2000). How does evolution build a complex brain? In G. R. Bock & G. Cardew (Eds.), *Novartis Foundation Symposium: Vol. 228. Evolutionary developmental biology of the cerebral cortex* (pp. 206–220). Chichester, England: Wiley.

KRUBITZER, L., MANGER, P., PETTIGREW, J., & CALFORD, M. (1995). The organization of somatosensory cortex in monotremes: In search of the prototypical plan. *Journal of Comparative Neurology, 351,* 261–306.

KUFFLER, S., & NICHOLLS, J. (1976). *From neuron to brain.* Sunderland, MA: Sinauer.

KUPERBERG, G. R. (2007). Neural mechanisms of language comprehension: Challenges to syntax. *Brain Research, 1146,* 23–49.

KUPERBERG, G. R., SITNIKOVA, T., CAPLAN, D., & HOLCOMB, P. (2003). Electrophysiological distinctions in processing conceptual relationships within simple sentences. *Cognitive Brain Research, 17,* 117–129.

KUPFERMANN, I. (1991). Localization of higher cognitive and affective functions: The association cortices. In E. R. Kandel, J. H. Schwartz, & T. M. Jessell (Eds.), *Principles of neural science* (pp. 821–838). Norwalk, CT: Appleton and Lange.

KURZBAN, R., TOOBY, J., & COSMIDES, L. (2001). Can race be erased? Coalitional computation and social categorization. *Proceedings of the National Academy of Sciences, USA, 98,* 15387–15392.

KUTAS, M., & FEDERMEIER, K. D. (2000). Electrophysiology reveals semantic memory use in language comprehension. *Trends in Cognitive Sciences, 4,* 463–470.

KUTAS, M., & HILLYARD, S. A. (1980). Reading senseless sentences: Brain potentials reflect semantic incongruity. *Science, 207,* 203–205.

LABAR, K. S., LEDOUX, J. E., SPENCER, D. D., & PHELPS, E. A. (1995). Impaired fear conditioning following unilateral temporal lobectomy in humans. *Journal of Neuroscience, 15,* 6846–6855.

LABAR, K. S., & PHELPS, E. A. (1998). Role of the human amygdala in arousal mediated memory consolidation. *Psychological Science, 9,* 490–493.

LABERGE, D. (1990). Thalamic and cortical mechanisms of attention suggested by recent positron emission tomographic experiments. *Journal of Cognitive Neuroscience, 2,* 358–372.

LADAVAS, E., PALADINI, R., & CUBELLI, R. (1993). Implicit associative priming in a patient with left visual neglect. *Neuropsychologia, 31,* 1307–1320.

LAENG, B. (1994). Lateralization of categorical and coordinate spatial functions: A study of unilateral stroke patients. *Journal of Cognitive Neuroscience, 6,* 189–203.

LAMME, V. (2003). Why visual attention and awareness are different. *Trends in Cognitive Sciences, 17,* 12–18.

LANE, R. D., FINK, G. R., CHAU, P. M., & DOLAN, R. J. (1997). Neural activation during selective attention to subjective emotional responses. *Neuroreport, 8,* 3969–3972.

LANGSTON, W. J. (1984). I. MPTP neurotoxicity: An overview and characterization of phases of toxicity. *Life Sciences, 36,* 201–206.

LÊ, S., CARDEBAT, D., BOULANOUAR, K., HENAFF, M. A., MICHEL, F., MILNER, D., ET AL. (2002). Seeing, since childhood, without ventral stream: A behavioural study. *Brain, 125*(Pt.1), 58–74.

LEBEDEV, M. A., & NICOLELIS, M. A. (2006). Brain-machine interfaces: Past, present and future. *Trends in Neurosciences, 29,* 536–546.

LE BIHAN, D. (2003). Looking into the functional architecture of the brain with diffusion MRI. *Nature Reviews Neuroscience, 4,* 469–480.

LEDOUX, J. E. (1991). Emotion and the limbic system concept. *Concepts in Neuroscience, 2,* 169–199.

LEDOUX, J. E. (1992). Emotion and the amygdala. In J. P. Aggleton (Ed.), *The amygdala: Neurobiological aspects of emotion, memory, and mental dysfunction* (pp. 339–351). New York: Wiley-Liss.

LEDOUX, J. E. (1994). Emotion, memory and the brain. *Scientific American, 270*(6), 50–57.

LEDOUX, J. E. (1995). In search of an emotional system in the brain: Leaping from fear to emotion and consciousness. In M. S. Gazzaniga (Ed.), *The cognitive neurosciences* (pp. 1047–1061). Cambridge, MA: MIT Press.

LEDOUX, J. E. (1996). *The emotional brain: The mysterious underpinnings of emotional life.* New York: Simon and Schuster.

LETTVIN, J. Y., MATURANA, H. R., MCCULLOCH, W. S., & PITTS, W. H. (1959). What the frog's eye tells the frog's brain. *Proceedings of the Institute of Radio Engineers, 47,* 1940–1951.

LEVELT, W. J. M. (1989). *Speaking: From intention to articulation.* Cambridge, MA: MIT Press.

LEVELT, W. J. M. (1994). The skill of speaking. In P. Bertelson, P. Eelen, & G. d'Ydewalle (Eds.), *International perspectives on psychological science: Vol. 1. Leading themes* (pp. 89–103). Hove, England: Erlbaum.

LEVELT, W. J. M. (1999). Models of word production. *Trends in Cognitive Sciences, 3,* 223–232.

LEVELT, W. J. M., ROELOFS, A., & MEYER, A. S. (1999). A theory of lexical access in speech production. *Behavioral and Brain Sciences, 22,* 1–75.

LEVY, D. A., HOPKINS, R. O., & SQUIRE, L. R. (2004). Impaired odor recognition memory in patients with hippocampal lesions. *Learning and Memory, 11,* 794–796.

LEWIS, D. A., & LUND, J. S. (1990). Heterogeneity of chandelier neurons in monkey neocortex: Corticotropin-releasing factor and parvalbumin-immunoreactive populations. *Journal of Comparative Neurology, 293,* 599–615.

LEY, R. G., & BRYDEN, M. P. (1982). A dissociation of right and left hemispheric effects for recognizing emotional tone and verbal content. *Brain and Cognition, 1,* 3–9.

LHERMITTE, F. (1983). "Utilization behaviour" and its relation to lesions of the frontal lobes. *Brain, 106,* 237–255.

LHERMITTE, F., PILLON, B., & SERDARU, M. (1986). Human autonomy and the frontal lobes. Part I: Imitation and utilization behavior: A neuropsychological study of 75 patients. *Annals of Neurology, 19,* 326–334.

LINEBARGER, M., SCHWARTZ, M., & SAFFRAN, E. (1983). Sensitivity to grammatical structure in so-called agrammatic aphasics. *Cognition, 13,* 361–392.

LISSAUER, H. (1890). Ein Fall von Seelenblindheit nebst einem Beitrage zur Theorie derselben. *Archiv für Psychiatrie, 21,* 222–270.

LIU, T., STEVENS, S. T., & CARRASCO, M. (2007). Comparing the time course and efficacy of spatial and feature-based attention. *Vision Research, 47,* 108–113.

LOCKHART, D. J., & BARLOW, C. (2001). Expressing what's on your mind: DNA arrays and the brain. *Nature Reviews. Neurosciece, 2,* 63–68.

LOFTUS, E., & GREENE, E. (1980). Warning: Even memory for faces may be contagious. *Law and Human Behavior, 4,* 323–334.

LOFTUS, E., MILLER, D., & BURNS, H. (1978). Semantic integration of verbal information into visual memory. *Journal of Experimental Psychology. Human Learning and Memory, 4,* 19–31.

LOOMIS, J. M., FUJITA, N., DA SILVA, J. A., & FUKUSIMA, S. S. (1992). Visual space perception and visually directed action. *Journal of Experimental Psychology, 18,* 906–921.

LORENZ, K., & TINBERGEN, N. (1957). Taxis and instinct: Taxis and instinctive action in the egg-retrieving behavior of the Graylag Goose. In C. H. Schiller (Ed. & Trans.), *Instinctive behavior: The development of a modern concept.* New York: International Universities Press. (Original work published in 1938 in *Zeitschrift für Tierpsychologie, 2,* 1–19.)

LUCIANI, LUIGI. *Fisiologia del Homo.* Firenze, Italy: Le Monnier, 1901–1911.

LUCK, S. J., FAN, S., & HILLYARD, S. A. (1993). Attention-related modulation of sensory-evoked brain activity in a visual search task. *Journal of Cognitive Neuroscience, 5,* 188–195.

LUCK, S. J., & HILLYARD, S. A. (1994). Spatial filtering during visual search: Evidence from human electrophysiology. *Journal of Experimental Psychology. Human Perception and Performance, 20,* 1000–1014.

LUPIEN, S. J., FIOCCO, A., WAN, N., MAHEU, F., LORD, C., SCHRAMEK, T., ET AL. (2005). Stress hormones and human memory function across the lifespan. *Psychoneuroendocrinology, 30,* 225–242.

MACDONALD, A. W., COHEN, J. D., STENGER, V. A., & CARTER, C. S. (2000). Dissociating the role of the dorsolateral prefrontal and anterior cingulate cortex in cognitive control. *Science, 288,* 1835–1838.

MACKAY, D. G. (1987). *The organization of perception and action: A theory for language and other cognitive skills.* New York: Springer.

MACLEAN, P. D. (1949). Psychosomatic disease and the "visceral brain": Recent developments bearing on the Papez theory of emotion. *Psychosomatic Medicine, 11,* 338–353.

MACLEAN, P. D. (1952). Some psychiatric implications of physiological studies on frontotemporal portion of limbic system (visceral brain). *Electroencephalography and Clinical Neurophysiology, 4,* 407–418.

MACLEOD, C. (1991). Half a century of research on the Stroop effect: An integrative review. *Psychological Bulletin, 109,* 163–203.

MACMILLAN, M. B. (1986). A wonderful journey through skull and brains: The travels of Mr. Gage's tamping iron. *Brain and Cognition, 5,* 67–107.

MACMILLAN, M. (2000). *An odd kind of fame: Stories of Phineas Gage.* Cambridge, MA: MIT Press.

MACRAE, C. N., MORAN, J. M., HEATHERTON, T. F., BANFIELD, J. F., & KELLEY, W. M. (2004). Medial prefrontal activity predicts memory for self. *Cerebral Cortex, 14,* 647–654.

MAGNO, E., & ALLAN, K. (2007). Self-reference during explicit memory retrieval: An event-related potential analysis. *Psychological Science, 18,* 672–677.

MAINLAND, J., & SOBEL, N. (2006). The sniff is part of the olfactory percept. *Chemical Senses, 31,* 181–196. [Epub, December 8, 2005]

MALMO, R. (1942). Interference factors in delayed response in monkeys after removal of frontal lobes. *Journal of Neurophysiology, 5,* 295–308.

MANGUN, G. R., & HILLYARD, S. A. (1991). Modulations of sensory-evoked brain potentials indicate changes in perceptual processing during visual-spatial priming. *Journal of Experimental Psychology. Human Perception and Performance, 17,* 1057–1074.

MANGUN, G. R., HOPFINGER, J., KUSSMAUL, C., FLETCHER E., & HEINZE, H. J. (1997). Covariations in PET and ERP measures of spatial selective attention in human extrastriate visual cortex. *Human Brain Mapping, 5,* 273–279.

MANN, J. J. (2003). Neurobiology of suicidal behavior. *Nature Reviews. Neuroscience, 4,* 819–828.

MARKOWITSCH, H. J., KALBE, E., KESSLER, J., VON STOCKHAUSEN, H. M., GHAEMI, M., & HEISS, W. D. (1999). Short-term memory deficit after focal parietal damage. *Journal of Clinical and Experimental Neuropsychology, 21,* 784–797.

MARKUS, H. (1977). Self-schemata processing information about the self. *Journal of Personality and Social Research, 35,* 63–78.

MARLER, P. (1991). Song-learning behavior: The interface with neuroethology. *Trends in Neurosciences, 14,* 199–206.

MAROIS, R., YI, D. J., & CHUN, M. M. (2004). The neural fate of consciously perceived and missed events in the attentional blink. *Neuron, 41,* 465–472.

MARR, D. (1982). *Vision: A computational investigation into the human representation and processing of visual information.* San Francisco: Freeman.

MARSLEN-WILSON, W., & TYLER, L. K. (1980). The temporal structure of spoken language understanding. *Cognition, 8,* 1–71.

MARSOLEK, C. J. (1995). Abstract visual-form representations in the left cerebral hemisphere. *Journal of Experimental Psychology. Human Perception and Performance, 21,* 375–386.

MARTIN, A., WIGGS, C. L., UNGERLEIDER, L. G., & HAXBY, J. V. (1996). Neural correlates of category specific behavior. *Nature, 379,* 649–652.

MATHER, M., HENKEL, L. A., & JOHNSON, M. K. (1997). Evaluating characteristics of false memories: Remember/know judgments and memory characteristics questionnaire compared. *Memory and Cognition, 25,* 826–837.

MATTINGLEY, J. B., RICH, A. N., YELLAND, G., & BRADSHAW, J. L. (2001). Unconscious priming eliminates automatic binding of colour and alphanumeric form in synaesthesia. *Nature, 410,* 580–582.

MAUNSELL, J. H. R., & VAN ESSEN, D. C. (1983). Functional properties of neurons in middle temporal visual area of the macaque monkey. I. Selectivity for stimulus direction, speed, and orientation. *Journal of Neurophysiology, 49,* 1127–1147.

MAZOYER, B., TZOURIO, N., FRAK, V., SYROTA, A., MURAYAMA, N., LEVIER, O., ET AL. (1993). The cortical representation of speech. *Journal of Cognitive Neuroscience, 5,* 467–479.

MCADAMS, C. J., & REID, R. C. (2005). Attention modulates the responses of simple cells in monkey primary visual cortex. *Journal of Neuroscience, 25,* 11023–11033.

MCCARTHY, G., PUCE, A., GORE, J. C., & ALLISON, T. (1997). Face-specific processing in the human fusiform gyrus. *Journal of Cognitive Neuroscience, 9,* 605–610.

MCCARTHY, R., & WARRINGTON, E. K. (1986). Visual associative agnosia: A clinico-anatomical study of a single case. *Journal of Neurology, Neurosurgery, and Psychiatry, 49,* 1233–1240.

MCCLELLAND, J. L. (2000). Connectionist models of memory. In E. Tulving and F. I. M. Craik (Eds.), *The Oxford handbook of memory* (pp. 583–596). New York: Oxford University Press.

MCCLELLAND, J. L., & RUMELHART, D. E. (1981). An interactive activation model of context effects in letter perception: Part 1. An account of the basic findings. *Psychological Review, 88,* 375–407.

MCCLELLAND, J. L., & RUMELHART, D. E. (1986). *Parallel distributed processing: Explorations in the microstructure of cognition: Vol. 2. Psychological and biological models.* Cambridge, MA: MIT Press.

MCCLELLAND, J. L., ST. JOHN, M., & TARABAN, R. (1989). Sentence comprehension: A parallel distributed processing approach. *Language and Cognitive Processes, 4,* 287–335.

MCGAUGH, J. L., CAHILL, L., & ROOZENDAAL, B. (1996). Involvement of the amygdala in memory storage: Interaction with other brain systems. *Proceedings of the National Academy of Sciences, USA, 93,* 13508–13514.

MCGAUGH, J. L., INTROINI-COLLISION, I. B., CAHILL, L., MUNSOO, K., & LIANG, K. C. (1992). Involvement of the amygdala in neuromodulatory influences on memory storage. In J. P. Aggleton (Ed.), *The amygdala: Neurobiological aspects of emotion, memory, and mental dysfunction* (pp. 431–451). New York: Wiley-Liss.

MCHENRY, L. C., JR. (1969). *Garrison's history of neurology.* Springfield, IL: Thomas.

MCNEIL, J. E., & WARRINGTON, E. K. (1993). Prosopagnosia: A face-specific disorder. *Quarterly Journal of Experimental Psychology. A, Human Experimental Psychology, 46,* 1–10.

MEADOWS, J. C. (1974). Disturbed perception of colours associated with localized cerebral lesions. *Brain, 97,* 615–632.

MERZENICH, M. M., & JENKINS, W. M. (1995). Cortical plasticity, learning and learning dysfunction. In B. Julesz and I. Kovacs (Eds.), *Maturational windows and adult cortical plasticity* (pp. 1–24). Reading, MA: Addison-Wesley.

MERZENICH, M. M., & KAAS, J. H. (1980). *Principles of organization of sensory-perceptual systems of mammals.* New York: Academic Press.

MERZENICH, M. M., KAAS, J. H., SUR, M., & LIN, C. S. (1978). Double representation of the body surface within cytoarchitectonic areas 3b and 1 in "SI" in the owl monkey (*Aotus trivirgatus*). *Journal of Comparative Neurology, 181,* 41–73.

MERZENICH, M. M., RECANZONE, G., JENKINS, W. M., ALLARD, T. T., & NUDO, R. J. (1988). Cortical representational plasticity. In P. Rakic and W. Singer (Eds.), *Neurobiology of neocortex* (pp. 41–67). New York: Wiley.

MESULAM, M. M. (2000). *Principals of behavioral and cognitive neurology.* New York: Oxford University Press.

METCALFE, J., FUNNELL, M., & GAZZANIGA, M. S. (1995). Right hemisphere superiority: Studies of a split-brain patient. *Psychological Science, 6,* 157–164.

MEYER-LINDENBERG, A., BUCKHOLTZ, J. W., KOLACHANA, B. R., HARIRI, A., PEZAWAS, L., BLASI, G., ET AL. (2006). Neural mechanisms of genetic risk for impulsivity and violence in humans. *Proceedings of the National Academy of Sciences, USA, 103,* 6269–6274.

MIDDLETON, F. A., & STRICK, P. L. (2000). Basal ganglia and cerebellar loops: Motor and cognitive circuits. *Brain Research. Brain Research Reviews, 31,* 236–250.

MIGAUD, M., CHARLESWORTH, P., DEMPSTER, M., WEBSTER, L. C., WATABE, A. M., MAKHINSON, M., ET AL. (1998). Enhanced long-term potentiation and impaired learning in mice with mutant postsynaptic density-95 protein. *Nature, 396,* 433–439.

MILLER, G. (1951). *Language and communication.* New York: McGraw-Hill.

MILLER, G. (1956). The magical number seven, plus-or-minus two: Some limits on our capacity for processing information. *Psychological Review, 101,* 343–352.

MILLER, G. (1962). *Psychology, the science of mental life.* New York: Harper & Row.

MILNER, B. (1995). Aspects of human frontal lobe function. *Advances in Neurology, 66,* 67–84.

MILNER, B., CORKIN, S., & TEUBER, H. (1968). Further analysis of the hippocampal amnesic syndrome: 14-year follow-up study of HM. *Neuropsychologia, 6,* 215–234.

MILNER, B., CORSI, P., & LEONARD, G. (1991). Frontal-lobe contributions to recency judgements. *Neuropsychologia, 29,* 601–618.

MISHKIN, M. (1978). Memory in monkeys severely impaired by combined but not by separate removal of amygdala and hippocampus. *Nature, 273,* 297–298.

MITCHELL, J. P. (2008). Activity in right temporo-parietal junction is not selective for theory-of-mind. *Cerebral Cortex, 18,* 262–271.

MITCHELL, J. P., BANAJI, M. R., & MACRAE, C. N. (2005). General and specific contributions of the medial prefrontal cortex to knowledge about mental states. *Neuroimage, 28,* 757–762.

MITCHELL, J. P., MACRAE, C. N., & BANAJI, M.R. (2004). Encoding-specific effects of social cognition on the neural correlates of subsequent memory. *Journal of Neuroscience, 24,* 4912–4917.

MITCHELL, J. P., MACRAE, C. N., & BANAJI, M.R. (2006). Dissociable medial prefrontal contributions to judgments of similar and dissimilar others. *Neuron, 50,* 655–663.

MOLNAR, Z. (2004). Thomas Willis (1621–1645), the founder of clinical neuroscience. *Nature Reviews Neuroscience, 5,* 329–335.

MONTALDI, D., SPENCER, T. J., ROBERTS, N., & MAYES, A. R. (2006). The neural system that mediates familiarity memory. *Hippocampus, 16,* 504–520.

MORAN, J., & DESIMONE, R. (1985). Selective attention gates visual processing in extrastriate cortex. *Science, 229,* 782–784.

MORAN, J. M., MACRAE, C. N., HEATHERTON, T. F., WYLAND, C. L., & KELLEY, W. M. (2006). Neuroanatomical evidence for distinct cognitive and affective components of self. *Journal of Cognitive Neuroscience, 18,* 1586–1594.

MORAY, N. (1959). Attention in dichotic listening: Effective cues and the influence of instructions. *Quarterly Journal of Experimental Psychology, 9,* 56–60.

MORGAN, M. A., & LEDOUX, J. E. (1999). Contribution of ventrolateral prefrontal cortex to the acquisition and extinction of conditioned fear in rats. *Neurobiology of Learning and Memory, 72,* 244–251.

MORUZZI, G., & MAGOUN, H. W. (1949). Brainstem reticular formation and activation of the EEG. *Electroencephalography and Clinical Neurophysiology, 1,* 455–473.

MOSCOVITCH, M., WINOCUR, G., & BEHRMANN, M. (1997). What is special about face recognition? Nineteen experiments on a person with visual object agnosia and dyslexia but normal face recognition. *Journal of Cognitive Neuroscience, 9,* 555–604.

MOTTER, B. C. (1993). Focal attention produces spatially selective processing in visual cortical areas V1, V2 and V4 in the presence of competing stimuli. *Journal of Neurophysiology, 70,* 909–919.

MOUNTCASTLE, V. B. (1976). The world around us: Neural command functions for selective attention. *Neurosciences Research Program Bulletin, 14*(Suppl.), 1–47.

MOZELL, M., KENT, P., & MURPHY, S. (1991). The effect of flow rate upon the magnitude of the olfactory response differes for different odorants. *Chemical Senses, 16,* 631–649.

MUELLER, N. G., & KLEINSCHMIDT, A. (2003). Dynamic interaction of object- and space-based attention in retinotopic visual areas. *Journal of Neuroscience, 23,* 9812–9816.

MÜNTE, T. F., HEINZE, H.-J., & MANGUN, G. R. (1993). Dissociation of brain activity related to semantic and syntactic aspects of language. *Journal of Cognitive Neuroscience, 5,* 335–344.

MÜNTE, T. F., SCHILZ, K., & KUTAS, M. (1998). When temporal terms belie conceptual order. *Nature, 395,* 71–73.

MUSHIAKE, H., MASAHIKO, I., & TANJI, J. (1991). Neuronal activity in the primate premotor, supplementary, and precentral motor cortex during visually guided and internally determined sequential movements. *Journal of Neurophysiology, 66,* 705–718.

NACEWICZ, B. M., DALTON, K. M., JOHNSTONE, T., LONG, M. T., MCAULIFF, E. M., OAKES, T. R., ET AL. (2006). Amygdala volume and nonverbal social impairment in adolescent and adult males with autism. *Archives of General Psychiatry, 63,* 1417–1428.

NAESER, M. A., PALUMBO, C. L., HELM-ESTABROOKS, N., STIASSNY-EDER, D., & ALBERT, M. L. (1989). Severe non-fluency in aphasia: Role of the medial subcallosal fasciculus plus other white matter pathways in recovery of spontaneous speech. *Brain, 112,* 1–38.

NAVON, D. (1977). Forest before trees: The precedence of global features in visual perception. *Cognitive Psychology, 9,* 353–383.

NETTER, F. H. (1983). *The CIBA collection of medical illustrations: Vol. 1. Nervous system, Part 1: Anatomy and physiology.* Summit, NJ: CIBA Pharmaceutical.

NEVILLE, H. J., & LAWSON, D. L. (1987). Attention to central and peripheral visual space in a movement detection task. III. Separate effects of auditory deprivation and acquisition of a visual language. *Brain Research, 405,* 284–294.

NISSEN, M. J., KNOPMAN, D. S., & SCHACTER, D. L. (1987). Neurochemical dissociation of memory systems. *Neurology, 37,* 789–794.

NIEUWLAND, M., & VAN BERKUM, J. (2005). Testing the limits of the semantic illusion phenomenon: ERPs reveal temporary semantic change deafness in discourse comprehension. *Cognitive Brain Research, 24,* 691–701.

NOBRE, A. C., ALLISON, T., & MCCARTHY, G. (1994). Word recognition in the human inferior temporal lobe. *Nature, 372,* 260–263.

NORMAN, D. A., & SHALLICE, T. (1986). Attention to action: Willed and automatic control of behavior. In R. J. Davidson, G. E. Schwartz, & D. Shapiro (Eds.), *Consciousness and self-regulation* (Vol. 4, pp. 1–18). New York: Plenum.

NORMAN, K. A., & SCHACTER, D. L. (1997). False recognition in younger and older adults: Exploring the characteristics of illusory memories. *Memory and Cognition, 25,* 838–848.

NORRIS, D., MCQUEEN, J., & CUTLER, A. (1995). Competition and segmentation in spoken word recognition. *Journal of Experimental Psychology. Learning, Memory, and Cognition, 21,* 1209–1228.

NORTH, N. T., & O'CARROLL, R. E. (2001). Decision making in patients with spinal cord damage: Afferent feedback and the somatic marker hypothesis. *Neuropsychologia, 39,* 521–524.

NOTTEBOHM, F. (1980). Brain pathways for vocal learning in birds: A review of the first 10 years. *Progress in Psychobiology and Physiological Psychology, 9,* 85–124.

NUNN, J. A., GREGORY, L. J., BRAMMER, M., WILLIAMS, S. C., PARSLOW, D. M., MORGAN, M. J., ET AL. (2002). Functional magnetic resonance imaging of synesthesia: Activation of V4/V8 by spoken words. *Nature Neuroscience, 5,* 371–375.

NYBERG, L., CABEZA, R., & TULVING, E. (1996). PET studies of encoding and retrieval: The HERA model. *Psychonomic Bulletin & Review, 3,* 134–147.

NYBERG, L., CABEZA, R., & TULVING, E. (1998). Asymmetric frontal activation during episodic memory: What kind of specificity? *Trends in Cognitive Sciences, 2,* 419–420.

NYBERG, L., MCINTOSH, A., CABEZA, R., HABIB, R., HOULE, S., & TULVING, E. (1996). General and specific brain regions involved in encoding and retrieval of events: What, where, and when. *Proceedings of the National Academy of Sciences, USA, 93*, 11280–11285.

OCHSNER, K. N., BEER, J. S., ROBERTSON, E. A., COOPER, J., GABRIELI, J. D. E., KIHLSTROM, J. F., ET AL. (2005). The neural correlates of direct and reflected self-knowledge. *Neuroimage, 28*, 797–814.

O'CONNOR, D. H., FUKUI, M. M., PINSK, M. A., & KASTNER, S. (2002). Attention modulates responses in the human lateral geniculate nucleus. *Nature Neuroscience, 5*, 1203–1209.

O'CRAVEN, K. M., DOWNING, P. E., & KANWISHER, N. (1999). fMRI evidence for objects as the units of attentional selection. *Nature, 401*, 584–587.

OJEMANN, G., OJEMANN, J., LETTICH, E., & BERGER, M. (1989). Cortical language localization in left, dominant hemisphere. *Journal of Neurosurgery, 71*, 316–326.

OSBORN, A. G., BLASER, S., & SALZMAN, K. L. (2004). *Diagnostic imaging. Brain.* Salt Lake City, UT: Amirsys.

OSGOOD, C. E., SUCI, G. J., & TANNENGAUM, P. H. (1957). *The measurement of meaning.* Urbana: University of Illinois Press.

OSTERHOUT, L., & HOLCOMB, P. J. (1992). Event-related brain potentials elicited by syntactic anomaly. *Journal of Memory and Language, 31*, 785–806.

PALLER, K., KUTAS, M., & MCISAAC, H. (1995). Monitoring conscious recollection via the electrical activity of the brain. *Psychological Science, 6*, 107–111.

PALFREMAN, J., & LANGSTON, J. W. (1995). *The case of the frozen addicts.* New York: Pantheon.

PALLIS, C. A. (1955). Impaired identification of faces and places with agnosia for colors. *Journal of Neurology, Neurosurgery, and Psychiatry, 18*, 218–224.

PAPEZ, J. W. (1937). A proposed mechanism of emotion. *Archives of Neurology and Psychiatry, 79*, 217–224.

PARR, L. A., DOVE, T., & HOPKINS, W. D. (1998). Why faces may be special: Evidence of the inversion effect in chimpanzees. *Journal of Cognitive Neuroscience, 10*, 615–622.

PASCUAL-LEONE, A., BARTRES-FAZ, D., & KEENAN, J. P. (1999). Transcranial magnetic stimulation: Studying the brain-behaviour relationship by induction of 'virtual lesions.' *Philosophical Transactions of the Royal Society of London. Series B, Biological Sciences, 354*, 1229–1238.

PASSINGHAM, R. E. (1982). *The human primate.* Oxford, England: Freeman.

PASSINGHAM, R. E. (1993). *The frontal lobes and voluntary action.* New York: Oxford University Press.

PAYNE, J., & NADEL, L. (2004). Sleep, dreams, and memory consolidation: The role of the stress hormone cortisol. *Learning and Memory, 11*, 671–678.

PELPHREY, K. A., SINGERMAN, J. D., ALLISON, T., & MCCARTHY, G. (2003). Brain activation evoked by perception of gaze shifts: The influence of context. *Neuropsychologia, 41*, 156–170.

PELPHREY, K. A., VIOLA, R. J, & MCCARTHY, G. (2004). When strangers pass: Processing of mutual and averted social gaze in the superior temporal sulcus. *Psychological Science, 15*, 598–603.

PENFIELD, W., & JASPER, H. (1954). *Epilepsy and the functional anatomy of the human brain.* Boston: Little, Brown.

PERANI, D., DEHAENE, S., GRASS, F., COHEN, L., CAPP, S. F., DUPOUX, E., ET AL. (1996). Brain processes of native and foreign languages. *Neuroreport, 7*, 2439–2444.

PERETZ, I., KOLINSKY, R., TRAMO, M., LABRECQUE, R., HUBLET, C., DEMEURISSE, G., ET AL. (1994). Functional dissociations following bilateral lesions of auditory cortex. *Brain, 117*, 1283–1301.

PERLMUTTER, J. S., & MINK, J. W. (2006). Deep brain stimulation. *Annual Review of Neuroscience, 29*, 229–257.

PERRETT, D. I., ORAM, M. W., HIETANEN, J. K., & BENSON, P. J. (1994). Issues of representations in object vision. In M. J. Farah and G. Ratcliff (Eds.), *The neuropsychology of high-level vision: Collected tutorial essays* (pp. 33–62). Hillsdale, NJ: Erlbaum.

PERRETT, S., RUIZ, B., & MAUK, M. (1993). Cerebellar cortex lesions disrupt learning-dependent timing of conditioned eyelid responses. *Journal of Neuroscience, 13*, 1708–1718.

PETERS, B. L., & STRINGHAM, E. (2006). No booze? You may lose: Why drinkers earn more money than nondrinkers. *Journal of Labor Research, 27*, 411–422.

PETERSEN, S. E., FIEZ, J. A., & CORBETTA, M. (1992). Neuroimaging. *Current Opinion in Neurobiology, 2*, 217–222.

PETERSEN, S. E., ROBINSON, D. L., & MORRIS, J. D. (1987). Contributions of the pulvinar to visual spatial attention. *Neuropsychologia, 25*, 97–105.

PETRIDES, M. (2000). Middorsolateral and midventrolateral prefrontal cortex: Two levels of executive control for the processing of mnemonic information. In S. Monsell and J. Driver (Eds.), *Control of cognitive processes: Attention and performance XVIII* (pp. 535–548). Cambridge, MA: MIT Press.

PHELPS, E. A., CANNISTRACI, C. J., & CUNNINGHAM, W. A. (2003). Intact performance on an indirect measure of race bias following amygdala damage. *Neuropsychologia, 41*, 203–208.

PHELPS, E. A., & GAZZANIGA, M. S. (1992). Hemispheric differences in mnemonic processing: The effects of left hemisphere interpretation. *Neuropsychologia, 30*, 293–297.

PHELPS, E. A., LABAR, D. S., ANDERSON, A. K., O'CONNOR, K. J., FULBRIGHT, R. K., & SPENCER, D. S. (1998). Specifying the contributions of the human amygdala to emotional memory: A case study. *Neurocase, 4*, 527–540.

PHELPS, E. A., O'CONNOR, K. J., CUNNINGHAM, W. A., FUNAYMA, E. S., GATENBY, J. C., GORE, J. C., ET AL. (2000). Performance on indirect measures of race evaluation predicts amygdala activity. *Journal of Cognitive Neuroscience, 12*, 729–738.

PHELPS, E. A., O'CONNOR, K. J., GATENBY, J. C., GRILLON, C., GORE, J. C., & DAVIS, M. (2001). Activation of the human amygdala to a cognitive representation of fear. *Nature Neuroscience, 4*, 437–441.

PHILLIPS, M. L., YOUNG, A. W., SCOTT, S. K., CALDER, A. J., ANDREW, C., GIAMPIETRO, V., ET AL. (1998). Neural responses to facial and vocal expressions of fear and disgust. *Proceedings of the Royal Society of London, Series B, 265*, 1809–1817.

PHILLIPS, M. L., YOUNG, A. W., SENIOR, C., BRAMMER, M., ANDREW, C., CALDER, A. J., ET AL. (1997). A specific neural substrate for perceiving facial expressions of disgust. *Nature, 389*, 495–498.

PINKER, S. (1994). *The language instinct.* New York: Morrow.

PINKER, S. (1997a). *How the mind works.* New York: Norton.

PINKER, S., & BLOOM, P. (1990). Natural language and natural selection. *Behavioral and Brain Sciences, 13*, 707–726.

PISELLA, L, GRÉA, H., TILIKETE, C., VIGHETTO, A., DESMURGET, M., RODE, G., ET AL. (2000). An 'automatic pilot' for the hand in human posterior parietal cortex: Toward reinterpreting optic ataxia. *Nature Neuroscience, 3*, 729–736.

PLANT, G. T., LAXER, K. D., BARBARO, N. M., SCHIFFMAN, J. S., & NAKAYAMA, K. (1993). Impaired visual motion perception in the contralateral hemifield following unilateral posterior cerebral lesions in humans. *Brain, 116*, 1303–1335.

PLOMIN, R., CORLEY, R., DEFRIES, J. C., & FULKER, D. W. (1990). Individual differences in television viewing in early childhood: Nature as well as nurture. *Psychological Science, 1*, 371–377.

PODGORNY, P., & SHEPARD, R. (1978). Functional representations common to visual perception and imagination. *Journal of Exper-*

imental Psychology. Human Perception and Performance, 4, 21–35.

POHL, W. (1973). Dissociation of spatial discrimination deficits following frontal and parietal lesions in monkeys. *Journal of Comparative and Physiological Psychology, 82,* 227–239.

POSNER, M. I. (1986). *Chronometric explorations of mind.* New York: Oxford University Press.

POSNER, M. I., & RAICHLE, M. E. (1994). *Images of mind.* New York: Freeman.

POSNER, M. I., SNYDER, C. R. R., & DAVIDSON, J. (1980). Attention and the detection of signals. *Journal of Experimental Psychology. General, 109,* 160–174.

POSNER, M. I., WALKER, J. A., FRIEDRICH, F. J., & RAFAL, B. D. (1984). Effects of parietal injury on covert orienting of attention. *Journal of Neuroscience, 4,* 1863–1874.

POSTLE, B. R., & CORKIN, S. (1998). Impaired word-stem completion priming but intact perceptual identification priming with novel words: Evidence from the amnesic patient H.M. *Neuropsychologia, 36,* 421–440.

PRABHAKARAN, V., NARAYANAN, K., ZHAO, Z., & GABRIELI, J. D. (2000). Integration of diverse information in working memory within the frontal lobe. *Nature Neuroscience, 3,* 85–90.

PREMACK, D., & WOODRUFF, G. (1978). Does the chimpanzee have a theory of mind? *Behavioral and Brain Sciences, 1,* 515–526.

PREUSS, T. M., & COLEMAN, G. Q. (2002). Human-specific organization of primary visual cortex: Alternating compartments of dense Cat-301 and calbindin immunoreactivity in layer 4A. *Cerebral Cortex, 12,* 671–691.

PREVIC, F. H. (1991). A general theory concerning the prenatal origins of cerebral lateralization in humans. *Psychological Review, 98,* 299–334.

PUCE, A., ALLISON, T., ASGARI, M., GORE, J. C., & MCCARTHY, G. (1996). Differential sensitivity of human visual cortex to faces, letterstrings, and textures: A functional magnetic resonance imaging study. *Journal of Neuroscience, 16,* 5205–5215.

PURVES, D., AUGUSTINE, G., & FITZPATRICK, D. (2001). *Neuroscience* (2nd ed.). Sunderland, MA: Sinauer.

RAICHLE, M. E. (1994). Visualizing the mind. *Scientific American, 270*(4), 58–64.

RAICHLE, M. E., FIEZ, J. A., VIDEEN, T. O., MACLEOD, A. K., PARDO, J. V., FOX, P. T., ET AL. (1994). Practice-related changes in human brain functional anatomy during nonmotor learning. *Cerebral Cortex, 4,* 8–26.

RAINE, A. (2002). Biosocial studies of antisocial and violent behavior in children and adults: A review. *Journal of Abnormal Child Psychology, 30,* 311–326.

RAINE, A., LENCZ, T., BIHRLE, S., LACASSE, L., & COLLETTI, P. (2000). Reduced prefrontal gray matter volume and reduced autonomic activity in antisocial personality disorder. *Archives of General Psychiatry, 57,* 119–127.

RAKIC, P. (1995a). Corticogenesis in human and nonhuman primates. In M. S. Gazzaniga (Ed.), *The cognitive neurosciences* (pp. 127–146). Cambridge, MA: MIT Press.

RAMACHANDRAN V. S. (1993). Behavioral and magnetoencephalographic correlates of plasticity in the adult human brain. *Proceedings of the National Academy of Sciences, USA, 90,* 10413–10420.

RAMACHANDRAN, V. S., & HUBBARD, E. M. (2001a). Psychophysical investigations into the neural basis of synaesthesia. *Proceedings of the Royal Society of London, Series B, 268,* 979–983.

RAMACHANDRAN, V. S., & HUBBARD, E. M. (2001b). Synaesthesia—A window into perception, thought and language. *Journal of Consciousness Studies, 8,* 3–34.

RAMACHANDRAN, V. S., & HUBBARD, E. M. (2003). Hearing colors, tasting shapes. *Scientific American, 288*(5), 52–59.

RAMIREZ-AMAYA, V., MARRONE, D. F., GAGE, F. H., WORLEY, P. F., & BARNES, C. A. (2006). Integration of new neurons into functional neural networks. *Journal of Neuroscience, 26,* 12237–12241.

RAMÓN Y CAJAL, S. (1909–1911). *Histologie du système nerveaux de l'homme et de vertébrés.* Paris: Maloine.

RANGANATH, C., & BLUMENFELD, R. S. (2005). Doubts about double dissociations between short- and long-term memory. *Trends in Cognitive Sciences, 9,* 374–380.

RANGANATH, C., YONELINAS, A. P., COHEN, M. X., DY, C. J., TOM, S. M., & D'ESPOSITO, M. (2004). Dissociable correlates of recollection and familiarity within the medial temporal lobes. *Neuropsychologia, 42,* 2–13.

RAO, S. C., RAINER, G., & MILLER, E. K. (1997). Integration of what and where in the primate prefrontal cortex. *Science, 276,* 821–824.

RAMPON, C., TANG, Y. P., GOODHOUSE, J., SHIMIZU, E., KYIN, M., & TSIEN, J. Z. (2000). Enrichment induces structural changes and recovery from nonspatial memory deficits in CA1 NMDAR1-knockout mice. *Nature Neuroscience, 3,* 238–244.

REICHER, G. M. (1969). Perceptual recognition as a function of meaningfulness of stimulus material. *Journal of Experimental Psychology, 81,* 275–280.

REICHERT, H., & BOYAN, G. (1997). Building a brain: Developmental insights in insects. *Trends in Neuroscience, 20,* 258–264.

REINHOLZ, J., & POLLMANN, S. (2005). Differential activation of object-selective visual areas by passive viewing of pictures and words. *Brain Research. Cognitive Brain Research, 24,* 702–714.

RENTSCHLER, I., TREUTWEIN, B., & LANDIS, T. (1994). Dissociation of local and global processing in visual agnosia. *Vision Research, 34,* 963–971.

REVERBERI, C., TORALDO, A., D'AGOSTINI, S., & SKRAP, M. (2005). Better without (lateral) frontal cortex? Insight problems solved by frontal patients. *Brain, 128,* 2882–2890.

RHODES, G., BYATT, G., MICHIE, P. T., & PUCE, A. (2004). Is the fusiform face area specialized for faces, individuation, or expert individuation? *Journal of Cognitive Neuroscience, 16,* 189–203.

RICH, A. N., WILLIAMS, M. A., PUCE, A., SYNGENIOTIS, A., HOWARD, M. A., MCGLONE, F., ET AL. (2006). Neural correlates of imagined and synaesthetic colours. *Neuropsychologia, 44,* 2918–2925. [Epub ahead of print, August 9]

RIDDERINKHOF, K. R., DE VLUGT, Y., BRAMLAGE, A., SPAAN, M., ELTON, M., SNEL, J., ET AL. (2002). Alcohol consumption impairs detection of performance errors in mediofrontal cortex. *Science, 298,* 2209–2211.

RIDDERINKHOF, K. R., ULLSPERGER, M., CRONE, E. A., & NIEUWENHUIS, S. (2004). The role of the medial frontal cortex in cognitive control. *Science, 306,* 443–447.

RIDDOCH, G. (1917). Dissociation of visual perceptions due to occipital injuries, with especial reference to appreciation of movement. *Brain, 40,* 15–47.

RIDDOCH, M. J., HUMPHREYS, G. W., GANNON, T., BOTT, W., & JONES, V. (1999). Memories are made of this: The effects of time on stored visual knowledge in a case of visual agnosia. *Brain, 122*(Pt.3), 537–559.

RILEY, B., & KENDLER, K. S. (2006). Molecular genetic studies of schizophrenia. *European Journal of Human Genetics, 14,* 669–680.

RILLING, J. K., GUTMAN, D. A., ZEH, T. R., PAGNONI, G., BERNS, G. S., & KILTS, C. D. (2002). A neural basis for social cooperation. *Neuron, 35,* 395–405.

RINGO, J. L., DOTY, R. W., DEMETER, S., & SIMARD, P. Y. (1994). Time is of the essence: A conjecture that hemispheric specialization arises from interhemispheric conduction delays. *Cerebral Cortex, 4,* 331–343.

RISSE, G. L., GATES, J. R., & FANGMAN, M. C. (1997). A reconsideration of bilateral language representation based on the intracarotid amobarbital procedure. *Brain and Cognition, 33,* 118–132.

RIZZOLATTI, G., GENTILUCCI, M., FOGASSI, L., LUPPINO, G., MATELLI, M., & CAMARDA, R. (1988). Functional organization of inferior area 6 in the macaque monkey. *Experimental Brain Research, 71,* 465–490.

ROBERTS, T. P. L., POEPPEL, D., & ROWLEY, H. A. (1998). Magnetoencephalography and magnetic source imaging. *Neuropsychiatry, Neuropsychology, and Behavioral Neurology, 11,* 49–64.

ROBERTSON, L. C., KNIGHT, R. T., RAFAL, R., & SHIMAMURA, A. P. (1993). Cognitive neuropsychology is more than single-case studies. *Journal of Experimental Psychology. Learning, Memory, and Cognition, 19,* 710–717.

ROBERTSON, L. C., LAMB, M. R., & KNIGHT, R. T. (1988). Effects of lesions of temporal-parietal junction on perceptual and attentional processing in humans. *Journal of Neuroscience, 8,* 3757–3769.

ROBERTSON, L. C., LAMB, M. R., & ZAIDEL, E. (1993). Interhemispheric relations in processing hierarchical patterns: Evidence from normal and commissurotomized subjects. *Neuropsychology, 7,* 325–342.

ROBINSON, D. L., & PETERSEN, S. (1992). The pulvinar and visual salience. *Trends in Neurosciences, 15,* 127–132.

ROBINSON, D. L., GOLDBERG, M. E., & STANTON, G. B. (1978). Parietal association cortex in the primate: Sensory mechanisms and behavioral modulation. *Journal of Neurophysiology, 41,* 910–932.

RODRIGUEZ-OROZ, M. C., OBESO, J. A., LANG, A. E., HOUETO, J. L., POLLAK, P., REHNCRONA, S., ET AL. (2005) Bilateral deep brain stimulation in Parkinson's disease: A multicentre study with 4 years follow-up. *Brain, 128,* 2240–2249.

ROEDIGER, H. L., & MCDERMOTT, K. B. (1995). Creating false memories: Remembering words not presented in lists. *Journal of Experimental Psychology. Learning, Memory, and Cognition, 21,* 803–814.

ROGERS, R. D., SAHAKIAN, R. A., HODGES, J. R., POLKEY, C. E., KENNARD, C., & ROBBINS, T. W. (1998). Dissociating executive mechanisms of task control following frontal lobe damage and Parkinson's disease. *Brain, 121,* 815–842.

ROGERS, T. B., KUIPER, N. A., & KIRKER, W. S. (1977). Self-reference and the encoding of personal information. *Journal of Personality and Social Psychology, 35,* 677–688.

ROLLS, E. T. (1992). Neurophysiological mechanisms underlying face processing within and beyond the temporal cortical visual areas. *Philosophical Transactions of the Royal Society of London. Series B, Biological Sciences, 335,* 11–20.

ROSE, J. E., HIND, J. E., ANDERSON, D. J., & BRUGGE, J. F. (1971). Some effects of stimulus intensity on response of auditory nerve fibers in the squirrel monkey. *Journal of Neurophysiology, 24,* 685–699.

ROSENBAUM, D. A., SLOTTA, J. D., VAUGHAN, J., & PLAMONDON, R. (1991). Optimal movement selection. *Psychological Science, 2,* 86–91.

ROSENBAUM, R. S., KOHLER, S., SCHACTER, D. L., MOSCOVITCH, M., WESTMACOTT, R., BLACK, S. E., ET AL. (2005). The case of K.C.: Contributions of a memory-impaired person to memory theory. *Neuropsychologia, 43,* 989–1021.

ROSER, M. E., FUGELSANG, J. A., DUNBAR, K. N., CORBALLIS, P. M., & GAZZANIGA, M. S. (2005). Dissociating processes supporting causal perception and causal inference in the brain. *Neuropsychology, 19,* 591–602.

ROTHWELL, J. C., TRAUB, M. M., DAY, B. L., OBESO, J. A., THOMAS, P. K., & MARSDEN, C. D. (1982). Manual motor performance in a deafferented man. *Brain, 105,* 515–542.

ROWAN, A. N., & ROLLIN, B. E. (1983). Animal research—For and against: A philosophical, social, and historical perspective. *Perspectives in Biology and Medicine, 27,* 1–17.

ROWE, D. C. (2001). *Biology of crime.* Los Angeles: Roxbury.

ROWLAND, L. P. (ED.). (1989). *Merritt's textbook of neurology* (8th ed.). Philadelphia: Lea & Febiger.

RUFF, C. C., BLANKENBURG, F., BJOERTOMT, O., BESTMANN, S., FREEMAN, E., HAYNES, J.-D., ET AL. (2006). Concurrent TMS-fMRI and psychophysics reveal frontal influences on human retinotopic visual cortex. *Current Biology, 16,* 1479–1488.

RUMELHART, D. E., MCCLELLAND, J. L., & PDP RESEARCH GROUP. (1986). *Parallel distributed processing: Explorations in the microstructure of cognition: Vol. 1. Foundations.* Cambridge, MA: MIT Press.

RUSSELL, J. A. (1979). Affective space is bipolar. *Journal of Personality and Social Psychology, 37,* 345–356.

RYAN, J. D., ALTHOFF, R. R., WHITLOW, S., & COHEN, N. J. (2002). Amnesia is a deficit in relational memory. *Psychological Science, 11,* 454–461.

SACKS, O. W. (1995). *An anthropologist on Mars: Seven paradoxical tales.* New York: Knopf.

SADATO, N., PASCUAL-LEONE, A., GRAFMAN, J., IBANEZ, V., DEIBER, M-P., DOLD, G., ET AL. (1996). Activation of the primary visual cortex by Braille reading in blind subjects. *Nature, 380,* 526–528.

SAGIV, N., & BENTIN, S. (2001). Structural encoding of human and schematic faces: Holistic and part-based processes. *Journal of Cognitive Neuroscience, 13,* 937–951.

SAKAI, K., & PASSINGHAM, R. E. (2003). Prefrontal interactions reflect future task operations. *Nature Neuroscience, 6,* 75–81.

SAMII, A., TURNBULL, I. M., KISHORE, A., SCHULZER, M., MAK, E., YARDLEY, S., ET AL. (1999). Reassessment of unilateral pallidotomy in Parkinson's disease: A 2-year follow-up study. *Brain, 122,* 417–425.

SAMS, M., HARI, R., RIF, J., & KNUUTILA, J. (1993). The human auditory sensory memory trace persists about 10 sec: Neuromagnetic evidence. *Journal of Cognitive Neuroscience, 5,* 363–370.

SANDER, D., GRANDJEAN, D., POURTOIS, G., SCHWARTZ, S., SEGHIER, M. L., SCHERER, K. R., ET AL. (2005). Emotion and attention interactions in social cognition: Brain regions involved in processing anger prosody. *Neuroimage, 28,* 848–858.

SANFEY, A. G., LOEWENSTEIN, G., MCCLURE, S., & COHEN, J. D. (2006). Neuroeconomics: Cross currents in research on decision-making. *Trends in Cognitive Sciences, 10,* 108–116.

SANFEY, A. G., RILLING, J. K., ARONSON, J. A., NYSTROM, L. E., & COHEN, J. D. (2003). The neural basis of economic decision-making in the ultimatum game. *Science, 300,* 1755–1758.

SAPIR, A., SOROKER, N., BERGER, A., & HENIK, A. (1999). Inhibition of return in spatial attention: Direct evidence for collicular generation. *Nature Neuroscience, 2,* 1053–1054.

SAPOLSKY, R. M. (1992). Stress, the aging brain, and the mechanisms of neuron death. Cambridge, MA: MIT Press.

SAPOLSKY, R. M., UNO, H., REBERT, C. S., & FINCH, C. E. (1990). Hippocampal damage associated with prolonged glucocorticoid exposure in primates. *Journal of Neuroscience, 10,* 2897–2902.

SATORI, G., & JOB, R. (1988). The oyster with four legs: A neuropsychological study on the interaction of visual and semantic information. *Cognitive Neuropsychology, 5*, 105–132.

SAUCIER, D., & CAIN, D. P. (1995). Spatial learning without NMDA receptor-dependent long-term potentiation. *Nature, 378*, 186–189.

SAVER, J. L., & DAMASIO, A. R. (1991). Preserved access and processing of social knowledge in a patient with acquired sociopathy due to ventromedial frontal damage. *Neuropsychologia, 29*, 1241–1249.

SAXE, R., & POWELL, L. J. (2006). It's the thought that counts: Specific brain regions for one component of theory of mind. *Psychological Science, 17*, 692–699.

SAXE, R., & WEXLER, A. (2005). Making sense of another mind: The role of the right temporo-parietal junction. *Neuropsychologia, 43*, 1391–1399.

SAYGIN, A. P., WILSON, S. M., DRONKERS, N. F., & BATES, E. (2004). Action comprehension in aphasia: Linguistic and non-linguistic deficits and their lesion correlates. *Neuropsychologia, 42*, 1788–1804.

SCHACHTER, S., & SINGER, J. (1962). Cognitive, social and physiological determinants of emotional state. *Psychological Review, 69*, 379–399.

SCHACTER, D. L. (1987). Implicit memory: History and current status. *Journal of Experimental Psychology. Learning, Memory, and Cognition, 113*, 501–518.

SCHACTER, D. L., GILBERT, D. T., & WEGNER, D. M. (2007). *Psychology.* New York: Worth.

SCHIRBER, M. (2005, February 18). Monkey's brain runs robotic arm. *LiveScience.* [Retrieved April 11, 2007, from http://www.livescience.com/technology/050218_monkey_arm.html]

SCHMIDT, R. A. (1987). The acquisition of skill: Some modifications to the perception-action relationship through practice. In H. Heuer and A. F. Sanders (Eds.), *Perspectives on perception and action* (pp. 77–103). Hillsdale, NJ: Erlbaum.

SCHNEIDER, G. E. (1969). Two visual systems. *Science, 163*, 895–902.

SCHOENEMANN, P. T., SHEEHAN, M. J., & GLOTZER, L. D. (2005). Prefrontal white matter volume is disproportionately larger in humans than in other primates. *Nature Neuroscience, 8*, 242–252.

SCHOENFELD, M., HOPF, J. M., MARTINEZ, A., MAI, H., SATTLER, C., GASDE, A., ET AL. (2007). Spatio-temporal analysis of feature-based attention. *Cerebral Cortex.* [Epub ahead of print, January 4]

SCOTT, S. K., YOUNG, A. W., CALDER, A. J., HELLAWELL, D. J., AGGLETON, J. P., & JOHNSON, M. (1997). Impaired auditory recognition of fear and anger following bilateral amygdala lesions. *Nature, 385*, 254–257.

SCOVILLE, W. B. (1954). The limbic lobe in man. *Journal of Neurosurgery, 11*, 64–66.

SCOVILLE, W. B., & MILNER, B. (1957). Loss of recent memory after bilateral hippocampal lesions. *Journal of Neurology, Neurosurgery, and Psychiatry, 20*, 11–21.

SEIDENBERG, M. S., & MCCLELLAND, J. L. (1989). A distributed, developmental model of word recognition and naming. *Psychological Review, 96*, 523–568.

SEJNOWSKI, T. J., & CHURCHLAND, P. S. (1989). Brain and cognition. In M. I. Posner (Ed.), *Foundations of cognitive science* (pp. 301–356). Cambridge, MA: MIT Press.

SEKULER, R., & BLAKE, R. (1990). *Perception* (2nd ed.). New York: McGraw-Hill.

SELFRIDGE, O. G. (1959). Pandemonium: A paradigm for learning. In *Proceedings of a symposium on the mechanisation of thought processes* (pp. 511–526). London: H. M. Stationary Office.

SERGENT, J. (1982). The cerebral balance of power: Confrontation or cooperation: *Journal of Experimental Psychology. Human Perception and Performance, 8*, 253–272.

SERGENT, J. (1985). Influence of task and input factors on hemispheric involvement in face processing. *Journal of Experimental Psychology. Human Perception and Performance, 11*, 846–861.

SERVOS, P., ENGEL, S. A., GATI, J., & MENON, R. (1999). fMRI evidence for an inverted face representation in human somatosensory cortex. *Neuroreport, 10*, 1393–1395.

SHADMEHR, R., & HOLCOMB, H. H. (1997). Neural correlates of motor memory consolidation. *Science, 277*, 821–825.

SHALLICE, T., & BURGESS, P. W. (1991). Deficits in strategy application following frontal lobe damage in man. *Brain, 114*, 727–741.

SHALLICE, T., BURGESS, P. W., SCHON, F., & BAXTER, D. M. (1989). The origins of utilization behaviour. *Brain, 112*, 1587–1598.

SHALLICE, T., & WARRINGTON, E. (1969). Independent functioning of verbal memory stores: A neuropsychological study. *Quarterly Journal of Experimental Psychology, 22*, 261–273.

SHAROT, T., RICCARDI, A. M., RAIO, C. M., & PHELPS, E. A. (2007). Neural mechanisms mediating optimism bias. *Nature, 450*, 102–105.

SHAW, P., GREENSTEIN, D., LERCH, J., CLASEN, L., LENROOT, R., GOGTAY, N., ET AL. (2006). Intellectual ability and cortical development in children and adolescents. *Nature, 440*, 676–679.

SHEINBERG, D. L., & LOGOTHETIS, N. K. (1997). The role of temporal cortical areas in perceptual organization. *Proceedings of the National Academy of Sciences, USA, 94*, 3408–3413.

SHEPHERD, G. M. (1991). *Foundations of the neuron doctrine.* New York: Oxford University Press.

SHEPHERD, G. M., WOOLF, T. B., & CARNEVALE, N. T. L. (1989). Comparisons between active properties and distal dendritic branches and spines: Implications for neuronal computations. *Journal of Cognitive Neuroscience, 1*, 273–286.

SHERRINGTON, C. S. (1935). Santiago Ramón y Cajal 1852–1934. *Obituary Notices of Fellows of the Royal Society, 4*, 425–441.

SHERRINGTON, C. S. (1947). *The integrative action of the nervous system* (2nd ed.). New Haven, CT: Yale University Press.

SHIMAMURA, A. P. (2000). The role of the prefrontal cortex in dynamic filtering. *Psychobiology, 28*, 207–218.

SHORS, T. J. (2004). Memory traces of trace memories: Neurogenesis, synaptogenesis and awareness. *Trends in Neurosciences, 27*, 250–256.

SHUREN, J. E., BROTT, T. G., SCHEFFT, B. K., & HOUSTON, W. (1996). Preserved color imagery in an achromatopsic. *Neuropsychologia, 34*, 485–489.

SIDTIS, J. J., VOLPE, B. T., HOLTZMAN, J. D., WILSON, D. H., & GAZZANIGA, M. S. (1981). Cognitive interaction after staged callosal section: Evidence for transfer of semantic activation. *Science, 212*, 344–346.

SINGER, T., SEYMOUR, B., O'DOHERTY, J., KAUBE, H., DOLAN, R. J., & FRITH, C. D. (2004). Empathy for pain involves the affective but not sensory components of pain. *Science, 303*, 1157–1162.

SINGER, W. (2000). Phenomenal awareness and consciousness from a neurobiological perspective. In T. Metzinger (Ed.), *Neural correlates of consciousness* (pp. 121–137). Cambridge, MA: MIT Press.

SMALL, D. M., ZATORRE, R. J., DAGHER, A., EVANS, A. C., & JONES-GOTMAN, M. (2001). Changes in brain activity related to eating chocolate. *Brain, 124*, 1720–1733.

SMILEK, D., DIXON, M. J., & MERIKLE, P. M. (2005). Synaesthesia: Discordant male monozygotic twins. *Neurocase, 11*, 363–370.

SMITH, A. P. R., STEPHAN, K. E., RUGG, M. D., & DOLAN, R. J. (2006). Task and content modulate amygdala-hippocampal connectivity in emotional retrieval. *Neuron, 49*, 631–638.

SMITH, E. E., JONIDES, J., & KOEPPE, R. A. (1996). Dissociating verbal and spatial working memory using PET. *Cerebral Cortex, 6*, 11–20.

SNODGRASS, J. G., & VANDERWART, M. (1980). A standardized set of 260 pictures: Norms for name agreement, image agreement, familiarity, and visual complexity. *Journal of Experimental Psychology. Human Learning and Memory, 6*, 174–215.

SOBEL, N., PRABHAKARAN, V., DESMOND, J. E., GLOVER, G. H., GOODE, R. L., SULLIVAN, E. V., ET AL. (1998). Sniffing and smelling: Separate subsystems in the human olfactory cortex. *Nature, 392*, 282–286.

SPELKE, E., HIRST, W., & NEISSER, U. (1976). Skills of divided attention. *Cognition, 4*, 215–230.

SPERRY, R. W., GAZZANIGA, M. S., & BOGEN, J. E. (1969). Interhemispheric relationships: The neocortical commissures; syndromes of hemisphere disconnection. In P. J. Vinken and G. W. Bruyn (Eds.), *Handbook of clinical neurology* (Vol. 4, pp. 273–290). Amsterdam: North-Holland.

SPEZIO, M. L., ADOLPHS, R., HURLEY, R. S. E., & PIVEN, J. (2007). Analysis of face gaze in autism using "Bubbles." *Neuropsychologia, 45*, 144–151.

SQUIRE, L. R., BLOOM, F. E., MCCONNELL, S. K., ROBERTS, J. L., SPITZER, N. C., & ZIGMOND, M. J. (EDS.). (2003). *Fundamental neuroscience* (2nd ed.). Amsterdam: Academic Press.

SQUIRE, L. R., & KNOWLTON, B. J. (1995). Memory, hippocampus, and brain systems. In M. S. Gazzaniga (Ed.), *The cognitive neurosciences* (pp. 825–837). Cambridge, MA: MIT Press.

SQUIRE, L. R., & SLATER, P. (1983). Electroconvulsive therapy and complaints of memory dysfunction: A prospective three-year follow-up study. *British Journal of Psychiatry, 142*, 1–8.

STEIN, B., & MEREDITH, M. (1993). The merging of the senses. Cambridge, MA: MIT Press.

STEIN, M. B., KOVEROLA, C., HANNA, C., TORCHIA, M. G., & MCCLARTY, B. (1997). Hippocampal volume in woman victimized by childhood sexual abuse. *Psychological Medicine, 27*, 951–959.

STERNBERG, S. (1966). High speed scanning in human memory. *Science, 153*, 652–654.

STERNBERG, S. (1975). Memory scanning: New findings and current controversies. *Quarterly Journal of Experimental Psychology, 27*, 1–32.

STEVEN, M. S., DORON, K. W., GAZZANIGA, M. S., & COLVIN, M. K. (2006). Subregion parcellation and topographic connectivity mapping of the human corpus callosum using diffusion tensor imaging. Poster presented at the Cognitive Neuroscience Society 2006 Annual Meeting. Cognitive Neuroscience Society Abstracts, No. A4.

STEVEN, M. S., & PASCUAL-LEONE, A. (2006). Transcranial magnetic stimulation and the human brain: An ethical evaluation. In J. Illes (Ed.), *Neuroethics: Defining the issues in theory, practice, and policy* (pp. 201–212). Oxford, England: Oxford University Press.

STONE, V. E., BARON-COHEN, S., & KNIGHT, R. T. (1998). Frontal lobe contributions to theory of mind. *Journal of Cognitive Neuroscience, 10*, 640–656.

STROOP, J. (1935). Studies of interference in serial verbal reaction. *Journal of Experimental Psychology, 18*, 643–662.

SUN, F. T., MILLER, L. M., & D'ESPOSITO, M. (2004). Measuring interregional functional connectivity using coherence and partial coherence analyses of fMRI data. *Neuroimage, 21*, 647–658.

SWAAB, T. Y., BROWN, C. M., & HAGOORT, P. (1997). Spoken sentence comprehension in aphasia: Event-related potential evidence for a lexical integration deficit. *Journal of Cognitive Neuroscience, 9*, 39–66.

SWANSON, L. W. (1983). The hippocampus and the concept of the limbic system. In W. Seifert (Ed.), *Neurobiology of the hippocampus* (pp. 3–19). London: Academic Press.

TANAKA, J. W., & FARAH, M. J. (1993). Parts and wholes in face recognition. *Quarterly Journal of Experimental Psychology. A, Human Experimental Psychology, 46*, 225–245.

TARR, M. J., BUELTHOFF, H. H., ZABINSKI, M., & BLANZ, V. (1997). To what extent do unique parts influence recognition across changes in viewpoint? *Psychological Science, 8*, 282–289.

TARR, M. J., & GAUTHIER, I. (2000). FFA: A flexible fusiform area for subordinate-level visual processing automatized by expertise. *Nature Neuroscience, 3*, 764–769.

TAUB, E., & BERMAN, A. J. (1968). Movement and learning in the absence of sensory feedback. In S. J. Freedman (Ed.), *The neuropsychology of spatially oriented behavior* (pp. 173–191). Homewood, IL: Dorsey.

TAYLOR, S. E., & BROWN, J. D. (1988). Illusion and well-being: A social psychological perspective on mental health. *Psychological Bulletin, 103*, 193–210.

TEATHER, L. A., PACKARD, M. G., & BAZAN, N. G. (1998). Effects of posttraining intrahippocampal injections of platelet-activating factor and PAF antagonists on memory. *Neurobiology of Learning and Memory, 70*, 349–363.

THIBAULT, C., LAI, C., WILKE, N., DUONG, B., OLIVE, M. F., RAHMAN, S., ET AL. (2000). Expression profiling of neural cells reveals specific patterns of ethanol-responsive gene expression. *Molecular Pharmacology, 58*, 1593–1600.

THOMPSON, R. F. (2000). *The brain: A neuroscience primer* (3rd ed.). New York: Freeman.

THOMPSON-SCHILL, S. L., D'ESPOSITO, M., AGUIRRE, G. K., & FARAH, M. J. (1997). Role of left inferior prefrontal cortex in retrieval of semantic knowledge: A reevaluation. *Proceedings of the National Academy of Sciences, USA, 94*, 14792–14797.

THOMPSON-SCHILL, S. L., D'ESPOSITO, M., & KAN, I. P. (1999). Effects of repetition and competition on activity in left prefrontal cortex during word generation. *Neuron, 23*, 513–522.

THOMPSON-SCHILL, S. L., SWICK, D., FARAH, M. J., D'ESPOSITO, M., KAN, I. P., & KNIGHT, R. T. (1998). Verb generation in patients with focal frontal lesions: A neuropsychological test of neuroimaging findings. *Proceedings of the National Academy of Sciences, USA, 95*, 15855–15860.

THORNDIKE, E. (1911). *Animal intelligence: An experimental study of the associative processes in animals.* New York: MacMillan.

TIGNOR, R. L. (2008). *Worlds together, worlds apart: A history of the world from the beginnings of humankind to the present* (2nd ed.). New York: Norton.

TOOLEY, K., TRAXLER, M., & SWAAB, T. (2007). Electrophysiological evidence of syntactic (not semantic) priming in sentence comprehension. Submitted for publication.

TOOTELL, R. B., HADJIKHANI, N., HALL, E. K., MARRETT, S., VANDUFFEL, W., VAUGHAN, J. T., ET AL. (1998). The retinotopy of visual spatial attention. *Neuron, 21*, 1409–1422.

TOOTELL, R. B., SILVERMAN, M. S., SWITKES, E., & DEVALOIS, R. L. (1982). Deoxyglucose analysis of retinotopic organization in primate striate cortex. *Science, 218*, 902–904.

TRANEL, D., & HYMAN, B. T. (1990). Neuropsychological correlates of bilateral amygdala damage. *Archives of Neurology, 47*, 349–355.

TREISMAN, A. M. (1969). Strategies and models of selective attention. *Psychological Review, 76,* 282–299.

TREISMAN, A., & GELADE, G. (1980). A feature-integration theory of attention. *Cognitive Psychology, 12,* 97–136.

TRIVERS, R. L. (1971). The evolution of reciprocal altruism. *Quarterly Review of Biology, 46,* 35–57.

TSAO, D. Y., FREIWALD, W. A., TOOTELL, R. B., & LIVINGSTONE, M. S. (2006). A cortical region consisting entirely of face-selective cells. *Science, 311,* 670–674.

TULVING, E. (1993). Self-knowledge of an amnesiac individual is represented abstractly. In T. K. Srull & R. S. Wyer (Eds.), *The mental representation of trait and autobiographical knowledge about the self* (pp. 147–156). Hillsdale, NJ: Erlbaum.

TULVING, E., HAYMAN, C. A., & MACDONALD, C. A. (1991). Long-lasting perceptual priming and semantic learning in amnesia. A case experiment. *Journal of Experimental Psychology, 17,* 595–617.

TULVING, E., KAPUR, S., CRAIK, F. I. M., MOSCOVITCH, M., & HOULE, S. (1994). Hemispheric encoding/retrieval asymmetry in episodic memory: Positron emission tomography findings. *Proceedings of the National Academy of Sciences, USA, 91,* 2016–2020.

TULVING, E., & SHACTER, D. L. (1990). Priming and human memory systems. *Science, 7,* 1–306.

TVERSKY, A., & KAHNEMAN, D. (1988). Rational choice and the framing of decisions. In E. D. Bell, H. Raiffa, & A. Tversky (Eds.), *Decision making: Descriptive, normative, and prescriptive interactions* (pp. 167–192). Cambridge, England: Cambridge University Press.

UMILTA, M. A., KOHLER, E., GALLESE, V., FOGASSI, L., FADIGA, L., KEYSERS, C., ET AL. (2001). I know what you are doing: A neuropysiological study. *Neuron, 31,* 155–165.

UNGERLEIDER, L. G., & MISHKIN, M. (1982). Two cortical visual systems. In D. J. Engle, M. A. Goodale, & R. J. Mansfield (Eds.), *Analysis of visual behavior* (pp. 549–586). Cambridge, MA: MIT Press.

VALENSTEIN, E. S. (1986). *Great and desperate cures: The rise and decline of psychosurgery and other radical treatments for mental illness.* New York: Basic Books.

VALLAR, G., & PERANI, D. (1986). The anatomy of unilateral neglect after right-hemisphere stroke lesions. A clinical/CT-scan correlation study in man. *Neuropsychologia, 24,* 609–622.

VANDER, A., SHERMAN, J., & LUCIANO, D. (2001). *Human physiology: The mechanisms of body function* (8th ed.). Boston: McGraw-Hill.

VAN TURENNOUT, M., HAGOORT, P., & BROWN, C. M. (1999). Brain activity during speaking: From syntax to phonology in 40 milliseconds. *Science, 280,* 572–574.

VARGHA-KHADEM, F., GADIAN, D. G., WATKINS, K. E., CONNELLY, A., VAN PAESSCHEN, W., & MISHKIN, M. (1997). Differential effects of early hippocampal pathology on episodic and semantic memory. *Science, 277,* 376–380.

VOLFOVSKY, N., PARNAS, H., SEGAL, M., & KORKOTIAN, E. (1999). Geometry of dendritic spines affects calcium dynamics in hippocampal neurons: Theory and experiments. *Journal of Neurophysiology, 82,* 450–462.

VOLPE, B. T., LEDOUX, J. E., & GAZZANIGA, M. S. (1979). Information processing of visual field stimuli in an "extinguished" field. *Nature, 282,* 722–724.

VUILLEUMIER, P., HENSON, R. N., DRIVER, J., & DOLAN, R. J. (2002). Multiple levels of visual object constancy revealed by event-related fMRI of repetition priming. *Nature Neuroscience, 5,* 491–499.

WAGER, T. D., & SMITH, E. E. (2003). Neuroimaging studies of working memory: A meta-analysis. *Cognitive, Affective & Behavioral Neuroscience, 3,* 255–274.

WAGNER A. D., SCHACTER, D. L., ROTTE, M. KOUTSTAAL, W., MARIL, A., DALE, A. M., ET AL. (1998). Building memories: Remembering and forgetting of verbal experiences as predicted by brain activity. *Science, 281,* 1188–1191.

WALKER, E. P. (1983). *Walker's mammals of the world* (4th ed., Vol. 1). Baltimore: Johns Hopkins University Press.

WANG, X. T. (1996). Domain-specific rationality in human choices: Violations of utility axioms and social contexts. *Cognition, 60,* 31–63.

WAPNER, W., JUDD, T., & GARDNER, H. (1978). Visual agnosia in an artist. *Cortex, 14,* 343–364.

WARRINGTON, E. K. (1982). Neuropsychological studies of object recognition. *Philosophical Transactions of the Royal Society of London. Series B, Biological Sciences, 298,* 13–33.

WARRINGTON, E. K. (1985). Agnosia: The impairment of object recognition. In P. J. Vinken, G. W. Bruyn, & H. L. Klawans (Eds.), *Handbook of clinical neurology* (pp. 333–349). New York: Elsevier.

WARRINGTON, E. K., & MCCARTHY, R. A. (1994). Multiple meaning systems in the brain: A case for visual semantics. *Neuropsychologia, 32,* 1465–1473.

WARRINGTON, E. K., & SHALLICE, T. (1984). Category specific semantic impairments. *Brain, 107,* 829–854.

WARRINGTON, E. K., & TAYLOR, A. M. (1978). Two categorical stages of object recognition. *Perception, 7,* 695–705.

WEICKERT, T. W., GOLDBERG, T. E., MISHARA, A., APUD, J. A., KOLACHANA, B. S., EGAN, M. F., ET AL. (2004). Catechol-O-methyltransferase val108/158met genotype predicts working memory response to antipsychotic medications. *Biological Psychiatry, 56,* 677–682.

WEINBERGER, D. R. (1988). Schizophrenia and the frontal lobes. *Trends in Neurosciences, 11,* 367–370.

WEISKRANTZ, L. (1956). Behavioral changes associated with ablation of the amygdaloid complex in monkeys. *Journal of Comparative and Physiological Psychology, 49,* 381–391.

WEISKRANTZ, L. (1986). *Blindsight: A case study and implications.* Oxford, England: Oxford University Press.

WELLER, W. L. (1993). SmI cortical barrels in an Australian marsupial, *Trichosurus vulpecula* (brush-tailed possum): Structural organization, patterned distribution, and somatotopic relationships. *Journal of Comparative Neurology, 337,* 471–492.

WERNICKE C. (1876). Das Urwindungssystem des menschlichen Gehirns. *Archiv für Psychiatrie und Nervenkrankheiten, 6,* 298–326.

WESSINGER, C. M., BUONOCORE, M. H., KUSSMAUL, C. L., & MANGUN, G. R. (1997). Tonotopy in human auditory cortex examined with functional magnetic resonance imaging. *Human Brain Mapping, 5,* 18–25.Whalen, P. J., Kagan, J., Cook, R. G., Davis, F. C., Kim, H., Polis, S., et al. (2004). Human amygdala responsivity to masked fearful eye whites. *Science, 306,* 2061.

WHALEN, P. J., RAUCH, S. L., ETCOFF, N. L., MCINERNEY, S. C., LEE, M. B., & JENIKE, M. A. (1998). Masked presentations of emotional facial expressions modulate amygdala activity without explicit knowledge. *Journal of Neuroscience, 18,* 411–418.

WHEELER, M. E., PETERSEN, S. E., & BUCKNER, R. L. (2000). Memory's echo: Vivid remembering reactivates sensory-specific cortex. *Proceedings of the National Academy of Sciences, USA, 97,* 11125–11129.

WHEELER, M. E., SHULMAN, G. L., BUCKNER, R. L., MIEZIN, F. M., VELANOVA, K., & PETERSEN, S. E. (2006). Evidence for separate perceptual reactivation and search processes during remembering. *Cerebral Cortex, 16,* 949–959.

WICHMANN, T., & DELONG, M. R. (1996). Functional and pathophysiological models of the basal ganglia. *Current Opinion in Neurobiology, 6,* 751–758.

WICKELGREN, W. A. (1974). *How to solve problems.* San Francisco: Freeman.

WICKER, B., KEYSERS, C., PLAILLY, J., ROYET, J.-P., GALLESE, V., & RIZZOLATTI, G. (2003). Both of us disgusted in my insula: The common neural basis of seeing and feeling disgust. *Neuron, 40,* 655–664.

WIESENDANGER, M., ROUILLER, E. M., KAZENNIKOV, O., & PERRIG, S. (1996). Is the supplementary motor area a bilaterally organized system? *Advances in Neurology, 70,* 85–93.

WILLIAMS, G. C. (1966). *Adaptation and natural selection.* Princeton, NJ: Princeton University Press.

WILLIAMSON, A., SPENCER, D. D., & SHEPHERD, G. M. (1993). Comparisons between the membrane and synaptic properties of human and rodent dentate granule cells. *Brain Research, 622,* 194–202.

WILLIS, J., & TODOROV, A. (2006). First impressions: Making up your mind after a 100-ms exposure to a face. *Psychological Science, 17,* 592–598.

WILSON, E. O. (1975). *Sociobiology, the new synthesis.* Cambridge, MA: Belknap Press of Harvard University Press.

WILSON, F. A., SCALAIDHE, S. P., & GOLDMAN-RAKIC, P. S. (1993). Dissociation of object and spatial processing domains in primate prefrontal cortex. *Science, 260,* 1955–1958.

WILSON, M. A., & MCNAUGHTON, B. L. (1994). Reactivation of hippocampal ensemble memories during sleep. *Science, 265,* 676–679.

WILSON, M. A., & TONEGAWA, S. (1997). Synaptic plasticity, place cells, and spatial memory: Study with second generation knockouts. *Trends in Neurosciences, 20,* 102–106.

WISE, R. J. (2003). Language systems in normal and aphasic human subjects: Functional imaging studies and inferences from animal studies. *British Medical Bulletin, 65,* 95–119.

WISE, S. P., DI PELLEGRINO, G., & BOUSSAOUD, D. (1996). The premotor cortex and nonstandard sensorimotor mapping. *Canadian Journal of Physiology and Pharmacology, 74,* 469–482.

WITELSON, S. F., KIGAR, D. L., & HARVEY, T. (1999). The exceptional brain of Albert Einstein. *Lancet, 353,* 2149–2153.

WITHERS, G. S., GEORGE, J. M., BANKER, G. A., & CLAYTON, D. F. (1997). Delayed localization of synelfin (synuclein, NACP) to presynaptic terminals in cultured rat hippocampal neurons. *Brain Research. Developmental Brain Research, 99,* 87–94.

WOLDORFF, M. G., GALLEN, C. C., HAMPSON, S. A., HILLYARD, S. A., PANTEV, C., SOBEL, D., ET AL. (1993). Modulation of early sensory processing in human auditory cortex during auditory selective attention. *Proceedings of the National Academy of Sciences, USA, 90,* 8722–8726.

WOLDORFF, M. G., & HILLYARD, S. A. (1991). Modulation of early auditory processing during selective listening to rapidly presented tones. *Electroencephalography and Clinical Neurophysiology, 79,* 170–191.

WOLFE, J. M., ALVAREZ, G. A., & HOROWITZ, T. S. (2000). Attention is fast but volition is slow. *Nature, 406,* 691.

WOLFORD, G., MILLER, M. B., & GAZZANIGA, M. (2000). The left hemisphere's role in hypothesis formation. *Journal of Neuroscience, 20,* RC64. Retrieved from http://www.jneurosci.org/cgi/content/full/20/6/RC64.

WOLPAW, J. R., LOEB, G. E., ALLISON, B. Z., DONCHIN. E., DO NASCIMENTO, O. F., HEETDERKS, W. J., ET AL. (2006). BCI Meeting 2005—Workshop on signals and recording methods. *IEEE Transactions on Neural Systems and Rehabilitation Engineering, 14,* 138–141.

WOODARD, J. S. (1973). *Histologic neuropathology: A color slide set.* Orange: California Medical Publications.

WOOLSEY, C. N. (1952). Pattern of localization in sensory and motor areas of the cerebral cortex. In *The biology of mental health and disease* (pp. 193–225). New York: Hoeber.

WOOLSEY, C. N. (1958). Organization of somatic sensory and motor areas of the cerebral cortex. In H. F. Harlow & C. N. Woolsey (Eds.), *Biological and biochemical bases of behavior* (pp. 63–81). Madison: University of Wisconsin Press.

WOOLSEY, T. A., WELKER, C., & SCHWARTZ, R. H. (1975). Comparative anatomical studies of the SmI face cortex with special reference to the occurence of "barrels" in layer IV. *Journal of Comparative Neurology, 164,* 79–94.

WURTZ, R. H., GOLDBERG, M. E., & ROBINSON, D. L. (1982). Brain mechanisms of visual attention. *Scientific American, 246*(6), 124–135.

XU, Y., LIU, J., & KANWISHER, N. (2005). The M170 is selective for faces, not for expertise. *Neuropsychologia, 43,* 588–597.

YINGLING, C. D., & SKINNER, J. E. (1976). Selective regulation of thalamic sensory relay nuclei by nucleus reticularis thalami. *Electroencephalography and Clinical Neurophysiology, 41,* 476–482.

YONELINAS, A., KROLL, N., DOBBINS, I., LAZZARA, M., & KNIGHT, R. T. (1998). Recollection and familiarity deficits in amnesia: Convergence of remember-know, process dissociation, and receiver operating characteristic data. *Neuropsychology, 12,* 323–339.

ZAMANILLO, D., SPRENGEL, R., HVALBY, O., JENSEN, V., BURNASHEV, N., ROZOV, A., ET AL. (1999). Importance of AMPA receptors for hippocampal synaptic plasticity but not for spatial learning. *Science, 284,* 1805–1811.

ZANGALADZE, A., EPSTEIN, C. M., GRAFTON, S. T., & SATHIAN, K. (1999). Involvement of visual cortex in tactile discrimination of orientation. *Nature, 401,* 587–590.

ZEKI, S. (1993). *A vision of the brain.* Oxford, England: Blackwell.

ZIEMANN, U., MUELLBACHER, W., HALLETT, M., & COHEN, L. G. (2001). Full text modulation of practice-dependent plasticity in human motor cortex. *Brain, 124,* 1171–1181.

ZIHL, J., VON CRAMON, D., & MAI, N. (1983). Selective disturbance of movement vision after bilateral brain damage. *Brain, 106,* 313–340.

ZIMMER, C. (2004). *Soul made flesh: The discovery of the brain—and how it changed the world.* New York: Free Press.

ZOLA-MORGAN, S., & SQUIRE, L. (1993). Neuroanatomy of memory. *Annual Review of Neuroscience, 16,* 547–563.

ZOLA-MORGAN, S., SQUIRE, L. R., CLOWER, R. P., & REMPEL, N. L. (1993). Damage to the perirhinal cortex exacerbates memory impairment following lesions to the hippocampal formation. *Journal of Neuroscience, 13,* 251–265.

ZORAWSKI, M., BLANDING, N. Q., KUHN, C. M., & LABAR, K. S. (2006). Effects of sex and stress on acquisition and consolidation of human fear conditioning. *Learning & Memory, 13,* 441–450.

ZWITSERLOOD, P. (1989). The locus of the effects of sentential-semantic context in spoken-word processing. *Cognition, 32,* 25–64.

CREDITS

Chapter 1: **1.1**: Reproduced with the permission of the Bodleian Library; University of Oxford; **1.2**: © The Print Collector/Alamy; **1.3**: Reproduced with the permission of the Bodleian Library, University of Oxford; **1.4a**: Bettmann/Corbis; **1.5a–c**: General Research Division, New York Public Library, Astor, Lenox and Tilden Foundations; **1.6a**: Mary Evans Picture Library; **1.6b**: From Luciani, Luigi. *Fisologia del Homo.* Le Monnier, Firenze, 1901–1911; **1.7**: Mary Evans Picture Library/Sigmund Freud Copyrights; **1.8a**: New York Academy of Medicine; **1.9a**: World Health Organization, Geneva, Switzerland; **1.9b**: World Health Organization, Geneva, Switzerland; **1.9c**: From *Arch. Anat. Physiol. Wiss. Medezin* (1852): 199–216; **1.10**: Brodmann, K., *Vergleichende Lokalisationslehre der Grosshirnrinde in ihren Prinzipien dargestellt auf Grund des Zellenbaues.* Leipzip: J.A. Barth, 1909; **1.11b**: From Golgi, Camillo, *Untersuchungen über den Flineren des Centralen und Peripherischen Nerven Systems.* Fisher, Jena, 1894; **1.12a**: Bettmann/Corbis; **1.12b**: From *Histologie du Système Nerveaux de l'Homme et de Vertébrés* by Santiago Ramón y Cajal. Maloine, Paris. 1909–1911; **p. 9, fig. 1a**: © Copyright Museum Boerhaave, Leiden. Photo: Science Photo Library/Photo Researchers, Inc.; **p. 9, fig. 1b**: Bettmann/Corbis; **p. 9, fig. 2**: Courtesy National Library of Medicine, Bethesda, Maryland; **1.14a**: Science Photo Library/Photo Researchers, Inc.; **1.15a**: Courtesy of Mary Brazier; **1.15b**: From Sigmund Freud's *Über den Bau der Nervenfasern und Nervenzellen beim Flusskrebs, Sitz. Akad. Wiss.* 85 (1882): 9–14. Wien, Austria; **1.16a**: McHenry, L.C., Jr., Garrison's History of Neurology. Springfield, Illinois: Charles C. Thomas, Publisher, 1969, p. 206. © 1969 by Charles C. Thomas, Publisher. Courtesy of Professor O.L. Zangwill, Cambridge; **1.16b**: From Budge, Julius, *Lehrbuch der Speciallen Physiologie des Menschen*, vol. 8 (1862); **p. 13a**: Reprinted from *The Physiologist* (1981) with permission; **p. 13b**: From *Biological Bulletin* 40 (1921); **1.17**: UPI-Bettmann/Corbis; **1.18a**: Underwood & Underwood-Betttmann/Corbis; **1.18b**: Benjamin Harris/University of New Hampshire; **1.19**: Courtesy of George A. Miller; **1.20**: Bettmann/Corbis.

Chapter 2: **2.1**: Courtesy of Michael Silverman and Gary Banker at Oregon Health Sciences University; **2.3**: Carpenter, M., *Human Neuroanatomy*, 7th edition. Baltimore, Maryland: William & Wilkins, 1976. © 1976 by Williams & Wilkins; **2.5**: Withers, G.S., George, J.M., Banker, G.A., and Clayton, D.F., Delayed localization of synelfin (synuclein, NACP) to presynaptic terminals in cultured rat hippocampal neurons, *Brain Research: Developmental Brain Research*, 99 (1997): 87–94; **2.6**: Adapted from Kandal, E.R. Schwartz, J.H., and Jessell, T.M. (Eds.), *Principles of Neural Science*, 3rd edition. Norwalk, Connecticut: Appleton & Lange, 1991. Copyright © 1991 by Appleton & Lange; **2.8**: Netter, F.H., *The CIBA Collection of Medical Illustrations. Vol I: Nervous System, Part 1: Anatomy and Physiology.* Summit, NJ: CIBA Pharmaceutical Company, 1983; **p. 31a–b**: From Haeusser, M., The Hodgkin-Huxley theory of the action potential, *Nature Reviews Neuroscience* 3 (2000): 1165; **p. 35**: Netter, F.H., *The CIBA Collection of Medical Illustrations. Vol I: Nervous System, Part 1: Anatomy and Physiology.* Summit, NJ: CIBA Pharmaceutical Company, 1983. Adapted with permission of Novartis, formerly CIBA; **2.15**: Netter, F.H., *The CIBA Collection of Medical Illustrations. Vol I: Nervous System, Part 1: Anatomy and Physiology.* Summit, NJ: CIBA Pharmaceutical Company, 1983; **2.17a**: Adapted from Kandal, E.R. Schwartz, J.H., and Jessell, T.M. (Eds.), *Principles of Neural Science*, 3rd edition. Norwalk, Connecticut: Appleton & Lange, 1991. Copyright © 1991 by Appleton & Lange; **2.17b**: Adapted from Kuffler, S., and Nicholls, J., *From Neuron to Brain.* Sunderland, MA: Sinauer Associates, 1976; **2.20**: Adapted from Kandal, E.R. Schwartz, J.H., and Jessell, T.M. (Eds.), *Principles of Neural Science*, 3rd edition. Norwalk, Connecticut: Appleton & Lange, 1991. Copyright © 1991 by Appleton & Lange; **2.22**: Adapted from Kuffler, S., and Nicholls, J., *From Neuron to Brain.* Sunderland, MA: Sinauer Associates, 1976; **2.23**: Copyright Dennis Kunkel; **2.26 and 2.27**: Doyle, et al., Figure from "The Structure of the Potassium Channel," *Science* 280: 69–77 (1998). Reprinted with permission from AAAS; **2.30**: Adapted from Kandal, E.R. Schwartz, J.H., and Jessell, T.M. (Eds.), *Principles of*

Neural Science, 3rd edition. Norwalk, Connecticut: Appleton & Lange, 1991. Copyright © 1991 by Appleton & Lange; **2.32 and 2.35**: Adapted from Purves, D., Augustine, G., and Fitzpatrick, D., *Neuroscience*, 2nd edition. Sunderland, MA: Sinauer Associates, 2001; **2.36**: Adapted from Gibson, J., Beierllein, M., and Connors, B. (1999), Two networks of electrically coupled inhibitory neurons in neocortex, *Nature* 402 (6757): 75–79.

Chapter 3: **3.1a–b**: DeArmond, S.J., Fusco, M.M., and Dewey, M.M., *The Structure of the Human Brain: A Photographic Atlas*, 2nd edition. New York: Oxford University Press, 1976; **3.2a**: Courtesy of Cindy Jordan, University of California, Berkeley; **3.2b,c and 3.3a,b**: Courtesy of Carla J. Shatz, University of California, Berkeley; **3.5a–c**: Woodward, J.S., *Histologic Neuropathology: A Color Slide Set*. Orange, CA: California Medical Publications, 1973; **3.7a–b**: Adapted from McClelland, J.L., and Rummelhart, D.E. (1986). *Parallel Distributed Processing: Explorations in the Microstructure of Cognition. Vol. 2: Psychological and Biological Models*. Cambridge, MA: MIT Press; **3.9b**: Courtesy of Allen Song, Duke University; **3.12c**: *The Brain: A Neuroscience Primer* by Richard F. Thompson. © 1985, 1993, 2000 by Worth Publishers. Used with permission. **3.13**: Bear, M.F., Connors, B.W., and Paradiso, M.A., *Neuroscience: Exploring the Brain*. Baltimore, Maryland: Willian & Wilkins, 1996; **p. 75a–b**: Courtesy of John Walker, University of California, San Francisco; **p. 75c, bottom**: Adapted from Ramachandran, V.S., Behavioral and magnetoencephalographic correlates of plasticity in the adult human brain, *Proc. Natl. Acad. Sci. U.S.A.* 90 (1993): 10413–10420; **3.16b**: Wessinger, C.M., Buonocore, M.H., Kussmaul, C.L., and Mangun, G.R., Tonotopy in human auditory cortex examined with functional magnetic resonance imaging, *Human Brain Mapping* 5 (1997): 18–25. New York: John Wiley & Sons, Inc., 1997; **3.19**: Adapted from Kandel, E.R., Schwartz, J.H., and Jessell, T.M. (Eds.), *Principles of Neural Science*, 3rd edition. Norwalk, Connecticut: Appleton & Lange, 1991; **3.20a**: Carpenter, M., Human Neuroanatomy, 7th edition. Baltimore, Maryland: William & Wilkins, 1976; **3.20b**: Courtesy of Allen Song, Duke University; **3.21**: Adapted from Kandel, E.R., Schwartz, J.H., and Jessell, T.M. (Eds.), *Principles of Neural Science*, 3rd edition. Norwalk, Connecticut: Appleton & Lange, 1991; **3.23**: Courtesy of David Amaral; **3.25 and 3.26**: Netter, F.H., *The CIBA Collection of Medical Illustrations. Vol I: Nervous System, Part 1: Anatomy and Physiology*. Summit, NJ: CIBA Pharmaceutical Company, 1983; **3.27b**: Courtesy of Allen Song, Duke University; **3.28–3.30**: Carpenter, M., Human Neuroanatomy, 7th edition. Baltimore, Maryland: William & Wilkins, 1976; **3.34**: Photograph © Garvis Keriman/Peter Arnold, Inc.; **3.36a**: Carpenter, M., *Human Neuroanatomy*, 7th edition. Baltimore, Maryland: William & Wilkins, 1976; **3.36b**: Lennart Nilsson/Bonnier Alba AB; **3.42**: © Bryan Reading/www.cartoonstock.com; **3.43 and 3.44**: Erikson, P.S., Perfilieva, E., Björk-Eriksson, T., Alborn, A., Nordborg, C., Peterson, D., and Cage, F., Neurogenesis in the adult hippocampus, *Nature Medicine* 4 (1998): 1312–1317; **3.46**: Adapted from Kandel, E.R., Schwartz, J.H., and Jessell, T.M. (Eds.), *Principles of Neural Science*, 3rd edition, Norwalk, Connecticut: Appleton & Lange, 1991; **3.47**: Adapted from Kandel, E.R. Schwartz, J.H., and Jessell, T.M. (Eds.), *Principles of Neural Science*, 3rd edition. Norwalk, Connecticut: Appleton & Lange, 1991; **3.50**: Karni, A., Meyer, G., Rey-Hipolito, C., Jezzard, P., Adams, M., Turner, R., and Ungerleider, L., The acquisition of skilled motor performance: Fast and slow experience-driven changes in primary motor cortex, *Proc. Natl. Acad. Sci.* U.S.A. 95 (1998): 861–868

Chapter 4: **p.123**: Courtesy of Foundation for Biomedical Research, Washington, D.C.; **4.9a**: Reprinted with permission from Tootell, R.B., Silverman, M.S., Switkes, E., and De Valois, R.L., Deoxcyglucose analysis of retinotopic organization in primate striate cortex, *Science* 218 (1982): 902–904. Copyright 1982 American Association for the Advancement of Science; **4.10**: Rampon, C., Tang, Y.P., Goodhouse, J., Shimuzu, E., Kyin, M., Tsien, J.Z., Enrichment induces structural changes and recovery from nonspatial memory deficits in CA1 NMDAR1-knockout mice, *Nature Neuroscience* 3 (2000): 238–244, used with permission; **4.12b**: Fig. 1-1 (A), Greenberg, J.O., and Adams, R.D. (Eds), *Neuroimaging: A Companion to Adams and Victor's Principles of Neurology*. New York: McGraw-Hill, Inc., 1995. Reprinted by permission of McGraw-Hill, Inc.; **4.13b**: Fig. 1-1 (B), (C), and (D), Greenberg, J.O., and Adams, R.D. (Eds.), *Neuroimaging: A Companion to Adams and Victor's Principles of Neurology*. New York: McGraw-Hill, Inc., 1995. Reprinted by permission of McGraw-Hill, Inc.; **4.14:** Images courtesy of Dr. Megan S. Steven, Karl Doron, and Adam Riggall. Scans were acquired at the Dartmouth Brain Imaging Center at Dartmouth College; **4.15**: DeArmond, S.J., Fusco, M.M., and Dewey, M.M., *The Structure of the Human Brain: A Photographic Atlas*, 2nd edition. New York: Oxford University Press, 1976. Copyright ©1976 by Oxford University Press, Inc. Reprinted with permission; **4.16, 4.17, and 4.18a–b**: Woodward, J.S., *Histologic Neuropathology: A Color Slide Set*. Orange, CA: California Medical Publications, 1973; **4.18c**: Fig. 8.24 (B) and (C), Greenberg, J.O., and Adams, R.D. (Eds.), *Neuroimaging: A Companion to Adams and Victor's Principles of Neurology*. New York: McGraw-Hill, Inc., 1995. Reprinted by permission of McGraw-Hill, Inc.; **4.19a**: Woodward, J.S., Histologic Neuropathology: A Color Slide Set. Orange, CA: California Medical Publications, 1973; **4.19b**: Holbourn, A.H.S., Mechanics of head injury, *The Lancet* 2: 177–180, © by The Lancet 1943; **4.21**: These cartoons appeared in *Life*, 3 March 1947. Used by permission of the estate of Mina Turner; **4.24**: Corthout, E., Uttl, B., Ziemann, U., Cowey, A., Hllett, M., Two periods of processing in the circum(striate) visual cortex as revealed by transcranial magnetic stimulation, *Neuropsychologia* 37 (1999): 137–145; **4.25**: From chapter "Transcranial magnetic stimulation & the human brain" by Megan Steven & Alvaro Pascual-Leone in "Neuroethics: Defining the Issues in Theory, Practice & Policy" edited by Illes, Judith, (2005). By permission of Oxford University Press; **4.32**: Roberts, T.P.L., Poeppel, D., and Rowley, H.A., *Magnetoencephalography and magnetic source imaging, Neuropsychiatry, Neuropsychology and Behavioral Neurology* 11 (1998): 49–64; **4.33a**: Courtesy of Marcus Raichle, M.D. School of Medicine, Washington University in St. Louis; **4.33b**: Posner, M.I., and Raiche, M.E., *Images of Mind*. New York: W.H. Freeman and Company, 1994; **4.34**: Figure 4, Fox et al., "Retinotopic Organization of Human Visual Cortex Mapped with Position-emission Tomography," *The Journal of Neuroscience* 7 (3): 918 (1987). Reprinted with permission of The Society for Neuroscience; **4.35**: Duong, T.Q., Kim, D.S., Ugurbil, K., and Kim, S.G., Spatiotemporal dynamics of the BOLD fMRI signals: Toward mapping submillimeter cortical columns using the early negative response, *Magnetic Resonance in Medicine* 44 (2000): 231–242; **4.37**: Wagner, A.D., Schacter, D.L., Rotte, M. Koutstaal, W., Maril, A., Dale, A.M., Rosen, B.R., and Buckner, R.L., Building memories: Remembering and forgetting of verbal experiences as predicted by brain activity, *Science* 281 (1998): 1188–1191; **4.38a**: Deibert, E., Kraut, M., Kremen, S., and Hart, J., Jr., Neural pathways in tactile object recognition, *Neurology* 52 91999): 1413–1417; **4.38b**: Zangaladze, A., Epstein, C.M., Grafton, S.T., and Sathian, K., Involvement of visual cortex in tactile discrimination of orientation, *Nature* 401 (1999): 587–590.

Chapter 5: **5.3**: Wessinger, C.M., Buonocore, M.H., Kussmaul, C.L., and Mangun, G.R., Tonotopy in human auditory cortex examined with functional magnetic: resonance imaging, *Human Brain Mapping* 5 (1997): 18–25; **5.7a**: Courtesy of N. Sobel; **5.7b**: Sobel, N., Prabhakaran, V., Desmond, J.E., Glover, G.H., Goode, R.L., Sullivan, E.V., and Gabrieli, J.D. (1998). Sniffing and smelling: separate subsystems in the human olfactory cortex. *Nature* 92: 282–286; **5.12a**: Charles Smith/Corbis; **5.12b**: LWA-Paul Chmielowiec/Corbis; **5.13**: Sekuler, R., and Blake, R., *Perception*, 2nd edition. New York: McGraw-Hill, Inc., 1990; **5.17**: Zeki, S.A., *A Vision of the Brain*. Oxford, UK: Blackwell Scientific, 1993; **5.18**: Adapted from Maunsell, J.H.R., and Van Essen, D.C., Functional properties of neurons in middle temporal visual area of the macaque monkey. I. Selectivity for stimulus direction, speed, and orientation, *Journal of Neurophysiology* 49 (1983): 1127–1147; **5.19 and 5.20**: Zeki, S., *A vision of the Brain*. Oxford, UK: Blackwell Scientific, 1993; **5.22 and 5.23**: Hadjikhani, N., Liu, A.K., Dale, A.M., Cavanagh, P., and Tootell, R.B., Retinotopy and color sensitivity in human visual cortical area V8, *Nature Neuroscience* 1 (1998): 235–241; **5.25**: Adapted from Heywood, C.A., Wilson, B., and Cowey, A., A case study of cortical colour blindness with relatively intact achromatic discrimination, *Journal of Neurology, Neurosurgery and Psychiatry* 50 (1987): 22–29; **5.26 and 5.27**: Gallant, J.L., Shoup, R.E., and Mazer, J.A., A human extrastriate area functionally homologous to macaque V4, *Neuron* 27 (2000): 227–235. © 2000, reprinted with permission from Elsevier Science; **5.28a**: Musée d'Orsay, Paris. Photo: Giraudon/Art Resource; **5.28b**: © 2008 Estate of Pablo Picasso/Artists Rights Society (ARS), New York; **5.30**: Beckers, G., and Zeki, S., The consequences of inactivating areas V1 and V5 on visual motion perception, *Brain* 118 (1995): 49–60; **5.34**: Esterman, Ivry, Robertson, & Verstynen, Figure from "Coming Unbound: Disrupting Automatic Integration of Synesthetic Color and Graphemes by Transcranial Magnetic Stimulation of the Right Parietal Lobe" from *Journal of Cognitive Neuroscience*, Vol. 18, pp. 1570–1576 (2006). Reprinted by permission of The MIT Press; **5.35**: Copyright © BBC.

Chapter 6: **6.2 left**: Roger Ressmeyer/Corbis; **6.2 right**: Carl & Ann Purcell/Corbis; **6.5**: Adapted from Robinson, D.L., and Petersen, S., The pulvinar and visual salience, *Trends in Neuroscience* 15 (1992): 127–132; **6.7**: Kohler, S., Kapur, S., Moscovitch, M., Winocur, G., and Houle, S., Dissociation of pathways for object and spatial vision: A PET study in humans, *Neuroreport* 6 (1995): 1865–1868; **6.8b**: Kanwisher, N., Woods, R., Iacobonie, M., and Mazziotta, J.C., A locus in human extrastriate cortex for visual shape analysis, *Journal of Cognitive Neuroscience* 9 (1997): 133–142; **6.9**: Grill-Spector, et al., Figure from "The lateral occipital complex and its role in object recognition," *Vision Research*, 41:10–11. Copyright 2001 by Elsevier Science & Technology Journals. Reproduced with permission of Elsevier Science & Technology Journals in the format Textbook via Copyright Clearance Center; **6.11**: Culham et. al. Ventral occipital lesions impair object guarantors brain. *Brain*, 2003, 126, 243–247, by permission of Oxford University Press; **6.19**: Sekuler, R., and Blake, R., Perception, 2nd edition. New York: McGraw-Hill, Inc., 1990. © 1990 by McGraw-Hill, Inc. Reprinted by permission of McGraw-Hill, Inc.; **6.23**: Adapted from Warrington, E.K., Agnosia: The Impairment of Object Recognition, in Vinken, P.J., Bruyn, G.W., and Klawans, H.L. (Eds.), *Handbook of Clinical Neurology*. New York: Elsevier Science, 1985, pp. 333–349; **6.24**: Adapted from Warrington, E.K., Neuropsychological studies of object recognition, *Philosophical Transactions of the Royal Society*, London, Section B298 (1982): 13–33; **6.25**: McCarthy, G., and Warrington, E.K., Visual associative agnosia: A Clinico-anatomical study of a single case, *Journal of Neurology, Neurosurgery and Psychiatry* 49 (1986): 1233–1240; **6.26a**: Adapted from Warrington, E.K., Neuropsychological studies of object recognition, *Philosophical Transactions of the Royal Society, London, Section B* 298 (1982): 13–33; **6.26b**: Warrington, E.K., and Taylor, A.M., Two categorical stages of object recognition, *Perception 7* (1978): 695–705; **6.28**: Adapted from Humphreys, G.W., Riddoch, M.J., Donnelly, N., Freeman, T., Boucart, M., and Muller, H.M., "Intermediate Visual Processing and Visual Agnosia" in Farah, M.J. and Ratcliff, G. (Eds.), *The Neuropsychology of High-Level Vision: Collected Tutorial Essays*. Lawrence Erlbaum Associates, 1994, pp. 63–102; **6.29**: Behrmann, M., et al., Figure from "Intact visual imagery and impaired visual perception in a patient with visual agnosia," *Journal of Experimental Psychology: Human Perception and Performance*, 20. Copyright © 1994 by the American Psychological Association. Reprinted by permission; **6.30**: Wapner, W., Judd, T., and Gardner, H., Visual agnosia in an artist, *Cortex* 14 (1978): 343–364. Copyright 1978 by the Assoicazione per lo Sviluppo delle Recerche Neuropsicologiche; **6.31**: Adapted from Warrington, E.K., and McCarthy, R.A., Multiple meaning systems in the brain: A case for visual semantics, *Neuropsychologia* 32 (1994): 1465–1473; **6.35**: Adapted from Brain Research 342, Baylis, G.C., Rolls, E.T., and Leonard, C.M., Selectivity between faces in the responses of a population of neurons in the cortex in the superior temporal sulcus of the monkey, pp. 91–102, © 1985 with kind permission of Elsevier Science-NL, Sara Burgerhartstr 25, 1055 KV Amsterdam, The Netherlands; **6.36**: Tsao, et al., Figures from "A Cortical Region Consisting Entirely of Face-Selective Cells," *Science* 311: 670–674 (2006).

Reprinted with permission from AAAS; **6.37a**: McCarthy, G., Puce, A., Gore, J.C., and Allison, T., Face-specific processing in the human fusiform gyrus, *Journal of Cognitive Neuroscience* 9 (1997): 605–610. © 1997 by the Massachusetts Institute of Technology, used with permission; **6.38:** Reprinted from *Cognition*, 83:1, Bentin & Carmel, "Domain specificity versus expertise: factors influencing distinct processing of faces," pp. 1–29, Copyright © 2002, with permission from Elsevier; **6.39**: Reprinted by permission from Macmillan Publishers Ltd: Julian Paul Keenan, Aaron Nelson, Margaret O'Connor, Alvaro Pascual-Leone (2001) Self-recognition and the right hemisphere. *Nature* Jan 18; 409(6818):305; **6.40**: Moscovitch, M., Winocur, G., and Behrmann, M., What is special about face recognition? Nineteen experiments on a person with visual object agnosia and dyslexia but normal face recognition, *Journal of Cognitive Neuroscience* 9 (1997): 555–604. © 1997 by the Massachusetts Institute of Technology, used with permission; **6.41**: McNeil, J.E., and Warrington, E.K., "Prosopagnosia: A Face Specific Disorder" in *The Quarterly Journal of Experimental Psychology* 46A (1993): 1–10. Copyright 1993. Reprinted by permission of The Experimental Psychology Society; **6.42**: Block, J.R., and Yuker, H.E., *Can You Believe Your Eyes: Over 250 Illusions and Other Visual Oddities.* Mattituck, New York: Amereon Press, 1992; **6.43**: Adapted from Farah, M.J., Specialization Within Visual objectRecognition: Clues from Prosopagnosia and Alexia, in Farah, M.J., and Ratcliff, G. (Eds.), *The Neuropsychology of High-Level Vision: Collected Tutorial Essays.* Hillsdale, NJ: Lawrence Erlbaum Associates, 1994, pp. 133–146; **6.44**: This article was published in *Cognitive Brain Research*, Vol. 24 Julia Reinholz, Stefan Pollmann, Differential activation of object-selective visual areas by passive viewing of pictures and words, 702–714. Copyright Elsevier 2005; **6.46**: Podgorny, P., and Shepard, R., Functional representations common to visual perception and imagination, Journal of Experimental Psychology: Human Perception and Performance 4 (1978): 21–35; **6.47**: Behrmann, M., Moscovitch, M., and Winocur, G., Intact visual imagery and impaired visual perception in a patient with visual agnosia, *Journal of Experimental Psychology: Human Perception and Performance* 20 (1994): 1068–1087. Copyright © 1994 by the American Psychological Association. Reprinted with permission; **6.48**: Sacks, O.W., *An Anthropologist on Mars: Seven Paradoxical Tales.* New York: Knopf, 1995. Reprinted with permission; **6.49**: Riddoch, M.J., Humphreys, G.W., Gannon, T., Bott, W., and Jones, V., Memories are made of this: The effects of time on stored visual knowledge in a case of visual agnosia, Brain 122 (1999): 537–559. Reprinted with permission.

Chapter 7: **7.1a**: From Lewis P. Rowland (Ed.), *Merritt's Textbook of Neurology*, 8th edition. Philadelphia: Lea & Febiger, 1989, p. 661. Copyright © 1989 by Lea & Febiger; **7.1b**: From Jon Palfreman and J. William Langston, *The Case of the Frozen Addicts.* New York: Pantheon Books, 1995. Photograph by Russ Lee, © Pantheon books, 1995. Used by permission; **7.8**: Adapted from Kandel, E.R., Schwartz, J.H., and Jessell, T.M. (Eds.), *Principles of Neural Science*, 3rd edition. Norwalk, Connecticut: Appleton & Lang, 1991; **7.9**: From Taub, E., and Berman, A.J., Movement and Learning in the Absence of Sensory Feedback. In S.J. Freedman (Ed.), *The Neuropsychology of Spatially Oriented Behavior.* Homewood, IL: Dorsey, 1968, Figs. 2 and 8. Reprinted with permission; **7.10**: Rothwell, J.C., Traub, M.M., Day, B.L., Obeso, J.A., Thomas, P.K., and Marsden, C.D., Manual motor performance in a deafferented man, *Brain* 105 (1982): 515-542; **7.11 and 7.12**: Bizzi, E., Accornero, N. Chapplel, W., and ; Hogan, N., Posture control and trajectory formation during arm movement, *The Journal of Neuroscience* 4: 2738-2744, (1984); **7.15 and 7.16, and 7.18**: Adapted from Georgopoulos, A.P., Neurophysiology of Reaching, in Jeannerod, M. (Ed.), *Attention and Performance XIII: Motor Representation and Control.* Hillsdale, NJ: Lawrence Erlbaum Associates, 1990, pp. 227–263; **7.17:** Kakei, et al., Figures from "Muscle and Movement Representations in the Primary Motor Cortex," *Science* 285: 2136–2139 (1999). Reprinted with permission from AAAS; **7.20**: Motorlab, University of Pittsburgh School of Medicine; **7.21a–c**: Reprinted by permission from Macmillan Publishers Ltd: Hochberg et al. (2006) Neuronal ensemble control of prosthetic devices by a human with tetraplegia. Nature July 13;442:164–171; **7.21d**: © Rick Friedman; **7.22**: Adapted from Graziano, M.S.A., and Gross, C.G., Mapping space with neurons, Current Directions in *Psychological Science* 3 (1994): 164–167; **7.23**: Desmurget, M., Epstein, C.M., Turner, R.S., Prablanc, C., Alexander, G.E., and Grafton, S.T., Role of the posterior parietal cortex in updating reaching movements to a visual target, *Nature Neuroscience* 2 (1999): 563–567; **7.24**: Shadmehr, R., and Holcomb, H.H., Neural correlates of motor memory consolidation, Science 277 (1997): 821–825; **7.26**: This article was published in Cerebral Cortex, Vol. 15 Calvo-Merino et al. (2005) Action Observation and Acquired Motor Skills: an fMRI Study with Expert Dancers, 1243–1249. Copyright Elsevier 2005; **7.28**: Adapted from Mushiake, H., Masahiko, I., and Tanji, J., Neuronal activity in the primate premotor, supplementary, and precentral motor cortex during visually guided and internally determined sequential movements, *Journal of Neurophysiology* 66 (1991): 705–718; **7.32**: Adapted from Heilman, K.M., Rothi, L.J., and Valenstein, E., Two forms of ideomotor apraxia, Neurology 32 (1982): 342–346; **7.33**: Johnson-Frey SH, Newman-Norlund R., Grafton ST (2004) A Distributed left hemisphere Network Active During Planning of Everyday Tool Use Skills from Cerebral Cortex 15:681–695; **7.35**: Adapted from Wise, S.P., Di Pellegrino, G., and Boussaoud, D., The premotor cortex and nonstandard sensorimotor mapping, *Canadian Journal of Physiology and Pharmacology* 74 (1996): 469–482; **p. 297**: Adapted from Franz, E., Eliassen, J., Ivry, R., and Gazzaniga, M., Dissociation of spatial and temporal coupling in the bimanual movements of callosotomy patients, *Psychological Science* 7 (1996): 306–310; **7.40 and 7.42**: Adapted from Wichmann, T., and DeLong, M.R., Functional and pathophysiological models of the basal ganglia, *Current Opinion in Neurobiology* 6 (1996): 751–758; **7.43**: Color plates 2 and 4 from Greenberg, J.O., and Adams, R.D. (Eds.), Neuroimaging: A Companion to Adams and Victor's Principles of Neurology. New York: MacGraw-Hill, Inc., 1995. Reprinted by permission of McGraw-Hill, Inc.; **7.45**: This Week in the Journal, *New England Journal of Medicine* Volume 345: September 27, 2001.

Chapter 8: **8.2**: Atkinson, R.C., and Shiffrin, R.M., Human Memory: A Proposed System and Its Control Processes, in Spence, K.W., and Spence, J.T. (Eds.), *The Psychology of Learning and Motivation*, Vol. 2. New York: Academic Press, 1968, pp. 89–195; **8.3**: Markowitsch, H.J., Kalbe, E., Kessler, J., Von Stockhausen, H.M., Ghaemi, M., and Heiss, W.D., Short-term memory deficit after focal parietal damage, *Journal of Clinical & Experimental Neuropsychology* 21 (1999): 784–797; **8.4**: Baddeley, A., and Hitch, G., Working Memory, in Bower, G.H. (Ed.), *The Psychology of Learning and Motivation*, Vol. 8. New York, Academic Press, 1974, pp. 47–89; **8.5b**: Adapted from Coren, S., Ward, L.M., and Enns, J.T., *Sensation and Perception*, 4th edition. Ft. Worth, TX: Harcourt Brace College Publishers, 1994; **8.6**: From J. Jonides; **8.8**: Drawing © Ruth Tulving, Courtesy the artist; **8.10**: Drachman, D.A., and Arbit, J., Memory and the hippocampal complex. II. Is memory a multiple process? *Archives of Neurology* 15 (1996): 52–61; **8.12**: Fig. 6.1, Corkin et al., "H.M.'s medial temporal lobe lesion: Findings from magnetic resonance imaging," *The Journal of Neuroscience* 17: 3964–3979, (1997); **8.14a–c**: Courtesy of David Amaral; **8.17**: Adapted from Squire, L.R., and Slater, P., Electroconvulsive therapy and complaints of memory dysfunction: A prospective three-year follow-up study, *British Journal of Psychiatry* 142 (1983): 1–8; **8.18**: Reprinted by permission from Macmillan Publishers Ltd: Corkin, S. (2002) What's new with the amnesic patient H.M.? Nature Reviews Neuroscience, Feb; 2(2):153–60; **8.19**: Tulving, E., Gordon Hayman, C.A., and MacDonald, C.A., Long-lasting perceptual priming and semantic learning in amnesia. A case experiment, *Journal of Experimental Psychology* 17 (1991): 595-617; **8.27**: Figs. 2, 4, and 6, Zola-Morgan et al., Damage to the perirhinal cortex exacerbates memory impairment following lesions to the hippocampal formation, *The Journal of Neuroscience* 13: 251–265, (1993); **8.29:** Ranganath, et al., Figure from "Dissociable correlates of recollection and familiarity within the medial temporal lobes," *Neuropsychologia*, 42:1. Copyright 2003 by Elsevier Science & Technology Journals. Reproduced with permission of Elsevier Science & Technology Journals in the format Textbook via Copyright Clearance Center; **8.30**: This article was published in *Neuropsychologia*, Vol. 42 Ranganath et. al., Dissociable correlates of recollection and familiarity within the medial temporal lobes, 2–13. Copyright Elsevier 2003; **8.31**: Reprinted by permission from Macmillan Publishers Ltd: Laura L. Eldridge, Barbara J. Knowlton, Christopher S. Furmanski, Susan Y. Bookheimer and Stephen A. Engel, (2000) Remembering episode: a selective role for the hippocampus during retrieval. *Nature Neuroscience*, (3) 11:1149–52; **8.32**: This article was published in *Neuropsychologia*, Vol. 42 Ranganath et. al., Dissociable correlates of recollection and familiarity within the medial temporal lobes, 2–13. Copyright Elsevier 2003; **p. 351**: McClelland, J.L., Connectionist Models of Memory. In: Tulving, E. and Craik, F.I.M. (Eds.), *The Oxford Handbook of Memory*, pp. 583–596. Oxford University Press: New York, 2000; **8.33**: Reprinted, with permission, from the *Annual Review of Neuroscience*, Volume 30 © 2007 by Annual Reviews www.annualreviews.org; **8.34**: Jennifer D. Ryan, Robert R. Althoff, Stephen Whitlow, Neal J. Cohen (2000) Amnesia Is a Deficit in Relational Memory, *Psychological Science* 11 (6), 454–461. Copyright © 2000, Blackwell Publishing Ltd; **8.35**: Mark E. Wheeler, Steven E. Petersen, and Randy L. Buckner, *Memory's echo: Vivid remembering reactivates sensory-specific cortex*, Proceedings of the National Academy of Sciences, USA. September 26, 2000, vol. 97, no. 20, 11125–11129; **8.36**: Courtesy of Roberto Cabeza; **8.37**: Reprinted by permission from Macmillan Publishers Ltd: Randy L. Buckner, William M. Kelley and Steven E. Petersen. (1999) Frontal cortex contributes to human memory formation. *Nature Neuroscience*, April 2; 311–314; **8.38**: Grafton, S., Hazeltine, E., and Ivry, R., Functional mapping of sequence learning in normal humans, *Journal of Cognitive Neuroscience* 7 (1995): 497–510. © 1995 by the Massachusetts Institute of Technology. Adapted with permission of MIT Press.

Chapter 9: **9.1 and 9.3**: Adolphs et. al. (1995) Fear and the Human Amygdala. *The Journal of Neuroscience*, 15(9):5878–5891. Reprinted with permission of The Journal of Neuroscience, http://www.jneurosci.org; **9.4**: Ekman, P., Cross-Cultural Studies in Facial Expression, in P. Ekman (Ed.), *Darwin and Facial Expressions: A Century of Research in Review*. New York: Academic Press, 1973; **9.5**: MacLean, P.D., Psychosomatic disease and the "visceral brain": Recent developments bearing on the Papez theory of emotion, *Psychosomatic Medicine* 11 (1949): 338–353; **9.6**: Davidson, R.J., Jackson, D.C., and Kalin, N.H., Emotion, plasticity, context, and regulation: Perspectives from affective neuroscience, *Psychological Bulletin* 126 (2000): 890–909; **9.7**: Davis, M., The Role of the Amygdala in Conditioned Fear, in J.P. Aggleton (Ed.), *The Amygdala: Neurobiological Aspects of Emotion, Memory and Mental Dysfunction* (pp. 225–306). New York: Wiley-Liss, 1992; **9.10**: Reprinted by permission from Macmillan Publishers Ltd: Adam K. Anderson & Elizabeth A. Phelps. (2001) Lesions of the human amygdala impair enhanced perception of emotionally salient events. *Nature*; May 17; 41:305–309; **9.13**: Reprinted by permission from Macmillan Publishers Ltd: Adolphs et al. (2005). A mechanism for impaired fear recognition after amygdala damage. *Nature*; January 6; 433:68–72; **9.14**: From Whalen, et. Al. Human Amygdala Responsivity to Masked Fearful Eye Whites. *Science* Vol. 306, p. 2061 (2004). Reprinted with Permission of AAAS; **9.15**: W. A. Cunningham, M. K. Johnson, C. L. Raye, J. C. Gatenby, J. C. Gore, & M. R. Banaji, (2004). Separable neural components in the processing of Black and White Faces. *Psychological Science*, 15, 806–813. Copyright © 2004, Blackwell Publishing Ltd; **9.16 and 9.17a**: R.J.R. Blair et. al. Dissociable neural responses to facial expressions of sadness and anger, *Brain*, 1999, 122, 883–893, by permission of Oxford University Press; **9.17b**: A.J. Calder, A.W. Young, D. Rowland, and D.I. Perrett, Computer-enhanced emotion in facial expressions. Proceedings. *Biological Sciences*. 1997 June 22; 264(1383): 919–925. © Royal Society of London, 1997.

Chapter 10: **10.7 and 10.8**: Swaab, Brown and Hagoort, "Spoken Sentence Comprehension in Aphasia: Event-related Potential Evidence for a Lexical Integration Deficit," *Journal of Cognitive Neuroscience*, 9:1. Reprinted by permission of MIT Press Journals; **10.10**: Binder, J.R., Frost, J.A., Hammeke, T.A., Bellgowan,

P.S.F., Springer, J.A., Kaufman, J.N., and Possing, E.T., Human temportal lobe activation by speech and non-speech sounds, *Cerebral Cortex* 10 (2000): 512–528; **10.12:** McClelland, James L., David E. Rumelhart, and PDP Research Group., *Parallel Distributed Processing, Volume 2: Explorations in the Microstructure of Cognition: Psychological and Biological Models*, figure: "Fragment of a Connectionist Network for Letter Recognition," © 1986 Massachusetts Institute of Technology, by permission of The MIT Press; **10.13**: Puce, A., Allison, T., Asgari, M., Gore, J.C., and McCarthy, G., Differential sensitivity of human visual cortex to faces, letterstrings, and textures: A functional magnetic resonance imaging study, Journal of Neuroscience 16 (1996): 5205–5215; **10.15**: Binder, J.R., Frost, J.A., Hammeke, T.A., Bellgowan, P.S.F., Springer, J.A., Kaufman, J.N., and Possing, E.T., Human temporal lobe activation by speech and non-speech sounds. Cerebral Cortex 10 (2000); **10.18:** E. Kaan and T.Y. Swaab, Figure from "Electrophysiological Evidence for Serial Sentence Processing", *Cognitive Brain Research*, 17. Copyright 2003 by Elsevier Science & Technology Journals. Reproduced with permission of Elsevier Science & Technology Journals in the format Textbook via Copyright Clearance Center; **10.19:** Schliz, Munte & Kutas, Figure from "When Temporal Terms Belie Conceptual Order," *Nature*, 395. Copyright 1998 by Nature Publishing Group (Permissions). Reproduced with permission of Nature Publishing Group (Permissions) in the format Textbook via Copyright Clearance Center; **10.20:** Hagoort, et al., Figure 1 from "Integration of Word Meaning and World Knowledge in Language Comprehension," *Science*, Vol. 304, pp. 438–441 (2004). Reprinted with permission from AAAS; **10.21**: From Peter Hagoort, Lea Hald, Marcel Bastiaansen, Karl Magnus Petersson, "Integration of Word Meaning and World Knowledge in Language Comprehension," Originally published in Science Express on 18 March 2004. *Science* 16 April 2004: Vol. 304. no. 5669, pp. 438–441. Reprinted with Permission of AAAS; **10.23**: Caplan, D., Alpert, N., Waters, G., and Olivieri, A., Activation of Broca's area by syntactic processing under conditions of concurrent articulation, *Human Brain Mapping* 9 (2000): 65–71; **10.24:** Courtesy of Nina Dronkers; **10.25**: Adapted from Levelt, W.J.M., The Architecture of Normal Spoken Language Use, in Blanken, G., Ditgtman, J., Grimm, H., Marshall, J.C., and Wallesh, C-W. (Eds.), *Linguistic Disorders and Pathologies: An International Handbook*. Berlin: Walter de Gruyter, 1993; **10.26 and 10.27:** Adapted from van Turennout, M., Hagoort, P., and Brown, C.M., Brain activity during speaking: From syntax to phonology in 40 milliseconds, *Science* 280 (1999): 572–574; **10.28a:** Courtesy Musée Depuytren, Paris; **10.35:** Kutas & Federmeier, Figure from "Electrophysiology Reveals Semantic Memory Use in Language Comprehension," *Trends in Cognitive Science*, 4:12. Copyright 2000 by Elsevier Science & Technology Journals. Reproduced with permission of Elsevier Science & Technology Journals in the format Textbook via Copyright Clearance Center; **10.36**: Adapted from Hagoort, P., Brown, C., and Groothusen, J., The syntactic positive shift (SPS) as an ERP measure of syntactic processing. Special issue: Event-related brain potentials in the study of language, *Language and Cognitive Processes* 8 (1993): 439–483; **10.37:** Munte, Heinze and Mangun, Figure from "Dissociation of Brain Activity Related to Syntactic and Semantic Aspects of Language," *Journal of Cognitive Neuroscience*, 5:3, Summer 1993. Reprinted by permission of MIT Press Journals; **10.38:** G.R. Kuperberg, Figure from "Neural mechanisms of language comprehension: Challenges to syntax", *Brain Research*, 1146. Copyright 2007 by Elsevier Science & Technology Journals. Reproduced with permission of Elsevier Science & Technology Journals in the format Textbook via Copyright Clearance Center.

Chapter 11: **11.3 and 11.4**: Michael Gazzaniga; **11.11a–b**: Abigail A. Baird, Mary K. Colvin, John D. VanHorn, Souheil Inati and Michael S. Gazzaniga. Functional Connectivity: Integrating Behavioral, Diffusion Tensor Imaging, and Functional Magnetic Resonance Imaging Data Sets, *The Journal of Cognitive Neuroscience*. 2005; 17:687–693; **11.15:** Haerer, A.F. (revised by), DeJong's The Neurologic Examination, 5th edition. Philadelphia, Pennsylvania: J.B. Lippincott Company; **11.16:** Adapted from Kingstone, A., & Gazzaniga, M. S. (1995). Subcortical transfer of higher order information: More illusory than real? *Neuropsychology*, 9, 321–328; **11.19**: Gazzaniga, M.S., Cerebral specialization and interhemispheric communication: Does the corpus callosum enable the human condition? *Brain* 123 (2000): 1293–1326; **11.23**: Efron, Robertson, & Delis, Figure from "Hemispheric Specialization of Memory for Visual Hierarchical Stimuli," *Neuropsychologia*, 24:2. Copyright 1985 by Elsevier Science & Technology Journals. Reproduced with permission of Elsevier Science & Technology Journals in the format Textbook via Copyright Clearance Center; **11.24a:** Adapted from Kimura, D., The Asymmetry of the human brain, *Scientific American* 228 (1973): 70–78; **11.25**: Adapted from Bartholomeus, B., Effects of task requirements on ear superiority for sung speech, *Cortex* 10 (1974): 215–223; **11.32**: Adapted from Kitterle, F., Christman, S., and Hellige, J., Hemispheric differences are found in identification, but not detection of low versus high spatial frequencies, *Perception and Psychophysics* 48 (1990), 297–306; **11.33**: Sergent, J., Influence of task and input factors on hemispheric involvement in face processing, *Journal of Experimental Psychology: Human Perception and Performance 11* (1958): 846–861; **11.35**: Kosslyn, S.M., Koening, O., Barret, A., Cave, C.B., Tang, J., and Gabrieli, J.D.E., Evidence for two types of spatial representations: Hemispheric specialization for categorical and coordinate relations, *Journal of Experimental Psychology: Human Perception and Performance* 15 (1989): 723–735; **11.39**: Marsolek, C.J., Abstract visual-form representations in the left cerebral hemisphere, *Journal of Experimental Psychology: Human Perception and Performance* 21 (1995): 375–386; **11.41**: Previc, F.H., A general theory concerning the prenatal origins of cerebral lateralization in humans, *Psychological Review* 98 (1991): 299–334.

Chapter 12: **12.2**: Courtesy National Library of Medicine, Bethesda, Maryland; **12.3a**: Bettmann/Corbis; **12.6**: Adapted from fig. 2, Broadbent, D.A., *Perception and Communications*. New York: Pergamon, 1958; **12.9:** Posner, M.I., Snyder, C.R.R., and Davison, J., Attention and the detection of signals, *Journal of Experimental*

Psychology: General 109 (1980): 160–174; **12.11:** Liu, et al., Figures from "Comparing the time course and efficacy of spatial and feature-based attention", Vision Research, 47:1. Copyright 2007 by Elsevier Science & Technology Journals. Reproduced with permission of Elsevier Science & Technology Journals in the format Textbook via Copyright Clearance Center; **12.12:** From Hernandez-Peon, et al. Modification of electrical activity in cochlear nucleus during "attention" in unanesthetized cats. *Science*, Vol. 123. (1956), pp. 331–332. Reprinted with Permission of AAAS; **12.13**: Adapted from Hillyard, S.A., Hink, R.F., Schwent, V.L., and Picton, T.W., Electrical signs of selective attention in the human brain, *Science* 182 (1973): 177–180; **12.14**: Adapted from Woldorff, M.G., Gallen, C.C., Hampson, S.A., Hillyard, S.A., Pantev, C., Sobel, D., and Bloom, F.E., Modulation of early sensory processing in human auditory cortex during auditory selective attention, *Proc. Natl. Acad. Sci.* U.S.A. 90 (1993): 8722–8726; **12.18**: Adapted from Hopfinger, J., and Mangun, G.R., Reflexive attention modulates visual processing in human extrastriate cortex. *Psychological Science* 9 (1998): 441–447; **12.20**: Hopf, J.M., Boelmans, K., Schoenfeld, M.A., Luck, S.J., Heinze, H.J. (2004) Attention to features precedes attention to locations in visual search; evidence from electromagnetic brain responses in humans. *The Journal of Neuroscience*, 24(8):1822–32. Reprinted with permission of The Journal of Neuroscience, http://www.jneurosci.org; **12.21:** Heinze, et al., Figure from "Combined spatial and temporal imaging of brain activity during visual selective attention in humans," *Nature*, 372. Copyright 1994 by Nature Publishing Group (Permissions). Reproduced with permission of Nature Publishing Group (Permissions) in the format Textbook via Copyright Clearance Center. **12.22:** Adapted from Mangun, G.R., Hopfinger, J., Kussmaul, C., Fletcher, E., and Heinze, H.J. Covariations in PET and ERP measures of spatial selective attention in human extrastriate visual cortex, *Human Brain Mapping* 5 (1997): 273–279; **12.23**: Tootell, R.B., Hadjikhani, N., Hall, E.K., Marrett, S., Vanduffel, W., Vaughan, J.T., and Dale, A.M., The retinocopy of visual spatial attention, *Neuron* 21 (1998): 1409–1422; **12.24 and 12.25**: Kastner, S., DeWeerd, P., Desimone, R., and Ungerleider, L.C., Mechanisms of directed attention in the human extrastriate cortex as revealed by functional MRI, Science 282 (1998): 108–111; **12.26**: Reprinted by permission from Macmillan Publishers Ltd: Daniel H. O'Connor, Miki M. Fukui, Mark A. Pinsk and Sabine Kastner. (2002) Attention modulates responses in the human lateral geniculate nucleus. *Nature Neuroscience*, Nov., 5(11): 1203–9; **12.28:** M. Schoenfeld, J.M. Hopf, A. Martinez, H. Mai, C. Sattler, A. Gasde, H.J. Heinze, S. Hillyard, Figures from "Spatio-temporal Analysis of Feature-Based Attention," *Cerebral Cortex*, 17:10. Copyright 2007 by Oxford University Press - Journals. Reproduced with permission of Oxford University Press-Journals in the format Textbook via Copyright Clearance Center; **12.29:** Mueller & Kleinschmidt, Figures from "Dynamic Interaction of Object- and Space-Based Attention in Retinotopic Visual Areas," *Journal of Neuroscience*, Vol. 23, No. 30, pp. 9812–6. Copyright 2003 by the Society for Neuroscience. Reprinted with permission from the Society for Neuroscience; **12.32, 12.33, and, 12.34**: Hopfinger, J.B., Buonocore, M.H., and Mangun, G.R., The neural mechanism of top-down attentional control, *Nature Neuroscience* 3 (2000): 284–291; **12.35**: Reprinted by permission from Macmillan Publishers Ltd: Corbetta, M. and Shulman, G. (2002) Control of goal-directed and stimulus-driven attention in the brain. *Nature Reviews Neuroscience*, March; 3(3):201–15; **12.37**: Adapted from Moran, J., and Desimone, R., Selective attention gates visual processing in extrastriate cortex, *Science* 229 (1985): 782–784; **12.38:** B. Motter, Figures from "Focal attention produces spatially selective processing in visual cortical areas V1, V2, and V4 in the presence of competing stimuli", *Journal of Neurophysiology*, 70:3. Copyright 1993 by American Physiological Society. Reproduced with permission of American Physiological Society in the format Textbook via Copyright Clearance Center; **12.39:** McAdams & Reid, Figures from "Attention Modulates the Responses of Simple Cells in Monkey Primary Visual Cortex," *Journal of Neuroscience*, Vol. 25, No. 47, pp. 11023–33. Copyright 2005 by the Society for Neuroscience. Reprinted with permission from the Society for Neuroscience; **12.41**: Adapted from Wurtz, R.H., Goldberg, M.E., and Robinson, D.L., Brian mechanisms of visuals attention, Scientific American 246 (1982): 124–135; **12.43**: Adapted from Robinson, D.L., and Petersen, S., The pulvinar and visual salience, Trends in *Neuroscience* 15 (1992): 127–132; **12.46:** Bisley, J.W., Goldberg, M.E., Figures from "Neural Correlates of Attention and Distractibility in the Lateral Intraparietal Area," *Journal of Neurophysiology*, 95:3. Copyright 1996 by American Physiological Society. Reproduced with permission of American Physiological Society in the format Textbook via Copyright Clearance Center; **12.47**: Reproduced from *Scientific American* 246 (1982), p. 134. © 1998 Artists Rights Society (ARS), New York/VG Bild-Kunst, Bonn; **12.51**: Fig. 2, Posner et al., "Effects of parietal injury on covert orienting of attention," *The Journal of Neuroscience* 4: 1863–1874, (1984); **12.54**: Reprinted by permission from Macmillan Publishers Ltd: Hans-Otto Karnath, Susanne Ferber & Marc Himmelbach. (2001) Spatial awareness is a function of the temporal lobe not the posterior parietal lobe. *Nature*; June 21, 411:950–953; **12.55**: Argye E. Hillis, *Neurobiology of Unilateral Spatial Neglect The Neuroscientist*, Vol. 12, No. 2, 153–163 (2006) Copyright © 2006, SAGE Publications; **12.58**: Grabowecky, M., Robertson, L.C., and Treisman, A., Preattentive processes guide visual search, *Journal of Cognitive Neuroscience* 5 (1993): 288–302; **12.61**: This article was published in *Neuron*, Volume 41, Issue 3, René Marois, Do-Joon Yi and Marvin M. Chun The Neural Fate of Consciously Perceived and Missed Events in the Attentional Blink, Pages 465–472. Copyright Elsevier 2004.

Chapter 13: **13.2 and 13.4**: Adapted from Fuster, J.M., *The Prefrontal Cortex: Anatomy, Physiology, and Neuropsychology of the Frontal Lobe*, 2nd edition. New York: Raven Press, 1989; **13.5**: Rao, S.C., Rainer, G., and Miller, E.K., Integration of what and where in the primate prefrontal lobe cortex, *Science* 276 (1997): 821–824; **13.7:** T. Jason Druzgal and Mark D'Esposito, Figure from "Dissecting Contributions of Prefrontal Cortex and Fusiform Face Area to Face Working Memory," *Journal of Cognitive Neuroscience*, 15:6. Copyright 2003 by MIT Press - Journals. Reproduced with permission of MIT Press - Journals in the format Textbook via Copyright

Clearance Center; **13.8**: Adapted from Milner, B., Corsi, P., and Leonard, G., Frontal-lobe contributions to recency judgements, *Neuropsychologia* 29 (1991): 601–618; **13.10**: Glisky, E.L., Polster, M.R., and Routhuieaux, B.C., Double dissociation between item and source memory, *Neuropsychology* 9 (1995): 229–235; **13.11:** Alan Baddeley, Figure from "Working Memory: Looking Back and Looking Forward," *Nature Reviews Neuroscience*, 4:10, October 2003. Reprinted by permission from Macmillan Publishers Ltd, Copyright © 2003, Nature Publishing Group; **13.12a–c:** Katsuyuki Sakai and Richard E. Passingham, Figures from "Prefrontal Interactions Reflect Future Task Operations," *Nature Neuroscience*, 6:1, January 2003. Reprinted by permission from Macmillan Publishers Ltd, Copyright © 2003, Nature Publishing Group; **13.14**: From Étienne Koechlin, Chrystèle Ody, and Frédérique Kouneiher, The Architecture of Cognitive Control in the Human Prefrontal Cortex, *Science*, Vol. 302. (2003) no. 5648, pp. 1181–1185. Reprinted with Permission of AAAS; **13.18b**: Thompson-Schill, S.L., D'Esposito, M., Aquirre, G.K., and Farah, M.J., Role of left interior prefrontal cortex in retrieval of semantic knowledge: A reevaluation, *Proc. Natl. Acad. Sci. U.S.A.* 94 (1997): 14792–14797; **13.18c**: Thompson-Schill, S.L., Swick, D., Farah, M.J., D'Esposito, M., Kan, I.P., and Knight, R.T., Verb generation in patients with focal frontal lesions: A neuropsychological test of neuroimagings findings, *Proc. Natl. Acad. Sci. U.S.A.* 95 (1998): 15855–15860; **13.19**: Rogers, R.D., Shahakian, R.A., Hodges, J.R., Polkey, C.E., Kennard, C., and Robbins, T.W., Dissociating executive mechanisms of task control following frontal lobe damage and Parkinson's disease, *Brain* 121 (1998): 815-842; **13.20b**: Konishi, S., Nakajima, K., Uchida, I., Kameyama, M., Nakahara, K., Sekihara, K., and Miyashita, Y., Transient activation of inferior prefrontal cortex during cognitive set shifting, *Nature Neuroscience* 1 (1998): 80–84; **13.27**: Adapted from Shallice, T., Burgess, P.W., Schon, F., and Baxter, D.M., The origins of utilization behavior, *Brain* 112 (1989): 1587–1598; **13.30**: Adapted from Gehring, W.J., Goss, B., Coles, M.G.H., Meyer, D.E., and Donchin, E., A neural system for error detection and compensation, *Psychological Science* 43 (1993): 385–390.

Chapter 14: **14.1**: From Damasio et. al. The Return of Phineas Gage: Clues about the brain from the skull of a famous patient. *Science* Vol. 264. No. 5162, pp. 1102–1105 (1994). Reprinted with Permission of AAAS; **14.6c:** Jennifer S. Beer, Oliver P. John, Donatella Scabini, and Robert T. Knight, Figure 5 from "Orbitofrontal Cortex and Social Behavior: Integrating Self-monitoring and Emotion-Cognition Interactions," *Journal of Cognitive Neuroscience*, 18:6 (June, 2006), pp. 871–879. © 2006 by the Massachusetts Institute of Technology. Reprinted by permission of MIT Press Journals; **14.7:** Mitchell et. al. (2004) Encoding-Specific Effects of Social Cognition on the Neural Correlates of Subsequent Memory. *The Journal of Neuroscience*, 24(21): 4912–4917. Reprinted with permission of The Journal of Neuroscience, http://www.jneurosci.org; **14.9a:** Courtesy Wychwood Editions; **14.9b–c**: Rebecca Saxe, Lindsey J Powell (2006) It's the Thought That Counts: Specific Brain Regions for One Component of Theory of Mind, *Psychological Science* 17 (8), 692–699. Copyright © 2006, Blackwell Publishing Ltd.; **14.11a**: Ami Klin, Warren Jones, Robert Schultz, Fred Volkmar, Donald Cohen. "Visual Fixation Patterns During Viewing of Naturalistic Social Situations as Predictors of Social Competence in Individuals with Autism." Archives of General Psychiatry 2002; 59:809–816. © 2002 American Medical Association. All rights reserved; **14.13a–b**: Reprinted by permission from Macmillan Publishers Ltd: M.L. Phillips et al. (1997) A specific neural substrate for perceiving facial expressions of disgust. *Nature*; October 2; 389:495–498; **14.15a**: This article was published in *Trends in Cognitive Sciences*, Volume 11, Issue 5, Jennifer S. Beer The default self: feeling good or being right? Pages 187–189. Copyright Elsevier 2007; **14.15b**: Jennifer S. Beer et al, Heerey, Keltner, Scabini, & Knight (2003) The Regulatory Function of Self-Conscious Emotion: Insights From Patients With Orbitofrontal Damage. *Journal of Personality and Social Psychology*, 85, (4) 594–604. Copyright © 2003 by the American Psychological Association, Inc.

Chapter 15: **15.4b**: Adapted from Catania, K.C., Northcutt, R.G., Kaas, J.H., and Beck, P.D., Nose stars and brain stripes, Nature 364 (1993): 493 and Catania, K.C., Northcutt, R.G., Kaas, J.H., Organization of the somosensory cortex of the star-nosed mole, *Journal of Comparative Neurology* 351 (1995): 549–567; **p. 642**: Bettmann/Corbis; **15.5**: Weller, W.L., SmI cortical barrels in an Australian marsupial, Trichosurus vulpecula (brush-tailed possum): Structural organization, patterned distribution, and somatotopic relationships, *Journal of Comparative Neurology* 337 (193): 471–492; **15.10b**: Florence, S.L., and Kaas, J.H., Large-scale reorganization at multiple levels of the somatosensory pathway follows therapeutic amputation of the hand in monkeys, *Journal of Neuroscience* 15 (1995): 8083–8095; **p. 654**: Adapted from Lettvin, J.Y., Maturana, H.R., McCulloch, W.S., and Pitts, W.H., What the frog's eye tells the frog's brain, *Proc. Insti. Radio Engineers* 47 (1959): 1940–1951; **15.13 and 15.14**: Adapted from Gaulin, S.J.C., and Fitzgerald, R.W., Sexual selection for spatial-learning ability, *Animal Behavior* 37 (1989): 322–331; **15.15**: Adapted from Jacobs, L.F., Gaulin, S.J.C., Sherry, D.F., and Hoffman, E.E., Evolution of spatial cognition: Sex-specific patterns of spatial behavior predict hippocampal size, *Proc. Natl. Acad. Sci.* U.S.A. 87 (1990): 6349–6352; **15.19**: Gallistel, C.R., The Replacement of General-Purpose Theories with Adaptive Specializations, in Gazzaniga, M.S. (Ed.), *The Cognitive Neurosciences.* Cambridge, MA: MIT Press, 1995, pp. 1255–1267. © 1995 Massachusetts Institute of Technology. Adapted with permission of MIT Press; **15.20**: Adapted from Harkness, R.D., and Maroudas, N.G., Central place foraging by an ant (Cataglyphis bicolor Fab.): A model of searching, *Animal Behaviour* 33 (1985): 916–928. Gallistel, C.R., The Replacement of General-Purpose Theories with Adaptive Specializations, in Gazzaniga, M.S. (Ed.), *The Congnitive Neurosciences*, Cambridge, MA: MIT Press, 1995, pp. 1255–1267. © 1995 Massachusetts Institute of Technology. Adapted with permission of MIT Press.

INDEX